Developing
CLIENT/SERVER
Applications with Visual Basic® 4

Dan Rahmel
Ron Rahmel

SAMS
PUBLISHING

201 West 103rd Street
Indianapolis, Indiana 46290

We would like to dedicate this book to the managers, designers, and programmers of Microsoft's Visual Basic and all the third-party manufacturers of Visual Basic components. Only five short years ago, application development was in the dark ages. Thanks to the Visual Basic community, where once there was darkness, now there is light.

Copyright © 1996 by Sams Publishing

FIRST EDITION

All rights reserved. No part of this book shall be reproduced, stored in a retrieval system, or transmitted by any means, electronic, mechanical, photocopying, recording, or otherwise, without written permission from the publisher. No patent liability is assumed with respect to the use of the information contained herein. Although every precaution has been taken in the preparation of this book, the publisher and author assume no responsibility for errors or omissions. Neither is any liability assumed for damages resulting from the use of the information contained herein. For information, address Sams Publishing, 201 W. 103rd St., Indianapolis, IN 46290.

International Standard Book Number: 0-672-30789-8

Library of Congress Catalog Card Number: 95-70101

99 98 97 96   4 3 2 1

Interpretation of the printing code: the rightmost double-digit number is the year of the book's printing; the rightmost single-digit, the number of the book's printing. For example, a printing code of 96-1 shows that the first printing of the book occurred in 1996.

Composed in AGaramond, Optima, Helvetica, and MCPdigital by Macmillan Computer Publishing

Printed in the United States of America

Trademarks

All terms mentioned in this book that are known to be trademarks or service marks have been appropriately capitalized. Sams Publishing cannot attest to the accuracy of this information. Use of a term in this book should not be regarded as affecting the validity of any trademark or service mark.

Visual Basic is a registered trademark of Microsoft Corporation.

Publisher and President	*Richard K. Swadley*
Acquisitions Manager	*Greg Wiegand*
Development Manager	*Dean Miller*
Managing Editor	*Cindy Morrow*
Marketing Manager	*Gregg Bushyeager*

Acquisitions and Development Editor
Sunthar Visuvalingam

Software Development Specialist
Steve Flatt

Production Editors
James Grass, Johnna VanHoose

Copy Editors
Nancy Albright, Margaret Berson, David Bradford, Kimberly K. Hannel, Greg Horman, Kris Simmons, Angie Trzepacz

Technical Reviewers
Vincent Mayfield, Brian Morgan

Editorial Coordinator
Bill Whitmer

Technical Edit Coordinator
Lynette Quinn

Formatter
Frank Sinclair

Editorial Assistants
Sharon Cox, Andi Richter, Rhonda Tinch-Mize

Cover Designer
Tim Amrhein

Book Designer
Alyssa Yesh

Production Team Supervisor
Brad Chinn

Production
Mary Ann Abramson, Carol Bowers, Michael Brumitt, Jeanne Clark, Terrie Deemer, Mike Dietsch, Judy Everly, Jason Hand, Mike Henry, Ayanna Lacey, Clint Lahnen, Kevin Laseau, Paula Lowell, Donna Martin, Steph Mineart, Casey Price, Nancy Price, Bobbi Satterfield, SA Springer, Andrew Stone, Susan Van Ness, Mark Walchle, Colleen Williams

Indexer
Chris Cleveland

Overview

	Introduction	xxiv
I	**Overview of Necessary Visual Basic and Client/Server Concepts**	
1	Overview of Visual Basic	3
2	Overview of Client/Server Concepts	25
3	Networks (Client/Server Foundation)	49
4	Overview of Database Concepts	95
5	Visual Basic Data Access	117
6	Object Programming Overview	147
7	Visual Basic 4	159
8	Constructing a Simple Client/Server System	187
II	**Constructing a Basic Client/Server System**	
9	Overview of a Client/Server System	209
10	Table Construction	225
11	Sales Client	263
12	Purchasing/Inventory Client	351
13	Management Client	449
14	Pseudo Server	499
15	Execution and Functioning of the Client/Server System	521
16	Access Security	545
III	**Using VBA for Client Front-Ends**	
17	Overview of Visual Basic for Applications (VBA)	577
18	Overview of Excel Objects	603
19	Excel Additions to the Client/Server System	629
IV	**Advanced Client/Server Topics**	
20	Structured Query Language (SQL) Primer	643
21	Upsizing to Microsoft SQL Server	667
22	Open Database Connectivity (ODBC)	689
23	Object Linking and Embedding (OLE)	711

	24	Creating an OLE Server	727
	25	Query Builder	753
	26	Remote Client/Server Access	789
	27	Telephony	851
	28	Security for Client/Server	873
	29	Third-Party Tools, Utilities, and Controls	911

V Appendixes

A	User Interface Guidelines	937
B	Error Handling	955
C	Sources	967
D	List of Acronyms and Terms	987
	Index	997

Contents

	Introduction	**xxiv**

I Overview of Necessary Visual Basic and Client/Server Concepts

1   Overview of Visual Basic   3

    Visual Basic Development System 4
        Who Should Read This Chapter? 4
        Visual Basic Language 4
        Visual Basic Program 6
        Event Orientation 11
        Projects (VBP or MAK) 12
        Different Versions of Basic 13
    Outside Resources 14
        Plug-In Components (DLL, VBX, and OCX) 14
        Windows API 16
        Help File Compiler 18
        Setup Wizard 19
        Crystal Reports 23
        VB Knowledge Base and Microsoft Developer's Network 23

2   Overview of Client/Server Concepts   25

    Structure 26
        Client 27
        Middleware 27
        Server 29
    Progression of Client/Server Systems 30
        File Server 31
        Database Server 31
        Groupware Server 32
        Object Servers 33
        Other Servers and Server Applications 34
    Client/Server Division of Labor 34
        Server Responsibilities 34
        Client Responsibilities 35
    Client/Server Structure 36
    Enterprise Information Systems 37
    Data Warehousing 37
    Three-Tier Client/Server Systems 38
    Distributed or Remote Processing 39
        What Is DCE? 40

Replication	41
Transaction Processing Monitors	42
E-mail and Embedded Messages	44
Network Operating System	45
Directory Services	45
Peer-to-Peer	46
This Book's Client/Server Focus	47

3 Networks (Client/Server Foundation)   49

Networks	50
Local Area Network (LAN)	51
Sample Network	51
Basic Network Terms	53
Network Topologies	53
Chain or Wave	53
Ring	54
Star	54
Bus or Bus-Wired	55
Cabling	55
10BASE-T (Twisted Pair)	56
10BASE-2 (Thinnet)	56
10BASE-5 (Thick)	56
100BASE-T (Twisted Pair)	57
Fiber	57
Transport Protocols	58
Ethernet	58
Token Ring	60
ARCnet	60
Fiber Distributed Data Interface (FDDI)	60
Data Transfer Protocol (Network Operating System)	61
IPX and SPX	61
TCP/IP (Transmission Control Protocol/Internet Protocol)	62
NetBEUI	64
System Network Architecture (SNA)	64
Network Hardware	64
Repeaters	64
Bridges	65
Routers	65
Gateways	65
Hubs	66
Network Operating Systems/File Servers	66
Windows NT 3.51	67
NetWare	70

Contents vii

        LAN Server 4.0 for OS/2 71
        AIX 71
        Solaris 71
    Network Interface Design 72
    Network Standards 72
    Wide Area Networks 73
    What Are Wide Area Networks? 73
    What Is ISDN? 74
        ISDN Overview 75
        Narrowband ISDN (Original) 81
        Broadband ISDN (B-ISDN) 87
    Asynchronous Transfer Mode (ATM) 89
        ATM Hardware 92
        Transmission Mechanism—SONET 92

4 Overview of Database Concepts   95

    Database Concepts 96
        Tables 96
        Indexes 98
    What Is a Relational Database? 99
        What Is a Key Field? 101
        Queries 102
        Joins 102
    What Is SQL? 104
        SQL Database Structure 106
        SQL Queries 106
    Normalization 106
        Five Normal Modes 109
    Guidelines for Distributed Data 109
        Data Dictionary 110
        Data Rule Integrity 111
        Data Integrity 111
        Data Concurrency 112
        Update Problems 114
        Transaction Consistency 114
        Referential Integrity 115
        Centralization/Decentralization 116

5 Visual Basic Data Access   117

    Data Access 122
        Data Control 122
        Data Access Objects (DAO) 126
        Remote Data Object (RDO) 128

ODBC API 129
   Custom Drivers 131
Data Access Technology 131
   JET Engine 131
   Open Database Connectivity (ODBC) 134
   Custom Driver Technology 135
Data Tools 136
   Data Manager 136
   Upsizing Tools 137
   OLE Automation and DDE 138
   Reporting Tools 138
Client/Server Features 139
   Using Indexes 139
   Using Queries 139
   Embedding OLE and Other BLOBs 140
   Transactions 141
   Null Fields 144
   `SQL PassThrough` 145
   The `Set` Object 145
   Database Connections 146

6 Object Programming Overview   147

Basic Object Programming 148
   Traditional Structured Programming 149
   Object Programming 149
   Classes 150
   Instances and Instantiation 150
   Framework 151
   Encapsulation 151
   Messages 152
   Visual Basic Object Programming 152
Advanced Object Programming 153
   Inheritance 153
   The Fragile Base Class 154
   Polymorphism 155
   Object Version Controls 155
Object Programming and Object Components 156
Problems with Objects 157
Objects in a Client/Server Environment 158

7 Visual Basic 4   159

Visual Basic Development Environment 160
Visual Basic 16- and 32-Bit Versions 161

Visual Basic for Applications 161
OLE Automation 162
    Class Modules 162
    Object Browser 163
    Visual Basic 4 Objects and Collections 163
OLE Custom Controls (OCX) 165
    Windows 95 Interface Support 166
Custom Controls and References 166
Menu and Toolbar Negotiation 168
Insertable Objects as Controls 168
Forms as Callable Objects 169
Creation of In-Process OLE Servers 169
    Making a Simulated DLL with VB 169
Data Access Engine 170
    Referential Integrity 170
    New Data-Bound Controls 171
Integrated Development Environment Improvements 172
    IDE Extensibility 172
    IDE Enhancements 173
    Creating Add-ins 175
    Resource Files 175
Language Enhancements 176
    Conditional Compilation 177
    Property Procedures 178
New Related Applications 178
    API Viewer 178
    New Data Manager 179
    Crystal Reports 181
    Visual SourceSafe Administrator and Explorer 182
    Component Manager 183
Remote Data Objects and Remote Data Control 184
Features Lacking in VB 4 184

8 Constructing a Simple Client/Server System   187

Using DDE to Demonstrate Concepts 188
    Why Use Dynamic Data Exchange? 189
    DDE Overview 191
The Server Application 193
    Server Form Setup 193
    Setting Server Properties 195
    Adding Server Code 197

    The Client Application 199
        Client Form Setup 199
        Setting Client Properties 200
        Adding Client Code 202
    Summary 206

II   Constructing a Basic Client/Server System

9   Overview of a Client/Server System   209

    Client Programs 212
        Sales Client 212
        Purchasing Client 215
        Management Reports Client 217
        Pseudo Server Client 220
    Application Tables 221
    Client Problems to Consider 223

10   Table Construction   225

    Constructing the Client/Server Tables 226
    Normalizing the C/S Tables 229
    Creating the Required Directories 230
    Creating the Tables 231
        Building the Sales Table 231
        Building the Inventory_Sales Table 234
        Building the Inventory_Parts Table 235
        Building the SalesItems Table 236
        Building the PseudoServer Table 238
        Building the Counter Table 239
        Building the Assembly Table 241
        Building the Customer Table 242
        Building the Supplier Table 244
        Building the Purchase Table 245
        Building the PurchaseItems Table 246
        Building the Location Table 247
        Building the Staff Table 248
    Visual Basic Code 250
    Summary 255

11   Sales Client   263

    Creating the Sales Client 264
    How the Sales Client Works 267
        Database Access 269
    Starting the Sales Project 270
        Creating the .INI File 271

Contents   xi

	Creating the Forms	273
	Creating the SALES.FRM	273
	Creating the CUST.FRM	288
	Creating the ITEM.FRM	295
	Creating the INVNTRY.FRM	298
	Adding Code to GLOBAL.BAS	301
	Adding Code to the SALES.FRM	305
	Adding Code to the ITEM.FRM	339
	Adding Code to the INVNTRY.FRM	342
	Adding Code to the CUST.FRM	344
	Summary	349
12	**Purchasing/Inventory Client**	**351**
	How the Purchase Client Works	355
	Database Access	357
	Starting the Purchase/Inventory Project	358
	Creating the Purchase .INI File	358
	Creating the Forms	359
	Creating the PURCHASE.FRM	359
	Creating the AUTOBILD.FRM	372
	Creating the LIST.FRM	376
	Creating the INVNTRY.FRM	379
	Creating the PART.FRM	382
	Creating the SUPPLIER.FRM	386
	Adding Code to the PURCHASE.FRM	392
	Adding Code to the AUTOBILD.FRM	427
	Adding Code to the INVNTRY.FRM	431
	Adding Code to the LIST.FRM	433
	Adding Code to the PART.FRM	437
	Adding Code to the SUPPLIER.FRM	442
	Summary	447
13	**Management Client**	**449**
	How the Management Client Works	452
	Database Access	453
	Starting the Management Project	453
	Creating the Manage.INI File	454
	Creating the Forms	454
	Creating the Manage.FRM	455
	Creating the Location.FRM	464
	Creating the Staff.FRM	469
	Adding Code to the Manage.FRM	476

		Adding Code to the Location.FRM 486
		Adding Code to the Staff.FRM 490
	Summary 497
14	**Pseudo Server**	**499**
	Starting the Pseudo Server Project 501
		Creating the .INI File 502
	Creating the Form 502
		Creating the PSERVER.FRM 503
		Adding Code to PSERVER.FRM 511
	Summary 518
15	**Execution and Functioning of the Client/Server System**	**521**
	Setup 522
		Creating the .EXE Files 522
		Putting Files in the Correct Place 523
		Creating Installation Disks 524
		Modifying the .INI Files 524
	Setting Up the System on a Network 526
	Execution 526
		Using the Sales Client 526
		Using the Purchasing and Inventory Client 531
		Creating a Purchase Order 532
		Adding Inventory to Sales or Parts 536
		Creating an Autobuild Item 537
		Autobuilding Sales Items 538
		Using the Management Client 539
		Using the Pseudo Server 542
16	**Access Security**	**545**
	Planning Database Security 546
	System Security Versus Database Security 547
		Windows for Workgroups Logon 547
		Windows 95 Logon 548
		Access Logon 548
		ODBC Access Logon 549
	Users and Groups 550
	Creating Access Accounts 553
		Access Workgroup Administrator 553
		Creating Groups 554
		Creating Users 555
		Adding Users to Groups 555
		Locking Database Objects 556

	Creating and Changing Ownership 557
	Types of Permissions 558
	Encryption of a Database 559
	Changing ODBC Options 559
Access Security from Access Basic 561
	Creating Users and Group Accounts 561
	Assigning Permissions to Objects 561
	Changing Ownership of Objects 562
	Changing and Clearing Passwords 563
	Using `CompactDatabase` to Encrypt 563
Printing a Security Report 564
Visual Basic/MS Access Security Interface 564
Modifying the Client/Server System 565
	Security on the Tables 565
	Program Logon 570
Object Security 574

III Using VBA for Client Front-Ends

17 Overview of Visual Basic for Applications (VBA)   577

Basic Languages 578
    Object Overview 578
Access Basic (for Access 2.0) 581
    Access Code Libraries 581
Visual Basic for Applications 583
    Language Specifics 583
    VBA in Microsoft Excel and Microsoft Project 590
Using OLE Automation 596
    Access Basic and OLE 597
    Word Basic Through OLE 597
    Excel Through OLE 598
    Project Through OLE 599
    Creating Objects in Visual Basic 601

18 Overview of Excel Objects   603

Excel Object Quickstart 604
    Recording an Excel Macro 604
    Creating a Form and Buttons 608
Interpreting an Object Chart 610
    Referencing the Objects 610
Excel Objects and Collections 612
    The `Application` Object 612
    General-Purpose Objects 615

	The `Workbook` Object/Collection	615
	The `Worksheet` Object	617
	The `RoutingSlip` Object	620
	The `Chart` Object	620
	Drawing Objects	621
	Built-In User Interface Objects	622
	The `DialogSheet` Object	624
	Excel Events	624
	Pasting into VB 4	626
19	**Excel Additions to the Client/Server System**	**629**
	Excel Additions	630
	Using OLE Automation	631
	Creating the Additions to the Management Client	633
	Creating the Routines	634
	Running the Export Chart Option	636
	Adding the New Form	637
	Adding the `DisplayXLChart()` Routine	638

IV Advanced Client/Server Topics

20	**Structured Query Language (SQL) Primer**	**643**
	Vendor-Specific Dialects	644
	Functions	645
	Stored Procedures and Triggers	646
	SQL Language	647
	The `SELECT` Command	647
	SQL Aggregate Functions	650
	`SELECT` with `ORDER BY`	652
	`SELECT` with `GROUP BY`	653
	The `UNION` Clause	655
	The `JOIN` Command	655
	Data Definition Language (DDL)	656
	Data Manipulation Language (DML)	656
	MS Access SQL Implementation	656
	MS Access Implementation	657
	ODBC SQL	660
	Core SQL Grammar	661
	Extended SQL Grammar	662
	ODBC Drivers	662
	SQL Server Implementation	663

21	**Upsizing to Microsoft SQL Server**	**667**
	The Upsizing Wizard	668
	Creating a SQL Server Database	668
	Creating the Device	669
	Creating the Database	669
	Setting Up an ODBC Connection	670
	Creating an ODBC Connection	670
	Upsizing the Database	672
	Preparing the Database File	672
	Beginning the Upsizing	674
	Examining the Upsized Database with Attached Tables	678
	Examining the Upsized Database with SQL Server Browser	678
	Examining the Upsized Database with SQL Object Manager	679
	Testing the Client/Server System	680
	Adding Users and Groups	681
	Granting Permissions	683
	Modifying the .INI Files	685
	Modifying the Clients	686
	Using ODBC to Port to Oracle, Sybase, and Other Database Servers	687
22	**Open Database Connectivity (ODBC)**	**689**
	Visual Basic ODBC Access	691
	ODBC Overview	693
	ODBC Administrator	694
	.INI Files	696
	Driver Architecture	697
	ODBC API	698
	Core Functions	699
	Level 1	701
	Level 2	702
	JET Engine ODBC Calls	704
	ODBC SQL	704
	Core SQL Grammar	704
	Extended SQL Grammar	705
	Using ODBC for Table Transfer	705
	Remote Data Objects	705
	The `rdoEngine` Object	706
	The `rdoEnvironment` Object	707
	The `rdoError` Object	707
	The `rdoConnection` Object/Collection	707
	The `rdoTable` Object/Collection	707

The `rdoColumn` Object/Collection 707
The `rdoPreparedStatement` Object/Collection 707
The `rdoParameter` Object/Collection 708
The `rdoRecordset` Object/Collection 708
`RegisterDatabase` 708
Upgrading the Management Client 708
Modifying the Sales Report 709

23 Object Linking and Embedding (OLE) 711

Component Object Model (COM) 714
Inheritance 715
Objects and Interfaces 716
OLE Fundamentals 719
OLE Implementation 720
Linking and Embedding 720
In-Place Activation 721
Uniform Data Transfer and Drag-and-Drop 721
Compound Files and Structured Storage 721
Monikers 722
Automation 724
Distributed or Remote OLE 724
Other Object Systems 725
Object-Oriented System Analysis and Design (OOA) 725

24 Creating an OLE Server 727

Making Pseudo Server an OLE Server 728
Creating the Class 729
Adding the Properties and Methods 730
Setting the Preferences 732
Using the Object Browser 734
Registering the OLE Server 734
Executing the OLE Server 735
Creating the OLE Client in Excel 735
Remote OLE 739
How Remote OLE Works 740
Remote OLE Applications 741
Converting the Pseudo Server 745
Designing OLE Automation Servers 748
Designing the Object Hierarchy 748
Handling OLE Errors 749
Version Control 749
OLE Registry 749
Using the Client Registration Utility 750

	Creating Remote Client Distribution Disks 751
	Using `ByRef` Versus `ByVal` 751
	OLE Remote Security 752

25 Query Builder 753
Tools Used to Construct the Query Builder 754
Overview of SQL Server 756
    Data Constructs 756
    System Administrator (SA) and Database Owner (DBO) 758
    System Tables 758
    Data Types 760
    Views 762
    SQL Indexes 763
    Transact-SQL, Stored Procedures, and Triggers 763
Laying the Foundation for the Table Builder 763
    Setting Up the Database in SQL Server 763
    Creating the ODBC Connection 768
    Creating the Table Builder Program 772
    Checking the Table 780
Creating the Query Builder 781
    Form Construction 782
    General Declarations 784
    Building the Query 784
    Suggestions for Improvements to Query Builder 786

26 Remote Client/Server Access 789
Modem (Direct to Server) Connection 791
    Modem or Serial Port Connection 791
    Future Direct Connection (TAPI and MAPI) 793
Adding Remote Access to the Client/Server System 796
    Additions to Pseudo Server 799
    Creating the Remote Client 806
    Creating the Remote Sales Client 807
Messaging 821
    Simple and Complex Messaging 823
    Messaging Interfaces 823
MAPI Architecture 827
    Simple MAPI 827
    Extended MAPI 828
    OLE Messaging 829
Visual Basic MAPI Interface 829
    MAPI Controls 830
    OLE Messaging Library Access 840

Messaging Clients and Servers 842
    cc:Mail 842
    Microsoft Mail 842
    Lotus Notes 843
    Microsoft Exchange Server 844
    Windows 95 Integrated Messaging 845
    Private Messaging and Public Messaging 846
Remote Access Service (RAS) 847
Connection Technologies 849
    WinSock 1.1 849
    WinSock 2.0 850

27 Telephony   851

An Overview of Telephone Systems 853
    Types of Telephony Systems 854
Telephony API Standards 856
    TAPI 858
    TSAPI 868
    Signal Computing System Architecture 870
    Universal Serial Bus 871
    Versit 872
Visual Basic Telephony 872

28 Security for Client/Server   873

Why Is Client/Server Security Important? 874
    What Are Security Risks and Threats? 875
What Security Standards Are Available? 878
    Internet Security 880
    Security or Integrity? 880
    Directory Services 883
    Current Operating System Security 887
    How Secure Is Windows NT 3.5? 887
    How Secure Is NetWare? 887
How Are Network Interfaces Made Secure? 888
    Passwords 888
    Database Security 889
    E-Mail Security 891
    Firewall Overview 895
    Firewall Design or Selection 895
    Planning Database Security 897
    Securing a Database 898
    Handling Security with Visual Basic 900

29	**Third-Party Tools, Utilities, and Controls**	**911**
	Help File Editors	913
	RoboHelp by Blue Sky Software Corporation	913
	VB Helpwriter by Teletech Systems	914
	Multiuser Databases	914
	Access by Microsoft	915
	Visual FoxPro by Microsoft	916
	Visual/db from AJS Publishing	916
	ROCKET (SIxBase) by SuccessWare International	916
	Components	917
	Printer and Report Components	918
	Links and Drivers	920
	VB/Link by Brainstorm Technologies	920
	Notes HiTest by Lotus	921
	Distinct TCP/IP SDK by Distinct Corporation	921
	VBSQL/DBLibrary	922
	Client/Server Developers' Kits	922
	Worldgroup by Galacticomm	922
	Mindwire by Durand Communication Network	922
	Database Tools	923
	Choreo 1.1 for VB by CenterView Software	923
	Oracle Power Objects	924
	Source Code Tools	924
	Visual Sourcesafe 4.0 by Microsoft	925
	VB/Rig Professional by Avanti Software	925
	Versions/VB by StarBase	926
	User Interface	926
	VSVBX by Videosoft	926
	VSFlex by Videosoft	927
	Spread/VBX by FarPoint Technologies	927
	LeadTools by Lead Technologies	928
	Imageknife/VBX by Media Architects	928
	Gantt/VBX by ADDSoft	928
	TrueGrid Pro by APEX Software Corporation	928
	Telephony	929
	Visual Voice by Stylus Innovation	929
	Visual Fax by Stylus Innovation	930
	VBVoice by Pronexus	930
	VBFax by Pronexus	931
	Installation Creators	931
	Install Shield by Stirling Technologies	931
	WISE Installation System by Great Lakes Business Solutions	932

Online Services 932
    Microsoft Network 932
    CompuServe 933
    America Online 933
    OLE Broker 933
The End 934

V   Appendixes

A   User Interface Guidelines   937

What Is Good User Interface Design? 938
Copy Other Programs 938
Remember to Be Consistent 939
Keep the User Informed 940
    Message Boxes 940
    Cursor Settings and Status Bars 941
Screen Layout 943
    Multiple Forms or Windows 944
    Design Flow 945
    Icons and Menu Items 947
    Tab Order 947
Help Options 948
    Help Files 949
    Context-Sensitive Help 950
    Hotspot or SHED Files 951
    Help Status Bar 952
    Tool Tips 953

B   Error Handling   955

Error Handling Routines 956
    Returned Error Processing 956
    System Error Checking 957
    Error Trapping 957
    Generating Errors 959
    Unanticipated Errors 959
    Error Events 961
Centralizing Error Handling 961
    Error Handling Dialog Boxes 961
    Simple Error Routines 962
    Error Logging 963
Client/Server Error Problems 964
    Values Out of Range 964
    Various Error Types 965
    Business Rules 965

C	**Sources**	**967**
	Books	968
	Magazines	970
	Technical Manuals	971
	Software Companies	972
	Data Access and Report Writers	972
	Graphics Utilities and Programs	983
	System Development and Integration Tools	983
	Online Support	985
D	**List of Acronyms and Terms**	**987**
	Index	**997**

Acknowledgments

A book, especially one of this size, can be written only with the help of many people. We would like to thank everyone who helped make this book possible by providing time, information, and experience.

The greatest thanks goes to the entire Rahmel family. Long nights, straining deadlines, and short tempers are often part of writing a book. They were definitely present during the writing of this one. With the help of our family, we survived. Thank you to both Marie Rahmel and Darlene Rahmel. Thanks also to David Rahmel, who lent extensive support and knowledge of networks, client/server implementations, SQL Server and Sybase implementations, and cross-platform development.

Thanks to Microsoft, who created a development environment that is a joy to work in. After the years we've spent slogging through C/C++ code, the quick and efficient creation of complete applications using VB is paradise. Also, the Microsoft Developer Network provided much of the technical information required to complete this book. We thank all the programmers, writers, and designers who constantly work to make MSDN a fantastic resource.

We'd like to thank the whole staff of Sams Publishing. This book was produced under a rigorous schedule and a dramatically changing Visual Basic landscape, so we thank them for their patience through many of the tense moments.

Thanks goes to the San Diego Visual Basic User's Group, a spectacular group of people who didn't mind answering many extensive questions. We'd like to thank all the user groups in San Diego and the people who run them. Running a user group is a tremendous amount of work and often fairly thankless, so we would like to thank these fine people who provide an invaluable resource.

Thanks to Don Murphy, Greg Mickey, George Sullivan, Jack Birchett, Dick Eger, George Helsten, Steve Wilson, the San Diego Police Department, Alex Tosheff, Bill Tosheff, Floyd Geis, Napoleon Hill, and Anthony Robbins.

About the Authors

Dan Rahmel, a product manager for Coherent Visual, lives in San Diego and has been involved in the microcomputer industry since 1978. He has a broad range of computer experience, including the ability to effectively program in eight languages (for both Windows and Macintosh); install complete Windows, Macintosh, and VAX-based systems; manage information systems; implement Geographic Information System technology; and develop pen-based computer software. He currently develops client/server systems for police departments and manages new product development for Coherent Visual's software for Apple's pen-based Newton handheld computer.

Ron Rahmel is a division manager at Science Applications International Corporation. He has more than 17 years of experience in hardware and systems design and the fabrication of components for military networking communications systems.

This is the second book coauthored by Dan Rahmel and Ron Rahmel. The first, *Interfacing to the PowerPC Microprocessor* (Sams Publishing, 1995), described both the complete workings of the PowerPC microprocessor and the numerous interfaces to which such a processor would be attached (such as PCI, 1394, parallel, serial, SCSI). This book also described PowerPC system design and the uses of PowerPC embedded processors.

Introduction

Client/server has changed the world of computing forever. The explosion of personal computers and Local Area Networks (LANs) has moved most computing power away from mainframe computers to individual desktop computers. Servers allow the information stored on these numerous desktop computers (clients) to be centralized and coordinated. This allows the power in individual personal computers to be leveraged. Client/server computing, and the concepts this field embodies, bring tremendous capability to information systems within an organization.

Visual Basic has become a leader in this revolution by providing one of the most exciting design applications available. The popularity of Visual Basic grew as the capabilities of database servers and LAN installations mushroomed. Visual Basic is at the forefront of the new application programming technology, which allows complete solutions to be created without the learning curve associated with traditional languages such as C and C++.

Visual Basic provides simplified design and rapid-application development for client/server systems. Visual Basic has long been ideal for front-end development. With the database integrated in the VB environment and access to Open Database Connectivity (ODBC), you can design and write a Visual Basic program to provide a complete application in a fraction of the time traditional developers have required. VBX and OCX components have provided compelling reasons for developers to use Visual Basic. Components are available that have substantially increased the functionality that was already included in the VB system.

In the past, Visual Basic was limited primarily to the creation of client programs. With the release of Visual Basic 4, a VB programmer can now create OLE Automation Servers. The Remote OLE system included with the enterprise edition allows Visual Basic to create a three-tier solution or network server with the same ease of implementation associated with earlier client development.

Our intention in writing this book was to provide a strategic overview of all of the technologies involved in client/server development. Not only are traditional database topics such as normalization and multiuser access covered, but also object development, Object Linking and Embedding (OLE), remote access, scaling to database servers, security, OLE automation, Dynamic Data Exchange (DDE), telephony, SQL, user interface guidelines, and many others. We have attempted to include every primary topic that we have encountered while implementing client/server systems based on Visual Basic.

How to Use This Book

This book was designed to provide a general overview of important concepts and specific code and implementation for a complete client/server system. Therefore, you can use this book best by progressing sequentially through the chapters. Concepts introduced in early chapters are built upon when the actual system is created.

We recommend that you read the chapters that detail all of the concepts inherent in designing and creating a database or client/server system.

If you're already familiar with client/server design, but unfamiliar with Visual Basic, we suggest that you also read the chapters specifically detailing Visual Basic itself.

We have included a separate chapter on the features of Visual Basic version 4 (Chapter 7). As 32-bit operating systems (Windows 95 and Windows NT) become more prevalent, organizations will convert all of their legacy applications written in VB 3.0 to the new 32-bit implementation. This chapter will help you understand what is new in Visual Basic 4. If you've been working with VB 3.0, Chapter 7 will explain the new features. If you started with VB 4, all of the features listed in this chapter will be missing from earlier versions, giving you a better idea of what must be added to or converted in legacy applications.

Part II, in which the actual client/server system is built, is progressive. Each of the clients works together on a common database. Therefore, these chapters must be covered as a unit.

Most of the other chapters are autonomous. Because they build on concepts introduced sequentially as you read through the book, the most effective way to cover the material is to read from the beginning to the end. However, most of the chapters are self-contained and may be read separately.

What This Book Covers

This book is divided into five parts. The first four parts contain chapters that describe technical concepts and Visual Basic code related to the topic.

Part I, "Overview of Necessary Visual Basic and Client/Server Concepts," covers all the concepts you should understand before attempting to implement a client/server system. Visual Basic itself is described, along with some of the features that make it an ideal development tool. Other topics include the progression of C/S systems, various system architectures, networking concepts, distributed data problems, normalization, and data consistency and concurrency. Object programming is described (detailing specific object concepts relevant to VB 4), as well as the features added to the newest version of Visual Basic. Finally, you will construct a simple set of client and server applications, using DDE to help you understand the various concepts that were described in earlier chapters.

In Part II, "Constructing a Basic Client/Server System," you will actually implement a complete client/server system. This system uses a Microsoft Access database stored on a file server that you access by constructing client programs. The Microsoft Access database used by the system will be upscaled to SQL Server later in the book, and the client programs (with a few minor modifications) will access the new data source.

Three client applications are constructed: the Sales client (which provides point-of-sale invoice entry), the Purchasing/Inventory client (which lets you create purchase orders and other inventory functions), and the Management client (which generates reports on the state of the business). You'll also build an application called the Pseudo Server, which acts as a partial server by watching the database and providing information to the other client applications.

After the system is created, you will use Microsoft Access to set security conditions so that the individual client programs can read and write only the data for which they need access.

Part III, "Using VBA for Client Front-Ends," details the Visual Basic for Applications (VBA) system built into most Microsoft Office applications. The Management client is then modified to use Excel as a reporting engine. Through VBA, the entire operation of an application can be controlled. The Management client is used to control Excel to create charts and enter data.

In Part IV, "Advanced Client/Server Topics," most of the advanced system techniques are explained. The database language SQL is described, as well as basic database server concepts. The process of upsizing the database (currently used by the client programs) into SQL Server is detailed. Once the database itself is converted to SQL Server, the client programs are modified to access the new data in two different ways: through Microsoft Access attached tables and through the Remote Data Objects in Visual Basic.

The Open Database Connectivity (ODBC) standard is explained, and basic ODBC access is demonstrated. ODBC provides an industry standard way of accessing heterogeneous data sources. The Remote Data Objects in Visual Basic dramatically reduce the difficulty of accessing ODBC.

Object Linking and Embedding (OLE) provides one of the key technologies included in Visual Basic 4: the ability to create OLE Automation Servers. The many facets of the OLE system are described. The Pseudo Server application is modified to act as both a local and a remote OLE Automation Server.

Remote access to a client/server system is often essential with the growth of geographically disparate users and portable systems. Services for this type of application are described, and the Pseudo Server client is modified to allow remote modem access to data. Also, a Remote client program is created to exchange information with the Pseudo Server addition.

Telephony, the integration of computers and telephone systems, is outlined. This field is rapidly expanding because of recent advances in the power of hardware, as well as the potential applications available when the telephony system is attached to a back-end database system.

This part of the book also explains the various security risks and threats, a vital topic in a world of distributed computing power. Security services, firewalls, encryption, and numerous other topics are covered.

The final chapter of Part IV describes several key products that can be used in Visual Basic development. The factor that makes VB one of the most cost-effective development environments on the market is the availability of a large number of third-party product additions. This chapter describes some of the most powerful tools in the field.

The four appendixes in Part V describe general topics for easy reference. Appendix A provides guidelines for user interface design. Error trapping, due to its specificity and complexity, is not included in the client applications constructed in this book. Appendix B describes how error routines are constructed and where they should be implemented. Appendix C lists resources for more information, including books, magazines, products, Internet sites, and other sources. Appendix D explains some common terms and acronyms.

Conventions Used in This Book

This book uses the following conventions:

- Notes, Tips, and Warnings, which appear in gray boxes, bring particular information to your attention.
- All code appears in a `monospace` font.
- Placeholders appear in an *`italic monospace`* font.
- When a line of code is too long to fit on one line of this book, it is broken at a convenient place and continued to the next line. The code continuation character (➥) appears at the beginning of that next line. You should type a line of code that is broken by a code continuation character as one long, unbroken line.

Client/Server Information

The client/server field is tremendously interesting. The power of personal computers now gives individual users access to significant amounts of information. By creating effective C/S systems, a designer can substantially increase the effectiveness and efficiency of an organization. Use this book to aid in creating systems that are user-friendly, powerful, and suited for the applications that users need.

With all of the technologies embraced by the client/server community, it's often difficult to keep up-to-date on important events and products that have been announced. The Internet has become a major clearinghouse of information. It provides instant access to the most current technical and product data available.

The Internet is huge, and it's often difficult or time-consuming to track down specific information. For this reason, we have set up a World Wide Web site to provide information and links to relevant client/server sites that are related to Visual Basic. Please visit our World Wide Web site at `http://www.electriciti.com/~cvisual`.

I

Overview of Necessary Visual Basic and Client/Server Concepts

1

Overview of Visual Basic

Visual Basic Development System

The Visual Basic system is a complete, integrated development environment. It includes a project-based file system, a window creator that gives double-click access to event code, automated menu building, an integrated debugger, a runtime environment, as well as access to outside features including plug-in components and the Windows API. This chapter provides a brief overview of the development system and the included utilities you will use to develop client/server applications.

Visual Basic grew from the original BASIC programming language to become a robust programming environment. With the capability to accept VBX plug-in components, the Visual Basic system, already powerful, became expandable. The further addition of the JET database engine, which allows complete database manipulation functions to manipulate a Microsoft Access database, made Visual Basic a client development tool of choice.

Microsoft added such tools as a help compiler for full online help and the Application Setup Wizard, which allowed quick and simple setup of distribution disks. These tools furthered the capabilities of enterprise deployment of an application written in Visual Basic.

Visual Basic 4 has substantially increased the viability of VB as an enterprise development tool. Team development, OLE Automation server manipulation, class creation, remote data objects, and a revised Data Manager have enhanced the system's capabilities. Now, it's possible to create full 32-bit applications with complete OLE capabilities and powerful remote data access using Visual Basic 4.

Who Should Read This Chapter?

Visual Basic is an ideal development environment for client/server and database applications. Readers of this book should already be familiar with the general use and programming of Visual Basic. This chapter will provide a general review of the Visual Basic system, as well as describe how the outside resources available can be used to produce a complete application.

We recommend, if you are a beginner-to-intermediate Visual Basic developer, that you read or at least skim this chapter. Many specifics of VB are covered that will be used throughout this book. Also, you may find many distinctions about VB and its included tools that are not immediately apparent without many hours of development time.

Although this chapter will be primarily a review for advanced users, we'd like to suggest that you glance at the tip boxes that provide general tips and checklists for particular tasks.

Visual Basic Language

Visual Basic is based on the evolving standard of Basic, which has been continually improving for almost 20 years. Because of its longevity, Basic is understood by literally millions of users.

Unfortunately, because of Basic's historical lack of power and simple implementation, the language's reputation has been that of an inferior development environment. Visual Basic is changing all of that.

Visual Basic is a structured version of Basic. This primarily means that it lacks the line numbers traditional in older forms of Basic and it also de-emphasizes the GOTO command. The GOTO command allows a program to jump instantly to another point in the executing code. This made program flow (the order of program execution) extremely difficult to follow and understand. If the program flow is difficult to follow, the program is extremely difficult and expensive to maintain. It also tends to make the program difficult to understand by anyone but the original programmer, which makes legacy applications almost impossible to maintain and dangerous to update (the new version might not work at all).

Basic is an interpreted language rather than a compiled one (like C or C++). This means that each Basic instruction is stored as an operation code, or *op-code*. An op-code is a number that represents a certain function (for example, 1 = Print to Screen, 36 = Save File, and so on.) A Basic program is a series of op-codes that execute sequentially. Each op-code is sent through the interpreter, which actually sends instructions. The instructions to the microprocessor then perform the requested task.

In comparison, C and other compiled languages turn programming code directly into microprocessor instructions (see Figure 1.1). Compiled languages take time to compile all of the separate code modules and then go through a linking phase, where the modules are linked into one complete piece of code.

FIGURE 1.1.
Basic versus C program execution.

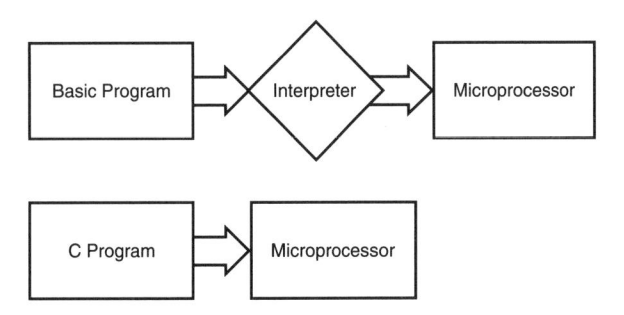

The problem with interpreted languages can be characterized in one word: speed. These languages tend to be slower than compiled languages because they have to pass through the interpreter (often called the *runtime program* or *library*) before the instructions actually execute on the processor. (See Figure 1.2.) Interpreted programs also require the presence of the interpreter program. In the past, the interpreter required a proportionally large amount of diskspace and memory when both were in short supply.

FIGURE 1.2.
Op-code execution.

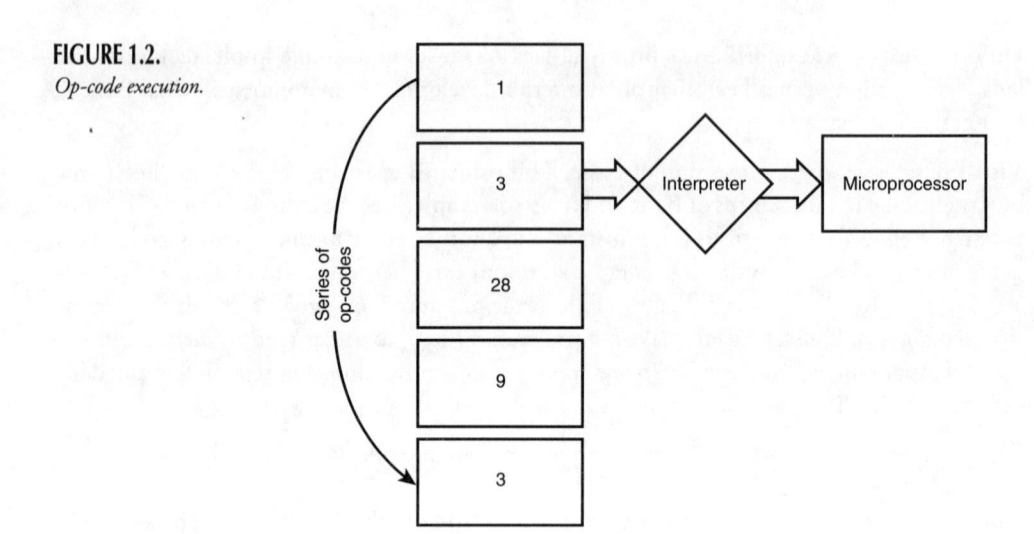

Although speed will forever be an issue, it has become less so because of the way development systems are evolving. Common processor-intensive tasks are increasingly becoming included in the operating system. To open a window, for example, a program calls a Windows routine to create and display the window. It rarely matters if it is a C program or a Basic program calling this routine. The execution time will be determined by the Windows routine, not the calling language.

Memory and disk space problems are much less of an issue than they were in the past. In the old days, when a disk could store merely 128KB, the runtime library (interpreter) would often take up 64KB to 80KB. This was a substantial percentage of disk space. Today however, disk storage and memory have dramatically increased, whereas the runtime libraries have not gotten much bigger. The Visual Basic runtime library is between 200KB and 300KB. On a hard disk of 80MB, this runtime DLL size is hardly an issue. Also, because there is only one runtime library required for all of the interpreted programs on a system to use, the size is largely inconsequential.

Visual Basic Program

Every Visual Basic program consists of a number of forms and modules. Forms hold the layout information of the window, code, and any controls that are to be displayed. Modules are files that contain only code with no visual component. Objects are memory structures that contain both basic code and variables. Objects are used to hold OLE objects, create multiple windows, or duplicate a given control with all of its properties and methods.

> **NOTE**
>
> Visual Basic has a wide variety of terms to describe a subroutine (which is essentially a delimited string of commands that are executed as a unit). In VB, a `Sub - End Sub` unit is a routine that can receive a value but does not return any. The `Sub - End Sub` pair, when found within an object, is called a method. This is traditional object-oriented terminology. A `Function - End Function` unit can receive a value and also return one.

To add to the confusion, when you double-click a control, the box shows the object and then labels the function or subroutine with a `Proc:`. (See Figure 1.3.) We assume this means procedure, which is a term often used to describe a subroutine. Throughout this book, we will use only the terms subroutine, function, and method.

FIGURE 1.3.
Proc: menu.

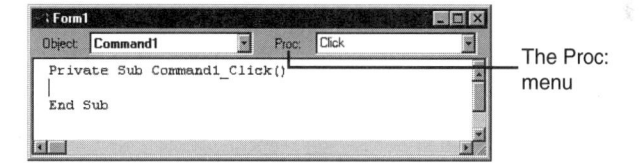

The Proc: menu

Forms (FRM and FRX) and Controls

Forms are a combination of a window, the controls it displays (such as scroll bars, text boxes and buttons), and the event code involved with the form and its controls. There are two types of form files: an .FRM file (which is a form file saved in TEXT format) and an .FRX file (which is a form saved in BINARY format). There is no functional difference between these two file types until you begin using outside programs to access your project files. (See the NOTE in the "Projects (VBP or MAK)" section that follows.)

A form is constructed by selecting a control from the Control Palette and drawing it on the form. (See Figure 1.4.) You can also automatically insert the control on the form by double-clicking its icon in the Control Palette. You can change a property across several controls by holding down the Shift key while selecting multiple controls. If you display the Properties window, then only the common fields will appear. Any change to a property affects all of the selected controls.

> **TIP**
>
> If you ever need information about one of the controls, simply click its icon on the Control Palette and press the F1 key. The Help file for that particular control will appear. This also works for most third-party VBX controls.

FIGURE 1.4.
The Control Palette.

When you double-click a control that has been placed on a form, the primary event code for that control is displayed. (See Figure 1.5.) If you double-click the form's background, the form's Load event method code will be displayed.

FIGURE 1.5.
A control's event code.

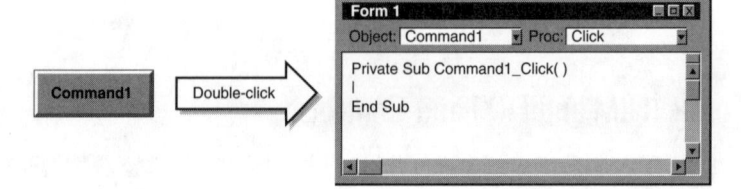

Any form-level variables should be declared in the General Declarations area. Declarations and subroutines that are in the General section of a form cannot be accessed from outside the form. The only exception to this rule is the ability to pass a variable, array, or object to a global subroutine.

> **TIP**
>
> When you change the name of a control in the Properties window, all of the code associated with that control does not automatically transfer with the name change. Any code associated with the control is put in the General subroutines section. From there, if you change the subroutine's name to the new control, the code is automatically reattached to the control.
>
> Also, if you delete a control from the screen, the code associated with it is not automatically removed. This is an excellent feature; it ensures you don't accidentally delete code when deleting a control from the screen (so-called *hidden code*). However, if you want the code deleted, make sure you enter the General subroutines area and delete any unused code that remains there. This will save disk space and compile time. It will also save confusion when you or someone else needs to update the application.

Modules (BAS)

Modules are code files. They contain code that is not associated with any form. They also include functions or subroutines that can be accessed from any other file. Variables may also be global in nature when stored in a module (.BAS) file.

Subroutines and functions may accept data passed to them by routines in other modules or in forms. A module is the place to store all of your code and variables that need to be shared. Variables need the keyword GLOBAL before their definition to make them accessible from any subroutine. Otherwise they can be used only by the subroutines contained within that module.

You may have heard of object-oriented programming (OOP), or you may even use it. OOP is a powerful new way of conceptualizing and implementing programs. One of the goals of OOP is to encapsulate all of the routines and variables of a given object (for example, a form).

In older styles of programming global variables and routines were accessible and changeable from anywhere in the program. This causes many problems. For example, one routine (we'll call it Sub A) might be using a variable to track a certain factor. Sub A then calls Sub B to perform another task. If Sub B modifies this global variable (the one Sub A is using), when execution returns to Sub A it may malfunction. By encapsulating the variables within the subroutines, Sub B cannot access and potentially harm the variables being used by Sub A. In the same way, if a global subroutine is used by many other subroutines, one change to the functioning of the routine may require all of the routines that depend on it to be rewritten.

Encapsulating the code and variables (that are required by the code) in an object means that they can work independently without fear of crashing the entire program with one change. This also makes coding much more clear, because code and variables directly associated with the object are kept with that object.

Because programming environments are moving toward object-oriented methodology, in this book we will seek to use global routines and variables only when necessary. All the subroutines and functions in this book will remain in the form that requires them unless all forms must have access to them. Programming in this way is not really a restriction, so much as a new way of approaching a project. Isolating variables and routines has great benefits for both debugging and maintenance.

Objects and Instances

In Visual Basic, most of the common items in a program are considered objects. Text boxes are objects. So are forms, scroll bars, list boxes, and other controls. An object is a structure in memory that has specific properties and, usually, associated subroutines.

A copy of an object in memory is called an instance. Installed with VB in the VB\SAMPLES\OBJECTS directory is an excellent sample project called OBJECTS.VBP. This example project creates additional instances of the same window every time you press the New

Instance button. Because a form is an object, when a new instance is created it has all of the same controls and procedures that exist in the original. This is ideal for creating an application that can open multiple documents. Each form can have routines and properties that are specific to that document. A new instance simply holds all the data important to that file.

Visual Basic lacks some of the specific requirements of a true, object-oriented language, but it follows many of the same rules and has many of the same advantages. For example, a programmer can create one prototype object on the screen and use that as a master. Additional instances can then be created, automatically retaining the same properties and behavior. Then those properties (such as the background color or screen position) can be modified to make the new instance slightly different.

Objects are becoming increasingly important. Implementation of OLE object support will soon be a dominant feature in major applications (see Chapter 15, "Overview of Application Integrated Basic Scripting"). Distributed objects are also predicted to be a major force in client/server computing (see Chapter 2, "Overview of Client/Server Concepts"). We will use many types of objects in constructing the client/server applications in this book.

Program Files

When a Visual Basic program is complete, an .EXE file can be created. The .EXE file contains all of the op-code instructions that make up your program and additional code to load the Visual Basic runtime library and begin program execution.

The simplest Visual Basic program is shown in Figure 1.6. Only two files need to be used to run the program on a machine: the program itself (.EXE) and the VB runtime library (VBxRUN.DLL). It is very rare for a VB program to consist of only two files.

FIGURE 1.6.
Simple VB program with two files.

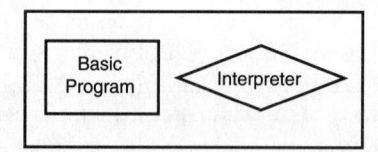

Usually, a completed and shipping program consists of numerous files, as shown in Figure 1.7. These .DLL (Dynamically Linked Library), .VBX (Visual Basic Extension), .INI (Initialize), and .HLP (Help) files are the most common types you'll include with almost any Windows programming project.

Plug-in components are one of the features that make Visual Basic so powerful. The VBX, the OCX, and the DLL are types of files called "plug-ins" that you can plug into your project to do specific things (see the section "Plug-In Components" later in this chapter). There are thousands of commercially available plug-ins that do everything from network communication to displaying toolbars.

FIGURE 1.7.

Typical VB program with many files.

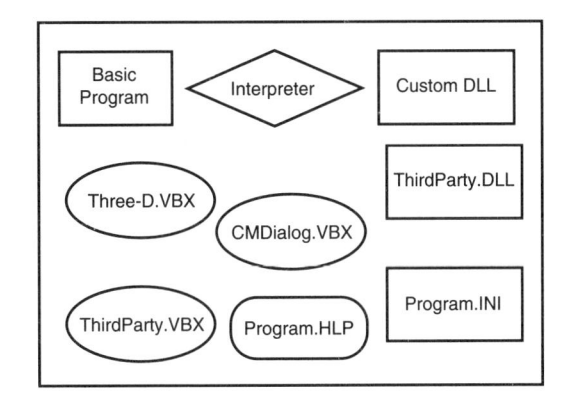

Visual Basic is an extremely powerful programming language that enables you to do nearly everything you could want to do from within Basic. However, plug-ins enable you to save time and money. On every programming project, numerous hours are used defining the problem and debugging the resultant solution. If a programmer earns $50 per hour, it doesn't take long to realize that paying $400 for a tested, commercial plug-in that does the functions your project needs is quite a bargain. Plug-ins are also often not that expensive.

Compared with traditional development environments, Visual Basic has often been known to cut development time by 75 percent on heavy user-interface applications (as most are these days). If an application has particular parts that are extremely processor intensive, one of the best ways to create the project is to use each development system's strength. You can use a C/C++ compiler, for example, to write a mathematical routine to plug in to your Visual Basic front-end program. You can create components as DLLs, VBXs, or OCXs. This provides the best of both worlds.

Event Orientation

A Visual Basic program functions by being *event-driven*. On older pre-GUI (Graphics User Interface) systems such as DOS, commands were (and still are) sent to the program through a command line or through a series of sequential menus. This made program flow extremely simple to follow. Typically, only one thing could happen at a time. For example, Menu 2 was accessible only after Menu 1 had been completed. If the `dir` command was typed in, the program (in this case, the operating system) determines which routine to call and executed the routine that printed the directory. Then it waited for another command. These user interfaces were extremely sequential; one thing followed another in a predictable way.

With the widespread use of GUI operating systems such as Windows, programming became much more complicated. At any moment, the user could have clicked with the mouse on a button, pulled down a menu, aborted a command, or typed a key. The Windows environment itself may have opened a window, refreshed part of the screen, received data from the keyboard or mouse, or any number of other events.

Programmers first attempted to handle all of the possible events with something called an event loop. The event loop received each event and routed the event and data to the proper routine. The problem was, the event loop had to be written by hand. Each new project varied slightly with the types of events it needed to receive and react to.

Visual Basic took a huge step forward by being event driven. Visual Basic provides the complete event loop, built in to the development system, as well as default routines to handle most common events. For example, when the cursor is in a text box and a key is pressed, the character is automatically inserted into the text box. (See Figure 1.8.) This saves tremendous amounts of time formerly spent on tedious details.

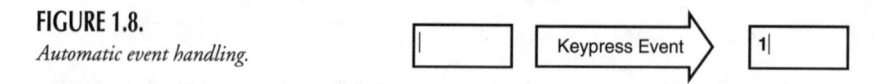

FIGURE 1.8.
Automatic event handling.

If you want to customize the application's reaction to a given event, simply customize the routine that is called when a particular event occurs. In the previous example of the key press, the key-press event might change a number in a calculation field. This means the screen must be updated. In Visual Basic, simply double-clicking the text box where the event will occur shows the code that will be executed when a change is made to the box. (See Figure 1.9.)

FIGURE 1.9.
Text box change event.

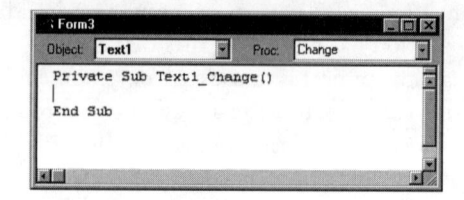

Projects (VBP or MAK)

As you probably already know, the Visual Basic development environment is based around a project metaphor. One project contains all of the files that will be used by that application. The types of files that can be included in a project include: .FRM, .FRX, .BAS, .VBX, and .OCX. The project itself is stored as a .VBP file (.MAK is the extension used by VB 3.0 projects).

The project metaphor provides an ideal way of keeping together all the files needed for an application. Files may be shared over the network for group project development. However, only one user may modify a given file at a time.

> **TIP**
>
> Any of the files in a project can be saved in binary or text-file format. The default format for saving files is binary. Although the files may be slightly larger, we highly

> recommend storing your files as text files. They are then saved as standard text files that may be opened by any text editors or the Notepad application included with Windows.
>
> Saving them in text format allows programs such as the Setup Wizard (see the section "Setup Wizard" later in this chapter) and Help-file compilers to access the data. It also enables you to do powerful search and replace functions (depending on your text editor) and you can even use macro programs to edit your program files.

A project will include all of the files that will later be "compiled" into your .EXE file. Plug-in components, it should be noted, will not compile into the .EXE. They remain separate files and must be installed along with the .EXE, runtime, and other files.

Different Versions of Basic

You may be confused by all of the different versions of Basic that are available. There is Visual Basic 3.0 Standard, Visual Basic 3.0 Professional, Visual Basic 4.0, Visual Basic for Applications (VBA), Access Basic, Word Basic, Quick Basic, Map Basic, and GW-Basic, to name a few. Many of these will be merging as time progresses, but because Visual Basic is a proprietary standard owned by Microsoft, more versions will probably appear.

The primary development environment for client/server developers is Visual Basic 4.0 Enterprise Edition. The Professional Edition contains many tools for enterprise development but lacks the remote data objects useful for attaching to remote data sources through ODBC. Visual Basic Standard Edition runs the same code but is missing many of the advanced tools such as the communications tools, the outline control, the multimedia control, and so on. Visual Basic 4.0 is the most recent version of VB. Its many new features are described in Chapter 7, "Visual Basic 4.0." The programming language itself remains largely unchanged from VB 3.0 except for the addition of object programming capabilities. Converting older software from VB 3.0 to VB 4.0 is not a difficult task.

Visual Basic for Applications is now the foundation that all Visual Basic applications are based on. Based on the Visual Basic language, it is built into Visual Basic 4.0 as well as the Microsoft Office applications such as Microsoft Excel, Microsoft Access, and Microsoft Project. It can accomplish many of the tasks that the complete VB 4.0 environment can, but it is a slimmed-down version. VBA cannot accept VBX plug-ins (although OCX-enabled applications should be able to access OCXs from VBA). VBA also has no forms or windows. Instead, communication with the user occurs through dialog boxes. VBA code cannot be compiled into a standalone application.

The VBA language, at the present time, is an excellent "Super-Macro" language (macro languages are often used in spreadsheets to duplicate common tasks). VBA can communicate with and control other applications that support OLE objects and automation. VBA programs also include the powerful capability of using the Macro Recorder, which will record actions the user does and code them in VBA. This way the user can start the Macro Recorder and do the general types of operations that are to be programmed. The VBA code is automatically created for easy examination and editing.

Access Basic, Word Basic, and Map Basic are versions of Basic found in the commercial applications: Microsoft Access, Microsoft Word, and MapInfo. These versions of Basic serve the same purpose as VBA, but they differ in some of the commands and functions available to the developer. More commercial applications will probably have their own customized dialects of Basic, as the idea of a programmable application becomes more popular and accepted.

QuickBasic and GW-Basic are the poorer cousins of Visual Basic. Not to be denigrated, these forerunners of Visual Basic run primarily under DOS, so they are compact. They lack many of the professional features required for professional development and are unsuitable for most commercial applications.

Outside Resources

One of the greatest advantages to being a Visual Basic programmer is the ability to use many resources outside the Visual Basic development environment to accomplish your programming task. These include the ability to use commercial or customized component plug-ins, the Setup Wizard (included with VB), the Shape Editor (included with VB), the Visual Basic Knowledge Base (included with VB), the Windows API (built into Windows), the Help Compiler (included with VB) and ODBC Drivers (many included with VB). These tools provide a wealth of possibilities to shrink the time it takes to develop a project, increase the number of features, and provide the ease of use required in a modern program.

Plug-In Components (DLL, VBX, and OCX)

Plug-in components are precompiled pieces of code that usually do one particular task very well. Visual Basic eXtension (.VBX) or OLE Custom Control (OCX) controls are added to your project and appear in the Control Palette. A Dynamically Linked Library (DLL) doesn't appear in the Control Palette but is individually called by your Visual Basic code.

The components can consist of protocol interfaces (such as TCP/IP extensions), API interfaces (such as the Lotus Notes plug-ins), user interface additions (such as VSVBX by Videosoft or ImageKnife by Media Architects) or client/server development aids (such as Choreo by Centerview Software). For more information on components and utilities, see Chapter 29, "Third-Party Tools, Utilities, and Controls." The CD-ROM included with this book contains many samples and demos of components.

DLLs are the simplest type of components. You must `Declare` what the access interface will be.

```
Declare Sub Scramble Lib "Puzzle.DLL" (ByVal Pieces As Integer)
```

The `Declare Sub` statement begins the declaration of a routine named `Scramble`. If the DLL returns a value, then a `Declare Function` statement must be used. The routine is stored in a DLL named `Puzzle`. It requires one integer parameter passed to it. Passing the `Pieces` variable with a `ByVal` statement makes VB pass the actual variable value instead of the variable reference. Then, the routine can be called in Visual Basic like an external function.

```
Call Scramble 5 [CR]
```

DLLs are simple to program in C, C++, FORTRAN, or other compiled languages. DLLs are ideal for simple plug-in routines such as math calculations and specific interfacing tasks. However, the DLL method is not very robust for doing complex interfacing with the Visual Basic development environment. DLLs do not provide properties that you can set from within the VB environment. They also do not include the capability to create objects that can be manipulated within the VB design environment (such as a custom list box or tab control).

VBXs and OCXs are more complicated to develop than DLLs but are extremely easy for the Visual Basic developer/component user to use. The VB developer adds the VBX/OCX to the current project. The VBX/OCX functionality can then be inserted into any window by drawing the VBX/OCX control on the form. For example, Videosoft produces a tabbed control that can be used in VB applications. If added to a project, the icon appears in the Control Palette and a tabbed control can be drawn onto the form. (See Figure 1.10.)

FIGURE 1.10.
Commercial VBX added to form.

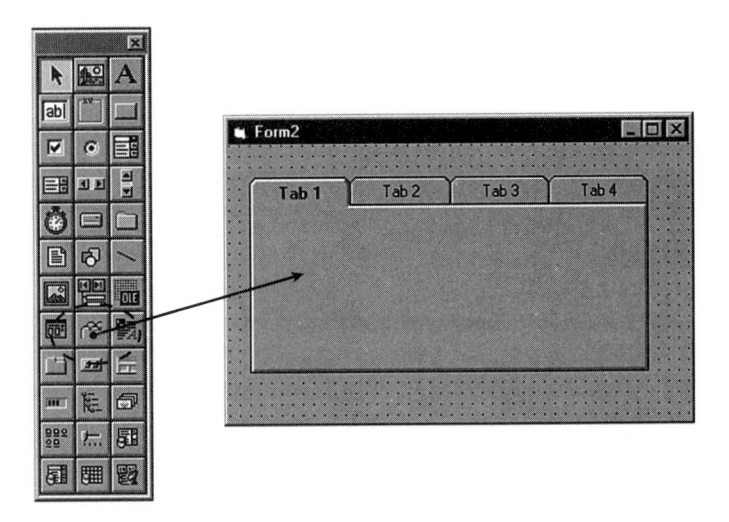

An OCX is the new, full-featured version of VBXs that will be dominant under the Windows 95 operating system. The OCX standard is more robust than that provided for VBXs. The standard was created to allow OCXs to be plugged into a number of development environments including C/C++ and applications such as MS Access (where VBXs were limited to augmenting Visual Basic). The new Windows 95 operating system supports use of the full,

32-bit processor commonly in use today. VBX controls are 16-bit based (as is the Windows 3.1 operating system). OCX controls, however, can be either 16-bit or 32-bit. This will make them faster and better able to take advantage of the processor's capabilities.

OCX controls can also be plugged into any programming language (with an IDE that supports them), including Visual Basic. They will even be usable from programs that support a macro language, such as Visual Basic for Applications. This will create an even broader market of available commercial controls.

The dominant area of component plug-ins is the commercial market. There are numerous components available for many of the most common tasks. For example, adding a print preview to your application (like those found in Microsoft products) would normally be expensive and time-consuming (if not completely impractical). You can, however, simply purchase a component that plugs into your project and gives you complete print-preview capabilities. You merely send the print commands to the Preview window, and the control does the rest! Visual Basic has created the first viable component market.

Another active area is the creation of customized plug-ins for a particular task. For example, if you needed to interface with a peculiar old mainframe or a specialized piece of medical equipment, you could create a customized interface component. This component might exchange information with the device on a low level, reading and writing data in a particular way.

This customized plug-in may be written in compiled C or C++ for speed or compiled FORTRAN if intense mathematical calculations are required. You can then use Visual Basic to write your complete program and simply call the interface component when information needs to be sent or received.

> **WARNING**
>
> You may include .VBX and .DLL files in your program directory, but this is not recommended. When the Visual Basic runtime executes, it first looks in the \WINDOWS\SYSTEM directory for the plug-in files used by your product. Therefore, if an older or perhaps incompatible version exists in the \WINDOWS\SYSTEM\ directory, it will be used.
>
> This could cause many potential problems for your application. We, therefore, recommend that your application installs to the \WINDOWS\SYSTEM\ directory.

Windows API

An API (Application Program Interface) is a generic way to interact with a given program. Essentially, an API exposes to the outside world the levers that cause a program to function. For example, you create a program to draw a square on the screen. You then compile the program, but you also provide an API for it. Through the API, other programs can call your square-drawing routine to draw squares where they want. The Windows API exposes routines such as event handlers, window handling, shape drawing, and other subroutines built into Windows.

The Windows API allows any programming language to pass parameters and execute routines built into the operating system. For example, to open a window, a program can call the `CreateWindow()` function, which will tell the operating system to create a window. There are hundreds of API functions available for the VB Developer to call.

Visual Basic normally masks the API calls for you by providing simpler commands (such as .Show to display a window) that are closely integrated with the Visual Basic environment. Windows API calls, generically, are called with C-based parameters. These can often differ from standard Visual Basic variables, so conversions sometimes must occur. With Visual Basic commands, this is not a worry of the programmer. Most conversion and most error trapping is done in the background by the VB language.

However, by simplifying the command set and shielding the user from complexity, Visual Basic also cuts off access to some complex but powerful functionality. Therefore, Visual Basic enables you to directly call the Windows API. This gives a Visual Basic programmer as much power as a C programmer, but it also increases the complexity of programming and the possibility of a lethal crash.

> **NOTE**
>
> When running in Visual Basic, the environment is well protected; seldom do you have a General Protection Fault (GPF). When an API call is used, however, the program steps out of the protective VB shell, and the chances of catastrophic failure are much greater.

Most VB programs, therefore, use traditional VB commands where they are available and then use the Windows API to access powerful functions missing in VB. Windows API functions are most often placed in a code module. Each API must be Declared. These declarations can be found using the API Viewer application. For example, to call the `CreatePolygon` API function, declare the function like this:

```
Declare Function CreatePolyPolygonRgn Lib "GDI" (lpPoints As POINTAPI,
  lpPolyCounts As Integer, ByVal nCount As Integer,
  ByVal nPolyFillMode As Integer) As Integer
```

To call the function, you must pass the required parameters:

```
hrgn% = CreatePolygonRgn(thePoly(0), NumCoords%, ALTERNATE)
```

This notation may seem foreign and slightly cryptic to a Visual Basic programmer, because it is. Visual Basic is made to be simple and understandable. If you do any type of advanced programming, however, you will eventually have to make at least some API calls.

Help File Compiler

Help files are one of the great bonuses included in the Windows system. If you've ever used the online help in Visual Basic, your word processor, or your spreadsheet, you know how convenient this help-at-your-fingertips can be. You can do searches for keywords, click on a highlighted word and have it give you more information, or even see a diagram or other nontextual object. Microsoft built the Help file engine into the Windows operating system. This means that any application can include a Help file complete with hypertext links. The help can be accessed with only a few lines of code, so it is economical to implement a robust Help system.

Visual Basic includes a Help Compiler so you can create a complete Help file to include with your program. Pressing the F1 key in most programs shows you context-sensitive help. This means that help is shown for the screen or the control that is currently displayed or selected. Visual Basic even includes a `HelpContextID` property in most of the Controls (as well as for each form) so you can easily implement this feature.

The Help Compiler is actually run from DOS and is used to compile an .RTF file that has been formatted in a particular way. You can read about creating the .RTF file in your Visual Basic manual, or you can get a Microsoft Word template to create Help .RTF files (see the section "Online Access" in Appendix C, "Sources"). Creating the Help file by using a word-processor template can be extremely complex and time-consuming.

We highly recommend you purchase a Help file creator program. There are many commercial and shareware versions available. These programs provide a complete user interface that automates the creation of a Help file, greatly simplifying its construction. These Help file creator programs range in price from $30 to $500. They also collapse the time required to create the Help file, giving you more time to ensure that your Help file is thorough and clear.

> **TIP**
>
> Choosing a Help file creator seems to be largely a matter of personal choice. It also depends on the intended application of the Help file. Here are some of the primary options you will want to look for when looking for a help file creator. You may not need many of these options, but you can determine whether the program provides them in case you need them at a later time:
>
> - Can you save the finished document to a word processor? This saves numerous hours if your Help file is also to be the basis of your program's manual.
> - Can the program insert or imbed bit-mapped graphics?
> - Can the program insert and reference hot spots or hot-spot files (often referred to as .SHG or SHED files)?
> - Can the program scan a VB project and create topics for all the major forms and controls?

> - Can the program generate a Visual Basic file for inclusion in your project that automates the context-sensitive help?
> - Can the program do multiple fonts and sizes on a single line (like a word processor), or are you limited to one style per paragraph?
> - Can the program do multiple columns?
> - Can you insert or imbed multimedia files (.WAV, Video for Windows, .AVI, or MIDI files)?
> - Will it automatically generate an index or a glossary?
> - Does it have a spelling checker?
> - Can you test individual pieces without compiling the whole Help file?

Hot Spot Editor

Included with Visual Basic is a program for creating images with hot spots. The Hot Spot Editor lets you import a bit map and place a rectangle of "hot spots" on it. These hot spots, when clicked, can jump to another part of the Help file. This type of linking is commonly known as *hypertext*.

For example, you could take a screen shot of your application. After loading the screen-shot bit map into the Hot Spot Editor, you can place a hot spot over each menu item as well as each window. You can then assign a hot spot a context ID. When the user brings up the Help file, he or she can click various parts of the bit map, which will automatically jump to the associated part of the Help file. Clicking a menu, for example, could jump to a complete description of the menu and all of its items.

The hot-spot files can contain any bit maps including maps, screen shots, diagrams, spatial layouts, and so on. This enables your Help file to be truly multimedia. You can use words, pictures, and sound to help users understand the client/server program that they must use.

You can also call the Help program to show any topic at any time. For example, you might include a Help button on a dialog box. When the user clicks on the button, simply call the Help engine to display information on that dialog box.

Setup Wizard

As a client/server developer, you will probably need to distribute your client application to a number of users. If you have more than a handful of computers to install the program on, installation can be tedious and expensive when done by hand. A typical program has a number of files that must be placed in different folders (or also known as directories).

To ease the task, Microsoft has included the Setup Wizard. This will create one or more install disks (depending on the number and size of the files) to copy all of the files used by the program into the correct directories. The install program that the Setup Wizard generates is similar to the setup programs you're probably already used to for installing Visual Basic, Word, Excel, Quattro Pro, or many other programs.

You'll want to use the latest version of the Setup Wizard. If you think your version might be older, download the newer version from any of the sources listed in Appendix C, "Sources." Microsoft is constantly removing bugs and adding features to this program.

NOTE

When we began developing in Visual Basic, we heard nothing but bad things about the Setup Wizard from other developers. The Setup Wizard is a very basic implementation of a setup program, but it does its simple job very well. If you need extra features the program lacks, you can modify it yourself as described later in this chapter, or you can purchase a commercial program (see Chapter 29, "Third-Party Tools, Utilities, and Controls").

TIP

When shopping for a commercial program, check to see if it has some of these features. Many of these features may not be important to you at the present time, but you should check in case you'll need them in the future:

- Compression of imaged files
- An UnInstall program (for the user to uninstall your program)
- Billboards (the screens that give product information on the screen during install)
- Does it scan your project file (for automatic file inclusion)?
- Does it create one .EXE (for uploading to online services) or does it use many files? Multiple file installs are preferable for disk-based installs, whereas a single .EXE is much better for online downloads.
- Does it display a ReadMe file?
- Does it define file groups and prompt the user for file grouping?
- Does it provide name and serial-number registration?

The Setup Wizard will take you step by step through creating installation disks. Before you begin, make sure you have several blank formatted disks handy (it will not format or erase files for you). Also, make sure you have saved your files in text-file format. The Setup Wizard can create the install disks if your files are in binary-file format, but it cannot scan the files for information it might need.

The actual install program that is written to the floppy is a VB program (which uses a compiled program to load it). You can, therefore, modify the SETUP program to do nearly anything you could want (including displays of billboards, folder creation, and so forth). You have two choices: you can modify the installation program for the one program you're installing, or you can modify the master file so that all new installations will be created using the new features you've added.

> **TIP**
>
> Before making any changes to the setup project, make sure to make a backup copy of all the setup project files. If you make any mistakes or simply want to reuse the original installation files, you can copy these from your backup files. You might create a directory named SETUPBAK and copy all of the files in the SETUP1 directory into it.

Modifying the Program's Installation Program

First, run Setup Wizard and create the install disks for your program. After you have created the installation disks, everything is ready for you to begin. The Setup Wizard, when creating the installation setup file, automatically runs Visual Basic to modify the setup project for the parameters that you requested. Therefore, the last project VB loaded was the setup program.

If you now double-click Visual Basic and click the file menu, #1 (or the most recent file accessed) should say \SETUPKIT\SETUP1\SETUP1A. If you click this project, the installation project opens, and you'll see that the project includes four forms and two modules. You can make any changes to any of the files that you want.

For example, maybe you want to change the application title it displays in the top-left corner of the window during the installation. If you view the code of SETUP1A.FRM and look in the General Declarations section, you'll see the APP NAME variable. You can change this to any string you want. You might change it to:

```
Const APPNAME = "Client Installation Program"
```

Now select Make EXE... under the File menu to save the program. You'll now have to compress this .EXE and copy it over the general .EXE on your installation disk. On the installation disk, the setup file is stored in compressed format.

To compress the file, return to DOS and at the standard C:> prompt type

```
COMPRESS C:\VB\SETUPKIT\SETUP1\SETUP1A.EXE [CR]
```

This compresses the .EXE file using the COMPRESS program included with DOS. The compress program simply adds an underline to the last character in the extension to show that it is compressed (SETUP1A.EXE is now SETUP1A.EX_). Now copy this compressed file to your first installation disk. Type

```
COPY C:\VB\SETUPKIT\SETUP1\SETUP1A.EX_ A:\ [CR]
```

Use this as the master, and copy as many installation disks from it as you require. One note: The next time you run Setup Wizard, any change you've made to the SETUP1A will be lost. For this reason, you may want to alter the master setup file.

Modifying the Master Installation Program

You may want to add some features to the master setup form so that all the installation disks you make have those features. This is accomplished by making changes to the SETUP1.VBP project in the \SETUPKIT\SETUP1\ directory.

Use Open Project... in the File menu and open SETUP1.VBP. In this project you will find several files, as shown in Figure 1.11.

FIGURE 1.11.
SETUP1 project files.

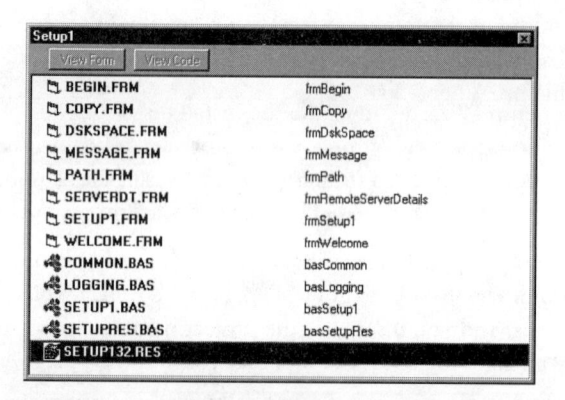

We recommend you don't make any complex changes to the project. Many simple changes can be made that will greatly enhance the look and usability of the install. You can alter the groups created at the Start menu (or Program Manager) level or simply include a tiled background bit map of your company logo. When you're finished modifying the project, save all of the changes. This is the project that will be duplicated any time the Setup Wizard creates new installation disks.

> **WARNING**
>
> Any changes you make to the setup project could potentially harm the installation process. Therefore, make sure you test your installation disks on a machine that doesn't have your program currently installed before you widely distribute the installation.

Crystal Reports

Crystal Reports is a report-generating piece of software included with Visual Basic. The included edition is somewhat limited, but it does enable you to generate reports from any connected database file.

If you begin developing applications using the Crystal Reports OCX, there is a powerful upgrade available. Crystal Reports Professional will handle almost any database-reporting needs.

VB Knowledge Base and Microsoft Developer's Network

Included with your Visual Basic Development System is a file called Knowledge Base (KB). This Help file contains technical notes, tips, programming suggestions, bug reports, and general help for developing applications. The Knowledge Base is updated nearly every month with new topics and help, so the version you received with VB will almost certainly be out of date. The most recent version is available at the download sites listed in the Appendix C, "Sources." Make sure you get the newest version!

Often a programmer spends hours reinventing the wheel. KB provides the built-up experience of thousands of programmers over several years. If you're experiencing a problem, the odds are good that someone else encountered it before you. The KB holds many answers to these common problems. When you download it, beware—it's huge! The unindexed version is around 2MB compressed, and the indexed version (which we recommend because you can do searches for topics) is around 4MB at the time of this writing. The KB is an essential source of information.

Another vital source of information is the Microsoft Developer's Network. The program costs between $500 per year (for level 2-Professional Development) and $1,200 (for level 3-BackOffice development) for a subscription to the network. It is worth every penny. For the level 2 membership, you receive more than 10 CD-ROMs of technical information and operating systems. This is over 6.5GB of information. This includes copies of all the Windows operating systems as well as numerous drivers and Software Development Kits (SDKs). The level 3 membership includes all the applications and support kits for BackOffice development (such as SQL Server, Mail Server, NT Server, and so on).

Using these CDs, you can discover nearly everything you need to know about your development platform. Once again, if you are doing professional client/server development, these developer programs are a must.

2
Overview of Client/Server Concepts

Client/server design is beginning to dominate all forms of network computing. Since local area network (LAN) implementations have become standard in the business community, people have sought new and more effective ways to share resources. Current client/server systems can share everything from data to processing power, distributing the responsibility for processes and data integrity to the software and hardware of both the client and the server.

The most commonly used client/server systems are currently database models. Usually, either a file server is used to facilitate multiuser access to a database file, or an actual database server is used to allow individuals within an organization to centralize and share data. Databases will continue to be the focus of most client/server efforts in the coming years. Therefore, database design methodology is crucial to the understanding of client/server systems. Database rules and design concepts have been evolving for more than 20 years.

Structure

All client/server systems can be divided into three parts: the client, the middleware, and the server. (See Figure 2.1.) This diagram is the model for the general framework for client/server systems in this book. Every client/server model can be defined by this diagram, which you can use as a conceptual tool for understanding any client/server system.

FIGURE 2.1.
The client-middleware-server diagram.

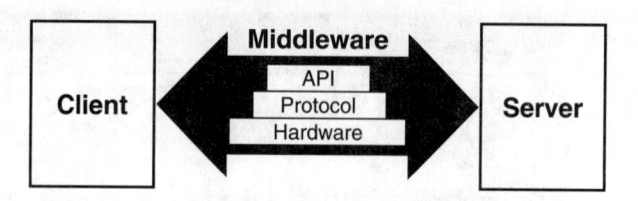

Client typically refers to a user front-end piece of software, which often uses a graphical user interface (GUI). The term client can also be used to refer to the particular machine accessing the system, or even the driver used to communicate with one or more servers.

Middleware sits between the client and the server and is often transparent to the user. Middleware is usually a combination of the three layers shown in Figure 2.1: hardware, protocols, and APIs. *Stacking* middleware means that several compatibility layers are used in unison to allow communication between the client and the server.

The *server* is most often the centralized program or machine. There are usually many clients for each server. A server can exist as one of many types: file server, database server, object server, and so on. Often, multiple server programs run on one server machine; for example, a file server, a mail server, and a SQL database server can all run on a single machine at the same time.

These three pieces of the client/server system can become extremely complicated, especially when the program definitions become blurred. In many situations, each machine is both a client and a server. (See Chapter 8, "Constructing a Simple Client/Server System.") In a peer-to-peer network, this is exactly the case. Many people think of the slash mark (/) in the term "client/server" as referring to middleware. This might make it easier for you to understand the model.

Client

Most of a user's time is spent interacting with a client program with a graphical front end. The client program hides the more complex parts of the client/server interaction and lets the user focus on finding a solution or completing a task. Building client programs is the primary professional use of Visual Basic.

A client does certain processing on the client hardware (such as displaying reports and simple calculations) but distributes difficult and specialized tasks to the server. For example, the client can request data from the server. The client then holds onto the data from the server and allows the user to do such things as search, graph, import, and otherwise manipulate the data. Also, if the client is constructed to do so, it can allow the user to modify the data. Sometimes the data is modified merely for "what if" purposes and is stored in a client-specific file (or deleted when it is no longer needed). The client may also send the updated data to the server and request that the main storage is modified to reflect the changes made by the user.

Client programs usually have a back end that the middleware plugs into. The *back end* is a common way of accessing the middleware (usually an API) that allows a single programming environment in which the client exists (for example, Visual Basic) to communicate with various pieces of middleware (for example, ODBC).

Middleware

The middleware between the client and the server is the most difficult and complex part of the client/server interaction. The term *middleware* is generally used to refer to the software that enables the client and the server to communicate. Often referred to as *glue*, this layer converts between one layer and another. Middleware is usually "stacked" with several layers and protocols used simultaneously. For example, for a VB client to communicate with a SQL server, the middleware involved might include WinSock, a TCP/IP stack, ODBC, and an ODBC driver.

Middleware is often transparent to the user and consists of a series of drivers or programs. As an example from the real world, a language interpreter could be thought of as a type of middleware. The interpreter, for example, might speak both English and German, allowing a person who speaks English to communicate with someone who speaks German. To further use this example, imagine that the interpreter doesn't speak German but rather English and French. Another interpreter is required who can speak French and German. Translation now must go through two interpreters (stacked middleware) for communication to occur. Each additional interpreter (piece of middleware) is "stacked" on top of the other one.

Now, for a client/server example, imagine that a mail server has a message for a user. The mail server must send the message over the local area network (LAN) to the client mail program. First, the server program calls an API. (See Figure 2.2.) In this case the API called is MAPI (Messaging Application Program Interface). There are literally thousands of standard APIs for everything from mail to video serving. Sometimes APIs are stacked on top of other APIs. In this case, the MAPI API sets up a connection using the protocol part of the stack.

FIGURE 2.2.
Messaging diagram.

[Diagram: Client ⟷ Middleware (MAPI / Named Pipes/TCP/IP / Thin Ethernet Cable) ⟷ Mail Server]

The protocol in this example is Named Pipes over TCP/IP (two protocols, one stacked on the other). The protocol layer defines the common language the client machine and the server machine use over the network. The protocol layer may consist of many different protocols translating each other. One form of protocol can even be sent over an incompatible network using a technique known as *encapsulation*, where one protocol is stored within another. (See Figure 2.3.)

FIGURE 2.3.
Packet encapsulation.

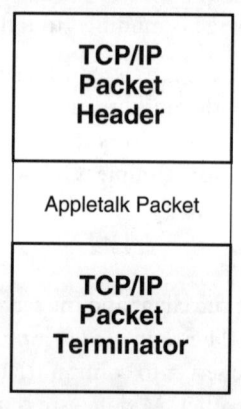

[Diagram: TCP/IP Packet Header / Appletalk Packet / TCP/IP Packet Terminator]

Using the MAPI API layer and the protocol layer, the mail server is able to send the message to a PC on the network that uses compatible middleware (MAPI capable and TCP/IP aware) for a client mail program to receive mail.

For better understanding of the client/server world, we include *hardware* at base of the middleware stack diagram shown in Figure 2.1, shown previously. Hardware is a factor that is largely assumed or implied by various descriptions of client/server systems, but it is of crucial importance to system designers. Hardware (cards, cabling, and interfaces) determines the throughput, security, and reliability of the client/server connection.

In terms of throughput, for example, a long, twisted-pair cable might not provide the bandwidth needed to use real-time multimedia servers. In terms of security, there is a world of difference between a point-to-point, fiber-optic line and a digital modem cellular link. The way system updates are verified, aborted, and resent depends largely on the hardware foundation over which the middleware connects the two (or more) parties. We have included hardware in this diagram to help you realize that it is an important factor to consider when designing your client/server system.

The hardware layer is always at the bottom. It can consist of the actual cabling as well as the electrical specification standards required for compatibility. For example, a TCP/IP packet can be transmitted over a standard ethernet coaxial cable or routed over a phone line via a modem. Multiple types of hardware might be used by any one transaction; for example, the packet could move through a network, over a phone line, and onto another network. The hardware layer, when described, usually consists of the type of material over which the signal is sent (coaxial, twisted-pair, fiber, and so on) and the electrical tolerances for correct transmission.

Middleware exists to enable different types of software or hardware to communicate effectively. It is often extremely expensive in resources to communicate with an uncommon type of device or software. Middleware can provide a common interface bridge to the uncommon interface.

Middleware does create certain performance penalties—each translation requires additional time and processor cycles. Middleware does, however, provide broad connectivity among heterogeneous systems, and you can always purchase additional pieces of middleware to plug into the back end for added capability with little or no additional programming.

Server

A server usually handles complex and calculation-intensive tasks. The term *server* is most often used to refer to a specific hardware machine running a server software program that responds to requests submitted over a network. The server's job is to process information and commands. For example, a database server receives requests for data from various clients, sends resultant sets of data to clients, makes updates to relational databases, and other various tasks.

A server rarely has a sophisticated user interface because most of its interactions are with other programs. This interaction usually occurs through its back end, its exposed interface for exchanging information. Most commands come through some type of communication link, network, or middleware. Typically, the only time the server has interaction with a user through the front end is during setup, configuration, and transaction monitoring. There are generally many clients for each server.

Examples of simple, single-machine servers include DDE servers, OLE servers, graphics servers, and various database engines. Common file servers include Netware, Windows NT, and UNIX. Database servers include Microsoft SQL Server, Sybase, Oracle, and Informix.

Server machines usually have a great amount of random access memory (RAM), so calculation is speeded. Also large disk storage capabilities are required to store centralized information and faster processors than the average desktop machine in order to handle excess processing loads. Servers are now beginning to include multiple processors. If these processors can work together, usually with the coordination of the operating system, the system is called a symmetrical multiprocessing (SMP) system. Servers, such as database servers, that take advantage of SMP technology are called *scalable servers*.

Progression of Client/Server Systems

The implementation of client/server systems can confuse any programmer and system integrator. Client/server systems are described in many specific ways. We have often heard people describe a particular system as "not *really* a client/server system" or "not a *true* client/server system." The reason for arguments over what a client/server system is, is largely historical. The definition of client/server systems has evolved slowly as new products have entered the market and new standards have been agreed upon. (See Figure 2.4.) The definition of client/server architecture expands as the capabilities of the systems increase. Therefore, what is considered cutting edge today in client/server applications will be considered rudimentary tomorrow.

FIGURE 2.4.
A timeline of the evolution of servers.

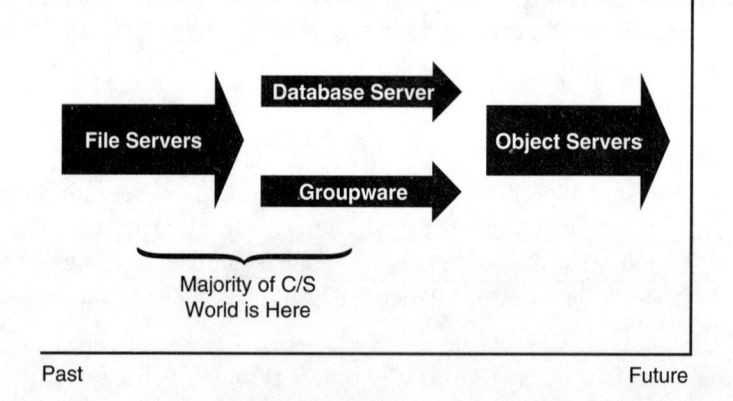

Currently, file-serving client/server implementations dominate the network world. Small as well as huge companies have embraced file sharing as a necessary business tool. Database servers and groupware are the most rapidly growing markets. With the falling expense of powerful servers and the increased need to share information, database servers and groupware provide the tools necessary for widespread effective client/server implementation.

File Server

As you can see in Figure 2.4, the primary notion of the function of a client/server program has been evolving. First, nearly all servers consisted of file-sharing servers, which allow many different machines on a network to upload files to a central server that can then be accessed by other users. On the DOS platform, this means that through software drivers another "virtual" drive is added to your system (such as N:).

File servers are still the dominant use of servers in small to medium size organizations. Many people can use this common network drive to access and update a stored database. Features such as record locking were added to databases to facilitate the use of a single database by multiple users. The client/server system we construct in Part 2 of this book is just such a system. It uses a network shared volume and a multiuser database so that all of the clients can access and update the database.

Database Server

As the use of multiuser databases became widespread and the server hardware became more powerful, companies began developing database servers. With file sharing, a file server can run on a central server machine and grant access to files and directories. When the user requests a copy of a file, the file server sends it to the client's machine.

Database servers run a server program that keeps all of the database tables in a common format, stored on the server machine. The client sends a request (for a query or update, for example) to the database server, and the server executes the request. The most dominant type of database servers are those based on the SQL language.

The database server market is one of the fastest growing market segments. Almost all large companies and institutions have some type of database server installed on their LANs or on bigger machines (VAX or IBM, for example).

> **NOTE**
>
> DB2 is a database server sold by IBM and is based on the SQL search engine. DB2 does not refer to dBase II or any of its descendants (such as dBase III and dBase IV). This is a common misunderstanding that occurs when the microcomputer and the database worlds meet. Please remember to clarify this when talking to someone unfamiliar with the database world—especially when referring to DB2. This will help prevent confusion and misunderstanding.

Groupware Server

With the rise of database servers also comes the rise of groupware applications. *Groupware* is a loose category in the client/server world that describes programs that are able to coordinate groups of documents or information over a network. For example, if a group of users is working together to publish a book, many types of documents might be required, and the group might need to interact and share information. Using groupware, the team can use the network to keep the CorelDRAW files, the MS Word files, and the CAD drawings together in a group, even if they exist on separate machines. The group can also use the groupware e-mail to track the progress of the project.

Currently most groupware applications are *document centric*, they coordinate various files stored on different machines around the network. Applications are beginning to develop that use specific API engines. This gives the user publishing capabilities for individual elements in a document. For example, if the head of a division needs the ongoing spending figures for a particular project from the various people working on it, groupware can publish the cells in a spreadsheet that each general manager is required to keep. The division manager can then input these particular cells.

You might ask, "Why not just keep all the necessary information in a central database so that data can be coordinated and easily accessed?" Here are a couple reasons why groupware should be used instead of a central database. First, it is difficult for a database to store all of the different file formats for convenient access. For example, how can a Visio drawing file be placed in a database? It is possible but inconvenient—it would have to be removed again to be used or edited.

A second reason is the ad hoc nature of groupware. Many projects have to be put together quickly, and a team might only exist for the duration of the project. The overhead time involved in setting up an accurate database, normalizing it, and then training the individual users can be tremendous. With groupware, people can share the information from the programs they already use in a format that is usable by all members. Additionally, groups can be set up, modified, altered, and eliminated in a very short time.

The most popular package in the groupware market is Lotus Notes. Notes has wide cross-platform support including Windows, OS/2, Unix, Macintosh, and other platforms. For extensive information on Lotus Notes, see Chapter 29, "Third-Party Tools, Utilities, and Controls."

Microsoft Exchange was in beta testing at the time of this writing. The first version appears to have a lot of potential. If your client/server development focuses on Microsoft-based installations, such as MS Office, BackOffice, VB, and so on, then there are compelling reasons to use Microsoft Exchange, given its close integration with the Windows and Windows NT operating systems. Cross-platform support, however, does not look to be available anytime soon.

Workflow Groupware

Workflow groupware is an increasingly common client/server category. Workflow uses other programs, such as groupware, to automate and monitor the progress of a particular project or group. For example, to get approval for a new budget, the budget might have to pass through many individuals or groups, to be approved at each stage before continuing to the next. With workflow applications, a set of documents can move through the organization, directed by user-defined rules and routes. Workflow analysis software can observe bottlenecks and other problems that can be examined and remedied. The same process can be used for designing a building, building a bridge, monitoring a software project, and so on.

Object Servers

Many watchers of the computer industry are predicting that *object servers* will become the dominant type of server in the next decade. An object server treats data, pictures, database objects, and procedures in nearly the same manner. Because each object is somewhat self-contained, a client can request a download or execution of a particular object from the server. The object has information about itself contained in its data; therefore, each object "knows" how to react to a command or request.

While this is an extremely simplified explanation, the interchangeability of objects is the strength of the object server. A single object server can handle multimedia serving (video and audio), database access, file sharing, mail, routines, and any other piece of data that can be encapsulated within an object.

The world of object standards can be extremely confusing. Standards are based on an object model which defines the format of the object itself. Microsoft has Component Object Model, or COM, while IBM and Apple support System Object Model (SOM). After an object model has been defined, additional standards for the access, activation, and storage of the objects that comply with these models are used (such as OLE and OpenDoc). There is then a third set of standards for object servers to use to broker objects, such as CORBA, DSOM, or Distributed OLE, over the network. For more information on these various aspects of objects, see Chapter 23, "Object Linking and Embedding (OLE)."

Object servers are not extremely popular right now because of the tremendous amount of network traffic and server-processing overhead involved with implementing them. They also require development environments and operating systems to interact with objects. Most of the operating systems and development environments currently only do so in a marginal fashion. Some form of object servers will likely be dominant in the future. When such an object server is available and what it will look like is difficult to say. The amount of data a network can handle is increasing, but new features, such as live video feed, quickly use up the bandwidth. Objects can also be difficult to coordinate over wide area networks such as the Internet. We'll have to wait and see.

> **NOTE**
>
> Visual Basic 4.0 has provided a dramatic step in the direction of object-based network systems. However, Remote OLE is extremely resource intensive on both the client and server machines at this time. With business only now beginning to widely endorse database servers and groupware application, industry adoption of object standards remains a ways off.

Other Servers and Server Applications

There are numerous other types of servers available, including report servers, mail servers, time servers, video servers, calendar servers, image servers, audio servers, and others. Many of these servers are either highly specialized or act as integrated functions included with other servers.

Specialized servers such as these are becoming less common. Because much of the overhead for building and implementing a server is the interface and API specifications, including additional functions such as these into existing servers is a fairly easy task. Groupware has also drained the market of the need for specialized servers—grouped documents and automated processes can often accomplish the same tasks.

Client/Server Division of Labor

The client and the server are designed to divide the processing workload. For example, a server is perfect for intense processing when a large number of shared resources must be brought together. A client, on the other hand, can do most of the processing specific to the user's needs, such as drawing a pie chart from collected data.

The division of labor facilitated by a client/server system is the great advance over the centralized processing of mainframe-based systems. Substantial processing power exists in each desktop computer, but the requirement of specialized processing and data centralization remains. Client/server methodology requires responsibilities to be divided between the client and server machines.

Server Responsibilities

The server centralizes data and responses to client commands and queries. Because the data is centralized at the server, the server is traditionally responsible for complete data backup and archiving, which can be accomplished by using a tape drive (the most common method) or a synchronize utility.

A server can use replication to ensure data security. Replication allows multiple data sources to synchronize and coordinate information. This allows a mirror of existing data to be kept in several different geographic locations. To accomplish replication, data at each of the mirror sights must be able to coordinate the individual data sets.

Data Coordination

The server is also responsible for data coordination. When a client/server setup is created, the existence of multiple copies of the same data must be tightly controlled. In the old days of master/slave systems using mainframe and dumb terminals, this was never a problem, because all data resided on the mainframe. In the client/server world, the client applications can download subsets of one or more tables, modify them, and then upload them to the server for updating, which creates problems with data concurrency and data consistency (see Chapter 4, "Overview of Database Concepts").

Stored Procedures

Lately there has been a push to increase the use of stored procedures by servers. *Stored procedures* are routines that stay native on the server and are executed when particular database conditions occur or when they are called.

There has been increasing interest in putting business rules as stored procedures on a central server. For example, in a traditional point-of-sale system, if an individual sale is higher than a specified amount (let's say $5,000) then the customer's credit is checked. Traditionally, each client program checks each sale to see if the amount is over $5,000. However, if the accounting department decides the cutoff should be at $7,000, all of the individual client programs have to be modified.

In this example, if the business rules are put online and can be called at the server to check the limit, then the business rule routine is the only thing that needs be changed. A stored procedure can be activated automatically when particular conditions occur. A *trigger* is the database feature used to check particular operations and call the stored procedure when conditions are met. The following *Distributed or Remote Processing* section contains more information on these types of distributed processing.

Client Responsibilities

A client program is responsible for the integrity of the data downloaded from the server. Many client programs that access mission-critical data do not have write privileges for the database. For security and data integrity reasons, as few clients as possible should have the capability to modify the databases. Many clients are simply constructed to do queries on the main database.

During updates sent from the client to the server, integrity is vitally important. For example, if a sale consists of 10 items, and the connection is broken after the sixth item is updated, the design of the client/server system must provide the ability to restart the transaction or abort the entire update in order to start over. Communication from the client to the server must be monitored and controlled to ensure the accuracy of the data. To ensure accuracy, database servers use a method known as *flat transaction* (see Chapter 4), which allows a client to encapsulate a transaction between `Begin Transaction` and `Commit Transaction` commands. If anything goes wrong during the transaction, all of the changes can be undone back to where the transaction began.

Other client/server systems use techniques such as data checksums to guarantee data integrity. There is no single system to prevent data corruption, but rather many proprietary implementations. Most include transaction processing, but the implementation of transaction processing widely varies.

> **NOTE**
>
> A checksum is a summary value of all the data that is to be sent. The checksum is then sent with the data. A new checksum is calculated on the receiving machine and compared with the original value. If they match, the data is apparently accurate. If not, the system requests the data to be resent.

Client/Server Structure

There are two common structures for a client/server system: decision support systems and online transaction processing systems (OLTP). The division between these types of systems is often fairly fuzzy, but they give a basic framework that can be used to evaluate a given system.

Decision support systems are most often used by management. These systems are designed to get information periodically (for example, each quarter) from other independent systems. From this periodic data *snapshot* or *freeze-frame*, a manager can then generate a summary of what has taken place and can make judgments on the direction to take next. It is unnecessary to have this data collected instantly. For example, when accounting closes out a year, they often spend several weeks collecting and compiling the proper data for the final summary. Because the report is generated over time, it is important that the data being worked from is a snapshot. For example, when reporting on inventory levels, if the report is generated from live data, then the report shows different figures when it is first run than when it is run later in the week.

Online transaction processing (OLTP) systems are used day to day. They rely on instantaneous response (or at least response within a few seconds) and must be constructed with this in mind. A point-of-sale system is an excellent example. When the salesperson is selling merchandise at a store, the item is entered and the price automatically appears on the screen. Then the item is deducted from the store inventory. The computer reaction must be instantaneous and accurate.

Enterprise Information Systems

Enterprise information systems (EIS) is a current buzz word that is carelessly used to label just about any system. While there is no strict definition for this concept, it does have a generally understood meaning. An EIS is a system that uses network technology to bring together information and processes important to an enterprise's function. For example, a system that uses a LAN to connect several databases (such as financial, accounting, and production databases) to make a division of a corporation profitable is an EIS.

An *enterprise* is a unit of organization that has a particular purpose such as producing a widget, supplying accurate figures, producing a profit, and so on. Also, an enterprise can be a company, a division of a company, a work group, or a loosely coordinated project. The primary reason for the creation of an EIS is to expand the reach of data communication and to make information available to the people in the enterprise who fulfill the enterprise's function. The information must therefore have relevance to the enterprise.

Visual Basic (and VBA) are becoming extremely popular tools to use in this area. The VB development system is simple enough that applications can be developed rapidly and installed in various parts of the enterprise. The users in each area can return feedback on what they need altered or what particular function the program is missing. The applications can be quickly changed to the users' specifications and then resubmitted for approval.

Because VBA is built into many of the popular applications, such as Excel, Project, and Access, power users in an organization can even create or modify these enterprise applications themselves. Programmers can take advantage of the advanced features already present in these programs and can leverage the technology.

Data Warehousing

Creating *data warehouses* for enterprise information is becoming an increasingly popular way of maximizing the usage of an organization's information. A data warehouse contains essential data (often summary, historical, or recent company data) that needs to be used to make decisions about the enterprise. For example, a chain of department stores might create a central data warehouse containing daily sales figures for all the stores. Reports could be generated and trends analyzed using the information stored in the data warehouse.

Centralizing the information into a single place decreases the load that would be placed on a system to do global information queries as well as providing instant access to necessary data. A traditional database server can be used to run a data warehouse. There are an increasing number of systems available that are specialized for the need of warehousing (such as databases created by CA-Ingres). Implementation of data warehouses by industry is beginning to leverage the use of the literally millions of pieces of data generated by an organization every day.

> **TIP**
>
> Creating a data warehouse is a very specialized task. Often hiring an expert in the field is a wise choice for implementation. Before implementation begins, however, consider how the warehouse should be used. Because it is a business analysis tool, make sure you state the goal of your data warehouse in business terms such as "improve net profits by 5 percent" or "decrease defects by 10 percent." These types of goals will allow you to determine exactly what data needs to be centralized. After the system is deployed, make sure data access patterns are monitored. Data that remains unused show be archived to make room for more useful data.

Three-Tier Client/Server Systems

Three-tier systems are becoming increasingly popular in the business world. The three tiers consist of the clients, an object tier, and the data source (usually a database server). Adding the object tier between the client and the traditional server allows for the inclusion of business rules or pre-processing before the data is entered into the data source.

For example, in a point-of-sale system, an object tier could be placed between the client machine run by the salesperson and the database server, which records the transaction. The object tier could check the credit card number entered into the invoice on the client and charge the amount to the credit card. Or the object tier could query a customer database to ensure the customer's credit was good.

These types of tasks cannot be easily incorporated into the database server through triggers or stored procedures. Incorporation into the client would mean a single change to a business rule would require updating each client, a tedious and expensive processing.

> **NOTE**
>
> Microsoft is seeking to make Distributed or Remote OLE the dominant system to implement three-tier systems. Setting up an OLE server on the network can provide the object tier. Visual Basic 4.0 can be used to accomplish setting up such a system and may become a popular way of doing it. VB is easy to program and easy to change, placing business rule development in the hands of many people. For more information, see Chapter 24, "Creating an OLE Server."

Distributed or Remote Processing

Distributed processing will grow substantially in the coming years. Distributed processing essentially outsources various processing tasks on a network. A database server is a simple example of distributed processing. The client program, for example, can send a SQL command to find a particular record on the server. The server does all of the processing and then returns a result. This same technique is being applied to tasks such as three-dimensional image rendering, mathematical calculations, business rules, transaction updates, as well as many other uses.

Distributed processing has two primary benefits: specialization and centralization. A process such as rendering can be very specialized and most appropriately done on a particular type of machine (an SGI Indigo machine, for example). Rather than doing a particular function on a general personal computer, the task can be sent to a machine that specializes in exactly that type of processing, which allows resources to be used in the most efficient way.

Distributed processing also allows resources to be centralized. As in the case of a database server, a single central database can exist on the server, and all of the processing occurs there rather than constantly distributing and updating data. It also decreases network traffic by processing the query and returning a small result set rather than sending the entire database to the client for processing.

There are various ways to activate remote processes. Some of the remote process activation occurs within the server itself, as is the case with a database server. Others are called to run within the operating system, often giving them access to all of the potential resources, including other applications and drivers stored on a particular machine.

A remote routine is called using a *remote procedure call* or RPC. An RPC is used to allow one type of system to call a routine on another machine. A standard is used that specifies how an RPC is to pass parameters and data correctly.

Database servers already use stored procedures or *triggers*—code stored on the database server that can either be called remotely or activated when certain prespecified conditions occur. The language that stored procedures are written in varies from vendor to vendor. Sybase and Microsoft have agreed to standardized on a single, embedded language. For more information on stored procedures, see Chapter 20, "A Structured Query Language (SQL) Primer."

On the operating system level, there are competing technologies attempting to become the standards. Already in place is the basic remote procedure call (RPC) on Unix platform machines. Microsoft is creating Distributed OLE, which uses the basic RPC format as a foundation yet provides many additional services. IBM and a consortium of other vendors have agreed on the basics of distributed system object model (DSOM), which is currently available on OS/2 platform machines. Both of these architectures use an object model in which objects can be called and activated across a network.

In the future, there are plans to implement a much broader distributed processing system. The concept is called *metacomputing* and is being pioneered by San Diego Supercomputer Center and other supercomputer installations around the globe. Metacomputing seeks to create an environment where a computer can access the resources it needs for any particular task. For example, a person can create a model of a molecular reaction on a PC. If the model is activated, the computer can automatically sense that it doesn't have the computing power needed to process such a huge task, and it can connect to a mainframe or supercomputer to farm out the task. The user doesn't need to know on which computer or where the process is being run. The PC simply shows the results.

It is called metacomputing because all computers become extensions of each other. A process set to run on a supercomputer in San Diego might be sent to a computer in Russia, which has more free processing cycles at that particular time. In fact, a process might be split and sent to many computers, each of which do their part of the task.

Metacomputing might seem to be in the distant future, but there are already PC-based, 3-D modeling programs that do metacomputing today. It is difficult to say when metacomputing will begin to bring real possibilities to the client/server world. However, with the tremendous advances taking place in 1995 in the field of distributed processing, common applications might be just around the corner.

Microsoft is advocating the use of OLE to implement such capabilities. (For more information, see Chapter 23, "Object Linking and Embedding (OLE).")

What Is DCE?

Distributed Computing Environment (DCE) is a set of standards that were developed by the Open Systems Foundation. DCE provides an overall foundation for a secure way to access resources that exist on various heterogeneous operating systems and machines. DCE provides a variety of services including remote procedure calls, distributed naming services, time synchronization, distributed file systems, and network security. Although primarily on Unix-based platforms right now, DCE is predicted to become a widely accepted cross-platform standard. For RPCs, DCE specifies a portable procedure language called IDL (Interface Definition Language). An IDL compiler then creates portable C code that can be compiled on and linked to RPC libraries that handle message exchange, network overhead, and the processing required to make the RPC routine available on the network. These RPC routines can then be run on any machine.

DCE is only partially supported by Novell, Microsoft, and Sun. Without these three major players on board, an industry standard seems unlikely. DCE technologies compete with proprietary standards produced by all three of these vendors; therefore, the level of support for the various parts of DCE varies. Most other manufacturers and system designers, including IBM, seek to make DCE a dominant standard. DCE offers many advantages (which are beyond the scope of this book), so partial industry implementation seems most likely.

Replication

Replication is the ability of a server (database server, file server, mail server, or groupware server) to duplicate and synchronize the data it has with another machine. For example, if you upload a file to a server in San Diego and that server had replication capabilities, it can automatically transfer a copy of the file to a mirror server in Chicago. This capability is essential to groupware applications in order for people to interact beyond the scope of a LAN.

Replication makes the widespread use of a wide area network (WAN) attractive. For example, in the application for creating a new budget (described in the section titled, "Workflow Groupware"), people can work through the approval process even though they are located in different geographic regions. The replication server can mirror one site to another. To the users at each end, the available files appear identical. When an update is made to one, the other is automatically updated. The WAN can hook together two geographically separate LANs inexpensively. (See Figure 2.5.) Using our common diagram, when LAN1 wants to update LAN2 they do so over the middleware Lotus Notes/Frame Relay/Packet Switching Network. (See Figure 2.6.)

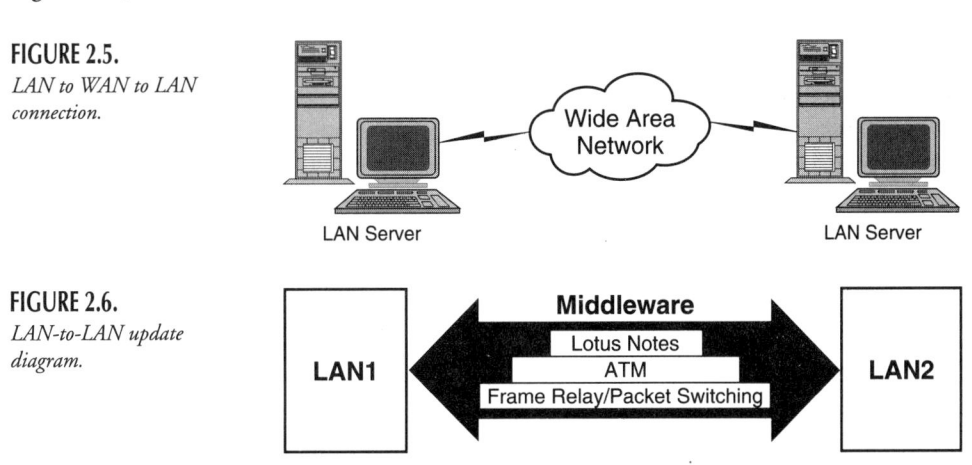

FIGURE 2.5.
LAN to WAN to LAN connection.

FIGURE 2.6.
LAN-to-LAN update diagram.

There are two types of replication: immediate replication and skulking (periodic replication). *Immediate replication* causes an update to mirror as soon as a change occurs. Immediate replication is usually used on connected LANs or over high-speed WANs, where updates are convenient, quick, and inexpensive. *Skulking* (the industry term for periodic replication) updates the mirror periodically with an entire group of changes. This periodic update can occur during off-peak telephone or rate hours. Skulking is used most where low-rate updates occur (such as over a telephone modem) or when extremely large amounts of data are concerned making immediate updates uneconomical. Skulking is often used by online services, such as America Online, which replicate picture or sound files onto your PC for easy access.

Problems occur with data concurrency on replication servers. The data on a mirror can quickly become obsolete, especially if periodic updates methods are used. See Chapter 4 for more information on data concurrency.

The distribution of messages was the first widely implemented use of replication. You might have heard of FidoNet-type bulletin board systems, where you can post a message or send e-mail, and, during off-peak telephone hours, the FidoNet calls other FidoNet boards to replicate your postings. On the Internet, Usenet news is a global bulletin board which uses replication to make messages posted from any site available around the world by replicating to numerous Internet hub sites. Also on the Internet are FTP or Gopher mirror sites, which are accessible file repositories that store replicated files of the most popular sites.

Novell also uses a type of replication on its servers to enable "mirroring" of a server to a backup server. The backup server has a duplicate set of files and records that the main server contains. If the main server fails, the mirror comes online with little or no loss in time and productivity.

Replication is therefore a powerful tool for client/server computing. Remote sites can share a common backbone of data. While replication provides a great number of new ways to access data, it also creates problems of its own.

Replication has to be properly set up so that it exchanges and synchronizes data and doesn't destroy it. A replication route must be created so that old data doesn't overwrite newer data. Replication can cause numerous data concurrency problems and so called "dirty read" errors. A replicated system requires much planning before implementation is attempted.

Intergalactic networks commonly use replication for data synchronization. Intergalactic networks allow two or more LANs to interface using a WAN as the middleware. With the growth of ATM and other packet-switching tools, intergalactic client/server applications might dramatically increase. Lotus is working with AT&T to create an intergalactic network for Lotus Notes. For more information on wide area networks (WAN) and their connectivity, see Chapter 3, "Networks (Client/Server Foundation)."

Transaction Processing Monitors

Transaction processing (TP) monitors run on a server and act as a traffic cop for transactions, regulating their flow and guiding them to their destinations. A TP monitor starts server processes, funnels work to the server, and monitors the workloads for the system. TP monitors are becoming widely used on transaction-intensive systems and are currently dominant on systems that require a great number of connections or terminals used intermittently. (See Figure 2.7.) They can coordinate systems with various applications and resources and can shuttle a transaction to the resource most able to complete the given task. In this way, TP monitors can dramatically increase the performance of a client/server system, because they can match the ideal resource for the specific task. They can also provide firewall protection for your network (see Chapter 28, "Security for Client/Server").

FIGURE 2.7.
TP monitor.

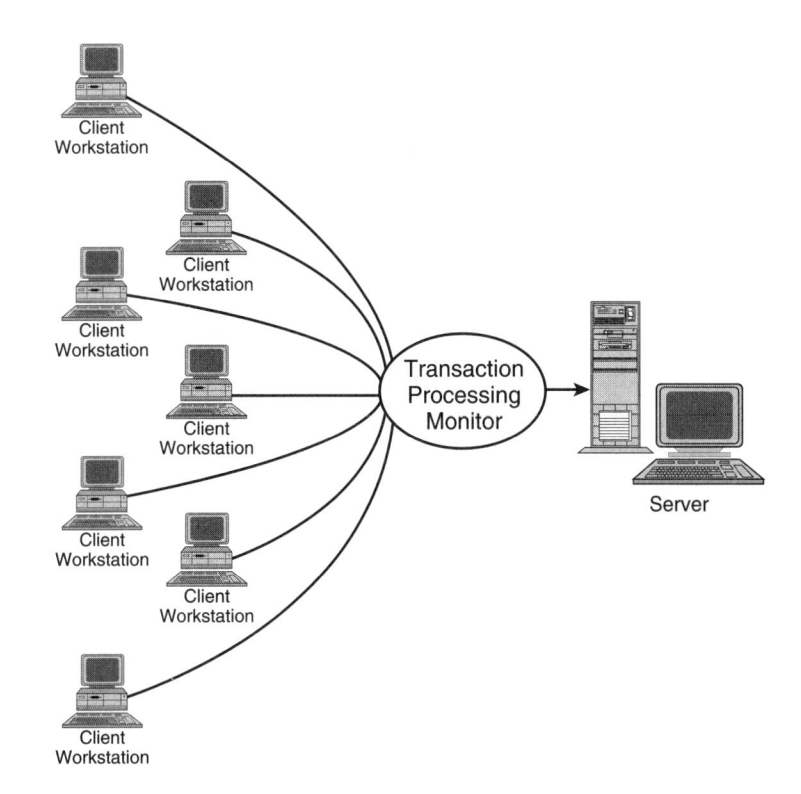

For example, a great number of ATM banking machines need to communicate secure transactions with the bank's main computer. These transactions, however, are sporadic; yet, they need immediate access to the financial database to carry out financial transactions (withdrawals, deposits, and so on) Having 1000 sessions for 1000 ATM machines constantly open to the server, incurs great amounts of overhead and waste, especially when a majority of the time these sessions are unused for transactions. The TP monitor sits between the server or servers and takes care of all of the overhead processing while routing the transactions to the needed servers. This process is often called *funneling*—the many connections are "funneled" down into just a few connections so that the server can appropriately deal with them.

TP monitors can also prioritize and queue transactions when resources are scarce. This can decrease the number of errors a client/server system experiences and therefore decrease downtime and user frustration—this also can save a tremendous amount of money. Usage loads that would have previously required the purchase of an additional server can now be leveled.

Using a separate application for TP monitoring is called *TP heavy*. Database vendors are beginning to build some of the TP functions directly into their databases: this is known as *TP lite*. The advantage of building such functions into the database is for the tightly coupled integration with actual database transactions. However, this does cause problems with accessing other resources and functions not used directly by the database.

E-mail and Embedded Messages

Messaging is a dominant technology in the client/server world. Because of the broad standardization, the available message bridges, and the affinity of users for electronic mail, messaging is used as a basic transport protocol by many applications. Messaging has become the most common use of network communication—with the addition of image, sound, and data embedding, the growth of this market could be phenomenal.

Users are familiar the common e-mail available through MCI Mail, Internet, American Online, CompuServe, and so on. Standard e-mail is a text document that contains a destination address (or a multiple address list) that is sent over a network. Recently, the online networks have begun to provide bridges so that a message sent from a CompuServe user can be received by an America Online or Internet user. Also, local messaging on LANs, and message funneling, which uses a mail server to funnel messages sent on a LAN to a WAN, are becoming widespread technologies.

These technologies enable an individual user to asynchronously communicate with another user almost anywhere in the world at any time. Messages sent are stored on mail servers until they can be retrieved by the destination user.

All of this messaging infrastructure has allowed vendors to begin implementation of advanced messaging systems that can store embedded data and other special information.

Groupware is a fundamental technology facilitated largely by the e-mail revolution. Groupware uses e-mail technology to provide information transfer, conferencing network bulletin boards, and occasional replication services.

E-mail provides an ideal point-to-point transfer system for client/server information and updates. For example, a salesman in the field can record various updates to a customer's account. At any time, the client program can use the MAPI interface to encapsulate the field updates in a message. The message can be sent to an automated mail server or a manager in charge of customer updates. This message can be sent on nearly any wide area network including Internet or over the wireless ARDIS network. When received, the mail server can automatically update the main database, or the manager can manually execute an update program. The possibilities are nearly endless.

Now there is a new generation of mail systems—Lotus Notes and Microsoft Exchange. These applications have complete groupware capabilities for facilitating database-like access to messages. They do this by relocating a majority of the message processing from the message client to the mail server. In current e-mail systems, a message remains on the mail server as long as the client is unavailable. When the client becomes available, all of the messages are downloaded to the client application. All message tracking, replies, and manipulation must be done by the client software.

This new wave of advanced mail servers keeps all of these functions on the mail server. The clients actively communicate with the servers rather than merely downloading specific messages. This provides the ability to browse mail stored on the server before it is downloaded. It also enables replication, remote access, and other groupware functions.

There are currently three primary APIs for message access: Messaging API (MAPI), Vendor Independent Messaging (VIM), and Common Mail Calls (CMC). MAPI and VIM are competing technologies. Luckily, CMC is a simpler protocol and is supported by both protocols. Therefore, for simple messaging, CMC allows the creation of one set of code that works with both API types.

MAPI is fully supported by all Microsoft products and is included as an OCX with Visual Basic Professional and Enterprise Editions. There is also Extended MAPI, which supports 90 more calls for advanced functionality. MAPI is included in Windows 95, and access is possible through Visual Basic 4 using OLE Messaging. MAPI has the support of many service providers and network tools manufacturers such as CompuServe, Banyan, HP, DEC, and SoftSwitch.

VIM is supported by a consortium that includes Lotus, Apple, IBM, Borland, MCI, Oracle, WordPerfect, and Novell. VIM has been receiving strong industry support. Discussions are underway for combining VIM with CMC to provide a complete open industry standard. However, MAPI has made tremendous inroads in the Client/Server industry, so two standards might still need to be supported.

For more information on messaging, see Chapter 26, "Remote Client/Server Access."

Network Operating System

A network operating system (NOS) provides the basic capabilities of file sharing. In the last few years network operating systems have begun to provide increasingly advanced services including server extensions, groupware services, directory services, replication, and interserver communication. See Chapter 3 for a complete description of the available commercial NOS architectures currently available.

Directory Services

Directory services enable multiple servers and networks to interact in a consistent manner. For example, without a directory service, a user would need an individual access privilege, a logon, and a password for each independent network connection. A directory service centralizes all of this information and keeps access privileges and information about various servers and machines in one place. This way, a user can simply logon to the directory service, which handles all of the validation, to request access to the servers.

Directory services have yet to become well established. There are several competing architectures, including those available for NetWare and the X.500 standard (see Chapter 3 for more information). Microsoft has yet to declare its intentions with regard to directory services. Because Windows NT Server is gaining substantial market acceptance, Microsoft's decision as to what directory services to use will have a major impact on any standard currently in place.

Peer-to-Peer

Peer-to-peer networking is extremely popular in smaller organizations or work groups. Peer-to-peer interaction occurs without the presence of a central server. The most popular implementation of peer-to-peer networks include LANtastic on PC-compatible machines and AppleTalk on the Macintosh platform. Windows for Workgroups includes many peer-to-peer features.

Peer-to-peer implementations essentially put both the client and the server programs on all machines. One user activates a client program to send e-mail to another user. The server program operates in the background on all of the machines. If a message comes across the network, the server on each machine checks to see if the message is intended for its client. If so, the server receives the message and signals the user that a message was received.

The most common uses of peer-to-peer exchanges include file transfer, e-mail services, and data-sharing. Windows for Workgroups provides various services through applications such as Schedule +, Remote Services, and even the File Manager. Windows 95 provides one of the most substantial sets of peer-to-peer services provided with an OS. Visual Basic has access to most of these services, and some are described in Chapter 26 and in Chapter 27, "Telephony."

There are several advantages of a peer-to-peer interaction. It is always cheaper than a standard server setup because a computer does not have to be purchased for dedicated server use. The setups often don't even have to be purchased separately—they are already built into many of the operating systems (Windows for Workgroups and Macintosh OS, for example). They occasionally reduce network traffic. For example, in a file transfer, the file is sent directly from machine to machine rather than uploaded to a server by one machine and then downloaded by another.

The disadvantages of the peer-to-peer architecture are numerous. Both machines that seek to communicate must be on at the same time. For example, if Joe needs to send a message to Patricia, but Patricia's machine is not on, the e-mail remains on Joe's machine, which will occasionally query to see if the other machine is now available. If Joe turns his machine off and Patricia later turns her machine on, the message is not sent but rather remains on Joe's powered-down machine until both machines are on at the same time.

Peer-to-peer access also lacks any type of centralization. It is difficult to set up a mission critical database when the network has no central point. Data tends to become fractured and unreliable because various versions of the database remain on the different machines. Because both the client and the server software must reside on each PC, peer-to-peer networking is taxing on system resources. More memory and processor time are used for handling transactions, which decreases the overall system speed.

Security is difficult and rarely implemented on a peer-to-peer network. Because these types of networks are often set up in an ad hoc fashion, little thought is given to access restrictions and possible data tampering or damage. Passwords are selected on a user-by-user basis, and there are often several "floating," unused passwords active on the system that can be accessed by anyone. For simplicity's sake, many users publish their machines and hard drives on the network in guest mode; therefore, anyone can access and change any information on their system.

In a peer-to-peer network, scaling is difficult. A peer-to-peer network usually reaches its usable capacity at between 10 and 30 users. Eight users is usually the optimal limit—network traffic, security, and network problems are still within a reasonable limit. For example, most peer-to-peer networks are created with a chain topology (see Chapter 3). If one of the nodes is unplugged the whole network ceases to function. With eight users, finding such a problem is still possible. With 30 users, it is a much more difficult exercise.

Cross-platform support is nearly nonexistent. Because peer-to-peer communications are built into most of the operating systems, the peer-to-peer services can most often only communicate with an identical OS. For example, the Macintosh peer-to-peer interface cannot communicate with Windows for Workgroups. Rarely do these system services provide interplatform communication.

Despite the disadvantages, peer-to-peer interaction is here to stay. These types of networks are extremely easy to set up, and because there is no central influence (a server), changing the network structure (adding new machines or printers) is very simple. Also, remote users adopt a much more peer-to-peer–like system where often the client and the server programs must exist on a single portable machine for convenience and flexibility.

Peer-to-peer networks can be used to your advantage. For example, they can be used as a type of rapid prototype of a future network. By installing a peer-to-peer network, you can gauge how much network power a particular workgroup will need before valuable time and resources are deployed in a poor arrangement.

An old builder's trick is to not put in any walkways after finishing construction of a building but rather to wait until the institution is opened and watch where people walk. The builder then puts the walkways in the paths created by the walkers. No one wants to install gleaming new walkways that no one uses. The same is true for network pathways.

This Book's Client/Server Focus

When developing this book, we had to make many decisions. Should we focus on the hot new categories, such as object servers, TP monitors, distributed processing, or on the more general uses? We've decided to split the difference and show you how to create applications using the file server and database server models. However, we do explain the object server (and more advanced technologies) and give examples in several of the chapters.

The more advanced technologies are in a stage of uncertainty at the moment. For example, will database servers be used for multimedia network applications? Will object servers impose too much of a performance penalty and therefore be modified into something different? Will the CORBA standard be widely used in object servers? Which companies conception of stored procedures will become dominant? None of these questions can be answered right now. This book provides the foundation necessary for you to understand the issues concerning these new standards and how they relate to your Visual Basic client/server applications.

3
Networks (Client/Server Foundation)

Networks

Client/server computing started from the idea that computers on a network could share information. Rather than the older master/slave methodology, new client/server ideas suggested that data and processing power could be shared among largely independent machines. A network would form a communication backbone that would make this sharing possible.

Networks essentially formed much of the middleware link, allowing communication between the client machines and software and their complementary servers. (See Figure 3.1.) The shared processing and data exchange formed by such a system is what makes up a Distributed Computing Environment (DCE). The client/server communication link can be made up of internal and/or external interfaces.

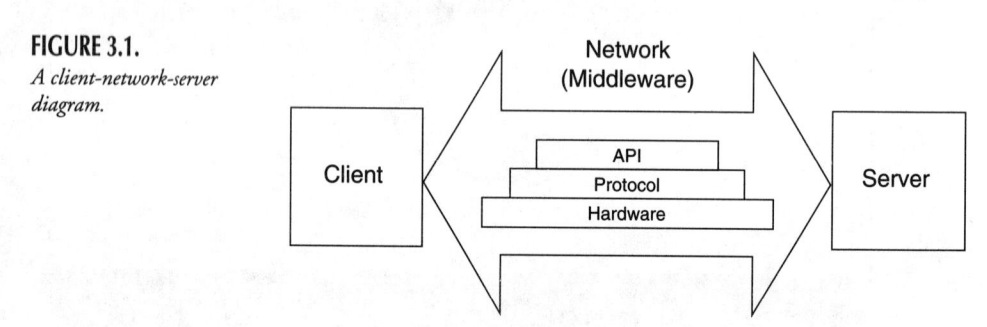

FIGURE 3.1.
A client-network-server diagram.

The network backbone is made up primarily of various Local Area Networks (LANs). These physically hook the various machines together. Protocols that run over the networks transport information between machines. On each server resides some type of server software, most often a general file server that comes in the form of a Network Operating System (NOS). Typical NOS configurations include Novell NetWare and Windows NT Server.

The LANs that allow the machines to communicate can themselves be used to communicate with other LANs using a Wide Area Network (WAN). Wide Area Networks might consist of something as simple as a point-to-point router hooked to a T1 line or as complex as an ATM carrier network.

This chapter reviews the concepts necessary to understand what is involved with creating the foundation for a local and wide-area client/server system. Most client/server designers are presented with a network that is already in place and must tailor the specific C/S system to work with existing legacy hardware. This chapter gives an overview of many of the various configurations that might be encountered on such a job. If you are already familiar with LAN and WAN concepts, skimming this chapter should provide a simple review.

Local Area Network (LAN)

Local Area Networks (LANs) have grown in number and size at a phenomenal rate, connecting a wide variety of computers: PCs, workstation, mainframes (or multiprocessing servers), and even supercomputer (or Massively Parallel Processor (MPP)) systems. As this technology grew, client/server and distributed computing technology provided more economical ways of sharing and distributing information than older mainframe-based systems. LANs have spread from large and small business offices, government facilities, schools, and universities into individual homes. Normally, LANs are installed in a single building spanning a few thousand meters. Multiple LANs are connected with repeaters, hubs, routers, bridges, and gateways to cover a large building or several buildings in one geographical area.

The greater the geographic distance a network spans, the more complex its implementation. Distances spanning from a few thousand meters to less than 50 kilometers are designated as Metropolitan Area Networks (MANs) by the Institute of Electrical and Electronic Engineers (IEEE) 802.6. While the IEEE can't mandate anything to the industry, it has taken on the task of defining and producing a set of standards for networks. The term MAN, however, is rarely used, and these medium-sized networks are often referred to as either large LANs or small WANs. Wide Area Networks span a state, a nation, or the world (see WAN section of this chapter). Generally speaking, most networks consist of multiple LANs connecting into WANs through bridges, gateways, routers, a modem, or an Integrated Services Digital Network (ISDN) or Asynchronous Transfer Mode (ATM) switch. This chapter addresses current LAN and WAN technologies and interfaces.

With the increasing use of LANs for business and personal use, it is crucial that C/S systems have the capability to easily and effectively interface to the customer and its user's LANs. How the C/S interfaces with the network is largely a function of the operating system the machine is running. The following is a general overview of some of the common technologies and structures of many of the LANs available today. The networking world is complex and often bewildering. This section provides a basic primer so you can understand how a network functions and, subsequently, how C/S systems use it.

Sample Network

Figure 3.2 diagrams many of the common components of a LAN. The diagram contains a backbone cable, two ring networks, two star networks, a Fiber Distributed Data Interface (FDDI) network, a router, some hubs, some bridges, a gateway, some concentrators, and a few servers.

FIGURE 3.2.
A sample LAN.

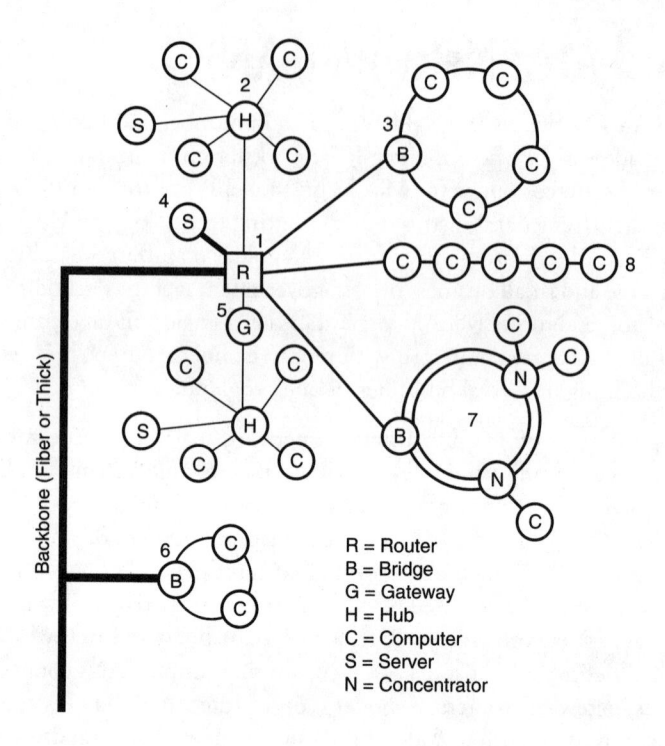

R = Router
B = Bridge
G = Gateway
H = Hub
C = Computer
S = Server
N = Concentrator

The thick line to the left of the diagram, labeled *Backbone*, provides a common link for an organization, building, or geographic area. The backbone is a high-speed transmission line (usually fiber or thick cable) that allows different networks to be connected effectively. A building, for example, might run a backbone up several floors so that the networks on each floor can communicate with the rest of the networks in the building. On a university campus, a fiber backbone is often used to connect the entire campus together.

In the network diagram, there are two junctions off the backbone. This is known as *tapping* the backbone. One of the taps goes directly into a bridge (#6) to a ring-topology network. The second tap interfaces with a router (#1). The router distributes packets to the various networks hooked to it. As the diagram shows, a router can interface with all of the various topologies.

The router interfaces with a star-topology network (#2). It also connects to a ring topology (#3), an FDDI network (#7), a chain or wave network (#8), and a gateway (#5) to another star network. A server (#4) may also be directly connected to the router with a high-speed line for quick access.

Rarely will any one network have all of these features and devices. However, a network will commonly have a number of them. Each piece of the network serves a crucial function. A network configuration is determined primarily by cost factors and the type and number of computer systems that need to be networked. Particular computer systems (and operating systems) work best for particular types of networks. For this reason, the systems you use are often a determining factor. For example, if the LAN needs to be interfaced to an IBM mainframe, a Token-Ring network is the optimal configuration.

Basic Network Terms

Node—A device connected to a network. Usually a computer system, workstation, or server. Occasionally a router, gateway, repeater, bridge, or hub.

Packet—The basic electronic-data building block of a network. A packet is a self-contained data structure that is sent over the network. A packet consists of two pieces: the header and the data. The header contains address information about the origination, destination, and type of packet. The data is a block of data. On a network, a packet is sent by one machine (or server) and is passed down the network. Each node checks the packet header information to see if its address is equal to the destination address. If the addresses match, the packet belongs to that node and it accepts the data. If not, the node will not read the data and pass the packet to the next node.

Network Topologies

The *network topology* describes a LAN's wires, cables, or fiber layout. Each type of topology is favored for particular applications depending on cable run length, number of computer systems, operating system being used, costs, network security, maintainability, and reliability.

Chain or Wave

The *chain* or *wave* topology, a low-cost and simple implementation, is shown in Figure 3.3. Packets (data) are passed down the daisy chain from computer to computer until they reach the end of the network. This topology structure is mainly used where Ethernet installations or Macintosh computer systems are installed; both designs were based on networks with the chain type structure, and part of the Macintosh line has built-in EtherTalk and AppleTalk capabilities.

Pros: Cheap, easy to set up; no hubs or other hardware required. Chain-structure networks can be extended with the installation of repeaters, routers, bridges, and so on. Used by AppleTalk and EtherWave.

Cons: Mostly for small groups of computers. No single point-to-point connection between computer systems generates a great amount of traffic, but a large amount (users' input and output traffic) does flow through each node, which slows down the network. If one of the nodes is disconnected and breaks the chain, all the other nodes down the line lose connection. Termination at the beginning and end of the chain is critical to it being able to function and operate properly.

FIGURE 3.3.
Chain or wave topology.

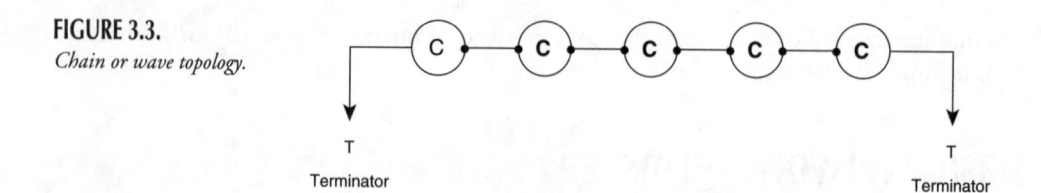

Ring

A ring-style topology is a serial-type chain of computers. (See Figure 3.4.) However, rather than terminating at the beginning and end of the chain, the ring must make a complete circle. Initially this topology, with its higher throughput capacity, was better for some business applications. This higher throughput correlates to minimal time delay between transmission and reception of data. In networked computer systems that deliver a large data output or where applications generate a large amount of network traffic, it is more efficient. If a substantial increase in network traffic continues, then the high-speed FDDI ring networks should be considered. They may become more prevalent in the future.

Pros: Compatibility with mainframe systems including SNA protocol. Has large base of legacy hardware. Large geographic area possible. Used by FDDI and Token-Ring networks.

Cons: Ring network cards tend to be more expensive than other topologies. Because the circle must be complete, the cabling is more expensive and can be more difficult to install. No single computer system generates a great amount of traffic, but a large amount (users input and output traffic) can be on the network—which then has to flow through each node, decreasing network throughput. If one of the nodes is disconnected and breaks the ring, all the other nodes go down in the network (exceptions include FDDI networks).

FIGURE 3.4.
Ring topology.

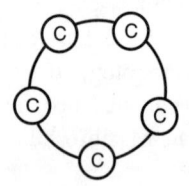

Star

A star topology is the most popular networking topology. All the nodes are hooked to a central hub in a star configuration. (See Figure 3.5.) A hub, or set of connected hubs, sits at the center of the star, and each computer has its own branch from the star connecting it to the hub. The computer connected to the star could also be the beginning or end computer in a chain or wave topology.

Pros: Less network traffic to each node. If a node is disconnected, it won't affect any of the other nodes on the network. Easy hook-up because only one line needs to be run to each node.

Cons: More expensive hardware because of the need for hubs.

FIGURE 3.5.
Star topology.

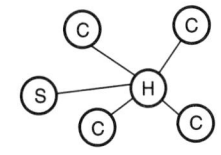

Bus or Bus-Wired

A bus or bus-wired network is commonly used for the baseband or backbone part of a network. Each computer is "tapped off" a common cable or bus. (See Figure 3.6.) Usually thin coaxial, thick coaxial, or fiber cables are used.

Pros: Inexpensive; easy to install and maintain because of the simple, single cable runs. Node can be disconnected from network without disrupting network operation. Often used by Ethernet networks.

Cons: Cable and connectors are more expensive than other networks that use twisted pair. Great amount of network traffic because common bus is shared. Damage to central cable can bring down part or all of system network.

FIGURE 3.6.
Bus-wired topology.

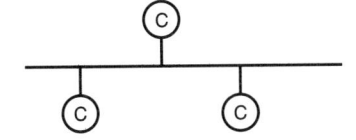

Cabling

The network cable selection is important to network operation. Environmental factors that will affect networking operation include distance, data rate, number of devices or nodes, topology, cost, and flexibility. There are some other important network cable factors to consider depending on area of installation and operation, such as shielding, crosstalk and interference concerns, upgrade or expansion potential, data security, and safety and performance requirements or standards. Crosstalk is when electrical signal energy traveling down one wire is absorbed by an adjacent wire, creating disturbance in its processing circuits (transmit or receive). Any concerns related to your network cabling and cable specifications should be discussed with a qualified cable supplier. Following is a list of network cable types available, with a brief overview of those used in current LAN installations.

10BASE-T (Twisted Pair)

10BASE-T is used to designate a baseband system that has a 10MB per second (10MB/second) data rate using twisted-pair cable as the medium of transmission. There are two types of twisted-pair cable: unshielded (UTP) and shielded (STP). UTP cable is normally installed by most telephone companies in buildings, even through it is more susceptible to outside electrical interference. Another potential concern with twisted-pair cable (whether shielded or unshielded) is crosstalk. Any concerns related to your network should be discussed with a qualified cable supplier.

Pros: Small, easy to install, and inexpensive. Because twisted-pair wiring is used by telephone systems, there is the possibility that the necessary cable is already installed. Cable cost is low, due to large usage and quantities sold.

Cons: Unknown quality of already installed cabling; twisted pair will not support high data-transfer rates. Susceptibility to outside interference. Possible security risk (compared to fiber).

10BASE-2 (Thinnet)

10BASE-2, also called Thinnet, is used to designate a baseband system that has a 10MB/second data rate. It has a maximum segment length of 185 meters (607 ft.) using 50 Ohm coaxial cable as the medium of transmission. Thinnet is basically an enhanced RG-58 coaxial cable that is used to connect computer systems inside a building or enclosed space with a short cable path. This is normally installed using a bus-wired topology.

Pros: Fairly inexpensive and easy to install. Medium to high data-transfer rates. Better resistance to outside interference (electrical noise) than 10BASE-T.

Cons: Higher cost of cabling (compared to 10BASE-T). Possible security risk (compared to fiber).

10BASE-5 (Thick)

10BASE-5 is used to designate a baseband system that has a 10 MB/second data rate with a maximum segment length of 500 meters (1640.5 ft.), 315 meters farther than Thinnet. It uses 50 Ohm coaxial trunk cable or thick coaxial cable as the medium of transmission. This cable is used mainly for a network communication backbones that require longer distances between nodes exist and better protection against electrical noise.

Pros: Medium to high data-transfer rates, better resistance to outside interference of outside electrical noise than 10BASE-2. Longer cable runs possible.

Cons: Higher cabling costs. Difficulty (larger in diameter and stiff not flexible to work with) of installation. No higher throughput than 10BASE-2. Possible security risk (compared to fiber).

100BASE-T (Twisted Pair)

100BASE-T Ethernet technology evolved quickly to meet the stresses placed on LANs due to the bandwidth requirements of multimedia applications. The 100BASE-T Ethernet is used to designate a baseband system that has a 100MB/second data rate. With its high data rate throughput and backward compatibility the 100BASE-T Ethernet created an interim bridge till ATM technology and costs can meet customers needs. For 100BASE-T Ethernet to meet its performance goals, network segment length limits were imposed. This provided the network with the capability to safely meet the response time required to detect collisions from any point in a repeater zone.

Each 100BASE-T Ethernet has a maximum segment length of 100 meters (328.1 ft.), between a node and its repeater hub. Other length limitations are defined in the IEEE standard 802.3u such as only two hubs can be tied together in a repeater zone and separated only by a five meter cable. This defines the maximum distance to be 205 meters between any two nodes. For larger networks, bridges or switching hubs are required that can regenerate every signal received and form boundaries between collision zones. Thus providing a workable solution to the timing problem.

Pros: High data transfer rates, specified to be able to support three different types of physical media: a two-pair cable, a four-pair cable, and optical fiber. Can run on the standard 10BASE-T cable (Category 3 wire). 100MB/second Ethernet equipment can communicate with 10MB/second equipment (the 100MB/second equipment adjusts its speed to 10MB/second).

Cons: Distance limitations. All connections within a repeater hub must be the same speed (either 100MB/second or 10MB/second). Increases equipment cost; to extend networks more than 205 meters, bridges and switching hubs are required which are more expensive than repeater hubs.

Fiber

Fiber optic is the most expensive network cabling solution. It is excellent for backbones or router links, due to the physical properties such as connectivity over extended lengths, light weight, and capability to provide a secure network communication interface. Fiber optic cable conducts light pulses that contain the transmitted data instead of electrical signals. The transmission rate of fiber optic cable can exceed 100MB/second. It has a possible segment length of two kilometers (6560 ft.) with fiber optic cable as the medium of transmission. Because the signal is in the form of a beam of light, transmission distance depends on strength of light sources and number of connections or splices in the cable. Cables may consist of a single fiber or multiple fiber lines.

The high throughput of current C/S computer systems more effectively matches the transfer rates possible in using a fiber cable. In the past, machines have rarely had the need for expensive high-speed network transfers. Now, with the high-speed processors available and the growth of local FDDI and ATM networks, fiber is becoming more of a necessity for implementing networked multimedia applications.

Pros: Very high data transfer rates, immune to electrical interference, no corrosion problems, long cable lengths. Cable is extremely secure from unauthorized tapping or eavesdropping. High transfer rates allow complete transmission of digitized video and audio signals. Used by Ethernet, FDDI, Token Ring, and other high-speed protocols.

Cons: High cost of hardware and cabling. Minimum security risk due to physical properties of the cable. When used in a star topology, two fibers are needed, one for inputs and one for outputs. These cables must be run to each computer system which can be fairly costly.

Transport Protocols

Transport protocols are the physical layer protocols for transmission and data handling over a network. Each protocol handles packet transmission, data collision, and line sensing.

Ethernet

Ethernet is the most common type of networking protocol. Each Ethernet packet consists of a preamble, a destination address, a source address, a type field, a data field, and a CRC checksum. (See Figure 3.7.)

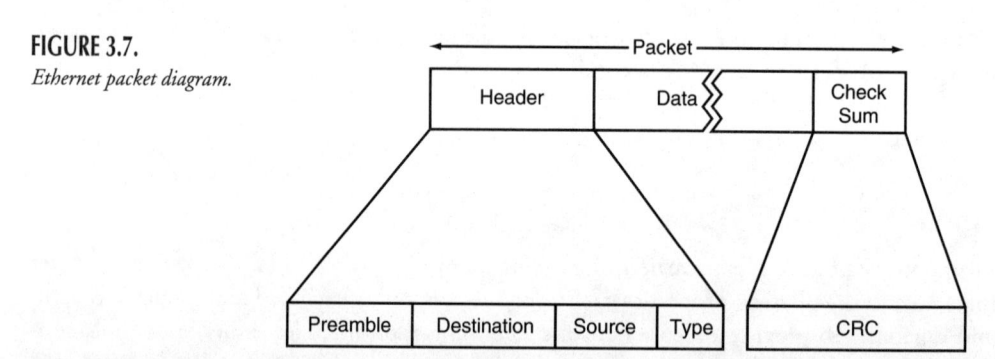

FIGURE 3.7.
Ethernet packet diagram.

The Ethernet protocol supports an industry standard called Carrier Sense Multiple Access with Collision Detection (CSMA/CD). This protocol ensures that data collision is handled in a fast and reliable way. For example, if two nodes begin transmitting packets at the same time, this causes a data collision on the network. All nodes on the network immediately stop transmitting data. Each of the nodes that transmitted the data that collided randomize a waiting time before they begin to broadcast again (this is called non-persistent protocol). This way, the node with the shorter wait time begins broadcasting and the other checks the bus, sees it's busy, and waits until the bus is once again free. A large number of data collision decreases the overall network speed.

Ethernet, in its standard implementation, can run at data transfer rates of 10MB/second. Due to increased demands on the network, Ethernet's transfer rates are reaching their limits and are unable to handle the large data loads efficiently. This can be seen in decreased network speed (throughput) and increased number of collisions. To solve this problem, a Fast Ethernet, IEEE 802.3u, implementation has been created. (See Figure 3.8.) Fast Ethernet has transmission rates of 100MB/second, 10 times the rate of normal Ethernet implementations. The new implementation retains the original CSMA/CD protocol. Many of the Fast Ethernet devices can also run at normal Ethernet speeds (10MB/second), enabling them to integrate seamlessly into a network.

FIGURE 3.8.
Wide transfer.

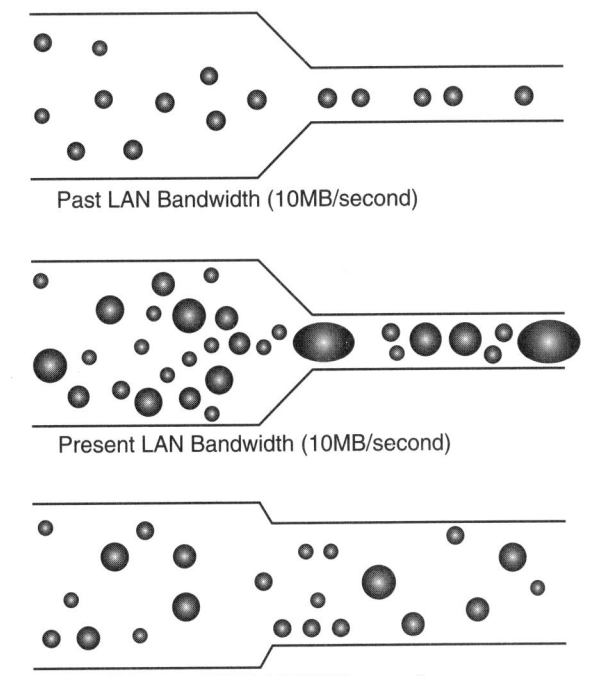

Past LAN Bandwidth (10MB/second)

Present LAN Bandwidth (10MB/second)

Fast Ethernet, FDDI (100MB/second)

> **NOTE**
>
> It is important to understand that all network equipment connected in a network segment (separated by a network repeater, hub, bridge, and so on) have to operate at the same speed. Network equipment interconnecting network segments operating at different transmission rates (10MB/second or 100MB/second) have to be designed to meet this requirement. Some of the new 100MB/second Ethernet adapter cards on the market are designed to automatically adjust the transfer rate to 10MB/second if installed in a 10 MB/second network segment.

Token Ring

A Token-Ring network uses a ring topology. Information is passed using the token-passing protocol. There are two types of packets (called *frames* in Token-Ring terminology): a message frame and a token frame. A frame is passed from node to node around the circle. Each node checks the frame to see whether it is a message or a token. If the frame is a token, it means that the network is idle and it can send a message frame. If the frame is a message, it checks the address to see if the message is intended for that node. If not, it relays the message frame to the next node.

Advancements in Token-Ring technology have made Token-Ring switches available that operate in the data link layer. These switches offer a boost in bandwidth through high port density that provides increased throughput based on the number of active ports. Through the use of source routing protocol, data is forwarded according to the route descriptor located in the frame header.

The majority of the existing Token-Ring networks that were developed to meet IEEE 802.5 specification are operating with data rates of about 4MB/second. Due to advances in technology, these systems are increasing their speed to 16MB/second. This requires adapter cards and cable (high-performance 150 Ohm twisted pair) designed to meet the 802.5 standard and the 16MB/second transmission rate. The segment cable distance for IBM Type 3 cable (4MB/second transmission rate) is a maximum of about 148 feet. The segment cable distances for IBM Types 1 and 2 cable (trunk cable with 16 MB/second transmission rate) are a maximum of 330 feet. An IBM Type 9 cable with a 16MB/second transmission rate has a maximum segment distance of 220 feet.

ARCnet

ARCnet is a protocol developed in the 1970s by Datapoint Corporation. The protocol uses a bus topology like Ethernet, but uses a token to determine which node can control the bus (like Token Ring). Each ARCnet node is assigned a node number. A token is passed consecutively from node to node. The node that currently has the token can then send data on the network.

Fiber Distributed Data Interface (FDDI)

FDDI is based on a Token-Ring standard. FDDI uses token passing to control sending access to the network. This protocol is primarily for high-speed, extremely reliable network systems. An FDDI network topology is set up like a dual ring. (See Figure 3.9.)

The extra ring provides redundancy. If one part of the ring is disabled or disconnected, the protocol automatically reconfigures itself to pass data around the disabled area. The concentrator supplies additional protection for the network by enabling nodes to be connected and disconnected from the system without interrupting network operation.

FIGURE 3.9.
FDDI network.

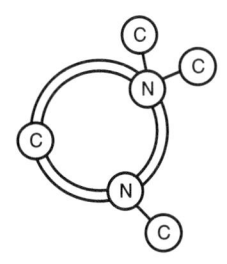

FDDI is implemented with fiber-optic cable and supports transmission rates of around 100MB/second.

Data Transfer Protocol (Network Operating System)

Tunneling is a way to transport packets of one Network Operating System (NOS) inside packets of another NOS (typically by using a router or gateway). For example, tunneling may be used if a Power Macintosh user running AppleTalk on the West Coast wants to send a file to a Power Macintosh user running AppleTalk on the East Coast. If they both hooked up to a WAN that is running TCP/IP, the connection between them would be TCP/IP. If both have routers capable of tunneling, the sending router will hide the AppleTalk packet inside a TCP/IP packet. When the other router receives the packet, it strips off the TCP/IP part of the packet and sends the AppleTalk packet on its way.

Simple Network Management Protocol (SNMP)—or alternatively, Simple Network Monitoring Protocol—is used to manage Internet, TCP/IP, and Ethernet networks. Often built into a network smart hub (and called an agent), this tracks the network packet activity, enabling network administrators to watch network traffic for particular area loads, and so on. The SNMP uses a special requester packet sent over the network's standard protocol. Special SNMP packet-retrieval software (called a manager) is necessary to retrieve this information.

IPX and SPX

Internetwork Packet Exchange (IPX) and Sequenced (or Sequential) Packet Exchange (SPX) are the standard packet protocol formats for connectionless and connection-oriented protocols used in Novell NetWare networks. Connectionless and connection-oriented protocols are focused on how the protocol handles errors. The connectionless protocol discards packets or frames where an error is detected, where connection-oriented protocols concentrate on providing a transfer medium that is error free. IPX and SPX packets are normally 576 bytes in length consisting of the header and data. New versions of NetWare allow larger packet sizes of about 1KB for Ethernet-based networks and 4KB for Token-Ring–based networks. The header size is 30 bytes for IPX and 42 bytes for SPX, which is made up of the 30-byte IPX header information and 12 bytes of additional header information.

Novell NetWare has implemented IPX as the protocol that provides communication functions between its clients and servers. These functions consist of managing the network and routing packets, along with providing programmatic interfaces for a connectionless protocol that can be used by application developers. IPX operational capabilities combine dynamic packet routing and internal bridging of file-server network adapters. In support of application developers, APIs are available for initialization and transmission of nonguaranteed datagram (datagrams with errors are discarded without sender or receiver being informed) messages using the connectionless protocol across the network.

SPX provides Novell NetWare with the capability of guaranteed delivery of packets within the NetWare environment. To accomplish this, SPX provides flow control, sequencing, full error checking, and point-to-point communication services to meet the requirement for guaranteed delivery of packets. In performing these function, additional delays are induced that increase packet delivery time between nodes. SPX functions in much the same way as TCP.

TCP/IP (Transmission Control Protocol/Internet Protocol)

The TCP/IP protocol is made up of three separate protocols: the Transmission Control Protocol (TCP), the User Datagram Protocol (UDP), and the Internet Protocol (IP). TCP/IP is the largest protocol standard, normally associated with networking in the UNIX environment. Additionally, it functions on both LANs and WANs, thus supporting free interoperability of heterogeneous networks. This protocol provides error checking, flow control (to prevent swamping another user by another faster or more powerful user), status and synchronization control.

> **NOTE**
>
> Data-packet fragmentation regularly occurs when transmitting large packets over a TCP/IP WAN. This normally does not occur within a LAN. Most user IP-compatible systems have the ability to reassemble fragments, since it is a requirement of IP stacks. To minimize fragmentation, set maximum limits on the Maximum Transfer Unit (MTU) and the Maximum Segment Size (MSS) for a data frame or packet traveling over an Ethernet. Recommended packet size, including the header, is MTU = 1,500 bytes or 1,492 bytes on IEEE Ethernet, and MSS = 1,456 bytes (IP packet minus header). For people using Serial Link Internet Protocol (SLIP), Compressed SLIP (CSLIP), or Point-to-Point Protocol (PPP) for serial IP connections, it is recommended to set MTU = 256 bytes and MSS = 212 bytes due to their reduced bandwidth.

TCP works with IP, and is organized into four conceptually different layers of control. These layers are: Application Layer, Transport Layer, Internet Layer, and Network Interface Layer. The Application Layer is above the Transport Layer, where application programs are activated using the services provided by TCP/IP. TCP operates and provides a common set of intercommunication functions in the Transport Layer for one application to communicate with another over the Internet. The Internet Layer provides the IP functions of the identification (address) of interconnecting hardware. The Network Interface Layer handles routing and delivery of IP Datagrams.

Transmission Control Protocol (TCP) provides circuit-oriented communication services that include end-to-end flow control, error control, connection setup, and status exchange. Its services correspond to those provided in the OSI Level 4, Transport Layer responsible for reliable communications between network nodes. The TCP header is about 20 to 24 bytes long containing the following information: source port, destination port, sequence number, destination address, data offset, control flags, windows, checksum, urgent pointer, and data.

User Datagram Protocol (UDP) is a protocol for connectionless services to provide nonguaranteed communications between network nodes. UDP efficiency is greater than TCP and is specially suited for short requests and responses. It has no provisions to provide a guaranteed delivery protocol, inherent sequencing or error recovery, or retransmission.

Internet Protocol (IP) is responsible for providing the routing and delivery communication services to move packets or datagrams through the network environment. The IP header appends the TCP header with an additional header about 20 to 24 bytes long containing the following information: version, header length, type of service, total length, identification, flags, fragment offset, time to live, protocol, checksum, source address, destination address, and data or TCP header. Other functions and services include name control and translation, status translation and communications, multisubnet routing and management.

The IP name control and translation service entails generating a useful naming convention that includes assigning network IDs and local host addresses to network users. Then the status and communication function provides the users with the status of Internet operations performed in an understandable format. There are four types of status messages: destination unreachable/invalid, timeout, parameter error, and redirect request (which could mean there is a shorter route to the destination through another router). With multisubnet routing, the Internet Protocol provides for the exchange of Gateway-to-Gateway Protocol (GGP) messages that determine the status of gateways and their networked hosts. The GGP can also evaluate the operability of each interface with "probes" that are sent out to perform this function. IP management provides a vehicle for control and information gathering of the Internet environment.

NetBEUI

In the process of trying to find a standard network interface, a set of protocols was developed called Network Basic Input/Output System (NetBIOS). This set of protocols was used by IBM and Microsoft in the creation of some LAN software in the 1980s. With the implementation of NetBIOS Extended User Interface (NetBEUI) protocol NetBIOS became a working network protocol suite. This network protocol suite was used by LAN Manager, LAN Server, and OS/2 LAN Server.

NetBIOS is also known as NetBIOS Frame (NBF) and NetBEUI. This protocol has the shortcoming of not being routable. To solve this problem, a format was created that tunnels NetBEUI blocks in TCP/IP blocks for routing. However, static routing tables must be created, making it difficult to use.

Although NetBEUI was the default protocol of Windows NT 3.1, Windows NT 3.51 has made TCP/IP its standard protocol. OS/2, however, upgraded the standard to remove many of its past limitations and supports it as a major OS/2 networking protocol.

System Network Architecture (SNA)

System Network Architecture (SNA) is primarily an IBM mainframe protocol that runs on the AS/400 and larger machines. This protocol is also available through AIX, and IBM has committed to continued support and expansion of this protocol. Typically, personal computers are interfaced to SNA through either a Token-Ring network or an SNA Terminal Emulator card.

Network Hardware

The network hardware addressed here is used to connect LANs to other LANs or connect LANs to WANs. This hardware may function as a simple amplifier such as a repeater to extend the length of an existing LAN or join two existing LANs together. Network hardware increases in capability and complexity starting with repeaters, bridges, routers, gateways, and hubs. These capabilities are implemented through additional internal electronic circuitry and software that provide features such as regeneration of packets, network management, routing and flow control.

Repeaters

Repeaters operate at the physical layer of the network model. To allow data to pass over extended distances, repeaters are installed, but this does induce a delay that is seen by the receiver of the packet. Some repeaters have the capability to retime and regenerate signals; this ensures that data packets are usable when they arrive at their destination.

Bridges

A bridge operates at both the physical layer and Media Access Control (MAC) sublayer of the data-link layer in the OSI model. These bridges enable the interconnection of networks that have the same Network Operating System (NOS) but different hardware. For example, a bridge can be placed between one Ethernet network using IPX packets and another Token-Ring network also using Ethernet packets in the IPX format. The IPX packets can flow freely between the two networks.

Bridges have the ability to learn which node addresses reside on which network. This provides them with the capability to control the network traffic coming in and leaving their network through a process called filtering and forwarding. This process, transparent to higher-level protocols, is a basic feature designed into bridges. Bridges generally have greater throughput, require less maintenance and administration time, and are less expensive than routers and gateways. Some of the advanced bridges have available such features as address lock-in/lock-out (which protects privacy and restricts user access), protocol-based filtering/forwarding (which filters network traffic based on user protocol requirements), backup routing (which establishes emergency automatic routing paths activated upon communication link failure only), and Simple Network Management Protocol (SNMP).

Routers

Routers are the next step above bridges, providing the user with expanded capability through programmability. Routers normally operate at the network layer in the OSI model, making them more expensive and difficult to install and manage. Routers are used to control and direct network traffic through the best route, thereby increasing throughput and reducing congestion. Some routers and protocols (such as DECnet Local Area Transport (LAT) and IBM NetBIOS) are not compatible, thus eliminating the ability to directly route packets using these protocols.

The more computers on a network, the more network traffic will cause slower transfers and more data collisions. Using a router, the network may be broken into little networks called zones. If the router receives a packet that needs to proceed to another zone, the router sends it to that zone. If the packet destination is in the same zone, the packet is never exposed to other zones. This limits traffic across the entire network.

Gateways

Gateways are similar to routers except that they add additional capability and are more complex by being able to perform protocol translation. Gateways can connect networks that use different NOS software and that may or may not have similar hardware. (See Figure 3.10.) A gateway transmission could entail the use of three separate protocols: the source protocol, the transmission-path protocol, and the destination-network protocol. For example, a gateway can enable a Token Ring running IPX packets and an Ethernet running TCP/IP packets to communicate freely. The gateway translates the packets to the NOS native to that network before passing the packet through.

FIGURE 3.10.
A gateway placement.

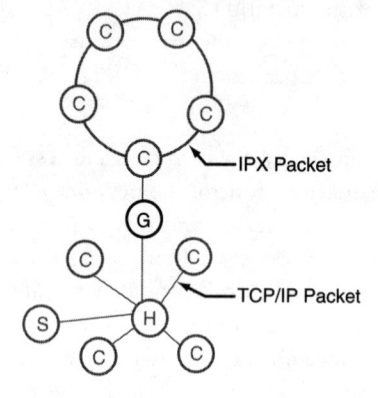

Gateways can also provide interfaces between various systems and database servers. For example, INTERSOLV, Inc. provides ODBC support for gateways such as IBM DDCS/2 and DDCS/6000, Micro Decisionware, Inc., Sybase-4 NetGateway, and Sybase-10 OmniSQL- Gateway. For more information, see Chapter 29, "Third-Party Tools, Utilities, and Controls."

Hubs

With the rapid growth of networks and the requirement to integrate more users and workstations, the first network-wiring concentrator or hub was developed. A hub is a central point where computers and/or networks are interconnected, traditionally for a star topology. These hubs can be physically made up of repeaters, bridges, routers, or a gateway. There are two types of hubs: passive and smart. A passive hub merely sits at the center of the star, connecting the various nodes. A smart hub, however, may be remotely controlled by the system operator and can send back packet-traffic information for analysis.

Network Operating Systems/File Servers

A server can be a simple file server that provides a central location for all of the nodes to store files, mail, data, and so on. A server may also monitor and govern network traffic, exchange data formats, perform print serving, do data queries, and so on.

There are many file servers available on the market. There are many different peer-to-peer solutions, and this market changes most often and dramatically. With the advent of Windows 95 and its extensive peer-to-peer functions, it is unclear what the future market will look like. For this reason, we have excluded information on these types of systems. For current information, check one of the popular magazines, such as *LAN Times*.

The file-server market is currently dominated by a single player: Novell. Between NetWare versions 3.*x* and 4.*x*, Novell is estimated to control between 70 and 80 percent of the current installed base. Microsoft is attempting to make strong inroads into this market with its product, Windows NT Server (also known as NT Advanced Server or NT AS). NT Advanced Server has the benefit of being well integrated with Microsoft's SQL Server product.

Following is a summary of the most common NOS systems. Although some of these systems may not seem relevant to Visual Basic client/server development, any configuration is possible through the use of ODBC drivers across a network. An overview may provide some insight into the system that you must use.

Windows NT 3.51

Windows NT 3.51 is a 32-bit advanced NOS that was designed for businesses and individuals needing advanced networking capabilities. It is made up of two parts, which are sold separately: Windows NT Workstation OS and Windows NT Server (was called Advanced Server) NOS. This can be fairly confusing, especially because people often refer to both NT Workstation and NT Server as simply NT (for example, "We're running NT as our file server").

Briefly, Windows NT Workstation is an advanced operating system. Windows NT supports multitasking, memory protection, and other advanced features that its simpler cousins (such as Windows 3.1 and Windows for Workgroups) lack. It will, however, run all software that runs on Windows 3.1 and WfW. Windows 95 includes many of NT's features, but still lacks the robustness of the NT operating system.

Windows NT Server, by contrast, is a complete file server and NOS. The confusion often arises because on a single machine, Windows Server runs under NT Workstation. (See Figure 3.11.) NT Server, therefore, appears as if it is a normal NT Workstation implementation with some extra utilities. In reality, NT Server handles numerous network protocols, file sharing, security, administration, and data-integrity functions.

Also, Microsoft SQL Server customers can purchase an NT SQL Server version that runs on the NT Server system. SQL Server is also available to run on top of the OS/2 operating system.

One of the design criteria of the Windows NT Workstation and NT Server products was to support computer systems having multiple processors. These computer systems are built with and use two or more processors or Central Processing Units (CPUs) simultaneously. Control of these systems (with multiple processors) is accomplished through the implementation of the concept called Symmetric MultiProcessing (SMP).

SMP is implemented through the use of hardware and software that is designed to coordinate tasks assigned to multiple processors. The Operating System (OS) divides up the tasks to be performed and distributes them as small subprocesses to different microprocessors to be executed simultaneously. To track the progress of the flow of subprocesses through multiple processors, the OS creates threads. A *thread* used in the SMP system is a technique implemented by an OS to keep track of the location and status of each process being executed by the different processors. These systems are using the multithreaded operating-system technologies.

FIGURE 3.11.
Windows NT Server setup.

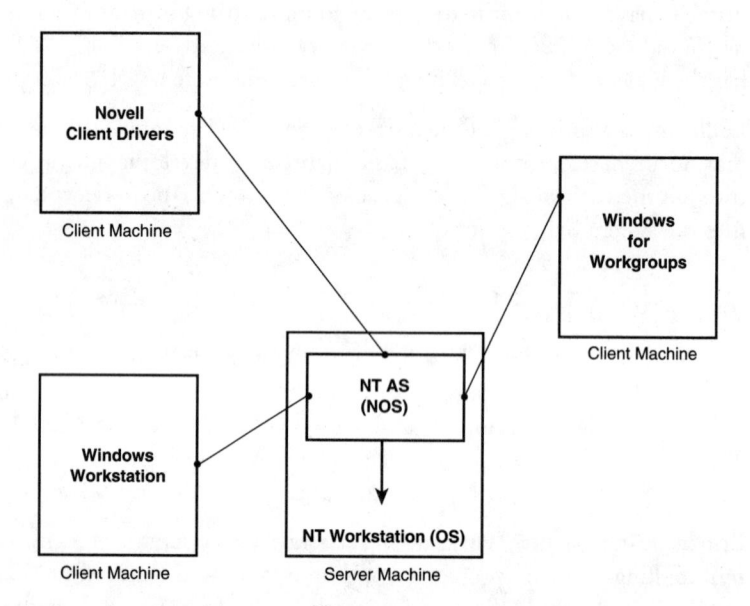

```
     Novell
  Client Drivers                                  Windows
                                                    for
                                                 Workgroups
   Client Machine
                                                Client Machine
                          NT AS
                          (NOS)
     Windows
    Workstation
                       NT Workstation (OS)
   Client Machine        Server Machine
```

Often the load on a single server is fairly great. As single-server machines perform more and more functions (such as database serving, file serving, etc.) the processing power required increases dramatically. The ability of NT Workstation, NT Server, and SQL Server to take advantage of these new SMP capabilities is often critical. Many servers are now judged by their scalability (ability to use an increasing number of processors) or lack thereof.

Windows NT has been ported to various hardware platforms including Intel 80*x*86, Pentium, and RISC (DEC Alpha, MIPS, and PowerPC). There are new Alpha-based workstations available running at 275 MHz and 300 MHz with Windows NT. Microsoft also has a version of Windows NT for the PowerPC. This prevents an organization from being locked into a single computer platform. A C/S system may be created freely by mixing and matching various machines for the best price/performance advantage.

Client/server programs developed with Visual Basic will run on any machine running NT. Windows NT provides an *x*86 emulation layer, so most programs will execute on any platform machine. Additionally, Microsoft has committed to recompile many of their applications (including the complete Microsoft Office) to run natively. With Windows NT running on many different platforms, a client/server system is not restricted to a single system vendor.

Windows NT supports a large number of protocols. The protocol support for NT 3.51 is IPX/SPX, enhanced support for TCP/IP, NetBIOS (NetBEUI) for LAN Manager compatibility, Data Link Control (DLC) for mainframe access, AppleTalk for Macintosh network integration, and Network File System, created by Sun. The NT 3.51 server also incorporates automatic configuration via the Dynamic Host Configuration Protocol (DHCP).

Windows NT Workstation

The following hardware lists were put together from minimum set requirements recommended by Microsoft for the Windows NT Workstation and Server. This equipment is needed for a user to operate Windows NT in the client/server enviroment.

- *Microprocessor*—80386 [other optional processors for high-end workstations are 80486, Pentium, or RISC (including PowerPC, MIPS R4000, MIPS R4400, DEC Alpha)]
- *Memory*—12MB (386 PC), 16 MB(RISC)
- *Hard Disk*—100MB or more (40MB hard disk space required)
- VGA high-resolution graphics
- Network adapter card
- CD-ROM (optional)

Windows NT Server (Advanced Server)

The NT Server minimum recommended configuration is

- *Microprocessor*—80386 [other optional processors are 80486, Pentium (1 or 2), or RISC (including PowerPC, MIPS R4000, MIPS R4400, DEC Alpha) (1 or 2)]
- *Memory*—12 MB (386 PC), 16MB (RISC)
- *Hard Disk*—300MB or more (90MB hard disk space required)
- VGA high-resolution graphics
- Network adapter card
- CD-ROM (optional)

NT Server 3.51 recommended RAM is 12MB–16MB. Through better design and memory management, NT 3.51 performance and speed have improved from 70 percent to 100 percent over an equal hardware system configuration operating Windows NT 3.1. Some additional performance increases would be seen with the addition of more RAM.

Remote Access Service (RAS) capabilities were enhanced with the inclusion of IPX/SPX rather than requiring additional software support. These capabilities were further enhanced by greater support for TCP/IP and NetBEUI protocols, additional or improved features such as PPP and SLIP, and encryption. Since Windows NT Workstation login restrictions were not incorporated as they were in NetWare, the login security feature is provided through a function called call-back. Call-back operation is performed by the server hanging up and calling back the client, thus providing toll call savings for remote clients along with security verification.

NetWare

Novell's NetWare has the largest installed based of server network systems. These systems were built around its fast, effective, and well-supported file and print servers. This experience with file and print servers and their database server for decision-support applications makes them an asset to Visual Basic client/server developers.

The NetWare Network Operating System was specially designed to take all memory and allocate it to NetWare cache. Through optimizing access to the file-cache portion, NetWare file servers have achieved their speed and performance by using this cache to manage files being serviced. NetWare Loadable Modules (NLMs) are parts of NetWare OS that provide hardware interfaces and utilities through server-based software executables. These NLMs also use memory-allocation routines to gain a portion of NetWare cache to service their application programs. The NetWare cache-memory pool can be accessed through many programmatic interfaces, causing memory-management problems. Novell recommends using ANSI-compatible APIs so that proper decisions are made in the allocation of this memory.

NetWare 3.11

NetWare 3.11 is Novell's designation for the version of NetWare 386. It was designed for file servers based on the Intel 80386 microprocessor. This networking software was mainly based around file servers, print servers, and a start, through the use of NetWare Loadable Modules (NLMs), in cross-platform compatibility. NetWare has been an Intel/PC-based networking system, where servers and users all had Intel/PC-based computer systems. The upgrade from NetWare 2.*x* was mainly to optimize the use of the 80386 microprocessor with Novell's NetWare software and provide the capability to store Macintosh files on a PC file server.

NetWare for the Macintosh came out in the time frame of version 2.15 as a value-added process. Macintosh support was left out of version 3.0 but added in version 3.1 through the use of an NLM. The NLM allowed Macintoshes to connect to a NetWare file server and store Macintosh files.

NLMs are part of the NetWare OS that is set aside to provide for extending the OS capabilities. These NLMs are located on the server along with NetWare OS. This area of the OS is where programmers implement developed applications that can provide new system services. These NLMs provide hardware interfaces, utilities, and server-based software execution with the capability of being loaded and unloaded while the server is in operation. NLMs are installed and become part of the NetWare OS.

In NetWare version 3.1, NLMs were a definite problem because they were causing unpredictable crashes and without resolution. These crashes were because of bugs in the application programs or conflicts between the NetWare OS and applications, sometimes shutting down the whole network. NetWare 3.1 had no memory protection for NLM applications, so when errors occurred it affected the entire system. Due to NetWare's lack of memory management, virtual-memory services are not supported; this eliminated paging code in and out of memory and limited the number of NetWare applications that could run on a server. The other limiting factor for operational users is the lack of preemptive multitasking, which prevents applications with higher priority from interrupting a running application.

NetWare 4.x

Novell NetWare 4.x includes many new features such as automatic data compression, significant online documentation, a new GUI interface, clients for DOS, Windows, and OS/2, support for SCSI jukeboxes, enhanced disk mirroring, and enhanced printing support.

Most significantly, the new version supports NetWare Directory Service (NDS). Initially, this new paradigm is difficult to set up and manage, but as networks become more integrated, directory services will become essential. Directory services allow the creation of a global naming service that lets users log onto a network, rather than onto each individual server. The naming services keep track of access privileges and resources, providing a global intermediary for the network.

LAN Server 4.0 for OS/2

OS/2 provides support for many of the standard formats, including the complete implementation of LAN Manager/Server data protocol, NetWare's IPX/SPX, and TCP/IP. LAN Server, the NOS available to run under OS/2, can take advantage of OS/2's SMP capabilities. LAN Server is a complete 32-bit NOS that features TCP/IP support, NetBIOS support, and numerous other protocols. LAN Server features most of the major features of the more dominant NOS programs. Like NT Server, however, it does lack global-naming capabilities.

AIX

AIX is a UNIX system, so AIX supports TCP/IP as its standard protocol. It also supports NetWare for AIX/6000 from IBM, which gives it IPX compatibility, FDDI networks, the Serial Optical Channel Converter (SOCC), and Enterprise System Connection (ESCON). The AIX/3270 host connection system allows the RS/6000 to be connected to a System/390 host computer using TCP/IP on SNA network protocols.

Solaris

The Solaris system supports TCP/IP. Solaris, developed by Sun, uses the Open Networking Computing (ONC) plus a family of protocols and distributed network services, including Network File System (NFS), Network Lock Manager, Automounter, Remote Execution service (REX), RPC Protocol Compiler, and so on. Additional protocols and formats will depend on implementation requirements.

Network Interface Design

The computer systems today must be capable of interfacing to networks that consist of portables, desktop systems, and workstations through the network servers. Generally these external interfaces are either Ethernet or Token Ring. The Ethernet standard (IEEE 802.3) or the Token-Ring standard (IEEE 802.5) define their electrical interfaces and connectors.

Network Standards

The ideal network is transparent to the hardware it interconnects. With a myriad of networking product manufacturers flooding the market with product, compatibility has become a real nightmare. The industry recognized this as a problem and became involved in creating and accepting performance standards. Layer standards have been created. (See Figure 3.12.)

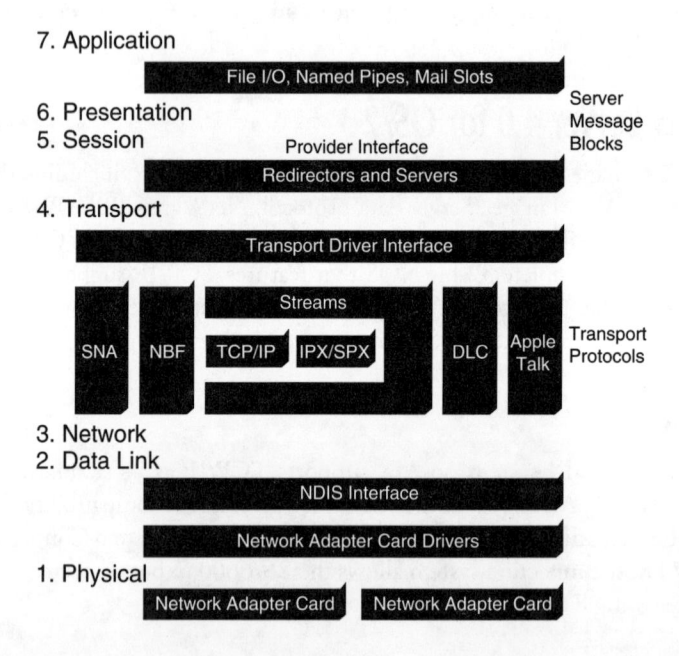

FIGURE 3.12.
Network layers.

7. Application
   - File I/O, Named Pipes, Mail Slots — Server Message Blocks
6. Presentation
5. Session
   - Provider Interface
   - Redirectors and Servers
4. Transport
   - Transport Driver Interface
   - Streams: SNA, NBF, TCP/IP, IPX/SPX, DLC, Apple Talk — Transport Protocols
3. Network
2. Data Link
   - NDIS Interface
   - Network Adapter Card Drivers
1. Physical
   - Network Adapter Card   Network Adapter Card

The Institute of Electronic and Electrical Engineers (IEEE) has undertaken the task of defining and producing a set of standards for networks using the International Standards Organization (ISO) seven-layer Open Systems Interconnection (OSI) model as the starting point. The IEEE published its first set of networking standards, the 802 series, in 1985 with standards 802.1 through 802.5. To try to keep up with technology there are proposed IEEE standards 802.6 through 802.10.

Wide Area Networks

Wide Area Networks (WANs) have become an increasingly hot topic in the last few years. With the growth of LANs and replication capabilities in file and database servers, people are beginning to look for convenient and widespread ways to hook LANs together over great geographic distances.

Replication of information in the C/S environment and in data warehousing is very important. It is the C/S system's alternative to the mainframe-centric central database (where all downloaded data comes from one common database). Replication services are a function of the server and its databases.

In the C/S environment, duplicate databases may be located on several servers. For example, three stores may wish to keep a single customer database. In the mainframe world, each store would have to keep a constant connection open to the central database. Using replication, three copies of the database may be kept: one at each location. The database server, at automatic intervals, connects to the other copies or mirrors of the database and synchronizes information. Replication services allow smaller servers to handle the load of a large organization through data coordination.

Replication services could also be known as automated replication management. Replication is particularly appropriate for use with Wide Area Networks. For example, each store in a geographically diverse location can keep its own copy of the database. At the end of the day, the server can automatically synchronize the data through a WAN such as the Internet. This is precisely the technique used by Usenet News servers on the Internet to coordinate message groups.

ATM and ISDN technologies are at the center of this push. They both provide extremely high bandwidth for network traffic—so high, in fact, that some people wonder whether all of this bandwidth is really necessary, considering the extra expense. ATM and ISDN are betting on the predicted multimedia explosion. Certainly, multimedia has exploded on the desktop in the last few years. Network-hardware manufacturers believe that users will have the same level of multimedia needs on the network: to send live video, to have video conferencing, to get mass data on demand, to send and receive video e-mail, and so forth.

What Are Wide Area Networks?

A Wide Area Network can be defined as a system for connecting computers over a large geographical area that provides for the sharing of information and hardware resources. These are what link the remote clients to the server containing their information. WANs may span the globe using satellite, microwave, fiber optic, and normal telephone communication links. The rapid growth in technology has begun the merging and integration of telephone communications and computer systems. Aspects of telecommunications such as teleconferencing, white boarding (interactive chalkboard talk on a computer display), and so on are being provided over WANs. This allows clients and customers to meet without spending large amounts of travel time and still communicate and transfer information stored in C/S system databases.

A wide range of technologies, equipment, protocols, and services are being used in support of C/S systems over WANs. The development of integrated systems and networks having the capability to transmit and process all types of data is emerging. Computing, switching, and digital-transmission technology, plus digitization techniques, are also being used for data, voice, and image transmission.

This section focuses only on WAN technology related to Integrated Services Digital Network (ISDN) and Asynchronous Transfer Mode (ATM). These two network technologies are most important to understand, because all future and some current C/S systems will be installed to work over ISDN and ATM networks. Therefore, focusing on computer, network-equipment, telephone, and multimedia interfaces will help C/S system developers to effectively design usable C/S systems. These technologies are also supporting the expansion of LANs and personal computers for broader information exchange.

The International Consultative Committee on Telegraphy and Telephony (Comite Consultatif International Telegraphique et Telephonique, or CCITT) is one of the most important organizations helping to define the standards for networking. The CCITT is trying to create a global networking standard so that all networks can intercommunicate. The CCITT is a branch of an arm of the United Nations. *Note:* The CCITT has changed its name to the International Telecommunications Union Telecommunication Standard Sector (ITU-TSS).

Most current computer systems do not create and process enough data to burden the data rates and the capacities of current LANs. However, transmission from LAN to LAN over geographic distances requires either expensive, dedicated lines or slow modems. WANs provide the capability to achieve LAN speeds over large geographic distances economically. With the coming of video data traffic, in addition to expanding normal data traffic, high-bandwidth, economical WANs will be required in the near future.

There are an incredible number of protocols and ways in which they are used. It becomes even more confusing when the industry freely mixes a protocol with an implementation. Therefore, be warned that the world of WANs is often confusing because people and companies use the same terms to mean different things.

What Is ISDN?

The CCITT established that ISDN was a network providing end-to-end digital connectivity in support of a wide range of services (as opposed to primarily standard analog phone lines). These services included digital voice and nonvoice services being made available to users. These services are accessible by using the limited set of standard, multipurpose user-network interfaces. In 1984, 1989, and 1991, the CCITT adopted a series of recommendations applying to

ISDN that attempted to keep ISDN specifications and goals current with technology and user needs. ISDN has a goal to standardize the operating parameters and interfaces so that a network can accommodate various mixed digital-transmission services. These services are a combination of digital data and digital voice or a mixture of lower-rate traffic transmissions over an ISDN channel.

So what is ISDN? It is a digital network made up of a variety of network technologies, architectures, structures, protocols, and services designed to provide data, voice, and image transmission among users through a standard interface. In an example implementation, an ISDN adapter card could be put into a PowerPC computer system at each end. (See Figure 3.13.) These machines could then freely exchange data at high speeds because the direct connection to the ISDN network is digital. The implementation of telecommunications technology in ISDN makes it possible to use these data services over an ISDN line. This capability helps provide a cost-effective and efficient way of delivering information faster and with greater accuracy, while providing connection stability.

ISDN Overview

The goal of the Integrated Services Digital Network (ISDN) is to be the worldwide digital telecommunication network through the development of integrated systems that can transmit and process all types of data. This network will encompass the existing public telecommunication networks and provide industry and the public with a broader range of services. The ISDN system uses reliable digital-transmission technology over high-quality, reliable transmission links. These links include many existing and future optical-fiber networks, some using technology like Synchronous Optical Network (SONET).

FIGURE 3.13.
An ISDN connection overview.

ISDN may use many transmission protocols or services, including ATM, Switched Multimegabit Data Service (SMDS), X.25, frame relay, and direct protocol. The ISDN network is essentially a free-form digital network, a transparent highway over which different protocols can share transport capability. (See Figure 3.14.) The protocols that can be used on it are essentially limitless and are mostly governed by the pursuit of compatibility. This incredible flexibility has been at the root of many of the complaints and much of the confusion surrounding ISDN. One device that attaches to ISDN needs either the same or a translatable protocol. Historically, ISDN has been a network in which numerous proprietary and public protocols exist, making communication compatibility often difficult.

FIGURE 3.14.
The ISDN cloud.

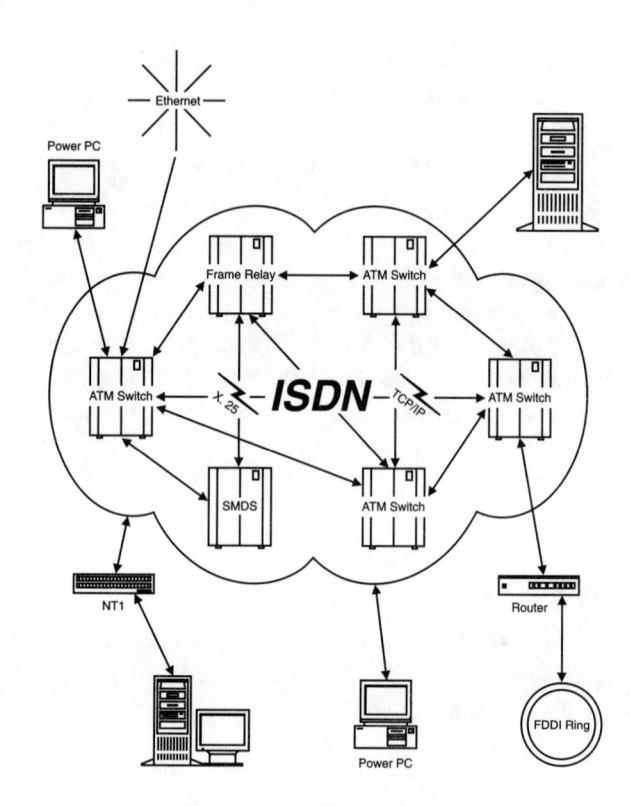

What Are the HDLC, X.25, Frame Relay, and SMDS Protocols?

The High Level Data Link Control (HDLC) is one of the most widely supported foundation protocols. HDLC is an internationally adopted ISO standard. It can be referred to as a bit-oriented protocol because messages are treated as a string of bits (called a frame), rather than a string of characters. It is the basis for the data link layers of ISDN, frame relay, V.42, X.25, and the link layer of SNA.

There are three types of frames: information or I frames, supervisory control sequences or S frames, and command/response or U frames. These frames all have the following basic format; each part is called a field, and each frame begins and ends with a flag or flag field with a specific bit pattern: 01111110. (See Figure 3.15.) Moving left to right in the figure, the next field over is the 8-bit address field, which contains the address of the destination unit for a control or information frame, and the source of the response for a response frame. The next field is the 8-bit control field, where each frame has a different control frame meaning. The information field, which exists only in the information frame, is not limited in length. This field is followed by a frame check field, which is 16 bits long. Ending the frame is the ending flag consisting of the following 8 bits: 01111110.

FIGURE 3.15.
HDLC frame format.

Begin Flag	Address	Control	Information	Frame Check	End Flag

The X.25 protocol (CCITT X.25) is a packet-switched protocol. This protocol is commonly used to set up X.25 networks. ISDN features the capability of transmitting and hooking into X.25 networks. X.25 protocol features three layers: Layer 1 (Physical Layer) is similar to RS-232, Layer 2 (Link Access Protocol) is Higher Data Link Control and Link Access Protocol Balanced (HDLC Lap B), and Layer 3 (Packet Layer) contains the rules for successful data transfer across public networks.

The X.25 protocol was designed for communication links (channels) with high bit-error rates (BER). CCITT X.25 describes the X.25 protocol interfaces and CCITT X.21 is the standard covering the physical interface. To provide a near-term solution to the high bit-error problem, link-level flow control and retransmission became part of the X.25 protocol.

The link-level flow control protocol manages the exchange of a data frame and an acknowledge frame. Part of the X.25 error-checking process uses an acknowledge system that follows all transmissions. The receiver of the transmission replies with an acknowledge (ACK) for packets accepted. It replies with a negative acknowledge (NAK) for packets not accepted due to error. The acknowledge-system process occurs at every hop point (retransmission point or node) between the source and destination along the WAN.

An X.25 frame contains control information and the actual X.25 packets. (See Figure 3.16.) The frame consists of a flag (1 byte), an address (1 byte), a control field (1 byte), a packet (3–131 bytes), field sequence check (2 bytes), and a final flag (1 byte). The packet itself contains 3 bytes of control information and up to 128 bytes of user data. (See Figure 3.17.)

FIGURE 3.16.
The X.25 frame format.

Flag	Address	Control	Packet	Field Sequence Check	Flag

FIGURE 3.17.
X.25 packet.

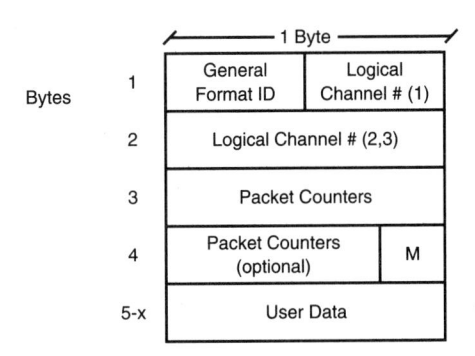

Bytes		
1	General Format ID	Logical Channel # (1)
2	Logical Channel # (2,3)	
3	Packet Counters	
4	Packet Counters (optional)	M
5-x	User Data	

(1 Byte width indicated across top)

In X.25, after an error was detected, the packet in error is retransmitted. Technological improvements seen in copper and fiber signaling channels have produced a significant reduction in BERs. Switching networks using the X.25 protocol are now burdened with the overhead involved with implementing the link-level flow control and retransmission process with drastically reduced benefits.

With the incorporation of reliable transmission technology, the error-checking and retransmission features of the X.25 packet-switching protocol make it less than optimal for use on ISDN. To provide a protocol that optimizes ISDN assets, frame relay protocol was developed.

Frame relay is a protocol based on the X.25. (See Figure 3.18.) One of its design goals was to reduce unnecessary overhead from X.25 error checking. Frame relay was to be used on highly reliable lines based on newer transmission technology than X.25 was created to handle. Frame relay will supplant X.25 as ISDN matures. Designed for use on ISDN, frame relay has become much more widely implemented in non-ISDN environments.

FIGURE 3.18.
The frame relay frame format.

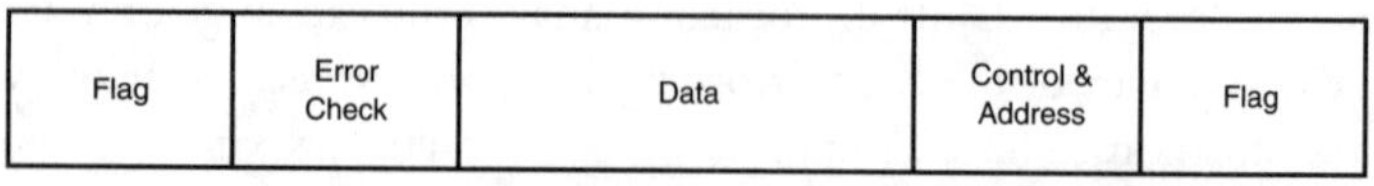

Flag	Error Check	Data	Control & Address	Flag

To achieve the lower overhead of the frame-relay protocol, the flow control and error correction through automatic retransmission were removed. Also, X.25 Layers 2 and 3 were combined as the multiplexing and switching of logical connections was placed in Layer 2. This technique eliminated an entire layer that had been present in X.25. Call-control signaling was also placed on a line separate from the data (see the section, "Narrowband ISDN (Original)," later in this chapter). If the frame relay occurs over a fixed line, the call-control signaling is not required.

Frame relay is a connection type protocol based on the X.25 standard protocol. Frame relay, like X.25, implements error checking on the data link level, although detected errors are handled differently. In frame-relay protocol, there is a Discard Eligibility (DE) bit sent with each frame. In X.25, every packet in error would be retransmitted. In frame relay, when an error is detected in a frame and the DE bit is set, the frame is simply discarded. The data source is not notified of the error or the discarded frame. If the DE bit is not set, a signal is sent to a higher level to retransmit the data.

Applying frame relay to certain applications that require high data-rate transfers can provide real-time benefits. Some services or applications include block interactive data programs, file transfer, multiplexing of low bit-rate channels, and character interactive traffic programs. The block interactive data transfer applications, like high-resolution videotex or CAD/CAM systems, require small delays and high data throughput to produce their high-resolution graphics.

When large data-file-transfer requirements are being looked at, high throughput is normally the critical parameter. Transfers must be completed in a reasonable amount of time. Frame relay can be used for transferring one large block of data.

This block consists of multiplexed data from a group of low bit-rate user applications requesting communication over a WAN. It is usually more economical to transfer larger amounts of data over a short period than to complete many slow, small individual transfers. Text editing done across the network, for example, consists of many small packets of information requiring transfer. These could be packaged as a single larger frame because they normally consist of short frames, low delays, and low throughput.

Frame-relay networks consist of a series of queues. Frames may stack up in a frame buffer, which can cause unacceptable delays for high-throughput applications. Therefore, frame-relay systems must rely on the network systems to implement a procedure of congestion control. There are two buffers for each frame device: a transmission and a reception buffer. When the reception buffer becomes too full, one of two strategies is activated; either some of the frames in the buffer are discarded, or the device sending the frames is signaled to slow down its transmission. The protocol to slow down the transmitting device is called congestion control.

Congestion control seeks to minimize the number of discarded frames and regulate the flow of traffic on the network. Regulating the flow of network traffic ensures that network resources can be fairly distributed and a single transmitter does not monopolize bandwidth. Because frame relay is optimized for high-throughput operations, only simple congestion-control functions are built in. Therefore, it is primarily the network's responsibility to monitor the network traffic and implement congestion control.

Switched Multimegabit Data Service (SMDS) is to be a high-speed connectionless service (Class D or 4) that will extend LAN-like performance outside the subscriber premises across the metropolitan area. SMDS is proposed to sit on top of the Distributed Queue Dual Bus (DQDB). Distributed Queue Dual Bus and FDDI are two types of High-Speed Local Area Networks (HSLANs) which have specified or proposed transmission rates of 100MB/second and use optical fiber as the transmission media. Offered by Bellcore, SMDS is offered at DS1 and DS3.

SMDS, like ATM, divides all data into small, 53-byte packets called slots. Unlike ATM, SMDS uses three physical layer formats for data transmission. The delays inherent in a system with this much overhead make it a poor candidate for real-time, data-transfer operations.

Data Transfer Rate Comparison—LAN, WAN, Modem, and I/O

Communications are becoming more data intensive every day. The need to transfer data at high speeds typically comes at a substantial cost. ISDN, however, promises to revolutionize this price/performance issue. The ISDN has been growing and expanding areas where access is available for almost 10 years.

The data-transfer rates of most typical data-communications devices are featured on a logarithmic scale. (See Figure 3.19.) You will notice that the speed of the WANs is approaching those of local I/O bus structures (SCSI, 1394, and so on). I/O buses, however, are not useful for long-distance data transfer. The Basic ISDN or Basic Rate Interface (BRI) ISDN is substantially faster than current 14.4K and 28.8K modems. With the low monthly cost of these

ISDN connections, they are extremely economical for even routine enterprise-data transfers. The Primary ISDN or Primary Rate Interface (PRI) ISDN achieves data rates unachievable with a standard modem, bringing transfer rates to about the speed of Ethernet LANs. This transfer rate is great enough for the large majority of standard data-transfer needs.

FIGURE 3.19.
Data transfer rates.

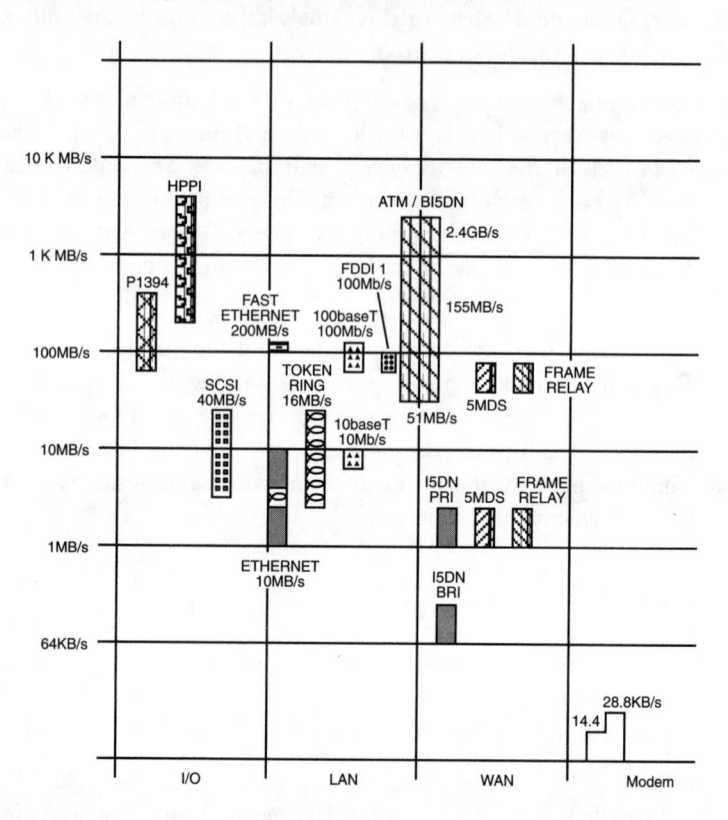

Broadband ISDN (B-ISDN) connections provide transfer rates suitable for organizations. The bandwidth is on par with ATM LANs and Fast Ethernet. These lines can be used for full digital-video transfer (multimedia applications), backbone communications, and complete LAN-to-LAN access. A B-ISDN connection requires a complete fiber-optic network from both the source (your service provider must have fiber capabilities) and the destination (your network must be able to accept a fiber line). This can become expensive and is usually possible only for organizations that can justify the need for such high data-transfer rates.

National ISDN-1,2 and Beyond

The creators of ISDN realized that they would need to create a international standard for implementation by providers. Agreed to under the sponsorship of the Corporation for Open Systems International (COS), the standard seeks to create levels of implementation. Each level specifies services and capabilities that the ISDN switches will support. It also defines the way devices interact and communicate with ISDN (telephone, terminals, and so on). These standards are known as National ISDN, with each level becoming more stringent as to the type of services the provider must supply.

The first level, National ISDN 1 (NI-1) requires implementation of uniform Basic Rate Interface (BRI) and critical supplementary services in the geographic area to be classified. It also requires the availability of Primary Rate Interface (PRI). National ISDN 1 is the most commonly implemented level around the U.S. today.

National ISDN-2 (NI-2) requires all of the specifications of NI-1, but also requires uniform deployment of PRI, consistent implementation of end-user services, and the availability of Multirate ISDN. Multirate ISDN (sometimes called Switched Fractional DS-1) is an alternative to the bonding architecture; it uses signal-call, circuit-switched technology to provide the next step in ISDN services. It provides flexible, dialable channels with transmission speeds up to 1.536MB/second. Bandwidth is negotiable and is determined at call origination.

National ISDN-3 (NI-3) is in only the preliminary stages at this point. It will provide additional end-user services as it matures in the next couple of years.

ISDN Codes

The vast variety of products and services available for ISDN can be confusing and often bewildering. Customers often don't know what questions to ask, let alone what the advantages of particular products are. In order to solve this problem, the Solutions '94 forum sought to make ISDN more accessible. It created something called ISDN ordering codes.

An ordering code is a preestablished set of network services associated with specific customer equipment for a specific application. These codes are based on the most popular configurations of ISDN equipment in use around the country. To place an order for an ISDN service, the customer must simply specify the code included on the current equipment. More than 40 vendors of ISDN Customer Premise Equipment (CPE) support ISDN codes, with over 100 codes already registered. Using an ordering code such as "Generic Data M," the ISDN service provider will configure the line so the equipment can work right out of the box.

Narrowband ISDN (Original)

Narrowband ISDN started with basic circuit-switch technology. It is using a switching unit as a 64Kb/second channel and carries variable-length packets. New client/server systems are coming on line in increasing numbers and these systems are demanding more network throughput and bandwidth.

To increase speeds on the narrowband ISDN, many systems currently include compression. This compresses the packet automatically at one LAN end, sends the packet, and the other LAN decompresses the packet and puts it on the network.

There are two forms of narrowband ISDN interface: BRI and PRI. (See Figure 3.20.) Both of these rates may be used over traditional twisted-pair lines. These means they are perfect digital networks for personal use and any small-to-medium sized organization. The ISDN communication channels could be called digital pipes that connect subscriber to subscriber. These pipes may vary in capacity do to size and the quantity of the channel needed for user to user transfers. There are three common type of ISDN channels, designated as B, D, and H; each has assigned bit-transmission rates as shown in Table 3.1.

Table 3.1. ISDN channel types and interface structures.

Channel	Bit Rate	Interface	Application
B	64Kb/second	Basic access	Basic user channel
H0	384Kb/second	Primary rate access	HO, H11, H12— Video, Private networking between PBXs and links between other networks
H11	1536Kb/second	Primary rate access	
H12	1920Kb/second	Primary rate access	
D16	16Kb/second	Basic access	Signal control information
D64	64Kb/second	Primary rate access	

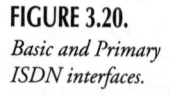

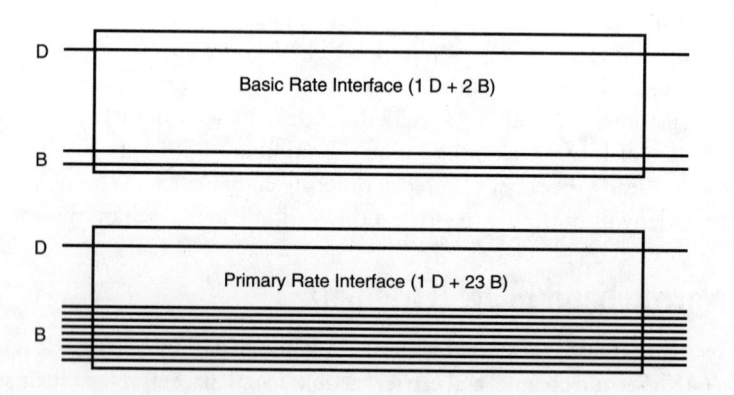

FIGURE 3.20.
Basic and Primary ISDN interfaces.

Basic Rate Interface (1 D + 2 B)

Primary Rate Interface (1 D + 23 B)

Narrow ISDN is divided into two basic channels: Bearer Channel (B Channel) and Data Channel (D Channel). This may be confusing, because the B Channel is the one that most often carries all of the data. Transfer rates of ISDN vary with the local ISDN supplier's implementation in your geographic area. (See Table 3.2.)

Table 3.2. Basic and primary narrowband ISDN transfer rates.

Interface	Gross Bit Rate	Structure
Basic access	192Kb/second	2B + D16
Primary rate access	1.544Mb/second	23B + D64
	1.544Mb/second	3H0 + D64
	1.544Mb/second	4H0
	2.048Mb/second	5H0 + D64
		H11 and so on
Primary rate access	2048Kb/second	30B + D64
		5H0 + D64
		H12 + D64
		and so on

D Channel carries the control and signaling information for the data on the B Channel. The channel runs at 16Kb/second when signaling information. Channel D is typically a low-bandwidth channel that is used to call for access to a connection, connect, and provide set-up information for the data transfer. This is called out-of-band signaling.

The D Channel is supported by its own protocol, called Common Channel Signaling System 7 (CCSS7). This defines how the D Channel will communicate. The channel handles the call signaling (call establishment), call progress monitoring, call termination, and enhanced telephone features. It does this in two parts: the message-transfer part and the user part. The message-transfer part provides the call establishment, disconnection, supervision, and billing. The user part accommodates user (or service provider) features or services. The user parts correspond to the higher layers of the OSI model. All call requests for use of the B channel are sent over the D channel. These signals request access to the B channel and pass signaling information to control circuit-switched calls. The D channel can be used for packet switching or low-speed telemetry. For this channel to be used efficiently, the signal flow is controlled by statistical multiplexing, which will allow the three types of signal to share the same channel.

In a traditional phone line, the same channel carries is used for signaling and voice/data information. (See Figure 3.21.) This wastes a portion of the bandwidth because, although the connection is active, extra bandwidth needed only for signaling remains in use. By separating the voice/data line from the signaling line, bandwidth isn't wasted during the connection.

D Channel may also be used to send X.25 packets. This allows ISDN to be used all over the world (where legacy X.25 networks exist). The X.25 packet transfer may be used for user messaging, small file transfers, transaction processing, remote telemetry, and a host of other applications.

FIGURE 3.21.
A phone line versus an ISDN line.

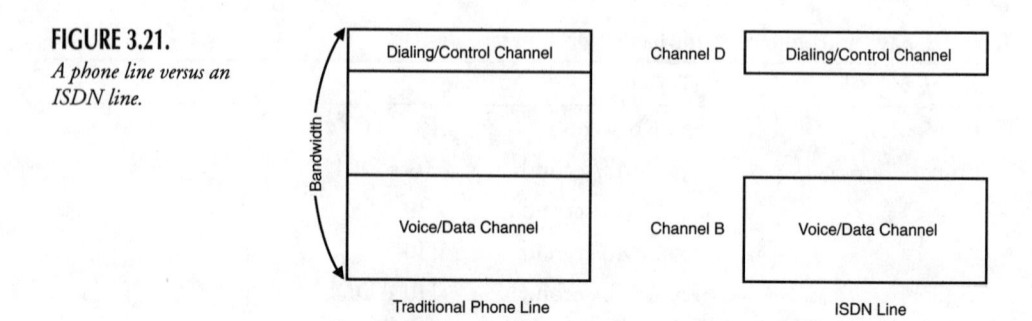

B Channel typically carries all of the data for the transmission. Multiple B Channels may be used together for higher single-channel bandwidth (see "What Is Bonding Architecture?" later in this chapter). Each Channel B can independently support individual data, voice, and video. When mixed traffic does occurs on the B channel, circuit switching is required and all of the traffic must be destined for the same destination.

A single Channel B line has a throughput of 64Kb/second. If a Signaling System 7 is unavailable in a remote area of the country, the B Channel can use some of its bandwidth to carry the control signaling. This reduces the line's possible throughput to 56Kb/second.

The B channel can be set up with three kinds of connections: a circuit-switched, a packet-switched, or a semipermanent. A circuit-switched connection is the same as the current-switched digital service, which uses a circuit-switched connection like the telephone to join two users together. The packet-switched connection is when a user is connected to a packet-switching node, and data is packetized using X.25 or frame-relay protocols prior to being transmitted between users. A semipermanent connection is similar to a leased line connection, where pre-arranged protocols are set up between users prior to making the call.

H Channel—a high-speed transparent digital channel roughly equivalent to current T carrier channels (expensive T1 & T3 data lines)—is not very common. This gives ISDN the capability to transfer data at up to 1.544MB/second.

Basic and Primary Rate Interface

BRI uses two B Channels and one D Channel. This is usually the most inexpensive and common service. BRI can use either B Channel for voice or data. The D Channel is for low-speed, low-priority signaling or packet-switched data. The total data rate is 192Kb/second, with 144Kb/second available to users.

A BRI supplies two 64Kb/second lines, which, if bonded (see below), allow transfer rates of 128Kb/second. This is almost nine times faster than the standard 14.4Kb/second modem and more than four times faster than a high-speed 28.8Kb/second modem. Additionally, modems reach their ideal throughput only on perfect lines. One of the greatest advantages of digital lines over the traditional analog phone lines is the constancy of quality. Through digital networks, a "bad line" is rarely a problem because line noise is virtually eliminated. Line noise is all too common in traditional phone lines, slowing down even the transfer rate of the modem because of required packet retransmission.

PRI is similar to BRI but contains 23 B Channel lines and one D Channel. Each B Channel can run up to 64Kb/second for a total throughput of 1472Kb/second. This gives the total throughput as 1.5Mb/second, which makes it compatible with the traditional T1 lines. *Note:* The European standard runs at a total throughput of 2Mb/second (which provides 30 B Channels and one D Channel). The PRI is designed for volume requirements such as large-scale computer connections, PBX services, and trunk lines.

What Is Bonding Architecture?

Bonding architecture allows B Channel lines to be aggregated to form one large bandwidth. If implemented with allocation on demand, this provides the ability to configure the bandwidth of the ISDN line as needed. For example, if in the morning high throughput is required for a video conference, 6 B Channels can be "bonded" to form one high-throughput line. After the conference is over, these lines can be released as lines for individual use.

Bonding provides an extremely powerful feature in order to allocate a service as needed. It offers wide-bandwidth ISDN users flexible configurable channels.

How to Hook Up to Narrowband ISDN

ISDN is most likely available from your local phone-system provider. If the phone company has set up ISDN switching circuits at its central station, ISDN can be wired with a standard twisted pair, shielded or unshielded.

To attach narrow ISDN to a computer or network, one of three devices may be used. The Network Termination Device (NT1) is an interface for each BRI connection, and it provides line testing and line-conversion capabilities. This is sometimes built into ISDN-compatible devices.

The terminal adapter attaches computer systems, workstations, and other devices to the ISDN line. Many ISDN telephone include a built-in terminal adapter.

An aggregation device is most often used to attach a LAN to ISDN. This device features bonding of multiple ISDN lines. It most often exists as an ISDN network bridge.

There are various ISDN devices available for ISA and PCMCIA slots. Motorola produces a BRI connection and terminal emulator in one card (PCTA 120). Dassault AT produces a BRI card for a type-2 PCMCIA slot (MCIA-FID). The ISDN product market is rapidly changing. It is nearly impossible for any published book to be current on all of the new hardware. Consult your local vendors and magazine for more current information.

Major ISDN vendors such as Intel, Inc. and Combinet, Inc. have ISDN network bridges available. These products vary in relation to security features, price, compression abilities, installation level, dynamic-channel allocation, console-administration tools, performance, and general compatibility.

Narrow ISDN in Remote Areas

ISDN is offered commonly in major metropolitan areas. Access from remote areas is growing, but it may be unavailable in the area needed. To ensure this isn't a key problem, it is possible to hook to an ISDN through Switched 56 services offered by both regional and interchange carriers.

Switched 56 links are single-channel, switched-data connections. They are capable of 56Kb/second transfer rate. Access is widely available throughout the US.

Switched 56 is often slightly more expensive than ISDN. It also cannot carry digital voice signals, making it inappropriate for single-connection, enterprise-wide services.

What Is Point-to-Point Protocol (PPP)?

Point-to-Point Protocol (PPP) is a nonproprietary protocol for any serial line links. It is based on the industry standard HDLC (see "What Are the HDLC, X.25, Frame Relay, and SMDS Protocols?" earlier in this chapter), so much of the standard definition work is already done. To the HDLC standard, PPP adds a section for protocol identification. (See Figure 3.22.) This allows packets to be conveniently and accurately identified making cross-network compatibility a possibility.

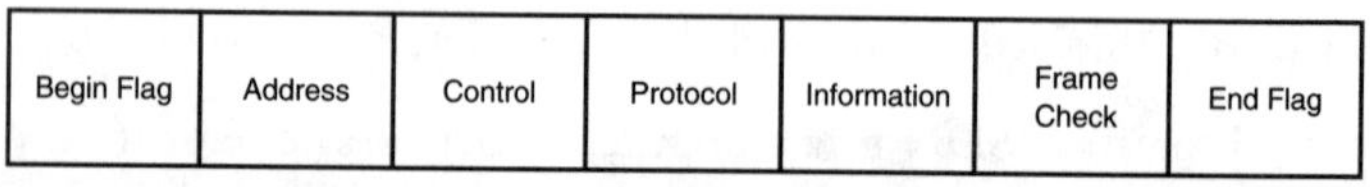

FIGURE 3.22.
A Point-to-Point Protocol packet.

Begin Flag	Address	Control	Protocol	Information	Frame Check	End Flag

PPP encapsulates traditional network-layer protocols inside a standard packet format, allowing remote tunneling of diverse packets. Protocols that may be encapsulated include IP (the network layer of TCP/IP), IPX (NetWare), Banyan Vines, and any implementation of the Open Systems Interconnection (OSI) network layer.

PPP can replace Serial Line Internet Protocol (SLIP) in many circumstances and is much more powerful. PPP is becoming the glue that allows many LANs to communicate over Narrow ISDN. The Internet Engineering Standard Group has officially approved the PPP as an open standard of datagrams across network links.

Broadband ISDN (B-ISDN)

The implementation of Broadband ISDN (B-ISDN) uses all of the protocol and connections of ATM to provide extremely high throughput transmission. B-ISDN lines are required to be fiber based and have transmission rates from 50MB/second to an estimated 2.4GB/second.

Broadband ISDN Reference Model

The reference model uses different conceptual planes to represent user, control, and management functions. (See Figure 3.23.) Structurally, this layered model is based on the same hierarchical framework as the traditional OSI-layer model. It is described as part of the ITU-TSS Recommendation I.320, the ISDN Protocol Reference model, and it provides a way to understand the different parts of the ATM protocol.

FIGURE 3.23.
The B-ISDN Protocol Reference model.

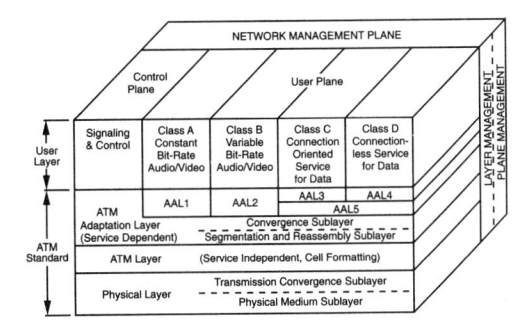

The user plane returns information to the user on the status of transfers. It can provide information about flow control and recovery of errors. The user plane can also transmit and receive user information.

The control plane handles all of the control and connection control functions. It performs the signaling necessary for connection setup, supervision, and call release.

The management plane provides interlayer and interplane management functions.

The highest level in the B-ISDN model varies with implementation. It supports high-level protocols such as Ethernet and Token Ring.

AAL has five different service classes. (See Table 3.3.) Each class is built around the allowable amount of transmission delay acceptable. ATM, by implementation, is typically connection-oriented. This means that a connection must be made before data transmission can begin. This is the basis of the ATM virtual channel. In contrast, LANs are connectionless in that they can send out packets to a node as soon as it is connected to the network. This makes it necessary for vendors to do extra work in order to design products that allow current LAN applications work across an ISDN WAN. Currently, no standard definition of this "LAN emulation" exists, so each implementation is vendor specific.

Table 3.3. Five specifications of AAL.

AAL 1—Class A	Connection-oriented
	Constant-rate data stream
	Strict timing requirement
	Applications: Full-motion video, audio
AAL 2—Class B	Connection-oriented
	Variable-rate data stream
	Strict timing requirement
	Common data type: compressed data
AAL 3—Class C	Connectionless-oriented
	Designed for use with protocols such as SMDS
	Loose timing requirement
	LAN emulation
	Common data type: intermittent, high-capacity data traffic
AAL4—Class D	Connectionless-oriented
	Designed for use with protocols such as SMDS
	Loose timing requirement
	Common data type: intermittent, high-capacity data traffic
AAL5—Class C	Connection-oriented
	Variable-rate data stream
	Very low cell overhead
	LAN emulation

The ATM Adaptation Layer (AAL) has two sublayers: the Convergence sublayer and the Segmentation and Reassembly layer (SAR). This layer maps the services from their native format to the ATM layer. The Convergence sublayer converts the user data buffer into an AAL structure. This sublayer adds any header or footer information required by the AAL. The Segmentation and Reassembly layer does the mapping of user data to ATM cells.

The ATM Layer deals only with information contained in the header, creating and extracting the header. This layer is common to all services. There are two types of ATM cells: User-to-Network Interface (UNI) and Network-to-Network Interface (NNI). UNI is used from a node to access an ATM switch. NNI is used to communicate with other ATM switches, and it also performs routing of cells, multiplexing, and flow control. After the cells are segmented, the header is added.

The physical layer has two sublayers: the Transmission Convergence (TC) sublayer and the Physical Medium (PMD) sublayer. The TC sublayer actually maps the ATM cells onto the transmission medium (that is, the transmission frame format). It is responsible for cell delineation and some simple cell-mapping functions. The TC calculates the final byte of the five-byte cell header, fills the frame with null cells (if necessary), and handles frame delineation.

The physical layer currently has four mediums specified: DS3 for 44.76MB/second transfer, multimode fiber for 100MB/second transfer, Block coded at 155MB/second (traditional ATM speed), and synchronous digital hierarchy framing at 155MB/second (the standard SONET implementation).

Transmission Mechanism: ATM

Asynchronous Transfer Mode (ATM), also known as cell relay, has been a major contributor in the development of technology supporting the broadband ISDN effort. ATM provides significant benefits over frame-relay–based transmission. ATM is capable of reaching gigabit transfer rates, whereas frame relay is limited in its current specification to around 2Mb/second. ATM was also designed for wide-bandwidth applications so it will support isochronous network traffic.

How to Hook Up to Broadband ISDN

Wide ISDN must be accomplished by hooking your ATM switchbox to the provider's switchbox. How this is done, and if it is available, depends on your local provider. There are, however, two common types of B-ISDN lines: Class A and Class C. Class A transfer is high-data-rate and constant-bit-rate audio/video. This is commonly used to implement guaranteed bandwidth applications such as video conferencing. Class C lines are typical high-speed data transfer, but are used where the persistent, time-based transfer of data is less crucial than Class A. Class A lines can cost about three times as much as a standard Class C, so this extreme cost must often be justified.

Both classes correspond to the AALs. AALs map the data from the native format into the AAL. This performs error checking, removes jitters, and discards corrupt information. Some AALs also ensure that data is received properly and signal the sender if the data has to be resent. You may find lines that correspond to AALs other than A or C, but they are far more rare.

Asynchronous Transfer Mode (ATM)

Asynchronous Transfer Mode (ATM) is a set of protocols and hardware that allow for extremely high speed, wide bandwidth data transfers. Transfer rates run the spectrum from 25MB/second to 2GB/second. ATM is a switched, connection-oriented technology available at both LAN and WAN levels. (See Figure 3.24.) ATM significantly improves price/performance ratios from past WAN solutions.

FIGURE 3.24.
ATM operational concept.

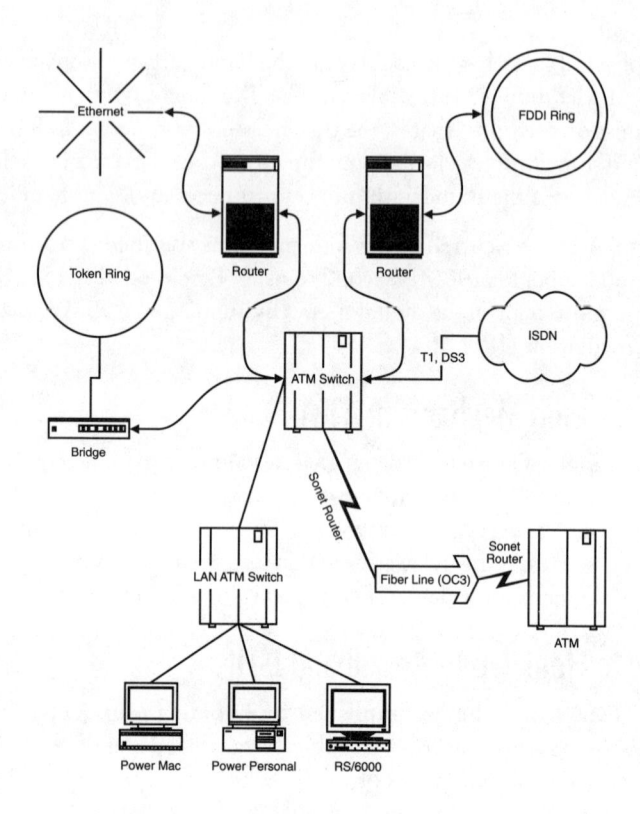

ATM networks operate in burst modes to send tremendous amounts of data over the network. (See Figure 3.25.) There are three key areas in which ATM differs from other network technology: parallel orientation, fixed-length cells, and virtual-channel connection capabilities.

FIGURE 3.25.
ATM network traffic.

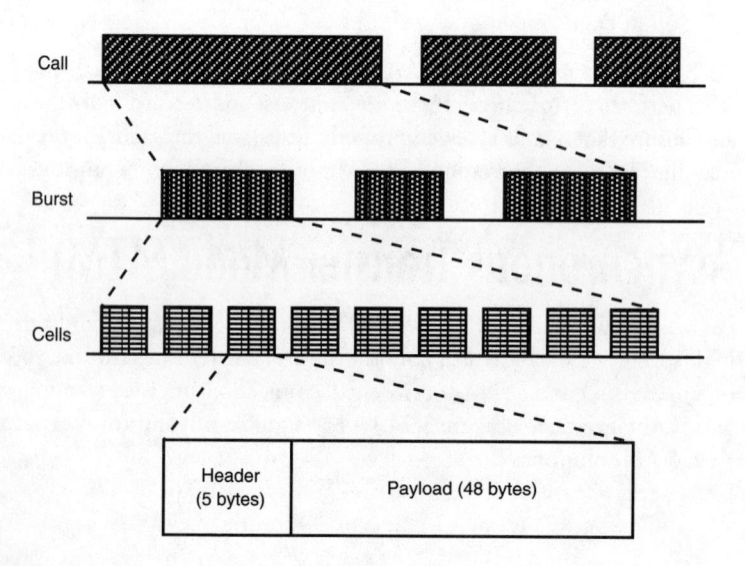

Parallel Orientation

Traditional LANs have a serial orientation. Ethernet, for example, has a transfer rate of 10MB/second. The network, however, can transmit only one packet at a time over the line, in a serial fashion. This means that the more network traffic there is, the slower the real transfer rate. For example, if an Ethernet network had 10 machines hooked up to it that were all transmitting at the same time, the transfer rate would be fairly low. Don't forget that only one packet may be on the network at one time. This means with 10 machines all sending data on a 10MB/second system, the actual transfer rate for each machine would be around 1MB/second. This is before you consider transfer overhead and slowdowns because of data collision. Even though a star network appears as if a line goes to each node, only one packet may be transmitted at a time.

ATM has no such problems. ATM is hooked up as a parallel network, meaning a truly individual line goes to each node. As more nodes and traffic are added to the ATM system, the throughput for each node remains the same. This becomes extremely important if multimedia network applications become prevalent.

Fixed Length Cells

A discrete data block on an ATM network is called a cell. Each cell has a definite length: 53 bytes. (See Figure 3.26.) Most networks use variable-length packets to transmit data. An ATM network maps data into fixed-length cells. When the cells reach their destination, they are reassembled into their original data (usually a tradition packet).

FIGURE 3.26.
ATM cell structure.

Generic Flow Control (4 bits)	Virtual Path Identifier (8 bits)	Virtual Channel Identifier (12 bits)	Payload Type (3 bits)	C L P	Header Error Check (8 bits)	Cell Payload (48 bytes)

Fixed-length cells are required for the technique of hardware switching. Switching is the foundation of ATM's phenomenal speed and high price/performance level. It also allows the constancy required for applications that will require "guaranteed bandwidth," such as live video transfer.

Virtual Channel Connection

ATM is a protocol that is connection-oriented. When the connection between a sender and a receiver is established, a virtual channel is created. It then provides a common path or channel from the sender to the receiver. This is one of the features that allows the ATM cells to be so small; they need to identify themselves only with a channel ID rather than a complete IP address, for example.

The virtual channel also enables networks managers (and service providers) to gain end-to-end data on the amount of data sent. This allows a provider, for example, to charge the sender only for the time that was actually used. These virtual channels also provide various paths through which the data is sent to provide network traffic load balancing and bandwidth allocation.

Because of virtual channels, ATM also provides redundancy. The source and destination are known by the channel, so if a link or switch fails, the traffic is automatically rerouted around the problem.

ATM Hardware

It is forecast that ATM will be key to future growth in interfacing desktop computer systems to the information superhighway. With the current increase in popularity of ATM, more products are becoming available such as adapter cards, bridges, concentrators, routers, and servers. Through technology advancements, products are currently available and are being developed that allow the integration of ATM into LANs and WANs, along with private and public networks.

The PC computer systems currently can be connected to Ethernet LANs and, through the LANs, to ATM networks. A PCI ATM adapter card is currently being built by IBM and will be available in the near future. Currently the PCI interface slots is being built into most desktop PC systems and some workstations. This provides the capability to interface directly to ATM network equipment through an adapter card. Thus providing users direct access to the ATM networks, bypassing the LAN interface. The other ATM products discussed here are to provide the reader with information to understand what may be required and incorporated when interfacing to a ATM network.

ATM Adapters

ATM hardware is becoming increasingly available and easy to find. Makers and brands proliferate daily. The following is a general overview of some of the available hardware. We don't seek to favor the IBM brand name; we have featured IBM models because the company is one of the most vocal and supportive proponents of the ATM standard. It has, in many areas, set the standard for ATM adoption. Fore Systems is also a pioneer in the ATM field. The ATM hardware to choose will likely depend on your needs and your wallet, so carefully review all the available vendors and models.

IBM has two ATM adapter cards on the market; one is for DOS/Windows-based desktop computer systems, and the other is for Novell servers. The IBM adapter cards available so far use standard ISA and MCA slot architectures. Additionally, IBM has committed to releasing PCI ATM cards in the coming year.

Transmission Mechanism—SONET

The SONET standard is the most common fiber hook-up for an ATM network. SONET lines typically transmit data at the base ATM rate of 155MB/second. In addition to ATM, SONET lines also support frame-relay transfers. SONET often provides the physical transfer layer for ATM fiber networks. The SONET standard works much like a modem except for optical lines.

(See Figure 3.27.) A modem must translate digital signals into audio signals for transmission over the phone line. The receiving modem then converts those audio signals back to the digital data and sends it to the computer. SONET lines work in a similar way, except that they translate digital signals into optical signals and back again.

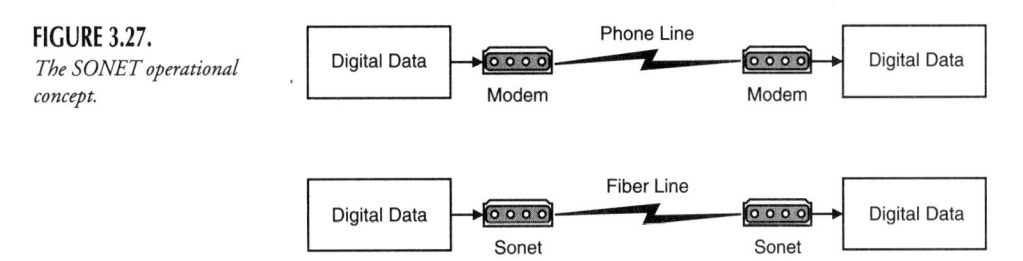

FIGURE 3.27.
The SONET operational concept.

For example, if a user needs to send data to a node on a remote ATM network, he sends the data to his ATM, which converts it using the AAL. The data, now a series of ATM cells, is sent to the TC process. Here the ATM cells are placed within a SONET frame for transmission. The SONET frame is then sent on the fiber-optic line, where it is received on the other end by a SONET receiver. (See Figure 3.28.) The data is then converted in a reverse process from the SONET frame to the ATM cells and back to the user data. All of this is done extremely quickly and with minimum latency.

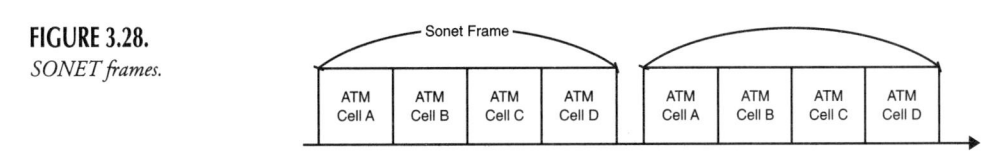

FIGURE 3.28.
SONET frames.

The SONET standard has its own packet-transmission encapsulation format and error checking. Data transfer may also occur on a UTP5 line. Fore Systems, Inc. is a current manufacturer of SONET interface boards.

4

Overview of Database Concepts

The client/server world is currently dominated by databases. Whether a file server is used to facilitate multiuser access to a database file or an actual database server is used, databases will remain the focus of most client/server efforts. Therefore, database design methodology is crucial to the understanding of client/server systems.

Database rules and design concepts have been evolving for more than twenty years. The distribution of data that has occurred in the last ten years has been unprecedented. Many of the traditional data concepts have been updated as relational data, groupware, and the connection of islands of data have taken place.

This chapter is divided into three parts: database concepts, normalization, and guidelines for distributed data. If you're already familiar with the basics of relational database creation and SQL, you may want only to skim the first section. Normalization is a technique critical to the design of relational systems; this section describes how a database is broken down into tables. The third section explains the methodology required to distribute data effectively—one of the more difficult aspects of client/server deployment. Data integrity, data concurrency, relational integrity, data dictionary creation, and other topics are explained.

Database Concepts

You are probably already familiar with the basic concepts of flat-file database design, so I'll just summarize some of the concepts. Pay particular attention to the row and column basis for the layout of a database. This row and column format is how SQL databases are formatted and accessed.

A database system is often referred to by the acronym DBMS, which stands for *Database Management System*. A database system is usually one or more tables created to fulfill a group of integrated purposes, such as business organization, accounting, inventory control, customer tracking, and vendor tracking.

Tables

A table is the most basic part of a database. Multiple tables can exist in a single database. (See Figure 4.1.) A single table is often referred to as a database. On personal computers, multiple tables once were used separately rather than integrated as a relational database, which is the case today.

FIGURE 4.1.
Multitable database.

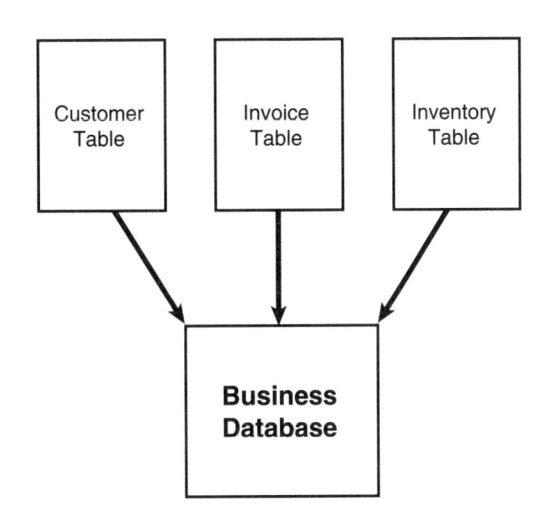

A simple example of a table is a traditional address book. Consider Table 4.1.

Table 4.1. Address book database.

LASTNAME	FIRSTNAME	ADDRESS	CITY	STATE	ZIP	PHONE
Lisbonn	Rick	1550 Keystone St.	Glendale	CA	91206	(818) 555-3344
Garnett	Lena	520 S. 8th St.	Reno	NV	89504	(702) 555-9121
Kafmanan	Lisa	1960 Lindley Ave.	Reseda	CA	91355	(818) 555-0300
Johnson	Jay	14234 Riverside	Riverside	CA	92504	(714) 555-6784
Collins	Sarah	303 W. Milford St.	Portland	OR	97219	(503) 555-0953

Each line that holds a person's information in Table 4.1 is known as a *record*. A record stores one set of information, just as a single card in a Rolodex contains one set of information. Each record is made up of many individual fields. A *field* is one piece of information, such as the last name or the city. The fields in a table define its structure. The *structure* determines what each field is named and what type of data it holds—text, integers, strings, and so forth. The structure of the fields is common to all the individual records.

There are typically two ways of showing a database. One way is to display the records in spreadsheet form, in which every row contains a record and every column defines a field, as in Table 4.1. Another way to display records, especially for data entry, is in a per record form, as in Table 4.2. In this format, records are paged through on the screen like you page through a normal book. Usually only one record is displayed on the screen at a time.

Table 4.2. Record shown in traditional format.

FIRSTNAME:	Rick
LASTNAME:	Lisbonn
ADDRESS:	1550 Keystone St.
CITY:	Glendale
STATE:	CA
ZIP:	91206
PHONE:	(818) 555-3344

A table is usually a file or a part of a file that contains the structure (including field names and exact field definitions) and the data itself (any number of records). Fields and records are the terms used by most personal computer databases to describe how a table is constructed. One or more tables make up a database.

Indexes

Indexes increase the speed of searches and maintain the integrity of a database. Indexes work just like the index to a book. An index to a book lists terms alphabetically and specifies on which pages each term is found. An index to a table references individual records in a table and creates an array of individual pointers to various records. This array of pointers may be ordered so that the table appears in alphabetical order.

The key word when describing an index is the word *appear*. An index does not really order a table. Instead, the index makes it appear that a table is sorted in a particular order. In older database designs, when all the records in a database needed to be sorted into alphabetical order, the records in the database were actually moved around until they were stored in the proper order. This was a slow and tedious process. If a sort malfunctioned, the original data file could be damaged. Whenever a new record was added, the table had to be resorted. If the user wanted the data to be sorted by city, for example, instead of by last name, the whole database had to be resorted. To restore the original order, this process had to be repeated.

Indexes solved these problems. When the table needs to be sorted by last name, the table data is never touched. An external index file that points to the various records in the table is created (see Figure 4.2). When a new record is added, a pointer is inserted into the index file.

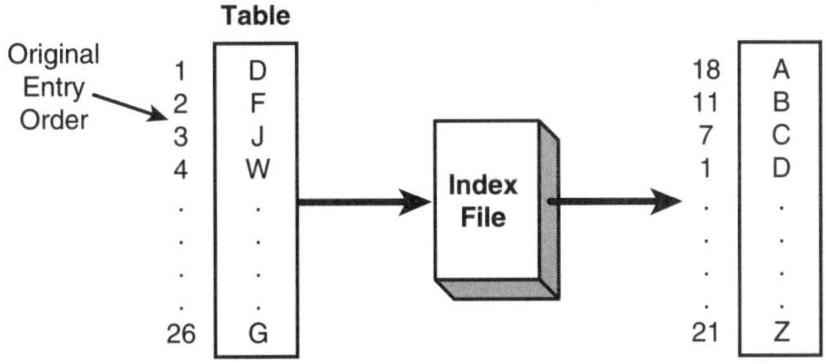

FIGURE 4.2.
An index to a table.

Searches (or queries) can be done with indexes to greatly enhance the speed of finding a particular record. A single table can have multiple indexes. Indexes greatly augment the flexibility of a database system.

What Is a Relational Database?

When a database consists of only one table, it is known as a *flat-file* or *flat* database. Flat-file databases are the simplest form of database. They are extremely fast and simple to use. Filemaker Pro by Claris Corporation is an example of a flat-file database program. These databases are ideal for beginners who need to create and access data quickly and easily.

A relational database is a database that contains multiple tables that are related to each other (see Figure 4.3). Relational databases are far more powerful than flat-file databases because their information can be stored and referenced in a much more usable format.

> **NOTE**
>
> A relation between two tables is a piece of reference data. For example, the Addresses table might be related to the Rentors table. One address may have multiple renters. Therefore, a relation is created between the Addresses and Rentors tables. The relation connects an address record in one table with one or more rentor's record in another table. Having both tables stored in a database with the specified relation creates a relational database.

FIGURE 4.3.

A relational database with eight tables.

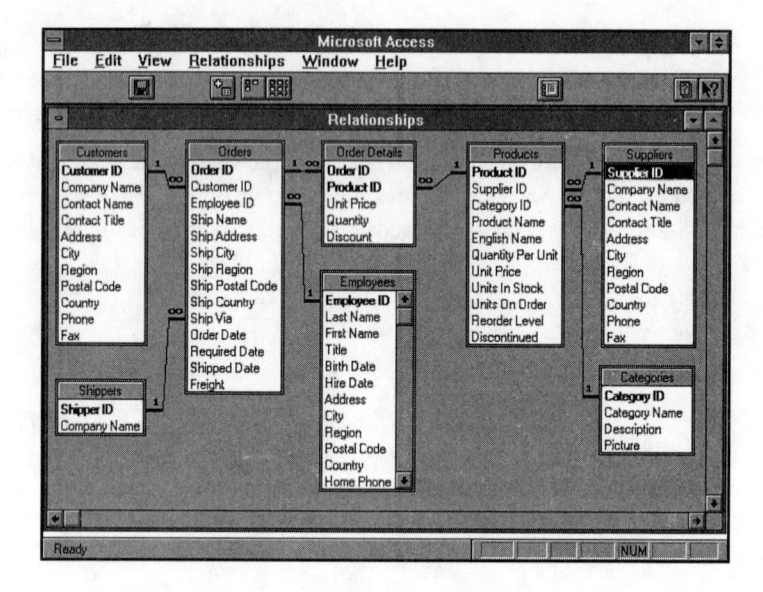

A sales application might require multiple, separate tables to store all the data needed to create a sales invoice. For an invoicing system, multiple tables are required. One table contains the information on the clients of the company (such as name and address); another table contains an inventory of the items stocked and sold; a final table contains the information for each sales invoice (the goods purchased, total sale, taxes, and so forth). These three different tables must be accessed for each invoice (see Figure 4.4).

FIGURE 4.4.

Sales invoice tables.

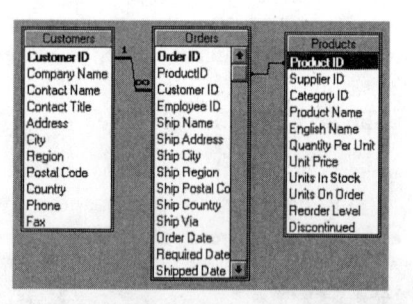

A relational database is, therefore, a set of several tables that can reference (or provide a relation) to each other. Keeping the different data in various tables reduces duplication, effort, and enables a much more robust system to be constructed. Every time the same customer buys goods, for example, the invoice table can reference the customer information table; no data needs to be entered. Finding all the sales made to that particular customer is as easy as referencing the customer table and using the relation to find all of the invoice records attached to it.

To relate two or more separate tables, a special field is usually created. This field holds the necessary information to find the linked record. The most common way to do this is to use a key field.

> **NOTE**
>
> The field used to relate two different tables is usually in the form of a number. A real world example is a person's social security number (SSN). In one table, your SSN might be used to locate your driver's license information. Another table could use the SSN to find employment information. These two tables could be related using the field containing the SSNs.

What Is a Key Field?

A *key field* is a field defined in the table that is used for referring to or referencing another database. There are two basic types of key fields: a *primary key field* and a *dependent* (or *foreign*) *key field*.

A primary field uses a unique identifier, such as a number or ID for each record. This unique identifier works like a person's Social Security number. There are never any duplicate Social Security numbers, so the information for two different people should never be confused. Similarly, the primary key is unique so that an individual record may be referenced by a different table. In a customer table, for example, CustID might be a field that contains the primary key, as in Table 4.3.

Table 4.3. A data table with a primary key field.

FirstName	LastName	CustID
John	Smith	12347
Joseph	Brown	12348
Jill	Johnson	12349

If another table needs to reference John Smith, only the number 12347 must be stored. The stored CustID is used to look up John Smith's information, such as his name and address.

When a table references another table's primary field, it uses a dependent (or foreign) key field to store the unique identifier of the primary field. For example, an invoice table that stores sales information and relates to the Customer table for the person who purchased the various goods would look something like the table shown in Table 4.4.

Table 4.4. A sales table.

CustID	Date	ItemName	Price
12347	1/5	Tomato	$ .24
12349	1/6	Bread	1.97
12349	1/6	Tomato	.24
12348	1/6	Soup	1.20
12347	1/9	Bread	1.97

In this table, the CustID field is a dependent field; it is used to find the correct customer record stored in the Customer Table. In a properly normalized relational database system, the items for sale (as well as their prices and descriptions) would be stored in another table and the Invoice table would reference it with the primary key of each item.

Key fields exist in nearly every data format. A primary key field might be product codes (such as CV-0008 or MA-6794-GC), or it might contain a simple counter (such as 1, 2, or 3). The only requirement is that each record's primary key field must not be duplicated within that table. A variety of techniques are used to ensure that each identifier is unique. They include using a large random number (which makes the chances of a duplicate number nearly impossible), a time stamp, or a counter that increments whenever a record is added.

Queries

A *query* is a search of a database for particular records or values. A query can be used to reference multiple tables. The data returned by a query is called the *resultant set*. For example, a query might search for all customers with the last name "Smith" or for all customers who have not purchased goods in 60 days so that a special mailer can be sent to them.

A query can use Boolean logical operators, such as AND, OR, and NOT. For example, you can search a table to find all the people in the database who are over 50 *and* who have an annual income exceeding $40,000.

Joins

In a multiple table environment, it is often necessary to do a query against more than one table. A *join* enables a query to search multiple fields across multiple tables for a resultant set. A join does not actually modify the tables; it is an external reference, like an index, that enables searches to be applied to it. A join makes multiple tables appear as though they were one table. (See Figure 4.5.)

FIGURE 4.5.
Diagram of a join.

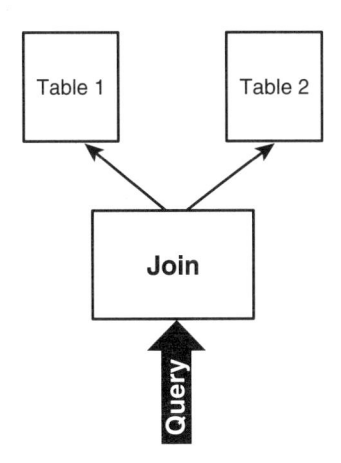

A join is usually sent as a variation of a standard query. Few databases use a literal JOIN command. Instead, a query that references multiple tables is done—the join is implied. For example, a SQL join might read:

SELECT Order_no, Staff.Staff_num, Lastname FROM Sales, Staff WHERE Sales.Staff_num = Staff.Staff_num

This command creates a join between the Sales and the Staff tables for all the records where the Staff_num field matches. The SQL database then creates references to the resultant set. In Microsoft Access, a join is created by clicking and dragging a reference from one field in a table to a field in another table (see Figure 4.6). This creates the necessary code for the query.

FIGURE 4.6.
A join in Microsoft Access.

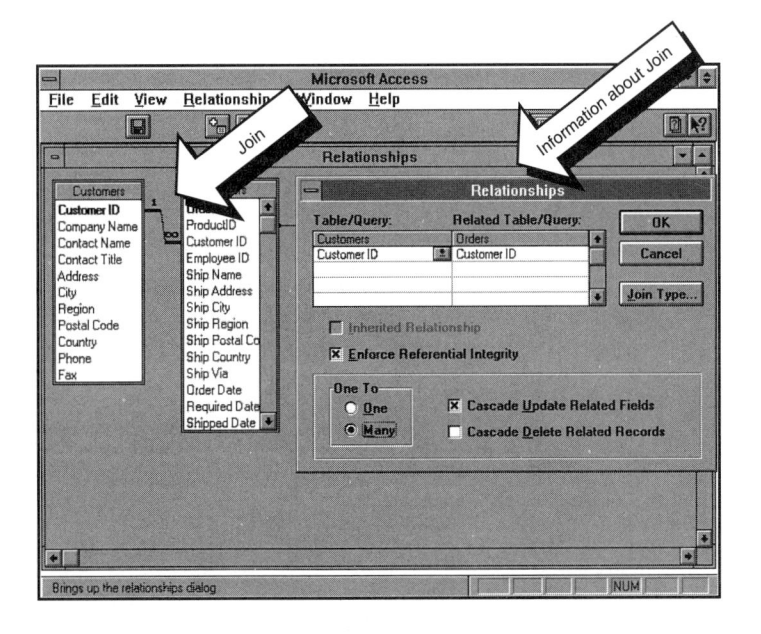

Joins are necessary in a relational system. They provide the glue needed to associate the various related tables. There are three types of joins: inner joins, outer joins, and self joins.

- **Inner joins.** Inner joins are the most common joins and are used by default. Inner joins create a resultant set of all the records that are related and fulfill the other join conditions imposed in the WHERE clause of the statement.
- **Outer joins.** Outer joins contain all the records in one table and all the related records in another table. If the database has referential integrity, the resultant sets from inner joins and outer joins are identical. However, if some of the records in the first table have no references to records in the second table, the outer join still includes them in the resultant set. These records are excluded in an inner join.
- **Self joins.** Self joins enable you to correlate data within a single table. For example, you can create a self join between supervisors and employees from an employee table. The employee's records could contain a dependent field that references their supervisor's primary key. A self join enables you to query this data.

Microsoft Access enables you to create all these types of joins. Join technology is becoming increasingly powerful as programs such as PowerBuilder and Visual FoxPro incorporate capabilities for all three join types into their database engines. More primitive database technology (such as xBase engines) required specific coding for most join types. Most of the work that had to be done by hand in the past is now automated because of these newer database tools.

What Is SQL?

SQL is essentially a common database programming language. SQL stands for Structured Query Language and is traditionally pronounced "sequel." Commands including update, insert, and search are sent to a SQL engine (or interpreter) and the desired process takes place. A SQL instruction line is sent to a SQL engine which searches the requested tables and returns the resultant data. (See Figure 4.7.)

FIGURE 4.7.
Example SQL engine search.

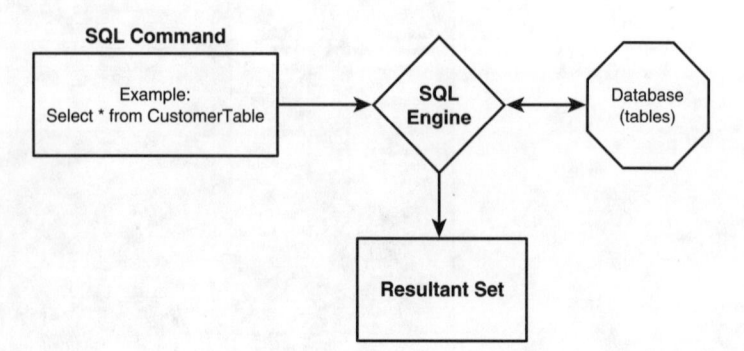

SQL is a simple language with only 32 commands. The many variations of the SQL language, however, make direct compatibility among various SQL engines (such as MS SQL Server, Oracle, and Sybase) difficult. Each vendor implements some commands differently. For example, the same command sent to two different implementations may return two slightly different resultant sets. This makes it important to understand what the various commands do on the specific systems being used.

Each vendor-specific variation to SQL is called a *dialect*. Just as there are variations of the Basic language—GW-Basic, Visual Basic, Access Basic, Word Basic, and so on—vendor-specific dialects of SQL have additional commands and command functions that operate slightly differently.

Additionally, each vendor stores the actual tables and relations among tables differently. The SQL language is essentially like an API for database engines. It provides a set of common commands for accessing a database, but the database can be stored in whatever format the vendor chooses (see Figure 4.8). There are programs available, such as Irwin or Infomodeler, that are specifically designed for porting tables and relations among SQL databases.

FIGURE 4.8.
Proprietary database formats.

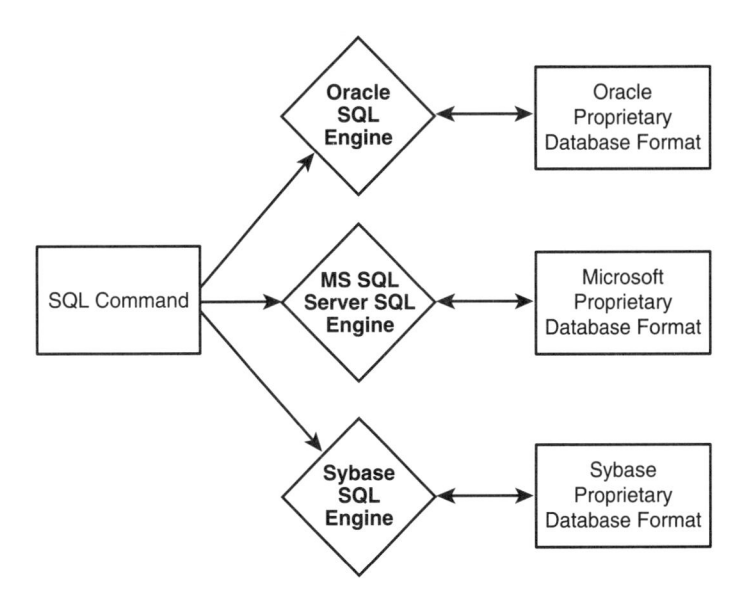

SQL has become a standard for the database community. Despite its various implementations, the SQL command set provides a foundation for databases and their custom implementations. It also provides the common vocabulary used to describe databases.

SQL Database Structure

Queries and commands are sent to various SQL engines, using *rows* and *columns* to describe the various parts of a database. Earlier you saw how a table's structure is described by a record, which defines the units of data, and fields, which define the individual pieces of data that make up a record.

SQL uses an analogy to a spreadsheet to describe a database. Each row contains a record and each column contains a field. (Just remember that *r*ow equals *r*ecord—two *r*'s.) All data tables are referenced by the SQL language in this fashion. The address book in Table 4.1 is an example of what a table looks like to a SQL engine.

SQL Queries

Most relations are created by using a standard query. The primary and dependent fields are set up in each table, and a query defines the connection. SQL has become the common language to create queries for all varieties of databases. You will use SQL queries extensively in Visual Basic to access the JET engine and the ODBC drivers. (See Chapter 5, "Visual Basic Data Access," for more information.)

When a database creates a relation on a SQL database server, it creates a join. A join makes it possible to access data items in either one of the joined tables quickly. When you use SQL, creating a join may take some time, especially if one of the tables contains a large number of records. After the join is complete, however, any queries sent to the joined set are extremely quick.

The UNJOIN command is used in systems that use a formal JOIN command. This command can be used to eliminate the join created between the two tables. At the time of this writing, implementation of these two commands is rare.

Normalization

Normalization is a technique used either to convert a large flat database into a relational database or to create a stable, well-formatted database from scratch. Data normalization provides rules on how to break tables or fields into several tables that conveniently reference one other.

Data normalization seeks to minimize duplication of data within a database by logically dividing a large table into several smaller tables. This makes the information more differentiated and usable as well. For example, instead of a single table for sales invoicing in which each record contains complete information on the customer (name, address, telephone number), items purchased (soup, Coca-Cola, paper towels), and payment information (credit terms, tax status, and so on), many smaller tables would be created; perhaps a Customer table, a Sales table, and a Credit table. Through data relations, these various tables can reference one other. This prevents many of the problems inherent in a single large flat-file database.

Some common problems in maintaining a single, flat-file database include:

- Duplication of information
- Large individual record size
- Difficult and lengthy queries
- Similar record confusion
- Increased data entry required
- Security

One of the biggest problems with a single flat-file database system is the duplication of information. For example, a flat invoicing system must contain all the fields shown in Table 4.5 for each invoice.

Table 4.5. A flat-file invoice system.

Field	Record Data
CustLastName	Smith
CustFirstName	John
CustAddress	2100 Melrose Place
CustCity	Beverly Hills
CustState	CA
CustZip	90210
CustPhone	(555) 555-1212
Date	1/5
ItemName	Tomato
Price	$.24
InvoiceNum	#1023

You can see that more fields must be defined for each item of the invoice than in a relational invoice system that contains only the CustID reference to the customer's record. Therefore, the first drawback of a flat-file database is the space it consumes.

Additionally, whenever this customer returns, all the address information must be re-entered for storage. Constantly re-entering this information can cause many problems. For example, if the salesperson were to type 90120 instead of 90210, the error might go unnoticed, but the data would be invalid. This can cause problems with data integrity, and taking care of this type of invalid data is called *data cleaning*. A database should be designed, however, to eliminate potential problems such as this one.

Another problem is the possible similarity of different data. For example, if you wanted to find all the purchases made by John Smith, you might make a search in which `FirstName=John` and `LastName=Smith`. What happens if there are two people named John Smith, one who lives in Beverly Hills and the other in Westwood? The search would find all of the transactions for both John Smiths. With a relational database, this problem would not occur. You first would search the customer database to locate the correct John Smith and then do a search on the invoice table for all the sales with the correct `CustID`.

Data normalization is also used when a variable number of fields is desired. For example, some businesses work with many customers that have multiple addresses. Including a field for each address (`address1`, `address2`, `address3`, and so on) can consume memory and disk space, especially if some businesses have only one address whereas others have three. The records for the customers with a single address must still hold the fields, `address2` and `address3`, even if they are not used. And what happens if a new customer has five addresses?

With data normalization, the fields required for an address (address, city, state, and ZIP code) can be broken off into another table. Each record in the new table contains the address fields and a dependent key that points to the main customer record. Under this normalized system, as many addresses as necessary can be added to the new table; each one simply references the same customer record.

Using properly normalized data tables helps ensure the integrity of the entire database. It also makes changes or additions of fields to a particular table much easier. If a table is used by group X, you can add a field without effecting any other group in the organization as long as the relations among fields remains the same. Under a flat-file system, any field change or addition would alter the central table, and every record would be affected.

Beware of over-normalizing your data. This means that tables are broken down too much, which results in sluggish performance and poor use of resources. There is a tendency to use data normalization whenever a designer sees duplicate data. Generally, however, fields should be normalized only if there is duplication in many cases.

Suppose, for example, that you need an inventory system that tracks cars stored on the lot and the current data table contains one field to record the car's color because 99 percent of the cars on the lot are a single color. If you get a few two-tone cars, there is no need to normalize the table. Just enter a second color field in the main table or permit descriptions such as "blue and tan" to be used in the single color field.

Whenever you add another related table to a database, the queries and joins become more complicated, slower, and more resource-intensive.

Knowing when to continue normalizing a table and when to stop can be learned only by experience. A few years ago when machines had less power and database servers did not exist, designers kept multiple tables to a minimum because of the performance penalties. Now a database server can handle a multiple table join or query more easily and effectively than an older multi-user database ever could. Therefore, the extent of normalization is determined by the capabilities of your target platform.

Five Normal Modes

Normalizing data is a documented methodology with strict rules. Few people, however, obey all these rules when they implement a system and, instead, use them as guidelines. The rules are extremely strict and describe an ideal world in which resources and processor speeds are no longer a problem. These rules are divided into five levels called *normal forms*. Knowing the normal forms is not extremely important. Most normalized databases comply with the first, second, and third forms. The fourth and fifth forms are more demanding and complicated. Generally, they arc only partially implemented—if at all.

- **First normal form.** Tables must be flat and contain no repeating groups. For example, the city and state should not be stored in the same field. Having the city and state in the same field puts two pieces of disparate data in the same field and violates the first normal form. For the same reason, an address field should not contain two lines. To normalize, you should create separate `Address1` and `Address2` fields.
- **Second normal form.** All data in non-key fields must be fully dependent on the primary key. This means that each record must contain a primary key that uniquely identifies it. Because each record has a primary key, it may be accessed and related through this field without the chance that the reference will address the wrong record.
- **Third normal form.** All data must be fully dependent on the primary key and must be independent of one other. This prevents a change in one piece of data in a non-key field from making the other fields of the record invalid.
- **Fourth normal form.** Independent data entries may not be stored in the same table when many-to-many relations exist between them. Therefore, a relation table must be created to store the actual many-to-many relations (rather than the relations being implicit through key fields). This requires that additional tables be created to hold these pointers to the tables. This can create sever performance penalties and is often not followed.
- **Fifth normal form.** It must be possible to reconstruct the original non-normalized table from the normalized tables. This can be a tedious process, but it provides error checking. If you normalize a table, reconstructing the original table using the normalized database enables you to ensure that no data was lost.

Guidelines for Distributed Data

Client/server systems are notorious for having a broad range of distributed data. With the widespread use of LANs came a torrent of independent data islands. An organization must coordinate these individual data islands. Essentially an organization seeks to convert a tremendous load of data with little inherent meaning into useful and dependable information.

Techniques have been developed to ensure that this process is achieved with the least amount of difficulty and the most integration. Keeping data relevant and connected is an ongoing and often laborious process. However, if you use data dictionary documentation, systems of data verification for data integrity, and other necessary processes, not only will the task be simplified, but the information it provides will be more relevant.

Data Dictionary

As you create an enterprise-wide data system or integrate disparate databases, you immediately run into dozens of problems with achieving clean data. *Clean data* refers to data that has been processed so that duplicates, typos in identical records, and incompatibilities in structure have been eliminated.

Unclean data undoubtedly exists everywhere in your organization. The growth of the personal computer has created a surge of individual users setting up their own databases and spreadsheets to store information critical to their areas of interest.

Coordinating this separate data can be a nightmare. Take, for example, a simple address list. In one data table, the field for the state might consist of a two-letter text field. Another data table might use a 15-byte text field with the name of each state typed out. To make matters worse, some users might have typed two letter abbreviations, whereas others typed the entire names. The state field would even be one of the more simple fields. Does the table store ZIP codes or ZIP+4 codes? Is the ZIP code stored as a number or as text? Is there a single name field, or both first and last name fields? You can see how difficult synchronizing even simple tables can be.

This description should not discourage you, but it does illustrate what must be done if an organization wants to best use all the information that it spends time and money creating. One of the best steps in coordinating this process is to decide which data is important enough to be shared. There is little use in working toward standardizing a database that only a few people need to use.

After you have a rough idea of what data needs to be coordinated, create a standards document. This describes the way newly created databases should be implemented. Table 4.6 contains an example of a standards document. If all new databases are created according to the methodology, the otherwise difficult task of linking them into the enterprise's data structure is greatly simplified.

Table 4.6. A data structure document.

Field	Field Type	Field Definition
FirstName	Text	20 Characters
LastName	Text	40 Characters

Field	Field Type	Field Definition
Address	Text	80 Characters
ZIP	Integer	
ZIP+4	Integer	

A formal document detailing this information and other data relationships is called a *data dictionary* or a *data resource dictionary*. At a minimum, you should create an informal data dictionary as you begin implementing your client/server system. Doing this documentation step helps you understand the strengths and weaknesses of the data structures that you choose. If developments are not documented at the beginning as they are created, returning to the system and creating the documentation later is typically difficult and time-consuming.

Data Rule Integrity

Depending on your database, there may be many rules that must be in place for the data itself to have integrity. For example, if your organization was formed in 1978, accounting records should have dates after this time. If a record has a date before 1978, it is either damaged or a typo must have occurred. This is called *data rule integrity*.

Not only data mistakes can make data useless. Too little data is also a problem. For example, if 1,200 records per geographic area are required for statistical significance in a test that your organization is conducting, only 200 records for an area can be misleading or even false to someone looking at a decision support data summary. Another example would be a calculation of average incomes when the query only finds one person who fits the search criteria.

Some of the new databases, such as Access, enable you to formalize data rules in the database so that incorrect data does not occur. Using Visual Basic, a designer can programmatically ensure that such rules are not violated. If these safeguards are not built into the basic framework of your client/server system, make sure that they are documented in the data dictionary document.

Data Integrity

Ensuring data integrity is an important issue when you create a database system. If the data is not secure, the consequences can be enormous. People in any enterprise rely on data to be accurate and well collected. If the data is haphazardly modified or corrupted, decisions will be made on this inaccurate information. Implementing data integrity controls ensures that data is not tampered with or modified intentionally or accidentally by unauthorized personnel. Data integrity also includes techniques to ensure that if a transaction (such as a data update or database modification) is corrupted, the modification is not committed to the database.

Flat transaction is the term used to identify a self-contained transaction. Flat transactions comply with ACID properties—Atomicity, Consistency, Isolation, and Durability. ACID properties ensure that a given transaction is a self-contained unit that can be undone if all operations are not correct.

> **NOTE**
>
> The four parts of the ACID transaction model are all fulfilled in a flat transaction. *Atomicity* requires all the actions to either succeed or fail. *Consistency* requires the system to be returned to a nominal state either through completion of the transaction or an abort. Therefore if the transaction fails, the system must be returned to its original state. *Isolation* requires the serialization of all access to shared resources. This isolates various transactions from each other. *Durability* requires that the changes are permanent after the transaction has been committed. There can be no rollbacks after a commit.

For example, when a bank transfers funds electronically, a certain amount is deducted from one account and added to another. These are two operations: subtracting the amount from one database record and adding the amount to another database record. If both of these operations are encapsulated in a flat transaction, they act as one unit.

Therefore, if the withdrawal of the money from one account succeeds but the deposit fails, the entire transaction is aborted. Flat transactions eliminate the danger of a partially completed update ruining the integrity of the database.

Data Concurrency

When data is distributed in client/server systems, some versions of data are more up-to-date than other versions. Multiple copies of data require that a system be put in place to retain the maximum degree of *data concurrency*. When a copy of data becomes old, it is known as *obsolete data*. Preventing obsolete data is difficult, especially on a client/server system.

The old mainframe systems did not have to be concerned with data concurrency. When data was entered into a terminal, it was instantly updated on the mainframe. Although updating was instantaneous, there was little distributed power or flexibility (see Figure 4.9). It also made network traffic constant because the terminal needed the mainframe to send all the display information and to handle all user input.

FIGURE 4.9.
Mainframe master/slave characteristics.

Data Currency	Network Traffic	Data Integrity	Distributed Processing	Flexibility
High ↑	High ↑	High ↑	Low ↓	Low ↓

With an older client/server file-sharing system, a data file was downloaded to the individual computer, updated, or modified, and then uploaded to the main server. Data concurrency was extremely low because the data file could remain on the machine for an extended duration and become obsolete (see Figure 4.10). This provided greater flexibility and data integrity, however, because only a single user could modify the file at a time. This often meant that most users had read-only privileges; the system administrator controlled the changes that were made to the data.

FIGURE 4.10.
File-sharing characteristics.

Data Currency	Network Traffic	Data Integrity	Distributed Processing	Flexibility
Low ↓	Low ↓	High ↑	High ↑	High ↑

Newer client/server systems are much more complex. Many of the factors increase in unison, making data concurrency decisions difficult. As data concurrency increases, network traffic and the required processing time also increase because processing is required whenever an update is made. Data concurrency needs vary with each situation. A stockbroker could not rely on stock quotes an hour old. On the other hand, an individual investor might need stock quote updates only once a day at most.

Data concurrency operates in much the same way as the mail system. If you absolutely, positively need it there overnight, you can send a package using FedEx. Sending an average letter overnight, however, costs you 36 times more than sending it via traditional mail (although it won't take three to five working days to arrive).

When you design your system, consider how quickly your data will become obsolete and what you will do if it does. Current database technology does some type of synchronization that compares two separate tables and updates the original with any records that have changed. This can be done with an update list, a flag that indicates a record modification, a date check (which might compare to records and use the newer one), and record checksums.

Providing for accurate updating of a multiuser database can be a tricky task. Two users might try to update the same record at the same time. A transaction that has 1,000 operations might fault on the 923rd. Creating a useful update system can often be as much art as science. Various techniques and tools are being developed to help deal with these problems.

Update Problems

Data collision occurs when two users attempt to update the same record at the same time. Systems usually use one of two methods to prevent this from happening. The table can be locked at some level so that two updates cannot take place at the same time. The other alternative is use of time stamps for transactions, allowing the system to determine the order of the transactions before updates occur.

The most commonly used prevention is to provide a lock on the data being updated. For example, user A wants to update a record, so he asks the database for record-locking permission and locks the record. The user with the record lock is the only person who can update this record; other users usually have read permission. When user A has finished updating, he releases the lock. Locking types include database-level, table-level, dynaset-level, record-level, page-level, pessimistic, and optimistic. You will use most of these locking schemes as you create Visual Basic and Access applications.

An alternative method to prevent data collision is to provide time stamps for transactions. Locking a record can create a bottleneck if a relatively long time is required for the update. A lock on an entire table is usually unacceptable. Instead, each update is provided with a separate time stamp. Attempted updates are put in sequential order, or *serialized,* according to their time stamps. Time stamping requires that the database server have this feature and control all transactions. For this reason, most client/server systems use simple record locking.

Other problems, such as read inconsistencies, can occur if you let a record be read while you have it locked for updating. For example, user A locks a record for updating. While he is entering new data, user B reads the record that contains the old, non-updated information. This is known as a *dirty read*. Time stamping can prevent this because a read can check for updates to the record in the time stamp queue.

Transaction Consistency

Simple flat transactions can be used effectively with many types of data updating. However, if the update requires changing a large number of records, putting each record within a separate transaction can cause a lot of overhead and waste processor time. For example, if 100,000 records in the database must be updated, beginning and committing each transaction could make the update take an unreasonably long period of time.

If all of the updates were contained in a single transaction, any error would cause the whole transaction to be revoked and the transfer that has taken place up to that point would be wasted. Most system designers break down the number of total operations into a suitable number of transactions so that errors causing a revoked transaction—called a *rollback*—would not waste too many operations. Database vendors have begun creating more advanced tools to solve this problem.

The simplest method that has been added is the use of *SyncPoints*. A SyncPoint enables you to place markers within a large transaction. You then can rollback to the last SyncPoint. SyncPoints, however, are merely a memory structure. If the server crashes, all the operations for the transaction are lost. Only with the `Commit` command is the data actually written into the database. With SyncPoints, you can rollback the entire transaction.

Chained transactions place incremental `Commits` without closing the transaction (thus saving all the overhead involved in opening and closing the transaction with each `Commit`). Chained transactions can rollback to the last `Commit`, but they cannot rollback the entire transaction.

Sagas are used like chained transactions, but they also have the ability to rollback the entire transaction. They do this by creating a string of offsetting transactions. For example, if the transaction added $100 to an account, the saga would store a subtract $100 transaction on the side until the transaction was complete. If the transaction needed a rollback, the string of offsetting transactions would be activated to reverse any updates that were made.

If databases in a single transaction require updating across multiple machines or databases, a two-phase `Commit` is used. It permits the synchronization of operations in different places so that they all either succeed or are set to rollback. For example, a sale transaction might include an operation to add money to the income accounting, to remove an item from inventory, and to credit a salesperson's quota account. These three operations might occur on three separate databases, and they must be coordinated to retain data integrity. TP monitors are primarily responsible for two-phase `Commits`. They can coordinate databases by using the OSI TP standard for implementation or their own proprietary methods.

Referential Integrity

A relational database environment offers many opportunities for poor data integrity. For example, in a sales database, one table might hold the customer list and another might hold the invoice list. Each invoice should reference a customer, even if a generic "Walk-in Customer" record must be used. This is called *referential integrity*. All entries in both tables are hooked together and contain accurate references.

If a customer is deleted from the customer table, there are now invoices that contain a reference to a non-existent customer. This would destroy the referential integrity of the database. In the past, client/server and database applications were expected to police the tables to make sure this did not occur.

Newer databases, such as Microsoft Access, provide functions that automatically take care of these problems and ensure referential integrity. There are two primary processes used to solve this problem: cascade delete and cascade update. With *cascade delete,* if a record is deleted from one table, all the records in a linked table that reference the entry can be automatically deleted. For example, if a customer is deleted, all the invoices connected to the customer are deleted as well. *Cascade update* works in much the same way. Any changes to the primary key field are automatically changed in the linked records to reflect the new primary field.

These functions can be overridden for special cases. For example, if a customer is deleted, you might want the invoices to remain. Therefore, to preserve the referential integrity of your database, you might change the relation of each of the customer's invoices to a general record such as "Unnamed Customers." In this way, you can retain referential integrity and keep a complete set of invoices.

Centralization/Decentralization

You might think that client/server architecture departs from centralization. Client/server architecture does not centralize data in the way an old mainframe/dumb terminal used to be wholly centralized. On these old systems, all the data and processing power was on the mainframe; the dumb terminal merely accessed the data. Client/server architecture should seek to distribute the computing power and data storage, but it by no means eliminates the need for centralization.

Client/server systems, however, can have multiple points of coordination. A system might have multiple servers of a specific types—for example, several file servers—or it might mix types of servers—for example, two database servers, one file server, and one time server.

Creating a data dictionary and other documentation is the first step toward centralizing mission-critical data. In-place groupware—that is, groupware already being used—often provides a good place to begin looking for data that needs to be shared. Groupware enables users to create ad hoc groups to share data they need. If a group is already sharing data, this need is already visible. Centralizing the data would merely be formalizing the data exchange process to provide wider access, security, data consistency, and data integrity.

5

Visual Basic Data Access

Visual Basic provides a variety of ways to access data. In addition to file reading and writing in sequential, binary, or random access modes (which are not covered in this book), Visual Basic supports a wide range of complete database interfaces.

The Visual Basic development system has a complete set of tools for the rapid prototyping of a client program with database access. This enables you to quickly implement an idea or project for a proof-of-concept example. Visual Basic also supports complete scalability so that existing code and structures are built upon, which enables you to use the prototype as a foundation without having to discard your work and begin again. That way, you can make the program more powerful and complex until it is fully functional.

To enable you to complete an application quickly, Visual Basic includes five standard ways of addressing data: the data control, data access objects (DAO), remote data objects (RDO), the open database connectivity (ODBC) API, and custom drivers. (See Figure 5.1.) With each increase in complexity comes an increase in power and capabilities. For a specific application project, you need a certain level of data-handling sophistication to make the application fulfill its designated role.

FIGURE 5.1.
The progression of data access.

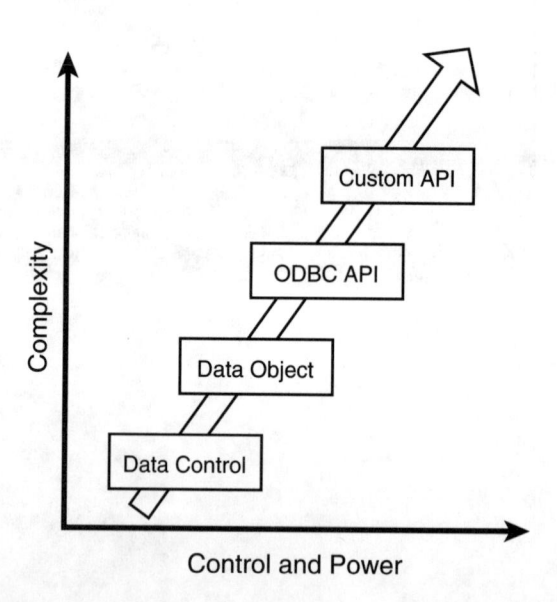

To create the system, the designer can start at any of the five levels of data access. The objectives and needs of a new project are often not clearly defined, and you don't recognize obstacles at the outset. Starting at a simpler level permits much more flexibility.

Working at a less complex level makes modification and changes inexpensive before you've invested numerous hours in the project, after which point making changes is difficult and painful. This scalable path of sophistication enables you to create a functioning prototype that can form the base of the larger completed project.

The *data control* is the simplest tool to implement complete database access. Included as a control in the Visual Basic palette, it enables you to draw the control on any form and connect database tables simply by modifying its properties. (See Figure 5.2.) Without writing one line of code, you can attach text fields and other controls that automatically display data.

FIGURE 5.2.
The data control in the palette.

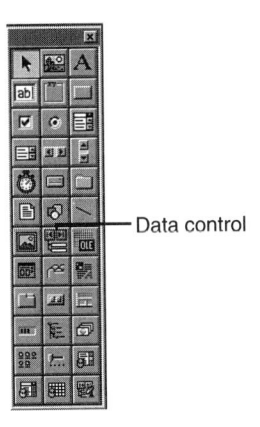

The controls that you can directly connect to a data control are known as *bound controls*. Bound controls enable automatic synchronization with a particular field in the attached table. They automatically page and update with any change made to the data control. Bound controls included with the Visual Basic 4.0 Professional and Enterprise Editions include the text box, image control, picture box, label, checkbox, masked edit, list box, combo box, DBList box, DBCombo box, and DBGrid. (See Figure 5.3.)

FIGURE 5.3.
Bound controls.

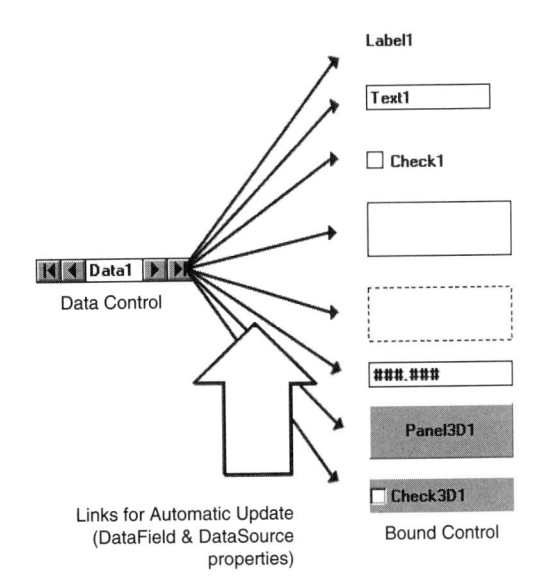

The *data access object (DAO)* is more sophisticated than the data control, but it requires more programming work to implement. The DAO enables programming access to all of the capabilities provided by the data control. Unlike the data control, it does not appear as a graphic on the form; however, it does accept many of the same commands that the data control uses. As a result, you can easily use the code written for the data control with a data object.

The *remote data object (RDO)* is an interface similar to the DAO but provides optimized access to ODBC data sources. Available only in the Enterprise Edition, the RDO provides a simple yet robust interface to ODBC data sources, including stored procedure access, cursors, and recordsets.

You can easily convert the code written for the DAO to use the RDO instead. The remote data control (RDC) works in the same manner as the traditional data control. You can bind all data-aware controls to the RDC.

> **NOTE**
>
> Both the data control and the (DAO) use a technology called the JET engine. The JET engine is the database interface engine that provides simple Visual Basic commands to manipulate a data source. The most common complaint against the JET engine is its lack of speed when it's not accessing native MS Access databases. If you're using an ODBC data source, using the RDO is much faster because it does not use the JET engine.

The *open database connectivity (ODBC) API* is a middleware layer that gives Visual Basic its true scalable database power. ODBC is a common API that is used to access any database that has an ODBC-compatible driver. (See Figure 5.4.) Some of the available ODBC drivers include FoxPro, Btrieve, xBase (the format of dBASE that is now in the public domain), Paradox 3.*x*, SQL Server, and Oracle.

FIGURE 5.4.
ODBC drivers.

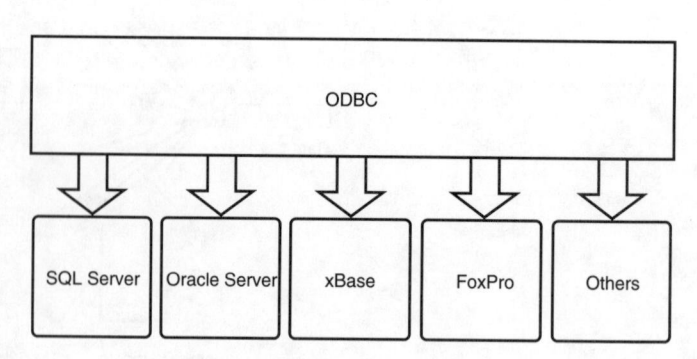

Numerous other drivers are available from third parties including ALLBASE, Btrieve 5 and 6.*x*, Clipper, DB2, DB2/2, DB2/6000, dBASE II through IV, Excel, FoxBase, FoxPro, Gupta SQLBase, IMAGE/SQL, INFORMIX 4 and 5, INGRES, Microsoft SQL Server, NetWare SQL 2.11 and 3.*x*, Oracle 6 and 7, Paradox 3 through 4.5, PROGRESS 6, SQL/400, SQL/DS, Sybase System 10, Sybase SQL Server 4, Teradata, text files, and XDB 2.41 and 3.0.

The ODBC API is the most complicated way to access a data source because you must use direct API calls to establish connections, maintain sessions, send commands, and so on. With the availability of remote data objects, you no longer need to use the ODBC API directly (to access either Microsoft or third-party ODBC drivers). The RDO provides only the slightest degradation of performance over direct API calls.

> **NOTE**
>
> At the time of this writing, no Microsoft Access ODBC drivers are commercially available. Because ODBC is cross-platform—it is available for the Macintosh—but Microsoft Access is not, there is no convenient way to retrieve information stored in an Access database using a Macintosh.
>
> If you want to create a client/server implementation in a mixed environment of PCs and Macintoshes, you should examine some of the alternatives, such as FoxPro. Most of the database servers have complete ODBC access available across platforms. They include SQL Server, Oracle, Informix, Ingres, and Sybase.
>
> The upsizing tools can scale an Access database into a complete SQL Server database. You can then access SQL Server from the Macintosh.

If you know exactly what type of database you want to access, many *custom drivers* are available that address the specific functions of particular database systems. Custom drivers include all types of commercial plug-ins in OCX, VBX, OCX, or DLL form that give a program specific low-level access to a particular type of database.

Custom drivers are often called *call-level APIs*. Oracle supplies an OCX plug-in that can access all the commands and objects in an Oracle system. Although an Oracle server might be accessible through the ODBC API with the correct driver, the Oracle custom driver enables specific and optimized access to all Oracle functions. Implementing a specific system—as opposed to using a general API such as ODBC—locks the application into a single vendor. The code is not easily reusable with another type of database, but it provides the best possible customized interface to a specific database system.

Data Access

Visual Basic provides several ways to access a database system. Using the data control requires the least programming, and you can easily connect each data control to bound controls. Data access objects (DAO) are flexible and fairly simple to control, but they require programming. Using the RDO also requires programming. Programming the ODBC API or custom drivers is more challenging, but they offer the quickest access and have many features that are not available with the other methods. Each form of access provides a step further in the path of complete application development.

Data Control

The data control is the most commonly used way to access a database. It is quick, convenient, and fairly powerful. It can be bound to controls such as text boxes that automatically update as the data control changes records. A data control can access all the databases that you can open with the more programming-intensive data objects. The data control also provides an already built user interface for navigating a database—including the Next Record, Previous Record, First Record, and Last Record buttons. The data control can use queries to display only the data specified by the query.

> **TIP**
>
> Although the data control is ideal for prototyping, it can be limiting as a development tool. Client/server developers typically opt for using the DAO or RDO to develop their applications.

A data control has eight properties that enable it to access a database: `Connect`, `DatabaseName`, `RecordSource`, `RecordsetType`, `BOFAction`, `EOFAction`, and `ReadOnly`. These properties define how and what database a data control will address. The three primary properties (`Connect`, `DatabaseName`, and `RecordSource`) determine the data source to access. The other properties specify particular characteristics of the access.

> **WARNING**
>
> Some of these properties (such as the `Connect` property) are passed parameters different from those of the equivalent properties in Visual Basic 3. Make sure you check your code if you are doing an upgrade to Visual Basic 4.

The `Connect` property is often the most variable of the three properties. This property specifies the type of database to which the data control is connected. The `Connect` property is a string that contains one of several text strings which direct the JET engine to use a particular driver.

If the data control is to interface with an Access database, the `Connect` property is left as an empty string (" ") or set to a semicolon (;). If the data control is connected to another type of database, such as FoxPro, the parameters vary based on the particular kind of database.

Table 5.1 describes the possible `DatabaseName` and `Connect` properties for various types of databases. Both of these properties must be set to strings containing the appropriate parameters. Note that the `Connect` property must end in a semicolon (;). This is a placeholder for the JET engine.

Table 5.1. `DatabaseName` and `Connect` properties for database connection.

Database Format	`DatabaseName` *Property*	`Connect` *Property*
Microsoft Access	drive:\path\filename.MDB	;
dBASE III	drive:\path	`dBASE III;`
dBASE IV	drive:\path	`dBASE IV;`
Paradox 3	drive:\path	`Paradox 3.x;`
Paradox 4	drive:\path	`Paradox 4.x;`
Btrieve	drive:\path\file.DDF	`Btrieve;`
FoxPro 2.0	drive:\path	`FoxPro 2.0;`
FoxPro 2.5	drive:\path	`FoxPro 2.5;`
FoxPro 2.6	drive:\path	`FoxPro 2.6;`
Excel 3.0	drive:\path\file.XLS	`Excel 3.0;`
Excel 4.0	drive:\path\file.XLS	`Excel 4.0;`
Excel 5.0	drive:\path\file.XLS	`Excel 5.0;`
Text	drive:\path\file	`Text;`
ODBC	Data source name or an empty string (" ")	*

* ODBC; DSN=*server*; DATABASE=*defaultdatabase*; UID=*user*; PWD=*password*; LoginTimeout=*seconds*

For an attached external ODBC table, the `Connect` property contains various parameters to enable the system to log in to access the external database. The `Connect` property then appears in the following format:

`ODBC;DSN=DataSourceName;UID=Userid;PWD=Password`

The `DatabaseName` property contains the name of the data file or data source to access. Some of the older databases (such as dBASE or Paradox) contain all the files needed for a database in a directory so a specific filename is unnecessary. With an ODBC data source, if the `DatabaseName` property is left empty (""), the user is prompted to select a data source from the traditional ODBC dialog box.

The `RecordSource` property determines the table or query from which the data control and the data object retrieve their records. From the Properties window, a popup shows the available tables for the database selected in the `DatabaseName` property. You can set the `RecordSource` property either at design time or runtime.

As you can see in Figure 5.5, only the tables are shown. You can access any query simply by typing the query name in the property box. For example, `MyQuery` was entered in Figure 5.5.

FIGURE 5.5.
Popup of available tables and a custom-typed `MyQuery`.

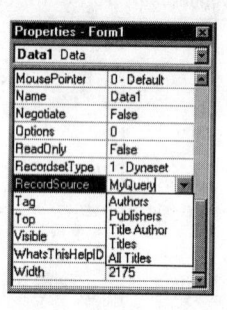

The other properties (`RecordsetType`, `BOFAction`, `EOFAction`, and `ReadOnly`) specify particular attributes of access to the database. You set the `RecordsetType` to one of the values shown in Table 5.2. This specifies the type of access object to use for the data control.

Table 5.2. Settings for `RecordsetType` property.

Setting	Value	Description
vbRSTypeTable	0	Table recordset
vbRSTypeDynaset	1	(Default) Dynaset recordset
vbRSTypeSnapshot	2	Snapshot recordset

The `BOFAction` and `EOFAction` properties determine the type of action taken when the beginning or end of file is reached (for example, it can generate a validate event). The `ReadOnly` property specifies read-only access to the data source (which is unnecessary if a snapshot is used).

As an interface becomes more full featured, you can hide the data control. A designer can create custom database controls (such as particular command buttons) that activate functions such as the Next Record and Previous Record. To hide a data control, set the `Visible` property to `False`.

Coding joins is done mostly through recordsets. A recordset can conveniently create a multiple table join with almost no coding; however, you should usually code joins through the DAO. Placing the joins into the code rather than properties gives you more control for future maintenance.

You can use the `Refresh` method to open or reopen a database if the `Connect`, `DatabaseName`, `ReadOnly`, or `Exclusive` properties have changed. Use `Refresh` to rebuild the recordset to which the data control is attached. You can also use it to flush the buffer, which might hold obsolete data.

For example, a data control might show a particular record with bound controls on a form. When another form is displayed and edits or updates this record, the record in memory shown by the original form is obsolete. When you activate the `Refresh` method for the data control on the older form, the new data is displayed.

Bound Controls

The data control has several shortcomings. Any bound controls must be bound at design time to a particular data control. The designer must know in advance what type of data will be accessed on that particular form so he can create multiple data controls for the necessary database access.

Visual Basic 4 added bound controls to complete the bound controls missing from Visual Basic 3. There is now a bound `List Box` control that enables you to display data in a hierarchical fashion.

The bound Grid control can load in data as it is viewed, providing a way to view large data tables without using tremendous amounts of memory. There is also a bound Combo control. All these bound controls enable a developer to complete an application without doing any of coding that was once required to connect data to controls such as the grid, list, or combo boxes.

Shortcomings of the Data Control

The largest restraint on using data controls for an entire application is that data controls are bound to a form. This makes it difficult to create a consistent data control system. By keeping each data control bound to a form, locating all the instances where data is accessed throughout a program becomes difficult. If you keep all data references and variables in one or more particular modules or classes, they are much easier to find, update, and maintain.

For example, in `Form1` a data control accesses `MyDB`. If a second form containing a data control that modifies `MyDB` opens, `Form1` is unaware of this modification until it is refreshed. This can cause numerous display and data consistency problems. Making sure data controls are linked properly can be an arduous task. VB 4 enables you to create a global data control, but it remains more difficult to use and less flexible than using the DAO.

Because a data control resides on a particular form, it must be initialized every time that form is loaded or unloaded. This requires a separate login (for security) to the database server for each control on the form whenever it is loaded. This can create unacceptable processing overhead and performance degradation, especially for forms that need to pop up and display a data field quickly.

> **NOTE**
>
> You can access a data control from another form as an object of the form on which it exists. In fact, any control can be accessed from a different form. For example, a statement line on `Form2` might read
>
> `Form1.Data1.Recordset.FindFirst "State = 'CA'"`
>
> We do not recommend this method. Its poor design makes maintenance, data consistency, and application expansion difficult. It also requires the form that stores the data control to remain in memory constantly, which is a poor use of system resources.

Data controls are ideal for either simple applications or rapid prototyping. You can also use the functions used with the data control with the data access objects, so scalability is ensured. In an application development cycle, you can use the data control to quickly prototype and test a concept without losing work when the project is upgraded to use the DAO.

Both the data control and the DAO have convenient commands for navigating a data set provided by a query. They include `FindFirst`, `FindLast`, `MoveFirst`, `MoveLast`, `MoveNext`, and `MovePrevious`.

Data Access Objects (DAO)

A DAO is a far more flexible programmer's tool for accessing a database than the data control. The data control essentially provides a front end for the data object.

In a client/server system, creating an application with data controls is cumbersome and difficult to maintain. When you design a system around central data objects rather than GUI controls, the entire program structure becomes more simple. Data access can be centralized to particular classes or modules. You can pass DAO references easily between routines and also create them in local variables, which provides added flexibility.

When designing a client/server system, you should have control over the data and its display and modification. For example, implementing an undo function is much more difficult using the data control.

Using the DAO means slightly more coding, but the benefits in terms of reliability and flexibility are often substantial. Also, some controls (including many third-party controls) cannot be bound to a data control. They require the same custom programming regardless of whether a data control or a data object is used to access the database.

Without using bound controls, the steps for editing data are as follows:

1. Create a table, recordset, or snapshot object of the data to be accessed.
2. Select the specific record for retrieval and make it the current record (usually with a search or query).
3. Invoke the EDIT method, which loads the record into memory and marks it for editing.
4. Load the data into a set of variables or arrays (often called a buffer).
5. Transfer the data from the buffer variables into the text controls and radio buttons on the screen.
6. The user can manipulate data on the form shown.
7. If the user presses the OK button, store the screen values into the buffer variables.
8. Update the record with the values in the buffer variables.
9. Invoke the UPDATE method, which writes the changes into the table.

This process might seem tedious, but it has many advantages. Once you've constructed the variable set to match the fields in the database, many operations can use the read and write variable routines. The buffer variables essentially create another middleware layer between the data that is shown to the user and the data record itself. This enables data manipulation and confirmation before transfer either from the record to the screen or from the screen to the record.

For example, the user might select multiple records and activate the editing form. The form might display empty text fields for all the fields in the database. The user can enter data into one or more of the fields to be changed.

When the user presses the OK button, the application updates only the filled fields for all the selected records. A For…Next loop can read each selected data record into the variable set and place the values in the filled text boxes on the screen in the appropriate data field. This provides quick and easy batch changes. It also enables the program to release access to the database or record while the user is editing the data.

> **TIP**
>
> Using buffer variables is also suitable when data is stored in a different format from that in which it is displayed. A simple example is a percentage variable. For mathematical reasons, a percentage might be stored as a decimal (such as .79) in a database field but presented to the user as a whole number (such as 79). Data conversion must happen both when the percentage is displayed to the user and when the user's changed value is saved to the record.

Tables, snapshots, and recordsets offer a variety of ways to access data stored in tables. Table 5.3 describes which situations make each structure ideal for a particular type of application.

Table 5.3. Table, recordset, and snapshot access.

Access	Subset of Data?	Read Only?	Joins?	Optimized for small table?	Optimized for Query?
Table	No	Optional	No	No	No
Recordset	Yes	Optional	Yes	No	Yes
Snapshot	Yes	Yes	Yes	Yes	Yes

A *snapshot* is a read-only subset of the records of a database for a given query. Snapshots are perfect for applications that need read-only manipulation of client/server data, such as the management client that is constructed later in this book.

Many applications make it possible to read a given set of data that can be used as the basis for what-if analysis. You can take a snapshot of the data and display it with no risk of damage to the data. Access to this data is fairly quick because once the data is read, no further accesses to the main database are required.

Recordsets enable the creation of a result set from a query. This set might consist of joins of multiple tables. Recordsets can be single user or shared. You can also create a recordset from another recordset, which provides for more flexibility in data selection and modification. Recordsets, like snapshots, are dynamic. If a record is added to the data source and the new record fits the criteria specified by the recordset, the record is automatically added to the set.

> **NOTE**
>
> Recordsets are the equivalent of dynasets from Visual Basic 3.0. Functionally, they work in nearly the same way. Recordsets, however, have the added flexibility of being part of the VB object model. Dynasets are included in VB 4.0 for backwards compatibility, but we recommend that all code be upgraded to use the new recordsets.

Remote Data Object (RDO)

The remote data objects (RDO) are used as traditional DAOs are. Recordsets, snapshots, and tables can be accessed through the RDO. Specialized commands are available for stored procedures, ODBC security, cursors settings, and so on. The RDO provides access to the ODBC API in the way traditional DAOs are used without the overhead of the JET engine. The remote data control is related to RDO in the same way that the data control is a visible user interface control for the DAO.

Functionally, you'll see little difference when your programs are upgraded from using the DAO to the RDO. For more complete information on the remote data control, see Chapter 22, "Open Database Connectivity (ODBC)."

ODBC API

The ODBC API can interface with any database that has an ODBC driver. ODBC drivers for Access, FoxPro, xBase, Btrieve, SQL Server, and Oracle are included with Visual Basic.

Unlike the standard JET engine access, you must call ODBC commands in the same way that you call the functions in a plug-in DLL. For example, to create a connection to an ODBC driver, you first must declare the SQLAllocConnect() function. All ODBC functions begin with the SQL prefix. The ODBC functions are generally declared in a separate module and appear as follows:

```
Declare Functions SQLAllocConnect Lib "odbc.dll" (ByVal henv&, phdbc&) as Integer
```

To call the function, simply use it as you would any other Visual Basic function.

```
result = SQLAllocConnect(henv,Connection(i).hdbc)
```

ODBC contains more than 100 commands. Table 5.4 describes some common ODBC commands. There are several levels of ODBC compliance. For more information on the various ODBC compliance levels, calls, and general interface, see Chapter 22.

Table 5.4. Core ODBC commands.

ODBC Command	Level	Description
SQLAllocConnect	Core	Creates a connection handle
SQLAllocEnv	Core	Creates an environment handle
SQLAllocStmt	Core	Creates a statement handle
SQLCancel	Core	Cancels a SQL statement
SQLConnect	Core	Connects to a specified driver
SQLColAttributes	Core	Returns attributes of a column in the resultant set
SQLBindCol	Core	Assigns storage to the resultant column and sets the data type
SQLBrowseConnect	Level 2	Returns connection values
SQLDataSources	Level 2	Returns a list of DataSources
SQLDrivers	Level 2	Returns a list of drivers and their attributes
SQLDescribeCol	Core	Describes a column in the resultant set
SQLDisconnect	Core	Closes the connection

continues

Table 5.4. continued

ODBC Command	Level	Description
SQLBindParameter	Level 1	Assigns storage for a parameter in a SQL statement
SQLDriverConnect	Level 1	Connects to a specified driver or prompts the user
SQLError	Core	Returns additional error or status information
SQLExecDirect	Core	Executes a statement
SQLExecute	Core	Executes a prepared statement
SQLFetch	Core	Returns a resultant row
SQLFreeConnect	Core	Releases the connection handle
SQLFreeEnv	Core	Releases the environment handle
SQLFreeStmt	Core	Ends a statement and frees the resources associated with it
SQLGetConnectOption	Level 1	Returns the value of a connection option
SQLGetData	Level 1	Returns part of the data from the resultant set
SQLGetInfo	Level 1	Returns information about a specific driver
SQLGetFunctions	Level 1	Returns the functions of a supported driver
SQLGetTypeInfo	Level 1	Returns information on supported data types
SQLGetStmtOption	Level 1	Returns the value of a statement option
SQLGetCursorName	Core	Returns the cursor name associated with a statement
SQLSetCursorName	Core	Specifies a cursor name to associate with a statement
SQLNumResultCols	Core	Returns the number of columns in a resultant set
SQLParamData	Level 1	Used with SQLPutData to supply parameters
SQLParamOptions	Level 2	Specifies the use of multiple values for parameters
SQLPrepare	Core	Prepares a SQL statement for later execution
SQLPutData	Level 1	Sends part or all of a data value for a parameter
SQLRowCount	Core	Returns the number of rows affected by an insert, an update, or a deletion
SQLSetConnectOption	Level 1	Sets a connection option
SQLSetStmtOption	Level 1	Sets a statement option
SQLSpecialColumns	Level 1	Returns special information on optimum columns for some commands
SQLStatistics	Level 1	Returns statistics on a table and its indexes

ODBC Command	Level	Description
SQLTables	Level 1	Returns the list of table names from a data source
SQLTransact	Core	Commits or rolls back a transaction

Custom Drivers

Custom drivers are available for database engines. These come in the form of a DLL, a VBX, or an OLE custom control (OCX). Some companies produce database drivers for simpler database formats in actual Visual Basic code. For more information on available custom drivers, refer to Chapter 29, "Third-Party Tools, Utilities, and Controls."

Data Access Technology

Visual Basic uses several primary technologies to create the functionality and ease of use available through the data controls and data objects. The JET engine is the interface layer between Visual Basic and most of the available database drivers. The JET engine interfaces with ISAM drivers, Access ISAM drivers, and ODBC drivers using a common set of Visual Basic programming commands.

The ISAM drivers are essentially the core database engine stored as a driver. For example, a dBASE ISAM driver contains all of the basic functions of the dBASE engine so you can query the database, edit data, and create tables. These drivers are custom built to work with the JET engine, and you can use them only through JET access.

JET Engine

The data access objects (DAO) and the data control use a common engine, the JET (Joint Engine Technology) database access engine. The *JET engine* is a middleware layer that connects Visual Basic to databases ranging from dBASE to ODBC data sources. Using simplified SQL statements, the JET engine controls the database and provides such features as recordsets and snapshots. The JET engine is primarily the same engine used in Microsoft Access.

The JET engine is a compatibility layer that enables Visual Basic to access three types of databases: ODBC databases (such as Oracle and Microsoft SQL Server), ISAM databases (xBase, Paradox, and Btrieve), and Microsoft Access databases. (See Figure 5.6.) The JET engine simplifies access to all these formats by providing a standard way to address them. The application's .INI file stores the configuration of parameters that affect how the JET engine is optimized. Table 5.5 shows some of these parameters.

FIGURE 5.6.
Visual Basic data access.

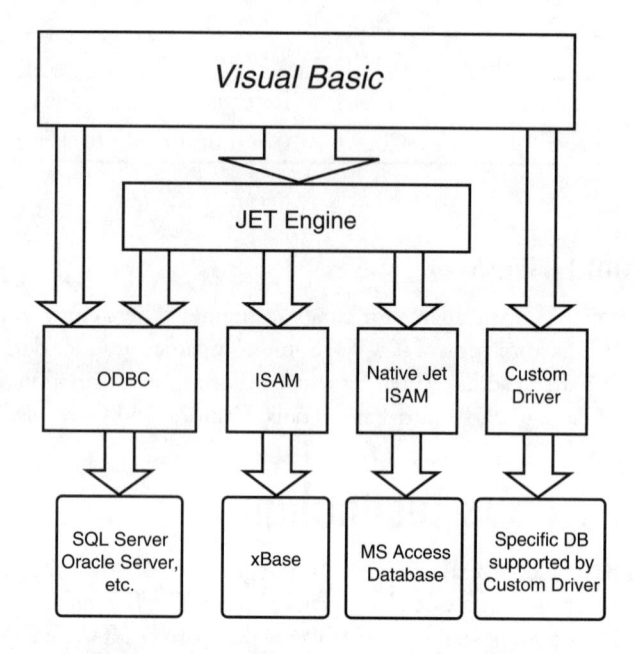

Table 5.5. JET engine default settings in the .INI file.

.INI Parameter Name	Default	Minimum	Maximum
MaxBufferSize	512	18	4096
ReadAheadPages	8	0	31
PageTimeout	5	0	2,147,483,647
LockedPageTimeout	5	0	2,147,483,647
LockRetry		20	
CommitLockRetry	20		

NOTE

Most applications have their own .INI files that contain various parameters and preferences that the applications need when they boot. For example, a client program might store the directory path and the name of the default database to open when it is executed. If the name of the database changes, you can change the name in the .INI file with a simple text editor.

If you use the JET engine, you must include an .INI file with your application. Place the .INI file in the WINDOWS directory, and name it to match the name of your

> application. For example, an application called MAIN.EXE would have an .INI file with a path that looked like the following:
> `C:\WINDOWS\MAIN.INI`
> This .INI file tells the JET engine where to find the JET drivers, and it contains information on various settings for the ISAM drivers.

Indexed Sequential Access Method (ISAM) drivers can handle databases, tables, indexes, and data types. To connect to Btrieve, dBASE III and IV, FoxPro 2.0 and 2.5, and Paradox 3.*x*, the JET engine uses the ISAM drivers. There are ODBC drivers available for these databases, but the JET engine uses the ISAM drivers to access these file types.

There are limitations to each of these ISAM drivers. For a complete description of the various specific limitations, consult the article entitled "Differences Among Installable ISAMs" found in the Visual Basic for Windows Knowledge Base. The most recent version of the Knowledge Base is available on many of the online services and from other sources listed in Appendix C, "Sources."

Functions such as `CompactDatabase` and `RepairDatabase` are usually not available through the ISAM/JET engine. For example, when a record is deleted from a dBASE table, the record is not removed. It is simply marked as deleted, and as a result, it still uses disk space. If many records are deleted, the table carries many "dead" records. `CompactDatabase` actually removes these files or creates a new database copy that contains only the current records. Custom drivers usually feature these functions. You should evaluate them if you have frequent storage problems.

The Visual Basic Compatibility Layer (VBCL), also known as JET 2.5/3.0, was an upgrade of the older JET 1.1 and 2.0 engine. JET 2.0 and higher provide links to databases in the Microsoft Access 2.0 format.

Since the release of JET 2.0, there has been another revision to add individual features. The newest update is JET 2.5/3.0, which includes bug fixes and increased functionality for database repair, as well as 32-bit support.

JET Engine 2.5/3.0

Between the original JET 1.1 engine and the current 2.5/3.0 version, a tremendous number of features were added. JET 2.5 and JET 3.0 are the new standard JET interfaces for 16 and 32 bit systems, respectively. Included in the new engine is the capability to use such features as validation rules, automatic entry of a default value, a `Required` flag, the new Rushmore query technology, and automatic relational features.

Access 2.0 enables you to use validation rules that ensure that the input data fulfills particular parameters. For example, a validation rule might specify that a sale quantity field cannot contain a number less than 1 or greater than 99. This is a field-level validation rule. Additionally, there is a record-level validation rule that can compare several fields to ensure validity.

You can automatically insert default values into a given field when a new record is added. For example, you might insert today's date into the invoice's date field or an incremental invoice number into the InvoiceNum field. In the past, each application had to programmatically enter data into these fields. This feature can keep the database consistent because the default value is kept with the database. Without this feature, consistency problems can occur, especially if the database is accessed from various client programs.

The new engine features a Required flag, which means that something must be entered into a given field for it to be recorded. This is especially useful if several fields must be filled. They might include fields that queries will use as a key. Using the Required flag is more convenient than individually checking each field, and you can create a single routine to handle the trapped empty field errors.

The new Rushmore technology, first included in the FoxPro database, is an engine to speed queries and sorts. Rushmore can coordinate multiple indexes to assure lightning-fast query set building. The older query technologies could use only a single index at a time.

Also included are sophisticated relational features such as cascade update, cascade delete, programmatic access to referential integrity, and programmatic access to security. One of the most useful and advanced features in the new JET engine is the capability to enforce referential integrity. (For more information, see Chapter 4, "Overview of Database Concepts.")

Open Database Connectivity (ODBC)

The open database connectivity (ODBC) API is a database-independent piece of middleware used to access various different database formats. For example, if a client program requests a query of data through the ODBC, it does not have to worry about what type of database is at the other end. The server might be a FoxPro driver or an Oracle driver. The calls made to the ODBC API remain the same despite the driver being called.

The ODBC standard has various levels of compliance. The Core level specifies that functions correspond to those compiled in the X/Open and SQL Access Group Call Level Interface specification. There are also Level 1 and Level 2 specifications. Many applications that use the ODBC driver require the drivers to meet at least Level 1 specifications. As a result, it is fairly safe to design an application to use Level 1 functions. To determine what conformance levels are supported, use the commands SQLGetInfo, SQLGetFunctions, and SQLGetTypeInfo. For more information on ODBC conformance levels, see Chapter 22. You can also examine Table 5.4, which details what level each of the common functions requires.

Custom Driver Technology

You can use custom drivers to access a data source with technology made specifically to use that data source. For example, Oracle sells a product that plugs into Visual Basic and is optimized specifically to work with Oracle databases.

Many of the custom drivers are available only as a Dynamically Linked Library (DLL). This requires that you use individual API calls rather than Visual Basic commands or controls. An API has functions that fall into two categories; it can either execute commands or select data (for reading, editing, or updating).

These two types of functions are treated differently because interacting with returned data (through data sets, cursors, and so on) requires special optimization. As a result, selecting data functions displays the most performance increase in an optimized driver.

For example, SQL Server can use stored procedures. *Stored procedures* are routines that can execute on the database server and return a result. You can activate these stored procedures through custom calls. Often, these stored procedures do not return any data (except perhaps an error code). Stored procedures therefore have the same performance on generic or custom drivers.

SQL Server can also do batch sets of commands so that several different queries are sent to the database server at the same time for efficient processing. That way, the server can return multiple resultant sets in rapid succession. You might have to do some specific programming, however, to receive the multiple data sets that are returned.

If the API is specific to the particular database, changing an application that uses it to access a different type of database can be a nightmare. You cannot easily port a program designed to use a custom call interface to work with another database. However, you can port such a program to another programming language (such as C or Fortran) because the calls remain the same.

One of the primary advantages of using a custom call is the capability to receive return codes. The data controls and data objects can call a stored procedure, but they cannot receive any information returned by it. For example, you might write a stored procedure to return the success or failure of a given task. The message cannot be received unless you use one of the API interfaces.

VBSQL (DB-Library)

VBSQL is a VBX plug-in designed to provide a call-level interface to Microsoft SQL Server and Sybase System 7. (For Sybase System 10 and higher, you must use third-party ODBC drivers.) VBSQL is also known as the SQL Server Programmer's Toolkit for Visual Basic or the DB-Library for SQL Server.

Using VBSQL offers relatively few advantages over using the ODBC drivers with SQL passthrough. Both systems are nearly identical in speed. You can optimize VBSQL to take better advantage of the SQL Server engine, but unless specific applications require the extra power, this tuning is not extremely important. ODBC has the advantage of broad compatibility, which makes access to heterogeneous databases possible.

VBSQL might be useful if the Visual Basic application will be ported into a C development environment. The VBSQL calls are identical in the C libraries except that each variable must be bound with each column or field. VBSQL also features real call-back handlers that are not available through the ODBC API.

Be sure to examine whether ODBC will fulfill your needs. If it can, the capability to attach to other types of foreign databases with little or no change in code is extremely compelling.

Data Tools

Several database tools are built into the Visual Basic development environment. They enable a designer to create complete client/server systems more easily. You can use the Data Manager to create and edit an entire database as well as set relations among tables. You can use the upsizing tools to port a desktop database system to a full database server. The reporting tools ease the creation of reports generated and printed by an application.

Data Manager

The Data Manager is a database creation utility included with Visual Basic. Accessible under the Add-Ins menu, the Data Manager enables you to create Access databases. It also enables you to open and modify the data for any table in the following formats: Microsoft Access 1.0, 1.1, and 2.0; Paradox 3, 3.5, and 4; dBASE III and IV; FoxPro 2.0, 2.5, and 2.6; and Btrieve. The Data Manager is provided to make quick access to these databases simple.

The Data Manager has been substantially rewritten from the version included with Visual Basic 3.0. It enables you to create tables, fields, indexes, QueryDefs, and relations and test SQL statements.

> **NOTE**
>
> A QueryDef is a powerful structure that enables you to store queries in a database with variables. When you need to run the query, the program can simply supply the values to particular variables and run the query. Like the move toward storing default values within the database itself, this enables the queries themselves to be centralized and contained with the data.

Visual Basic includes the Data Manager to enable you to begin constructing databases quickly. The Data Manager is excellent for creating a database and making slight modifications. It is not meant to be the cornerstone of anything but the most rudimentary development effort. Although it has the capability to access the complete features of Access, it does not have the modeling, updating, or data modeling capabilities of systems such as Infomodeler or Irwin.

We use the Data Manager to create the database for our client/server system in the second part of this book. All the data from our system is stored in an Access database until we upsize the data into SQL Server.

As with many of the tools included with Visual Basic, the Data Manager is provided for scalability. It enables you to design a database within the Visual Basic environment quickly and conveniently. If necessary, you can then upsize the construction to a more powerful environment.

Microsoft makes available the source code for the Data Manager. A developer can add the features needed to create a specialized tool. The source code is available through the online services provided by Microsoft (see Appendix C, "Sources").

The new Data Manager included with Visual Basic 4 has Access 2.0 as its default database format. You can use it to modify fields after they have been created (a feature lacking in the earlier version). The new Data Manager can still manipulate the data stored in the older format (Access 1.1).

Upsizing Tools

One of the most powerful scaling features of a Microsoft Access-based database is a tool called the Upsizing Wizard. Usually, to scale up to a full database server from a desktop database requires completely reconstructing the tables, queries, relations, and other attributes of a database. Once the structure is in place, you can import the data. The only alternative to this laborious process is buying an expensive tool that could do the translation automatically, such as Irwin.

Microsoft provides the Upsizing Wizard for a fairly small fee (approximately $100 at the time of this writing and free to developers). This application converts a Microsoft Access database into a complete Microsoft SQL Server database, including its table structure, data, and attributes.

> **NOTE**
>
> At the time of this writing, the upsizing tool for Access 95 is not scheduled to be available for almost half a year. For this reason, we used the Access 2.0 Upsizing Wizard for our upsizing demonstration.

OLE Automation and DDE

Although not generally considered in the category of data access, OLE and DDE provide powerful tools for data that is not stored in traditional formats. If the client program supports OLE automation or a DDE interface, you can probably access the data stored in that program for use in a client/server system.

Visual Basic supports the complete DDE interface. Using Visual Basic, you can create both DDE client and DDE server programs. (Chapter 8, "Constructing a Simple Application," contains a complete example of DDE usage.) Spreadsheets, geographic information systems (GIS) programs, and various third-party programs include a DDE interface. These commercial programs often do not list in their application manuals what specific DDE connectivity commands they support. If there is a program that could enhance your client/server system, check with the manufacturer to see whether a DDE interface exists.

Increasingly integrated into application programs (everything from CAD to financial analysis tools), OLE automation is the wave of the future. Most major applications will support OLE Automation in the next two years. A program with OLE Automation can access the complete data stored in Microsoft Excel, Project, Word, and Access. Visual Basic 4.0 enables you to create your own OLE server applications. For more information on OLE, see Chapter 23, "Object Linking and Embedding (OLE)."

Reporting Tools

Visual Basic includes Crystal Reports Version 3.0. Crystal Reports enables you to create reports from any database conveniently. The capabilities of this version are severely limited. The Crystal Reports generator operates largely outside the Visual Basic programming environment. All the data must exist in a database file. Fields calculated by Visual Basic must be written into a database before you can use them.

The Crystal Reports included with Visual Basic provides an excellent starting engine. If you need reports generated from a database, Crystal Reports can automatically generate the reports and provide complete printing capabilities. The report can appear in a form in your application as an integrated component. The Crystal Reports plug-in makes access to the reporting engine transparent to the user.

If you need more than rudimentary reports, we suggest that you consider Crystal Reports Version 4.5 Professional, which is available commercially. This product has the power of a substantial reporting tool. It can use the reports that you have already created using the simpler version included with Visual Basic. Chapter 29, "Third Party Tools, Utilities, and Controls," lists other third-party reporting tools.

Client/Server Features

Visual Basic contains many features that make the development of a client/server system easier and make the finished application more powerful. Using indexes can speed various queries. Visual Basic provides many ways to create and store indexes on the database server.

Visual Basic now supplies the capability to automatically store an OLE object in a database. You can write other formatted data to a database using the raw data storage functions. Transaction processing (TP) is possible with Visual Basic because it incorporates opening, committing, and aborting transaction functions as well as a variety of locking mechanisms (see Chapter 4 for information on TP).

Using Indexes

Using an index is a way to speed database querying access. Refer to Chapter 4 for a complete description of indexes. You can create an index by using the Data Manager, or you can create it as an index object from within Visual Basic. Indexes are stored in the database.

A database that contains many indexes must update each index whenever a record is added or changed. Too many indexes can actually slow down overall performance of a database. Make sure that you create only the indexes that are needed. If you create temporary indexes, remove them when their function is no longer necessary.

Creating an index for a table that contains many records can be a slow process. The creation of an index requires much of the work that is normally done by a sort. Therefore, some of the processing for searches and sorts is done up front, increasing performance when a query executes.

These warnings are merely tips on the judicious use of indexes. According to Microsoft, around 80 percent of the databases created with Access do not contain indexes. In most cases, they increase the speed of a system so substantially that they should be included in a database. Indexes can be extremely powerful tools, but they might also constrain the performance of your client/server system if they're used poorly.

Using Queries

Visual Basic is ideal for creating any type of query. Not only can it access prebuilt queries stored in various databases, but it also can construct a query on the fly. Because all queries that use Visual Basic tools—including JET, ODBC, data object, and data control—are string-based, you can construct queries that use all the common string functions.

You can store a query as a query object and append it to the existing database. In Visual Basic, this is a `QueryDef` object. Essentially, a `QueryDef` object is a compiled SQL query stored in the database.

Embedding OLE and Other BLOBs

It is often convenient to have a database store large amounts of formatted data—often called a Binary Large Object (BLOB). For example, in a product table, one field could store a .TIFF image of each particular item. A system might also require that you store a large amount of raw data—from a data acquisition system, for example—in a record with other information.

For raw data, Visual Basic includes an `AppendChunk` function, which enables a chunk of raw data to be added to the binary or memo field of a table. `AppendChunk` is passed a data object that it inserts into the referenced field. For example, the following code stores an OLE object into a binary field of a database. You could modify this same basic code to store any large binary file.

```
Sub PasteBigFile (FName As String)
    Dim TotalSize As Long, CurChunk As String
    Dim I As Integer, FNum As Integer, ChunkSize As Integer
    ChunkSize = 12000     ' Set size of chunk.
    Data1.RecordSet.Edit  ' Enter Edit mode.
    Data1.RecordSet.Fields("Comments") = ""  ' Clear Comments field.
    FNum = FreeFile       ' Get free file number.
    Open FName For Binary As #FNum      ' Open the file.
    TotalSize = LOF(FNum)
    Do While Not EOF(FNum)
        If TotalSize - Seek(FNum) < ChunkSize Then
            ChunkSize = TotalSize - Seek(FNum) + 10
        End If
        CurChunk = String$(ChunkSize + 1, 32)
        Get #FNum, , CurChunk        ' Read chunk from file.
        If InStr(CurChunk, Chr$(0)) > 0 Then
            CurChunk = Left$(CurChunk, InStr(CurChunk, Chr$(0)) - 1)
        End If
' Append chunk to Comments field.
        Data1.RecordSet.Fields("Comments").AppendChunk (CurChunk)
    Loop
    Data1.RecordSet.Update       ' Save the record.
    Close FNum          ' Close the file.
End Sub
```

> **NOTE**
>
> The `AppendChunk` command and other binary field storage is implemented robustly for Microsoft Access data tables. Standard ODBC database engines have some severe limitations when describing general data. It is sometimes possible to put this raw data into a memo field, which is a resizable field stored in an external file. The database then holds a reference to a particular address in this external file, which is accessed when the field is manipulated.

> However, at the time of this writing, the ODBC drivers for FoxPro and other databases can access only one memo-type field per table. Often, this memo field is used by a catch-all field, such as Notes or Description, and is not available for the use of data.
>
> A possible workaround might include creating a table specifically to store various BLOBs, each with a unique identification. You can then reference these entries from the other table by their IDs.

Transactions

Visual Basic includes commands to implement a transaction-based system. These commands can encapsulate update operations within a transaction so the various operations are treated as one command. Using a transaction, all the updates must be successful or none are committed to the database. This prevents partially successful updates from destroying the integrity of the database.

The BeginTrans command sets up a transaction. Further update operations (such as modifying data) are contained within the transaction. When the application has completed the operations contained within the transaction, a CommitTrans command is executed. If an error occurs during the transaction, a Rollback command revokes all the changes contained in the transaction.

You can use these commands to ensure the data integrity of several operations. For example, records can be deleted, edited, and created within a single transaction. That transaction can then be committed or revoked.

Some drivers do not support transactions. Before using these commands, the application should check the Transactions property for the data object or recordset. The application might then warn the user that if transaction processing is not supported, the database integrity could be corrupted. If Transactions = False, the BeginTrans, CommitTrans, and Rollback statements are ignored for databases that support them. If you are updating multiple databases, make sure that they all support transactions, or a Rollback command might revoke the updates on only some of the databases. If that happens, it could destroy the data consistency and integrity that a particular database had before the partial entries.

Database-Level Locking

Database-level locking locks the entire database, an entire table, or all the tables that are accessed by a particular recordset. For example, by setting the lock properties on a recordset, you lock all the tables associated with that transaction, even if they are located among different database files.

With database-level locking, you can deny read access to prevent dirty reads. A *dirty read* occurs when an application reads a record just prior to an update. The application, therefore, reads old data. If a series of record updates are in progress, an application might get a dirty read on one record and read an updated record on another read. This situation compromises the entire data set read by the application. Setting a lock at the database level is also known as the *exclusive access method.*

To set exclusive access to a table, database, or recordset, use the `Exclusive` parameter. This is the second parameter passed to the `OpenDatabase` method.

```
Set TestDB = OpenDatabase("TestDB.MDB",True)
```

A recordset is slightly more complicated. It has several options to provide various types of access privileges.

To create a recordset, you can include the `Options` parameter.

```
Set TestRecordset = TestDB.CreateRecordset (SQLQuery, Options)
```

In this statement, the `Options` parameter would consist of one or more ORed values from Table 5.6.

Table 5.6. Option values for `CreateRecordset`.

Option	Value	Description
DB_DENYWRITE	1	Locks all the records in a recordset for modification by other applications.
DB_READONLY	4	Permits read-only access to the records in a recordset.
DB_APPENDONLY	8	Appends but does not read or write to recordset records.
DB_INCONSISTENT	16	Permits an update to apply to all the fields of a recordset, even if the update affects other rows of the recordset.
DB_CONSISTENT	32	Default setting. Update applies only to those fields that do not affect other records of the recordset.

We recommend that you use database-level locking if your database will be used by a single user. Access is faster because the engine does not have to do the more complex searching required for a more refined locking method. It also does not require that the client system have the SHARE.EXE file installed, which is required for multiuser database access. This can save system overhead. In a client/server system, this level of locking is rarely used.

Page-Level Locking: Optimistic and Pessimistic

The Microsoft Access database engine and many database servers use an advanced data structure that enables fields to vary in size. For example, in an advanced system, when a text field contains a null value—that is, it does not contain a string—it uses no room in memory or on disk.

This type of dynamic record storage uses *variable-length fields*. More traditional databases allocate the space of the string field in every record, whether the string is empty or not. Having variable-length fields enables individual tables to contain a variety of fields without requiring a great amount of space for each empty record.

To record variable-length records, the database stores the data by using a series of pages. A *page* is a block of disk space that can contain a record, a part of a record, or multiple records, depending on what fits in that amount of space. For Access, a page equals 2000 bytes (2KB).

Page locking enables you to lock a particular page. The advantage of page locking is apparent when you must lock a series of sequential records at one time. Instead of locking each record individually, you can lock the entire page, which substantially increases the speed and decreases the amount of processing required. You use page locking primarily with databases that feature variable-length records, such as Microsoft Access or SQL Server.

Optimistic and pessimistic locks refer to how transactions are treated in regard to locking pages.

Pessimistic locking—the default method used by Visual Basic—locks the pages of a database when an application executes a `BeginTrans` or `EDIT` command. With pessimistic locking, the user can invoke the `EDIT` command for a particular record, and all users are locked out for updating that record or any other record in the page where the record is stored. This prevents two programs from updating the same piece of data simultaneously, which would cause an update conflict (refer to Chapter 4). The `LockEdits` property determines whether locking is pessimistic or optimistic. In the default setting—pessimistic locking—`LockEdits` is set to `True`.

Optimistic locking locks pages only when a `CommitTrans` or `UPDATE` is executed. Optimistic locking is perfect for client/server-type access. Although pessimistic locking locks the page when the `EDIT` method is invoked, optimistic locks the page only during the few milliseconds that the actual update occurs. If two users invoke an `EDIT` on the same record, the first user to send the `UPDATE` command updates the record. When the other user attempts to update the record, an error is returned. The application then decides how to proceed. Should the user's changes be dumped? Should the application record over the other user's changes? Should the user be prompted about which record to keep? Because it is unlikely that two users will modify the same field in the same record simultaneously, you can merge the two records to include both sets of data. The designer of the application must decide.

You can set optimistic locking at the table, recordset, or recordset level. Simply set the `LockEdits` property to `False`.

```
TestRecordset.LockEdits = False
TestTable.LockEdits = False
Data1.Recordset.LockEdits = False
```

If an UPDATE has already taken place and the client program attempts to update the same record, an error code of type 3197—`Data has changed, operation stopped`—is generated. You can intercept this with an `On Error Goto` routine.

Record-Level Locking

Record locking is the most common form of locking in traditional databases. Record locking locks access to individual records so that update conflicts do not occur. Record locking is used mostly by databases that feature fixed-length fields, such as xBase or FoxPro.

> **NOTE**
>
> Many of the more advanced database systems such as Oracle provide record-level locking. One of the most common criticisms of Microsoft SQL Server 6.0 is that record-level locking is still not provided (it uses page-level locking). Microsoft has promised to provide record-level locking sometime in the future. Be aware of this shortcoming when designing your client/server system.

Null Fields

Null fields are a potential minefield for the client/server developer. If you attempt to perform an action on a string field in a database that contains a null value, an error is generated. In many cases, the standard JET engine automatically takes care of this problem. If the system accesses a foreign database, however, the program might terminate because of an error.

> **NOTE**
>
> A null value is not the same as a null (or empty) string. A null string is a string that equals "". It is a string whose length is zero. A null value is not a string at all; it is a null value where a string pointer would normally exist.

Fortunately, there are several ways to remedy this problem. The most common is to use the function `IsNull()`, which requires that you programmatically check each string for a null value. If a string is a null value, it cannot be processed.

Consider the following code. It shows how an application can test a string and make it into a null string so that it does not cause errors when it is used by other parts of the program.

```
If IsNull(LastName) Then
        MsgBox "LastName is a Null."
        LastName = ""
End If
```

Another clever way to accomplish the same result is to use the & operator. The & operator concatenates, or joins, two strings to create a new string. Using the & operator between a zero-length string and a null value creates a zero-length string. If a string is already stored in the particular field, nothing happens to it. The following code is an example of how you might implement this.

```
' This prevents an error if NameField is set to Null
txt_Name.Text = "" & MyRS!NameField
```

SQL PassThrough

Many databases use a particular dialect of SQL to implement specific functions such as embedded commands. A typical JET engine accepts SQL commands and converts them to generic SQL calls to the ODBC engine. This does not permit convenient access to server-specific functions.

The remote data objects can call many of the functions and stored procedures but not all of them. Therefore, ODBC provides a function called SQL PassThrough. SQL PassThrough enables a program to pass an uninterpreted SQL command directly to the engine of the special database.

Whenever you use the SQL PassThrough function in a system-specific implementation, the portability of the client/server system is threatened. Other database servers might not contain the same commands, or they might implement them differently. If you use the SQL PassThrough function, make sure to document a description of the function of the call in the source code. When the code must be ported to another system, the programmer for the new system might be unfamiliar with the commands used in the old system. If you document the commands in the source code, you can eliminate some of the time the new programmer must spend studying system documentation.

The Set Object

The Set command is an extremely useful tool in Visual Basic. It enables you to set the reference to an object in a variable or to create a new instance of that object. Because recordsets, queries, snapshots, and indexes are stored as objects, the Set function is used extensively in a client/server system.

The following example sets the TestDB database object to represent the TestDB.MDB database file. You can then use the TestDB object for any access or manipulation needs.

```
Dim TestDB as DATABASE

Set TestDB = OpenDatabase("TestDB.MDB",True)
```

Database Connections

When you develop a Visual Basic client/server application, be sure to consider how the user will interact with the program and how the client program must relate to the server. If the user takes a long time browsing and editing a large number of records, these records might be locked away from other users. If the user accesses a group of records and leaves work for the day with the records still reserved on his machine, those records might remain inaccessible until his connection is terminated.

The simplest solution is to read the data into memory or a temporary storage table and close the connection to the main database. This solution is appropriate when the data is not constantly updated or when the user needs primarily to analyze the data—not to modify it. The client machine must have the appropriate storage available to accommodate the data.

If this solution is not appropriate for a particular client program, another option exists. Visual Basic includes the Timer control, shown in Figure 5.7. The Timer control activates a routine after a given amount of time has passed. For example, you can write a client program that checks for inactivity and breaks the connection after a given duration. When the user returns, the program can automatically reconnect to the database in a way that's transparent to the user.

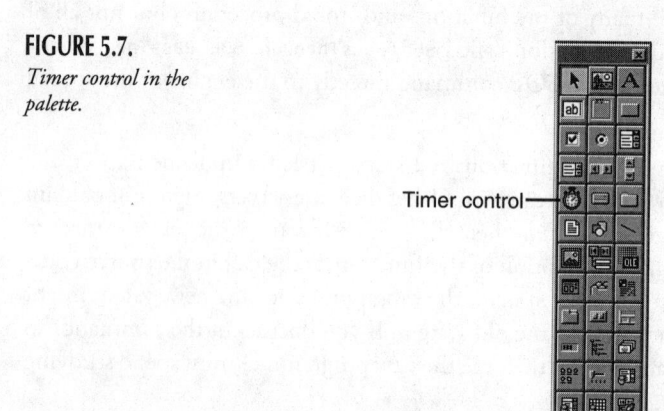

FIGURE 5.7.
Timer control in the palette.

If you are using the DAO or the RDO for data access, you must set all the objects that contain the connections to Nothing to sever the connection. ODBC data sources can connect and disconnect only at the API level. This enables the objects to remain in place while the connection is eliminated. Different ODBC drivers react to connection creation and destruction in different ways. Be sure to check the drivers you are using to determine if this will cause any problems.

6

Object Programming Overview

If you are involved in the programming, development, or client/server industries, you have probably heard about object-oriented programming (OOP). Because the basic concepts of object programming coordinate so well with client/server strategies, they are the ideal building blocks for the new client/server computer world.

Objects promise to allow for easier maintenance of systems, reusable code and modules, and productivity increases as object systems become widely adopted. Visual Basic 4 has turned to an increasingly object-based development environment. Although VB 3 had the basic capability to create and use objects, the VBA engine included in Visual Basic 4 is based on the object metaphor.

Object programming is perfect for client/server development. It enables you to create code for reusability so you can easily create various client programs from the same components. Distributed objects are the cornerstone of future object databases and network systems.

The entire client/server community is moving toward both object component implementation and object programming concepts. By providing reusable components and reusable classes, objects should provide the productivity increase that client/server computing has been promising.

Object-oriented programming is sometimes difficult to understand for traditional programmers. However, as a Visual Basic programmer, you are already familiar with many of the concepts. The controls placed on forms are objects. They have properties (such as `BackColor` and `Caption`) and they have methods (such as `Show` and `Unload`). This chapter discusses basic object concepts and advanced object concepts. Because object programming is such a large and varied field, we have included all the essential information that you need.

Basic Object Programming

Object-oriented programming uses all the standard constructs—`if...then`, `for...next`, and so forth—that you expect from a programming language. There are also new commands that deal with object inheritance and other concepts.

The real difference, however, from standard procedural programming is conceptual. It will take some time to get used to thinking about how objects are used and how they work together. If you have been programming for a while, you may remember the change from common global variables, which existed across a system, to private variables, which exist only within code modules and routines. Learning where and when to pass variables and how to do it required a new way of looking at how programs must be built.

Object-oriented programming, likewise, requires you to adjust to the new concepts. When to place routines and variables inside an object is a difficult decision when you first start using object programming. Most C programmers don't know when to take advantage of the C++ object features. Don't worry—Visual Basic makes object programming fairly pleasant.

Chapter 6 ■ Object Programming Overview

Traditional Structured Programming

Traditional structured or procedural programming contains two basic and separate pieces: routines (or code) and variables (see Figure 6.1). Routines handle all the interactions, do all the processing, and manipulate the data. Data can be stored in a variety of variables that can be freely exchanged among routines.

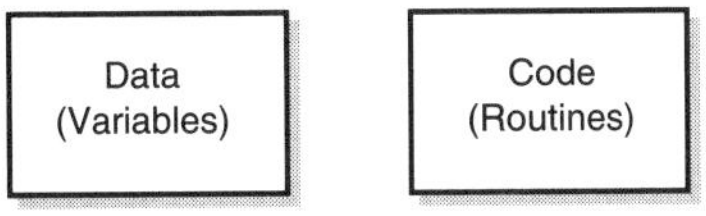

FIGURE 6.1.
A traditional procedural program structure.

```
Data              Code
(Variables)       (Routines)
```

Variables have rudimentary definitions (such as integer or string), but it is largely up to the programmer in a procedural programming system to address specifically a particular routine to a particular variable. For example, the integer variable `Timer` might hold the time since the clock struck midnight. To use this variable in a program, the programmer must send it specifically to a time conversion routine to get the time printed correctly on the screen. The variable `Timer` and its function—displaying the time—are not coupled together.

This is difficult for maintenance because a programmer who didn't originally write the program can examine the source code and not understand what a variable is supposed to represent. It also makes changes to code or variables uncertain because it is unclear what other parts of the program need the variable structure in its original form. Maintenance is further complicated by the fact that a variable and a routine that uses it might be located in completely different places in the program. For example, one might be in a form and another in a module. This often makes definitions difficult to find.

Object Programming

Object programming seeks to solve these problems by coupling the variables with the routines that use and manipulate them (see Figure 6.2). For instance, the timer example explained previously becomes a `Timer` object that contains both the variable and the function that displays it.

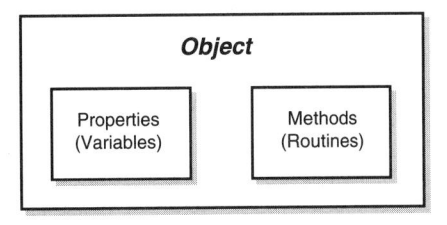

FIGURE 6.2.
An object-oriented program structure.

```
Object
  Properties       Methods
  (Variables)      (Routines)
```

This enables routines—called *methods*—that directly manipulate, affect, or display the data variables—called *properties*—to be stored together to unify the programming construct. You can add more methods to do various time calculations, to display different clock faces, or to carry out other relevant routines.

Therefore, an object becomes a self-contained unit that contains data and all the routines that manipulate this data. By keeping the two pieces together, the object becomes portable. For example, once a programming object is created, it can be cut and pasted into another program without the worry of leaving an important variable or routine behind. Likewise, the object can be published on a network for use as a type of black box. Other programmers have to know only basic methods and properties in order to use it.

Classes

In object programming, the terms *object* and *class* are often used almost interchangeably. That is because the object needs the class to be created. An *object* is an actual structure in memory. A *class* is a template used to create the object. Therefore, an object is a concrete instance of a class.

The difference between a class and an object might be difficult to understand until you think in terms of the computer memory used. Imagine that you need a Timer object like the one described previously. The Timer object requires one integer variable (property), but it requires ten different drawing routines (methods). In an object, the methods and the properties are coupled together. If the integer took two bytes of memory and the drawing routines required a total of 5KB, each Timer object would require 5002 bytes.

The solution to this problem is to use a template for the object, called a class. The object itself is a memory construct that holds all the information that *differs* from the template, or class. Therefore, the class construct must be loaded into memory once, holding all the methods and prototypes of the properties (see Figure 6.3). Objects created from the class need only the memory required to hold a pointer to the object class and the space required to hold the values of the properties. The values of the properties are presumed to be different from the prototypes in the class.

Instances and Instantiation

Each presence of an object in memory is called an *instance*. When loaded into memory, the Excel spreadsheet application becomes an object. Therefore, using two CreateObject() commands for Excel loads two copies—two instances—of Excel. The process of making an object actually become a live memory construct is called *instantiation*. A class is used to instantiate an object in memory. In the previous example, two separate sessions of Excel are instantiated.

FIGURE 6.3.
Multiple object instantiation from a class.

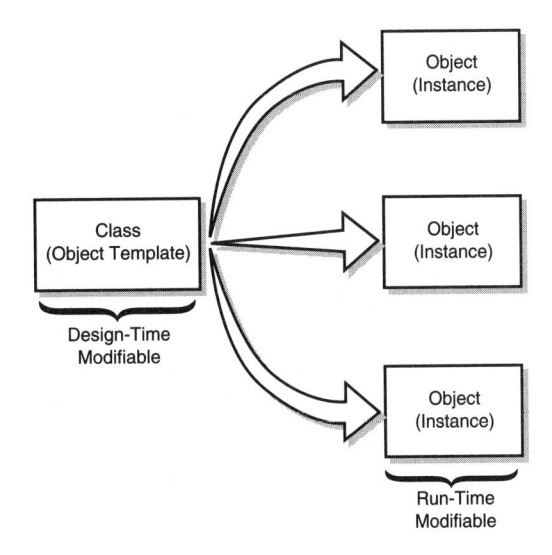

Framework

Numerous classes can be brought together in a hierarchy called a *framework*. Frameworks are the structures used to bring together classes for overall generalized solutions. The classes are structured hierarchically, which provides a clear organization of how classes relate to each other. For example, Excel is a spreadsheet object framework. All the classes for Excel objects exist to provide the common functionality of a spreadsheet.

Operating systems are increasingly made up of object frameworks. For example, an operating system can contain a disk access framework, a display framework, a security framework, and so on. All these frameworks describe objects that can be instantiated for use. Some operating systems contain more than 100 unique frameworks for all the necessary system services.

Frameworks are also used to construct applications. Microsoft Foundation Class (MFC), Think Class Libraries (TCL), and MacApp are all object frameworks used to build applications in C/C++. They provide the classes for objects, such as windows, controls, and memory structures. By providing common objects for all programs to use, development time for individual applications—the time spent declaring variables and calling specific functions—is dramatically reduced.

Encapsulation

Keeping the data and the routines packed together is called *encapsulation*. Encapsulation is used to describe the coupling of data and routines to provide a programmer's black box. None of the variables, except the variables passed into and out of the object, are accessible to the system. This enables all the workings of the methods and the internal properties to be hidden. This technique is also known as *information hiding*. It makes the object as simple as possible, and it prevents tampering with properties that are important to the object functioning correctly.

In creating an object, using private properties is the first level of abstraction toward a black box. Eliminating the exposure of variables outside the object is the next step. The object uses methods such as Visual Basic's `Property Get` and `Property Set` to restrict all access of variables to routines that exist specifically for this purpose. This way, values can always be checked to ensure that they are in the proper range before they are sent to routines.

For example, a routine might require a property named `tempProp` to be used in a division routine. If `tempProp` is set to zero, the routine generates a divide-by-zero error. If you provide a set of gatekeeper routines when the property is originally set, it can be rejected as an inappropriate value. This helps ensure that the methods of the object do not crash because of erroneous property values.

Encapsulation hides data that is important to the object but irrelevant to the programmer using the object. The object provides only the information necessary for interfacing, sending messages, and so on.

Messages

In the world of object-oriented programming, you often hear the term *messages* used in the context of "send a release message to the object." Messages refer to manipulating an object, whether it is calling a method or setting a property. A release message, for example, could instruct a particular object to release a portion of memory. The message concept is a holdover from earlier object-oriented systems. As network objects become more prevalent, messages to objects will be sent to objects located on remote machines.

For example, an object might be located on another machine. Sending it a message to identify itself might be conceptually easier to understand than calling one of its methods through a remote procedure call. You will likely encounter the messaging terminology in many object-oriented discussions.

Visual Basic Object Programming

You might be asking where Visual Basic 4 fits into this object methodology? Visual Basic 4 enables you to create classes that include both methods and properties. As with many Microsoft applications, Visual Basic can rest on top of the Microsoft Foundation Class (MFC). This means that although a Visual Basic programmer does not directly access the objects of the Windows framework, the Visual Basic methods, such as the `Form.Show` method, access the appropriate methods.

When you use the Insert menu to create a new class module, you can use a class module to create objects. You can use those objects within your own programs, or they can be published with the OLE server feature for use by other applications. Other programs can then instantiate the objects that you created in Visual Basic and call methods for them.

Visual Basic also uses the VBA object framework. It includes the VBA classes:

- Collection
- Constants
- Conversion
- DateTime
- FileSystem
- Financial
- Information
- Interaction
- Math
- Strings

You can examine these classes by using the Object Browser built into Visual Basic 4.

Advanced Object Programming

Object programming becomes increasingly complex once you move past the basic object concepts. The field of object programming is currently undergoing dramatic change, just like the client/server world. The industry is struggling with learning the best features and the most appropriate way of implementing object technology given the limitations of speed, memory, storage, and connectivity.

Topics such as inheritance, polymorphism, object reusability, and object version control are primary topics of debate. These topics in many ways define how an object implementation is set up. Visual Basic implements Microsoft's beliefs in these various implementation details of course, but it is important to understand the underlying technological issues.

Inheritance

Inheritance is a hotly contested topic in the object community because the very nature of inherited characteristics means that a single change to a class can have far-reaching effects on all the children defined from that class. Object languages like SmallTalk and C++ objects can inherit methods, properties, and behaviors from objects above them in the object hierarchy. For example, the difference between a rectangle and a rounded rectangle is only an additional property—the corner radius. A rectangle object must have coordinates for the top-left corner and the bottom-right corner. A rounded rectangle also has a property that defines how rounded the corner on the rectangle will be.

Using inheritance, a rounded rectangle is defined as a subclass of the rectangle (see Figure 6.4). The rounded rectangle class inherits the properties of the rectangle—that is, the coordinates. The extra corner radius property is added to the properties inherited from the rectangle class.

FIGURE 6.4.
Rounded rectangle inheritance.

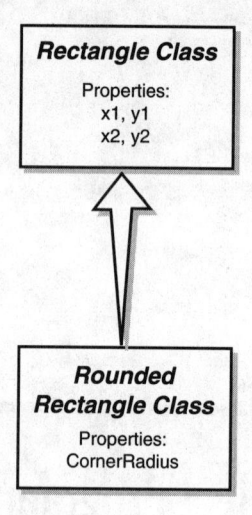

```
┌─────────────────┐
│ Rectangle Class │
│   Properties:   │
│     x1, y1      │
│     x2, y2      │
└─────────────────┘
         ▲
         │
┌─────────────────┐
│     Rounded     │
│ Rectangle Class │
│   Properties:   │
│   CornerRadius  │
└─────────────────┘
```

In this way, an entire framework can be built. If a class does not have all the features that are needed for a particular program, you can create a subclass, which inherits all the features from the original class and also adds the missing features. Methods that must be changed can be named the same as the method higher in the hierarchy.

In the previous example, a Draw method might be used to draw the rectangle. In the rounded rectangle class, a method called Draw is created that draws the rounded rectangle.

When you access methods or properties, execution moves up the object hierarchy until the method or property is found. To override a method or property, simply give it the same name as the one that needs to be overridden.

The Fragile Base Class

Some object models want to extend the inheritance capability to their system objects for complete inheritance across the system—for example, IBM's System Object Model. If the object must be modified, an additional subclass can be added to provide the needed features. This provides for a dynamically modifiable object system. This type of inheritance is known as *implementation inheritance*.

There is a problem with this system, however. Some people refer to it as the fragile base class problem. Because all the subclasses are based on an original class, what happens if that class is modified? Like a set of dominoes, all the subclasses defined from the base class are affected. In an object system, a missing base object would cause all the objects defined from it to collapse.

Some vendors claim that the benefits outweigh the potential side-effects. After all, how often will the base classes be modified? The advantages are a hugely extensible system. Other vendors have built various controls into their object systems to minimize the chances of problems occurring.

Microsoft's Component Object Model (COM), described in Chapter 23, "Object Linking and Embedding (OLE)," does not include object or class inheritance in its system object model. Instead, COM provides a technique called *aggregation* or component inheritance, which enables objects that might appear as a single object to be grouped together. This does not provide the type of extensibility that occurs in an inherited system, but it also does not suffer the potential drawbacks.

Visual Basic 4.0 also does not support implementation inheritance. Instead, it supports component inheritance. This enables you to create a class that can use objects from other created classes within its definition. This type of aggregation is the type of inheritance you will notice in object frameworks such as the Excel object chart. Collections are often a dominant feature used in component inheritance.

Polymorphism

Polymorphism signifies a fairly simple technique. It is the ability to use a method with the same name on different objects with the effect appropriate to that object. For example, a rectangle object might have a Draw method to draw it to the screen. A rounded rectangle might also have a Draw method to draw it to the screen. Both objects have different methods for screen drawing, but sending a Draw message to either object causes it to be displayed.

This technique offers potential for increasing productivity. For example, a loop can send Draw commands to a group of heterogeneous objects, and they each use their own routines to display themselves on the screen. Sending them all Clear messages causes them to remove themselves from memory. Polymorphism is also known as *overloading*.

Object Version Controls

Version control is an important issue in an object system. OLE objects can be created with a specified version, and multiple versions of an object can be stored on the same system. Most of the details of the version control fall under the implementation of the OLE object registry.

One of the technologies that Microsoft has implemented to dramatically decrease the problem of version malfunctions of a new object after it is deployed as a component (such as an OCX) is the QueryInterface. OLE has the capability of querying an object for the methods and properties that are supported. In some cases, therefore, a program can ignore the version number and simply make sure that the proper object characteristics are available.

Object Programming and Object Components

Object programming, which has been around nearly two decades, was the genesis of reusable objects in a system. The use of objects as interchangeable components and plug-ins at the operating system level has occurred only within the last ten years. These *object component* technologies, such as OLE, OpenDoc, and NeXTSTEP, are bringing the real power of object manipulation to user platforms.

Although there is some cross-over, particularly in programmer implementation, the fields of object programming and object component technologies have remained fairly distinct. Objects available to an operating system use an object model to provide common object access (see Figure 6.5).

FIGURE 6.5.
An object model on top of an OS.

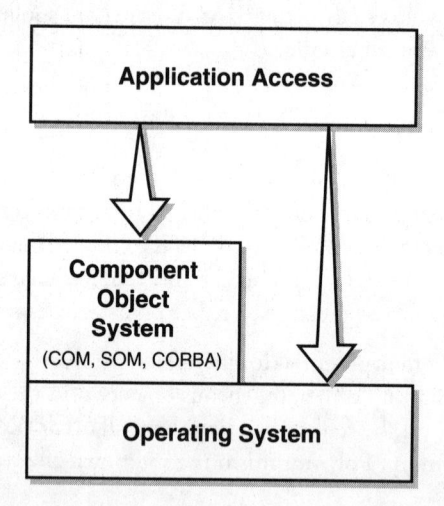

The cross-over between the worlds of object programming and object components occurs mostly in the plug-in control market. OLE Custom Controls (OCXs), the successors of VBXs, can be plugged into applications such as Access and Word for implementation by the user. The presence of VBA blurs the line between general (cross-application) programming and macro development within individual applications. For the foreseeable future, however, the requirements for programming objects and component objects will probably remain different.

Problems with Objects

Because of the fantastic possibilities of object-based design, many people speak of objects as a cure-all. Before we begin to explain object programming, we want to mention some of the drawbacks to these new implementations.

When an object system is implemented, different objects created by many people must be pulled together and placed in a single project. You have probably already seen the time and expense of upgrading any major application and the incompatibilities and bugs in a new version. Now imagine 50 objects in one project, all made and supported by 50 different vendors. One object upgrade can affect the functioning of the system and, consequently, all the other objects. Imagine upgrading the operating system that the machine is running. This might require a new version for each object, which means all the headaches involved with upgrading 50 different pieces.

Another problem comes with the lack of control while objects are used. Visual Basic programmers using VBXs have already encountered this situation. If the control has a bug in it, the project might have to wait until the manufacturer provides an upgrade. This loss of control can be substantial if the project is mission-critical.

This situation does not occur just with commercial products. It also occurs with objects produced in-house by a different department, which might not be interested in perfecting the specific operation of the object that you need. In fact, it might even be unwilling to provide the source code or modification control.

Objects tend to take up much more memory and require more processing than traditional procedural equivalents.

Ten years ago when we first examined object-oriented programming systems, such as SmallTalk, the memory and processing requirements made them unfeasible. Today, with the increase in machine power and substantial drops in computer prices, objects are beginning to catch on. Although the machines have gotten much faster and object implementation has become much more sophisticated, objects still exact a performance penalty. The implementation of an object system or framework must, therefore, be justified by the increased value and productivity potential.

An object is not as simple as it sounds. There is not just one object format, but many: OLE objects, OpenDoc objects, CORBA objects, NeXTSTEP objects, and so on. Therefore, object-to-object compatibility is not a simple task. There are object converters, gateways, and compatibility proposals. Even so, interobject communication can be as difficult as many of the client/server communications, middleware, and other compatibility layers. In object programming, a C++ object is not directly compatible with Visual Basic. That is, without the necessary linking, interface, and foundation codes and utilities, Visual Basic could not interact with a C++ object.

Most objects are based on a hierarchical metaphor. For this reason, the planning involved in a hierarchical system can often be far more important than in a typical procedural system. A poorly designed hierarchy can have disastrous effects and may straightjacket a project into a poor implementation.

Objects in a Client/Server Environment

Objects are becoming increasingly popular in the client/server development world. The distribution of power through a client/server system makes objects perfect because of their encapsulated black-box-like nature. This enables objects stored on either the client or the server to contain both data and the code that acts upon that data.

Objects facilitate advanced team development. By programming with classes, individual team members can be assigned work on particular classes. The input and output properties can be simulated so they can do sample builds for simulated prototyping.

Using components (such as OCX or VBX plug-ins) substantially reduces the development time of numerous client programs. By adopting information-hiding techniques, you can protect variables from corruption.

Distributed objects provide three-tier client/server architectures. You can implement business rules and distributed computing by creating objects to filter information before it is stored in a central database. Distributed objects enable a server to provide most of the processing power while a client can easily access the data and execute the object methods. By creating appropriate objects, a programmer can essentially create a custom server to provide specialized services to networked clients.

Microsoft has made objects crucial to its future programming and operating system strategy. Object Linking and Embedding (OLE) provides the fundamental object technology for the Windows operating system. OLE technology is accessed through object references. For more information on OLE, see Chapter 23, "Object Linking and Embedding (OLE)."

7

Visual Basic 4

Visual Basic Development Environment

Visual Basic 4 is the upgrade to VB 3 that has been two years in the making. (See Figure 7.1.) The VB environment has dramatically shifted from standard, procedure-based programming to an emphasis on an object environment.

FIGURE 7.1.
The Forms, Properties, and Project windows.

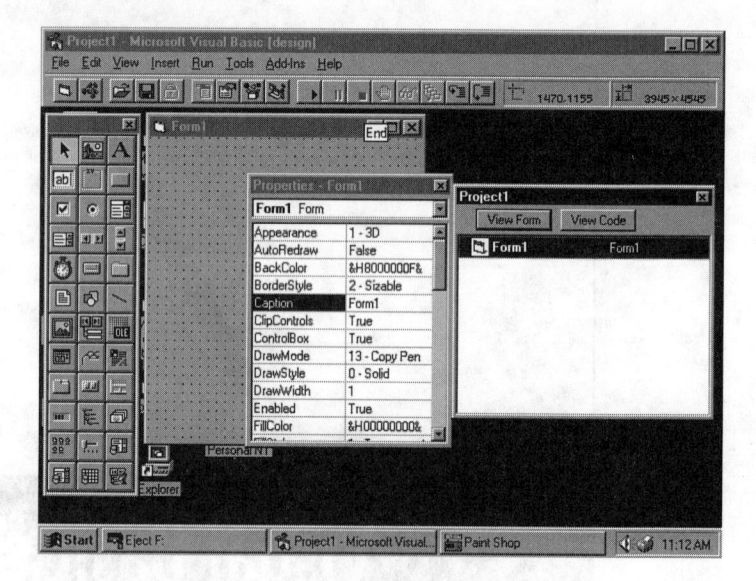

Visual Basic has long been used for the creation of client/server systems. The VB 4 development has added significant features to aid in system development.

There are three different versions of Visual Basic 4 available: Standard Edition, Professional Edition, and Enterprise Edition. The Standard Edition is available only in a 32-bit version, which encourages people to upgrade to Windows 95 or at least use the Win32s extensions. The Professional Edition and the Enterprise Edition each include both 16- and 32-bit versions of the development environment.

The Standard Edition contains all of the new VB language features, but it doesn't contain many of the advanced controls and tools supplied with the other editions. The Standard Edition cannot be used effectively for client/server development.

The Professional Edition includes all of the Custom Controls, a new version of Crystal Reports, the Hot Spot Editor, and ODBC drivers for SQL Server and Oracle. The Professional Edition 4.0 is essentially the updated equivalent of VB 3.0 Professional.

The Enterprise Edition is a new level of Visual Basic packaging and includes significant extra features for the client/server developer. Complete remote object tools are provided for system setup and maintenance of Remote OLE. SourceSafe is included, which is a source librarian tool that allows team project development on a program. The Remote Data Objects and Remote Data Control are included for optimized access to ODBC data sources.

Using the Remote OLE server tools, Visual Basic can be used to create either an advanced three-tier client/server solution, or it can provide simple functions, business rules, and data serving across the network. The SetupWizard even provides the necessary tools to create installation disks (including the OLE Registration components) or network install setup applications.

The Enterprise Edition will clearly be the choice of most client/server developers. The extra features that simplify and expand data-access capabilities are dramatic. The difference in cost between the Professional and Enterprise Editions will be quickly made up in time savings for C/S system development. In this book we will focus on the use of the Enterprise Edition.

Visual Basic 16- and 32-Bit Versions

The 16-bit version of VB 4.0 will run on Windows 3.1, Windows for Workgroups, Windows NT, and Windows 95. However, the new custom controls that are used in Windows 95 (such as the property tab sheet, the slider, and so forth) are not available in the 16-bit version.

The 32-bit version will run only on Windows 95 or Windows NT 3.51 or later. The standard 16-bit VBX custom controls cannot be used in the 32-bit version of VB 4. VB 4 is structured to use the new OLE Custom Controls (OCXs) exclusively. The 32-bit version can use either 16- or 32-bit versions of an OCX. Applications created with the 32-bit version will not run on Win32s.

Conditional compilation helps to enable a single code base to be maintained with 16- and 32-bit versions.

Visual Basic for Applications

One of the most important new features added to Visual Basic (VB) 4 is the Visual Basic for Applications language engine, version 2.0 (VBA). Version 2 was designed to be backward-compatible with previous standalone versions of VB and VBA 1.0 that were included in MS Excel 5.0 and MS Project 4.0.

With the inclusion of VBA in these programs, Object Linking and Embedding (OLE) Automation objects and VB code are easily transferred between applicable programming environments. As improvements continue to be made in VBA, they are reflected in the VB language and the development environment. Other new features or expanded capabilities are described in the following paragraphs.

OLE Automation

OLE automation provides a defined interface through which programs can communicate. Through the OLE automation structure, the application objects of one program are made available to other applications to use. In part or whole, the functions of an application are exposed so they may be executed across applications. An application may make available to the OLE system one or more objects with exposed properties and methods. Using the functions provided by another program, the objects can form building blocks to create new applications with more capabilities, more quickly and easily.

Visual Basic 4 (32-bit only) provides the user with the capability to create both in-process and out-of-process OLE servers. Creating OLE servers allows the capabilities to provide exposed functions to other programs, which was previously impossible in Visual Basic.

> **NOTE**
>
> VB 4 allows the creation of two types of OLE Automation Server: in-process (also known as OLE DLLs) and out-of-process. Out-of-process are the more common type. These programs execute in their own memory space, rather than the space allocated to an executing application. In-process servers execute within the same memory space as the application that calls it. In-process servers are faster (because the application bounds do not have to be crossed), but do not allow a single instance of the application to be shared and also cannot be run on distributed OLE. The capability requirements of an in-process server are also more strict. See the VB manual for information on the Use OLE DLL Restrictions in the options dialog box.

Class Modules

To create OLE servers, Visual Basic 4 now includes class modules. A class module appears identical to a traditional module, but instead of defining a routine it is used to define objects. The class module allows the creation of `Public` variables that become the `properties` of the class. Public routines that are created become the `methods` of the class. For more information on object-oriented programming, see Chapter 6, "Object Programming Overview."

OLE servers are implemented by creating classes that may be published. The classes that have been created in a Visual Basic class module can then be instantiated from another program. Any OLE Automation client (such as VBA in Excel or a custom C++ program) can access the objects published by the VB Class Module.

Object Browser

The Object Browser provides the user with the tools to search and display object information from object libraries, objects you created, OLE Automation objects, or even objects made available from other applications. (See Figure 7.2.) The Object Browser allows viewing of any object libraries selected in the Custom Controls dialog box. Object information is stored and retrieved from within the Visual Basic object library of the Object Browser. Activation of the Object Browser is either from the View Menu in VB 4 or the Object Browser button on the toolbar.

FIGURE 7.2.
The Object Browser screen display.

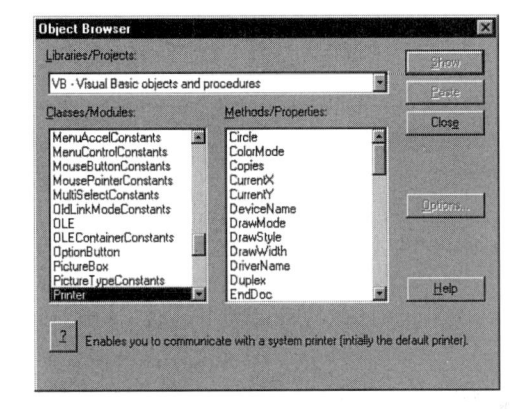

The Object Browser display enables the programmer to view classes, properties, and methods of defined objects in a hierarchical order from object libraries. Included on the display are object descriptions and links to the objects' native help files. This information is valuable and available for use during the development of a client application.

Other object information, such as a constant name and its corresponding number, is also available. Any of these objects may be selected, and through the cut-and-paste function of the browser's Edit menu, they can be inserted into the application code.

Visual Basic 4 Objects and Collections

Objects are the primary unit in an object-oriented system. A collection allows the creation of essentially an array of objects. Many objects of the same type may be kept in a collection for reference and manipulation. For example, a number of child windows on an MDI form can be stored in a collection. The collection can then be accessed to tile the various windows contained in it. VB 4 has added several commands to handle collections because of the great number of objects added to the new environment.

Part I ■ Overview of Necessary Visual Basic and Client/Server Concepts

With an emphasis on object-oriented programming, most of Visual Basic has been changed in structure to an object foundation. Listing 7.1 is a reference of many of the object groups for data access. Below each object are the methods that are directly associated with the object or collection. These are the new methods that have been added in VB version 4.

You can see that collections are used extensively for the new data object interface. Methods and properties of the collection itself are accessed with the plural form (that is, `columns` is used to access a collection of `column` objects).

Listing 7.1. Object groups for data access.

```
Column, Columns
    Column Object, Columns Collection:   Legend
        CellText
        CellValue
        Insert
        Item
        Remove
DBEngine
    DBEngine Object
        CompactDatabase
        CreateWorkspace
        Idle
        RegisterDatabase
        RepairDatabase

Document, Documents
    Document Object, Docments Collection:   Legend
        Refresh

Error, Errors
    Error Object, Error Collection Properties:   Legend
        Count
        Description
        HelpContext
        HelpFile
        Number
        Source

Group, Groups
    Group Object, Groups Collection:   Legend
        Append
        CreateUser
        Delete
        Refresh

Index, Indexs
    Index Object, Indexs Collection:   Legend
        Append
        CreateField
        CreateProperty
        Delete
        Refresh
```

```
Parameter, Parameters
    Parameter Object, Parameters Collection:   Legend
        Refresh

Property, Properties
    Property Object, Properties Collection:   Legend
        Append
        Delete
        Refresh

QueryDef, QueryDefs
    QueryDef Object, QueryDefs  Collection:   Legend
        Append
        Close
        CreateProperty
        Delete
        Execute
        OpenRecordset
        Refresh

Recordset, Recordsets
    Recordset Object, Recordsets Collection

Relation, Relations
    Relation Object, Relations  Collection:   Legend
        Append
        CreateField
        Delete
        Refresh

User, Users
    User Object, Users Collection:   Legend
        Append
        CreateGroup
        Delete
        NewPassword
        Refresh

Workspace, Workspaces
    Workspace Object, Workspaces Collection:   Legend
        BeginTrans
        Close
        CommitTrans
        CreateDatabase
        CreateGroup
        CreateUser
        OpenDatabase
        Refresh
        Rollback
```

OLE Custom Controls (OCX)

Visual Basic 4 is constructed to use the new OLE Custom Controls (OCX) instead of the older Visual Basic extension (VBX). The new OLE controls are available in both 16- and

32-bit versions. (For more information see the previous section, "Visual Basic 16- and 32-Bit Versions.")

Visual Basic contains the complete environment for hosting OLE Custom Controls. Unlike VBXs, which were limited to use with Visual Basic, OLE Custom Controls can be plugged into a variety of programs. The same OLE Custom Controls can be used in MS Access, Delphi, and a variety of other programs. Therefore, there will be a broader market and a much larger supply of OCX controls than there have been of VBX controls in the past.

Windows 95 Interface Support

Visual Basic 4 supports the new controls that are standard with Windows 95. (See Figure 7.3.) These include the Rich Text object, the property sheet tab strip, the toolbar control, the status bar control, the progress bar control, the treeview control (which provides an outline with pictures or icons), the imagelist control, the listview control, and the slider control.

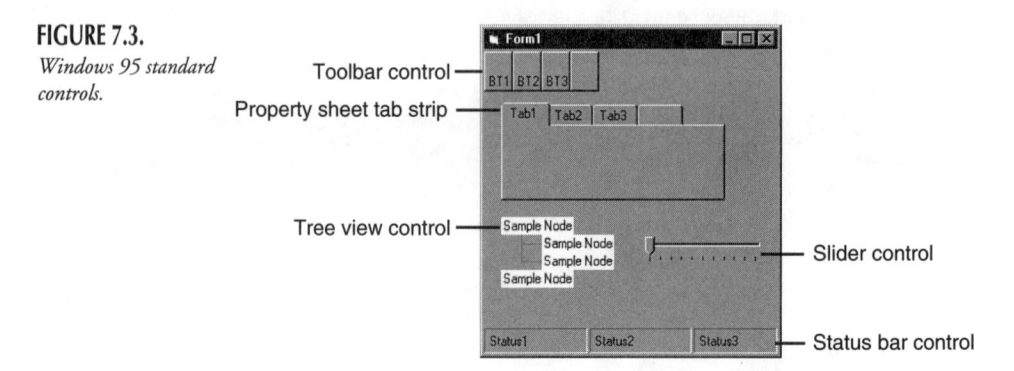

FIGURE 7.3.
Windows 95 standard controls.

The imagelist control is perhaps one of the most powerful new interface controls. It allows multiple images to be stored in a convenient data structure. This structure can then be passed to other controls such as the tab strip, treeview control, or the listview control for display.

> **NOTE**
>
> These controls can be used only in the 32-bit version of Visual Basic 4. They cannot be used in any applications that will be running in a 16-bit environment.

Custom Controls and References

In VB 3, any custom controls were added through the project. Visual Basic 4 provides complete user-interface access to all of the objects that may be used in a project, including OLE

Custom Controls and insertable objects. Under the Tools menu, the options Custom Controls... and References... are used to determine which controls and OLE objects are available in the current programming environment.

The References dialog box allows determination of what objects from another application will be added to the current program's object library. (See Figure 7.4.) Files that may be added to the References section include Type Libraries (*.TLB, *.OLB), executable files (*.EXE), and OLE Custom Controls (*.OCX). The Browse button allows selection of files that are not registered in the OLE Registry.

FIGURE 7.4.
The References dialog box.

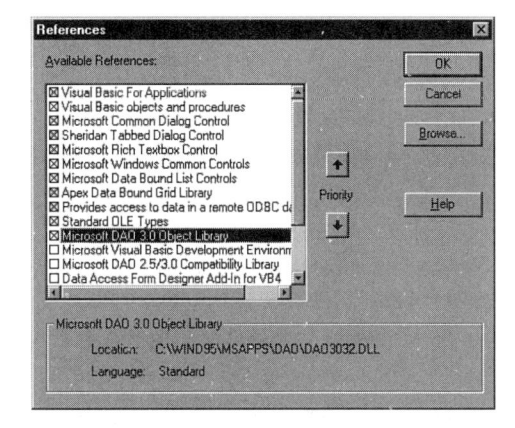

The Browse button also allows the setting of the available object's priority. When an object reference is made in a program's code, the object libraries must be searched to find the appropriate object. By moving a particular object library up in the References dialog, the library is searched sooner rather than later. This enables you to select the libraries that are used most often, and put them higher in the search list for optimization of the program's throughput.

The Custom Controls dialog box allows addition of any insertable objects to the project's toolbox palette. (See Figure 7.5.) In VB 3, controls were added to a project by selecting the Add File... option and selecting the VBX from the proper directory. The new method in VB 4 is far more elegant. Objects that will appear in the palette (and your final compiled application) have a checkmark to the left of the entry name. The Show frame enables the display to be altered to show only Insertable Objects, Controls, or Selected Items.

> **NOTE**
>
> All of the controls that appear in the Custom Controls dialog box must be available in the references section. Therefore, make sure that you've added the control in the References dialog (unless the control needs to be used only in this project).

FIGURE 7.5
The Custom Controls dialog box.

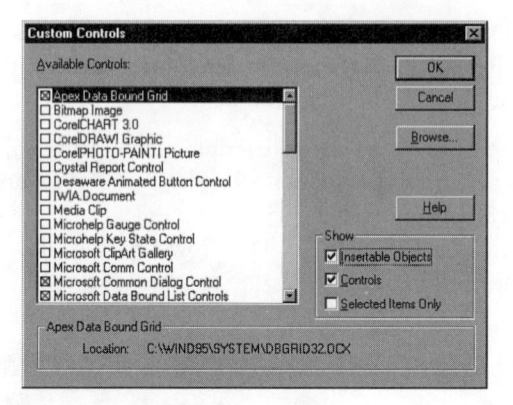

Menu and Toolbar Negotiation

If an OLE object is inserted into the container in a Visual Basic application, double-clicking the object will activate it. With in-place activation capabilities, the menus may have to change to accommodate the menu options of the OLE server application. Visual Basic 4 provides the ability to control how the menus for activated objects will appear in relation to current menus.

The appearance of the menu and the toolbar may now be negotiated, because Visual Basic added the capability to create the OLE server; they can now be linked to—or embedded in—an application. This process is called *user-interface negotiation*, and it is important due to the limited space available on the objects form.

This negotiation determines how the menus and toolbar will be displayed on the OLE server and is controlled by setting the NegotiateMenus property of the form. The NegotiatePosition property of a form also modifies how the menus are affected during activation. This property determines whether the activated menu appears not at all, to the right, to the left, or in the middle of current menus. If the NegotiateMenus property is set to False, the NegotiatePosition property is not used.

> **TIP**
>
> The menu's NegotiatePosition may also be set in the Menu Editor. This enables the setting to be changed at design time.

Insertable Objects as Controls

Objects from any program that may act as an OLE server application may be inserted into a Visual Basic form as an object that may be manipulated programmatically. For example, in a word-processing program, the menu command `Insert Object` may be used to insert an Excel chart. Now, Visual Basic can access and manipulate OLE objects at both design time and runtime.

Forms as Callable Objects

Forms are now objects that may be accessed from other forms. For example, under Visual Basic 3 it was impossible to execute a routine stored in one form from code in another form. With the addition of the *Public* suffix to a routine definition, routines may now be exposed to other forms.

Creation of In-Process OLE Servers

The Enterprise Edition features the ability to create OLE in-process servers. In-process servers are stored as DLLs in the \WINDOWS\SYSTEM\ directory. They are used to provide encapsulated programming code for team project development, to create Wizards and Add-Ins for Visual Basic, to create OLE Automation Servers to be accessed from other programs (such as Excel), or to break down a large project into more manageable pieces.

An in-process server is created by using the Make OLE DLL option under the File menu. This option will save the VB file as a .DLL file, which can then be copied into any machine's \WINDOWS\SYSTEM\ directory along with the VB40032.DLL file. For more information on OLE server, see Chapter 24, "Creating an OLE Server."

> **NOTE**
>
> A program may not run as an in-process server while in the debugging environment of Visual Basic. It must be run normally and tested with a client accessing it in a normal manner with another instance of VB. However, in the Options dialog box under the Advanced Options tab, the setting Use OLE DLL Restrictions is available. When this option is checked, the VB program will run with all the restrictions of a DLL, allowing testing in a simulated in-process environment.

Making a Simulated DLL with VB

Visual Basic 4 still does not compile code, so DLLs may not be created directly from within VB. However, VB 4 provides a way to simulate DLL capabilities using OLE. This enables other programs and languages to call and access routines written in Visual Basic. The calls to a VB DLL must be made through the OLE framework.

You cannot access a VB DLL using a `Declare` statement. It must be used through the OLE engine. The fact that it is a DLL means that it may be copied to a client machine and used by other programs on that machine as an OLE Automation Server.

The advantages of writing separate DLLs in C/C++ are still numerous. VB DLLs require the OLE foundation (DLLs, and so on) to be installed on the system before the VB DLLs can be accessed. This creates a great deal of memory and processing overhead. Also, a process that you need in a DLL may require the fast execution of a compiled language.

> **NOTE**
>
> DLLs created in Visual Basic are also not multithreaded. This means that they cannot spawn a separate process when running under a multithreaded operating system such as Windows NT. For example, if one program calls the DLL and then another calls the same DLL, two entire instances of the VB DLL and the VB runtime must be loaded into memory. This means that a minimum (before your DLL is loaded) of approximately 500K of memory is used for each instance. That much memory usage can strain even a powerful machine. With a C/C++ DLL designed for multithreading, a new instance can take a mimimal amount of memory because the same code can be used.

Data Access Engine

Visual Basic 4 contains a new JET database engine (version 3.0) and data access objects (DAO). JET 3.0 is a 32-bit database engine that delivers increased performance while providing new features such as programmability of security and relations, and cascading updates and deletes.

Referential Integrity

VB 4 now supports programmatic access to referential integrity. Referential integrity ensures that records in related tables remain consistent with referential rules that are created. For more information on referential integrity, see Chapter 4, "Overview of Database Concepts."

To support these capabilities, cascade-update and cascade-delete features have been added to VB 4. These features have been standard to MS Access 2.0 but were not accessible previously from Visual Basic.

Referential integrity is created using the `Attributes` property that exists in the `Field`, `Relation`, and `TableDef` objects. This property is used to set whether a relation is a one-to-one relation, an inherited relation, a left-join relation, or a right-join relation. It allows settings for cascade updates and deletes.

> **NOTE**
>
> A cascade relation indicates that modification to a linked record affects the other records that are related to it. For example, a Customer data table may be related to an Orders data table with cascade delete set to TRUE. When a customer is deleted, all of the orders that were made by that customer are also deleted.

New Data-Bound Controls

VB 4 has several more controls having the added capability of being easily bound to a data or remote-data control. These are bound controls that have three new properties, which are referred to as data-aware properties. *Data-aware properties* are used in characterizing bound controls. These new data-aware properties, along with a description of their operational function, are shown in the following list.

Property	Description
DataChanged	Identifies the values that are in a bound control that have changed.
DataField	Defines the field name that resides in the recordset constructed by the data control.
DataSource	Defines the data control name to which it is bound.

The data-bound controls consist of the data-bound list and combo, data-bound grid, and the data outline control. These controls (data-bound list and combo, data-bound grid) are in addition to the intrinsic (or standard) bound controls and are listed under Custom Controls or OLE Custom Controls (.OCX).

Under OLE data-bound controls, there is the OLE container control. Through more use of data-bound controls in applications, operational efficiency is increased. This occurs with the control's capability to provide the application with automatic list management and instantaneous read-write access to external data. The following list includes the three data controls that were added to VB 4 and their basic functions.

Class Name	Description
Data-bound list	The data-bound list box control (.OCX) provides many of the characteristics and properties of the standard list-box control, with additional data-access capabilities. This control has the capability of automatically being filled with information from a database field that is bound to its data control. Additionally, there is an option that allows a selected field to be passed to a

continues

Class Name	Description
	second data control— a powerful tool that can be used in look-up table applications.
Data-bound combo	The data-bound combo box control (.OCX) provides many of the characteristics and properties of the standard combo-box control with basically the same data-access capabilities as the data-bound list box control. The main difference between these controls is that the combo-box control provides a text box where the selected field of data is copied and can be edited.
Data-bound grid	The data-bound grid box control (.OCX) provides many of the characteristics and properties of the standard grid-box control, with additional data access capabilities. It displays the characteristics of a spreadsheet-bound control, with multiple rows and columns depicting records and fields of a `Recordset` object.

Integrated Development Environment Improvements

The Integrated Development Environment (IDE) has gone through substantial revisions to make it more powerful and easier to use. The environment has become extensible, additional layout capabilities have been added, there is more control over the environment itself, and the debugger has been revised.

> **TIP**
>
> All of the changes make the IDE more professional and useful, but tend to use more screen space. We recommend the use of a bigger screen or higher resolution (greater than 640×480) for your development machine. The floating palettes, multiple VB instances, new debugging capabilities, and the Object Browser tend to quickly fill the screen. Therefore, development is more productive if a great amount of time is not spent shuffling screen elements.

IDE Extensibility

The VB 4 IDE can be managed through the use of the OLE Automation interface, or extended through the addition of new menu items to an Add-Ins menu.

The Add-In Manager can be used to add customized environment editions (such as programming tools), Wizards, and tools constructed within Visual Basic. (See Figure 7.6.) By opening the environment to third-party modification, Microsoft has provided the ability to create a far more robust development system. Specialized text editors and macro creators are just two of the possible third-party enhancements you will see soon.

FIGURE 7.6.

The Add-In Manager window.

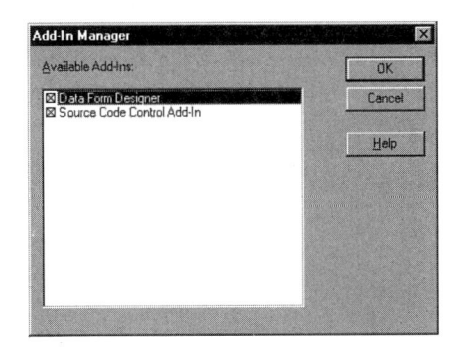

IDE Enhancements

Enhancements to the development system environment include such things as Control Lock, which gives the developer the capability to *lock* controls, preventing their movement through the user interface (UI). Control Nudge gives the developer excellent control in creating, moving, and sizing controls. Using Shift and Control with the arrow keys, an object can be moved or sized in increments of one pixel or grid unit at a time.

To expand the use of the mouse in the Windows environment, context menus (also referred to as right-mouse-button pop-up menus) are supported for use on forms, controls, and code modules when implemented at design time. Context menus show only the menu selections appropriate to the control, form, or object that was selected. Context menus have been gradually added to Microsoft Office and other applications, and with the release of Windows 95, have become an accepted part of the user interface.

ToolTips now are on the toolbox and toolbar to help users identify icon functions. The yellow rectangles that appear when the mouse pointer is over the icon or button are the ToolTips. Inside each yellow rectangle is the name of that control or icon. ToolTips are created by using the MouseMove event with a timer control in conjunction with a text box to display the names of controls or buttons.

The IDE now includes a color palette for easy coloring of controls. (See Figure 7.7.) Programmers who in the past have used the tedious property-sheet method of coloring a screen will appreciate this feature addition.

The debugger has also been enhanced for easier viewing of variables. (See Figure 7.8.) The debugger is more similar to the debugger included in the MS Excel and Project applications than the older version of Visual Basic. Object features have been added, so objects may be examined in the Immediate window.

FIGURE 7.7.
The color palette.

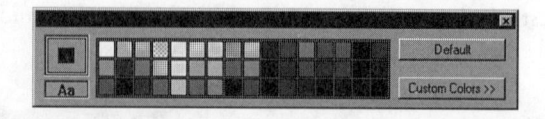

FIGURE 7.8.
The Debug window.

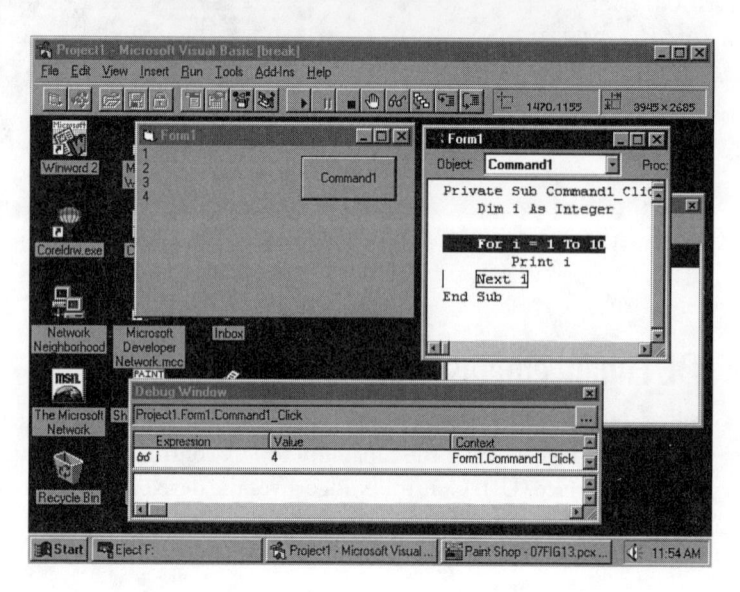

A new project-file extension was added to assist developers in identifying VB project files from source files used by other development tools. The new Visual Basic project-file extension is .VBP in place of .MAK.

> **TIP**
>
> Despite the existence of the new project extension (.VBP), the old project extension (.MAK) may still be used. We recommend that any of the projects that you are upgrading to VB 4 be changed to use the new extension. This way upgraded projects can be readily identified.

Positioning features have been greatly enhanced by the new IDE. Objects drawn on a form may now be locked down so that accidental repositioning does not occur. Objects may be moved by designated increments so that exact positioning is possible.

Also supported in VB 4 is the capability of executing multiple instances of the Visual Basic environment. This allows multiple VB applications to be executing in memory with debugger capabilities at the same time.

This is particularly ideal when developing OLE client and OLE server applications. The client and server may be executing on different instances of the VB environment. This enables each to be watched (execution, variable values, and so on) at the same time. Interaction between the two may be closely examined.

Incremental Compile

The new incremental-compile feature is fantastic for programs with many forms and modules. The VB 4 will compile as much code as is required to get the system functioning and begin execution. Other forms and modules continue to compile in the background as the program is running.

Incremental compile has two options: background compile and compile on demand. Background compiling can occur in the background as the application is executing. Compile on demand compiles the forms and modules only as they are accessed. In a large program, this can mean substantial time savings when execution has to be frequently stopped and restarted.

> **NOTE**
>
> It is important to note that the incremental compile can have negative effects when creating OLE Automation servers. If a client tries to access a method through OLE that is not yet compiled, a crash can occur. Therefore, Microsoft suggests that the option be turned off when creating an OLE server. This will ensure that all of the code is compiled for the server before execution begins and partial compilation problems will be avoided.

Creating Add-ins

The Professional Edition and Enterprise Edition also enable the developer to create his or her own add-ins. There are three types of objects that may be used to create add-ins to the VB environment: menu objects, file objects, and forms/controls objects. Menu objects enable new menus to be added and response routines to individual selections to be set. Files objects enable creating, opening, and closing files contained within a project. The forms/controls objects enable complete manipulation of the forms and controls used in a project.

Resource Files

Resource files are general files used to contain string literals, pictures, and data that need to be separated from the main application. These files can be used to provide customization and localization of the application. Resources stored in a file can be loaded on demand, so memory is conserved until a particular resource is needed.

For example, all of the text to be used in a program's dialog boxes could be placed in a resource file. To localize a program for another language, a different resource file could be activated (for example, one that contained the text in Spanish) and the application recompiled with the new definitions. Alternate definitions could also be stored in a single resource file that may be accessed depending on a preferences setting.

> **NOTE**
>
> Creation of a resource file (.RES is the filename extension) is done using a development product such as AppStudio, which contains a resource editor and compiler and is part of the Microsoft Visual C++ development system.

Each project is limited to one resource file. Resource files are added to a project like any other file using the Add File command under the File menu. To access the items in a resource file, the functions `LoadResString`, `LoadResPicture`, and `LoadResData` have been added to Visual Basic.

Language Enhancements

The language enhancements that have been added to VB 4 parallel the features provided in VBA. Visual Basic 4 and VBA are now directly code compatible. Code from a VBA application may be pasted directly into a VB 4 application. Following is a list of language enhancements and a description of their function.

Enhancement	*Description*
Line continuation character	The line-continuation character enables the use of an underscore character preceded by a space (_)at the end of a line. The next line will be compiled as if it were on the preceding line.
`With…End With`	The `With` statement allows action to be taken on a series of statements addressing a specific object without requalifying the name of that object.
`For Each…Next`	The `For Each` statement provides for repeating a group of statements for each element in a collection.
`Collection object`	The `Collection` data type gives an application the capability of constructing its own group of objects that can be identified and assigned keys.
`Error object`	The `Err` object now provides more information when errors occur and the specific error types that are returned from OLE servers. With OLE server enhancements and the ability to create an OLE server in VB, an error code with a rich set of information is important. It allows a program to react effectively and specifically to a problem instead of sending it to a generic handling routine.

Conditional Compilation

Conditional compilation was added to make VB more versatile by enabling it to meet the open system and multiplatform software compatibility requirements. Certain parts of a program can now be selectively compiled. This feature allows the software designer to develop different versions of an application program that can run on different platforms with specific features for that platform.

At compile time, the designer selectively compiles the parts of the program needed for that version and platform. These specific features could be required for the program to run on different platforms, use currency display filters or changing of dates for distribution in multiple languages.

> **TIP**
>
> Conditional compilation will be used extensively when a single code base is needed for both 16- and 32-bit versions of an application. By using the conditional compilation features, alternate `Declare` statements, variables settings, and so on, a single project for both 16- and 32-bit applications can be used.

To use conditional compiling, the conditional parts of the code have to be enclosed between the `#If… #Then` and `#EndIf` statements, which perform a branching test with the use of Boolean constants. If the code segment is to be part of the compiled code, the Boolean constant value has to be set to -1 (`True`). For example, for a conditional `Declare` statement, the following code could be used:

```
#If Win32 Then
    ' Declare Win32 function
#Else
    ' Declare 16 bit function
#Endif
```

Note that the compiler constant `Win32` is used in the above statement. There are two constants, `Win16` and `Win32`, that may be used to determine the type of compilation that is taking place. If 32-bit compilation is taking place, the `Win32` constant will be set to `TRUE` and `Win16` set to `FALSE`. Compiling under a 16-bit version sets the constants exactly opposite.

> **NOTE**
>
> Constants for conditional compilation are set in the Options dialog box under the Tools menu. The constant values may be set in the Conditional Compilation Arguments field under the Advanced Options tab, or on a command line using the /d switch to enter the constants.

Property Procedures

Property procedures have been added to the language, the same as are available through VBA. A *property procedure* is a method by which an object can have data members (such as properties) where code is executed upon retrieving or assigning one of those properties. For example, to set a variable StartDay, a Property Let procedure could be written. The routine could be passed the variable for Monday and determine the actual date for the most recent Monday and store this in the field. This is an example of processing that can take place before the value of the variable is set. It ensures the user does not set the variable to a value that would be inaccurate or cause an application error.

Using property procedures allows for information hiding (fully described in Chapter 6). Information hiding prevents the user from directly accessing the variables that the routine or class use, but instead allows access and manipulation through a specific routine.

Using property procedures can allow range checking, data verification, and subroutine activation possible whenever a property is set.

New Related Applications

Visual Basic has always included external applications such as the Hot-Spot Editor to aid in product development. VB 4 includes numerous utilities as well as upgrades to older applications. The new applications include the API Viewer, Data Manager, Crystal Reports, Visual SourceSafe, and Component Manager.

Some of the applications— the Hot-Spot Editor, for example—have not had substantial changes. They have been primarily upgraded to use the new Windows 95 interface.

API Viewer

The API Viewer provides the definitions for all of the constants, Declare statements, and types that are common to VB. (See Figure 7.9.) This includes Declare statements for the WinAPI, both in 16- and 32-bit versions.

> **NOTE**
>
> These constants and declare statements had to be accessed using a normal text editor and were stored in such files as CONSTANT.TXT. Using the API Viewer is more convenient because the entire constant file does not have to be used, saving code size and compile time.

FIGURE 7.9.
The API Viewer.

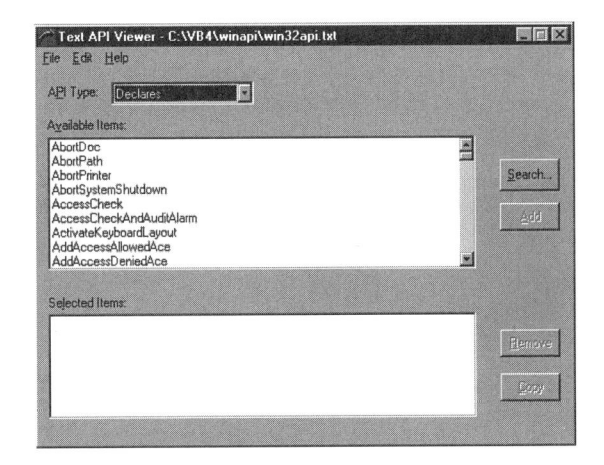

New Data Manager

The Data Manager application has been revised to have more features and appears substantially more efficient. (See Figure 7.10.) The new Data Manager can access Microsoft Access 2.0 database files, Paradox files, dBase III and IV, FoxPro 2.0 and 2.5, Btrieve, and ODBC data sources.

FIGURE 7.10.
Data Manager with tables.

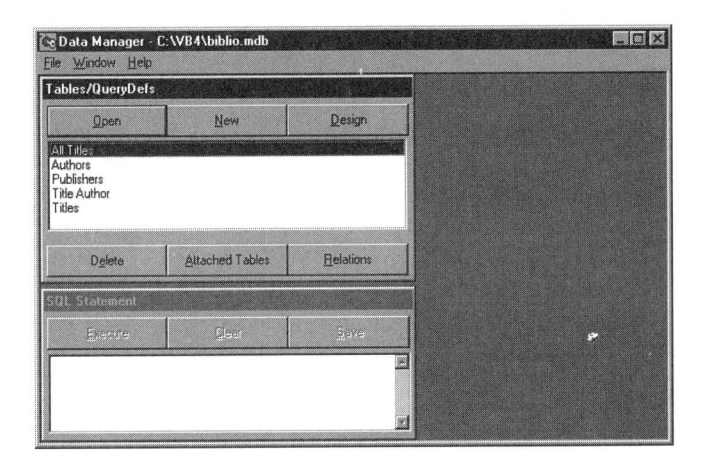

When a table is opened, the screen is not much different from the Data Manager included with Visual Basic 3 (except for the cleaner Windows 95 look). Likewise, the window that allows data editing is not radically different. (See Figure 7.11.)

The design screen is vastly more powerful. (See Figure 7.12.) Field characteristics can now be edited. All of the extra MS Access specific features for fields have now been added to the Data Manager's capabilities. Fields can be added, edited, and removed without the need for an extra database.

FIGURE 7.11.
Data Manager editing.

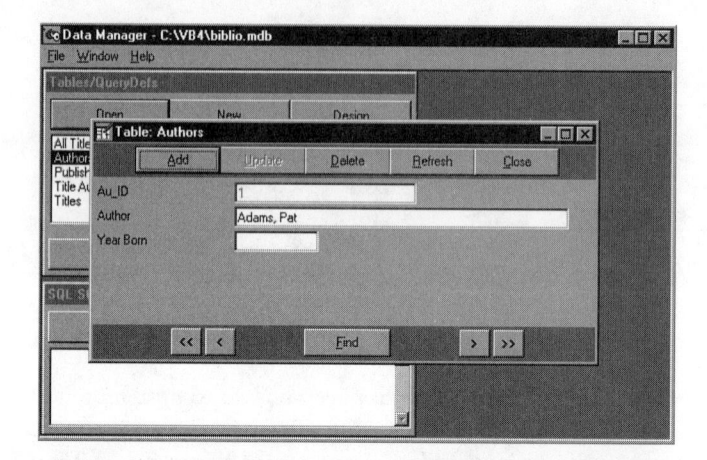

FIGURE 7.12.
The Data Manager with table editor.

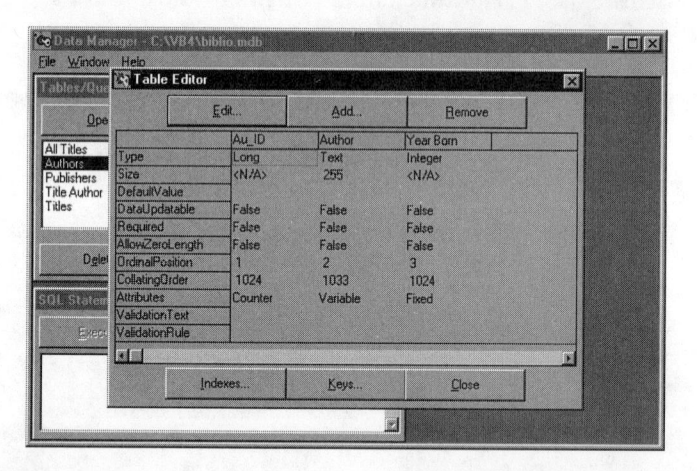

Other databases may now become attached tables in a database (like the attached tables in MS Access). Relations may be created among various fields in the tables of a database file. (See Figure 7.13.)

SQL queries may be added to the database and executed from the Data Manager. In the BIBLIO.MDB database included with VB, the All Titles query definition has been created in SQL. This query may be edited in the SQL Statement window and executed within the Data Manager. (See Figure 7.14.) This provides easy testing of SQL queries without executing MS Access. It also allows stored SQL queries to be conveniently edited and modified.

FIGURE 7.13.
The Data Manager (Relations button) window.

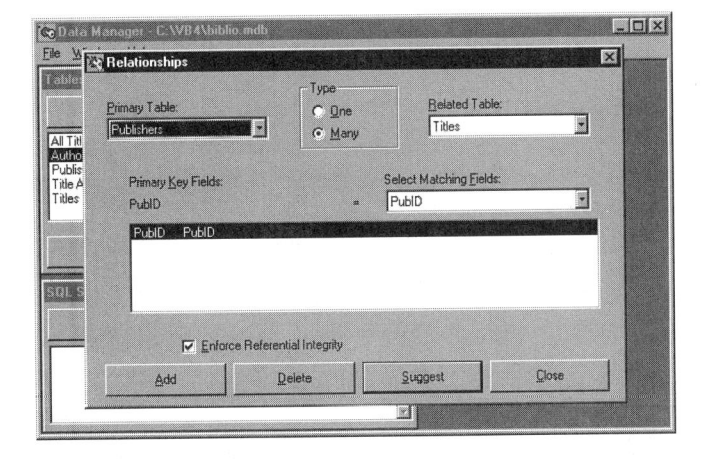

FIGURE 7.14.
Data Manager Tables/ Query Defs. All Titles.

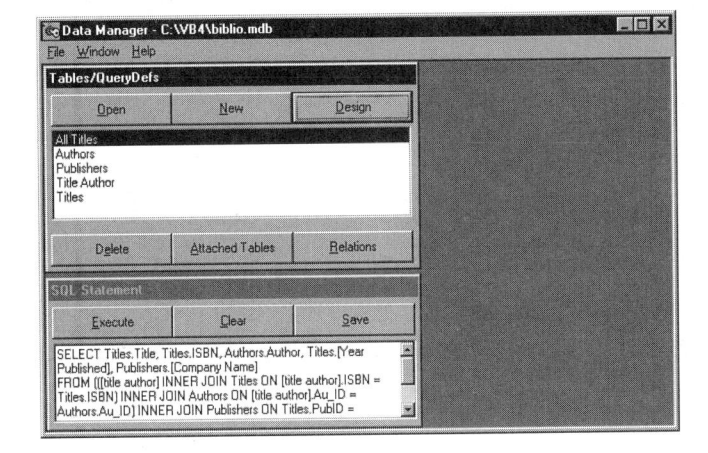

Crystal Reports

The Crystal Reports engine has been updated for Windows 95. (See Figure 7.15.) It also includes new features such as insertion of OLE objects and bit-mapped graphics. The reporting functionality has become more powerful to include such features as Cross Tab reports.

Like its predecessor supplied in VB 3, Crystal Reports still relies on a completed database, however, from which it draws information. This sacrifices some convenience for outputting program-generated data. All data generated by the program must be written into another database before a report may be generated. This can consume time and disk space that would be unnecessary if the engine could accept data directly or if a custom output routine is used.

FIGURE 7.15.
The Crystal Reports (sample).

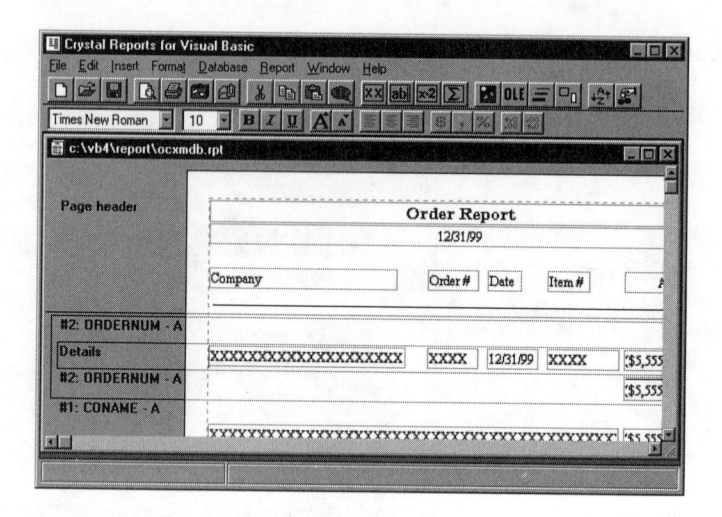

For basic database reporting, it is a fantastic engine to begin creating reports. Crystal Reports Professional is far more powerful and should be examined for professional applications. (For more information, see Chapter 29, "Third-Party Tools, Utilities, and Controls.")

Visual SourceSafe Administrator and Explorer

The Visual SourceSafe system is used to provide team project coordination. Two applications, the Administrator and the Explorer, are used to manage a programming project. Visual SourceSafe allows individual file tracking as well as code-module storage for reuse.

The Administrator is used to manage a project over the network. (See Figure 7.16.) Files may be checked in and checked out. SourceSafe also keeps track of version control. The Administrator application allows setting up various users with states of control, all projects to be added, files deleted, administrator check-in, and so on.

There are four different capability levels users may have: read privileges, check-out privileges (which enables file modification), add privileges (the user can modify the file list), and destroy privileges. The Administrator is used strictly to set up the user accounts and assign privilege levels.

The Explorer application is used by individual programmers to check resources available to them. (See Figure 7.17.) All resources are stored in hierarchical formats. An organization could therefore publish entire sets of code for shared use on the network. Individual Explorer users could access these code resources and use them in different projects. There are two versions of Visual SourceSafe for Windows: 16- and 32-bit.

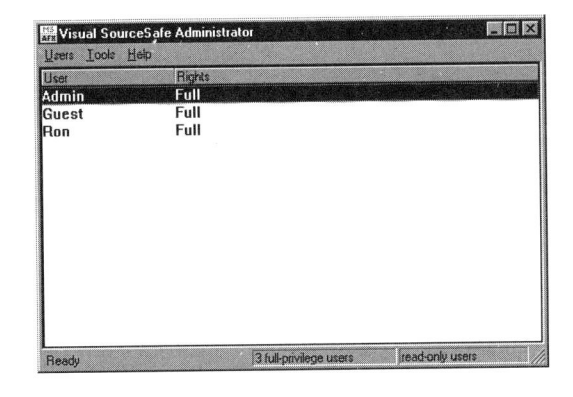

FIGURE 7.16.
The Visual SourceSafe 4.0 Admin—32-bit.

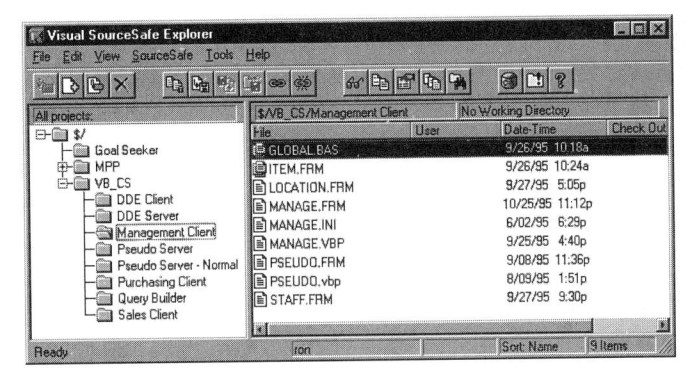

FIGURE 7.17.
Visual SourceSafe 4.0 Explorer—32-bit.

Component Manager

The Component Manager that is included with the Enterprise Edition is a breakthrough in client/server computing. (See Figure 7.18.) It enables distributing and sharing objects over a network. This enables you to create an OLE Automation server in Visual Basic (for business rules, and so on) that may be accessed by any OLE-capable machine on a network.

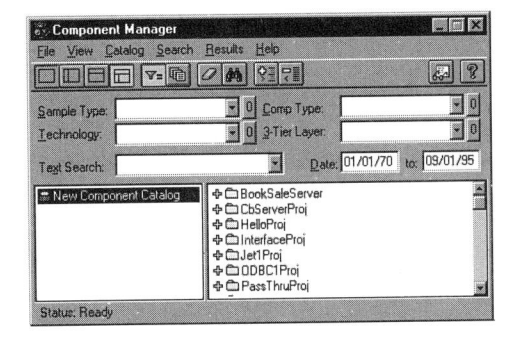

FIGURE 7.18.
The Component Manager.

The Component Manager application allows OLE servers (such as other Component Managers, SQL Server 6.0, and so on) on the network to be accessed, OLE server catalogs to be created, registration of various OLE servers for network access, and retrieval of information on a particular OLE server.

Component catalogs contain the registration information on each OLE object and server available to the system. A component catalog can be stored on the local machine or in any ODBC data source.

For more information on the Component Manager, see Chapter 24, "Creating an OLE Server."

Remote Data Objects and Remote Data Control

The Enterprise Edition includes a new data object model called remote data objects. *Remote data objects* (RDO) parallel the uses of the data access objects (DAO) that are traditional to Visual Basic. The new RDO system allows optimized access to ODBC data sources. Therefore, the ODBC API does not need to be used to achieve effective ODBC access speeds. The RDO system is specifically optimized to use database servers with sophisticated query engines such as Microsoft SQL Server 6.0 and Oracle. Various query cursor features are included to provide effective access options.

The remote data control acts like the standard data control, including the ability to bind data-aware controls to it. (See Figure 7.19.) The remote data control uses the RDO system to interface with ODBC data sources. When loading the 32-bit Enterprise Edition of VB 4, the remote data objects reference is checked by default instead of the DAO in the other editions of the package. The RDO system is most likely to be used with client/server development.

FIGURE 7.19.
The remote data control.

For more information on the RDO system, see Chapter 22, "Open Database Connectivity (ODBC)." The chapter explains the RDO system as well as providing sample code showing how it may be used.

Features Lacking in VB 4

Visual Basic 4 is a significant upgrade to Visual Basic 3, but it is not perfect. For the client/server developer, it is almost as important to understand what a development system cannot do as what it can do before beginning a project.

VB 4 features no compilation. Through OLE Automation server capabilities, other programs can access code developed in Visual Basic in a way similar to the use of a traditional DLL. However, Visual Basic is interpreted and therefore cannot produce a true DLL. It also cannot be used to produce a VBX or OCX. A development system such as Visual C++ must be used to create these extensions.

VB 4 provides no thread support for the multitasking provided for Windows 95 and Windows NT. This means that individual routines in a Visual Basic program cannot be set aside in the processing engine to have particular processing priority and demarcated processing time. A Visual Basic program is treated as a single giant thread. Microsoft hopes that OCX producers will create extensions that provide multithreading for particular processes.

Although Visual Basic 4 can be an OLE Automation server, it cannot be an actual OLE server. This means that it cannot create objects that may be linked or embedded into a document. An OLE Automation server may accept commands set by other applications (such as VBA) and create objects in memory, but does not provide an encapsulated object that another application can save for reuse. For example, a drawing program that could create a diagram to be embedded in a word processing document could *not* be created using Visual Basic 4.

Visual Basic 4 is now available in three different editions: Standard, Professional, and Enterprise. The Standard Edition is not practical for use on any substantial size project and also cannot generate 16-bit code. The Professional Edition is perfect for application developers and designers who have no need for team project development, effective access to remote data sources (through the RDO and RDC), and have no need to create Remote OLE Automation servers. Access to remote data sources is possible through the JET engine (like the earlier VB 3.0), but is not the optimized ODBC API. The Enterprise Edition contains all the necessary tools for complete c/s system deployment and will be the package of choice among client/server developers.

8

Constructing a Simple Client/Server System

Using DDE to Demonstrate Concepts

You might have a hard time understanding the client/server concepts described so far if you have never seen a client/server system operating. In this chapter, we demonstrate some of the basic concepts of client/server design by creating both a client application and a server application. To make the system as simple as possible, the programs run on the same machine—as separate applications—and use dynamic data exchange (DDE) to communicate. The DDE link acts as middleware for this client/server implementation. (See Figure 8.1.)

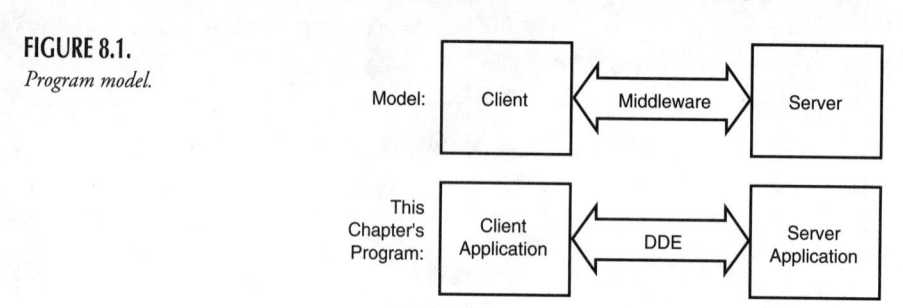

FIGURE 8.1.
Program model.

These client/server applications are not intended to be demonstrations of a complete implementation of a DDE application or a client/server system. You construct these applications to provide a hands-on model of client/server computing. Once you understand the basics of how a client/server system is constructed, adding to that base of knowledge will be a simpler task.

Feel free to modify these programs to learn more. You might choose to add Distributed or Network DDE capabilities—a fairly simple process. Many articles that describe how to do this are available through the Microsoft Developer Network. You might also modify the server to accept multiple client links. If you want to understand more about DDE, both of these additions to the existing client and server programs are recommended.

The client/server system that you will create consists of a server program and a client program. The server program receives commands from the client application, as shown in Figure 8.2. If the client sends an ADD command by clicking on the Add button, the data from the client program's text box is stored in the list box on the server screen. This works in much the same way in which updates are sent to a database server—for instance, a SQL server—for storage. The server program also accepts Query and Beep commands.

Additionally, the server program watches the data that is input from the client program. When more than five entries are stored in the list, the server program notifies the client program that this condition exists. This entry tracking is an excellent example of a proactive server application that can notify clients of events that have taken place. In SQL, covered in depth in later chapters, a subroutine that executes when a certain condition is met is known as a *trigger*.

FIGURE 8.2.
Server application.

A common example of a proactive server is a mail server on a local area network (LAN). Mail can be received and stored by the mail server. When your machine becomes available on the network—for example, when you turn on your machine—the server automatically notifies you that mail is waiting in your mailbox.

The client application fulfills most of the common roles of a client application. (See Figure 8.3.) It enables the user to input data that can be sent to the server. A client application handles most of the user-interface interaction without bothering the server. When the update is ready—in this case, a piece of text has been entered—the user can click a button and the new information is sent to the server. The client program can send commands to the server program, telling it to add records, beep the speaker, and search for a particular record.

FIGURE 8.3.
Client application.

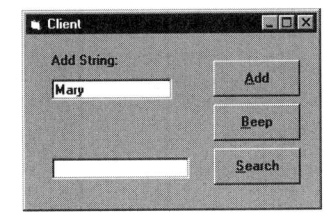

Information is exchanged by the client and server program by using a variety of DDE commands. Visual Basic has complete DDE link access built in. Text, pictures, and binary data can be exchanged between two or more running applications.

Why Use Dynamic Data Exchange?

If you are familiar with the Microsoft programming world, you might ask, "Why not use OLE for this example? After all, DDE is being phased out in favor of OLE." Although this statement is true, DDE will be around for a long time. Many existing applications can already communicate through a DDE interface. DDE has several advantages over OLE automation when you're creating a simple demonstration application.

> **NOTE**
>
> The DDE interface as well as network DDE requires substantially less overhead than an equivalent OLE-based application. The advantages of smaller resource requirements are clear, especially in applications that use less powerful remote portable computers. If your remote machines are running Windows for Workgroups and have minimal RAM configurations, it is a good idea to examine the DDE system and determine if you can live with its limitations.

DDE is a simple interapplication communication interface that can easily demonstrate basic client/server concepts. DDE is built into all versions of Visual Basic, so the examples can be used with either Visual Basic 4.0 or Visual Basic 3.0 Professional. There are four main reasons why DDE is still widely used:

- Distributed OLE requires vastly greater overhead than an equivalent DDE system.
- Visual Basic 3.0 Professional (with its huge installed base of VBXs) lacks OLE server capabilities.
- A great number of legacy applications incorporate DDE.
- The DDE interface is much simpler and does not require complex system interaction, such as the OLE registry.

As of this writing, Distributed OLE has just been officially released. Distributed DDE is widely available and currently used in many client/server applications. Network DDE—sometimes called Distributed DDE—enables a program to have a live data link with a program running on another computer, which means that these simple demonstration programs are scalable to provide examples for more complex client/server solutions.

Distributed OLE is much more robust and feature laden, but any standard takes time to become established. We do, however, recommend the use of OLE for more complex program interaction. DDE is not the future; Microsoft seeks to make OLE the primary linking standard. For more information on OLE, see Chapter 23, "Object Linking and Embedding (OLE)."

Most of the DDE interface is accessible through the Visual Basic properties of a control or the LINK subroutines built into the controls. Many applications have DDE communication built in, including Windows' Program Manager, MS Word, MS Excel, Arc/Info, and MS Access. DDE enables your current client/server programs to exchange data with many programs that have not yet been upgraded to take advantage of the new OLE features. Upgrades to OLE automation might happen slowly because of the complexity involved in implementing the OLE features.

The next section provides a brief overview of how DDE functions. As OLE slowly replaces DDE, these concepts will remain important because the OLE protocol is built on top of the DDE protocol. While you use OLE, knowing DDE will enable you to understand what is taking place beneath the interface.

DDE Overview

DDE provides synchronous communications between applications. This requires that both applications be open at the same time. There are two types of DDE applications: client and server. The server application must be open before the client application executes.

> **NOTE**
>
> Requiring the server application to be open before the client is a feature specific to OLE. By requiring a live link, it makes the DDE system simpler. However, OLE's capability to dynamically load and unload makes OLE more powerful.

As shown in Figure 8.4, DDE uses three pieces of information to open a link between two applications: an application name, a topic, and an item. The *application name* is the unique filename of the application to be connected with—for instance, EXCEL for EXCEL.EXE or SERVER for the SERVER.EXE application example. The *topic* defines the type of data being exchanged over the link. The topic is merely a text string such as `"TOPIC!R1C4"` that denotes a spreadsheet cell in an Excel DDE link. There is no standard for how a topic string is formatted, so your DDE applications can use any topic string to communicate. The client and server applications, however, must use a consistent topic designation or they are not able to communicate. The *item* is the actual data that is exchanged.

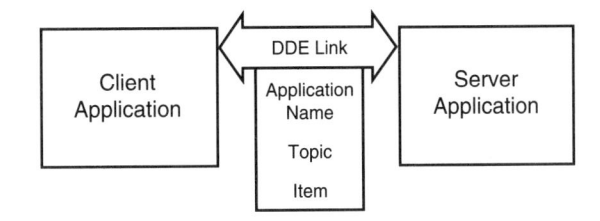

FIGURE 8.4.
DDE link.

There are three types of links that may be created with DDE: automatic, manual, and notify. *Automatic links* update linked data automatically with no interaction from the program. For example, two text boxes could be linked using DDE. When something is typed into one of the text boxes, it is instantly updated in the other linked box, ensuring that the text in both remains the same. *Manual links* exchange updated data only when the client requests an update.

We will use the notify type of link in the client/server example. With a *notify link,* the server application notifies the client application of a change to the data but does not automatically send the new data. This enables you to create a `LinkNotify` routine that is automatically called when the data has changed. You then can prepare to receive the new data and request that it be sent. As the new data is received, the client application displays it.

You access DDE from Visual Basic by using a combination of event routines, methods, and properties, which are described in Tables 8.1, 8.2, and 8.3. The implementation of these factors varies, depending on whether the application is a client or a server. For example, the `LinkTopic` property in the server can be set to any topic. In the client application, it must also contain the name of the server application to which it is linked.

Table 8.1. DDE events.

Event	Description
LinkClose	Activates when a DDE connection terminates
LinkError	Activates when an error in connection occurs; error code is returned
LinkExecute	Activates when the server application receives a command string
LinkNotify	Activates when the source that is linked (such as a text box) changes
LinkOpen	Activates when a DDE connection begins

Table 8.2. DDE methods.

Method	Description
LinkExecute	Sends a command string to the server
LinkPoke	Transfers the contents of a control to the server
LinkRequest	Asks the source to update the contents of a control
LinkSend	Transfers the contents of a picture control to the server

Table 8.3. DDE properties.

Property	Description
LinkItem	Contains the data for the item part of the DDE transmission
LinkMode	Specifies the mode of the link: manual, automatic, notify, or none
LinkTimeout	Specifies the amount of time to wait for a response to a DDE message before aborting
LinkTopic	Contains the data for the topic part of the DDE transmission

The Server Application

To start the project, you must first create the server application. You will follow the basic methodology described in Chapter 1, "Overview of Visual Basic."

1. Create the interface.
2. Set the properties.
3. Write the code and event routines.

To achieve maximum benefit, you should sit in front of your computer as you build the application in the steps described. Doing so will help you understand what you are reading.

The server application receives and stores data that is sent over the DDE link by using the ADD command, which you will define. It also executes commands such as Beep (which you will name BEP) and Search (which you will name SRH). Commands are handled by the LinkExecute event routine. The client calls the LinkExecute method and the LinkExecute event in the server application runs, as shown in Figure 8.5.

FIGURE 8.5.
LinkExecute method and LinkExecute event.

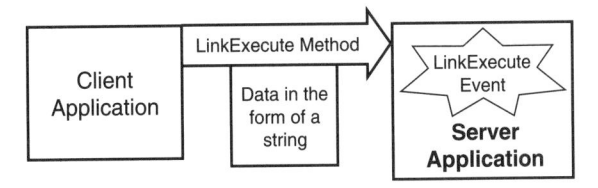

In the case of the server application, the data is received from the client in the form of a string. The string's first three characters contain a command, followed by a space, and end with any data relevant to the command. For example, sending a string such as "SRH Joe" activates the Search routine to search for the name Joe. This will become clearer as you construct the application.

Server Form Setup

Begin by constructing the application. To construct the application, follow these steps:

1. Double-click to execute Visual Basic. You will see a blank Form1 in a new project. Give this form a name. Name it frm_Server.
2. Select the Properties window under the View menu, or press the F4 button to bring it up.
3. Scroll down and highlight the Name property, which currently says Form1. Change the property to frm_Server. (See Figure 8.6.)

FIGURE 8.6.

frm_Server name property.

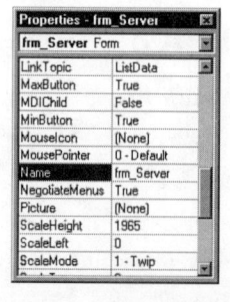

> **NOTE**
>
> Microsoft has naming conventions for all variables, forms, and controls. The purpose of a naming convention is to make code easier to read and maintain. Forms, controls, and variables are given a prefix that identifies what they are. For example, a form that shows a find box is named `frmFind`. The first three letters, `frm`, identify what the name refers to. They should be typed in lowercase to make the code more readable. For example, a command such as `frmFind.Show` displays a form—not a text box or button, which can also be named `Find`.
>
> Variables can also use this convention. For example a long integer number might be named `lUniqueID`. This makes type mismatch errors much less likely. It also shows when type conversions are occurring—for instance, `lUniqueID = sTempID`.
>
> A complete guide to the Microsoft naming conventions is available from Microsoft, included on the developer CD-ROM, and available for downloading through one of the online resources listed in Appendix C, "Sources." It is not essential that you follow the Microsoft naming conventions strictly, as long as naming conventions are standardized within your organization. As you will see, the following examples make a slight variation to the MS conventions by adding an underscore (_) character between the prefix and the variable name. We believe that it makes code more readable.

4. Change the `Caption` property of the form to `Server`, which changes the name in the title bar of the form. This title makes it easy to identify which window contains the server application when both the client and the server are running.

5. Because both the client and the server applications will be running on the same screen, you must shrink the size of the server form. Click the server form and move to the bottom right corner, where the cursor changes to a diagonal double-arrow. This is the same as resizing any window. Now click and drag the form edge until the form is approximately four inches wide by three inches tall. You could also set the size of the form more precisely using `Width` and `Height` properties.

Now add two controls to the form—a list box and a text box—as shown in Figure 8.7. The list box contains the data sent to the server by the client application. The text box contains the actual DDE link between the two applications. We will set a property so the text box will not appear on the screen in the running server application. You want it to be invisible so that the user does not accidentally modify it.

FIGURE 8.7.
Adding a list box and a text box to the form.

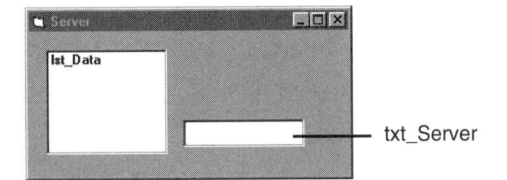

6. To create the list box, select the List Box tool from the Control palette. (See Figure 8.8.) Click the button while the cross-hair cursor is on the form, and drag it until it is approximately the size of the one shown in Figure 8.7. Create the text box in the same way. Click the Text Box tool, and draw a text box approximately the same size as the one shown in Figure 8.7.

FIGURE 8.8.
The List Box, Text Box, Three-D command button, and Command Button tools from the Control palette.

Now that the visual aspects of the form have been created, you need to modify some of the properties of the controls to access them from DDE.

Setting Server Properties

1. Select the form itself by clicking any area that is not occupied by a control. You want to set the properties so that the application can act as a DDE server. Press F4 to bring up the Properties window, and modify the following two properties:

   LinkMode property—Change it from 0 (none) to 1 (Source).

   LinkTopic property—Change it from Form1 to ListData.

   Now you must modify the list box so that it has a name that describes it.

> **NOTE**
>
> Naming the various items in your project as soon as you create them is a good programming habit. Naming takes only moments, and it saves much debugging time and frustration later. Likewise, once code that calls the item by a particular name is implemented, it is time-consuming to go through and change all the code. For example, if eighteen routines access a text box named `Text1`, changing the name requires replacing all eighteen references to the old name. This can be frustrating and time-consuming. It is much easier to name the control or variable when it is first created.

2. Select the list box with the arrow cursor. Bring up the Properties window, and modify the following two properties:

   `Name` property—Change it from `List1` to `lst_Data`.

   `Sorted` property—Change it from `False` to `True`.

3. Now select the text box. It is the conduit to the client application through which messages are sent. You want to make the text box invisible because messages sent to the client application do not need to show on the server screen. Bring up the Properties window, and modify the following three properties:

   `Name` property—Change it from `Text1` to `txt_Server`.

   `Text` property—Change it from `Text1` to `' '` (an empty string).

   `Visible` property—Change it from `True` to `False`.

   The server application user interface is now complete. To make sure that you do not lose anything, save the project to your hard disk.

4. Under the File menu, select the Save Project... selection. Visual Basic asks you for the name of the project and the name of the form that you have created. Name the project SERVER.VBP and the form SERVER.FRM. You will save everything again when you are finished.

> **NOTE**
>
> The default file extension for projects in Visual Basic 4.0 is now .VBP (under VB 3.0 it was .MAK). Visual Basic 4.0 can still use the .MAK extension but emphasizes using the .VBP extension to avoid confusion with a specific type of C program file that also uses the .MAK extension.

You can execute the server program now if you want.

5. To start the server program, select the `Start` option under the `Run` menu or press the F5 key. The server program displays the empty list box; notice that the `txt_Server` field does not appear because you set its `Visible` property to `False`. Most traditional

servers have little user interface compared to client applications. The server's responsibility is largely that of processing commands and data. Therefore, the user interface is usually limited to monitoring, installation, and preferences windows.

6. After you have executed the program, stop execution by closing the window or clicking the Stop button on the VB toolbar. Visual Basic should return to design mode where you can begin adding the server code.

Adding Server Code

You now construct the heart of the server application—the routine that receives and processes the commands and data. You construct a simple routine that breaks the string received from the client through DDE into two pieces: the command and the data. The command consists of a three-character command, followed by a space and the data.

1. Double-click the mouse button on the form (any area not occupied by an item). The code window appears and shows the Object: as Form and the Proc: as Load.

2. Click the Proc: combo box, and select the LinkExecute event routine. This routine is executed when the LinkExecute method is called by the DDE client. Notice that the LinkExecute event routine accepts two parameters, cmdstr and cancel, as in

    Private Sub Form_LinkExecute(CmdStr As String, Cancel As Integer)

    The CmdStr is the string of data sent from the client application. The Cancel variable indicates to the client whether the server processed the command. The default value of Cancel is True (−1), which means that the LinkExecute event did not handle the execution. This is the case by default if the client calls for a LinkExecute and no code is in the event routine. In that case, the client knows that the CmdStr was not processed. Your routine, therefore, must set the Cancel value to 0 so that the client knows that you have processed the command.

3. Type the following code into the LinkExecute routine:

```
Private Sub Form_LinkExecute(cmdstr As String, Cancel As Integer)
    Dim tempcmd$, tempdata$

    tempcmd$ = Left$(cmdstr, 3)
    tempdata$ = Right$(cmdstr, Len(cmdstr) - 4)
    Select Case tempcmd$
        Case "ADD"
            lst_Data.AddItem tempdata$
            If lst_Data.ListCount > 5 Then
                txt_Server.Text = "Over 5"
            End If
        Case "BEP"
            Beep
        Case "SRH"
            For i = 0 To lst_Data.ListCount - 1
                If lst_Data.List(i) = tempdata$ Then
                    txt_Server.Text = "Found, Item#" & Str$(i) & "," &
➥lst_Data.List(i)
```

```
                    Exit For
                End If
            Next i
        Case Else
            ' Command was not found, do nothing
    End Select
    Cancel = 0
End Sub
```

Notice that after the two variables are defined, the CmdStr is split into two parts. The first three letters are the command that is sent from the client; they are stored in the variable tempcmd$. You can now easily process this small string. The rest of the CmdStr is stored in the tempdata$ variable, which is evaluated with a SELECT CASE statement to determine what command was sent. The sample server program accepts three commands: ADD, BEP, and SRH. You can add a flagging or error routine in the CASE ELSE area to signal the client that the command has not been found.

The ADD command adds the data sent to the server in the tempdata$ to the list in the list box. This is a much simplified example of what a SQL server does when it receives an update command from a client. The server then checks whether the number of items in the list is greater than five.

If the lst_Data has more than five items, the text Over 5 is stored to the txt_Server field. Remember that the txt_Server text box is linked to the client program through DDE to show the status of the transaction. Therefore, a change to the txt_Server box sends a LinkNotify event to the client application. The client can get the new information from the server to display it.

This provides a good example of a server program that can actively send information about the state of data set to individual clients. For example, a server might flag a purchasing client program when inventory on a particular item gets low.

The alternative is to have the client constantly request information from the server to check on the condition of the data. This means lots of inefficiency and an unnecessary increase in network traffic.

The second command, BEP, beeps the speaker on the server. If the client program and the server program were running on separate machines, a BEP command from the client would cause the server speaker to beep.

This BEP command is an example of a client activating a routine that runs on the server. A more complex routine might be called to do a calculation or perform an intensive routine. A client program might make a remote procedure call (RPC) to run such a subroutine on the server or on another client machine. For more information on RPCs, see Chapter 23, "Object Linking and Embedding (OLE)."

The final command that is accepted by the server program is a data search, SRH. The SRH command takes the data sent by the client program (tempdata$) and searches the current data list (lst_Data) for its occurrence. If it is found, the server sends back a message through the `txt_Server` box link that the data was found. It also sends back the number in the list that the added data item occupies.

In a real database client/server application, the client would send a query to the server program. The server would do the search and return a resultant set—a data set that contains all the records that match the criteria specified in the query. The client could update the data and send it back to the server.

4. The server program is now complete. You might want to execute the program to make sure that there are no typing mistakes. The program should run and look no different from the first time you executed it. Stop the server program by double-clicking in the close box in the upper-left corner of the window.

5. Now save the program to an .EXE file so that you can execute it at the same time as the client application. Under the File menu, select the Make EXE file... command. Name the .EXE file SERVER.EXE. You must reference the application from the client program by the name of its .EXE. Therefore, if you want to name it something else, make sure that you change the filename in the `LinkTopic` field in the client application.

The Client Application

The client application accepts input from the user. The program can send this data to the server application across the DDE link. The client can send a `Beep` command and a `Search` command to find a particular string in the data list. It can receive messages from the server application on the status of the list and results of a `Search` command.

Notice that very little data is kept in the client application. The data list exists entirely within the server. Meanwhile, the client application handles all the user interaction and general user-interface controls. Typically, this is a delicate balance in client/server applications.

Client Form Setup

Now you will construct the client program.

1. Under the File menu, select New Project..., which opens a blank form named `Form1`, just as when you constructed the server program. Resize the form so that it is approximately the same size as the server form, but move it to the lower half of the screen. This will provide enough room so that both windows can be displayed.

2. You need to draw three buttons on the form, as shown previously in Figure 8.3. To draw the buttons, called *command buttons,* use the Command Button tool, as shown in Figure 8.8. The function of each button is to send a message and some data to the server application through the DDE link.

> **NOTE**
>
> You might have noticed that the Command Button tool used to create the preceding example is not the Sheridan Three-D icon button normally used with the Visual Basic Professional edition. (See Figure 8.8.) The appearance of both is similar under Windows 3.1. The Sheridan Three-D button can also display an icon—something that the command button cannot.
>
> When running under Windows 95, however, the form has the new 3-D look—including beveled edges and shadows. The traditional command button takes on the new Windows 95 3-D look. The traditional command buttons also have the `Default` and `Cancel` properties that automatically simulate a button press when the Enter and Esc keys are pressed. These properties are useful for implementing the OK and Cancel buttons in a dialog box or window.
>
> The Three-D command button does not support the `Default` and `Cancel` properties. Additionally, if you use the Three-D command button in your program, you must distribute the Sheridan OCX, which takes up approximately 100KB of disk space and memory. This is not a large sacrifice if you use the other 3D controls, such as the Frame or Ribbon controls.
>
> You can use either control to create the buttons on your form. Just make sure that you consistently use one type. Otherwise, when your application runs under Windows 95 or Windows NT 3.51, buttons on the same form might look different.

Now that the three buttons are on the screen and labeled, you can add the text boxes. Add one text box toward the top of the form and one toward the bottom, as shown in Figure 8.3. The top text box holds any names that you enter before you add them to the server application's data list. The bottom text box receives any status messages from the server application and displays them.

You might also want to add labels over the text boxes to denote what they are. We have added the `Add String:` and `Status:` labels, as you can see. To modify the string for labels, change the `Caption` property.

You have now constructed all the visual aspects of the client program. To save the project to your hard disk, select Save Project... under the File menu. Name the project CLIENT.VBP and the form CLIENT.FRM. You will save everything again when you are finished.

Setting Client Properties

1. Select the form itself by clicking any area that is not occupied by a control. You now want to set the properties so that the application can act as a DDE client. Bring up the Properties window by pressing F4, and modify the following two properties:

Caption property—Change it from Form1 to Client.

Name property—Change it from Form1 to frm_Client.

Don't change any of the Link properties for the form. On the client, you are going to use a text box to link to the server application. Using the Link property on a control provides a simple conduit to pass information such as text. The control merely has to be modified to send the data across the DDE link.

2. You must change the names and titles that appear on the buttons. Select each button by clicking it. Display the Properties window, and change the properties for the three buttons. Change the following on the button labeled Command1:

    Caption property—Change it from Command1 to &Add.

    Name property—Change it from Command1 to btn_Add.

    Change the following on the button labeled Command2:

    Caption property—Change it from Command2 to &Beep.

    Name property—Change it from Command2 to btn_Beep.

    Change the following on the button labeled Command3:

    Caption property—Change it from Command3 to &Search.

    Name property—Change it from Command3 to btn_Search.

3. Now, change some of the properties of the text boxes. To demonstrate a different technique, in the code section, set some of the properties using executing code. This is called setting values at runtime (whereas setting properties in the VB IDE is called design-time modification). The LinkMode property, for example, should be set at runtime.

4. Select the top text box, which is labeled Text1. Change the following two properties:

    Text property—Change it from Text1 to ' ' (an empty string).

    Name property—Change it from Text1 to txt_AddString.

5. Select the bottom text box, which is labeled Text2. Change the following two properties:

    Text property—Change it from Text2 to ' ' (an empty string).

    Name property—Change it from Text2 to txt_Client.

6. Now you only need to add the client program access code and your client/server system is finished.

> **TIP**
>
> The & symbol in the previous command button captions is one of the advanced tools in Visual Basic. In the `Caption` property of command buttons, radial buttons, check boxes, and labels, an & symbol creates an underscore character (_) under the character it precedes. For example, the Add button appears as A̲dd. The character that is underlined is called the *access key*.
>
> This means that pressing the access key while simultaneously holding down the Alt key activates the given control. Pressing Alt+A is the same as clicking the Add button. This enables users to access part of the user interface quickly, without having to move their hands away from the keyboard to the mouse.
>
> We recommend that you make extensive use of this feature, especially for client programs that might run on a portable, for which a track ball or mouse key makes quick access difficult. A word of warning, though: Make sure that you watch for conflicts among access keys. If you have a button that has the same access key as a menu, for example, the user will be unable to access one or the other from the keyboard.
>
> If you place a label control (which is static text) with a `TabIndex` property that is one number less than the `TabIndex` number of a text control (which is editable text), hitting the access key for the label highlights the text control. For example, you could create a label control with a `Caption` property of `&Name` and a `TabIndex` property of `0`. You then could create a text control with a `TabIndex` property of `1`. When the user presses Alt+N, the text cursor appears in the text control edit region.

Adding Client Code

DDE links, unlike OLE links, must be live. This means that when the client program attempts a link, the server application must be running. OLE can automatically execute an unloaded program. Therefore, you cannot set the `LinkMode` of the client control—in this case, the `txt_Client` text box—at design time because no server is running.

1. You must connect the link between the two DDE applications at runtime. In the `Form_Load` event routine—which you get to by double-clicking an empty space on the form—place the following code:

```
Private Sub Form_Load ()
    txt_Client.LinkTopic = "Server|ListData"
    txt_Client.LinkItem = "txt_Server"
    txt_Client.LinkMode = 3      ' Link Notify
End Sub
```

The first line of code defines the `LinkTopic` property. If you refer back to when you created the server application, the first modifications to the properties were to set up the server form's `Link` settings. You set the `LinkTopic` property to the string `ListData`.

In the client program, you must set the property to what is called a *compound link,* which contains the server application's name and the LinkTopic property separated by a pipe character (¦). On the left side of the pipe is the application name, indicating the SERVER.EXE file. On the right is the LinkTopic property that you defined in the server application as ListData. After you have finished entering the code, close the Code window.

The second line of code sets the item that will be linked. In this case, the LinkItem property is set to equal txt_Server, which is the name of the text box on the server program's form. Communication will occur between the txt_Client and the txt_Server text boxes.

The third line of code sets the LinkMode property of the txt_Client text box to Notify mode. This means that whenever a change occurs to the DDE linked data, the LinkNotify event subroutine for the txt_Client text box is executed. You will use it to display a message that an update has been received. After you receive notification, you will manually retrieve the new information.

2. Now double-click the text box at the bottom of the screen—that is, the txt_Client text box. By default, this text box shows the code for the Change event. Click the Proc: menu, and change the selection to the LinkNotify event code. Enter the following code:

```
Sub txt_Client_LinkNotify ()
    MsgBox "Link Notify - Data from Server", , "Link Notify"
    txt_Client.LinkMode = 2      ' Set the mode to Manual data retrieval
    txt_Client.LinkRequest       ' Request the updated data
    txt_Client.LinkMode = 3      ' Return the mode to LinkNotify
End Sub
```

The first line of code displays a message box that tells the user that the client program received an update event from the server program. In a typical client/server program, this type of event might ask a question. For example, with an e-mail program, the client application might signal that new mail has been received and ask whether the user wants to read it immediately or leave it until later.

The second line of code sets the link to receive the new data. To do this, the DDE client must be placed in Manual mode to receive the transmission. Then the client program executes the LinkRequest method for the txt_Client text box. This method receives the updated data from the server program and inserts it into the client's linked text box.

Finally, the program resets the LinkMode to 3. This returns the txt_Client text box to Notify mode. It can now receive and react to the next change notification.

3. You must now add the code to the various buttons to make them send commands to the server application. Double-click the Add button. You will see the event code for the Click routine. Enter the following code:

```
Private Sub btn_Add_Click()
    On Error Resume Next
```

```
    txt_Client.LinkExecute "ADD " & txt_AddString.text
End Sub
```

This routine calls the `LinkExecute` method of the `txt_Client` text box to send the `ADD` command to the server application. This `ADD` command adds the data sent to the data list box. In addition to the `ADD` command, the text from the `txt_Addstring` text box is sent. Any text in this text box is added to the server's data.

4. Close the code window, and double-click the Beep Command button. In the `Click` event routine, enter the following code:

```
Private Sub btn_Beep_Click()
    On Error Resume Next

    txt_Client.LinkExecute "BEP "
End Sub
```

This routine sends a command to the server application to execute the `Beep` routine.

5. Close the code window, and double-click the Search button. Enter the following code:

```
Private Sub btn_Search_Click()
    Dim result$
    On Error Resume Next

    result$ = InputBox$("Please enter the string for the Server to find.",
➥"Find String")
    If result$ <> "" Then
        txt_Client.LinkExecute "SRH " & result$
    End If
End Sub
```

The first line of code creates a string variable that will receive whatever string the user types. The second line of code ensures that the application will continue executing if an error occurs. The next line actually presents the user with an input box to enter a string to be searched for. Note that the string entered must exactly match the data in the server's data set—including capitalization. For instance, if the data in the server is `Joe`, the search string `Joe` will be found, whereas `joe` will not. This situation is easily remedied with an automatic capitalization or other routine, but it serves no purpose for this demonstration.

The fourth line of code ensures that there is data to be searched for. If the user entered no data or pressed the Cancel button, the `result$` would equal "" (an empty string) and there is no point in doing a search. Otherwise, `txt_Client`'s `LinkExecute` method is called, and the server is sent the `SRH` command with the data entered by the user.

6. When you have entered the code, save the project once more. Now make an .EXE file of the client application. Select Make EXE file... under the File menu, and create the file CLIENT.EXE.

7. You can now execute both programs. The easiest way to do this is by running the Explorer under the Start menu. Select the folder in which CLIENT.EXE and SERVER.EXE are located. As you can see in Figure 8.9, the project, form, and .EXE files were placed in a folder named DDE inside a folder labeled CLNTSRVR.

FIGURE 8.9.
Client and server files.

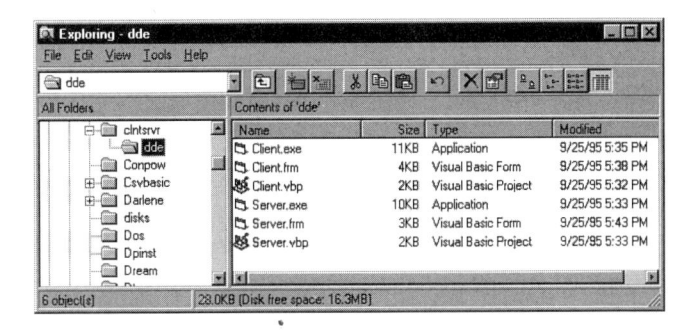

8. Double-click the SERVER.EXE icon. The server application executes. Remember that the server must be running before the client program runs. Otherwise, DDE will generate an error when the client attempts to make the link.

9. Double-click the client application. You have a mini-client/server system running on your machine. Use Alt+Tab to show the server application. Next press Alt+Tab again to show the client application. This way, both applications should be showing on the screen at the same time. You can now type text into the top text box on the client application. Clicking the Add button sends the data to the server. The data then appears in the server list box. (See Figure 8.10.) Add several different pieces of text to the list data in the server.

FIGURE 8.10.
Add some data to the server list.

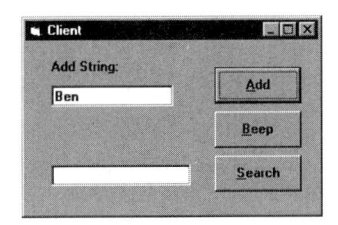

10. Click the Beep button. The beep will sound. Don't forget that this is not the client program that is simply beeping, but rather the server after it receives a client command. If you were using Distributed DDE, the client and the server programs could be located on different machines. In that case, clicking the client Beep button would cause the server machine to beep.

11. Finally, you can click the Search button. An input box appears and asks you for a search string. Enter text that matches one of the items in the server's list data. Clicking the OK button sends the search to the server. If the server program locates the string that you requested, it returns a Found notification and the number in the list of the item and the name data. The client program is sent a `LinkNotify` event, and it displays a notification box. After you click OK, the text appears in the lower text box.

That's it! You now have a rudimentary set of client and server programs. Now that you have a fundamental understanding of client and server concepts, you can construct a complete client/server program that uses clients, a server, and a database foundation.

Summary

These two sample programs should give you a good basic foundation of how a client application and a server application relate to each other. The basic dynamics shown by these two programs are present in all client/server implementations. Although they might be obscured by the many layers of complexity, these simple relations are always present.

A client application usually provides most of the user interface. Each client program usually executes on a desktop machine or a workstation. Typically, there are many client programs accessing the server program. It would be more difficult, for example, but you could have multiple client programs adding data to the single server program's data list.

A server application is usually used to centralize data storage and to handle transaction processing. For example, it might handle a SQL query or execute a mathematical routine. The server program that you created in this chapter accepts queries, centralizes data, and executes a remote routine. Because the server is simple, little user interface is provided. The server's user interface often must give access to records or files, monitor transactions, and grant various user requests.

II

Constructing a Basic Client/Server System

9

Overview of a Client/Server System

The best way to learn about client/server development is to implement an actual client/server system. In Part II of this book, you implement a set of three client programs and a Pseudo Server program that accesses a multi-user Microsoft Access database created in Visual Basic. Access is not required in Part II. The clients are a Sales Invoicing client, a Purchasing and Inventory client, and a Management Reports client (see Figure 9.1). These programs interact through the database and share information.

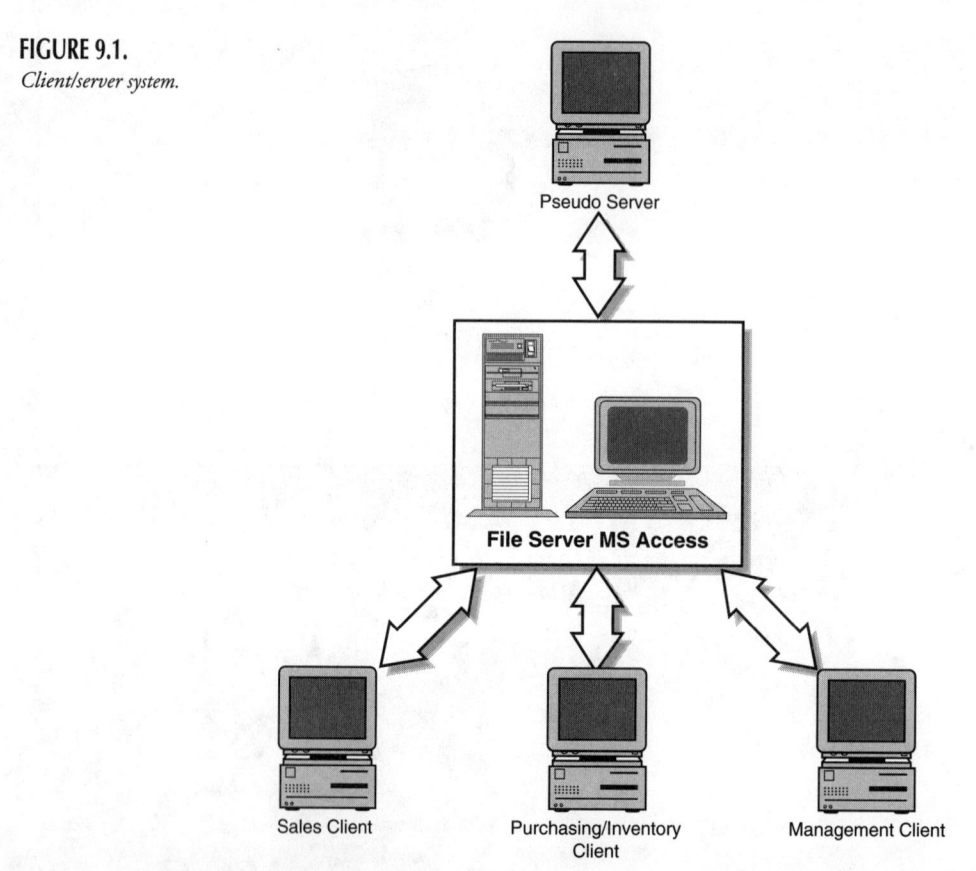

FIGURE 9.1.
Client/server system.

Visual Basic is used best in conjunction with other programs. For example, Visual Basic lacks the capability to create security settings for an Access database (its native format). However, it can take advantage of security setup in Access. Therefore, you can enhance the client applications by using Access and Excel to provide additional advanced features. Using VBA, OLE Automation, and Excel to supplement the C/S system will be demonstrated in Part III.

In Part IV, we will upsize the database and applications to work with Microsoft SQL Server for complete database server access. The ability to change the data access to use the remote data objects (RDO) to access the data through an ODBC data source instead of the data access objects

(DAO) will be demonstrated. Using the RDO dramatically increases performance during interaction with SQL Server.

In Part II, you begin by creating a client/server system implementation. This implementation consists of a file server that holds the database file that handles multi-user database access (see Figure 9.2). You create multi-relational tables that are stored in Access format, the native format of the JET engine. All the necessary tables are created using the Data Manager application included with Visual Basic. Also included is the code for creating each table programmatically through Visual Basic or SQL.

FIGURE 9.2.
Abstract diagram of the client/server system.

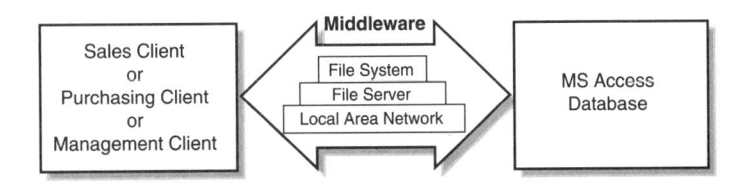

These applications are not meant to be examples of excellent user interface capabilities or aesthetic excellence. (For information on designing user interfaces, see Appendix A, "User Interface Guidelines.") We have found it far more constructive to build an application step-by-step; this enables you to observe the process and implementation. This process should be more instructive than a ready-made program. In Visual Basic, code is hidden behind buttons and various controls; it makes sense only within the context of its event-driven environment. By providing the construction details, the functions of the client programs should be easier to understand.

> **NOTE**
>
> In these client applications, most of the error checking routines are missing. Error checking is vital to all client/server systems. To recover from a malfunction automatically is crucial to enabling users to trust the system. Error checking, however, involves many lines of similar code that must be typed; therefore, for the purposes of demonstration, we have left out the error routines in order to focus on specific client/server code implementation. For error checking concepts, examine Appendix B, "Error Handling," which provides information on creating a complete error trapping system. In our implementations, we use VB/Rig Pro from Avanti Software to create most of the basic error checking that we need. See Chapter 29, "Third-Party Tools, Utilities, and Controls," for more details.

Given these constraints, we have attempted to construct useful programs that help you to understand the underlying Visual Basic concepts and that provide a foundation from which you can work. Many of the best user interface enhancements can be achieved simply by plugging in a component described in Chapter 29.

Client Programs

The three client programs—the Sales Invoicing client, the Purchasing and Inventory client, and the Management Reports client—consist of a variety of forms and controls. The Pseudo Server consists of a single form. The programs are constructed as separate projects in Visual Basic and are compiled into four different .EXE files.

The three client programs can all run on the same machine or on networked machines. They access a database stored on a file server and a designated shared drive. For simplicity of construction, you will create all the programs on drive C. This is the ideal way to test a client/server system during design stage, because you don't need to deal with network and configuration problems.

Be aware that network conditions (routers, gateways, and so on) and throughput variables (network traffic, server speed, and so on) can dramatically affect performance. Unfortunately, with the variety of configurations in place in the computer industry, there is no accurate way to judge these performance difficulties. Experience through implementation is the only way to get a good feel for how these factors will affect the system.

> **NOTE**
>
> These programs have been tested running under Windows, Windows for Workgroups, and Windows 95 as clients. For the file server, both a Novell NetWare Server and a Windows NT Advanced Server were tested. Any Windows-compatible machine (including the PowerPC, DEC Alpha, and MIPS-based machines) should be capable of executing these programs.

Sales Client

The Sales client program, shown in Figure 9.3, is the point-of-sale client of the client/server system. This application is an example of an online transaction processing (OLTP) system. An OLTP system relies on quick response to activity because it is being used in real-time. Someone using this client typically enters a sale while the customer waits. This demands immediate data access so that the invoice can be completed and printed. If the quantity of an item on the invoice does not exist in inventory, the Sales client knows immediately and flags the user.

To ensure data integrity, the Sales client implements transaction processing after the invoice has been approved. This ensures that all the table modifications created by the invoice either succeed or fail without the risk of a partial update, which could corrupt the database.

FIGURE 9.3.

The Sales Invoice client screen.

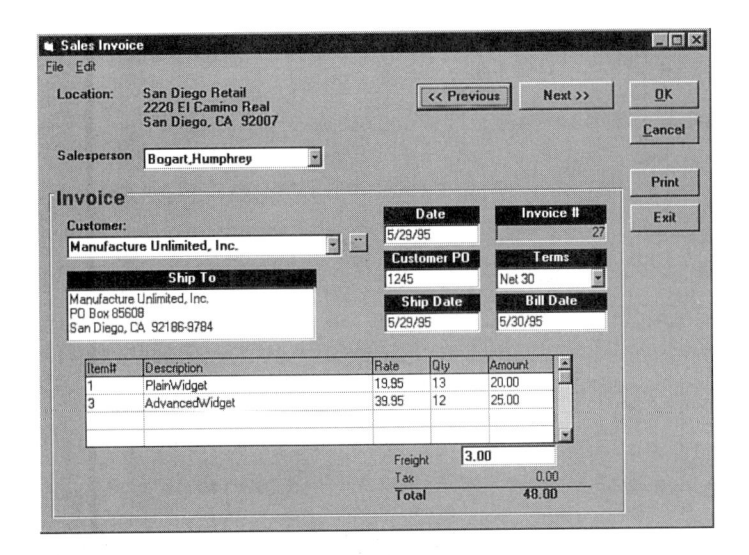

The application is based on an invoice system in which each sale is entered as an individual invoice. Every invoice requires a customer name to be chosen from the Customer table using the drop-down combo menu. If a name is entered that is not stored in the Customer table, the Customer form shown in Figure 9.4 appears. This form enables the user to enter a new name, which is added to the table.

FIGURE 9.4.

The Customer screen.

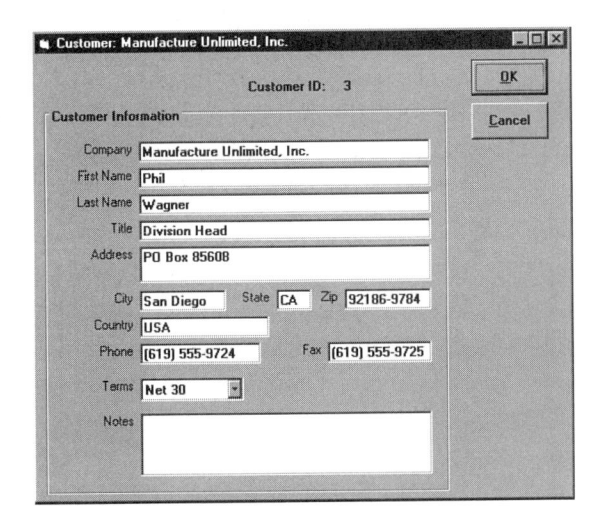

The combo is filled with all the individuals and companies listed in the Customers table. If the user types in a Customer name not found in the list, the Sales client asks the user whether this is a new customer. If the user selects Yes, a form that enables the user to enter all the specific customer information appears. This information entered into the new customer form is then added to the customer list.

The invoice is assigned an invoice number by accessing the Counter table, which stores all the incremental numbers used by the client/server system. The record in the Counter table with a `TableName` field that equals `Sales` holds the next available invoice value.

The `Date`, `Ship To`, `Customer PO`, `Bill Date`, and `Terms` fields are all modifiable by the user, so they can be changed for a particular invoice. These changes are stored in the Sales table.

Individual sale items are entered in the grid at the bottom of the invoice. When the Item column is selected, a command button appears that allows access to a list of the available sales items (see Figure 9.5). Items are entered with a quantity, unit cost, and final price.

FIGURE 9.5.
The Sales Item screen.

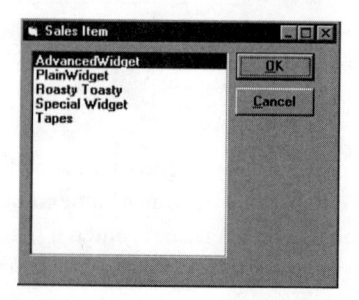

The Grid control, however, does not enable the user to edit values within the individual cells. To solve this problem, a text box control is placed on the form and set to be invisible. When the user clicks a particular cell, the text box is moved over that cell, sized to the cell's width and height, input with the cell's current contents, and made visible. It appears to the user as though he is editing the cell. In reality, the cell's contents are being edited in the text box. When the user moves to a different cell, the contents of the text box are copied back to the cell.

As the quantity for each item is entered, the total and the sales tax are automatically calculated. They include the value entered in the `Freight` field for the invoice.

As an item is entered on the invoice, it is automatically removed from the inventory and placed in the reserve items field to ensure that no other user sells them. The Pseudo Server returns the reserved items to the inventory if anything like a shutdown or crash prevents the Sales client from canceling and returning the items.

The buttons on the right of the invoice form produce the functions that they traditionally represent. The OK button writes the invoice data to the appropriate tables and creates a new invoice in which information can be entered. The Cancel button clears the invoice and starts over. The Next and Previous buttons enable the user to page through the currently available invoices.

The Print button enables the user to print an invoice from the receipt currently shown on the screen. Invoices are printed with text commands by using the Visual Printer object. Although the Crystal Reports included with Visual Basic could be used, the output is only slightly better than the results available through the Printer object.

Likewise, the Crystal Reports included with Visual Basic are memory-intensive and must print from a database file. This means that print information must be written into a scratch database or a complex query setup. For this reason, we suggest that you look at the available report generator add-ons described in Chapter 29. Many of them offer professional printing capabilities in a fraction of the amount of time that it takes to write a custom report yourself.

Purchasing Client

The Purchasing client is the largest and the most complicated client program because it must create purchase orders, track inventory, accept new supplies purchases, assemble units for sale from a variety of raw materials items, add or edit supplier records, and add new items (sales or parts) to inventory.

This client, like the Sales client, is also an OLTP application. Items received into inventory must be updated instantly so that the Sales client can have access to the data. The Purchasing client can also edit or add parts available to the Sales client.

The main Purchase Order screen, shown in Figure 9.6, acts much like the Sales Invoice screen does. The Purchase Order form does not, however, reserve items from the inventory, because it is set up to purchase items *for* inventory. Items are not actually entered into inventory until the Received button is clicked to accept the purchase order.

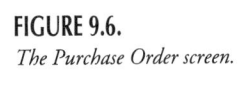

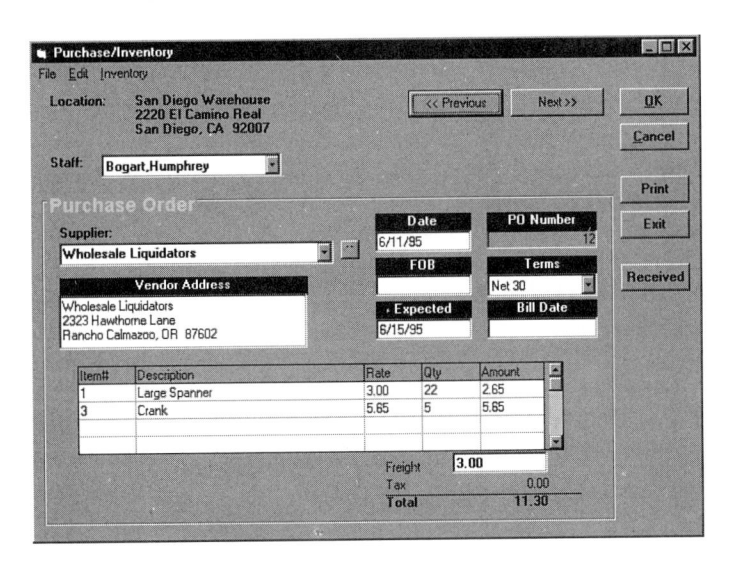

FIGURE 9.6.
The Purchase Order screen.

Entering suppliers is nearly the same as entering customers. If a particular supplier is not found in the Supplier table, it can be entered. Every purchase order requires a supplier.

The Purchasing client is responsible for inventory management. Items received on a purchase order are not entered into the sales inventory, but rather the parts inventory. This enables the various parts required for construction to be totaled separately to determine final unit costs and the manufacturer's pricing.

To enter an item in the sales inventory, that sales item must be constructed from the raw materials stored as parts. These finished items are created from assembly records that define all the parts and quantities required to assemble a final unit. The number of parts can be automatically removed from the parts inventory for each sales item constructed.

You use the Autobuild Edit form, shown in Figure 9.7, to construct these relations. All the available parts—crank, spanner, whistle—are listed in the box on the right side of the form. With the Item combo, select the sales item whose autobuild definition is to be created or edited. From the parts list, select individual parts, and enter the quantity required. Using the Add button, add it to the Sales item's autobuild definition.

FIGURE 9.7.
The Autobuild Edit screen.

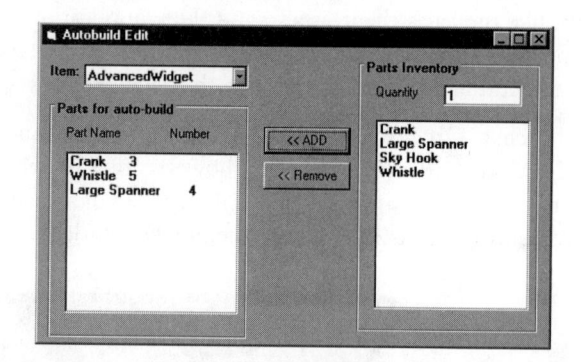

The Remove button enables you to remove items from the item's autobuild definition. There is no way to edit the quantity required. Therefore, you must remove the item from the autobuild list and add it again with the new required quantity.

Once you create a definition, you can build a quantity of sale items. Using the Autobuild Sales Item form (see Figure 9.8), specify a quantity of sale items. When you click the OK button, the program removes the proper number of each type of part from the parts inventory and adds the total quantity of the sales items to the sales inventory.

The user can also add or edit sales or parts in the inventory. The Parts Inventory form, shown in Figure 9.9, can be used to examine the quantities of the parts held in stock as well as the number below which the item should be reordered. The number of items in the inventory and the total units is summarized at the bottom of the window.

FIGURE 9.8.
The Autobuild Sales Item screen.

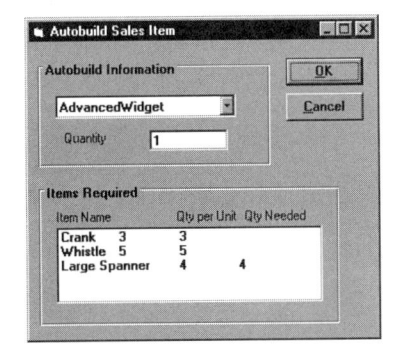

FIGURE 9.9.
Parts Inventory form.

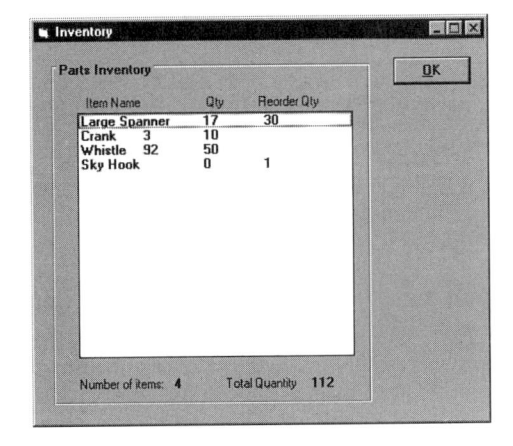

Management Reports Client

The Management Reports client, shown in Figure 9.10, generates reports and information about the status of sales data, purchasing data, inventory data, and overall figures. This application is a decision support system (DSS) application. The data necessary for the reports generated from the database is essentially a snapshot of a period of time.

Decision support systems need summary information, in contrast to an OLTP's system, which demands instant access to information. Few management reports need to know how many widgets are being sold as the day progresses, but many reports require the sales information once the day is through. Decision support systems provide summary data and trend analysis so that management can make accurate risk assessments for future action.

Often, a DSS allows a subset of the overall data to be downloaded to an individual client program and manipulated using "what-if" analysis. Once the data is analyzed, it is not uploaded to the server but is discarded.

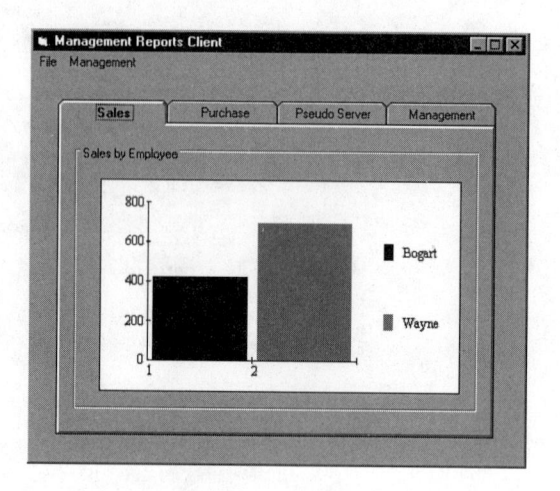

FIGURE 9.10.
The Management Reports Client.

The Management client displays summary information from all the tables used by the other clients. Each piece of summary data is retrieved by using a SnapShot object (which is read-only) to query the database and retrieve information. This client provides many examples of summary queries and various ways in which the information can be displayed.

The Sales report in Figure 9.10 creates a bar chart of the total sales for every employee. Each bar is labeled with the name of an employee. This report must access various tables, including the Staff and SalesItems tables. The routines are an example of using the Visual Basic Graph control and of creating a multi-table coordinated query.

The Purchase report, shown in Figure 9.11, uses a grid to display unit cost data for various parts. The grid is generated by using a query that sums all the individual costs of the parts in the parts inventory for each sales item. This report uses both inventory tables and the Assembly table to coordinate the aggregate function.

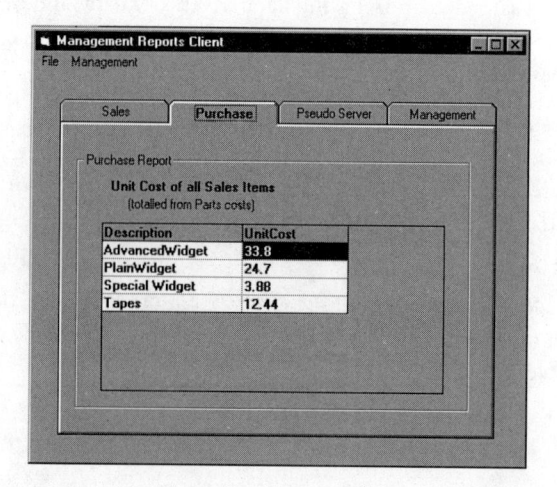

FIGURE 9.11.
The Purchase report.

The Pseudo Server report, shown in Figure 9.12, displays the various flags and their values. These flags are summary information about the database itself or the tables contained within it. The Pseudo Server can track various aspects of the system and provide summary information. This report displays some of this summary information.

FIGURE 9.12.
The Pseudo Server report.

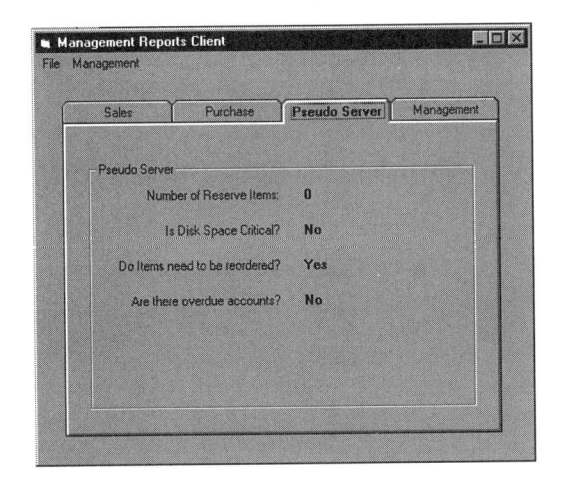

The Management report shows a variety of information, including average sales per employee, today's sales, average sales per invoice, and the item with the most sales (see Figure 9.13). This report uses numerous queries to determine many different types of information from some of the tables. A Management Reports section of an application usually provides overview data that an executive can use to see the big picture.

FIGURE 9.13.
The Management report.

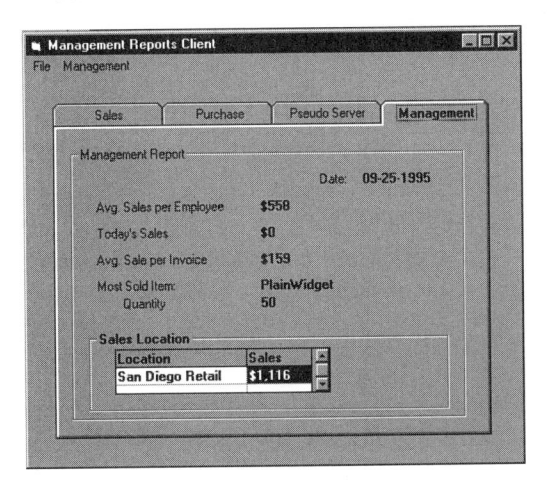

The Management client itself also allows various management-centered OLTP operations. It enables employee information and salary levels to be entered. Each reports section displays information in a convenient format relevant to the running of an organization. A Management DSS frequently must be rewritten as needs and business change—for instance, to record and display information for new management techniques such as just-in-time inventory and Total Quality Management (TQM).

Pseudo Server Client

The Pseudo Server client, shown in Figure 9.14, is a program used to demonstrate various facets of the client/server world. In the example system that you are constructing, the file server is the true server that various clients access. The database file is stored on this file server to enable common access.

FIGURE 9.14.
The Pseudo Server screen.

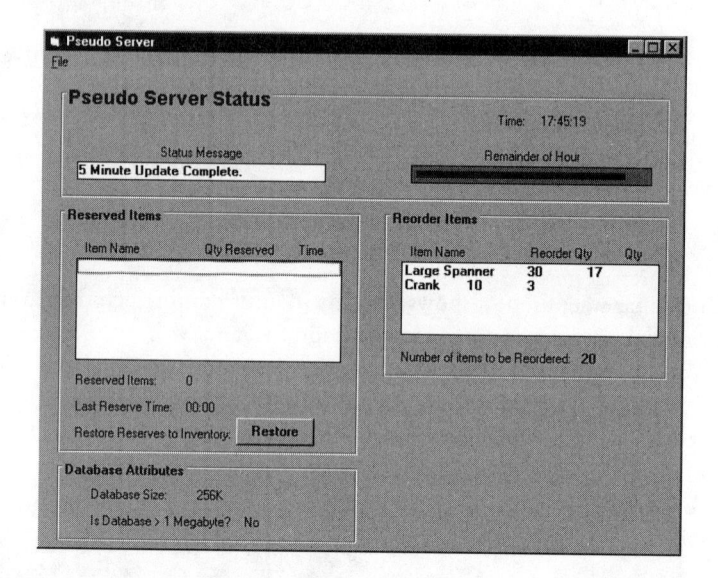

The Pseudo Server does not process client requests as a traditional server would. Instead, it monitors the database for certain conditions and signals the clients by changing flags in a common-read table. Presumably, the Pseudo Server program would run on the main file server and watch for particular conditions, thereby freeing the client programs to focus their available processing power on functions more relevant to the client computers.

The Pseudo Server, in addition to the flags that it sets or resets, also watches the SalesInventory table for items left in reserve. After a given amount of time—thirty minutes in the application—the Pseudo Server returns these reserved units to the inventory. This prevents a user from reserving a number of units and then incorrectly canceling the invoice—for example, by using the reset key or by turning the power off—which would leave the reserved items in limbo.

Application Tables

Begin creating the client/server system by setting up the database file that all the applications will access and share. You will construct a complete set of tables to handle all the traditional management tasks for a company, Widget Co. For this, you need to construct 13 different tables:

- Location table
- Staff table
- Customer table
- Suppliers table
- Counter table
- Sales inventory table
- Parts inventory table
- Sales table for invoices
- SalesItems table
- Purchase table
- PurchaseItems table
- Assembly table
- PServer table

Table 9.1 briefly describes each table.

Table 9.1. Tables stored in WIDGETCO.MDB.

Table Names	Descriptions
Location	Company locations, stores, and warehouses
Staff	Employees
Customer	Customer information
Supplier	Supplier information
Counter	Counters for unique IDs of new invoices, purchase orders, and so on
Inventory_Parts	All items that are purchased or used in manufacturing
Inventory_Sales	All items sold through the Sales client
Sales	General information of each sales invoice
SalesItems	Line items for each sales invoice

continues

Table 9.1. continued

Table Names	Descriptions
Purchase	General information on each purchase order
PurchaseItems	Line items for each purchase order
Assembly	Contains relations between parts and sales items for autobuilding
PServer	Flags and information for the Pseudo Server

These tables are related to one another through various ID and UniqueID numbers. (See Chapter 10, "Table Construction," for a complete explanation of the table relations and structures.)

The Location table tracks various sites of the business, such as retail outlets, franchises, warehouses, distribution hubs, and headquarters. The Staff table is linked to a location so that employees can be tracked correctly. Each sales invoice also contains the location of the sales so that location-by-location figures can be compiled. All inventoried items are also tracked through the LocationID field. If items are low at one location, they can be redistributed to another location.

The Staff table holds the names, salaries, and other information about the employees. Each invoice in the Sales client and each purchase order in the Purchasing client require a StaffID for easy tracking. Therefore, an employee must exist in the Staff table for either an invoice or a purchase order to be created.

The Customer table holds all the information on each customer. Because this is a simple flat database, there are no related tables to store multiple addresses, phone numbers, contacts, and so forth. Adding the extra related tables for each customer is a relatively simple addition. By the time the Widget Co. Client/server system has been constructed, you should have the skills to create this yourself. Further normalization, however, can increase the complexity and decrease the performance of the program. Before you add another related table, make sure that you don't merely need an additional phone number field that you could have added to the table definition.

The Supplier table keeps track of all the vital information that applies to suppliers of materials used in manufacturing of Widget's products. This table also keeps the terms used with the supplier to provide information for cash-flow analysis.

The Counter table holds the values of the last number inserted in many of the tables. It holds the last invoice number, the last purchase order number, the last assigned parts inventory item number, and so on.

The Inventory_Sales table contains all the items stocked for sale in inventory. The Inventory_Parts table is separate from the Sales_Inventory table because parts have different requirements. Rarely does a company sell as merchandise the various parts that it uses to create its product. The Inventory_Parts table contains all the items stocked for use in autobuilding the final sales items in inventory.

The Sales table holds all the general information for each sales invoice. For data normalization, only the summary information is stored in this record. The individual items from the invoice are stored in a related table, SalesItems. Each invoice record holds other relations to tables, including the Location table, the Customer table, and the Staff table.

The SalesItems table holds all the sales transactions that occur on a sales invoice. Each item is stored with a relation to the Inventory_Sales table, which holds information on every item. This table stores each entry with a primary key that relates it to the Sales table and a secondary line item value that stores the invoice line on which the item is located.

The Purchase and PurchaseItems tables serve roles similar to the Sales and the SalesItems tables. These tables store each purchase order record and the line items of the purchase order.

The Assembly table contains all the parts needed to assemble an individual item. This enables parts to be tracked and resupplied individually as a unit is created. It also enables the client program to calculate the total unit cost of an assembled item from the costs of all its component parts.

The PServer table contains flags for all the values tracked by the Pseudo Server. Clients can access these flags to obtain summary information on the state of the database. Particular client programs can also have write access to particular flag fields so that they can reset them.

All these tables are stored in the WIDGETCO.MDB database. You join tables by using SQL statements and queries. All but two of the tables (the PServer and Counter tables) have fields with relations to other tables.

Client Problems to Consider

With numerous clients accessing the same database, numerous problems can occur. This section describes some common problems the designer of a client/server system might encounter. The individual client programs contain solutions to some of these problems but not all of them. Problems occur in different ways for enterprises of different sizes.

For example, a large company with many salespeople must implement a system that often handles data collision—two or more people attempting to update a record at the same time. Therefore, these system designers might spend a large amount of time creating an update queue or a time-based update retry system.

On the other hand, a small company might have only one or two people actually making sales, and the retry system might consist of a simple form that asks the user if the update should be reattempted. This is the method implemented by the example Sales client.

Besides common data collision problems, a number of data concurrency problems face the client program. Suppose, for example, that there are ten widgets in inventory at the present time. Salesperson1 makes a sale for eight widgets and begins to construct an invoice. If Salesperson2 wants to sell seven widgets, his client program checks the inventory, which registers that ten widgets are available. Once Salesperson1 presses the OK button, only two widgets remain—not enough for SalesPerson2 to complete his sale.

The Sales client solves this problem by containing a reserved field. When the Sales client originally requests a quantity of items for sale, this number is removed from the OnHand field in the table and is placed in the Reserved field in the table. Other clients that query see only the number remaining after the reserve. Additionally, the time of the reserve is stored with the items. The Pseudo Server checks the reserved field. After thirty minutes, it returns the reserved widgets to the OnHand quantity if the invoice has not been completed or approved.

A simpler but less flexible option would be to lock the record off from access by other clients while one of the client programs uses it. This would clearly be unacceptable in this application, where multiple Sales clients might need to access this data simultaneously. In some applications, though, multiple, simultaneous access is not required. Other applications demand strict controls so that this type of record or page locking is the only option.

Data concurrency problems are some of the most insidious problems that a client/server system can have. The moment that data is downloaded from the server to the client, it begins to lose its currency. When you design a system, make sure to take these potential problems into account.

Client/server design is one of the most rigorously difficult fields in which to create an application because of the amount of interconnection. In this field, experience counts for everything. Brochures and advertisements promise the world, but they rarely deliver. There is a great deal at stake when creating a client/server system. Often the organization will rely on the system for mission critical data. Be sure to test a system thoroughly before you deploy it.

The client/server system presented in the following chapters will lead you through the various aspects of system development. By following the construction of each piece of the overall system, many of the problems that can hamstring deployment are described. The various client programs themselves such as the Purchasing client or the Management Reports client may be used as a foundation upon which a complete solution can be constructed.

> **TIP**
>
> Without experience, setting up a client/server system is incredibly difficult. Building the client/server system in this book will introduce you to some of the problems that you will face. We suggest that you should actually attempt to deploy this system on the network on which your own final system will reside. It will provide an excellent test bed for you to begin to see potential missing links in the chain of systems required to fulfill your task.

10

Table Construction

Before you can construct the client programs, you must first create the database that will provide the foundation for this system. The central database holds all of the tables that contain related information for the system. You use the Data Manager included with Visual Basic to create the various tables stored within the database.

Constructing the Client/Server Tables

Thirteen tables must be constructed (see Table 10.1 and Figure 10.1). Each table will be accessed by various clients and different client programs. For example, the Inventory_Sales table is accessed by all three client programs and the Pseudo Server program as well.

Table 10.1. Widget Co. Tables.

Table	Access By
PServer	Purchasing client, Pseudo Server
Sales	Sales client, Management client
SalesItems	Sales client, Management client
Purchase	Purchasing client
PurchaseItems	Purchasing client
Assembly	Purchasing client
Counter	Sales client, Purchasing client
Customer	Sales client
Supplier	Purchasing client
Staff	Sales client, Purchasing client
Inventory_Sales	Sales client, Purchasing client, Management client, Pseudo Server
Inventory_Parts	Purchasing client, Management client
Location	Sales client, Purchasing client

Many tables are related. Figure 10.2 shows the basic relations among the tables. These relations might seem complicated at first. As each client program is constructed, though, you will clearly see how the relations work among the tables. Figure 10.3 shows the relations among the tables used by the Sales client program. The tables used by the Purchasing client are shown in the Figure 10.4. Both applications access many of the same tables and share information.

The lines that connect the various tables denote connections between the key fields. In the upper left corner, you will notice the Location table. The LocationID field in the Location table—the primary key—is related to all the LocationID fields in the other tables—foreign keys. The beginning and the end of each connecting line have the same type of shape. For example, if the connection begins at the field of one table with a dark arrowhead, the connection will end at another table with the same type of arrowhead. This makes tracking the connections easier.

FIGURE 10.1.
Widget Co. tables.

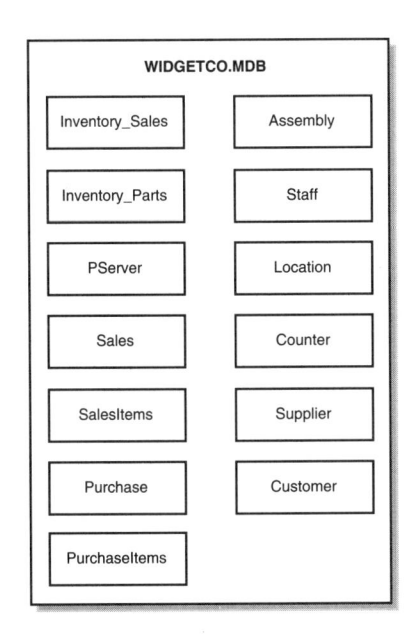

```
WIDGETCO.MDB

Inventory_Sales      Assembly

Inventory_Parts      Staff

PServer              Location

Sales                Counter

SalesItems           Supplier

Purchase             Customer

PurchaseItems
```

Notice that the Counter table and the PseudoServer table do not have any relations with the other tables. This is because these tables are accessed individually by client programs and are not directly connected with a particular table. For example, the Counter table holds the last invoice number that was used. This table is not connected to any of the tables, but instead is read directly by the Sales client program. The client retrieves a number from this table, increments the last invoice number, and creates a new invoice. This new invoice, however, does not need to reference the Counter table and therefore needs no relation.

Once you have created the database, you are ready to begin building the tables. The following examples use the Data Manager to construct the tables. For an example of how to use SQL statements to construct tables, see Chapter 25, "Constructing a Query Builder."

After you construct each, you will use the Data Manager to enter sample information. Type this information as it is listed so that the examples, queries, and reports that follow in the book will match those that you replicate on your machine.

FIGURE 10.2.
Widget Co. table relations.

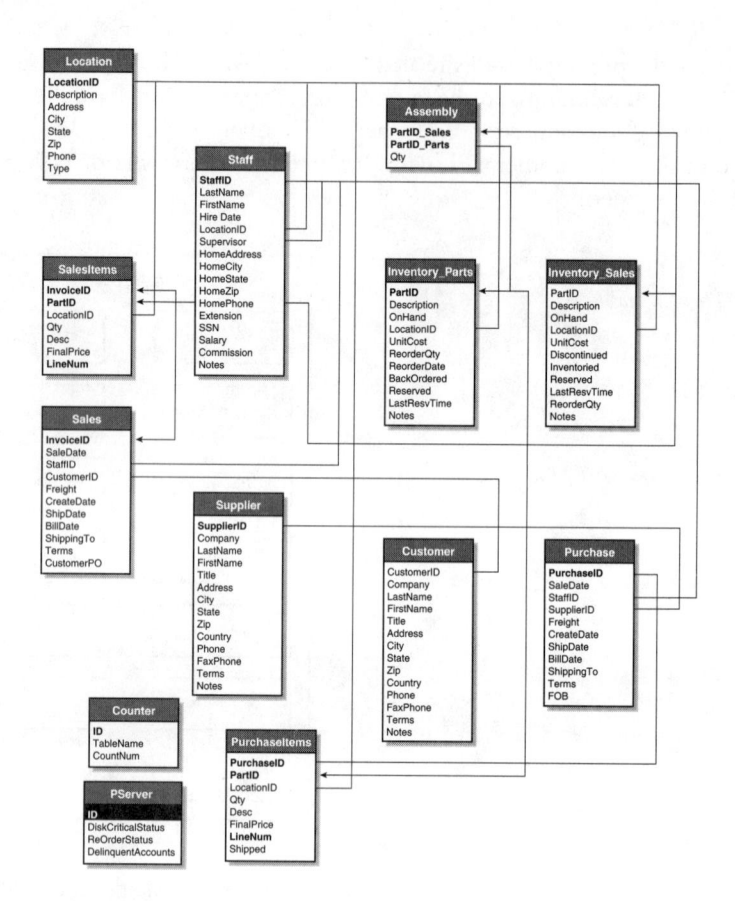

FIGURE 10.3.
Sales client tables.

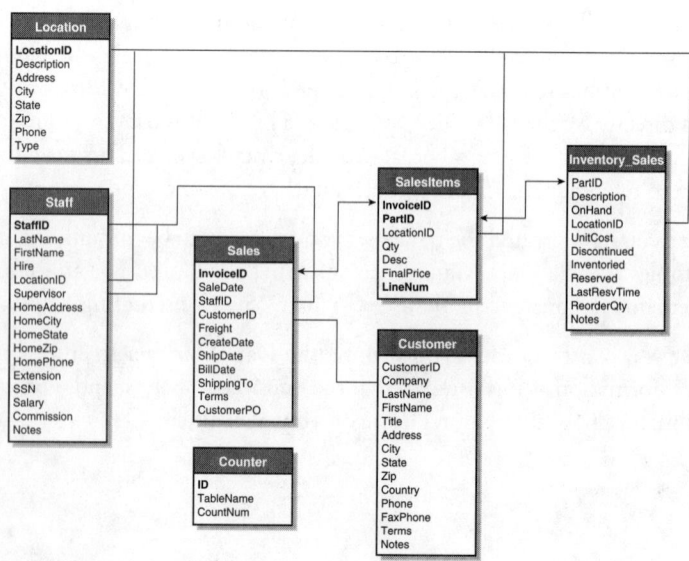

FIGURE 10.4.
Purchasing client tables.

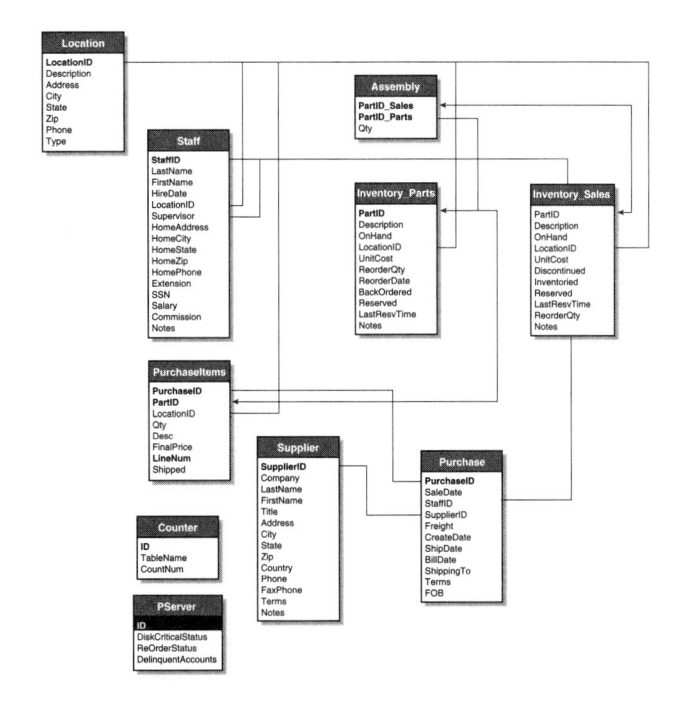

Normalizing the C/S Tables

The degree of normalization required by a database varies with the complexity and speed requirements of the individual application. (For more information on normalization, see Chapter 4, "Overview of Database Concepts.") With this database, we have sought to normalize the data to the generally appropriate level. Choosing the appropriate level is a judgement call based on experience. As you normalize more databases, the level required will become apparent based on the system and application the database will be deployed with.

Each part in the inventory tables—Inventory_Sales and Inventory_Parts—is stored separately, and the relations between these tables and the others are quite clear. The PartID field is used to identify each part uniquely.

The Customer and Supplier tables contain all the information in a flat-file form. If multiple contacts existed for a single company or even many phone numbers for a single contact, further normalization of this table would be required. Be sure that adding more related tables (such as a table for phone numbers) is actually necessary. They add complexity and decrease general performance. Therefore, make sure the needed extra information is the rule rather than the exception. Occasional extra information (such as a third phone number) can be stored in the Notes field.

One of the best implementation tips in regard to normalization is to reevaluate the tables after they have been in use for a few weeks. If many phone numbers or addresses are required for each individual, you will observe data proliferating in the Notes field.

Users often store information about a customer that won't fit in ordinary fields in the Notes field so that the data won't be lost. The data is not usable information, however, if it remains in the Notes field—searching is difficult, and correlating among unformatted data is nearly impossible. Therefore, make sure that commonly required data is given its own field or table.

Creating the Required Directories

For all the various projects, forms, files, and the database, you need specific directories in which store the information. You will create two sets of directories: a central directory for the final .EXE files and another directory for all the project, form, and module files.

The client server directory (CLNTSRVR), shown in Figure 10.5, holds the database and four folders that contain the .EXE file directories. Use either the Explorer or My Computer icon to create the necessary folders. Create the following directories:

> C:\CLNTSRVR\SALES
> C:\CLNTSRVR\PURCHASE
> C:\CLNTSRVR\MANAGE
> C:\CLNTSRVR\PSERVER

FIGURE 10.5.
The CLNTSRVR directory.

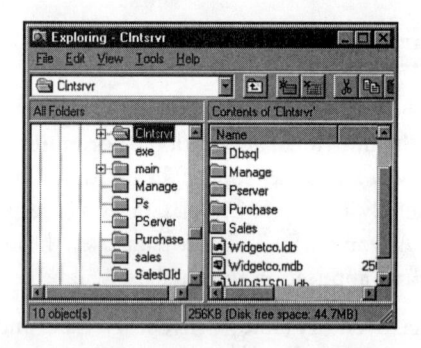

To create the directories to hold the project, form, module, and .INI files, use the same process. The main directory in this case is the client/server Visual Basic (CS_VB) directory, which is shown in Figure 10.6. Create the following directories:

> C:\CS_VB
> C:\CS_VB\SALES
> C:\CS_VB\PURCHASE
> C:\CS_VB\MANAGE
> C:\CS_VB\PSERVER

Chapter 10 ■ Table Construction

FIGURE 10.6.
The CS_VB directory.

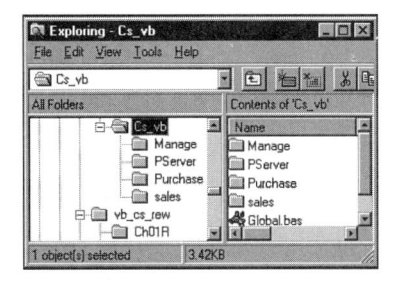

> **NOTE**
>
> You will use the individual source files that will be shared in common (ITEM.FRM and GLOBALS.BAS) directly in CS_VB. All the other files specific to each project—other forms, .INI files, and so forth—will be stored in the individual project folders.

Creating the Tables

Now use the Data Manager to create the database. Execute Visual Basic, and select the Data Manager option from the Add-Ins menu. Select New Database... under the File menu (see Figure 10.7). This enables you to create an Access database.

FIGURE 10.7.
New database.

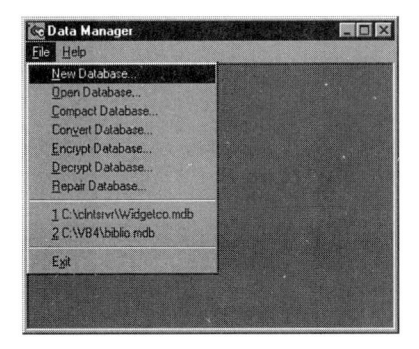

Type in the filename `WIDGETCO.MDB`, placing it in the CLNTSRVR directory. The database will now be created, and the Data Manager displays the main navigation window. From this window, you can add tables and queries to the database.

Building the Sales Table

To create the Sales table described in the following section, click the New button. The table editing window appears. For the table Name field, type `Sales` (see Figure 10.8). This is the name used within a query to access the data in this table.

FIGURE 10.8.
Adding a new table.

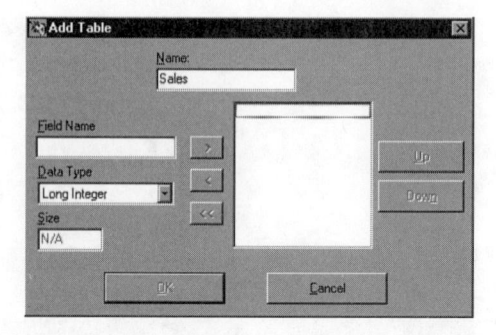

Enter all the fields for the table listed in Table 10.2 (see Figure 10.9). This table includes the name, type, and size of the field. For most of the fields, the size is unimportant because the data type has a predetermined size. For example, Long is 4 bytes. Type each field name into the Field Name text box. Enter the type and, if applicable, the size. Click the right arrow (>) to add the field to the table.

FIGURE 10.9.
Adding a new field.

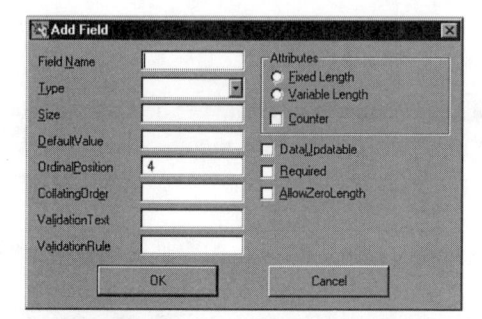

> **NOTE**
>
> In each of these tables, we have included the field type programming constant—for instance, dbLONG. These constants are included in Visual Basic and should be helpful if you need to add these data tables programmatically to a database server not directly specified in this book, such as Informix.

After you have added all the fields, the table window should look roughly like the one shown in Figure 10.10. Feel free to change the order with the Up and Down buttons of any of the fields. None of the client programs constructed in this book rely on accessing the fields by their index number.

FIGURE 10.10.
The Sales table screen.

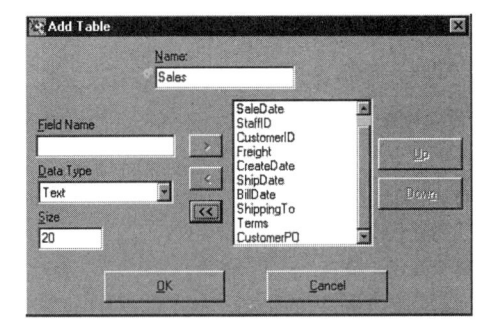

> **TIP**
>
> It is usually poor programming practice to rely on a field's position in the table. For example, a field can be referenced by using an index such as `temp = MyDS.Fields(0)`. It is a much better to use the field name. Thus, if the order ever changed within the data dictionary, the client program will continue to function properly.

Enter the Data into Various Tables

As you build the various client programs in this book, you will no longer have to enter the information directly into the database. Instead, the client programs will provide custom front-ends from which you can enter the information. For now, enter some data so that the client programs have something to display.

Table 10.2. Sales table definition.

Field Name	Constant Type	Field Type	Field Length
*InvoiceID	dbLONG	Long	4
SaleDate	dbDATE	Date/Time Variant	8
StaffID	dbLONG	Long	4
CustomerID	dbLONG	Long	4
Freight	dbCURRENCY	Currency Double	8
CreateDate	dbDATE	Date/Time Variant	8
ShipDate	dbDATE	Date/Time Variant	8
BillDate	dbDATE	Date/Time Variant	8
ShippingTo	dbTEXT	TextString	200
Terms	dbINTEGER	Integer	2
CustomerPO	dbTEXT	TextString	20

* Indicates the key field

After you have finished creating the table, close the table window. Select the table, and click the Open button. This will display all the fields of the database. Click the Add button for each record in Table 10.3 at the end of the chapter, and enter the information. Once you have entered the information, close the window and create the next table.

> **NOTE**
>
> This data is informal filler data used to demonstrate the various features of the client programs. However, please enter this information as listed. The exact data is not as important as the formatting and the existence of data in the proper fields. When data is entered into the individual client programs, error checking is done to ensure that inappropriate data is not stored to the database. Few error routines, however, are included to catch errors in data read from the database. Therefore, incorrectly entered data can cause problems.

Building the Inventory_Sales Table

The Inventory_Sales table contains all the items that are sold through the Sales client. This table lists the number of the items remaining in inventory, descriptions of each item, part numbers, the number of reserved items, the last reserve update, inventoried and discontinued flags, and Notes fields for additional information about the items.

Build this table in the same way as you constructed the Sales table. The table definition in Table 10.4 lists the field name, the constant type, the field type, and the field length (see Figure 10.11). For most of the fields, the size is unimportant because the data type has a predetermined size. For example, Long is 4 bytes. After you have constructed the table, enter the sample data that the client programs will use.

FIGURE 10.11.
The Inventory_Sales table screen.

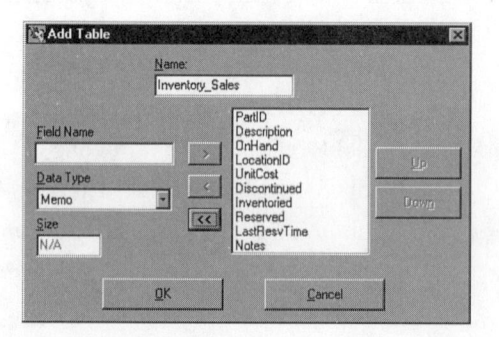

Table 10.4. Inventory_Sales table definition.

Field Name	Constant Type	Field Type	Field Length
*PartID	dbLONG	Long	4
Description	dbTEXT	TextString	50
OnHand	dbLONG	Long	4
LocationID	dbLONG	Long	4
UnitCost	dbCURRENCY	Currency Double	8
Discontinued	dbBOOLEAN	True/False Integer	1
Inventoried	dbBOOLEAN	True/False Integer	1
Reserved	dbLONG	Long	4
LastResvTime	dbDATE	Date/Time Variant	8
Notes	dbMEMO	Memo	0

* Indicates the key field

After you created the table, close the table window. Select the table, and click the Open button. This will display all the fields of the database. Click the Add button for each record in Table 10.5 at the end of the chapter, and enter the information. Once you have entered the information, close the window and create the next table.

Building the Inventory_Parts Table

The Inventory_Parts table contains all the items that can be purchased by the Purchasing client and assembled into the finished product to be sold by the company. This table is kept separate from the Inventory_Sales table because rarely does a company sell the raw materials that are used in producing its products. The Purchasing client enables the user to autobuild a number of parts stored in the Inventory_Parts table and to create a finished unit, which is placed in the Inventory_Sales table (see Figure 10.12).

> **NOTE**
>
> Figure 10.12 is an example of the table after it has been opened using the Design button. This view enables the table definition to be edited once it has been created.

Build this table in the same way as you constructed the Sales table. The table definition in Table 10.6 lists the field name, the constant type, the field type, and the field length. For most of the fields, the size is unimportant because the data type has a predetermined size. For example, Long is 4 bytes. After you have constructed the table, enter the sample data that the client programs will use.

FIGURE 10.12.
The Inventory_Parts table screen Design.

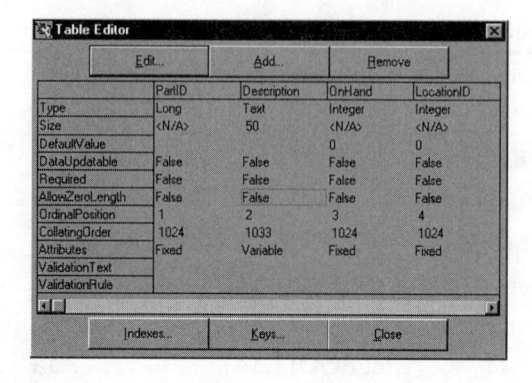

Table 10.6. Inventory_Parts table definition.

Field Name	Constant Type	Field Type	Field Length
*PartID	dbLONG	Long	4
Description	dbTEXT	TextString	50
OnHand	dbINTEGER	Integer	2
LocationID	dbINTEGER	Integer	2
UnitCost	dbCURRENCY	Currency Double	8
ReorderQty	dbINTEGER	Integer	2
ReorderDate	dbDATE	Date/Time Variant	8
BackOrdered	dbINTEGER	Integer	2
Reserved	dbLONG	Long	4
LastResvTime	dbDATE	Date/Time Variant	8
Notes	dbMEMO	Memo	0

* Indicates the key field

After you have created the table, close the table window. Select the table, and click the Open button. This will display all the fields of the database. Click the Add button for each record in Table 10.7 at the end of the chapter, and enter the information. Once you have entered the information, close the window and create the next table.

Building the SalesItems Table

The Items table contains all the information for a single line in the Sales client invoice. The Items table has relations to the Sales table, the Inventory_Sales table, and the Location table. Each Items table record consists of

    The part number for the item being sold

    The invoice number of the invoice on which the sale is occurring

Chapter 10 ■ Table Construction 237

The quantity of the item being sold

The final price of the item—the user can override the calculated value

A description of the item if the user overrode the standard description

The line number on the invoice on which the item occurs

Build this table in the same way as you constructed the Sales table. The table definition in Table 10.8 lists the field name, the constant type, the field type, and the field length. For most of the fields, the size is unimportant because the data type has a predetermined size. For example, Long is 4 bytes.

After you have constructed the table, the Data Manager window should look roughly like the one shown in Figure 10.13. Don't forget to put an index on the key field for speed. Enter the sample data that will the client programs will use.

Table 10.8. SalesItems table definition.

Field Name	Constant Type	Field Type	Field Length
*InvoiceID	dbLONG	Long	4
*PartID	dbLONG	Long	4
LocationID	dbLONG	Long	4
Qty	dbINTEGER	Integer	2
Desc	dbTEXT	TextString	50
FinalPrice	dbCURRENCY	Currency Double	8
*LineNum	dbINTEGER	Integer	2

* Indicates the key fields

FIGURE 10.13.
The SalesItems table screen.

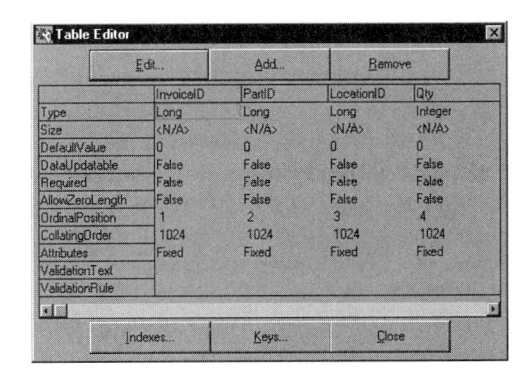

After you have created the table, close the table window. Select the table, and click the Open button. This will display all the fields of the database. Click the Add button for each record in Table 10.9, and enter the information. Once you have entered the information, close the window and create the next table.

Table 10.9. SalesItems table sample data.

InvoiceID	PartID	LocationID	Qty	Desc	FinalPrice	LineNum
25	1	1	1		19.9500	1
25	4	1	23		56.3500	2
25	3	1	3		119.8500	3
26	1	1	26	PlainWidget with a twist	518.7000	1
27	1	1	13	PlainWidget	20.0000	1
27	3	1	12		25.0000	2
26	3	1	6		0.0000	2
26	4	1	5		0.0000	3
24	3	1	7	AdvancedWidget	20.0000	1
24	4	1	1		26.0000	2
28	1	1	1		19.9500	1
29	1	1	9		179.5500	1
30	2	1	5		149.7500	1

Building the PseudoServer Table

The PseudoServer table consists of a series of flags. The PseudoServer client sets these flags, and other clients can read or reset them. The PseudoServer can do complex queries and other processes, and it can summarize this data for the other clients. For example, the Purchasing client needs to know only that items must be reordered. The client does not need to do an extensive check each time. Instead, a single variable, set by the Pseudo Server, can be examined by the client.

Build this table in the same way as you constructed the Sales table. The table definition in Table 10.10 lists the field name, the constant type, the field type, and the field length. For most of the fields, the size is unimportant because the data type has a predetermined size. For example, Long is 4 bytes.

After you have constructed the table, the Data Manager window should look roughly like the one shown in Figure 10.14. Don't forget to put an index on the key field for speed. Enter the sample data that the client programs will use.

Table 10.10. PseudoServer table definition.

Field Name	Constant Type	Field Type	Field Length
*ID	dbLONG	Long	4
DiskSpaceStatus	dbDOUBLE	Double	8
InventoryStatus	dbDOUBLE	Double	8
DelinquentAccount	dbTEXT	TextString	1

* Indicates the key field

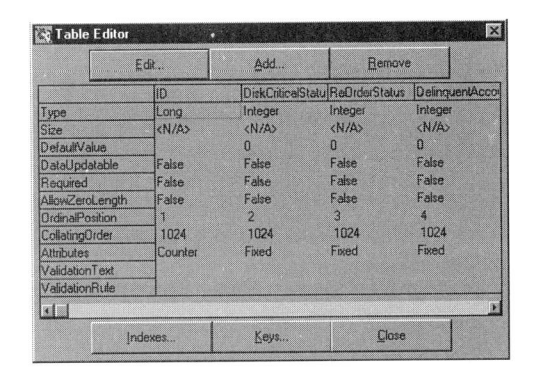

FIGURE 10.14.
The PServer table screen.

After you have created the table, close the table window. Select the table, and click the Open button. This will display all the fields of the database. Click the Add button for each record in Table 10.11, and enter the information. Once you have entered the information, close the window and create the next table.

Table 10.11. PseudoServer table sample data.

ID	DiskCriticalStatus	ReOrderStatus	DelinquentAccounts
1	0	−1	0

Building the Counter table

The Counter table consists of many long integer values that are kept for some of the individual tables. Counters are kept to track the largest invoice numbers, part numbers, and purchase order numbers. Some simpler client/server systems count the number of records that exist and create the new entry from this number. This procedure can cause many problems if records are deleted.

Suppose, for example, that a table contains three records labeled 1, 2, and 3. When a fourth record is inserted, it would be labeled 4. However, if record 2 is deleted and a new record is added, the fourth record added would be labeled 3. This means that two records would be labeled 3, which violates the requirement that each label in a primary key filed must be unique. You must, therefore, use a different type of counter.

Access provides an automatic counter field, which automatically tracks and assigns a unique number to each record so that individual programs don't have to supply this function. This automatic counter is not upsizable to the SQL Server. Therefore, you must use your own table to track the unique ID numbers for all the clients.

Build this table in the same way as you constructed the Sales table. The table definition in Table 10.12 lists the field name, the constant type, the field type, and the field length. For most of the fields, the size is unimportant because the data type has a predetermined size. For example, Long is 4 bytes.

After you have constructed the table, the Data Manager window should look roughly like the one shown in Figure 10.15. Don't forget to put an index on the key field for speed. Enter the sample data that the client programs will use.

Table 10.12. Counter table definition.

Field Name	Constant Type	Field Type	Field Length
*ID	dbLONG	Long	4
TableName	dbTEXT	TextString	50
CountNum	dbLONG	Long	4

* Indicates the key field

FIGURE 10.15.
The Counter table screen.

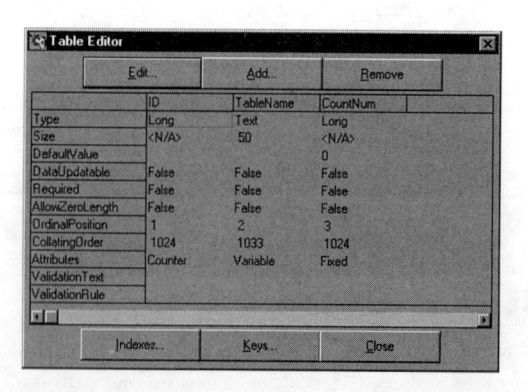

After you have created the table, close the table window. Select the table, and click the Open button. This will display all the fields of the database. Click the Add button for each record in Table 10.13, and enter the information. Once you have entered the information, close the window and create the next table.

Table 10.13. Counter table sample data.

ID	TableName	CountNum
1	Sales	31
2	Customer	16
3	SalesItems	1
4	Supplier	14
5	Purchase	13
7	Inventory_Sales	6
8	Inventory_Parts	5
9	Location	3

Building the Assembly Table

The Assembly table holds all the references to the parts contained in the Inventory table that must be assembled to create a single unit, which will be placed in the Inventory_Sales table. By using these records to reference both the Inventory_Parts and the Inventory_Sales tables, information such as the total unit cost per assembled item can be determined.

Build this table in the same way as you constructed the Sales table. The table definition in Table 10.14 lists the field name, the constant type, the field type, and the field length. For most of the fields, the size is unimportant because the data type has a predetermined size. For example, Long is 4 bytes.

After you have constructed the table, the Data Manager window should look roughly like the one shown in Figure 10.16. Don't forget to put an index on the key field for speed. Enter the sample data that the client programs will use.

Table 10.14. Assembly Table definition.

Field Name	Constant Type	Field Type	Field Length
*PartID_Sales	dbLONG	Long	4
*PartID_Parts	dbLONG	Long	4
Qty	dbINTEGER	Integer	2

* Indicates the key fields

After you have created the table, close the table window. Select the table, and click the Open button. This will display all the fields of the database. Click the Add button for each record in Table 10.15, and enter the information. Once you have entered the information, close the window and create the next table.

FIGURE 10.16.
The Assembly table screen.

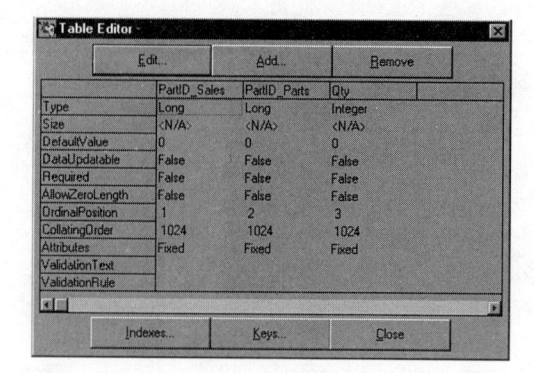

Table 10.15. Assembly table sample data.

PartID_Sales	PartID_Parts	Qty
1	1	5
1	2	10
2	2	4
3	3	3
4	2	7
3	2	5
3	1	4
4	3	1

Building the Customer Table

The Customer table contains all the information on every customer to whom a sales is made through the Sales client. This table contains the company name, contact name, address, phone number, fax number, notes, and several flags regarding the customer's account.

Note that the phone number and ZIP code, traditionally stored as number fields, are here stored as text strings. This is done to add flexibility to the field. For example, the ZIP code for a particular customer might instead be a postal code used in Canada which uses alphanumerics (letters) in the code. A number field would make placing a postal code in this field impossible. Likewise, a phone number field can store letters for a number such as 1-800-FLOWERS.

Build this table in the same way as you constructed the Sales table. The table definition in Table 10.16 lists the field name, the constant type, the field type, and the field length. For most of the fields, the size is unimportant because the data type has a predetermined size. For example, Long is 4 bytes.

After you have constructed the table, the Data Manager window should look roughly like the one shown in Figure 10.17. Don't forget to put an index on the key field for speed. Enter the sample data that the client programs will use.

Table 10.16. Customer table definition.

Field Name	Constant Type	Field Type	Field Length
*CustomerID	dbLONG	Long	4
Company	dbTEXT	TextString	50
LastName	dbTEXT	TextString	50
FirstName	dbTEXT	TextString	30
Title	dbTEXT	TextString	30
Address	dbTEXT	TextString	60
City	dbTEXT	TextString	20
State	dbTEXT	TextString	2
Zip	dbTEXT	TextString	10
Country	dbTEXT	TextString	15
Phone	dbTEXT	TextString	24
FaxPhone	dbTEXT	TextString	24
Terms	dbINTEGER	Integer	2
Notes	dbMEMO	Memo	0

* Indicates the key field

After you have created the table, close the table window. Select the table, and click the Open button. This will display all the fields of the database. Click the Add button for each record in Table 10.17 at the end of the chapter, and enter the information. Once you have entered the information, close the window and create the next table.

FIGURE 10.17.
The Customer table screen.

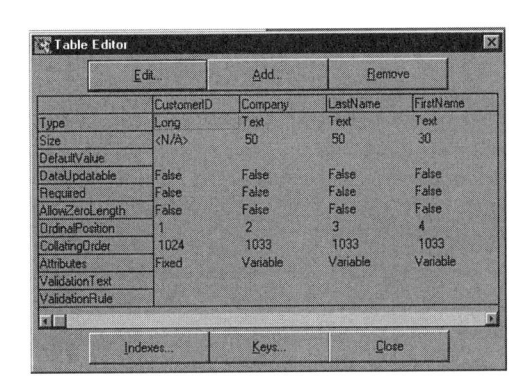

Building the Supplier Table

The Supplier table is nearly identical to the Customer table in respect to the information that it contains. These two tables are often combined into a single table with a field specifying the entry type. For instance, Entry_Type = Customer and Entry_Type = Supplier.

We recommend splitting the tables for the sake of security. Rarely do the users in the Manufacturing or Purchasing departments need to know the names and addresses of the customers, and the Sales department rarely needs to know the information about the suppliers. By separating the information into two different tables, access can be given on a case-by-case basis.

Build this table in the same way as you constructed the Sales table. The table definition in Table 10.18 lists the field name, the constant type, the field type, and the field length. For most of the fields, the size is unimportant because the data type has a predetermined size. For example, Long is 4 bytes.

After you have constructed the table, the Data Manager window should look roughly like the one shown in Figure 10.18. Don't forget to put an index on the key field for speed. Enter the sample data that the client programs will use.

Table 10.18. Supplier table definition.

Field Name	Constant Type	Field Type	Field Length
*SupplierID	dbLONG	Long	4
Company	dbTEXT	TextString	50
LastName	dbTEXT	TextString	50
FirstName	dbTEXT	TextString	30
Title	dbTEXT	TextString	30
Address	dbTEXT	TextString	60
City	dbTEXT	TextString	20
State	dbTEXT	TextString	2
Zip	dbTEXT	TextString	9
Country	dbTEXT	TextString	15
Phone	dbTEXT	TextString	24
FaxPhone	dbTEXT	TextString	24
Terms	dbINTEGER	Integer	2
Notes	dbMEMO	Memo	0

* Indicates the key field

After you have created the table, close the table window. Select the table, and click the Open button. This will display all the fields of the database. Click the Add button for each record in

Table 10.19 at the end of this chapter, and enter the information. Once you have entered the information, close the window and create the next table.

FIGURE 10.18.
The Supplier table screen.

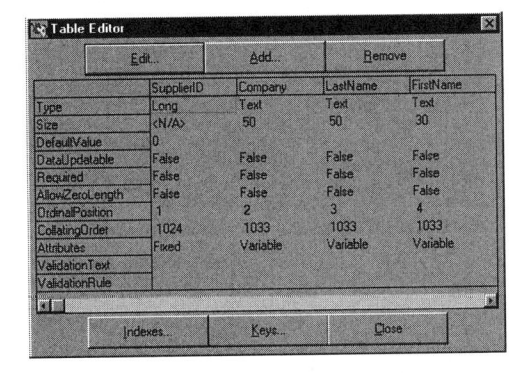

Building the Purchase Table

The Purchase table holds the general information for each purchase order. It operates much like the Sales client, and it is integrated with the PurchaseItems table. The Purchase table contains the overall data on a purchase order, whereas the PurchaseItems table retains all the line items. Both tables are related by the primary key PurchaseID. The Purchase table contains fields such as the ID of the supplier to whom the PO will be issued, the bill date, sale date, creation date, and the ship date.

Build this table in the same way as you constructed the Sales table. The table definition in Table 10.20 lists the field name, the constant type, the field type, and the field length. For most of the fields, the size is unimportant because the data type has a predetermined size. For example, Long is 4 bytes.

After you have constructed the table, the Data Manager window should look roughly like the one shown in Figure 10.19. Don't forget to put an index on the key field for speed. Enter the sample data that the client programs will use.

Table 10.20. Purchase Table definition.

Field Name	Constnat Type	Field Type	Field Length
*PurchaseID	dbLONG	Long	4
SaleDate	dbDATE	Date/Time Variant	8
StaffID	dbLONG	Long	4
SupplierID	dbLONG	Long	4
Freight	dbCURRENCY	Currency Double	8
CreateDate	dbDATE	Date/Time Variant	8

continues

Table 10.20. continued

Field Name	Constnat Type	Field Type	Field Length
ShipDate	dbDATE	Date/Time Variant	8
BillDate	dbDATE	Date/Time Variant	8
ShippingTo	dbTEXT	TextString	200
Terms	dbINTEGER	Integer	2
CustomerPO	dbTEXT	TextString	20

* Indicates the key field

After you have created the table, close the table window. Select the table, and click the Open button. This will display all the fields of the database. Click the Add button for each record in Table 10.21 at the end of this chapter, and enter the information. Once you have entered the information, close the window and create the next table.

FIGURE 10.19.
The Purchase table screen.

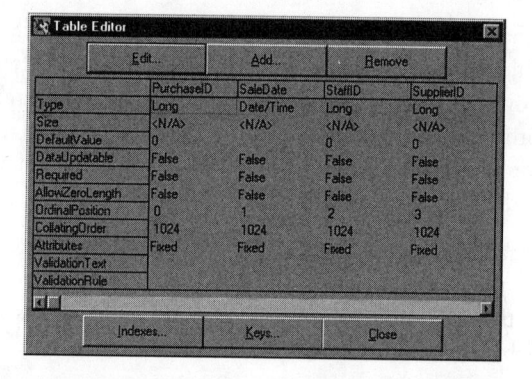

Building the PurchaseItems Table

The PurchaseItems table contains all the line items for each purchase order (see Figure 10.20). Each line item has two user override fields: FinalPrice and Description. The FinalPrice field is automatically calculated by multiplying the quantity by the unit cost, or the user can input a custom price. The Description field remains null unless the user modifies the description from the Inventory_Parts database. In that case, the edited description is saved with the line item.

Build this table in the same way as you constructed the Sales table. The table definition in Table 10.22 lists the field name, the constant type, the field type, and the field length. For most of the fields, the size is unimportant because the data type has a predetermined size. For example, Long is 4 bytes.

After you have constructed the table, the Data Manager window should look roughly like the one shown in Figure 10.21. Don't forget to put an index on the key field for speed. Enter the sample data that the client programs will use.

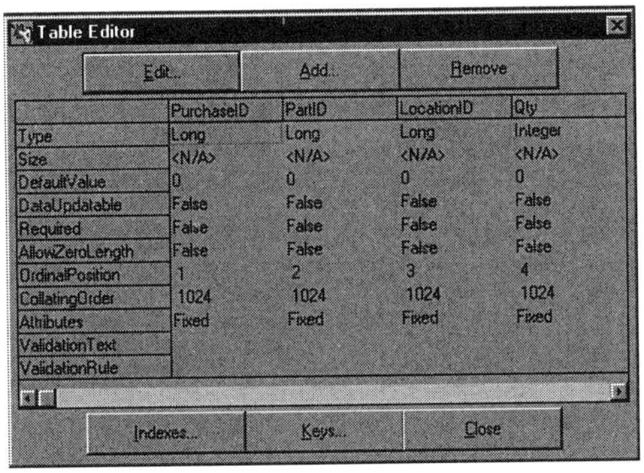

FIGURE 10.20.
The PurchaseItems table screen.

Table 10.22. PurchaseItems Table Definition

Field Name	Constant Type	Field Type	Field Length
*PurchaseID	dbLONG	Long	4
*PartID	dbLONG	Long	4
LocationID	dbLONG	Long	4
Qty	dbINTEGER	Integer	2
Desc	dbTEXT	TextString	50
FinalPrice	dbCURRENCY	Currency Double	8
*LineNum	dbINTEGER	Integer	2
Shipped	dbLONG	Long	4

* Indicates the key fields

After you have created the table, close the table window. Select the table, and click the Open button. This will display all the fields of the database. Click the Add button for each record in Table 10.23 at the end of the chapter, and enter the information. Once you have entered the information, close the window and create the next table.

Building the Location Table

The Location table holds all the locations owned by the enterprise. A single company might have a retail store, a warehouse, management offices, and branch offices. Sales, purchases, expenses, and inventories are often evaluated on a store-by-store basis. For this reason, the location table can be used to store locations. The INI file of each client program contains the default location that the client will save on the forms.

Build this table in the same way as you constructed the Sales table. The table definition in Table 10.24 lists the field name, the constant type, the field type, and the field length. For most of the fields, the size is unimportant because the data type has a predetermined size. For example, Long is 4 bytes.

After you have constructed the table, the Data Manager window should look roughly like the one shown in Figure 10.21. Don't forget to put an index on the key field for speed. Enter the sample data that the client programs will use.

Table 10.24. Location table definition.

Field Name	Constant Type	Field Type	Field Length
*LocationID	dbLONG	Long	4
Description	dbTEXT	TextString	100
Address	dbTEXT	TextString	50
City	dbTEXT	TextString	50
State	dbTEXT	TextString	2
Zip	dbTEXT	TextString	9
Phone	dbTEXT	TextString	50
Type	dbTEXT	TextString	3

* Indicates the key field

FIGURE 10.21.
Location table screen.

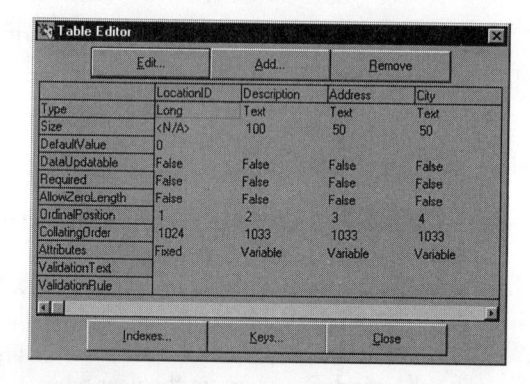

After you have created the table, close the table window. Select the table, and click the Open button. This will display all the fields of the database. Click the Add button for each record in Table 10.25 at the end of the chapter, and enter the information. Once you have entered the information, close the window and create the next table.

Building the Staff Table

The Staff table contains information on the employees within the organization, such as name, address, and phone.

The Staff table is different from the other tables in that it relates to itself. The Supervisor field can hold the StaffID of the current employee's supervisor. This makes the reference an internal table reference, also called a self-join. This type of relation is often not recommended in normalization guidelines because looping, integrity faults, and other problems are possible. In this case, though, it enables the table to roughly show the management hierarchy.

Build this table in the same way as you constructed the Sales table. The table definition in Table 10.26 lists the field name, the constant type, the field type, and the field length. For most of the fields, the size is unimportant because the data type has a predetermined size. For example, Long is 4 bytes.

After you have constructed the table, the Data Manager window should look roughly like the one shown in Figure 10.22. Don't forget to put an index on the key field for speed. Enter the sample data that the client programs will use.

Table 10.26. Staff Table definition.

Field Name	Constant Type	Field Type	Field Length
*StaffID	dbLONG	Long	4
LastName	dbTEXT	TextString	50
FirstName	dbTEXT	TextString	30
HireDate	dbDATE	Date/Time Variant	8
LocationID	dbLONG	Long	4
Supervisor	dbLONG	Long	4
HomeAddress	dbTEXT	TextString	60
HomeCity	dbTEXT	TextString	30
HomeState	dbTEXT	TextString	2
HomeZip	dbTEXT	TextString	10
HomePhone	dbTEXT	TextString	24
Extension	dbTEXT	TextString	4
SSN	dbTEXT	TextString	11
Salary	dbCURRENCY	Currency Double	8
Commission	dbDOUBLE	Double	8
Notes	dbMEMO	Memo	0

* Indicates the key field

After you have created the table, close the table window. Select the table, and click the Open button. This will display all the fields of the database. Click the Add button for each record in Table 10.27 at the end of the chapter, and enter the information. Once you have entered the information, close the window and create the next table.

FIGURE 10.22.
The Staff table screen.

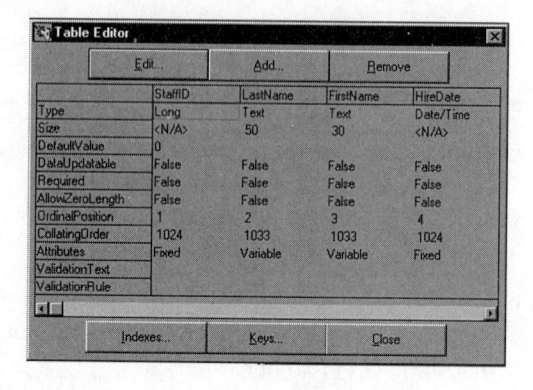

Visual Basic Code

In many instances, using an automated table-creation program offers greater advantages than creating the data structure by hand. A program like this can be reused, and it can create the same tables in many different database formats and database servers. For this reason, we have included automated routines that use Visual Basic commands to create the 13 tables in this chapter.

> **NOTE**
>
> These routines do not add the sample data. You must still do that by hand. You can use the Data Manager to enter the data, or you can use the specific tool included with the data source into which the tables will be written.

The routine that creates the tables is `MakeDB()`. It accepts a single parameter—the name of the database. In this case, the program calls the routine with the function command, as in `MakeDB("C:\CLNTSRVR\WIDGETCO.MDB")`. Add this routine to a simple form, and call it when a command button is clicked. All the tables will be automatically created and formatted.

Listing 10.1 shows the `MakeDB()` routine. It uses the `ExecuteSQL` command to implement the creation. This command is useful for sending SQL commands that do not require a resultant set to be returned.

Listing 10.1. The `MakeDB()` routine.

```
Sub MakeDB (cDBName As String)
    Dim db        As Database
    Dim tDef      As New TableDef
    Dim cSQL      As String
    Dim qd        As QueryDef
```

Chapter 10 ■ Table Construction

```
    On Error GoTo CreateError

    Set db = CreateDatabase(cDBName, dbLANG_GENERAL)

    '*** TABLE: Assembly ***
    cSQL = "CREATE TABLE [Assembly] ("
    cSQL = cSQL + "[PartID_Sales] LONG,"
    cSQL = cSQL + "[PartID_Parts] LONG,"
    cSQL = cSQL + "[Qty] SHORT"
    cSQL = cSQL + ")"
    db.Execute cSQL

    cSQL = "CREATE UNIQUE INDEX [PrimaryKey] ON [Assembly] ([PartID_Sales],
➥[PartID_Parts]) WITH PRIMARY"
    db.Execute cSQL



    '*** TABLE: Counter ***
    cSQL = "CREATE TABLE [Counter] ("
    cSQL = cSQL + "[ID] COUNTER,"
    cSQL = cSQL + "[TableName] TEXT( 50),"
    cSQL = cSQL + "[CountNum] LONG"
    cSQL = cSQL + ")"
    db.Execute cSQL

    cSQL = "CREATE UNIQUE INDEX [PrimaryKey] ON [Counter] ([ID]) WITH PRIMARY"
    db.Execute cSQL


    '*** TABLE: Customer ***
    cSQL = "CREATE TABLE [Customer] ("
    cSQL = cSQL + "[CustomerID] LONG,"
    cSQL = cSQL + "[Company] TEXT( 50),"
    cSQL = cSQL + "[LastName] TEXT( 50),"
    cSQL = cSQL + "[FirstName] TEXT( 30),"
    cSQL = cSQL + "[Title] TEXT( 30),"
    cSQL = cSQL + "[Address] TEXT( 60),"
    cSQL = cSQL + "[City] TEXT( 20),"
    cSQL = cSQL + "[State] TEXT( 2),"
    cSQL = cSQL + "[Zip] TEXT( 10),"
    cSQL = cSQL + "[Country] TEXT( 15),"
    cSQL = cSQL + "[Phone] TEXT( 24),"
    cSQL = cSQL + "[FaxPhone] TEXT( 24),"
    cSQL = cSQL + "[Terms] SHORT,"
    cSQL = cSQL + "[Notes] LONGTEXT"
    cSQL = cSQL + ")"
    db.Execute cSQL



    '*** TABLE: Inventory_Parts ***
    cSQL = "CREATE TABLE [Inventory_Parts] ("
    cSQL = cSQL + "[PartID] LONG,"
    cSQL = cSQL + "[Description] TEXT( 50),"
    cSQL = cSQL + "[OnHand] SHORT,"
    cSQL = cSQL + "[LocationID] SHORT,"
```

continues

Listing 10.1. continued

```
    cSQL = cSQL + "[UnitCost] CURRENCY,"
    cSQL = cSQL + "[ReorderQty] SHORT,"
    cSQL = cSQL + "[ReorderDate] DATETIME,"
    cSQL = cSQL + "[BackOrdered] SHORT,"
    cSQL = cSQL + "[Reserved] LONG,"
    cSQL = cSQL + "[LastResvTime] DATETIME,"
    cSQL = cSQL + "[Notes] LONGTEXT"
    cSQL = cSQL + ")"
    db.Execute cSQL

    cSQL = "CREATE UNIQUE INDEX [PrimaryKey] ON [Inventory_Parts] ([PartID]) WITH
➥PRIMARY"
    db.Execute cSQL

'*** TABLE: Inventory_Sales ***
    cSQL = "CREATE TABLE [Inventory_Sales] ("
    cSQL = cSQL + "[PartID] LONG,"
    cSQL = cSQL + "[Description] TEXT( 50),"
    cSQL = cSQL + "[OnHand] LONG,"
    cSQL = cSQL + "[LocationID] LONG,"
    cSQL = cSQL + "[UnitCost] CURRENCY,"
    cSQL = cSQL + "[Discontinued] BIT,"
    cSQL = cSQL + "[Inventoried] BIT,"
    cSQL = cSQL + "[Reserved] LONG,"
    cSQL = cSQL + "[LastResvTime] DATETIME,"
    cSQL = cSQL + "[ReorderQty] SHORT,"
    cSQL = cSQL + "[Notes] LONGTEXT"
    cSQL = cSQL + ")"
    db.Execute cSQL


'*** TABLE: Location ***
    cSQL = "CREATE TABLE [Location] ("
    cSQL = cSQL + "[LocationID] LONG,"
    cSQL = cSQL + "[Description] TEXT( 100),"
    cSQL = cSQL + "[Address] TEXT( 50),"
    cSQL = cSQL + "[City] TEXT( 50),"
    cSQL = cSQL + "[State] TEXT( 2),"
    cSQL = cSQL + "[Zip] TEXT( 9),"
    cSQL = cSQL + "[Phone] TEXT( 50),"
    cSQL = cSQL + "[Type] TEXT( 3)"
    cSQL = cSQL + ")"
    db.Execute cSQL

    cSQL = "CREATE UNIQUE INDEX [PrimaryKey] ON [Location] ([LocationID]) WITH
➥PRIMARY"
    db.Execute cSQL


'*** TABLE: PServer ***
    cSQL = "CREATE TABLE [PServer] ("
    cSQL = cSQL + "[ID] COUNTER,"
    cSQL = cSQL + "[DiskCriticalStatus] SHORT,"
    cSQL = cSQL + "[ReOrderStatus] SHORT,"
    cSQL = cSQL + "[DelinquentAccounts] SHORT"
    cSQL = cSQL + ")"
    db.Execute cSQL
```

Chapter 10 ■ Table Construction

```
    cSQL = "CREATE UNIQUE INDEX [PrimaryKey] ON [PServer] ([ID]) WITH PRIMARY"
    db.Execute cSQL


    '*** TABLE: Purchase ***
    cSQL = "CREATE TABLE [Purchase] ("
    cSQL = cSQL + "[PurchaseID] LONG,"
    cSQL = cSQL + "[SaleDate] DATETIME,"
    cSQL = cSQL + "[StaffID] LONG,"
    cSQL = cSQL + "[SupplierID] LONG,"
    cSQL = cSQL + "[Freight] CURRENCY,"
    cSQL = cSQL + "[CreateDate] DATETIME,"
    cSQL = cSQL + "[ShipDate] DATETIME,"
    cSQL = cSQL + "[BillDate] DATETIME,"
    cSQL = cSQL + "[ShippingTo] TEXT( 200),"
    cSQL = cSQL + "[Terms] SHORT,"
    cSQL = cSQL + "[CustomerPO] TEXT( 20)"
    cSQL = cSQL + ")"
    db.Execute cSQL

    cSQL = "CREATE UNIQUE INDEX [PrimaryKey] ON [Purchase] ([PurchaseID]) WITH
➥PRIMARY"
    db.Execute cSQL


  '*** TABLE: PurchaseItems ***
    cSQL = "CREATE TABLE [PurchaseItems] ("
    cSQL = cSQL + "[PurchaseID] LONG,"
    cSQL = cSQL + "[PartID] LONG,"
    cSQL = cSQL + "[LocationID] LONG,"
    cSQL = cSQL + "[Qty] SHORT,"
    cSQL = cSQL + "[Desc] TEXT( 50),"
    cSQL = cSQL + "[FinalPrice] CURRENCY,"
    cSQL = cSQL + "[LineNum] SHORT,"
    cSQL = cSQL + "[Shipped] LONG"
    cSQL = cSQL + ")"
    db.Execute cSQL

    cSQL = "CREATE INDEX [InvoiceID] ON [PurchaseItems] ([PurchaseID])"
    db.Execute cSQL
    cSQL = "CREATE UNIQUE INDEX [PrimaryKey] ON [PurchaseItems]
➥([PurchaseID],[PartID],[LineNum]) WITH PRIMARY"
    db.Execute cSQL


    '*** TABLE: Sales ***
    cSQL = "CREATE TABLE [Sales] ("
    cSQL = cSQL + "[InvoiceID] LONG,"
    cSQL = cSQL + "[SaleDate] DATETIME,"
    cSQL = cSQL + "[StaffID] LONG,"
    cSQL = cSQL + "[CustomerID] LONG,"
    cSQL = cSQL + "[Freight] CURRENCY,"
    cSQL = cSQL + "[CreateDate] DATETIME,"
    cSQL = cSQL + "[ShipDate] DATETIME,"
    cSQL = cSQL + "[BillDate] DATETIME,"
    cSQL = cSQL + "[ShippingTo] TEXT( 200),"
    cSQL = cSQL + "[Terms] SHORT,"
```

continues

Listing 10.1. continued

```
    cSQL = cSQL + "[CustomerPO] TEXT( 20)"
    cSQL = cSQL + ")"
    db.Execute cSQL

    cSQL = "CREATE UNIQUE INDEX [PrimaryKey] ON [Sales] ([InvoiceID]) WITH PRIMARY"
    db.Execute cSQL


'*** TABLE: SalesItems ***
    cSQL = "CREATE TABLE [SalesItems] ("
    cSQL = cSQL + "[InvoiceID] LONG,"
    cSQL = cSQL + "[PartID] LONG,"
    cSQL = cSQL + "[LocationID] LONG,"
    cSQL = cSQL + "[Qty] SHORT,"
    cSQL = cSQL + "[Desc] TEXT( 50),"
    cSQL = cSQL + "[FinalPrice] CURRENCY,"
    cSQL = cSQL + "[LineNum] SHORT"
    cSQL = cSQL + ")"
    db.Execute cSQL

    cSQL = "CREATE INDEX [InvoiceID] ON [SalesItems] ([InvoiceID])"
    db.Execute cSQL
    cSQL = "CREATE UNIQUE INDEX [PrimaryKey] ON [SalesItems]
➥([InvoiceID],[PartID],[LineNum]) WITH PRIMARY"
    db.Execute cSQL


'*** TABLE: Staff ***
    cSQL = "CREATE TABLE [Staff] ("
    cSQL = cSQL + "[StaffID] LONG,"
    cSQL = cSQL + "[LastName] TEXT( 50),"
    cSQL = cSQL + "[FirstName] TEXT( 30),"
    cSQL = cSQL + "[HireDate] DATETIME,"
    cSQL = cSQL + "[LocationID] LONG,"
    cSQL = cSQL + "[Supervisor] LONG,"
    cSQL = cSQL + "[HomeAddress] TEXT( 60),"
    cSQL = cSQL + "[HomeCity] TEXT( 30),"
    cSQL = cSQL + "[HomeState] TEXT( 2),"
    cSQL = cSQL + "[HomeZip] TEXT( 10),"
    cSQL = cSQL + "[HomePhone] TEXT( 24),"
    cSQL = cSQL + "[Extension] TEXT( 4),"
    cSQL = cSQL + "[SSN] TEXT( 11),"
    cSQL = cSQL + "[Salary] CURRENCY,"
    cSQL = cSQL + "[Commision] DOUBLE,"
    cSQL = cSQL + "[Notes] LONGTEXT"
    cSQL = cSQL + ")"
    db.Execute cSQL

    cSQL = "CREATE UNIQUE INDEX [PrimaryKey] ON [Staff] ([StaffID]) WITH PRIMARY"
    db.Execute cSQL

'*** TABLE: Supplier ***
    cSQL = "CREATE TABLE [Supplier] ("
    cSQL = cSQL + "[SupplierID] LONG,"
    cSQL = cSQL + "[Company] TEXT( 50),"
    cSQL = cSQL + "[LastName] TEXT( 50),"
    cSQL = cSQL + "[FirstName] TEXT( 30),"
```

```
    cSQL = cSQL + "[Title] TEXT( 30),"
    cSQL = cSQL + "[Address] TEXT( 60),"
    cSQL = cSQL + "[City] TEXT( 20),"
    cSQL = cSQL + "[State] TEXT( 2),"
    cSQL = cSQL + "[Zip] TEXT( 9),"
    cSQL = cSQL + "[Country] TEXT( 15),"
    cSQL = cSQL + "[Phone] TEXT( 24),"
    cSQL = cSQL + "[FaxPhone] TEXT( 24),"
    cSQL = cSQL + "[Terms] SHORT,"
    cSQL = cSQL + "[Notes] LONGTEXT"
    cSQL = cSQL + ")"
    db.Execute cSQL

    cSQL = "CREATE UNIQUE INDEX [PrimaryKey] ON [Supplier] ([SupplierID]) WITH
➥PRIMARY"
    db.Execute cSQL

    db.Close

    Exit Sub

CreateError:
    MsgBox "Could not create database: " + Error$, 16
    Exit Sub
End Sub
```

Summary

If you have followed through with the actions from this chapter, the tables are complete and the sample data has been entered. You now can construct the client applications. Each client program functions separately, but all the applications work together to form a complete system by using the common database. Although you can create the clients in any order, we do not recommend it. The client applications in this book build on the concepts of the others. Each one employs new features and Visual Basic techniques.

> **WARNING**
>
> If you do decide not to construct one of the client programs, make sure that you create the Global.BAS module and the ITEM.FRM files are described in Chapter 11, "Sales client." These files are shared and used by all the clients. Because of the sample data that you entered in this chapter, all the clients can execute without any additional data.

Table 10.3. Sales table sample data.

InvoiceID	SaleDate	StaffID	CustomerID	Freight	CreateDate
24	5/26/95 0:00:00	1	6		5/26/95 17:01:22
25	5/29/95 0:00:00	2	6	3.0000	5/29/95 0:12:57
26	5/29/95 0:00:00	1	4	3.0000	5/29/95 0:13:58
27	5/29/95 0:00:00	2	3	3.0000	5/29/95 11:23:45
28	5/29/95 0:00:00	1	8	3.0000	5/29/95 16:06:11
29	5/30/95 0:00:00	2	6	3.0000	5/30/95 18:04:42
30	6/1/95 0:00:00	1	9	8.0000	6/1/95 16:43:56

Table 10.5. Inventory_Sales table sample data.

PartID	Description	OnHand	LocationID	UnitCost
1	PlainWidget	1	0	19.9500
2	Special Widget	20	0	29.9500
3	AdvancedWidget	92	0	39.9500
4	Tapes	44	0	2.4500
5	Roasty Toasty	0	0	10.0000

Table 10.7. Inventory_Parts table sample data.

PartID	Description	OnHand	LocationID	UnitCost
1	Large Spanner	17	0	3.0000
3	Crank	3	0	5.6500
2	Whistle	92	0	0.9700
4	Sky Hook	0	0	2.0000

Chapter 10 ■ Table Construction

ShipDate	BillDate	ShippingTo	Terms	CustomerPO
		Taylor,John 761 Tremor St. San Francisco, CA 98075	0	
		Taylor,John 761 Tremor St. San Francisco, CA 98075	0	
		Smithy,John 206 N. Wincott Ave. Pawling, NY 12564-1409	0	
5/29/95 0:00:00	5/30/95 0:00:00	Manufacture Unlimited, Inc. PO Box 85608 San Diego, CA 92186-9784	1	1245
		Hartman,Phil,	0	
		Jones,George,	0	
		Hartman,Phil,	0	

Discontinued	Inventoried	Reserved	LastResvTime	ReorderQty	Notes
0	1	-3		50	
0	1	0		20	
0	1	0		100	
0	0	0		35	
0	0	0		5	This item is on backorder

ReorderQty	ReorderDate	BackOrdered	Reserved	LastResvTime	Notes
30					
10					
50					
			0		

Table 10.17. Customer table sample data.

CustomerID	Company	LastName	FirstName	Title	Address
1	Cutting Edge	Burt	Ron	CIO	2354 W. Covina
2	Interactive Multimedia	Goldman	Jonathan	Editor	955A McLean Dr.
3	Manufacture Unlimited, Inc.	Wagner	Phil	Division Head	PO Box 85608
4		Smithy	John		206 N. Wincott Ave.
5		Dog		Head Honcho	
6		Taylor	John		761 Tremor St.
7	WorldWide Resources	Phillips	Beth Ann	Sales Manager	1818 Mexico Way
8		Nakamura	Takahashi	Independent Consultant	
9	General Foods				Rte 1

Table 10.19. Supplier table sample data.

SupplierID	Company	LastName	FirstName	Title	Address
10	Wholesale Liquidators				2323 Hawthorne Lane
11		Appleseed	Johnny		8284 Virginia Ct.
12	Choise Enteprises				
13	Griffin Inc.	Joel	Griffin	Owner	555 Main Stewart Way D-14

City	State	Zip	Country	Phone	FaxPhone	Terms	Notes
Encinitas	CA	92024	USA	(619) 555-1234	(619) 555-1235	0	
Beumont	TX	77707	USA	(710) 555-7512		0	
San Diego	CA	92186-9784	USA	(619) 555-9724	(619) 555-9725	1	
Pawling	NY	12564-1409	USA	(432) 555-0023		0	
			USA			0	
San Francisco	CA	98075	USA	(803) 555-4903		0	
Dallas	TX	09876	USA	(708) 555-0992	(708) 555-0993	0	She is an extremely industrious person and a pleasure to work with.
			USA			0	
Orem	UT	84048-6418	USA			0	

City	State	Zip	Country	Phone	FaxPhone	Terms	Notes
Rancho Calmazoo	OR	87602	USA	714-555-6262		0	They call as soon as the bill is late. Make sure to pay on time.
Frevell	VI	43002	USA	810-555-2664		0	
						0	
Hinesville		GA	31313	USA	772-555-9251	0	

Table 10.21. Purchase table sample data.

PurchaseID	SaleDate	StaffID	SupplierID	Freight	CreateDate
10	5/30/95 0:00:00	1	10	3.0000	5/30/95 0:48:53
11	5/30/95 0:00:00	2	10	3.0000	5/30/95 19:22:28
12	6/11/95 0:00:00	1	10	3.0000	6/11/95 0:36:39

Table 10.23. PurchaseItems table sample data.

PurchaseID	PartID	LocationID	Qty	Desc
10	1	1	1	
10	2	1	1	
11	3	1	1	Crank-hello
12	3	1	5	
12	1	1	22	

Table 10.25. Location table sample data.

LocationID	Description	Address
1	San Diego Retail	2220 El Camino Real
2	San Diego Warehouse	2220 El Camino Real

Table 10.27. Staff table sample data.

StaffID	LastName	FirstName	HireDate	LocationID	Supervisor	HomeAddress	HomeCity
1	Wayne	John	5/5/94 0:00:00	0	0	1818 Sunset Blvd.	Hollywood
2	Bogart	Humphrey	5/9/94 0:00:00	0	0	1819 Sunset Blvd.	Hollywood

ShipDate	BillDate	ShippingTo	Terms	FOB
		Wholesale Liquidators,	0	
		Wholesale Liquidators		
		2323 Hawthorne Lane,	0	
6/15/95 0:00:00		Wholesale Liquidators		
		2323 Hawthorne Lane		
		Rancho Calmazoo, OR 87602	1	

FinalPrice	LineNum	Shipped
2.6500	1	0
0.9700	2	0
5.6500	1	0
5.6500	1	0
2.6500	2	0

City	State	Zip	Phone	Type
San Diego	CA	92007	(619) 555-6715	1
San Diego	CA	92007	(619) 555-7189	2

HomeState	HomeZip	HomePhone	Extension	SSN	Salary	Commission	Notes
CA		(310) 555-7862		563-67-9212	40000000.0000	0	
CA		(310) 555-9162		389-65-0861	35000000.0000	0	

11

Sales Client

Creating the Sales Client

The sales client provides a simple point-of-sale client program that you can run on one or more client machines. You create a sales invoice using standard Windows controls, and all of the information is saved into the central client/server database. (See Figure 11.1.) This client provides examples of database editing, relational synchronization, SQL statements, reservations to avoid multiple user interference, and front-end user interface interaction.

FIGURE 11.1.
The Invoice screen.

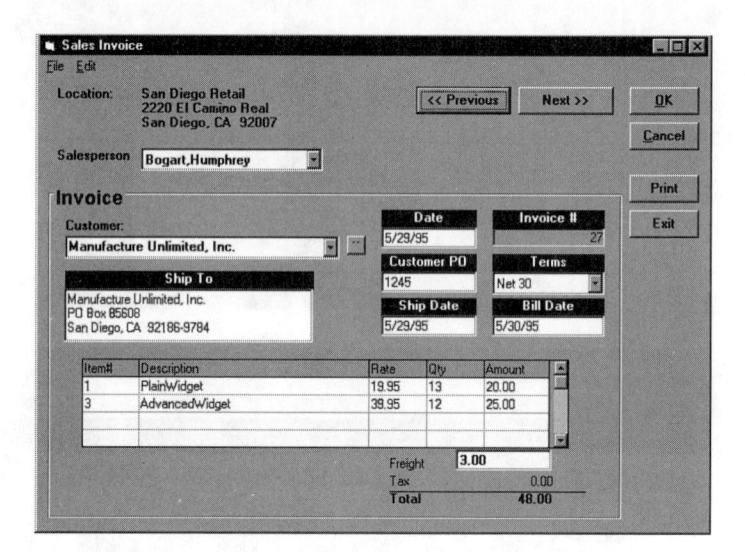

For each invoice, the user can select a customer from the customer list (the Customer table) or add a new customer. Much of the invoice information about the customer, such as the Ship To Address, is stored in the main database. This information is retrieved from the server (in this case, the database file) and placed in editable text fields, where the user can change it for each particular invoice.

The user can make changes to certain fields on the invoice that are saved only to that invoice. This information is not written back into the central database record. As a result, the user has the flexibility to address special-case situations without corrupting the central database.

For example, it is easy to add "Attn: Joe Smith" to the Ship To Address for printing on the current invoice. Doing this will not change the original Ship To Address stored with the customer record. Also, fields such as the Terms field are set to the default setting placed in the customer record, but the user can freely change them for each invoice. (See Figure 11.2.)

FIGURE 11.2.
The Terms popup.

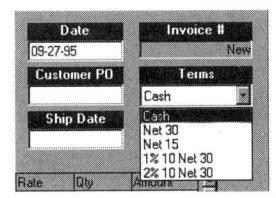

The user enters the individual items for each invoice by their item numbers. The data on each item is retrieved from the Sales Item list. (See Figure 11.3.) Once the information for a particular item is retrieved from the server, the user can edit most of the information (such as the Description) for additional comments or other reasons. The client program automatically enters the sales price and description found in the SalesInventory table.

FIGURE 11.3.
The Sales Item screen.

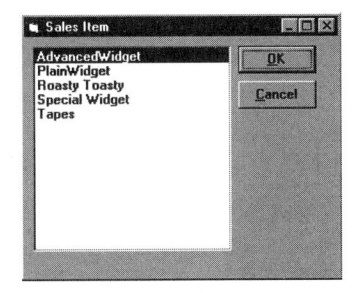

The user sets the quantity of the item, which defaults to 1 when an item is entered. The application automatically calculates the total and tax by multiplying the quantity by the unit price.

When the user enters a particular quantity for an item, the client program automatically reserves this number of items on the main database, subtracting the amount from the OnHand field. This practice ensures that another client does not sell these particular items while the main client completes the invoice. When the invoice is completed, the client program clears the reserved field because these units are sold and no longer in inventory.

Checking the number of inventoried items for any particular sales item is easy. The Sales Inventory form shows all the items contained in the Inventory_Sales table with their available quantities. (See Figure 11.4.) It also displays the minimum quantity that prompts a reorder (in the Purchasing client) of the item when the inventory dips too low. Note that reserved items do not appear in this list, so if a user creates and then cancels an invoice, the quantities increase.

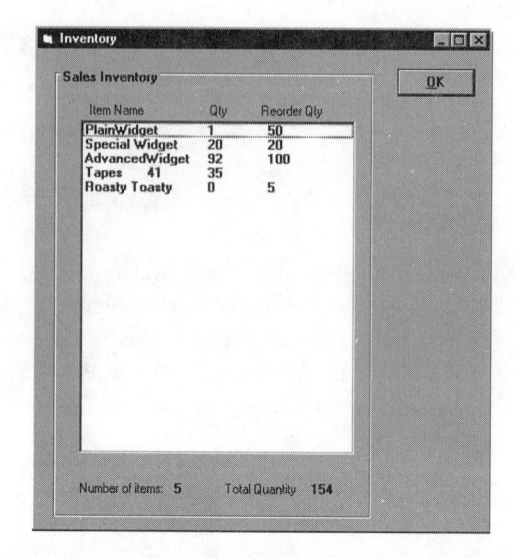

FIGURE 11.4.
The Sales Inventory screen.

> **NOTE**
>
> Usually, choosing Cancel returns the items to inventory. However, for our purposes, the sales client Cancel button does not return the items to inventory so we can demonstrate the Pseudo Server's timed capability to return forgotten reserves to inventory. For more information on the Pseudo Server, see Chapter 14, "Pseudo Server."

Once the invoice is completed, the user can click the OK button. The client program first checks the invoice to make sure the selected customer information is stored in the Customer table. If it isn't, the program requests that the user enter information about the new customer or choose a customer who is already in the database. (See Figure 11.5.)

After the customer name is confirmed, the sale items are confirmed. The client program will not save the invoice if it has any inaccurate entries (such as missing item numbers). The user is notified of the error and returned to the invoice.

Once all the entries in the invoice are appropriate, the various items of the invoice are stored to the database. All of the update operations that take place for this invoice are encapsulated within a single transaction. This ensures there are no partial updates of the database tables.

The client program clears the reserved items fields that are holding reserves for this invoice. The items have been sold and there is no further need to return them to inventory. Next, the client program stores the individual sales lines for the invoice and updates the invoice number and other information. After all the database updates have been completed, the transaction is committed.

FIGURE 11.5.
The Customer screen.

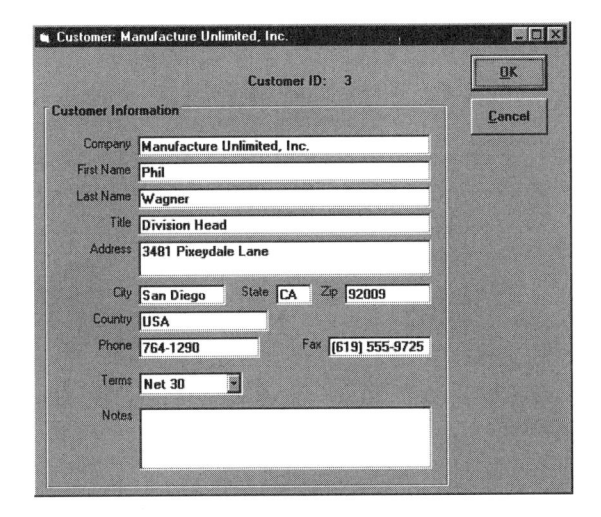

You can view and edit any previously entered invoices using the Next and Previous command buttons. Any modification to a stored invoice activates the OK button so you can save the new modifications.

The preceding description details how the user experiences the sales client program. As a client/server developer, you should understand not only how this program functions, but also what considerations you must make if multiple sales client programs will be accessing the same data. If you learn how all the pieces of this system work together, creating a consistent system is a much simpler process.

How the Sales Client Works

The sales client consists of five primary files:

> frm_Invoice (stored as SALES.FRM)—Primary form. Shows all invoice information, accepts user input, and enables individual invoice creation.
>
> frm_Item (stored as ITEM.FRM)—Displays various items stored in the SalesInventory table. The user can select items for insertion into the selected invoice.
>
> frm_Customer (stored as CUST.FRM)—Enables the user to add a new customer to the Customer table or edit the information of an existing one.
>
> frm_Inventory (stored as INVNTRY.FRM)—Shows all the existing Sales Inventory with descriptions, on-hand quantities, and reorder quantities.
>
> GLOBAL.BAS—Holds all the global code and variables for the program.

The sales project is named SALES.VBP and holds all five files. (See Figure 11.6.) The frm_Invoice form is the startup form that is first executed and displayed to the user. The startup form is set in the Project tab in the Options dialog box. The Options dialog box is available under the Tools menu. The user accesses all the other forms with menu options and command buttons.

FIGURE 11.6.
The Sales project.

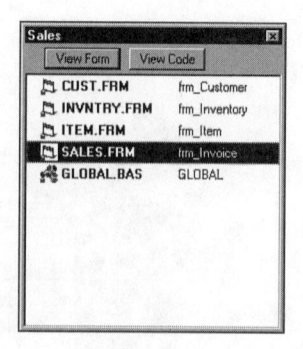

The sales client must have access to various tables constructed in Chapter 10, "Table Construction." When the client is first executed, it makes the connection with the particular database (in this case, the WIDGETCO.MDB). The .INI file for the application stores the information regarding the central database (in this case, the SALES.INI). The .INI stores the path of the central database.

All the data for each invoice is stored in the main database. When the user commits an invoice, the sales client writes the general invoice information to the Sales table. The individual line transactions are written to the SalesItems table.

The `OpenDatabase` command performs any writes to a data table. `OpenDatabase` creates a database object in memory connected to the specified database. The program must also pass the parameters that set `Exclusive` and `ReadOnly` to `FALSE` (all of the client programs need access to the database).

> **NOTE**
>
> As in other clients, the sales client uses the `OpenDatabase` command without any workspace information (such as `Set MyDb = OpenDatabase("WIDGETCO.MDB")`). Visual Basic provides the workspace information automatically. If you wanted a complete reference, it would look like the following:
>
> `Set MyDb = DBEngine.Workspaces(0).OpenDatabase("WIDGETCO.MDB")`
>
> A workspace reference is necessary when adding security to an application. In Chapter 16, "Access Security," a secure workspace is added when the client program logs onto the database.

When the Invoice form is first loaded, it creates a snapshot of the current Customer table. It uses the SQL command `ORDER BY` to automatically sort the various customer entries into alphabetical order. If there is no entry in the Company field, the program creates a LastName, FirstName field to sort by.

The program cycles through each of the Customer table records, adding the name of the customer to the combo box list and storing the customer's CustomerID field in the corresponding ItemData field. When the invoice entry is created, the client program doesn't have to requery the CustomerID because the information for all the names in the customer base is already in the table. The user can conveniently edit the information for a particular customer if he selects the ... button to the right of the combo box.

After the combo box is filled, its main edit field is set to `""`. if there is nothing in this field, the user can easily enter a new or existing customer's name or use the combo box to select an existing customer.

When the user selects a customer, the client program accesses the Customer table to read all of the pertinent information. Information such as the Ship To Address, Credit Terms, and the Customer PO fields are automatically entered into the appropriate fields on the invoice.

After all of this preliminary initialization, the program waits for user interaction. The user can then enter items into the `grd_Main` by choosing an item button or directly typing in an item number.

> **NOTE**
>
> You might notice that this sales client and other client programs do not use the `FindFirst` method to do a subsearch of a current dynaset. For example, if a dynaset contains all the inventory's parts, the program can use the `FindFirst` method to find a particular part record. Instead, these clients create a new dynaset subset of the original dynaset that contains only the record we need.
>
> The problem with using the `FindFirst` method is its incompatibility with the `SQL PassThrough` function. You cannot use the `FindFirst` method when the program is passing the SQL statements directly to the server. This dramatically limits the possible portability of an application. Keep this in mind while designing your client applications.
>
> Alternatives to using dynasets include using a specific `QueryDef` to find the resultant set or using the `SEEK` method on a single table. Check the documentation of the server you will be using to determine how these commands affect it.

Database Access

The sales client needs to access numerous related tables. (See Figure 11.7.) The diagram shows each table and how they are related. The client uses the Location, Staff, Sales, SalesItems, Customer, Inventory_Sales, and Counter tables.

FIGURE 11.7.
Sales client data access.

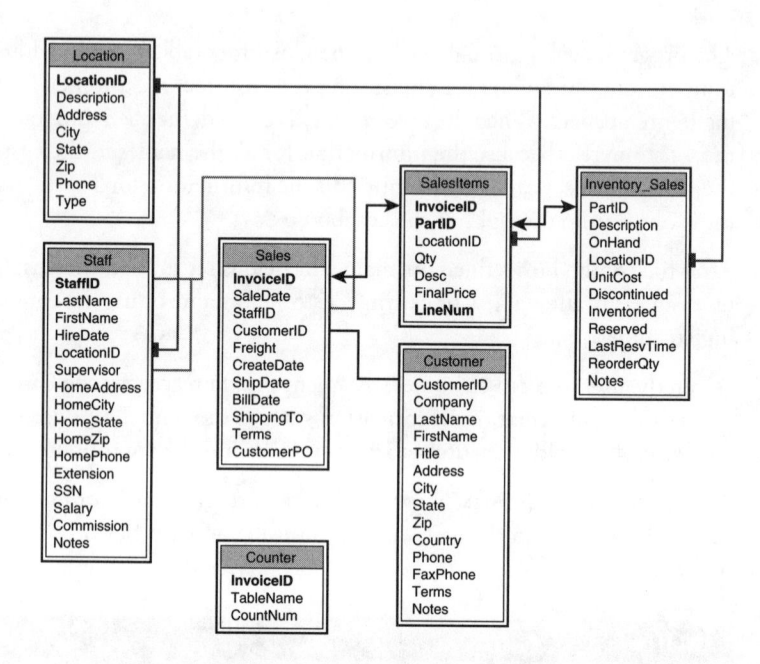

Location
- **LocationID**
- Description
- Address
- City
- State
- Zip
- Phone
- Type

Staff
- **StaffID**
- LastName
- FirstName
- HireDate
- LocationID
- Supervisor
- HomeAddress
- HomeCity
- HomeState
- HomeZip
- HomePhone
- Extension
- SSN
- Salary
- Commission
- Notes

Sales
- **InvoiceID**
- SaleDate
- StaffID
- CustomerID
- Freight
- CreateDate
- ShipDate
- BillDate
- ShippingTo
- Terms
- CustomerPO

SalesItems
- **InvoiceID**
- **PartID**
- LocationID
- Qty
- Desc
- FinalPrice
- **LineNum**

Customer
- CustomerID
- Company
- LastName
- FirstName
- Title
- Address
- City
- State
- Zip
- Country
- Phone
- FaxPhone
- Terms
- Notes

Inventory_Sales
- PartID
- Description
- OnHand
- LocationID
- UnitCost
- Discontinued
- Inventoried
- Reserved
- LastResvTime
- ReorderQty
- Notes

Counter
- **InvoiceID**
- TableName
- CountNum

All these tables are used by the Sales Invoice form. The Location field shows where the invoice is created. The Staff table stores the StaffID of the salesperson with each invoice. The Sales table holds each invoice, whereas the SalesItems table holds the individual line items of the invoice. The Customer table holds all of the customer information, and the CustomerID is stored with each invoice. The Counter table is not related to any of the tables directly but is used to store the incremental values (such as the last added invoice number, last item number, and so on). Finally, the Inventory_Sales contains the information of each item that can be sold.

The Item form accesses the Inventory_Sales table and enables the user to select an item. The Inventory form also displays the items from the Inventory_Sales table. The Customer form enables the user to view, edit, and add all of the customer records stored in the Customer table.

Starting the Sales Project

The sales client project in our example is stored in the directory C:\CS_VB\SALES. You should have already created the necessary directories as described in Chapter 10, "Table Construction." The finished .EXE and .INI files we create when the application is complete will be stored in the C:\CLNTSRVR\SALES directory.

> **NOTE**
>
> It is not important that you name your directories the same names we chose. However, make sure that the .INI file is stored in the same directory as the project. Each client program accesses the necessary information from the .INI file of the same name stored in the project directory. In a real world client application, the application's .INI file is placed in the \WINDOWS\ directory.

Creating the .INI File

Before we can execute the application, we must construct the .INI file. An .INI file is used to store various parameters about a given program, such as the type of database, the driver types, the directory of the stored database, and so forth.

> **NOTE**
>
> Microsoft encourages developers to use the Windows Registration file to store file information. At the present time, however, REGEDIT.EXE (the main program for editing registration variables) is fairly clumsy and difficult to use. Because client/server applications are often widely distributed, an .INI file provides a much more elegant solution. In the future, Microsoft might make the use of Windows Registration more effective, warranting its widespread use.

INI files are extremely useful because you can create and edit them with any text editor (such as the Notepad application included with Windows). You can keep several versions of an .INI file for various configurations and simply copy them into the correct directory to use them. Additionally, they can hold parameters (such as the database directory pathway) that you can easily change without adding complicated setup code for an application.

We create the .INI file using the Notepad utility found in the Accessories program group in Windows. (See Figure 11.8.) Note that the name of the .INI should match the name of the .EXE application file. For example, an application with a filename SALES.EXE should have an .INI file named SALES.INI.

FIGURE 11.8.
Notepad showing SALES.INI.

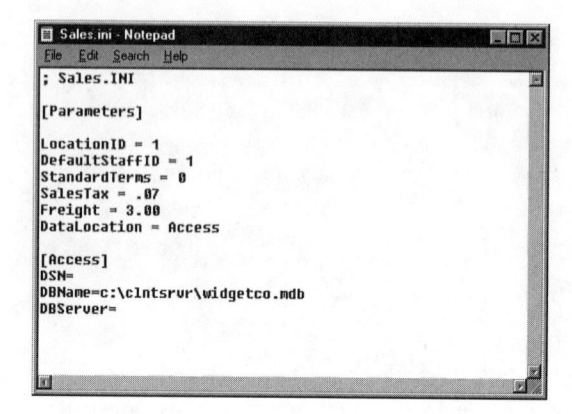

```
; Sales.INI

[Parameters]

LocationID = 1
DefaultStaffID = 1
StandardTerms = 0
SalesTax = .07
Freight = 3.00
DataLocation = Access

[Access]
DSN=
DBName=c:\clntsrvr\widgetco.mdb
DBServer=
```

Within an .INI file, a ; character denotes a comment. The .INI file can store parameters in subdivided sections. The [...] denotes a section of parameters. Each section is used to subdivide the .INI file for easy access. When you use the Windows API to access individual parameters in an .INI file, you must supply the section where the parameter is stored. The .INI file in Figure 11.8 has [Parameters] and [Access] sections.

Create the .INI file by opening the Notepad program. Enter the information from Listing 11.1. Save the file as SALES.INI in the Sales directory. The client program will read all of this information when execution begins. The Notepad or other text editing program can be used to edit any of the fields (such as SalesTax and Freight) during client deployment.

Listing 11.1. SALES.INI file.

```
; Sales.INI

[Parameters]

LocationID = 1
DefaultStaffID = 1
StandardTerms = 0
SalesTax = .07
Freight = 3.00
DataLocation = Access

[Access]
DSN=
DBName=c:\CLNTSRVR\WIDGETCO.mdb
DBServer=
```

Creating the Forms

The first step toward building an application is drawing the various forms. This way, you can rapidly prototype an application and show it to various potential users for critique and input. This stage is often the most fun and the quickest to do.

> **TIP**
>
> When you're demonstrating a rapid prototype to a user, make sure the user understands the amount of work still required after the prototype is running. With RAD tools, you can create a basic working application in an extremely short period of time. Programmers as well as users fall into the trap of believing that 80 percent of the work is done. In reality, with Rapid Application Development (RAD) tools such as Visual Basic, only 10 to 15 percent of the time on a typical project is spent on the user interface.

Before you place any code on a form, you can execute and operate the application autonomously. This enables the designer to easily add a few SHOW commands to various buttons in order to simulate operation. As a result, you can create a proof-of-concept demo application before any actual coding is done. For this reason, you first construct all the forms necessary for the project, which you can compile and save before entering all the code.

Creating the SALES.FRM

The Invoice form is the main form of the sales client application. From this form, a user can create an invoice, examine an existing invoice, or access either the Customer Entry or the Items forms. The menu options also enable the user to cut, copy, and paste information, view inventory quantities, and exit the program.

The Invoice form consists of a combo box control to access the customer list, a set of editable text fields to change information regarding the currently displayed invoice, a grid control that contains the items that the invoice actually describes, and a series of buttons along the right side that control the rest of the display.

When constructing the sales form you should draw the Items command button (the small button to the left of the grid) at approximately the x or horizontal place it will appear when the form is shown. The vertical placement is not critical, however, because the program will automatically align this button with the particular line that the user is editing.

As you can see in Figure 11.9, the Sales form is fairly complex. This description leads you step-by-step through creating this form. After you construct this form, you will have the necessary skills to create the additional forms with the help of the screenshots, figures, and property tables supplied in each form construction section.

FIGURE 11.9.

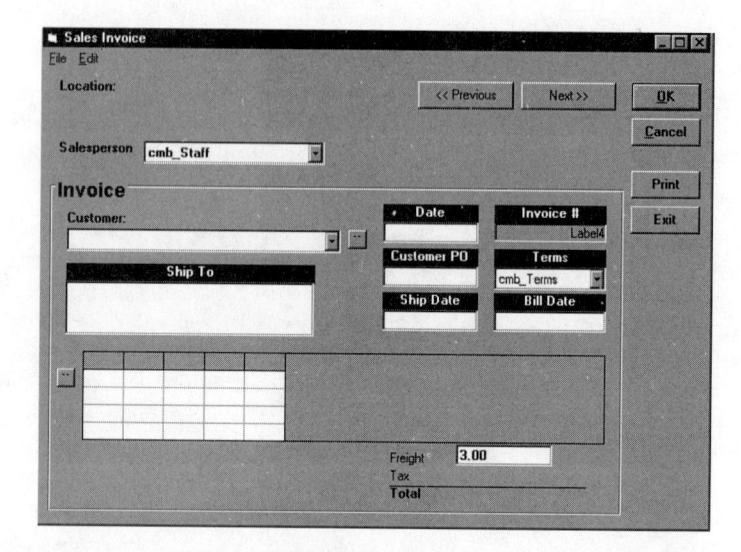

The Invoice form.

> **NOTE**
>
> The various label controls that appear on the form are not included in the following tables of controls. You should add labels to each form as they appear in the figures. Including the labels here would be a meaningless waste of space because they are very simple, consisting of a Caption property, x and y coordinates, and a background color. Place the labels in approximately the space shown in the figure and then add the text for the label.
>
> There are a few special cases when constructing these forms. For example, the label for the current invoice number is made to look like a read-only text box but is really a label. The labels that look like text boxes are included with their various property descriptions.

Figure 11.10 shows the Name properties of all the significant controls on the form shown in Figure 11.9. Use this figure as a reference for creating the controls and relating them to the various control tables.

Figure 11.11 contains four controls that are hidden on the final form. These controls are used for background manipulation and should not be seen by the user. The text boxes include the txt_GridText control used to give the user the appearance of editing individual grid cells. The other two text controls capture the user pressing the Tab key or the Shift+Tab keys to move the txt_GridText control appropriately. These simulate the traditional key commands of a spreadsheet.

Chapter 11 ■ *Sales Client*

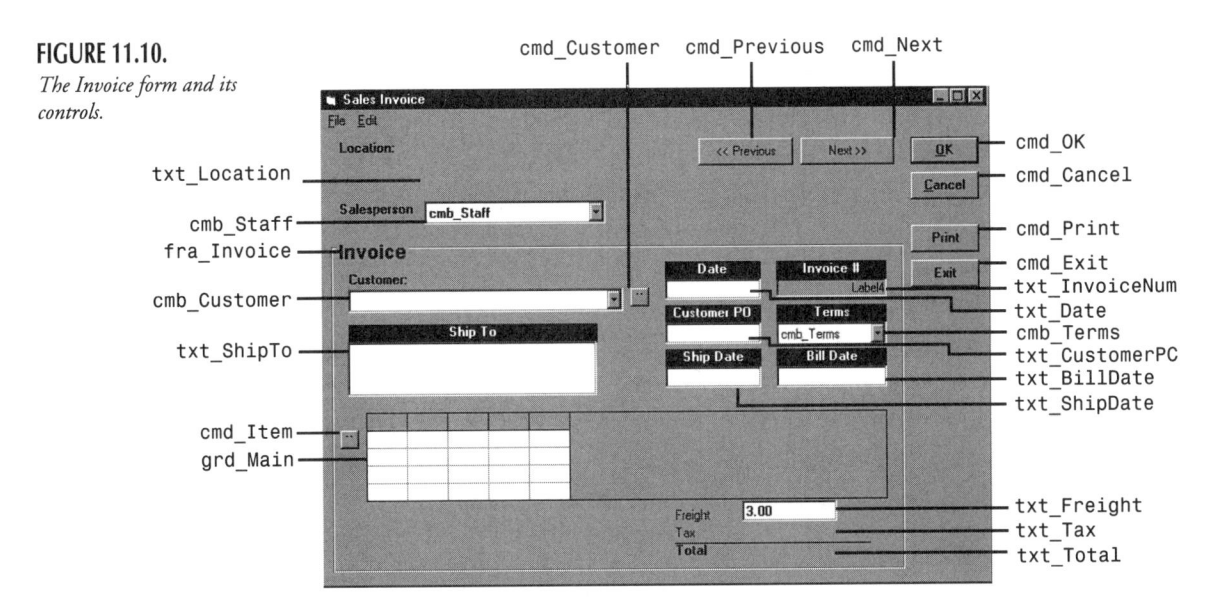

FIGURE 11.10.
The Invoice form and its controls.

Callouts (clockwise from top): cmd_Customer, cmd_Previous, cmd_Next, cmd_OK, cmd_Cancel, cmd_Print, cmd_Exit, txt_InvoiceNum, txt_Date, cmb_Terms, txt_CustomerPC, txt_BillDate, txt_ShipDate, txt_Freight, txt_Tax, txt_Total, grd_Main, cmd_Item, txt_ShipTo, cmb_Customer, fra_Invoice, cmb_Staff, txt_Location

FIGURE 11.11.
Hidden controls on the Sales form.

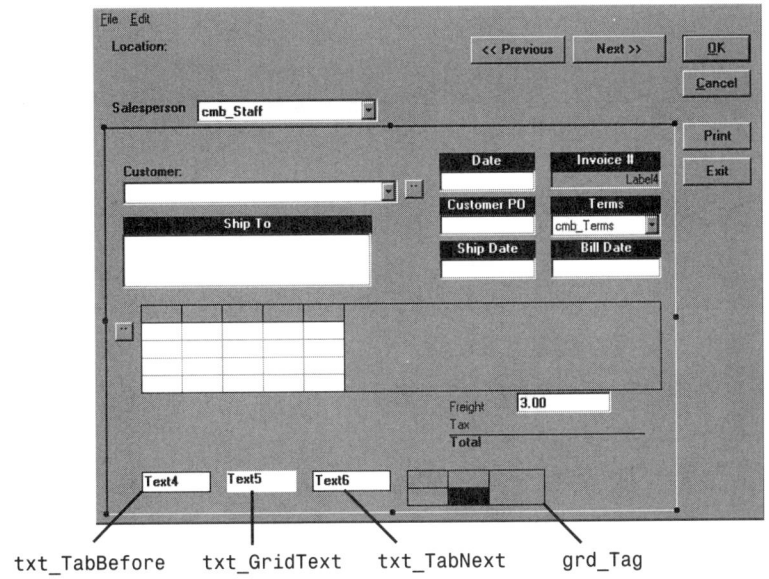

Callouts: txt_TabBefore, txt_GridText, txt_TabNext, grd_Tag

The grid control provides a mirror of the grd_Main grid. Called the grd_Tag (because it fulfills the same function as the Tag property in the text fields), the values of any loaded Invoice are stored here. When the user clicks the OK button, the program compares the contents of grd_Tag to the contents of grd_Main in order to save only the differences.

To begin your form, start a new project. If you double-clicked the Visual Basic application, a default project and form should be showing. Otherwise, select New Project under the File menu. Start by saving the project. You should have already created the various necessary directories as described in Chapter 10. If you haven't, do that now.

Select the Save Project option under the File menu. First, you are prompted for the name of the base form. Select the CS_VB\SALES directory and name the form SALES.FRM. Name the project SALES.VBP. Now that you've saved these two things, additional form saving is less confusing.

Select the Form1 and set the properties listed in Table 11.1. You might want to wait until later to set the Top, Left, Width, and Height. It is usually most convenient to resize and move a form when you're setting up all of the various controls so that the various palettes such as the Control Palette (called the Toolbox) remain visible.

There are six commands buttons on the outer form: the Next, Previous, OK, Cancel, Print, and Exit buttons. Create each command button as shown in Figure 11.9. Then, set the properties according to Tables 11.1 through 11.7.

Table 11.1. The `frm_Invoice` form.

BackColor	&H00C0C0C0&
Caption	Sales Invoice
ClientHeight	6195
ClientLeft	1785
ClientTop	2370
ClientWidth	9375
Height	6885
Left	1725
LinkTopic	Form1
ScaleHeight	6195
ScaleWidth	9375
Top	1740
Width	9495

Table 11.2. The `cmd_Prev` command button.

Caption	<< Previous
Height	375
Left	5280

TabIndex	3
Top	120
Width	1335

Table 11.3. The `cmd_Next` command button.

Caption	Next >>
Height	375
Left	6720
TabIndex	2
Top	120
Width	1335

Table 11.4. The `cmd_OK` command button.

Caption	&OK
Default	-1 'True
Height	375
Left	8280
TabIndex	4
Top	120
Width	975

Table 11.5. The `cmd_Cancel` command button.

Cancel	-1 'True
Caption	&Cancel
Height	375
Left	8280
TabIndex	5
Top	600
Width	975

Table 11.6. The `cmd_Print` command button.

Caption	Print
Height	375
Left	8280
TabIndex	0
Top	1320
Width	975

Table 11.7. The `cmd_Exit` command button.

Caption	Exit
Height	375
Left	8280
TabIndex	12
Top	1800
Width	975

Create the label to hold the selected sales location and the drop-down list to select the employee who made the sale on this invoice. Set the properties to those listed in Tables 11.8 and 11.9. Both the location and the default employee value are stored in the .INI file.

Table 11.8. The `txt_Location` label.

BackColor	&H00C0C0C0&
Height	735
Left	1440
TabIndex	13
Top	120
Width	2535

Table 11.9. The `cmb_Staff` combo box.

Height	300
Left	1440
Style	2 'Dropdown List

TabIndex	20
Top	960
Width	2535

Create the frame that will contain the information from the invoice. You'll have to enlarge the form to handle the size of the frame and all the information it contains. Set the properties to those listed in Table 11.10. All the controls that follow should be created inside this frame control.

Table 11.10. The fra_Invoice frame.

Caption	Invoice
FontBold	-1 'True
FontItalic	0 'False
FontName	Arial
FontSize	13.5
FontStrikethru	0 'False
FontUnderline	0 'False
ForeColor	&H00FF0000&
Height	4575
Left	120
ShadowColor	1 'Black
TabIndex	22
Top	1440
Width	8055

Next, draw the grid that will hold all of the invoice information. Call this grid by the Name property of grd_Main. This grid holds all the individual sales items for each invoice. Set the various properties to those listed in Table 11.11.

Table 11.11. The grd_Main grid.

BackColor	&H00FFFFFF&
Cols	5
FixedCols	0
FontBold	0 'False

continues

Table 11.11. continued

FontItalic	0 'False
FontName	MS Sans Serif
FontSize	8.25
FontStrikethru	0 'False
FontUnderline	0 'False
ForeColor	&H00000000&
Height	1215
HighLight	0 'False
Left	480
Rows	5
ScrollBars	2 'Vertical
TabIndex	36
Top	2400
Width	7335

Create a small command button to the left of the grid as shown in Figure 11.9. Set the properties to those listed in Table 11.12. This button will be used to put a sales item from the inventory on the invoice. Vertical placement of this button is unimportant because the program moves the button vertically to match the invoice line that is selected. The button remains invisible (Visible = False) until the user selects the item column of an invoice.

Table 11.12. The cmd_Item command button.

Caption	...
Height	255
Left	120
TabIndex	28
Top	2640
Visible	0 'False
Width	255

Inside the frame (fra_Invoice), draw seven labels that will appear as the titles for their particular fields: Date, Invoice Number, Customer PO, Terms, Bill Date, Ship Date, and Customer Address. They can consist of a label array. Place them in approximately the positions where you see them in Figure 11.9. Table 11.13 shows the properties for the Date label. Notice that the traditional ForeColor and BackColor settings have been reversed to make the text appear white on black. Also, set the Alignment property to Center so the label is easier to align.

Table 11.13. The Date label.

Alignment	2 'Center
BackColor	&H00000000&
Caption	Date
ForeColor	&H00FFFFFF&
Height	255
Index	0
Left	4680
TabIndex	7
Top	360
Width	1335

Now, create the text box controls that actually represent these fields. You only need to create five of these text boxes. (See Tables 11.14 through 11.18.) The Invoice Number field is a label so the user can't edit it. The Terms field is a combo box drop-down selector, cmb_Terms. (See Table 11.20.) The Customer Address is the biggest text box, for it must hold the multiple lines on the shipping address. (See the properties in Table 11.15.)

Table 11.14. The txt_ShipTo text box.

FontBold	0 'False
FontItalic	0 'False
FontName	MS Sans Serif
FontSize	8.25
FontUnderline	0 'False
Height	735
Left	225
MultiLine	-1 'True
TabIndex	35
Top	1440
Width	3495

Table 11.15. The txt_Date text box.

FontBold	0 'False
FontItalic	0 'False
FontName	MS Sans Serif
FontSize	8.25
FontUnderline	0 'False
Height	285
Left	4680
TabIndex	34
Top	600
Width	1335

Table 11.16. The txt_CustomerPO text box.

FontBold	0 'False
FontItalic	0 'False
FontName	MS Sans Serif
FontSize	8.25
FontUnderline	0 'False
Height	285
Left	4680
TabIndex	33
Top	1200
Width	1335

Table 11.17. The txt_ShipDate text box.

FontBold	0 'False
FontItalic	0 'False
FontName	MS Sans Serif
FontSize	8.25
FontUnderline	0 'False
Height	285
Left	4680

TabIndex	25
Top	1800
Width	1335

Table 11.18. The `txt_BillDate` text box.

FontBold	0 'False
FontItalic	0 'False
FontName	MS Sans Serif
FontSize	8.25
FontUnderline	0 'False
Height	285
Left	6240
TabIndex	24
Top	1800
Width	1575

The text boxes (except the `txt_ShipTo` control) should not have the MultiLine property set to TRUE and should be nearly the same in all respects. Line up these text controls under the labels created earlier so the screen looks like that in Figure 11.9. There should be empty spaces under the Invoice Number and Terms headings.

The Invoice Number is created by the client program itself, and the program cannot enable the user freely edit it. However, it must be displayed with all the other information vital to that particular invoice in a place the user would look for it. Therefore, modify a label to appear as if it were a read-only text box. (See Table 11.19.) You could have made a read-only text box using a variety of techniques (such as using the KeyPress events to eliminate the key stroke or various calls to the Windows API), but this technique is the least complicated.

Table 11.19. The `txt_InvoiceNum` label.

Alignment	1 'Right Justify
BorderStyle	1 'Fixed Single
FontBold	0 'False
FontItalic	0 'False
FontName	MS Sans Serif
FontSize	8.25

continues

Table 11.19. continued

FontUnderline	0 'False
Height	255
Left	6240
TabIndex	17
Top	600
Width	1575

Draw the Terms combo selection box. Create the combo box under the Terms heading and name it `cmb_Terms`. Set the properties listed in Table 11.20 to their proper settings. If you set the Style to Dropdown List, the user cannot edit the text in the control.

Table 11.20. The `cmb_Terms` combo box.

FontBold	0 'False
FontItalic	0 'False
FontName	MS Sans Serif
FontSize	8.25
FontUnderline	0 'False
Height	300
Left	6240
Style	2 'Dropdown List
TabIndex	32
Top	1200
Width	1575

Now, you must add the customer selection to the form. Draw another combo box and set the properties to those listed in Table 11.21. This time you leave the style to the default Dropdown Combo. This way a user can enter the name of a customer into the text field of the combo box. When the user clicks the OK button, the list is searched for the customer name. If it's in the list, that customer is automatically selected. If not, the user can enter a new customer.

Table 11.21. The `cmb_Customer` combo box.

Height	300
Left	240
TabIndex	26
Top	720
Width	3855

To enable the user to edit the customer in the customer list, create a command button and name it `cmd_Customer`. Set the properties to those listed in Table 11.22. The user can click this button to show the Customer form.

Table 11.22. The `cmd_Customer` command button.

Caption	...
Height	255
Left	4200
TabIndex	27
Top	720
Width	255

You now construct the items at the bottom of the grid that summarize the invoice. Create a text box for the Freight value (Table 11.23) and two labels (for the Tax in Table 11.25 and the Total in Table 11.26). Set the properties equal to those listed in their tables. The user can customize the Freight value, but the program calculates the Tax and the Total values. The Tax rate is stored in the .INI file. Place a line under the Freight field by selecting the shapes object in the VB palette and drawing the line in the space below the Freight field (see Table 11.24).

Table 11.23. The `txt_Freight` text box.

Height	285
Left	5730
TabIndex	38
Text	3.00
Top	3630
Width	1350

Table 11.24. The Line1 line.

X1	4800
X2	7560
Y1	4200
Y2	4200

Table 11.25. The txt_Tax label.

Alignment	1 'Right Justify
BackColor	&H00C0C0C0&
FontBold	0 'False
FontItalic	0 'False
FontName	MS Sans Serif
FontSize	8.25
FontStrikethru	0 'False
FontUnderline	0 'False
Height	255
Left	5760
TabIndex	14
Top	3960
Width	1335

Table 11.26. The txt_Total label.

Alignment	1 'Right Justify
BackColor	&H00C0C0C0&
Height	255
Left	5760
TabIndex	15
Top	4200
Width	1335

Finally, add the controls that are hidden at the bottom of the frame. (See Figure 11.11.) The easiest way to accomplish this is to stretch the fra_Invoice frame so it is larger than the needed size, insert the controls, and then decrease the frame height until they are no longer showing.

The three text box controls enable the user to edit the information in the grid `grd_Main`. The grid `grd_Tag` stores the original information of an invoice so the program can determine whether the user made any changes.

Create the three text box controls with the properties listed in Tables 11.27, 11.28, and 11.29. Notice that the `txt_GridText` has slightly different property values from the other two because it appears on the screen positioned over the grid. Also add the `grd_Tag` at the bottom screen as shown and set the properties to those listed in Table 11.30.

Table 11.27. The `txt_TabNext` text box.

Height	285
Left	2880
TabIndex	31
Text	Text6
Top	4680
Width	1095

Table 11.28. The `txt_TabBefore` text box.

Height	285
Left	480
TabIndex	29
Text	Text4
Top	4680
Width	975

Table 11.29. The `txt_GridText` text box.

BorderStyle	0 'None
Height	285
Left	1680
TabIndex	30
Text	Text5
Top	4680
Visible	0 'False
Width	975

Table 11.30. The grd_Tag grid.

Height	495
Left	4200
TabIndex	23
Top	4680
Width	1935

Adding the Menus

Creating the menus is as simple as using the Menu Designer included with Visual Basic. Select Menu Editor from the Tools menu. You see a window for creating and editing the menus. Create all the menus shown in Figure 11.12. The figure labels the menu names that you will enter into the second text field in the dialog box.

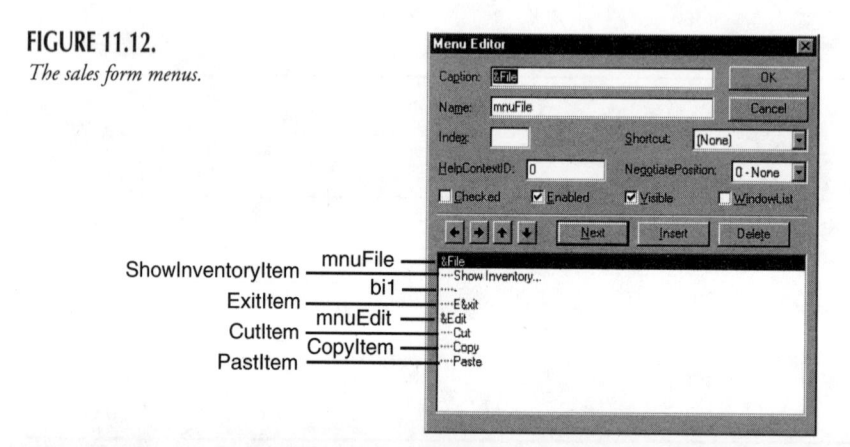

FIGURE 11.12.
The sales form menus.

> **CAUTION**
>
> Do not use the Close box in the upper-left corner of the Menu Design window. Unfortunately, using this Close box is not the same as clicking the OK button but instead activates the Cancel action, which will discard any changes you have made to the menus.

Creating the CUST.FRM

The Customer form is used to examine or edit information in the Customer table. Creating the Customer form is fairly straightforward compared to creating the Invoice form. The form itself consists mostly of edit fields, a frame, and the OK and Cancel buttons. Figure 11.13 shows the completed form after all the controls have been added. Figure 11.14 shows the Name properties of the individual controls.

FIGURE 11.13.
The Customer form.

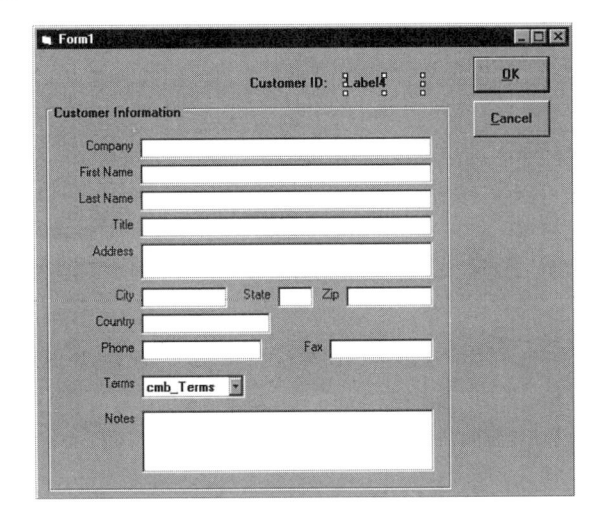

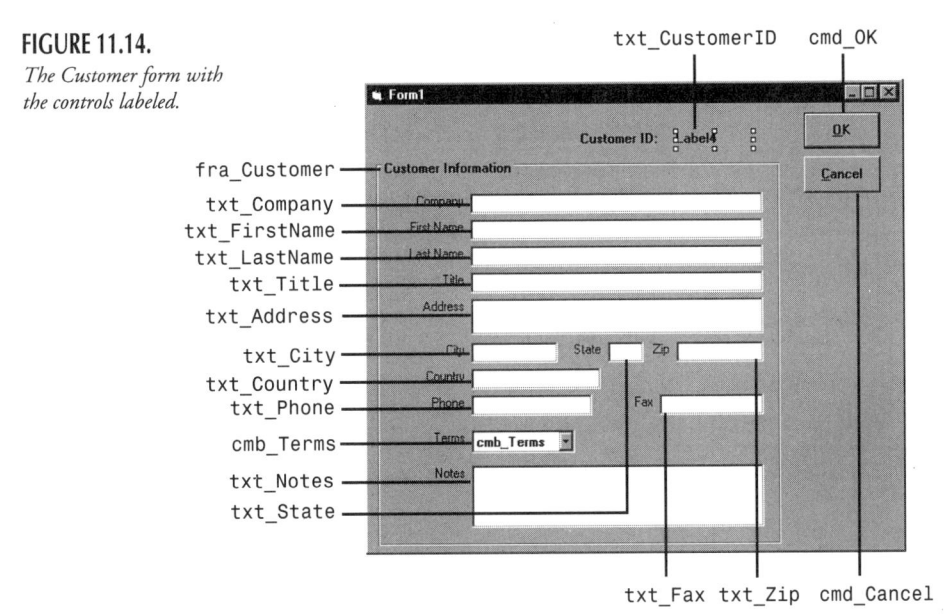

FIGURE 11.14.
The Customer form with the controls labeled.

Create each control on the form and set the properties to match the properties listed in the table for that control.

Table 11.31 lists all the individual controls and their various locations. The Location denotes whether they should appear on the form itself or within a particular frame. The table lists all the tables of properties for constructing the Customer form.

Table 11.31. Controls for the Customer form.

Table	Control	Location
Table 11.32	frm_Customer	
Table 11.33	fra_Customer	Form
Table 11.34	txt_State	fra_Customer
Table 11.35	txt_Zip	fra_Customer
Table 11.36	txt_Phone	fra_Customer
Table 11.37	txt_Fax	fra_Customer
Table 11.38	txt_Country	fra_Customer
Table 11.39	cmb_Terms	fra_Customer
Table 11.40	txt_Notes	fra_Customer
Table 11.41	txt_FirstName	fra_Customer
Table 11.42	txt_LastName	fra_Customer
Table 11.43	txt_Address	fra_Customer
Table 11.44	txt_City	fra_Customer
Table 11.45	txt_Company	fra_Customer
Table 11.46	txt_Title	fra_Customer
Table 11.47	cmd_Cancel	Form
Table 11.48	cmd_OK	Form
Table 11.49	txt_CustomerID	Form

Table 11.32. The frm_Customer form.

BackColor	&H00C0C0C0&
Caption	Form1
ClientHeight	6075
ClientLeft	1290
ClientTop	870
ClientWidth	7485
Height	6480

Left	1230
LinkTopic	Form1
ScaleHeight	6075
ScaleWidth	7485
Top	525
Width	7605

Table 11.33. The `fra_Customer` SSFrame.

Caption	Customer Information
Height	5295
Left	120
TabIndex	22
Top	720
Width	5655

Table 11.34. The `txt_State` text box.

Height	285
Left	3240
TabIndex	7
Top	2520
Width	495

Table 11.35. The `txt_Zip` text box.

Height	285
Left	4200
TabIndex	8
Top	2520
Width	1215

Table 11.36. The txt_Phone text box.

Height	285
Left	1320
TabIndex	10
Top	3240
Width	1695

Table 11.37. The txt_Fax text box.

Height	285
Left	3960
TabIndex	11
Top	3240
Width	1455

Table 11.38. The txt_Country text box.

Height	285
Left	1320
TabIndex	9
Top	2880
Width	1815

Table 11.39. The cmb_Terms combo box.

Height	300
Left	1320
Style	2 'Dropdown List
TabIndex	14
Top	3720
Width	1455

Table 11.40. The txt_Notes text box.

Height	855
Left	1320
MultiLine	-1 'True
TabIndex	12
Top	4200
Width	4095

Table 11.41. The txt_FirstName text box.

Height	285
Left	1320
TabIndex	2
Top	840
Width	4095

Table 11.42. The txt_LastName text box.

Height	285
Left	1320
TabIndex	3
Top	1200
Width	4095

Table 11.43. The txt_Address text box.

Height	495
Left	1320
MultiLine	-1 'True
TabIndex	5
Top	1920
Width	4095

Table 11.44. The `txt_City` text box.

Height	285
Left	1320
TabIndex	6
Top	2520
Width	1215

Table 11.45. The `txt_Company` text box.

Height	285
Left	1320
TabIndex	1
Top	480
Width	4095

Table 11.46. The `txt_Title` text box.

Height	285
Left	1320
TabIndex	4
Top	1560
Width	4095

Table 11.47. The `cmd_Cancel` command button.

Cancel	-1 'True
Caption	&Cancel
Height	495
Left	6120
TabIndex	13
Top	720
Width	1095

Table 11.48. The `cmd_OK` command button.

Caption	&OK
Default	-1 'True
Height	495
Left	6120
TabIndex	0
Top	120
Width	1095

Table 11.49. The `txt_CustomerID` label.

BackColor	&H00C0C0C0&
Caption	Label4
Height	255
Left	4320
TabIndex	30
Top	360
Width	1095

Creating the ITEM.FRM

The Item form is the simplest form of the project. It consists of a list box control and the OK and Cancel buttons. Figure 11.15 shows the completed form after all the controls have been added. Figure 11.16 shows the Name properties of the individual controls.

FIGURE 11.15.
The Item form.

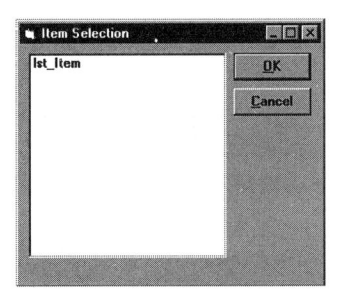

FIGURE 11.16.
The Item form with the controls labeled.

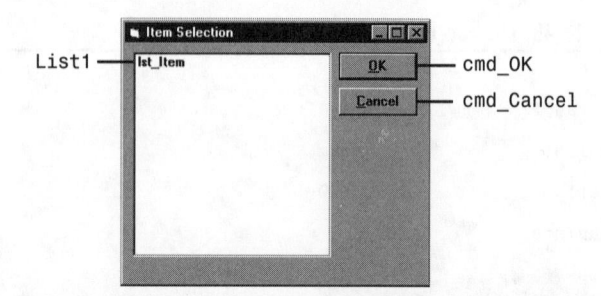

Create each control on the form and set the properties to match the properties listed in the table for that control. You can set the list box to any size appropriate for adequately viewing the data it will display.

Table 11.50 lists all the individual controls and their various locations. The Location denotes whether they should appear on the form itself or within a particular frame. The table also lists all the tables of properties for constructing the Item form.

> **NOTE**
>
> The Item form, like the GLOBAL.BAS file, should be stored in the project root directory (CS_VB) rather than the project directory (CS_VB\SALES). The Item form is a reusable component that you can add to different projects. The other client programs in this book (the Purchasing client and the Management client) use this same source code file for their projects. It displays a list of queried items and returns the item selected.

Table 11.50. Controls for the Item form.

Table	Control	Location
Table 11.51	`frm_Item`	
Table 11.53	`List1`	Form
Table 11.54	`cmd_Cancel`	Form
Table 11.55	`cmd_OK`	Form

Table 11.51. The `frm_Item` form.

`BackColor`	`&H00C0C0C0&`
`Caption`	`Item Selection`
`ClientHeight`	`3765`

ClientLeft	2145
ClientTop	1770
ClientWidth	4650
Height	4170
Left	2085
ScaleHeight	3765
ScaleWidth	4650
Top	1425
Width	4770

Table 11.52. The `List1` list box.

Height	2955
Left	360
TabIndex	3
Top	360
Width	2295

Table 11.53. The `cmd_Cancel` command button.

Cancel	-1 'True
Caption	&Cancel
Height	375
Left	3360
TabIndex	1
Top	720
Width	1095

Table 11.54. The `cmd_OK` command button.

Caption	&OK
Default	-1 'True
Height	375
Left	3360

continues

Table 11.54. continued

TabIndex	0
Top	240
Width	1095

Creating the INVNTRY.FRM

The Inventory form uses a list box to display inventory items in columns. It does not permit user input. You don't define the columns with properties but instead with a Windows API routine to set the tab parameters. For more information, see the "Adding Code to GLOBAL.BAS" section later in this chapter. Figure 11.17 shows the completed form after all the controls have been added. Figure 11.18 shows the Name properties of the individual controls.

FIGURE 11.17.
The Inventory form.

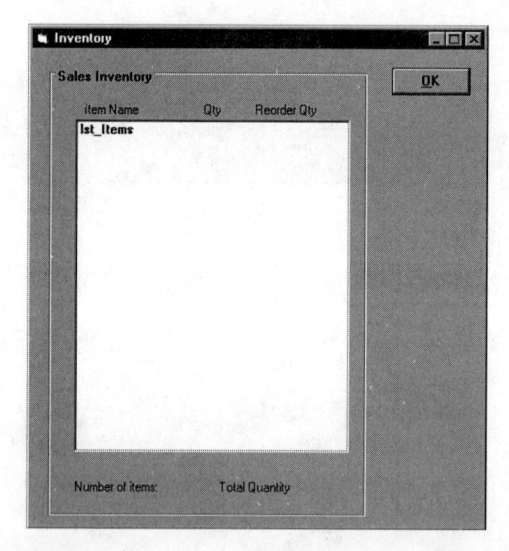

Create each control on the form and set the properties to match the properties listed in the table for that control.

Table 11.56 lists all the individual controls and their various locations. The Location denotes whether they should appear on the form itself or within a particular frame. This table lists all the tables of properties for constructing the Inventory form.

Chapter 11 ■ Sales Client

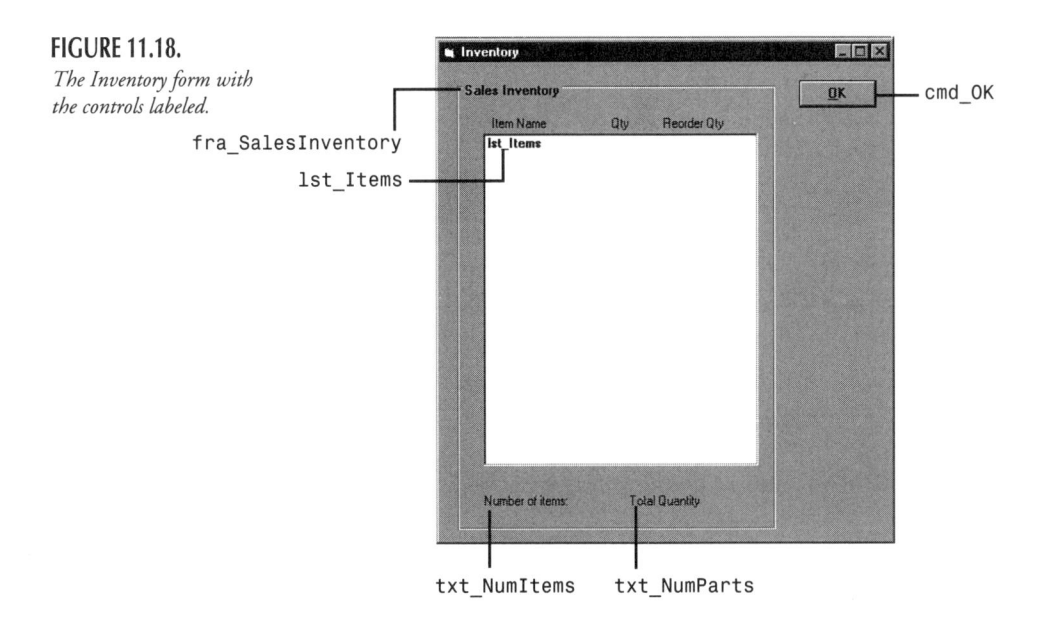

FIGURE 11.18.
The Inventory form with the controls labeled.

Table 11.55. Controls for the Inventory form.

Table	Control	Location
Table 11.56	frm_Inventory	
Table 11.57	cmd_OK	Form
Table 11.58	fra_SalesInventory	fra_Inventory
Table 11.59	lst_Items	fra_Inventory
Table 11.60	txt_NumParts	fra_Inventory
Table 11.61	txt_NumItems	fra_Inventory

Table 11.56. The `frm_Inventory` form.

BackColor	&H00C0C0C0&
Caption	Inventory
ClientHeight	6510
ClientLeft	2415
ClientTop	615
ClientWidth	6330
Height	6915

continues

Table 11.56. continued

Left	2355
LinkTopic	Form2
ScaleHeight	6510
ScaleWidth	6330
Top	270
Width	6450

Table 11.57. The cmd_OK command button.

Caption	&OK
Default	-1 'True
Height	375
Left	5040
TabIndex	7
Top	240
Width	1095

Table 11.58. The fra_SalesInventory SSFrame.

Caption	Sales Inventory
Height	6135
Left	240
TabIndex	0
Top	240
Width	4455

Table 11.59. The lst_Items list box.

Height	4710
Left	360
TabIndex	1
Top	720
Width	3855

Table 11.60. The `txt_NumParts` label.

BackColor	&H00C0C0C0&
Height	255
Left	3600
TabIndex	9
Top	5640
Width	615

Table 11.61. The `txt_NumItems` label.

BackColor	&H00C0C0C0&
Height	255
Left	1680
TabIndex	2
Top	5640
Width	495

Adding Code to GLOBAL.BAS

All the applications of the client/server system created in this book use the GLOBAL.BAS file. You can create the code and duplicate the file with the Explorer or File Manager, or all the applications can share the same source file. The only limitation to sharing a single source file is that only one user can edit the file at a time.

The Global module contains all the variables and routines that need to be accessed by the entire application. For example, you can create the variable for the main database object as a global variable. Once you've created this object, any form can create dynaset and snapshot objects from it.

Create the GLOBAL.BAS file by selecting the Module option from the Insert menu. Save this file as GLOBAL.BAS in the root code directory (CS_VB). This makes it more convenient for all the applications to share it.

One note about using shared files: any changes made to the shared file are reflected in all the shared applications. Be careful about making haphazard changes. They will affect all of the projects.

General Declarations

You should place all of these variables and function definitions in the General Declarations section of the GLOBAL.BAS module. The `Database` and `Recordset` variables are used by all the clients to access their particular tables. Most of the variables are used by the various clients in different ways, primarily to store data outside a particular form so it can be accessed by all of the forms in the project.

There are variables provided for all the major configuration variables that are read from the INI files. The constants have been included for sending the `cut`, `copy`, `paste`, and `settabstops` system messages.

The `Declare` section is used to define all of the Windows API calls the applications will use. Notice the conditional compilation programming structure. This `#If...Then...#Else...#End If` structure only compiles the API calls for the appropriate system. Therefore, if the project is compiled in the 16-bit version of VB 4.0, those calls are used. Otherwise, the 32-bit `Declares` are used.

The `Declare` statements define three Windows API functions: `GetPrivateProfileString`, `WritePrivateProfileString`, and `SendMessage`. The `Get` and `Write` profile string routines are used to read and write information to an INI file, respectively. The `SendMessage` API call is used to activate the cut, copy, and paste commands as well as setting the tab stops in list box controls.

```
Global MyDB As Database
Global MyDS As Recordset
Global MySS As Recordset
Global MyWorkspace As Workspace
Global SQLStmt As String
Global SQL$

Global g_CurrentInvoice As Long
Global g_PartNum As Long
Global SalesItemFlag As Integer

Global g_LoadCustFlag As Integer
Global g_ClearCustFlag As Integer
Global g_LoadPartFlag As Integer
Global g_ClearPartFlag As Integer

Global g_CustomerID As Long
Global g_SupplierID As Long
Global g_InvoiceDirty As Integer
Global INIPath As String

' INI Variables
Global g_CurrentLocation As Integer
Global g_DefaultStaffID As Integer
Global g_StandardTerms As Integer
Global g_SalesTax As Integer
Global g_Freight As Double
Global g_DataLocation As String
Global g_DBName As String
```

```
Global g_OKFlag As Integer
Global i As Integer, j As Integer
Global Const err_ODBCItemConnect = 3151
Dim testsingle As Single
Dim testlong As Long

Global Const WM_USER = &H400
Global Const WM_CUT = &H300
Global Const WM_COPY = &H301
Global Const WM_PASTE = &H302
Global Const EM_UNDO = (WM_USER + 23)
Global Const LB_SETTABSTOPS = (WM_USER + 19)
Public Const LBS_USETABSTOPS = &H80&

Global Const ASC_ENTER = 13          ' ASCII code of ENTER key.

' WinAPI calls differ for 16-bit compile and 32-bit compile
#If Win16 Then
Declare Function GetPrivateProfileString Lib "Kernel" (ByVal AppName As String, ↦
ByVal KeyName As String, ByVal default As String, ByVal ReturnedString As String,
↦ByVal MAXSIZE As Integer, ByVal filename As String) As Integer

    Declare Function WritePrivateProfileString Lib "Kernel" (ByVal AppName As ↦
String, ByVal KeyName As String, ByVal NewString As String, ByVal filename As↦
String) As Integer

    Declare Function SendMessage Lib "User" (ByVal hWnd As Integer, ByVal wMsg As
↦Integer, ByVal wParam As Integer, lParam As Any) As Long

#Else
    Declare Function GetPrivateProfileString Lib "kernel32" Alias ↦
"GetPrivateProfileStringA" (ByVal lpApplicationName As String, ByVal lpKeyName As↦
 Any, ByVal lpDefault As String, ByVal lpReturnedString As String, ByVal nSize As
↦Long, ByVal lpFileName As String) As Long

    Declare Function WritePrivateProfileString Lib "kernel32" Alias↦
 "WritePrivateProfileStringA" (ByVal lpApplicationName As String, ByVal lpKeyName
As↦
Any, lpString As Any, ByVal lpFileName As String) As Long

    Declare Function SendMessage Lib "user32" Alias "SendMessageA" (ByVal hWnd As
↦Long, ByVal wMsg As Long, ByVal wParam As Integer, ByVal lParam As Long) As Long

#End If
```

General Routines

All of the routines we discuss in this section belong in the General section of the form. Code in the General section is available to all routines within the form. To create a new routine, select Procedure from the Insert menu. A dialog box asks you whether the routine should be a Sub, Function, or Property.

For each of the following routine sections, the type of procedure (either Sub or Function) is given in the title. Type in the routine name and click the OK button. For example, the name of the first subroutine is CenterForm. A window will open and show the begin and end routine structure. Type the text found in the following section.

> **NOTE**
>
> Don't forget to include the parameters that appear between and after the parentheses in some of the routines. These parameters specify values that are passed to or returned from the routine. For example, the CenterForm routine requires that a form variable be passed to it.

Sub CenterForm (TempForm As Form)

The center form routine will center any form on the screen. Centering is useful when the width of the user's screen is unknown. This routine uses the properties of the Screen variable and the form's width and height to determine the center.

> **TIP**
>
> Do not center all of the forms in an application. This makes the forms stack up in the center of the screen. Not only is this unappealing, but often a user will want to read information off one of the back forms. When they're all centered, it's difficult to examine any form but the primary one.

```
Sub CenterForm(TempForm As Form)
    TempForm.Move ((Screen.Width - TempForm.Width) \ 2),➥
    ((Screen.Height - TempForm.Height) \ 2)
End Sub
```

Function GetAppPath ()

The GetAppPath function returns the path name of the directory in which the application is executing. It ensures that the path string ends with the \ character so you can add to the string simply by using the & character to access a file.

```
Function GetAppPath () As String
    Dim Path$

    Path$ = App.Path
    If Right$(Path$, 1) <> "\" Then Path$ = Path$ + "\"
    GetAppPath = Path$
End Function
```

Function ReadINI (AppName, KeyName, filename As String)

The `ReadINI` routine reads the information from an .INI file. The section of the .INI is addressed by entering a KeyName appropriate to the section (in the SALES.INI, Access is one of the section names that you could use). You use the Windows API function `GetPrivateProfileString()` to read the information from the .INI file. The information is returned as a string.

```
Function ReadINI(AppName, KeyName As String, filename As String) As String
    Dim INIReturn As String

    INIReturn = String(255, Chr(0))
    ReadINI = Left(INIReturn, GetPrivateProfileString(AppName, ➥
      ByVal KeyName, "", INIReturn, Len(INIReturn), filename))
End Function
```

Sub SendEditMessage (Action As Integer)

You use the `SendEditMessage` routine to activate the cut, copy, and paste (CC&P) routines from menu items. For a normal edit field, the CC&P keys are accepted (Ctrl+X, Ctrl+C, and Ctrl+V), but you cannot simply implement them from a menu option (where a user often looks). This routine uses the Windows API function `SendMessage()` to send the necessary action message to the control so these functions can be activated programmatically.

```
Sub SendEditMessage(Action As Integer)
    Dim lRC As Long ' Result Code.
    On Error Resume Next
    lRC = SendMessage(Screen.ActiveForm.ActiveControl.hWnd, Action, 0, 0)
End Sub
```

Sub WriteINI (sAppname, sKeyName, sNewString, sFileName As String)

The `WriteINI` routine writes a value for a parameter in the .INI file. This way, you can save preferences from within a program into the .INI file. This works in virtually the same way as the `ReadINI` routine.

```
Sub WriteINI(sAppname, sKeyName As String, sNewString, sFileName As String)
    Dim flag As Integer

    flag = WritePrivateProfileString(sAppname, sKeyName, sNewString, sFileName)
End Sub
```

Adding Code to the SALES.FRM

Adding the code to the form is a routine task. First, you need to create any form level routines. These routines are not activated by an event (such as a mouse click) but are called by other parts of the code. These routines appear in the General section of the code menus. (See Figure 11.19.)

FIGURE 11.19.
The General routines.

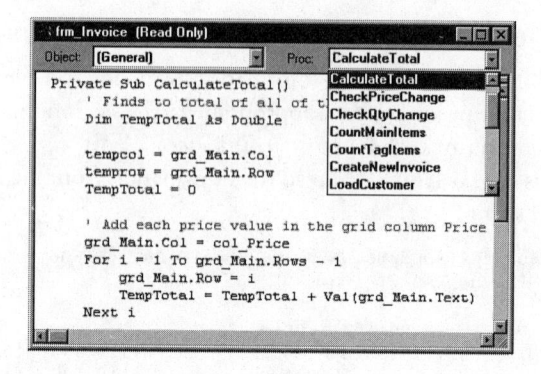

```
frm_Invoice (Read Only)
Object: (General)              Proc: CalculateTotal
                                     CalculateTotal
Private Sub CalculateTotal()         CheckPriceChange
    ' Finds to total of all of t     CheckQtyChange
    Dim TempTotal As Double          CountMainItems
                                     CountTagItems
    tempcol = grd_Main.Col           CreateNewInvoice
    temprow = grd_Main.Row           LoadCustomer
    TempTotal = 0

    ' Add each price value in the grid column Price
    grd_Main.Col = col_Price
    For i = 1 To grd_Main.Rows - 1
        grd_Main.Row = i
        TempTotal = TempTotal + Val(grd_Main.Text)
    Next i
```

General Declarations

First, enter the variables in Listing 11.2 into the General Declarations section. They include variables to track the row and column of the grid that the user is editing, three recordset object variables to store the various dynasets that the routines need to access, and constants used to access the various columns of the grid.

Listing 11.2. General Declarations.

```
Dim gRow As Integer
Dim gCol As Integer

Dim CurrentInvoice As Integer
Dim OriginalItems As Integer
Dim InvoicesDS As Recordset
Dim PartsDS As Recordset
Dim SalesItemsDS As Recordset

' Grid Column Types
Const col_ItemNum = 0
Const col_Desc = 1
Const col_UnitCost = 2
Const col_Qty = 3
Const col_Price = 4
Const col_LineNum = 5
Const col_Reserved = 6
Const col_OrigQty = 7
```

These grid constants make the code much more readable. They are used to specify a column number on the invoice grid where the various pieces of SalesItem information are stored.

> **TIP**
>
> We highly recommended that you frequently use such constants instead of raw numbers when you're designing an application. Code that doesn't use constants

> (grid.col = 4) is harder to read and maintain than code that does (grid.col = col_Price). There is no performance penalty, and they greatly improve readability and maintainability.

General Routines

All the routines we discuss in this section are added to the General section of the form. Code in the General section is available to all routines within the form. To create a new routine, select New Procedure under the View menu. A dialog box asks you whether the routine should be a Sub or a Function.

For each of the following routines, the type is given in the title. Type in the routine name (without the open and close parentheses) and click the OK button. A window will opens and shows the begin and end routine structure. Type the text found in each section.

Sub CalculateTotal ()

You use the `CalculateTotal` routine to total up all the items in the invoice and present a sum in the `txt_Total` text control. There are a number of different events that make the program retotal the invoice: a change in the quantity, modification of the final price, change in the freight, or the change to a different invoice.

The total calculation also fills in the `txt_Tax` field. The amount of the tax is read from the .INI file where it is stored as a parameter. This makes it convenient for a system administrator to change a parameter in a single .INI file and copy this file to all the client machines, rather than completely recompile the application.

```
Private Sub CalculateTotal()
    ' Finds to total of all of the items stored in the grid
    Dim TempTotal As Double

    tempcol = grd_Main.Col
    temprow = grd_Main.Row
    TempTotal = 0

    ' Add each price value in the grid column Price
    grd_Main.Col = col_Price
    For i = 1 To grd_Main.Rows - 1
        grd_Main.Row = i
        TempTotal = TempTotal + Val(grd_Main.Text)
    Next i

    ' Multiply total by SalesTax read from the INI file
    txt_Tax = Format(TempTotal * g_SalesTax, "##0.00")
    txt_Total = Format(TempTotal + (TempTotal * g_SalesTax) +➥
       Val(txt_Freight), "##0.00")
' Restore column and row positions
    grd_Main.Col = tempcol
    grd_Main.Row = temprow
End Sub
```

Sub CheckPriceChange ()

The `CheckPriceChange` routine checks whether user has modified the Price column. If he has, the total is then recalculated. This prevents needless recalculations that slow down client access. Notice how the selected column is first checked to determine whether it is the price column. This routine is called by a `LostFocus` event of the grid text box to determine whether the user has finished editing the column.

```
Private Sub CheckPriceChange()
    ' Check for user modification of qty or price that requires
    ' recalculation of invoice total

    ' First, check if user was modifying the Price column
    If grd_Main.Col = col_Price Then
        grd_Main.Col = col_UnitCost
        grd_Tag.Col = col_UnitCost
        ' Make grd_Tag access the same row as grd_Main
        grd_Tag.Row = grd_Main.Row

        If grd_Main.Text <> grd_Main.Tag Then
            CalculateTotal
        End If
    End If
End Sub
```

Sub CheckQtyChange ()

The `CheckQtyChange` routine is more complicated than the `CheckPriceChange` routine because any changes must be registered with the database. If the quantity has changed, the program calculates the difference between the old reserved quantity and the new quantity. The number of additional reserve items is removed from inventory and placed in the reserved column.

The program then updates the Tag values and recalculates the totals. If there are not enough items for the new quantity in inventory, the program alerts the user and aborts the update, restoring the original quantity value to the cell.

```
Private Sub CheckQtyChange()
    ' If qty changed, additional units will have to be Reserved
    Dim TempQty$, TempUnitCost$, SQL$

    ' Check if modification occurred on qty column
If grd_Main.Col = col_Qty Then
        TempQty$ = grd_Main.Text

        grd_Main.Col = col_UnitCost
        grd_Tag.Col = col_UnitCost
        ' Make grd_Tag access the same row as grd_Main
        grd_Tag.Row = grd_Main.Row
        TempUnitCost$ = grd_Main.Text
        ' Check to make sure quantity and unit cost are numbers
        If IsNumeric(TempQty$) And IsNumeric(TempUnitCost$) Then
            grd_Main.Col = col_Qty
            grd_Tag.Col = col_Qty
            ' Check if old qty and new qty are different
```

```
                If Val(grd_Main.Text) <> Val(grd_Tag.Text) Then
                    ' Reserve items in table so other client's won't➥
                    ' sell same inventory
numchange = Val(grd_Main.Text) - Val(grd_Tag.Text)
                    grd_Main.Col = col_ItemNum
                    SQL$ = "Select * from Inventory_Sales where PartID = "➥
                        & grd_Main.Text
Set PartsDS = MyDB.OpenRecordset(SQL$, dbOpenDynaset)
                    PartsDS.LockEdits = False
                    If PartsDS!OnHand > numchange Then
                        PartsDS.Edit
                        PartsDS!OnHand = PartsDS!OnHand - numchange
                        PartsDS!Reserved = PartsDS!Reserved + numchange
                        PartsDS!LastResvTime = Now
                        PartsDS.Update
                        ' Saved the number of reserved items
                        grd_Tag.Col = col_Reserved
                        grd_Tag.Text = Val(grd_Tag.Text) + numchange
                        ' Update grd_Tag quantity value
                        grd_Tag.Col = col_Qty
                        grd_Main.Col = col_Qty
                        grd_Tag.Text = grd_Main.Text
                        ' Save off new price
                        grd_Main.Col = col_Price
                        grd_Tag.Col = col_Price
                        grd_Main.Text = Format$(Val(TempQty$) *➥
                            Val(TempUnitCost$), "####.#0")
'grd_Tag.Text = grd_Main.Text
                    Else
                        MsgBox "There are only " & PartsDS!OnHand &➥
                            " items in stock. Please order more and re-attempt sale."
' Restore old quantity
                        grd_Main.Col = col_Qty
                        grd_Tag.Col = col_Qty
                        grd_Main.Text = grd_Tag.Text
                    End If
                    CalculateTotal
                End If
            End If
            ' Reset back to original column
            grd_Main.Col = col_Qty
        End If
End Sub
```

Function CountMainItems()

You use the CountMainItems routine to determine the number of items stored in the invoice. To confirm the existence of an item in the particular row of a grid, the routine checks the Price column (although it can choose an ItemNum field chosen instead).

A CountMainItems routine is necessary because when the invoice is approved by the user, the client checks whether this is an older invoice being edited or a new invoice. If it is an old invoice, the program must compare the current number of invoice items with the old number to determine if it must add additional line item records to the SalesItems table.

```
Private Function CountMainItems()
    Dim numItems As Integer
    
    ' Determine how many items are stored in invoice
    numItems = 0
    For i = 1 To grd_Main.Rows - 1
        grd_Main.Col = col_Price
        grd_Main.Row = i
        If IsNumeric(grd_Main.Text) Then
            numItems = numItems + 1
        End If
    Next
    CountMainItems = numItems
End Function
```

Function CountTagItems ()

The `CountTagItems` routine is the parallel routine of the `CountMainItems` routine. You use it to compare the old number of items when the invoice was originally loaded and the new items stored in grd_Main. Using a For...Next loop, the routine compares each of the items in the tag column with those in the price column.

Because this function is only different from the `CountMainItems` function in that it accesses a separate grid, you can use a single routine that passes the grid control as a parameter. We didn't do this in the example because the code is slightly easier to understand as separate routines.

```
Private Function CountTagItems()
    Dim numItems As Integer
    
    numItems = 0
    For i = 1 To grd_Tag.Rows - 1
        grd_Tag.Col = col_Price
        grd_Tag.Row = i
        If IsNumeric(grd_Tag.Text) Then
            numItems = numItems + 1
        End If
    Next
    CountTagItems = numItems
End Function
```

Sub CreateNewPO (numitems As Integer)

The program calls the `CreateNewPO` routine to create an entirely new invoice (versus modifying an existing entry). Notice that the entire invoice creation is enclosed by `BeginTrans` and `CommitTrans` statements. This means the multiple stages of creating an invoice are either all completed or rolled back. The three stages include assigning an invoice number, adding the invoice general information to the Sales table, and adding all the individual items to the SalesItems table.

If any one of these stages fail, the program can revoke the entire transaction so a partial update doesn't occur. Enclosing multiple operations within a transaction (such as adding all the individual invoice items) also dramatically increases performance because the updates can all occur at once instead of individually.

> **NOTE**
>
> Notice that all the updates occur within this single procedure. Unfortunately, Visual Basic requires that all EDIT, UPDATE, and ADDNEW commands enclosed in a transaction must occur within a single procedure. This means that you cannot call another routine to do some of the updates within a transaction. The transaction cannot track these updates, and an error sometimes occurs upon CommitTrans.
>
> This requirement decreases the readability and often the maintainability of an application. For this reason, you should use the SQL transaction processing commands if you're using a database server for your project. This is not only much more efficient (a TP Monitor, for example, can level transaction calls), but it also enables various routine to add to the update. Transaction processing implementation varies among different SQL implementations. Check the manual for the one you will be using.

To create a new invoice, you must first assign a invoice number. The Counter table contains all the record counters, including the next available invoice number. The program increments the table to include the invoice currently being added.

Next, the program creates a new invoice record in the Sales table and writes all the invoice summary information. Notice that with the cmb_Staff and cmb_Customer combo boxes, the ItemData field is accessed based on the currently selected item (determined by the ListIndex property).

Finally, the program stores all the individual items in the invoice. Notice that the Description field is only stored if it is different from the standard description of the PartID. This technique is extremely useful because it makes the application both storage conscious and user friendly.

By storing any changed description, the program enables the user to make any required specific changes to the item's description. If no changes are made, however, the field is left as a NULL value—meaning it doesn't take up any space in the actual record. These variable fields are a recent improvement to desktop databases and also exist in SQL implementations.

Finally, the program eliminates the items in the Reserve field. There is no need to change the OnHand field in the inventory table because the items were deducted from the inventory when they were reserved. We also do not set the Reserved time to NULL because there might be other clients with items still stored in the Reserve field that need timing. For more information on the maintenance of the Reserve field, see Chapter 14, "Pseudo Server."

```
Private Sub CreateNewInvoice(numItems As Integer)
    Dim TempTable As Table
    Dim ScratchDS As Recordset
    Dim TempItemNum As Long
    Dim tempInvoiceNum As Long
```

```
BeginTrans
    ' Get the invoice number counter
    SQL$ = "Select * from Counter where TableName = 'Sales'"
    Set ScratchDS = MyDB.OpenRecordset(SQL$, dbOpenDynaset)
    tempInvoiceNum = ScratchDS!CountNum
    ' increment Invoice number
    ScratchDS.Edit
    ScratchDS!CountNum = tempInvoiceNum + 1
    ScratchDS.Update

    ' Create invoice record
    InvoicesDS.AddNew
    InvoicesDS!InvoiceID = tempInvoiceNum
    InvoicesDS!SaleDate = txt_Date.Text
    InvoicesDS!StaffID = cmb_Staff.ItemData(cmb_Staff.ListIndex)
    InvoicesDS!CustomerID = cmb_Customer.ItemData(cmb_Customer.ListIndex)
    InvoicesDS!Freight = txt_Freight
    InvoicesDS!CreateDate = Now
    InvoicesDS!ShipDate = txt_ShipDate.Text
    InvoicesDS!BillDate = txt_BillDate.Text
    InvoicesDS!ShippingTo = txt_ShipTo.Text
    InvoicesDS!Terms = cmb_Terms.ListIndex
    InvoicesDS!CustomerPO = txt_CustomerPO.Text
    InvoicesDS.Update

    For i = 1 To numItems
        ' Set row(record) to save
        grd_Main.Row = i
        grd_Tag.Row = i
        ' Create invoice record
        SalesItemsDS.AddNew
        SalesItemsDS!InvoiceID = tempInvoiceNum
        SalesItemsDS!Linenum = i
        grd_Main.Col = col_ItemNum
        SalesItemsDS!PartID = Val(grd_Main.Text)
        SalesItemsDS!LocationID = g_CurrentLocation
        grd_Main.Col = col_Qty
        SalesItemsDS!Qty = Val(grd_Main.Text)
        grd_Main.Col = col_Desc
        grd_Tag.Col = col_Desc
        grd_Tag.Row = i
        ' Do we have to save the description or
        ' is it identical to the item desc.?
        If grd_Main.Text <> grd_Tag.Text Then
            SalesItemsDS!Desc = grd_Main.Text
        End If
        grd_Main.Col = col_Price
        SalesItemsDS!FinalPrice = Val(grd_Main.Text)
        SalesItemsDS.Update
        ' Eliminate any reserved items
        grd_Tag.Col = col_Reserved
        If Val(grd_Tag.Text) > 0 Then
            ' Eliminate reserved items
            grd_Main.Col = col_ItemNum
            SQL$ = "Select * from Inventory_Sales where PartID = "
                & grd_Main.Text
```

```
Set ScratchDS = MyDB.OpenRecordset(SQL$, dbOpenDynaset)
                ScratchDS.Edit
                ScratchDS!Reserved = ScratchDS!Reserved - Val(grd_Tag.Text)
                ScratchDS!LastResvTime = Null
                ScratchDS.Update
            End If
        Next i
    CommitTrans
End Sub
```

Sub LoadCustomer()

The LoadCustomer routine loads the address information about the selected customer into the txt_ShipTo field. This field is actually saved with the invoice record so the user can make modifications from the standard address stored in the Customer database.

The program reads the information about the customer that is currently selected by the cmb_Customer combo box. Notice that once again, the program uses the ItemData property to obtain the CustomerID for the selected customer. The program then creates a snapshot of the single record to read the information.

> **NOTE**
>
> The following code uses both a Chr$(13) (carriage return) and a Chr$(10) (line feed). This signals the text engine to put the following statements on the next line. You must use both the carriage return and the line feed, or the statements that follow appear on the same line.

```
Private Sub LoadCustomer()
    Dim l_CustID As Long
    Dim s_CustID As Single

    ' Has no customer been selected?
    If cmb_Customer.ListIndex = -1 Then
        cmb_Customer.Text = ""
    Else
        l_CustID = cmb_Customer.ItemData(cmb_Customer.ListIndex)
        SQLStmt = "Select * FROM Customer WHERE CustomerID = " & l_CustID
        Set MySS = MyDB.OpenRecordset(SQLStmt, dbOpenSnapshot)
        txt_ShipTo.Text = cmb_Customer.Text & Chr$(13) & Chr$(10)➥
            & MySS!Address & Chr$(13) & Chr$(10) & MySS!City &➥
            ", " & MySS!State & "   " & MySS!Zip
cmb_Terms.ListIndex = MySS!Terms
    End If
End Sub
```

Sub LoadCustomerPopup ()

The `LoadCustomerPopup` routine loads the combo box that holds all the names of the Customers. The user can select a particular customer from this list. The list also determines if a customer name that the user typed manually into the combo box already exists in the Customer table.

Because Customers can be either individuals or companies, the ORDER BY statement in the SQL query effectively categorizes them. If the Company field is left blank, the ORDER BY command moves it to the front of the list.

As a result, all individuals appear together, alphabetized by LastName, at the top of the combo box list. If you want a different order, simply changing the ORDER BY statement will alter how they appear in the combo box without any new programming!

```
Private Sub LoadCustomerPopup()
    Dim numfields As Integer
    Dim fieldTitle As String
    Dim s As String, qnum As Integer
    Dim CustID As Single

    ' Read all customer and add to Combo Box
    SQLStmt = "Select * FROM Customer ORDER BY Company,LastName"
    Set MySS = MyDB.OpenRecordset(SQLStmt, dbOpenSnapshot)

    cmb_Customer.Clear
    ' Reset record counter
    i = 0
    Do Until MySS.EOF      ' Until end of file.
        Add$ = ""
        If "" & MySS!Company <> "" Then
            Add$ = Add$ & MySS!Company
        Else
            Add$ = MySS!LastName & "," & MySS!FirstName
        End If
        cmb_Customer.AddItem Add$
        CustID = MySS!CustomerID
        cmb_Customer.ItemData(cmb_Customer.NewIndex) = CustID

        i = i + 1
        MySS.MoveNext      ' Move to next record.
    Loop
End Sub
```

Sub LoadInvoiceNum()

You can use the `LoadInvoiceNum` routine to either set the Invoice number to new for a new invoice or display the latest invoice number if you need to generate one. This routine is not used to generate an invoice number at the first creation of an invoice because the user might cancel it, leaving the invoice number reserved. As a result, there would be gaps in the generated invoice numbers that would be unacceptable to most organizations' record keepers.

```
Private Sub LoadInvoiceNum()
    ' Place the appropriate number in the InvoiceNumber field on the screen
    If g_CurrentInvoice = -1 Then
        txt_InvoiceNum = "New"
    Else
        SQLStmt = "Select * FROM Counter"
        Set MySS = MyDB.OpenRecordset(SQLStmt, dbOpenSnapshot)
        txt_InvoiceNum = MySS!InvoiceCount
    End If
End Sub
```

Sub LoadLocation()

The `LoadLocation` routine finds the record of the current location read from the .INI file. If you store the location information in an .INI file, this is the only file you need to modify for the program to record sales at various locations. Because the location doesn't change once the client program is executed, the location information is stored in a label field. Unlike the Salesperson or Customer fields, which obviously must be selected for each invoice, the location remains fixed for the duration of the client program's execution.

> **TIP**
>
> In this client/server system, the information on each location is contained within the main database in the Location table. You should store location information in a separate file. That way, if new stores are added, you can update this file independently.

```
Private Sub LoadLocation()
    ' Display the location where the invoice is being generated
    SQLStmt = "Select * FROM Location WHERE LocationID =" & g_CurrentLocation
    Set MySS = MyDB.OpenRecordset(SQLStmt, dbOpenSnapshot)

    txt_Location = MySS!Description & Chr$(13) & Chr$(10) & MySS!Address ↩
& Chr$(13) & Chr$(10) & MySS!City & ", " & MySS!State & "   " & MySS!Zip
End Sub
```

Sub LoadStaffPopup ()

You use the `LoadStaffPopup` routine to enter all the staff names from the Staff table into a combo box and select the default staff member in the box. Often, one particular staff member uses a client program first. You can set the default staff ID number in the .INI file that the client reads on startup. After the program inserts all the staff into the combo box, it selects that person's ID.

The SQL select statement uses the ORDER BY command to automatically alphabetize the employees. The alternative is to use the SORTED property of the combo box. If there are many staff members, however, it seems a better idea to make the database or the database server handle the processing. This way, you could include other information in the text entries for the combo box list without destroying the order. (A combo box entry might include the first name first and remain sorted by the last name, for example.)

```
Private Sub LoadStaffPopup()
    Dim numfields As Integer
    Dim fieldTitle As String
    Dim s As String, qnum As Integer
    Dim StaffID As Long, SelStaff As Integer

    SQLStmt = "Select * FROM Staff ORDER BY LastName,FirstName"
    Set MySS = MyDB.OpenRecordset(SQLStmt, dbOpenSnapshot)

    SelStaff = -1
    ' Reset record counter
    i = 0
    Do Until MySS.EOF      ' Until end of file.
        Add$ = MySS!LastName & "," & MySS!FirstName
        cmb_Staff.AddItem Add$
        StaffID = MySS!StaffID
        cmb_Staff.ItemData(cmb_Staff.NewIndex) = StaffID
        If StaffID = g_DefaultStaffID Then
            SelStaff = i
        End If

        i = i + 1
        MySS.MoveNext      ' Move to next record.
    Loop
    ' Set staff to equal default staff member
    If SelStaff <> -1 Then
        cmb_Staff.ListIndex = SelStaff
    Else
        cmb_Staff.ListIndex = 0
    End If
End Sub
```

Sub MoveTextBox (Grid As Control, TextBox As Control)

The `MoveTextBox` routine is used to move the text box `txt_GridText` into place over the grid so the user has the illusion of editing the grid cell. Note that this routine does not size the text box to the size of the current row and column. The resizing of the `txt_GridText` control occurs in the `SetCell()` routine.

Because of the different background colors for the Fixed Columns and Fix Rows as well as their traditional content (which is not editable by the user), the editing routine automatically skips these rows and columns. When the X and Y coordinates are determined, the `txt_GridText` moves to that location.

Additionally, the `cmd_Item` button moves to the Y coordinate of this new edit row. The `cmd_Item` button is only visible when the item column is selected, and then it appears to the left of the row that is selected.

```
Private Sub MoveTextBox(grid As Control, TextBox As Control)
    ' Move a text box to the position of the current cell in a grid:
    Dim X As Single
    Dim Y As Single
    Dim i As Integer
    ' Skip grid border
    X = grid.Left
    Y = grid.Top
    If grid.BorderStyle = 1 Then
        X = X + Screen.TwipsPerPixelX
        Y = Y + Screen.TwipsPerPixelY
    End If
    ' Skip fixed columns and rows
    For i = 0 To grid.FixedCols - 1
        X = X + grid.ColWidth(i)
        If grid.GridLines Then
            X = X + Screen.TwipsPerPixelX
        End If
    Next
    
    For i = 0 To grid.FixedRows - 1
        Y = Y + grid.RowHeight(i)
        If grid.GridLines Then
            Y = Y + Screen.TwipsPerPixelY
        End If
    Next
    ' Find current data cell
    For i = grid.LeftCol To grid.Col - 1
        X = X + grid.ColWidth(i)
        If grid.GridLines Then
            X = X + Screen.TwipsPerPixelX
        End If
    Next
    For i = grid.TopRow To grid.Row - 1
        Y = Y + grid.RowHeight(i)
        If grid.GridLines Then
            Y = Y + Screen.TwipsPerPixelY
        End If
    Next
    ' Move the Text Box, and make small adjustments
    TextBox.Move X + Screen.TwipsPerPixelX, Y + Screen.TwipsPerPixelY
    cmd_Item.Move cmd_Item.Left, Y + Screen.TwipsPerPixelY
End Sub
```

Sub RecordToScreen (TempDS As Dynaset)

RecordToScreen reads all the information from a record for an invoice and places the data in the appropriate controls on the screen. This is the central routine for the Next and Previous buttons to page through the available invoices.

> **NOTE**
>
> The `RecordToScreen` and `ScreenToRecord` routines create a layer between the actual record information and the screen. This layer enables the user to modify the data by batch or do the processing before actual database entry. This is in contrast to the simpler direct connection formed by bound controls and the data control.

First, the general information of the invoice is read and placed in each control. The routine then creates a dynaset of all the items that are stored for that invoice. Using a `Do...Until` loop, the program finds and places all the records in both the `grd_Main` and the `grd_Tag`. After the program reads all the items, it uses a `For...Next` loop to find the Unit Cost and the Description (for items that don't have a user-modified description) of all the invoice items. Finally, it stores the Tag fields for the general information for checking later changes and calculating the total of the invoice.

```
Private Sub RecordToScreen(TempDS As Recordset)
    Dim ScratchDS As Recordset

    txt_InvoiceNum.Caption = TempDS!InvoiceID

    txt_Date.Text = TempDS!SaleDate

    ' Set Staff combo to show proper employee for record
    For i = 0 To cmb_Staff.ListCount - 1
        If cmb_Staff.ItemData(i) = TempDS!StaffID Then
            cmb_Staff.ListIndex = i
        End If
    Next i

    cmb_Staff.ListIndex = TempDS!StaffID - 1
    txt_Freight = Format(TempDS!Freight, "##0.00")
    txt_ShipDate.Text = "" & TempDS!ShipDate
    txt_BillDate.Text = "" & TempDS!BillDate

    ' Store till later, loading Customer will set default Terms
    TempTerms = TempDS!Terms
    txt_CustomerPO.Text = "" & TempDS!CustomerPO
    CustID = TempDS!CustomerID

    For i = 0 To cmb_Customer.ListCount - 1
        If CustID = cmb_Customer.ItemData(i) Then
            cmb_Customer.ListIndex = i
            Exit For
        End If
    Next i

    tempShip = "" & TempDS!ShippingTo
    If tempShip = "" Then

    Else
        txt_ShipTo.Text = tempShip
    End If
```

```
    ' Enter individual invoice items into the grid
    SQL$ = "Select * From SalesItems where InvoiceID = " & TempDS!InvoiceID
    Set ScratchDS = MyDB.OpenRecordset(SQL$, dbOpenDynaset)
    grd_Main.Rows = 1
    grd_Main.Rows = 20
    grd_Tag.Rows = 1
    grd_Tag.Rows = 20
    grd_Main.FixedRows = 1
    i = 1
    Do Until ScratchDS.EOF
        grd_Tag.Row = i
        grd_Main.Row = i

        grd_Tag.Col = col_ItemNum
        grd_Tag.Text = ScratchDS!PartID
        grd_Main.Col = col_ItemNum
        grd_Main.Text = ScratchDS!PartID

        grd_Tag.Col = col_Desc
        grd_Tag.Text = "" & ScratchDS!Desc
        grd_Main.Col = col_Desc
        grd_Main.Text = "" & ScratchDS!Desc

        grd_Tag.Col = col_Qty
        grd_Tag.Text = ScratchDS!Qty
        grd_Tag.Col = col_OrigQty
        grd_Tag.Text = ScratchDS!Qty
        grd_Main.Col = col_Qty
        grd_Main.Text = ScratchDS!Qty

        grd_Tag.Col = col_Price
        grd_Tag.Text = Format$(ScratchDS!FinalPrice, "###0.00")
        grd_Main.Col = col_Price
        grd_Main.Text = Format$(ScratchDS!FinalPrice, "###0.00")

        ScratchDS.MoveNext
        i = i + 1
    Loop
    OriginalItems = i - 1
    For j = 0 To i
        grd_Main.Row = j
        grd_Main.Col = 0
        If grd_Main.Text <> "" And IsNumeric(grd_Main.Text) Then
            SQL$ = "Select * from Inventory_Sales WHERE PartID = " _
                & grd_Main.Text
Set PartsDS = MyDB.OpenRecordset(SQL$, dbOpenDynaset)
            grd_Main.Col = col_Desc
            grd_Main.Text = PartsDS!Description
            grd_Main.Col = col_UnitCost
            grd_Main.Text = Format$(PartsDS!UnitCost, "###0.00")

            grd_Tag.Col = col_Desc
            grd_Tag.Text = PartsDS!Description
            grd_Tag.Col = col_UnitCost
            grd_Tag.Text = Format$(PartsDS!UnitCost, "###0.00")
        End If
    Next j
    cmb_Terms.ListIndex = TempTerms
```

```
        ' Save Tag items for later compare
        txt_Date.Tag = txt_Date.Text
        cmb_Customer.Tag = cmb_Customer.Text
        cmb_Staff.Tag = cmb_Staff.Text
        txt_Freight.Tag = txt_Freight.Text
        txt_ShipDate.Tag = txt_ShipDate.Text
        txt_BillDate.Tag = txt_BillDate.Text
        txt_CustomerPO.Tag = txt_CustomerPO.Text

        ' Calculate the total for all displayed items
        CalculateTotal
End Sub
```

Sub SetCell ()

The SetCell routine prepares the txt_GridText box for editing. It calls the MoveTextBox() routine to position the box over the proper grid cell. The current grid row and column are saved to variables so that when these change, later routines will know where to store the edited information. The routine then sizes the text box to fit the current grid and column and transfers the content of the grid cell to the text box.

Next, the routine sets various properties of the text box control. Note that the ZOrder property is set to 0. The ZOrder property sets the front-to-back order of a particular control to other controls on the form. Setting the ZOrder to 0 ensures that the text box will appear on top of all the other controls (preventing the text box from hiding behind the grid, for example).

Finally, the routine checks the selected column number. If the column number is equal to col_ItemNum, the button to select items should become visible.

```
Private Sub SetCell()
       ' Move the text box over the current grid cell
       MoveTextBox grd_Main, txt_GridText
       ' Save the position of the row and column
       gRow = grd_Main.Row
       gCol = grd_Main.Col
       ' Make the text box the same size as current cell
       txt_GridText.Width = grd_Main.ColWidth(grd_Main.Col) ↵
           - 2 * Screen.TwipsPerPixelX
       txt_GridText.Height = grd_Main.RowHeight(grd_Main.Row) ↵
           - 2 * Screen.TwipsPerPixelY
    ' Place the grid cell text into the text box
       txt_GridText.Text = grd_Main.Text
       ' Show the text box
       txt_GridText.Visible = True
       txt_GridText.ZOrder 0
       ' Set the focus on the text box
       txt_GridText.SetFocus
       If gCol = 0 Then
          cmd_Item.Visible = True
       Else
          cmd_Item.Visible = False
       End If
End Sub
```

Sub SetupDefaultScreen ()

The `SetupDefaultScreen` routine simply resets all the screen control values to default values. It essentially creates a blank invoice. This routine is called on first execution after the user clicks the OK button and a new invoice is displayed. Notice that the Tag fields are set to the blank values.

Although this routine is not strictly necessary (because in a new invoice, all the information is saved and the tags are not checked), using it is good design practice so that unmaintained or "dirty" values are not sitting in memory, where they can possibly cause a forgotten routine to return unintended results.

```
Private Sub SetupDefaultScreen()
    ' Set Terms combo box
    cmb_Terms.ListIndex = g_StandardTerms
    grd_Main.Col = 0
    grd_Main.Row = 1
    grd_Tag.Col = 0
    grd_Tag.Row = 1
    SetupGrid
    txt_Date.Text = Format$(Now, "mm-dd-yy")
    LoadInvoiceNum
    cmb_Customer.ListIndex = -1
    txt_ShipTo = ""
    txt_CustomerPO = ""
    txt_ShipDate = ""
    txt_BillDate = ""
    txt_Freight = Format(g_Freight, "##0.00")
    CalculateTotal
End Sub
```

Sub SetupGrid ()

`SetupGrid` sets up the grid control for column titles, column width, and row width. The routine formats both the `grd_Main` and the `grd_Tag` controls for the number of rows and other specifications. After this is complete, the routine determines the width of all the grid columns. The routine then sets the Width property of the entire grid to accommodate all the columns. Without adjusting the width to accomodate all the columns on a single screen, the horizontal scroll bar appears. Having a scrollbar on an invoice screen does not allow the user to see all the critical information at a glance and is a bad interface in this case.

```
Private Sub SetupGrid()
    Dim tempwidth As Integer

    grd_Main.Cols = 5
    ' clear the Main grid completely
    grd_Main.Rows = 1
    ' Make the Tag grid bigger for extra Tag values
    grd_Tag.Cols = 8
    'clears the Tag grid completely
    grd_Tag.Rows = 1
```

```
        grd_Main.Row = 0
        grd_Main.Col = 0
        ' Set column titles
        grd_Main.ColWidth(0) = 800
        grd_Main.Text = "Item#"
        grd_Main.Col = 1
        grd_Main.ColWidth(1) = 3200
        grd_Main.Text = "Description"
        grd_Main.Col = 2
        grd_Main.ColWidth(2) = 800
        grd_Main.Text = "Rate"
        grd_Main.Col = 3
        grd_Main.ColWidth(3) = 800
        grd_Main.Text = "Qty"
        grd_Main.Col = 4
        grd_Main.ColWidth(4) = 900
        grd_Main.Text = "Amount"
        grd_Main.Rows = 5
        grd_Main.FixedRows = 1
        grd_Main.FixedCols = 0
        grd_Tag.Rows = 5
        grd_Tag.FixedRows = 1
        grd_Tag.FixedCols = 0

    tempwidth = 0
    For i = 0 To grd_Main.Cols - 1
        tempwidth = tempwidth + grd_Main.ColWidth(i)
    Next i
    ' Add a little so Scrollbar doesn't overlap last column
    grd_Main.Width = tempwidth + 340
End Sub
```

Sub UpdateInvoice(mainitems As Integer)

UpdateInvoice stores any changes to the current invoice. You can divide the routine into three different pieces: update any changed summary information, add additional line items in the invoice, and update all the invoice lines. The entire routine uses data that was stored when the invoice was originally loaded to determine the new information versus the old.

The first part of the routine checks each text value against the original property stored in the Tag property. Notice that this comparison occurs with the combo box controls as well. The combo box controls have a Text property that mirrors the ListIndex item selected.

The second section of UpdateInvoice checks for items that were added to the original invoice. If there have been additions, the routine adds records to accommodate the new items. Notice that the only information added to these new records is the key fields such as InvoiceID and LineNum. This enables the third section (the update routine) to update all the records, new and old.

Whenever designing an application, try to keep the number of procedures that update or edit data to a minimum and eliminate all unnecessary duplicate routines. When you add new fields to a table or change the functionality, it is extremely easy to overlook a hidden routine and cause endless problems for a client.

The third section of the UpdateInvoice routine updates all the line items that have changed since the invoice was loaded. The routine checks each value against the value held in the grd_Tag. If the value is different, the record is updated. After the update occurs, the values in grd_Tag are updated to those in grd_Main. This ensures that any further editing does not reupdate the same values. The routine then calls the UPDATE command to save the operation.

Finally, the routine activates the CommitTrans command to write all the changes out to the database. The routine sets the variable g_CurrentInvoice to -1, which displays a new invoice.

```
Private Sub UpdateInvoice(mainitems As Integer)
    Dim SQL$
    Dim RecordDS As Recordset
    Dim ScratchDS As Recordset
    Dim TagItems As Integer

    TagItems = CountTagItems()

    BeginTrans
' Check Invoice fields against Tag values
        ' Create Recordset containing invoice record
        SQL$ = "Select * from Sales WHERE InvoiceID = " & txt_InvoiceNum.Caption
        Set RecordDS = MyDB.OpenRecordset(SQL$, dbOpenDynaset)
        RecordDS.Edit
        If txt_Date.Text <> txt_Date.Tag Then
            RecordDS!SaleDate = txt_Date.Text
        End If
        If cmb_Staff.Text <> cmb_Staff.Tag Then
            RecordDS!StaffID = cmb_Staff.ItemData(cmb_Staff.ListIndex)
        End If
        If cmb_Customer.Text <> cmb_Customer.Tag Then
            RecordDS!CustomerID = cmb_Customer.ItemData(cmb_Customer.ListIndex)
        End If
        If txt_Freight.Text <> txt_Freight.Tag Then
            RecordDS!Freight = txt_Freight.Text
        End If
        If txt_ShipDate.Text <> txt_ShipDate.Tag Then
            RecordDS!ShipDate = txt_ShipDate.Text
        End If
        If txt_BillDate.Text <> txt_BillDate.Tag Then
            RecordDS!BillDate = txt_BillDate.Text
        End If
        If txt_ShipTo.Text <> txt_ShipTo.Tag Then
            RecordDS!ShippingTo = txt_ShipTo.Text
        End If
        If cmb_Terms.Text <> cmb_Terms.Tag Then
            RecordDS!Terms = cmb_Terms.ListIndex
        End If
        If txt_CustomerPO.Text <> txt_CustomerPO.Tag Then
            RecordDS!CustomerPO = txt_CustomerPO.Text
        End If
        RecordDS.Update

        ' Are there more items than the original invoice?
        If mainitems > OriginalItems Then
            ' Add slots for new items
            SQL$ = "Select * From SalesItems Where InvoiceID = "➥
                & txt_InvoiceNum
```

```
            Set ScratchDS = MyDB.OpenRecordset(SQL$, dbOpenDynaset)
                For i = 1 To (mainitems - OriginalItems)
                    ScratchDS.AddNew
                    ScratchDS!InvoiceID = Val(txt_InvoiceNum)
                    ScratchDS!Linenum = OriginalItems + i
                    ScratchDS!LocationID = g_CurrentLocation
                    ScratchDS.Update
                Next i
            End If
            For i = 1 To mainitems
            '   any changes from old items check against grd_Tag
                grd_Main.Row = i
                grd_Tag.Row = i

                SQL$ = "Select * From SalesItems Where InvoiceID = " ⮕
                    & txt_InvoiceNum & " and LineNum = " & I
            Set ScratchDS = MyDB.OpenRecordset(SQL$, dbOpenDynaset)
                ScratchDS.Edit

                ' --- ItemNum
                grd_Main.Col = col_ItemNum
                grd_Tag.Col = col_ItemNum
                If grd_Tag.Text <> grd_Main.Text Then
                    ScratchDS!PartID = Val(grd_Main.Text)
                    grd_Tag.Text = grd_Main.Text
                End If

                ' --- Quantity
                grd_Main.Col = col_Qty
                grd_Tag.Col = col_OrigQty
                If grd_Tag.Text <> grd_Main.Text Then
                    ScratchDS!Qty = Val(grd_Main.Text)
                    grd_Tag.Text = grd_Main.Text
                End If

                ' --- Description
                grd_Main.Col = col_Desc
                grd_Tag.Col = col_Desc
                If grd_Tag.Text <> grd_Main.Text Then
                    ScratchDS!Desc = grd_Main.Text
                    grd_Tag.Text = grd_Main.Text
                End If

                ' --- FinalPrice
                grd_Main.Col = col_Price
                grd_Tag.Col = col_Price
                If grd_Tag.Text <> grd_Main.Text Then
                    ScratchDS!FinalPrice = Val(grd_Main.Text)
                    grd_Tag.Text = grd_Main.Text
                End If

                ScratchDS.Update
            Next i
        CommitTrans
        g_CurrentInvoice = -1
End Sub
```

Control Code

You must add all the code in this section to the individual controls. Simply double-click the control on the Sales form and the relevant code box appears. Then, in the drop-down combo box labeled Proc:, select the event the code belongs to.

For example, the first code we discuss in this section belongs to the combo box named cmb_Customer and should be placed in the Click event procedure. The name of the control is followed by a final _ character and then the name of the event.

Sub cmb_Customer_Click ()

The cmb_Customer_Click routine is activated if the user selects a customer from the customer combo box control. The routine calls the LoadCustomer() routine, which fills the Ship To text box, terms, and other fields specific to the customer. The update flag (g_InvoiceDirty) is set to TRUE so if the user clicks the Cancel button, the application knows that information on the invoice will be lost. The application can then prompt the user to make sure he wants to discard the changes.

> **TIP**
>
> Prompting the user to stop accidentally activated commands is one of the most difficult user interface design problems. If the application prompts the user too much, it becomes annoying. If you don't prompt enough, data gets lost unintentionally. Make sure you give some thought to this problem and check back with users a short time after system deployment. They can tell you what is good and what is missing.

```
Private Sub cmb_Customer_Click()
    LoadCustomer
    g_InvoiceDirty = True
End Sub
```

Sub cmb_Customer_LostFocus ()

The application calls the cmb_Customer_LostFocus routine if the combo box has lost the focus. This routine essentially selects the entry that holds the Customer name in the case that the user types the name instead of selecting it. The routine searches the list, sets the ListIndex to the appropriate value, and loads the customer record.

```
Private Sub cmb_Customer_LostFocus() '
    ' Is current value in the customer list?
    For i = 0 To cmb_Customer.ListCount - 1
        If cmb_Customer.Text = cmb_Customer.List(i) Then
            ' Customer is in list, select customer
```

```
            cmb_Customer.ListIndex = i
            LoadCustomer
            Exit Sub
        End If
    Next i
End Sub
```

Sub cmb_Terms_Change ()

The `cmb_Terms_Change` routine simply sets the update flag (`g_InvoiceDirty`) to TRUE if the user has made a change to the selected terms.

```
Private Sub cmb_Terms_Change()
    g_InvoiceDirty = TRUE
End Sub
```

Sub cmd_Cancel_Click ()

If the user clicks the Cancel button, the `cmd_Cancel_Click` routine is activated. It first checks for changes to the invoice that would be lost if the Cancel operation is executed. It then prompts the user to confirm that the changes can be discarded. The `MsgBox()` routine returns the number 1 if the user clicks the OK button.

The routine then sets the `g_CurrentInvoice` variable to -1, which indicates this is a new invoice and executes the `SetupDefaultScreen()` routine. The routine resets the invoice form to a blank form.

```
Private Sub cmd_Cancel_Click()
    ' If flag is dirty, make sure user wants to discard changes
    If g_InvoiceDirty = True Then
        result = MsgBox("Are you sure you want to eliminate all of the " &Â
            "changes you've made to this invoice?", 33, "Cancel Invoice")
If result = 1 Then
            g_CurrentInvoice = -1
            SetupDefaultScreen
        End If
    End If
End Sub
```

Sub cmd_Customer_Click ()

The application executes the `cmd_Customer_Click` routine if the user clicks on the `cmd_Customer` button that is to the right of the `cmb_Customer` control. When the user clicks this button, he wants to either edit the customer selected in the combo box or create a new customer.

The routine first checks the combo box for any selection at all. If no selection is indicated, the variable `NewSupplier` is set to TRUE. Later in the routine, this variable flags code to indicate that a new customer record needs to be processed.

If there is a selection, the routine searches all the listings in the combo box for an entry that matches the text typed into the combo box. The listing is searched by the text rather than by selection (`ListIndex`) because the user might have typed in the name instead of selecting it from the list. In that case, the routine must find the item number.

If the Supplier is not found, the routine creates a new record and shows the frm_Supplier form. Otherwise, the routine sets the g_SupplierID variable to the SupplierID number and shows the frm_Supplier. The frm_Supplier itself, upon loading, checks the variables and determines whether to retrieve any data or fill any fields.

```
Private Sub cmd_Customer_Click()
    Dim NewCustomer As Integer
    Dim CustomerSlot As Integer

    NewCustomer = False
    CustomerSlot = -1

    ' Is there a selection in the combo box?
    If cmb_Customer.ListIndex = -1 Then
        NewCustomer = True
    Else
        ' No selection, search for manually keyed entry
        For i = 0 To cmb_Customer.ListCount - 1
            If cmb_Customer.Text = cmb_Customer.List(i) Then
                CustomerSlot = i
                Exit For
            End If
        Next i
        If CustomerSlot = -1 Then
            NewCustomer = True
        End If
    End If

    If NewCustomer = True Then
        ' Setup blank record
        g_LoadCustFlag = False
        g_ClearCustFlag = True
        frm_Customer.Caption = "New Customer"
        frm_Customer.Show 1
    Else
        ' Load selected customer info
        g_LoadCustFlag = True
        g_ClearCustFlag = False
        g_CustomerID = cmb_Customer.ItemData(cmb_Customer.ListIndex)
        frm_Customer.Caption = "Customer: " & cmb_Customer.Text
        frm_Customer.Show 1
    End If

    ' Reload the customer popup in case any information has been changed
    ' or customer has been added.
    LoadCustomerPopup
End Sub
```

Sub cmd_Item_Click ()

The application activates the cmd_Item_Click routine when the user clicks the cmd_Item (which is the button to the left of the first grid column that is labeled ...). This can only occur when the focus is in the first column of the invoice (otherwise, the button is not visible). The routine displays the Item form to enable the user to choose a Sales item.

All the clients use the Item form; therefore, you provide public variables (properties) to set what the list displays. For example, the property ListQuery defines the SQL query that is used to find all the items to fill the list box. The results of the user's selection are placed in the ListResult property for the calling application to retrieve.

The number 1 with the Show method (frm_Item.Show 1) prevents the user from selecting another window until the frm_Item is closed. Using the number 1 after a Show command makes the form resemble a modal dialog box; the user cannot access other windows until the form is dismissed or hidden.

If the user does not cancel the Item form (indicated by a part value of -1), then the information for that item is entered into the invoice. The g_PartNum is stored in the column 0. The routine then creates a snapshot object to get all of the information about the item entry.

After this information is retrieved and stored in the grd_Main, the routine recalculates the invoice's total. The routine then selects the quantity of this line item and returns control to the system.

```
Private Sub cmd_Item_Click()
    Dim tempsingle As Single

    On Error GoTo SearchError
    g_PartNum = -1
    frm_Item.ListTitle = "Item Selection"
    frm_Item.ListQuery = "Select * FROM Inventory_Sales ORDER BY Description"
    frm_Item.ListItem1 = "Description"
    frm_Item.ListItem2 = ""
    frm_Item.ListIDField = "PartID"
    frm_Item.Show 1
    DoEvents
    If frm_Item.ListResult <> -1 Then
        g_PartNum = frm_Item.ListResult
        grd_Main.Col = 0
        grd_Main.Text = g_PartNum

        grd_Tag.Col = 0
        grd_Tag.Row = grd_Main.Row
        'grd_Tag.Text = g_PartNum

        SQLStmt = "Select * FROM Inventory_Sales WHERE PartID = " _
            & g_PartNum & ";"

        Set MySS = MyDB.OpenRecordset(SQLStmt, dbOpenSnapshot)
        grd_Main.Col = 1
        grd_Main.Text = MySS!Description
        grd_Main.Col = 2
        grd_Main.Text = MySS!UnitCost
        grd_Main.Col = 4
        grd_Main.Text = MySS!UnitCost
        grd_Main.Col = 3
        grd_Main.Text = 1

        grd_Tag.Col = 1
        grd_Tag.Text = MySS!Description
        CalculateTotal
```

```
        DoEvents
        SetCell
        'txt_GridText.SetFocus   ' Set focus back to grid, see Text_LostFocus.
    End If
    g_InvoiceDirty = True
    Exit Sub
SearchError:
    Msg = "Error# " & Err & ":" & Error(Err)
    MsgBox Msg   ' Display message.
Exit Sub
End Sub
```

Sub cmd_Next_Click ()

All the invoices available in the database are accessible from the Sales client. The user chooses the cmd_Next button to display to the next invoice. If the currently shown invoice is the "new" invoice, the application displays a message alerting the user that there are no further stored invoices.

When the user clicks the button, the InvoiceDS (the global dynaset for the invoices) moves to the next record if the current invoice is not a blank invoice. If the next record is an invoice, the application calls the RecordToScreen() routine to move the invoice information and all the invoice line items onto the screen. The routine also sets the global invoice value to indicate this selected invoice. If the routine reaches the end-of-file, it shows a new invoice and clears the screen of values.

```
Private Sub cmd_Next_Click()
    If g_CurrentInvoice = -1 Then
        MsgBox "There aren't any newer invoices than the current invoice. " &Â
           "Please use the 'Prev' button to access other invoices.",Â
           16, "No Next Invoices"
    Else
        InvoicesDS.MoveNext
        ' If last invoice, show blank invoice
        If InvoicesDS.EOF = True Then
            g_CurrentInvoice = -1
            SetupDefaultScreen
        Else
            ' Load new invoice
            RecordToScreen InvoicesDS
            g_CurrentInvoice = Val(txt_InvoiceNum)
        End If
    End If
End Sub
```

Sub cmd_OK_Click ()

When the user clicks the OK button, the application records the current invoice to the database. Before this can be done, the cmd_OK_Click routine must make many checks on the validity of the data entered into the invoice by the user. It checks the customer name to make sure one is entered and then to make sure the entered name exists in the Customer table. The application does not save the invoice if the customer is not valid.

Providing the customer is valid, the routine proceeds to check the individual line items. The routine makes sure that some items are entered on the invoice by calling the `CountMainItems()` routine.

If the invoice is valid, the routine determines whether the invoice itself is a new invoice or an update. The routines must be separate because creating a record from scratch has far different needs than updating an existing invoice. Finally, the routine creates a new blank invoice.

```vb
Private Sub cmd_OK_Click()
    Dim CustomerSlot As Integer
    Dim result As Integer, numItems As Integer
    Dim ScratchDS As Recordset, TempTable As Table

    CustomerSlot = -1
    ' Make sure a customer is selected
    If cmb_Customer.Text = "" Then
        MsgBox "A Customer name is required for an invoice. " & _
            "Please select a customer from the list", _
            16, "Empty Customer Name"
Exit Sub
    End If
    ' Make sure that customer is in the customer list
    For i = 0 To cmb_Customer.ListCount - 1
        If cmb_Customer.Text = cmb_Customer.List(i) Then
            CustomerSlot = i
            Exit For
        End If
    Next i

    If CustomerSlot = -1 Then
        result = MsgBox("The customer name is not in the Customer list. " & _
            "Would you like to add it?", 33, "Add New Customer?")
If result = 1 Then
            ' Setup blank record
            g_LoadCustFlag = False
            g_ClearCustFlag = True
            frm_Customer.Caption = "New Customer"
            frm_Customer.Show 1
            LoadCustomerPopup
            MsgBox "Now please select the customer and click on " & _
                "the 'OK' button again to save the invoice.", 64
' User must now select the customer
            Exit Sub
        Else
            Exit Sub
        End If
    End If

    ' Make sure that items have been entered on the invoice
    ' & items are listed in SalesInventory table
    numItems = CountMainItems()

    If numItems = 0 Then
        MsgBox "There are no items with prices in this invoice. " & _
            "Please enter an item before saving the invoice.", _
            16, "Blank Invoice"
```

```
        Exit Sub
    End If

    If txt_InvoiceNum = "New" Then
        CreateNewInvoice numItems
    Else
        UpdateInvoice numItems
    End If

    SetupDefaultScreen
End Sub
```

Sub cmd_Prev_Click ()

The user clicks the `cmd_Prev` button to show previous invoices. The client program is designed so that conceptually a blank invoice follows the last existing invoice. As a result, if the user clicks the `cmd_Prev` button while a new invoice is displayed, this routine displays the last available invoice record.

If the client is displaying the very first invoice, the routine displays a message alerting the user that there are no further stored invoices. If the current invoice is not a blank invoice, the InvoiceDS (the global dynaset for the invoices) moves to the previous record.

The application calls the `RecordToScreen()` routine to move the invoice information and all the invoice line items onto the screen. It also sets the global invoice value to indicate this selected invoice.

```
Private Sub cmd_Prev_Click()
    ' Is a blank invoice being shown?
    If g_CurrentInvoice = -1 Then
        ' Move to last invoice in the file
        InvoicesDS.MoveLast
    Else
        InvoicesDS.MovePrevious
        If InvoicesDS.BOF = True Then
            MsgBox "No previous invoices", 16, "No previous invoices"
InvoicesDS.MoveNext
        End If
    End If
    RecordToScreen InvoicesDS
    g_CurrentInvoice = Val(txt_InvoiceNum)
End Sub
```

Sub cmd_Print_Click ()

The application activates the `cmd_Print_Click` routine if the user clicks the `cmd_Print` button. The routine prints the current invoice to the printer object. This routine is merely a basic demonstration; we recommend that you use a third-party report generator or preview tool. They provide far most robust capabilities and tools that will dramatically decrease your report development time. For more information, see Chapter 29, "Third Party Tools, Utilities, and Controls."

> **NOTE**
>
> Although very simple, the printer object does have some uses. It will print to any printer, graphics enabled or not. It is also fairly speedy to use.
>
> We most often use the printer object when we need to use carbon forms in the printer. A laser printer cannot use the three-ply forms that many companies require. The printer object prints to a daisy wheel or dot-matrix printer quickly and effectively. Also, the data sent to the printer object can be sent to a form instead for on-screen viewing of the soon-to-be printed information.

```
Private Sub cmd_Print_Click()
    On Error GoTo ErrorHandler

    Printer.FontBold = True
    Printer.Print "WidgetCo."
    Printer.FontBold = False
    ' Location Address/Phone
    Printer.Print frm_Invoice.txt_Location
    Printer.Print
    ' Print Invoice Number
    Printer.Print "Invoice # " & frm_Invoice.txt_InvoiceNum
    Printer.Print
    ' Print Bill To & Ship To
    Printer.FontBold = True
    Printer.Print "Ship To:"
    Printer.FontBold = False
    Printer.Print frm_Invoice.txt_ShipTo
    Printer.Print
    ' Print Salesperson Name
    Printer.Print "Salesperson: " & frm_Invoice.cmb_Staff.Text;
    ' Print Customer PO
    Printer.Print Tab(35); "Cust PO:" & frm_Invoice.txt_CustomerPO;
    ' Print Ship Date
    Printer.Print Tab(55); "Ship Date: " & frm_Invoice.txt_ShipDate
    ' Print Terms
    Printer.Print "Terms:" & frm_Invoice.cmb_Terms.Text;
    ' Print Date invoice was entered
    Printer.Print Tab(35); "Date: " & frm_Invoice.txt_Date
    Printer.Print

    ' Print Invoice Item Headings
    Printer.Print "Item #"; Tab(12); "Description"; Tab(40); ➥
        "Price"; Tab(50); "Qty."; Tab(60); "Total"
    Printer.Line (0, Printer.CurrentY + 6) - ➥
        (Printer.Width, Printer.CurrentY + 6)
Printer.Print
    ' Print Invoice Items
    For i = 1 To frm_Invoice.grd_Main.Rows - 1
        frm_Invoice.grd_Main.Row = i
        frm_Invoice.grd_Main.Col = 0
        If frm_Invoice.grd_Main.Text <> "" Then
            Printer.Print frm_Invoice.grd_Main.Text; Tab(12);
            frm_Invoice.grd_Main.Col = 1
```

```
            Printer.Print frm_Invoice.grd_Main.Text; Tab(40);
            frm_Invoice.grd_Main.Col = 2
            Printer.Print Format$(Val(frm_Invoice.grd_Main.Text),➥
                "$####.#0"); Tab(50);
frm_Invoice.grd_Main.Col = 3
            Printer.Print frm_Invoice.grd_Main.Text; Tab(60);
            frm_Invoice.grd_Main.Col = 4
            Printer.Print Format$(Val(frm_Invoice.grd_Main.Text), "$####.#0")
        End If
    Next i
    Printer.Line (0, Printer.CurrentY + 6)-➥
        (Printer.Width, Printer.CurrentY + 6)
Printer.Print
    ' Print Shipping
    Printer.Print Tab(45); "Freight:"; Tab(60);
➥Format$(Val(frm_Invoice.txt_Freight), "$###0.00")
    ' Print Sales Tax
    Printer.Print Tab(45); "Sales Tax:"; Tab(60); Format$(Val(frm_Invoice.txt_Tax),
➥ "$###0.00")
    ' Print Total
    Printer.FontBold = True
    Printer.Print Tab(45); "Total:"; Tab(60); Format$(Val(frm_Invoice.txt_Total),➥
"$###0.00")
    Printer.FontBold = False
    Printer.EndDoc
    Exit Sub

ErrorHandler:
    MsgBox "There was a problem printing to your printer."
Exit Sub

End Sub
```

Sub Form_Activate ()

The `Form_Activate` routine simply selects the Customer combo box for editing. This routine is a very useful event to update information when a form is selected. If the update routines are placed in the `Paint` event, they are activated every time a redraw occurs whether the window is selected or not.

```
Private Sub Form_Activate()
    cmb_Customer.SetFocus
End Sub
```

Sub Form_Load ()

The `Load` event causes the Invoice form to initialize. The default values are read from the .INI file for the current location, central database path, and so on.

The routine creates the primary form-level dynasets and snapshots that the invoice engine will access. Notice that the dynasets are created with the `LockEdits` property set to `FALSE`. This creates optimistic locking for the record updating. For more information on optimistic and pessimistic record locking, see Chapter 5, "Visual Basic Data Access."

The routine initializes the various combo boxes from the database file to include the necessary data. After all the parameters are initialized, the routine creates a blank invoice and sets the update invoice flag (g_InvoiceDirty) to False. The Me command is a handy Visual Basic command that returns the name of the form that the control is on. You could place this same statement on any form without modification, and it will close the window.

```
Private Sub Form_Load()
    CenterForm Me

' Setup path of INI file with location of project or executable
    INIPath = GetAppPath() & "Sales.INI"

    ' Point access engine to look for INI file in application directory
    DBEngine.INIPath = INIPath

    ' Read global parameters for default values
    g_CurrentLocation = Val(ReadINI("Parameters", "LocationID", INIPath))
    g_DefaultStaffID = Val(ReadINI("Parameters", "DefaultStaffID", INIPath))
    g_StandardTerms = Val(ReadINI("Parameters", "StandardTerms", INIPath))
    g_SalesTax = Val(ReadINI("Parameters", "SalesTax", INIPath))
    g_Freight = Val(ReadINI("Parameters", "Freight", INIPath))
    g_DataLocation = ReadINI("Parameters", "DataLocation", INIPath)
    g_DBName = ReadINI(g_DataLocation, "DBName", INIPath)

    ' Open connection to Database
    Set MyDB = OpenDatabase(g_DBName, False, False)

    ' Setup recordsets for invoice browing
    Set InvoicesDS = MyDB.OpenRecordset("Select * from Sales", dbOpenDynaset)
    InvoicesDS.LockEdits = False
    InvoicesDS.MoveLast

    Set SalesItemsDS = MyDB.OpenRecordset("Select * from SalesItems", Â
        dbOpenDynaset)
SalesItemsDS.LockEdits = False

    ' Initialize variables
    g_CurrentInvoice = -1
    LoadCustomerPopup
    LoadStaffPopup
    LoadLocation

    cmb_Terms.AddItem "Cash"
    cmb_Terms.AddItem "Net 30"
    cmb_Terms.AddItem "Net 15"
    cmb_Terms.AddItem "1% 10 Net 30"
    cmb_Terms.AddItem "2% 10 Net 30"
    SetupDefaultScreen
    g_InvoiceDirty = False
End Sub
```

Sub Form_Unload (Cancel As Integer)

The application calls the Form_Unload routine as the main form (SALES.FRM) is unloaded. An END statement finishes execution and quits the program. You can use the Unload event for all of the program's housekeeping. It can unload variables, close files, release objects, and perform any other end maintenance that needs to be done before execution ends.

> **NOTE**
>
> Putting an END in the Unload event of the main form is crucial to the proper operation of your applications. Visual Basic 4.0 does not automatically close all the forms for the application when the main form is closed. If the user uses the close window drop-down menu to close the main form while other forms are hidden, the application will remain open. This causes a "phantom application;" the application appears in the Alt+Tab and the Ctrl+Esc task list but does not show a window.
>
> If you put an END statement in the Unload event of the main form, the application will shut down when the main form is closed.

```
Private Sub Form_Unload(Cancel As Integer)
    End
End Sub
```

Sub grd_Main_Click ()

If the user clicks the grd_Main, the grd_Main_Click routine calls SetCell (which places the text box over the selected cell for editing) and then sets the focus to the text control txt_GridText. This gives the user the illusion that he is editing the cell itself inside the grid.

In reality, txt_GridText is sized to fit the cell that was clicked and moved into place over it, and the grid cell's contents are copied into the text box. The routine also sets the parameter g_Dirty to TRUE so the application will save the invoice when the user clicks the OK button.

> **TIP**
>
> This use of the grid is an excellent example of ingenuity in Visual Basic design. The original Microsoft programmer who came up with this technique should be rewarded. However, for a professional application, we recommend that you purchase an editable grid control. These controls also have powerful database and display capabilities. See Chapter 29, "Third-Party Tools, Utilities, and Controls," for more information.

```
Private Sub grd_Main_Click()
    ' Set text box over select cell
    SetCell
    ' Set focus to text box
    txt_GridText.SetFocus
    g_InvoiceDirty = True
End Sub
```

Sub grd_Main_KeyPress (KeyAscii As Integer)

The application calls the `grd_Main_KeyPress` routine when the grid has the focus and the user presses a key. If the user presses the Enter key, the key press is sent to the `txt_GridText` control for handling.

> **TIP**
>
> If you ever need to nullify a key press event, a program can set the `KeyAscii` variable to `0` and then exit this routine. This is one technique that you can use to make a text box read-only or to trap out specific keystrokes.

```
Private Sub grd_Main_KeyPress(KeyAscii As Integer)
    SetCell
    ' Redirect this KeyPress event to the text box:
    If KeyAscii <> ASC_ENTER Then
        SendKeys Chr$(KeyAscii)
    End If
End Sub
```

Text Control Change Event Routines

The `txt_BillDate_Change ()`, `txt_CustomerPO_Change ()`, `txt_Date_Change ()`, `txt_ShipDate_Change ()`, and `txt_ShipTo_Change ()` routines are all activated if the user makes a change to the text. If the user changes the text, the update invoice flag (`g_InvoiceDirty`) is set to `True`. This enables the routines to check if any changes have been made to the invoice.

```
Sub txt_BillDate_Change ()
    g_InvoiceDirty = True
End Sub
Sub txt_CustomerPO_Change ()
    g_InvoiceDirty = True
End Sub
Sub txt_Date_Change ()
    g_InvoiceDirty = True
End Sub

Sub txt_Freight_LostFocus ()
    CalculateTotal
End Sub

Sub txt_ShipDate_Change ()
    g_InvoiceDirty = True
End Sub

Sub txt_ShipTo_Change ()
    g_InvoiceDirty = True
End Sub
```

Sub txt_GridText_GotFocus ()

The `txt_GridText_GotFocus` routine selects all the text currently stored in the `txt_GridText` control. The routine is activated when the user selects a particular cell. By selecting the contents, the user can replace the current text by simply beginning to type.

```
Private Sub txt_GridText_GotFocus()
    txt_GridText.SelStart = 0
    txt_GridText.SelLength = 32000
End Sub
```

Sub txt_GridText_KeyPress (KeyAscii As Integer)

The `txt_GridText_KeyPress` routine captures a carriage-return key and resets the focus to the `grd_Main`. By setting the `KeyAscii` to `0` in the `KeyPress` event, no other routines react to the KeyPress.

```
Private Sub txt_GridText_KeyPress(KeyAscii As Integer)
    If KeyAscii = ASC_ENTER Then
        grd_Main.SetFocus    ' Set focus back to grid, see Text_LostFocus.
        KeyAscii = 0         ' Ignore this KeyPress.
    End If
End Sub
```

Sub txt_GridText_LostFocus ()

If the text control `txt_GridText` loses the focus, the user must have selected something else. This routine transfers the text that is stored in the text control back to the cell of the grid it was displayed over.

After this is finished, the routine must check the quantity. If the user changed the quantity, the program must reserve additional items. The routine must also check for price changes. If the user changed a price, the program must recalculate the total and tax.

```
Private Sub txt_GridText_LostFocus()
    Dim tmpRow As Integer
    Dim tmpCol As Integer
    ' Save current settings of Grid Row and col. This is needed only if
    ' the focus is set somewhere else in the Grid.
    tmpRow = grd_Main.Row
    tmpCol = grd_Main.Col
    ' Set Row and Col back to what they were before Text1_LostFocus:
    grd_Main.Row = gRow
    grd_Main.Col = gCol
    grd_Main.Text = txt_GridText.Text   ' Transfer text back to grid.
    
    CheckQtyChange
    CheckPriceChange
    
    txt_GridText.SelStart = 0        ' Return caret to beginning.
    txt_GridText.Visible = False     ' Disable text box.
```

```
    ' Return row and Col contents:
        grd_Main.Row = tmpRow
        grd_Main.Col = tmpCol
End Sub
```

Sub txt_TabBefore_GotFocus ()

Capturing tabs from Visual Basic is not a simple process. Pressing the Tab key automatically moves the focus to the control that has a TabIndex property one greater than the current item's TabIndex. Pressing the Shift+Tab does exactly the opposite, subtracting 1.

The invoice in the Sales client should work in a way that is familiar to users. In a traditional spreadsheet or database, the Tab and Shift+Tab key presses move the selected cell box forward and backward, respectively. We have simply created two text box controls with a TabIndex one less and one more than that of the `txt_GridText` control.

> **WARNING**
>
> Make sure the two text boxes created earlier have TabIndex properties that numerically "straddle" that of the `txt_GridText` control. Otherwise, the Tab and Shift+Tab routines will not work correctly. For example, if the TabIndex property of `txt_GridText` is set to 5, the `txt_TabBefore` control should have a TabIndex of 4 and the `txt_TabNext` control should have a TabIndex value of 6.

When this routine receives the focus, it moves the selected cell one to the left and returns the focus to `txt_GridText`. If the cell is in column 0 when the user presses the Shift+Tab key, the selected cell is set to the far-right column of the row above. This is a simple solution to the problem of providing a familiar user interface.

```
Private Sub txt_TabBefore_GotFocus()
    ' Make sure that the selected cell is not on the very first rectangle
    If Not (grd_Main.Col = 0 And grd_Main.Row = 1) Then
        If grd_Main.Col > 0 Then
            grd_Main.Col = grd_Main.Col - 1
        Else
            grd_Main.Col = grd_Main.Cols - 1
            grd_Main.Row = grd_Main.Row - 1
        End If
    End If
    SetCell
    txt_GridText.SetFocus    ' Set focus back to grid, see Text_LostFocus.
End Sub
```

Sub txt_TabNext_GotFocus ()

When the `txt_TabNext_GotFocus` routine receives the focus, it moves the selected cell one to the right and returns the focus to `txt_GridText`. If the cell is in last column when the user presses the Tab key, the selected cell is set to the first column of the row below. It provides the opposite function of the `txt_TabBefore` control.

```
Private Sub txt_TabNext_GotFocus()
    If grd_Main.Col + 1 < grd_Main.Cols Then
        grd_Main.Col = grd_Main.Col + 1
    Else
        grd_Main.Col = 0
        grd_Main.Row = grd_Main.Row + 1
    End If
    SetCell
    txt_GridText.SetFocus    ' Set focus back to grid, see Text_LostFocus.
End Sub
```

Menu Items Code

You enter the following code after you first select the item from the menu on the Invoice form. You can also enter the event code by selecting the particular menu object and then the Proc: in the code editing window. The following routines simply exit, cut, copy, paste, and display a form.

```
Sub cmd_Exit_Click ()
    End
End Sub

Sub CopyItem_Click ()
    SendEditMessage WM_COPY
End Sub

Sub Cutitem_Click ()
    SendEditMessage WM_CUT
End Sub

Sub ExitItem_Click ()
    End
End Sub

Sub PasteItem_Click ()
    SendEditMessage WM_PASTE
End Sub

Sub ShowInventoryItem_Click ()
    frm_Inventory.Show
End Sub
```

Adding Code to the ITEM.FRM

The Item form is a general form used to display a list of items that the user can select. The form itself was designed to be reusable. In order to accomplish this goal, we used a new feature in Visual Basic 4: public variables. A form can now have public variables (or properties) that other forms and modules can access.

Once these properties are set, these values are used to fill the list box when the form is activated. The user can specify the title of the list box, the query used to display the information, the field stored in each item's ItemData, and the fields displayed in the box. The user's selection is returned in one of the properties.

To create the form, enter the variable definitions in the General Declarations portion of the form. Then, add any form level routines to the General section of the code. Finally, include all the code for the various events supported by the form.

General Declarations

All the variables in the declarations section of this form are public variables, which makes them available to other forms and modules as properties. For example, to set the ListTitle property, another form might contain the code `frm_Item.ListTitle = "My List"`. All the properties except ListResult are input properties so that they return the result of the user's selection.

```
Public ListTitle As String
Public ListQuery As String
Public ListItem1 As String
Public ListItem2 As String
Public ListIDField As String
Public ListResult As Integer
```

General Routines

All of the routines in this section belong in the General section of the form. Code you place in the General section is available to all routines within the form. To create a new routine, select New Procedure under the View menu. A dialog box asks whether the routine should be a Sub or Function.

For each of the following routines, the type is in the title. Type in the routine name (without the open and close parentheses) and click the OK button. A window opens and shows the begin and end routine structure. Type the text found in each of the following sections.

Sub LoadItemList ()

The `LoadItemList` routine loads the list control named `List1` with data from the query. The caption to the list box is passed in the ListTitle property. The query itself must be stored in the ListQuery property, from which a dynaset is created.

The program's `Do...Until` loop cycles through each record in the dynaset and displays the fields specified in the ListItem1 and ListItem2 properties. If ListItem2 is set to an empty string (`""`), the routine displays only one field. If both properties contain values, the routine displays two fields separated by a comma. The routine stores set the value of the field specified in the ListIDField property to the ItemData array for each item. For example, the ListIDField may specify the PartID field in the table, and the PartID number for the selected record is stored for each item in the list.

```
Private Sub LoadItemList()
    ' Set caption of form to ListTitle property
    Me.Caption = ListTitle
```

```
    ' Get query from public property
    SQL$ = ListQuery
    Set MySS = MyDB.OpenRecordset(SQL$, dbOpenSnapshot)

    ' Clear list box
    lst_Item.Clear
    ' Reset record counter
    i = 0

    ' Process all of the records until the end of the file
Do Until MySS.EOF
    If ListItem2 = "" Then
        ' Add the item description to the listbox
lst_Item.AddItem MySS.Fields(ListItem1)
    Else
        ' Add the item decription to the listbox
        lst_Item.AddItem MySS.Fields(ListItem1) &Â
            ", " & MySS.Fields(ListItem2)
End If
    ' Store the PartID into the related ItemData field. When
    ' the user selects the item from the list, the record in the
    ' database can be instantly accessed by searching for the
' equivalent PartID
    PartID = MySS.Fields(ListIDField)
    lst_Item.ItemData(lst_Item.NewIndex) = PartID

    i = i + 1
    MySS.MoveNext      ' Move to next record.
    Loop
    lst_Item.ListIndex = 0
End Sub
```

Control Code

You must add all of the code in this section to the individual controls. Simply double-click the control on the Item form, and the relevant code box appears. Then, in the drop-down combo box labeled `Proc:`, select the event the code belongs to.

Sub cmd_Cancel_Click ()

If the user clicks the Cancel button, the window needs to notify the `cmd_Cancel_Click` routine that the user canceled without selecting an item. This is accomplished by setting the ListResult property to -1.

```
Private Sub cmd_Cancel_Click()
    ListResult = -1
    Me.Hide
End Sub
```

Sub cmd_OK_Click ()

If the user clicks the OK button, the `cmd_OK_Click` routine sets the ListResult property to the ItemData value of the currently selected item. This provides the calling routine with instant access to the key of the record that was selected.

```
Private Sub cmd_OK_Click()
    ListResult = lst_Item.ItemData(lst_Item.ListIndex)
    Me.Hide
End Sub
```

Sub Form_Activate ()

The Activate event code is executed every time the user activates the form. It first sets the ListResult to -1, which signifies no return value. This is important because if the user clicks the close box instead of the Cancel button, the Cancel routine that normally sets the value to -1 will not be activated. An item the user didn't select could be accidentally returned. By setting the value here, we avoid such a possibility.

The routine then calls the LoadItemList() routine to fill the list box with items from the query. All the necessary properties (such as the ListItem1, ListItem2, and ListIDField variables) must be set in order for the list box to fill properly.

```
Private Sub Form_Activate()
    ListResult = -1
    LoadItemList
End Sub
```

Sub List1_DblClick ()

When the user double-clicks an item, the program activates the OK button click routine. This is an excellent user interface and programming device. Users are accustomed to double-clicking for a shortcut to operations.

This routine does not directly "okay" the item but instead calls the main OK routine. This enables the routine to remain centralized, which is good programming practice. This reference makes all the OK operations accessible using a single routine call.

It is a good idea to use this type of call activation for any on-screen buttons that have parallel menu items. Then, it is necessary to maintain only one set of code.

```
Private Sub lst_Item_DblClick()
    cmd_OK_Click
End Sub
```

Adding Code to the INVNTRY.FRM

The Inventory form displays a list of the current sales inventory as well as two summary numbers. Adding the code to the Inventory form is straightforward because the form itself accepts no user input. Very few event routines are required. First, you create any form level routines, putting them in the General section of the code. These routines are not activated by an event (such as a mouse click) but are called by other parts of the code.

Control Code

You must add all the code discussed in this section to the individual controls. Simply double-click the control on the Inventory form, and the relevant code box appears. Then, in the drop-down combo box labeled `Proc:`, select the event the code belongs to.

Sub cmd_OK_Click ()

Because the Inventory form is strictly informational, it doesn't need a Cancel button. The OK button needs only to hide the current form.

```
Private Sub cmd_OK_Click()
    Me.Hide
End Sub
```

Sub Form_Load ()

The `Load()` routine sets up the tabs in the list box using the `SendMessage()` Windows API call. The routine also calls the `CenterForm()` routine in order to center the form on the user's screen.

```
Private Sub Form_Load()
   Dim NumOftabs As Integer
   ReDim Tabs(3) As Long

    ' Setup tabs for lst_Reserved
    NumOftabs = 3
    Tabs(0) = 70
    Tabs(1) = 115
    Tabs(2) = 190

    ' Use Windows API call to set tab stops
    temp = SendMessage(lst_Items.hWnd, LB_SETTABSTOPS, NumOftabs, Tabs(0))

    CenterForm Me
End Sub
```

Sub Form_Paint ()

The `Paint()` routine actually gathers the inventory data for display and adds it to the list box. The routine creates a snapshot that contains all the records in the Inventory_Sales table. The `Do…Until` loop then adds each item to the list. The `Form_Load()` event already created the width of the tab settings. Finally, the routine stores the total number of items (how many different types of items are in inventory) as well as the total quantity of items (the number of units for all of the items) in text box controls at the bottom of the form.

> **TIP**
>
> Note that you should calculate the total number of items with a SQL aggregate function. Using the aggregate commands places the processing demand on the server where it belongs. This is only an example to show how you might cycle through the

> entire database. For examples of more complex queries that use aggregate functions, see the queries for the management client in Chapter 13.

```
Private Sub Form_Paint()
    Dim ScratchSS As Recordset
    Dim numItems As Integer, numParts As Integer

    ' Query entire database
    SQL$ = "Select * from Inventory_Sales"
    Set ScratchSS = MyDB.OpenRecordset(SQL$, dbOpenSnapshot)

    lst_Items.Clear
    numItems = 0
    numParts = 0

    ' Add each record to sum
    Do Until ScratchSS.EOF
        lst_Items.AddItem ScratchSS!Description & Chr$(9)Â
            & Str$(ScratchSS!OnHand) & Chr$(9) & Str$(ScratchSS!ReOrderQty)
numParts = numParts + ScratchSS!OnHand
        numItems = numItems + 1
        ScratchSS.MoveNext
    Loop
    txt_numItems = numItems
    txt_numParts = numParts
End Sub
```

Adding Code to the CUST.FRM

The Customer form enables a user to add a customer or edit the information of an existing customer. This form begins by creating a dynaset that contains only the record that the user will edit. The application then copies the data to the fields of the form and each control's tag field so the program can check for any changes to the original data.

When the user is done editing the form, the application checks the various fields for accuracy (ensuring there are no letters in the numeric fields, for example) and copies them into a variable structure. This variable structure is then written into the record.

Adding the code to the form is a routine task. First, you create the form level routines, placing them in the General section of the code. These routines are not activated by an event (such as a mouse click) but are called by other parts of the code.

General Declarations

There is only a single general declaration for this form. Enter the CustomerDS variable in the General Declarations section. This is used to create a single record recordset that points to the record of the selected customer.

```
Dim CustomerDS As Recordset
```

General Routines

You add all the routines discussed in this section to the General section of the form. Code in the General section is available to all routines within the form. To create a new routine, select Procedure under the Insert menu. Enter the routine name and type, and click the OK button. The code window opens and shows the begin and end routine structure. Type the text from the following sections.

Sub CopyTags ()

The application uses the `CopyTags` routine to set all the Tag properties of the controls that hold data equal to the text properties that contain the actual data. As changes are made to the text properties, the application can compare them with the tags to determine which ones have changed.

```
Private Sub CopyTags()
    ' Set Tags equal to Text
    txt_Company.Tag = txt_Company.Text
    txt_LastName.Tag = txt_LastName.Text
    txt_FirstName.Tag = txt_FirstName.Text
    txt_Title.Tag = txt_Title.Text
    txt_Address.Tag = txt_Address.Text
    txt_City.Tag = txt_City.Text
    txt_State.Tag = txt_State.Text
    txt_Zip.Tag = txt_Zip.Text
    txt_Country.Tag = txt_Country.Text
    txt_Phone.Tag = txt_Phone.Text
    txt_Fax.Tag = txt_Fax.Text
    cmb_Terms.Tag = cmb_Terms.Text
    txt_Notes.Tag = txt_Notes.Text
End Sub
```

Sub RecordToScreen (TempDS As Recordset)

The `RecordToScreen` routine copies all the fields from the record into the various controls on the screen. Notice the values that are set with a `""` and the `&` command. These fields might contain NULL values, and this prevents an error from occurring. Setting a control property to a NULL creates an error.

```
Private Sub RecordToScreen(TempDS As Recordset)
    ' The double quotes will eliminate an error if field is Null
    txt_Company.Text = "" & TempDS!Company
    txt_LastName.Text = "" & TempDS!LastName
    txt_FirstName.Text = "" & TempDS!FirstName
    txt_Title.Text = "" & TempDS!Title
    txt_Address.Text = "" & TempDS!Address
    txt_City.Text = "" & TempDS!City
    txt_State.Text = "" & TempDS!State
    txt_Zip.Text = "" & TempDS!Zip
    txt_Country.Text = "" & TempDS!Country
    txt_Phone.Text = "" & TempDS!Phone
    txt_Fax.Text = "" & TempDS!FaxPhone
    cmb_Terms.ListIndex = Val(TempDS!Terms)
```

```
    txt_Notes.Text = "" & TempDS!Notes
    txt_CustomerID.Caption = g_CustomerID
End Sub
```

Sub ScreentoRecord (TempDS As Recordset)

The `ScreentoRecord` routine takes all the values from the screen and writes off any changes to the selected record. The routine calls the EDIT method to activate the Edit mode. Then, the routine compares each value against the Tag values for any differences. Because the Tag properties were originally set to equal the record values, any changes the user made are reflected in the text fields.

```
Private Sub ScreentoRecord(TempDS As Recordset)
    TempDS.Edit

    ' Compare each field to original value, only save if changed
    If txt_Company.Text <> txt_Company.Tag Then
        TempDS!Company = txt_Company.Text
    End If
    If txt_LastName.Text <> txt_LastName.Tag Then
        TempDS!LastName = txt_LastName.Text
    End If
    If txt_FirstName.Text <> txt_FirstName.Tag Then
        TempDS!FirstName = txt_FirstName.Text
    End If
    If txt_Title.Text <> txt_Title.Tag Then
        TempDS!Title = txt_Title.Text
    End If
    If txt_Address.Text <> txt_Address.Tag Then
        TempDS!Address = txt_Address.Text
    End If
    If txt_City.Text <> txt_City.Tag Then
        TempDS!City = txt_City.Text
    End If
    If txt_State.Text <> txt_State.Tag Then
        TempDS!State = txt_State.Text
    End If
    If txt_Zip.Text <> txt_Zip.Tag Then
        TempDS!Zip = txt_Zip.Text
    End If
    If txt_Country.Text <> txt_Country.Tag Then
        TempDS!Country = txt_Country.Text
    End If
    If txt_Phone.Text <> txt_Phone.Tag Then
        TempDS!Phone = txt_Phone.Text
    End If
    If txt_Fax.Text <> txt_Fax.Tag Then
        TempDS!FaxPhone = txt_Fax.Text
    End If
    If txt_Notes.Text <> txt_Notes.Tag Then
        TempDS!Notes = txt_Notes.Text
    End If
    If cmb_Terms.Text <> cmb_Terms.Tag Then
        TempDS!Terms = cmb_Terms.ListIndex
    End If
```

```
    TempDS.Update
End Sub
```

Sub SetupDefaultScreen ()

The `SetupDefaultScreen()` sets the controls in the form to empty values. This prevents a previously hidden form from showing old information. The routine then calls `CopyTags()` to synchronize the Tag properties to the new empty values.

```
Private Sub SetupDefaultScreen()
    txt_Company.Text = ""
    txt_LastName.Text = ""
    txt_FirstName.Text = ""
    txt_Title.Text = ""
    txt_Address.Text = ""
    txt_City.Text = ""
    txt_State.Text = ""
    txt_Zip.Text = ""
    txt_Country.Text = ""
    txt_Phone.Text = ""
    txt_Fax.Text = ""
    cmb_Terms.ListIndex = 0
    txt_Notes.Text = ""
    txt_CustomerID.Caption = "New"
    ' Make sure tags are reset as well
    CopyTags
End Sub
```

Control Code

You must add all the code discussed in this section to the individual controls. Simply double-click the control on the Customer form, and the relevant code box appears. Then, in the drop-down combo box labeled `Proc:`, select the event the code belongs to.

Sub cmd_Cancel_Click ()

The `cmd_Cancel_Click` routine sets the `g_OKFlag` to `False`. This variable is checked by the routine that originally activated the form. If set to `False`, the calling routine recognizes that the user chose the Cancel button instead of the OK button. The routine then hides the form using the Hide command.

```
Private Sub cmd_Cancel_Click()
    g_OKFlag = False
    Me.Hide
End Sub
```

Sub cmd_OK_Click ()

The `cmd_OK_Click` routine saves the Customer data to the customer record. If the customer is new, the routine creates and selects the record. It calls the `ScreenToRecord()` routine to write the new information into the database. The `OKFlag` is set to `True` to notify the routine that activated the form that the user clicked the OK button.

```
Private Sub cmd_OK_Click()
    Dim ScratchDS As Recordset
    Dim ScratchTable As Recordset

    g_OKFlag = True
    Me.Hide
    If txt_CustomerID = "New" Then
        ' Get the customer number counter
        SQL$ = "Select * from Counter where TableName = 'Customer'"
        Set ScratchDS = MyDB.OpenRecordset(SQL$, dbOpenDynaset)
        g_CustomerID = ScratchDS!CountNum
        ' increment Invoice number
        ScratchDS.Edit
        ScratchDS!CountNum = g_CustomerID + 1
        ScratchDS.Update

        ' Create customer record
        Set ScratchTable = MyDB.OpenRecordset("Customer", dbOpenTable)
        ScratchTable.AddNew
        ScratchTable!CustomerID = g_CustomerID
        ScratchTable.Update
        ' Create Recordset for editing
        SQL$ = "Select * from Customer where CustomerID = " & g_CustomerID
        Set CustomerDS = MyDB.OpenRecordset(SQL$, dbOpenDynaset)
    End If
    ScreentoRecord CustomerDS
End Sub
```

Sub Form_Load ()

The `Form_Load` routine simply creates the Terms combo box by loading all the possible options. Note that the `RecordToScreen` routine sets the Terms combo box to its current value.

```
Private Sub Form_Load()
    ' Setup Terms combo control
    cmb_Terms.AddItem "Cash"
    cmb_Terms.AddItem "Net 30"
    cmb_Terms.AddItem "Net 15"
    cmb_Terms.AddItem "1% 10 Net 30"
    cmb_Terms.AddItem "2% 10 Net 30"
End Sub
```

Sub Form_Activate ()

The application uses the `Form_Activate` routine to load the form. If the `g_LoadCustFlag` or `g_ClearCustFlag` are `True`, the routine reformats the form. The flags are then set to `False` after the formatting occurs.

> **NOTE**
>
> When designing an application, be sure to put the form-loading routines in the `Form_Activate` routine so it will be executed every time the window is reactivated. If you put the loading routines in the `Load()` event, the routines are activated only the

> first time the form is loaded. If the displayed result set changes in a different client program, the changes are not reflected on the screen. Another way to solve this problem is to unload the form after every deactivation, but it dramatically slows down the application to reload the form every time.
>
> The other alternative is to put the load routine in the `Paint()` event. Putting the load routines here will require the same flag checks; otherwise, if the current form displays a child form, the reactivation will obliterate any changes the user made.

```
Private Sub Form_Activate()
    If g_LoadCustFlag = True Then
        ' Find the customer record in the database
        SQL$ = "Select * from Customer where CustomerID = " & g_CustomerID
        Set CustomerDS = MyDB.OpenRecordset(SQL$, dbOpenDynaset)
        RecordToScreen CustomerDS
    ElseIf g_ClearCustFlag = True Then
        SetupDefaultScreen
    End If
    ' Reset flags
    g_LoadCustFlag = False
    g_ClearCustFlag = False
End Sub
```

Summary

The application is now complete. The sales client can now be used to enter invoices into the database system. This client demonstrates the use of the grid control, overlaying a text control to simulate grid editing, menu selections, item reservations, and database techniques. Database techniques such as optimistic record locking, dynaset creation, record edits and editions, record searching, incremental unique ID counters, and joins. Studying the code for each of these techniques supplies a foundation of code on which to build future applications.

The sales client can add invoices, add customers, enter items, edit older invoices, take items out of inventory, check a list of the inventory, and print the invoice. All these capabilities should provide an understanding of how a client program can be implemented for a multi-user environment. The reservations of items, relevant field checking, invoice counter increments, and other code designed to make the system work effectively are used and in many ways enhanced in the other client programs you will create in this book.

If you've created the tables in Chapter 10 and entered the default values, press the F5 key to execute the program. To compile the program as a stand-alone .EXE, make sure that either the .INI file is placed in the same directory that the application is executing, or change the path in the Invoice Form_Load routine to search in the new directory.

12

Purchasing/Inventory Client

The Purchasing/Inventory Client is a program that maintains the data of all of the items produced by the enterprise, inventory levels, purchase orders, and production of items. This type of client application would be used on the floor at the purchasing department, the shipping and receiving center, and the manufacturing center. Each department would need access to this common data.

The Purchase Client generates purchase orders for any number of items listed from the Inventory_Parts table. (See Figure 12.1.) This PO is automatically given a specific PO number (when the OK button is clicked). Each PO can then be entered into the database system where it is used for inventory management, PO invoicing, shipment receipts, and provides data the Management Client can use.

FIGURE 12.1.
Purchase Order screen.

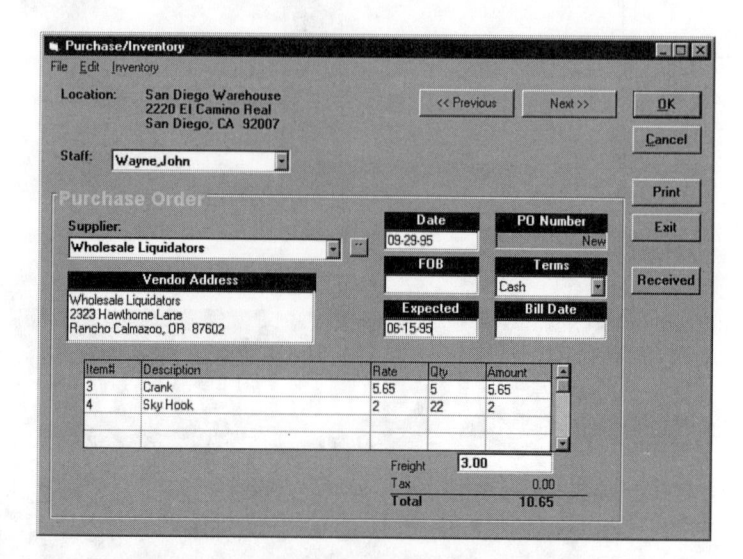

The Purchasing Department can track the progress and arrival of inventory parts by creating POs for items that need to be ordered (see Figure 12.2). The items are stored in the database's ordered fields. Using this client, the shipping and receiving department can check what items are inbound or should have already arrived.

Items may be added to both the parts and the sales inventories using this client (see Figure 12.2). The items in the sales inventories are seen and used by the Sales Client program. The parts items are used by the manufacturing division of the enterprise to be assembled into the finished product which is stored in the sales inventory. Through this client, an assembly record may be constructed to build any final sales product from several inventory items.

The manufacturing department can use this client program to document the completion of finished items and the depletion of inventory levels. Through the Autobuild Edit form (see Figure 12.3), specifications may be made to determine the quantity of various raw materials parts that must be used to assemble each finished good.

FIGURE 12.2.
Sales or Parts Add/Edit Item.

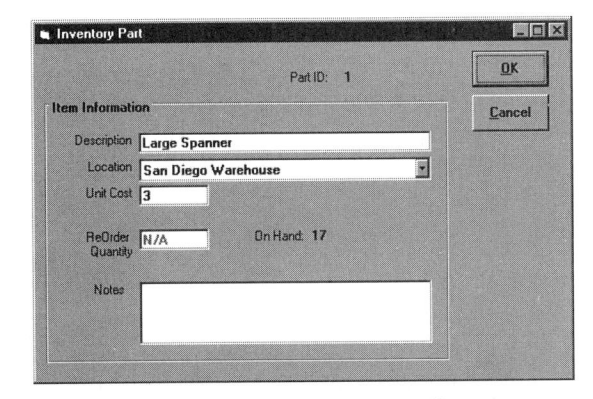

FIGURE 12.3.
Autobuild Edit screen.

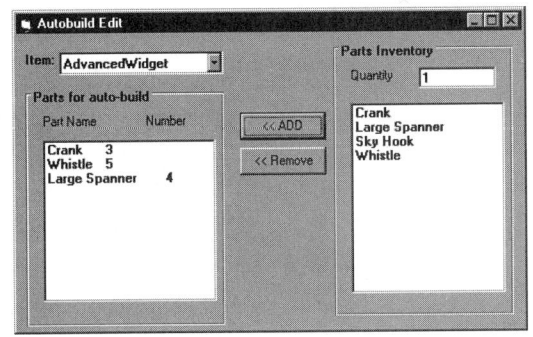

After the relation for materials to finished goods has been produced, the AutoBuild form is used to build a specified quantity of the item (see Figure 12.4). The necessary parts items are removed from the parts inventories and the specified number of finished goods are recorded in the sales inventory.

FIGURE 12.4.
Autobuild Sales Item.

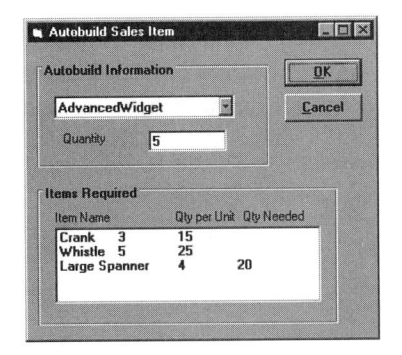

For each PO, individual parts are entered by item number. The data on each item is retrieved from the Part Item list (see Figure 12.5). Once the information for a particular item is retrieved from the server, most of the information (such as the Description) can be edited. The client program automatically enters the cost and description found in the Inventory_Parts table.

FIGURE 12.5.
Part Item Select screen.

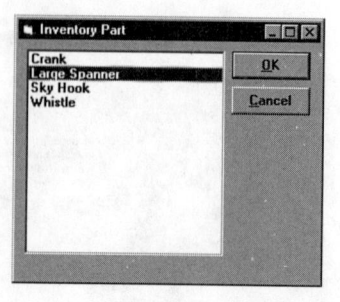

To check the number of inventoried items for any particular part is easy. The Inventory form (see Figure 12.6) shows all the items contained in the Inventory_Parts table and the quantities available for each item. Note that any ordered items do not appear in this list until the Received button has been pressed.

FIGURE 12.6.
Inventory screen.

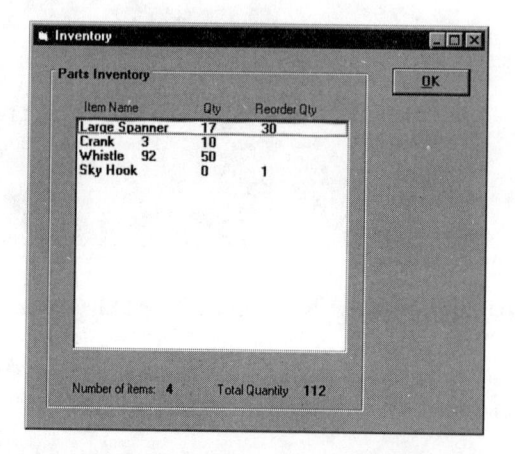

For each PO, the user can select a supplier from the supplier list (the Supplier table) in the combobox or add a new one. Much of the PO information about the supplier, such as the Ship To address, is stored in the main database. This information is retrieved from the server (in this case the database file), placed in editable text fields, and may be changed for each particular invoice. The user can edit or add new suppliers by clicking on the Supplier button to the right of the combobox. This shows the Supplier edit form (see Figure 12.7).

When the Purchase Client is first executed, it checks a flag to determine whether items need to be reordered (or newly built). The Counter table is checked and if the Reorder flag is set, the reorder notice (see Figure 12.8) appears. This alerts purchasers when sales items have fallen below reorder levels.

Any previously entered PO may be edited and viewed using the Next and Previous command buttons. Any modification to a stored invoice activates the OK button so the new modifications can be saved.

FIGURE 12.7.
Supplier screen.

FIGURE 12.8.
Reorder Warning screen.

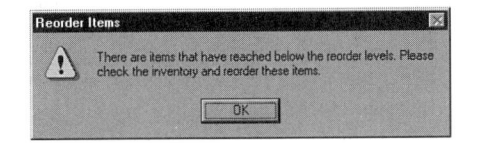

How the Purchase Client Works

The Purchase Client consists of eight primary files:

frm_Purchase (stored as PURCHASE.FRM)—Primary form. Allows the user to create purchase orders and save the information to the tables.

frm_AutobuildEdit (Stored as LIST.FRM)—Setup of a finished item (SalesItem) from a number of raw materials (Parts). Definition used to Autobuild items.

frm_Part (stored as PART.FRM)—Allows the user to add a new part to either the Inventory_Parts or Inventory_Sales table or edit the information of an existing one.

frm_Item (stored as ITEM.FRM)—Displays various items stored in the Inventory_Parts table. Items may be selected for insertion into the selected PO. This is a shared file and must be added to the project. See Chapter 11, "Sales Client," for its construction.

frm_Supplier (stored as SUPPLIER.FRM)—Allows the user to add a new supplier to the Supplier table or edit the information of an existing one.

frm_Autobuild (stored as AUTOBILD.FRM)—Assembles the number of items specified in the Assembly form into a unit that is added to the Inventory table.

frm_Inventory (stored as INVNTRY.FRM)—Shows all the existing Sales Inventory with descriptions, onhand quantities, and reorder quantities.

Global.BAS—Holds all the global code and variables for the program. This is a shared file and must be added to the project. See Chapter 11, "Sales Client," for its construction.

The Purchase Project is named Purchase.VBP and holds all eight of these files (see Figure 12.9). All these files are created from scratch except the ITEM.FRM and the Global.BAS files which should have been created in Chapter 11 (and which should be added to the project). The frm_Purchase form is the startup form set in the Project... tab of the Options dialog. All the other forms are accessed by menu options and command buttons.

FIGURE 12.9.
Purchase.VBP Project screen.

The Purchase client must have access to various tables constructed in Chapter 10, "Table Construction." When the Client is first executed, the connection with the particular database is made (in this case the WIDGETCO.MDB). The information regarding the central database is stored in the application's INI file (in this case the Purchase.INI).

All the data for each PO is stored in the main database in various tables. When the user commits to an invoice, the Purchase Client writes the general invoice information to the Purchase table. The individual line transactions are written to the PurchaseItems table.

Any writes to the data table are accomplished with an OpenDatabase command. The OpenDatabase creates in memory a Database Object connected to the specified database. The program must also pass the parameters setting the Exclusive parameter to FALSE (you need all the clients to access the database) and also the ReadOnly parameter to FALSE. These two parameters may be omitted because they both default to FALSE.

When the Purchase form is first loaded, it creates a snapshot of the current Supplier table. It uses the SQL command ORDER BY to automatically sort the various Supplier entries into alphabetical order. If there is no entry in the Company field, the program creates a LastName, FirstName field to be sorted by.

The program cycles through each of the Supplier table records adding the name of the supplier to the combobox list and storing the supplier's SupplierID field in the corresponding ItemData field of the combobox. This way, when the invoice entry is created, the SupplierID does not have to be retrieved through another database search.

The UniqueID information for all the names in the supplier base has already been entered into the table. This also allows convenient editing of a particular supplier if the user selects the '...' button to the right of the combobox.

After the combobox is filled, its main edit field is set to "". By having nothing in this field, the user may easily enter a new supplier name, a previous supplier name, or use the combobox to select an existing supplier.

If a supplier has been selected, the Supplier table is accessed to read all the additional information. Information such as the Ship To address, Credit Terms, and SupplierID fields are automatically entered into their assigned fields on the PO.

After all this preliminary initialization, the program waits for user interaction. The user may then enter any items into the `grd_Main` by using the item button.

Database Access

The Purchase Client needs to access numerous related tables (see Figure 12.10). The diagram shows each table and how they are related. The lines and arrows denote various related fields among the tables. Note that the shape at the beginning and end of the relation match (that is, an arrow-head occurs on both ends of a line). This should help to see which fields are connected despite overlapping lines.

The Purchase Client uses 10 of the 13 total tables: Location, Staff, Purchase, PurchaseItems, Supplier, Assembly, PServer, Inventory_Sales, Inventory_Parts, and Counter. The Purchase Client handles all inventory management (including sales through the Autobuild function) and so needs access to most of the tables.

Most of these tables are used by the Purchase form. The Location field must be taken to show where the PO is created. The Staff table is used to store the StaffID of each PO's creator. The Purchase table holds each invoice, while the PurchaseItems table holds the individual line items of the PO. The Supplier table holds all the supplier information and the SupplierID is stored with each PO. The Counter table is not related to any of the tables directly, but is used to store the incremental values (such as the last added PO number, last item number, and so on) Finally, the Inventory_Parts contains the information of each item that may be sold.

The Item form accesses the Inventory_Parts table and allows the user to select an item for purchase. The Inventory form also displays the items from the Inventory_Parts table. The Supplier form allows viewing, editing, and adding all the supplier records stored in the Supplier table. The Assembly table holds the relations for final units' construction between the parts in the Inventory_Parts table and the items in the Inventory_Sales table. The PServer holds the ReorderFlag used to signal the Purchase Client user that reorders are necessary.

FIGURE 12.10.
Purchase Client data access diagram.

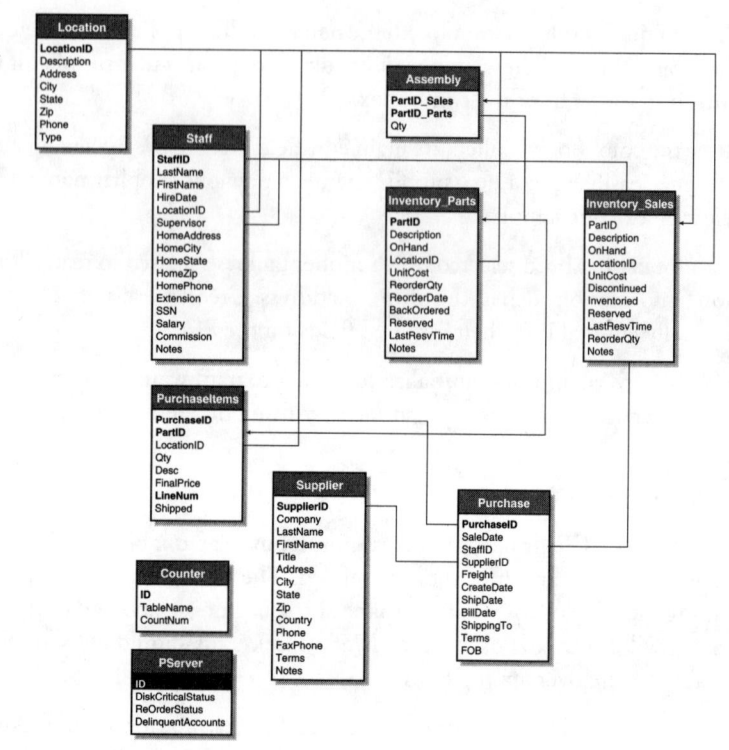

Location
LocationID
Description
Address
City
State
Zip
Phone
Type

Assembly
PartID_Sales
PartID_Parts
Qty

Staff
StaffID
LastName
FirstName
HireDate
LocationID
Supervisor
HomeAddress
HomeCity
HomeState
HomeZip
HomePhone
Extension
SSN
Salary
Commission
Notes

Inventory_Parts
PartID
Description
OnHand
LocationID
UnitCost
ReorderQty
ReorderDate
BackOrdered
Reserved
LastResvTime
Notes

Inventory_Sales
PartID
Description
OnHand
LocationID
UnitCost
Discontinued
Inventoried
Reserved
LastResvTime
ReorderQty
Notes

PurchaseItems
PurchaseID
PartID
LocationID
Qty
Desc
FinalPrice
LineNum
Shipped

Supplier
SupplierID
Company
LastName
FirstName
Title
Address
City
State
Zip
Country
Phone
FaxPhone
Terms
Notes

Purchase
PurchaseID
SaleDate
StaffID
SupplierID
Freight
CreateDate
ShipDate
BillDate
ShippingTo
Terms
FOB

Counter
ID
TableName
CountNum

PServer
ID
DiskCriticalStatus
ReOrderStatus
DelinquentAccounts

Starting the Purchase/Inventory Project

The Purchase Client program in our example is stored in the CS_VB\PURCHASE directory. You should have created the directory structure necessary in Chapter 10, "Table Construction." If you haven't, please do so now.

For simplicity, and because we are not using an installer program, the Purchase Client looks for the INI file in the same folder in which the application executed. This also provides a sample routine, GetAppPath, in the Global.BAS file, which you can reuse for various applications in the future. In a real world client application, the application's .INI file would be placed in the \WINDOWS\ directory.

Creating the Purchase .INI File

Before the application can be executed, we must construct the .INI file. An .INI file is used to store various parameters about a given program, such as the type of database to be accessed, the driver types, the directory of the stored database, and so on. The Purchase.INI file contains many parameters in common with the Sales Client .INI.

Within an .INI file, the ';' character denotes a comment. The .INI file can store parameters in subdivided sections. The [...] denotes a section of parameters. This .INI file has the Parameters and the Access sections.

Create the .INI file by opening the Notepad program found in the Accessories program group. Enter the information below in Listing 12.1. Save the file as Purchase.INI in the Purchase directory.

Listing 12.1. Purchase.INI.

```
; Purchase.INI

[Parameters]

LocationID = 2
DefaultStaffID = 1
StandardTerms = 0
SalesTax = .07
Freight = 3.00
DataLocation = Access

[Access]
DSN=
DBName=c:\clntsrvr\WidgetCo.mdb
DBServer=
```

Creating the Forms

The first step toward building an application is drawing the various forms necessary. This way an application can be rapidly prototyped and shown to the various users for critique and input.

Also, before code is placed on a form, it should operate autonomously. That allows the designer to easily add a few SHOW commands to various buttons in order to simulate operation. For this reason, you will first construct all the forms necessary for the project which you may compile and save before you begin entering all the code.

Creating the PURCHASE.FRM

The Purchase Form has many controls but is fairly similar to the Sales Form created in Chapter 11. Figure 12.11 shows what the completed form looks like after all the controls have been added. Note the callouts to those controls. The figure also shows the Name properties of all the individual controls. Create each control on the form and set the properties to match the properties listed in the table for that control's property.

Like the Sales Form, the Purchase Form also contains the four hidden controls shown in Figure 12.12. The three textbox controls are used for manipulation of the PO data, while the grd_Tag retains a PO's original information to check for user changes.

FIGURE 12.11.
Purchase Form - Controls.

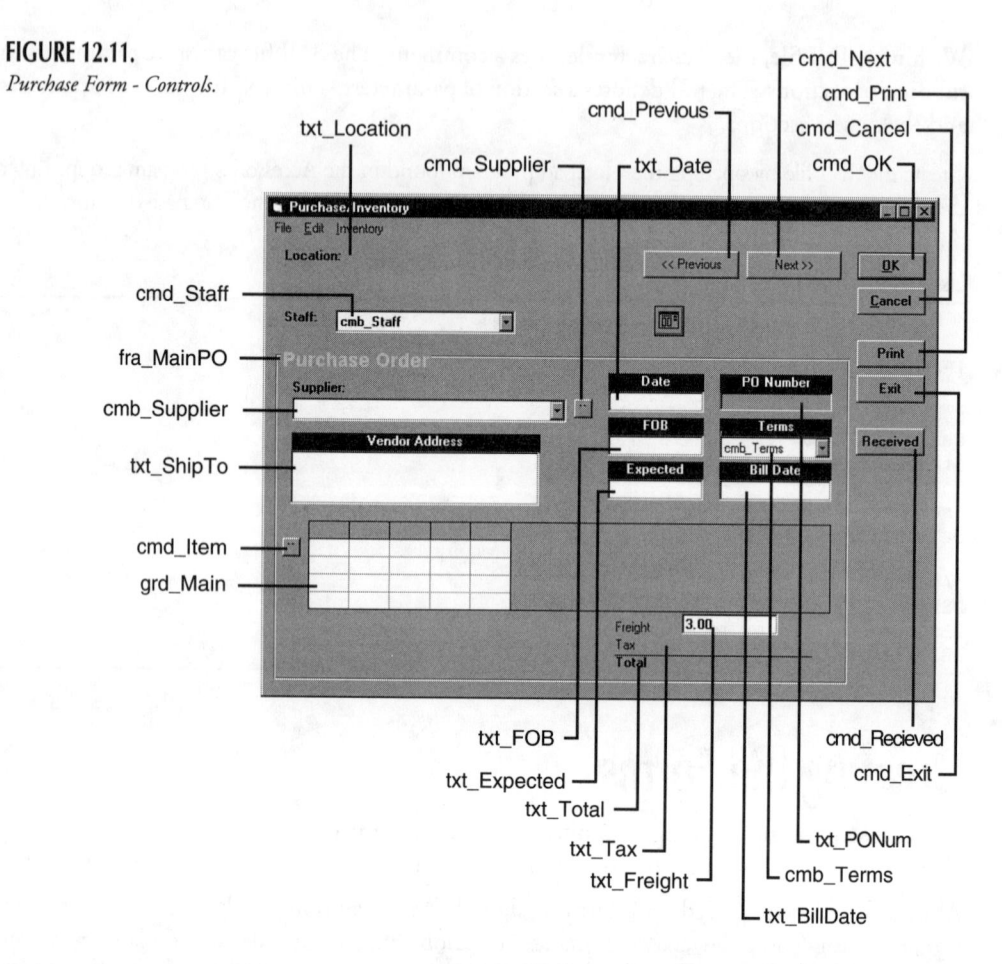

The following contains a list of all the controls that need to be added to the form. The table holding the control's property data is listed as well as the location at which the control should be placed. For example, if the location is listed as fra_Purchase, the item should be created in that frame. If the location is listed as Form, place the control on the form itself.

FIGURE 12.12.
Hidden Controls on Purchase Form.

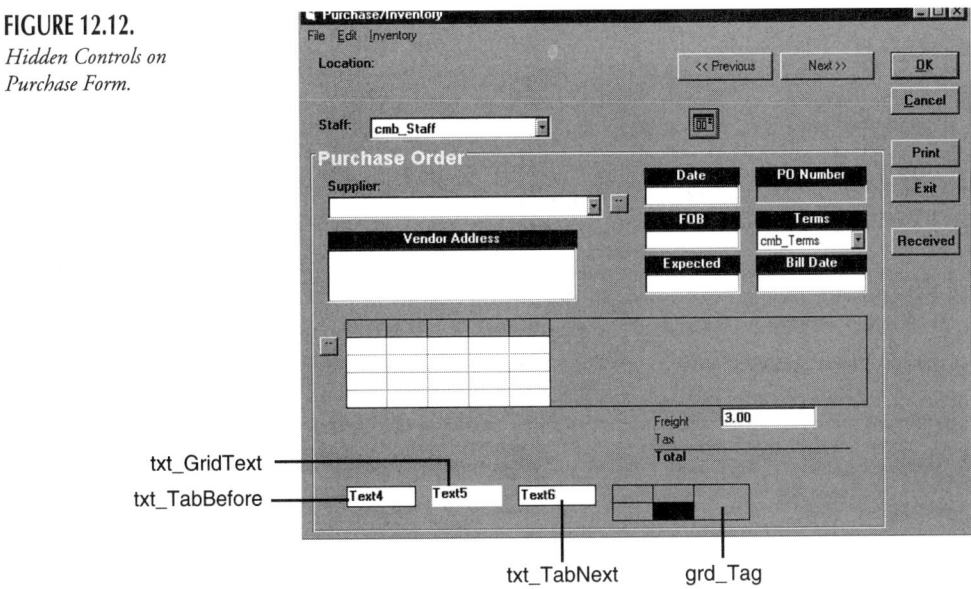

Table	Control	Location
Table 12.1.	Form frm_Purchase	
Table 12.2.	CommonDialog CMDialog1	Form
Table 12.3.	CommandButton cmd_Received	fra_Purchase
Table 12.4.	SSFrame fra_MainPO	fra_Purchase
Table 12.5.	TextBox txt_Freight	fra_Purchase
Table 12.6.	Grid grd_Main	fra_Purchase
Table 12.7.	TextBox txt_ShipTo	fra_Purchase
Table 12.8.	TextBox txt_Date	fra_Purchase
Table 12.9.	TextBox txt_FOB	fra_Purchase
Table 12.10.	ComboBox cmb_Terms	fra_Purchase
Table 12.11.	TextBox txt_TabNext	fra_Purchase
Table 12.12.	TextBox txt_GridText	fra_Purchase
Table 12.13.	TextBox txt_TabBefore	fra_Purchase
Table 12.14.	CommandButton cmd_Item	fra_Purchase
Table 12.15.	CommandButton cmd_Supplier	fra_Purchase
Table 12.16.	ComboBox cmb_Supplier	Form
Table 12.17.	TextBox txt_Expected	Form
Table 12.18.	TextBox txt_BillDate	Form
Table 12.19.	Grid grd_Tag	fra_Purchase
Table 12.20.	Line Line1	fra_Purchase
Table 12.21.	Label txt_Tax	fra_Purchase
Table 12.22.	Label txt_Total	fra_Purchase

continues

Table	Control	Location
Table 12.23.	Label txt_PONum	fra_Purchase
Table 12.24.	ComboBox cmb_Staff	fra_Purchase
Table 12.25.	CommandButton cmd_Exit	Form
Table 12.26.	CommandButton cmd_Print	Form
Table 12.27.	CommandButton cmd_Cancel	Form
Table 12.28.	CommandButton cmd_OK	Form
Table 12.29.	CommandButton cmd_Prev	Form
Table 12.30.	CommandButton cmd_Next	Form
Table 12.31.	Label txt_Location	Form

Table 12.1. Form frm_Purchase.

BackColor	=	&H00C0C0C0&
Caption	=	Purchase/Inventory
ClientHeight	=	6195
ClientLeft	=	450
ClientTop	=	3420
ClientWidth	=	9375
Height	=	6885
Left	=	390
LinkTopic	=	"Form1"
ScaleHeight	=	6195
ScaleWidth	=	9375
Top	=	2790
Width	=	9495

Table 12.2. CommonDialog CMDialog1.

Left	=	5400
Top	=	840

Table 12.3. CommandButton cmd_Received.

Caption	=	Received
Height	=	375
Left	=	8280
TabIndex	=	40
Top	=	2520
Width	=	975

Table 12.4. SSFrame `fra_MainPO`.

Caption	=	Purchase Order
FontBold	=	-1 'True
FontItalic	=	0 'False
FontName	=	Arial
FontSize	=	13.5
FontStrikethru	=	0 'False
FontUnderline	=	0 'False
ForeColor	=	&H0000FFFF&
Height	=	4575
Left	=	120
ShadowColor	=	1 'Black
TabIndex	=	22
Top	=	1440
Width	=	8055

Table 12.5. TextBox `txt_Freight`.

Height	=	285
Left	=	5730
TabIndex	=	38
Text	=	3.00
Top	=	3630
Width	=	1350

Table 12.6. Grid `grd_Main`.

BackColor	=	&H00FFFFFF&
Cols	=	5
FixedCols	=	0
FontBold	=	0 'False
FontItalic	=	0 'False
FontName	=	MS Sans Serif
FontSize	=	8.25
FontStrikethru	=	0 'False

continues

Table 12.6. continued

FontUnderline	=	0 'False
ForeColor	=	&H00000000&
Height	=	1215
HighLight	=	0 'False
Left	=	480
Rows	=	5
ScrollBars	=	2 'Vertical
TabIndex	=	36
Top	=	2400
Width	=	7335

Table 12.7. TextBox txt_ShipTo.

FontBold	=	0 'False
FontItalic	=	0 'False
FontName	=	MS Sans Serif
FontSize	=	8.25
FontStrikethru	=	0 'False
FontUnderline	=	0 'False
Height	=	735
Left	=	225
MultiLine	=	-1 'True
TabIndex	=	35
Top	=	1440
Width	=	3495

Table 12.8. TextBox txt_Date.

FontBold	=	0 'False
FontItalic	=	0 'False
FontName	=	MS Sans Serif
FontSize	=	8.25
FontStrikethru	=	0 'False
FontUnderline	=	0 'False

Height	=	285
Left	=	4680
TabIndex	=	34
Top	=	600
Width	=	1335

Table 12.9. TextBox txt_FOB.

FontBold	=	0 'False
FontItalic	=	0 'False
FontName	=	MS Sans Serif
FontSize	=	8.25
FontStrikethru	=	0 'False
FontUnderline	=	0 'False
Height	=	285
Left	=	4680
TabIndex	=	33
Top	=	1200
Width	=	1335

Table 12.10. ComboBox cmb_Terms.

FontBold	=	0 'False
FontItalic	=	0 'False
FontName	=	MS Sans Serif
FontSize	=	8.25
FontStrikethru	=	0 'False
FontUnderline	=	0 False
Height	=	300
Left	=	6240
Style	=	2 'Dropdown List
TabIndex	=	32
Top	=	1200
Width	=	1575

Table 12.11. TextBox txt_TabNext.

Height	=	285
Left	=	2880
TabIndex	=	31
Text	=	Text6
Top	=	4680
Width	=	1095

Table 12.12. TextBox txt_GridText.

BorderStyle	=	0 'None
Height	=	285
Left	=	1680
TabIndex	=	30
Text	=	Text5
Top	=	4680
Visible	=	0 'False
Width	=	975

Table 12.13. TextBox txt_TabBefore.

Height	=	285
Left	=	480
TabIndex	=	29
Text	=	Text4
Top	=	4680
Width	=	975

Table 12.14. CommandButton cmd_Item.

Caption	=	...
Height	=	255
Left	=	120
TabIndex	=	28
Top	=	2640
Visible	=	0 'False
Width	=	255

Table 12.15. CommandButton `cmd_Supplier`.

Caption	=	...
Height	=	255
Left	=	4200
TabIndex	=	27
Top	=	720
Width	=	255

Table 12.16. ComboBox `cmb_Supplier`.

Height	=	300
Left	=	240
TabIndex	=	26
Top	=	720
Width	=	3855

Table 12.17. TextBox `txt_Expected`.

FontBold	=	0 'False
FontItalic	=	0 'False
FontName	=	MS Sans Serif
FontSize	=	8.25
FontStrikethru	=	0 'False
FontUnderline	=	0 'False
Height	=	285
Left	=	4680
TabIndex	=	25
Top	=	1800
Width	=	1335

Table 12.18. TextBox `txt_BillDate`.

FontBold	=	0 'False
FontItalic	=	0 'False
FontName	=	MS Sans Serif

continues

Table 12.18. continued

FontSize	=	8.25
FontStrikethru	=	0 'False
FontUnderline	=	0 'False
Height	=	285
Left	=	6240
TabIndex	=	24
Top	=	1800
Width	=	1575

Table 12.19. Grid grd_Tag.

Height	=	495
Left	=	4200
TabIndex	=	23
Top	=	4680
Width	=	1935

Table 12.20. Line Line1.

X1	=	4800
X2	=	7560
Y1	=	4200
Y2	=	4200

Table 12.21. Label txt_Tax.

Alignment	=	1 'Right Justify
BackColor	=	&H00C0C0C0&
FontBold	=	0 'False
FontItalic	=	0 'False
FontName	=	MS Sans Serif
FontSize	=	8.25
FontStrikethru	=	0 'False
FontUnderline	=	0 'False
Height	=	255

Left	=	5760
TabIndex	=	14
Top	=	3960
Width	=	1335

Table 12.22. Label txt_Total.

Alignment	=	1 'Right Justify
BackColor	=	&H00C0C0C0&
Height	=	255
Left	=	5760
TabIndex	=	15
Top	=	4200
Width	=	1335

Table 12.23. Label txt_PONum.

Alignment	=	1 'Right Justify
BorderStyle	=	1 'Fixed Single
FontBold	=	0 'False
FontItalic	=	0 'False
FontName	=	MS Sans Serif
FontSize	=	8.25
FontStrikethru	=	0 'False
FontUnderline	=	0 'False
Height	=	255
Left	=	6240
TabIndex	=	17
Top	=	600
Width	=	1575

Table 12.24. ComboBox cmb_Staff.

Height	=	300
Left	=	960

continues

Table 12.24. continued

Style	=	2 'Dropdown List
TabIndex	=	20
Top	=	960
Width	=	2535

Table 12.25. CommandButton `cmd_Exit`.

Caption	=	Exit
Height	=	375
Left	=	8280
TabIndex	=	12
Top	=	1800
Width	=	975

Table 12.26. CommandButton `cmd_Print`.

Caption	=	Print
Height	=	375
Left	=	8280
TabIndex	=	0
Top	=	1320
Width	=	975

Table 12.27. CommandButton `cmd_Cancel`.

Cancel	=	-1 'True
Caption	=	&Cancel
Height	=	375
Left	=	8280
TabIndex	=	5
Top	=	600
Width	=	975

Table 12.28. CommandButton cmd_OK.

Caption	=	&OK
Default	=	-1 'True
Height	=	375
Left	=	8280
TabIndex	=	4
Top	=	120
Width	=	975

Table 12.29. CommandButton cmd_Prev.

Caption	=	<< Previous
Height	=	375
Left	=	5280
TabIndex	=	3
Top	=	120
Width	=	1335

Table 12.30. CommandButton cmd_Next.

Caption	=	Next >>
Height	=	375
Left	=	6720
TabIndex	=	2
Top	=	120
Width	=	1335

Table 12.31. Label txt_Location.

BackColor	=	&H00C0C0C0&
Height	=	735
Left	=	1440
TabIndex	=	13
Top	=	120
Width	=	2535

Adding the Menus

Creating the menus is as simple as using the Menu Designer included with Visual Basic. Select Menu Editor from the Tools menu. You see a window for creating and editing the menus. Create all the menus shown in Figures 12.13a and 12.13b. The figures label the menu names that you will enter into the second text field in the dialog box that specifies the object name of the menu item.

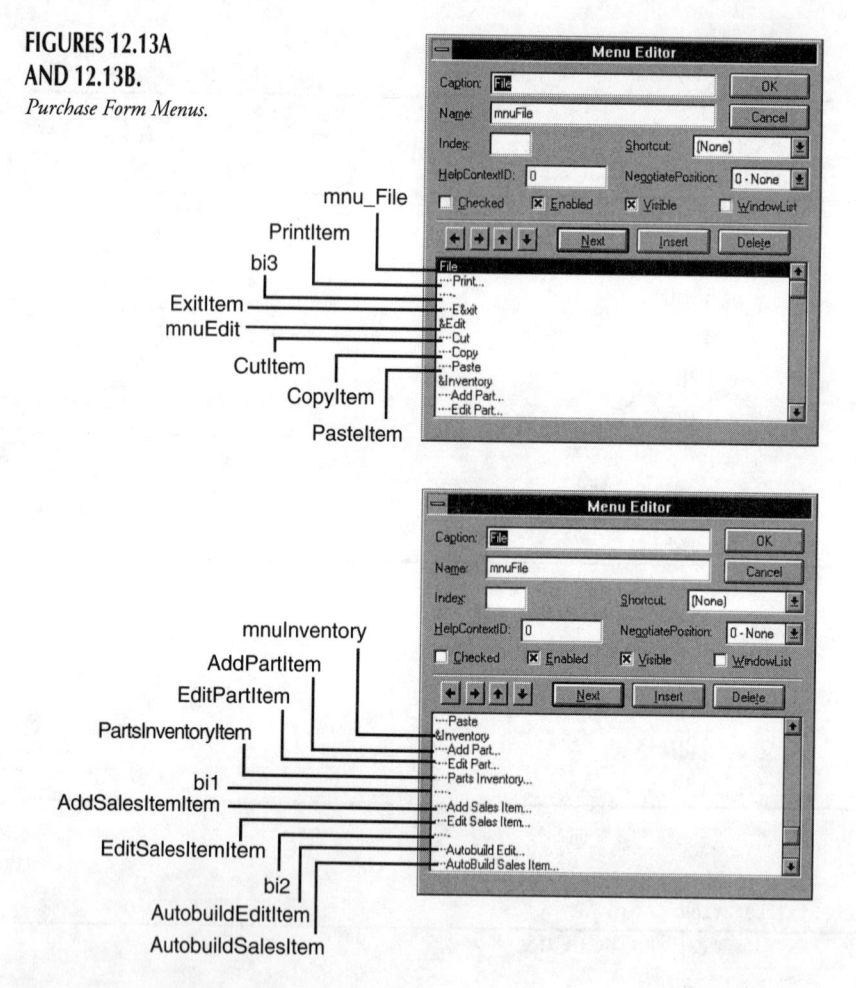

FIGURES 12.13A AND 12.13B.
Purchase Form Menus.

Labels for first Menu Editor (File menu):
- mnu_File
- PrintItem
- bi3
- ExitItem
- mnuEdit
- CutItem
- CopyItem
- PasteItem

Menu items shown:
- File
  - Print...
  - E&xit
- &Edit
  - Cut
  - Copy
  - Paste
- &Inventory
  - Add Part...
  - Edit Part...

Labels for second Menu Editor (Inventory menu):
- mnuInventory
- AddPartItem
- EditPartItem
- PartsInventoryItem
- bi1
- AddSalesItemItem
- EditSalesItemItem
- bi2
- AutobuildEditItem
- AutobuildSalesItem

Menu items shown:
- Paste
- &Inventory
  - Add Part...
  - Edit Part...
  - Parts Inventory...
  - Add Sales Item...
  - Edit Sales Item...
  - Autobuild Edit...
  - AutoBuild Sales Item...

Creating the AUTOBILD.FRM

Creating the Autobuild Form is fairly straightforward. Figure 12.14 shows what the completed form looks like after all the controls have been added. Note the pointers to those controls. The figure also shows the Name properties for all the individual controls. Create each control on the form and set the properties to match the properties listed in the table for each control's property.

FIGURE 12.14.
Autobuild Form - Controls.

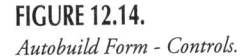

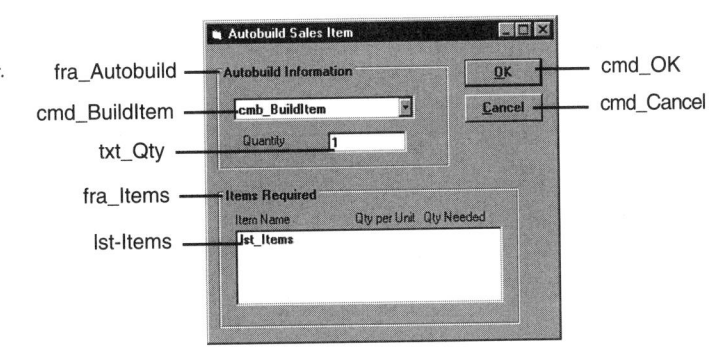

The following contains a list of all the controls that need to be added to the form. The table holding the control's property data is listed as well as the location at which the control should be placed. For example, if the location is listed as fra_Autobuild, the item should be created in that frame. If the location is listed as Form, place the control on the form itself.

Table	Control	Location
Table 12.32.	Form frm_Autobuild	
Table 12.33.	SSFrame fra_Items	Form
Table 12.34.	ListBox lst_Items	fra_Autobuild
Table 12.35.	SSFrame fra_AutoBuildInfo	fra_Autobuild
Table 12.36.	TextBox txt_Qty	fra_Autobuild
Table 12.37.	ComboBox cmb_BuildItem	fra_Autobuild
Table 12.38.	CommandButton cmd_Cancel	fra_Autobuild
Table 12.39.	CommandButton cmd_OK	fra_Autobuild

Table 12.32. Form frm_Autobuild.

BackColor	=	&H00C0C0C0&
Caption	=	Autobuild Sales Item
ClientHeight	=	4020
ClientLeft	=	1875
ClientTop	=	1545
ClientWidth	=	4860
Height	=	4425
Left	=	1815
LinkTopic	=	Form3
ScaleHeight	=	4020
ScaleWidth	=	4860

continues

Table 12.32. continued

Top	=	1200
Width	=	4980

Table 12.33. SSFrame `fra_Items`.

Caption	=	Items Required
ForeColor	=	&H00000000&
Height	=	1935
Left	=	120
ShadowColor	=	1 'Black
TabIndex	=	6
Top	=	1920
Width	=	4215

Table 12.34. ListBox `lst_Items`.

Height	=	1200
Left	=	240
TabIndex	=	7
Top	=	600
Width	=	3735

Table 12.35. SSFrame `fra_AutoBuildInfo`.

Caption	=	Autobuild Information
ForeColor	=	&H00000000&
Height	=	1455
Left	=	120
ShadowColor	=	1 'Black
TabIndex	=	3
Top	=	240
Width	=	3255

Table 12.36. TextBox `txt_Qty`.

Height	=	285
Left	=	1560
TabIndex	=	2
Text	=	1
Top	=	960
Width	=	1095

Table 12.37. ComboBox `cmb_BuildItem`.

Height	=	300
Left	=	240
Style	=	2 'Dropdown List
TabIndex	=	4
Top	=	480
Width	=	2535

Table 12.38. CommandButton `cmd_Cancel`.

Cancel	=	-1 'True
Caption	=	&Cancel
Height	=	375
Left	=	3600
TabIndex	=	1
Top	=	720
Width	=	1095

Table 12.39. CommandButton `cmd_OK`.

Caption	=	&OK
Default	=	-1 'True
Height	=	375
Left	=	3600
TabIndex	=	0
Top	=	240
Width	=	1095

Creating the LIST.FRM

The Autobuild form is used to create items for the Inventory_Sales from items in the Inventory_Parts table. Creating the List Form (Autobuild Edit Form) is fairly straightforward. Figure 12.15 shows what the completed form looks like after all the controls have been added. Note the pointers in the figure. It also shows the Name properties of all the individual controls. Create each control on the form and set the properties to match the properties listed in the table for that property.

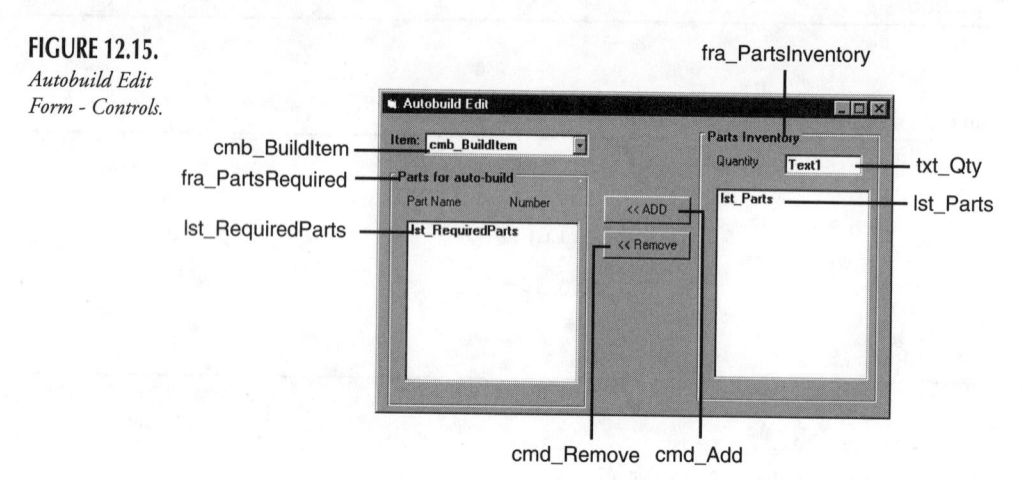

FIGURE 12.15.
Autobuild Edit Form - Controls.

The following contains a list of all the controls that need to be added to the form. The table holding the control's property data is listed as well as the location at which the control should be placed. For example, if the location is listed as fra_AutobuildEdit, the item should be created in that frame. If the location is listed as Form, place the control on the form itself.

Table	Control	Location
Table 12.40.	Form frm_AutobuildEdit	
Table 12.41.	ComboBox cmb_BuildItem	Form
Table 12.42.	SSFrame fra_PartsRequired	fra_AutobuildEdit
Table 12.43.	ListBox lst_RequiredParts	fra_Purchase
Table 12.44.	SSFrame fra_PartsInven	fra_Purchase
Table 12.45.	TextBox txt_Qty	fra_Purchase
Table 12.46.	ListBox lst_Parts	fra_Purchase
Table 12.47.	CommandButton cmd_Remove	fra_Purchase
Table 12.48.	CommandButton cmd_Add	fra_Purchase

Table 12.40. Form `frm_AutobuildEdit`.

BackColor	=	&H00C0C0C0&
Caption	=	Autobuild Edit
ClientHeight	=	4020
ClientLeft	=	1305
ClientTop	=	1650
ClientWidth	=	7110
Height	=	4425
Left	=	1245
LinkTopic	=	Form2
ScaleHeight	=	4020
ScaleWidth	=	7110
Top	=	1305
Width	=	7230

Table 12.41. ComboBox `cmb_BuildItem`.

Height	=	300
Left	=	600
Style	=	2 'Dropdown List
TabIndex	=	9
Top	=	240
Width	=	2295

Table 12.42. SSFrame `fra_PartsRequired`.

Caption	=	Parts for auto-build
ForeColor	=	&H00000000&
Height	=	3255
Left	=	120
TabIndex	=	7
Top	=	720
Width	=	2775

Table 12.43. ListBox lst_RequiredParts.

Height	=	2370
Left	=	240
TabIndex	=	8
Top	=	720
Width	=	2415

Table 12.44. SSFrame fra_PartsInven.

Caption	=	Parts Inventory
Height	=	3735
Left	=	4440
TabIndex	=	3
Top	=	120
Width	=	2535

Table 12.45. TextBox txt_Qty.

Height	=	285
Left	=	1200
TabIndex	=	5
Text	=	Text1
Top	=	360
Width	=	1095

Table 12.46. ListBox lst_Parts.

Height	=	2760
Left	=	240
TabIndex	=	4
Top	=	840
Width	=	2175

Table 12.47. CommandButton cmd_Remove.

Caption	=	<< Remove
Height	=	375
Left	=	3120
TabIndex	=	1
Top	=	1560
Width	=	1215

Table 12.48. CommandButton cmd_Add.

Caption	=	<< ADD
Height	=	375
Left	=	3120
TabIndex	=	0
Top	=	1080
Width	=	1215

Creating the INVNTRY.FRM

The Inventory form is used to display both sales and parts inventory lists with the number of items in stock. Creating the Inventory Form is fairly straightforward. Figure 12.16 shows what the completed form looks like after all the controls have been added. Note the pointers to the controls. The figure also shows the Name properties of all of the individual controls. Create each control on the form and set the properties to match the properties listed in the table for that property.

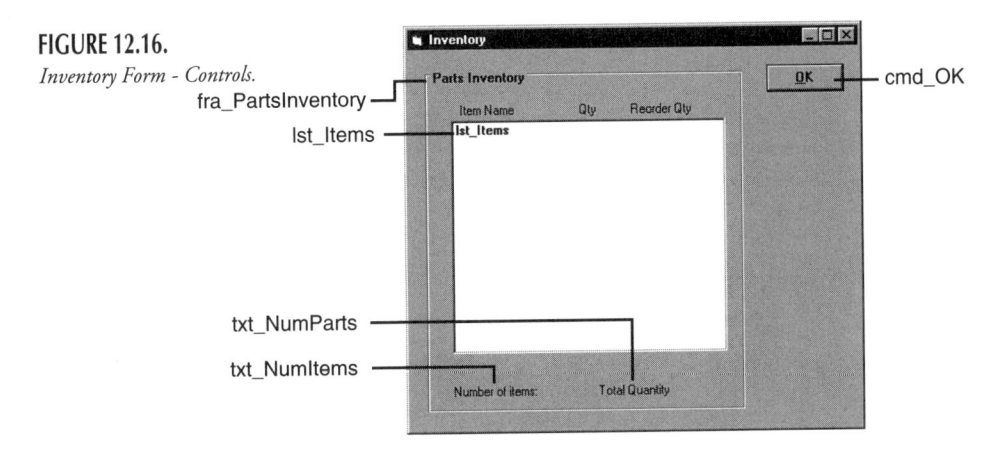

FIGURE 12.16.
Inventory Form - Controls.

The following is a list of all the controls that need to be added to the form. The table holding the control's property data is listed as well as the location at which the control should be placed. For example, if the location is listed as fra_Inventory, the item should be created in that frame. If the location is listed as Form, place the control on the form itself.

Table	Control	Location
Table 12.49.	Form frm_Inventory	
Table 12.50.	CommandButton cmd_OK	Form
Table 12.51.	SSFrame fra_PartsInventory	fra_Inventory
Table 12.52.	ListBox lst_Items	Form
Table 12.53.	Label txt_NumParts	Form
Table 12.54.	Label txt_NumItems	fra_Purchase

Table 12.49. Form frm_Inventory.

BackColor	=	&H00C0C0C0&
Caption	=	Inventory
ClientHeight	=	6510
ClientLeft	=	2415
ClientTop	=	615
ClientWidth	=	6330
Height	=	6915
Left	=	2355
LinkTopic	=	"Form2"
ScaleHeight	=	6510
ScaleWidth	=	6330
Top	=	270
Width	=	6450

Table 12.50. CommandButton cmd_OK.

Caption	=	&OK
Default	=	-1 'True
Height	=	375
Left	=	5040
TabIndex	=	7
Top	=	240
Width	=	1095

Table 12.51. SSFrame `fra_PartsInventory`.

Caption	=	Parts Inventory
Height	=	6135
Left	=	240
TabIndex	=	0
Top	=	240
Width	=	4455

Table 12.52. ListBox `lst_Items`.

Height	=	4710
Left	=	360
TabIndex	=	1
Top	=	720
Width	=	3855

Table 12.53. Label `txt_NumParts`.

BackColor	=	&H00C0C0C0&
Height	=	255
Left	=	3600
TabIndex	=	9
Top	=	5640
Width	=	615

Table 12.54. Label `txt_NumItems`.

BackColor	=	&H00C0C0C0&
Height	=	255
Left	=	1680
TabIndex	=	2
Top	=	5640
Width	=	495

Creating the PART.FRM

The Part form is used to create a new part for addition to the Inventory_Parts table. The Part form consists of a few textboxes, buttons, and a combobox, so construction is fairly straightforward. Figure 12.17 shows what the completed form looks like after all the controls have been added. Note the pointers to the controls. The figure also shows the Name properties of all of the individual controls. Create each control on the form and set the properties to match the properties listed in the table for that property.

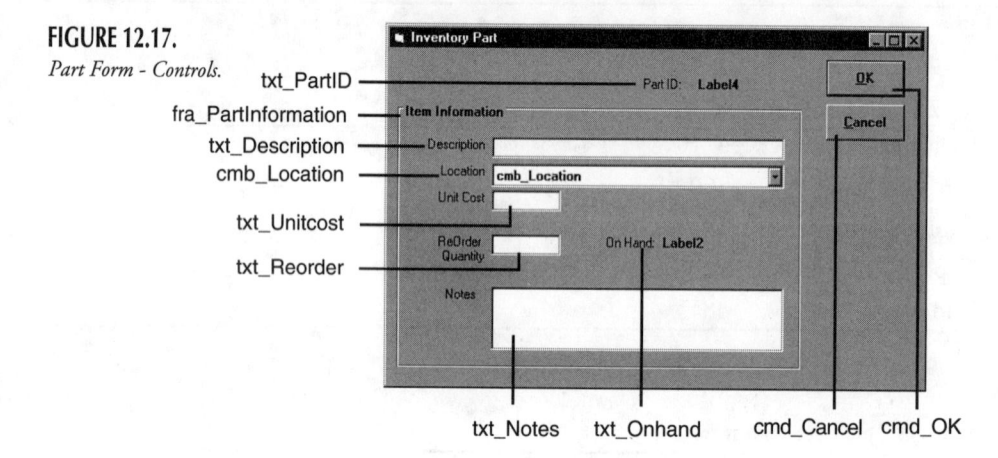

FIGURE 12.17.
Part Form - Controls.

The following is a list of all the controls that need to be added to the form. The table holding the control's property data is listed as well as the location at which the control should be placed. For example, if the location is listed as fra_Part, the item should be created in that frame. If the location is listed as Form, place the control on the form itself.

Table	Control	Location
Table 12.55.	Form frm_Part	
Table 12.56.	SSFrame fra_PartInformation	Form
Table 12.57.	ComboBox cmb_Location	fra_Part
Table 12.58.	TextBox txt_Notes	Form
Table 12.59.	TextBox txt_UnitCost	Form
Table 12.60.	TextBox txt_Description	fra_Part
Table 12.61.	Label txt_OnHand	fra_Part
Table 12.62.	CommandButton cmd_Cancel	fra_Part
Table 12.63.	CommandButton cmd_OK	Form
Table 12.64.	Label txt_PartID	Form

Table 12.55. Form `frm_Part`.

BackColor	=	&H00C0C0C0&
Caption	=	Inventory Part
ClientHeight	=	4560
ClientLeft	=	1290
ClientTop	=	870
ClientWidth	=	7485
Height	=	4965
Left	=	1230
LinkTopic	=	Form1
ScaleHeight	=	4560
ScaleWidth	=	7485
Top	=	525
Width	=	7605

Table 12.56. SSFrame `fra_PartInformation`.

Caption	=	Inventory Part Information
Height	=	3615
Left	=	120
TabIndex	=	12
Top	=	720
Width	=	5655
Begin TextBox txt_Reorder		
Height	=	285
Left	=	1320
TabIndex	=	5
Top	=	1800
Width	=	975

Table 12.57. ComboBox cmb_Location.

Height	=	300
Left	=	1320
Style	=	2 'Dropdown List
TabIndex	=	6
Top	=	840
Width	=	2175

Table 12.58. TextBox txt_Notes.

Height	=	855
Left	=	1320
MultiLine	=	-1 'True
TabIndex	=	3
Top	=	2520
Width	=	4095

Table 12.59. TextBox txt_UnitCost.

Height	=	285
Left	=	1320
TabIndex	=	2
Top	=	1200
Width	=	975

Table 12.60. TextBox txt_Description.

Height	=	285
Left	=	1320
TabIndex	=	1
Top	=	480
Width	=	4095

Table 12.61. Label txt_OnHand.

BackColor	=	&H00C0C0C0&
Caption	=	Label2
Height	=	255
Left	=	3720
TabIndex	=	7
Top	=	1800
Width	=	975

Table 12.62. CommandButton cmd_Cancel.

Cancel	=	-1 'True
Caption	=	&Cancel
Height	=	495
Left	=	6120
TabIndex	=	4
Top	=	720
Width	=	1095

Table 12.63. CommandButton cmd_OK.

Caption	=	&OK
Default	=	-1 'True
Height	=	495
Left	=	6120
TabIndex	=	0
Top	=	120
Width	=	1095

Table 12.64. Label `txt_PartID`.

BackColor	=	&H00C0C0C0&
Caption	=	Label4
Height	=	255
Left	=	4320
TabIndex	=	16
Top	=	360
Width	=	1095

Creating the SUPPLIER.FRM

The Supplier form is used to add a new vendor to the Supplier table. Figure 12.18 shows what the completed form looks like after all the controls have been added. Note the callouts to those controls. The figure also shows the Name properties of all of the individual controls. Create each control on the form and set the properties to match the properties listed in the table for that property.

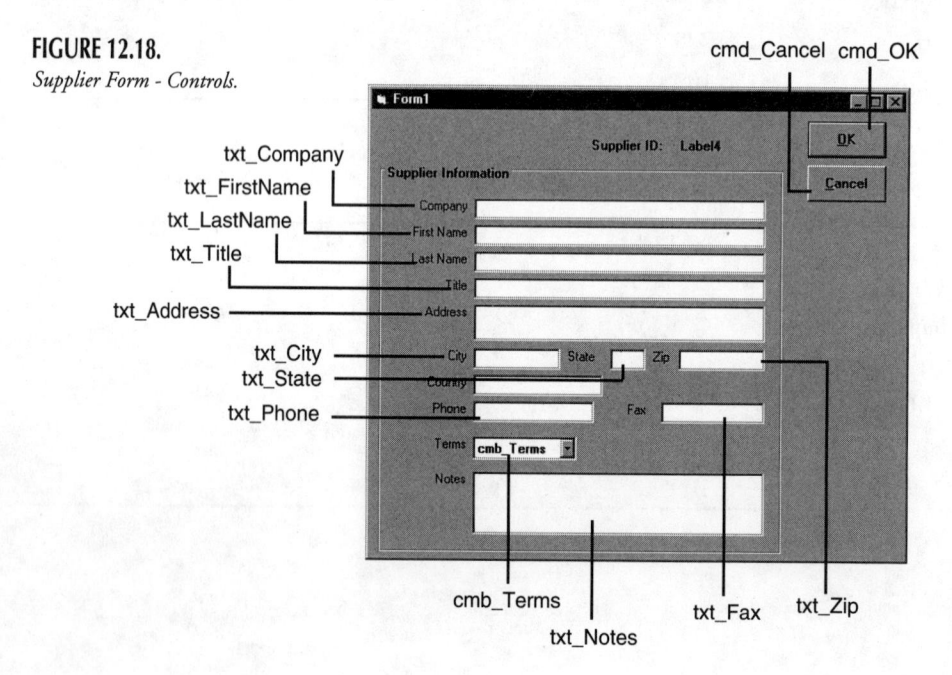

FIGURE 12.18.
Supplier Form - Controls.

The following is a list of all the controls that need to be added to the form. The table holding the control's property data is listed as well as the location at which the control should be placed. For example, if the location is listed as fra_Supplier, the item should be created in that frame. If the location is listed as Form, place the control on the form itself.

Table	Control	Location
Table 12.65.	Form frm_Supplier	
Table 12.66.	SSFrame fra_SupplierInfo	Form
Table 12.67.	TextBox txt_State	fra_Supplier
Table 12.68.	TextBox txt_Zip	Form
Table 12.69.	TextBox txt_Phone	Form
Table 12.70.	TextBox txt_Fax	fra_Supplier
Table 12.71.	TextBox txt_Country	fra_Part
Table 12.72.	ComboBox cmb_Terms	fra_Part
Table 12.73.	TextBox txt_Notes	Form
Table 12.74.	TextBox txt_FirstName	Form
Table 12.75.	TextBox txt_LastName	Form
Table 12.76.	TextBox txt_Address	Form
Table 12.77.	TextBox txt_City	fra_Supplier
Table 12.78.	TextBox txt_Company	fra_Part
Table 12.79.	TextBox txt_Title	fra_Part
Table 12.80.	CommandButton cmd_Cancel	Form
Table 12.81.	CommandButton cmd_OK	Form
Table 12.82.	Label txt_SupplierID	Form

Table 12.65. Form frm_Supplier.

BackColor	=	&H00C0C0C0&
Caption	=	Form1
ClientHeight	=	6075
ClientLeft	=	1290
ClientTop	=	870
ClientWidth	=	7485
Height	=	6480
Left	=	1230
LinkTopic	=	Form1
ScaleHeight	=	6075
ScaleWidth	=	7485
Top	=	525
Width	=	7605

Table 12.66. SSFrame `fra_SupplierInfo`.

Caption	=	Supplier Information
Height	=	5295
Left	=	120
TabIndex	=	22
Top	=	720
Width	=	5655

Table 12.67. TextBox `txt_State`.

Height	=	285
Left	=	3240
TabIndex	=	7
Top	=	2520
Width	=	495

Table 12.68. TextBox `txt_Zip`.

Height	=	285
Left	=	4200
TabIndex	=	8
Top	=	2520
Width	=	1215

Table 12.69. TextBox `txt_Phone`.

Height	=	285
Left	=	1320
TabIndex	=	10
Top	=	3240
Width	=	1695

Table 12.70. TextBox txt_Fax.

Height	=	285
Left	=	3960
TabIndex	=	11
Top	=	3240
Width	=	1455

Table 12.71. TextBox txt_Country.

Height	=	285
Left	=	1320
TabIndex	=	9
Top	=	2880
Width	=	1815

Table 12.72. ComboBox cmb_Terms.

Height	=	300
Left	=	1320
Style	=	2 'Dropdown List
TabIndex	=	14
Top	=	3720
Width	=	1455

Table 12.73. TextBox txt_Notes.

Height	=	855
Left	=	1320
MultiLine	=	-1 'True
TabIndex	=	12
Top	=	4200
Width	=	4095

Table 12.74. TextBox txt_FirstName.

Height	=	285
Left	=	1320
TabIndex	=	2
Top	=	840
Width	=	4095

Table 12.75. TextBox txt_LastName.

Height	=	285
Left	=	1320
TabIndex	=	3
Top	=	1200
Width	=	4095

Table 12.76. TextBox txt_Address.

Height	=	495
Left	=	1320
MultiLine	=	-1 'True
TabIndex	=	5
Top	=	1920
Width	=	4095

Table 12.77. TextBox txt_City.

Height	=	285
Left	=	1320
TabIndex	=	6
Top	=	2520
Width	=	1215

Table 12.78. TextBox txt_Company.

Height	=	285
Left	=	1320
TabIndex	=	1
Top	=	480
Width	=	4095

Table 12.79. TextBox txt_Title.

Height	=	285
Left	=	1320
TabIndex	=	4
Top	=	1560
Width	=	4095

Table 12.80. CommandButton cmd_Cancel.

Cancel	=	-1 'True
Caption	=	&Cancel
Height	=	495
Left	=	6120
TabIndex	=	13
Top	=	720
Width	=	1095

Table 12.81. CommandButton cmd_OK.

Caption	=	&OK
Default	=	-1 'True
Height	=	495
Left	=	6120
TabIndex	=	0
Top	=	120
Width	=	1095

Table 12.82. Label txt_SupplierID.

BackColor	=	&H00C0C0C0&
Caption	=	Label4
Height	=	255
Left	=	4320
TabIndex	=	30
Top	=	360
Width	=	1095

Adding Code to the PURCHASE.FRM

Now that the Purchase form has been created, the code to make it function must be added. Much of this code also requires the other forms to be functioning as well, Therefore, if you attempt to execute it when it is partially constructed, it may generate an error in certain operations. However, these errors will not hurt anything so don't be afraid to attempt different executions.

Adding the code to the form is a routine task. The variables that remain at the Form level are added to the General Declaration area. Then, any Form level routines are created in the General Routines area using the Procedure...option under the Insert Menu. These routines are not activated by an event (such as a mouse click), but are called by other parts of the code.

These routines appear in the (General) section of the code menus. Finally, routines are added to the specific events of particular controls. These routines are activated when the particular event occurs, usually caused by a user action.

General Declarations

First, enter the variables in Listing 12.2 into the General Declarations section. They include variables to track the row and column of the grid the user is editing, three recordset Object variables to store the various dynasets that need to be accessed by the routines, and constants used to access the various columns of the grid.

These grid constants make the code much more readable. It is highly recommended that when designing an application you frequently use such constants instead of raw numbers. There is no performance penalty and they greatly improve readability and maintainability.

Listing 12.2. General Declarations.

```
Dim gRow As Integer
Dim gCol As Integer

Dim OriginalItems As Integer
Dim PurchaseDS As Recordset
Dim PartsDS As Recordset
Dim PurchaseItemsDS As Recordset

' Grid Column Types
Const col_ItemNum = 0
Const col_Desc = 1
Const col_UnitCost = 2
Const col_Qty = 3
Const col_Price = 4
Const col_LineNum = 5
Const col_Reserved = 6
Const col_OrigQty = 7
```

General Routines

The routines represented in the following section heads are all added to the General section of the form. Code placed in the general section is available to all routines within the form. The following section titles are routine types. Select the Procedure and type in the routine name (without the open and close parentheses or the Sub or Function text) and click the OK button. The window opens showing the begin and end routine structure.

Sub CalculateTotal ()

The `CalculateTotal` routine is used to total all the items in the PO and present a sum in the `txt_Total` text control. There are a number of different events that cause the invoice to re-total: a change in the quantity, modification of the final price, change in the freight, or the change to a different invoice.

The total calculation also fills in the `txt_Tax` field. The tax amount is read from the INI file where it is stored as a parameter. This makes it convenient for a system administrator to change a parameter in a single INI file and copy this file to all the client machines, rather than requiring a complete application recompile.

```
Private Sub CalculateTotal()
    ' Finds to total of all of the items stored in the grid
    Dim TempTotal As Double

    tempcol = grd_Main.Col
    temprow = grd_Main.Row
    TempTotal = 0
```

```
    grd_Main.Col = col_Price
    For i = 1 To grd_Main.Rows - 1
        grd_Main.Row = i
        TempTotal = TempTotal + Val(grd_Main.Text)
    Next i

    ' Multiply total by SalesTax read from the INI file
    txt_Tax = Format(TempTotal * g_SalesTax, "##0.00")
    txt_Total = Format(TempTotal + (TempTotal * g_SalesTax) + Val(txt_Freight), "##0.00")

    ' Restore column and row positions
    grd_Main.Col = tempcol
    grd_Main.Row = temprow
End Sub
```

Sub CheckPriceChange ()

This routine checks if the Price column has been modified. If it has, the total is recalculated. This prevents needless recalculations that slow down client access. Notice how the selected column is first checked to determine whether it is the Price column. This routine is called by a LostFocus event of the Grid textbox to determine the user has finished editing the column.

```
Private Sub CheckPriceChange()
    ' Check for user modification of qty or price that requires
    ' recalculation of PO total

    ' First, check if user was modifying the Price column
    If grd_Main.Col = col_Price Then
        grd_Main.Col = col_UnitCost
        grd_Tag.Col = col_UnitCost
        ' Make grd_Tag access the same row as grd_Main
        grd_Tag.Row = grd_Main.Row

        If grd_Main.Text <> grd_Main.Tag Then
            CalculateTotal
        End If
    End If
End Sub
```

Sub CheckPServer ()

This routine is executed at the beginning of the program. It checks a flag set by the Pseudo Server program to determine if items need to be reordered. If so, the user is notified so he or she may check the inventory lists. This is an example of using the Pseudo Server to do some of the processor intensive work and provide a simple flag to the client so it can avoid the tedious processing work.

```
Private Sub CheckPServer()
    Dim ScratchDS As Recordset

    SQL$ = "Select * from PServer"
    Set ScratchDS = MyDB.OpenRecordset(SQL$, dbOpenDynaset)
    ' Check if items need to be reordered
    If ScratchDS!ReOrderStatus = True Then
        MsgBox "There are items that have reached below the reorder levels. Please check the inventory and reorder these items.", 48, "Reorder Items"
    End If
End Sub
```

Function CountMainItems ()

The `CountMainItems` routine is used to determine the number of items stored in the invoice. To confirm the existence of an item in the particular grid row, the routine checks the Price column (although the ItemNum field may have been chosen instead).

A `CountMainItems` routine is necessary because when the invoice is approved by the user, the client checks if this is an older invoice being edited or a new invoice. If it is an old invoice, the current number of invoice items must be compared with the old number to determine if additional line item records must be added to the PurchaseItems table.

```
Private Function CountMainItems()
    Dim numItems As Integer

    numItems = 0
    ' Cycle through all price columns to determine # of items
    For i = 1 To grd_Main.Rows - 1
        grd_Main.Col = col_Price
        grd_Main.Row = i
        If IsNumeric(grd_Main.Text) Then
            numItems = numItems + 1
        End If
    Next
    CountMainItems = numItems
End Function
```

Function CountTagItems ()

This routine is the parallel routine of the `CountMainItems` routine used to compare the old number of items when the invoice was originally loaded and the newer items stored in `grd_Main`. Because this function is only different from the `CountMainItems` function in that it accesses a separate grid, a single routine might be used that passed the grid control as a parameter. Including a separate routine was done in this example strictly because the code appears slightly clearer as separate functions.

```
Private Function CountTagItems()
    Dim numItems As Integer

    numItems = 0
    For i = 1 To grd_Tag.Rows - 1
        grd_Tag.Col = col_Price
```

```
            grd_Tag.Row = i
            If IsNumeric(grd_Tag.Text) Then
                numItems = numItems + 1
            End If
        Next
        CountTagItems = numItems
End Function
```

Sub CreateNewPO (numitems As Integer)

This routine is called if an entirely new PO must be created (versus modifying an existing entry). The CreateNewPO routine creates the actual PO record but uses the same routine used by the UpdatePO routine to record actual information. By using the same routine, the extra time and problems created by maintaining two pieces of code are avoided.

Notice the entire PO creation is enclosed by BeginTrans and CommitTrans statements. This creates a situation in which the multiple stages of creating a PO are either all completed or all changes are discarded (using the Rollback command). The three stages include: assigning an invoice number, adding the PO general information to the Purchase table, and adding all the individual items to the PurchaseItems table.

If any one of these stages fails, the entire transaction can be revoked so a partial update won't occur. Enclosing multiple operations within a transaction (such as adding all the individual PO items) also dramatically increases performance because the updates can all occur at once instead of individually.

To create a new PO, first a PO number must be assigned. The Counter table contains all the record counters including the next available PO number. The table is incremented to include the PO currently being added.

Next, a new PO record is created in the Purchase table and all the PO summary information is written. Notice that in the case of the combos cmb_Staff and cmb_Supplier the ItemData field is accessed based on the currently selected item (determined by the ListIndex property).

After the PO record has been created, all of the individual items in the PO are stored. Notice that the Description field is only stored if it is different from the standard Description of the PartID. This technique is extremely useful because it allows the application to be both storage conscious and user friendly. By storing any changed description, it allows the user to make any required specific changes to the items description. If no changes are made, however, the field is left as a NULL value, meaning it doesn't take up any space in the actual record. These variable fields are a recent improvement to desktop databases and also exist in SQL implementations.

Finally, the items in the Reserve field are eliminated. There is no need to change the OnHand field in the inventory table because the items were deducted from the inventory when they were reserved. We also do not set the Reserved time to NULL because there may exist other clients with reserved items that are still stored in the Reserve field that need timing. For more information on the maintenance of the Reserve field, see Chapter 14, "Pseudo Server."

```
Private Sub CreateNewPO(numItems As Integer)
    Dim ScratchDS As Recordset
    Dim tempPONum As Long

    BeginTrans
        ' Get the PO number counter
        SQL$ = "Select * from Counter where TableName = 'Purchase'"
        Set ScratchDS = MyDB.OpenRecordset(SQL$, dbOpenDynaset)
        tempPONum = ScratchDS!CountNum
        ' increment PO number
        ScratchDS.Edit
        ScratchDS!CountNum = tempPONum + 1
        ScratchDS.Update

        ' Create PO record
        PurchaseDS.AddNew
        PurchaseDS!PurchaseID = tempPONum
        PurchaseDS!SaleDate = txt_Date.Text
        PurchaseDS!StaffID = cmb_Staff.ItemData(cmb_Staff.ListIndex)
        PurchaseDS!SupplierID = cmb_Supplier.ItemData(cmb_Supplier.ListIndex)
        PurchaseDS!Freight = txt_Freight
        PurchaseDS!CreateDate = Now
        PurchaseDS!ShipDate = txt_Expected.Text
        PurchaseDS!BillDate = txt_BillDate.Text
        PurchaseDS!ShippingTo = txt_ShipTo.Text
        PurchaseDS!Terms = cmb_Terms.ListIndex
        PurchaseDS!FOB = txt_FOB.Text
        PurchaseDS.Update

        ' Store individual PO items
        For i = 1 To numItems
            ' Set row(record) to save
            grd_Main.Row = i
            grd_Tag.Row = i
            ' Create PO record
            PurchaseItemsDS.AddNew
            ' The PurchaseID references the PO to which the item belongs
            PurchaseItemsDS!PurchaseID = tempPONum
            PurchaseItemsDS!Linenum = i
            grd_Main.Col = col_ItemNum
            PurchaseItemsDS!PartID = Val(grd_Main.Text)
            ' g_CurrentLocation is stored in the PURCHASE.INI file
            PurchaseItemsDS!LocationID = g_CurrentLocation
            grd_Main.Col = col_Qty
            PurchaseItemsDS!Qty = Val(grd_Main.Text)
            grd_Main.Col = col_Desc
            grd_Tag.Col = col_Desc
            grd_Tag.Row = i
            ' Do we have to save the description or is it identical to the item desc.?
            If grd_Main.Text <> grd_Tag.Text Then
                PurchaseItemsDS!Desc = grd_Main.Text
            End If
            grd_Main.Col = col_Price
            PurchaseItemsDS!FinalPrice = Val(grd_Main.Text)
            PurchaseItemsDS.Update
        Next i
```

```
        CommitTrans
End Sub
```

Sub DoPrint()

The DoPrint routine generates a simple PO using the printer object. Once again, we recommend purchasing a report generator or full-featured printer control rather than struggling to make the VB printer object function the way you need it to function.

```
Private Sub DoPrint()
    Dim Msg As String

    On Error GoTo ErrorHandler

    CMDialog1.CancelError = True
    CMDialog1.FromPage = 1
    CMDialog1.ToPage = 1
    CMDialog1.Flags = PD_ALLPAGES
    ' Display Print Dialog
    CMDialog1.Action = 5
    If Err = 0 Then
        Printer.FontBold = True
        Printer.Print "WidgetCo."
        Printer.FontBold = False
        ' Location Address/Phone
        Printer.Print frm_Purchase.txt_Location
        Printer.Print
        ' Print PO Number
        Printer.Print "PO # " & frm_Purchase.txt_PONum
        Printer.Print
        ' Print Bill To & Ship To
        Printer.FontBold = True
        Printer.Print "Ship To:"
        Printer.FontBold = False
        Printer.Print frm_Purchase.txt_ShipTo
        Printer.Print
        ' Print Salesperson Name
        Printer.Print "Staff: " & frm_Purchase.cmb_Staff.Text;
        ' Print Customer PO
        Printer.Print Tab(35); "FOB:" & frm_Purchase.txt_FOB;
        ' Print Ship Date
        Printer.Print Tab(55); "Expected Date: " & frm_Purchase.txt_Expected
        ' Print Terms
        Printer.Print "Terms:" & frm_Purchase.cmb_Terms.Text;
        ' Print Date PO was entered
        Printer.Print Tab(35); "Date: " & frm_Purchase.txt_Date
        Printer.Print

        ' Print PO Item Headings
        Printer.Print "Item #"; Tab(12); "Description"; Tab(40); "Price"; Tab(50); "Qty."; Tab(60); "Total"
        Printer.Line (0, Printer.CurrentY + 6)-(Printer.Width, Printer.CurrentY + 6)
        Printer.Print
        ' Print PO Items
        For i = 1 To frm_Purchase.grd_Main.Rows - 1
```

```
                frm_Purchase.grd_Main.Row = i
                frm_Purchase.grd_Main.Col = 0
                If frm_Purchase.grd_Main.Text <> "" Then
                    Printer.Print frm_Purchase.grd_Main.Text; Tab(12);
                    frm_Purchase.grd_Main.Col = 1
                    Printer.Print frm_Purchase.grd_Main.Text; Tab(40);
                    frm_Purchase.grd_Main.Col = 2
                    Printer.Print Format$(Val(frm_Purchase.grd_Main.Text), "$####.#0");
Tab(50);
                    frm_Purchase.grd_Main.Col = 3
                    Printer.Print frm_Purchase.grd_Main.Text; Tab(60);
                    frm_Purchase.grd_Main.Col = 4
                    Printer.Print Format$(Val(frm_Purchase.grd_Main.Text), "$####.#0")
                End If
            Next i
             Printer.Line (0, Printer.CurrentY + 6)-(Printer.Width, Printer.CurrentY + 6)
            Printer.Print
            ' Print Shipping
            Printer.Print Tab(45); "Freight:"; Tab(60);
Format$(Val(frm_Purchase.txt_Freight), "$###0.00")
            ' Print Sales Tax
            Printer.Print Tab(45); "Sales Tax:"; Tab(60);
Format$(Val(frm_Purchase.txt_Tax), "$###0.00")
            ' Print Total
            Printer.FontBold = True
            Printer.Print Tab(45); "Total:"; Tab(60);
Format$(Val(frm_Purchase.txt_Total), "$###0.00")
            Printer.FontBold = False
            Printer.EndDoc
    End If
    Exit Sub

ErrorHandler:
    MsgBox "There was a problem printing to your printer."
Exit Sub
End Sub
```

Sub LoadLocation ()

LoadLocation finds the record of the current location read from the INI file. Because the location will not change (most likely), once the Client program is installed, the location information is stored in a label field. Unlike the Salesperson or Supplier fields which obviously must be selected for each PO, the location remains fixed for the duration of the Client program's execution.

```
Private Sub LoadLocation()
    ' Retrieve location record from table
    SQL$ = "Select * FROM Location WHERE LocationID =" & g_CurrentLocation
    Set MySS = MyDB.OpenRecordset(SQL$, dbOpenSnapshot)

    ' Get location address
    txt_Location = MySS!Description & Chr$(13) & Chr$(10) & MySS!Address & Chr$(13)
& Chr$(10) & MySS!City & ", " & MySS!State & "  " & MySS!Zip
End Sub
```

Sub LoadStaffPopup ()

The `LoadStaffPopup` routine is used to enter all the staff names in the Staff table into a combobox and selects the default staff member in the box. Often one particular staff member uses a Client program (the head of purchasing, a central employee, and so on) to fill out purchase orders. This allows the default staff ID number to be set in the INI file from which the client reads on startup. After all the staff has been inserted into the combobox, that person is selected.

The SQL Select statement uses the ORDER BY command to automatically alphabetize the employees. The alternative is to use the SORTED property of the combobox. If there are many staff members, however, it seems a better idea to allow the database or the Database Server to handle the processing. This way other information could be included in the text entries for the combo list without destroying the order (a combo entry might include the first name first while remaining sorted by the last name, for example, "John Smith.")

```
Private Sub LoadStaffPopup()
    Dim StaffID As Long, SelStaff As Integer

    SQL$ = "Select * FROM Staff ORDER BY LastName,FirstName"
    Set MySS = MyDB.OpenRecordset(SQL$, dbOpenSnapshot)

    SelStaff = -1
    ' Reset record counter
    i = 0
    Do Until MySS.EOF       ' Until end of file.
        Add$ = MySS!LastName & "," & MySS!FirstName
        cmb_Staff.AddItem Add$
        StaffID = MySS!StaffID
        cmb_Staff.ItemData(cmb_Staff.NewIndex) = StaffID
        If StaffID = g_DefaultStaffID Then
            SelStaff = i
        End If

        i = i + 1
        MySS.MoveNext       ' Move to next record.
    Loop
    ' Set staff to equal default staff member
    If SelStaff <> -1 Then
        cmb_Staff.ListIndex = SelStaff
    Else
        cmb_Staff.ListIndex = 0
    End If
End Sub
```

Sub LoadSupplier ()

This routine loads the selected supplier's address information into the txt_ShipTo field. The information about the supplier currently selected by the cmb_Supplier combo is read. Notice that once again the `ItemData` is used to obtain the SupplierID for the selected supplier. A snapshot of the single record is then created to read the information.

```
Private Sub LoadSupplier()
    Dim SupplierID As Long
```

```
    If cmb_Supplier.ListIndex = -1 Then
        cmb_Supplier.Text = ""
    Else
        ' Find supplier ID
        SupplierID = cmb_Supplier.ItemData(cmb_Supplier.ListIndex)
        ' Find supplier record
        SQL$ = "Select * FROM Supplier WHERE SupplierID = " & SupplierID
        Set MySS = MyDB.OpenRecordset(SQL$, dbOpenSnapshot)

        ' Load supplier address
        txt_ShipTo.Text = cmb_Supplier.Text & Chr$(13) & Chr$(10) & MySS!Address & Chr$(13) & Chr$(10) & MySS!City & ", " & MySS!State & "   " & MySS!Zip
        cmb_Terms.ListIndex = MySS!Terms
    End If
End Sub
```

Sub LoadSupplierPopup ()

This routine loads the combobox holding all the suppliers names. Because suppliers may be either individuals or companies, the ORDER BY statement in the SQL query effectively categorizes them. If the Company field is left blank, the ORDER BY command moves it to the front of the list.

Therefore, all individuals appear together, alphabetized by LastName, at the top of the combo list. If a different order is desired, simply changing the ORBER BY statement alters without any new programming how they appear in the combo box.

> **NOTE**
>
> It is sensible to do as much processing as possible with the query (rather than programatically). A SQL query is mostly a text string, which makes modification much easier than changing a program's execution flow. The ORDER BY, GROUP BY, and VIEW BY commands allow the data to be returned in the order that is desired. Using these SQL commands instead of sorting the data after it has been downloaded is preferable because the processing then takes place on the server rather than the client machine.
>
> A SQL query might even be included in the INI file, allowing ordering changes to be made without any necessary re-compile. This saves a dramatic amount of redeployment time if the database changes slightly. A new .INI file can simply be copied to each machine.
>
> Using the SQL ordering commands also allows a Database Server to optimize the query and therefore send only the data necessary for display. This decreases network traffic compared with sending all the data across the connection to have the client sort it later. Using the query commands maximizes the implementation of an effective client/server system.

```
Private Sub LoadSupplierPopup()
    Dim SQL$
    Dim SupplierID As Long

    SQL$ = "Select * FROM Supplier ORDER BY Company,LastName"
    Set MySS = MyDB.OpenRecordset(SQL$, dbOpenSnapshot)

    cmb_Supplier.Clear
    ' Reset record counter
    i = 0
    Do Until MySS.EOF         ' Until end of file.
        Add$ = ""
        If "" & MySS!Company <> "" Then
            Add$ = Add$ & MySS!Company
        Else
            Add$ = MySS!LastName & "," & MySS!FirstName
        End If
        cmb_Supplier.AddItem Add$
        SupplierID = MySS!SupplierID
        cmb_Supplier.ItemData(cmb_Supplier.NewIndex) = SupplierID

        i = i + 1
        MySS.MoveNext    ' Move to next record.
    Loop
End Sub
```

Sub MoveTextBox (grid As Control, TextBox As Control)

This routine is used to move the textbox txt_GridText into place over the grid so the user has the illusion of editing the grid cell. Note that this routine does not size the textbox to the size of the current row and column. The resizing of the `txt_GridText` control occurs in the `SetCell()` routine.

Because of the different background colors for the fixed columns and fixed rows, as well as their traditional content, the editing routine automatically skips these routines. When the desired X and Y coordinates are determined, the `txt_GridText` is moved to that location.

Additionally, the cmd_Item button is moved to the Y coordinate of this new edit row. The cmd_Item button is only visible when the item column is selected and then appears to the left of the selected row.

```
Private Sub MoveTextBox(grid As Control, TextBox As Control)
    ' Move a text box to the position of the current cell in a grid:
    Dim X As Single, Y As Single

    ' Skip grid border
    X = grid.Left
    Y = grid.Top
    If grid.BorderStyle = 1 Then
        X = X + Screen.TwipsPerPixelX
        Y = Y + Screen.TwipsPerPixelY
    End If

    ' Skip fixed columns and rows
    For i = 0 To grid.FixedCols - 1
```

```
            X = X + grid.ColWidth(i)
            If grid.GridLines Then
                X = X + Screen.TwipsPerPixelX
            End If
        Next

        For i = 0 To grid.FixedRows - 1
            Y = Y + grid.RowHeight(i)
            If grid.GridLines Then
                Y = Y + Screen.TwipsPerPixelY
            End If
        Next

        ' Find the X value of the current data cell
        For i = grid.LeftCol To grid.Col - 1
            X = X + grid.ColWidth(i)
            If grid.GridLines Then
                X = X + Screen.TwipsPerPixelX
            End If
        Next
        ' Find the Y value of the current data cell
        For i = grid.TopRow To grid.Row - 1
            Y = Y + grid.RowHeight(i)
            If grid.GridLines Then
                Y = Y + Screen.TwipsPerPixelY
            End If
        Next
        ' Move the Text Box, and make small adjustments
        TextBox.Move X + Screen.TwipsPerPixelX, Y + Screen.TwipsPerPixelY
        cmd_Item.Move cmd_Item.Left, Y + Screen.TwipsPerPixelY
End Sub
```

Sub RecordToScreen (TempDS As Recordset)

`RecordToScreen` reads all the information from a record for a purchase order and puts it in the appropriate controls on the screen. This is the central routine for the Next and Previous buttons to page through the available POs.

First the PO's general information is read and placed in each control. The routine then creates a dynaset of all the items that are stored for that PO. Using a `Do...Until` loop, all the records are found and placed in both the `grd_Main` and the `grd_Tag`.

After all the items have been read, a `For...Next` loop is used to find the Unit Cost and the Description (for items that don't have a user modified description) of all the PO items. Finally, the Tag fields are set to equal the current general information fields so these fields may be later compared to determine any changes made by the user. The total of the PO is then calculated.

```
Private Sub RecordToScreen(TempDS As Recordset)
    Dim ScratchDS As Recordset
    Dim TempTerms As Integer, SupplierID As Long

    ' Store simple text values
    txt_PONum.Caption = TempDS!PurchaseID
```

```
txt_Date.Text = TempDS!SaleDate
cmb_Staff.ListIndex = TempDS!StaffID - 1
txt_Freight = Format(TempDS!Freight, "##0.00")
txt_Expected.Text = "" & TempDS!ShipDate
txt_BillDate.Text = "" & TempDS!BillDate
' Store till later, loading Supplier will set default Terms
TempTerms = TempDS!Terms
txt_FOB.Text = "" & TempDS!FOB
SupplierID = TempDS!SupplierID

' Search the Supplier combo for the correct supplier and select
For i = 0 To cmb_Supplier.ListCount - 1
    If SupplierID = cmb_Supplier.ItemData(i) Then
        cmb_Supplier.ListIndex = i
        Exit For
    End If
Next i

tempShip = "" & TempDS!ShippingTo
If tempShip = "" Then
    ' Read Supplier address
Else
    txt_ShipTo.Text = tempShip
End If

SQL$ = "Select * From PurchaseItems where PurchaseID = " & TempDS!PurchaseID
Set ScratchDS = MyDB.OpenRecordset(SQL$, dbOpenDynaset)

' Reset grd_Main and grd_Tag to load PO items
grd_Main.Rows = 1
grd_Main.Rows = 20
grd_Tag.Rows = 1
grd_Tag.Rows = 20
grd_Main.FixedRows = 1
i = 1

' Find all item records which belong to the PO
Do Until ScratchDS.EOF
    grd_Tag.Row = i
    grd_Main.Row = i

    grd_Tag.Col = col_ItemNum
    grd_Tag.Text = ScratchDS!PartID
    grd_Main.Col = col_ItemNum
    grd_Main.Text = ScratchDS!PartID

    ' If Desc is blank, we'll fill it in with Part# info below
    grd_Tag.Col = col_Desc
    grd_Tag.Text = "" & ScratchDS!Desc
    grd_Main.Col = col_Desc
    grd_Main.Text = "" & ScratchDS!Desc

    grd_Tag.Col = col_Qty
    grd_Tag.Text = ScratchDS!Qty
    grd_Tag.Col = col_OrigQty
    grd_Tag.Text = ScratchDS!Qty
    grd_Main.Col = col_Qty
    grd_Main.Text = ScratchDS!Qty
```

```
            grd_Tag.Col = col_Price
            grd_Tag.Text = Format$(ScratchDS!FinalPrice, "###0.00")
            grd_Main.Col = col_Price
            grd_Main.Text = Format$(ScratchDS!FinalPrice, "###0.00")

        ScratchDS.MoveNext
        i = i + 1
    Loop
    OriginalItems = i - 1

    ' This loop takes each PO item and inserts the description & UnitCost
    For j = 0 To i
        grd_Main.Row = j
        grd_Main.Col = 0
        If grd_Main.Text <> "" And IsNumeric(grd_Main.Text) Then
            SQL$ = "Select * from Inventory_Parts WHERE PartID = " & grd_Main.Text
            Set PartsDS = MyDB.OpenRecordset(SQL$, dbOpenDynaset)
            grd_Main.Col = col_Desc
            grd_Tag.Col = col_Desc

            ' Check if there is already a description stored in field
            If grd_Main.Text = "" Then
                grd_Main.Text = PartsDS!Description
                grd_Tag.Text = PartsDS!Description
            End If

            ' Store unit cost
            grd_Main.Col = col_UnitCost
            grd_Main.Text = Format$(PartsDS!UnitCost, "###0.00")

            grd_Tag.Col = col_UnitCost
            grd_Tag.Text = Format$(PartsDS!UnitCost, "###0.00")
        End If
    Next j
    ' Now save off the Terms
    cmb_Terms.ListIndex = TempTerms

    ' Save Tag items for later compare
    txt_Date.Tag = txt_Date.Text
    cmb_Supplier.Tag = cmb_Supplier.Text
    cmb_Staff.Tag = cmb_Staff.Text
    txt_Freight.Tag = txt_Freight.Text
    txt_Expected.Tag = txt_Expected.Text
    txt_BillDate.Tag = txt_BillDate.Text
    txt_FOB.Tag = txt_FOB.Text

    ' Calculate the total of the PO
    CalculateTotal
End Sub
```

Sub SetCell ()

The SetCell routine prepares the txt_GridText box for editing. It calls the MoveTextBox() routine to position the box over the proper grid cell. The current grid row and column are saved to variables so that when these change later routines will know where to store the edited information. The textbox is then sized to fit the current grid and column. The content of the grid cell is transferred to the textbox.

Various properties are now set on the textbox control. Note that the ZOrder property is set to 0. The ZOrder property sets the front-to-back order of a particular control to other controls on the form. Setting the ZOrder to 0 ensures the textbox will appear on top of all the other controls (preventing, for example, the textbox from being hidden behind the grid).

Finally the selected column number is checked. If the column number is equal to `col_ItemNum`, then make the button to select items visible.

```
Private Sub SetCell()
    ' Move the text box to the current grid cell:
    MoveTextBox grd_Main, txt_GridText
    ' Save the position of the grids Row and Col for later:
    gRow = grd_Main.Row
    gCol = grd_Main.Col
    ' Make text box same size as current grid cell:
    txt_GridText.Width = grd_Main.ColWidth(grd_Main.Col) - 2 * Screen.TwipsPerPixelX
    txt_GridText.Height = grd_Main.RowHeight(grd_Main.Row) - 2 * Screen.TwipsPerPixelY
    ' Transfer the grid cell text:
    txt_GridText.Text = grd_Main.Text
    ' Show the text box:
    txt_GridText.Visible = True
    txt_GridText.ZOrder 0
    txt_GridText.SetFocus
    If gCol = col_ItemNum Then
        cmd_Item.Visible = True
    Else
        cmd_Item.Visible = False
    End If
End Sub
```

Sub SetupDefaultScreen ()

This routine simply resets all the screen control values to default values. It essentially creates the blank purchase order. This routine is called at first execution, and after the user clicks the OK button and a new PO is displayed. Notice that the Tag fields are set to equal the blank values.

Although this is not strictly necessary (because in a new PO all the information is saved and the Tags are not checked), this is a good design so unmaintained or "dirty" values are not sitting in memory, possibly causing a forgotten routine to return unintended results.

```
Private Sub SetupDefaultScreen()
    cmb_Terms.ListIndex = g_StandardTerms
    grd_Main.Col = 0
    grd_Main.Row = 1
    grd_Tag.Col = 0
    grd_Tag.Row = 1
    SetupGrid
    txt_Date.Text = Format$(Now, "mm-dd-yy")
    txt_PONum = "New"
    cmb_Supplier.ListIndex = -1
    txt_ShipTo.Text = ""
    txt_FOB.Text = ""
```

```
        txt_Expected.Text = ""
        txt_BillDate.Text = ""
        txt_Freight.Text = Format(g_Freight, "##0.00")

        ' Reset Tag information
        cmb_Terms.Tag = cmb_Terms.Text
        txt_Date.Tag = txt_Date.Text
        txt_PONum.Tag = txt_PONum.Caption
        cmb_Supplier.Tag = cmb_Supplier.Text
        txt_ShipTo.Tag = txt_ShipTo.Text
        txt_FOB.Tag = txt_FOB.Text
        txt_Expected.Tag = txt_Expected.Text
        txt_BillDate.Tag = txt_BillDate.Text
        txt_Freight.Tag = txt_Freight.Text
End Sub
```

Sub SetupGrid ()

SetupGrid sets up the Grid control for column titles, width, column width, row width. Both the grd_Main and the grd_Tag controls are formatted for the number of rows, and so on. When this is complete, the width of all the grid columns is determined. The Width property of the entire grid is set to accommodate all the columns. Without adjusting the width, the horizontal scroll bar appears.

> **TIP**
>
> On an invoice or PO, a horizontal scrollbar is a poor design and user interface because it doesn't allow all the item's parameters to be viewed at once. If, in an application, your design is too wide for a single grid line, consider what information the user must frequently consult. Make sure this information appears as one of the first columns.
>
> Also consider using a different user interface technique. For example, a listbox with all the item names that may be double-clicked showing a form containing all the information for that item.

```
Private Sub SetupGrid()
    Dim tempwidth As Integer

    grd_Main.Cols = 5
    grd_Main.Rows = 1         'clears the grid completely
    grd_Tag.Cols = 8          ' Make bigger for extra Tag values
    grd_Tag.Rows = 1          'clears the grid completely

    grd_Main.Row = 0
    grd_Main.Col = 0
    grd_Main.ColWidth(0) = 800
    grd_Main.Text = "Item#"
    grd_Main.Col = 1
    grd_Main.ColWidth(1) = 3200
    grd_Main.Text = "Description"
    grd_Main.Col = 2
    grd_Main.ColWidth(2) = 800
```

```
        grd_Main.Text = "Rate"
        grd_Main.Col = 3
        grd_Main.ColWidth(3) = 800
        grd_Main.Text = "Qty"
        grd_Main.Col = 4
        grd_Main.ColWidth(4) = 900
        grd_Main.Text = "Amount"
        grd_Main.Rows = 5
        grd_Main.FixedRows = 1
        grd_Main.FixedCols = 0
        grd_Tag.Rows = 5
        grd_Tag.FixedRows = 1
        grd_Tag.FixedCols = 0

        tempwidth = 0
        For i = 0 To grd_Main.Cols - 1
            tempwidth = tempwidth + grd_Main.ColWidth(i)
        Next i
        ' Add a little so Scrollbar doesn't overlap last column
        grd_Main.Width = tempwidth + 340
End Sub
```

Sub UpdatePO (main items As Integer)

UpdatePO stores any changes to the current PO. The routine can be divided into three different pieces: update any changed summary information, add additional line items in the invoice, and update all the invoice lines. The entire routine uses data that was stored when the invoice was originally loaded in order to determine the new versus the old.

> **NOTE**
>
> Handling user changes to current data and updating those changes is often the most challenging implementation task faced by the client/server designer. There is no single way to accomplish this task and often the implementation varies depending on the required results.
>
> Often an array of some sort is used to read a complete record and the data is then transferred to the screen. This can be extremely effective when updating multiple records at once or when multiple records must be kept in memory at once. The primary disadvantage of this technique is the lack of conceptual proximity between the original data and the structure. For example, if another field is added to the table, all the implementations of the array must be updated to reflect these changes. This is extremely easy to overlook, especially in a complex project.
>
> In this application we have used the Tag property fields to store the original data for all the text fields. This keeps the original data within the same structure as the changed data. We have also used a grid (grd_Tag) that parallels the original grid (grd_Main). The two grids can then be examined at update time for any differences.
>
> Both of these techniques are appropriate to different implementations and are often mixed and matched in a single application. Consider which is best for the task at hand.

The first part of the routine checks each text value against the original property stored in the Tag property. Notice that this occurs with the combo controls as well. The combo controls have a Text property which mirrors the ListIndex item selected.

The second section of `UpdatePO` checks for items that were added to the original invoice. If there have been additions, records are added to accommodate the new items. Notice that none of the information is added to these new records except the values placed in the key fields of the record (fields such as PurchaseID and LineNum). This allows the third section (the update routine) to update all the records, new and old.

When designing an application, try to keep the `Update` or `Edit` procedures to a minimum and eliminate all unnecessary duplicate routines. When new fields are added to a table, or the functionality has changed, it is extremely easy to overlook a hidden routine and cause endless problems for a client.

The third section updates all the line items that have changed since the load of the PO. Each value is checked against the value held in the grd_Tag. If the value is found to be different, the record is updated. After the update occurs, the values in grd_Tag are updated to equal those in grd_Main. This ensures that any further editing does not re-update the same values. The `Update` command is then called to save the operation.

Finally, the `CommitTrans` command is activated to write all the changes out to the database. The variable g_CurrentInvoice is then set to equal -1 which displays a new PO for entry.

```
Private Sub UpdatePO(mainitems As Integer)
    Dim SQL$
    Dim RecordDS As Recordset
    Dim ScratchDS As Recordset
    Dim TagItems As Integer

    TagItems = CountTagItems()

    BeginTrans
    ' Check PO fields against Tag values
        ' --- Summary Info Section
        ' Create Recordset containing PO record
        SQL$ = "Select * from Purchase WHERE PurchaseID = " & txt_PONum.Caption
        Set RecordDS = MyDB.OpenRecordset(SQL$, dbOpenDynaset)
        RecordDS.Edit
        If txt_Date.Text <> txt_Date.Tag Then
            RecordDS!SaleDate = txt_Date.Text
        End If
        If cmb_Staff.Text <> cmb_Staff.Tag Then
            RecordDS!StaffID = cmb_Staff.ItemData(cmb_Staff.ListIndex)
        End If
        If cmb_Supplier.Text <> cmb_Supplier.Tag Then
            RecordDS!CustomerID = cmb_Supplier.ItemData(cmb_Supplier.ListIndex)
        End If
        If txt_Freight.Text <> txt_Freight.Tag Then
            RecordDS!Freight = txt_Freight.Text
        End If
```

```
            If txt_Expected.Text <> txt_Expected.Tag Then
                RecordDS!ShipDate = txt_Expected.Text
            End If
            If txt_BillDate.Text <> txt_BillDate.Tag Then
                RecordDS!BillDate = txt_BillDate.Text
            End If
            If txt_ShipTo.Text <> txt_ShipTo.Tag Then
                RecordDS!ShippingTo = txt_ShipTo.Text
            End If
            If cmb_Terms.Text <> cmb_Terms.Tag Then
                RecordDS!Terms = cmb_Terms.ListIndex
            End If
            If txt_FOB.Text <> txt_FOB.Tag Then
                RecordDS!FOB = txt_FOB.Text
            End If
            RecordDS.Update
            
            ' --- New Items Section
            ' Are there more items than the original PO?
            If mainitems > OriginalItems Then
                ' Add slots for new items
                SQL$ = "Select * From PurchaseItems Where PurchaseID = " & txt_PONum
                Set ScratchDS = MyDB.OpenRecordset(SQL$, dbOpenDynaset)
                For i = 1 To (mainitems - OriginalItems)
                    ScratchDS.AddNew
                    ScratchDS!PurchaseID = Val(txt_PONum)
                    ScratchDS!Linenum = OriginalItems + i
                    ScratchDS!LocationID = g_CurrentLocation
                    ScratchDS.Update
                Next i
            End If
            
            ' ---- Update Records Section
            For i = 1 To mainitems
                ' any changes from old items check against grd_Tag
                grd_Main.Row = i
                grd_Tag.Row = i
                
                SQL$ = "Select * From PurchaseItems Where PurchaseID = " & txt_PONum & _
" and LineNum = " & i
                Set ScratchDS = MyDB.OpenRecordset(SQL$, dbOpenDynaset)
                ScratchDS.Edit
                
                ' --- ItemNum
                grd_Main.Col = col_ItemNum
                grd_Tag.Col = col_ItemNum
                If grd_Tag.Text <> grd_Main.Text Then
                    ScratchDS!PartID = Val(grd_Main.Text)
                    grd_Tag.Text = grd_Main.Text
                End If
                
                ' --- Quantity
                grd_Main.Col = col_Qty
                grd_Tag.Col = col_OrigQty
                If grd_Tag.Text <> grd_Main.Text Then
                    ScratchDS!Qty = Val(grd_Main.Text)
                    grd_Tag.Text = grd_Main.Text
                End If
```

```
            ' --- Description
            grd_Main.Col = col_Desc
            grd_Tag.Col = col_Desc
            If grd_Tag.Text <> grd_Main.Text Then
                ScratchDS!Desc = grd_Main.Text
                grd_Tag.Text = grd_Main.Text
            End If

            ' --- FinalPrice
            grd_Main.Col = col_Price
            grd_Tag.Col = col_Price
            If grd_Tag.Text <> grd_Main.Text Then
                ScratchDS!FinalPrice = Val(grd_Main.Text)
                grd_Tag.Text = grd_Main.Text
            End If

            ScratchDS.Update
        Next i
    CommitTrans
    g_CurrentInvoice = -1
End Sub
```

Control Code

All the code represented by the following section heads must be added to the individual controls. Simply double-click the control on the Purchase form and the relevant code box appears. Then, in the drop-down combo labeled Proc:, select the event that is specified. Enter the code given for the particular event.

Sub cmb_Terms_Change ()

This routine sets the update flag for the PO (g_InvoiceDirty) to True. When the user seeks to cancel the PO, discarding changes can be confirmed. This routine is activated when the combo for the PO payment terms is changed.

```
Private Sub cmb_Terms_Change()
    g_InvoiceDirty = True
End Sub
```

Sub cmd_Cancel_Click ()

If the user clicks on the Cancel button, this routine is activated. It first checks if there have been any changes to the PO which would be lost if the Cancel operation is executed. If so, the user is prompted to confirm that the changes may be discarded. The MsgBox() routine returns the number 1 if the user clicked on the OK button.

The g_CurrentInvoice variable is the set to -1 which indicates this is a new PO and the SetupDefaultScreen() routine is executed.

```
Private Sub cmd_Cancel_Click()
    Dim result As Integer

    result = 1
    ' Are there any entries on the PO?
    If g_InvoiceDirty = True Then
        result = MsgBox("Are you sure you want to eliminate all of the changes you've made to this PO?", 33, "Cancel PO")
    End If
    ' Should we discard entries?
    If result = 1 Then
        g_CurrentInvoice = -1
        SetupDefaultScreen
    End If
End Sub
```

Sub cmd_Supplier_Click ()

This routine is executed if the user clicks on the cmd_Supplier button that is to the right of the cmb_Supplier Combo control. When the user clicks on this button, he either wants to edit the supplier selected in the combobox or create a new one.

The combo is first checked for any selection at all. The combo box may have a ListIndex setting of -1 which indicates no values are selected. If no selection is indicated, the variable NewSupplier is set to True. This variable tells the routine to process a new supplier record later in the execution.

If there is an item selected in the combo box, all the listings in the combo are searched for an entry matching the text typed into the text field of the control. The list of the combo is searched for an equivalent of the typed text rather than by simply looking at the selected item (ListIndex) because the user may have typed in the name by hand after selecting an item. This would make the typed name differ from the selected item. In that case, the item number must be found.

If the supplier is not found, a new record is created and the frm_Supplier form is shown. Otherwise the g_SupplierID variable is set to the SupplierID number and the frm_Supplier is shown. The frm_Supplier itself, upon loading, checks the variables and determines any data that must be retrieved and fields that must be filled.

> **CAUTION**
>
> Determining where data will be loaded is an extremely important decision when designing a client/server system. In the code below, data retrieval is done by the form itself with outside routines setting variables to indicate what to load. This essentially *localizes* the loading routine to the form that actually uses it.
>
> In contrast, the data might have been loaded by the outside routine and the data structure simply passed to the form through one or more variables. This *externalizes* the routine from the form using the data.

> Lastly, an external routine may be *globalized* and put into a module so that many routines may access it. This provides one central routine that all other routines can access.
>
> Choosing the access style is important in the design stage. If a particular data set needs to be loaded by many routines, it should be global so that when the data changes, only one routine needs to be altered. Keeping it localized, however, has the advantage of keeping the loading code directly with the code that must use the loaded data. If the access needs are not considered before implementation takes place, bugs and re-coding are often far more prevalent.

```
Private Sub cmd_Supplier_Click()
    Dim NewSupplier As Integer
    Dim SupplierSlot As Integer

    NewSupplier = False
    SupplierSlot = -1
    If cmb_Supplier.ListIndex = -1 Then
        NewSupplier = True
    Else
        For i = 0 To cmb_Supplier.ListCount - 1
            If cmb_Supplier.Text = cmb_Supplier.List(i) Then
                SupplierSlot = i
                Exit For
            End If
        Next i
        If SupplierSlot = -1 Then
            NewSupplier = True
        End If
    End If

    If NewSupplier = True Then
        ' Setup blank record
        g_LoadCustFlag = False
        g_ClearCustFlag = True
        frm_Supplier.Caption = "New Supplier"
        frm_Supplier.Show 1
    Else
        ' Load selected supplier info
        g_LoadCustFlag = True
        g_ClearCustFlag = False
        g_SupplierID = cmb_Supplier.ItemData(cmb_Supplier.ListIndex)
        frm_Supplier.Caption = "Supplier: " & cmb_Supplier.Text
        frm_Supplier.Show 1
    End If

    LoadSupplierPopup
End Sub
```

Sub cmd_Item_Click ()

The routine is activated when the user clicks on the cmd_Item. This may only occur when the focus is in the first column of the invoice (otherwise the button is not visible). The rm_Item is shown to enable the user to choose a Sales item. The number "1" following the Show method prevents the user from selecting another window until the frm_Item is closed.

If the user does not cancel the Item Form (indicated by a part value of -1), then the information for that item is entered into the invoice. The g_PartNum is stored in the column 0. A Snapshot object is then created to get all the information about the item entry.

After this information is retrieved and stored in the grd_Main, the invoice's Total is recalculated. The quantity of this line item is then selected and control is returned to the system.

```
Private Sub cmd_Item_Click()
    On Error GoTo SearchError

    g_PartNum = -1
    ' Setup properties for list box display
    frm_Item.ListTitle = "Inventory Part"
    frm_Item.ListQuery = "Select * FROM Inventory_Parts ORDER BY Description"
    frm_Item.ListItem1 = "Description"
    frm_Item.ListItem2 = ""
    frm_Item.ListIDField = "PartID"
    frm_Item.Show 1
    ' Did the user select an item?
    If frm_Item.ListResult <> -1 Then
        g_PartNum = frm_Item.ListResult
        grd_Main.Col = 0
        grd_Main.Text = g_PartNum

        grd_Tag.Col = 0
        grd_Tag.Row = grd_Main.Row
        'grd_Tag.Text = g_PartNum

        SQL$ = "Select * FROM Inventory_Parts WHERE PartID = " & g_PartNum & ";"
        Set MySS = MyDB.OpenRecordset(SQL$, dbOpenSnapshot)

        grd_Main.Col = 1
        grd_Main.Text = MySS!Description
        grd_Main.Col = 2
        grd_Main.Text = MySS!UnitCost
        grd_Main.Col = 4
        grd_Main.Text = MySS!UnitCost
        grd_Main.Col = 3
        grd_Main.Text = 1

        grd_Tag.Col = 1
        grd_Tag.Text = MySS!Description
        CalculateTotal
        DoEvents
        SetCell
        'txt_GridText.SetFocus    ' Set focus back to grid, see Text_LostFocus.
    End If
    g_InvoiceDirty = True
    Exit Sub
```

```
SearchError:
    Msg = "Error# " & Err & ":" & Error(Err)
    MsgBox Msg   ' Display message.
    Exit Sub
End Sub
```

Sub cmd_Next_Click ()

The cmd_Next button is used to jump to the next invoice. If the currently shown invoice is a new invoice, a message is displayed alerting the user that there are no further stored invoices. If the current invoice is not a blank invoice, the InvoiceDS (the global dynaset for the invoices) is moved to the next record. If the end-of-file has been reached, a New invoice is shown.

If the next record is an invoice, the RecordToScreen() routine is called to move the invoice information and all the invoice line items onto the screen. The global invoice value is also set to indicate this selected invoice.

```
Private Sub cmd_Next_Click()
    ' Is there a current PO?
    If g_CurrentInvoice = -1 Then
        MsgBox "There aren't any newer POs than the current PO. Please use the
'Prev' button to access other POs.", 16, "No Next POs"
    Else
        PurchaseDS.MoveNext
        If PurchaseDS.EOF = True Then
            g_CurrentInvoice = -1
            SetupDefaultScreen
        Else
            RecordToScreen PurchaseDS
            g_CurrentInvoice = Val(txt_PONum)
        End If
    End If
End Sub
```

Sub cmd_OK_Click ()

If the OK button is pressed, the invoice is recorded to the database. Before this can be done, many checks must ensure the data the user entered into the invoice is valid. The Supplier name is checked to make sure one is entered, and then to make sure the entered name exists in the Supplier table. The saving of the invoice is stopped if the Supplier is not valid.

If the supplier is valid, the routine proceeds to check the individual line items. The routine makes sure that some items are entered on the invoice by calling the CountMainItems() routine.

If the PO is proven to be valid, the PO itself is determined to be either a new invoice or an update of an existing one. The routines must be separate because creating a record from scratch has far different implications than updating an existing PO. The update or creation routine is then called. Finally, the routine creates a new blank purchase order.

```
Private Sub cmd_OK_Click()
    Dim SupplierSlot As Integer
    Dim result As Integer
    Dim numItems As Integer

    SupplierSlot = -1
    If cmb_Supplier.Text = "" Then
        MsgBox "A Supplier name is required for a PO. Please select a supplier from the list", 16, "Empty Supplier Name"
        Exit Sub
    End If
    ' Make sure that supplier is in the supplier list
    For i = 0 To cmb_Supplier.ListCount - 1
        If cmb_Supplier.Text = cmb_Supplier.List(i) Then
            SupplierSlot = i
            Exit For
        End If
    Next i
    If SupplierSlot = -1 Then
        result = MsgBox("The supplier name is not in the Supplier list. Would you like to add it?", 33, "Add New Supplier?")
        If result = 1 Then
            ' Setup blank record
            g_LoadCustFlag = False
            g_ClearCustFlag = True
            frm_Supplier.Caption = "New Supplier"
            frm_Supplier.Show 1
            LoadSupplierPopup
            MsgBox "Now please select the supplier and click on the 'OK' button again to save the PO.", 64
' User must now select the supplier
            Exit Sub
        Else
            Exit Sub
        End If
    End If

    ' Make sure that items have been entered on the PO
    ' & items are listed in SalesInventory table
    numItems = CountMainItems()

    If numItems = 0 Then
        MsgBox "There are no items with prices in this PO. Please enter an item before saving the PO.", 16, "Blank PO"
Exit Sub
    End If

    If txt_PONum = "New" Then
        CreateNewPO numItems
    Else
        UpdatePO numItems
    End If

    SetupDefaultScreen
End Sub
```

Sub cmd_Prev_Click ()

The cmd_Prev button is used to show previous invoices. The Client program is made so that, conceptually, a blank invoice follows the last existing invoice. Therefore, if the user clicks the cmd_Prev button while a new invoice is displayed, this routine displays the last available invoice record.

If the Client is displaying the very first invoice, a message is displayed alerting the user that there are no further stored invoices. If the current invoice is not a blank invoice, the InvoiceDS (the global dynaset for the invoices) is moved to the previous record.

The `RecordToScreen()` routine is called to move the invoice information and all the invoice line items onto the screen. The global invoice value is also set to indicate this selected invoice.

```
Private Sub cmd_Prev_Click()
    ' Is there a current PO?
    If g_CurrentInvoice = -1 Then
        PurchaseDS.MoveLast
    Else
        PurchaseDS.MovePrevious
        If PurchaseDS.BOF = True Then
            MsgBox "No previous POs", 16, "No previous POs"
            PurchaseDS.MoveNext
End If
    End If
    RecordToScreen PurchaseDS
    g_CurrentInvoice = Val(txt_PONum)
End Sub
```

Sub cmd_Print_Click ()

Execute the simple printing routine created earlier.

> **TIP**
>
> The Common Dialog control included with Visual Basic supports the Printer Setup dialog boxes. If you need to allow the user to configure the printer, simply add this control and set the properties correctly. See the documentation on the Common Dialog control for more information.

```
Sub cmd_Print_Click ()
    DoPrint
End Sub
```

Sub cmd_Received_Click ()

This routine takes all the saved items from a PO and enters the items into the Inventory_Parts. In a business, a Purchase Order is usually created to order particular items. Those items are received after the PO has been issued. This button actually receives the items into inventory.

First the routine checks to make sure this is not a new invoice. A dynaset is created to store all the line items of the PO. A `Do...Until` loop is created to cycle through each line item and add the amount not currently received in inventory.

```
Private Sub cmd_Received_Click()
    Dim PurchaseItemsDS As Recordset
    Dim PartItemsDS As Recordset
    Dim tempqty As Long

    If txt_PONum = "New" Then
        MsgBox "Cannot enter items as received because PO has not been saved into the system. Click the 'OK' button, reselect the invoice, and then press 'Received'.", 16, "PO Not Saved"
    Else
        ' Open a dynaset with all invoice items
        SQL$ = "Select * from PurchaseItems where PurchaseID = " & txt_PONum
        Set PurchaseItemsDS = MyDB.OpenRecordset(SQL$, dbOpenDynaset)

        ' Cycle through all items stored for PO
        Do Until PurchaseItemsDS.EOF
            ' Open a dynaset to  the Inventory_Parts
            SQL$ = "Select * from Inventory_Parts where PartID = " & PurchaseItemsDS!PartID
            Set PartItemsDS = MyDB.OpenRecordset(SQL$, dbOpenDynaset)

            ' Calculate difference between qty and shipped fields
            tempqty = PurchaseItemsDS!Qty - PurchaseItemsDS!Shipped

            If tempqty > 0 Then
                ' Add PO value to Inventory_Parts
                PartItemsDS.Edit
                PartItemsDS!OnHand = PartItemsDS!OnHand + tempqty
                PartItemsDS.Update

                ' Update the quantity that was received
                PurchaseItemsDS.Edit
                PurchaseItemsDS!Shipped = PurchaseItemsDS!Shipped + tempqty
                PurchaseItemsDS.Update
            End If

            PurchaseItemsDS.MoveNext
        Loop
    End If
End Sub
```

Sub cmb_Supplier_Click ()

This button allows the selection of a Supplier which automatically enters the necessary information in the ShipTo text field. The `LoadSupplier` routine is called to fill in the information. The dirty flag is set to indicate a change to the purchase order.

```
Private Sub cmb_Supplier_Click()
    LoadSupplier
    g_InvoiceDirty = True
End Sub
```

Sub cmb_Supplier_LostFocus ()

This routine attempts to find a supplier entered by hand into the text field of the combobox. If the user selected a supplier, and then typed over the supplier name, the text will differ from the supplier selected in the combo box. The list of suppliers is searched to select the appropriate supplier in the list.

```
Private Sub cmb_Supplier_LostFocus()
    For i = 0 To cmb_Supplier.ListCount - 1
        If cmb_Supplier.Text = cmb_Supplier.List(i) Then
            cmb_Supplier.ListIndex = i
            LoadSupplier
            Exit Sub
        End If
    Next i
End Sub
```

Sub cmd_Exit_Click ()

The Exit command button ends the execution of the VB program. It also removes any hidden forms from memory.

```
Private Sub ExitItem_Click()
    End
End Sub
```

Sub Form_Activate ()

This routine simply selects the Supplier combobox for editing. This allows the user to begin entering a supplier into a blank PO when the form is activated.

```
Private Sub Form_Activate()
    cmb_Supplier.SetFocus
End Sub
```

Sub Form_Load ()

The Load event causes the Invoice Form to initialize. The default values are read from the .INI file, the primary form-level dynasets and snapshots are created, and all the comboboxes are initialized. Notice that the dynasets are created with the LockEdits property set to false. This creates *optimistic locking* for the record updating.

A blank invoice is created and the update invoice flag (g_InvoiceDirty) is set to False. The CheckPServer routine is called to determine if any items need to be reordered and to signal the user if items are short.

```
Private Sub Form_Load()
    Dim INIPath As String

    ' Setup path of INI file
    INIPath = GetAppPath() & "Purchase.INI"
```

```
' Set path for custom INI for Access engine
DBEngine.INIPath = INIPath

' Read global parameters for default values
g_CurrentLocation = Val(ReadINI("Parameters", "LocationID", INIPath))
g_DefaultStaffID = Val(ReadINI("Parameters", "DefaultStaffID", INIPath))
g_StandardTerms = Val(ReadINI("Parameters", "StandardTerms", INIPath))
g_SalesTax = Val(ReadINI("Parameters", "SalesTax", INIPath))
g_Freight = Val(ReadINI("Parameters", "Freight", INIPath))
g_DataLocation = ReadINI("Parameters", "DataLocation", INIPath)
g_DBName = ReadINI(g_DataLocation, "DBName", INIPath)

' Open connection to Database
Set MyDB = OpenDatabase(g_DBName, False, False)

SQL$ = "Select * from Purchase"
Set PurchaseDS = MyDB.OpenRecordset(SQL$, dbOpenDynaset)
PurchaseDS.LockEdits = False

SQL$ = "Select * from PurchaseItems"
Set PurchaseItemsDS = MyDB.OpenRecordset(SQL$, dbOpenDynaset)
PurchaseItemsDS.LockEdits = False

' Initialize variables
g_CurrentInvoice = -1
LoadSupplierPopup
LoadStaffPopup
LoadLocation

cmb_Terms.AddItem "Cash"
cmb_Terms.AddItem "Net 30"
cmb_Terms.AddItem "Net 15"
cmb_Terms.AddItem "1% 10 Net 30"
cmb_Terms.AddItem "2% 10 Net 30"
SetupDefaultScreen
g_InvoiceDirty = False
CenterForm Me

' Check for reorder items to alert user
CheckPServer
End Sub
```

Sub Form_Unload (Cancel As Integer)

The routine is called as the main form (PURCHASE.FRM) is unloaded. An End statement finishes execution and quits the program.

> **TIP**
>
> Putting an END in the main form's Unload event is crucial to the proper working of your applications. Visual Basic 4.0 does not automatically close all the forms for the application when the main form is closed. This means that if the user uses the close window pop-down menu to close the main form and other forms are hidden, the application remains open. This causes the Phantom Application effect to occur. This effect causes the application to appear in the Alt+Tab list and the taskbar, but does not allow the application window to be shown.
>
> By putting an END statement in the main form's Unload event, the application shuts down when the main form is closed.

```
Private Sub Form_Unload(Cancel As Integer)
    End
End Sub
```

Sub grd_Main_Click ()

If the user clicks on the grd_Main, this routine calls SetCell routine (which places the text box over the selected cell for editing) and then sets the focus to the text control txt_GridText. This provides the user with the illusion that the cell itself is being edited inside the grid.

In reality, txt_GridText is sized to fit the cell, moved into place over it, and the grid's contents are copied into the textbox. The parameter g_Dirty is also set to TRUE so the PO is saved when the user clicks the OK button.

```
Private Sub grd_Main_Click()
    ' Set text box to appear over selected cell
    SetCell
    txt_GridText.SetFocus   ' Set focus back to grid, see Text_LostFocus.
    g_InvoiceDirty = True
End Sub
```

Sub grd_Main_KeyPress (KeyAscii As Integer)

This routine is called when the grid has the focus and a key is pressed. If the key is the Enter key, the KeyPress is sent to the txt_GridText control for handling.

> **TIP**
>
> If you ever need to nullify a KeyPress event, a program can set the KeyAscii variable to 0 and then exist this routine. This is one technique that can be used to make a textbox read-only or to trap out particular key strokes.

```
Private Sub grd_Main_KeyPress(KeyAscii As Integer)
    SetCell
    ' Redirect this KeyPress event to the text box:
    If KeyAscii <> ASC_ENTER Then
        SendKeys Chr$(KeyAscii)
    End If
End Sub
```

Menu Items Code

The following code represented by the section heads is entered by selecting the item from the menu on the form and entering the code. They may also be entered by selecting the control and the Proc: in the code editing window.

Sub AddPartItem_Click ()

This routine is used to add a part to the Inventory_Parts table. Because this is a part, the `SalesItemFlag` is set to FALSE. The clear flag is set so the form, when shown, will have empty text fields. The Part Form is then shown.

```
Private Sub AddPartItem_Click()
    g_PartNum = -1
    SalesItemFlag = False
    g_LoadPartFlag = False
    ' Set clear flag to show blank form
    g_ClearPartFlag = True
    frm_Part.Show
End Sub
```

Sub AddSalesItemItem_Click ()

This routine is used to add a Sales item to the Inventory_Sales table. Because this is a Sales item, the `SalesItemFlag` is set to True. The Part Form is then shown.

```
Private Sub AddSalesItemItem_Click()
    g_PartNum = -1
    ' This is a Sales item, not a part
    SalesItemFlag = True
    g_LoadPartFlag = False
    g_ClearPartFlag = True
    frm_Part.Show 1
    SalesItemFlag = False
End Sub
```

Sub EditPartItem_Click ()

This routine is used to edit a part from the Inventory_Parts table. First, the Item Form is shown to enable the user to select the item to edit. The `SalesItemFlag` is set to False to enable editing of an inventory part.

> **TIP**
>
> The DoEvents() routine is often useful when attempting to automate user interaction. The routine creates a system pause that enables the operating system to handle waiting events (such as screen update, mouse events, and so on).
>
> In this case, if the user double-clicks on the Item Form, the event is carried over so the click selects the main form. This sends the newly displayed frm_Part to be hidden behind the main form. The DoEvents takes the click out of the event queue and the program operates normally.

```
Private Sub EditPartItem_Click()
    g_PartNum = -1
    SalesItemFlag = False
    ' Setup fields for Item form
    frm_Item.ListTitle = "Select Edit Part"
    frm_Item.ListQuery = "Select * FROM Inventory_Parts ORDER BY Description"
    frm_Item.ListItem1 = "Description"
    frm_Item.ListItem2 = ""
    frm_Item.ListIDField = "PartID"
    frm_Item.Show 1
    DoEvents
    If frm_Item.ListResult <> -1 Then
        g_PartNum = frm_Item.ListResult
        g_LoadPartFlag = True
        g_ClearPartFlag = False
        frm_Part.Show 1
    End If
End Sub
```

Sub EditSalesItemItem_Click ()

This routine is used to edit a part from the Inventory_Sales table. First, the Item Form is shown to enable the user to select the item to edit. The SalesItemFlag is set to True to enable a Sales item to be edited.

```
Private Sub EditSalesItemItem_Click()
    g_PartNum = -1
    SalesItemFlag = True
    g_LoadPartFlag = True
    g_ClearPartFlag = False
    ' Setup fields for Item form
    frm_Item.ListTitle = "Select Sales Item"
    frm_Item.ListQuery = "Select * FROM Inventory_Sales ORDER BY Description"
    frm_Item.ListItem1 = "Description"
    frm_Item.ListItem2 = ""
    frm_Item.ListIDField = "PartID"
    frm_Item.Show 1
    DoEvents
    If frm_Item.ListResult <> -1 Then
        g_PartNum = frm_Item.ListResult
        SalesItemFlag = True
        frm_Part.Show 1
```

```
        End If
        SalesItemFlag = False
End Sub
```

Sub ExitItem_Click ()

This event occurs if the Exit option is selected under the File menu. The routine ends the execution of the program and exits.

```
Sub ExitItem_Click ()
    End
End Sub
```

Sub PartsInventoryItem_Click (), Sub AutobuildEditItem_Click (), and Sub AutoBuildItem_Click ()

These routines display their appropriate forms.

```
Private Sub PartsInventoryItem_Click()
    frm_Inventory.Show
End Sub

Private Sub AutobuildEditItem_Click()
    frm_AutobuildEdit.Show
End Sub

Private Sub AutoBuildItem_Click()
    frm_Autobuild.Show
End Sub
```

Sub PrintItem_Click ()

Activates the DoPrint() routine to print the PO to the currently selected printer.

```
Private Sub PrintItem_Click()
    DoPrint
End Sub
```

Cut, Copy, and Paste

These three menu routines simply call the SendEditMessage routine to send the Windows API the correct message.

```
Private Sub CopyItem_Click ()
    SendEditMessage WM_COPY
End Sub

Private Sub Cutitem_Click ()
    SendEditMessage WM_CUT
End Sub

Private Sub PasteItem_Click ()
    SendEditMessage WM_PASTE
End Sub
```

Sub txt_BillDate_Change (), Sub txt_Expected_Change (), Sub txt_Date_Change (), Sub txt_FOB_Change (), and Subtxt_Freight_Change ()

These routines set the g_InvoiceDirty flag to True if any change was made. This activates the OK button so the Purchase Order can be updated. Any change to the text in the Text controls activates this event.

The program should prevent the user from quitting or erasing the form unintentionally. Therefore, a flag that is set to True indicates that changes have been made to the item. The user should be prompted on whether these changes should be abandoned.

```
Private Sub txt_BillDate_Change ()
    g_InvoiceDirty = True
End Sub

Private Sub txt_Expected_Change ()
    g_InvoiceDirty = True
End Sub

Private Sub txt_Date_Change ()
    g_InvoiceDirty = True
End Sub

Private Sub txt_FOB_Change ()
    g_InvoiceDirty = True
End Sub

Private Sub txt_Freight_Change ()
    g_InvoiceDirty = True
End Sub

Private Sub txt_ShipTo_Change()
    g_InvoiceDirty = True
End Sub
```

Sub txt_Freight_LostFocus ()

If the Freight control has lost the focus, recalculate the PO total because the user may have altered the Freight value.

```
Private Sub txt_Freight_LostFocus()
    CalculateTotal
End Sub
```

Sub txt_GridText_GotFocus ()

This routine selects all the text currently stored in the txt_GridText control. The routine is activated when the user Tabs to or clicks on a particular cell. By selecting the contents, the user can replace the current text just by typing.

```
Private Sub txt_GridText_GotFocus()
    txt_GridText.SelStart = 0
    txt_GridText.SelLength = 32000
End Sub
```

Sub txt_GridText_KeyPress (KeyAscii As Integer)

The `KeyPress` routine captures an Enter key and resets the focus to the grd_Main. By setting the KeyAscii to 0 in the KeyPress event, no other routines react to the KeyPress.

```
Private Sub txt_GridText_KeyPress(KeyAscii As Integer)
    If KeyAscii = ASC_ENTER Then
        grd_Main.SetFocus    ' Set focus back to grid, see Text_LostFocus.
        KeyAscii = 0         ' Ignore this KeyPress.
    End If
End Sub
```

Sub txt_GridText_LostFocus ()

If the text control txt_GridText loses the focus, the user must have selected something else. This routine must transfer the text stored in the text control back to the cell of the grid it is displayed over.

After this is completed, the Quantity must be checked. If the user changed the Quantity, additional items must be reserved. The Price change must also be checked. If the user changed the price, the Total and the Tax must be recalculated.

```
Private Sub txt_GridText_LostFocus()
    Dim tmpRow As Integer
    Dim tmpCol As Integer
    ' Save current settings of Grid Row and col. This is needed only if
    ' the focus is set somewhere else in the Grid.
    tmpRow = grd_Main.Row
    tmpCol = grd_Main.Col
    ' Set Row and Col back to what they were before Text1_LostFocus:
    grd_Main.Row = gRow
    grd_Main.Col = gCol
    grd_Main.Text = txt_GridText.Text   ' Transfer text back to grid.

    CheckPriceChange

    txt_GridText.SelStart = 0           ' Return caret to beginning.
    txt_GridText.Visible = False        ' Disable text box.
    ' Return row and Col contents:
    grd_Main.Row = tmpRow
    grd_Main.Col = tmpCol
End Sub
```

Sub txt_TabBefore_GotFocus ()

Capturing tabs from Visual Basic is not a simple process. Hitting the Tab key automatically moves the focus to the control with a `TabIndex` property one greater than the current item's `TabIndex`. Hitting the Shift-Tab does exactly the opposite, subtracting 1.

The Invoice should work in a way with which users are familiar. In a traditional spreadsheet, the Tab and Shift-Tab key presses move the selected cell box forward and backward, respectively. We have therefore simply created two textbox controls with a TabIndex one less and one more than the txt_GridText control.

When this routine receives the focus, it moves the selected cell one to the left and returns the focus to txt_GridText. If the cell is in column 0 when the Shift-Tab key is pressed, the selected cell is set to the far right column of the row above.

This provides a simple solution to the problem of good user interface.

```
Private Sub txt_TabBefore_GotFocus()
    ' Make sure that the selected cell is not on the very first rectangle
    If Not (grd_Main.Col = 0 And grd_Main.Row = 1) Then
        If grd_Main.Col > 0 Then
            grd_Main.Col = grd_Main.Col - 1
        Else
            grd_Main.Col = grd_Main.Cols - 1
            grd_Main.Row = grd_Main.Row - 1
        End If
    End If
    SetCell
    txt_GridText.SetFocus   ' Set focus back to grid, see Text_LostFocus.
End Sub
```

Sub txt_TabNext_GotFocus ()

When this routine receives the focus, it moves the selected cell one to the right and returns the focus to txt_GridText. If the cell is in the last column when the Tab key is pressed, the selected cell is set to the first column of the row below.

```
Private Sub txt_TabNext_GotFocus()
    If grd_Main.Col + 1 < grd_Main.Cols Then
        grd_Main.Col = grd_Main.Col + 1
    Else
        grd_Main.Col = 0
        grd_Main.Row = grd_Main.Row + 1
    End If
    SetCell
    txt_GridText.SetFocus   ' Set focus back to grid, see Text_LostFocus.
End Sub
```

Adding Code to the AUTOBILD.FRM

The Autobuild form contains all the code necessary to build Inventory_Sales parts from Inventory_Parts records. Adding the code to the Autobuild form is a routine task. The variables accessible at the Form level are added to the General Declarations area. Then any Form level routines belonging in the General Routines area are created using the Procedure... option. These routines are not activated by an event (such as a mouse click), but are called by other parts of the code.

These routines will appear in the (General) section of the code menus. Finally, routines are added to the specific events of particular controls. These routines are activated when the particular event occurs, usually caused by a user action.

General Declarations

Add these variables to the General Declarations area of the Form. These variables must be modified by various routines of the form.

The `PartsArray` is used to determine the parts and the parts quantity required to complete the Autobuild. The three constants all denote constants specifying columns in the array. The `BldQtyUnit` holds the number of parts required for one unit. The `BldQtyTotal` holds the BldQtyUnit multiplied by the number of units to be built. The `BldPartID` stores the PartID of the part to be used in the Autobuild.

```
Dim PartsArray()
Dim AssemblyDS As Recordset

Const BldQtyUnit = 0
Const BldQtyTotal = 1
Const BldPartID = 2
```

General Routines

All the routines in the following section heads are added to the General section of the Form. Code placed in the general section is available to all routines within the form. Create the routine by selecting the Procedure…. Type in the name of the routine and select the type of routine (for example, sub, function, private, and so on). Enter the code listed for the particular routine.

Sub LoadBuildList (num As Integer)

This routine builds the listbox containing all the items needed for construction of the select Sales item, the quantity of parts required, and the number of parts in the inventory.

```
Private Sub LoadBuildList(num As Integer)
    Dim PartID As Long
    Dim SQL$
    ReDim PartsArray(50, 3)

    SQL$ = SQL$ & " SELECT b.Description, a.Qty, a.PartID_Parts"
    SQL$ = SQL$ & " FROM Assembly AS a, Inventory_Parts AS b"
    SQL$ = SQL$ & " WHERE a.PartID_Sales = " &
cmb_BuildItem.ItemData(cmb_BuildItem.ListIndex)
    SQL$ = SQL$ & " and (a.PartID_Parts = b.PartID)"
    Set AssemblyDS = MyDB.OpenRecordset(SQL$, dbOpenDynaset)

    lst_Items.Clear
    ' Reset record counter
    i = 0
    Do Until AssemblyDS.EOF    ' Until end of file.
        PartsArray(i, BldQtyUnit) = AssemblyDS!Qty
        PartsArray(i, BldQtyTotal) = num * PartsArray(i, BldQtyUnit)
        ' This line will print the item, qty per unit, and total qty required
        s = AssemblyDS!Description & Chr$(9) & PartsArray(i, BldQtyUnit) & Chr$(9)
& PartsArray(i, BldQtyTotal)
        lst_Items.AddItem s
```

```
        PartsArray(i, BldPartID) = AssemblyDS!PartID_Parts
        lst_Items.ItemData(lst_Items.NewIndex) = PartsArray(i, BldPartID)

        i = i + 1
        AssemblyDS.MoveNext      ' Move to next record.
    Loop
End Sub
```

Sub LoadItemList ()

This routine creates a list of all the available Sales items. This list is added, item-by-item, to the combobox for the user to select the desired item to autobuild. The items are alphabetized (using the SQL ORDER BY statement) by their Description field.

> **NOTE**
>
> Each item to be selected for autobuild must include an assembly record in the Assembly table to describe the items needed from construction. This record may be created using the List.FRM (frm_AutobuildEdit). This form does not verify that such a record exists until the user clicks the OK button. A possible enhancement to this form would be to add only the Sales items which have assembly records.

```
Private Sub LoadItemList()
    Dim PartID As Long

    SQLStmt = "Select * FROM Inventory_Sales ORDER BY Description"
    Set MySS = MyDB.OpenRecordset(SQLStmt, dbOpenSnapshot)

    ' Reset record counter
    i = 0
    Do Until MySS.EOF      ' Until end of file.
        cmb_BuildItem.AddItem MySS!Description
        PartID = MySS!PartID
        cmb_BuildItem.ItemData(cmb_BuildItem.NewIndex) = PartID

        i = i + 1
        MySS.MoveNext      ' Move to next record.
    Loop
End Sub
```

Control Code

All the code represented in the following section heads must be added to the individual controls. Simply double-click the control on the Autobuild form and the relevant code box will appear. Then, in the drop-down combo labeled Proc:, select the event belonging to the following code.

Sub cmd_Cancel_Click ()

This routine hides the form if the user clicks on the Cancel button. The form remains in memory so the next time the form is accessed it does not have to be retrieved from the disk.

```
Private Sub cmd_Cancel_Click()
    Me.Hide
End Sub
```

Sub cmd_OK_Click ()

This routine checks all the necessary parameters and activates the autobuild if the user clicks the OK button. First, the Assembly table is checked to ensure that a record exists for the selected Sales item. The quantity is then checked to determine that it is a numeric entry and has a value greater than zero.

If the user's autobuild selection is OK, the routine activates to load the item list which checks if enough inventory items exist to sustain the autobuild. If not, the user is altered and may decrease the quantity requested or cancel the autobuild.

Finally, the individual parts are removed from the Inventory_Parts in the appropriate quantities and the autobuild items are added to the Inventory_Sales.

```
Private Sub cmd_OK_Click()
    Dim result As Integer

    result = True
    'Check if item exists in Assembly
    If result = False Then
        MsgBox "This item does not have an assembly parts list. Use the 'Autobuild Edit...' option to create one.", 16, "No Assembly Record"
Exit Sub
    End If
    ' Make sure Qty is a number
    If Not (IsNumeric(txt_Qty) And Val("" & txt_Qty) > 0) Then
        MsgBox "Quantity must be a number greater than 0.", 16, "Quantity Error"
Exit Sub
    End If

    ' Move through assembly list and build up list box
    LoadBuildList Val(txt_Qty)

    ' Check each item in the parts inventory
    BeginTrans
    If Qty < qtyneeded Then
        MsgBox "There are not enough '" & AssemblyDS!Description & "' items in inventory.", 16, "Not Enough Inventory"
' Eliminate all previous edits for this transaction
        Rollback
        Exit Sub
    End If

    CommitTrans
    'Me.Hide
End Sub
```

Sub Form_Load ()

This routine initializes the tab values that are needed by the listbox lst_Items to display the parts required to build the items and the quantities. It also creates the item list combo to allow the user to select the Sales Item to autobuild. The form is then centered on the screen.

```
Private Sub Form_Load()
   Dim NumOftabs As Integer
   ReDim Tabs(3) As Long

   NumOftabs = 3
   Tabs(0) = 70
   Tabs(1) = 115
   Tabs(2) = 190

   ' Setup tabs for lst_Items
   temp = SendMessage(lst_Items.hWnd, LB_SETTABSTOPS, NumOftabs, Tabs(0))
   ' Load the combobox with all sales items that may be built
   LoadItemList
   cmb_BuildItem.ListIndex = 0
   CenterForm Me
End Sub
```

Adding Code to the INVNTRY.FRM

The code for the Inventory form is fairly simple because it does not require any user interaction. The form retrieves the various inventory levels and displays them in a listbox. All Form level routines are created in the General Routines area using the Procedure... option. These routines are not activated by an event (such as a mouse click), but are called by other parts of the code.

These routines appear in the (General) section of the code menus. Finally, routines are added to the specific events of particular controls. These routines are activated when the particular event occurs, usually caused by a user action.

Control Code

All the code represented in the following section heads must be added to the individual controls. Simply double-click the control on the Inventory form and the relevant code box will appear. Then, in the dropdown combo labelled Proc:, select the event belonging to the following code.

Sub cmd_OK_Click ()

Because this form is strictly informational, there is no Cancel button necessary. Therefore, the OK button only needs to hide the current form.

```
Private Sub cmd_OK_Click()
    Me.Hide
End Sub
```

Sub Form_Load ()

The `Load()` routine sets up the tabs in the listbox using the `SendMessage()` Windows API call. The routine also calls the `CenterForm()` routine in order to center the form on the user's screen.

```
Private Sub Form_Load()
    Dim NumOftabs As Integer
    ReDim Tabs(3) As Long

    ' Setup tabs for lst_Reserved
    NumOftabs = 3
    Tabs(0) = 70
    Tabs(1) = 115
    Tabs(2) = 190

    ' Use Windows API call to set tab stops
    temp = SendMessage(lst_Items.hWnd, LB_SETTABSTOPS, NumOftabs, Tabs(0))

    CenterForm Me
End Sub
```

Sub Form_Paint ()

The `Paint()` routine actually gathers the inventory data for display and adds it to the listbox. A SnapShot is created which contains all the records in the Inventory_Sales table. The `Do...Until` loop then adds each item to the List. The width of the tab settings were created previously in the `Form_Load()` event. Finally, the totals of the number of items as well as the totals of the quantities of items are stored in textbox controls at the bottom of the form.

```
Private Sub Form_Paint()
    Dim ScratchSS As Recordset
    Dim numItems As Integer, numParts As Integer

    SQL$ = "Select * from Inventory_Parts"
    Set ScratchSS = MyDB.OpenRecordset(SQL$, dbOpenSnapshot)

    lst_Items.Clear
    numItems = 0
    numParts = 0

    ' Add inventory information to list box
    Do Until ScratchSS.EOF
        lst_Items.AddItem ScratchSS!Description & Chr$(9) & Str$(ScratchSS!OnHand) & Chr$(9) & Str$(ScratchSS!ReOrderQty)
        numParts = numParts + ScratchSS!OnHand
        numItems = numItems + 1
        ScratchSS.MoveNext
    Loop
    txt_numItems = numItems
    txt_numParts = numParts
End Sub
```

Adding Code to the LIST.FRM

The Autobuild form is used to create the Assembly definitions to create sales parts from inventory parts. The code demonstrates manipulation of listboxes, data search routines, and record construction. Each part of the code base is placed at specific areas of the project. The variables remaining at the Form level are added to the General Declaration area. Then any Form level routines will be created in the General Routines area using the Procedure… option. These routines are not activated by an event (such as a mouse click), but are called by other parts of the code.

These routines appear in the (General) section of the code menus. Finally, routines are added to the specific events of particular controls. These routines are activated when the particular event occurs, usually caused by a user action.

General Declarations

There is only a single General Declaration for this form. Enter the AssemblyDS variable in the declarations section. This is the general dynaset object used in constructing the assembly record.

```
Dim AssemblyDS As Recordset
```

General Routines

All the routines represented by the following section heads are added to the General section of the Form. Code placed in the general section is available to all routines within the form. To create a new routine, select Procedure…. Enter the procedure name, type, and choose the public or private setting. When the procedure has been created, enter the routine code.

Sub LoadBuildList ()

The LoadBuildList() routine is used to add all the parts (with their quantities) needed to build a Sales item into the listbox lst_Required parts. A dynaset is created that has the description of each part, the quantity needed, and its PartID as the dynaset's resultant columns. These items are added to the listbox. The ItemData for each part is filled with the related PartID number.

```
Private Sub LoadBuildList()
    Dim PartID As Long

    SQL$ = SQL$ & " SELECT b.Description, a.Qty, a.PartID_Parts"
    SQL$ = SQL$ & " FROM Assembly AS a, Inventory_Parts AS b"
    SQL$ = SQL$ & " WHERE a.PartID_Sales = " &
cmb_BuildItem.ItemData(cmb_BuildItem.ListIndex)
    SQL$ = SQL$ & " and (a.PartID_Parts = b.PartID)"
    Set AssemblyDS = MyDB.OpenRecordset(SQL$, dbOpenDynaset)

    lst_RequiredParts.Clear
    ' Reset record counter
    i = 0
    ' Enter all Assembly items into the ListBox
```

```
        Do Until AssemblyDS.EOF    ' Until end of file.
            s = AssemblyDS!Description & Chr$(9) & AssemblyDS!Qty    'Description
            lst_RequiredParts.AddItem s
            PartID = AssemblyDS!PartID_Parts
            lst_RequiredParts.ItemData(lst_RequiredParts.NewIndex) = PartID

            i = i + 1
            AssemblyDS.MoveNext      ' Move to next record.
        Loop
End Sub
```

Sub LoadItemList ()

This routine is used to fill the combo cmb_BuildItem with all the possible Sales items. The user can select one of these sales items to create an Assembly record containing all the necessary parts to construct a unit.

```
Private Sub LoadItemList()
    Dim PartID As Long

    SQLStmt = "Select * FROM Inventory_Sales ORDER BY Description"
    Set MySS = MyDB.OpenRecordset(SQLStmt, dbOpenSnapshot)

    ' Reset record counter
    i = 0
    Do Until MySS.EOF      ' Until end of file.
        cmb_BuildItem.AddItem MySS!Description
        PartID = MySS!PartID
        cmb_BuildItem.ItemData(cmb_BuildItem.NewIndex) = PartID

        i = i + 1
        MySS.MoveNext       ' Move to next record.
    Loop
End Sub
```

Sub LoadPartList ()

This routine fills the lst_Parts listbox control with all the parts that may be used to construct a Sales item. The parts come from the Inventory_Parts table. The PartID is added to the ItemData of the Listbox for each item.

```
Private Sub LoadPartList()
    Dim PartID As Long

    SQLStmt = "Select * FROM Inventory_Parts ORDER BY Description"
    Set MySS = MyDB.OpenRecordset(SQLStmt, dbOpenSnapshot)

    ' Reset record counter
    i = 0
    Do Until MySS.EOF      ' Until end of file.
        lst_Parts.AddItem MySS!Description
        PartID = MySS!PartID
        lst_Parts.ItemData(lst_Parts.NewIndex) = PartID
```

```
        i = i + 1
        MySS.MoveNext      ' Move to next record.
    Loop
End Sub
```

Control Code

All the code represented by the following section heads must be added to the individual controls. Simply double-click the control on the Purchase form and the relevant code box appears. Then, in the drop-down combo labelled Proc:, select the event that belongs to the particular routine. Enter the code for that routine that follows.

Sub cmb_BuildItem_Click ()

This routine is activated when the user changes the selected Sales item. The `LoadBuildList()` routine searches the Assembly table for the required assembly parts for the newly selected Sales item and displays them in the Listbox.

```
Private Sub cmb_BuildItem_Click()
    ' The user made a change to the combobox
    LoadBuildList
End Sub
```

Sub cmd_Add_Click ()

When the cmd_Add button is clicked, this routine transfers the item selected in the lst_Parts ListBox with the quantity specified in the txt_Qty Text Box into the required parts to construct a Sales item.

After the selection of an item and the numeric quantity of the txt_Qty field are verified, the list is checked to ensure the part does not already exist in the parts list. Because it is one of the key fields, there cannot be two Assembly records describing the same part.

If the part does not already exist in the list, a new Assembly record is created. The `cmd_Build_Click` routine is then called to rebuild the Combo lst_RequiredParts to show the new part.

```
Private Sub cmd_Add_Click()
    Dim TempTable As Recordset

    ' Make sure an item is selected for adding
    If lst_Parts.ListIndex = -1 Then
        MsgBox "There is no item selected to add to the build list. Please select an item, set the quantity and ADD again.", 16, "Nothing Selected"
Exit Sub
    End If
    ' Check if quantity is a good value
    If Not IsNumeric(txt_Qty.Text) Then
        MsgBox "The quantity entry is not a number. Please set the quantity and ADD again.", 16, "Quantity Error"
Exit Sub
    End If
```

```
    ' Make sure the item doesn't already exist in the build list
    AddItemID = lst_Parts.ItemData(lst_Parts.ListIndex)
    For i = 0 To lst_RequiredParts.ListCount - 1
        If lst_RequiredParts.ItemData(i) = AddItemID Then
            MsgBox "The selected item already exists in the build list. Please
REMOVE the item if you wish a new selection.", 32, "Item Exists"
Exit Sub
        End If
    Next i

    ' Create new assembly record
    Set TempTable = MyDB.OpenRecordset("Assembly", dbOpenTable)
    TempTable.AddNew
    TempTable!Qty = Val(txt_Qty.Text)
    TempTable!PartID_Sales = cmb_BuildItem.ItemData(cmb_BuildItem.ListIndex)
    TempTable!PartID_Parts = lst_Parts.ItemData(lst_Parts.ListIndex)
    TempTable.Update
    cmb_BuildItem_Click
End Sub
```

Sub cmd_Remove_Click ()

When the cmd_Remove button is clicked by the user, this routine is called to remove a part from the Assembly list. First, the routine verifies the user has selected a part in the lst_RequiredParts to remove.

A dynaset is then created containing a single record of the item that was selected in the listbox. The Delete method is used to remove the record from the Assembly table. The cmd_Build_Click routine is then called to rebuild the Combo lst_RequiredParts to show the remaining items.

```
Private Sub cmd_Remove_Click()
    Dim ScratchDS As Recordset

    ' Make sure an item is selected for removal
    If lst_RequiredParts.ListIndex = -1 Then
        MsgBox "There is no item selected to remove from the build list. Please
select an item and REMOVE again.", 32, "Nothing Selected"
Exit Sub
    End If

    SQL$ = "Select * From Assembly Where PartID_Sales = " &
cmb_BuildItem.ItemData(cmb_BuildItem.ListIndex)
    SQL$ = SQL$ & " and PartID_Parts = " &
lst_RequiredParts.ItemData(lst_RequiredParts.ListIndex)
    Set ScratchDS = MyDB.OpenRecordset(SQL$, dbOpenDynaset)
    ScratchDS.Delete
    cmb_BuildItem_Click
End Sub
```

Sub Form_Load ()

This Load() routine activates routines to fill the lst_Parts listbox control and cmb_BuildItem combo control. The ListIndex property of the cmb_BuildItem is set to the first item. The Form is centered on the screen. This routine also sets the tab stops for the lst_RequiredParts listbox control.

```
Private Sub Form_Load()
   Dim NumOftabs As Integer
   ReDim Tabs(3) As Long

      LoadItemList
      LoadPartList
      cmb_BuildItem.ListIndex = 0
      txt_Qty = 1
      CenterForm Me

   NumOftabs = 1
   Tabs(0) = 60
   Tabs(1) = 90
   Tabs(2) = 110
   Tabs(3) = 140

      temp = SendMessage(lst_RequiredParts.hWnd, LB_SETTABSTOPS, NumOftabs, Tabs(0))
End Sub
```

Adding Code to the PART.FRM

The Part form is used to add or edit an inventory part record. Adding the code to the form is a routine task. The variables remaining at the Form level are added to the General Declaration area. Then any Form level routines are created in the General Routines area using the Procedure… option. These routines are not activated by an event (such as a mouse click), but are called by other parts of the code.

These routines will appear in the (General) section of the code menus. Finally, routines are added to the specific events of particular controls. These routines are activated when the particular event occurs, usually caused by a user action.

General Declarations

There is only a single General Declaration for this form. Enter the PartDS variable in the declarations section. The variable holds a dynaset type recordset used to enter or modify a part record.

```
Dim PartDS As Recordset
```

General Routines

All the routines represented by the following section heads are added to the General section of the Form. Code placed in the general section is available to all routines within the form. To create a new routine, select Procedure… option. A dialog box appears prompting whether the routine should be a Sub, Function, or Property. Select the appropriate type specified in the code. For each routine below, the type is given in the title.

Type in the routine name (without the open and close parentheses) and click the OK button. The window opens showing the begin and end routine structure. Type the text found below into the code area.

Sub CopyTags ()

This routine sets the Tag properties of all the controls on the form to equal the primary properties (text properties, and so on) The Tag values can then be used after the user has clicked the OK button to determine which primary properties have changed and need to be updated.

```
Private Sub CopyTags()
    ' Duplicate text field tags
    txt_Description.Tag = txt_Description.Text
    cmb_Location.Tag = cmb_Location.Text
    txt_UnitCost.Tag = txt_UnitCost.Text
    txt_Reorder.Tag = txt_Reorder.Text
    txt_Notes.Tag = txt_Notes.Text
End Sub
```

Sub LoadLocation ()

`LoadLocation` finds the record of the current location read from the INI file. Because the location does not change (most likely) once the Client program is installed, the Location information is stored in a label field. Unlike the Salesperson or Supplier fields which obviously must be selected for each PO, the location remains fixed for the duration of the Client program's execution.

```
Private Sub LoadLocation()
    Dim SQL$
    Dim LocationID As Long, SelLocation As Integer

    SQL$ = "Select * FROM Location ORDER BY Description"
    Set MySS = MyDB.OpenRecordset(SQL$, dbOpenSnapshot)

    SelLocation = -1
    ' Reset record counter
    i = 0
    Do Until MySS.EOF     ' Until end of file.
        Add$ = MySS!Description
        cmb_Location.AddItem Add$
        LocationID = MySS!LocationID
        cmb_Location.ItemData(cmb_Location.NewIndex) = LocationID
        If LocationID = g_CurrentLocation Then
            SelLocation = i
        End If

        i = i + 1
        MySS.MoveNext     ' Move to next record.
    Loop
    ' Set location to equal current location read from INI file
    If SelLocation <> -1 Then
        cmb_Location.ListIndex = SelLocation
    Else
        cmb_Location.ListIndex = 0
    End If
End Sub
```

Sub RecordToScreen (TempDS As Recordset)

This routine copies all the fields from the record into the various controls on the screen. Notice the values set with a "" and the & command. These fields may contain NULL values, and this prevents an error from occurring. Setting a control property to a NULL creates an error.

```
Private Sub RecordToScreen(TempDS As Recordset)
    txt_Description.Text = "" & TempDS!Description
    txt_UnitCost.Text = "" & TempDS!UnitCost
    If SalesItemFlag = True Then
        txt_Reorder.Text = "" & TempDS!ReOrderQty
    Else
        txt_Reorder.Text = "N/A"
    End If
    txt_OnHand = "" & TempDS!OnHand
    txt_Notes.Text = "" & TempDS!Notes
    txt_PartID = g_PartNum
End Sub
```

Sub ScreentoRecord (TempDS As Recordset)

This routine takes all the values from the screen and writes off any changes to the selected record. The Edit method is called to activate the Edit mode. Then each value is compared against the Tag values for any differences. The Tag properties were originally set to equal the record values. Any changes the user made would be reflected in the Text fields.

```
Private Sub ScreentoRecord(TempDS As Recordset)
    TempDS.Edit

    txt_PartID.Caption = g_PartNum

    If txt_Description.Text <> txt_Description.Tag Then
        TempDS!Description = txt_Description.Text
    End If
    If txt_UnitCost.Text <> txt_UnitCost.Tag Then
        TempDS!UnitCost = txt_UnitCost.Text
    End If
    If SalesItemFlag = True Then
        If txt_Reorder.Text <> txt_Reorder.Tag Then
            TempDS!ReOrderQty = txt_Reorder.Text
        End If
    End If
    If txt_Notes.Text <> txt_Notes.Tag Then
        TempDS!Notes = txt_Notes.Text
    End If

    TempDS.Update
End Sub
```

Sub SetupDefaultScreen ()

The SetupDefaultScreen() sets the controls in the form to empty values. This prevents a form that was previously hidden from showing old information. The routine CopyTags() is then called to synchronize the Tag properties to the new empty values.

```
Private Sub SetupDefaultScreen()
    txt_PartID = "New"
    txt_OnHand = "0"

    txt_Description.Text = ""
    txt_UnitCost.Text = ""
    If SalesItemFlag = False Then
        txt_Reorder.Text = "N/A"
    Else
        txt_Reorder.Text = ""
    End If
    txt_OnHand = ""
    cmb_Location.ListIndex = 0
    txt_Notes.Text = ""
    txt_PartID.Caption = "New"
    CopyTags
End Sub
```

Control Code

All the code represented in the following section heads must be added to the individual controls. Simply double-click the control on the Purchase form and the relevant code box appears. Then, in the drop-down combo labeled Proc:, select the event the code belongs to. Enter the code into the particular event.

Sub cmd_Cancel_Click ()

This routine sets the g_OKFlag to false for any routine that originally activated this form to know that the Cancel button was used to close it instead of the OK button. The form is hidden using the Me command. This command activates the method (Hide) of the form that is currently executing the routine.

```
Private Sub cmd_Cancel_Click()
    g_OKFlag = False
    Me.Hide
End Sub
```

Sub cmd_OK_Click ()

This routine is activated when the user clicks the OK button to record the part shown on the form. This routine handles both Sales items and Inventory parts. The form is checked to determine if a new part record must be created or an existing part was being edited.

If the record is new, the appropriate Count table record (Inventory_Sales or Inventory_Parts) is incremented. The ScratchTable recordset variable is created and a new record is added. Only the PartID of the record is added, leaving the ScreentoRecord() routine to store the values. The ScreenToRecord() routine is activated to write the data that has changed (by comparing the Tag fields) to the data table.

```
Private Sub cmd_OK_Click()
    Dim ScratchDS As Recordset
    Dim ScratchTable As Recordset

    g_OKFlag = True
    Me.Hide
    If txt_PartID = "New" Then
        ' Get the item number counter
        If SalesItemFlag = False Then
            SQL$ = "Select * from Counter where TableName = 'Inventory_Parts'"
            Set ScratchDS = MyDB.OpenRecordset(SQL$, dbOpenDynaset)
        Else
            SQL$ = "Select * from Counter where TableName = 'Inventory_Sales'"
            Set ScratchDS = MyDB.OpenRecordset(SQL$, dbOpenDynaset)
        End If
        g_PartNum = ScratchDS!CountNum
        ' increment item number
        ScratchDS.Edit
        ScratchDS!CountNum = g_SupplierID + 1
        ScratchDS.Update

        ' Create item record
        If SalesItemFlag = False Then
            Set ScratchTable = MyDB.OpenRecordset("Inventory_Parts", dbOpenTable)
        Else
            Set ScratchTable = MyDB.OpenRecordset("Inventory_Sales", dbOpenTable)
        End If
        ScratchTable.AddNew
        ScratchTable!PartID = g_PartNum
        ScratchTable.Update
        ' Create Recordset for editing
        If SalesItemFlag = False Then
            SQL$ = "Select * from Inventory_Parts where PartID = " & g_PartNum
            Set PartDS = MyDB.OpenRecordset(SQL$, dbOpenDynaset)
        Else
            SQL$ = "Select * from Inventory_Sales where PartID = " & g_PartNum
            Set PartDS = MyDB.OpenRecordset(SQL$, dbOpenDynaset)
        End If
    End If
    ' Write information to record
    ScreentoRecord PartDS
End Sub
```

Sub Form_Load ()

The LoadLocation routine is called to fill the cmb_Location combo so the user can select where the part exists. The Form is then centered on the screen before display.

```
Private Sub Form_Load()
    LoadLocation
    CenterForm Me
End Sub
```

Sub Form_Paint ()

The `Paint()` routine is used to either load or clear the displayed data if either flag is set. The g_LoadPartFlag sets up the dynaset to access either the Inventory_Parts table or the Inventory_Sales table. The record is then loaded using the `RecordToScreen()` routine.

If the screen needs to be cleared, the `SetupDefaultScreen()` is executed. Both flags are then cleared so the `Paint()` routine does not redo the same operation next time form painting occurs.

```
Private Sub Form_Paint()
    If g_LoadPartFlag = True Then
        ' There is no reorder qty for Parts, so dim selection
        If SalesItemFlag = False Then
            Me.Caption = "Inventory Part"
            txt_Reorder.Enabled = False
            SQL$ = "Select * from Inventory_Parts where PartID = " & g_PartNum
            Set PartDS = MyDB.OpenRecordset(SQL$, dbOpenDynaset)
        Else
            Me.Caption = "Sales Item"
            txt_Reorder.Enabled = True
            SQL$ = "Select * from Inventory_Sales where PartID = " & g_PartNum
            Set PartDS = MyDB.OpenRecordset(SQL$, dbOpenDynaset)
        End If
        RecordToScreen PartDS
    ElseIf g_ClearPartFlag = True Then
        SetupDefaultScreen
    End If
    g_LoadPartFlag = False
    g_ClearPartFlag = False
End Sub
```

Adding Code to the SUPPLIER.FRM

The Supplier form allows entry and editing of vendor records. A vendor that is stored in the database must be selected in order for a PO to be created. Adding the code to the Supplier form is a routine task much like the Part form above. The variables remaining at the Form level are added to the General Declaration area. Then any Form level routines are created in the General Routines area using the Procedure… option. These routines are not activated by an event (such as a mouse click), but are called by other parts of the code.

These routines will appear in the (General) section of the code menus. Finally, routines are added to the specific events of particular controls. These routines are activated when the particular event occurs, usually caused by a user action.

General Declarations

There is only a single General Declaration for this form. Enter the SupplierDS variable in the declarations section. The SupplierDS variable is used to hold the recordset of the record that is being created or modified.

```
Dim SupplierDS As Recordset
```

General Routines

All the routines represented by the following section heads are added to the General section of the Form. Code placed in the general section is available to all routines within the form. To create a new routine, select Procedure.... A dialog box appears prompting whether the routine should be a sub, function, or property. For each routine below, the type is given in the title.

Type in the routine name (without the open and close parentheses) and click the OK button. The window opens showing the begin and end routine structure. Now enter the code specified for each routine below.

Sub CopyTags ()

This routine sets the Tag properties of all the controls on the form to equal the primary properties (text properties, and so on). The Tag values can then be used after the user has clicked the OK button to determine which primary properties have changed and need to be updated.

```
Private Sub CopyTags()
    txt_Company.Tag = txt_Company.Text
    txt_LastName.Tag = txt_LastName.Text
    txt_FirstName.Tag = txt_FirstName.Text
    txt_Title.Tag = txt_Title.Text
    txt_Address.Tag = txt_Address.Text
    txt_City.Tag = txt_City.Text
    txt_State.Tag = txt_State.Text
    txt_Zip.Tag = txt_Zip.Text
    txt_Country.Tag = txt_Country.Text
    txt_Phone.Tag = txt_Phone.Text
    txt_Fax.Tag = txt_Fax.Text
    cmb_Terms.Tag = cmb_Terms.Text
    txt_Notes.Tag = txt_Notes.Text
End Sub
```

Sub RecordToScreen (TempDS As Recordset)

This routine copies all the fields from the record into the various controls on the screen. Notice the values set with a "" and the & command. These fields may contain NULL values and this prevents an error from occurring. Setting a control property to a NULL creates an error.

```
Private Sub RecordToScreen(TempDS As Recordset)
    txt_Company.Text = "" & TempDS!Company
    txt_LastName.Text = "" & TempDS!LastName
    txt_FirstName.Text = "" & TempDS!FirstName
    txt_Title.Text = "" & TempDS!Title
    txt_Address.Text = "" & TempDS!Address
    txt_City.Text = "" & TempDS!City
    txt_State.Text = "" & TempDS!State
    txt_Zip.Text = "" & TempDS!Zip
    txt_Country.Text = "" & TempDS!Country
```

```
    txt_Phone.Text = "" & TempDS!Phone
    txt_Fax.Text = "" & TempDS!FaxPhone
    cmb_Terms.ListIndex = Val(TempDS!Terms)
    txt_Notes.Text = "" & TempDS!Notes
    txt_SupplierID.Caption = g_SupplierID
End Sub
```

Sub ScreentoRecord (TempDS As Recordset)

This routine takes all the values from the screen and writes off any changes to the selected record. The Edit method is called to activate the Edit mode. Then each value is compared against the Tag values for any differences. The Tag properties were originally set to equal the record values. Any changes the user made would be reflected in the text fields.

```
Private Sub ScreentoRecord(TempDS As Recordset)
    TempDS.Edit

    If txt_Company.Text <> txt_Company.Tag Then
        TempDS!Company = txt_Company.Text
    End If
    If txt_LastName.Text <> txt_LastName.Tag Then
        TempDS!LastName = txt_LastName.Text
    End If
    If txt_FirstName.Text <> txt_FirstName.Tag Then
        TempDS!FirstName = txt_FirstName.Text
    End If
    If txt_Title.Text <> txt_Title.Tag Then
        TempDS!Title = txt_Title.Text
    End If
    If txt_Address.Text <> txt_Address.Tag Then
        TempDS!Address = txt_Address.Text
    End If
    If txt_City.Text <> txt_City.Tag Then
        TempDS!City = txt_City.Text
    End If
    If txt_State.Text <> txt_State.Tag Then
        TempDS!State = txt_State.Text
    End If
    If txt_Zip.Text <> txt_Zip.Tag Then
        TempDS!Zip = txt_Zip.Text
    End If
    If txt_Country.Text <> txt_Country.Tag Then
        TempDS!Country = txt_Country.Text
    End If
    If txt_Phone.Text <> txt_Phone.Tag Then
        TempDS!Phone = txt_Phone.Text
    End If
    If txt_Fax.Text <> txt_Fax.Tag Then
        TempDS!FaxPhone = txt_Fax.Text
    End If
    If cmb_Terms.Text <> cmb_Terms.Tag Then
        TempDS!Terms = cmb_Terms.ListIndex
    End If
```

```
        If txt_Notes.Text <> txt_Notes.Tag Then
            TempDS!Notes = txt_Notes.Text
        End If

        TempDS.Update
End Sub
```

Sub SetupDefaultScreen ()

The `SetupDefaultScreen()` sets the controls in the form to empty values. This prevents a form that was previously hidden from showing old information. The routine `CopyTags()` is then called to synchronize the Tag properties to the new empty values.

```
Private Sub SetupDefaultScreen()
    ' Clear all text and tag properties
    txt_Company.Text = ""
    txt_LastName.Text = ""
    txt_FirstName.Text = ""
    txt_Title.Text = ""
    txt_Address.Text = ""
    txt_City.Text = ""
    txt_State.Text = ""
    txt_Zip.Text = ""
    txt_Country.Text = ""
    txt_Phone.Text = ""
    txt_Fax.Text = ""
    cmb_Terms.ListIndex = 0
    txt_Notes.Text = ""
    txt_SupplierID.Caption = "New"
    CopyTags
End Sub
```

Control Code

All the code represented by the following section heads must be added to the individual controls. Simply double-click the control on the Supplier form and the relevant code box appears. Then, in the drop-down combo labeled Proc:, you should see each event specified below. Select the proper event and enter the code shown below.

Sub cmd_Cancel_Click ()

This routine sets the g_OKFlag to `False` for any routine that originally activated this form to know that the Cancel button was used to close it instead of the OK button. The form is hidden using the `Me` command which sends the method to the form the routine is currently executing in.

```
Private Sub cmd_Cancel_Click()
    g_OKFlag = False
    Me.Hide
End Sub
```

Sub cmd_OK_Click ()

This routine saves the Supplier data off to the supplier record. If the supplier is new, the record is first created and selected. The `ScreenToRecord()` routine is called to write the new information into the database.

```
Private Sub cmd_OK_Click()
    Dim ScratchDS As Recordset
    Dim ScratchTable As Recordset

    g_OKFlag = True
    Me.Hide
    If txt_SupplierID = "New" Then
        ' Get the customer number counter
        SQL$ = "Select * from Counter where TableName = 'Supplier'"
        Set ScratchDS = MyDB.OpenRecordset(SQL$, dbOpenDynaset)
        g_SupplierID = ScratchDS!CountNum
        ' increment Invoice number
        ScratchDS.Edit
        ScratchDS!CountNum = g_SupplierID + 1
        ScratchDS.Update

        ' Create customer record
        Set ScratchTable = MyDB.OpenRecordset("Supplier", dbOpenTable)
        ScratchTable.AddNew
        ScratchTable!SupplierID = g_SupplierID
        ScratchTable.Update
        ' Create Recordset for editing
        SQL$ = "Select * from Supplier where SupplierID = " & g_SupplierID
        Set SupplierDS = MyDB.OpenRecordset(SQL$, dbOpenDynaset)
    End If
    ScreentoRecord SupplierDS
End Sub
```

Sub Form_Load ()

This routine simply creates the Terms combo by loading all the possible options. The Terms combobox is used for selecting the default credit terms extended to a vendor.

```
Private Sub Form_Load()
    cmb_Terms.AddItem "Cash"
    cmb_Terms.AddItem "Net 30"
    cmb_Terms.AddItem "Net 15"
    cmb_Terms.AddItem "1% 10 Net 30"
    cmb_Terms.AddItem "2% 10 Net 30"
End Sub
```

Sub Form_Paint ()

The `Paint` routine is used to load the form. If the `g_LoadCustFlag` is `True` or the `g_ClearCustFlag` is `True`, the form is reformatted. The flags are then set to `False` after the formatting occurs.

```
Private Sub Form_Paint()
    ' Load a supplier into form?
    If g_LoadCustFlag = True Then
        SQL$ = "Select * from Supplier where SupplierID = " & g_SupplierID
        Set SupplierDS = MyDB.OpenRecordset(SQL$, dbOpenDynaset)
        RecordToScreen SupplierDS
    ElseIf g_ClearCustFlag = True Then
        SetupDefaultScreen
    End If
    ' Reset flags
    g_LoadCustFlag = False
    g_ClearCustFlag = False
End Sub
```

Summary

The application is now complete. The Purchasing client can now be used to create and receive purchase orders, assemble sales items from inventory parts, add suppliers, add and edit inventory parts, and examine current inventories. This client demonstrates the use of the grid control, overlaying a text control to simulate grid editing, menu selections, item reservations, and database techniques. Database techniques such as optimistic record locking, dynaset creation, record edits and additions, record searching, incremental unique ID counters, and joins are demonstrated. Studying the code for each of these techniques will supply a foundation of code on which to build future applications.

The Purchasing client can be used as an Online Transaction Processing (OLTP) system for daily use and tracking. All the capabilities the client demonstrates should provide an understanding of how a client program can be implemented for a multi-user environment. The autobuild from the multi-relation assembly record, single record dynaset editing, relevant field checking, purchase order numbers and various fields' counter increments, and other code designed to make the system work effectively. All of these techniques can be used to create a robust client/server implementation for your organization.

If you've created the tables in Chapter 10, "Table Construction," and entered the default values, press the F5 key to execute the program. To compile the program as a standalone EXE, make sure that either the INI file is placed in the same directory that the application is executing or change the path in the Invoice Form Load() event routine to search in the new directory.

13

Management Client

The Management Client is a Decision Support System application. It brings together information from all parts of the enterprise for examination and analysis. The Management Client is a tool to analyze data, unlike the other two clients, which create and act on data. This client queries the data for specific summary information and presents only the information important to governing the enterprise.

Figure 13.1 shows a display of the Sales information: a bar chart of Sales per Employee. The Management Client has four summary or report sections, available through the four tabs, each of which contains a report. These reports include the Sales Report, the Purchase Report, the Pseudo Server Report, and the Management Report (a summary of varying data). The user clicks one of the tabs to activate the query and display the resulting report.

FIGURE 13.1.
Management Client with Sales Report shown.

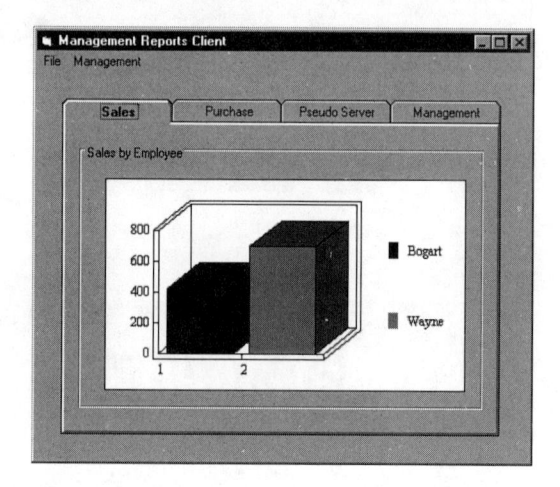

The Sales Report (refer to Figure 13.1) calculates all the sold item totals and categorizes the sales by employee. The results are presented in bar chart format with each bar representing an employee.

The Purchase Report (see Figure 13.2) displays the total cost of each sales item in the inventory. The total of the item is figured by summing the costs of all the individual parts required to create a finished unit.

The Pseudo Server Report (see Figure 13.3) displays the three flags maintained by the Pseudo Server. Their status is displayed as well as the total number of items reserved in the Sales inventory. The Pseudo Server automatically returns all reserves that have remained on reserve for more than one hour. This figure represents the items currently held on an invoice or in limbo.

The Management Report (see Figure 13.4) is a compilation of some typical information required by an executive. Values such as the average sales per employee, the day's sales figures, the average sales per invoice, and the item most frequently sold and its quantity are shown. Additionally, the grid at the bottom contains a report showing the amount of sales for each location.

Chapter 13 ■ Management Client 451

FIGURE 13.2
Management Client with Purchase Report shown.

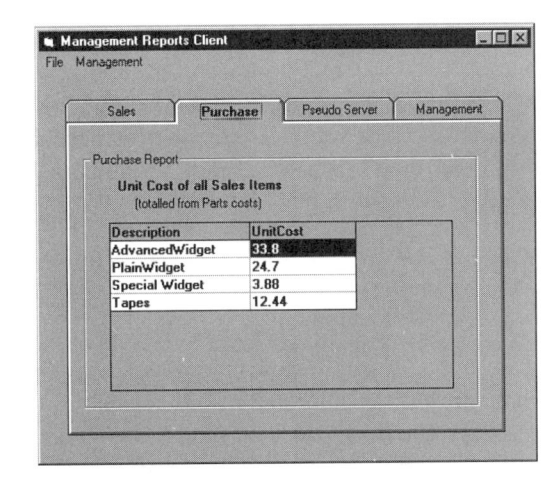

FIGURE 13.3.
Management Client with PServer Report shown.

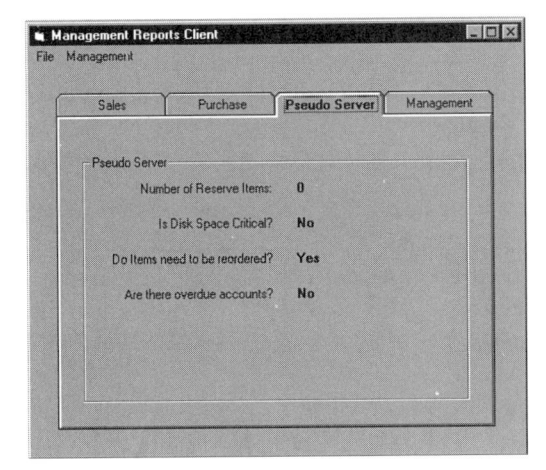

FIGURE 13.4.
Management Client with Management Report shown.

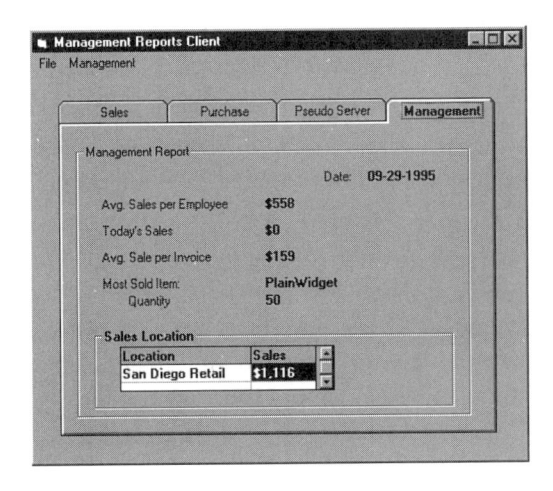

This client, in addition to containing useful sample queries, demonstrates several useful Visual Basic techniques. Techniques for optimizing an application are of crucial importance to bring a project in on time and on budget. It is important not only to provide enough programming time to create system critical routines, but also to plan the design of an application to minimize complexity and the amount of programming required to complete it.

All the reports are on a single form rather than in multiple windows. The reports are activated when the user clicks the particular tab. Having all the controls for all the reports on a single form can cut down on screen resources, which are limited in Windows 3.1 (this is not a problem in Windows 95 or Windows NT).

Using tabs is a more difficult documentation task, because a single form essentially contains multiple windows worth of information and controls. This complicates documentation and may make it difficult to find particular information for users who are not at ease with the tab control. Finally, having all the controls on a single form can make the application slower because the event loop decreases in speed with more controls on the form.

The advantage of using a single form with tabs is the flexibility it provides without resorting to the complexity of a multi-window (multi-form) application. It provides the user with an interface that is simple to use and understand—an interface that is far more complex to duplicate with multiple windows.

Another technique used is the inter-form access used by the Edit Staff... and Edit Location... selections under the Management menu. These routines use the public properties provided by the Item form to set up a list of available options from the Manage form. This remote manipulation can greatly simplify coding of certain routines (although it may make documentation more difficult).

How the Management Client Works

The Management Client consists of five primary files:

> frm_Manage (stored as MANAGE.FRM)—Primary form. Contains all the reports for the client in frames. A report is visible or invisible based on which button was clicked.
>
> frm_Location (stored as LOCATION.FRM)—Enables creation and editing of company locations. Uses Location passed in the g_CustomerID variable.
>
> frm_Staff (stored as STAFF.FRM)—Enables the management user to add a new Staff member to the Staff table or edit the information of an existing one.
>
> frm_Item (stored as ITEM.FRM)—Displays various items from either the Location or the Staff tables for selection. These are displayed for selection and use in the editing options. This is a shared file and must be added to the project. See Chapter 11, "Sales Client," for details on how to construct this file.

GLOBAL.BAS—Holds all the global code and variables for the program. This is a shared file and must be added to the project. See Chapter 11 for details on how to construct this file.

The Management Project is named Manage.VBP and holds all five of these files (see figure 13.5). All these files are created from scratch except GLOBAL.BAS and ITEM.FRM, which should have been created in Chapter 11 (and which should be added to the project). The `frm_Manage` form is the Startup form set in the Project tab under the Options dialog box. All the other forms are accessed by menu options and command buttons.

FIGURE 13.5.
Manage.VBP Project.

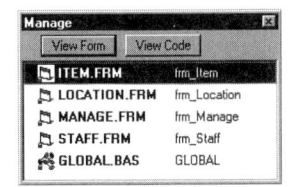

The Management Client must have access to various tables constructed in Chapter 10, "Table Construction." When the client is first executed, the connection with the particular database is made (in this case, the WIDGETCO.MDB). The information regarding the central database is stored in the application's .INI file (in this case the Manage.INI).

Database Access

The Management Client should have read access to nearly every table in the particular area of business study. This access is necessary to create an overview of the current situation. The current client returns data and information from almost all the tables in the system. Specific Management Clients may be created that can access data only from a particular location.

The implementation of a Management Client is largely determined by the enterprise and the needs of the enterprise. This client should provide an example of some of the information that can be obtained.

Starting the Management Project

The Management Client project in the example should be stored in the directory CS_VB\MANAGE. In Chapter 10, you should have created all the folders needed for the clients. If you haven't done so, refer to that chapter for instructions. Make sure the .INI file is placed in the same directory because the Management Client looks for the .INI file in the same folder in which the application executed.

Creating the Manage.INI File

First, construct the .INI file, which is used to store various parameters about a given program such as the type of database to be accessed, the driver types, the directory of the stored database, and so on. The Manage.INI file contains many parameters in common with the Sales Client .INI.

Within an .INI file, a ';' character denotes a comment. The .INI file can store parameters in subdivided sections. The '[...]' denotes a section of parameters. This .INI file has the [Parameters] and the [Access] sections.

Create the .INI file by opening the Notepad program found in the Accessories program group. Enter the information shown in Listing 13.1. Save the file as Manage.INI in the MANAGE directory.

Listing 13.1. MANAGE.INI file.

```
; Manage.INI

[Parameters]

LocationID = 1
DefaultStaffID = 1
StandardTerms = 0
SalesTax = .07
Freight = 3.00
DataLocation = Access

[Access]
DSN=
DBName=c:\clntsrvr\widgetco.mdb
DBServer=
```

Creating the Forms

The first step toward building an application is drawing the various necessary forms. The Management forms are far simpler than the previous Sales and Purchasing clients. The Management Client is the most malleable of all the clients. In a real application, the necessary management reports differ dramatically depending on the application. These simple reports give you a basis for how a reporting engine might appear.

Also, before code is placed on a form, the form can operate autonomously. Thus, the designer can easily add a few SHOW commands to various buttons in order to simulate operation. For this reason, you will first construct all the forms necessary for the project, which you can compile and save before you begin entering all the code.

Creating the Manage.FRM

Figure 13.6 shows what the completed form looks like after all the controls have been added. Figure 13.7 shows the Name properties of all of the individual controls. Create each control on the form and set the properties to match the properties listed in the table for that property.

FIGURE 13.6.
Manage form.

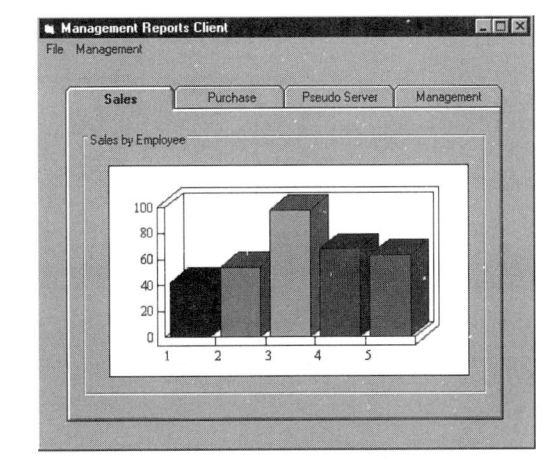

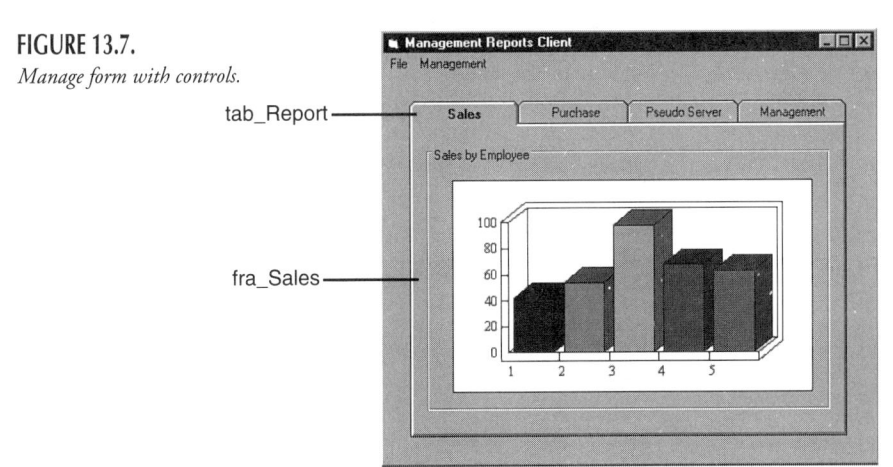

FIGURE 13.7.
Manage form with controls.

tab_Report

fra_Sales

To construct the Management Client, first you must add a tab control. You will place all the other controls into the tab control to display the information. There will be four tabs, one for each report.

In Figure 13.6, the Sales tab is selected and all the controls are shown for that tab. Once the appropriate tab is selected, a frame is added to the tab area. All the controls are then added to the frame, and the frame's properties are specified (see Table 13.19).

To create the next tab, the Purchase Report, click on the Purchase tab. This selects the Purchase Report and brings it to the front. Add the purchase frame, and then add the necessary controls (see Figure 13.8).

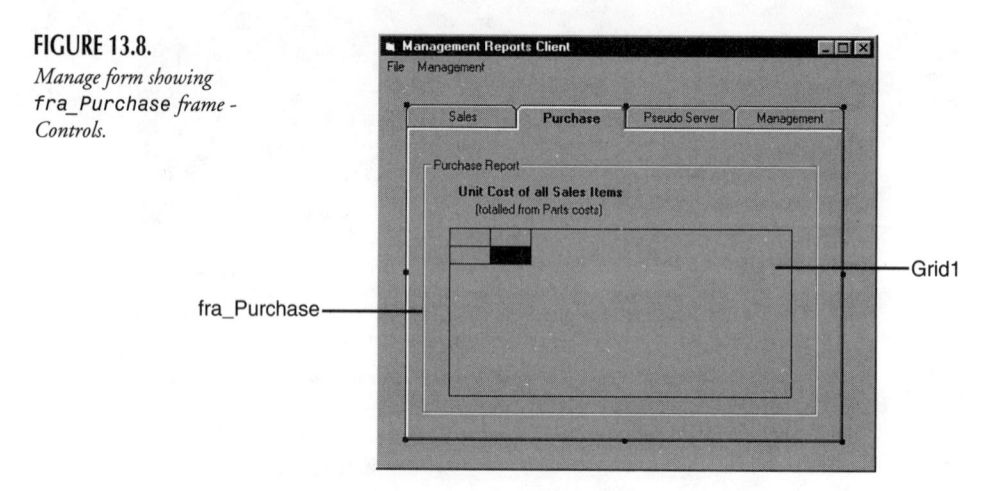

FIGURE 13.8.
Manage form showing `fra_Purchase` *frame - Controls.*

Following this same procedure, create the Pseudo Server tab (see Figure 13.9) and the Management tab (see Figure 13.10). The Sales Report tab is activated by default at the application's startup.

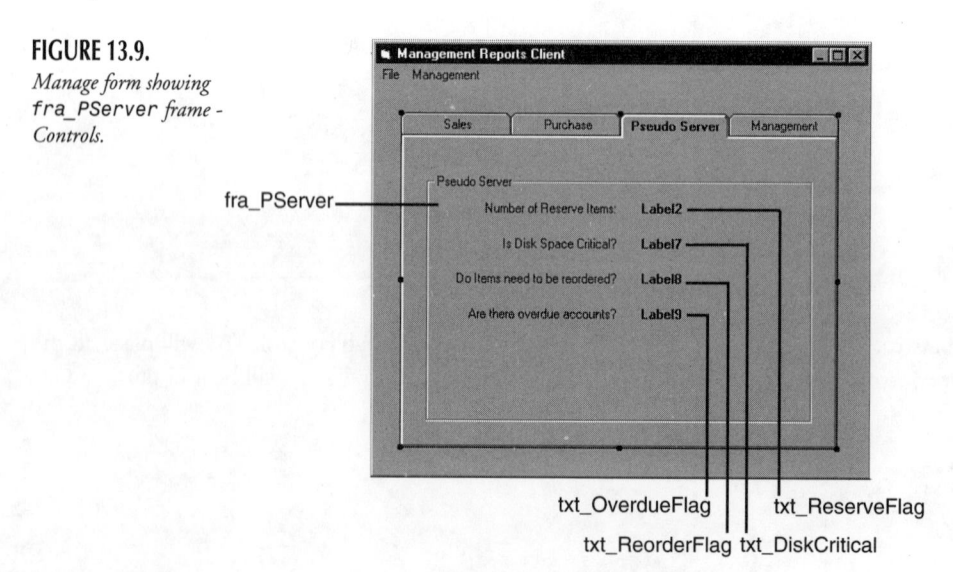

FIGURE 13.9.
Manage form showing `fra_PServer` *frame - Controls.*

Chapter 13 ■ Management Client   457

FIGURE 13.10.
Manage Form showing `fra_Management` *frame-Controls.*

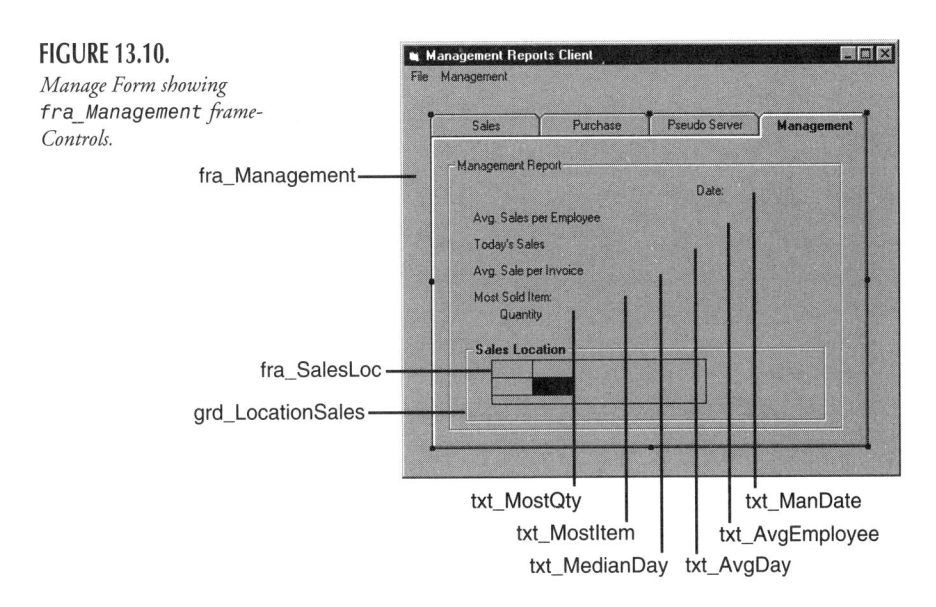

[Figure: Manage Form with callouts labeling fra_Management, fra_SalesLoc, grd_LocationSales, txt_MostQty, txt_MostItem, txt_MedianDay, txt_AvgDay, txt_ManDate, txt_AvgEmployee]

Table 13.1 shows all the controls for the form. It also shows the location at which the control should be created. If the location says "Form," then it should be created on the form. If a frame name is specified (that is, `fra_`), the control should be created within this frame.

Table 13.1. Controls for the Manage form.

Table	Control	Location
Table 13.2.	Form `frm_Manage`	
Table 13.3.	SSFrame `fra_Management`	Manage tab
Table 13.4.	SSFrame `SalesLoc`	`fra_Management`
Table 13.5.	Grid `grd_LocationSales`	`fra_Management`
Table 13.6.	Label `txt_MostQty`	`fra_Management`
Table 13.7.	Label `txt_MostItem`	`fra_Management`
Table 13.8.	Label `txt_MedianDay`	`fra_Management`
Table 13.9.	Label `txt_AvgDay`	`fra_Management`
Table 13.10.	Label `txt_ManDate`	`fra_Management`
Table 13.11.	Label `txt_AvgEmployee`	`fra_Management`
Table 13.12.	SSFrame `fra_PServer`	Pseudo Server tab
Table 13.13.	Label `txt_OverdueFlag`	`fra_Pserver`
Table 13.14.	Label `txt_ReorderFlag`	`fra_Pserver`

continues

Table 13.1. continued

Table	Control	Location
Table 13.15.	Label txt_DiskCritical	fra_Pserver
Table 13.16.	Label txt_ReserveFlag	fra_Pserver
Table 13.17.	SSFrame fra_Purchase	Purchase tab
Table 13.18.	Grid Grid1	fra_Purchase
Table 13.19.	SSFrame fra_Sales	Sales tab
Table 13.20.	Graph Graph1	fra_Sales
Table 13.21.	SSTab control tab_Report	Form

Table 13.2. Form frm_Manage.

BackColor	&H00C0C0C0&
Caption	Management Reports Client
ClientHeight	5220
ClientLeft	1365
ClientTop	1605
ClientWidth	7245
Height	5910
Left	1305
LinkTopic	Form1
ScaleHeight	5220
ScaleWidth	7245
Top	975
Width	7365

Table 13.3. SSFrame fra_Management.

Caption	Management
ForeColor	&H00000000&
Height	735
Left	2640
TabIndex	10

Top	4320	
Visible	0 'False	
Width	4335	

Table 13.4. SSFrame SalesLoc.

Caption	Sales per Location
ForeColor	&H00000000&
Height	1935
Left	240
TabIndex	18
Top	2640
Width	3975

Table 13.5. Grid grd_LocationSales.

Height	1215
Left	120
TabIndex	19
Top	480
Width	3615

Table 13.6. Label txt_MostQty.

BackColor	&H00C0C0C0&
Height	255
Left	2640
TabIndex	29
Top	2280
Width	1215

Table 13.7. Label txt_MostItem.

BackColor	&H00C0C0C0&
Height	255
Left	2640
TabIndex	24
Top	2040
Width	1215

Table 13.8. Label txt_MedianDay.

BackColor	&H00C0C0C0&
Height	255
Left	2640
TabIndex	23
Top	1680
Width	1215

Table 13.9. Label txt_AvgDay.

BackColor	&H00C0C0C0&
Height	255
Left	2640
TabIndex	22
Top	1320
Width	1215

Table 13.10. Label txt_ManDate.

BackColor	&H00C0C0C0&
Height	255
Left	2880
TabIndex	21
Top	360
Width	1215

Table 13.11. Label txt_AvgEmployee.

BackColor	&H00C0C0C0&
Height	255
Left	2640
TabIndex	20
Top	960
Width	1215

Table 13.12. SSFrame fra_PServer.

Caption	Pseudo Server
ForeColor	&H00000080&
Height	1095
Left	2640
TabIndex	9
Top	3000
Visible	0 'False
Width	4335

Table 13.13. Label txt_OverdueFlag.

BackColor	&H00C0C0C0&
Caption	Label9
Height	255
Left	3000
TabIndex	35
Top	1920
Width	735

Table 13.14. Label txt_ReorderFlag.

BackColor	&H00C0C0C0&
Caption	Label8
Height	255

continues

Table 13.14. continued

Left	3000
TabIndex	34
Top	1440
Width	735

Table 13.15. Label txt_DiskCritical.

BackColor	&H00C0C0C0&
Caption	Label7
Height	255
Left	3000
TabIndex	33
Top	960
Width	735

Table 13.16. Label txt_ReserveFlag.

BackColor	&H00C0C0C0&
Caption	Label2
Height	255
Left	3000
TabIndex	12
Top	480
Width	615

Table 13.17. SSFrame fra_Purchase.

Caption	Purchasing/Inventory
ForeColor	&H0000FFFF&
Height	1155
Left	2640
TabIndex	7
Top	1680

Visible	0 'False	
Width	4410	

Table 13.18. Grid Grid1.

Height	795
Left	480
TabIndex	8
Top	960
Width	3510

Table 13.19. SSFrame fra_Sales.

Caption	Sales
ForeColor	&H00FF0000&
Height	1425
Left	2565
TabIndex	5
Top	150
Visible	0 'False
Width	4440

Table 13.20. GRAPH Graph1.

GraphType	4 '3D Bar
GridStyle	1 'Horizontal
Height	3870
Labels	3 'Y Labels only
Left	345
RandomData	0 'Off
TabIndex	6
Top	720
Width	3780

Table 13.21. SSTab control tab_Report.

Height	4575
Left	360
TabIndex	0
Top	360
Width	6135
TabsPerRow	4
Tab	0
TabOrientation	0
Tabs	4
TabHeight	529
TabCaption(0)	Sales
TabCaption(1)	Purchase
TabCaption(2)	Pseudo Server
TabCaption(3)	Management

Creating the Location.FRM

The Location form is used to add a new location or edit an existing one. Figure 13.11 shows what the completed form looks like after all the controls have been added. Figure 13.12 shows the Name properties of all the individual controls. Create each control on the form and set the properties to match the values listed in the table.

FIGURE 13.11.
Location Form.

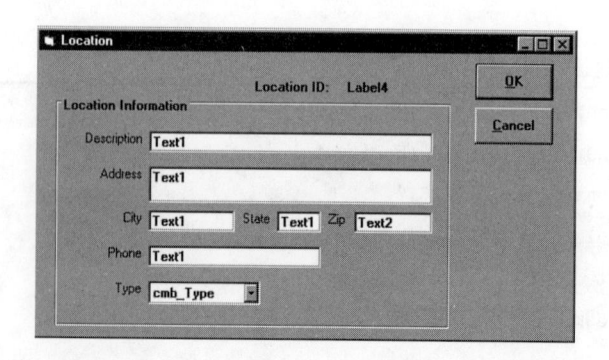

Table 13.36 shows all the controls for the form. It also shows the location at which the control should be created. If the location says Form, then it should be created on the form. If a frame name is specified (that is, fra_...), the control should be created within this frame.

FIGURE 13.12.
Location Form - Controls.

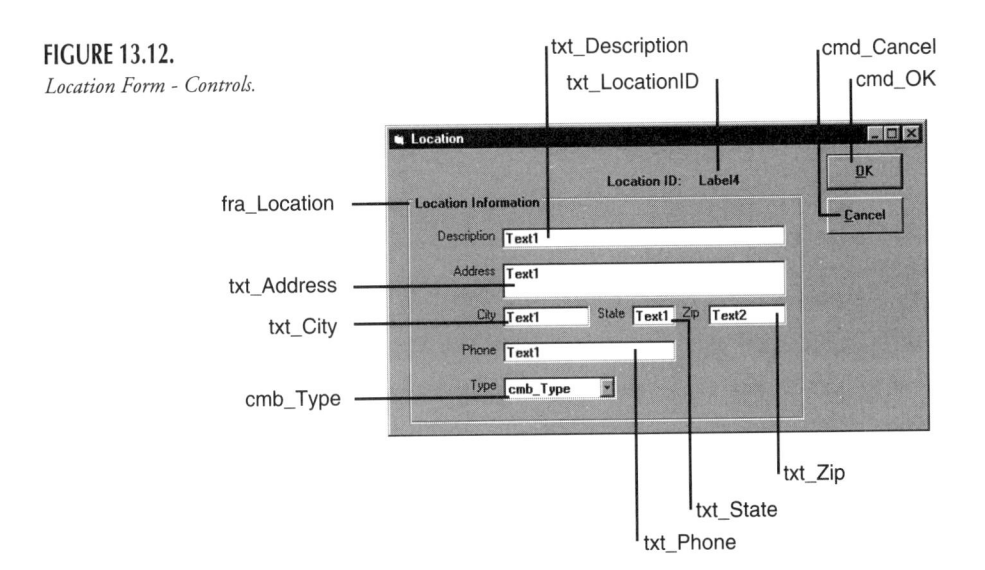

Table 13.26. Controls for the Location form.

Table	Control	Location
Table 13.27.	Form frm_Location	
Table 13.28.	SSFrame fra_Location	Form
Table 13.29.	TextBox txt_State	fra_Location
Table 13.30.	TextBox txt_Zip	fra_Location
Table 13.31.	TextBox txt_Phone	fra_Location
Table 13.32.	ComboBox cmb_Type	fra_Location
Table 13.33.	TextBox txt_Address	fra_Location
Table 13.34.	TextBox txt_City	fra_Location
Table 13.35.	TextBox txt_Desc	fra_Location
Table 13.36.	CommandButton cmd_Cancel	Form
Table 13.37.	CommandButton cmd_OK	Form
Table 13.38.	Label txt_LocationID	Form

Table 13.27. Form frm_Location.

BackColor	&H00C0C0C0&
Caption	Location
ClientHeight	4095
ClientLeft	1290
ClientTop	870
ClientWidth	7485
Height	4500
Left	1230
LinkTopic	Form1
ScaleHeight	4095
ScaleWidth	7485
Top	525
Width	7605

Table 13.28. SSFrame fra_Location.

Caption	Location Information
Height	3135
Left	120
TabIndex	16
Top	720
Width	5655

Table 13.29. TextBox txt_State.

Height	285
Left	3240
TabIndex	4
Top	1560
Width	495

Table 13.30. TextBox txt_Zip.

Height	285
Left	4200
TabIndex	5
Top	1560
Width	1215

Table 13.31. TextBox txt_Phone.

Height	285
Left	1320
TabIndex	6
Top	2040
Width	1695

Table 13.32. ComboBox cmb_Type.

Height	300
Left	1320
Style	2 'Dropdown List
TabIndex	8
Top	2520
Width	1455

Table 13.33. TextBox txt_Address.

Height	495
Left	1320
MultiLine	-1 'True
TabIndex	2
Top	960
Width	4095

Table 13.34. TextBox txt_City.

Height	285
Left	1320
TabIndex	3
Top	1560
Width	1215

Table 13.35. TextBox txt_Desc.

Height	285
Left	1320
TabIndex	1
Top	480
Width	4095

Table 13.36. CommandButton cmd_Cancel.

Cancel	-1 'True
Caption	&Cancel
Height	495
Left	6120
TabIndex	7
Top	720
Width	1095

Table 13.37. CommandButton cmd_OK.

Caption	&OK
Default	-1 'True
Height	495
Left	6120
TabIndex	0
Top	120
Width	1095

Table 13.38. Label `txt_LocationID`.

BackColor	&H00C0C0C0&
Caption	Label4
Height	255
Left	4320
TabIndex	18
Top	360
Width	1095

Creating the Staff.FRM

The Staff form is used to add a new staff member or edit an existing one. This form enables the specification of typical information fields (such as name, address, and so on) as well as a field to specify a supervisor. This field provides the capability of the table to join to itself. The supervisor is recorded as a StaffID from the table in which the employee is being added or edited.

Figure 13.13 shows what the completed form looks like after all the controls have been added. Figure 13.14 shows the Name properties of all the individual controls. Create each control on the form and set the properties to match the values listed in the table.

FIGURE 13.13.
Staff Form.

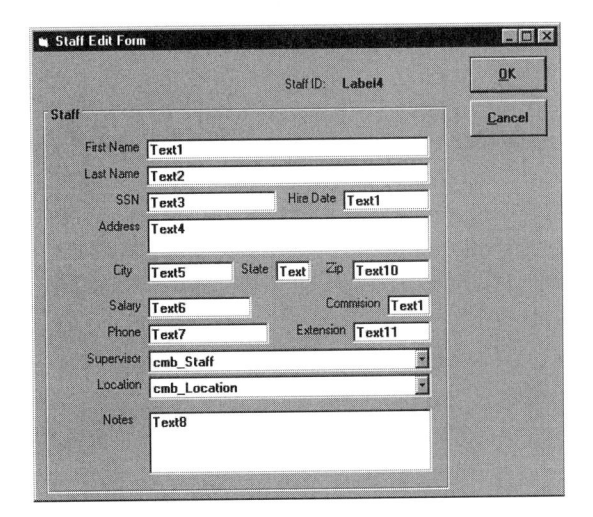

Part II ■ Constructing a Basic Client/Server System

FIGURE 13.14.
Staff Form - Controls.

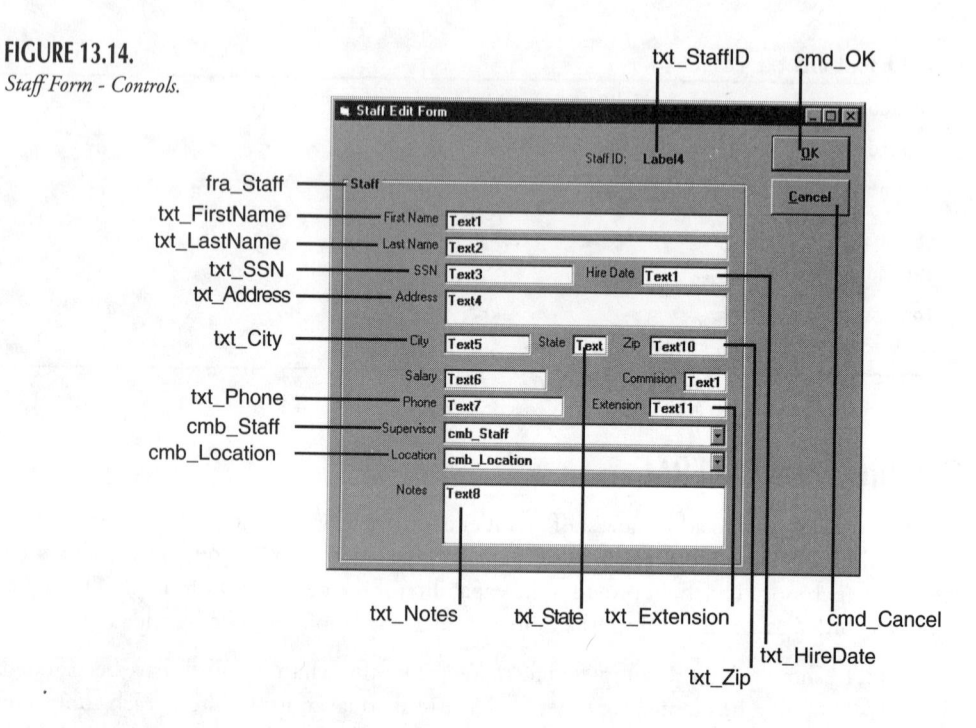

Table 13.39 shows all the controls for the form. It also shows the location at which the control should be created. If the location says Form, then it should be created on the form. If a frame name is specified (that is, fra_...), the control should be created within this frame.

Table 13.39. Controls for the Staff form.

Table	Control	Location
Table 13.40.	Form `frm_Staff`	
Table 13.41.	SSFrame `fra_Staff`	Form
Table 13.42.	TextBox `txt_HireDate`	`fra_Staff`
Table 13.43.	ComboBox `cmb_Location`	`fra_Staff`
Table 13.44.	TextBox `txt_State`	`fra_Staff`
Table 13.45.	TextBox `txt_Zip`	`fra_Staff`
Table 13.46.	TextBox `txt_Phone`	`fra_Staff`
Table 13.47.	TextBox `txt_Extension`	`fra_Staff`
Table 13.48.	TextBox `txt_Commission`	`fra_Staff`
Table 13.49.	ComboBox `cmb_Staff`	`fra_Staff`
Table 13.50.	TextBox `txt_Notes`	`fra_Staff`
Table 13.51.	TextBox `txt_FirstName`	`fra_Staff`

Table	Control	Location
Table 13.52.	TextBox txt_LastName	fra_Staff
Table 13.53.	TextBox txt_Address	fra_Staff
Table 13.54.	TextBox txt_City	fra_Staff
Table 13.55.	TextBox txt_Salary	fra_Staff
Table 13.56.	TextBox txt_SSN	fra_Staff
Table 13.57.	CommandButton cmd_Cancel	Form
Table 13.58.	CommandButton cmd_OK	Form
Table 13.59.	Label txt_StaffID	Form

Table 13.40. Form frm_Staff.

BackColor	&H00C0C0C0&
Caption	Form1
ClientHeight	6075
ClientLeft	1290
ClientTop	870
ClientWidth	7485
Height	6480
Left	1230
LinkTopic	Form1
ScaleHeight	6075
ScaleWidth	7485
Top	525
Width	7605

Table 13.41. SSFrame fra_Staff.

Caption	Staff Information
Height	5295
Left	120
TabIndex	22
Top	720
Width	5655

Table 13.42. TextBox `txt_HireDate`.

Height	285
Left	4080
TabIndex	33
Top	1200
Width	1335

Table 13.43. ComboBox `cmb_Location`.

Height	300
Left	1320
Style	2 'Dropdown List
TabIndex	31
Top	3720
Width	4095

Table 13.44. TextBox `txt_State`.

Height	285
Left	3240
TabIndex	7
Top	2160
Width	495

Table 13.45. TextBox `txt_Zip`.

Height	285
Left	4200
TabIndex	8
Top	2160
Width	1215

Table 13.46. TextBox txt_Phone.

Height	285
Left	1320
TabIndex	10
Top	3000
Width	1695

Table 13.47. TextBox txt_Extension.

Height	285
Left	4320
TabIndex	11
Top	3000
Width	1095

Table 13.48. TextBox txt_Commission.

Height	285
Left	4800
TabIndex	9
Top	2640
Width	615

Table 13.49. ComboBox cmb_Staff.

Height	300
Left	1320
Style	2 'Dropdown List
TabIndex	14
Top	3360
Width	4095

Table 13.50. TextBox txt_Notes.

Height	855
Left	1320
MultiLine	-1 'True
TabIndex	12
Top	4200
Width	4095

Table 13.51. TextBox txt_FirstName.

Height	285
Left	1320
TabIndex	2
Top	480
Width	4095

Table 13.52. TextBox txt_LastName.

Height	285
Left	1320
TabIndex	3
Top	840
Width	4095

Table 13.53. TextBox txt_Address.

Height	495
Left	1320
MultiLine	-1 'True
TabIndex	5
Top	1560
Width	4095

Table 13.54. TextBox `txt_City`.

Height	285
Left	1320
TabIndex	6
Top	2160
Width	1215

Table 13.55. TextBox `txt_Salary`.

Height	285
Left	1320
TabIndex	1
Top	2640
Width	1695

Table 13.56. TextBox `txt_SSN`.

Height	285
Left	1320
TabIndex	4
Top	1200
Width	1335

Table 13.57. CommandButton `cmd_Cancel`.

Cancel	-1 'True
Caption	&Cancel
Height	495
Left	6120
TabIndex	13
Top	720
Width	1095

Table 13.58. CommandButton cmd_OK.

Caption	&OK
Default	-1 'True
Height	495
Left	6120
TabIndex	0
Top	120
Width	1095

Table 13.59. Label txt_StaffID.

BackColor	&H00C0C0C0&
Caption	Label4
Height	255
Left	4320
TabIndex	30
Top	360
Width	1095

Adding Code to the Manage.FRM

The Management form is this client's central form. The code for this form provides all the queries and displays all the results of those queries. Adding the code to this form is a routine task. First, any form-level routines need to be created. These routines are not activated by an event (such as a mouse click), but are called by other parts of the code. These routines appear in the (General) section of the code menus.

The tabs on the Management Client activate the various reports. When clicked, each tab merely calls the particular report query routine to create the report.

Putting the routines as General Routines rather than having them embedded in the code of the tab control is a good idea for several reasons. Keeping the code separate from the control increases code clarity because all the routines can be accessed in a central place. Finding code embedded in controls often requires searching many controls every time a routine needs to be located.

If you place them as separate routines, you can easily scale them to be placed in global modules or classes. You can also specify input and output parameters (which is not possible in an event routine). Finally, if you place the routines in the general routines section, multiple other routines can call the function without having to simulate the event.

General Declarations

The only form-level variable is the temporary dynaset variable. Enter it into the General Declarations section.

```
Dim ScratchSS As Recordset
```

General Routines

All the routines shown in this section are added to the General section of the form. Code placed in the general section is available to all routines within the form. To create a new routine, select Procedure... under the Insert menu. Select the type of procedure according to the proper heading. The window opens showing the code window for the routine with the basic begin-and-end structure. Type the text found in each code section into the corresponding code area.

> **NOTE**
>
> When entering the code for each routine, be sure to enter the parameters that are to be received by the routine (shown in the definition parentheses ( )) and those returned by the routine (following the parentheses). For example, if the routine header is shown as:
>
> ```
> TestRoutine(num as Integer) As Double
> ```
>
> This function requires one parameter (num) passed to it, and returns another parameter (as variable type Double).

Sub ManagementReport ()

The `ManagementReport()` routine is activated when the user clicks the Management tab. This report uses a wide variety of queries to present executive summary information. Each query begins with a comment (') to describe it. The Management Report includes queries on the average sales per employee, total sales for today, average sales per invoice, and the item most frequently sold. It also fills the grid with Sales per location.

Each of these queries demonstrates a particular SQL command or type of query (using multiple tables, aggregate commands, AVG(), GROUP BY, and so on). By examining each query, you have a structural model of how queries to complete various actions are accomplished.

```
Private Sub ManagementReport()
    Dim ScratchSS As Recordset
    Dim num As Integer

    ' Find Average Sales per Employee
```

```
SQL$ = ""
SQL$ = SQL$ & " SELECT c.LastName, sum(b.finalprice) as SalesTotal"
SQL$ = SQL$ & " From Sales as a, SalesItems as b, Staff as c"
SQL$ = SQL$ & " Where (a.InvoiceID = b.InvoiceID) and (a.StaffID = c.StaffID)"
SQL$ = SQL$ & " Group by c.LastName"
Set ScratchSS = MyDB.OpenRecordset(SQL$, dbOpenSnapshot)

' Calculate Average
AvgTotal = 0
i = 0     Do Until ScratchSS.EOF
    AvgTotal = AvgTotal + ScratchSS!SalesTotal
    i = i + 1
    ScratchSS.MoveNext
Loop
' Place average in txt_AvgEmployee field
txt_AvgEmployee = Format$(AvgTotal / i, "$###0")

' Find Total sales for Today
SQL$ = ""
SQL$ = SQL$ & " SELECT  sum(b.finalprice) AS SalesTotal"
SQL$ = SQL$ & " FROM Sales AS a, SalesItems AS b"
SQL$ = SQL$ & " WHERE  (a.InvoiceID = b.InvoiceID) and a.SaleDate = #" & Date$
    & "#"
Set ScratchSS = MyDB.OpenRecordset(SQL$, dbOpenSnapshot)

' This will make sure a 0 exists if there are no sales for today
num = Val("" & ScratchSS!SalesTotal)
txt_AvgDay = Format$(num, "$###0")

' Find Average Sales per invoice
SQL$ = ""
SQL$ = SQL$ & " SELECT sum(b.finalprice) AS InvoiceTotal"
SQL$ = SQL$ & " FROM Sales AS a, SalesItems AS b"
SQL$ = SQL$ & " WHERE (a.InvoiceID = b.InvoiceID)"
SQL$ = SQL$ & " Group By a.InvoiceID"
Set ScratchSS = MyDB.OpenRecordset(SQL$, dbOpenSnapshot)

AvgTotal = 0
i = 0
Do Until ScratchSS.EOF
    AvgTotal = AvgTotal + ScratchSS!InvoiceTotal
    i = i + 1
    ScratchSS.MoveNext
Loop
txt_MedianDay = Format$(AvgTotal / i, "$###0")

' Find Most Sold Item
SQL$ = ""
SQL$ = SQL$ & " SELECT c.Description, sum(b.Qty) as QtySold"
SQL$ = SQL$ & " FROM Sales as a, SalesItems as B, Inventory_Sales as c"
SQL$ = SQL$ & " WHERE (a.InvoiceID = b.InvoiceID) and (b.PartID = c.PartID)"
SQL$ = SQL$ & " GROUP BY c.Description"
SQL$ = SQL$ & " Order BY 2 DESC"
Set ScratchSS = MyDB.OpenRecordset(SQL$, dbOpenSnapshot)

' Set text fields to show final query columns
txt_MostQty = ScratchSS!QtySold
txt_MostItem = ScratchSS!Description
```

Chapter 13 ■ Management Client 479

```
    ' Fill grid with Sales per Location

    txt_ManDate = Date$
    grd_LocationSales.Cols = 2
    ' Setting the Rows to 1 and then 20 clears any old data stored in grid
    grd_LocationSales.Rows = 1
    grd_LocationSales.Rows = 20
    ' One fixed row will show column titles
    grd_LocationSales.FixedRows = 1
    grd_LocationSales.FixedCols = 0

    ' Set column titles
    grd_LocationSales.Row = 0
    grd_LocationSales.Col = 0
    grd_LocationSales.Text = "Location"
    grd_LocationSales.ColWidth(0) = (grd_LocationSales.Width) * 0.6
    grd_LocationSales.Col = 1
    grd_LocationSales.Text = "Sales"
    grd_LocationSales.ColWidth(1) = (grd_LocationSales.Width) * 0.3

    SQL$ = ""
    SQL$ = SQL$ & " SELECT c.Description, sum(b.finalprice) AS SalesTotal"
    SQL$ = SQL$ & " FROM Sales AS a, SalesItems AS b, Location AS c"
    SQL$ = SQL$ & " WHERE (a.InvoiceID = b.InvoiceID) and (b.LocationID =
➥c.LocationID)"
    SQL$ = SQL$ & " GROUP BY c.Description;"

    Set ScratchSS = MyDB.OpenRecordset(SQL$, dbOpenSnapshot)

    ' Populate the grid control with sales location data
    i = 1
    Do Until ScratchSS.EOF
        grd_LocationSales.Row = i
        grd_LocationSales.Col = 0
        grd_LocationSales.Text = "" & ScratchSS!Description
        grd_LocationSales.Col = 1
        grd_LocationSales.Text = Format$(ScratchSS!SalesTotal, "$#,##0")
        i = i + 1
        ScratchSS.MoveNext
    Loop
End Sub
```

Sub PServerReport ()

This routine is activated when the user clicks the Pseudo Server tab. The routine queries the PServer table for the various flags and sets the appropriate Text controls to display their settings. It also finds and displays the number of reserved items. Although this is not strictly part of the Pseudo Server's table, it is part of the responsibility of the Pseudo Server application.

```
Private Sub PServerReport()
    Dim ScratchSS As Recordset
    Dim SQL$

    SQL$ = "Select * from PServer"
    ' Create Recordset of PServer record
    Set ScratchSS = MyDB.OpenRecordset(SQL$, dbOpenSnapshot)
```

```
    ' Show various flags in text fields
    If ScratchSS!ReOrderStatus = True Then
        txt_ReorderFlag = "Yes"
    Else
        txt_ReorderFlag = "No"
    End If
    If ScratchSS!DiskCriticalStatus = True Then
        txt_DiskCritical = "Yes"
    Else
        txt_DiskCritical = "No"
    End If
    If ScratchSS!DelinquentAccounts = True Then
        txt_OverdueFlag = "Yes"
    Else
        txt_OverdueFlag = "No"
    End If

    ' Find how many items are reserved in inventory

    SQL$ = "Select * from Inventory_Sales WHERE Reserved > 0"
    Set ScratchSS = MyDB.OpenRecordset(SQL$, dbOpenSnapshot)

    numReserved = 0

    Do Until ScratchSS.EOF
        numReserved = numReserved + ScratchSS!Reserved
        ScratchSS.MoveNext
    Loop
    txt_numReserved = numReserved
End Sub
```

Sub PurchaseReport ()

This routine is activated when the user clicks the Purchase/Inventory tab. The routine uses a complex query across three tables to generate the cost of each Sales item. From the Assembly table, it retrieves the number and types of parts required to make a Sales item unit. From the Inventory_Parts table, it retrieves all the costs of the individual parts. Finally, it totals the cost of all of these parts (SUM) and labels them by their description in the Inventory_Sales table.

The description in the preceding paragraph is approximately what happens in a step-by-step manner. SQL does not function this way. As you can see in the code, the SELECT statement generates a resultant set of two columns: one containing the description field from the sales inventory table (c=Inventory_Sales) and another with the SUM aggregate function for the unit costs. The GROUP BY clause actually selects all the various Sales items values so the SUM aggregate function may be used.

The final results are then placed in a grid control. The grid control is perfect for displaying dynamic amounts of information (any number of items could be displayed).

This query is an excellent example of the difference between the SQL language and a traditional sequential step language like BASIC. This query specifies the basic results needed from the query. It does not specify step by step how this can be accomplished. This way, the database server can optimize the query to complete the task in the most efficient way depending on the server's resources, including sending the query to another machine to process.

SQL's results-based syntax is what makes the language perfect for database queries but far from ideal for business rules or stored procedures. The OLE Remote server is made to complement an SQL system to provide the pieces to a client/server system that is not suited to a general database.

```
Private Sub PurchaseReport()
    Dim numfields As Integer
    Dim fieldTitle As String

    ' Clear old data
    Grid1.Rows = 1
    Grid1.Rows = 20
    Grid1.FixedRows = 1
    Grid1.FixedCols = 0

    ' Setup query to find unit cost
    SQL$ = ""
    SQL$ = SQL$ & " SELECT c.Description, sum(b.UnitCost * a.Qty) as UnitCost"
    SQL$ = SQL$ & " FROM Assembly AS a, Inventory_Parts AS b,  Inventory_Sales AS
➥c"
    SQL$ = SQL$ & " WHERE (a.PartID_Parts = b.PartID) And (a.PartID_Sales =
➥c.PartID)"
    SQL$ = SQL$ & " GROUP BY  c.Description;"
    Set ScratchSS = MyDB.OpenRecordset(SQL$, dbOpenSnapshot)

    numfields = ScratchSS.Fields.Count

    ' Give grid enough columns to store all fields
    Grid1.Cols = numfields

    ' For..Next loop will place field titles for all columns
    For j = 0 To numfields - 1
        Grid1.Row = 0
        Grid1.Col = j
        fieldTitle = ScratchSS.Fields(j).Name
        ' Set column heading to field name
        Grid1.Text = fieldTitle
        ' Make the column wide enough so the field name can be read
        Grid1.ColWidth(j) = Me.TextWidth(fieldTitle) * 2
    Next j

    ' For..Next loop will place data in the grid
    ' Reset record counter
    i = 0
    Do Until ScratchSS.EOF
        ' Set number of rows to accomodate all records
        Grid1.Rows = i + 2

        ' Enter all fields for this record in Grid
        For j = 0 To ScratchSS.Fields.Count - 1
            Grid1.Row = i + 1
            Grid1.Col = j
            ' Enter field value into Grid
            Grid1.Text = ScratchSS.Fields(j).Value
```

```
            Next j

        i = i + 1
        ScratchSS.MoveNext
    Loop
End Sub
```

Sub SalesReport ()

The `SalesReport()` routine is activated when the user clicks the Sales tab. This routine uses a three-table query to total all the sales by each salesperson. Once the query has generated a resultant set, each record will be inserted into the graph. The Legend text of each piece of data is set to the LastName field of the employee, so the legend shows which staff member each bar represents.

The routine also sets the number of bars (set to 20 by default) to equal the number of employees. Note that a graph cannot have less than two values. In that unlikely circumstance (that the enterprise has only one employee, but needs this report) the default is set to 2. In the chart, the second bar shows as a zero.

```
Private Sub SalesReport()
    ' Setup query for Sales per Employee
    SQL$ = ""
    SQL$ = SQL$ & " SELECT c.LastName, sum(b.finalprice) as SalesTotal"
    SQL$ = SQL$ & " From Sales as a, SalesItems as b, Staff as c"
    SQL$ = SQL$ & " Where (a.InvoiceID = b.InvoiceID) and (a.StaffID = c.StaffID)"
    SQL$ = SQL$ & " Group by c.LastName"
    Set ScratchSS = MyDB.OpenRecordset(SQL$, dbOpenSnapshot)

    ' Set the graph to some default characteristics
    Graph1.GraphType = 4      ' Three-D Bar Chart
    Graph1.NumPoints = 20
    Graph1.NumSets = 1
    Graph1.AutoInc = 0

    ' Suspend updating the graph until all data is inserted.
    ' This will improve the speed of the application
    Graph1.DrawMode = 0

    ' variable i will how the current bar number
    i = 1
    Do Until ScratchSS.EOF
        ' Set data for each bar
        Graph1.ThisPoint = i
        Graph1.GraphData = ScratchSS!SalesTotal
        Graph1.LegendText = ScratchSS!LastName
        ' Move to next query row
        ScratchSS.MoveNext
        i = i + 1
    Loop
    ' Minimum of 2 bars required for bar chart. Therefore, if one
    ' employee sold everything, a blank second bar is required.
    If i < 3 Then
        Graph1.NumPoints = 2
```

```
    Else
        Graph1.NumPoints = i - 1
    End If

    ' Reset the drawing mode to show the changes
    Graph1.DrawMode = 2
End Sub
```

Control Code

All of the code shown in this section must be added to the individual controls. Simply double-click the control on the Management form, and the relevant code box appears. Then, in the drop-down combobox labeled 'Proc:', select the event to which the code belongs.

Sub tab_Report_Click(PreviousTab As Integer)

This routine is activated when the user clicks one of the tabs on the tab control. The routine simply distributes the click to the appropriate report routine. The tab control is named tab_Report, and the property Tab holds the number of the tab that was selected.

```
Private Sub tab_Report_Click(PreviousTab As Integer)
    Select Case tab_Report.Tab
        Case 0   ' Sales Tab
            SalesReport
        Case 1   ' Purchase Tab
            PurchaseReport
        Case 2   ' PServer Tab
            PServerReport
        Case 3   ' Manage Tab
            ManagementReport
    End Select
End Sub
```

Sub Form_Load ()

The Load() event accesses the .INI file to retrieve the information it needs. In this case, with the reports included, it needs only the database settings. After it has retrieved the database path and name, it creates a globally available database object. It then centers the form on the screen.

Finally, it activates the tab_Report_Click routine. This simulates the user clicking on the tab control. Whatever tab is selected in the code (in this case, tab 0 by default), the report for that tab is shown. Any of the four tabs may be used as the default report. If some of the reports require extensive time to activate a query, they should be avoided as the startup report.

```
Private Sub Form_Load()
    Dim INIPath As String

    ' Setup path of INI file
    INIPath = GetAppPath() & "Manage.INI"

    ' Set path for custom INI for Access engine
    DBEngine.INIPath = INIPath
```

```
' Read global parameters for default values
g_DataLocation = ReadINI("Parameters", "DataLocation", INIPath)
g_DBName = ReadINI(g_DataLocation, "DBName", INIPath)

' Open connection to Database
Set MyDB = OpenDatabase(g_DBName, False, False)

' Center the form on the screen
CenterForm Me
' Activate the first report by simulating a mouse click on the button
tab_Report_Click 0
End Sub
```

Sub Form_Unload (Cancel As Integer)

The routine is called as the main form (MANAGE.FRM) is unloaded. An END statement finishes execution and quits the program. This routine is used to ensure that all the hidden forms are unloaded so that a phantom application does not remain.

```
Private Sub Form_Unload(Cancel As Integer)
    End
End Sub
```

Menu Items Code

The code shown in this section is entered by selecting the item from the menu on the form and entering the code. The routines may also be selected by choosing the particular menu object in the code window.

Sub AddLocationItem_Click ()

This routine displays the Location form for adding a location. Notice that the flags are set to tell the Location form to clear the record and not to load a current record.

```
Private Sub AddLocationItem_Click()
    ' Set flags to show new location
    g_LoadCustFlag = False
    g_ClearCustFlag = True
    ' Display the Location form
    frm_Location.Show 1
End Sub
```

Sub AddStaffItem_Click ()

This routine displays the Staff form for adding additional staff members. The Loading flag is set to FALSE, and the Clear flag is set to TRUE, so a blank form will be shown.

```
Private Sub AddStaffItem_Click()
    ' Set flags to show new staff member
    g_LoadCustFlag = False
    g_ClearCustFlag = True
    ' Display the Staff form
    frm_Staff.Show 1
End Sub
```

Sub EditLocationItem_Click ()

This routine is used to call and edit a Location record from the Location table. All the properties must be set for the Item form to display the proper location fields. The ListTitle, ListQuery, ListItem1, and ListID fields are all set to display the locations available for editing. Next, the Item form is shown to allow the user to select the location to edit.

If the user selects a location, the ListResults property returns the LocationID. The Location form is then shown to enable the location record to be edited.

```
Private Sub EditLocationItem_Click()
    ' Setup properties for List Box filling
    frm_Item.ListTitle = "Locations"
    frm_Item.ListQuery = "Select * FROM Location ORDER BY Description"
    frm_Item.ListItem1 = "Description"
    frm_Item.ListItem2 = ""
    ' LocationID will be the number returned by the ListBox if the user selects an
➥item
    frm_Item.ListIDField = "LocationID"
    ' Display the form as a modal dialog box
    frm_Item.Show 1
    DoEvents
    ' Make sure the user did not cancel or close the form without selecting an item
    If frm_Item.ListResult <> -1 Then
        ' Set flags to load location
        g_CustomerID = frm_Item.ListResult
        g_LoadCustFlag = True
        g_ClearCustFlag = False
        ' Display the Location form
        frm_Location.Show 1
    End If
End Sub
```

Sub EditStaffItem_Click ()

This routine is used to call and edit a Staff member record from the Staff table. Functionally, this routine is identical to the `EditLocationItem` routine.

```
Private Sub EditStaffItem_Click()
    ' Setup properties for List Box filling
    frm_Item.ListTitle = "Staff"
    frm_Item.ListQuery = "Select * FROM Staff ORDER BY LastName,FirstName"
    frm_Item.ListItem1 = "LastName"
    frm_Item.ListItem2 = "FirstName"
    ' StaffID will be the number returned by the ListBox if the user selects an
➥item
    frm_Item.ListIDField = "StaffID"
    ' Display the form as a modal dialog box
    frm_Item.Show 1
    DoEvents
    ' Make sure the user did not cancel or close the form without selecting an item
    If frm_Item.ListResult <> -1 Then
        ' Set flags to load location
        g_CustomerID = frm_Item.ListResult
        g_LoadCustFlag = True
```

```
        g_ClearCustFlag = False
        frm_Staff.Show 1
    End If
End Sub
```

Sub ExitItem_Click ()

This routine is activated if the user selects the Exit command from the File menu. This ends execution and unloads the application. Any hidden forms are flushed from memory.

```
Private Sub ExitItem_Click()
    End
End Sub
```

Adding Code to the Location.FRM

The Location form contains fields for all the information stored in a record from the Location table. Adding the code to the form is a routine task. First, any form-level routines are created. These routines are not activated by an event (such as a mouse click), but are called by other parts of the code. These routines appear in the (General) section of the code menus.

General Declarations

The only form-level variable is the temporary recordset variable. Enter it into the General Declarations section.

```
Dim LocationDS As Recordset
```

General Routines

All of the routines described in this section are added to the General section of the form. Code placed in the general section is available to all routines within the form. To create a new routine, select Procedure... under the Insert menu. Enter the name of the routine and select the specified type (sub or function). Then type the text found in the corresponding section into the code window.

Sub CopyTags ()

This routine sets the Tag properties of all the controls on the form to equal the primary properties (Text properties and so forth). The Tag values can then be used after the user has clicked the OK button to determine which primary properties have changed and need to be updated.

```
Private Sub CopyTags()
    ' This routine copies the information stored in the text
    ' field to the object's tag field for later comparison.
    txt_Desc.Tag = txt_Desc.Text
    txt_Address.Tag = txt_Address.Text
    txt_City.Tag = txt_City.Text
    txt_State.Tag = txt_State.Text
    txt_Zip.Tag = txt_Zip.Text
```

```
        txt_Phone.Tag = txt_Phone.Text
        cmb_Type.Tag = cmb_Type.Text
End Sub
```

Sub RecordToScreen (TempDS As Recordset)

This routine copies all the fields from the record into the various controls on the screen. Notice the values that are set with "" and the & command. These fields may contain NULL values, and this prevents an error from occurring. Setting a control property to a NULL creates an error.

```
Private Sub RecordToScreen(TempRS As Recordset)
    ' Retrieve record info and place in text box fields
    txt_Desc.Text = "" & TempRS!Description
    txt_Address.Text = "" & TempRS!Address
    txt_City.Text = "" & TempRS!City
    txt_State.Text = "" & TempRS!State
    txt_Zip.Text = "" & TempRS!Zip
    txt_Phone.Text = "" & TempRS!Phone
    cmb_Type.ListIndex = TempRS!Type
    txt_LocationID.Caption = g_CustomerID
End Sub
```

Sub ScreentoRecord (TempDS As Dynaset)

This routine takes all the values from the screen and writes off any changes to the selected record. The Edit method is called to activate the Edit mode. Then each value is compared against the Tag values for any differences. The Tag properties were originally set to equal the record values. Any changes the user made are reflected in the Text fields.

```
Private Sub ScreentoRecord(TempRS As Recordset)
    ' Begin the edit on the passed row
    TempRS.Edit

    ' Only store the changes to the database. The tag property is
    ' originally set equal to the field value. Any differences will
    ' appear when the two are compared.
    If txt_Desc.Text <> txt_Desc.Tag Then
        TempRS!Description = txt_Desc.Text
    End If
    If txt_Address.Text <> txt_Address.Tag Then
        TempRS!Address = txt_Address.Text
    End If
    If txt_City.Text <> txt_City.Tag Then
        TempRS!City = txt_City.Text
    End If
    If txt_State.Text <> txt_State.Tag Then
        TempRS!State = Left$(txt_State.Text, 2)
    End If
    If txt_Zip.Text <> txt_Zip.Tag Then
        TempRS!Zip = txt_Zip.Text
    End If
    If txt_Phone.Text <> txt_Phone.Tag Then
        TempRS!Phone = txt_Phone.Text
    End If
```

```
        TempRS!Type = cmb_Type.ListIndex

    ' Store any changes to the record
    TempRS.Update
End Sub
```

Sub SetupDefaultScreen ()

The `SetupDefaultScreen()` routine sets the controls in the form to empty values. This prevents a previously hidden form from showing old information. The routine `CopyTags()` is then called to synchronize the Tag properties to the new empty values.

```
Private Sub SetupDefaultScreen()
    ' Blank all of the dialog fields so old data does not remain
    txt_Desc.Text = ""
    txt_Address.Text = ""
    txt_City.Text = ""
    txt_State.Text = ""
    txt_Zip.Text = ""
    txt_Phone.Text = ""
    cmb_Type.ListIndex = 0
    txt_LocationID.Caption = "New"
    ' Copy the empty fields to the Tag properties
    CopyTags
End Sub
```

Control Code

All the code shown in this section must be added to the individual controls. Simply double-click the control on the Location form and the relevant code box appears. Then, in the drop-down combobox labeled 'Proc:', select the event for which the code is intended. Then enter the code in the event code area.

Sub cmd_Cancel_Click ()

This routine sets the `g_OKFlag` to `False`. Any routine that originally activated this form can detect that the Cancel button was used to close the form instead of the OK button. The form is hidden using the `Me` command. This command activates the method (Hide) of the form that is currently executing the routine.

```
Private Sub cmd_Cancel_Click()
    g_OKFlag = False
    Me.Hide
End Sub
```

Sub cmd_OK_Click ()

This routine is activated when the user clicks the OK button to record the location shown on the form. The OK routine is stores the new location or updates to a current location.

The `txt_LocationID` field is checked to determine if the location is new. If the location is new, the Counter table is addressed and the value is incremented. A new record is added to the

Location table with the LocationID number just acquired from the Counter table. The LocationDS recordset object is then set to contain the newly created record.

Finally, the LocationDS recordset is passed to the ScreenToRecord() routine, which stores the fields to the database. If the record had not been new, the LocationDS would have already pointed to the record that was being edited.

```
Private Sub cmd_OK_Click()
    Dim ScratchDS As Recordset
    Dim ScratchTable As Recordset

    g_OKFlag = True
    Me.Hide
    If txt_LocationID = "New" Then         ' Get the customer number counter
        SQL$ = "Select * from Counter where TableName = 'Location'"
        Set ScratchDS = MyDB.OpenRecordset(SQL$, dbOpenDynaset)
        g_CustomerID = ScratchDS!CountNum
        ' increment Invoice number
        ScratchDS.Edit
        ScratchDS!CountNum = g_CustomerID + 1
        ScratchDS.Update

        ' Create customer record
        Set ScratchTable = MyDB.OpenRecordset("Location", dbOpenTable)
        ScratchTable.AddNew
        ScratchTable!LocationID = g_CustomerID
        ScratchTable.Update
        ' Create Recordset for editing
        SQL$ = "Select * from Location where LocationID = " & g_CustomerID
        Set LocationDS = MyDB.OpenRecordset(SQL$, dbOpenDynaset)
    End If
    ScreentoRecord LocationDS
End Sub
```

Sub Form_Load ()

This routine loads the combo box to show the various types of locations. A location might be a retail establishment, a warehouse, and so forth. The cmb_Type combo box enables users to choose the type of location for the current record.

```
Private Sub Form_Load()
    ' Add the available location types to the combo box
    cmb_Type.AddItem "Branch Outlet"
    cmb_Type.AddItem "Retail"
    cmb_Type.AddItem "Warehouse"
    cmb_Type.AddItem "Office"
    cmb_Type.AddItem "Plant"
End Sub
```

Sub Form_Activate ()

The Activate() routine checks the g_LoadCustFlag (which is actually used to load a Location) and the g_ClearCustFlag (which signals a new location record). If either of these flags are set to TRUE, the appropriate routine is activated. Both flags are cleared at the end of the routine.

```
Private Sub Form_Activate()
    ' Should a customer record be loaded?
    If g_LoadCustFlag = True Then
        SQL$ = "Select * from Location where LocationID = " & g_CustomerID
        Set LocationDS = MyDB.OpenRecordset(SQL$, dbOpenDynaset)
        RecordToScreen LocationDS
    ElseIf g_ClearCustFlag = True Then
        SetupDefaultScreen
    End If
    ' Reset Flags
    g_LoadCustFlag = False
    g_ClearCustFlag = False
    ' Place cursor in starting box
    txt_Desc.SetFocus
End Sub
```

Adding Code to the Staff.FRM

The Staff form displays a staff record's information. Either a new staff record can be added to the Staff table, or a current record can be edited. To add the code to the Staff form, first add any form-level routines that need to be created. These routines are not activated by an event (such as a mouse click), but are called by other parts of the code. These routines will appear in the (General) section of the code menus.

General Declarations

The only form-level variable is the temporary recordset variable. Enter it into the General Declarations section.

```
Dim StaffDS As Recordset
```

General Routines

All the routines described in this section are added to the General section of the form. Code placed in the general section is available to all routines within the form. Create each subroutine or procedure and add the appropriate code. Be sure to add the parameters that need to be passed to and received from the routines.

Sub CopyTags ()

This routine sets the Tag properties of all the controls on the form to equal the primary properties (Text properties, and so on). The Tag values can then be used after the user has clicked the OK button to determine which primary properties have changed and need to be updated.

```
Private Sub CopyTags()
    txt_LastName.Tag = txt_LastName.Text
    txt_FirstName.Tag = txt_FirstName.Text
    txt_SSN.Tag = txt_SSN.Text
    txt_HireDate.Tag = txt_HireDate.Text
    txt_Address.Tag = txt_Address.Text
```

```
        txt_City.Tag = txt_City.Text
        txt_State.Tag = txt_State.Text
        txt_Zip.Tag = txt_Zip.Text
        txt_Salary.Tag = txt_Salary.Text
        txt_Phone.Tag = txt_Phone.Text
        txt_Extension.Tag = txt_Extension.Text
        txt_Commision.Tag = txt_Commision.Text
        cmb_Staff.Tag = cmb_Staff.Text
        cmb_Location.Tag = cmb_Location.Text
        txt_Notes.Tag = txt_Notes.Text
End Sub
```

Sub LoadLocationPopup ()

This routine loads the Location combobox. The location of each staff member must be stored in the database for billing and sales records. The Staff record records the LocationID selected in the Location combo box.

```
Private Sub LoadLocationPopup()
    Dim LocationID As Long, SelStaff As Integer
    
    SQL$ = "Select * FROM Location ORDER BY Description"
    Set MySS = MyDB.OpenRecordset(SQL$, dbOpenSnapshot)
    
    SelStaff = -1
    ' Reset record counter
    i = 0
    Do Until MySS.EOF     ' Until end of file.
        cmb_Location.AddItem MySS!Description
        LocationID = MySS!LocationID
        cmb_Location.ItemData(cmb_Location.NewIndex) = LocationID
        
        i = i + 1
        MySS.MoveNext     ' Move to next record.
    Loop
    
    cmb_Location.ListIndex = 0
End Sub
```

Sub LoadStaffPopup ()

This routine loads the Staff combo box for the Supervisor field on the form. For each staff record, a Supervisor may be chosen for a hierarchy in the organization. All the records are loaded from the Staff table. Note that the combobox cannot be set to the same StaffID as the record being shown. Such an equivalency would create a circular reference, which is not allowed for the join.

```
Private Sub LoadStaffPopup()
    Dim StaffID As Long, SelStaff As Integer
    
    SQL$ = "Select * FROM Staff ORDER BY LastName,FirstName"
    Set MySS = MyDB.OpenRecordset(SQL$, dbOpenSnapshot)
    
    SelStaff = -1
    ' Reset record counter
```

```
    i = 0
    Do Until MySS.EOF      ' Until end of file.
        Add$ = MySS!LastName & "," & MySS!FirstName
        cmb_Staff.AddItem Add$
        StaffID = MySS!StaffID
        cmb_Staff.ItemData(cmb_Staff.NewIndex) = StaffID
        If StaffID = g_DefaultStaffID Then
            SelStaff = i
        End If

        i = i + 1
        MySS.MoveNext       ' Move to next record.
    Loop
    ' Set staff to equal default staff member
    If SelStaff <> -1 Then
        cmb_Staff.ListIndex = SelStaff
    Else
        cmb_Staff.ListIndex = 0
    End If
End Sub
```

Sub RecordToScreen (TempDS As Recordset)

`RecordToScreen` reads all the information from a record for a Staff member and puts it in the appropriate controls on the screen. The general information of the Staff member is read and placed in each control. The Tag fields for the general information are stored for later checking of any alterations.

Notice that both the Supervisor and Location combo boxes require special handling. The StaffID of the supervisor and the LocationID of the location are the numbers actually stored in the Staff record. These ID numbers can be found in the ItemData arrays of the combo boxes.

```
Private Sub RecordToScreen(TempDS As Recordset)
    txt_StaffID.Caption = g_CustomerID
    txt_LastName.Text = "" & TempDS!LastName
    txt_FirstName.Text = "" & TempDS!FirstName
    txt_SSN.Text = "" & TempDS!SSN
    txt_HireDate.Text = "" & TempDS!HireDate
    txt_Address.Text = "" & TempDS!HomeAddress
    txt_City.Text = "" & TempDS!HomeCity
    txt_State.Text = "" & TempDS!HomeState
    txt_Zip.Text = "" & TempDS!HomeZip
    txt_Salary.Text = "" & TempDS!Salary
    txt_Phone.Text = "" & TempDS!HomePhone
    txt_Extension.Text = "" & TempDS!Extension
    txt_Commision.Text = "" & TempDS!Commision

    ' Find proper staff member in combo list
    cmb_Staff.ListIndex = -1
    If TempDS!Supervisor Then
        For i = 0 To cmb_Staff.ListCount - 1
            If cmb_Staff.ItemData(i) = TempDS!Supervisor Then
                cmb_Staff.ListIndex = i
                Exit For
            End If
        Next i
    End If
```

```
    ' Find proper location in combo list
    cmb_Location.ListIndex = 0
    If TempDS!LocationID Then
        For i = 0 To cmb_Location.ListCount - 1
            If cmb_Location.ItemData(i) = TempDS!LocationID Then
                cmb_Location.ListIndex = i
                Exit For
            End If
        Next i
    End If
    txt_Notes.Text = "" & TempDS!Notes
End Sub
```

Sub ScreentoRecord (TempDS As Recordset)

This routine stores any changes the user has made to the selected Staff record. All the Tag properties are checked against the Text properties to determine if any changes have been made.

```
Private Sub ScreentoRecord(TempDS As Recordset)
    TempDS.Edit

    If txt_LastName.Text <> txt_LastName.Tag Then
        TempDS!LastName = txt_LastName.Text
    End If
    If txt_FirstName.Text <> txt_FirstName.Tag Then
        TempDS!FirstName = txt_FirstName.Text
    End If
    If txt_SSN.Text <> txt_SSN.Tag Then
        TempDS!SSN = Left$(txt_SSN.Text, 11)
    End If
    If txt_HireDate.Text <> txt_HireDate.Tag Then
        TempDS!HireDate = txt_HireDate.Text
    End If
    If txt_Address.Text <> txt_Address.Tag Then
        TempDS!HomeAddress = txt_Address.Text
    End If
    If txt_City.Text <> txt_City.Tag Then
        TempDS!HomeCity = txt_City.Text
    End If
    If txt_State.Text <> txt_State.Tag Then
        TempDS!HomeState = Left$(txt_State.Text, 2)
    End If
    If txt_Zip.Text <> txt_Zip.Tag Then
        TempDS!HomeZip = txt_Zip.Text
    End If
    If txt_Salary.Text <> txt_Salary.Tag Then
        TempDS!Salary = txt_Salary.Text
    End If
    If txt_Phone.Text <> txt_Phone.Tag Then
        TempDS!HomePhone = txt_Phone.Text
    End If
    If txt_Extension.Text <> txt_Extension.Tag Then
        TempDS!Extension = txt_Extension.Text
    End If

    If txt_Commision.Text <> txt_Commision.Tag Then
        TempDS!Commision = txt_Commision.Text
    End If
```

```
    If cmb_Staff.Text <> cmb_Staff.Tag Then
        If cmb_Staff.ListIndex <> -1 Then
            TempDS!Supervisor = cmb_Staff.ItemData(cmb_Staff.ListIndex)
        Else
            TempDS!Supervisor = Null
        End If
    End If

    TempDS!LocationID = cmb_Location.ItemData(cmb_Location.ListIndex)
    If txt_Notes.Text <> txt_Notes.Tag Then
        TempDS!Notes = txt_Notes.Text
    End If

    TempDS.Update
End Sub
```

Sub SetupDefaultScreen ()

This routine simply resets all the screen control values to default values. Notice that the Tag fields are set to equal the blank values. Note that the cmb_Staff control is set to a value of –1. This control designates the supervisor of the staff member. A particular supervisor might not be specified, or the employee may be an owner. For these reasons, the combo box is set to an empty value.

```
Private Sub SetupDefaultScreen()
    txt_StaffID.Caption = "New"
    txt_LastName.Text = ""
    txt_FirstName.Text = ""
    txt_SSN.Text = ""
    txt_HireDate.Text = ""
    txt_Address.Text = ""
    txt_City.Text = ""
    txt_State.Text = ""
    txt_Zip.Text = ""
    txt_Salary.Text = 0
    txt_Phone.Text = ""
    txt_Extension = ""
    txt_Commision.Text = ""
    cmb_Staff.ListIndex = -1
    cmb_Location.ListIndex = 0
    txt_Notes.Text = ""
    CopyTags
End Sub
```

Control Code

All the code described in this section must be added to the individual controls. Double-click the control on the Purchase form, and the relevant code box appears. Then, in the drop-down combobox labelled 'Proc:', select the event to which the code belongs and enter the corresponding code.

Sub cmb_Staff_Click ()

The `cmb_Staff_Click` routine is activated if the user selects a Supervisor for the currently displayed Staff member. The StaffID of the selected Supervisor stored in the ItemData array of the combobox is checked against the current StaffID. The routine ensures that the Supervisor field is not set to equal the current StaffID. Such an equivalency would create a circular relationship and violate the Normalization standards of the database.

```
Private Sub cmb_Staff_Click()
    ' Check to make sure the supervisor is not set to himself
    If txt_StaffID <> "New" And cmb_Staff.ListIndex <> -1 Then
        If cmb_Staff.ItemData(cmb_Staff.ListIndex) = Val(txt_StaffID) Then
            MsgBox "Supervisor and Staff member cannot be the same person. Please select a different supervisor.", 16, "Self-Reference Error"
cmb_Staff.ListIndex = -1
        End If
    End If
End Sub
```

Sub cmd_Cancel_Click ()

This routine hides the form if the user clicks the Cancel button. It also sets the `g_OKFlag` to FALSE so that any routines that called the form can determine if the user canceled.

```
Private Sub cmd_Cancel_Click()
    g_OKFlag = False
    Me.Hide
End Sub
```

Sub cmd_OK_Click ()

This routine is activated when the user clicks the OK button to record the Staff member shown on the form. The OK routine stores the new Staff member record or updates the current one.

The `txt_StaffID` field is checked to determine if the member is new. If this is a new record, the Counter table is addressed and the value is incremented. A new record is added to the Staff table with the StaffID number just acquired from the Counter table. The StaffDS recordset object is then set to contain the newly created record.

Finally, the StaffDS recordset is passed to the `ScreenToRecord()` routine, which stores the fields to the database. If the record had not been new, the StaffDS would have already pointed to the record that was being edited.

```
Private Sub cmd_OK_Click()
    Dim ScratchDS As Recordset
    Dim ScratchTable As Recordset

    g_OKFlag = True
    Me.Hide
    If txt_StaffID = "New" Then
```

```
        ' Get the staff number counter
        SQL$ = "Select * from Counter where TableName = 'Staff'"
        Set ScratchDS = MyDB.OpenRecordset(SQL$, dbOpenDynaset)

        g_CustomerID = ScratchDS!CountNum
        ' increment staff number
        ScratchDS.Edit
        ScratchDS!CountNum = g_CustomerID + 1
        ScratchDS.Update

        ' Create Staff member record
        Set ScratchTable = MyDB.OpenRecordset("Staff", dbOpenTable)
        ScratchTable.AddNew
        ScratchTable!StaffID = g_CustomerID
        ScratchTable.Update
        ' Create Recordset for editing
        SQL$ = "Select * from Staff where StaffID = " & g_CustomerID
        Set StaffDS = MyDB.OpenRecordset(SQL$, dbOpenDynaset)
    End If
    ScreentoRecord StaffDS
End Sub
```

Sub Form_Load ()

This routine calls the `LoadStaffPopup()` routine to fill the `cmb_Staff` combo control. The combo box is used to select the Supervisor for the selected staff member. The Load routine also fills the Location combo box to select the location where the staff member works.

```
Private Sub Form_Load()
    LoadLocationPopup
    LoadStaffPopup
End Sub
```

Sub Form_Activate ()

The `Activate()` routine checks the `g_LoadCustFlag` (which is actually used to load a Staff member) and the `g_ClearCustFlag` (which signals a new Staff record). If either of these flags are set to TRUE, the appropriate routine is activated. Both flags are cleared at the end of the routine.

```
Private Sub Form_Activate()
    If g_LoadCustFlag = True Then
        SQL$ = "Select * from Staff where StaffID = " & g_CustomerID
        Set StaffDS = MyDB.OpenRecordset(SQL$, dbOpenDynaset)
        RecordToScreen StaffDS
    ElseIf g_ClearCustFlag = True Then
        SetupDefaultScreen
    End If
    g_LoadCustFlag = False
    g_ClearCustFlag = False
    ' Place cursor in first field
    txt_FirstName.SetFocus
End Sub
```

Summary

The application is now complete. The Management Client can now be used to examine reports on the state of sales, purchasing, Pseudo Server status, and management decision support factors. This client demonstrates the use of the graph control, the grid control, advanced SQL querying, the tab control, and database techniques such as SQL aggregate functions, record searching, and multi-table joins are demonstrated. Studying the code for these techniques will supply a foundation of code on which to build decision support systems and other database reporting system. In Chapter 19, "Excel Additions to the Client/Server System," the Management client is augmented to use Microsoft Excel to provide further reporting capabilities.

If you've created the tables in Chapter 10 and entered the default values, press the F5 key to execute the program. To compile the program as a standalone .EXE, make sure that you either place the .INI file in the same directory that the application is executing or you change the path in the Manage Form Load() event routine to search in the new directory.

14

Pseudo Server

The Pseudo Server application is an application running on the server that watches the database and returns information to the system administrator and the various client applications (see Figure 14.1). The Pseudo Server does not act in the capacity of a true server, because it does not send information to the client programs directly. Instead, the PServer application uses the common database to which the clients are connected to provide information.

FIGURE 14.1.

The Pseudo Server screen.

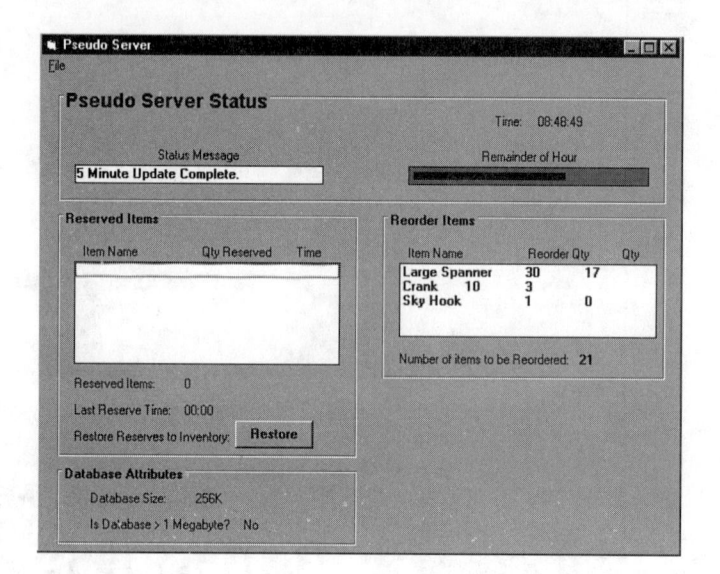

A server's job is often to free the individual client programs from tedious processing, which the server can do because it has more processing power, resources, or time. Our PServer, for example, watches for reserved items that are suspended in the reserve column. Normally, if an invoice is canceled, the Sales client program returns any reserved items back to the inventory. What happens if the machine is reset or turned off before a cancel is done? The items remain locked in the reserve column.

The PServer has the task of periodically checking the reserve fields of the sales items. If the reservation has remained for over an hour, the PServer assumes that the transaction has been aborted or that the client program can no longer fulfill its duty. It moves the items back to the general inventory.

This application is just one example of the myriad of applications that can use the Timer control for periodic processing. This application timer activates only once every 5 minutes, using very little processor time or resources.

The PServer can fulfill tasks that would be very complicated to do from the individual client applications. For example, the PServer can run on only the server machine and be given privileged access to various tables or system resources. It can then provide clients with summary information that is not restricted. Be careful, though, when you implement any type of program that bridges secure data sources. You don't want the program to become a gateway for inappropriate access of information.

A PServer-type program can be used for any time-based application in which it would be inconvenient or ineffective to implement in the client software and unavailable as a server feature. It can even be made to do other tasks, such as watching the phone line and accepting remote modem-based updates. The application possibilities are nearly limitless.

The PServer program can access any of the tables in the database. Because of the role fulfilled by the Pseudo Server, it is granted access to any table that it needs to complete its job. In the case of this implementation, all the tables can be accessed and used.

> **TIP**
>
> In a real application, such a program should be limited to only the databases that it needs. Otherwise, it becomes a gateway for potential security problems.

Starting the Pseudo Server Project

The PServer program in our example is stored in the directory PSERVER. Use Explorer to create a folder for the program. It is not crucial to name the directory the same as we have done; however, make sure that the .INI file is stored in the same directory. In a real world application, the application's .INI file would be placed in the \WINDOWS\ directory.

For the sake of simplicity, because we are not using an installer program, the Pseudo Server looks for the .INI file in the same folder in which the application executed. This also provides a sample routine, GetAppPath, in the GLOBAL.BAS file that you can reuse for various applications in the future.

To create the PServer, start a new project. If you double-clicked the Visual Basic application, a default project and form should be showing. Otherwise, select New Project under the File menu. Start by saving the project. You should have already created the various necessary directories as described in Chapter 10. If you haven't, do that now.

Select the Save Project option under the File menu. You are first prompted for the name of the base form. Select the CS_VB\PSERVER directory and name the form PSEUDO.FRM. Name the project PSEUDO.VBP. When all the files have been added to the project, the project window should look like the one shown in Figure 14.2.

FIGURE 14.2.
The PSERVER.VBP project.

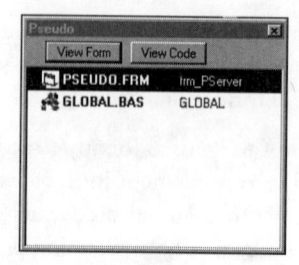

Creating the .INI File

Before the application can be executed, you must construct the .INI file. The INI file will hold various parameters used by the PServer application. For a complete explanation of creating an .INI file, see Chapter 11, "Sales Client."

When you create the .INI file, the name of the file should match the name of the final .EXE application file. For example, an application with a filename PSERVER.EXE will have an .INI file named PSERVER.INI. Open the Notepad application and type the .INI file in Listing 14.1. Save the .INI file in the PSERVER folder as PSERVER.INI.

Listing 14.1. PSERVER.INI.

```
; PServer.INI

[Parameters]

LocationID = 1
DefaultStaffID = 1
StandardTerms = 0
SalesTax = .07
Freight = 3.00
DataLocation = Access
 [Access]
DSN=
DBName=c:\clntsrvr\widgetco.mdb
DBServer=
```

Creating the Form

The first step in building an application is drawing the form. The PServer application uses only a single form because a server's work is mostly done in the background. There is little user interaction. Execute Visual Basic, and begin constructing the PServer form on the default Form1.

Creating the PSERVER.FRM

The Pseudo Server form consists primarily of labels and indicators used to let the system administrator know what is happening. Figure 14.3 shows what the completed form looks like after all the controls have been added. Figure 14.4 shows the Name properties of all the individual controls. Create each control on the form, and set the properties to match the properties listed in the table for that property.

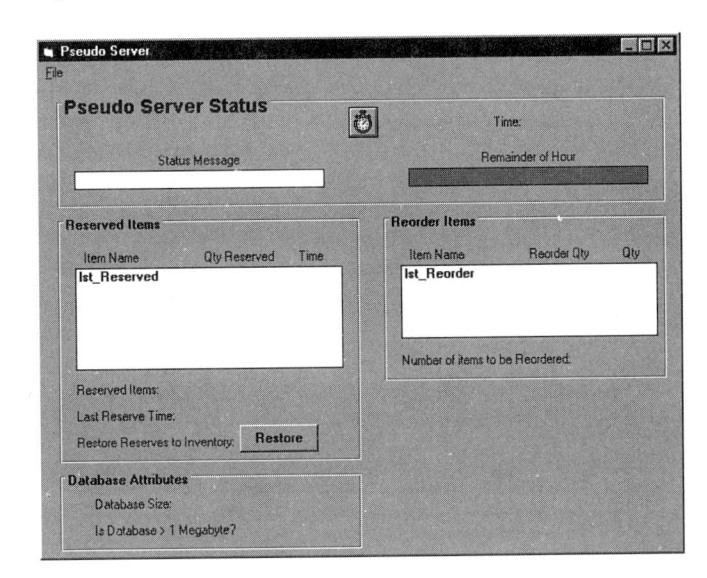

FIGURE 14.3.
The Pseudo Server form.

> **NOTE**
>
> The space on the form in the lower right corner is intentionally left blank. This space is left open to accommodate progress indicators and controls for the remote additions to the Pseudo Server presented in Chapter 26, "Remote Client/Server Access." Remote capabilities are added to receive a modem call and exchange information with a remote client.

To some of the labels that appear clear in Figure 14.3, we have added callouts in Figure 14.4 to describe them. However, your final form should appear like the one in Figure 14.3.

Table 14.1 contains a list of all the controls that need to be added to the form. The table holding the control's property data is listed as well as the location at which the control should be placed. For example, if the location is listed as fra_Attributes, the item should be created in that frame. If the location is listed as Form, place the control on the form itself.

Part II ■ *Constructing a Basic Client/Server System*

FIGURE 14.4.
The Pseudo Server form with controls described.

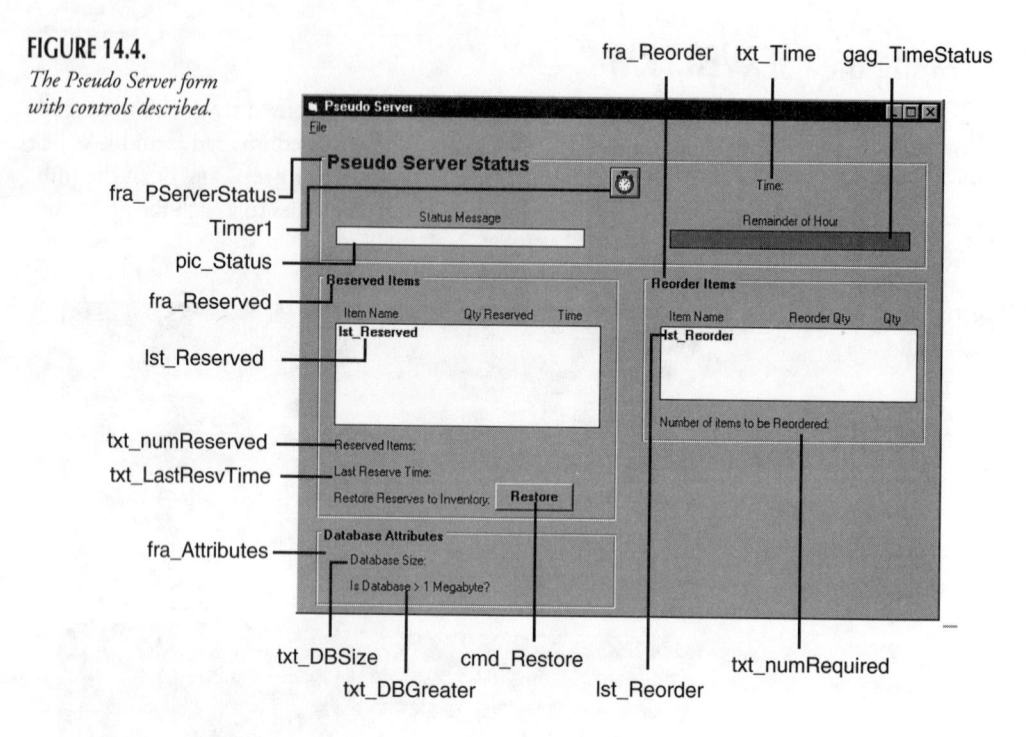

Table 14.1. Controls for the PServer form.

Table	Control	Location
Table 14.2	Form frm_PServer	
Table 14.3	SSFrame fra_Attributes	fra_Attributes
Table 14.4	Label txt_DBGreater	fra_Attributes
Table 14.5	Label txt_DBSize	fra_Attributes
Table 14.6	Label Timer Timer1	fra_PServerStatus
Table 14.7	SSFrame fra_PServerStatus	fra_PServerStatus
Table 14.8	Gauge gag_TimeStatus	fra_PServerStatus
Table 14.9	PictureBox pic_Status	fra_PServerStatus
Table 14.10	Label txt_Time	fra_PServerStatus
Table 14.11	SSFrame fra_Reorder	fra_Reorder
Table 14.12	ListBox lst_Reorder	fra_Reorder
Table 14.13	Label txt_numRequired	fra_Reorder
Table 14.14	SSFrame fra_Reserved	fra_Reserved
Table 14.15	CommandButton cmd_Restore	fra_Reserved

Table	Control	Location
Table 14.16	ListBox lst_Reserved	fra_Reserved
Table 14.17	Label txt_LastResvTime	fra_Reserved
Table 14.18	Label txt_numReserved	fra_Reserved

Table 14.2. Form frm_PServer.

BackColor	&H00C0C0C0&
Caption	Pseudo Server
ClientHeight	805
ClientLeftt	55
ClientTop	455
ClientWidtth	955
Height	495
Left	95
LinkTopic	orm1
ScaleHeight	805
ScaleWidth	955
Top	25
Width	075

Table 14.3. SSFrame fra_Attributes.

Caption	Database Attributes
ForeColor	&H00000000&
Height	1335
Left	4800
TabIndex	25
Top	4200
Width	3975

Table 14.4. Label txt_DBGreater.

BackColor	&H00C0C0C0&
FontBold	0'False
FontItalic	0'False
FontName	MS Sans Serif
FontSize	8.25
FontStrikethru	0'False
FontUnderline	0'False
Height	255
Left	2640
TabIndex	29
Top	720
Width	735

Table 14.5. Label txt_DBSize.

BackColor	&H00C0C0C0&
FontBold	0'False
FontItalic	0'False
FontName	MS Sans Serif
FontSize	8.25
FontStrikethru	0'False
FontUnderline	0'False
Height	255
Left	1920
TabIndex	27
Top	360
Width	1575

Table 14.6. Label Timer Timer1.

Interval	60000
Left	4320
Top	360

Table 14.7. SSFrame fra_PServerStatus.

Caption	Pseudo Server Status
FontBold	-1 'True
FontItalic	0 'False
FontName	Arial
FontSize	13.5
FontStrikethru	0 'False
FontUnderline	0 'False
ForeColor	&H00000080&
Height	1575
Left	240
TabIndex	6
Top	120
Width	8535

Table 14.8. Gauge gag_TimeStatus.

Autosize	-1 'True
BackColor	&H00808080&
Height	255
InnerBottom	5
InnerLeft	5
InnerRight	5
InnerTop	5
Left	4920
Max	60
NeedleWidth	1
TabIndex	8
Top	1080
Width	3375

Table 14.9. PictureBox pic_Status.

Height	255
Left	240
ScaleHeight	225
ScaleWidth	3465
TabIndex	7
Top	1080
Width	3495

Table 14.10. Label txt_Time.

BackColor	&H00C0C0C0&
FontBold	0'False
FontItalic	0'False
FontName	MS Sans Serif
FontSize	8.25
FontStrikethru	0'False
FontUnderline	0'False
Height	255
Left	6720
TabIndex	17
Top	360
Width	1695

Table 14.11. SSFrame fra_Reorder.

Caption	Reorder Items
Height	2295
Left	4800
TabIndex	4
Top	1800
Width	3975

Table 14.12. ListBox lst_Reorder.

Height	1005
Left	240
TabIndex	5
Top	720
Width	3615

Table 14.13. Label txt_numRequired.

BackColor	&H00C0C0C0&
Height	255
Left	2760
TabIndex	24
Top	1920
Width	855

Table 14.14. SSFrame fra_Reserved.

Caption	Reserved Items
Height	3735
Left	240
TabIndex	2
Top	1800
Width	4215

Table 14.15. CommandButton cmd_Restore.

Caption	Restore
Height	375
Left	2520
TabIndex	11
Top	3120
Width	1095

Table 14.16. ListBox lst_Reserved.

Height	1395
Left	240
TabIndex	3
Top	720
Width	3735

Table 14.17. Label txt_LastResvTime.

BackColor	&H00C0C0C0&
FontBold	0'False
FontItalic	0'False
FontName	MS Sans Serif
FontSize	8.25
FontStrikethru	0'False
FontUnderline	0'False
Height	255
Left	1800
TabIndex	19
Top	2760
Width	1215

Table 14.18. Label txt_numReserved.

BackColor	&H00C0C0C0&
FontBold	0'False
FontItalic	0'False
FontName	MS Sans Serif
FontSize	8.25
FontStrikethru	0'False
FontUnderline	0'False
Height	255
Left	1800
TabIndex	18
Top	2400
Width	1215

Adding Code to PSERVER.FRM

The PServer form is used to provide information to the system administrator. It is not made for regular interaction. First add the general declarations; they define all the variables used by the application. Next enter all the general routines, which are accessed by controls on the form. Then enter all the code that is actually placed inside the various controls to handle events.

General Declarations

Enter the variables in Listing 14.2 in the general declarations section. They include variables that track the timer for extended durations and a recordset variable. Most of the variables used by the PServer routines actively use local variables to ensure that all the various routines don't misuse a value and collide. Note that with any server, reliability and stability are usually emphasized over speed and convenience.

Listing 14.2. General declarations.

```
Dim TimerExtend As Integer
Dim InvoicesDS As Recordset
```

General Routines

The following routines are added to the general section of the form. Code placed in the general section is available to all the routines within the form. Enter the code after selecting Procedure... under the Insert menu to create each routine.

Sub DoFiveMinUpdate()

The `DoFiveMinUpdate` routine is activated every five minutes by the Timer1 control. This routine is constructed for short-term updates. It calls three other routines: `FindReservedItems`, `FindReorderItems`, and `FindDBInfo`. These routines actually update the various parts of the form and check for necessary events.

```
Private Sub DoFiveMinUpdate()
    FindReservedItems
    FindReorderItems
    FindDBInfo
End Sub
```

Sub DoHourUpdate()

This routine is called once an hour. The long duration between calls makes this routine ideal for checking data that needs only hourly updating—more would be overkill. It also provides a place to put processor intensive routines so that the server is inconvenienced only once an hour.

The beep is included so that you can hear when the activation occurs. The `RestoreReservedItems()` routine checks for items that have remained on reserve for over an hour and returns them to the general inventory.

```
Private Sub DoHourUpdate()
    ' This beep is just for demonstration purposes. Feel free to delete
    Beep
    RestoreReservedItems
End Sub
```

Sub FindDBInfo()

The `FindDBInfo()` routine is called every five minutes to check the size of the database. This routine could do nearly anything; it is simply an example of how the Pseudo Server program can watch the server and return information not normally available. The remaining free space in an SQL database could be examined to ensure that there is never danger of a partition full error.

If the routine finds that the WidgetCo database is over 1000K, the `DiskCriticalStatus` flag in the PServer table is marked `True`. This enables other clients with access to the PServer table, such as the Management client, to examine the summary information stored there.

```
Private Sub FindDBInfo()
    Dim ScratchDS As Recordset
    Dim DBSize As Long

    DBSize = Int(FileLen(g_DBName) / 1024)
    txt_DBSize = Str$(DBSize) & "K"

    SQL$ = "Select * from PServer"
    Set ScratchDS = MyDB.OpenRecordset(SQL$, dbOpenDynaset)

    ScratchDS.Edit
    If DBSize > 1000 Then
        ' Set flag to indicate disk condition
        ScratchDS!DiskCriticalStatus = True
        txt_DBGreater = "Yes"
    Else
        ScratchDS!DiskCriticalStatus = False
        txt_DBGreater = "No"
    End If
    ScratchDS.Update
End Sub
```

Sub FindReorderItems()

This routine checks the various parts in inventory and determines whether they need to be reordered. A snapshot of the Inventory_Parts table is used with a WHERE clause to determine whether the `OnHand` quantity is lower than `ReOrderQty`. All the items that need reordering are returned in the `ScratchSS` resultant set. Each reorder item is added to the Pseudo Server list box control, lst_Reorder.

Also, the ReOrderStatus flag in the PServer is set if there are any items to reorder. During each load, the Purchasing client checks this flag and notifies the user if reorders are required. This enables the Purchase client to do one simple table access instead of having to check the entire data set with each load. This is exactly the type of work for which the Pseudo Server is made—simplifying the processing needs of the other clients.

```
Private Sub FindReorderItems()
    Dim ScratchSS As Recordset
    Dim ScratchDS As Recordset
    Dim numRequired As Integer

    SQL$ = "Select * from Inventory_Parts WHERE OnHand < ReOrderQty"
    Set ScratchSS = MyDB.OpenRecordset(SQL$, dbOpenSnapshot)

    lst_Reorder.Clear
    numRequired = 0

    Do Until ScratchSS.EOF
        ' Add entry to list box
        lst_Reorder.AddItem ScratchSS!Description & Chr$(9) &
        Str$(ScratchSS!ReOrderQty) & Chr$(9) & Str$(ScratchSS!OnHand)
        ' Keep running total of reorder items
        numRequired = numRequired + (ScratchSS!ReOrderQty - ScratchSS!OnHand)
        ScratchSS.MoveNext
    Loop
    txt_numRequired = numRequired

    ' Set ReOrderStatus to TRUE if any items need to be reordered
    SQL$ = "Select * from PServer"
    Set ScratchDS = MyDB.OpenRecordset(SQL$, dbOpenDynaset)
    ScratchDS.Edit
    If numRequired > 0 Then
        ScratchDS!ReOrderStatus = True
    Else
        ScratchDS!ReOrderStatus = False
    End If
    ScratchDS.Update
End Sub
```

Sub FindReservedItems()

This routine is used to check all the reserved items and to display them in the lst_Reserved Pseudo Server list box. A snapshot, ScratchSS, is created to find all the Sales items that have quantities held in their reserve columns. The reserved items, quantities of reservation, and reserve times are displayed.

The last reserve time is also displayed so that the administrator of the Pseudo Server can determine whether there is currently activity on the client/server system. The item with the most recent reserved time is probably from the most recently updated invoice.

```
Private Sub FindReservedItems()
    Dim ScratchSS As Snapshot
    Dim numReserved As Integer
    Dim LastResvTime
```

```
            SQL$ = "Select * from Inventory_Sales WHERE Reserved > 0"
            Set ScratchSS = MyDB.OpenRecordset(SQL$, dbOpenSnapshot)

            lst_Reserved.Clear
            numReserved = 0
            LastResvTime = 0

            Do Until ScratchSS.EOF
                ' Add reserved item entry to list box
                lst_Reserved.AddItem ScratchSS!Description & Chr$(9) & _
                    Str$(ScratchSS!Reserved) & Chr$(9) & _
                    Format$(ScratchSS!LastResvTime, "hh:nn")
    numReserved = numReserved + ScratchSS!Reserved
                ' Keep track of the latest reserve time
                If ScratchSS!LastResvTime > LastResvTime Then
                    LastResvTime = ScratchSS!LastResvTime
                End If
                ScratchSS.MoveNext
            Loop

            txt_numReserved = numReserved
            txt_LastResvTime = Format$(LastResvTime, "hh:nn")
End Sub
Private Sub FindReservedItems()
            Dim ScratchSS As Snapshot
            Dim numReserved As Integer
            Dim LastResvTime

            SQL$ = "Select * from Inventory_Sales WHERE Reserved > 0"
            Set ScratchSS = MyDB.OpenRecordset(SQL$, dbOpenSnapshot)

            lst_Reserved.Clear
            numReserved = 0
            LastResvTime = 0

            Do Until ScratchSS.EOF
                ' Add reserved item entry to list box
                lst_Reserved.AddItem ScratchSS!Description & Chr$(9) & _
                    Str$(ScratchSS!Reserved) & Chr$(9) & _
                    Format$(ScratchSS!LastResvTime, "hh:nn")
    numReserved = numReserved + ScratchSS!Reserved
                ' Keep track of the latest reserve time
                If ScratchSS!LastResvTime > LastResvTime Then
                    LastResvTime = ScratchSS!LastResvTime
                End If
                ScratchSS.MoveNext
            Loop

            txt_numReserved = numReserved
            txt_LastResvTime = Format$(LastResvTime, "hh:nn")
End Sub
```

Sub RestoreReservedItems()

This routine is called once an hour to flush all the items reserved for over an hour back into inventory. It assumes that after an hour of reservation, the system that reserved the items is either inactive or has been reset without revoking the items that it reserved.

FlushTime is the time prior to this moment that reserve times are checked against. If LastResvTime is older than FlushTime, the items are returned to inventory.

> **NOTE**
>
> To determine FlushTime, we used the Visual Basic DateAdd function. This function enables a program to add or subtract a particular quantity to a date or time value. In this example, DateAdd subtracts one hour (h) from the value returned by the function Now. Using this routine simplifies the difficulties that you experience when you manipulate dates such as leap years and the roll-over at midnight.

A recordset that contains all the records with LastResvTime values older than FlushTime is created. The Do...Until loop retrieves each record of the resultant set, adds the reserved items to the inventory, and resets LastResvTime to null.

```
Private Sub RestoreReservedItems()
    Dim ScratchDS As Recordset

    ' FlushTime is equal to 1 hour before the present
    FlushTime = DateAdd("h", -1, Now)

    ' Find all items that need to be restored
    SQL$ = "Select * from Inventory_Sales WHERE LastResvTime < #" & FlushTime & "#"
    Set ScratchDS = MyDB.OpenRecordset(SQL$, dbOpenDynaset)
    ScratchDS.LockEdits = False

    Do Until ScratchDS.EOF
        ScratchDS.Edit
        ' Return reserved items to onhand
        ScratchDS!OnHand = ScratchDS!OnHand + ScratchDS!Reserved
        ScratchDS!Reserved = 0
        ScratchDS!LastResvTime = Null
        ScratchDS.Update
        ScratchDS.MoveNext
    Loop
End Sub
```

Control Code

All the code below must be added to the individual controls. Simply double-click the control on the PServer form; the relevant code box will appear. In the drop-down combo labeled Proc:, select the event whose label the code matches the section heading below.

Sub cmd_Restore_Click()

The Restore command button on the PServer form provides a way for the administrator to return items to inventory on hand. Clicking the Restore button executes the following code, which restores all the reserved items to inventory on hand without waiting for the proper restore update time.

```
Private Sub cmd_Restore_Click()
    ' Find all items that need to be restored
    SQL$ = "Select * from Inventory_Sales WHERE Reserved > 0"
    Set ScratchDS = MyDB.OpenRecordset(SQL$, dbOpenDynaset)
    ScratchDS.LockEdits = False

    ' Return all reserved items to inventory
    Do Until ScratchDS.EOF
       ScratchDS.Edit
       ScratchDS!OnHand = ScratchDS!OnHand + ScratchDS!Reserved
       ScratchDS!Reserved = 0
       ScratchDS!LastResvTime = Null
       ScratchDS.Update
       ScratchDS.MoveNext
    Loop
End Sub
```

Sub Form_Load()

This `Load()` routine sets up the variables and display characteristics. It calls the GLOBAL.BAS routine, `CenterForm`, to place `Me` (frm_PServer) in the center of the screen. The `TimerExtend` variable is set to zero minutes so that the timer can begin timing updates. The location of the database is read from the .INI file and is stored in a global variable (g_DBName). The main database object structure is created to serve as a basis for future dynaset and snapshot construction. General dynasets are created for global use.

Finally, the tab-stop values for the two list box controls are set up. The list box lst_Reserved displays reserved items and lst_ReOrder displays all the items in the Inventory_Parts table that need to be reordered. Setting tab stops allows a list box to have multiple columns.

```
Private Sub Form_Load()
   Dim NumOftabs As Integer
   ReDim Tabs(3) As Long

   CenterForm Me

   ' Reset counter for incremental timing
   TimerExtend = 0

   ' Setup path of INI file
   INIPath = GetAppPath() & "Pseudo.INI"

   ' Set path for custom INI for Access engine
   DBEngine.INIPath = INIPath

   ' Read global parameters for default values
   g_DataLocation = ReadINI("Parameters", "DataLocation", INIPath)
   g_DBName = ReadINI(g_DataLocation, "DBName", INIPath)

   Set MyDB = OpenDatabase(g_DBName, False, False)

   SQL$ = "Select * from Sales"
   Set InvoicesDS = MyDB.OpenRecordset(SQL$, dbOpenDynaset)
   InvoicesDS.LockEdits = False
   InvoicesDS.MoveLast
```

```
    ' Setup tabs for list boxes
    NumOftabs = 3
    Tabs(0) = 80
    Tabs(1) = 115
    Tabs(2) = 190

    ' Use Windows API call to set tab stops
    temp = SendMessage(lst_Reserved.hWnd, LB_SETTABSTOPS, NumOftabs, Tabs(0))
    temp = SendMessage(lst_Reorder.hWnd, LB_SETTABSTOPS, NumOftabs, Tabs(0))
End Sub
```

Sub Form_Unload(Cancel As Integer)

The Unload event contains an End command to close the program and to terminate execution. This prevents a phantom application problem. For more information on the Unload event, refer to the information box provided in Chapter 11, "Sales Client."

```
Private Sub Form_Unload(Cancel As Integer)
    End
End Sub
```

Sub Timer1_Timer()

The timer is the crucial control that makes the Pseudo Server easy to implement. The Timer control automatically activates and calls the Timer() routine at intervals specified with the Interval property.

Unfortunately, the Timer control has a maximum interval setting of approximately a minute. This is too frequent a duration for the Pseudo Server to work effectively in the background without stealing unnecessary processing power from the server machine. To resolve this problem, use a TimerExtend variable.

By setting the interval to activate every minute—a value of 60000—you can add 1 to the TimerExtend variable. This turns the TimerExtend into a minute counter, which enables the program to activate a routine at any long interval.

You can update the clock on the screen every minute so that the Pseudo Server looks active. TimerExtend is divided by five, and the routine subtracts the integer of the division from the floating point result of this difference. If the interval is not a five-minute interval, the result of the subtraction is a fraction. If it is a five-minute interval, the result is zero and various routines are activated. The status bar is updated as well as the TimeStatus gauge. The DoFiveMinUpdate() routine is then activated.

If TimerExtend exceeds 60, the hour update is activated and the TimerExtend variable is reset to zero to begin the cycle again.

```
Private Sub Timer1_Timer()
    TimerExtend = TimerExtend + 1
    txt_Time = Time$
    If (TimerExtend / 5) - Int(TimerExtend / 5) = 0 Then    ' 5 Minutes
        pic_Status.Cls
```

```
        pic_Status.Print "5 Minute Update..."

        ' Set status bar to show new progress
        gag_TimeStatus.Value = TimerExtend

        DoFiveMinUpdate

        ' Update status message
        pic_Status.Cls
        pic_Status.Print "5 Minute Update Complete."
    End If
    If TimerExtend > 60 Then      ' 60 Minutes
        TimerExtend = 0
        pic_Status.Cls
        pic_Status.Print "1 Hour Update..."

        DoHourUpdate

        ' Display Hourly Values
        pic_Status.Cls
        pic_Status.Print "1 Hour Update Complete."
    End If
End Sub
```

Menu Items Code

To enter the following code, select the item from the menu on the form. In this case, there is only one menu item, ExitItem. ExitItem is used to quit the PServer application and to clear the memory that it was occupying.

> **TIP**
>
> In every application, try to include the File menu with the Exit command. Every commercial program includes this option. By including it in all programs, the user always knows where to look to exit the program.

```
Sub ExitItem_Click ()
    End
End Sub
```

Summary

The application is now complete. The Pseudo Server is unique and differs greatly from the other clients you've constructed. It operates autonomously with little administrator interaction. The PServer can return items held in the reserved columns back to on hand inventory, track reorder items, set flags for the clients to examine conditions of the database, and provide the administrator with general information on the system. Database techniques such as SQL aggregate statements, date field checking, optimistic record locking, dynaset creation, record edits, record searching, batch record changes, and joins are demonstrated.

The Pseudo Server also uses the Timer control to provide a model for timed updates and queries. By scheduling timed automatic maintenance of the database, the engine could be used for nearly anything. Reports could be generated at specific intervals, remote data synchronization could take place, or a variety of other recurring events. The application also provides a suitable foundation for extension. In Chapter 24, "Creating an OLE Server," you will extend the PServer application to be an OLE Automation Server providing controlled information on the database to OLE Automation clients. In Chapter 26, "Remote Client/Server Access," the application is again extended to answer the modem on the system and provide remote interaction with a client over the telephone lines. These two applications turn the Pseudo Server into an actual server of information.

If you created the tables in Chapter 10 and entered the default values, pressing the F5 key executes the program. To compile the program as a standalone .EXE, make sure that either the .INI file is placed in the same directory in which the application is executing or change the path in the PServer Form Load() event routine to search in the new directory.

> **NOTE**
>
> The timer value has an interval set at 60000 milliseconds, which means it is activated once a minute. For testing, we recommend that you decrease this amount to 1000 so that real-time results can be observed.

15

Execution and Functioning of the Client/Server System

The client/server system is now complete. Each individual client can access, edit, and store data. The pseudo server can autonomously monitor the database and the necessary transactions. The tables are normalized and accessible through the JET engine or ODBC calls.

Although the construction of each application has been explained, the actual use of the system has not been described. This chapter explains how each client is used by members of the enterprise. All the functions and menu items are detailed.

Setup

This section explains how each client application can be configured. It includes compilation, modifying the proper .INI files, and placing all the files in their specific folders. Setting up the clients on a Windows NT Advanced Server-based network is also explained.

Creating the .EXE Files

Test to make sure that each of the individual programs works independently under Visual Basic. Select all the options and menus to make sure that everything is working properly. After each one has been tested, exit Visual Basic to clear all the excess data structures.

> **NOTE**
>
> Before you create an .EXE file for any project, be sure to quit Visual Basic and re-execute it to bring the project up fresh before you compile. Visual Basic is notorious for including lots of junk or extra structures in an .EXE file that was created after the project was executed. Data remaining in memory that was not cleaned out after execution was completed is written into the final .EXE file.
>
> The size of the final .EXE file can be up to 20 percent smaller if it is generated from a clean boot. Therefore, for speed, size, and safety, make sure that you quit and re-execute Visual Basic between each final compile.

Execute Visual Basic again so that the first project can be compiled. Load the SALES.VBP project file. You might want to add an icon of some type to the main form (under the Icon property of the form) so that the icon is used when the application is added to the taskbar or shown on the disk. If you do not select an icon, Visual Basic uses the generic form icon.

Under the File Menu, select the Make EXE file... option. Click the Options button to display the Options dialog box. For an Application Title, type `Sales Client`. For the icon field selection, select the main form. Click the Auto Increment version number option. This way, every time a compile is made, a new version number is automatically placed in the .EXE. Also enter any comments about the project. Click the OK button when you are finished.

Type `Sales.EXE` for the final filename. When you click the OK button, the file is compiled into the final .EXE file. Give the .EXE files any name you want. However, make sure that the .INI filename matches that of the .EXE. We gave the .EXE filenames that parallel the project names. For example, Sales.VBP has Sales.EXE.

Follow the same steps, and compile and save the .EXE files of the other three projects. Save the Purchasing client as Purchase.EXE, the Management client as Manage.EXE, and the Pseudo Server as PServer.EXE. These are the final .EXE files for distribution in the client/server system.

TIP

Although all the support files are required for full distribution, changes to the main project require you to distribute only a new .EXE file. This enables the network to be used to distribute updates across all the client machines without a complicated new install. Using a network install saves a company's IS department a great amount of time.

Putting Files in the Correct Place

Each Client program should be stored in its own folder or directory. This keeps clutter and confusion to a minimum. Place each compiled .EXE file in the proper folder shown in Figure 15.1. The main CLNTSRVR directory and the various application folders were created in Chapter 10, "Table Construction." SALES.EXE is stored in the Sales directory, and so forth. Place SALES.EXE and SALES.INI in the \CLNTSRVR directory. Make sure that the matching .INI files exist in the same directory as the application.

FIGURE 15.1.
Client/server application directories.

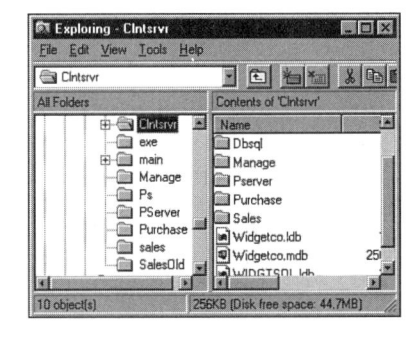

Now make sure that the WIDGETCO.MDB database file is in the \CLNTSRVR directory, where all the clients can access it. The system should function correctly now. After adding all the .EXE files, you can execute any of the clients.

If you want to use the database on a network drive, copy the WIDGETCO.MDB to the network drive. Each .INI file for the client programs must be changed to be redirected to the new path. The central drive also must be shared so that each client machine has access to it.

> **TIP**
>
> It is often a good idea to include a README text file that will be distributed with each install. The README file should provide recent information on the client. This file should be placed in the application folder. Users can also look at the README file for known bugs, updated features, and incompatibilities.

Creating Installation Disks

If each client will be executing on a separate Client machine, installation disks need to be created. Using the Application Setup wizard, you can create install disks for each client. If you don't know how to use the Setup wizard, see your Visual Basic manuals or Chapter 1, "Overview of Visual Basic," for a complete explanation.

Modifying the .INI Files

Each .INI file contains various information relating to the default configuration when the application executes. For example, the location is coded into the .INI file as a parameter. A client program is rarely moved from location to location. The semipermanence of such a variable is called for, instead of there being a combo box selection in each application.

> **NOTE**
>
> In creating parameters used by a program, there are three basic levels of permanence: constants where the value is hard-coded into the .EXE, .INI parameters that are semipermanent because they require some expertise to modify, and program preferences that can be changed on screen or in a dialog box. Consider placing parameters that might need to be changed in the .INI. Then they can easily be either hard-coded or added to the user interface.

All the parts of the .INI file are divided into different sections. The Sales.INI shown in listing 15.1 is divided into two sections: parameters and access. *Parameters* define variables that the program uses on execution to startup in a default state. The *access section* determines the information about the data source.

Each client program has its own .INI file. Therefore, you can change the `LocationID`, `DefaultStaffID`, `StandardTerms`, and so on, for the individual station. The added flexibility of modifying parameters on site without a recompile is substantial. You can also customize your installation program to make automatic modifications when the client program is installed.

> **WARNING**
>
> Having information such as sales tax, standard terms, and other values stored in an individual .INI file is a double-edged sword. It allows individual values to be set (for instance, if sales tax varies by county) if the clients are in different geographic regions, for example. However, when one of these values changes (state sales tax, for example), all the other similar clients must be coordinated. Therefore, in particular situations, it may be more beneficial to create a table in the central database that holds these values. Centralizing these values allows a single change to the table to be automatically reflected in all of the clients accessing the system. Whether these values should be centralized or dispersed depends on the system that needs to be deployed.

The `DBName` parameter under the [Access] section must be modified to suit the database name and the directory in which the database will be located. If a network drive is used, simply set this parameter to the path of the drive. If the database file is moved to a different directory, the `DBName` parameter must be altered to reflect this change.

Listing 15.1 is provided as a brief overview of the structure of the files in the event that you don't review the actual construction details, but instead execute the finished applications.

Listing 15.1. SALES.INI.

```
; Sales.INI

[Parameters]

LocationID = 1
DefaultStaffID = 1
StandardTerms = 0
SalesTax = .07
Freight = 3.00
DataLocation = Access

[Access]
DSN=
DBName=c:\clntsrvr\widgetco.mdb
DBServer=
```

Setting Up the System on a Network

Setting up the client systems on a network is as simple as setting up the proper networked and shared drive and changing the .INI files. This can be done with any common file server, such as Novell Netware or Windows NT Advanced Server. The system can be set up using peer-to-peer file sharing on a system such as Windows for Workgroups or Windows 95, but we do not recommend it. For more information on network and their software, see Chapter 3, "Networks (Client/Server Foundation)."

The file server runs the Pseudo Server and holds the main database file (WIDGETCO.MDB) that will be shared. The Windows 3.1, Windows for Workgroups, Windows 95, or Windows NT can be used to run the Management, Sales, and Purchasing clients.

> **NOTE**
>
> A Windows NT Advanced Server can be configured as either a normal server or the domain controller. If the server machine is the sole or primary server on your network, you will want to make it the domain server.
>
> Unfortunately, for security reasons, once the Advanced Server has been configured for either a server or a domain controller, there is no way to reconfigure it without completely reinstalling the entire server. This eliminates any users, groups, and other settings that you may have created.
>
> If you have yet to install Windows NT Advanced Server, make sure that you have decided what role it should fill. If the server is to be the only server on the LAN, configure it as a primary domain controller.

Execution

Each of the client applications may execute separately. The following sections describe the use of the particular client. Note that the connection with the database is made at the beginning of the client program execution and is maintained throughout the program's activation. Any connection problems will, therefore, be apparent as soon as the application is double-clicked.

Using the Sales Client

The Sales client is used to create customer invoices and to record the sale of various items. The main screen is the invoice screen on which a customer is selected and sales items are entered (see Figure 15.2).

FIGURE 15.2.

A blank sales invoice screen.

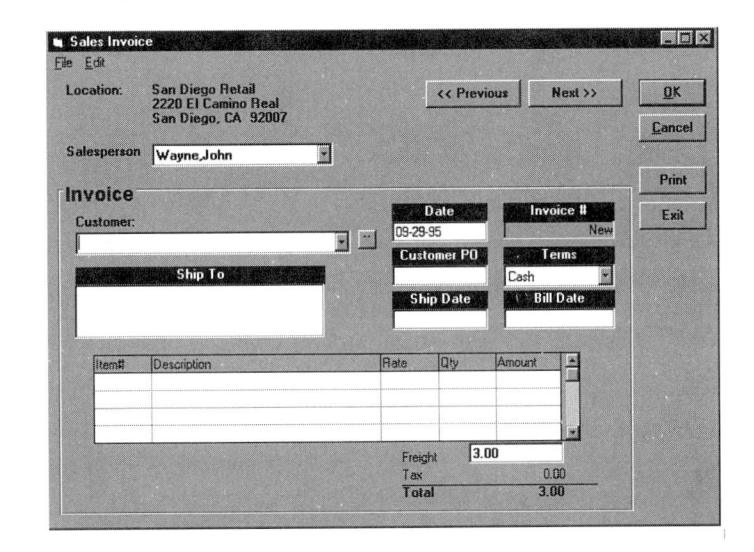

The Location field at the top of the screen shows the address of the location where the sale occurs. This location is specified in the .INI file for this client. This location name and address are printed on the finished sales invoice.

The Salesperson combo box is used to select the staff member making the sale for this invoice. All the available staff members are automatically added to this list. The default staff member is designated in the .INI file. Any employee who is selected will remain the selected employee until the program is exited or a new invoice is written with another employee. Therefore, an employee can select his name and it will remain selected while multiple invoices are created.

Creating a Sales Invoice

Once the Salesperson is selected, it is necessary to enter information for the specific invoice. All the information presented in the invoice frame is stored as an invoice record. The line items are stored individually with a reference to the invoice record.

A customer must be selected for the invoice. The customer must be contained in the Customer table. The combo box shows the names of all the customers contained in the Customer table. If the customer is not in the list, a new customer record must be added to the Customer table.

There are several ways to enter a new customer. When the user clicks the Customer button—the small button to the right of the combo box labeled ...—a New Customer record appears. If the user enters a name in the Customer field that does not exist in the customer list, the program prompts him to enter a new customer when he clicks the OK button on the form.

The data—address, city, and so on—from the selected customer is automatically entered in the Ship To address field. It can be modified by the user; all modifications are saved with the invoice record.

In the top right portion of the invoice are various fields related to the displayed invoice. The Date field automatically contains today's date, but may be modified to contain another date.

The Invoice # field is not editable. Because the client/server system can have many Sales clients, enabling the user to modify the invoice number could corrupt the data integrity; multiple invoices could be created with the identical numbers. Likewise, for security reasons, once an invoice is created, the invoice number should remain inviolable.

Sales are often made to other companies. The Customer PO field can store the purchase order number of a customer to simplify records. The customer purchase order number is stored as text because the purchase order can be any combination of alphanumerics used by a company.

The Terms combo box enables the user to select the terms extended to this customer on this sale. A customer might not have to pay immediately but, instead, at the end of thirty days. When the customer record is created, a default Terms field is included to determine the normal payment method for that customer. The Terms field on the invoice enables the user to override the default.

Suppose, for example, that the customer normally enjoys Net 30 terms. Because this order is small, the terms might be selected to equal Cash. The invoice is then recorded to be paid in cash.

The fields Ship Date and Bill Date can be entered on the invoice. The Ship Date should contain the date on which the sales items actually ship. This field can be filled in with the current date if the sale is made over the counter, or it can be edited later to enter the date on which the shipment takes place. The Bill Date enables the date on which the bill is sent (if the terms include some type of net payment) to be entered. This enables the company to track the actual billing dates. If payments have not been received, the Bill Date can be checked to determine when the bill was originally sent.

Items are entered on each line of the grid. Each item must be selected from the sales items table (Inventory_Sales). Items are specified by clicking the Item button (the small button to the left of the combo box labeled ...), which becomes visible when the text cursor is in the Item # column of the grid (see Figure 15.3).

Clicking the button shows the list of items available for sale. The user can select an item by clicking it (see Figure 15.4) and then clicking the OK button, or by simply double-clicking the item.

FIGURE 15.3.
The Sales Item button.

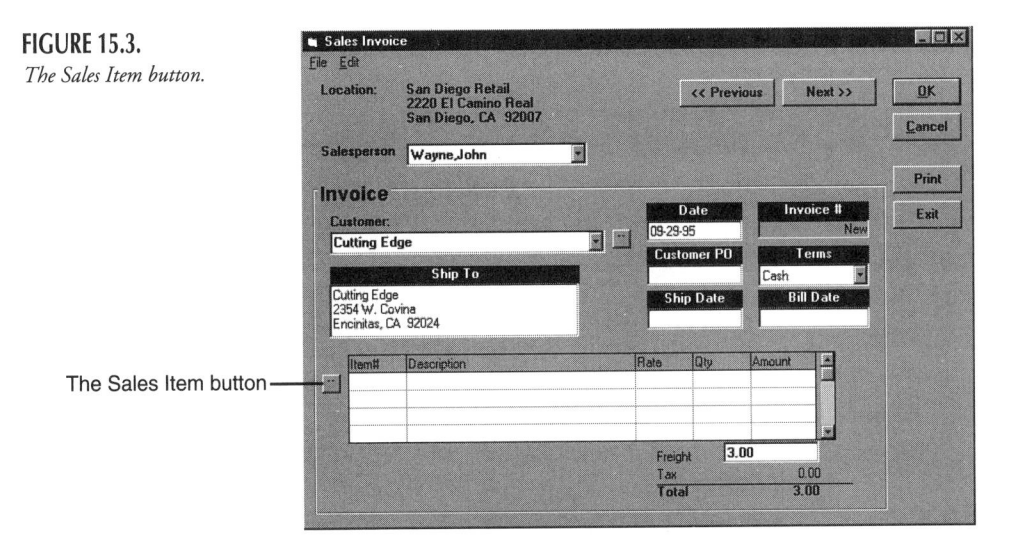

The Sales Item button

FIGURE 15.4.
The Sales Item screen.

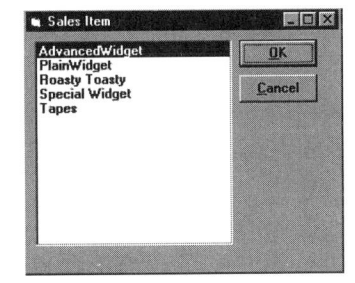

> **TIP**
>
> Currently only inventoried items are stored in this sales system. An excellent modification would be to include service items, such as consulting hours, which would not be reserved or subtracted from inventory.
>
> All items are also currently taxed. A routine might be added to check nontaxable items, such as food, and to exclude them from the calculation of the sales tax.

The information on the item now appears on the selected invoice item line (see Figure 15.5). The quantity field is selected. Any quantity entered is automatically checked against the inventory to ensure that enough items are in stock to fill the order. The specified quantity is then reserved so that other clients cannot sell these same items while the invoice is being completed. The user can alter the description, quantity, and amount by pressing the Tab key or by clicking the desired cell.

FIGURE 15.5.
The filled-in sales item line.

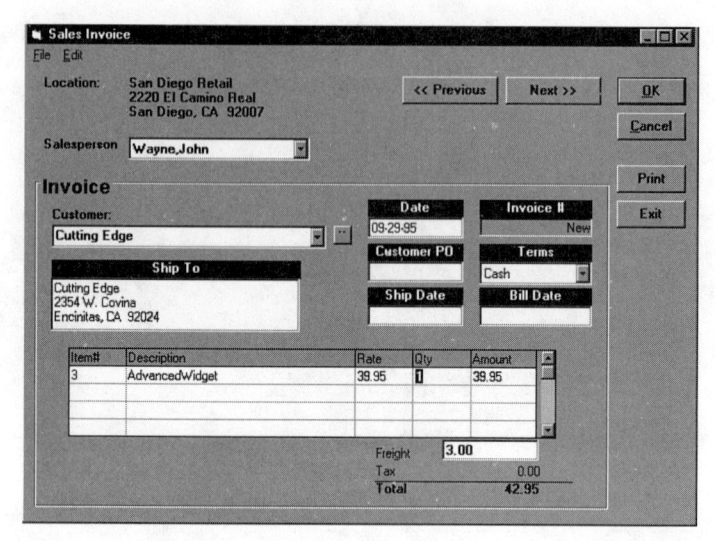

The Freight field can be modified. The default value is stored in the .INI file for the client. Modifying the Freight field automatically causes a recalculation of the total for the invoice.

Completing the invoice is done by clicking the OK button. If the invoice is flawed in some way or should be aborted, clicking the Cancel button confirms that the information should be discarded. After the user clicks the OK button—that is, discards changes—the invoice is cleared.

Clicking the Print button while an invoice is showing prints it. The invoice is sent with a number of PRINT statements to the currently selected printer.

The Previous and Next buttons enable the user to navigate through earlier invoices. Clicking the Previous button displays the invoice previous to the one currently displayed. With a new invoice on the screen, the previous invoice shows the last invoice created. Paging backward enables the user to examine each invoice back to the first one. Clicking the Previous button while the first invoice is being shown generates an error and warns the user that the first invoice is being shown.

The Next button moves forward through the invoices. When the most recent invoice is reached, clicking the Next button shows a new invoice for invoice creation. If the user clicks the Next button again, a warning appears to notify the user that the current record is the most recent invoice.

The File menu contains two items: Show Inventory... and Exit. The Exit selection exits the Sales client, just like the Exit button. The Show Inventory... selection shows the current inventory levels for all the sales items.

Selecting the Show Inventory menu item displays the Inventory form (see Figure 15.6). Each sales item is shown along with the quantity currently in stock and the reorder quantity. Two text fields at the bottom show the total number of distinct items in the sales inventory and the total quantity of parts. Clicking the OK button closes the form.

FIGURE 15.6.
The Sales Inventory screen.

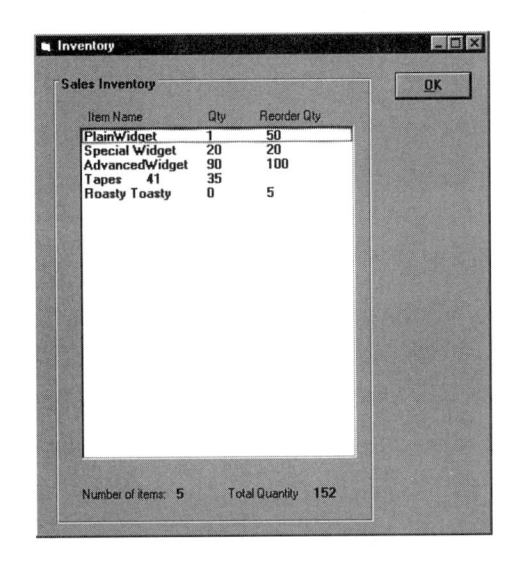

Any part of the text fields on the main invoice form can be cut, copied, or pasted. The Edit Menu contains all three commands. Additionally, the standard control keys can be used—Ctrl+X for Cut, Ctrl+C for Copy, and Ctrl+V for Paste.

The Sales client can be used to create, edit, and examine sales invoices for the client/server system. Sales items are removed from inventory as they are sold. Each invoice can be printed to the default printer selected in the Windows system.

Using the Purchasing and Inventory Client

The Purchasing client is used to generate purchase orders, purchase inventory items, and autobuild sales items. It is also used to check inventory levels, add sales or inventory parts, and print any purchase orders. The Purchasing client functions in a way similar to the Sales client, but it contains many more options and is created to bring items into the enterprise (through purchases and autobuilds) rather than to transfer items out of the enterprise (through sales).

Execute the Purchasing client on your machine. If the Pseudo Server has noticed that a reorder is required for any item, a flag has been set in the database. The Purchasing client checks this flag when it is executed, and if the flag is set, the reorder message box appears before any other form is shown (see Figure 15.7).

FIGURE 15.7.
The Reorder warning screen.

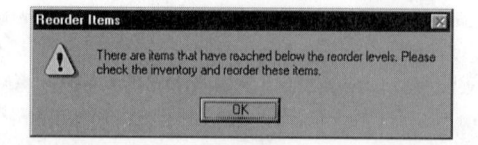

After you click the OK button to acknowledge the condition, a blank purchase order appears (see Figure 15.8). The blank purchase order enables the user to create a purchase order invoice to detail the purchase of inventory part supplies.

FIGURE 15.8.
A blank Purchase Order screen.

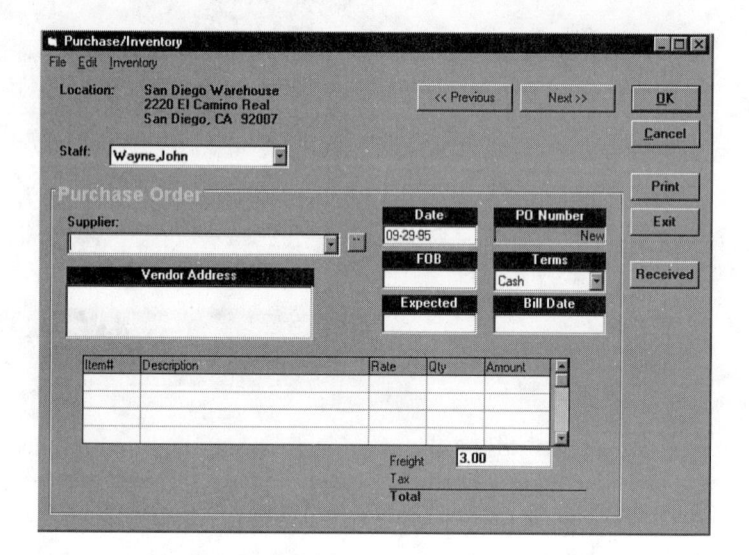

If you click the Previous button, a previous purchase order is shown. You can continue to click the Previous button until the client shows a message alerting you that there are no more purchase orders to view. Click the Next button to page back through the purchase orders until the purchase order number displays New.

Creating a Purchase Order

Now enter a purchase order. You might want to change the employee who is creating the order. Use the Staff combo box to select a different staff member (see Figure 15.9).

Now enter a new supplier. Click the ... button just to the right of the combo box. The Supplier form appears with the title New Supplier. Enter the company name Choice Enterprises, as shown in Figure 15.10. Enter any other information that you want, such as the mailing address or phone number. When you are finished, click the OK button. The supplier will be added to the Supplier table.

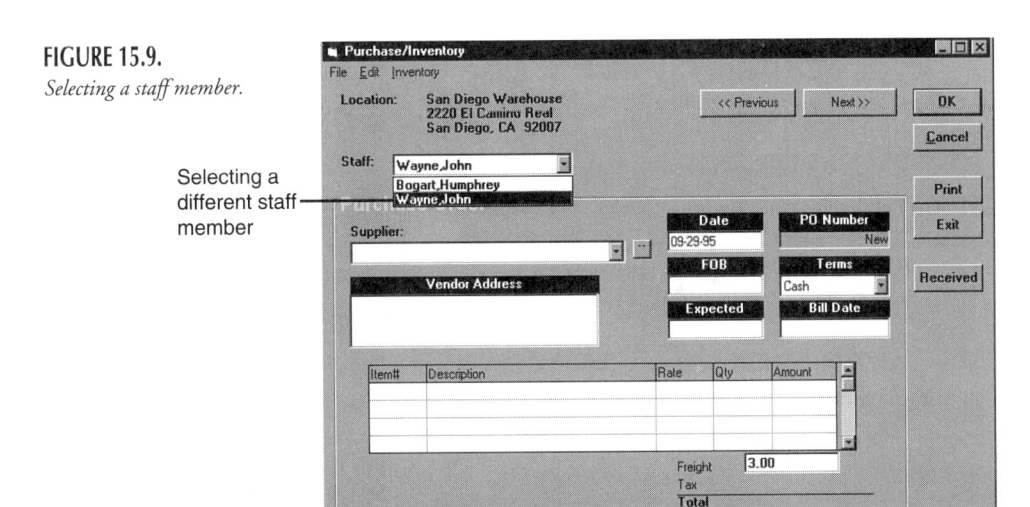

FIGURE 15.9.
Selecting a staff member.

FIGURE 15.10.
Choice Enterprises supplier entry.

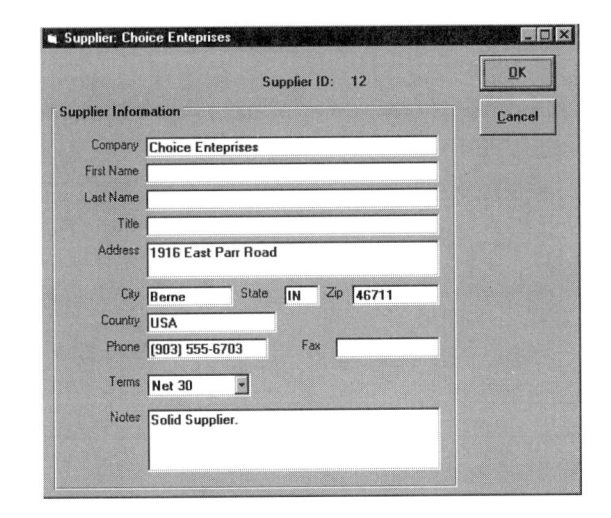

Click the combo box arrow to show the list of suppliers. Choice Enterprises should now appear in the list. Select a company; the Vendor Address field is automatically filled in (see Figure 15.11).

The Date field is automatically filled in with today's date. Click the Expected field, and enter a date approximately a week from today. Click the Terms combo list, and select Net 30. Finally, set the bill date to approximately 30 days from today.

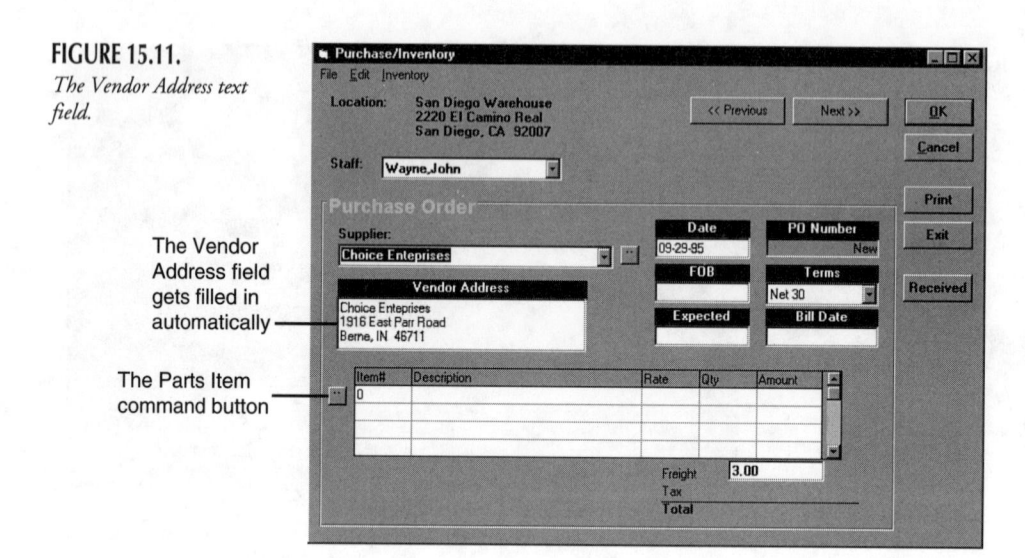

FIGURE 15.11.
The Vendor Address text field.

The Vendor Address field gets filled in automatically

The Parts Item command button

Now that you have entered all the base information, select items for the purchase order. Click the top left invoice cell below the grid titles. The Items command button should appear. It enables you to select an item from the parts inventory—the Inventory_Parts table—for purchase.

Click the Items button; the Item Select list appears (see Figure 15.12).

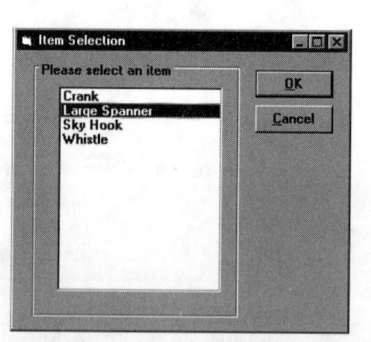

FIGURE 15.12.
The parts Item Selection screen.

Select an item from the item list and click the OK button. (You can also double-click the item to select it.) The item information should appear on the purchase order line. The quantity cell is automatically selected. Type in the quantity 3, and press the Tab key. This moves the editing box to the amount cell. Press the Tab key again, and the edit box appears on the next item line.

Enter another item. You will see that the tax and the total values at the bottom of the screen adjust automatically. Now select the Freight field, and change it from the default value of $3 to $2. Your completed purchase order should now look like the one shown in Figure 15.13.

FIGURE 15.13.
A completed purchase order.

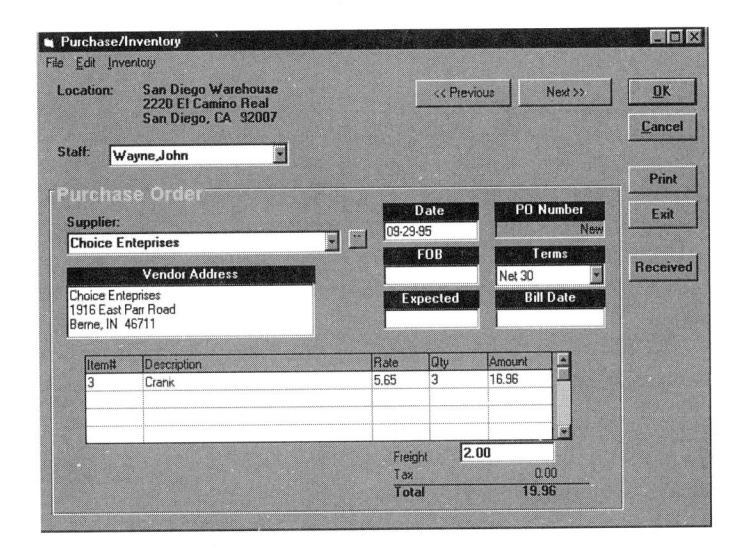

Clicking the OK button enters the purchase order record into the system and modifies the necessary tables. After all the entries from the purchase order have been saved, a new blank invoice appears.

The purchase order is currently outstanding because, presumably, the items have been ordered but not received. None of the items from the purchase order are recorded into inventory. Before you receive the items from the purchase order, check the inventory to see the current stock levels of the items.

Select Parts Inventory... under the Inventory menu. It displays the current inventory of all the items contained in the Inventory_Parts table and the quantities in stock, as shown in Figure 15.14. Note the inventory levels of each of the items that appeared on the purchase order that you just created. When you receive the items, the numbers on the purchase order are entered into inventory and the numbers that you are currently examining will increase. Click the OK button to remove the Inventory form from the screen.

To see the purchase order that you have just entered, click the Previous button. The purchase order is read from the database and is displayed in the form. You can now edit the purchase order; click the OK button to save the changes.

Click the Received button, which marks the purchase order as received and transfers the items on the purchase order into inventory. Now select Parts Inventory... under the Inventory menu again. The inventory increases by the amount of each item in the purchase order.

FIGURE 15.14.
The Parts Inventory screen.

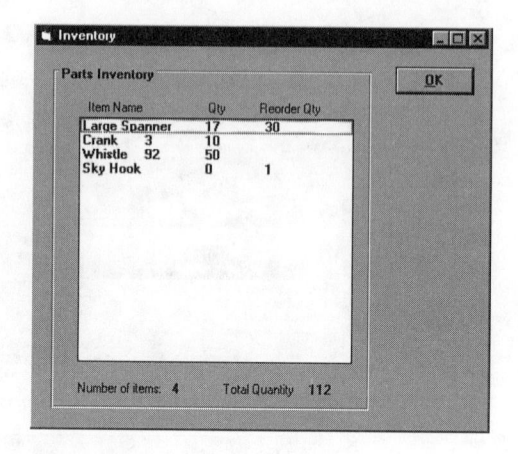

Adding Inventory to Sales or Parts

Items can be added or edited from either the Sales or the Parts lists. The options under the Inventory Menu include both adding and editing commands: Add Part..., Edit Part..., Add Sales Item..., and Edit Sales Item....

Now add to the Inventory_Parts table a part that can be used to autobuild another item. Select Add Part... under the Inventory menu. The Part form appears. It enables you to create an inventory item (see Figure 15.15).

FIGURE 15.15.
The Part form.

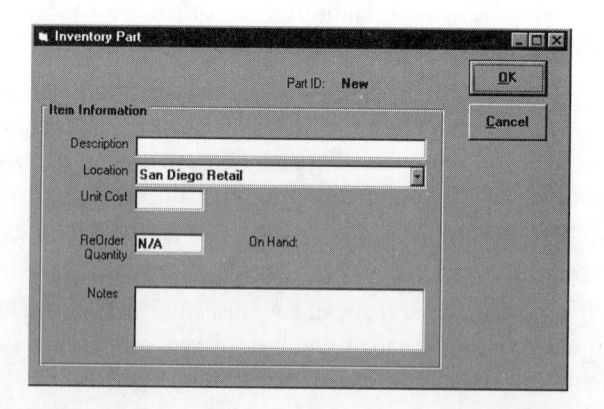

Create a new part—for example, the Wang Doodler. Fill in the Description, Unit Cost, Reorder Quantity, and Notes fields. Select a location where the part will be located. Click the OK button when you are finished. The part is saved into the parts inventory table (Inventory_Parts).

Creating an Autobuild Item

Creating an autobuild item enables you to construct a sales item from numerous inventory parts (see Figure 15.16). This enables all the individual parts costs and inventory levels to be tracked independently and combined to form the final sales unit.

FIGURE 15.16.
The Autobuild Edit screen.

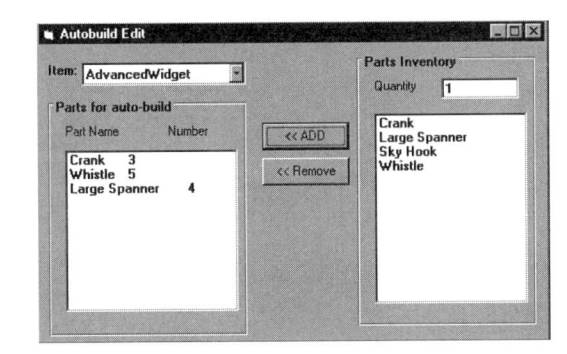

The combo box shows all the available sales items for which assembly records have been created. Selecting an item shows the parts required for its assembly.

In the Parts Inventory frame, all the available inventory parts are available for construction. The text field determines the quantity of each part required to create a single sales item. Select an item, enter a quantity, and click the Add button. This adds the selected item and quantity requirements to the assembly definition for the sales item selected in the combo box.

> **NOTE**
>
> Note that the Autobuild Edit form does not add or subtract any quantities from either inventory table. Autobuild Edit creates the assembly record used by the Autobuild form, which does affect inventory.

A part cannot be added to inventory more than once—a given part must be a distinct entry in the assembly record. If the quantity required for a particular part changes, use the Remove button to remove the entry and add it again with the new value.

The Remove button removes a part from the assembly definition. Select the part that needs to be removed, and click the Remove button.

> **NOTE**
>
> Currently no quantities can be added to the sales items inventory without autobuilding the item. If the enterprise resells items, an autobuild record could contain merely a one-to-one relation between the inventory part and the sales item. When additional sales items are received, the Autobuild essentially transfers one of the equivalent inventory items into the sales inventory.

Autobuilding Sales Items

Now that an autobuild assembly record has been created, the client can autobuild a sales item. Select the Autobuild... option from the Inventory menu to show the autobuild form (see Figure 15.17).

FIGURE 15.17.
The Autobuild screen.

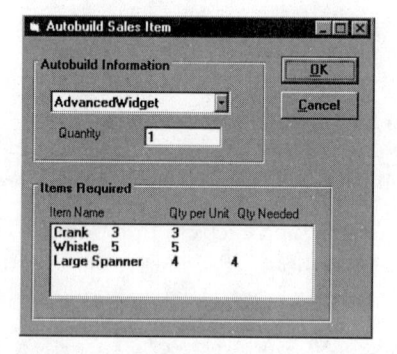

The combo box is used to select the item to be built. The text field holds the quantity of the final units to be constructed. The list box displays the various items needed for construction, the number of items needed to create the entered quantity, and the total number of each particular part required to build all the units specified.

After selecting an item and entering a quantity, click the OK button to build the items. If the number of parts required for the autobuild exceeds the number of parts in inventory, a message notifies the user and the list box is filled.

To test the routine, select an item and enter the quantity 100. This quantity requires more parts than there are available. Click the OK button. The warning message appears. Click the OK button to remove the message.

The list box now shows all the parameters of the failed autobuild (see Figure 15.18). Each part required to create the sales item is listed. The two columns also display the information on the required parts. The first number column shows the total quantity of each part needed to construct each sales item. The second number column shows the total quantity of the item needed to build the specified number of units. For each failed autobuild, one or more of the parts will have fewer parts in stock than those required for the autobuild.

FIGURE 15.18.
A failed autobuild.

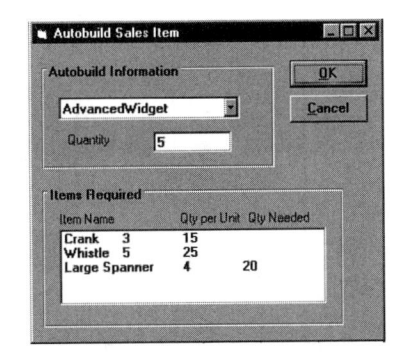

Parts are added to the inventory by creating a purchase order with the needed items, entering the purchase order, and then receiving the purchase order. You can reduce the quantities of the needed final units in the Autobuild form until a quantity is reached that is within inventory limits.

Using the Management Client

You can use the Management client to generate reports on the interactions of all the different clients. It summarizes data into a concise set of information for an overall look at the operations of the enterprise. The reports are actually executed when you click the respective report tab.

Checking Management Reports

The tabs in the tab strip enable you to navigate among the various reports. Clicking a particular tab shows the appropriate report. Each time you select a tab, the query to retrieve the necessary report data is activated. To update the report with new information, simply click the same report tab again. The query report is re-executed.

Clicking the Sales tab brings up the Sales report, shown in Figure 15.19. This report consists of a 3D bar chart of employee sales. Every staff member is represented as a bar on the chart. The legend to the right shows the names of the employees. The colors of the bars represent individual staff members.

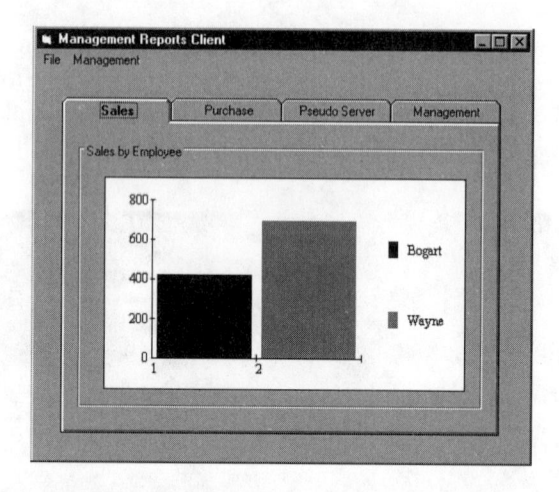

FIGURE 15.19.
The Management client with the Sales report shown.

> **NOTE**
>
> The bar chart does not differentiate among locations, types of employees, or time periods. You can add these options by modifying the query that generates the data placed in the bar chart. For management, the employee's salary might be superimposed as a second set of bars on the chart to determine sales versus salary.

Clicking the Purchasing/Inventory tab brings up the Purchasing/Inventory frame, shown in Figure 15.20. This report consists of a grid that shows the total cost of all the sales items. The cost is calculated by tabulating the individual costs of each part required to construct the sales item. The assembly record created using the Purchasing client is used to generate the list of assembly costs.

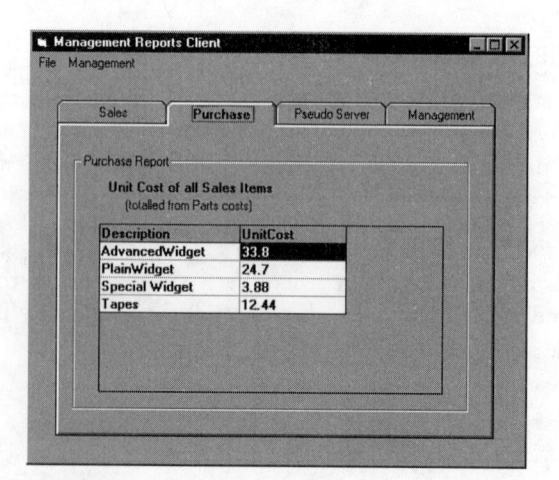

FIGURE 15.20.
The Management client with the Purchase report shown.

Chapter 15 ■ Execution and Functioning of the Client/Server System

Clicking the Pseudo Server tab brings up the Pseudo Server frame, shown in Figure 15.21. This report contains four status text fields. The first field totals the number of items that are currently on reserve. The Pseudo Server's job is to watch and remove these items from the reserve section after an hour of inactivity. The second text field shows the critical Disk Space flag. A value is set in the Pseudo Server program to switch this flag when the file size of the database exceeds a particular value. The Reordered Items text field signals that items in the parts inventory need to be reordered. Items can be reordered through the Purchasing client.

FIGURE 15.21.

The Management client with the Pseudo Server report shown.

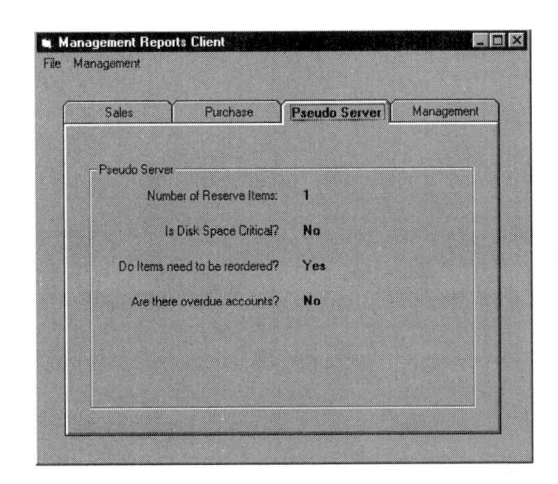

The overdue accounts is an example flag. This flag can signal when sales accounts, such as Net 30 days, are overdue. The Sales client does not actually activate this flag because a billing client is typically done separately by a different department.

Clicking the Management tab brings up the Management frame, shown in Figure 15.22. This report has the most varied fields of all the reports. To get a broad overview, management typically needs reports that relate to all the parts of the business. The first text field displays the average sales per employee. This enables managers to examine employee productivity. The Today's Sales text field shows the total sales volume for the day. This figure does not differentiate among locations.

The Average Sales per Invoice field shows the average of the totals of all the invoices. This figure enables management to determine the characteristics of the business. Is it more of a high volume but low total revenue business, or is it a low volume but high total revenue business? Figures like these can often surprise day-to-day managers who think that they have a feel for the typical customer and business transaction.

The Most Sold Item field shows the Sales item that has sold the most in quantity. The field directly below it shows the quantity sold.

FIGURE 15.22.
The Management client with the Management report shown.

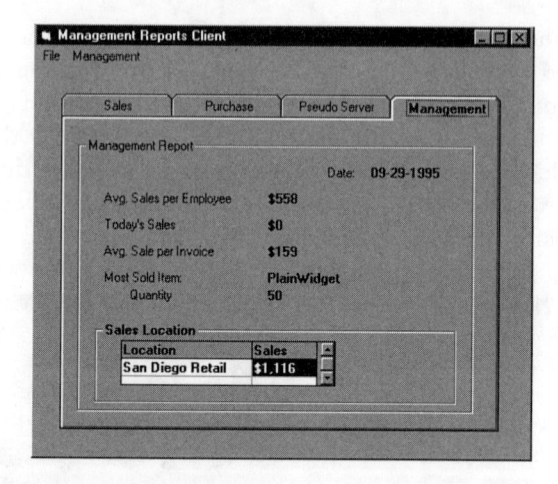

> **NOTE**
>
> The Most Sold Item field is often more appropriate as a list that shows the items in descending order of quantity sold. This enables management to determine which products to discontinue because of lack of scale. Likewise, this field is calculated purely by quantity. Sometimes it is better calculated on sales price, thereby listing the item that provides the most revenue.

The Sales per Location frame contains a grid that shows the sales at each location. Note that this query is not bounded by any time or date functions. Therefore, it displays the overall total sales.

Using the Pseudo Server

The Pseudo Server is self-maintaining. Simply execute the application to activate the PServer (see Figure 15.23). Once every five minutes, the screen is updated as the system does its check. A complete check is activated every hour for more intensive queries and maintenance.

The Reserved Items frame contains a list box, two text status fields, and a Restore button. In the list box, all the reserved items in inventory are listed. The reserve list is checked every hour. Items that have been reserved for over an hour are returned to the sales inventory. If the Restore button is pressed, the reserved items are immediately returned to inventory.

The two text fields below the reserved items list box show the total number of reserved items and the last time when an item was reserved. By observing these figures, a system administrator can informally watch the load and frequency of reserved items.

FIGURE 15.23.

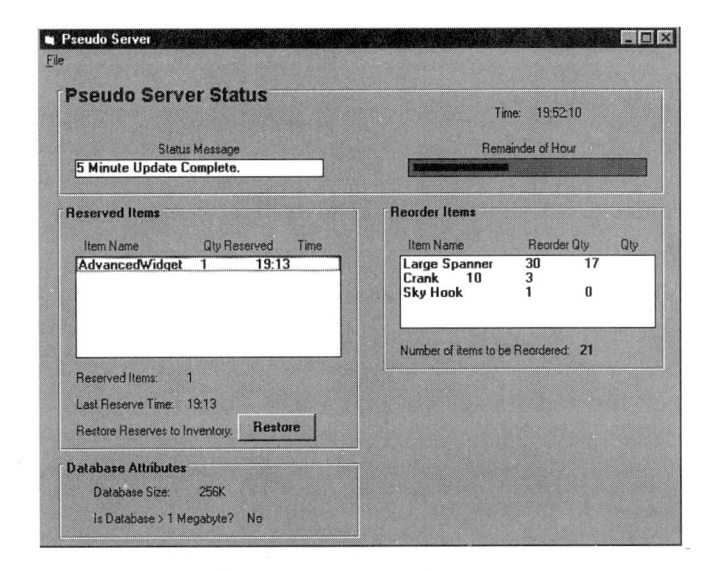

The Pseudo Server screen.

[Figure: Pseudo Server screen showing Pseudo Server Status with Time 19:52:10, Status Message "5 Minute Update Complete.", Reserved Items frame listing AdvancedWidget 1 19:13, Reorder Items frame listing Large Spanner 30 17, Crank 10 3, Sky Hook 1 0, Number of items to be Reordered: 21, Reserved Items: 1, Last Reserve Time: 19:13, Restore Reserves to Inventory button, Database Attributes: Database Size: 256K, Is Database > 1 Megabyte? No]

> **TIP**
>
> One of the enhancements that you might make to the Pseudo Server would be to store the reserved items and the reserve time with a time stamp in a Pseudo Server table. That way, you could add a report to the Management client to determine on average how often and how long items remain on reserve.
>
> You could also record the number of items flushed back into inventory every hour. Examining how often items remain suspended in reserve for over an hour helps when you want to adjust the system or the processes of the enterprise.

The Reorder Items frame contains a list of parts and the total number of parts to be reordered. This list is generated from the Inventory_Parts table to determine the number of parts that the Purchasing department must reorder. Every part that must be reordered is listed along with the quantity currently in inventory and the threshold below which reorders are required.

The text field with the number of items to be reordered shows the quantity needed to bring the inventory up to minimum levels. Because this number represents the minimum quantity required, more items than the number listed should be ordered.

The Database Attributes frame contains information about the database itself. The database size indicates the actual file size of the database stored on the hard disk or the network drive. Given the number of users and active transactions, any growth or upscaling can be determined by the current size of the database.

> **TIP**
>
> Tracking growth and increasing the user base is an area that can benefit dramatically from a log and an attached Management report. Databases and transactions often grow more rapidly than the original deployment plan anticipated. By periodically logging the database size with a time stamp—and perhaps the number of users—you can more easily predict the growth of the database.

The Pseudo Server can be left running indefinitely. Because of the updates every five and 60 minutes, few processor cycles are used by the application. It can easily be run on the central server machine without performance degradation.

16

Access Security

Visual Basic does not have the capability to create a secure database. Microsoft Access, on the other hand, is fully capable of creating and maintaining a secure database. If you have created the security for the database with Access, Visual Basic can use all of the security embedded in the database. Using Access in conjunction with Visual Basic enables you to create complete, secure client/server systems.

Microsoft Access can be used with the following Network Operating Systems (NOS): Microsoft LAN Manager, Windows for Workgroups (and Windows 95), NT Advanced Server, Novell NetWare, and LANtastic. Databases can be secured either through the security and logon procedures of the NOS itself for database file security, or through the Access application for individual table security.

Security measures are to protect data not only from prying eyes and purposeful corruption, but also from unintentional mistakes and data currency problems. When the amount of data a user can access is limited, so are his responsibilities for the system's data. With unlimited access, a single mistake could bring down the entire system. With limited access, it is only possible for the user to harm a specific area.

This chapter uses Microsoft Access to create security for the client/server system that was created in the earlier chapters (WIDGETCO.MDB). The changes include using Access to set up groups and users, modifying the .INI file to hold the necessary passwords and usernames, and having each client log onto the Access database.

Before beginning the modification, you need to review some essentials of this client/server project and Access security construction. For a more complete overview of security information, see Chapter 28, "Security for Client/Server."

Planning Database Security

Planning specific database security from the beginning is vitally important and should be in place before any deployment of the system occurs. This ensures that users understand the data is secure—both for their peace of mind and to make them understand that security is a topic the enterprise takes seriously. It also creates a standard logon procedure to which users will become accustomed. If security is part of the usage procedure, it will become routine. Adding it later requires more training, frustration, and technical-support headaches.

Make sure that you plan security access around groups rather than around individual users. For example, all of the sales force would be in the Sales group, whereas managers would be in various Management groups. *Groups* (also called *workgroups*) enable you to centralize security around a particular type of user. Basing security around groups essentially creates data permission rules, to which exceptions can be added. This is more flexible than viewing each user as his own rule.

With the groups created and well defined, adding a new staff member is as easy as adding him to the group. Otherwise, you must create independent permissions for each user. Group creation significantly decreases the maintenance required for a system.

It is recommended that a typical database has a maximum of five to six groups. This limit is not a technical one, but provides the maximum ease of use and the least confusion. With too many groups, group distinction and access privileges become unclear, which can lead to accidental granting of permission to inappropriate areas.

System Security Versus Database Security

It is a good idea to have any networked system with three or more users secured with passwords and accounts. The requirements will vary based on the needs and the maintenance costs that can be sustained by the enterprise. The simplest type of security is that which is provided by the NOS that is running (NetWare, NT Advanced Server, Windows for Workgroups, and so on).

You can set *system-level* security to give specific users and groups access to various files and directories. This baseline method is ideal for document sharing or when specific database tables are stored in separate files. The sections that follow provide examples of Windows for Workgroups and Windows 95 security procedures.

System-level security is an excellent solution for separate databases or low-level database usage. However, often a number of tables must be centralized in a single database file that must be accessed by many users. Therefore, access for users must be limited to specific tables within the database. For this reason, Access has its own *database-level* security system. Users must log onto the database so that access is possible only to the necessary tables and data.

Windows for Workgroups Logon

Windows for Workgroups creates a peer-to-peer network in which various users can access other users' hard drives. Either at the time of first booting or by executing the Log On/Off application, the user can log onto the Workgroups network (see Figure 16.1). After getting onto the network, the user can access shared files and printers as well as send mail.

FIGURE 16.1.
The Windows for Workgroups logon.

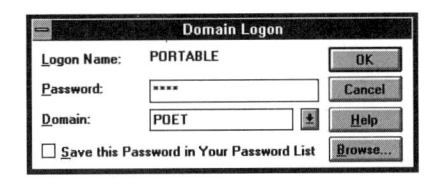

Because the Windows for Workgroups network is in a peer-to-peer format, there is no primary server in this peer-to-peer group. Each machine must keep track of all users and groups that might be logged onto the machine. Peer-to-peer systems do not allow security or security procedures to be centralized, making security maintenance more difficult than with a server-based system.

Specific files and printers can be shared on the network, each utilizing a password for different levels of access. For example, the WIDGETCO.MDB database file could be placed on the C: drive and shared using the File Manager. The program could give read-only access to all users, whereas read/write access is granted only with the use of a password.

In this way, a client/server database can be shared over a network. However, the machine that contains the database file must remain on for the other machines to access the file. If the machine were to crash, other users would be cut off from data access.

Windows 95 Logon

Windows 95 is fully compliant with the Windows for Workgroups protocol. Either upon boot or by executing the Log On/Off application, a Windows 95 user can function as a Workgroups peer or log onto a file server (see Figure 16.2). A Windows for Workgroups machine can also mount a volume that is shared on the Windows 95 machine.

FIGURE 16.2.
The Windows 95 system logon.

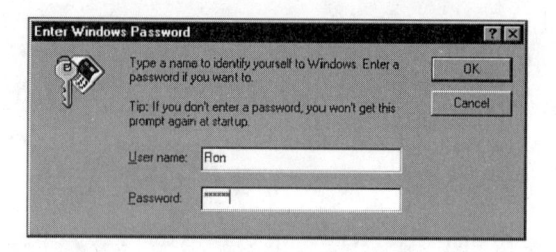

Windows 95 can also access password-protected shared folders from another peer-to-peer workstation (see Figure 16.3). When you double-click the shared folder, a window appears that asks for a password. If the password is verified, shared access is granted.

FIGURE 16.3.
Windows 95 shared folder password logon.

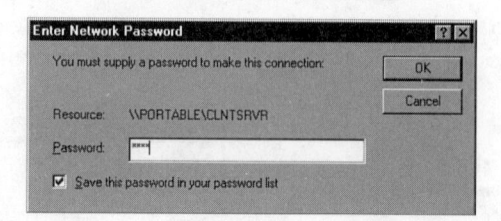

Access Logon

Logging into an Access database is very similar to creating a connection to a workgroup or a server. When Access is first executed, a password box appears through which the user logs onto the system. (See Figure 16.4). Any databases that are opened in Access after this point will check the username against the list of users who have access to the database and to the various objects within it. Each user or group has specifically delineated permissions, either through individual permissions or permissions for the group(s) to which the user belongs.

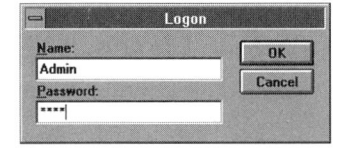

FIGURE 16.4.
Access logon.

> **WARNING**
>
> The MS Access security engine is not completely secure if implemented in a certain way. The JET database engine, once loaded into memory, is shared by all applications that access it. A trojan horse DLL or in-process OLE Server can be created to cycle through all of the Workspace objects until it locates the workspace being used by your application. It then has access to all of the secure information (databases, tables, and so on) that the currently logged on user does.
>
> You can avoid this security loophole by creating a specific Workspace object and not appending it to the Workspaces collection. Your workspace is then invisible to other code on the system.

Before any databases are secured, the Access logon window does not appear when the program is first executed. This is because the Access program defaults to logging the user as the default username Admin with no password (""). In the "Locking Database Objects" section later in this chapter, you will see how to secure the Access system so it does not provide a generic "back door" with which any user can retrieve information from secure databases.

> **NOTE**
>
> In Access, user and group names are not case-sensitive when used to start a session. However, you must match the name of the user or group account exactly if re-creating the account with the same name because of the way Access stores the names of the users and groups.

ODBC Access Logon

You can also address an Access database through the ODBC interface. Figure 16.5 shows the creation of a connection to an Access database.

FIGURE 16.5.
ODBC Login.

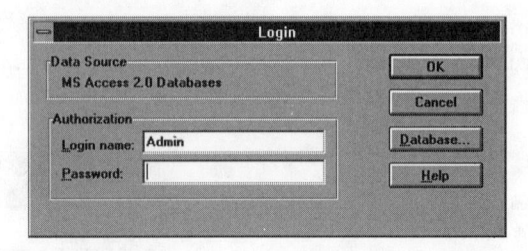

In this dialog box, the system database is selected by default. This is the SYSTEM.MDW file, which contains the users, groups, and passwords. If a system file is not selected, the default logon (`Admin`, `""`) is used. If the database is properly secured, this logon will not work and access to the secure database will be denied.

Users and Groups

A database can be placed on the network and used concurrently by many different users. Users may each have individual security permission options or they may belong to a group (or workgroup) that has defined security privileges. Security is created by the system administrator on the machine that will serve the workgroup.

Figure 16.6 shows a basic diagram of both users and groups. Remember that users and groups are created separately. A group cannot operate independently from users (for example, a group cannot log onto a database), but individual users can have permissions not available in any group.

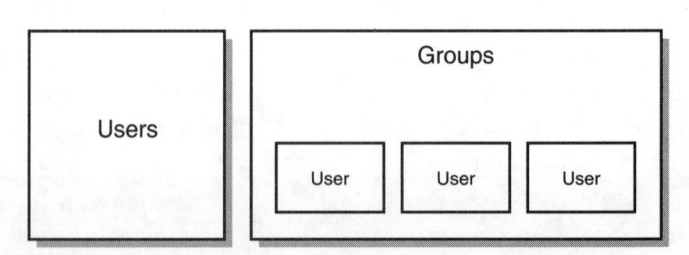

FIGURE 16.6.
Relationships between users and groups.

> **NOTE**
>
> With the new JET engine, the security filename has been changed from SYSTEM.MDA to SYSTEM.MDW.

Each user and group in Access has a unique *Security ID code* (SID). All of the SID codes are stored in the MSysAccounts table of the Access database SYSTEM.MDW (see Figure 16.7), which contains all of the users and groups as well as their passwords. This is the file that is accessed when a user logs onto Access. Any groups or user definitions added in Access become part of the system and appear regardless of which Access database is opened.

FIGURE 16.7.
The SYSTEM.MDW Access file.

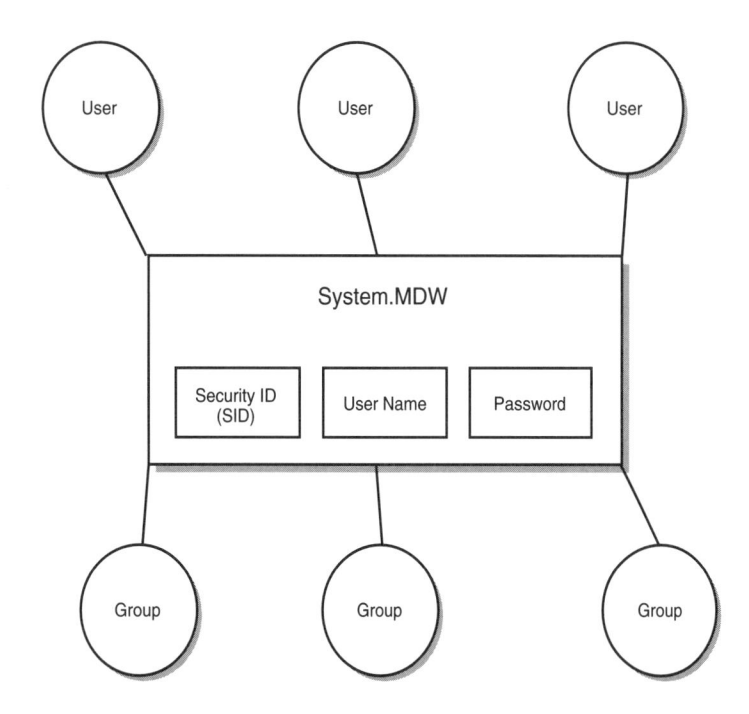

> **NOTE**
>
> All the SID codes are stored in the SYSTEM.MDW database. If this database is accidentally lost or deleted, access to all protected databases is also lost. Therefore, it is important to back up the SYSTEM.MDW file in addition to the database file to ensure that accidental damage will not eliminate access to your protected data.

Not all of the security for an Access database is stored in the SYSTEM.MDW file. It is important to realize that although all of the users, groups, and passwords are stored in the SYSTEM.MDW file, the permissions to various database objects (such as tables, queries, forms, and so on) are stored in the particular database file. They are referenced to the security user's profiles (in SYSTEM.MDW) by the SID created for each user.

Figure 16.8 shows an example of security settings that could be stored in the WIDGETCO database. In the diagram, User1 has a particular SID used to relate to the SYSTEM.MDW database. User1 has full access to Sales, read-only access to SalesItems, and full access to the Assembly table. All access to objects within the database is stored in the database.

When creating a secure system, it is often a good idea to follow a specific protocol. Figure 16.9 shows the recommended order for implementing the security on a database. This is the procedure used in this chapter to secure the client/server system. First the groups are created, followed by all of the user accounts. The users are then placed in the appropriate groups. Lastly,

Part II ■ Constructing a Basic Client/Server System

the various groups are given specific security privileges appropriate to that group. Following this order helps to clarify just what type of access is being granted to groups and users.

FIGURE 16.8.
Security settings stored in the database file.

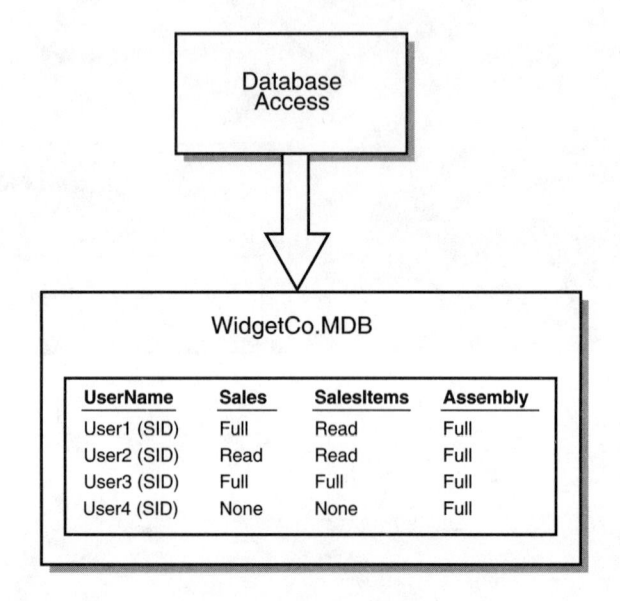

```
         Database
          Access
             |
             v
   WidgetCo.MDB

   UserName    Sales   SalesItems   Assembly
   User1 (SID) Full    Read         Full
   User2 (SID) Read    Read         Full
   User3 (SID) Full    Full         Full
   User4 (SID) None    None         Full
```

FIGURE 16.9.
Security setup order.

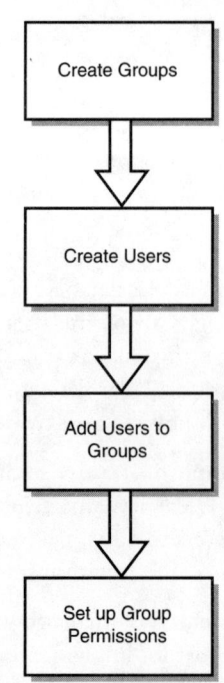

```
   Create Groups
        |
        v
   Create Users
        |
        v
   Add Users to
      Groups
        |
        v
   Set up Group
    Permissions
```

Creating Access Accounts

Most of the security features (except database encryption) can be found under the Security menu in Access. All of the Access system security is stored in the SYSTEM.MDW file. The Workgroup Administrator application, explained in the next section, enables the creation of a particular workgroup or the addition of users to that workgroup. From Access, all users, groups, and permissions can then be created, edited, or granted.

Access Workgroup Administrator

In the Access program group, note the icon for the MS Access Workgroup Administrator program. This program is used to either create SYSTEM.MDW files (known as a workgroups) or to join another workgroup (a SYSTEM.MDW located in a different directory), which allows access to all of the users and groups stored in another file.

Executing the Workgroup Administrator displays a window that shows the currently used system database (SYSTEM.MDW) and enables the creation or joining of a different one (see Figure 16.10). This Administrator program configures the version of Access running on your machine to open the selected workgroup when Access is executed.

FIGURE 16.10.
The MS Access Workgroup Administrator program.

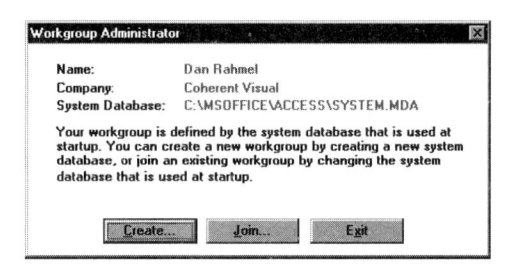

When you install Access, a default SYSTEM.MDW is created in the C:\Access folder (or in whatever directory in which you installed Access). If you want to create a new Workgroup, clicking the Create… button enables you to enter the owner information. (See Figure 16.11.) After this information is entered, the Administrator prompts you for the location and the name of the new system database. (See Figure 16.12.) Clicking the OK button creates this new group and sets the Access application to use it upon execution.

FIGURE 16.11.
Workgroup owner information.

FIGURE 16.12.
Workgroup system database.

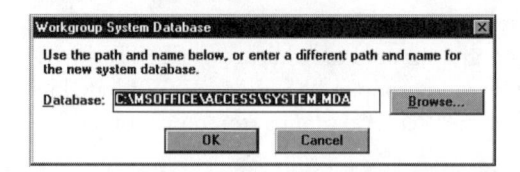

Creating Groups

To add a group, first start up Access. Open the database (for example, WIDGETCO.MDB) to which you want to add the group. Select the Groups… option from the Security menu.

The Groups window, shown in Figure 16.13, appears, enabling you to add or delete groups. Type a new group title into the text field. Don't worry about overwriting the one shown; you can create and delete groups, but you cannot edit the group name.

FIGURE 16.13.
Adding a new group.

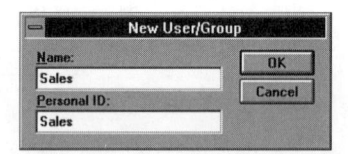

After entering a group name, click the New… button. The group name is shown, as well as the PersonalID. The PersonalID is how the group is referenced by the database (just like a LocationID or CustomerID field in one of the tables you created for the C/S system). Type a PersonalID and click the OK button. The group is now created and users and permissions relating to it can be selected.

> **TIP**
>
> It's a good idea to write down the PersonalID and Name of the group for each that is created. We recommend (if the Group Name is long enough) entering the exact text used for the Name of the group in the PersonalID. Note the case of each letter

(lowercase or uppercase) is important. That way if the group ever has to be recreated, it will be entered exactly as it originally appeared.

Creating Users

The process for creating users is nearly identical to that of creating groups. Select the Groups... option under the Security menu. The Users window appears (see Figure 16.14). Type the name of a user and click the New button. The program prompts you for a Personal ID to reference this user. Type a Personal ID and click the OK button. The user is then added to the user list.

FIGURE 16.14.
Adding a new user.

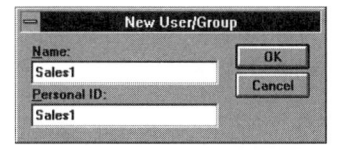

Note that the database administrator can also clear the password of any user. This is convenient if the user forgets or loses his password because you can assign a new password without creating a new account from scratch.

Adding Users to Groups

You use the bottom half of the User... window to add users to groups. The available groups are listed on the left, and groups to which the user belongs are in the right list box.

To add the user to a new group, simply select the group name in the left list box and click the Add button (see Figure 16.15). The selected group then appears in the right text box.

FIGURE 16.15.
Adding a user to a group.

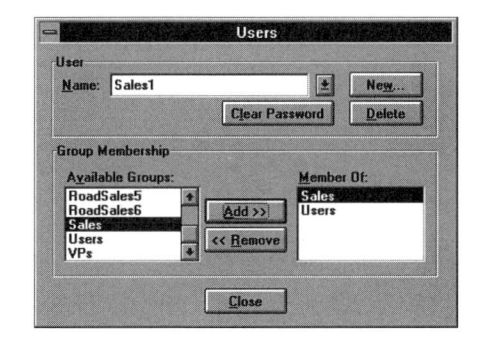

> **NOTE**
>
> By default, the Admin user is assigned to the Admins group and all users are assigned to the Users group. There must be at least one user belonging to the Admins group so that maintenance on the database can occur. It does not have to be the Admin user, however; you can create another user and added it to the Admins group, after which you can remove the Admin user.
>
> The Users group designation signifies belonging to the particular workgroup. Therefore, users cannot be removed from the Users workgroup. For this reason, be sure to closely track the security permissions of the Users group. Improperly set privileges for this group can create a tremendous security hole.

Locking Database Objects

After users and groups have been created, permission can be granted to all of the various objects in a database. Figure 16.16 shows the Permissions window that enables you to grant all of the security access.

FIGURE 16.16.
The Access Permissions window.

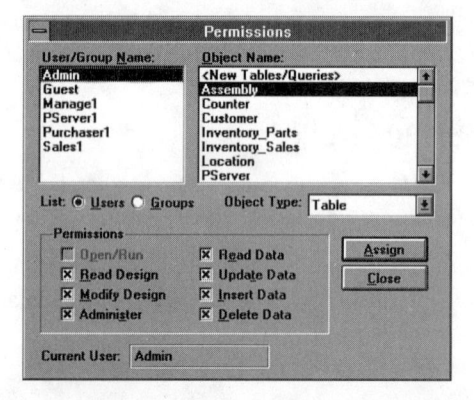

The list box in the top left of the window displays all of the available users or groups. You use the radio buttons that appear directly below the list to select whether the list displays users or groups. Except for special exceptions, it is recommended that you assign all privileges to the various groups; permission to individual users is then inherited from the groups to which the user is assigned. Setting the privileges for groups is a better security policy than assigning each individual user permissions, which becomes difficult to track and maintain.

All of the objects available to the current database are shown in the right list box. In addition to these objects, the default permissions of new objects can be set (which appear under the categories New Tables/Queries, New Forms, New Reports, New Macros, and New Modules).

The type of objects that appear in the right list box is determined by the selection of the combo box labeled Object Type that appears directly below the list box. Changing the object type changes the objects shown in the list box.

The Permissions box holds all of the actual permissions settings. The Permissions box displays the permissions set for the user or group selected in the left box pertaining to the database object selected in the right box. Note that multiple objects can be selected in the right list box to which permissions can be assigned.

The administrator can change permissions by selecting the proper object or objects and clicking the check boxes to set the access privilege level allowed to the user or group.

> **NOTE**
>
> Note that changes to the permissions are cumulative until the Assign or Close button is pressed. For example, the administrator might select the Sales group and select Read Data and Update Data permissions. Then the administrator might select another group and begin assigning permissions. At this point the access privileges for the Sales group have not yet been assigned to it. This does not occur until you click the Assign button, at which point all of the changes made to all of the objects are updated.
>
> Therefore, remember that privileges won't get assigned until you click the Assign button to close the window. Closing the window without clicking the Assign button might make you think changes were made when they were never saved.

Creating and Changing Ownership

For security reasons, you should specify the ownership of each database object. You can do this in one of three ways: creating a new database, importing an existing database, or changing the ownership of each individual object.

Creating a new database is certainly the easiest way to ensure complete ownership of the database objects by the proper user. Execute Access and logon as the appropriate user. Create a new database using the New Database... command under the File menu. Now all objects that are created will belong to this user.

Creating a new database is often not practical because often the database to which you must add ownership information already exists. Therefore, execute Access and log on as the appropriate user. Create a new database using the New Database... command under the File menu. Next select the Import... command under the File menu. Now all of the tables can be imported and the ownership will be designated as the user whose account is currently running.

If specific object ownership must be changed or all of the ownership is to be changed by hand, select the Change Owner... command under the Security menu. This brings up the Change

Owner window. (See Figure 16.17.) All of the objects for the database are listed in the list box, as well as each of the current owners of the objects. The combo box below the list box shows the types of objects currently being displayed. You can select one or more of the objects in the list box to change the ownership.

FIGURE 16.17.
Changing ownership.

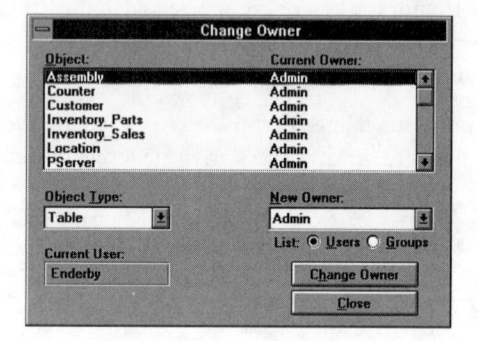

To select a new owner (user or group), select the new owner in the New Owner combo box. Clicking the Change Owner button reassigns the owner of the selected object or objects.

Types of Permissions

There are various types of permissions available for each user. A user can have read-only access, or permission to access a specific query but not another. Access is extremely flexible in its capability to define what each user and group can and cannot do within a database. Table 16.1 lists all of the possible access options and a brief description of what each option entails.

Table 16.1. Permission types.

Permission Type	Description
Open/Run	Opens a database, form, or report, or runs a macro.
Open Exclusive	Opens a database with exclusive access.
Read Design	Read access for tables, queries, forms, reports, macros, and modules.
Modify Design	Changes or deletes tables, queries, forms, reports, macros, and modules.
Administer	Can assign permissions and has full access to tables, queries, forms, reports, macros, and modules.
Read Data	Read access to tables and queries.
Update Data	Read and modify access to tables and queries, but cannot insert or delete data.

Permission Type	Description
Insert Data	Read and insert access to tables and queries, but cannot modify or delete data.
Delete Data	Read and delete access to tables and queries, but cannot modify or insert data.

Encryption of a Database

Encryption is used to make information unviewable by utilities and word processors that could read the data of the database file directly rather that through standard database-opening techniques. It makes the file appear scrambled to the utility or word processor.

To encrypt an Access database, the file must be rewritten to the hard disk. Encrypting uses the same basic interactions that the `Compact Database` command uses. The database is copied from its source into its new encrypted format. All databases must be closed before the encryption menu option is available.

Select the Encrypt/Decrypt option under the File menu. You must select a database to be encrypted and then enter a filename to which the encrypted version will be saved. If the identical filename is given, the new file is created and if successful, replaces the older file. Security to the encrypted file is through the same method (username and password) by which other secured access occurs.

Changing ODBC Options

You might need to change the options used for ODBC connections for the particular database that the client/server system needs to access. Select Options... under the View menu. In the category box, scroll down and select the Multiuser/ODBC option set. (See Figure 16.18.) These are all of the options that apply to Multiuser or ODBC access to this Access database.

FIGURE 16.18.
ODBC link options.

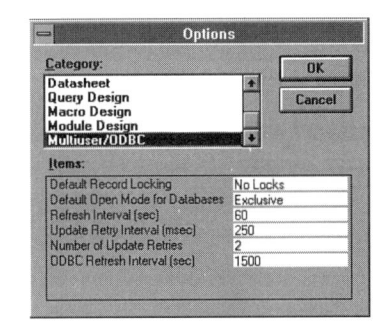

You can change all of these options from their default values. (See Table 16.2 for the list of options.) Following the table are descriptions of each option.

Table 16.2. Multiuser/ODBC MS Access options.

Option	Possible Values
Default Record Locking	No Locks, All Records, or Edited Record
Default Open Mode for Databases	Exclusive or Shared
Refresh Interval (sec)	1 to 32,766
Update Retry Interval (msec)	0 to 1000
Number of Update Retries	0 to 10
ODBC Refresh Interval (sec)	1 to 3600

Default Record Locking enables the selection of the locking strategy. The No Locks option is *optimistic locking*. The record is actually locked, but only for the milliseconds it takes for a connection to update the record. The Edited Record is optimistic locking that actually locks the whole page on which the record exists while an edit is taking place. The All Records option locks all records while a database is being accessed.

Default Open Mode for Databases opens the database as either Exclusive or Shared. Usually, while designing or making actual modifications to the database structure, you should use Exclusive access. Otherwise, on a multiuser system, Shared access is a much better idea.

Refresh Interval governs how often the records in memory are refreshed from the database. In a multiuser environment, other users will make alterations to the data that will be transparent to the user until an update occurs. The Refresh option under the Records menu enables the user to refresh the records manually at any time.

Update Retry Interval determines the amount of time the Access engine will wait before retrying an update on a record after an updating error has occurred on that record. The record might be in the middle of an update for another user, so the retry will attempt to update after the user has finished. The record might also be locked because an update is occurring on a record that exists on the same page as the desired record.

Number of Update Retries determines the number of times a retry is attempted. This number should not be too high; otherwise the user must sit without any status update. A better interface is to leave the retry number low and when the update fails, offer the user a choice of what to do (retry, abort, or ignore).

ODBC Refresh Interval is the same basic type as the Refresh Interval value except that it relates only to attached ODBC data sources.

Access Security from Access Basic

Most of the security options available in MS Access are also available programmatically through Access Basic or VBA. Permissions, ownership, User accounts, Group accounts, and passwords may be assigned through Access Basic or VBA. You can also encrypt a database using the `CompactDatabase()` command.

The Access Basic commands use the objects built into MS Access to change these various attributes. For more information on Access Object access, see Chapter 17, "Overview of Visual Basic for Applications (VBA)."

Creating Users and Group Accounts

The `Workspace` object includes the `CreateUser()` and `CreateGroup()` methods, which enable a program to create new users and groups. The routine in Listing 16.1 demonstrates creating a new group and new users. Notice the objects `Group` and `User` are created using the proper method. They are then appended to the collection of other similar objects (users or groups).

Listing 16.1. Creating users and groups with Access Basic.

```
Sub CreateSalesUsers ()
    Dim WS As WorkSpace
    Dim RoadSales As Group
    Dim TempUser As User
    Dim i

    Set WS = DBEngine.Workspaces(0)
    ' CreateGroup (GroupName, PersonalID)
    Set RoadSales = WS.CreateGroup("RoadSales", "RoadSales")
    WS.Groups.Append RoadSales

    For i = 2 To 10
        ' CreateUser(UserName,PersonalID, Password)
        Set TempUser = WS.CreateUser("Sales" & i, "Sales" & i, "")
        WS.Users.Append TempUser
    Next i
End Sub
```

Assigning Permissions to Objects

Access Basic also provides you with complete control over security permissions to objects in the database. By cycling through the containers, access can be automatically granted to all people in the Management group. Listing 16.2 shows an example of the `Permissions` property change to include full access.

Listing 16.2. Setting permissions of objects with Access Basic.
```
Sub SetPermission ()
    Dim MyDb As Database
    Dim i As Integer, j As Integer

    ' Set MyDB object to current database
    Set MyDb = DBEngine.Workspaces(0).Databases(0)

    ' Give full permission to the Management group for all objects
    For i = 0 To MyDb.Containers.Count - 1
        For j = 0 To MyDb.Containers(i).Documents.Count - 1
            MyDb.Containers(i).Documents(j).UserName = "Management"
            MyDb.Containers(i).Documents(j).Permissions = DB_SEC_FULLACCESS
        Next j
    Next i
End Sub
```

Changing Ownership of Objects

If any of the techniques for changing the ownership of object by hand are too specialized or not appropriate for the current database application, Access Basic can automate the process. As shown in Listing 16.3, the ownership of an object can be changed by altering the Owner property.

Listing 16.3. Setting ownership of an object with Access Basic.
```
Sub SetOwnership ()
    ' If an error occurs, move to the next object
    On Error Resume Next

    Dim MyDb As Database, MyCont As Container, MyDoc As Document
    Dim i As Integer, j As Integer

    ' Set MyDB object to current database
    Set MyDb = DBEngine.Workspaces(0).Databases(0)

    ' Set all objects to owner: MyOwner
    For i = 0 To MyDb.Containers.Count - 1
        Set MyCont = MyDb.Containers(i)
        For j = 0 To MyCont.Documents.Count - 1
            Set MyDoc = MyCont.Documents(j)
            MyDoc.Owner = "MyOwner"
        Next j
    Next i
End Sub
```

Changing and Clearing Passwords

Access Basic can also alter passwords programmatically. It is not recommended that you use these commands unless you're building a system administrator program, however. It is very easy to change many passwords this way, which creates possible security loopholes if password generation is not approached methodically.

The code in Listing 16.4 shows two ways of setting a password. The first two lines of code demonstrate using the `NewPassword` method to change the Admin account from the default empty password to `AdminPwd`. The second set of code sets the password as the user is created. The user `JohnHoward` is created with a password of `Password`.

Listing 16.4. Setting the password to an account with Access Basic.
```
Sub SetPasswords ()
    Dim WS As WorkSpace
    Dim TempUser As User

    Set WS = DBEngine.Workspaces(0)
    WS.Users("Admin").NewPassword "", "AdminPwd"

    Set TempUser = WS.CreateUser("JohnHoward", "JohnHoward", "Password")
    WS.Users.Append TempUser
End Sub
```

Using *CompactDatabase* to Encrypt

The `CompactDatabase` method from the `DBEngine` object can encrypt or decrypt a database. Listing 16.5 is a routine to encrypt the WIDGETCO.MDB into a new database called ENCRYPT.MDB. The last value in the `CompactDatabase` method determines the encryption. If omitted, the new database will have the same encryption (encrypted or not) as the original database. If set to `DB_ENCRYPT`, it will be encrypted, whereas `DB_DECRYPT` will decrypt the specified database.

Listing 16.5. Encryption in Access Basic.
```
Sub EncryptWidget()
    DBEngine.CompactDatabase "C:\CLNTSRVR\WIDGETCO.MDB",
    ➥"C:\CLNTSRVR\ENCRYPT.MDB", DB_LANG_GENERAL, DB_ENCRYPT
End Sub
```

Printing a Security Report

Microsoft Access enables the system administrator to print a security report to see all of the users and groups and their permission levels. The security report feature is available to anyone in the Admins group.

To print the report, select the Print Security... option under the Security menu. A preview of the Security Report is displayed. The report can be either printed or exported to Microsoft Word or Microsoft Excel.

Visual Basic/MS Access Security Interface

Visual Basic can use the Workspace object to address an MS Access database that has built-in security. Visual Basic can only access tables and queries in an Access database; therefore, privileges and permissions defined for the other database objects (such as Access forms, reports, modules, and so on) are not important to a Visual Basic-based system.

> **NOTE**
>
> Using the Workspace object is new in VB 4. In Visual Basic 3.0, the commands SetDataAccessOption and SetDefaultWorkspace are used to set security access. The functionality, however, remains essentially the same.

You can set the INIPath property if the .INI file for the application is not stored in the \WINDOWS directory with a name that matches the name of the .EXE file (for example, Sales.INI for Sales.EXE). This statement must appear before any data access calls are made or forms with data controls are loaded. For example, the following code sets the data access engine to look for the Sales.INI file in the Sales directory:

```
DBEngine.IniPath = "C:\CLNTSRVR\SALES\SALES.INI"
```

You can use the Workspace object to create a DBEngine workspace with a username and password for session access to password-protected tables. If specific Workspace-object creation is excluded, Visual Basic sends the generic administrator name and password to the JET engine. The DefaultUsername property is set to Admin; the DefaultPassword is set to "". You can set these properties in the DBEngine object so that all new Workspace objects created will use the new settings.

> **NOTE**
>
> Visual Basic must reference the SYSTEM.MDW file in order for the Access security mechanisms to be used in an effective way. Make sure that the Admin password has been altered from its default as ""; otherwise, any general logon can have administrator access.

Each logon-and-password combination is stored in the SYSTEM.MDW file with a unique SID. Any data-access call activates the SYSTEM.MDW file, which is checked for the username and password that were sent by the accessing Workspace object. If the database is not secured, the username and password properties in the workspace are ignored.

Modifying the Client/Server System

The client/server system can use the security features provided by MS Access with only slight modifications. For example, the Sales client has no reason to access the Purchase or PurchaseItems tables. You therefore create four different groups in the security settings: Sales, Purchase, Management, and PServer. You can then create individual users and add them to the groups and give the groups access permission to the necessary tables.

Then the various client applications and .INI files can be modified to use the new security features. The client/server system is then a complete, secure implementation.

Security on the Tables

Each table should be accessible by a particular type of user. Therefore, you create a group for each type of client in the client/server system: Sales, Purchase, Management, and PServer.

Table 16.3 contains a list of each of the tables that are included in the client/server system and indicates which clients have access to each table. Because you have not yet added any specific Access queries to the database that might be called from the client programs (each query is coded in the client), there is no need to set query permissions.

Table 16.3. Client program's access to tables.

TableName	Sales	Client Access Purchase	Management	PServer
Sales	Yes	No	Yes	No
SalesItems	Yes	No	Yes	No
Purchase	No	Yes	Yes	No

continues

Table 16.3. continued

TableName	Sales	Client Access Purchase	Management	PServer
PurchaseItems	No	Yes	Yes	No
Assembly	No	Yes	Yes	No
Inventory_Sales	Yes	Yes	Yes	Yes
Inventory_Parts	No	Yes	Yes	Yes
Customer	Yes	No	Yes	No
Supplier	No	Yes	Yes	No
PServer	No	Yes	Yes	Yes
Counter	Yes	Yes	Yes	No
Location	Yes	Yes	Yes	No
Staff	Yes	Yes	Yes	No

Here the Management client has access to all of the tables. This is simply an example; often you create different Decision Support System applications, each with its own access privileges necessary to produce the reports it generates. The Pseudo Server only has access to the tables that are used by the program. You could make the Pseudo Server program cover more areas of responsibility, which would require increased permissions to access the necessary data.

Access to data from any one client program should be kept to a minimum. For the safety and the integrity of the data, only those clients that need access to particular areas should have it. For example, although the Management client has access to all of the tables, most of its access is limited to read-only. The Management client does not need full access; providing it would be inappropriate.

Adding security might seem like extra work, but in the long run, it pays for itself by preventing costly corrupted-data problems. If each machine has password protection and each database is secured, the chances of accidental data corruption or illegal system access are greatly reduced.

Creating the Groups

You need to create four groups to define the access privileges of all of the users. Creating groups is an extremely simple process.

Select the Groups... option under the Security menu. The Groups window appears on the screen. Click the New... button to add a group. Type Sales in both the Name and PersonalID fields for the Sales client group. Click the OK button to create the group. Do the same for each of the following groups: Purchase, PServer, and Management. For easy reference, make the PersonalID the same as the group name.

After you have created all of the groups, close the Groups window; the groups are now created. Now you can add users to the system and assign each to a particular group.

Creating the Users

Now create four users for the system, one for each client program. The user names are nearly identical to the group names and are entered into the .INI files of the individual clients. Name the four users Sales1, Purchase1, Management1, and PServer1. Feel free to change the user names, but make sure the parameters in the .INI files match the names you use.

Select the Users... option under the Security menu. The Users window appears on the screen. Click the New... button to add a user. Type Sales1 in the Name and the PersonalID fields for the Sales client. Click the OK button to create the user.

The Sales1 user is automatically selected in the Users window. The Groups box below the list box on the right side (Member Of:) should show the Users group. This group is automatically added to the new user list. The list box on the right of the Groups box should contain all of the available groups. Because this is the Sales user, select the Sales group and click the Add button to add the group to the member list.

Do the same for each of the following users: Purchase1, PServer1, and Management1. For easy reference, make the PersonalID the same as the User name. Add the appropriate groups to each member list (that is, Purchase1 should have the Purchase group added, and so on).

Now that you have created all of the users and groups and the users have been added to the appropriate groups, you can begin to add the permissions. You set all of the permissions at the Group level, and also reset the permissions of the Users group to which each of the users belongs.

Eliminating the Users Group's Permissions

Because most users are added to the Users group, the complete access privileges of this group should be eliminated. You can then add access for all of the appropriate tables to a specific group. Having a group that all users belong to has the great advantage of giving the administrator the capability to quickly add or remove access for particular database objects for all user accounts. However, such a broadly powerful group can be dangerous to security because users might have permission to more tables than they should. In these cases, it is often best to eliminate all access and begin from scratch. This prevents access being given unknowingly.

Select Permissions... under the Security menu. Click the Groups radio button to show the available groups and select the Users group. (See Figure 16.19.) In the Object Names list box on the right, select all of the available tables by clicking and holding down the mouse button while moving the cursor downward. You can also select it by clicking the first table name, using the scrollbar until the final table is shown, and holding down the Shift key while clicking the last table.

FIGURE 16.19.
Resetting the Users group's permissions.

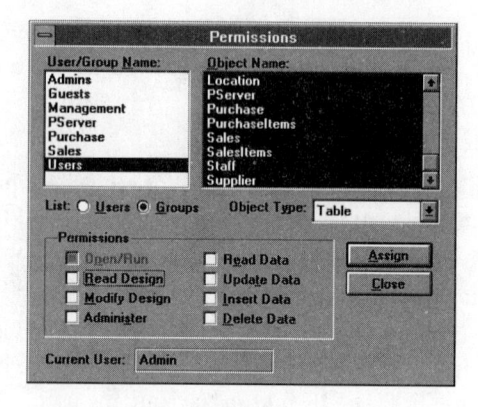

Now that all of the tables are selected, all of the check boxes in the Permissions box should be gray. Click any of the options and all of the boxes should turn white or empty, as shown in Figure 16.19. With all of the boxes empty, the Users group has no permissions to any of the tables.

Click the Assign button to set the Users group. Now you can select any individual table and give permission for the whole group. In this example, the Users group is left without any permissions. The Users group provides an excellent way to provide universal access to a database object.

Setting Up a New Administrator

Before you set up the permissions for the client/server system, it is a good idea to make the database secure. By default, any Visual Basic logon to an Access database uses the username of Admin and a blank password (""). To make the system secure, you have to change the Admin password so a Visual Basic program can't just jump past the security and access the database.

Log onto Access as the Admin user. If you have yet to create any password access, simply execute Access. Select the Change Password... option from the Security menu. The Change Password form is shown. Leave the Old Password field blank because the current Admin password is blank ("").

Enter a password into the New Password and Verify fields. Make the password something you'll remember and also write it down. Write it someplace you'll be able to find it, perhaps even on the inside cover of this book. To change any security you must have access to the Admin account in the future.

Click the OK button and the new password is saved. Exit and reexecute the application and notice you have to logon to Access. Type in the username of Admin and then type the password you just created. The database is now secure from backdoor access.

Setting Client/Server Permissions

Now you must set the permissions for each group. Table 16.4 lists all of the permissions from each table. You set permissions from the Permissions window. Select the Permissions... option from the Security menu. The window should show all of the users in the list box on the left and all of the tables in the list box on the right. Click the Groups radio button to show the groups in the left list box.

Select the Sales group. First, make sure that the group has no permissions. Select all of the tables in the right list box, clear the settings, and click the Assign button. (For more information on how to clear settings, see the "Eliminating the Users Group's Permissions" section.) Now that all of the permissions for the group have been cleared, you can begin assigning them.

Table 16.4. Client program's access to tables.

TableName	Sales	Client Access Purchase	Management	PServer
Sales	Full	None	ReadOnly	None
SalesItems	Full	None	ReadOnly	None
Purchase	None	Full	ReadOnly	None
PurchaseItems	None	Full	ReadOnly	None
Assembly	None	Full	ReadOnly	None
Inventory_Sales	Update	Full	ReadOnly	Update
Inventory_Parts	None	Full	ReadOnly	ReadOnly
Customer	Full	None	ReadOnly	None
Supplier	None	Full	ReadOnly	None
PServer	None	ReadOnly	ReadOnly	Full
Counter	Update	Update	ReadOnly	None
Location	ReadOnly	ReadOnly	Full	None
Staff	ReadOnly	ReadOnly	Full	None

Table 16.4 shows all of the permissions for the Sales group in the first column. Each specified permission setting (such as Full) determines which of the check boxes in the Permissions box should be checked. None of the groups will have the Read Design, Modify Design, or Administer boxes checked. Leave all of the table structure and other modifications for the Admin user.

If the permission setting is Full, then all four check boxes should be checked (Yes). With a ReadOnly setting, all of the check boxes should remain blank except for the Read Data check box.

Select each table for each group and set the permissions according to Tables 16.4 and 16.5. When this is finished, all of the groups should have the access that they need. Because the users have already been added to each group, they inherit the permissions settings.

Table 16.5. Access type reference.

Access Type	Read Data	Update Data	Insert Data	Delete Data
Full	Yes	Yes	Yes	Yes
ReadOnly	Yes	No	No	No
Update	Yes	Yes	No	No
None	No	No	No	No

Program Logon

To complete each client program's capability to access the secure database, you have to add code to each of the clients for proper logon. The Load() event for each form logs the client onto the system. The .INI files also have to be modified to support the new security. The username and password are added to the .INI files.

Modifying the Client .INI Files

First, modify each of the client .INI files. In many client/server systems, individual logon is not necessary nor advantageous. A particular user always uses the client program on his machine, or many people use the program but always for the same function. For this reason the username and password are added to the .INI file. The program then automatically logs onto the system when it is executed. This saves tedious password entry for a client that is always used in the same way.

If individual password protection is desired, it would be a fairly simple matter to make a password form that shows before any other form and prompts for the username and password. The construction of this form is left up to you.

Listing 16.6 shows the modification to the Sales.INI file. All of the code that appears in bold after the DBServer= setting should be added to the file with a text editor (such as Notepad.EXE). The UserName and Password parameters have been added to the [Access] section of the .INI file.

Notice that the Password parameter has been left blank. You did not give a password to the user in MS Access security, so this remains blank. If a password had been used, if would appear here.

A new section, [Options], has been added. This tells the Access/JET engine where to look for the system data security settings file. These statements must be present in the .INI file to enable use of the passwords. If these parameters cannot be found be the JET engine, access is completely denied. The parameters direct the engine to find these two files in the C:\ACCESS\ directory. This is for simplicity. In a real distributed client/server system, you would probably want to include these files in the application folder and set these parameters accordingly.

Listing 16.6. Sales.INI modified for security.

```
[Access]
DSN=
DBName=c:\clntsecu\clntsrvr\widgetco.mdb
DBServer=
UserName=Sales1
Password=

[Options]
SystemDB=C:\ACCESS\SYSTEM.MDW
UtilityDB=C:\ACCESS\UTILITY.MDA
```

These same modifications must be made to each of the other client .INI files. The Purchase.INI in Listing 16.7 has a UserName of Purchase1. The password is left blank as it was when the user was constructed.

Listing 16.7. Purchase.INI modified for security.

```
[Access]
DSN=
DBName=c:\clntsecu\clntsrvr\widgetco.mdb
DBServer=
UserName=Purchase1
Password=

[Options]
SystemDB=C:\ACCESS\SYSTEM.MDW
UtilityDB=C:\ACCESS\UTILITY.MDA
```

The Manage.INI in Listing 16.8 has a UserName of Management1. The password is left blank as it was when the user was constructed.

Listing 16.8. Manage.INI modified for security.

```
[Access]
DSN=
DBName=c:\clntsecu\clntsrvr\widgetco.mdb
DBServer=
UserName=Management1
Password=

[Options]
SystemDB=C:\ACCESS\SYSTEM.MDW
UtilityDB=C:\ACCESS\UTILITY.MDA
```

The PServer.INI in Listing 16.9 has a UserName of PServer1. The password is left blank as it was when the user was constructed.

Listing 16.9. PServer.INI modified for security.

```
[Access]
DSN=
DBName=c:\clntsecu\clntsrvr\widgetco.mdb
DBServer=
UserName=PServer1
Password=

[Options]
SystemDB=C:\ACCESS\SYSTEM.MDW
UtilityDB=C:\ACCESS\UTILITY.MDA
```

Modifying the Clients

The code in Listing 16.10 must be added to each of the clients in the `Form_Load()` event in the main form. The listing shows the modification to the `frm_Invoice` from the Sales client. The code in bold is added after the last reading of the .INI file and before any data access occurs.

The code creates two local variables: `UserName` and `Password`. These are used to read the name and the password from the .INI files.

> **NOTE**
>
> These variables are created at a procedure level instead of the global level (as the other .INI values are) for security reasons. In this implementation the password is stored in the .INI file, so the system is unsecured. If a password form were added, keeping the password in a local variable would be important. After the verification has taken place, if stored in a global variable, the password remains in memory for possible detection by a hacker. Setting it in a local variable ensures the system will flush the variables when the routine completes execution.

The `Workspace` object is used after the `ReadINI()` commands read the values from the .INI file to log the username and password into the system. Any databases that are now opened by this application are provided with this information. Enter this code into each of the client applications. No modifications are necessary because the unique parameters have been added to each .INI file.

Listing 16.10. Modified `Form_Load()` in `frm_Invoice` in the Sales project.

```
g_DBName = ReadINI(g_DataLocation, "DBName", INIPath)

Dim UserName As String, Password As String
Dim NewWorkspace As Workspace

' Read username and password from INI file
UserName = ReadINI(g_DataLocation, "UserName", INIPath)
Password = ReadINI(g_DataLocation, "Password", INIPath)

' Set up new secure workspace -- do not append to other workspaces
Set NewWorkspace = DBEngine.CreateWorkspace("NewWorkspace", UserName,
➥Password)

' Open connection to Database
Set MyDB = DBEngine.Workspaces("NewWorkspace").OpenDatabase(g_DBName,
➥False, False)

' Set up recordsets for invoice browsing
Set InvoicesDS = MyDB.OpenRecordset("Select * from Sales", dbOpenDynaset)
```

Testing the System

Now the system should be ready to use. First, test the system to make sure all of the security is in place: Execute MS Access and logon with the username of Sales1. The password was never set, so it can remain blank.

Double-click the Assembly table to open it. A `Permission Denied` message should appear (see Figure 16.20) that states you have no permission to use that table. Now double-click the Sales table; it should open perfectly. Try this with various other tables. Exit Access and log back on as the various users to make sure that each has the access granted and is denied permission where no privileges have been set.

FIGURE 16.20.
No permission to table from Access.

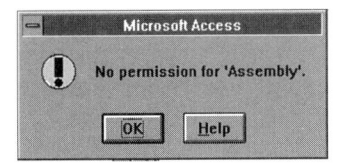

Now exit Access and execute one of the applications. Each application should execute perfectly. There should be no apparent change in their functioning. The programs themselves are designed to access only the data they need.

To make sure the security is working, change the username or password in one of the .INI files. When the application is executed, the error box shown in Figure 16.21 should appear. When you click the OK button the application will exit, letting you know that the username and password are actually being checked and that the system is secure.

FIGURE 16.21.
No permission to table from Visual Basic.

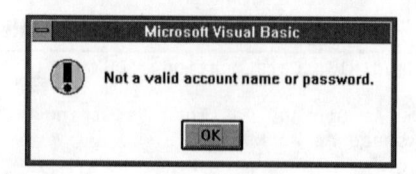

Object Security

With all of the MS Office applications moving toward complete OLE object compliance, security for objects and distributed processing is important. With the coming of technologies such as OLE DB, which provides OLE database and transaction capabilities of a network, security will be a very large issue. For more information on OLE and the security it uses, see Chapter 23, "Object Linking and Embedding (OLE)."

III

Using VBA for Client Front-Ends

17

Overview of Visual Basic for Applications (VBA)

Basic Languages

Visual Basic for Applications (VBA) is used in the following chapters to enhance the client/server system constructed thus far in the book. The version of Visual Basic for Applications that is included with Visual Basic 4 and with many of the Microsoft Office applications is fairly different from the version of Basic used by Visual Basic 3.0, so if you're just upgrading to VB 4, you should familiarize yourself with the changes. The language remains essentially the same, but greatly enhanced object features have been added.

This chapter will describe the basic features of VBA and its implementation in Excel and MS Project. Access Basic (the language used in Access 2.0) will also be briefly mentioned because of the amount of legacy code that will be slowly converted to the VBA language that is included with Access 95. As applications convert to a VBA-compatible language to provide their macro scripting and automation capabilities, understanding VBA will allow a client/server designer to leverage this new technology.

Objects are becoming increasingly important to the development world. VBA uses objects extensively, especially for database access. This chapter first provides an overview of the basic concepts of objects and their usage, including a description of the basic development environments of VBA in the current versions of the Microsoft Excel and Project applications. VBA is implemented differently depending on the base environment. You'll see how VBA is integrated into the main application and how that affects the way you interact with the environment.

Object Overview

VBA relies on objects for representation of many of its basic structures. For this reason, it is important to briefly explain how objects work. For a more complete explanation of objects, see Chapter 6, "Object Programming Overview." For a description of the role of objects in OLE and future computer development, see Chapter 23, "Object Linking and Embedding (OLE)."

Objects are the next great revolution in programming and design. They are easiest to explain in terms of older programming structures, yet the way they can be used opens entire new worlds of possibility.

On a very basic level, a program consists of routines and the data the routines use. These two pieces can be called procedures and data. Objects combine procedures and the data that relates to them into a single memory structure (see Figure 17.1). The procedures are called *methods* and the data is called *properties*. Both the methods and the properties are directly related to that particular object.

For example, a `Rectangle` object might contain properties such as `Left`, `Top`, `Right`, `Bottom`, `ForeColor`, `BackColor`, and so on, and contain methods such as `Move`, `Show`, `Draw`, `Paint`, and others. Because all of the data and the routines that manipulate that data are stored within the same structure (an object), objects are modular, unlike the traditional separation between routines and variables. All of the important information regarding an object is bound within it.

FIGURE 17.1.
The structure of an object.

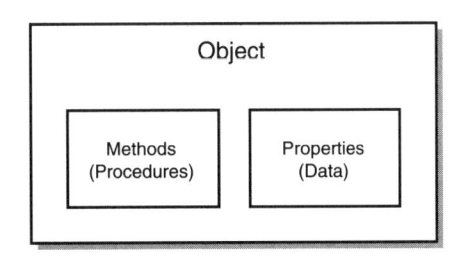

```
┌─────────────────────────────────────┐
│              Object                 │
│                                     │
│   ┌──────────────┐ ┌──────────────┐ │
│   │   Methods    │ │  Properties  │ │
│   │ (Procedures) │ │    (Data)    │ │
│   └──────────────┘ └──────────────┘ │
└─────────────────────────────────────┘
```

As a Visual Basic programmer, you are probably used to many object concepts. A *form*, for example, is an excellent example of a basic object with various properties (such as `Caption`, `Enabled`, `Top`, and `Left`) and methods (`Show`, `Cls`, `Move`, and so on). Interacting with a more complex object is very similar to interacting with a form.

In Visual Basic, you can create and manipulate objects in a hierarchical order, almost like a relational database. For example, you can have a form (one object) with additional objects placed on it and other objects placed within those objects. Many objects require the definition of other objects for their creation (these are called *dependent objects*).

Figure 17.2 shows a diagram of objects you are probably already familiar with through programming Visual Basic. *Data Access Objects* (DAO) are a collection of objects with their own properties and methods. VBA is structured to be entirely object-oriented. Even constants are included in the object metaphor as read-only properties.

FIGURE 17.2.
Microsoft Visual Basic objects.

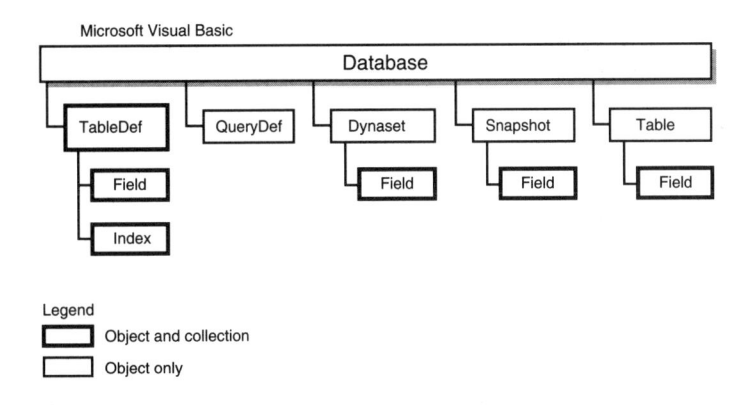

Figure 17.3 shows all of the objects available through the newest JET engine. Everything from fields to queries to security is represented as an object or object properties. In the figure, notice that each layer in the hierarchy becomes more specific.

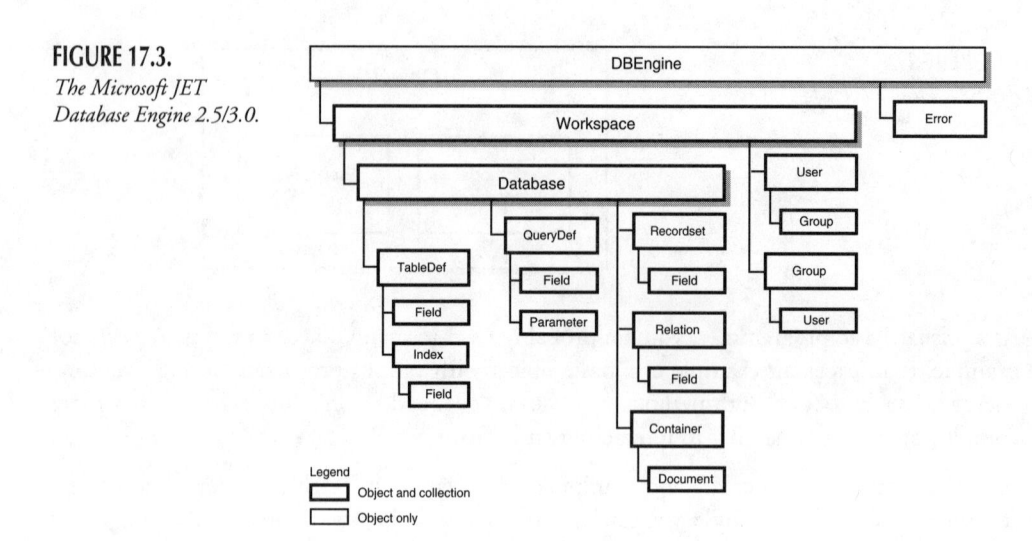

FIGURE 17.3.
The Microsoft JET Database Engine 2.5/3.0.

Collections

Multiple objects of the same type can be stored in collections (see Figure 17.4). For example, a `Worksheet` collection is made up of numerous individual worksheets. Collections can be addressed in one of three ways: using the exclamation point (!), using the object name, or using the object's index.

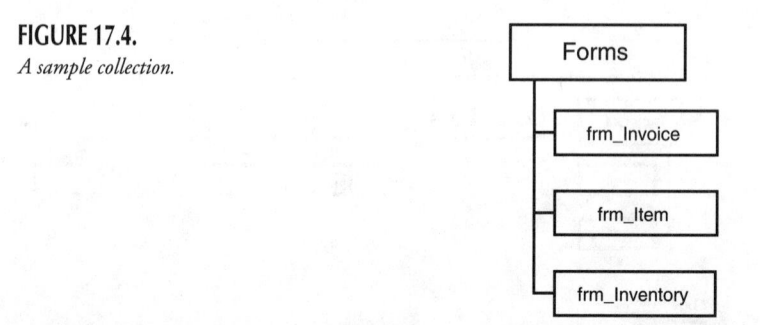

FIGURE 17.4.
A sample collection.

To access `frm_Invoice` in a collection of forms, you can use any of these three methods. For example:

```
Forms![frm_Invoice]
Forms("frm_Invoice")
Forms(0)
```

Note that the brackets in the first statement are optional unless the object name contains a space or punctuation (for example, if the form name is "Big Form"). The third example assumes that `frm_Invoice` is the first form in the collection.

Each collection contains a Count property that holds the number of objects in the collection. Listing 17.1 is an example of using the Count property with the index references to show all of the forms in the collection.

Listing 17.1. Using the Count property.
```
For i = 0 to Forms.Count
    Forms(i).Show
Next i
```

It is often a better idea to use the For...Each command (described in the section "For...Each...Next") to move through a collection. The objects might be nonsequential, which can cause an error if you do not use this command. Collection objects are accessed using the plural of the normal object name. For example, the collection named Worksheets is a collection of Worksheet objects. To access a single object in a collection, you must use an index value (in the same way an item is selected in an array). For example, Workspaces(0) accesses a single workspace in the Workspaces collection.

Access Basic (for Access 2.0)

Access Basic is the implementation of the BASIC language in the Microsoft Access 2.0 application. Although Access Basic is obsolete with the introduction of Access 95 (which contains the VBA engine), a great amount of legacy code has been created in the Access Basic dialect. The implementation of Access Basic is about 80 percent identical to Visual Basic. Code written in VB and Access Basic is nearly portable and compatible, allowing conversion without substantial difficulty.

In general, all of the BASIC implementations embedded in these applications (Access, Excel, Project, and so on) function as macro languages for each application. They can access all of the functionality and user-interface capabilities of the host program. Access Basic, for example, can send queries to the Access engine or print a particular report.

As demonstrated in Chapter 16, "Access Security," Access Basic (and now VBA in Access) has complete programmatic access to database security. Visual Basic does not include any user, group, or permission commands. Access Basic contains objects for complete creation and manipulation of all Access security features.

Access Code Libraries

Code libraries are one of the most crucial factors needed to improve productivity of application programming. These libraries store code that can be shared across a programming project.

For example, you can store a routine such as form centering in the library. Each application can then access the common code to save time developing and debugging. This helps cut down on reinventing the wheel.

MS Access includes the capabilities of a code library. A library in MS Access can contain more than just code, however; it is a standard database that has been modified to be used globally. It can therefore contain forms, reports, code, tables, and so on, thus enabling the creation of Wizards, general tables, and shared code. Functions in the code library should be general purpose and should contain code that is generic enough to be reused. To create a library, two steps are required:

1. Change the database extension from .MDB to .MDA.
2. Add an entry to the Libraries section of the MSACC20.INI file that denotes the library database. Put the entry in the form `filename=[rw¦ro]`.

To change the filename, simply execute File Manager and select the file. Use the Rename... option under the File menu. All library databases will have the .MDA extension. After a database is loaded as a library, it cannot be opened as a database anymore.

To change the .INI file, execute the Notepad application. Select the Find... option under the Search menu. Search for the string `[Libraries]`. Entries similar to the one shown in Listing 17.2 should already be under the section heading. These are the libraries already used by MS Access.

Listing 17.2. Default .INI settings.

```
[Libraries]
wzlib.mda=rw
wzTable.mda=rw
wzQuery.mda=rw
wzfrmrpt.mda=rw
wzbldr.mda=rw
WZCS.MDA=rw
```

An entry might specify that the library is read-only (ro) or read-write (rw). Using read-only libraries is faster, so determine if your library must have write access. Move the cursor to the end of the last entry of the section and press the Enter key. Now type the name of your new library followed by a read-only or read-write specification. Listing 17.3 provides an example of MyLib.MDA entered into the library.

Listing 17.3. New .INI settings.

```
[Libraries]
wzlib.mda=rw
wzTable.mda=rw
wzQuery.mda=rw
```

```
wzfrmrpt.mda=rw
wzbldr.mda=rw
WZCS.MDA=rw
MyLib.MDA=ro
```

Save the .INI file and re-execute MS Access. All of the library objects should now be globally available. If you are using this on a shared network drive with a team, be sure to document the library well. Although libraries are accessible from within any database, they do not appear as part of the database.

Visual Basic for Applications

VB 4 uses the essential VBA engine. Therefore, all of the features described in this chapter are also contained in the newest implementation of VB, as well as in any application that supports VBA. For a complete list of Visual Basic 4 features, see Chapter 7, "Visual Basic 4."

At the time of this writing, Microsoft had stated that it has no plans to release VBA for incorporation into third-party applications. Languages touted as VBA-compatible that can be added to a program for VBA compatibility are already beginning to appear (see Appendix C, "Sources"). These tools allow developers to add a VBA compatibility (such as VBA macros, automation, and a development environment) into their programs.

In many applications, VBA routines will be labeled as *macros*. Spreadsheets were the first applications to popularize macros, which are an executable string of commands—like a miniature programming language. As computers became more powerful, macro languages did as well, rivaling the power of a complete programming language. BASIC derivatives (VBA and compatibles) have begun to supplant these application-specific macro languages, but some of the terminology remains. As such, where appropriate this chapter describes the programs as macros (function macros, procedural macros, and so on).

Language Specifics

VBA includes new language commands and structures. Operations such as new ways to treat the scope of variables, For...Each...Next commands, With...EndWith statements, and While...Wend commands all make VBA a powerful language. The language even includes a line-continuation character. New property commands that provide information-hiding capabilities are included in VBA.

The new Property statements (Let, Get, and Set) provide tremendous additional potential for designing user-friendly and error-preventing code. These statements provide structured access to various properties, allowing a program to do pre-processing.

> **NOTE**
>
> Unlike Visual Basic 4, the versions of VBA included in the MS Office applications (other than Access) are not currently event-based. This means that programming VBA has to be approached slightly differently. Whereas Visual Basic activates the Form_Click() routine when a mouse click is made on a form, VBA provides no such structure. This is mainly because most applications have different environments, making specific event procedures difficult.

The Scope of Variables

In traditional Visual Basic, the scope of a created variable is typically easy to identify. If created in a routine, it is local to that routine. If created in the Declarations section of a form, it is local to all routines in the form. If created in the Declarations sections of a module, it is local to that module unless it begins with the keyword GLOBAL, in which case it is global in scope. You can access a global variable from any code in the project.

Because of the embedded nature of VBA, programs are usually stored in macros in an indeterminate place and can be called from anywhere in the controlling application. The difference of the fundamental location of code (individual macros versus a project) requires a slightly different approach to the scope of variables.

A variable with a *procedure-level scope* can only be accessed from within a routine. This works the same as the Visual Basic local variable. The routine in Listing 17.4 demonstrates this local scope. The TempVar variable cannot be accessed by any other macro.

Listing 17.4. Procedure-level variable.

```
Sub ProcedureVar ()
     Dim TempVar as Integer
     TempVar = 5
End Sub
```

For a variable with *module-level scope*, the variable definition must be placed outside the routine and before any procedure definitions. This is similar to placing a variable in the General Declarations area of a form or module in Visual Basic. Listing 17.5 shows an example of a variable accessible by all of the routines within that module.

Listing 17.5. Module-level variable.

```
Dim ModuleVar as Integer

Sub Proc1 ()
    ModuleVar = 3
End Sub

Sub Proc2 ()
    ModuleVar = ModuleVar + 3
End Sub
```

A variable with a *project-level scope* can be created in any module and can be accessed by any module in the project (or any worksheet collection, in the case of Excel). The variable is created using the keyword Public instead of the traditional Dim keyword. Listing 17.6 declares the project-level variable for global access by all of the modules.

Listing 17.6. Project-level variable.

```
Public GlobalVar as Integer

Sub Proc1 ()
    GlobalVar = 3
End Sub
```

Static Variables

Static variables are essentially local variables that do not lose their values when the routine completes execution. Listing 17.7 shows a traditional local variable. After the ProcedureVar() routine completes execution, the TempVar variable is discarded and the value it contains is lost.

Listing 17.7. Traditional local variable.

```
Sub ProcedureVar ()
    Dim TempVar as Integer
    TempVar = 5
End Sub
```

With a static variable, like a module-level variable, the value remains after execution is complete. As a static variable, however, it can still only be accessed by the routine that declares it. Listing 17.8 shows two routines that access a static TempVar variable. Notice that while the InitVar() routine initializes the variable, the ProcedureVar() routine adds 5 to the already existing number. Therefore, every time ProcedureVar() is called, 5 is added to the sustained value of the variable.

Listing 17.8. Static variable.

```
Sub InitVar ()
    Static TempVar as Integer
    TempVar = 5
End Sub

Sub ProcedureVar ()
    Static TempVar as Integer
    TempVar = TempVar + 5
End Sub
```

> **NOTE**
>
> The scopes of variables described in the section "Scope of Variables" are all available in Visual Basic, where scope is more easily determined and coded because of the environment. In VBA, scope is less obvious, making it a more important detail to consider.

For...Each...Next

The `For...Each...Next` commands provide a loop that steps through all of the objects in a collection or elements in an array. It can therefore act as a more powerful `For...Next` loop that can modify or access each of the elements within the structure in the same way.

For example, you can use the `For...Each...Next` loop to cycle through each worksheet in the `ActiveWorkbook` collection (which holds all of the worksheet objects in Excel) to change their titles to sequential numbers.

With...End With

You use the `With` statement to abbreviate object references. The command is used to set a particular object that all of the directly following statements will use. For example, Listing 17.9 shows setting the font and style of a particular range of Excel spreadsheet cells. In every line you'll notice that the `ActiveWorkbook.Worksheets(1).Range("A1").Font` portion is identical. This is because the same object is being referenced in the same way. The `With` statement enables you to make many references to a single object in a much simpler fashion.

Listing 17.9. Traditional object reference.

```
ActiveWorkbook.Worksheets(1).Range("A1").Font.Name = "Times New Roman"
ActiveWorkbook.Worksheets(1).Range("A1").Font.Bold = True
ActiveWorkbook.Worksheets(1).Range("A1").Font.Italic = True
ActiveWorkbook.Worksheets(1).Range("A1").Font.Size = 22
```

Listing 17.10 shows the same operation, but using the With command instead of all the typing. You can dramatically simplify the coding by using the With...End With commands. The amount of typing required for the more traditional method also increases the chance that a typo will misreference an object. In addition to reducing the amount of typing required, it can also improve performance over the literal listing of the object path.

Listing 17.10. With...End With object reference.
```
With ActiveWorkbook.Worksheets(1).Range("A1").Font
     .Bold = True
     .Italic = True
     .Size = 22
End With
```

The With statement can be used effectively when two or more properties or methods for a single object must be accessed. With statements can also be nested. In Listing 17.11, the ActiveWorkbook.Worksheets(1) object is accessed with calls to both the Select and Unprotect methods. If you use a nested With statement, the object may also be used to set the font values of the range.

Listing 17.11. Nested With object reference.
```
With ActiveWorkbook.Worksheets(1)
     .Select
     .Unprotect
     With .Range("A1").Font
          .Bold = True
          .Italic = True
          .Size = 22
     End With
End With
```

The With statement may be freely used with other Visual Basic programming commands. There are no essential limitations to which commands you can use within a With...End With command bracket. The use of the With statement in a For...Next loop is shown in Listing 17.12.

Listing 17.12. With...End With and other commands.
```
Sub WithRoutine ()
    With ActiveWindow
        For i = 0 to 10
            .Height = .Height + 10
        Next i
        TempVar = TempVar + 1
    End With
End Sub
```

While...Wend

VBA contains the While...Wend commands which provide a loop that is opposite in function to the traditional Visual Basic Do...Until. The While...Wend commands create a loop that continues while the condition is TRUE. Listing 17.13 provides an example of a While...Wend loop in which the loop continues while the variable i does not equal 7.

Listing 17.13. While...Wend loop.

```
Sub WhileWendTest ()
    Dim i As Integer
    i = 0
    While i <> 7
        i = i + 1
    Wend
End Sub
```

The Line-Continuation Character

A feature that has been missing from Visual Basic since its creation is a line-continuation character. This enables a single command line to extend beyond the length of a text editor line. A single line of Visual Basic code may now be continued on two or more lines in the Code Editor window. Both VBA and Visual Basic 4 support the use of this character (the underline) to extend a program line.

In the past, a single BASIC line could sometimes extend for nearly 200 to 300 characters to complete the whole statement. With the great amount of typing for object references, lines promise to become even longer. Breaking a single long line into multiple continued lines will dramatically improve the readability of the code.

Fortunately, VBA supplies a line-continuation character that enables you to extend a single command across multiple text lines. Using the continuation character is extremely simple. Enter a space followed by an underline character (_) at the end of the line that you want to continue. The next line becomes a continuation of the statement.

Property Procedures (Let, Get, and Set)

The new Property commands (Property Let, Property Get, and Property Set) provide great programming power by enabling you to shield the user from direct access to a properties variable. When you select Procedure from the Insert menu and choose the Property radio button, a Get and Let pair of procedures is created that does all of the property access. These two routines enable you to verify or convert any property before it is stored to or retrieved from the property location. The internal implementation of any property can be effectively shielded from the user.

The `Property Let` command creates a routine that sets the value of a property. The `Property Get` command creates a routine that returns the value of a property. The `Property Set` command creates a routine that sets a reference to an object. These three routines allow the handling of a property for an object.

The `Property Get` routine, for example, could return the text of a number value. In Listing 17.14, the string of status is returned by creating a `Property Get` routine. The `Get` statement could have also done calculation or verified the value of the requested property.

Listing 17.14. Property Get routine.

```
Dim CurrentStatus As Integer
Const Good = 0, Bad = 1, Ugly = 2

' Returns the current status of the variable as a string
Property Get Status() As String
     Select Case CurrentStatus
          Case Good
               Status= "Good"
          Case Bad
               Status= "Bad"
          Case Ugly
               Status= "Ugly"
     End Select
End Property

' This routine gets the status string by calling the Get routine
StatusStr = Status()
```

The `Property Let` routine is activated when the user wants to set the value of a property. For example, perhaps a shipping charge is only added if the item costs more than $100. In an Excel macro the current cell would be automatically set with the proper number when a cost is entered (see Listing 17.15).

Listing 17.15. Property Let routine.

```
Property Let ShipPrice(ByVal ItemCost)
     If ItemCost <= 100 Then
          ActiveCell.Value = ItemCost
     Else
          ActiveCell.Value = ItemCost + 10
     End If
End Property

Invoice.ShipPrice = 135
```

Event Handling

Unlike Visual Basic, VBA has no built-in event-driven foundation. Only VB 4 and Access 95 supplement the VBA engine by adding event-driven capabilities. When an event such as a `Click` on a form occurs in Visual Basic, the `Form_Click` event routine is automatically executed. This provides the event-driven architecture for which VB is famous.

VBA does not inherently contain events. The language is essentially procedure-driven, meaning it can poll events and react to them, but this is not done automatically. In Excel, for example, you can create a button to call a VBA macro, but there aren't such things as `MouseMove()` or `MouseDown()` events.

Lacking Features

VBA, as implemented in applications, can only be expanded using custom controls as the environment supports. At the time of this writing, only VB 4 and Access 95 could support OCX controls. Therefore, a control available in VB might not be accessible in a VBA environment.

VBA implementations cannot create a standalone executable. Only VB can create a final .EXE that can execute without a parent application. Access 95 now provides a runtime (which is an .EXE of Access that has all of the programming capabilities removed) that enables distribution of Access applications without complete installation of Access on each client machine. However, all of the other VBA applications (Excel, Project, and so on) require the actual application to execute the VBA code.

There are also no specific form-designing methods in VBA. Programs in which VBA are embedded (such as MS Access) sometimes provide indigenous user-interface features (such as an Access form), but this will not be standard across VBA implementations.

VBA in Microsoft Excel and Microsoft Project

VBA is currently included in three of the MS Office applications: Access 95, Excel, and Project. All of these applications have a robust object implementation. Access 95 provides its own programming and development environment, but reviewing it is beyond the scope of this book.

Excel and Project, however, integrate the VBA engine into their application environments. When you are familiar with the basic applications, the development environments are extremely simple to use.

Macro Recorder

The Macro Recorder is one of the most powerful ways of developing code. The Macro Recorder enables the user to activate the recorder, manually do a series of operations, and stop the recorder. All of the operations performed by the user are recorded in VBA code. This code can then be edited, copied, pasted, or otherwise modified.

Chapter 17 ■ Overview of Visual Basic for Applications (VBA) 591

To learn how to program on a particular application, there is no better way than the direct feedback this type of system provides. Let's create a small macro to demonstrate how the Macro Recorder works in Microsoft Excel.

Select the Record New Macro… option under the Tools menu (see Figure 17.5). This allows VBA to record the commands of any action that takes place. Type in the title of the new macro as `Test Macro`.

FIGURE 17.5.
The Excel Record New Macro… command.

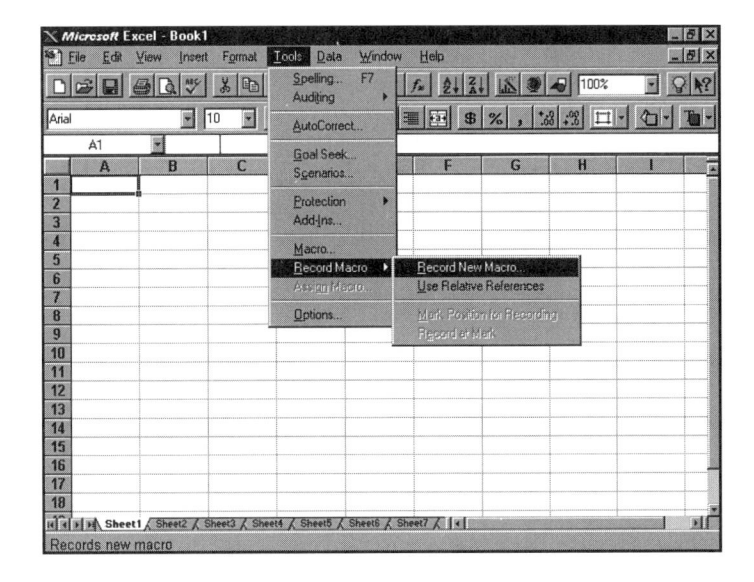

Now that the macro is recording, click in some of the cells in the spreadsheet and enter some numbers. You can see the numbers 1 through 4 have been entered in some of the cells by clicking on each cell. When a macro has begun recording, a Stop button appears on the left side of the screen (see Figure 17.6). After you've made some modifications to the spreadsheet, click the Stop button. The macro is now finished and the code can be edited.

Select the Macro… option from the Tools menu to display all of the macros currently available in this spreadsheet (see Figure 17.7). Note that in Excel, because only a single macro has been recorded, it is the only one that appears. In MS Project, many macros have already been included in a blank document and appear in the Macro window.

You can run the TestMacro, which duplicates exactly the actions done earlier. To edit the macro, select TestMacro from the list and click the Edit button. This shows the code of any available VBA macro.

When the TestMacro is edited (see Figure 17.8), the code is shown as well as the code toolbar. Notice that in Excel, the new VBA macro is added to appear as another tab along the bottom where the worksheets appear. You can access it simply by clicking the tab to view it.

FIGURE 17.6.
Recording a macro.

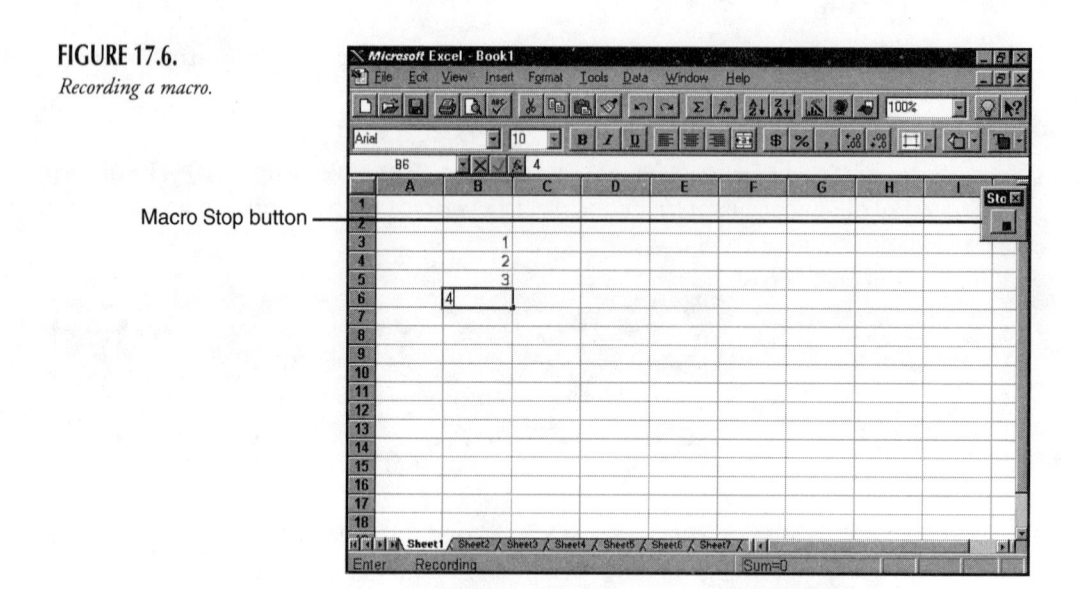

Macro Stop button

FIGURE 17.7.
The Edit macro.

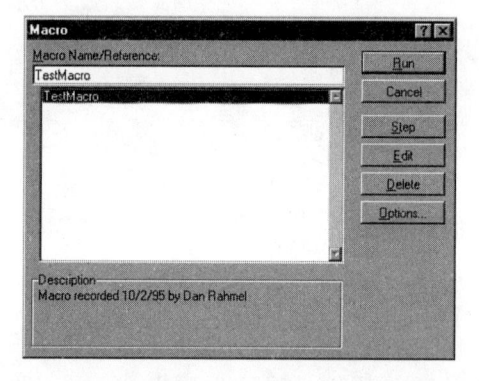

TestMacro is defined as a `Sub...End Sub` routine because no values are returned. All of the code necessary to re-create the actions recorded in the macro appears in the `TestMacro` routine. You can modify the code, add loops and variables to it, or call it from another routine. Creating macros and viewing the VBA code is probably the single best way to learn VBA. Experiment and see what code is generated.

FIGURE 17.8.
The TestMacro code window.

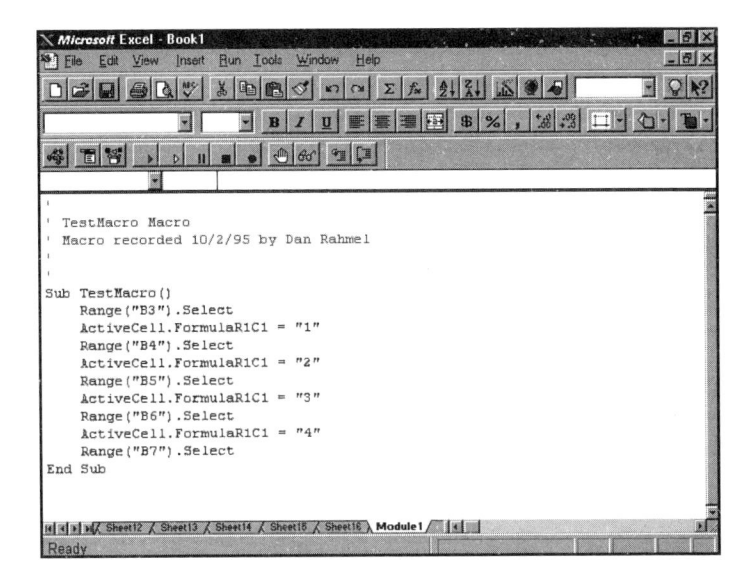

```
' TestMacro Macro
' Macro recorded 10/2/95 by Dan Rahmel
'
Sub TestMacro()
    Range("B3").Select
    ActiveCell.FormulaR1C1 = "1"
    Range("B4").Select
    ActiveCell.FormulaR1C1 = "2"
    Range("B5").Select
    ActiveCell.FormulaR1C1 = "3"
    Range("B6").Select
    ActiveCell.FormulaR1C1 = "4"
    Range("B7").Select
End Sub
```

Object Browser

The Object Browser is another powerful tool for working with VBA. It can only be accessed while a VBA code window is showing, either by selecting Object Browser under the View menu or using the Object Browser icon on the code toolbar. In Figure 17.9 the only object available is `Module1` and the only method under `Module1` is TestMacro.

FIGURE 17.9.
Object Browser showing TestMacro.

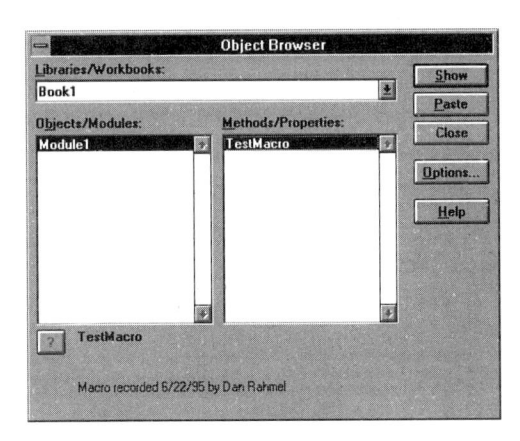

Select the Libraries/Workbooks popup menu at the top of the screen and change the selection to Excel. The list of all the objects available in Excel are listed in the Objects/Workbooks box. Clicking an object displays all of the methods and properties for that object. In Figure 17.10, the `Worksheet` object was clicked, followed by a click on the `Application` property of the object.

FIGURE 17.10.
The Excel Object Browser.

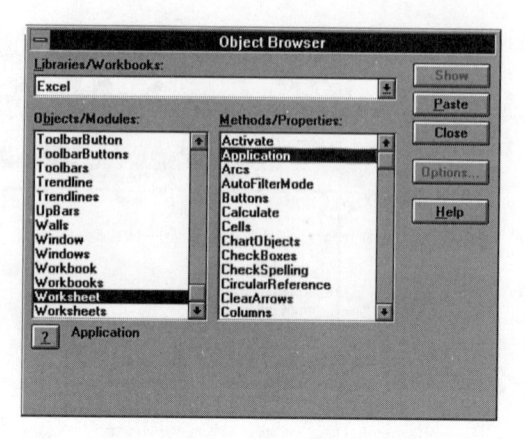

Notice at the bottom of the window there appears the name of the selected property to the right of the ? button. Clicking the ? button provides a complete description of that property or method.

The Object Browser is an excellent tool that enables the examination of all of the objects available in the VBA environment. In future versions, the Object Browser will probably become more graphical as object-oriented design and implementation become the standards.

Editing and Debugging Tools

VBA enables you to do complete runtime editing and debugging. Variables can be watched, breakpoints can be set, and most of the commonly featured debugging tools are available. There is now a breakpoint set on the first line of the TestMacro constructed earlier; note in Figure 17.11 that execution has halted at the first line.

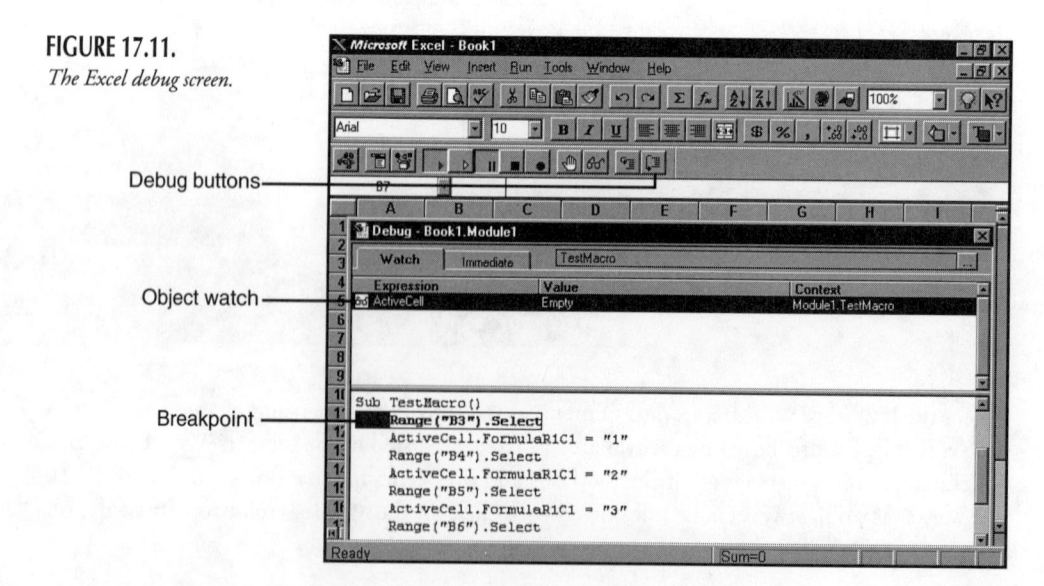

FIGURE 17.11.
The Excel debug screen.

Chapter 17 ■ Overview of Visual Basic for Applications (VBA) | 595

In the toolbar are the traditional buttons that enable you to set line stepping, breakpoints, and watches. The Debug window contains two different tabs: Immediate and Watch. The Immediate tab enables you to enter commands directly into the system, as does VB's Debug window. The Watch tab shows all variables that have a watch set on them. In the figure there is a watch set on the ActiveCell object.

The debug environment is a complete source-level debugger. It is nearly as full-featured as the debuggers in the complete Visual Basic development system. Given the command-line debugging, the Object Browser, the macro recorder, and the stepping capabilities, creating and debugging a simple program in this environment is rudimentary.

The MS Project Environment

So far, all of the figures and macro creation have shown the VBA implementation in Excel. The VBA engine in MS Project is nearly identical and runs in the same way. Figure 17.12 shows MS Project's macro window running under Windows 95. You can see that the box is identical to the Excel implementation.

FIGURE 17.12.
The MS Project macro window.

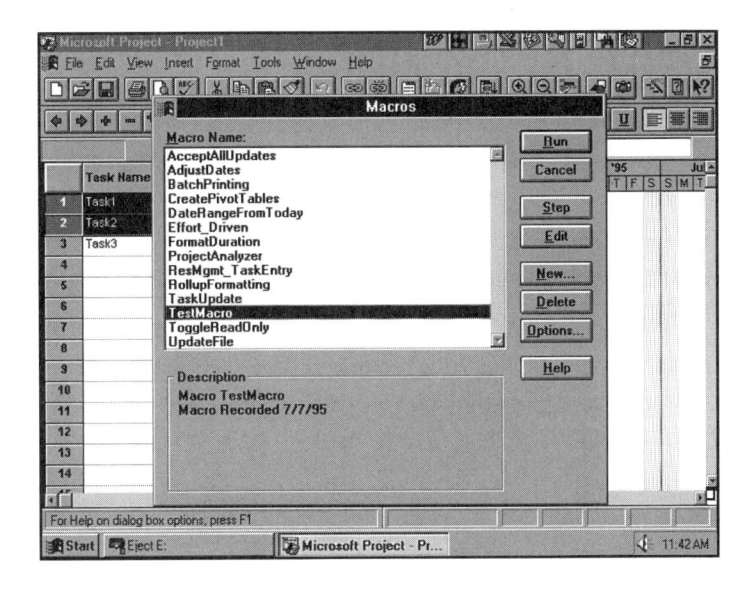

The development environment is also identical, with the same toolbars and code window. (See Figure 17.13.) The only item fundamentally different between the two environments is the lack of the tabs at the bottom of the window in Project to select the macros. They must be selected through the Macro window.

FIGURE 17.13
The MS Project development environment.

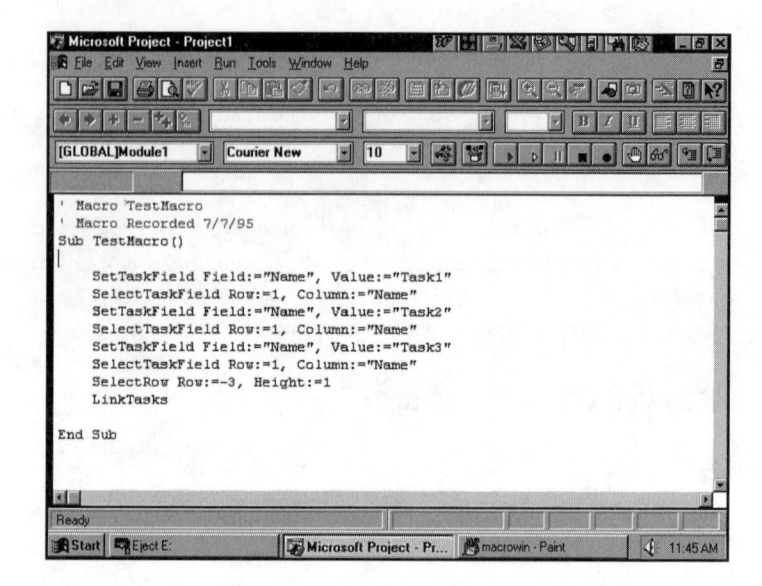

```
' Macro TestMacro
' Macro Recorded 7/7/95
Sub TestMacro()

    SetTaskField Field:="Name", Value:="Task1"
    SelectTaskField Row:=1, Column:="Name"
    SetTaskField Field:="Name", Value:="Task2"
    SelectTaskField Row:=1, Column:="Name"
    SetTaskField Field:="Name", Value:="Task3"
    SelectTaskField Row:=1, Column:="Name"
    SelectRow Row:=-3, Height:=1
    LinkTasks

End Sub
```

Using OLE Automation

OLE Automation enables you to access various OLE objects from other programs. For example, using OLE Automation, a Project VBA module could execute a function in Excel or create a new workbook. For a complete explanation of OLE Automation, see Chapter 23.

The Microsoft Office products have differing levels of OLE Automation capabilities. OLE Automation works on the client/server model: A client application (such as Visual Basic) calls a server application (such as Excel), as shown in Figure 17.14. The client can tell the server to activate a function, create a data object, or anything the server is capable of doing. A server is said to *expose* part of its interface that can be accessed through OLE Automation. Each application is exposed to varying degrees.

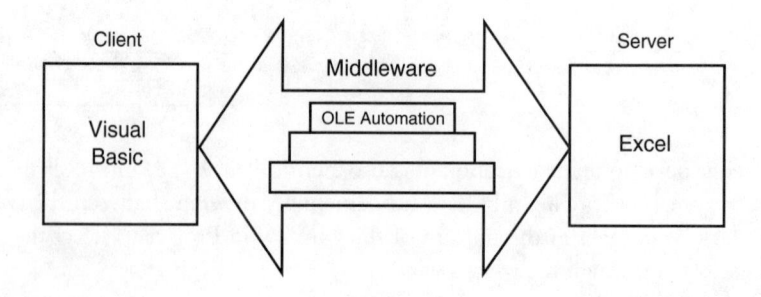

FIGURE 17.14.
OLE Automation Middleware.

Access Basic and OLE

Until the current version, Access could only be used as an OLE Automation client. Access Basic itself works on the complete object metaphor. Figure 17.15 shows all of the objects that Access creates and uses. With the release of Access 95, these objects are now exposed (through VBA) to allow other OLE Automation applications to control the Access 95 application.

FIGURE 17.15.
Microsoft Access objects.

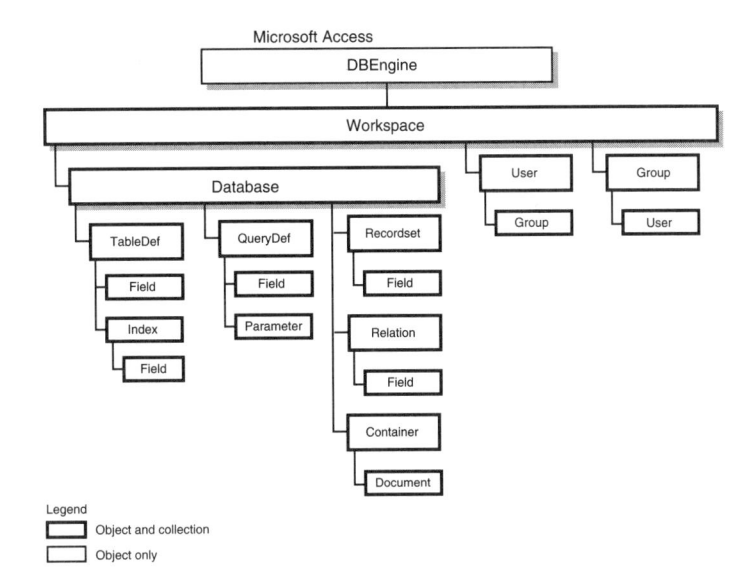

Word Basic Through OLE

Microsoft Word exposes only one object, Word Basic. You can send various Word functions to Word Basic to be executed. This is not a complete object implementation, but does enable full-featured creating and editing of a Word document.

Listing 17.16 is a demonstration of Visual Basic code that creates a blank document, enters two lines of text, and saves the file automatically. This code can be executed in a Visual Basic program and automatically loads Word if it is not currently in memory.

Listing 17.16. Sample Word automation.

```
Sub Command_Click()
    Dim TempDocument as Object

    Set TempDocument = CreateObject("Word.Basic")
    TempDocument.FileNew "Test",0
    TempDocument.Insert "Hello World!"
    TempDocument.InsertPara
    TempDocument.Insert "OLE Automation Test"
    TempDocument.FileSaveAs "MyTest.Doc"
    Set TempDocument = Nothing
End Sub
```

The commands sent as methods to the Word Basic object match those used in Word Basic. Use the same statements and functions you would use directly in Word. There are certain commands that you cannot use, including control structures (such as `While...Wend`, `If...Then`, and so on), variable declarations (such as `Dim`), the `FileExit` command, commands associated with custom dialog boxes, and routines that require array variables as arguments.

Strings also cannot be passed with the `$` suffix (such as `Parameter$`). Either eliminate the `$` from the variable name or enclose the keyword within brackets.

Excel Through OLE

Excel exposes all of its objects for complete access from OLE Automation. Figure 17.16 shows an overview of the basic objects and collections. As you can see, an object implementation is very hierarchical.

FIGURE 17.16.
Microsoft Excel objects.

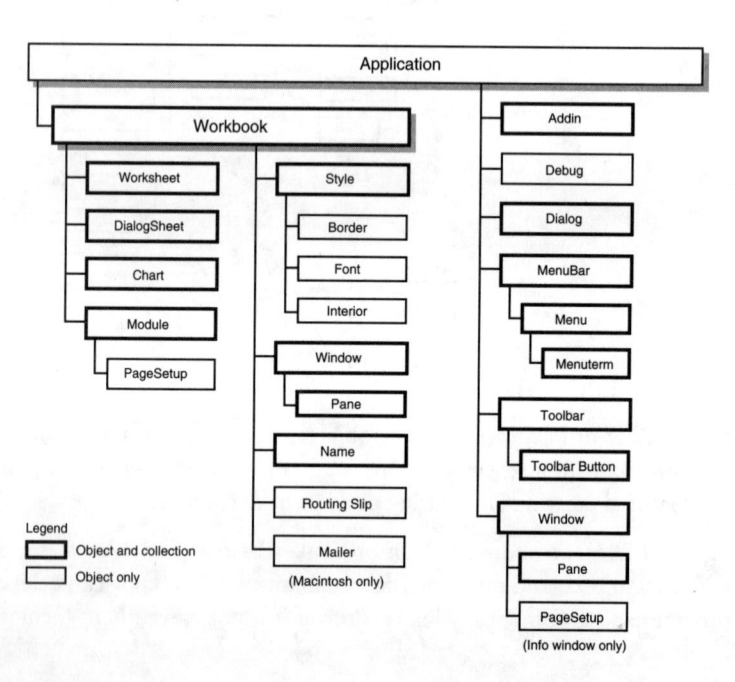

Listing 17.17 shows the code to create an Excel workbook, enter information, and save the document. The code shows moving down the Excel hierarchy by first activating Excel, creating a new workbook, and finally addressing the active worksheet.

Notice the final code sets the objects to a value of `Nothing`. This is good housekeeping. It tells the OLE system that the program is finished with the objects and the memory can be reallocated for other uses. You should set objects to `Nothing` anytime the objects no longer need to be used.

Listing 17.17. Sample Excel automation.

```
Sub Command_Click()
    Dim AppExcel as Object
    Dim Excel as Object
    Dim WS as Object

    Set AppExcel = GetObject(,"Excel.Application")
    Set Excel = AppExcel.Application
    Excel.Workbooks.New
    Set WS = Excel.ActiveSheet
    WS.Range("A1").Value = 25.3
    WS.Range("A2").Value = 3.3
    WS.Range("A3").Value = 32.2
    WS.Range("A4").Value = 9.8
    Excel.ActiveWorkbook.SaveAs "MyTest.XLS"
    Set WS = Nothing
    Set Excel = Nothing
    Set AppExcel = Nothing
End Sub
```

Excel is extremely deep in its object-oriented OLE Automation implementation. For this reason, an entire chapter in this book describes the Excel implementation for later construction of an add-on to the client/server project created in Part II. See Chapter 18, "Overview of Excel Objects," for a complete description of the Excel interface.

Project Through OLE

MS Project also exposes all of its objects to the OLE Automation interface. Figure 17.17 is a complete diagram of all of the objects available through OLE Automation access.

With resource allocation and complete task management, Project enables you to create an entire project through automation. The calendar is also an object that you can manipulate. The potential of using the automation of projects with database access and workgroups is staggering.

Listing 17.18 is a sample application that creates a new project, creates two tasks in the project, assigns resources and durations, and links the two tasks together. Notice that the code extensively uses the property name form of setting the object's properties (using a string containing the name of the property that is to be set), specifically addressing the `Name`, `Duration`, and `Resource` properties. To get information on these properties, use the Object Browser in MS Project to look at the desired objects.

The two tasks, after they are created, are linked with the `LinkTasksEdit` method. A project can work in a similar way to a spreadsheet. Notice that `LinkTasksEdit` uses the numbers 1 and 2 in order to specify the task numbers. Each task is stored in a row, and this row defines the task number. You might also notice that after creating the first task, simply moving to the `Name` task field starts a new task.

FIGURE 17.17.
Microsoft Project 4 objects.

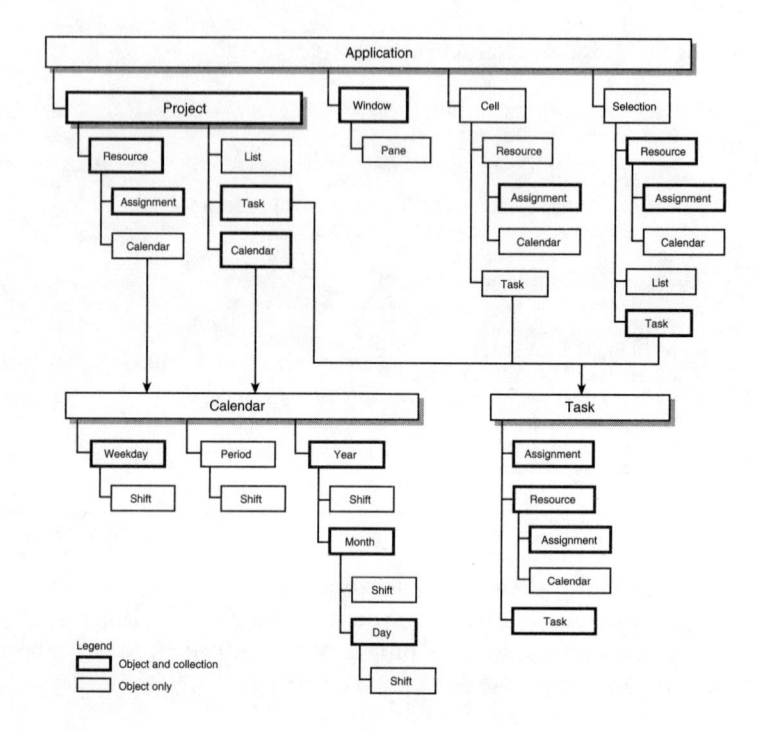

Listing 17.18. Sample project automation.

```
Sub Command_Click()
    Dim TempProject As Object

    Set MyProject = CreateObject("MSProject.Application")

    TempProject.FileNew (0)
    ' Set Task Name field
    TempProject.SetTaskField "Name","Construct Building"
    ' Set Resources for task
    TempProject.SetTaskField "Resources Names", "Builder"
    ' Set duration for task
    TempProject.SetTaskField "Duration",3

    ' Begin new task
    TempProject.SetTaskField 1,"Name"

    TempProject.SetTaskField "Name","Paint Building"
    TempProject.SetTaskField "Resources Names", "Painter"
    TempProject.SetTaskField "Duration",5

    ' Link the two tasks together
    TempProject.LinkTasksEdit 1,2

    TempProject.FileSaveAs "MyProjct.MPP"
End Sub
```

Creating Objects in Visual Basic

Visual Basic provides an excellent interface to OLE Automation that enables VB programs to reach out and create objects in any client program that supports VBA. VB 3.0 can only act as an OLE Automation client. VB 4 has full OLE Server capabilities, including the capability to create an OLE in-process server. For more information on VB 4, see Chapter 7.

In Visual Basic, you create an object with the CreateObject() command (as shown in most of the code in the various sections of this chapter). This creates the memory space of the specified object (Excel Object, Project Object, and so on). Through this object, you can activate methods and set properties.

The object should be reset to Nothing when the program is finished using them to conserve memory (Set Object = Nothing). OLE Automation can use a tremendous amount of memory, which is often at a premium. With Distributed OLE on the horizon, memory requirements promise to increase.

You can use the GetObject() function in two different ways: either to load a specific object or to load an OLE Server application to which commands can be sent. The GetObject() function has two parameters: filename and class. If the filename is included, that file is loaded through the OLE Server:

```
Set MyObject = GetObject("C:\WORDPROC\DOCS\OLETEST.DOC")
```

If the filename is not specified, the OLE Server is loaded:

```
Set MyProject = CreateObject("MSProject.Application")
```

After it is loaded, all of the OLE methods and properties of that object are available for use.

Visual Basic allows the use of VBA (through OLE Automation) to extend the range and capabilities of client programs. Programs that normally had to rely on the specific functions available to a development environment can now reach out and use the capabilities of a third-party product (such as Excel financial functions or MS Project scheduling).

18

Overview of Excel Objects

Microsoft Excel provides an extremely robust implementation of objects. Through the use of OLE Automation, Excel can become the ideal reporting tool for a client/server application. Because of the complete range of financial functions, graphing capabilities, page printing and tiling engines, and general-purpose object functions, Excel can effectively create most reports and automate presentation material.

If you are unfamiliar with the Excel application's capabilities, please examine, test, and copy before you begin reading this chapter. This chapter assumes familiarity with basic Excel structures, including worksheets, charts, user interface tools, and spreadsheet styles (such as column width, style, and so forth).

The Excel object model provides 77 objects that may be accessed through OLE. The main objects can be divided into a few primary categories: worksheet objects, charting objects, drawing objects, built-in user interface objects, user-defined objects, and general-purpose objects.

This chapter provides a Quickstart Tutorial to build a simple VB/Excel interacting program and then describes all the various objects available in Excel. Don't worry if at first you do not understand how the sample application works with all the various objects. As you spend more time interacting with the objects and referencing their definitions, their functions become clear.

Excel Object Quickstart

Interacting with unfamiliar objects can often be a difficult and frustrating experience. Objects interact in different ways and often must be used in a particular way that fits with the structure of the application's document. For example, an individual worksheet is not useful outside of a workbook that contains it.

Therefore, as a way of learning how to interact with a new object-based program, you should always first attempt to find sample source code. It is often the easiest way to learn to find a complete and working implementation of a function before attempting to create your own.

Secondly, you should liberally use the macro recorder built into many object programs. The code of the function that was recorded in the macro can then be examined. Try recording another slightly different macro and see how it works. This experimentation will show how the objects are created and used.

Interacting with a program's object externally (through VBA and OLE Automation) is only slightly more difficult than using the objects from within the program itself. In this chapter, you will first use Visual Basic to create a simple spreadsheet and imbed a chart. This will provide a base example of how Excel is accessed and can be used as a framework for later, more complex, applications.

Recording an Excel Macro

To demonstrate a VBA macro, let's create a simple macro to enter five numbers into the current worksheet and then create another macro to draw a simple pie chart based on this data (see Figure 18.1).

FIGURE 18.1.
Numbers entered for macro VB_Test.

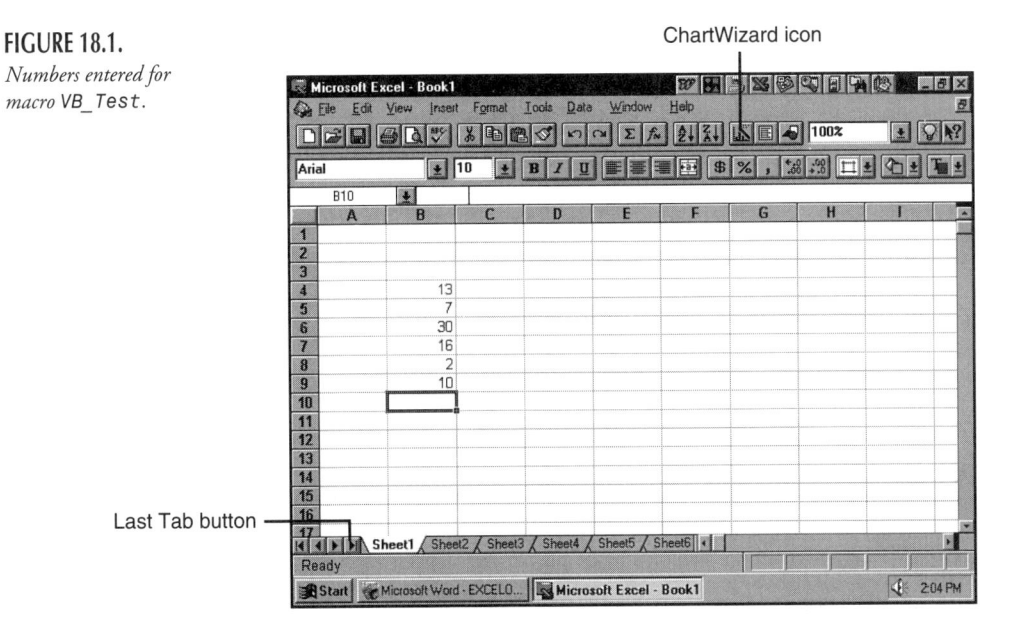

Execute MS Excel and a blank spreadsheet should appear. Start the macro recording by selecting Record New Macro… from the Record Macro option in the Tools menu. Title the macro VB_Test. The macro recording stop box should appear on the screen to indicate that a macro is being recorded.

Click the B4 cell and type 13. Click the subsequent cells and enter the following numbers: 7, 30, 16, 2, and 10. The spreadsheet should now look like Figure 18.1.

Click the Stop Recording button or select Stop Recording Macro from the Record Macro option in the Tools menu. To test and make sure that the macro executes properly, select a blank sheet by clicking the Sheet2 tab at the bottom of the workbook window. Now select the Macro… option from the Tools menu. The list of macros should appear containing only the VB_Test macro. Double-click this item.

The macro will execute and insert all the numbers as if you had just selected and typed them. Let's examine the VBA code for this macro. Click the Last Tab arrow button at the bottom of the screen (see Figure 18.1). Then click the tab labeled Module1. This module stores the code for the macro you just recorded.

The code that appears in the window should match Listing 18.1. If not, change any of the different values so that they match the listing. The code consists of two basic operations: the appropriate cell is selected, and the value for the active cell is set. This code can be cut and pasted (with slight modifications) directly into VB 4, as you will learn later.

Listing 18.1. The VB_Test macro.

```
Sub VB_Test()
    Range("B4").Select
    ActiveCell.FormulaR1C1 = "13"
    Range("B5").Select
    ActiveCell.FormulaR1C1 = "7"
    Range("B6").Select
    ActiveCell.FormulaR1C1 = "30"
    Range("B7").Select
    ActiveCell.FormulaR1C1 = "16"
    Range("B8").Select
    ActiveCell.FormulaR1C1 = "2"
    Range("B9").Select
    ActiveCell.FormulaR1C1 = "10"
    Range("B10").Select
End Sub
```

Now let's record the second macro, which creates a 3D Pie chart from the data. Scroll back to the Sheet2 tab and select it. Select the Record New Macro... option again, but this time, name the macro ChartTest. The Stop Recording button should appear to indicate recording has begun.

Click the first cell holding a number and drag the mouse down until all the cells with numbers are selected. This should leave the area from B4 through B9 selected. These are the cells used for creating the chart.

Now click the ChartWizard icon in the toolbar (see Figure 18.1). When you move the cursor down into the worksheet area, it should now show thin crosshairs.

In an area to the right of the selected numbers, click and drag the cursor until enough space is enclosed to fill most of the remaining space in the window. A dialog box for the ChartWizard should appear. This display should specify that the range equals $B$4:$B$9.

Click the Next button and select the 3D Pie chart selection (see Figure 18.2). Click the Next button again. At this point, you have no further modifications to make to the chart, so click the Finish button.

The chart should now appear and the window should look like the one shown in Figure 18.3. Select the Stop Recording Macro... option to complete the creation of the macro. To test the macro, click the Sheet1 tab. This should display the original numbers that were used to create the first macro.

Select the Macro... option under the Tools menu. Double-click the ChartTest macro and the chart should be created in the same location as the chart you recorded! You now have two fully working macros that are stored as VBA code. To examine the code for ChartTest, click the Last Tab button and again select the Module1 tab.

The code for both macros should be stored in the module. If you scroll down from the VB_Test macro, you should see the ChartTest macro directly beneath it. The macro code should appear the same as the code listed in Listing 18.2 (with the possible exception of the coordinate values).

FIGURE 18.2.
The 3D Pie chart selection in ChartWizard.

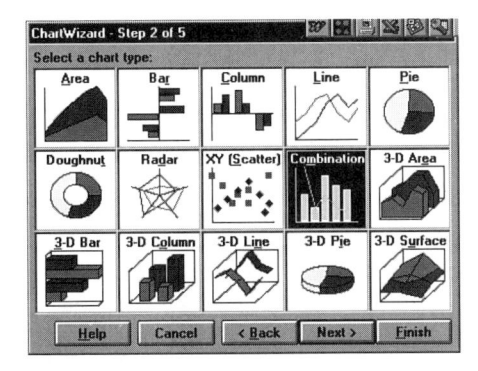

FIGURE 18.3.
A worksheet with a 3D Pie chart.

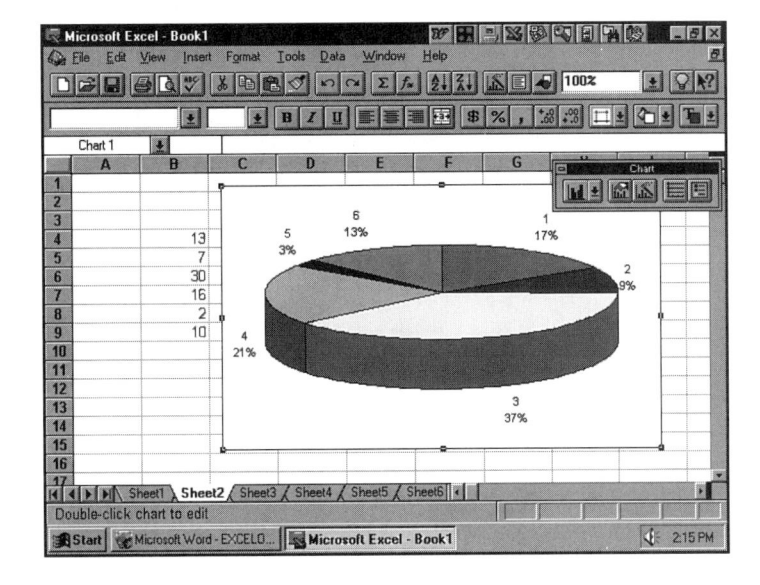

Listing 18.2. The ChartTest macro.

```
Sub ChartTest()
    Range("B4:B9").Select
    ActiveSheet.ChartObjects.Add(105, 9, 309, 180).Select
    Application.CutCopyMode = False
    ActiveChart.ChartWizard Source:=Range("B4:B9"), Gallery:=xl3DPie, _
        Format:=7, PlotBy:=xlColumns, CategoryLabels:=0, SeriesLabels _
        :=0, HasLegend:=1
End Sub
```

Now that the macros have been completed, switch to a blank worksheet by clicking the Sheet3 tab. Leave Excel executing, but collapse the application into the Task bar. You will now execute Visual Basic and use it to run the VB_Test macro by using OLE Automation.

Creating a Form and Buttons

Execute Visual Basic, which automatically opens a new project. First, you will create a form with three buttons, each of which will use VBA and OLE Automation in a different way. On Form1, the default form, draw three simple command buttons (as shown in Figure 18.4).

FIGURE 18.4.
Form1 with three command buttons.

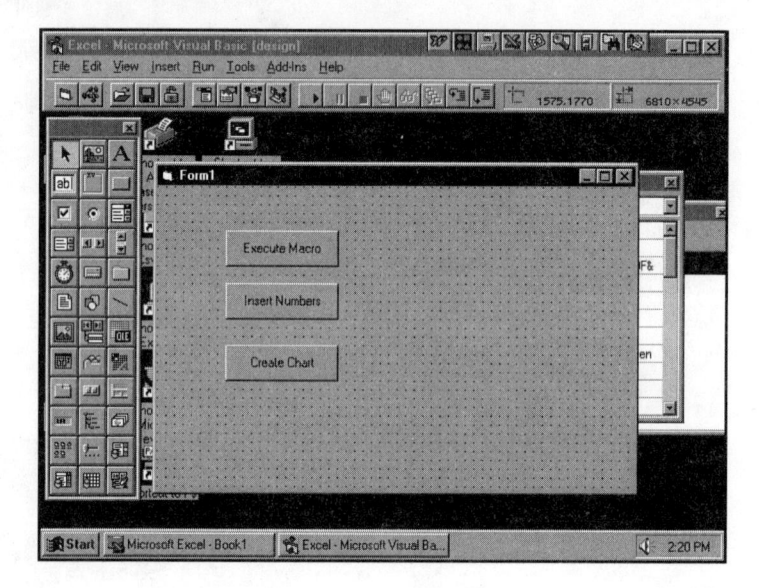

Label the first button Execute Macro, the second one Insert Numbers, and the third button Create Chart. The first button will execute the macro you just created in Excel, the second button will insert several numbers into the currently active sheet, and the third button will create a new chart.

When a VBA routine is executing within an application, an object reference can be made without any preceding object reference. For example, the `ActiveSheet` property may be referenced without any precursor:

```
Set a = ActiveSheet
```

However, from Visual Basic this same command generates an error because there is no `ActiveSheet` function in Visual Basic. To resolve this problem, merely include an object reference before the command. You can do this by creating an Excel object and then referencing it by hand:

```
Set xlApp = GetObject(,"Excel.Application")
Set a = xlApp.ActiveSheet
```

The easier way, especially with several lines of code to be transferred into Visual Basic, is to use the `With...End With` construction. Then only a dot (.) must be added in front of the reference for it to address the proper object accurately.

```
Set xlApp = GetObject(,"Excel.Application")
With xlApp
    Set a = .ActiveSheet
End With
```

To make the Visual Basic application function properly, you have to insert the appropriate object definitions to access the Excel objects. Double-click an empty space of the form. Enter the General Declarations section of the form, then enter the following variable definition:

```
Dim xlApp as Object
```

This object is used by the routines in the form to access the Excel object. Change the code window to show the definition of the `Form_Load()` event, then enter the code shown in Listing 18.3. This code creates the Excel object upon execution so that each routine can use it.

Listing 18.3. The `Form_Load` event code.

```
Private Sub Form_Load()
    Set xlApp = GetObject(, "excel.application")
End Sub
```

> **TIP**
>
> To simplify programming the Excel object, it is a good idea to give the Object Browser in VB 4 access to the Excel objects. This enables examination of all the Excel objects for quick reference.
>
> Select the References... option under the Tools menu. The References window should appear with a list box of current references. If Excel is installed on the machine, the Microsoft Excel Objects selection should appear in the list. Make sure a check appears in the check box to the left of the Excel entry. This enables all the object, method, and property definitions of Excel to be accessible from the VB Object Browser.

Make sure that Excel is still available with the macros you created earlier (MS Excel should appear at the bottom of the screen on the Task Bar). Switch to Excel by clicking the Excel Task Bar button and select a blank worksheet. Switch back to Visual Basic. Double-click the first command button and enter the code in Listing 18.4.

Listing 18.4. The `Command1_Click()` event code.

```
Private Sub Command1_Click()
    xlApp.Application.Run "VB_Test"
End Sub
```

This button code executes the `VB_Test` macro from Visual Basic. Execute the Visual Basic application. Click the first command button. You can switch to Excel and see that the macro has executed and the numbers have been inserted into the sheet.

You now know how to use Visual Basic and OLE Automation to execute a VBA macro in Excel. Excel contains numerous objects that make this sort of execution possible. The following sections review the most important object in the Excel object framework. Then you will transfer the code of the two macros into Visual Basic for execution in the second two command buttons.

Interpreting an Object Chart

Object charts are a standard part of object programming. Object charts demonstrate a hierarchical relationship between all the various objects. As you can see in Figure 18.5, the Workbook object is listed below the Application object. The Application object, in this case, is Excel, and the Workbook object is contained within the object.

The hierarchy in object-oriented programming defines relationships. For each step downward in the hierarchy, there are often multiple instances of each object. For example, the Application object defines MS Excel, of which there is one. However, there may be several workbook documents open from the Excel Application object. This means that there are several instances of the Workbook object, one for each open workbook. The Worksheet object is below the Workbook object in the hierarchy. Therefore, there may be (and usually are) multiple instances of the Worksheet object for every workbook.

You might understand this better if you examine Figure 18.6. The Excel application is positioned at the top of the other objects. Two workbooks are open in this application (MyWB.XLS and Sample1.XLS). Multiple worksheets are open in each workbook (Sheets 1 and 2). This is the way an Excel application organizes its objects.

Referencing the Objects

Now that you understand how the object charts represent the object hierarchy, the chart shows how to reference each object instance. Every level that is accessed is separated by a dot (.). For example, to set the name of a range of cells, the entire hierarchy may be invoked with dot commands:

```
Application.Workbooks("MyWB.XLS").Worksheets("Sheet1").Range("A1").Name =
➥"MyCells"
```

If you examine the object chart, you can see how each object steps down another level with the dot command. Of course, you rarely need all these references. Most of them are assumed. If the references are missing, the Active objects are used. For example, a single range command may be used:

```
Range("A1").Name = "MyCells"
```

In this example, the reference uses the Active application object, Workbook object, and Worksheet object to specify the range. This is particularly useful for macros in which specific table access is not required; instead, access occurs on any active worksheet.

Chapter 18 ■ Overview of Excel Objects 611

FIGURE 18.5.
Microsoft Excel objects.

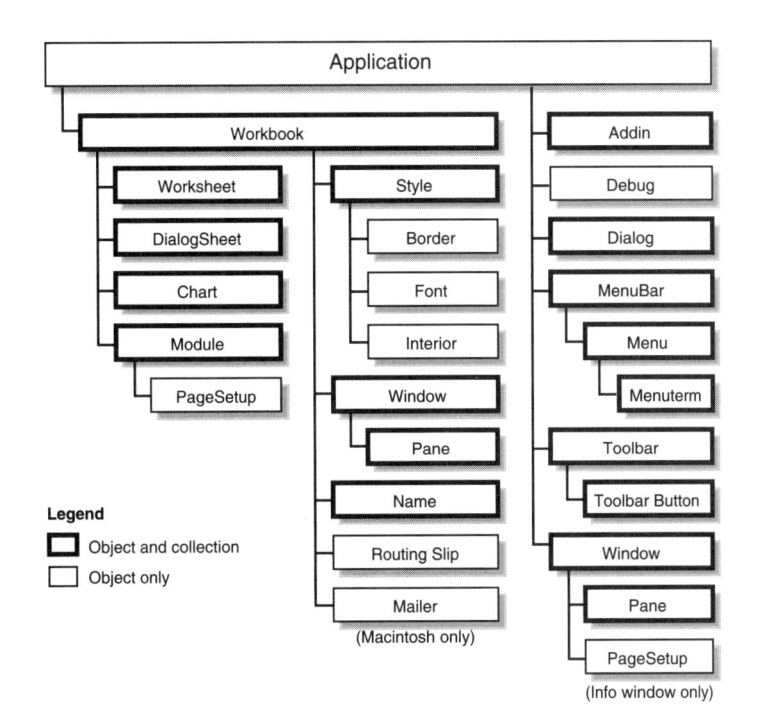

FIGURE 18.6.
The main object hierarchy.

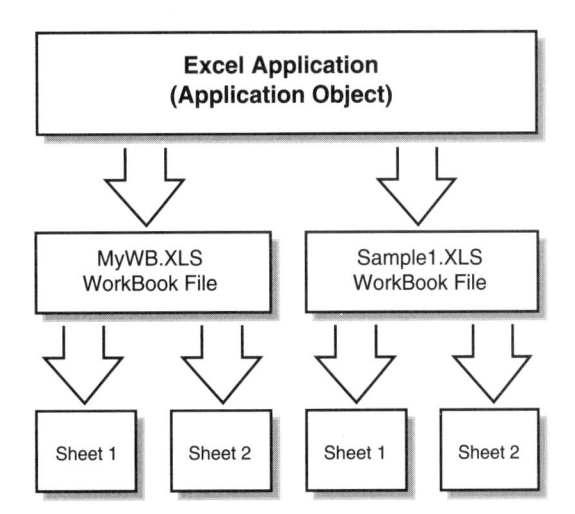

Excel Objects and Collections

Excel has a robust set of objects to create a spreadsheet document. The `Application` object sits at the top of the object hierarchy. All the other objects filter downward like an upside-down tree. Any collection of objects that exists enables individual members to be referenced either through an index value or by sending the particular name. An object that holds a collection may be referenced by using its plural name (for example, you reference a `Workbook` collection by using `Workbooks`).

The following are some of the more important objects and collections in the Excel application. Some of the properties and methods for each are also listed. This section is not exhaustive—that is beyond the scope of this book. Rather, this section gives an overview of some of the objects you will work with in this book as you construct Excel additions to the current client/server system.

The *Application* Object

Recall that the `Application` object is the top object in the Excel object hierarchy. The `Application` object is initialized when the application is originally executed. Changes made to the `Application` object affect all the other objects in the Excel environment. Through the `Application` object, other applications, such as Visual Basic, can execute macro commands in Excel.

The `Application` object has over 100 properties and methods, including five required properties: `Application`, `FullName`, `Name`, `Parent`, and `Visible`. The other properties are optional. All the object properties and methods are available online through the Object Browser. Let's review a few of the more important properties and methods.

Many of the methods and properties are specific to the application being used, and others (such as `Caption` and `ScreenUpdating`) are common to most OLE server applications. All the mathematical methods (such as `Average`, `Ceiling`, and so forth) are stored in the `Application` object, as well as all the references to the other primary objects, such as `Workbooks`, `Charts`, and `Worksheets`.

The *Application* Property

The `Application` property holds a string that identifies the program that created this object. This is a string that holds the text `Microsoft Excel` if the `Application` object is an Excel object. This value may be retrieved by using the `Application` or `Workbook` object. The following is an example:

```
Print myObject.Application.Value
```

This code displays the owner of the object.

The *Caption* Property

The Caption property contains the string stored in the caption of the main Excel window. Changing this value may be especially appropriate when the user must interact with Excel rather than only through the client application. For example, setting the caption to client Reporting Mode at least notifies users that they are not working strictly in Excel.

If this property is not set or is set to Empty, the property defaults to Microsoft Excel. To reset the caption, set it to empty:

```
Application.Caption = Empty
```

The *ClipboardFormats* Property

The ClipboardFormats property returns an array of numeric values that specify what formats are contained on the clipboard. The clipboard may hold an image in bitmap, binary, CGM, PICT, or other format. A spreadsheet may be stored as a SYLK, RTF, or Table format. There are over 32 possible formats that the clipboard may hold. Consult the online documentation for more information.

The *DisplayAlerts* Property

The DisplayAlerts property determines whether prompts and alerts are displayed. It is an excellent idea, if Excel is to be used in the background by a VB application, to set this value to False. A False value ensures that the user is not disturbed while a macro is running and automatically selects the default for prompts (such as the OK button).

If this value is set to False, Excel automatically sets it back to True (the default condition) when the macro has completed running. Therefore, a programmer should include setting this value at the beginning of an important routine.

The *ScreenUpdating* Property

The ScreenUpdating property determines whether updates are made to the screen as the macro is running. Setting this property to False dramatically increases the speed at which the macro executes. Unless there is a pressing need for the user to see what is occurring in the macro, set this value to False from your client application.

The *StatusBar* Property

The StatusBar property enables overriding of the status bar that appears at the bottom of the screen in Excel. As with the Caption property, this is a good place to insert text to notify the user that more than just Excel is running. For example, this code tells the user the client application is running:

```
Application.StatusBar = "Reporting Tool for Client Application"
```

The *WindowState* Property

The `WindowState` property stores the status of the Application window. The property can have one of three values: `xlNormal`, `xlMaximized`, and `xlMinimized`.

The *Calculate* Method

The `Calculate` method is fairly powerful because it enables you to specify when and where recalculation occurs. For an application that adds many numbers and formulas, suspending calculation speeds execution. The application can then call the recalculation after all the operations are complete.

For the `Application` object, executing the `Calculate` method recalculates all the formulas on all open worksheets. Merely call the method:

```
Application.Calculate
```

The *Help* Method

The `Help` method can be used to display a particular help topic. As described earlier in this book, each topic in a help file has a `HelpContextID`. This method takes two parameters (the help file and the `contextID`) and displays the appropriate topic:

```
Application.Help "MyApp.HLP",213
```

If the help file is not specified, the default help file is displayed (in Excel, this means the Excel help file). If the `HelpContextID` is not specified, the Contents page of the help file is displayed.

The *Run* Method

The `Run` method runs an Excel VBA macro, an Excel macro language macro, a DLL function, or an XLL function. The `Run` method can be used from Visual Basic to execute a method that has already been constructed in Excel. This will be demonstrated later when you execute the Excel VBA macro `VB_Test` from Visual Basic.

The *Quit* Method

The `Quit` method quits the Excel application. Note that if any changes are made to a workbook, the user is asked whether saving the changes is necessary.

> **WARNING**
>
> If the `DisplayAlerts` property (described previously) is set to `False`, the user is not prompted and the unsaved file is closed without saving the changes.

If the documents need to be saved before quitting without prompting the user, it is best to save all documents automatically by using the `For Each` loop. Here is an example of code to save all open workbooks and then exit:

```
For Each wb in Application.Workbooks
    wb.Save
Next wb
Application.Quit
```

General-Purpose Objects

The following objects are used by many of the other objects wherever necessary throughout the application.

The `Border` object enables a border for a cell, text box, and so forth to be kept. The `Border` object has no methods and contains the following seven properties: `Application`, `Color`, `ColorIndex`, `Creator`, `LineStyle`, `Parent`, and `Weight`. Each property helps determine the appearance of the border. Check the online help for a description of each.

The `Font` object also has no methods. It specifies all the font attributes, such as font name, size, color, style, and so forth. It contains 17 properties: `Application`, `Background`, `Bold`, `Color`, `ColorIndex`, `Creator`, `FontStyle`, `Italic`, `Name`, `OutlineFont`, `Parent`, `Shadow`, `Size`, `Strikethrough`, `Subscript`, `Superscript`, and `Underline`.

The `Interior` object specifies the interior of a cell or graphic. This object has no methods and eight properties: `Application`, `Color`, `ColorIndex`, `Creator`, `Parent`, `Pattern`, `PatternColor`, and `PatternColorIndex`.

The `Name` object is a defined name, which in Excel can specify a category, a cell range, a macro, and various other references. The `Name` object has a single method, `Delete`, which eliminates the object on which the method executes. The `Name` object has 16 properties, including `Application`, `Category`, `CategoryLocal`, `Creator`, `Index`, `MacroType`, `Name`, `NameLocal`, `Parent`, `RefersTo`, `RefersToLocal`, `RefersToR1C1`, `RefersToR1C1Local`, `ShortcutKey`, `Value`, and `Visible`.

The `PageSetup` object contains all the page setup attributes, such as paper size, margins, first page number, and so forth. This object has no methods but contains over 32 properties. These properties include `Application`, `BlackAndWhite`, `BottomMargin`, `CenterFooter`, `CenterHeader`, `CenterHorizontally`, `CenterVertically`, `ChartSize`, `Creator`, `Draft`, `FirstPageNumber`, `FitToPagesTall`, `FitToPagesWide`, `FooterMargin`, `HeaderMargin`, `LeftFooter`, `LeftHeader`, `LeftMargin`, `Order`, `Orientation`, `PaperSize`, `Parent`, `PrintArea`, `PrintGridlines`, `PrintHeadings`, `PrintNotes`, `PrintQuality`, `PrintTitleColumns`, `PrintTitleRows`, `RightFooter`, `RightHeader`, `RightMargin`, `TopMargin`, and `Zoom`.

The *Workbook* Object/Collection

The `Workbook` object is the central object for an Excel document. A `Workbook` object can contain worksheets, dialog sheets, charts, VBA modules, and Excel macros (see Figure 18.7). A single Workbook object can contain numerous objects, limited only by disk space, processor speed, and memory.

FIGURE 18.7.
Workbook *objects*.

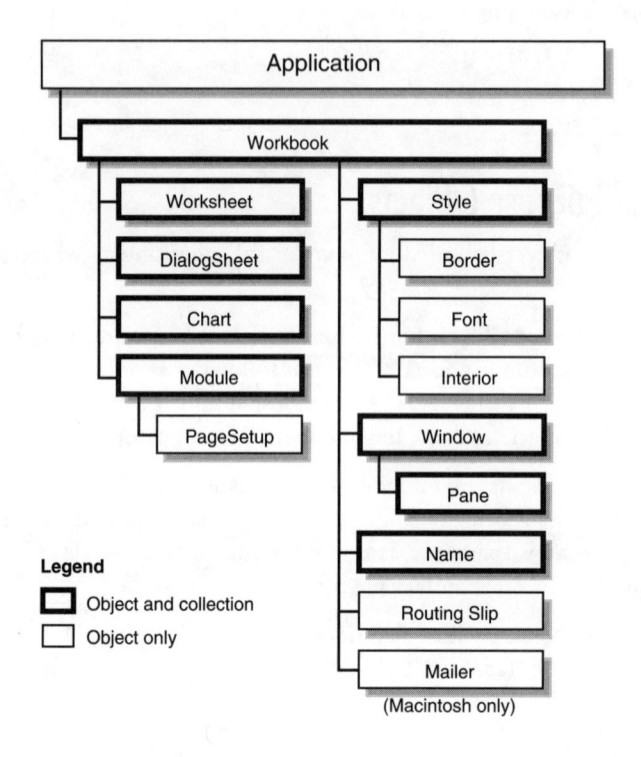

```
Application
└── Workbook
    ├── Worksheet
    ├── DialogSheet
    ├── Chart
    ├── Module
    │   └── PageSetup
    ├── Style
    ├── Border
    ├── Font
    ├── Interior
    ├── Window
    │   └── Pane
    ├── Name
    ├── Routing Slip
    └── Mailer
        (Macintosh only)
```

Legend:
- ▓ Object and collection
- ☐ Object only

A Workbook object also contains the collection of objects that make up a workbook. The Workbook collection is accessed by using the plural form Workbooks. The Workbook collection enables the use of the For Each loop to move through each object in the collection.

The *Name* Property

The Name property indicates the name of the file under which the Workbook is stored. If the file has not been previously saved, this property may be used to assign a filename:

```
ActiveWorkBook.Name = "MyWB.XLS"
```

The *Author* Property

The Author property holds the name of the author stored in the Summary Info... dialog box accessible under the File menu within Excel. This property may be used to track creation information in a client/server project.

```
Print Workbooks("MyWB.XLS").Author
```

The *Activate* Method

The `Activate` method enables a particular workbook from all the workbooks available to the `Application` object. It brings the specified workbook window to the front:

```
Workbooks("MyWB.XLS").Activate
```

The *Close* Method

The `Close` method can be used to close a workbook. Note that if the workbook has been changed, Excel prompts the user if saving is desired. This can be avoided in the same way as it is done with the `Application.Exit` discussed previously:

```
Workbooks("MyWB.XLS").Close
```

The *Count* Method

The `Count` method must be used with the plural form of `Workbook` (`Workbooks`). It returns the number of items in a collection. For example, this code returns the number of objects contained in the workbook:

```
result = Workbooks.Count
```

The *Worksheet* Object

The `Worksheet` object is a single spreadsheet in a workbook file. The `Worksheet` object is the data structure into which all the values, formulas, strings, and so forth are actually entered. A `Worksheet` object contains a number of other objects, including `Range` objects, `Outline` objects, `PivotTable` objects, `PageSetup` objects, `Scenario` objects, and `Drawing` objects (see Figure 18.8).

The `Range` object is probably one of the objects that you will use the most when creating an Excel VBA application, because it specifies a particular range of cells. The `Range` object is used to select cells, specify the cells for chart creation, delete cell functions, and so on.

The `Outline` object controls the characteristics of the worksheet's outline.

The `PivotTable` object is a complete data manipulation object that enables manipulation of large amounts of data. This data can be summarized, have fields selected, and have columns expanded and collapsed.

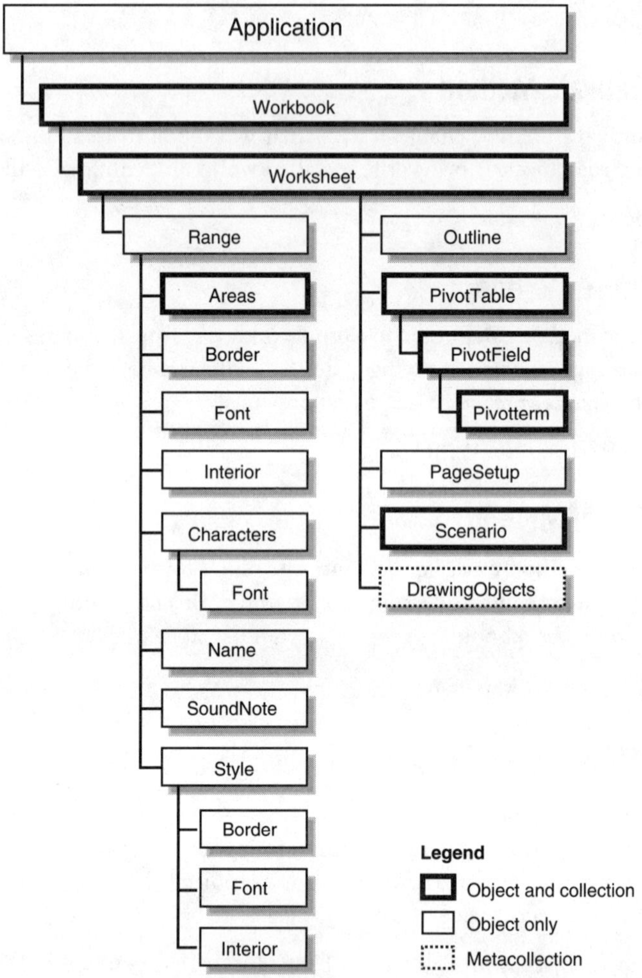

FIGURE 18.8.
Excel `Worksheet` *objects.*

```
Application
  └── Workbook
        └── Worksheet
              ├── Range
              │     ├── Areas
              │     ├── Border
              │     ├── Font
              │     ├── Interior
              │     ├── Characters
              │     │     └── Font
              │     ├── Name
              │     ├── SoundNote
              │     └── Style
              │           ├── Border
              │           ├── Font
              │           └── Interior
              ├── Outline
              ├── PivotTable
              │     └── PivotField
              │           └── Pivotterm
              ├── PageSetup
              ├── Scenario
              └── DrawingObjects
```

Legend:
- Object and collection
- Object only
- Metacollection

The `Scenario` object enables the specification of a set of named cells within a workbook. The `Scenario` object is often used for "what-if" analysis and also used in conjunction with the `PivotTable` object.

The `Worksheet` object itself has many important properties and methods. For a complete list of these object qualities, execute the Object Browser that is included with Excel or consult the online documentation.

The *Name* Property

The `Name` property is important because it is the means of specifying references to the particular worksheet if an index number is not specified. This property also is used for the display of the worksheet name on the Tab at the bottom of the Excel window.

The *Next* and *Previous* Properties

The Next and Previous properties return the worksheets that appear following and preceding, respectively, the currently selected worksheet. These properties can be used to get the characteristics of the sheets that surround the current sheet. This code shows how the worksheet following the current sheet may be selected:

```
Worksheets("Sheet1").Next.Activate
```

The *Visible* Property

The Visible property is useful for extensive updates. By setting Visible to False, none of the updates requires any processing power for the screen updates. This speeds program execution. The property may also be set to the Excel constant of xlVeryHidden:

```
Worksheets("Sheet1").Visible = xlVeryHidden
```

If set to this value, there is no way for the user to unhide the worksheet. The Worksheet.Visible property must be set to True to give the user access again.

The *Protect* Method

The Protect method can be used to protect the specified worksheet from user input. This method is perfect for setting before a complex macro. Possible user interruption can destroy all the progress made by the program. There are four levels that can be set for a worksheet: Password (requires password before worksheet modification), DrawingObjects (protects Drawing objects), Contents (protects cells), and Scenarios (protects Scenario objects).

To use this method to protect a worksheet with a password, the following code demonstrates the use of the method on the Sheet1 worksheet. The three True values that follow the password parameter specify the protection of the Drawing, Contents, and Scenarios objects.

```
Worksheets("Sheet1").Protect "SamplePass", True, True, True
```

The *Unprotect* Method

The Unprotect method removes protection from all the settings of the worksheet. If a password has been specified, the method takes the password as its only parameter. Therefore, if only partial unprotection is required, specific protections must be reset after an Unprotect method has been executed. The following is an example of the Unprotect method:

```
Worksheets("Sheet1").Unprotect "SamplePass"
```

The *RoutingSlip* Object

The `RoutingSlip` object is a powerful workgroup function built into MS Excel. It enables a copy of a `Workbook` object to be attached to an e-mail message that may be sent to multiple destinations. The messages may be sent one after another or all at once.

Routing enables a `Workbook` object to be tracked as it moves from one destination to the next and then returns to you after the routing is completed. This enables each subsequent user to make changes or additions to the routed `Workbook` object, and the completed `Workbook` object returns to the originator.

The `RoutingSlip` object enables the programmatic creation of a routing slip. This object has only one method, `Reset`, which resets the routing slip so that new routing may be created using the same slip. Note that the routing for this slip must have been completed or an error is generated.

The `Routing Slip` object has 10 properties: `Application`, `Creator`, `Delivery`, `Message`, `Parent`, `Recipients`, `ReturnWhenDone`, `Status`, `Subject`, and `TrackStatus`. Setting up a `RoutingSlip` object is fairly straightforward. After the various properties of the routing slip have been defined, the slip is sent by using the workbook method `Route`. This example routes the workbook `MyWB` to four different people, one after the other.

```
Workbooks("MyWB.XLS").HasRoutingSlip = True
With Workbooks("MyWB.XLS").RoutingSlip
    .Delivery = xlOneAfterAnother
    .Recipients = Array("George Washington", "John Adams", "Ben Franklin",
    ➥"Thomas Jefferson")
    .Subject = "Country Budget Draft #2"
    .Message = "This is the newest budget draft. Make any needed modifications."
End With
Workbooks("MyWB.XLS").Route
```

The *Chart* Object

The `Chart` object contains all the necessary objects to show a chart (bar, line, scatter, and so forth). This object contains 11 primary objects, listed hierarchically: `ChartGroup`, `ChartTitle`, `Legend`, `Axis`, `ChartArea`, `PlotArea`, `Floor`, `Walls`, `Corners`, `PageSetup`, and `DrawingObjects` (see Figure 18.9).

`ChartGroup` is the most important object because it contains the actual data or references to data required to create the chart. It contains all the other objects that define the data, such as the `Series` objects, `DataLabel` objects, `Point` objects, and `Trendline` objects, as well as various other data specifiers.

`DrawingObjects` (discussed in the next section) can contain any number of shapes or pictures. It can be used to create arrow-based callouts, additional free floating labels, OLE insertions, and so forth.

FIGURE 18.9.
Excel `Chart` *objects.*

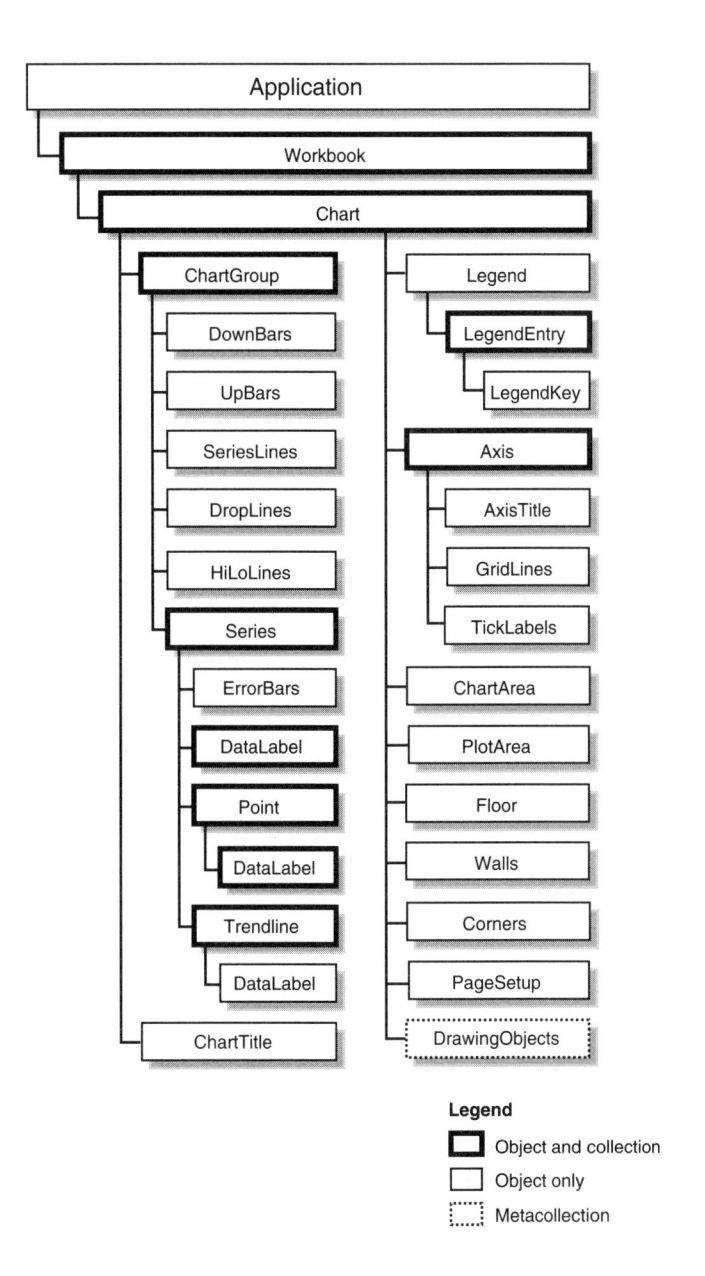

```
Application
  └── Workbook
        └── Chart
              ├── ChartGroup                    ├── Legend
              │     ├── DownBars                │     └── LegendEntry
              │     ├── UpBars                  │           └── LegendKey
              │     ├── SeriesLines             ├── Axis
              │     ├── DropLines               │     ├── AxisTitle
              │     ├── HiLoLines               │     ├── GridLines
              │     └── Series                  │     └── TickLabels
              │           ├── ErrorBars         ├── ChartArea
              │           ├── DataLabel         ├── PlotArea
              │           ├── Point             ├── Floor
              │           │     └── DataLabel   ├── Walls
              │           └── Trendline         ├── Corners
              │                 └── DataLabel   ├── PageSetup
              └── ChartTitle                    └── DrawingObjects
```

Legend
- Object and collection
- Object only
- Metacollection

Drawing Objects

A drawing object is a broadly used object. It can be used in a worksheet, a chart, or a dialog sheet. The `DrawingObjects` object is a collection of objects, including `ChartObject`, `GroupObject`, `Arc`, `Line`, `Oval`, `Picture`, `Rectangle`, `TextBox`, `Drawing` (which is a collection of drawing objects), `Button`, `CheckBox`, `DropDown`, `GroupBox`, `Label`, `ListBox`, `OptionButton`, `ScrollBar`, and `Spinner` (see Figure 18.10).

FIGURE 18.10.
Excel DrawingObjects objects.

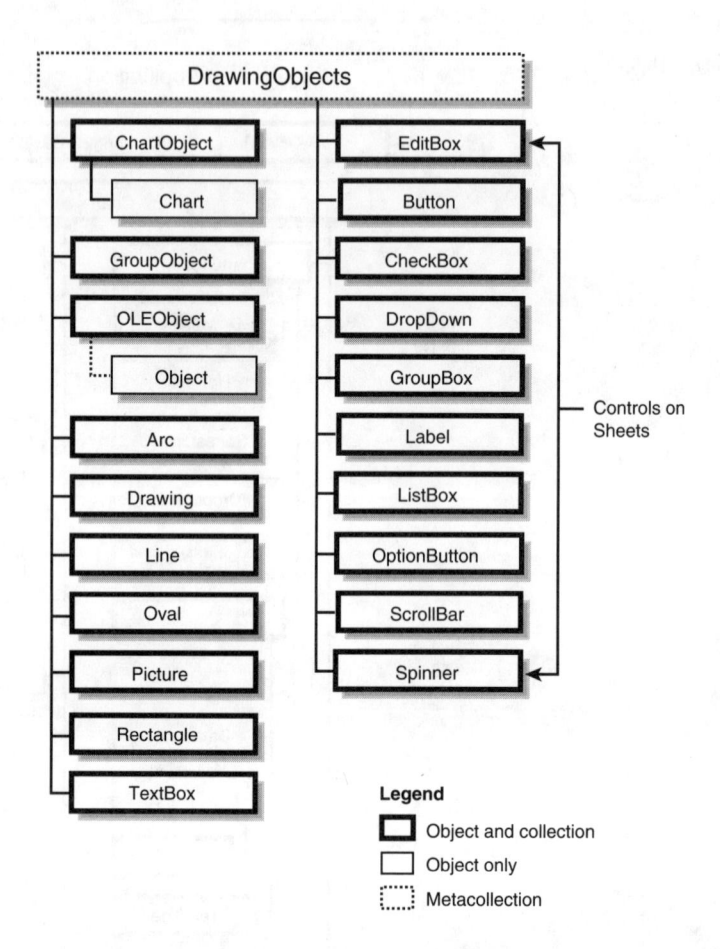

A drawing object is usually a fairly simple object, with only minimal properties and a few methods. Methods usually consist of `BringToFront`, `Copy`, `CopyPicture`, `Cut`, `Delete`, `Duplicate`, `Select`, and `SendToBack`. Additional methods are particular to the type of object. Use the `Add` method for an object collection to add a particular `Drawing` object. In this example, a rectangle is added to the current sheet:

```
ActiveSheet.Rectangles.Add 0,0,72,72
```

Built-In User Interface Objects

The user interface objects are used to define how the actual application will appear (see Figure 18.11). For example, the `MenuBar` object specifies all the menus that appear at the top of the window. By altering these objects, the look of Excel may be changed. For example, the `Add` method may be used to add a new menu to the window:

```
MenuBars(xlWorksheet).Menus.Add caption:="MyMenu"
```

FIGURE 18.11.
User interface objects.

```
                    Application
                         |
          ┌──────────────┼──────────────┐
          ├── Addin
          ├── Debug
          ├── Dialog              Legend
          ├── MenuBar             ▓ Object and collection
          │    └── Menu           ☐ Object only
          │         └── Menuterm
          ├── Toolbar
          ├── Toolbar Button
          ├── Window
          │    └── Pane
          └── PageSetup
              (Info window only)
```

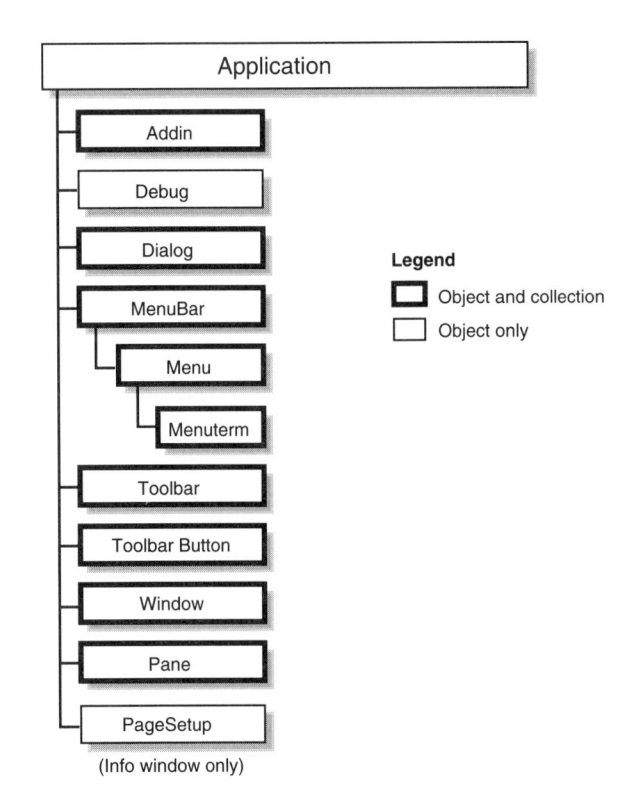

The `Addin` object includes files that can be installed to add functions to Excel. This object provides programmatic access to the add-ins under the Add-in menu.

The `Dialog` object is a general dialog that is included as a built-in element of the Excel user interface. This object is a very simple object with only one method (`Show`) and three properties (`Application`, `Creator`, and `Parent`).

The `MenuBar` object contains all the `Menu` objects. The `Menu` object holds all the `MenuItem` objects that define various options under that particular menu. Each `MenuItem` object has a `Caption` property that holds the text of how the `MenuItem` will appear. The ampersand (`&`) may be used to activate the underline/Alt access.

The `Toolbar` object contains all the information for both built-in and user-definable toolbars. A toolbar button may be added to any toolbar by using the `Add` method. Note that the number for specifying each button that is inserted is listed in Appendix D of the *Visual Basic Users Guide*. The following is sample code to add a button to the first toolbar in the collection:

```
Toolbars(1).ToolbarButtons.Add(101)
```

The `Window` object contains the window definitions of each window displayed by MS Excel. All the windows are stored in the `Windows` collection. The most recent window may be accessed by using the `ActiveWindow` object.

The *DialogSheet* Object

The `DialogSheet` object may be used to define a dialog box for displaying or inputting information (see Figure 18.12). Excel VBA does not contain the capability of using forms as used in Visual Basic. The dialog box, however, does provide a custom way that user input may be acquired.

FIGURE 18.12.
Excel `DialogSheet` objects.

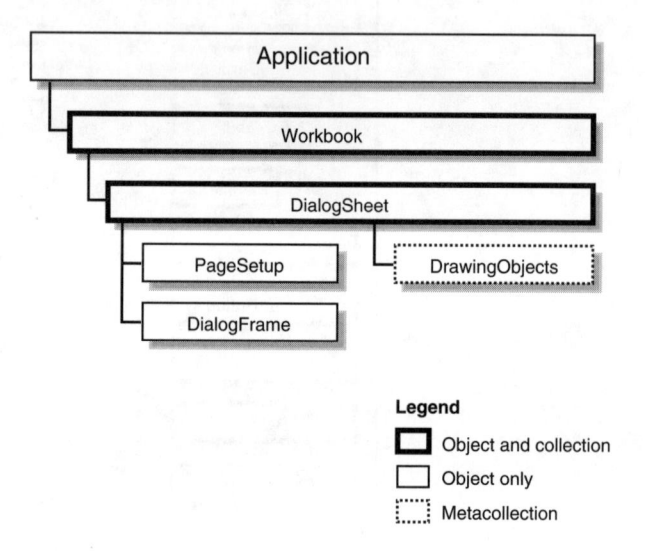

```
Application
 └── Workbook
      └── DialogSheet
           ├── PageSetup        DrawingObjects
           └── DialogFrame
```

Legend:
- Object and collection
- Object only
- Metacollection

An object unique to the `DialogSheet` object is the `DialogFrame` object. This object defines the position, size, and caption of the dialog box itself. The `DialogFrame` object has four methods, including `Characters`, `CheckSpelling`, `CopyPicture`, and `Select`. It also has 13 properties, including `Application`, `Caption`, `Creator`, `Height`, `Left`, `Locked`, `LockedText`, `Name`, `OnAction`, `Parent`, `Text`, `Top`, and `Width`.

The `OnAction` property enables setting a macro to call when the object is clicked. This property is found in many other objects (such as `DrawingObjects`, `Labels`, `CheckBoxes`, and so forth) and works in the same manner.

A `DialogSheet` object also may contain other objects, such as `Button` objects, `CheckBox` objects, `EditBox` objects, `GroupBox` objects, `ListBox` objects, `Label` objects, `ScrollBar` objects, `Spinner` objects, `TextBox` objects, `DropDown` objects, and `Drawing` objects.

Excel Events

Excel objects can respond to events that are sent to the system (such as mouse clicks, opening a document, and so forth). Each event is stored as a property. By setting the property to the name of the VBA macro that should be executed when the event occurs, a number of important events can be trapped to execute custom routines.

Excel has two types of event routines: automatic procedures that are executed when an event occurs for a workbook or worksheet, and event routines that are executed when a particular object receives an event.

All the automatic procedures are shown in Table 18.1. To create a procedure that is automatically activated, add a Sub routine that is named the same as the automatic procedure name to the necessary object. This routine is executed when the event occurs.

Table 18.1. Automatic procedures.

Object	Automatic Procedure Name
Workbook	Auto_Open, Auto_Close
Worksheet	sheetname!Auto_Open
Worksheet	sheetname!Auto_Activate, sheetname!Auto_Deactivate, sheetname!Auto_Close

Event routines are activated that have been set in the appropriate object's property. For example, this code sets the myRoutine macro to be executed when the application activates the specified Workbook:

```
Application.OnSheetActivate = ActiveWorkbook.Name & "!Module1.myRoutine"
```

Table 18.2 holds the names of all the events in Excel and the objects to which they apply.

Table 18.2. Excel events.

Event	Objects
OnAction	Arc, Arcs, Button, Buttons, CheckBox, CheckBoxes, DialogFrame, Drawing, Drawings, DrawingObjects, DropDown, DropDowns, EditBox, EditBoxes, GroupBox, GroupBoxes, GroupObject, GroupObjects, Line, Lines, ListBox, ListBoxes, OLEObject, OLEObjects, OptionButton, OptionButtons, Oval, Ovals, Picture, Pictures, Rectangle, Rectangles, ScrollBar, ScrollBars, Spinner, Spinners, TextBox, TextBoxes, ToolbarButton
OnCalculate	Application, Worksheet
OnData	Application, Worksheet
OnDoubleClick	Application, Chart, Dialogsheet, Worksheet
OnEntry	Application, Worksheet
OnKey	Application

continues

Table 18.2. continued

Event	Objects
OnRepeat	Application
OnSheetActivate	Application, Chart, Dialogsheet, Module, Workbook, Worksheet
OnSheetDeactivate	Application, Chart, Dialogsheet, Module, Workbook, Worksheet
OnTime	Application
OnUndo	Application
OnWindow	Application, Window

Pasting into VB 4

Now that you are familiar with the object framework of Excel, let's port the macros you created earlier into the command buttons of the VB project. Once an Excel macro has been created, it can be pasted directly into VB 4. Visual Basic 4 uses the VBA engine, enabling complete compatibility. There are only a few modifications that must be made because of object references.

Transferring the VB_Test macro is simple. Switch to Excel and select the Module1 tab. Select the code of VB_Test and copy it to the clipboard (with either the Copy option in the Edit menu or the key combination Ctrl+C). Now click Visual Basic in the Task Bar to activate the development system and bring it to the front.

Double-click the Insert Numbers command button. Select the Paste option in the Edit menu to paste the necessary code into the Command2 Click event. The code that was just pasted runs in the Excel application environment. Therefore, any object references automatically assume the Excel Application object at the top of the hierarchy. However, because you will run the macro commands from within Visual Basic, that basic assumption does not hold true.

You must add the reference to the Excel Application object. The easiest way to accomplish this task is to use the With...End With clause. Then you can encapsulate the entire macro so that every dot (.) reference automatically references the Excel object. This also is far more efficient programming than recreating the Excel Application reference with each line.

Look at Listing 18.5. The With xlApp command is at the beginning, which uses the xlApp object created in the Form_Load event. A dot command appears before each Range and ActiveCell method to make it access the object specified in the With definition. Finally, the End With command ends the object references.

Listing 18.5. A modified VB_Test in VB.

```
Private Sub Command2_Click()
    With xlApp
        .Range("B4").SELECT
```

```
        .ActiveCell.FormulaR1C1 = "13"
        .Range("B5").SELECT
        .ActiveCell.FormulaR1C1 = "7"
        .Range("B6").SELECT
        .ActiveCell.FormulaR1C1 = "30"
        .Range("B7").SELECT
        .ActiveCell.FormulaR1C1 = "16"
        .Range("B8").SELECT
        .ActiveCell.FormulaR1C1 = "2"
        .Range("B9").SELECT
        .ActiveCell.FormulaR1C1 = "10"
        .Range("B10").SELECT
    End With
End Sub
```

Enter these changes in the code that you've pasted from the VB_Test macro. After the changes are complete, execute the application. By clicking the Insert Numbers command button, these values are automatically inserted into the active worksheet as if the macro was executed from within Excel.

Now you will port the more complicated ChartTest macro. Stop the VB programming from running by closing the application window or clicking the Stop Toolbar icon. Switch to Excel and select the Module1 tab. Select all the code that makes up the ChartTest macro and copy the code. Click one of the tabs to select a worksheet that has the necessary data on it. If a pie chart for the data is already present, delete it—the VB macro you will create re-creates the chart.

Switch back to Visual Basic and double-click the third Command button. Paste the macro code into the Click event of the Command button. This code requires more modifications because of its complexity. If you look at the macro code, notice that the ChartWizard method line uses Named Arguments. With Named Arguments, rather than passing a number of parameters to a function in the required order, the individual parameters may be named and passed in any order.

For example, a simple function may require the passing of three values (SimpleF(x,y,z)). Parameters are passed in order (SimpleF(1,2,3)). With Named Arguments, each parameter may be named and passed in any order (SimpleF y:=2, x:=1, z:=3). Named Arguments provides better documented code and more flexibility with optional parameters.

If necessary, each name and := symbol may be deleted if the parameters are passed in the correct order.

VB 4 supports the use of Named Arguments (unlike VB 3.0), but methods and other parameters may be hidden by the extra typing. In this code example, there are two problems with a direct port from the ChartTest code: the Range method embedded in the arguments and an Excel constant.

The first Named Argument that is passed to the ChartWizard method is the Source parameter. This parameter uses the Range method to return a Range object. You must add the necessary object reference. Therefore, place a dot before the Range method. This references the object you will set up by using the With command.

> **TIP**
>
> The main part of the VBA code that doesn't work when directly pasted into Visual Basic is any reference to constants. Constants (properties with permanent values) are local to the system they run in. MS Excel has over 100 constants that can be used from within Excel but are not transferred with a cut and paste.
>
> There are two ways to add these constants. If the Excel Objects section in the References dialog box (selected under the Tools menu) has Excel Objects selected, the constants may be used in the project. Also available are the VB constants files that are included with the Office Developer's Kit (ODK). Many are freely available online. The Excel constants file is named XLCONST.BAS. This file must be added to the project in order for the constants to be used directly. If neither of these methods is used, the values represented by the given constants must be entered by hand.

The Gallery Named Argument is set to xl3DPie. This is an Excel constant that does not normally exist in Visual Basic (see previous Tip). Therefore, if you have the XLCONST.BAS file, add the file to the project. If not, the constant xl3DPie is equal to -4102. Enter this number instead of xl3DPie.

As you did with the first macro, you now add the With...End With clause to encapsulate the macro as well as the dot commands before each reference. After this is complete, the code should look like the code shown in Listing 18.6.

Listing 18.6. A modified ChartTest in VB.

```
Private Sub Command3_Click()
    With xlApp
        .Range("B4:B9").SELECT
        .ActiveSheet.ChartObjects.Add(144, 39.75, 219, 129.75).SELECT
        .Application.CutCopyMode = False
        .ActiveChart.ChartWizard Source:=.Range("B4:B9"), CategoryLabels:=0, _
        SeriesLabels:=0, HasLegend:=2, Title:="HelloChart", CategoryTitle:="", _
        ValueTitle:="", ExtraTitle:="", Gallery:=-4102
    End With
End Sub
```

Now execute the Visual Basic application. Clicking the third Command button creates the chart in Excel! With this overview, you can see some of the potential power for using the Excel application as a client tool.

One of the powerful objects contained in the Excel object hierarchy is the PivotTable object. This tool is not covered extensively because most of the data handling in the client/server system is accessed through Visual Basic's more robust and malleable features. If you are going to create Excel-based clients, however, examine the PivotTable object.

19

Excel Additions to the Client/Server System

This chapter adds to the client/server (C/S) system by adding reporting capabilities to the Management Client. Excel provides the capabilities for the ideal reporting tool because of its comprehensive financial, mathematical, and graphing functions. Therefore, you use OLE Automation to control Excel to provide enhanced features to your application.

There are traditionally two ways in which client applications are extended using other programs:

- The creation of new documents that a user can edit
- Using the application's interface (forms, menus, and so on) to make the object appear seamlessly as part of the client

An example of the first type of extension is the creation of a spreadsheet with values output from the client program. A client program uses OLE Automation to insert values, equations, or charts into a spreadsheet file. This file can be edited by the user. A user is, therefore, able to use a spreadsheet that is familiar to him to manipulate information that the client program is suited to output.

The exchange can go two ways. With the output to a spreadsheet, the user edits the spreadsheet, and the client application reads the new values from the spreadsheet. Using OLE Automation in this fashion can make information available to users for manipulation in a program they are accustomed to. OLE Automation can be used to construct not only spreadsheets but also form letters (MS Word), drawings (Visio), maps (ARC/Info), and just about anything else.

The second type of extension is the seamless integration of another program so that its functions appear as though they belong to the client program itself. An example of this is the in-place activation of a Visio drawing within an MS Word document.

Double-clicking an embedded Visio drawing activates the drawing directly within the Word document. Only the toolbar and a few of the menus change. Clicking another part of the document returns the user to the standard Word toolbars and menus.

Excel Additions

In this chapter, we will make two additions to the Management Client application: an Excel spreadsheet that contains a chart using OLE Automation and an Excel chart that appears within a Visual Basic form.

The first addition executes Excel, starts a new workbook, adds all the figures from the Purchase report, and creates a chart from these figures. (See Figure 19.1.) Excel is left open so that users can switch to Excel and make any edits they desire.

The second edition creates a linked OLE object that appears in a standard Visual Basic form. (See Figure 19.2.) From the user's point of view, the chart appears as though it were created within the client application itself. This enables the client to use all the power of Excel for enhanced reporting capabilities.

Chapter 19 ■ Excel Additions to the Client/Server System | 631

FIGURE 19.1.
A chart created in Excel using OLE Automation.

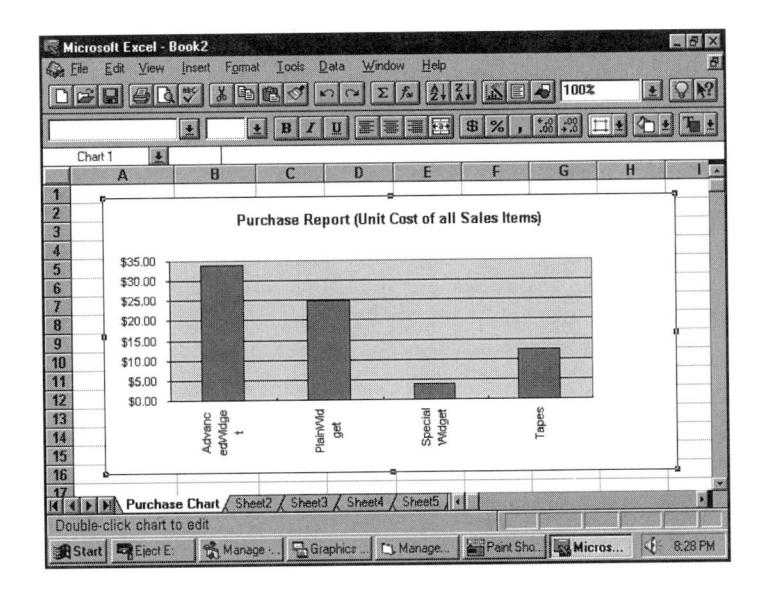

FIGURE 19.2.
An Excel chart object.

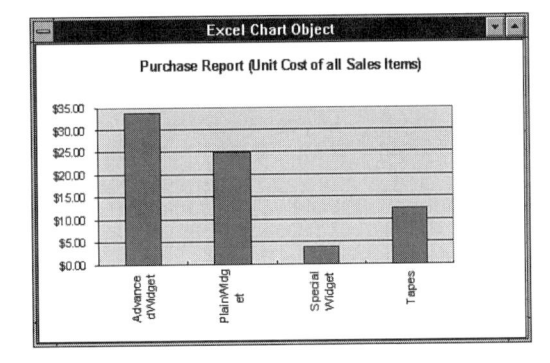

Using OLE Automation

To create a complete report within Excel, you can use the OLE Automation engine. In this way, Visual Basic can control the Excel application and insert and manipulate any part of the Excel worksheet or graph.

By using the objects that Excel exposes for automation (described in Chapter 18, "Overview of Excel Objects"), Visual Basic can completely manipulate the Excel environment. This means that spreadsheets can be created and that charts and data can be read from an existing worksheet.

> **TIP**
>
> You might work in an organization that uses standard spreadsheets such as Quattro Pro or Lotus 1-2-3, which at the time of this writing do not have OLE Automation capabilities. Organizations are often hesitant—rightly so, for support reasons—to introduce a different program.
>
> In these circumstances, we recommend presenting Excel as simply a reporting tool. It will save the worksheets and graphs into most commonly available formats, so translation should not be a problem. Until the other programs catch up in their capabilities, using Excel as a reporting engine is the most effective way of providing this type of presentation without violating organizational standards by introducing another spreadsheet.

OLE Automation tends to incur a great deal of overhead processing while executing. For this reason, it is extremely important for the designers of the system to implement every technique to optimize the particular program so that processing and memory needs are minimized.

Whenever an object is accessed through dot (.) commands, OLE requires the object path to be recreated. In a typical statement such as `APPXL.Application.Workbooks.Add`, an object reference is created at each dot separation, only to be destroyed after the command finishes. The previous statement creates and destroys three object references every time it executes. Therefore, you should minimize the number of dot commands that your programs contain.

Two commands can dramatically reduce the number of dot commands required, thereby increasing performance. They are the `With` command and the `Set` command. Both are employed when the same object is used repeatedly.

The `With` command in Visual Basic increases performance by building the object reference once and then repeatedly accessing the single instance. For example, the following code creates and destroys numerous object references, which causes a great deal of overhead:

```
ws.Cells(1,1).Value = "TestData"
ws.Cells(1,1).Font.Bold = True
ws.Cells(1,1).Font.Size = 12
```

Using the `With` command, you can eliminate almost two-thirds of the overhead of that code. To accomplish the same operations using the `With` command, you would write

```
With ws.Cells(1,1)
    .Value = "TestData"
    .Font.Bold = True
    .Font.Size = 12
End With
```

This code operates in an identical manner, but it is substantially faster and requires fewer system resources. The `Set` command (used to create objects) can be used in the same way to conserve memory and optimize performance. If you create objects that use the `Set` command at various parts of the program, the object remains created and is not eliminated at the end of each statement. An object variable could be set to hold the extended reference so that it does not have to be rebuilt every time. For example:

```
Set tempCells = we.Cells(1,1)
tempcells.Value = "TestData"
```

Creating the Additions to the Management Client

You will add a new menu to the Management Client to provide access to these new additions. (See Figure 19.3.) This new OLE menu has two options to activate the OLE additions. The first option uses automation to create a document that remains within Excel. The second option displays an Excel chart from within Visual Basic.

FIGURE 19.3.
A new OLE menu.

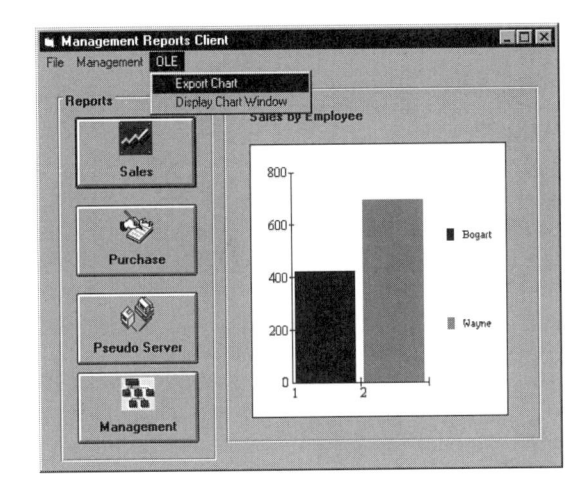

It is usually better to isolate OLE features to a particular part of the screen or a specific menu. Because of resource limitations, many client machines cannot effectively load several OLE applications. By isolating the OLE options, the user can understand which commands are particularly resource-intensive.

Load the Management Client project into Visual Basic. Activate the Menu Editor for the main window. Add a menu with a caption of OLE that has a Name property of mnuOLE. Add two items under the OLE menu: an Export Chart item with the name ExportChartItem and a Display Chart Window item with the name ChartWindowItem. Click the OK button on the Menu editor to add the menus.

After you have added the menus, open the References dialog box available under the Tools Menu. If Excel is installed and registered properly on your computer, you should see the Microsoft Excel 5.0 Object Library included in the available references list. Click the box to the left of this item so that the item is checked.

Creating the Routines

OLE Automation provides powerful capabilities in an extremely small amount of code. Therefore, you need to create only two routines to handle all the additions to the Management Client. The routines themselves contain numerous commented lines to help you understand what is taking place when the code executes.

Adding the *CreateXLChart()* Routine

The CreateXLChart() routine uses the Excel object base to create an Excel spreadsheet and chart in the Excel application. Select Procedure from the Insert Menu to create a new subroutine named CreateXLChart. Enter the code shown in Listing 19.1. This routine retrieves the Excel application object, creates a new workbook, adds data values retrieved from the Purchasing report to the first worksheet, and creates a bar chart from this data.

Listing 19.1. CreateXLChart().

```
Public Function CreateXLChart()
    Dim APPXL As Object
    Dim xl As Object
    Dim ws As Object
    Dim objChart1 As Object

    ' While processing OLE Automation, display watch
    Screen.MousePointer = 11

    ' GetObject will use Excel if already loaded, will load if necessary
    Set APPXL = GetObject(, "Excel.Application")

    Set xl = APPXL.Application
    ' Add a new workbook where chart and figure are added
    xl.Workbooks.Add
    Set ws = xl.ActiveSheet
    ' Set the name of the current worksheet to Purchase Client
    ws.Name = "Purchase Chart"

    ' Setup Purchasing Report SQL query
    ' This is the same query used with the Purchasing button
    s = ""
    s = s & " SELECT c.Description, sum(b.UnitCost * a.Qty) as UnitCost"
    s = s & " FROM Assembly AS a, Inventory_Parts AS b,  Inventory_Sales AS c"
    s = s & " WHERE (a.PartID_Parts = b.PartID) And (a.PartID_Sales = c.PartID)"
    s = s & " GROUP BY  c.Description;"

    ' Create Recordset to read values
    Set ScratchRS = MyDB.OpenRecordset(s, dbOpenDynaset)

    ' Determine the number of items in unit cost report
    numfields = ScratchRS.Fields.Count

    ' For..Next loop will place field titles for all columns
    MaxWidth = 0
    For j = 1 To numfields
```

Chapter 19 ■ Excel Additions to the Client/Server System

```vb
            fieldTitle = ScratchRS.Fields(j - 1).Name
            ' Set column heading to field name
            ' Put headings below where chart will appear
            With ws.Cells(35, j)
                ' Set cell value
                .Value = fieldTitle
                ' Make the column titles bolder than normal text will be
                .Font.Bold = True
                .Font.Size = 12
            End With
            ' Make the column wide enough so the field name can be read
            ws.Columns(j).EntireColumn.AutoFit
        Next j

    ' Set row starting point off of the screen (row 36). Data will be recorded
    ' in the lower part of the worksheet. This way the chart will only
    ' be directly visible.
    i = 36
    Do Until ScratchRS.EOF     ' Until end of file.

        ' Enter all fields for this record in Grid
        For j = 1 To ScratchRS.Fields.Count
            ' Enter field value into cell
            ws.Cells(i, j).Value = ScratchRS.Fields(j - 1).Value
        Next j

        i = i + 1
        ScratchRS.MoveNext     ' Move to next record.
    Loop

    ' Define Name of range for use by the Chart
    ws.Parent.Names.Add "CostRange", "=" & "A36:B39"
    Set objChart1 = ws.ChartObjects.Add(31.5, 9.75, 372.75, 204.75)
    With objChart1.Chart
        .SeriesCollection.Add "CostRange"
        ' xlColumn is a constant stored in the Excel object model
        ' Adding the Excel Object Library under References, this
        ' is accessible
        .Type = xlColumn
        .HasTitle = True
        .HasLegend = False
        .ChartTitle.Text = "Purchase Report (Unit Cost of all Sales Items)"
    End With

    ' Document is created in Excel, objects are no longer necessary
    ' Good housekeeping to set objects to Nothing
    Set APPXL = Nothing
    Set xl = Nothing
    Set ws = Nothing
    Set objChart1 = Nothing

    ' Reset mouse cursor
    Screen.MousePointer = 0
End Function
```

Running the Export Chart Option

Now that you have created the Export Chart code, add the code in Listing 19.2 to the Export Chart menu item. This code merely activates the `CreateXLChart` routine for the OLE Automation. A message is displayed when the routine has completed its tasks. Now run the Management Client application. To do this, select the Export Chart option from the OLE menu.

Listing 19.2. `ExportChartItem_Click`.

```
Private Sub ExportChartitem_Click()
    CreateXLChart
    ' The process may have taken a long time so notify the user
    ' that the operation is complete.
    MsgBox "Export to Excel complete. Use Alt-Tab or Task Bar to change to Excel
➥for editing or modification.", 64, "Export Complete"
End Sub
```

If it has any problems gaining control of Excel—such as the presence of a Tips dialog box—the OLE system displays a dialog box like the one shown in Figure 19.4. It notifies the user that the OLE Server is busy and allows a choice of options. Switch to the application and clear the obstruction; execution will continue.

FIGURE 19.4.
The Server Busy dialog box.

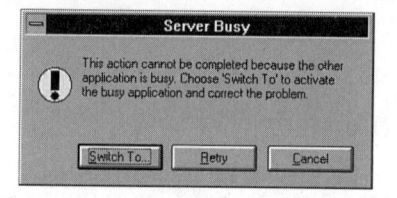

Once execution completes, a message box like the one shown in Figure 19.5 is displayed. Switch to the Excel application; you will see the chart that the OLE Automation has created. If you scroll down to the 35th row, you can see the data from which the chart was created.

FIGURE 19.5.
The Export Complete dialog box.

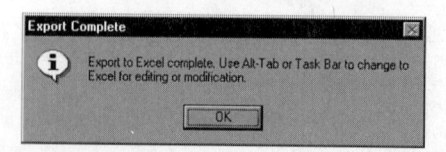

To display the graph in Visual Basic, you simply create a link to the file that you have created here. Save the workbook as MyChart.XLS to the same directory in which the project is located. The application will look in this folder and link to the chart.

Adding the New Form

Return to Visual Basic and stop execution of the Visual Basic application. You now will add a new form to display the chart and the code needed to activate it. Select the Form option from the Insert Menu. Name the form frm_OLEChart. Set the Caption property to Excel Chart Object. Set the background color to white. Because the default background in Excel is white, bleed-through will not be a problem.

Once the form has been created, add an OLE object by using the OLE tool from the palette, shown in Figure 19.6. Select the OLE tool, and click and drag a rectangle about three inches square. The size is not important, because it is automatically resized to fill the window.

FIGURE 19.6.
The OLE control.

After you have created the OLE object, a dialog box is automatically displayed that shows possible objects to insert at design time. (See Figure 19.7.) This enables the designer to define a particular object and prevents the object from having to be defined at runtime through program code. On this project, however, you want to construct the object manually at runtime. Therefore, click the Cancel button to close the dialog box.

FIGURE 19.7.
An Excel object form design.

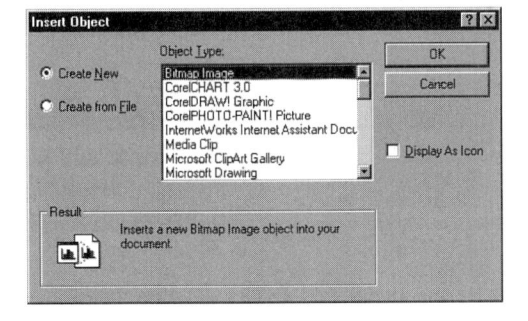

Now select the OLE object so that you can adjust its properties. Set Appearance to 0 (Flat), AutoActivate to 0 (Manual), BorderStyle to 0 (None), Caption to Excel Chart Object, Name to oleChart, and SizeMode to 2 (AutoSize). Once all these properties are set, the form should look approximately like the one shown in Figure 19.8.

With the form itself created, double-click a blank area to add the necessary code. Enter the code in Listing 19.3 into the Form_Load event.

FIGURE 19.8.
An Excel Chart Object form.

Listing 19.3. Form_Load for frm_OLEChart.

```
Private Sub Form_Load()
    DisplayXLChart
End Sub
```

Adding the *DisplayXLChart()* Routine

You now will create the code that actually links the OLE object on the form to the MyChart.XLS file. The chart is then displayed within the Visual Basic form. Select the Procedure option under the Insert menu. Type in the code for DisplayXLChart(), shown in Listing 19.4.

Listing 19.4. DisplayXLChart().

```
Private Sub DisplayXLChart()
    On Error GoTo ChartClickError
    Dim APPXL As Object
    Dim xl As Object
    Dim ws As Object
    Dim objChart1 As Object

    ' Get the application objects
    Set APPXL = GetObject(, "Excel.Application")
    Set xl = APPXL.Application
    Set ws = xl.ActiveSheet

    gstrWorksheet = "Purchase Chart"
    gstrChartObject = "Chart 2"

    ' To show a hidden Excel chart through the OLE control,
    ' use the control's Activate method. This is not the same
    ' as the OLE Activate that causes in-place editing.

    ws.ChartObjects(1).Activate
```

```
    ' Set the object type to linked so the chart will be
    ' read frin the file we created earlier
    oleChart.OLETypeAllowed = OLE_LINKED

    ' The App.Path is used to retrieve the chart from the same directory
    ' in which the application is executing
    oleChart.SourceDoc = App.Path & "\" & "MyChart.XLS"

    ' Set the path in the workbook to the chart itself
    ' Notice that we reference the chart by index of 1. We know there is only
    ' a single chart in the workbook. With multiple charts, a program would
    ' probably specify by name.
    oleChart.SourceItem = gstrWorksheet & "![" & gstrWorkbook & "]" &
➥gstrWorksheet & " " & ws.ChartObjects(1).Name

    ' Create the link.
    oleChart.Action = OLE_CREATE_LINK

    ' This activate will display the newly created link
    oleChart.object.Activate

    ' Set the chart to fit the current window size
    Me.Width = oleChart.Width
    Me.Height = oleChart.Height '= Me.ScaleHeight

    ' Eliminate the objects
    Set APPXL = Nothing
    Set xl = Nothing
    Set ws = Nothing
    Set objChart1 = Nothing

    Exit Sub

ChartClickError:
    ' Display any errors
    MsgBox Err & " - " & Error, MB_ICONEXCLAMATION
    Exit Sub
End Sub
```

The final step is to add the proper code to display the form. Once again, display the main form, frm_Manage. Under the Display Chart Window option, enter the code in Listing 19.5. It displays the chart in the Visual Basic form.

Listing 19.5. ChartWindowItem_Click.

```
Private Sub ChartWindowItem_Click()
    ' Display the OLE form
    frm_OLEChart.Show
End Sub
```

Execute the application and select the Display Chart Window option. The form will display the Excel chart created in the previous section. You can easily modify the Export Chart function to save the chart for linking automatically. This depends on which type of user interface you plan to implement for your client applications.

In past chapters, all the client programs were constructed strictly using Visual Basic. The additions in this chapter added to the Management client and demonstrated the power of using OLE Automation to extend a program's capabilities. The explosion of OLE Automation spreadsheets, word processors, e-mail programs, CAD programs, 3-D rendering programs, and many more provide a hint of the capabilities that are accessible.

By using the strong points of another product, you may fill in gaps in a particular client program that could not otherwise be created within budget. Although the cost savings are significant, be sure to check the memory requirements when using an OLE Automated solution. Memory on the individual machines on which the programs must be installed will be the primary restriction to widespread deployment of clients that take advantage of these features.

IV

Advanced Client/Server Topics

20

Structured Query Language (SQL) Primer

Structured Query Language (SQL) is a query programming language. Because of all the products that use the name SQL, the beginning client/server developer is often confused as to what exactly the term SQL describes. A simple SQL statement looks something like this:

```
Select * From TestTable Where Parameter = 1
```

This is one of the simplest types of SQL statements. A SQL statement is sent to a SQL-based query engine that generates a resultant set of data values. The resultant set comes in the form of rows (records) and columns (fields).

There are various "dialects" of SQL. A dialect is a SQL version that executes specific commands. For example, Microsoft SQL Server has one dialect, and Oracle Server has a different dialect. These dialects primarily supplement the commands that have been generally agreed upon in the SQL standards.

A SQL standards committee exists that attempts to standardize the common commands of SQL, making dialects unnecessary. Unfortunately, the SQL world moves so fast that the standards always seem to be years behind the features currently available in commercial products. The first widespread standard was called SQL 86 (ANSI X3.135-1986). Since then, the standards have been upgraded to SQL 89 (ANSI X3.135-1989) and the current standard SQL 92 (ANSI X3.135-1992).

There are now typically three levels that products describe themselves by: Entry SQL, Intermediate SQL, and Full SQL. Entry SQL complies with the 1986 standard, which is very rudimentary and does not include referential integrity.

Intermediate SQL is compliant with the 1989 standard and provides support for Dynamic SQL, partial referential integrity, enhanced set operations, improved transaction processing, and other features. The commands UNION JOIN, INTERSECT, and EXCEPT have been added to enable more control and flexibility when using multiple tables in conjunction with one query.

Full SQL describes a much more robust implementation, including scrollable cursors, complete table manipulation, full referential integrity, internationalization, temporary table support, and other features. Full SQL adds the commands DROP, ADD, and ALTER, which are used to control (and delete) entire tables.

Vendor-Specific Dialects

In addition to any type of SQL standard, SQL product producers add commands that make SQL nonstandard. These can usually be combined into two categories: functions and stored procedures and triggers (SP&T).

> **NOTE**
>
> The actual process of executing SQL code has three different forms:
>
> Dynamic SQL is the SQL implemented on all database programs. A SQL statement is sent to the SQL engine and the query is run. SQL acts like a language interpreter, wherein the code is created and issued at runtime.
>
> Static SQL is the SQL compiled and stored on the database server. This is ideal for queries that must be run frequently. The server can optimize the query because it is precompiled.
>
> Stored procedures and triggers (SP&T) store compiled code (like Static SQL) but can also accept variables, execute automatically given particular conditions, and so forth. None of the current ANSI standards cover SP&T SQL. This is why each vendor has an implementation of its own SP&T procedural language. Examples include Microsoft and Sybase using TRANSACT-SQL. Oracle uses PL/SQL, and DB2 uses platform-specific DLLs. These languages essentially augment normal SQL by adding additional commands for SQL compiling and optimization.

Functions

Functions are added by the manufacturer to simplify SQL programming, often adding capabilities that are impossible by using only SQL. Achieving the same functionality traditionally requires large data set downloads and customer parsing by a C program or equivalent. Oracle SQL has an extremely useful function called the DECODE function. Let's use this as an example of a task that this enhanced function makes more easier.

The DECODE function can, while the query is running, substitute a value and return another in the resultant set. In the client/server system you built in Part II, the Terms field held a number that related to the predefined constant determining the kind of terms the customer received (1 = Cash, 2 = Net 30 Days, and so forth). The DECODE statement can automatically substitute the text for a value and return this in the resultant set:

```
Select Terms from Customer
```

This statement returns a table that looks like this:

```
Terms
1
3
2
1
1
```

Using this `DECODE` statement:

```
Select DECODE(Terms, 1, 'Cash', 2, 'Net 30', 3, 'Net 15') from Customer
```

the returned table looks like this:

```
Terms
Cash
Net 15
Net 30
Cash
```

The `DECODE` statement is even more powerful because it can combine values (2 = Net Pay, 3 = Net Pay). When using `GROUP BY` statements, this value combining can be very useful.

Each vendor-specific SQL dialect has its own functions that the developers believed were important. Many of the functions are often impossible with traditional SQL. Function categories include string and substring handling, mathematical functions (such as median and statistical functions), conversion (date, number, hexadecimal, and so forth), and various comparison functions.

Stored Procedures and Triggers

As the SQL database server grew in popularity, users needed to shift more of the processing from the client to the server. Instead of downloading tremendous sets of data to the client for processing on each machine, it was much more efficient to give the server more capabilities so that the resultant set contained only the necessary data. SQL statements execution was still very slow because all the compiling had to be done at runtime.

Stored procedures solve this problem. *Stored procedures* are general SQL statements that can accept input and output parameters and remain partially compiled on the database server. A client sends the server various parameters and calls the stored procedure. It quickly executes because it is precompiled and optimized for that particular server.

Triggers provide even greater power. These are stored procedures that automatically activate when certain conditions exist. For example, when inventory drops below a reorder quantity, the trigger can automatically call a stored procedure to flag a database. A trigger can be automatically called when a `DELETE`, `INSERT`, or `UPDATE` command is used by a SQL statement. Triggers can also be used to force referential integrity.

In specific circumstances, a specific type of trigger is called a *rule*. A rule is a trigger that is used to perform simple checks on tables. Rules are used to enforce specific value integrities (for example, a Salary field must be between $0 and $4,000,000).

Trigger implementation is fairly nonstandard. Microsoft SQL Server supports one trigger per `DELETE`, `INSERT`, or `UPDATE`. Oracle allows up to 12 triggers per table. Check the current implementation of the system that you'll be using for exact specifications.

SQL Language

Any SQL command sent to a SQL engine typically begins with one of the following commands: SELECT, CREATE, DROP, ALTER, INSERT, DELETE, or UPDATE. These commands are used to manipulate a resultant set by selecting, editing, and maintaining a data set.

The SELECT command is used to create a query and retrieve a resultant set. This is the most common SQL command used. The SELECT command generates a resultant set of columns of one or more tables from a database.

CREATE, DROP, and ALTER are all used to manipulate entire tables. CREATE creates a table, DROP deletes a table, and ALTER is used to allocate additional storage for a database. These commands are occasionally missing from desktop computer SQL implementations. They often require the use of their standard UI to use these features.

INSERT, DELETE, and UPDATE are used on individual rows (records). INSERT is used to create a new row. DELETE removes an existing row. UPDATE alters particular columns of a given record.

All these commands are traditionally available in most complete SQL implementations. The table manipulation commands (CREATE, DROP, and ALTER) often can be used only by those given permission by the system administrator. This keeps tables from being created or modified indiscriminately.

SQL statements may also begin with a declaration of variables or parameters. Parameters are not supported in the baseline SQL standard and may not be supported in your SQL engine, but most implementations do support them. A common SQL statement has three parts:

```
[parameter-declaration] manipulative-statement [option-declaration] [;]
```

With some implementations, batch sequences of SQL statements may be sent to the SQL engine. This enables multiple related commands to be optimized by the engine. Often, only database servers feature batch SQL features.

The *SELECT* Command

SELECT is the command used to retrieve data. The SELECT statement is used to select what columns (fields) will be displayed as the resultant set. For example, this code selects every column in the table:

```
Select * from TestTable
```

The asterisk (*) is a wildcard character that selects all possible columns. Putting a specific column name in the SELECT statement returns only those fields. Here is an example:

```
Select LastName, FirstName from TestTable
```

This SELECT statement returns only the FirstName and LastName values from the table. Trying to access other fields from this resultant set generates an error.

The FROM command that follows the SELECT clause tells what table or tables from which to retrieve data. Many tables may be specified with the FROM statement. This code:

```
Select LastName, FirstName from Customers, Suppliers
```

selects all the LastName and FirstName values from both the Customers and Suppliers tables and returns them all as a single resultant set. If specific fields are in a particular table, the field may be specified by using the dot (.) command:

```
Select Customers.LastName, Suppliers.Company from Customers, Suppliers
```

This retrieves the LastName value from the Customers table and the Company value from the Suppliers table. SQL provides a simplified way to address various tables known as an *alias*, a variable that represents the table name. This can dramatically reduce the amount of typing required to specify a table (thereby reducing syntax errors). In this example:

```
Select a.LastName, b.Company from Customers a, Suppliers b
```

the SELECT statement accepts a table name, followed by a space, followed by the alias. Another common syntax for expressing an alias is to use the AS keyword. This is optional in most cases, but is often used to clarify code. Here is an example:

```
Select a.LastName, b.Company from Customers AS a, Suppliers AS b
```

An alias may also be used to change the name of the returned column (field). This is especially useful for labeling a column upon which a calculation is run. This example:

```
Select (GrossSales - Costs) NetProfit from MySales
```

returns a resultant set with one column named NetProfit containing the difference of the columns GrossSales and Costs that exist in the table MySales. Using an alias for a column that has many calculations greatly increases the maintainability of the SQL code.

The SELECT statement has many commands in addition to the FROM statement. The overall SELECT statement framework looks like this:

```
SELECT <clause>
    [DISTINCT]
    [INTO <clause>]
FROM <clause>
    [WHERE <clause>]
    [GROUP BY <clause>]
    [HAVING <clause>]
    [UNION subselect]
    [ORDER BY <clause> [ASC] [DESC] ]
    [SAVE TO TEMP <clause>]
    [;]
```

The SELECT and FROM statements are required for any query, but all other commands are optional. All SELECT statements may end with a semicolon (;), but this is usually optional.

SELECT with DISTINCT

The DISTINCT command returns only the first occurrence of a given value in a field in the resultant set. If a Customer table contains many different people with the same last name, it returns only distinct records or one record of each matching type. In this example:

```
Select Distinct LastName from Customer
```

the code does not return two records with the same LastName field. This command is often useful when a given record has multiple key fields and only individual items are needed. For example, in an Inventory file, multiple records might be kept for each item with an additional key field identifying the location of the item. By using the DISTINCT command, you can generate a list of items without any duplicate entries due to multiple locations.

SELECT with a WHERE clause

The WHERE clause is probably the most important optional statement in the SQL language. It enables specific conditions to be specified for the resultant set. The WHERE clause selects the rows that meet the clause conditions. This SELECT statement:

```
Select LastName, FirstName from Customer where State = 'WA'
```

returns all the rows that contain Washington in the State column. The WHERE clause can do many comparisons (see Table 20.1 for the comparison operators defined in ANSI SQL).

In standard SQL implementations, the = and <> comparison operators can be used on strings as well as numbers. Characters or strings should be enclosed with a single quote (').

Table 20.1. Comparison operators.

Operator	Meaning
=	Equals
>	Greater than
<	Less than
<=	Less than or equal to
>=	Greater than or equal to
<>	Not Equal

Logical operators can also be used in the WHERE clause (see Table 20.2 for those that are traditionally available). Some implementations of SQL have additional logical operators or ways of representing them. Please consult the manuals of your particular database program for details.

When using logical operators, use parentheses to clarify the evaluation order. Especially with multiplication and division, a misplaced parenthesis or a misjudgment of precedence order can return a subtle incorrect resultant set.

Table 20.2. Logical operators (in order of precedence).

Operator	Function
Not	Selects those that do not meet the criteria
And	Both conditions must qualify the row
Or	One or both of the conditions must be true to qualify the row

Using these commands together in a WHERE clause is much like traditional Visual Basic programming. To return a resultant set of all the staff members located in the state of California with salaries over $20,000 is a relatively simple query:

```
Select * from Staff Where State = 'CA' and Salary > 20000
```

SQL Aggregate Functions

Aggregate functions can collect data from many different rows and total this data into a final result. Aggregate functions include Count, Sum, Avg, Min, and Max. The parameter given to an aggregate function must be a column name. The asterisk (*) symbol may be used to include all columns.

The Count() function is used to count the number of records that comply with specified criteria. This example:

```
Select Count(*) from Staff
```

returns a single row and column that contains the total number of rows in the Staff table. Most often, the Count() function is used with other commands, such as the WHERE clause. This example:

```
Select Count(*) from Customer where State = 'CA'
```

returns the number of customer records that have a State field value that matches the one specified.

The Sum() function totals all the values in the selected rows. The Avg() function finds the average of the values, and Min() and Max() find the minimum and maximum of the values. This SELECT statement:

```
Select Min(Salary), Max (Salary), Avg(Salary) from Staff
```

returns the minimum, maximum, and average salary for all the employees contained in the Staff table. Aggregate functions can save a lot of network traffic and vastly increase program efficiency by not requiring each client to download a data set to do these operations by hand.

SELECT with BETWEEN, IN, and LIKE

BETWEEN, IN, and LIKE are commands that enable more complicated comparisons than the traditional comparison operators listed in Table 20.1. These three commands are called predicates because the resultant set of the WHERE clause is determined (or predicated) by the result of these commands.

The BETWEEN statement may be used effectively to specify high and low limits for a resultant set. The BETWEEN command requires a lower and upper value separated by an and operator (BETWEEN ... and ...). Here is an example:

```
Select LastName, FirstName, Salary from Staff
    Where Salary between 20000 and 40000
```

The BETWEEN predicate may be used with Character, Date, and Numeric columns. With Character columns, the strings are evaluated using their individual character values, which makes them case-sensitive.

> **CAUTION**
>
> The BETWEEN predicate varies dramatically with the vendor implementation of SQL. The function of BETWEEN can be either inclusive (including the begin and end values) or exclusive (not including the begin and end values). Therefore, two queries that appear identical may be run on the same data on varying systems and produce different results.
>
> On older versions of Oracle when you use the BETWEEN command on dates, the function changes between inclusive and exclusive depending on whether the two dates included one or many days! Therefore, refer to the server documentation and use a test set of data on your implementation platform to determine the exact operation of the BETWEEN command.

The IN predicate tests a column value against a series of other values and is included only if the values match. It can be used in place of multiple OR statements. This example:

```
Select * from Customer where State In ('CA','IN','WI')
```

returns all rows that have State field values that match those listed. The IN predicate is often used in conjunction with the NOT operator to exclude records containing certain values. This SELECT statement:

```
Select * from Customer where State Not In ('CA','IN','WI')
```

produces a resultant set that has all records that do not have a State column value of CA, IN, or WI. This IN command may also be used with Date and Numeric type values.

The LIKE predicate compares two strings in a similar way as the = comparison operator. Additionally, the LIKE command accepts wildcard characters, such as the underscore character (_) and the percent character (%). The underscore matches any single character and the percent symbol matches any number of characters. An underscore might be used to search a Phone number field:

```
Select * from Customer where Phone like '___-555-1212'
```

The three underscore characters create a wildcard section to find all the 555-1212 phone numbers regardless of their prefix. In contrast, the percent symbol looks for any number of characters. This SELECT statement:

```
Select * from Customer where Phone like '%555-1212%'
```

finds any string that has 555-1212, including 1-555-1212, extension 386. Therefore, the underscore is most appropriate when the exact format is known. The percent symbol is far more wide-ranging.

SELECT with *ORDER BY*

Using the ORDER BY statement, a SELECT command can specify how the resultant set is ordered. Normally, the rows are returned in the data set in the same order they were added. This statement:

```
Select * from Customer ORDER BY LastName, FirstName
```

returns a data set that is alphabetically sorted by the LastName field and then the FirstName field. Any columns used in the ORDER BY clause must be included in the SELECT clause.

The ORDER BY statement, by default, orders the field values in ascending order. Table 20.3 shows an example of ascending salary values. These same salary values could be sorted in descending order (see Table 20.4). The ORDER BY command may be told explicitly whether the values are to be ascending or descending. In this example:

```
Select * from Customer ORDER BY LastName DESC, FirstName
```

the DESC command returns the data set in descending order, and nothing (default is ascending) or explicit ASC returns the data in ascending order. Including the ASC command may make the code easier to understand.

Ascending and descending order can be specified for each field in the ORDER BY statement. This statement:

```
Select * from Customer ORDER BY LastName DESC, FirstName ASC
```

sorts the rows by last names in descending order and the second tier sort puts the first names in ascending order. This feature can be useful, for example, to sort a Sales table, with each sale sorting by ascending Zip code field with a descending TotalSales amount.

Table 20.3. Ascending salaries.

Row	Salary
1	$22,000
2	$27,000
3	$38,000
4	$40,000
5	$79,000

Table 20.4. Descending salaries.

Row	Salary
1	$79,000
2	$40,000
3	$38,000
4	$27,000
5	$22,000

SELECT with GROUP BY

One of the most powerful and time-saving commands for SQL queries is the GROUP BY command. This command enables specific criteria to be used to group rows in which particular columns have the same value. The grouped rows can then be used with aggregate functions to generate results by group. For example, the GROUP BY command could be used on the State field in conjunction with the SUM() aggregate function to return TotalSales by state. This could be done with a single SELECT statement:

```
Select Sum(TotalSales) from Sales Group By State
```

In the client/server system we built in Part II, each individual invoice line item was stored separately in the SalesItems table. A GROUP BY statement can generate the totals of each invoice quickly and simply:

```
Select InvoiceID, sum(FinalPrice) from SalesItems Group By InvoiceID
```

This SQL code generates a resultant set wherein the first column contains the InvoiceID and the second column contains the sum of all the items in that invoice (see Table 20.5). The GROUP BY command can be used for any type of grouping: numerical, character, or date. It can be used in conjunction with the ORDER BY clause because the grouped resultant set is not automatically ordered. This statement:

```
Select Sum(TotalSales) from Sales Group By State Order By State
```

returns a sum of total sales per state listed in alphabetical order.

Table 20.5. Sample SalesItems Query resultant set.

Column1	Column2
25	$196.15
26	$518.70
27	$45.00
28	$19.95
29	$179.55

> **TIP**
>
> Some SQL implementations require that each column name named in the SELECT statement must also be included in the GROUP BY statement. MS Access and SQL Server do not have this limitation, but if you experience any problems with using the GROUP BY statement with your database program, check the documentation to see whether this is the case.

The *HAVING* Clause

The HAVING clause is typically used with the GROUP BY clause to determine exactly what data returned by the GROUP BY clause will be displayed. The HAVING clause is like the WHERE clause because it specifies conditions that the data must meet before it is included in the resultant set. This query:

```
Select Sum(TotalSales) from Sales Group By State Having Sum(TotalSales) > 50
```

shows only the states that have a total sales of over 50 dollars. Once again, this assigns more of the processing work to the server, which returns to the client only the data that is specifically necessary.

> **NOTE**
>
> The HAVING clause is usually used with the GROUP BY clause, but it can be used alone. It must, however, be used with aggregate functions. Therefore, with a GROUP BY clause, it treats the entire data set to the aggregate function (SUM, AVG, and so forth). This occasionally can be useful to generate a true or false value on the entire data set. Otherwise, there are few applications wherein the HAVING clause is used alone.

The *UNION* Clause

The UNION clause enables multiple SELECT statements to be linked together to create one complete set. The resultant set eliminates duplicate rows so that a single data set is returned. Here is an example:

```
Select * from PurchaseItems UNION
```

> **NOTE**
>
> The way a database program handles a UNION set is widely variable. The standard SQL-89 first outlined how to handle two or more unionized result sets that did not have matching columns—for example, set A has columns named TotalSales and State, and set B has columns named TotalItems and State. Older SQL engines did not allow mismatched data sets.
>
> Most current database programs fill the missing column with a zero or null value. The resultant set of the previous example would look like this:
>
> | TotalSales | TotalItems | State |
> |---|---|---|
> | $2489.37 | 0 | CA |
> | 0 | 724 | CA |
>
> Consult the manual of your database for how UNIONs are handled.

The *JOIN* Command

A JOIN is a form of the SELECT statement that selects columns from two or more tables. JOIN is rarely an actual command (when it is, it creates a new table consisting of the tables in the JOIN statement). Joins are selected in the FROM clause of a SELECT statement. This example:

```
Select Sales.InvoiceID FROM Sales, Customers WHERE Sales.CustomerID =
↳Customers.CustomerID
```

joins the tables Sales and Customers to produce a resultant set wherein the CustomerID in each must be equal. The WHERE clause is optional to a JOIN and determines how the rows of the tables are combined.

This example is called a *simple join* or an *equi-join*. This is the most common type of join used in SQL design. Joins on individual machines tend to require quite a bit of processing power. Therefore, joins are most appropriate on a database server.

There are also joins called *outer joins*, which return all the matching values from the WHERE clause as well as the rows from one of the tables that have no direct match. An outer join is not supported by all SQL engines, and the syntax for activating an outer join varies. Check the manual of the SQL engine on which implementation will occur.

Data Definition Language (DDL)

The commands in SQL that create and modify databases, tables, and relations (such as CREATE TABLE, ALTER TABLE, and so forth) are known collectively as the Data Definition Language (DDL). SQL documentation frequently refers to various levels of DDL implementation. This refers to the types of commands for actual data structure definition that are supported by that particular SQL implementation.

Data Manipulation Language (DML)

Like DDL, Data Manipulation Language (DML) is a defined set of SQL commands. DML is used for accessing, updating, and maintaining the actual information in a database. Commands such as SELECT, INSERT, and UPDATE are included in a DML command set. Support for DDL varies widely but most SQL engines support the common DML commands.

MS Access SQL Implementation

In a perfect world, a SQL implementation would fit nicely into a category such as Full SQL or Intermediate SQL. Unfortunately, Microsoft Access has some features of each category and lacks other commands. Microsoft Access and the JET engine contain their own versions of SQL that can be used to query a database. These implementations are amazingly complete for bringing unheard-of power to the desktop level. They do, however, lack some of the commands and functionality available in complete database server implementations.

In Visual Basic, while using the JET engine, SQL commands are used to find data. For example, when using the data control, the DatabaseName property must be set to the database, and the RecordSource property is set to the table that is to be accessed. If you want to access a table called TestTable, the RecordSource is set to this string. When the method FindFirst is used, the program must send a query such as the following:

```
Data1.Recordset.FindFirst "State = 'WI'"
```

This query generates an entire SQL statement, which actually reads:

```
"Select * from TestTable where State = 'WI'"
```

To construct a Dynaset with this set of data, the program must set up a SQL string to create a Dynaset from a database that is set up to access that set of tables. The code to do so looks like this:

```
SQL$ = "Select * from TestTable where State = 'WI'"
MyDS = MyDB.CreateDynaset(SQL$)
```

This creates a Dynaset of all the records that meet the specified criteria. This Dynaset is automatically updated as records are added to the set. For example, if another record is added that includes the State column equal to 'WI', this record automatically is added to the Dynaset. This is not the case with Snapshots. It also is the reason that Dynasets are described as "dynamic."

> **WARNING**
>
> To compare dates, make sure the date is encapsulated by number signs (#). For example, if a table has a date field titled InvoiceDate, the following query won't generate the appropriate resultant set:
>
> ```
> Select * from TestTable where InvoiceDate = 1/3/95
> ```
>
> Here is the correct version:
>
> ```
> Select * from TestTable where InvoiceDate = #1/3/95#
> ```
>
> Forgetting the #/# can lead to hours of fruitless debugging because the problem is right in front of you. This happens most often when creating a SQL string such as the following:
>
> ```
> SQL$ = " ... where InvoiceDate = " & Date$
> ```
>
> This is the correct version:
>
> ```
> SQL$ = " ... where InvoiceDate = #" & Date$ & "#"
> ```

MS Access Implementation

Microsoft Access has its own implementation of the SQL engine. Both the Access application and the JET engine share a language implementation called Access SQL. The MS Access application contains one of the best ways to learn SQL query construction and prototype SQL queries for use in client/server applications.

MS Access has a Query window (also know as QBE) that enables the creation of queries with all the tables or attached tables in the database (see Figure 20.1). Notice in the figure that the

Design View toolbar button is depressed. A query may be created in the Query Builder grid and then the resultant set may be viewed by clicking the Datasheet View toolbar button.

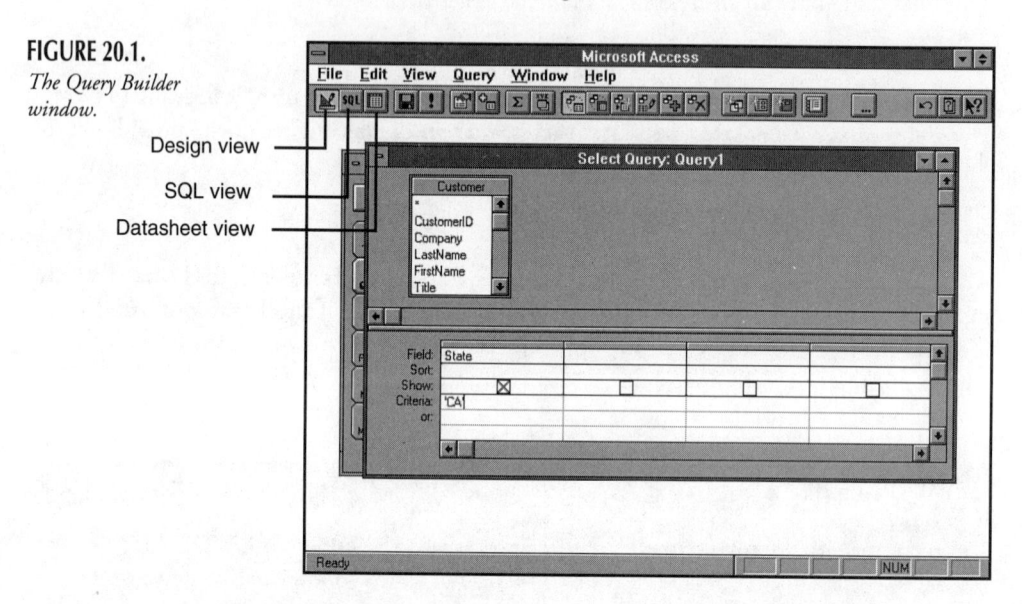

FIGURE 20.1.
The Query Builder window.

Design view
SQL view
Datasheet view

After a query has been constructed to fulfill the needs of the project, the Access SQL code may be examined and modified (see Figure 20.2). The code is accessed by clicking the SQL View button in the toolbar. You may change the SQL code and reactivate the Datasheet View to examine the results. Once SQL code is perfected, it can be COPYed and PASTEd into a Visual Basic code window. The SQL code can then be sent to the JET engine for the creation of a Dynaset or Snapshot object.

FIGURE 20.2.
The Access SQL code window.

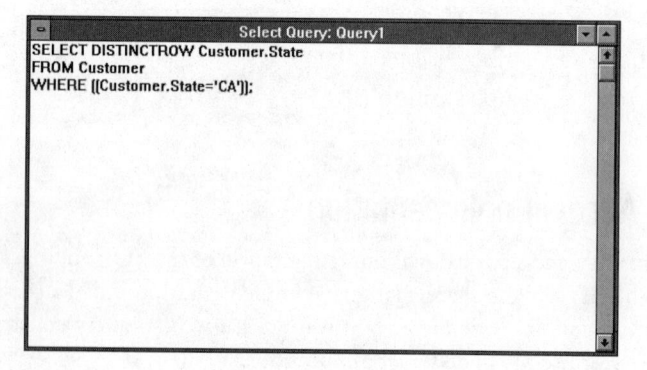

> **WARNING**
>
> Beware of changing back to the Design View from the SQL View. The Design View reinterprets any changes made to the SQL code and displays a Query Builder grid that most closely approximates the SQL code. When the SQL view is reentered, the SQL code is rebuilt from the Design View.
>
> This can destroy your query! Any SQL statements the Design View cannot interpret will be lost when the code is recreated in the SQL View. Optimization can also be destroyed, because the Access program builds a query that is not minimized but, instead, uses all explicit SQL commands. If you want to look at a modified SQL query in the Design View, make sure to copy the SQL source so that your original code will not be lost.

Access SQL is based on the SQL standard (ANSI-86, ANSI-89, and ANSI-92), but it does not support all the commands described in these standards. It also provides various extension commands as well as the capability of accepting various Access Basic commands and variables from within a query.

The following is a list of all the Access SQL commands. In the three standards that Access SQL is based on, there are over 200 key words that are defined. Needless to say, Access SQL is a subset. However, because Access can use Access Basic functions inside a query (such as string manipulation, conversion, and so forth), many commands are not necessary. Unfortunately, Access Basic commands are not portable to other SQL implementations.

ALL	HAVING	PARAMETERS
AS	IEEESINGLE	PIVOT
ASC	IN	PROCEDURE
BINARY	INNER	REAL
BIT	INSERT	RIGHT
BY	INT[EGER]	SELECT
CHAR[ACTER]	INTO	SET
CURRENCY	JOIN	SHORT
DATABASE	LEFT	SMALLINT
DATETIME	LEVEL	TABLEID
DELETE	LONG	TEXT
DESC	LONGBINARY	TRANSFORM
DISTINCT	LONGTEXT	UPDATE
DISTINCTROW	OPTION	VALUE
FLOAT	ORDER	WHERE
FROM	OWNERACCESS	WITH
GROUP		

Access SQL does not support subqueries. Instead, it enables the creation of multiple nested queries. It also does not support the ALTER, CREATE, and DROP DDL statements. These operations must be done by hand by using the MS Access user interface.

One of the most limiting shortcomings of Access is that it is incapable of using the DISTINCT command inside an aggregate function. For example, when using the SUM() aggregate function to total all the costs of an inventory table, nondistinct (duplicate) inventory item records are totaled together rather than being added to the sum only once.

> **NOTE**
>
> When using SQL Aggregate functions, the Access SQL engine has several important limitations. It cannot do a complex aggregate (in other words an aggregate of an aggregate). For example, if a program requires an average of sales in each state and then wants an overall average of these averages (producing a weighted average), the SQL code uses an Avg(Avg(TotalSales)) with a GROUP BY statement for the state. Access can do only one level of aggregation. The primary aggregate resultant set has to be downloaded to the client and averaged from there.
>
> Access also cannot use the DISTINCT function within an aggregate. Therefore, a statement such as Select Count(Distinct City) from Customer will not work.

Access SQL did include a few extra commands for greater querying power. Features implemented in MS Access SQL that are unavailable in ANSI standards include both inner and outer joins. The TRANSFORM statement can be used for crosstab queries. Additional aggregate functions have been added, including STDev and VarP. The PARAMETERS command enables the use of variables within a query.

Familiarity with the SQL engine is essential for VB client/server development if you plan to use the JET engine. However, the JET engine does have performance penalties. Using the ODBC SQL might be an effective (although more complex) alternative.

ODBC SQL

The Open Database Connectivity uses API calls from Visual Basic to interpret SQL commands. The SQL is converted by the particular ODBC driver (SQL Server, Oracle, and so forth) into commands that the database can understand. For more information on ODBC, see Chapter 23, "Object Linking and Embedding (OLE)," where you convert one of the client applications to access the database via ODBC.

The ODBC SQL implementation is divided into two parts: Core functions and Extended functions. The Core functions are based on the X/Open and SQL Access Group (SAG) SQL

CAE draft specification of 1992. Extended functions support such features as scrollable cursors and asynchronous processing.

> **CAUTION**
>
> ODBC has two separate types of conformance: API conformance and SQL Grammar conformance. The API consists of three levels of conformance: Core API, Level 1 API, and Level 2 API. ODBC SQL Grammar consists of only two levels: Core functions and Extended functions. The SQL Grammar also defines what SQL data types are supported.
>
> When you purchase ODBC drivers, be sure to check both types of conformance levels in order to understand what the limitations of that driver entail. These ODBC support levels are described in more detail in Chapter 23.

The conformance levels of a particular driver may actually be detected using an ODBC API call. This way, an application can enable use of any ODBC data source that supports all the functions the program requires.

Core SQL Grammar

The Core SQL Grammar compliance is the common level of ODBC driver. There is a Minimum SQL Grammar compliance level, but it is so simple that the Core SQL level has become the *de facto* standard. Here are the commands required for DDL compatibility:

```
CREATE TABLE
DROP TABLE
ALTER TABLE
CREATE INDEX
DROPINDEX
CREATE VIEW
DROP VIEW
GRANT
REVOKE
```

For DML capabilities, you must implement these commands:

```
SELECT
INSERT
UPDATE SEARCHED
DELETE SEARCHED
```

Simple expressions and comparisons, such as A + B > C, must be supported within a query. Subqueries and aggregate functions such as SUM and MIN must also be available.

The Core SQL implementation must support particular data types. This enables known data conversion between the program accessing the ODBC driver and any data format used by the data source. These data types include CHAR, VARCHAR, LONG VARCHAR, DECIMAL, NUMERIC, SMALLINT, INTEGER, REAL, FLOAT, and DOUBLE PRECISION.

Extended SQL Grammar

Extended SQL ODBC drivers are much less common because of the advanced commands required for compliance. If the driver supports Extended SQL Grammar, all Core SQL Grammar and data types must be supported. This ensures scaling possibilities for code.

Various DML commands have been added to increase the power of the SQL access. These include commands for outer joins, positioned UPDATE, positioned DELETE, SELECT FOR UPDATE, and unions.

Advanced functions such as SUBSTRING and ABS are supported. Data manipulation functions to work with data types such as date, time, and timestamp literals are also supported. The Extended ODBC driver must enable the use of batch SQL statements to increase flexibility and throughput. To support precompiled SQL code (such as Static SQL), the driver must also provide the capability of making embedded SQL procedure calls.

In addition to the data types supported by the Core SQL level, additional more powerful types must be implemented. These data types include BIT, TINYINT, BIGINT, BINARY, VARBINARY, LONG VARBINARY, DATE, TIME, and TIMESTAMP.

ODBC Drivers

ODBC drivers are also described as either single-tiered or multiple-tiered. With a single-tiered driver, the particular database program that the ODBC SQL statement is being sent to is a SQL-based Server. The single-tier driver takes care of basic formatting and conversion and merely sends a SQL statement to the data source. A multiple-tier driver is used when the database program does not directly support SQL and therefore must be converted through multiple tiers to be used by the database.

The ODBC specification defines most of the necessary data types available (see Table 20.6). With the advent of object databases and multimedia extensions, new data types may be added.

Table 20.6. ODBC SQL data types.

Data Type	Description
SQL_BIT	Single-bit binary data
SQL_TINYINT	Whole number between 0 and 255, inclusive
SQL_SMALLINT	Whole number between + and −32,767, inclusive
SQL_INTEGER	Whole number between + and −2,147,483,647, inclusive
SQL_REAL	Floating point with 7-digit precision; 3.4E +/− 38
SQL_FLOAT, SQL_DOUBLE	Floating point with 15-digit precision; 1.7E +/− 308
SQL_TIMESTAMP, SQL_DATE	Date and time data
SQL_TIME	Time data
SQL_CHAR	Character string; maximum = source-dependent
SQL_VARCHAR	Variable length character size; maximum = 255 characters
SQL_BINARY	Fixed-length binary data
SQL_VARBINARY	Variable-length with a maximum of 255 bytes
SQL_LONGVARBINARY	Variable-length binary data; maximum = source-dependent
SQL_LONGVARCHAR	Variable-length character data; maximum = source-dependent
SQL_DECIMAL, SQL_NUMERIC	Signed, exact, numeric value with a precision and a scale

An ODBC data source can support more SQL commands than those defined by a specification. If the ODBC driver cannot interpret the SQL command, the query is passed directly to the data source without any additional processing. In this way, vendor-specific SQL extensions can be used through the ODBC interface.

For information on the specific SQL statements supported by an ODBC driver, see the online help or text file supplied with the driver. For example, the Oracle ODBC driver included with VB explains its support and limitations in a .TXT file installed with the driver.

SQL Server Implementation

SQL Server is a standard implementation of the SQL language common to both the Microsoft SQL Server and the Sybase SQL Server. These two products are beginning to diverge, with

Microsoft SQL Server 6.0 soon to be released, and the changes could be significant. However, the basic implementation should remain the same.

> **TIP**
>
> The ODBC drivers for the Sybase and SQL Server implementations are different. At the time of this writing, there was no available ODBC driver for the Sybase System 10 OmniShare Server. Although it is supposed to be released soon, remember that ODBC drivers are often tailored to a specific system. Therefore, it is not enough to know what type of server will be accessed (for example, Sybase), but also what version of the database server system is being run (for example, System 7, System 10, and so forth).
>
> Because of the expense of database server maintenance and upgrades, enterprises often use an older-than-current version of a database server. Make sure a driver is available for the system version that must be accessed.

In addition to support for standard SQL commands and functions, SQL Server also includes a complete control-of-flow language known as Transact-SQL. This language enables the creation of complete query programs that can include branching, looping, breaks, and change in the execution order. There are a complete set of control-of-flow commands available to SQL Server.

The DECLARE command is available to create local variables or parameters that can be used by a SQL statement. SQL Server also includes a number of global variables that are available to gain information about the SQL Server system.

The COMPUTE statement can be used in conjunction with aggregate functions to provide a report-style resultant set. The results of a query that includes a COMPUTE clause are displayed with both detail and summary rows.

SQL Server supports defaults and rules. A default can set a default value for a column when a new row is created. A rule ensures that the value entered in a column remains within certain limits. A rule may also be used to restrict an entire data type.

SQL Server supports various error-handling techniques. These include the capability of retrieving a status value returned by an executed stored procedure, defining customized return values from stored procedures, the capability of passing parameters from a procedure to a stored procedure, and accessing global variables. A global variable such as @@ERROR can contain an error that may be passed to the user through the RAISERROR or PRINT commands.

The SET command enables the display of processing statistics, customizing the display of returned results, and monitoring and debugging display parameters. The SHUTDOWN statement is available to the system administrator to shut down the SQL Server from within a SQL statement.

SQL Server supports stored procedures and triggers. Included with SQL Server are various system-supplied procedures called system procedures. Triggers may be nested up to 16 levels deep.

> **CAUTION**
>
> Microsoft SQL differs from ANSI SQL in several ways, but often one of the subtle, hard-to-find problems is with the wildcard character. ANSI SQL uses the percent sign (%) to specify wildcards (including Oracle Servers). Microsoft implementations use the asterisk (*). When converting a query, be sure to change all the wildcard characters, or your resultant set will be vastly different.

With both Microsoft and Sybase poised to introduce new versions of their database servers, vast technical information presented here would be quickly outdated. Chapter 21, "Upsizing to Microsoft SQL Server," demonstrates more of the SQL engine for the database server. For information on where to get details on the new implementations, see Appendix C, "Sources."

21

Upsizing to Microsoft SQL Server

The Upsizing Wizard

Microsoft has created a powerful tool, the Upsizing Wizard, for its Access application. The Upsizing Wizard moves the structures that make up a database from an Access database to a SQL Server database. These structures include tables, relationships, indexes, default values, validation rules, and timestamp fields. This lets an organization upscale all of the databases created in MS Access to a complete database server, thus preserving an investment in desktop database information and technology.

The Upsizing Wizard also enables you to scale individual tables or other parts of the database (such as indexes, default values, and so on) at any time. This enables you to migrate a database to SQL Server over time and also provides for easy testing of individual tables to determine what might be lost in the translation (for example, any Access-specific functions will not be ported).

In this chapter you will use Microsoft Access 2.0 and the Microsoft Access Upsizing Wizard to convert all of the database tables and structures in the C/S system we've created in this book into a complete Microsoft SQL Server database. Note that you must have table and database creation access (such as a System Administrator (sa) account) to a Microsoft SQL Server in order to create the database on the database server itself. If you don't have this type of database creation access, ask the system administrator to create the database for you.

> **NOTE**
>
> We used Access 2.0 and not Access 95 for this upsizing because at the time of this writing, the upsizing tools for Access 95 were not available. The primary concepts of upsizing the Access database will undoubtedly remain the same, as will most of the options available to the Upsizing Wizard. Therefore, this chapter will still be usable when the Upsizing Tools are available for Access 95.

The Upsizing Wizard is included on the Solutions Development Kit CD-ROM and the Microsoft Development Library CD-ROM (sent to Microsoft Developers Level 1 and 2). It is also available for purchase directly from Microsoft. In this chapter, we will be using it to upsize the client/server database WIDGETCO.MDB, created in earlier chapters.

Creating a SQL Server Database

Before the database can be upsized to the SQL Server, you must create a device and a database on the database server to hold the tables and data. The device holds the database and log used by the system. The database holds all of the tables you are upsizing (Sales, SalesItems, Customer, and so on). When you're finished the database will be accessible to any machine on the network with an ODBC connection to the SQL Server and correct access permissions.

Creating the Device

SQL Server stores all databases and logs within *devices*. Therefore, you need to create a new device to hold the client/server system database. By creating an independent device for this database, the size and backup options can be strictly specified to the needs of this particular system.

To create a device, the SQL Administrator Win32 application must be executed. This application enables the creation of devices, databases, users, and groups. Click on the button labeled Devices to show all of the current devices. Select the Devices option under the Manage menu and then select the Create… hierarchical option. The Create Device window is then displayed (see Figure 21.1).

FIGURE 21.1.
The SQL Administrator Create Device window.

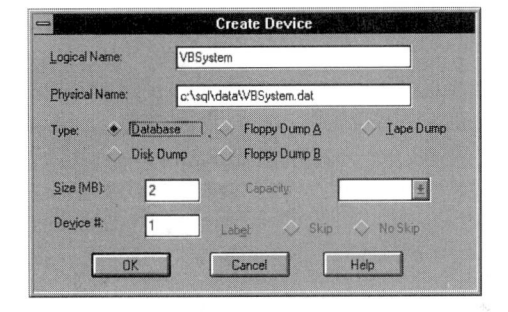

For the logical name of the device, type VBSystem. The physical name is then automatically created to mirror the logical name. Change the path if the device should be stored somewhere else (it won't matter to any of the programs that access the database server). Select Database as the device Type. The Size and Device # are automatically created.

Click the OK button to create the device. The SQL Administrator displays a message notifying you that the device was created. The Device Management window should now show the device, its filename, the size, space available, and other relevant information. Now that the device has been created to hold the database, it's time to create the database to hold the tables.

Creating the Database

The database for the client/server system is named CS_System. In this database will be stored all of the tables when they are upsized (Sales, Customer, Supplier, and so on). The CS_System database is the only database that is going to be stored in the VBSystem device.

In the SQL Administrator Win32, click the button labeled DB. Select Database under the Manage menu and then select the Create Database… hierarchical option. The Create Database window is displayed (see Figure 21.2). Enter the Database Name as CS_System. Specify the Data Device as VBSystem. Leave the Log Device set to none, which means the log is stored in the same device as the database.

FIGURE 21.2.
The SQL Administrator Create Database window.

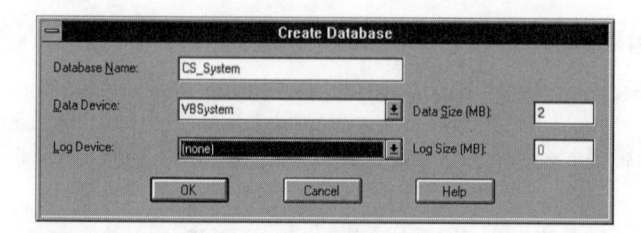

Click the OK button and the database is created. The program displays how many pages have been allocated to contain the database (see Figure 21.3). You can now use the device and the database to store the new tables.

FIGURE 21.3.
SQL Administrator successful database creation.

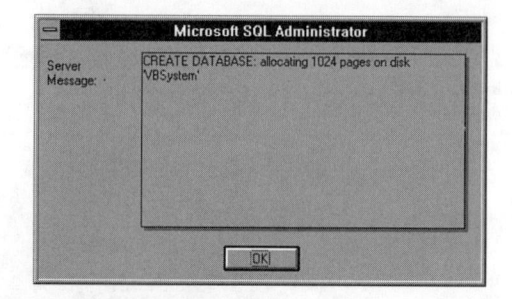

Setting Up an ODBC Connection

You must also create an ODBC connection to the database. The Upsizing Wizard uses an ODBC data source to connect to the SQL Server and create the necessary database structures. This data source performs best if in place before the upsizing begins.

The ODBC Administration utility is used to create the connections. It can often be found in the Control Panel. If it does not appear in the Control Panel, search your hard disk for the ODBCADM.EXE (16-bit) or ODBCAD32.EXE (32-bit), which are often stored in the \WINDOWS\SYSTEM directory.

If you cannot locate the ODBC Administrator utility, perhaps ODBC has not been installed on your machine. In this case, you can use Visual Basic to install the ODBC drivers needed to access numerous databases, including SQL Server and Oracle. Check the VB Program Group and look for the Data Access Setup icon. This program installs the necessary ODBC drivers. If the icon cannot be located, execute the Visual Basic SETUP.EXE. Do a custom install and the program will enable the installation of the necessary Data Access and ODBC drivers.

Creating an ODBC Connection

Execute the ODBC Administrator tool. If you already have an ODBC data source created that has table-creation and -modification capabilities on your server, use that source for the upsize.

Otherwise, click the Add... button to add a data source. Select the SQL Server or the SQL Server (32-bit) option from the list and click the OK button.

Now the ODBC SQL Server Setup window should appear as shown in Figure 21.4. For the Data Source Name, enter `CS_System`. This is the name of the ODBC connection; it won't be used by the server database. Type a description like the one shown in the figure. ODBC data sources tend to accumulate, and it is often difficult later to determine what role the data source filled and if it is safe to delete it. The more thorough the description now, the more helpful it will be later.

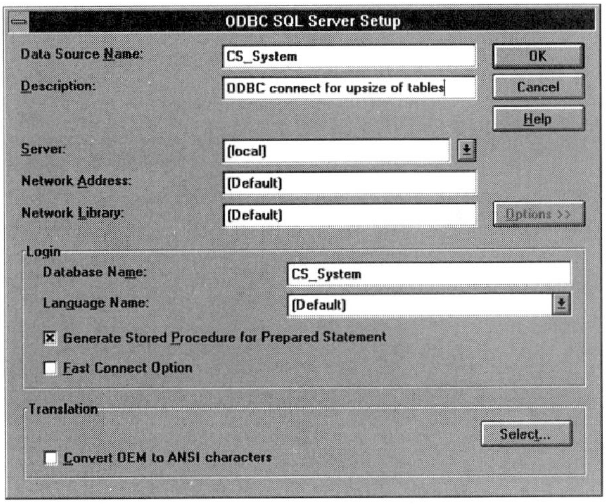

FIGURE 21.4.
Creating the ODBC connection.

In the Server field, enter the name of the database server to be accessed (or select local). Enter the Network Address and Library if necessary. Click on the Options button to show additional fields for the data source connection.

One of these fields determines what is the main login database. Enter the database name of the one created earlier called CS_System. Enter `CS_System` into the field so that this database is used as the default when the connection is made. With ODBC sources, you can change the database to which the connection is hooked at any time, although you can only select one database at a time.

When all of the fields have been entered, click the OK button to save the data source. The information is stored to the two ODBC .INI files. The connection can now be used by any program that can access the ODBC interface. This connection is used by the Upsizing Wizard to reconstruct the database on the SQL Server.

For more information about ODBC, see Chapter 22, "Open Database Connectivity (ODBC)," which provides a complete explanation of the ODBC interface as well as a demonstration on how to upgrade one of the client applications to make direct ODBC calls without having to access the JET engine.

Upsizing the Database

Now that all of the initial structures are in place, you can upsize the WIDGETCO.MDB database. After the database is upsized, as long as the Access file remains, the client program can continue to use the same routines (with only slight modifications) to access the tables. MS Access enables *attached tables* (those attached to the SQL Server tables) to act just as if they were local to the file.

Before the Wizard is activated, the tables must be prepared so they remain within the capabilities of SQL Server. After the upsizing occurs, the tables must be verified to ensure they were re-created correctly on the SQL Server. You can do this either through the SQL Browser add-in to MS Access or through the SQL Server Administration utilities themselves.

Preparing the Database File

The Upsizing Wizard can either create a new Access database that contains links to the newly created SQL Server database or add the links to the current database. In order to compare the results of before and after the upsizing, let's create the links inside an existing database. You don't want to have the potential of corrupting the WIDGETCO.MDB database, so you'll use a copy of it.

Execute the Explorer or File Manager and select the WIDGETCO.MDB file. Select the Copy... option under the File menu. Copy the file into the same directory and type `WIDGTSQL.MDB` as the filename. The system should now have two copies of the same database in the CLNTSRVR folder.

When the database is opened, check the Exclusive access box (see Figure 21.5) to ensure that no other users attempt to use it while the upsizing is taking place. Unpredictable results can occur if other users attempt access during the process.

FIGURE 21.5.
Opening the database with exclusive access.

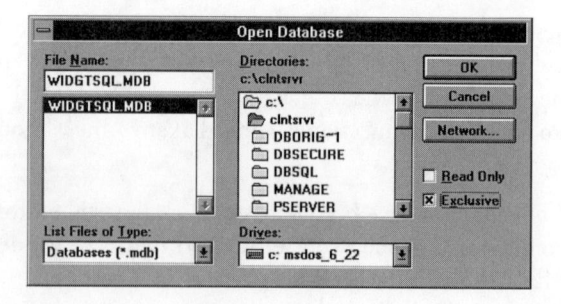

The Visual Basic Data Manager does not require the designer to enter a primary key for each table. Therefore, all of the tables created for the client/server project lack specified key fields. For the table to upsize correctly, you must specify a primary key.

Selecting keys is a fairly simple process. Execute the MS Access application and load the WIDGTSQL.MDB file. Select the first database, Assembly, and click the Design command button. Table 21.1 contains all of the designations for the key fields for the tables in the database. Notice that the key fields for the table are `PartID_Sales` and `PartID_Parts`. Both of these fields together become the keys for the table.

Table 21.1. Key field specifications.

Table Name	Key Field(s)
Assembly	PartID_Sales, PartID_Parts
Counter	ID
Customer	CustomerID
Inventory_Parts	PartID
Inventory_Sales	PartID
Location	LocationID
PServer	ID
Purchase	PurchaseID
PurchaseItems	PurchaseID, LineNum
Sales	InvoiceID
SalesItems	InvoiceID, LineNum
Staff	StaffID
Supplier	SupplierID

Select both of these fields by clicking and dragging the empty box to the left of each field entry. You can also extend the selection of fields by pressing the Shift or Ctrl keys (as used by standard list boxes). With the fields selected, click the key icon in the toolbar. Small key icons appear in the empty boxes to the left of the field names (see Figure 21.6). Close the window. You will be prompted to save the changes. Click the Yes button.

Set the keys for all of the database tables as specified in Table 21.1. For the multiple field keys, use the Ctrl and Shift keys to specify both fields as keys. Once all of the keys are set, the database is ready to be upsized.

FIGURE 21.6.
Setting the key fields for the Assembly table.

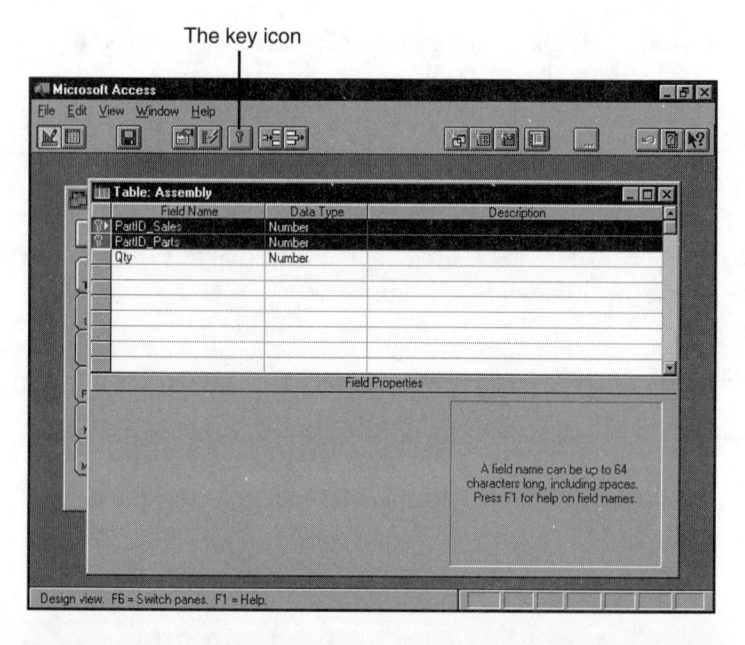

> **WARNING**
>
> Make sure you add a primary key to all of the tables created with the Visual Basic Data Manager. If there is no primary key for each table in the database, the upsizing will work perfectly but you will not be able to write to the upsized table.
>
> In Visual Basic, the programmer is expected to worry about all of the relations housekeeping (including setting all of the primary and foreign keys). The VB system does not require the programmer to select the field(s) that will be the primary key. When the database created with the VB Data Manager is loaded into Access, no errors occur. When the database is upsized, no error occurs. However, when an attempt is made to write to a table lacking a primary key, a No Write Permission error occurs.
>
> Therefore, when using Access with a database created in VB, make sure to specify the proper keys. If the SQL Server generates this error, check to make sure the upsized table contains a primary key.

Beginning the Upsizing

The Upsizing Wizard acts similarly to most of the other wizards available in the MS Office products. A series of four pages, each containing more detailed information about the coming process, enables the user to select various options relevant to the Wizard operation. When all of the selections are made, the user clicks the Finish button and the Wizard begins to complete its task.

To activate the Upsizing Wizard, select the Add-ins option under the File menu and choose the Upsizing Wizard (see Figure 21.7). The first of the Upsizing Wizard step screens is displayed. Notice that at any time you can click the Hint button or press the F1 key to obtain online help information on the selected screen.

FIGURE 21.7.
The Upsizing Wizard menu selection.

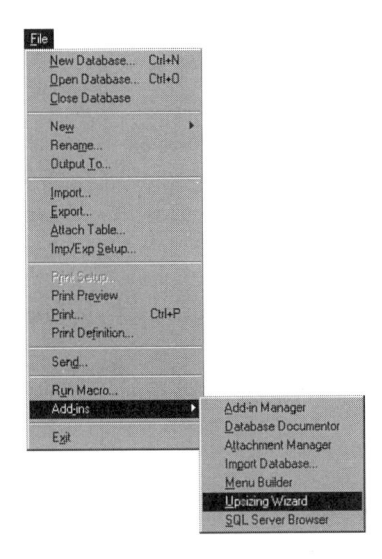

The Wizard screen 1, shown in Figure 21.8, asks the user to select either creating a new database or using an existing one. Note that this creates a new database *on the SQL Server*. This does not refer to the attaching of tables to the current Access database. Because you have already created the CS_System database on the server, leave the default setting of Use Existing Database. Click the Next button on the bottom of the window.

FIGURE 21.8.
Wizard Step 1: new or existing database.

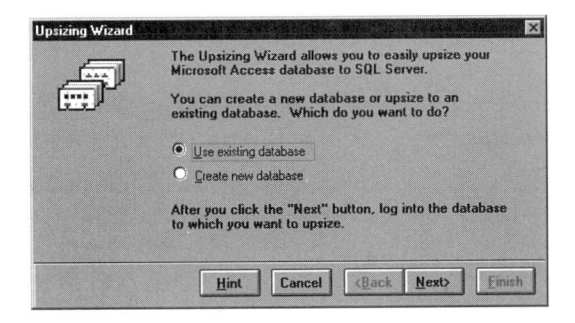

Step 2 allows the user to choose which tables should be upsized (see Figure 21.9). This allows selective upsizing and provide a way to upsize individual tables later. Any table may be selected and clicking the button with the single arrow (>) will move the table into the Export to SQL Server list box.

FIGURE 21.9.
Wizard Step 2: select tables to upsize.

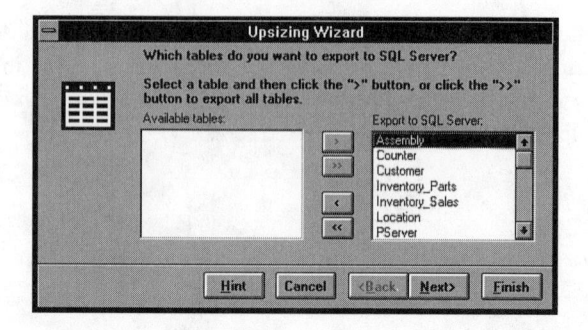

For the client/server system, you need all 13 of the tables to be upsized into the SQL Server. Click the double arrow (>>) button, which moves all of the table names into the Export list box. The Upsizing Wizard exports the entire table structure (field names and data types), as well as its data. Click the Next button to continue to the next step.

> **NOTE**
>
> After the upsize has been completed, the original tables are renamed to include a `_local` suffix. These tables do appear in the table list to be exported. To upsize these tables again, you must rename each of them to eliminate the `_local` suffix. The tables will then appear in the Available tables list box.

Step 3 provides for all of the options that will be used to process the upsized tables. (See Figure 21.10.) The top frame controls the upsizing process. Should the indexes be duplicated in the SQL Server? Should validation rules, default values, and table relationships by upsized with the database? Should timestamp fields be added? Timestamp fields are used by the database to determine if the record has been changed since it was last buffered, improving performance of the database (which would otherwise have to check each record).

FIGURE 21.10.
Wizard Step 3: upsizing options.

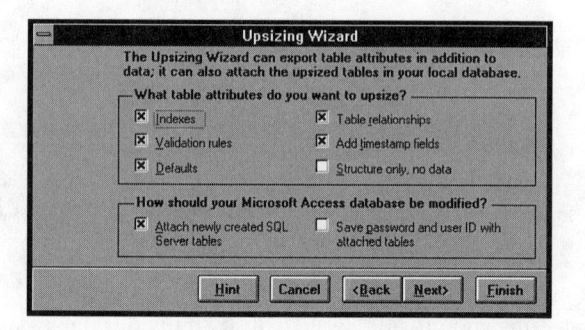

The final check box enables the structure of each table to be upsized without the data, thus enabling the creation of a virgin database on the server. If the data file you are upsizing is large, you can use this option to ensure the structure ports in correctly before the large amount of time is used loading in the data itself. For this project, these are all options you leave set to their defaults.

The bottom frame modifies the MS Access database file that is being upsized. Attached tables that link to the newly created SQL Server database can be automatically created. These table links in Access are called *attached tables*. Also, you can specify that security be automatically placed on the attached tables. Because security is going to be handled on the SQL database server itself, leave this option empty.

All of the default settings are appropriate for the client/server system database because you want to upsize both the data and the data structure itself. Click the Next button to continue.

The final step before the upsizing actually takes place enables the user to select an upsizing report. (See Figure 21.11.) This report is generated as the upsizing takes place and details any errors that might have occurred, all of the tables and structures that were created by the Upsizing Wizard, and other important maintenance information. This report can then be printed, saved as an MS Word document, or saved as an Excel document.

FIGURE 21.11.
Wizard Step 4: finish/ upsizing report.

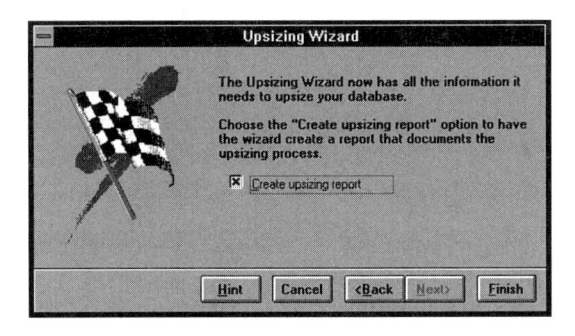

The authors strongly suggest that you create an *upsizing report*—a document that tells what was done and when—every time you upsize a major database. If the original tables must ever be consulted, this document provides a paper trail for each of the tables now on the SQL Server.

Click the Finish button to begin upsizing the database. Because WIDGTSQL.MDB has little data and few tables, the upsizing only takes about a minute. A status box appears (see Figure 21.12) to show the progress of the upsizing. If any errors are encountered, the Wizard halts, notifies you of the error, and asks if you want to continue. Few errors cause the Wizard to abort and require you to start over.

When the upsizing is complete, the Wizard beeps and displays a message box describing any errors that may have occurred. The report of the various factors of the upsized database is then generated. Print this report or save it to Excel or Word. The Database window should then reappear on the screen.

FIGURE 21.12.
Upsizing Wizard progress.

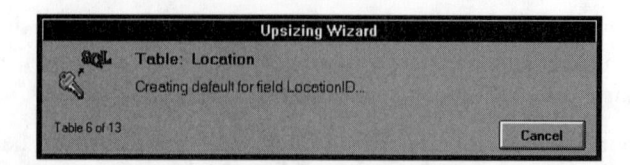

Examining the Upsized Database with Attached Tables

After the database has been upsized, each table can be examined as if it were a local tables. Figure 21.13 shows how the Access Database window now appears. You can see that all of the original table names have an Earth icon with an arrow to their left. This icon represents an attached table. All of the original tables have been renamed to include the extension `_local` and retain their icons. All of the attached tables have been named to match the original table names.

FIGURE 21.13.
Access Database window with attached tables.

Double-click on either the local or the SQL Server Assembly table and the same records are shown. You can edit them in the same way as well. Check each table to make sure the attachment works correctly and the data now in the SQL Server is identical to the original data. After the data has been checked for integrity on the SQL Server, you can feel free to delete the original tables.

Examining the Upsized Database with SQL Server Browser

A utility named the SQL Server Browser is included with the Access Upsizing Wizard. This tool enables you to browse any databases on the SQL Server as if they were Access databases. This enables you to examine and modify SQL Server tables without having to use SQL Server tools or attach each table that is to be viewed.

As shown in Figure 21.14, the SQL Server Browser is made to resemble the MS Access interface, both in display and interaction. This helps users who might be unfamiliar with the SQL Server Administrator tools to access a SQL database in a familiar way. The SQL Server Browser can access tables, views, defaults, rules, and stored procedures. A link to the SQL Server is made by using ODBC connections. You can use the same ODBC connection you created to upsize the database.

FIGURE 21.14.
SQL Server Browser.

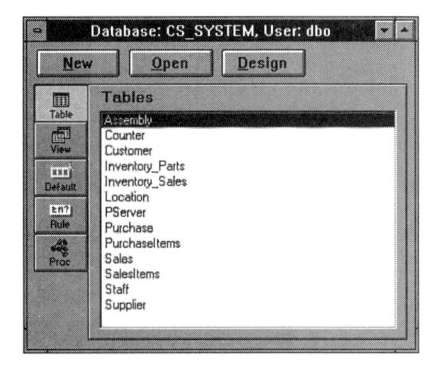

To run the SQL Server Browser, select it under the Add-ins option in the File menu. The program then asks for an ODBC data source to use for the connection. After you enter it, you must login with your password login. The connection is then opened and the browser is shown.

You can use the browser to examine any of the tables, views, defaults, rules, or procedures stored in the database. You can also use it to create new instances of any of these structures using the New option under the File menu. Under the View menu is an Ad-Hoc SQL… option that enables direct entry and execution of SQL and Transact-SQL commands, which is useful to test a new procedure or attempt a new query.

> **NOTE**
>
> The SQL Browser in MS Access is limited to viewing tables with a maximum of 40 fields. If a table has more than 40 fields, the Browser generates an error. If your table uses more than 40 fields, either attach the table to a database or use the browser included with SQL Server to examine the table.

Examining the Upsized Database with SQL Object Manager

You can also examine the structure of the tables in the SQL database by using direct SQL tools. Execute the SQL Object Manager program. After you have connected, change the database to CS_System using the Current Database drop-down combo box. (See Figure 21.15.) Now click on the Objects icon to show all of the objects contained in this database.

FIGURE 21.15.
Selecting the database.

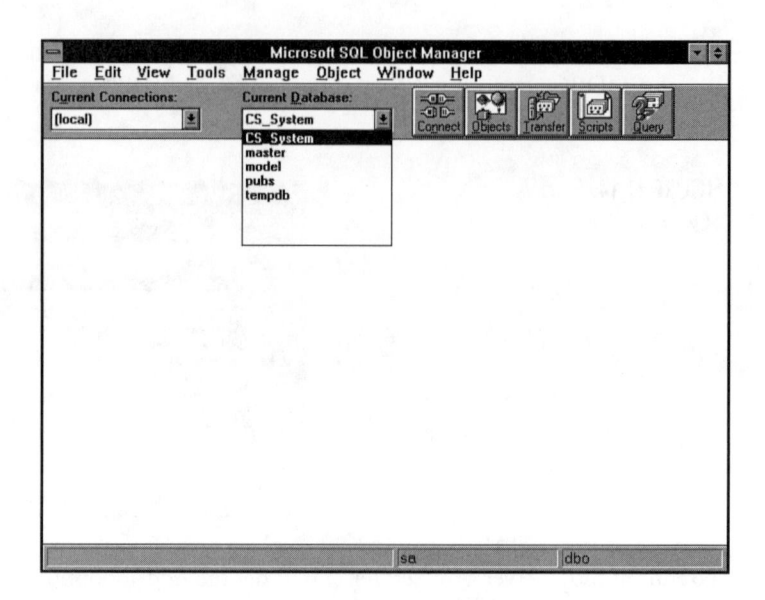

The Object list window for the CS_System database displays the names of all of the tables created by the Upsizing Wizard. (See Figure 21.16.) Double-clicking any of the table names displays the complete structure of the table. Also, selecting the table and selecting the Object Properties... option under the Object menu displays all of the statistics regarding the table including the table size, number of rows, indexes, triggers, and other information.

FIGURE 21.16.
Table objects in CS_System.

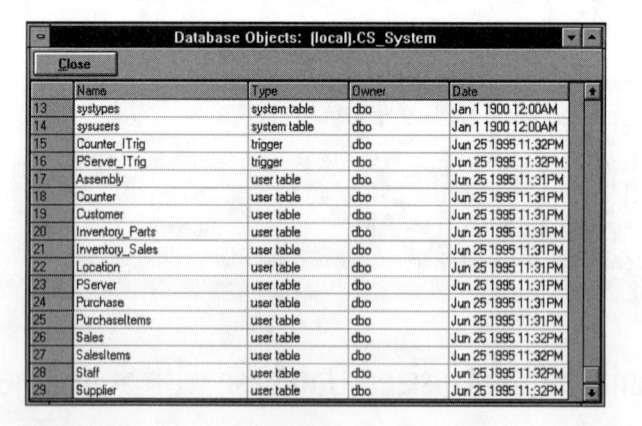

Testing the Client/Server System

Now that the upsizing is complete, you must test each of the client applications to ensure they can still access the necessary tables and data. Instead of accessing a shared database on a file server, now all of the clients (Sales client, Purchasing client, and so on) can access the SQL database server. (See Figure 21.17.) You can do this directly through the ODBC interface (demonstrated in Chapter 22) or through attached tables in the Access-based database file.

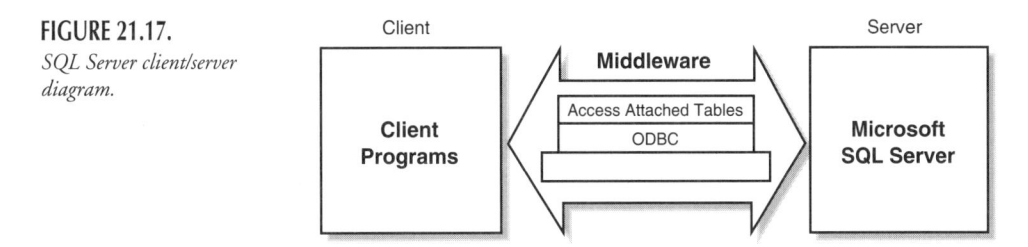

FIGURE 21.17.
SQL Server client/server diagram.

Adding Users and Groups

In order to activate the system, you must first add all the users logins so each client application can logon to the SQL Server properly. For security reasons discussed fully in Chapter 16, "Access Security," you need to create groups and grant each group permissions. Users are then added to these groups, and the individuals inherit the groups' access privileges.

Adding Groups

Execute the SQL Administrator 32 application to set users and groups. After logging on, select the Databases option from the Manage menu. When the Database Management window is showing, the Users and Groups window is accessible. Select the Users option under the Manage menu and then select the hierarchical option Users/Groups to display the window of all of the users and groups that relate to the CS_System database.

You must add your four primary groups like you did in Access security. Select the Add Group… option under the Manage menu. The Group Membership window appears (see Figure 21.18), which enables you to create the group and add various users. You add the users after all of the groups have been created.

FIGURE 21.18.
Adding a group.

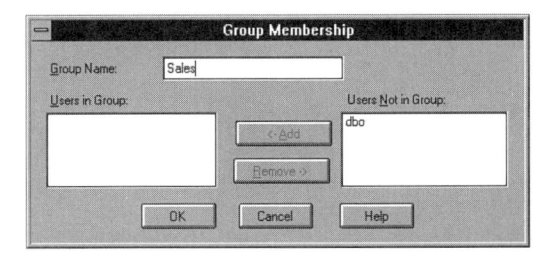

Type `Sales` for the group name and click the OK button to add the group to the database. (See Figure 21.19.) Add the other three required groups (Purchase, Management, and PServer) in the same way. After all four groups are added to the database, you can begin adding users.

FIGURE 21.19.
The Sales group is added.

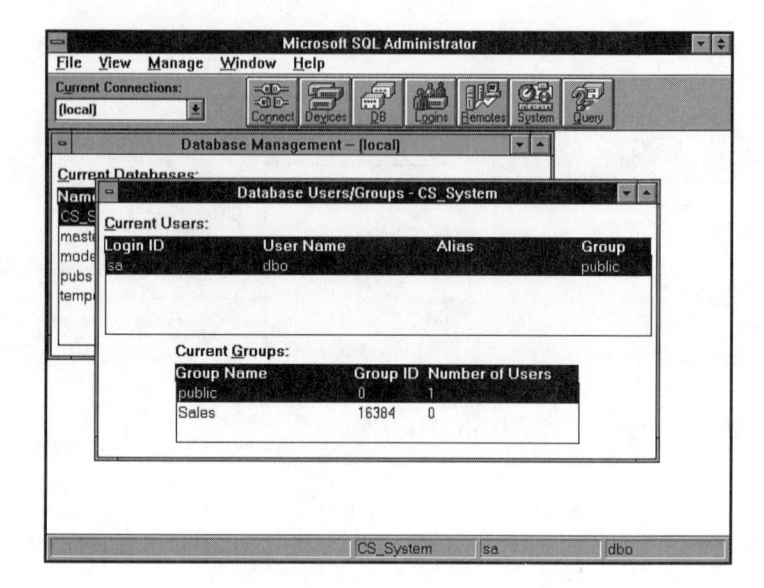

Adding Users

Close the Group Membership window. The Database Management—(local) window should be selected again. Click the button labeled Logins to display the System Logins Management window. The window shows all of the currently available user logins. You are going to add your four standard users to these logins.

Select the Add Login... option from the Manage menu. The new login window is displayed. (See Figure 21.20.) Enter `Sales1` as the Login ID and leave the password field blank. (This will be consistent with the name and password created for the MS Access security.) Set the Database field to CS_System to make the user's default database the one you're using for the client/server system. Finally, set the User Name the same as the Login ID: Sales1. Click the OK button and the user is created.

FIGURE 21.20.
Adding a new login.

Using the same technique, create each of the following users: Purchase1, PServer1, and Management1. For easy reference, leave the password blank and set the user name the same as the login ID. After all of the users have been added, close the window.

Putting Users in Groups

Select the Database Management—(local) window again. Select the Users option under the Manage menu and then select the hierarchical option Users/Groups. The bottom list box (Current Groups) should display all of the groups that have been added. Double-click the Management group.

The Group Membership window should appear showing the Management group. You need to add the Management1 user to the group. Click the Management1 selection in the list box (Users Not in Group) on the right. Click on the Add button and the User will be added to the group. (See Figure 21.21.) Click the OK button to accept the group.

FIGURE 21.21.
Adding the Management1 user to the group.

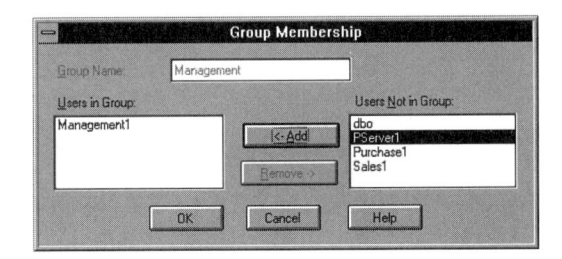

The window closes and the user is now entered into the system. The Management group in the Users/Groups window should now show that the Group contains one user.

Add each of the other users to the appropriate groups (Sales1 to the Sales group, and so on). When this has been completed, all of the users and groups should be set up. Now, when you have to add other users, they can be easily created and added to the appropriate group. Now you must set the security permissions for each group to provide the level of access appropriate for each type of client.

Granting Permissions

Now that you have created the user accounts on the SQL Server, you must grant the accounts permission to use the particular tables. See Table 21.2 (reprinted from Chapter 14, "Pseudo Server") for all of the permission settings for the various client accounts. Permissions for each group must be set to the levels shown in the table.

Table 21.2. Client programs' access to tables.

Table Name	Sales	Purchase	Group Access Management	PServer
Sales	Full	None	ReadOnly	None
SalesItems	Full	None	ReadOnly	None
Purchase	None	Full	ReadOnly	None
PurchaseItems	None	Full	ReadOnly	None
Assembly	None	Full	ReadOnly	None
Inventory_Sales	Update	Full	ReadOnly	Update
Inventory_Parts	None	Full	ReadOnly	ReadOnly
Customer	Full	None	ReadOnly	None
Supplier	None	Full	ReadOnly	None
PServer	None	ReadOnly	ReadOnly	Full
Counter	Update	Update	ReadOnly	None
Location	ReadOnly	ReadOnly	Full	None
Staff	ReadOnly	ReadOnly	Full	None

What each of the table access-type definitions denotes (Full, ReadOnly, and so on) is slightly different in SQL Server (see Table 21.3). Although in this implementation you won't take advantage of this feature, SQL Server enables you to set permissions for individual fields (columns) within a SQL table. This enables you to hide particular data (such as salaries) from most users while the table's other information (such as name and address) remains accessible.

Table 21.3. Access type reference.

Access Type	Select?	Update?	Insert?	Delete?
Full	Yes	Yes	Yes	Yes
ReadOnly	Yes	No	No	No
Update	Yes	Yes	No	No
None	No	No	No	No

To set up the needed permissions, execute the SQL Object Manager. After you've logged on, select the CS_System database. Select an individual table (such as Assembly) and select the Object Permissions... option under the Object menu. The Object Permissions window is then displayed (see Figure 21.22), enabling you to grant and revoke all of the permissions for each table.

FIGURE 21.22.

The Permissions window.

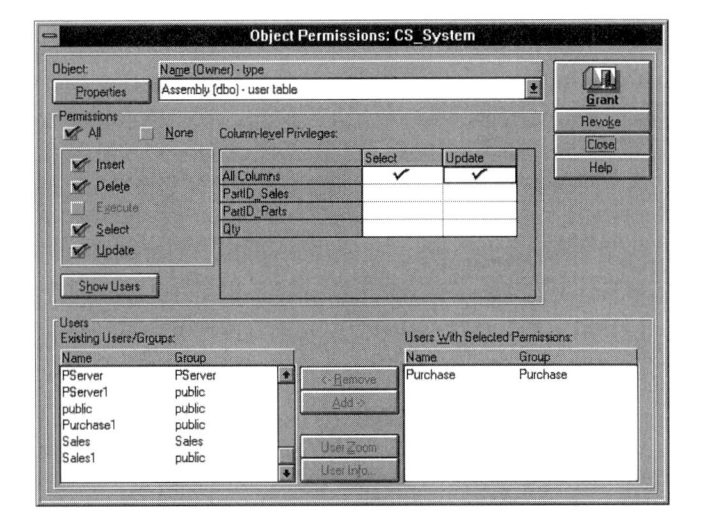

Notice that the Assembly table is selected in the combo box at the top of the window. Use this to select the table for which permissions must be set. From Table 21.2, you can see that the Purchase group is given full access to the Assembly table. Therefore, select the Purchase group in the bottom-left list box. Clicking the User Zoom... button displays which privileges have been granted to that group. Notice that the None check box in the permission frame is selected. The Purchase group has no access to the Assembly table.

The Purchase group should still be selected. Click the Add button to move the group into the area of groups or users to be modified. Now click the All check box to give the group complete permission to the table. You will notice that the Grant button in the top-right corner is now active. Click the Grant button to give the group the permissions to this table.

In the same way, add the necessary security to each of the tables for each group as listed in the above tables. When the tables are secure, you'll modify the clients so they can access them.

Modifying the .INI Files

The database file you have upsized is now called WIDGTSQL.MDB. You should still have the client/server database intact on your machine (WIDGETCO.MDB). All of the .INI files now have to be modified to access the new database.

The original Access code portion of the .INI file should appear as it does in Listing 22.1. The `DBName` parameter must be changed to access the new database. In Listing 21.2, the `DBName` is changed to the WIDGTSQL.MDB database, which contains attached tables that access the proper SQL Server database. Changing the database reference is all that is required for altering the data access. Modify this parameter on each of the clients and in the PServer .INI files.

Listing 21.1. Original .INI file.

```
[Access]
DSN=
DBName=c:\clntsrvr\widgetco.mdb
DBServer=
```

Listing 21.2. Attachment modified .INI file.

```
[Access]
DSN=
DBName=c:\clntsrvr\WIDGTSQL.mdb
DBServer=
```

Modifying the Clients

Very little modification is required for the client programs. The only modification that really must be made is to alter the approach in which new records are created. The dbOpenTable command is the fastest way to add new record to a table, but this command is not supported when the table is attached in the Access database. Therefore, you must modify all of the dbOpenTable commands to instead use the dbOpenDynaset command, which can be used with attached tables.

Table 21.4 shows the location of each of the routines that use the dbOpenTable command. The command is used only when records are added. Open the project, and then open the form and use the Find command to search for the text dbOpenTable. The Visual Basic Find dialog box will show the precise location of each instance of dbOpenTable in the code window, allowing you to modify the routines to the new code.

Table 21.4. Routines that use dbOpenTable.

Program	Form	Routine
Sales	frm_Customer	cmd_OK_Click()
Purchase	frm_Part	cmd_OK_Click()
Purchase	frm_AutobuildEdit	cmd_Add_Click()
Purchase	frm_Supplier	cmd_OK_Click()
Manage	frm_Location	cmd_OK_Click()
Manage	frm_Staff	cmd_OK_Click()

Listing 21.3 shows how the code must be modified. The dbOpenTable line has been commented out at the top of the listing and a dbOpenDynaset command has been entered on the following line. All references must then be changed to address the dynaset instead of the table. This means

changing the object to of each reference (in this case from ScratchTable to ScratchDS). Note that this is for good documentation purposes. ScratchTable is defined as a recordset, so it will work without any changes.

Listing 21.3. cmd__OK__Click () from the Cust.Frm in the Sales client.

```
' Create customer record
      ' Set ScratchTable = MyDB.OpenRecordset("Customer", dbOpenTable)
      Set ScratchDS = MyDB.OpenRecordset("Customer", dbOpenDynaset)
ScratchDS.AddNew
ScratchDS!CustomerID = g_CustomerID
ScratchDS.Update
' an alterative is to use direct SQL statements as shown below:
      'SQL$ = "INSERT INTO Customer (CustomerID) VALUES (" & g_CustomerID & ")"
      'MyDB.Execute SQL$
```

Modify all the routines listed in the table to use the new dbOpenDynaset command. Also included in Listing 21.3 is sample SQL code to accomplish the same record creation. If you desire to use SQL, this code works in the Listing 21.3 code and can be easily modified to work with the other code areas.

After you have made these modifications, the client programs should all work perfectly, using the SQL Server database as the data source. Test each one individually, and then compile them into .EXE files and test those files. If the whole system works, the upsizing was a success!

After you have verified that the Clients work through the attached tables, feel free to eliminate the local tables stored in the database. For safety and testing, the local databases were not removed from the Database file, but instead renamed with the _local extension. With the new tables working, keeping noncurrent data is a waste of resources and can cause later confusion.

Now that the files are list of attached tables, it is a good idea to take the Access database containing the attachments off of the file server. This should improve network performance for overall access.

Using ODBC to Port to Oracle, Sybase, and Other Database Servers

MS Access can port complete tables and queries to almost any SQL database that has an ODBC driver available. In addition to the Upsizing Wizard, Access supports extensive exporting capabilities including traditional formats such as Lotus Worksheets, Excel, Text (Delimited), and Text (Fixed Width), among others. Access also supports exporting directly to a SQL database through ODBC, provided the database server supports the SQL commands such as Create Table needed to replicate the table. You can then attach exported tables through the ODBC connection.

To export a table to an ODBC SQL source, select the Export... option under the File menu. One of the formats that appears at the bottom of the list box is SQL Database. This export uses SQL commands to create the exported table and populate the database. Click the SQL Database option and then click OK to accept the selection.

You must now select the table or query to export (as MyTable is selected in Figure 21.23). Note that you can only export a single table or query at one time. If the database to port consists of numerous tables, be sure to set aside a fair amount of time. Otherwise, you might want to use one of the third-party utilities discussed in Chapter 29, "Third-Party Tools, Utilities, and Controls," to simplify the process.

FIGURE 21.23.
Export table selection.

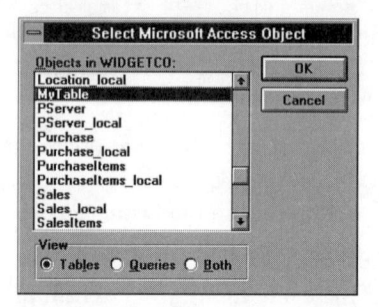

Access then prompts you for the name by which the database will be called when it is created on the ODBC data source. (See Figure 21.24.) If a table by that name already exists, the program will ask later whether the existing table should be written over. Therefore, don't worry about accidentally overwriting a table with the same name.

FIGURE 21.24.
Entering the export table destination name.

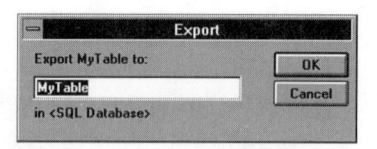

Next you must choose the ODBC data source that will do the actual transfer. Check with the vendor to make sure it is compatible with the Access exporting engine. (Most ODBC drivers support the core capabilities of ODBC and should work fine.)

After you've selected the data source and set the necessary options, the table is generated on the ODBC source and any errors are reported. If there are no errors, the table can be attached to the Access database and freely used and edited, nearly as easily as if it were stored in the local database.

Select the Attach Table... option under the File menu. Select the same ODBC data source that you used to port the table. A list of the tables available on that data source appears. Select the table and the attached table reference then appears in the MS Access table list.

22

Open Database Connectivity (ODBC)

Open Database Connectivity (ODBC) is an open standard for the creation of database drivers. As you can see in Figure 22.1, an application accesses ODBC through a set of standard commands: the ODBC API. A particular ODBC driver is used that matches the data source type that needs to be accessed. For example, a Sybase ODBC driver can be used to access a Sybase Server. An application can be written that accesses the standardized ODBC commands and can access any data source that has an available ODBC driver. After a program has been written calling the ODBC API, different data sources can be accessed by the program without any code modifications.

FIGURE 22.1.
An overview of ODBC.

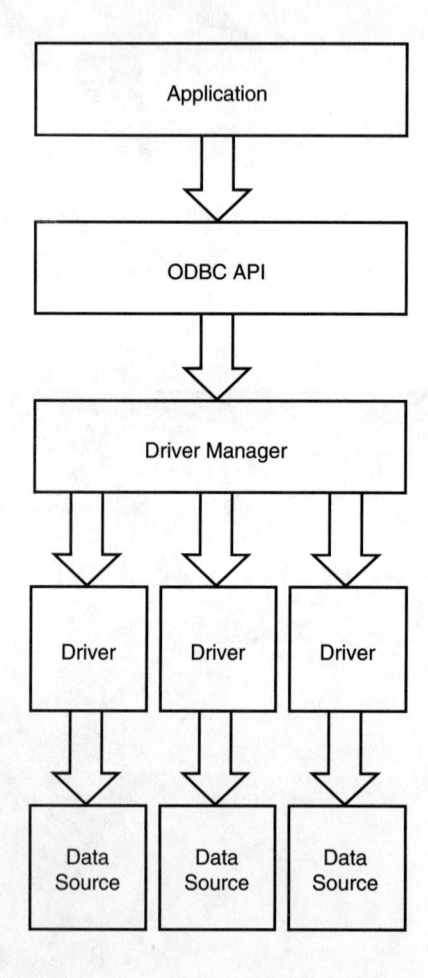

```
┌─────────────────┐
│   Application   │
└────────┬────────┘
         ▼
┌─────────────────┐
│    ODBC API     │
└────────┬────────┘
         ▼
┌─────────────────┐
│ Driver Manager  │
└──┬──────┬──────┬┘
   ▼      ▼      ▼
┌─────┐┌─────┐┌─────┐
│Drive││Drive││Drive│
│  r  ││  r  ││  r  │
└──┬──┘└──┬──┘└──┬──┘
   ▼      ▼      ▼
┌─────┐┌─────┐┌─────┐
│Data ││Data ││Data │
│Source││Source││Source│
└─────┘└─────┘└─────┘
```

This chapter provides examples of and information on accessing the ODBC interface, which is used primarily to access non-Microsoft Access data sources. When you use the JET engine through the Data Control or Data Access Objects to access a database server (such as Oracle or

SQL Server), you are indirectly using the ODBC drivers. When you access the ODBC interface directly, significant performance increases are possible. Therefore, in this chapter, we will use the new features in Visual Basic 4.0 Enterprise Edition to optimize this access.

The ODBC standard itself is becoming increasingly accepted. ODBC is a standard created by Microsoft and a league of independent groups and developers. ODBC acts as middleware between an application and any data source with an appropriate ODBC driver. (See Figure 22.2.) Rather than a programmer having to interact with numerous different APIs and proprietary search languages, ODBC provides a common API set that can be used to access many heterogeneous data sources.

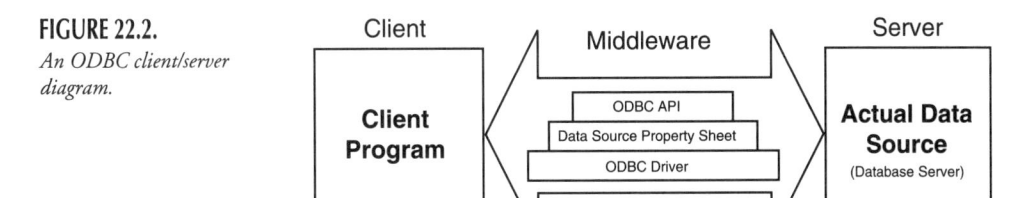

FIGURE 22.2.
An ODBC client/server diagram.

ODBC offers such capabilities as system table transparency (system tables are automatically modified by the driver), scrollable cursors (one or both ways, depending on the data source), transactions, asynchronous calling, array fetch and update, dynamic driver information, and stored procedures for SQL databases.

ODBC is an SQL-based standard that accepts all its query information through SQL command strings. Commands are provided for scalar functions, outer joins, stored procedures, complex data types (such as `date`, `time`, `timestamp`, and `binary`), and SQL pass-through to enable system-specific functions.

Visual Basic ODBC Access

Visual Basic has long provided a standard way to access ODBC drivers through the JET engine via the Data Control or Data Access Objects. ODBC could even be used indirectly by accessing attached tables in an Access database. These solutions tended to be either slow or memory-hungry. With the introduction of Visual Basic 4, Microsoft has provided a whole new streamlined way to access ODBC data sources.

Visual Basic 4 provides three ways to access ODBC: through the standard Data Access Objects (DAO); through the Remote Data Objects (RDO); or directly using the ODBC API. Visual Basic 3.0 allowed access to ODBC data sources either through the JET engine using the DAO (which tended to be slow) or through direct API calls. Remote Data Objects are new to Visual Basic 4. The RDO system provides optimized access to ODBC data sources with all the convenience of the traditional DAO.

Processing database queries through the JET engine (for non-Microsoft Access data sources) is often sluggish, especially with large result sets or frequent queries. Although the JET engine provides excellent database independence, for that functionality it does extensive preprocessing of queries and commands. This tends to slow standard data access.

Because of the JET engine's lack of speed, many client/server developers choose to make direct calls to the ODBC API. ODBC calls can be twice as fast as a similar query sent to the JET engine. Calling the ODBC API is more tedious than using the DAO and therefore is both more difficult to implement and more expensive to maintain.

Calling the ODBC API requires including the ODBC declaration functions (in a global module). Accessing ODBC through the API is known as using the ODBC Call-Level Interface. Figure 22.3 shows a Visual Basic call to the ODBC interface, which loads the necessary ODBC driver to access the particular data source. By using ODBC, some of JET's advanced features, such as dynasets and snapshots, are sacrificed. Connection to an ODBC data source requires more preparation and programming than the similar JET calls.

FIGURE 22.3.
ODBC calls to driver.

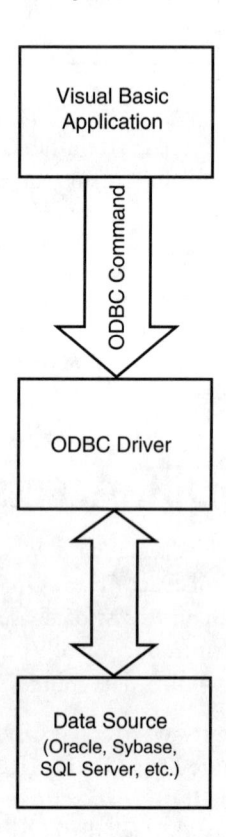

With the Visual Basic 4.0 Enterprise Edition, Remote Data Objects have been created to provide the best of both worlds to a client/server designer. The RDO system is used in nearly the same way as the traditional DAO (JET engine). Various database objects are used to access a database. The RDO is optimized to work with ODBC calls, unlike the JET engine, which provides a more generalized function.

Like the Data Control, there is also a Remote Data Control to which objects with Data Source and Data Field properties (such as text boxes) can be bound. (See Figure 22.4.) The Remote Data Control is added to a form and bound to individual objects in the same way the traditional Data Control is used. This gives instant access and prototyping capabilities to a system designer. As with the Data Control, the Remote Data Control is somewhat restrictive for complete project implementation.

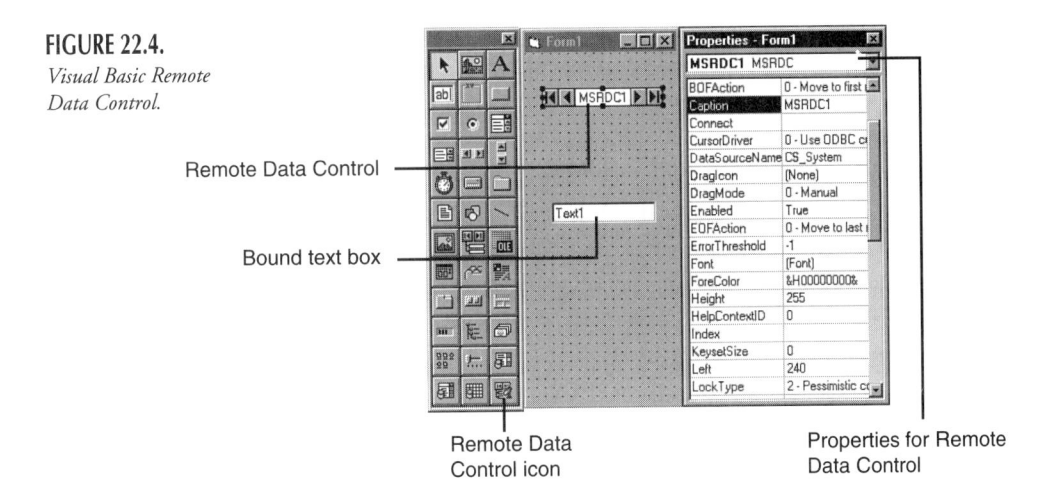

FIGURE 22.4.
Visual Basic Remote Data Control.

ODBC Overview

The ODBC system itself consists of several DLLs, .INI files, and applications. ODBC might seem complex at first, but once the system is in place, it is fairly straightforward. We recommend obtaining the latest ODBC Software Development Kit (SDK) from Microsoft. (See Appendix C, "Sources.") This provides the latest drivers, API declarations, and administrative utilities.

The entire ODBC system is organized around data sources. A data source holds the actual data that needs to be accessed, such as an Oracle Server or an SQL Server. A data source entry is created in the ODBC system that points to the actual data source. An application calls the ODBC interface with the data source entry name, and the ODBC system loads the appropriate driver and attempts to connect to the data source.

ODBC works by using a series of connections. Each connection defines a data source and (usually) contains the name of a default database to load. The connection provides the pathway between the API calls and the data source.

If the connection is successful, calls can be made to the ODBC API to retrieve data, update data, call stored procedures, and so forth. Each call to the API is converted by the particular ODBC driver into a protocol the data source can understand and use. Data sent from the data source is translated and manipulated through the ODBC system and returned to the application in a standard format.

The ODBC system accepts commands as normal SQL statements. These statements are parsed by the specific ODBC drivers to specific instructions for the database being accessed by the driver. If the data source is SQL-based, little conversion is required, whereas a non-SQL source requires extensive processing.

This brief description provides a general overview of how the ODBC system works, but the details of the system are extremely important for actual implementation. When an ODBC connection does not work, it is often because of a lack of understanding of the fundamentals and compatibility levels of the ODBC system.

Therefore, it is important to understand the entire ODBC system. The system is broken up into several components or categories: the ODBC API (which an application accesses), the ODBC Driver Manager (the DLL that loads the drivers), ODBC Drivers (database-specific drivers), and the data source administration applications.

Because the ODBC standard has various levels of compliance (for example, there are three levels of driver compliance), capabilities of a particular data source may vary. It is therefore important to understand the capabilities and functions that are available for the drivers a client/server system must use.

Before describing the actual ODBC architecture, it is important to understand how ODBC exists and is configured on a system. Drivers must be installed, data source connections set up, and .INI files configured. Because ODBC sits in the background and acts as middleware, these files are the only visible manifestations of ODBC on a computer system.

ODBC Administrator

The ODBC Administrator application is used to create and maintain the registered data sources. There are both 16- and 32-bit versions of ODBC data sources; therefore, two Administrator applications exist to maintain the different formats.

The term data source is used indiscriminately to specify either the ODBC property sheet that points to a database or the database itself. For example, the ODBC Administrator maintains data sources, which are the specific ODBC information used to interact with a database. The database itself is often called the data source because the ODBC property sheet only points to the actual data source.

The ODBC data source property sheet acts as a type of middleware (see Figure 22.5) between the ODBC API and the actual data source. Description of a data source can be confusing if you cannot determine whether it is referring to the actual data source or the registered property sheet in the ODBC system that points to the data source.

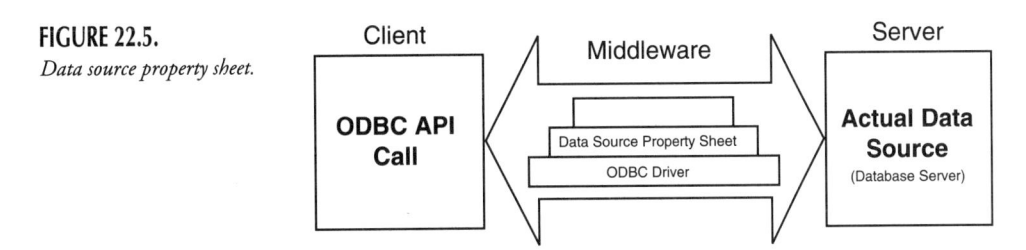

FIGURE 22.5.
Data source property sheet.

When the ODBC Administrator is executed, it displays all the data source property sheets that are available on a system (see Figure 22.6). Each connection can have one or more property sheets (each might access a different default table, and so forth). When a program accesses a data source, it uses the property sheet name.

FIGURE 22.6.
The ODBC Administrator.

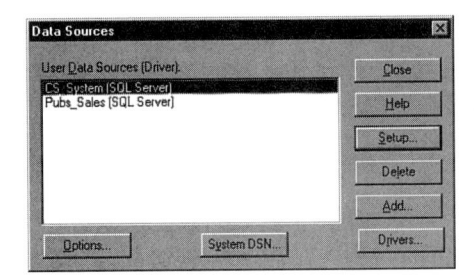

The information contained in a data source entry is shown by selecting one and clicking the Setup button. (See Figure 22.7.) The information includes the name of the data source property sheet (Data Source Name), the Server and server information, and the default database to access when a connection is created using the data source.

ODBC Connections

An application must open a connection to an ODBC data source. Multiple connections can be opened by a single application and can be used to query multiple databases. When the connection is originally opened, the ODBC system prompts the user for a username and password.

This information is sent to the data source for confirmation. This way all the security native to the data source is preserved. The connection then has the access to data allowed by the data source.

FIGURE 22.7.
ODBC connection settings.

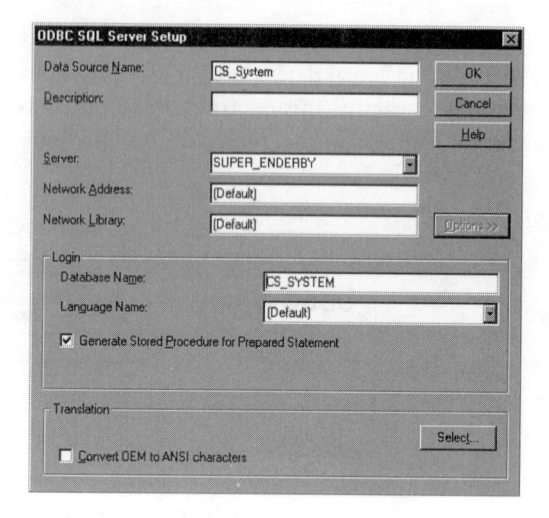

.INI Files

ODBC uses two .INI files to track information about the state of the driver setup on the machine: ODBC.INI and ODBCINST.INI.

The ODBC.INI file contains all the connection information for all the data sources. Entries are added to this .INI file each time an additional data source is added through the ODBCADM.EXE program or programmatically. The Data Source Name (DSN) parameter in the CONNECT string sent during an OpenDatabase() command is equal to an entry in this .INI file.

The ODBCINST.INI file contains information on all the installed ODBC drivers. If ODBC has never been installed on your machine, this file does not exist. An entry is created for each ODBC driver (SQL Server, Oracle, FoxPro, and so on) that can be used to create a data source connection.

WARNING

The ODBC.INI file contains all the connection information for the ODBC connections used by a machine. If an install program simply copied the .INI file to the \WINDOWS directory, it might eliminate all the current ODBC connections the user has created.

We recommend using an additional setup disk to install the ODBC drivers and libraries.

If you want to examine the ODBC data source property sheets that have been created, you can examine these .INI files. You can also modify the files to add additional data source property sheets, although this is not recommended. If you need to add additional connections to a data source programmatically, use the `RegisterDatabase` command, described later.

Driver Architecture

The actual construction of an ODBC driver largely depends on the format of the data source. For example, a relational SQL Database Server requires a different access method than a desktop database existing on a file server. Therefore, there are various tiers of driver construction.

These are important to the Visual Basic programmer primarily to understand performance limitations of various drivers. Generally, the more tiers a driver requires, the slower the connections and the individual dispatches will execute and return information.

Single-Tier Driver

Single-tier drivers are usually used with non-SQL data sources. The driver actually does all the translation of the ODBC commands and executes the necessary commands on the data. Therefore, the ODBC command is executed by the driver itself rather than being passed to a database program or server for processing.

A single-tier driver is used to interact with text files, xBase files, and other fundamental data formats. The single-tier driver is typically faster than multiple-tier drivers in operations such as connections. However, single-tier drivers tend to be slower in actually processing the searches, because they have not been optimized as a traditional database engine has been.

In a single-tier driver, the driver itself knows everything about the particular data format. Therefore, the Client machine has to do all the processing for a particular command. Because the driver itself must contain code for all the necessary searching routines, single-tier drivers tend to be larger than connection-oriented multiple-tier drivers.

Multiple-Tier Drivers

Multiple-tier drivers are used when the primary driver doesn't execute such operations as query commands itself, but instead sends the commands to another program or driver (such as a Database Server). Multiple-tier drivers tend to be much more client/server-oriented, because the Client simply has to place the required command in the proper format and the Server does the actual command processing. For this reason, connection commands take longer than a single-tier driver, but data requests are more quickly fulfilled.

A two-tier driver does some parsing before sending the ODBC command to the appropriate data source.

Three-tier (gateway) drivers use an intermediary machine, driver, or gateway for secondary translation between the original ODBC API calls or SQL commands and the final system interaction.

ODBC API

The ODBC API is available to any programming language that can call external Dynamic Link Libraries (DLLs). The API is divided into three levels of compliance. Each additional compliance level that the driver achieves allows more functionality and capability. The API itself is based on standards set by the X/Open and SQL Access Group Call-Level Interface specification.

With the advent of Remote Data Objects, Visual Basic programmers will use the ODBC API far less than in the past. However, the ODBC API gives a programmer access to more low-level capabilities (such as querying the capabilities of the driver itself) than are available through the RDO interface. Understanding the ODBC API can be important in understanding how the entire system works (the nuts and bolts under the RDO system).

Standard ODBC API interaction occurs in the order shown in Figure 22.8. First, an ODBC handle and connect must be allocated. As soon as the connection is created, each ODBC statement is sent to the driver. When all the statements have been executed, the program deallocates the created ODBC environment. If you aren't going to use the ODBC API directly, learning the technical steps involved with interfacing to ODBC isn't necessary. When the RDO interface accesses the ODBC data source, it is essentially making these same calls in the background.

The ODBC API is broken into three separate sets of command functions: Core, Level 1, and Level 2. One of the most important API calls is the `SQLGetInfo()` call. It returns the level of ODBC conformance so that a program knows what functions are supported by the particular driver.

FIGURE 22.8.
ODBC API standard call order.

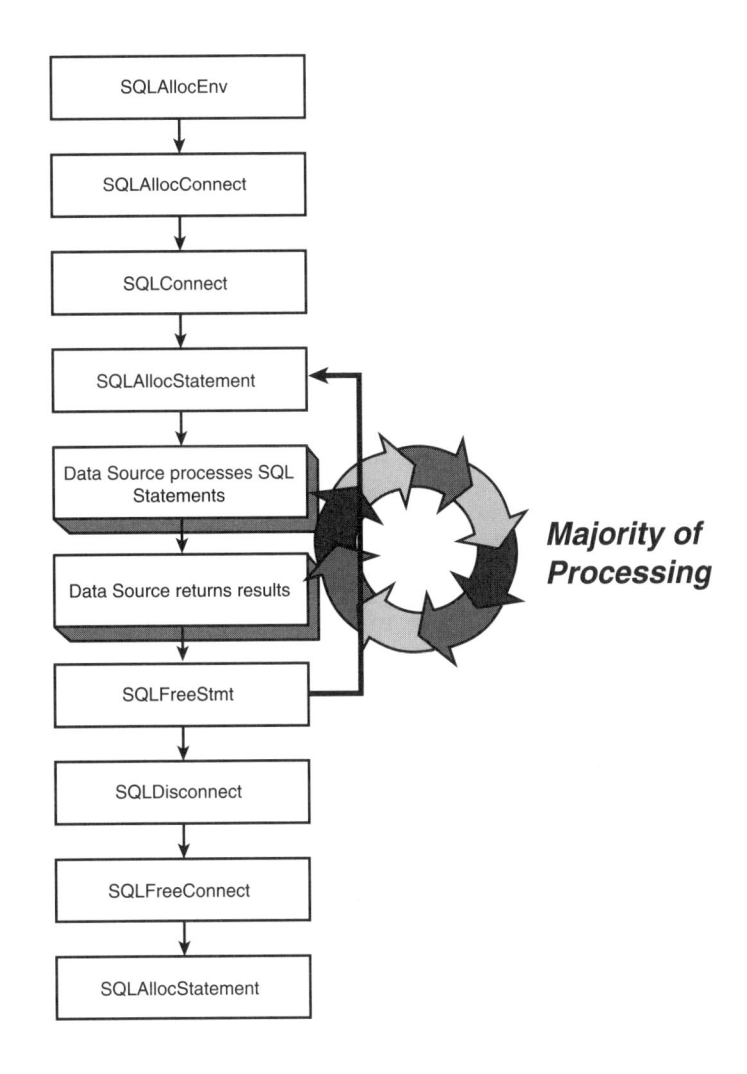

```
SQLAllocEnv
    ↓
SQLAllocConnect
    ↓
SQLConnect
    ↓
SQLAllocStatement ←┐
    ↓              │
Data Source processes SQL
Statements         │         Majority of
    ↓              │         Processing
Data Source returns results
    ↓              │
SQLFreeStmt ───────┘
    ↓
SQLDisconnect
    ↓
SQLFreeConnect
    ↓
SQLAllocStatement
```

Core Functions

The Core functions of the API provide the lowest base level of ODBC conformance. Typically a driver supports at a minimum both Core functions and Level 1 functions. Because the Core functions support only the basic operations of data access, most Core-function-only ODBC drivers are inappropriate for wide deployment.

Core functions allow calls to allocate and eliminate various ODBC resources such as environment, connections, and statement handles. They allow connection to various data sources. Once a connection has been established, multiple statements can be sent to the data source. Storage parameters for SQL statements and resultant fields can be set. Data can be retrieved from and about the resultant set. Basic transactions are supported—including commit and rollback. Finally, error information is available about the connection, statement, or environment.

The Core functions provide basic access to a data source. Table 22.1 includes all the individual API calls for the Core level. They are separated by type so each function's operation can be seen.

Table 22.1. Individual API calls for the Core level.

Function	Description
Connecting to a Data Source	
SQLAllocEnv	Creates an environment handle
SQLAllocConnect	Creates a connection handle
SQLConnect	Connects to a specific driver by data source name, user ID, and password
Preparing SQL Requests	
SQLAllocStmt	Creates a statement handle
SQLPrepare	Prepares an SQL statement for later execution
SQLGetCursorName	Returns the cursor name associated with the specified statement
SQLSetCursorName	Sets a cursor name
Submitting Requests	
SQLExecute	Executes a prepared statement
SQLExecDirect	Executes a statement
Retrieving Results and Information About Results	
SQLRowCount	Returns the number of rows affected by an insert, update, or delete request
SQLNumResultCols	Returns the number of columns in the resultant set
SQLDescribeCol	Returns information on a column in the resultant set
SQLColAttributes	Returns attributes of a column in the resultant set
SQLBindCol	Assigns storage and specifies the data type for a result column
SQLFetch	Returns a result row (record)
SQLError	Returns error or status information
Eliminating a Statement	
SQLFreeStmt	Terminates statement processing and frees all resources associated with the statement
SQLCancel	Cancels an SQL statement
SQLTransact	Commits or rolls back a transaction

Function	Description
	Eliminating a Connection
SQLDisconnect	Closes the connection passed as a handle
SQLFreeConnect	Releases the connection handle
SQLFreeEnv	Releases the environment handle

Level 1

Level 1 is the standard for ODBC functionality. It contains all the functions listed in the Core functions specification, with enhanced connection control, scalability, and data access capabilities.

The Level 1 drivers provide driver-specific dialog boxes for data sources so they can be appropriately configured by the user. Parameter values and resultant sets can be more effectively manipulated. Catalog information from the Server itself can be retrieved as well as information on the driver and the data source. This information can include stored procedure names, supported data types, scalar functions, or individual ODBC functions.

The Level 1 functions provide greater control over both the access to the data and the data source itself. Table 22.2 includes all the individual API calls for Level 1. They are separated by type so each function's operation can be seen.

Table 22.2. Individual API calls for Level 1.

Function	Description
	Connecting to a Data Source
SQLDriverConnect	Connects to a specific driver by connection string or, if blank, displays a dialog box
	Obtaining Information About Drivers
SQLGetInfo	Returns information about a specific driver and data source
SQLGetFunctions	Returns supported driver functions
SQLGetTypeInfo	Returns information about supported data types
	Setting and Retrieving Driver Options
SQLSetConnectOption	Sets a connection option
SQLGetConnectOption	Returns the value of a connection option
SQLSetStmtOption	Sets a statement option
SQLGetStmtOption	Returns the value of a statement option

continues

Table 22.2. continued

Function	Description
Preparing SQL Requests	
SQLBindParameter	Assigns storage for a parameter in an SQL statement
Submitting Requests	
SQLParamData	Used with SQLPutData to supply parameter data at execution time
SQLPutData	Sends part or all of a data value for a parameter
Retrieving Results and Information About Results	
SQLGetData	Returns part or all of one column of the selected row of a resultant set
Information About the Data Source's System Tables	
SQLColumns	Returns the list of column names for specified tables
SQLSpecialColumns	Returns information about the optimal set of columns that uniquely identifies a row in a specified table
SQLStatistics	Returns information about a single table and the associated list of indexes
SQLTables	Returns the list of table names stored in a data source

Level 2

Level 2 functionality is becoming increasingly common. The Remote Data Objects can use many of the features provided by a Level 2 driver. The Core and Level 1 functions must be included with the Level 2 driver.

Additionally, more access is provided to the entire client/server system on which the ODBC driver is operating. Increased connection information is available in addition to a list of available data sources. One of the most significant features of a Level 2 driver is the availability of cursors. This allows scrolling forward (and sometimes backward) through a resultant set. Scrolling allows for much more effective use of network and memory resources.

Other features are included, such as the capability to receive the SQL code after it has been processed by the driver (to examine the system-specific code actually used for the query). Catalog information is available that includes privileges, keys, and procedures. The driver can provide the capability to call a translation DLL, giving the data source extra flexibility.

The Level 2 functions provide advanced access to a data source that can make interactions much more efficient. Table 22.3 includes all the individual API calls for Level 2. They are separated by type so each function's operation can be seen.

Table 22.3. Individual API calls for Level 2.

Function	Description
Connecting to a Data Source	
SQLBrowseConnect	Returns successive levels of connection attributes and valid attribute values
Obtaining Information About a Driver and Data Source	
SQLDataSources	Returns the list of available data sources
SQLDrivers	Returns the list of installed drivers and their attributes
Preparing SQL Requests	
SQLParamOptions	Specifies the use of multiple values for parameters
SQLSetScrollOptions	Sets cursor behavior variables
Submitting Requests	
SQLNativeSql	Returns the text of the SQL translated by the driver
SQLDescribeParam	Returns the information for a specific parameter in a statement
SQLNumParams	Returns the number of parameters in a statement
Retrieving Results and Information About Results	
SQLExtendedFetch	Returns multiple resultant rows
SQLGetData	Returns part or all of one column of the selected row of a result set
SQLSetPos	Positions a cursor within a fetched block of data
SQLMoreResults	Determines if there are more result sets available; if so, initializes for the next result set
Information About the Data Source's System Tables	
SQLColumnPrivileges	Returns a list of columns and associated privileges for one or more tables
SQLForeignKeys	Returns a list of column names that comprise foreign keys
SQLPrimaryKeys	Returns the list of column names that comprise the primary key for a table
SQLProcedureColumns	Returns the list of input and output parameters, as well as the columns that make up the result set for the specified procedures
SQLProcedures	Returns the list of procedure names stored in a specific data source
SQLTablePrivileges	Returns a list of tables and the privileges associated with each table

JET Engine ODBC Calls

For the JET engine to use a particular ODBC driver, the driver must support the ODBC calls listed next. All the calls are from the Core or Level 1 specifications. Therefore, if the driver you need to use does not support any of the listed functions, you will have to use the ODBC API directly for access to the data source.

SQLAllocConnect	SQLExecDirect	SQLParamData
SQLAllocEnv	SQLExecute	SQLPrepare
SQLAllocStmt	SQLFetch	SQLPutData
SQLBindParameter	SQLFreeConnect	SQLRowCount
SQLCancel	SQLFreeEnv	SQLSetConnectOption
SQLColumns	SQLFreeStmt	SQLSetStmtOption
SQLDescribeCol	SQLGetData	SQLSpecialColumns
SQLDisconnect	SQLGetInfo	SQLStatistics
SQLDriverConnect	SQLGetTypeInfo	SQLTables
SQLError	SQLNumResultCols	SQLTransact

ODBC SQL

ODBC receives all its statements in the SQL language. The SQL grammar that can be used by a program is divided into two groups: Core Grammar and Extended Grammar. Core Grammar largely complies with the SQL CAE specification set by the X/Open and SQL Access Group in 1992. Extended Grammar provides many of the functions that are common to proprietary SQL dialects.

Core SQL Grammar

The Core SQL Grammar provides the basic capability to create and manipulate tables as well as perform basic queries. Core level is required for any type of ODBC compliance.

The commands in the Core SQL Grammar specifications include Create Table, Drop Table, Select, Insert, Update Searched, Delete Searched, Alter Table, Create Index, Drop Index, Create View, Drop View, Grant, and Revoke.

Simple expressions and comparisons such as A > B + C are supported, as well as subquery expressions and set functions (such as Sum and Min).

Data types supported include Char, VarChar, Long VarChar, Decimal, Numeric, SmallInt, Integer, Real, Float, and Double Precision.

Extended SQL Grammar

Extended SQL Grammar is much more robust. The Core Grammar functions and data types must be supported. Additionally, such advanced features as outer joins, positioned Update, positioned Delete, and Select for Update are supported. The Union command is also supported to produce unified result sets.

Expressions that allow manipulation of particular types of data have been included, such as SubString, Abs, and Date, Time, and Timestamp literals. New data types supported include Bit, TinyInt, BigInt, Binary, VarBinary, Long VarBinary, Date, Time, and Timestamp.

Extended Grammar supports batch SQL statements as well as static procedure calls. Most of the professional ODBC drivers support the Extended SQL Grammar feature set. It allows nearly complete access to the data source's native functionality.

Using ODBC for Table Transfer

The ODBC framework allows Visual Basic to be the perfect conversion engine from one type of database to another. For example, a VB program could open a connection to a DB2 Database Server, read a record from a DB2 table, and then write that same record to an SQL Server database, or vice versa. Visual Basic allows convenient access of any particular data files.

Now with the advent of Groupware such as Lotus Notes and the available Visual Basic interfaces, data can be transported from any format to any other format. (See Chapter 29, "Third-Party Tools, Utilities, and Controls.") This allows a single Visual Basic program to send and receive data from dissimilar data sources in any number of formats and protocols.

Remote Data Objects

Now that you understand the basics of the ODBC API, the new Remote Data Objects (RDO) in Visual Basic 4 provides a much easier way to access ODBC. RDO is a set of objects and collections that are used in a similar way to Visual Basic's Data Access Objects (DAO). Like DAO, they use recordsets, tables, and other objects to provide access to result sets. The RDO, however, is optimized strictly for use with ODBC data sources without any of the speed decreases normally associated with the JET engine.

> **TIP**
>
> Although the RDO interface is much easier to use than direct API calls, this does not mean that the ODBC API is no longer relevant. If you are planning to port the application you have created in Visual Basic to another language or another machine, it would be wise to continue to use the API.

> The ODBC API is available on different non-Windows machines (such as the Macintosh) and therefore provides cross-platform support not available using RDO. Additionally, any programming language (such as C, C++, FORTRAN, or COBOL) that can access outside calls can interact with the ODBC API. Therefore, code constructed in VB using the API can much more easily be rewritten for another language.

The RDO data objects and collections are used to create an ODBC connection to a data source, create recordsets and tables, access and modify data, execute stored procedures, and receive any RDO errors. Figure 22.9 shows a diagram of the data object model of the RDO. The objects of the RDO are described in the following sections.

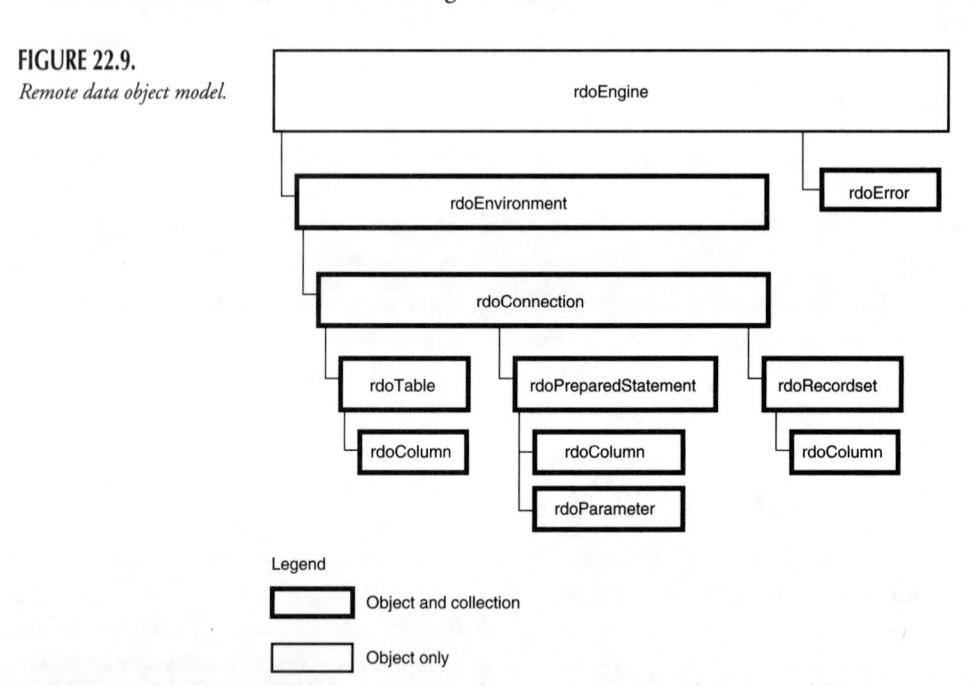

FIGURE 22.9.
Remote data object model.

```
rdoEngine
├── rdoEnvironment
│   └── rdoConnection
│       ├── rdoTable
│       │   └── rdoColumn
│       ├── rdoPreparedStatement
│       │   ├── rdoColumn
│       │   └── rdoParameter
│       └── rdoRecordset
│           └── rdoColumn
└── rdoError
```

Legend:
- Object and collection
- Object only

The *rdoEngine* Object

The rdoEngine object is functionally identical to the dbEngine object for traditional data access. Initializing the rdoEngine object initializes the RDO system and allows the subsequent creation of other objects hierarchically related (such as connections and recordsets).

The *rdoEnvironment* Object

The rdoEnvironment object provides the foundation for which multiple connections, databases, and transactions can be accessed for a particular user ID. It also provides the basis for transactions, especially across multiple connections. Note that transactions can be nested only five levels deep.

The *rdoError* Object

The rdoError object contains all the information on any error that occurs while accessing an ODBC data source. Descriptions of the error, the error code number, and the SQLState and SQLRetCode are provided for clear analysis of the error.

The *rdoConnection* Object/Collection

The rdoConnection object is the backbone of the ODBC system. Before any manipulation or access to a remote data source can be accomplished, a connection must first be established. Multiple connection objects can be created to access multiple heterogeneous data sources by the same program at the same time.

The *rdoTable* Object/Collection

The rdoTable object represents either an actual table on the remote data source or an SQL view. The rdoTable object allows modification to the actual structure of the table (such as adding columns and changing data types).

The OpenResultset method can be used to create an rdoResultset object.

The *rdoColumn* Object/Collection

The rdoColumn object is the reference to the columns or fields in a resultant set. Used by rdoTable objects, rdoPreparedStatement objects, and rdoRecordset objects, the rdoColumn collection represents a collection of data with common data types and property types. The Count method can be used to determine the number of objects in the collection.

The *rdoPreparedStatement* Object/Collection

For creation and access to stored procedures, the rdoPreparedStatement object allows SQL to be compiled and stored on the server for execution. The object can be used to execute already prepared stored procedures.

Additionally, the rdoPreparedStatement object can be used to check whether the procedure is still executing. The StillExecuting property tells a program whether the procedure has completed.

The *rdoParameter* Object/Collection

The `rdoParameter` object is used to pass and receive information from the stored procedure in the `rdoPreparedStatement` object.

The *rdoRecordset* Object/Collection

The `rdoRecordset` object is the functional equivalent of the traditional `Recordset` object used by the JET engine.

RegisterDatabase

Prompting the user to create the connection (as we have done in this chapter and in Chapter 25, "Query Builder") is simple and flexible, but programs often need to be self-configuring. The `RegisterDatabase` method can be used to install ODBC connection data sources. Additional data source information is added to the ODBC.INI file.

Listing 22.1 contains an example of using the `RegisterDatabase` method to create `SampleConnect`, an ODBC data source property sheet. The information created with this method is then used to open the database on the SQL Server. Note that all the parameters are passed to the method in the same basic string format normally used by an .INI file.

Listing 22.1. `RegisterDatabase` sample code.

```
Dim MyDB As Database
Dim S As String
' Set up a string with the proper parameters for the method
S = "Description=Sample data source creation" & Chr$(13)
S = S & "OemToAnsi=No" & Chr$(13)
S = S & "Network=" & Chr$(13)
S = S & "Address=\\SUPER_ENDERBY" & Chr$(13)
S = S & "Database=CS_System"
' Update the ODBC.INI.
DBEngine.RegisterDatabase "SampleConnect", "SQL Server", True, S
' Open the database.
Set MyDB = Workspaces(0).OpenDatabase("SampleConnect", False, False, "ODBC;")
```

Upgrading the Management Client

To demonstrate the capabilities of the RDO, we will upgrade the Sales report query in the Management Client application (constructed in Chapter 13, "Management Client"). The new query uses the Remote Data Objects to interact with a database through an ODBC data source.

Using the Remote Data Objects will dramatically increase the speed of data source access to a database server such as SQL Server or Oracle Server. Additional advantages include asynchronous queries. Your application can submit a query and return control to the user until an event routine signals the completion of the query. Also, stored procedure access, cursors, and other functions specific to the server are available through the Remote Objects. These enhanced capabilities may be used to provide additional capabilities in your client applications.

We have not coded into the source a specific ODBC data source. This enables you to select or create a property sheet to a particular data source. That data source can be the standard Access database file, the upsized SQL Server database created in Chapter 21, "Upsizing to Microsoft SQL Server," or any data source that has an available ODBC driver and the proper data.

ODBC data sources for SQL Server, Oracle, MS Access, FoxPro, text files, and others are included with Visual Basic. Not all drivers are created equal. There is a vast difference between a driver that is ODBC-compliant and one that is actually efficient. If, for example, your client/server system requires access to an Oracle data source, we recommend buying a driver instead of using the one included with VB. For sources of commercial ODBC drivers, see Appendix C.

Always examine the licensing agreements before distributing the drivers to the various Client machines. Each set of drivers has its own licensing agreements and might have per-seat charges. Be sure to check with your vendor before distributing them.

Modifying the Sales Report

Open the Management Client project. Double-click the Sales Report button. Enter the code shown in Listing 22.2. This code contains the same query that is used through the DAO in the previous version.

Instead of the DAO, RDO is used to connect through ODBC. Because the Sales Report is the first report shown when the application executes, the program prompts the user for an ODBC data source as soon as the application is double-clicked. If the entire application used the ODBC data source, the connection might be set up once in a global object, and all the queries could then access it.

Listing 22.2. `SalesReport()`.

```
Public Sub SalesReport()
    Dim dbsCSSystem As rdoConnection
    Dim rstSales As rdoResultset
    Dim i, j As Integer
    Dim tmpVar As Variant, tempVal As Double
    Dim BeginTime As Variant, EndTime As Variant

    BeginTime = Now
    'Use "" to allow the user to select data source
```

continues

Listing 22.2. continued

```
    Set dbsCSSystem = rdoEngine.rdoEnvironments(0).OpenConnection("")
    'Open a resultset with SQL statement and ForwardOnly Cursor
    s = ""
    s = s & " SELECT Staff.LastName, sum(SalesItems.FinalPrice) as SalesTotal"
    s = s & " From Sales as a, SalesItems as b, Staff as c"
    s = s & " Where (Sales.InvoiceID = SalesItems.InvoiceID) and (Sales.StaffID =
➥Staff.StaffID)"
    s = s & " Group by Staff.LastName"
    Set rstSales = dbsCSSystem.OpenResultset(s, rdOpenForwardOnly)

    Graph1.NumPoints = 20
    Graph1.NumSets = 1
    'GraphForm.Graph1.ThisPoint = 1
    Graph1.AutoInc = 0
    i = 1
    Do Until rstSales.EOF
        'form1.Data1.Recordset.FindFirst srchstr
        Graph1.ThisPoint = i
        tempVal = rstSales.rdoColumns("SalesTotal").VALUE
        Graph1.GraphData = tempVal
        tmpVar = rstSales.rdoColumns("LastName").VALUE
        Graph1.LegendText = tmpVar
        rstSales.MoveNext
        i = i + 1
    Loop
    ' Minimum of 2 bars required for bar chart. Therefore, if one
    ' employee sold everything, a blank second bar is required.
    If i < 3 Then
        Graph1.NumPoints = 2
    Else
        Graph1.NumPoints = i - 1
    End If
    Graph1.DrawMode = 2
    Set rstSales = Nothing
    Set dbsCSSystem = Nothing
End Sub
```

The ODBC interface, when accessing non-Microsoft Access databases, can be dramatically faster than traditional access through the JET engine. The addition of the Remote Data Objects and Remote Data Control that are included with the Visual Basic Enterprise Edition provide a simple and powerful way to access ODBC. This access comes without the complexity and significant learning curve typically associated with using the ODBC API.

23

Object Linking and Embedding (OLE)

Object linking and embedding—OLE, pronounced "olay"—is the first step towards a complete object-oriented operating system. Based on an object model called the *Component Object Model* (COM), OLE enables objects to be embedded, linked, stored, and manipulated throughout a system and over a network.

In the past, most data on an operating system was handled strictly as blocks of memory that had to be manipulated by the program that created them. By making objects available to the system, programs can exchange, manipulate, and use objects created by other programs.

The most common demonstration of OLE is the ability to embed a spreadsheet object, for example, into a word processor. In the past, to import or place a spreadsheet into a word processor required the word processor to be able to read and understand the file format or clipboard format of the spreadsheet. Once the sheet was imported into the word processor, it was no longer accessible from the spreadsheet (unless the word processor could export in the proper format). Through these various translations, imported data often lost its formatting, including font, style, and column width.

OLE enables a program to insert an object into a document. The word processor does not have to know what type of object is inserted, as long as it conforms to the OLE object format. The object might be a bitmap created by Microsoft Excel, a drawing created in Visio, or a piece of music recorded as a .WAV file. The program that accepts the inserted object—in this case, a word processor—is called the *container* application. The application supplying the object is the *server* application.

OLE provides much more than this simple but powerful function. Instead of embedding the object, it is possible to create a link. This means that the object is stored in another file, and you can reference it for positioning and printing. This enables the object to stay in its default file format. For example, a link could be created to a CorelDRAW file stored on a network drive. This drawing would appear in the word processing document, but the drawing itself would remain in the CorelDRAW file. Therefore, edits to the drawing could be made with CorelDRAW, which would automatically appear in the word processing document the next time it was opened.

As shown in Figure 23.1, there are nine facets to OLE. They are

- Embedding
- Linking
- In-place activation
- Drag-and-drop
- Uniform data transfer
- Compound files
- Monikers
- Automation
- Component Object Model

As you can see in Figure 23.1, most of these pieces of OLE interact in one way or another. The entire OLE system provides a thorough and consistent approach to working with objects.

FIGURE 23.1.
The nine technologies of OLE.

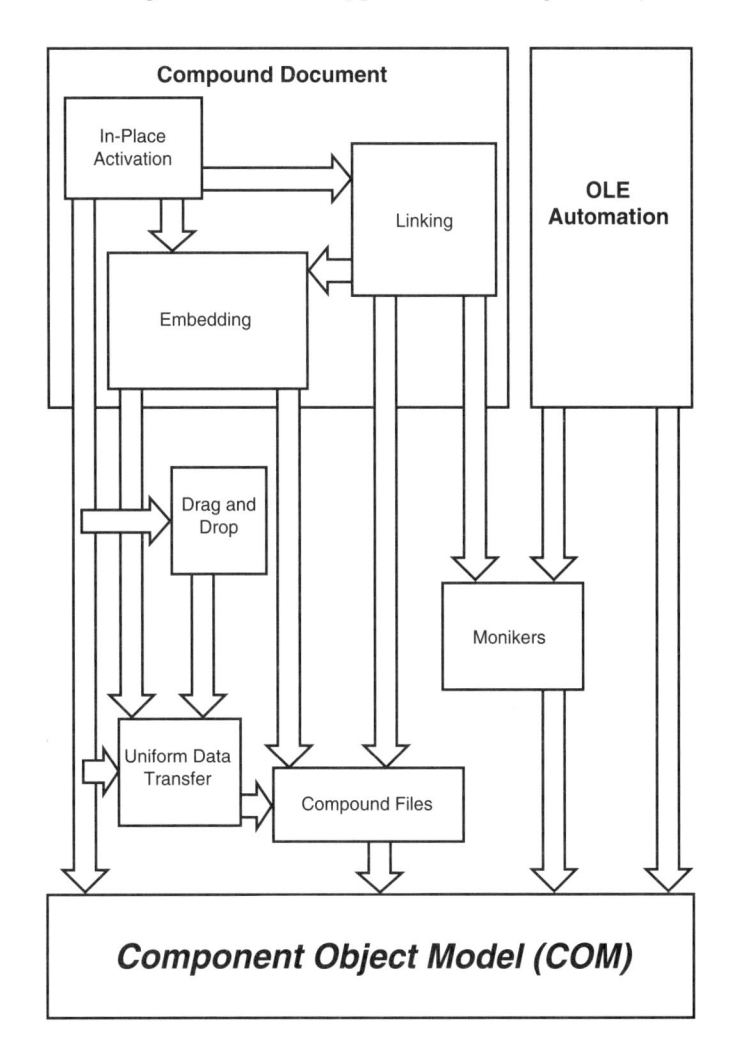

You can see three of the technologies in the compound document box—embedding, linking, and in-place activation. Embedding and linking place an object (or object reference) in another document, as just described. This document becomes known as a *compound document.* If the OLE Server application—the application or the DLL that created the object—supports in-place activation, you can double-click the object. You then can edit an object in its exact place in the document. Depending on the OLE Server, the toolbar or menus may change, but otherwise the activation of the OLE Server is transparent. The user can even believe that the object is being edited within the word processor (or other application) in which it is embedded.

Normally, OLE objects are created by using the Insert Object... menu option or by using the clipboard for copying and pasting. Uniform data transfer provides a standard way by which objects can be stored for transfer through the clipboard, through files, or through drag-and-drop user manipulation. The drag-and-drop capabilities enable an object to be dragged on the screen from the window of an application and dropped into the window of an OLE container application. This skips the intermediate step of transferring the object to the clipboard (by using the Cut or Copy commands) and then moving the object from the clipboard into the container document (by using the Paste command). With the OLE drag-and-drop interface, certain user interface elements can be simplified, and the extra memory and disk space required for the intermediate clipboard step is eliminated.

Compound files are OLE's method of storing one or more objects in a document. For example, in a word processing document, it is convenient to store the embedded object in a separate file because any changes to the word processing document require the object to be moved in the final stored file, and any changes to the object require the entire word processing document to be saved. Instead, compound files are stored as though they are files within files. Multiple objects can be read, written, and manipulated in a single document. OLE objects can be stored in any way the programmer wants, but OLE compound files provide a flexible, fast, and single way to store as many objects as are linked or embedded in a single file.

Monikers are another OLE technology that can be stored within an OLE compound document. *Monikers* are data structures that are used to identify relations. These relations can be between two objects, an object and a file, an object and a database record, or a specific programmer-built relation. Currently, monikers are typically used for linking an object to a file. The next major revision to Windows NT, however, will extend the relations created with monikers into the operating system itself.

The OLE automation interface through VBA has been used in previous chapters. Automation operates separately from linking and embedding, but because it is based on the object model and the OLE technologies, it is considered part of the overall OLE object framework.

The Component Object Model (COM) provides the foundation for the entire OLE system. COM provides the basic interfaces through which all the other parts of the OLE object framework can be accessed. Because COM provides the basis for the OLE system, all the other capabilities can best be understood by first understanding the COM system.

Component Object Model (COM)

The Component Object Model (COM) is the foundation of OLE. The COM standard defines objects and how they fundamentally interact with each other. The COM code is actually stored in COMPOBJ.DLL. All the API functions for creating and managing component objects are stored in the DLL. This library also contains all the lightweight remote procedure calls (LRPC) that are used to communicate between programs and objects.

There are four types of objects:

- Private
- In-process
- Local
- Remote

Private objects are created and used within an application. In-process objects exist in a DLL and can be used by the system or other applications. Local objects are contained within an .EXE but are accessible to other applications on the system. Remote objects can be stored on another machine across a network.

> **NOTE**
>
> The COM foundation to OLE is important for someone who wants to understand the technical operations of OLE. If you are planning to do all your implementation from Visual Basic, you can skip the following COM sections. However, if you will have to deal with DLLs and objects from C or C++, or if you seek to understand the inner workings of the OLE framework, this section provides an overview of the COM structure.

An object is created in memory using a Class template. COM provides something called a `ClassFactory`, which is used to instantiate an object from a class. Either COMPOBJ.DLL can be called to instantiate the new objects, or the `ClassFactory` for a particular class can be retrieved by the DLL so that your program can call it specifically every time a particular type of object needs to be created. Each class has a specific class ID (CLID).

Inheritance

Inheritance found in programming systems is not found in the COM interface. There is no inheritance in COM. Because of the fragile base-class problem described in Chapter 6, "Object Programming Overview," Microsoft does not include what it calls *implementation inheritance* in COM. Implementation inheritance means that objects can be defined as subclasses of a class; therefore, they inherit the methods and properties of the superclass above them.

Microsoft claims that this type of inheritance prevents objects from being freely interchanged or autonomously upgraded because of the web of relations that this structure creates. Because of the numerous class inheritance relationships, individual objects are not encapsulated.

Instead, the COM interface allows for aggregation. Aggregation lumps several objects together so that they are contained within a single object. Microsoft calls aggregation *component inheritance*. This avoids the creation of implicit relationships such as those generated by traditional subclassing. An aggregation is essentially a compound object—that is, the programming equivalent of a compound document. One of the best examples of this aggregation is the addition of OLE custom controls (OCXs) to a Visual Basic project.

Objects and Interfaces

To create an object or to access an object by using COM, the object must be interacted with through a COM interface. An interface is a collection of functions. The interface is the base level of interaction between COM and subsequent OLE interface. The program calls one of the functions stored in the interface table to get or set properties, call methods, or otherwise manipulate the object. Figure 23.2 shows an example of the pointer access that occurs when an OLE client makes a call to an OLE object. The object must be interacted with through the various interface functions; the actual data of the object is never accessible to the program.

FIGURE 23.2.

The interface function table.

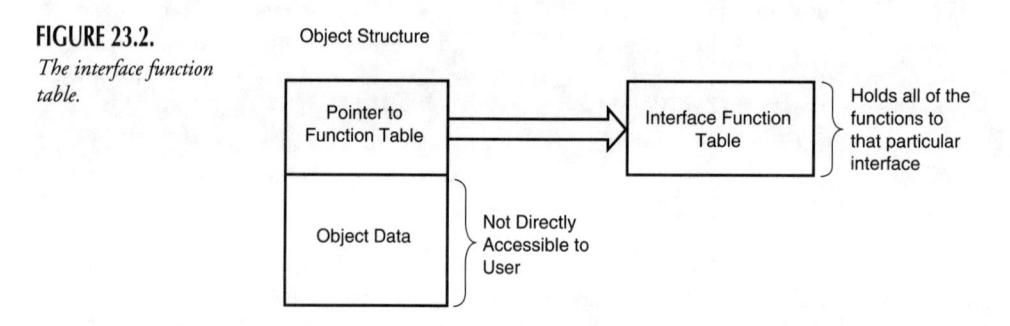

Table 23.1 contains some of the basic interfaces used with OLE. For example, when an in-place activation occurs, all in-place method calls or property setting takes place through one of the in-place interfaces.

Table 23.1. OLE interfaces.

Interface Name	Type
IOLEWindow	In-place activation
IOLEInPlaceFrame	In-place activation
IOLEInPlaceObject	In-place activation
IOLEInPlaceWindow	In-place activation
IOLEInPlaceSite	In-place activation

Interface Name	Type
IOLEInPlaceActiveObject	In-place activation
IOLEItemContainer	Linking
IOLEContainer	Linking
IRunningObjectTable	Linking
IPersistFile	Linking
IOLELink	Linking
IParseDisplayName	Linking
IOLEObject	Embedding
IPersistStorage	Embedding
IOLEClientSite	Embedding
IOLEAdviseHolder	Embedding
IDropSource	Drag-and-drop
IDropTarget	Drag-and-drop
IDataObject	Uniform data transfer
IAdviseSink	Uniform data transfer
IViewObject	Uniform data transfer
IDataAdviseHolder	Uniform data transfer
IDispatch	Automation
IStorage	Compound files
IStream	Compound files
ILockBytes	Compound files
IMoniker	Monikers
IBindCtx	Monikers
IUnknown	Component Object Model
IMalloc	Component Object Model
IClassFactory	Component Object Model

From C or C++, these interfaces can be called directly through pointers. Using VBA, each call goes through translation to a particular interface routine. In Figure 23.3, you can see the progress of a method as it is sent to an Excel worksheet object. Two translations occur before the actual IDispatch interface routine is activated.

FIGURE 23.3.

Automatic execution.

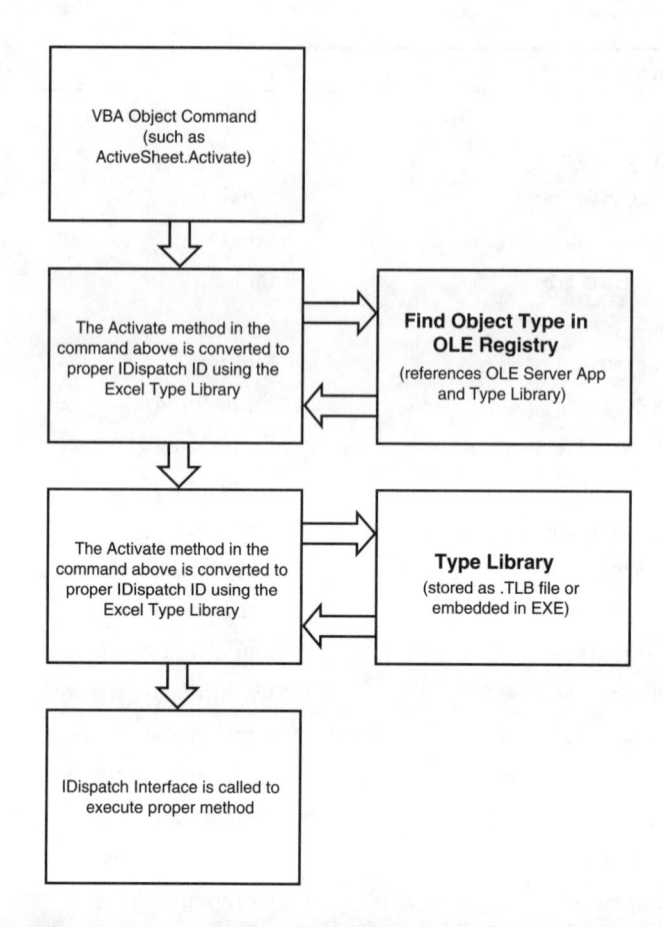

```
         ┌─────────────────────────┐
         │   VBA Object Command    │
         │       (such as          │
         │   ActiveSheet.Activate) │
         └───────────┬─────────────┘
                     ▼
 ┌──────────────────────────────┐      ┌──────────────────────────┐
 │  The Activate method in the  │─────▶│  Find Object Type in     │
 │ command above is converted to│      │     OLE Registry         │
 │  proper IDispatch ID using the│◀────│ (references OLE Server App│
 │      Excel Type Library      │      │    and Type Library)     │
 └──────────────┬───────────────┘      └──────────────────────────┘
                ▼
 ┌──────────────────────────────┐      ┌──────────────────────────┐
 │  The Activate method in the  │─────▶│      Type Library        │
 │ command above is converted to│      │  (stored as .TLB file or │
 │ proper IDispatch ID using the│◀─────│     embedded in EXE)     │
 │      Excel Type Library      │      │                          │
 └──────────────┬───────────────┘      └──────────────────────────┘
                ▼
        ┌────────────────────────┐
        │ IDispatch Interface is called to │
        │   execute proper method │
        └────────────────────────┘
```

> **NOTE**
>
> VB 4 supports the creation of only OLE automation servers. It cannot create objects for in-place editing and the like. In the interfaces table, you can see that OLE automation has only a single simple interface (`IDispatch`), while all the other linking and embedding portions of OLE have multiple complex interfaces. This is the reason that only automation serving is available at this time.

Interfaces are just function tables. The object still maintains the data. An object can have multiple interfaces. An object must include a different pointer to a function table for each interface.

The structure and definition of an interface is stored in a type library. Information about OLE automation files are typically stored in type library files—.TLB or .OLB extensions. The OLE Registry holds references to these type library files. VBA references these files to obtain the information needed to translate a text VBA call to the necessary `IDispatch` interface call. (See Figure 23.4.)

FIGURE 23.4.
VBA automation execution.

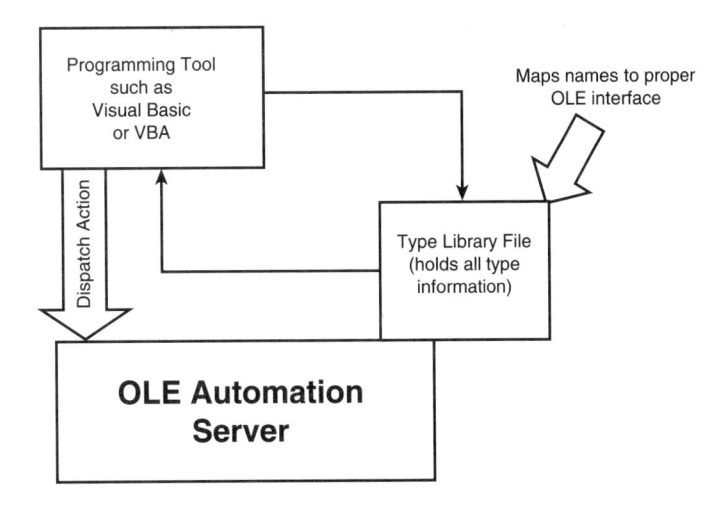

OLE Fundamentals

All objects contain a reference count. A reference count controls the object's lifetime. For example, whenever a variable that references the object is created, the count is incremented. This ensures that a variable will not be eliminated from memory while it is using the object. When a variable containing an object reference is destroyed—because the routine that created it ends, a form that contained it is unloaded, or it is set to nothing—the reference count is decremented. If the reference count reaches zero and the release function is called (often automatically), the object may delete itself.

All OLE objects must have the IUnknown function implemented. The IUnknown function sits at the top of the object hierarchy. All other interfaces inherit from the IUnknown interface. The AddRef(), Release(), and QueryInterface() functions must be supported.

QueryInterface() function allows the addition of other interfaces. IID is the integer number used to reference a particular interface. The IID parameter is passed to the QueryInterface() function to obtain a reference to the function. QueryInterface() allows the discovery of the objects functions at runtime.

AddRef() and Release() are two functions that are used to create a reference to an object. These two routines increment and decrement the reference count, respectively. When the reference count is zero, the object system knows that there are no references to the object, so it may be destroyed.

All OLE objects feature a global unique identifier (GUID). The GUID of each object is unique. An algorithm is used to generate the ID. This guarantees unique ID numbers even across the millions of objects that might occur on a distributed system.

> **TIP**
>
> In the OLE SDK, a routine is included to generate these IDs. They are automatically generated for you. If you want to examine the routine, however, you can see how these ID numbers are created.

OLE Implementation

Visual Basic 4 provides extensive use of OLE. With the release of Visual Basic 4, programmers of Visual Basic could finally create OLE automation servers. This enables other programs, through OLE automation, to instantiate objects by using classes that are defined in Visual Basic. For example, a business rule object can be created in Visual Basic and accessed from Excel, Access, C and C++, and any other OLE automation-capable application or programming language.

> **NOTE**
>
> It is important to note that Visual Basic still does not have the ability to be a general OLE Server. In Figure 23.1, which shows all the OLE services, you can see that OLE automation is separate from the other OLE functions. Visual Basic 4 provides the complete capability to be an OLE automation server.
>
> However, Visual Basic cannot create objects that may be linked or embedded into compound documents. Therefore, without additional DLL or OCX support, a Visual Basic program cannot, for example, generate a custom bar chart object to be embedded in a word processing compound document.

Linking and Embedding

Linking and embedding technology dramatically increases the productivity of a worker. Almost any type of object can be embedded directly into a document. A spreadsheet can be embedded in e-mail; a current sales chart can be placed in presentation material; a voice annotation can be embedded in a spreadsheet; or a complete video can be embedded in a word processing document.

At the present time, this technology is gaining rapid acceptance. Constrained in the past by slow processing speeds and lack of RAM, people now enjoy increased capabilities in both areas that enable them conveniently to embed many different objects into a single compound document.

In-Place Activation

In-place activation is a technology that users, after they are exposed to it, quickly become excited about. Instead of having to leave their word processor to edit a drawing or leave their drawing program to edit a chart, users can double-click an object and edit it in-place in the document they are working on.

Uniform Data Transfer and Drag-and-Drop

To transfer data between applications in the past, there were basically only three choices: clipboard, DDE, and file export/import. The standard clipboard is fairly fundamental and primitive. It can transfer only limited types, amounts, and structures of data. DDE has severe connection problems because of its basic implementation, and it cannot transfer formatted data. File import/export requires that all the data be stored on disk and both the sender and the receiver of the data must have a common format in order for the data to be exchanged.

Uniform data transfer provides the mechanism to transport an object between two or more applications through the clipboard, through drag-and-drop, or through a file.

Compound Files and Structured Storage

The OLE structured storage is one of the most exciting technologies in OLE for programmers. Whereas normal files are a sequential number of bytes that must be read and written in an application-specific manner, structured storage creates essentially an object hierarchy within a file. Microsoft often describes structured storage as a file system within a file. In the same way in which a directory holds subdirectories, each object holds subobjects. This allows multiple stream access for each file. The complete file does not have to be read or written to access a single part. For example, in a file that contained five bitmaps, the program could load a single bitmap without having to load the entire file. Multiple programs can access the same file, and multiple user overwrite protection is supplied. Individual objects within the can have different access privileges. Additionally, all compound documents contain summary header information.

OLE structured storage has been included as part of the Windows system for quite a while. Under Windows, the STORAGE.DLL file contains the compound document storage functions. Microsoft Word, Excel, and other common applications already store all their documents in structured storage files.

OLE documents are completely cross-platform. An OLE compound document can be loaded on either the Macintosh (running OLE services) or a Windows machine. The Macintosh standard picture format (PICT) and the Windows metafile (WMF) are automatically converted to present the picture correctly on each platform.

> **NOTE**
>
> On the Macintosh, the byte ordering is reversed compared to an Intel-based machine. Although the user rarely sees the byte ordering, the inverse byte order between Macintosh and Intel means that data transport between the two platforms requires a data conversion.
>
> Structured storage files are stored in Intel byte order, on both the Macintosh and Windows machines. Macintosh OLE does the transposition on-the-fly. This enables easy exchange of files between the two platforms.

Structured storage also provides file-like functions for the objects stored within the file, such as `CopyTo()`, `MoveElementTo()`, and `Clone()`, to move an object within the object hierarchy.

Structured storage provides something completely new to file storage operations: transaction processing. Changes to a file can be stored in a buffer and written only when the changes are committed, which enables changes to be revoked or committed after the complete write has been buffered. This dramatically decreases the number of corrupted files on a system because partial writes or crashes during storage are eliminated.

You can use DocFile Viewer (included with the OLE SDK as DFVIEW.EXE) to examine a structured storage object. Using DocFile Viewer, you can examine the hierarchy of an entire compound document. Use Microsoft Word to create a file with various objects embedded or linked; then open the document using the viewer. Each object appears as a separately defined entry in the compound document.

> **TIP**
>
> DocFile Viewer can read only files that are 64KB or smaller. Other tools, such as DocFile Explorer (DFEXPL.ZIP), are available from the online services. For serious structured storage work, we suggest that you acquire one of these tools.

There are two ways of writing to a Structured Storage file: `IStorage` and `IStream`. `IStorage` enables objects to be written into the file, so it can therefore act as a type of object database. Objects can be read or written independently. `IStream` works more like a traditional file with reads, writes, and seeks. `IStream` uses a continuous sequential data stream (as opposed to a hierarchical file format) like a traditional data file.

Monikers

Monikers exist to describe relationships between objects. A moniker can point from an object reference to the object's location on a hard disk. Monikers can be used to point to a location or record in a database.

Monikers are typically used to point to things such as paths to linked files. For example, if a compound document is created in a page layout program, such as PageMaker or Microsoft Publisher, to contain the picture of a CAD drawing (in AutoCAD), it is more appropriate to create a link than to embed the picture. The CAD drawing can continue to be edited, and the changes are reflected in the page layout document.

The page layout document, however, needs to know where to find the linked object on the hard disk or network. A moniker can save both an absolute path (for example, C:\CADFILES\mydraw.pcx) and a relative path (...\CADFILES\mydraw.pcx). Therefore, if the entire directory is moved, the object can still be found.

Monikers can even be customized to reference anything needed in an application. There are five types of monikers:

- File
- Item
- Pointer
- Composite
- Anti

File, item, and pointer monikers actually hold specific reference information and are called *simple monikers*. The composite and antimonikers are used in the process of grouping simple monikers together.

A file moniker is used to store either an absolute or a relative path. This is a simple moniker because it can hold only one path per moniker. An item moniker contains a string that is custom to the application or object that created it. A pointer moniker is used to bind to a memory or disk storage reference. Therefore, the object related by a pointer moniker can be either on disk or in memory.

Composite Monikers

A composite moniker, sometimes called a *generic composite,* is a group of other monikers. This moniker collects multiple monikers together into a collection. These simple monikers are stored in left-to-right order, and each is followed step-by-step to reach the desired reference.

For example, if each simple moniker held in the composite moniker symbolized one directory path level (in the path hierarchy), the complex moniker \ole\sample\dll\ would consist of three simple monikers. These monikers would have to be referenced to reach the destination directory in the hierarchy.

An antimoniker is used to eliminate the moniker in the path before it. This is needed because a composite moniker can only be appended; monikers cannot be freely inserted. Therefore, either the composite moniker must be destroyed and reconstructed, or the antimoniker can be used to eliminate select entries for the relation path.

Automation

OLE automation is a powerful feature in Visual Basic, and it is one that is used often by Visual Basic designers. For example, through OLE automation, Visual Basic can be used to control Excel and to create automatically a spreadsheet based on data acquired from various sources. Likewise, it can take this same data and, by using a geographic information system (GIS), such as Arc/Info or Map/Info, that is aware of automation, create a custom map that shows statistical areas in different colors.

Automation is no longer limited to C-based program. With Visual Basic 4 automation, the objects of your program can be used by application users. An Excel user, knowing rudimentary VBA skills, can activate your Visual Basic program, execute methods, and retrieve data.

Automation operates through the fairly simple IDispatch interface. IDispatch is used by an OLE application to get or set a property, invoke a method (by using IDispatch::Invoke), or query an object (by using IDispatch::GetInfo). IDispatch is used to manipulate an instance.

Distributed or Remote OLE

Distributed, or Remote, OLE enables the execution and manipulation of objects on remote systems. Remote functionality is perfect for distributing a processor-intensive task (such as graphics rendering or scientific calculation) or for providing shared access to common objects (such as business rules or programming objects).

One of the most important aspects of Remote OLE is its transparency to the user and the programmer alike. If a program is designed to work with traditional OLE 2.0, it automatically works with remote OLE. To the program that is accessing the OLE object, the latter seems to be on the machine on which the program is executing, because all remote access takes place in the background.

The foundation of Remote OLE is the remote procedure call (RPC). Earlier you briefly saw the lightweight RPC (LRPC), which can exchange and manipulate objects across object boundaries on a single machine. RPCs extend these capabilities by enabling the object to exist on another machine or on several other machines.

Distributed Computing Environment (DCE) is becoming increasingly popular as a distributed environment. Distributed OLE claims compatibility with certain levels in the specification, such as RPC calls. If DCE continues to grow in popularity, OLE compatibility with the specification will likely increase.

Other Object Systems

Now that there is an OLE object standard, you might think that applications will be able to exchange data freely among machines and platforms. There is not just one object format but many—OLE objects, OpenDoc objects, CORBA objects, NeXTSTEP objects, and so forth. Therefore, object-to-object compatibility is not a simple task.

There are object converters, gateways, and compatibility proposals. Even so, inter-object communication can be as difficult as many of the client/server communications, middleware, and other compatibility layers. As objects become increasingly popular, client/server designers will have to ensure that the objects can be exchanged, converted, and used by various object systems.

Common Object Request Broker Architecture (CORBA), created by the Object Management Group (OMG) consortium, is the likely object definition to be used on OS/2 and UNIX platforms. Luckily for programmers using OLE, there are currently 13 proposed standards to enable OLE objects to be exchanged with CORBA objects.

Microsoft is working with Digital Equipment Corporation to use the ObjectBroker product to provide an active gateway between CORBA and OLE objects. CORBA has yet to release a final specification, however, and implementations of various CORBA-compliant applications vary in compatibility. Therefore, check with the developer of the CORBA that needs to be interfaced with before you choose an interface solution.

Object-Oriented System Analysis and Design (OOA)

You might encounter the term *object-oriented analysis* (OOA) as you read about client/server concepts in regards to object implementation. This term has come into widespread use to indicate reengineering an organization's setup and data structure around object methodology.

The process attempts to deploy object technology to improve business processes and work flow. This technology primarily applies to the new distributed object systems that are used across a network.

With the release of object-based SQL Server 6.0, OLE Component Manager, and Remote OLE, this industry will probably change dramatically. In the past, distributed objects have been limited to workstations and powerful UNIX or mainframe-based machines. Because of the level of machines required to run the technology, it was rarely deployed enterprise-wide.

Now that distributed object technology can be used on a personal computer, organizations can use objects to streamline even their common operations. Appendix C, "Sources," lists some of the places from which you can obtain information on object reengineering.

24

Creating an OLE Server

There are many benefits for a client/server system that uses OLE Automation. With the release of Remote or Distributed OLE, objects can now be published on a network. This provides access of important information to users of applications such as MS Access, Excel, and Word. For more information about OLE Automation and Remote OLE, see Chapter 23, "Object Linking and Embedding (OLE)."

An OLE client that accesses an OLE Automation server is called an *OLE Automation Controller* in much of Microsoft's documentation. For simplicity's sake, this book refers to an application that controls an OLE Automation server as an OLE client. An OLE client is any program that can control and manipulate an OLE Server, including programs written by using Visual C++, Visual Basic, or VBA.

Visual Basic 4 now has the capability of creating complete OLE Automation Servers, both in-process and out-of-process. This is the most powerful feature in the new VB 4 version. Creation of OLE Automation servers opens a whole range of applications that was unavailable before.

> **NOTE**
>
> Only the Enterprise Edition can create in-process servers. An OLE in-process server is merely an OLE server that runs in the same memory space (a DLL) compared with an out-of-process server that runs in its own memory space (an .EXE). This makes execution of the in-process server much faster, because all the application (.EXE) overhead is not incurred. Note that there cannot be an in-process Remote OLE server created with VB 4.

VB 4 can also create Remote OLE servers. This enables an OLE Automation server to be placed on a server machine where it actually executes. This further enables the placement of business rule servers or processor-intensive routines on a high-power server machine and the execution of tasks for the client programs.

Making Pseudo Server an OLE Server

In order to demonstrate the VB 4 OLE Automation server features, you're going to modify the Pseudo Server application constructed in the previous chapters to be an OLE server. Not only can the Pseudo Server run normally, but it can also provide information to other clients on the system. Using the OLE capabilities in VB 4, you can create a three-tier client/server system (see Chapter 2, "Overview of Client/Server Concepts").

There are four steps to creating an OLE Automation server in Visual Basic:

1. Add classes to the project from which the object can be instantiated.
2. Define properties and methods in classes to be `Public`.

3. Set appropriate project preferences.
4. Make an .EXE that is registered in the OLE Registry.

First, you add a class to the Pseudo Server called `SalesInfo` that will provide information to other OLE clients. You then create several properties and methods that will be exposed for use by other applications. The preferences for the project will be set so that the application will compile as an OLE server. Finally, you compile the final application.

Creating the Class

Classes that are defined in an application may be defined to be used only within the application itself (`Private`), or they may be exposed for use by other applications (`Public`). Some of the variables you will make private so that you can practice information hiding (see Chapter 6, "Object Programming Overview"). There will be specific `Property Let` and `Property Get` statements to set and retrieve information from these variables. You will make other properties and methods public so that they are accessible to other programs.

One class module is used to define a single class. Therefore, if the server is meant to create multiple object types, several classes must be created. Each class module contains the name of the object that will be created, local methods, exposed methods, local properties (variables), and exposed properties.

Start by loading your Pseudo Server application into Visual Basic. You will add the class to the project. Pull down the Insert menu and select the Class Module option. A window should appear that looks the same as a traditional module window.

> **TIP**
>
> Make a backup of your completed Pseudo Server application before making any additions or modifications. This prevents both accidental damage to the code and a version that contains only the original pieces for study.

Click the right mouse button inside the Class window and a context menu should appear. Select the Properties option, which shows the various properties for the class. Change the `Instancing` property to 2 (`Creatable MultiUse`), the `Name` property to `SalesInfo`, and the `Public` property to `True`.

The `Instancing` property enables OLE clients to create multiple instances of the OLE object. This means that many objects can be created at the same time from the single class. If you wish only one instance to be created from a class, you may set it from the `Instancing` property.

> **WARNING**
>
> Note that when creating a Visual Basic out-of-process OLE server, the overhead for each instance of the server is about 500KB of memory. Therefore, the proliferation of VB OLE Servers can strain the available memory in a computer.

The Name property is used when creating an object from this server. For example, the class name for the Excel application is Application. and the Project Name is Excel. Therefore, creating an object requires code such as the following:

```
Set tempobj = CreateObject ("Excel.Application").
```

In the same way, your objects are instantiated with a command such as this:

```
Set tempobj = CreateObject ("Pseudo.SalesInfo").
```

Finally, the Public property specifies whether the class itself is visible to other applications. If set to False, the class may still be used by the program itself. To expose the class to the OLE Automation engine, this property must be set to True.

If you display the Project window, the Pseudo Server project should now appear as shown in Figure 24.1. Notice that the icons for the class differentiate it from normal modules. Now you need to add the various properties and methods to make the server operational.

FIGURE 24.1.
The Pseudo Server project.

Adding the Properties and Methods

First, let's add the necessary properties for the class. Enter all the variables listed in Listing 24.1. The TotalSales property will be exposed to any OLE client for direct access. Note that the TotalSales property does not comply with the rules of information hiding. It is a variable used internally that is exposed to the outside environment. Use Public properties with caution.

The other three variables, varBeginDate, varEndDate, and varLocation, are all defined as Private properties. These properties are exposed to the OLE environment only through a series of Property Let and Property Get statements.

Listing 24.1. Properties of the SalesInfo class.

```
Public TotalSales As Double

Private varBeginDate As Date
Private varEndDate As Date
Private varLocation As Integer
```

Property Get ReorderItems

This routine reads the variable setting provided by the Pseudo Server program that is stored in the txt_numRequired Text control. The Property Get statement shields any internal variables used by the server and returns the final value in the same way as a traditional VB function does.

Notice the Public designation that appears before the Property Get definition. This may be typed before the definition, or the method may be selected as Public when it is being inserted:

```
Public Property Get ReorderItems()
    ' Retrieve the reorder items from the text control field of the
    ' PServer form.
    ReorderItems = Val(frm_PServer.txt_numRequired.Caption)
End Property
```

GetTotalSales()

This routine returns a simulated value of the total sales for a location. Although the routine returns only a random number for the total sales, the proper query code can easily be retrieved from the Management Client. For understanding and simplicity, it is easier to see what is happening with a simpler routine.

Before any value is returned, the parameters are checked to determine whether they fall within the acceptable bounds. This is a good example of possible business rule checking. This routine could be made to check whether a selected client has not paid a bill previously or has bad credit. Just as easily, a credit authorization routine could be run.

If the verification is unsuccessful, a False value is returned to the calling routine. The return value could be made to include a specific error code that the OLE client could process:

```
Public Function GetTotalSales() As Double
    ' Make sure that the date and location variables are within limits
    If varBeginDate > CVDate("1/1/70") And varEndDate < Now And varLocation <
    ➥3 Then
        ' Randomize the total sales. In a real program, a query would be used
        ' like the one provided in the Management Client
        TotalSales = Int(100000 * Rnd) / 100
        ' Calculation was successful
        GetTotalSales = True
    Else
        ' There was an error with the input variables
        GetTotalSales = False
        TotalSales = 0
```

```
    End If
End Function
```

Property Get and *Let* Routines

The routines in Listing 24.2 are all `Property Let` and `Get` statements that isolate the properties used internally from the external OLE Automation environment. Enter each of these statements to provide proper information hiding access to the OLE clients.

Listing 24.2. `Property` `Let` **and** `Get` **statements.**

```
Public Property Get EndDate() As Date
    BeginDate = varEndDate
End Property

Public Property Get Location() As Integer
    Location = varLocation
End Property

Public Property Get BeginDate() As Date
    BeginDate = varBeginDate
End Property

Public Property Let EndDate(vNewValue As Date)
    varEndDate = vNewValue
End Property

Public Property Let Location(vNewValue As Integer)
    varLocation = vNewValue
End Property

Public Property Let BeginDate(vNewValue As Date)
    varBeginDate = vNewValue
End Property
```

Setting the Preferences

Now that the class with all the necessary methods and procedures has been created, the project must be configured to create an OLE server. There are three settings in the Project Preferences dialog box that must be adjusted: Project Name, StartMode, and Application Description. Select the Options selection on the Tools menu. In the options dialog, select the Project tab, shown in Figure 24.2.

FIGURE 24.2.
The Options Project tab.

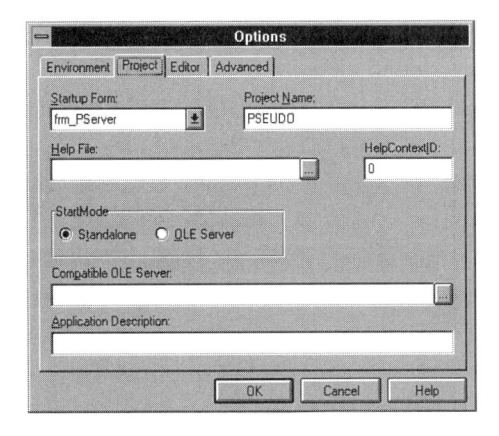

> **NOTE**
>
> The Startup Form option must also be set if you do not want a form to be displayed when an instance of one of the server's objects are instantiated. The subroutine `Sub Main()` may instead be activated, which may or may not display a form at your discretion. In the case of the Pseudo Server, the dialog provides appropriate server information.

First set the Project Name field to `Pseudo`. This is the name that the object will be referenced by (`CreateObject("Pseudo.SalesInfo")`). Next, set the StartMode field to OLE Server. This makes the application register itself as an OLE Server when it is running or when installed.

> **TIP**
>
> The `StartMode` property can be checked at runtime through the `App` object. This property enables you to detect whether an OLE Automation client created the instance or the user double-clicked the application. If started by OLE Automation, there is probably no need to show a user interface.
>
> If `App.StartMode` equals `vbSModeStandalone`, the application was started as a standalone application. If the property equals `vbSModeAutomation`, it was started as a server. These constants can be found in the VB library in the Object Browser.

You will not set the Compatible OLE Server field because there are no previous servers that are compatible with your server. Type a brief application description in the description field. The description that is entered in this field will appear in the Object Browser dialog box describing the server.

Finally, click the Advanced tab, shown in Figure 24.3. You must turn off Compile on Demand and Background Compile to ensure that the OLE server will work properly. Click the Compile On Demand option. The Background Compile option will automatically dim.

FIGURE 24.3.
The Options Advanced tab.

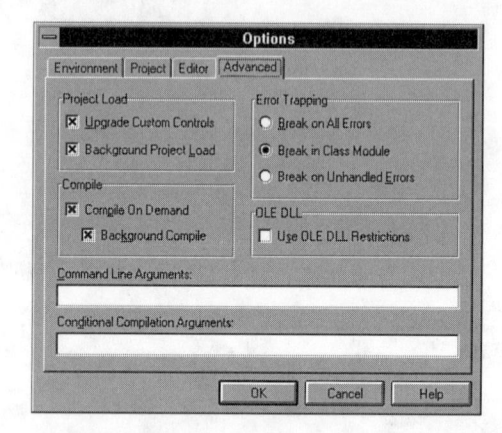

> **NOTE**
>
> Under the Advanced tab in the Enterprise Edition, you may notice the Use OLE DLL Restrictions option. Because you will not be making the Pseudo Server an OLE in-process server in this example, there is no need to check this box. However, if you are creating an in-process server, checking this option enables testing under conditions similar to the final server deployment.

Using the Object Browser

The Object Browser can now be used to examine the objects that have been created in the Class module. It may also be used to set a description and HelpContextID for the properties, methods, and classes shown in the Browser dialog box. If you execute the Object Browser, all the class SalesItems and all its components will appear.

Registering the OLE Server

An OLE Automation server must be listed with the OLE Registry in order to be accessible from other applications. This common registry is accessed when an OLE object call occurs. The registry is searched for the appropriate object type and calls the OLE Server that can provide and instantiate that object.

When an application is executed, it automatically registers itself on the machine for the duration of the execution. VB automatically registers the application when an .EXE is created. The

Application Setup Wizard also automatically registers the application when installed on a new machine. You will be using this capability later as you place the client on a remote machine.

Executing the OLE Server

Now execute the application. There will be no noticeable difference in functioning between this version (see Figure 24.4) and the normal .EXE version. Leave the application executing and minimize it into the task bar. You will now execute Excel and create the client that will access your new server.

FIGURE 24.4.
The Pseudo Server form.

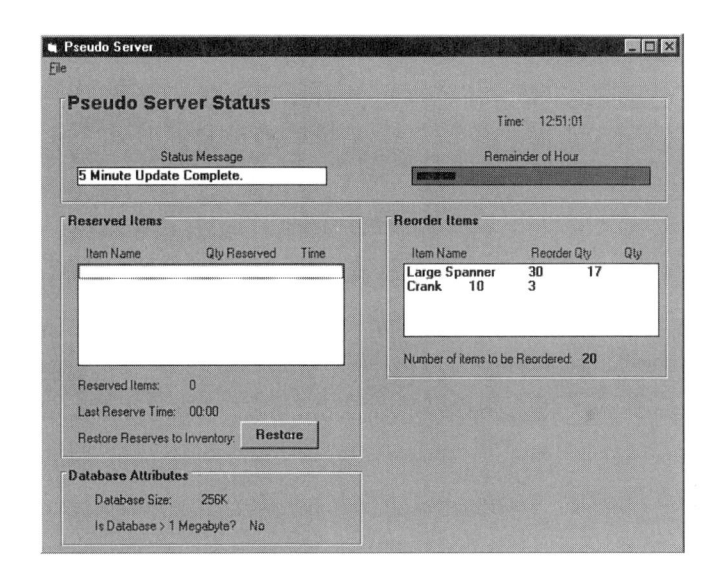

Creating the OLE Client in Excel

Now that you have an OLE Automation server, you will create an OLE client that can instantiate objects made available by the server. You will use Microsoft Excel to create your basic client to provide an example of real-world OLE Automation server access. It is extremely common for C/S developers to expose classes created in an application for use by other applications that provide OLE client access (such as MS Word, Access, Excel, Project, and so forth).

> **NOTE**
>
> Because standard object commands are used to access the OLE server, even code written in VB 3.0 can use a server created in VB 4. Therefore, if you have any legacy applications that have not yet been converted to VB 4, they may still access newly created servers.

To do this, you will use the traditional OLE commands `GetObject()` and `CreateObject()`. These will be used to instantiate the object `SalesInfo` provided by your OLE Automation server.

Execute the Excel application. Once Excel is available, create a spreadsheet that looks like the one shown in Figure 24.5. Be sure to place the dates and other information in the appropriate cells. The client program looks for the values in these locations. To create the button, select the Toolbars... option under the View menu. Click the Forms check box to show the toolbar that contains the Command Button tool. Click the OK button and the proper palette should appear.

FIGURE 24.5.
The Excel OLE client spreadsheet.

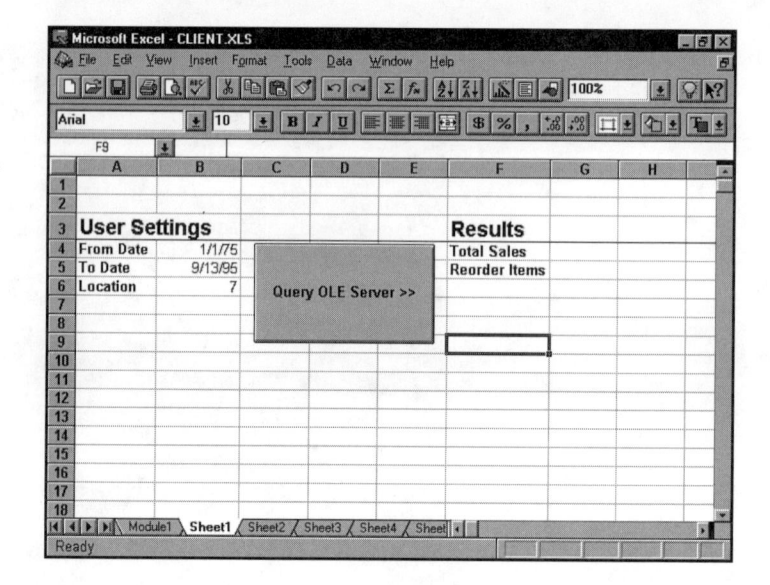

Select the Command Button tool just as you do in Visual Basic, and draw the button on the spreadsheet. When the button is drawn, a dialog box appears enabling you to assign a macro to the button. For the moment, cancel the dialog box because you have not yet created your macro.

Now that the spreadsheet has been created, you will create your VBA routine to make Excel into an OLE client of the Pseudo Server. Under the Insert menu, select the Macro menu and the Module option. The VBA editing window will appear. Enter the code in Listing 24.3. This is all the code that is required to access the OLE server. With the code entered in the macro, the form should appear as shown in Figure 24.6.

FIGURE 24.6.
Excel client macro code.

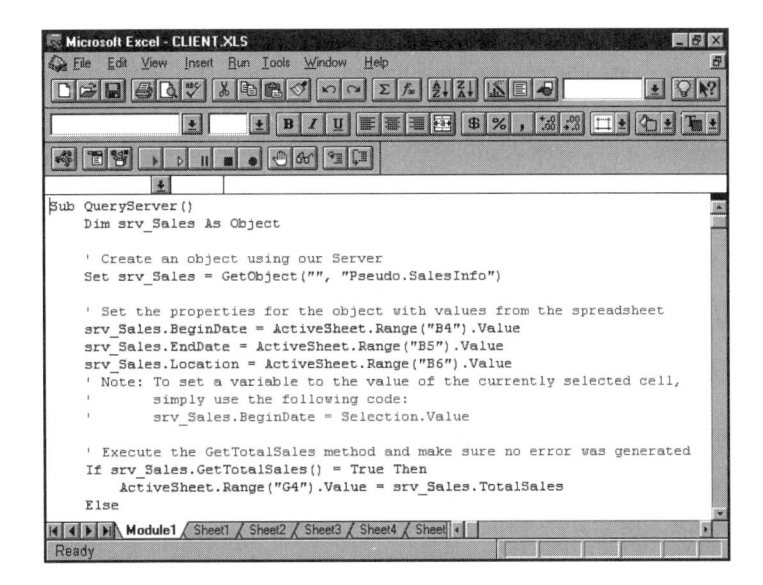

```
Sub QueryServer()
    Dim srv_Sales As Object

    ' Create an object using our Server
    Set srv_Sales = GetObject("", "Pseudo.SalesInfo")

    ' Set the properties for the object with values from the spreadsheet
    srv_Sales.BeginDate = ActiveSheet.Range("B4").Value
    srv_Sales.EndDate = ActiveSheet.Range("B5").Value
    srv_Sales.Location = ActiveSheet.Range("B6").Value
    ' Note: To set a variable to the value of the currently selected cell,
    '        simply use the following code:
    '        srv_Sales.BeginDate = Selection.Value

    ' Execute the GetTotalSales method and make sure no error was generated
    If srv_Sales.GetTotalSales() = True Then
        ActiveSheet.Range("G4").Value = srv_Sales.TotalSales
    Else
```

Listing 24.3. Client module code.

```
Sub QueryServer()
    Dim srv_Sales As Object

    ' Create an object using our Server
    Set srv_Sales = GetObject("", "Pseudo.SalesInfo")

    ' Set the properties for the object with values from the spreadsheet
    srv_Sales.BeginDate = ActiveSheet.Range("B4").Value
    srv_Sales.EndDate = ActiveSheet.Range("B5").Value
    srv_Sales.Location = ActiveSheet.Range("B6").Value
    ' Note: To set a variable to the value of the currently selected cell,
    '        simply use the following code:
    '        srv_Sales.BeginDate = Selection.Value

    ' Execute the GetTotalSales method and make sure no error was generated
    If srv_Sales.GetTotalSales() = True Then
        ActiveSheet.Range("G4").Value = srv_Sales.TotalSales
    Else
        ' One of the input values was not within the specified ranges
        MsgBox "There was a problem with the input dates or location. Dates must
        ➥be between 1/1/70 and today. Location must be less than 3.", 16,
        ➥"Date/Location Error"
    End If

    ' Retrieve the number of items that need to be reordered
    ActiveSheet.Range("G5").Value = srv_Sales.ReorderItems
End Sub
```

To return to the spreadsheet, click the Sheet1 spreadsheet tab. Click the right mouse button on the command button you inserted into the worksheet. Select the Assign Macro... option from the context menu. Now select the QueryBuilder macro you created and click OK.

The Pseudo Server should still be running, so the client can be used immediately. Click the command button to execute the macro. If the dates are between 1/1/70 and the current date, and the location number is less than 3, the results will automatically appear in the correct cells (see Figure 24.7).

FIGURE 24.7.
A successful OLE client query.

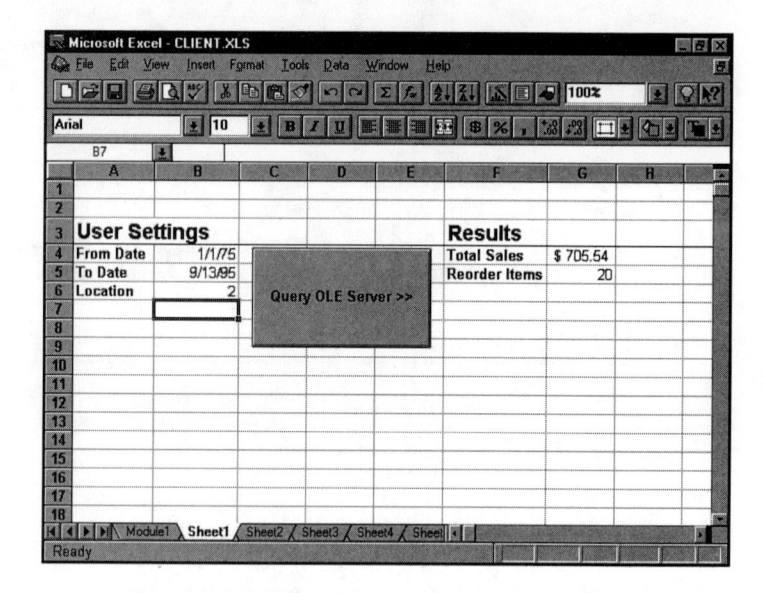

If the numbers supplied are outside this range, the client will notify the user of this problem (see Figure 24.8). This client routine provides an excellent example of the type of error checking that might be done by both the client and the server. The client is responsible for the actual user interface (such as displaying a descriptive dialog box) and the server examines the data and ensures that it is correct before returning a result.

FIGURE 24.8.
The Date/Location Error dialog box.

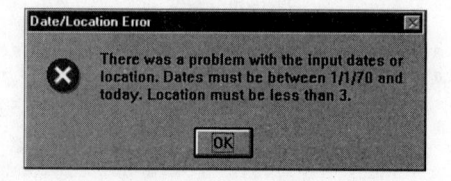

You now have a complete OLE client/server system! The system can be easily expanded to provide many of the features needed. This should provide a building foundation on which to create OLE server systems. Be sure to look at the examples included with Visual Basic for more sample code.

Remote OLE

Now that you've created an OLE Automation server, you will modify the server to be used over a network. This is done by using Remote OLE or Remote Automation. Remote OLE is transparent to the user and provides access to OLE components over a network. For more general information on Remote OLE, see Chapter 23.

> **NOTE**
>
> Remote OLE server applications can run only on 32-bit operating systems such as Windows 95 or Windows NT. The Remote OLE client application can run on a 16- or 32-bit operating system.

Although the user won't notice a difference when the resource is on the local machine or across the network (except for performance issues), the system designer has to do a significant amount of extra work.

The entire process of publishing and activating remote components must be carefully designed and constructed. Remote automation files must be added to both the client and the server machines. The components must be registered and security must be set up to handle access.

Microsoft has provided a number of programs with the Enterprise Edition to facilitate Remote OLE access. These programs provide a graphical user interface to registration services, component catalogs, and Remote OLE drivers.

> **NOTE**
>
> Remote OLE Automation servers can be created only with the Visual Basic Enterprise Edition. It includes particular capabilities as the .EXE file is being created that are not included in the Professional Edition. However, the Professional Edition can create Remote OLE clients. This is done primarily by the Application Setup Wizard when the install disks are being created.

An OLE server may be established anywhere on a network. Because numerous network protocols are supported, a server may be located nearly anywhere. A client can even access another OLE server that is running on the Internet! This widespread distribution provides the first feasible implementation possibilities of a practical three-tier client/server system.

> **WARNING**
>
> A single OLE server cannot be used as both a local and remote OLE server on the same machine. Each application that is registered in the OLE Registry has a setting determining a server's type. Therefore, to use the same type of component, save and install the object under a different object name.

How Remote OLE Works

Remote OLE works by providing an application called the Automation Manager (see Figure 24.9). The Automation Manager needs to be installed on the server machine. This provides the middleware between the OLE services on both machines. When an object is designated as Remote in the OLE Registry and the Automation Manager is executing on the server machine, the OLE system makes the connection to the Remote OLE server through standard network packets.

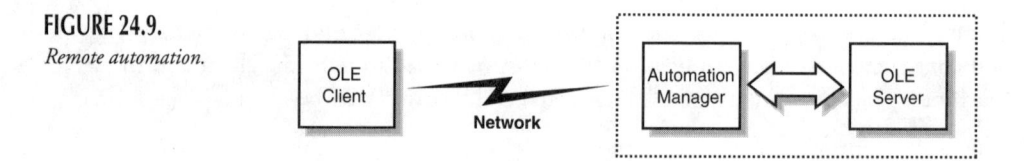

FIGURE 24.9.
Remote automation.

All the communication between the Remote OLE server and the OLE client takes place through the Automation Manager. When you double-click this program, it establishes the necessary services and minimizes itself. If the Automation Manager window is expanded, it shows the number of connections and number of objects currently being used over the remote connection (see Figure 24.10).

FIGURE 24.10.
The Automation Manager.

For a machine that always needs remote access, the Automation Manager can be placed in the Start folder for auto-execution on boot. Often servers can automatically execute the necessary application such as the Automation Manager on startup.

> **WARNING**
>
> Avoid using the JET engine remotely. If you locate the JET DAO on a remote machine, every call to the engine must be passed over the network, and every returned piece of data comes as a separate OLE message. This means that for a query, every record retrieved is sent as a separate OLE entry, bringing performance on a network to a crawl. Instead, create a simple server application to reside on the remote machine and do all the queries. The resultant data can be sent back as a single large string or array.

Remote OLE Applications

Other than the Automation Manager, two programs are used in the Remote OLE system:

- Remote Automation Connection Manager (RACM) manages the OLE Registry and is used to set an OLE server's local or remote connections
- Component Manager manages various catalogs of available objects

The Automation Manager and the Remote Automation Connection Manager are used directly together. They enable access and designation of various OLE objects. The Component Manager is more of an administration tool. If a client machine is set up for a particular user, it is not even necessary to include the Component Manager on that machine.

Using the Remote Automation Connection Manager (RACM)

The Remote Automation Connection Manager (RACM) is used to display all the classes registered in a particular system's OLE Registry (see Figure 24.11). The RACM enables remote access to be set for each class. Network addresses, protocols, and security may be set for a class. A context menu is provided when the right mouse button is clicked in the OLE Classes list box.

An OLE class can be changed from a local to a remote server. Clicking a class in the list box displays an icon in the Server Connection tab as either a local server or a remote server.

The tabs on the right, Server Connection and Client Access, are used to display and modify particular data of classes selected from the list box on the left. The Server Connection tab enables the server access to be easily changed. An OLE server may be tested on a local machine and, by using this utility, may be reconfigured to work on a network.

The Client Access tab enables particular security for the selected class to be specified (see Figure 24.12). The class may be set to `Disallow All Remote Clients`, `Allow Remote Creates by Key` (which allows access if the Remote Activation box is checked), `Allow Remote Creates by ACL` (which applies to Windows NT only), or `Allow All Remote Creates`. The `Allow Remote`

Creates by ACL class provides individual user security. Only users included in the Access Control List in the Windows Registry can access the object.

FIGURE 24.11.
RACM—the Server Connection tab.

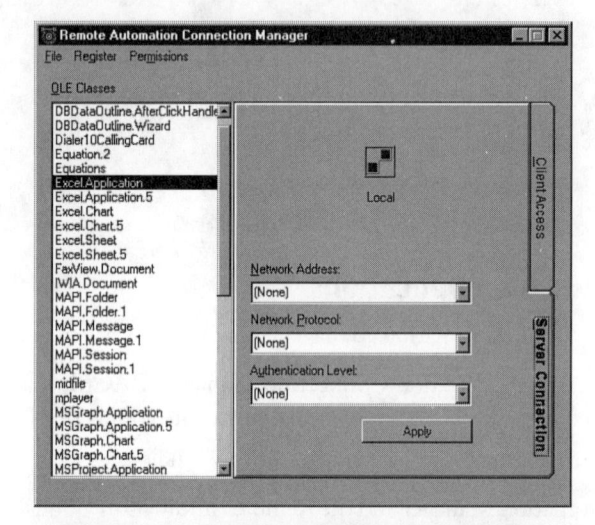

FIGURE 24.12.
RACM—the Client Access tab.

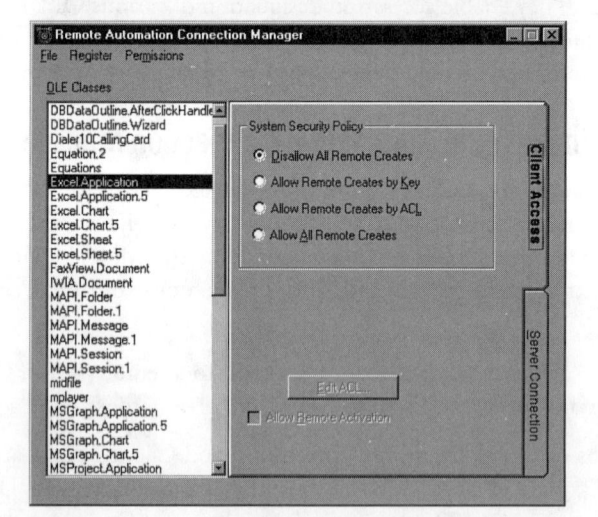

Using the Component Manager

The Component Manager is used to publish OLE objects over a network or track objects within a machine (see Figure 24.13). This application is included in the Enterprise Edition of Visual Basic. It creates component catalogs that may also be created to categorize objects for easy access.

FIGURE 24.13.
The Component Manager.

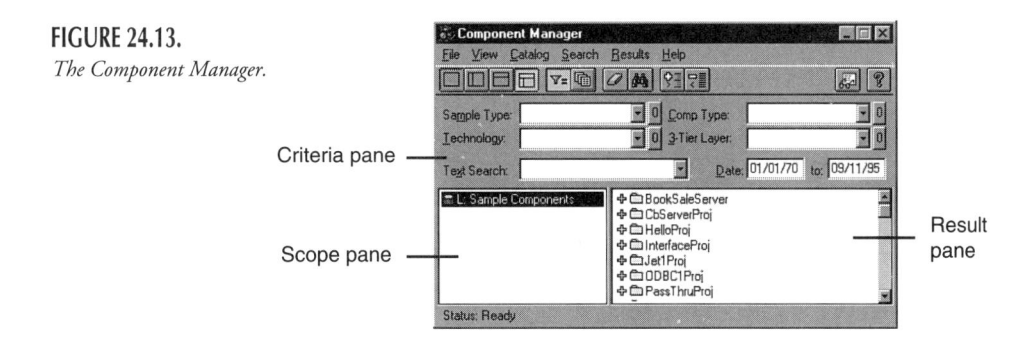

With the Component Manager, you can publish, over the network, the classes provided by the server you just created. In this section, you will publish your OLE Automation server on the network and use the client program on a remote machine to access these objects.

> **TIP**
>
> In addition to objects, information that explains the objects operation and use may also be published with the Component Manager. This especially enables an intermediate user the ability to find and use a particular object. For example, documentation and sample code could be included to show use of the object from an Excel VBA macro.
>
> Under the Component Manager, select an object and select the Properties option under the Results menu. The Usage Notes field can hold any information you want to provide.

Component Manager Catalogs hold all the lists of available components. A catalog may be stored on a local machine or in any ODBC data source. The Component Manager does not actually store the OLE servers. It merely provides a database that points to each server and contains information relating to the server, including registration files, specifications, tag information, versions, and associated files.

Component Manager Window

The screen of the Component Manager is broken into three different areas or panes: the Result pane, the Scope pane, and the Criteria pane. By default, all the panes are shown (as seen in Figure 24.13). Using the icons in the toolbar or the Layout options under the View menu, individual panes may be viewed or hidden. Both the Result and Scope panes have context menus available by clicking the right mouse button while an item is selected.

The Result pane contains all the available objects and documents in the selected catalog. The components displayed here are those from the catalog selected in the Scope pane that comply with the specifications set in the Criteria pane.

The Scope pane contains all the catalogs available to the current machine. Catalogs may be added as either Remote Catalogs (through an ODBC data source), Local Catalogs (stored as a catalog file), or new catalogs (which can be created).

The Criteria pane shows the parameters used to select the available components in the current catalog. For example, a date range may be specified to show only objects created between a begin and end date. This can be convenient in narrowing the possible versions of components that are displayed.

The four fields in the Criteria pane that show combo boxes are used to select the type of objects displayed by their *tags*. Tags are identical to keywords used in most indexes and online services. A class is specified to be referenced by certain tags that may be used in a search.

For example, a car dealership might create an OLE server to provide the bluebook value for each car. Therefore, there may be a Honda Prelude class, a Ford Mustang class, and so forth. The dealer may also have numerous other objects in a component catalog. A tag `Bluebook Cars` can be created. All the appropriate objects can be tagged with this designation. When the `Bluebook Cars` tag is specified in the Criteria pane, only those classes that are designated with this tag will be shown.

Tags are sorted into four categories: Sample Type, Technology, Comp Type, and 3-Tier Layer. Each category of tags has a combo box that contains all the tags assigned to that category. Selecting a particular tag in the combo box shows only the components that are properly tagged.

To the right of each combo box is a button that enables the sort order to be selected, as shown in Figure 24.14. By selecting a number other than zero, you may select the sort order for each of the four categories. When the results are displayed in the Result pane, they are sorted as specified.

FIGURE 24.14.
The sort order pop-up menu.

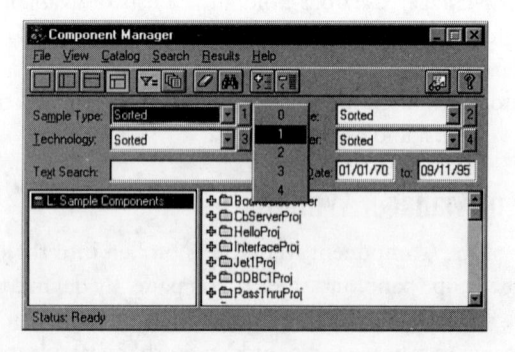

You set a tag by selecting an object in the Results pane and displaying its properties sheet (by using the context menu, double-clicking the object, or with the Properties option under the Results menu). The Property Tags tab, shown in Figure 24.15, shows all the tags that are selected for the item. In the figure, the `Basic Concepts`, `Out-Of-Process Server`, and `SingleUse Instancing` tags are selected. Searches for any of these three tags includes this class in the Results pane.

FIGURE 24.15.
The Property Tags tab.

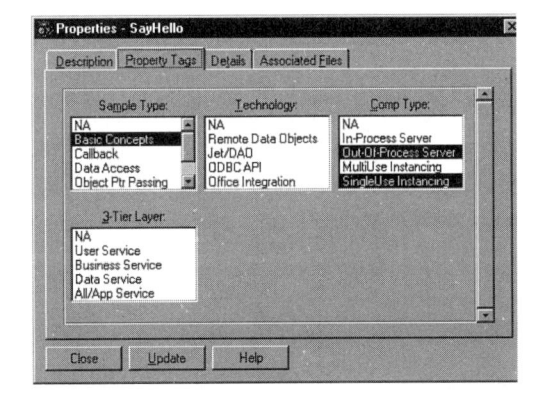

Converting the Pseudo Server

Once an OLE Automation server has been created in Visual Basic 4, adding Remote OLE capabilities requires no additional programming. There are only five steps to making a VB OLE Automation server accessible from a remote client:

1. Recompile the VB application for Remote server usage.
2. Create install disks for the server machine.
3. Install on the server machine.
4. Execute RACM on the server machine and specify remote access on the object.
5. Run the server application on the client machine to register in the OLE Registry.
6. Execute RACM and designate the object as remote.

To be a Remote OLE server a Visual Basic .EXE, must include additional routines. To convert the Pseudo Server into an OLE server, you must first set the project to compile in a particular way. Execute Visual Basic and load the Pseudo Server project. Select the Make EXE... option under the File menu.

Rename the executable PseudoR.EXE. Now click the Options... button. Check the Remote Server Support Files option so that the .EXE will compile as a Remote OLE server. Add any version information or comments that you think are appropriate. Click the OK button to accept these changes. Click the OK button to compile the .EXE file.

Now that the application is recompiled, you need to create install disks to install it on a remote machine. Execute the Application Setup Wizard. On the seventh step, for the Deployment

Model, select Install as an OLE automation shared component. Click the check box to install the remote OLE Automation server components.

After you create the installation disk, install the Pseudo Server application on the server machine. The installation should register the server in the OLE Registry and install the application, as well as the Remote Automation Connection Manager (RACM) and the Automation Manager applications.

Execute the RACM application. Select the Pseudo.SalesInfo object in the OLE Classes list box. Click the Client Access tab to show the remote access options. Leave the System Security Policy for the object to Allow Remote Creates by Key. Click the Allow Remote Activation option to enable remote user access.

Finally, execute the Automation Manager. This sets up the various necessary protocols so that the server can provide object access over the network. The Automation Manager will remain running in minimize to provide server access.

The Remote OLE server is now ready! Any client machines on the network that have the proper OLE Registration and remote access driver can now address the Pseudo Server's objects.

To allow the client access, first double-click the original compile .EXE of the server (the same one from which the installation disks were created). This installs an entry for the server objects into the OLE Registry. Quit the Pseudo Server application after it executes.

Execute the RACM utility on the client machine. Select the class Pseudo.SalesInfo, which should appear in the list box. Now you must specify the Network Address of the computer on which the OLE Automation server resides. In the case of your machine, the server name is SUPER_ENDERBY, which you enter in this field. Select the Network Protocol for the next field (we use NetBIOS over NetBEUI, standard on Windows 95 & NT).

Finally, click the right mouse button on the Pseudo.SalesInfo entry in the list box. A context menu will appear (see Figure 24.16) from which you must select Remote. This tells the OLE system that when this class is accessed, it should look on the network for the Network Address and Network Protocol specified to locate the object.

When you clicked the Remote menu option, the icon for that entry should have changed to appear as the one shown in Figure 24.17. You can now exit the RACM application. The system is now configured. Any program that uses the Pseudo Server's object can reference the class that is based on the server.

If you execute the Excel client you constructed earlier, it can access the Remote OLE server without any changes in code. If you expand the Automation Manager while it is running on the server machine and the objects are being accessed, the number of connections and object usage are displayed.

Chapter 24 ■ Creating an OLE Server

FIGURE 24.16.
Remote connection configuration in RACM.

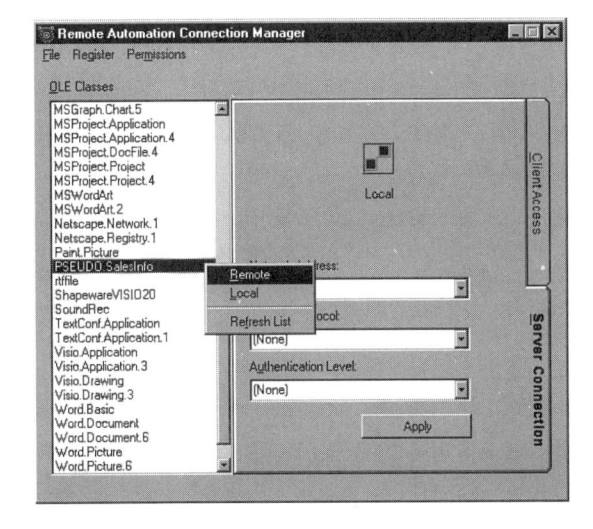

FIGURE 24.17.
The Remote component icon.

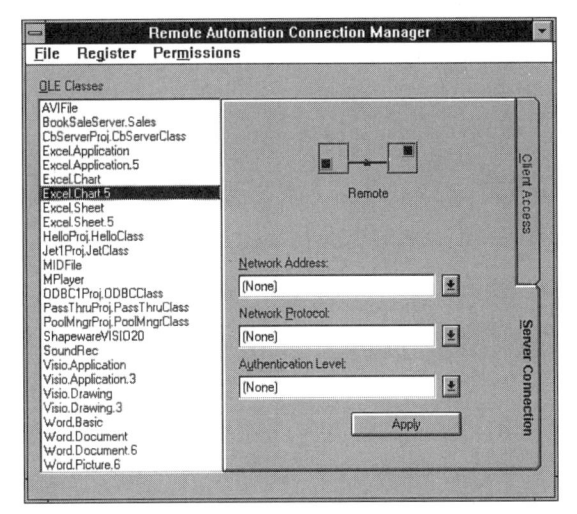

> **NOTE**
>
> The OLE service seems to initialize for each application as it is originally booted. Therefore, any changes you make in RACM may not appear to have taken place in an application until it is quit and reexecuted.

Designing OLE Automation Servers

Now that you have created your first OLE client/server system, there are some general guidelines to remember when designing such a system. By planning how your system will act, many of the deployment pitfalls can be avoided.

Sometimes OLE servers have no visible user interface. You should employ a status user interface such as that implemented in the Pseudo Server application. This provides the SA with an idea of the status of the system. With the inclusion on Windows 95 status bars in your user interface, the administrator can easily be kept informed of many operations.

> **CAUTION**
>
> Deployment of widespread access to objects is an *extremely* new endeavor. Because of Distributed OLE's recent release, there are few time-tested factors to judge how such a system will operate. Questions such as "How will normal usage of distributed objects affect network traffic?" have not yet been adequately answered. Therefore, be careful when using Distributed OLE in a production environment until you have a first-hand understanding of how the system will affect performance.
>
> Also test the performance of writing OLE objects into SQL Server 6.0 and Microsoft Exchange Server to determine whether widespread storage and exchange of objects is possible. Without testing these solutions, you will not be able to determine whether your use of distributed objects will be scalable.

Designing the Object Hierarchy

The object hierarchy of the system has to be considered carefully before work begins on a system. Poor design of this single component can make performance, usability, and expansion either extremely painful or painless. The object hierarchy consists of objects that are dependent upon one another.

For example, a project may contain two classes: one named Room and the other named Table. The Table class may be for use only by other objects within the project while the Room class is exposed. If the Room class uses or instantiates objects of the Table class, the Table class is dependent on the creation of a Room class. The Room class objects are said to be external objects.

Every increase in the number of hierarchy levels tends to increase the overhead of creating the external objects. Yet like a normalized database, a properly organized hierarchy can provide exactly the structure and extensibility necessary for the task.

Spend time evaluating and designing which objects will be necessary to the system now and in the future before jumping in and throwing something together. Consult the Visual Basic manual for extensive guidelines to follow when creating the hierarchy.

Handling OLE Errors

Normally, the OLE system has its own set of commands for errors. Visual Basic 4 has grafted these error returns into the main VB error engine, and they may be trapped as other VB errors are. When designing an OLE Server, try to make sure that the methods return as many error verification codes as possible. This enables clients to better inform their users about what has occurred on the system.

Version Control

As objects proliferate, there will be increasing problems of keeping all the programs that use a particular object working properly as that object is upgraded. Therefore the capability of tracking versions of an OLE server is built into the OLE system. This enables a set of objects to be upgraded, although the newer upgrade version may be used only by programs that are compatible with it.

If the OLE server supports backward compatibility with older versions of the server, the programs that use its objects can access the new version. If not, the older version can be left in the system and the objects that cannot handle the new version can access the previous compatible one.

OLE Registry

One of the most complex, and often most frustrating, parts of installation under Windows NT and Windows 95 is the OLE Registry. All OLE applications that can provide objects for use by other applications must be registered in the OLE Registry. When an application makes a call to an object, the system searches the registry for the appropriate reference.

This is done by using the ClassID, which is a textual representation of the object. For example, the ClassID of the Excel application is `Excel.Application`. From the registry, the ClassID is found, and what is called a *registry key* is returned. A key can contain one or more values. In the case of an object reference, the key points to the information required to load the OLE server (either an application or a DLL).

Applications and OLE servers must therefore be registered in the OLE Registry in order for a call from an OLE client to activate them. The registry is also used to store parameters instead of a traditional .INI file.

> **NOTE**
>
> In a client/server environment, individual users often have problems that require the reinstallation of the Windows system. If you are using the Windows API or working in C or C++ and doing your own registry entries, provide the user with the capability of repairing the application's registry entries. For example, if the system must be reinstalled and the registry is destroyed, the program can enable the user to rebuild the registry information without having to reinstall your application completely.

There are five basic ways to register a Visual Basic application in the OLE Registry:

- Install the OLE Server using disks created with the Application Setup Wizard.
- Run an OLE Server. When you run it the first time, it automatically registers the application.
- Select the OLE Server in the References dialog box in Visual Basic.
- Run the application from the command line, followed by the text /REGSERVER.
- Use the Client Registration Utilities.

The fourth way to register is provided specifically for Visual Basic programs. When the OLE Server compiles, code is added at the front of the application to detect command-line variables. If the /REGSERVER argument is encountered, the application registers itself.

Using the Client Registration Utility

When setup disks are created, the setup application automatically registers the application being installed. However, there are often times for testing or system reconstruction when it is convenient to register an application manually.

Registration is done by using the Client Registration Utilities. There are both 16- and 32-bit versions of the registration utilities named CLIREG16 and CLIREG32, respectively. They both require the specification of a .TLB or .VBR file to create the registration. These files specify the various OLE services and parameters. When building an OLE server, Visual Basic 4 automatically creates a .VBR file to be used with the server. The Application Setup Wizard automatically includes the appropriate registration utility when distribution disks are created.

The registration is done with a command-line interface and must be passed various parameters. Table 24.1 lists all the parameters that may be sent to the registration program. The format of the command line is the following:

```
CLIREGnn vbrfile -s {s} | -p {p} | -a {a} | -t {t} | -u | -q | -1 | -nologo | -[h
 | ?]
```

The *nn* that follows the `CLIREG` is either `16` or `32`, depending on the type of operating system being used. The *vbrfile* can be the filename of a Visual Basic registration file generated automatically when an application is compiled as an OLE server. The other parameters can be found in the table.

Table 24.1. Client Registration Utility parameters.

Parameter	Description
s	Sets the network address
p	Sets the network protocol
a	Sets the security authentication level (0 to 6)
t	Sets the typelib file
u	No information dialogs or error messages
l	Logs error information to file CLIREG.LOG
nologo	Doesn't display copyright information
h or ?	Shows the help screen of the available parameters

Creating Remote Client Distribution Disks

Remote client applications access a Remote OLE server. The Application Setup Wizard aids in creating distribution disks, which automatically have all the registration and component information to access the Remote server upon install. The drivers required for OLE are automatically added to the installation files.

Using *ByRef* Versus *ByVal*

When using Distributed OLE across a network, try to pass parameters that will not be modified to methods using the `ByVal` command. Although using the `ByRef` command on a local machine is far more efficient, it is dramatically slower over a network. This is because `ByRef` passes a pointer to a routine, and pointers cannot be used over a network.

Therefore, the OLE mechanism has to make a complete copy of the array or memory structure pointed to, send it over the network, and receive a complete copy back when the method is completed. Using the `ByVal` command, however, sends the data only one way. This decreases the amount of network traffic.

OLE Remote Security

Security for OLE Remote Servers is nearly as important as traditional file security. By allowing access to objects on the network to nearly everyone, the potential for breached security dramatically increases. The Remote OLE system can use the security capabilities of Windows NT. The access for particular objects can be restricted by the use of the NT User Registration Database. See information available from Microsoft for the definition of the NT security capabilities.

25

Query Builder

Many applications do not require a complete client/server application, but do require some type of Query Builder front-end to retrieve information from an existing table. A Query Builder application enables the user to select various characteristics to search a database and then execute a query. Often, the user of this type of application needs only read access and the capability of taking the resultant data and placing it into a spreadsheet or word processing application.

In this chapter, you create a Query Builder and Table Builder in Visual Basic, which constructs and retrieves information from a Microsoft SQL Server database. Table Builder creates a table, inserts sample records, and creates indexes for those records. In Query Builder, the user makes the various selections from the check boxes and text fields, then presses the Query command button. The Query button constructs a SQL query, connects to the SQL Server, creates a Recordset from the results, and displays this information to a Grid Control.

There are several sample tables included with SQL Server in the pubs database that may be used for joins, queries, and so forth. The Table Builder application creates its own tables of randomized data that it will query. By using sample data provided with the system, you gain an understanding of how the query engine works, but learn little about actually constructing the tables and inserting information. The Table Builder provides a good working foundation from which data creation and a storage engine may be built.

There are several pieces required to implement these two applications: a SQL Server Database Table to Query, an ODBC connection to the database that contains the table, and the Visual Basic Data Access Objects (DAO) to connect to the table. You will use tools included with SQL Server and Visual Basic to build the sample applications.

Tools Used to Construct the Query Builder

The Query Builder will be constructed by using a single platform running both Windows NT Advanced Server and NT SQL Server. ODBC drivers will be used to connect to the SQL Server database. The application assumes that the user has SA (system administrator) access with a password.

If this is not the case, the SA has to grant privileges to create a device, database, and table. Alternatively, the administrator must create them for you. The code must also be modified to fit the particular circumstances, including the user name, password, and ODBC connection. Most parts of the program can be developed from a remote terminal by using the ODBC connection over a network link. Operationally, this implementation is no different than a program created on a single machine, with the possible exception of network performance and connection variables.

In the construction of the Query Builder, the following applications are used:

- Windows NT Server: The server NOS on which the SQL Server will be installed.
- Microsoft SQL Server: The database server that accepts SQL commands and stores devices, databases, and procedures. SQL Server comes with a number of other utilities, including various command line programs (see Figure 25.1). The ones listed are the only programs necessary to construct the Query Builder (consult the SQL Server manual or online help for information on the programs not described). The following is a list and short description of the utilities you will be using to construct your SQL Server example:

    SQL Object Manager: A tool for creating, editing, and deleting database objects on the SQL Server. It is used to grant and revoke permission to various objects.

    SQL Administrator Win32: A graphical tool for administrating a SQL Server. It is used to create and manage devices, databases, segments, system logins, remote servers, system resources, database backup, database recovery, and transaction logs, and to provide the same query tools available from the iSQL/w application.

    iSQL/w: A rudimentary tool for sending SQL queries to the SQL Server. This provides a good testbed to create the basic queries that the Query Builder will eventually use. It also enables a user to watch performance and organization features of the operation of a particular query. This may help you optimize how you want to implement the query.

FIGURE 25.1.
Necessary SQL Server programs.

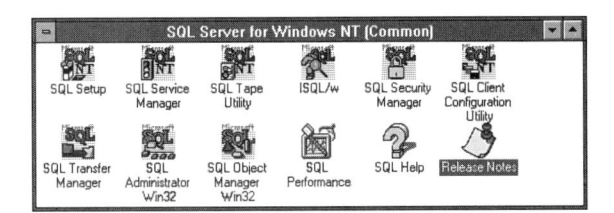

- Visual Basic Professional 4.0 or Enterprise Edition: May be used to construct all the forms and applications. The necessary ODBC drivers and programs are included with Visual Basic. They also come with Microsoft Access and other programs. Check with the individual products for various licensing requirements for any distribution of the ODBC drivers:

    ODBC Manager: Used to add, delete, or configure data connections accessed by the ODBC driver, called *data sources*. It also enables additional ODBC drivers to be installed. The ODBC Manager can be automatically invoked from Visual Basic, but you will use the program itself to demonstrate its accessibility.

    ODBC Driver Library: Drivers for the SQL Server libraries, which you will use through the JET engine to access the Database table.

Most of the code and the applications should work with any ODBC-compliant system. Configuration of the actual device and database may be different, so consult the individual reference manual of the database server you'll be using.

This chapter provides two ways of creating the structure and format of the table in the SQL Server database. You will use the SQL Object Manager and include the programmatic technique to create the table automatically. It also can be constructed by using the Microsoft Access database for creating the structures (as demonstrated in Chapter 21, "Upsizing to Microsoft SQL Server") and upsized to a SQL Server database. This chapter uses the tools that come with SQL Server and Visual Basic in order to familiarize and describe the various aspects of the system that will become the heart of your database effort.

The Table Builder program uses the database, device, and ODBC connections to fill the table with sample data and create two indexes. This is done largely with randomized loops generating data that is inserted into each record. First, it is important to understand the basics of Microsoft SQL Server. If you are already familiar with SQL Server, feel free to skip to the section that begins the database construction.

Overview of SQL Server

Microsoft SQL Server is a complete SQL Server engine. In addition to providing a complete query engine that is largely ANSI SQL-92 compliant, it also boasts a complete on-board SQL language called Transact-SQL. Transact-SQL has special functions for data manipulation and provides a language that can be used for stored procedures and trigger routines. Transact-SQL is the same language used on Sybase SQL Servers.

SQL Server databases are accessed primarily through ODBC drivers because of their widespread availability. You will access the SQL database and the programs included with the server through Visual Basic DAO. A SQL Server is constructed slightly differently from a traditional multi-user desktop database. Besides lacking most of the front-end creation tools built into a desktop database (such as the forms construction in MS Access), the storage structures operate differently. SQL Server uses various types of data storage constructs that are specialized for numerous users and enterprise-wide database use.

Data Constructs

SQL Server uses its own disk allocation to ensure that the greatest performance is achieved. As shown in Figure 25.2, there are three primary levels in which information is stored: a device, a database, and a table.

FIGURE 25.2.
SQL Server data structures.

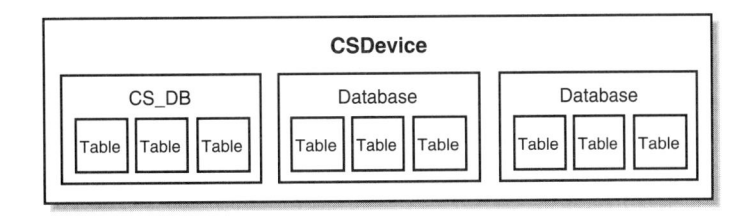

```
┌─────────────────────────────────────────────────────────────┐
│                          CSDevice                            │
│  ┌───────────────────┐ ┌───────────────────┐ ┌───────────────────┐ │
│  │      CS_DB        │ │     Database      │ │     Database      │ │
│  │ ┌─────┐┌─────┐┌─────┐ │ ┌─────┐┌─────┐┌─────┐ │ ┌─────┐┌─────┐┌─────┐ │
│  │ │Table││Table││Table│ │ │Table││Table││Table│ │ │Table││Table││Table│ │
│  │ └─────┘└─────┘└─────┘ │ └─────┘└─────┘└─────┘ │ └─────┘└─────┘└─────┘ │
│  └───────────────────┘ └───────────────────┘ └───────────────────┘ │
└─────────────────────────────────────────────────────────────┘
```

The *device* is a contiguous section of storage allocated on the hard disk of the server. A device is used to store databases and transaction logs. A database cannot be created until a device is created where it will be stored. A database can be stored across multiple devices.

The administrator of the server allocates an amount of storage that the server uses to a device file. The server can then optimize performance by expanding and shrinking the databases stored within the device file partition without having to use the OS native filing structure. When a device is created, the type of device is specified. In addition to database devices, database backup devices may also be created including a disk dump (hard disk backup), floppy dump A & B (floppy disk), and tape dump (tape backup).

The database holds all the various tables created, either by using the SQL Object Manager Win32 program or directly from SQL. A database is allocated within a device. A database object can hold numerous tables. An ODBC data source connection can conveniently access only one database at a time. Therefore, tables that must be related are most often stored within a single database.

Usually stored in the same place as the database is the *transaction log* to the database. A transaction log is used to buffer transactions for later database updating. (For more information on transactions, see Chapter 2, "Overview of Client/Server Concepts.") A transaction log is, by default, created within the same device as the database that it will be buffering. However, a transaction log may be placed within its own device if that becomes either necessary or advantageous.

For example, a transaction log becomes a crucial feature when you are attempting to back up (to tape drive or mirror to another machine) a server. Backing up databases is a problem because during the backup, clients may seek to update records in the database that is being copied. If the user updates both record 30 and record 100, but the backup system has copied only to record 60, the backup might contain both old data and data that was updated while the backup was occurring.

The simplest solution to this problem is to shut down the database system, making user access and potential problem updates impossible. Although this may be a possibility in some organizations, many need access to their data 24 hours a day, seven days a week. This makes weekly backups a problem.

Transactions logs solve this problem. Any updates after the backup begins are merely buffered in the transaction log, and the database is updated after the backup is complete. If the system requires a large number of transactions to be buffered as the backup occurs, the device that holds the database may run out of room. Therefore, a device may be created that both holds the transaction log for a database and may be sized independently of the database.

For the database being constructed here, transaction logs are not of crucial importance and are left to their defaults. However, when creating a client/server system, attention should be paid to how these are implemented.

System Administrator (SA) and Database Owner (DBO)

The system administrator (*SA* or *sa*) and database owner (*DBO* or *dbo*) are two primary designations of user status. They both have more power to modify structures than a traditional user. For the Table Builder, you need SA permission to construct the various devices and databases.

When the SQL Server is first installed, only the SA has the capability of creating new databases. The SA may grant permission to other users depending on what is necessary. The SA has exclusive use of the commands DISK INIT, DISK REINIT, DISK REFIT, KILL, and RECONFIGURE. The commands CREATE DATABASE, ALTER DATABASE, and DROP DATABASE may be granted to other users. The SA has unlimited power over the SQL Server system and may choose to modify nearly anything available to the system resources.

A DBO is granted special privileges for access to the database. The creator of a database is given the status of DBO and is responsible for administrating it. The SA may transfer the DBO designation of a database to another user. The DBO has the exclusive use (other than the SA) to execute the commands CHECKPOINT, DBCC, DROP DATABASE, GRANT (*statement*), REVOKE (*statement*), LOAD DATABASE, LOAD TRANSACTION, and SETUSER. The commands CREATE TABLE, CREATE VIEW, CREATE DEFAULT, CREATE RULE, CREATE PROCEDURE, DUMP DATABASE, and DUMP TRANSACTION may be granted to other users.

System Tables

There are various tables created by the SQL Server to track all the user-created tables and configurations. This is called the *System Catalog*, and it contains all the information on the user logins, IDs, access capabilities, devices, and other server databases. These tables are stored in the "master" database. By default, all users have access to the information in the System Catalog except for fields that contain permission or password data. Normally, none of these tables may be altered directly. Instead, procedures exist to make most of the modifications that are necessary indirectly. The System Catalog has 13 tables:

- syscharsets: A record for each character set and sort order used by SQL Server.
- sysconfigures: Data on various parameters set by the user. It also contains the values that take effect when the SQL Server issues a RECONFIGURE command.

- syscurconfigs: Values of the user parameters during the current session or query.
- sysdatabases: Information on each database on the server. When SQL Server is first installed, only the records for the master, model, and tempdb databases are stored here.
- sysdevices: A record for each device on the system.
- syslanguages: A record for all languages known to SQL Server except U.S. English, which SQL Server includes by default.
- syslocks: A record containing access privileges (such as Exclusive, Shared, Exclusive Intent, and so forth) for each page being used. Unlike other tables, this table is built dynamically when a query occurs.
- syslogins: All user accounts information and passwords. Indexed on the server user ID (suid) field.
- sysmessages: A record for every error that can be returned by SQL Server. Included in each record is the error number, severity level, and description of the error.
- sysprocesses: Information about server processes. Built dynamically like the syslocks table.
- sysremotelogins: A record for each remote user who can call a remote stored procedure.
- sysservers: A record for each Remote SQL Server that the SQL Server can call to invoke stored procedures.
- sysusages: Disk allocation information used to govern the structure of a device. It contains a record for each page number connected to a database.

Additionally, each database (including the master database), automatically contains 13 tables that are used to describe it. This is called a *database catalog* or a *data dictionary*. Included is such information as information about the system's database objects (tables and views), users, permissions, and so forth.

All the information about the server is stored within accessible databases. This enables a system administrator to examine the construction of the system for all the current system configurations. It also provides a way to create analysis programs that can automatically obtain necessary information on the system.

The Pseudo Server program that you constructed in Part II is just such an analysis program. These programs can obtain information about the way the system is used and provide data to the system administrator about how the system might be optimized. The Database Catalog also consists of 13 tables:

- sysalternates: Used for alternate users not stored in the sysusers table. Permission routines first check the sysusers table and, if not found, search the sysalternates table.
- syscolumns: A record for each column in every table and view, as well as a record for each parameter in a stored procedure.

- syscomments: Comment entries for all the views, rules, defaults, triggers, and stored procedures.
- sysdepends: Cross-reference data, including a record for each procedure, view, or table that is referenced by another procedure, view, or table.
- sysindexes: A record for each clustered index, unclustered index, table that has no clustered index, and table that contains text or image fields.
- syskeys: Records for all the keys of the databases, including Primary, Foreign, or Common keys.
- syslogs: The entire transaction log for the database.
- sysobjects: A record for each database object, which includes system table, user table, view, log, stored procedure, rule, default, trigger, and extended stored procedure.
- sysprocedures: A record for each view, default, rule, trigger, and stored procedure.
- sysprotects: User permissions information, including a record for each GRANT and REVOKE command that has been sent.
- syssegments: A record for each segment.
- systypes: A table of all the available data types. It contains a record for each general system type and any user-defined data type.
- sysusers: A record for each user allowed to access the database.

Data Types

SQL Server enables the use of 14 data types and the creation of user-defined data types. Choosing the correct data type for a particular field (or column) is important. SQL Server data types provide the basis for the table that you'll construct.

Integer types include int, smallint, and tinyint. Floating point types include float and real. Money data types include money and smallmoney. Character data may be stored as char(n), varchar(n), and text. Binary types include binary(n), varbinary(n), and image. Dates and time may be represented with datetime or smalldatetime types. Other data types include bit, timestamp, and sysname. Table 25.1 contains a short description of all the various data types supported by SQL Server.

Table 25.1. SQL Server data types.

Name	Data Type	Size	Description
char(n)	Character	n (nondynamic)	Holds up to 255 letters, symbols, and numbers.

Name	Data Type	Size	Description
varchar(n)	Character	Size of data, maximum specified by n	Holds up to 255 letters, symbols, and numbers.
int	Integer	4 bytes	Holds numbers between 2,147,483,647 and −2,147,483,648, inclusive.
smallint	Integer	2 bytes	Holds numbers between 32,767 and −32,768, inclusive.
tinyint	Integer	1 byte	Holds numbers between 0 and 255, inclusive.
float	Floating-point	8 bytes	Holds numbers between $1.7E-308$ and $1.7E+308$.
real	Floating-point	4 bytes	Holds numbers between $3.4E-38$ to $3.4E+38$.
binary(n)	Binary	n (nondynamic)	Holds up to 255 bytes of fixed-length data.
varbinary(n)	Binary	size of data, maximum specified by n	Holds up to 255 bytes of fixed-length data.
bit	Other	1 bit	Stores either a 1 or a 0.
money	Money	8 bytes	Holds numbers between 922,337,203,685,477.5807 and −922,337,203,685,477.5808.
smallmoney	Money	4 bytes	Holds numbers between 214,748.3647 and −214,748.3648.

continues

Table 25.1. continued

Name	Data Type	Size	Description
datetime	Date and time	8 bytes: 4 bytes for date and 4 bytes for time	Date number represents number of days before or after 1/1/1900; number represents time number of milliseconds after midnight.
smalldatetime	Date and time	4 bytes: 2 bytes for date and 2 bytes for time	Date number represents number of days before or after 1/1/1900; time number represents number of minutes after midnight.
text	Character		Holds up to 2,147,483,647 characters.
image	Other		Holds up to 2,147,483,647 bytes of binary data.
timestamp	Other		Updates every time record is INSERTed or UPDATEd.
sysname	Other	NOT NULL	Used by the system tables.

Views

A *view* is a type of virtual table that doesn't really exist as an object but can be treated as if it does for queries and updates. A view is the SQL counterpart to a Visual Basic Recordset. A view can be made up of various columns and rows from underlying tables known as *base tables*.

You will not use view in the Query Builder application, but views often are useful for Query Builder applications. For example, a single view might be created to correlate a number of disparate tables. Because the server handles all the overhead, this is an effective way for the query engine to access a single view to gain all the necessary information needed. For more information on building a view, consult the SQL Server manuals.

SQL Indexes

Like most databases, SQL Server allows particular fields to be indexed in order to speed a query. SQL used a balanced tree (or B-tree) structure to store its indexes. SQL Server enables several indexes to be created for a single table, and each index may be multitiered (for example, first sorted by field LastName and then sorted by field FirstName).

Your Table Builder application will create two indexes from within Visual Basic to demonstrate their use. SQL Server automatically uses an index when it speeds a query. Therefore, common sorting patterns should be created as indexes. However, avoid creating too many indexes or the database will show performance penalties. Each time a record is INSERTed or UPDATEd, each index must be updated as well.

Transact-SQL, Stored Procedures, and Triggers

SQL Server enables code to be stored on the server. This code is written in Transact SQL and is stored in precompiled form in the server's data dictionary. Transact SQL is a common language across Microsoft SQL Server and Sybase Server databases. These commands do not work with other systems, such as an Oracle Server.

Recall that a trigger is a stored procedure that is automatically executed when particular conditions are met. The conditions are checked every time an INSERT, UPDATE, or DELETE command is activated.

In the interest of compatibility and portability, both the Query Builder and the Table Builder programs do not use any database-specific commands, stored procedures, or triggers. All the SQL statements sent to the engine are JET/ODBC command-compliant so that they may be run against any compatible server.

Laying the Foundation for the Table Builder

Table Builder serves three functions: it can create the QueryTable for later access by Query Builder, it can insert the data into QueryTable, and it can create indexes for QueryTable. Before construction on Table Builder begins, however, the device, database, and ODBC structures must be created so Table Builder can access them. A SQL Server system is set up by creating the various levels (see Figure 25.3). You will follow this methodology to create your tables.

Setting Up the Database in SQL Server

In order to create the tables that the Query Builder will search, the various constructs in which you will place the tables need to be created. First, you must create a device into which the sample database will be stored. Within the device, you'll create the database that will store the sample table.

FIGURE 25.3.
Building with SQL Server.

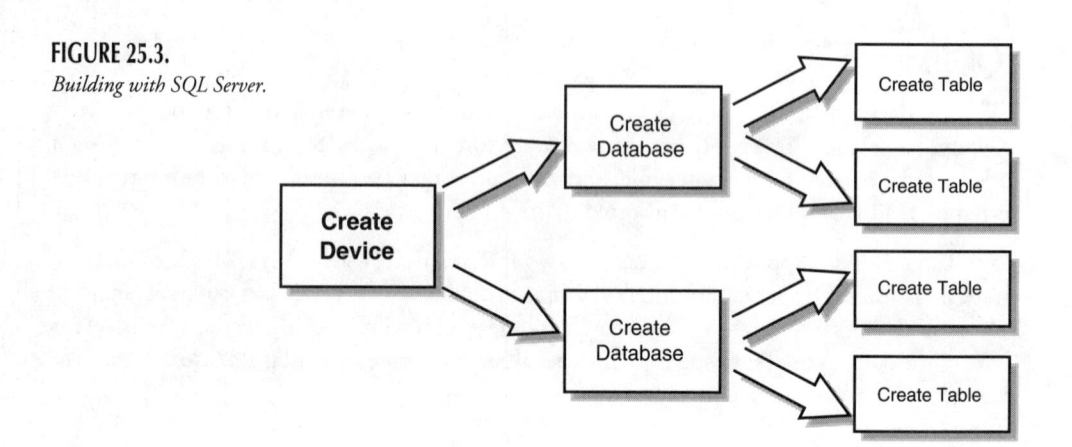

You use SQL Administrator to set up the device and the database. Navigation is easiest by using the large icons at the top of the screen (see Figure 25.4). This program supports nearly all the SQL Server Configuration operations except actual table construction (field definition, table creation, and so on).

FIGURE 25.4.
SQL Administrator icons.

Creating the Device

To create the device, execute the SQL Administrator Win32 application. The first window requests that a user name and password be entered and then a connection be made with SQL Server. After the program accepts your password and login ID, click the Devices button or select Devices from the Manage menu. This displays the Devices window, which contains all the devices currently available to the system. Note that, depending on which window is currently active, the menus that are accessible from the menubar change. This can sometimes become confusing when you are looking for a particular option but the correct window is not active.

Select the Manage menu again and you'll see that the menu has changed. Select the Devices option and then the Create... option, as shown in Figure 25.5. This displays the Create Device window wherein all information about the new device is entered.

FIGURE 25.5.
Creating a new device.

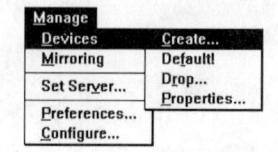

In the Logical Name field, type CSDevice, which is the name of the device where your databases will be stored (see Figure 25.6). When the selection is moved to the next field, the physical name is automatically entered into that box. The physical name includes the default SQL device path and the filename with the extension .DAT.

FIGURE 25.6.
The Create Device window.

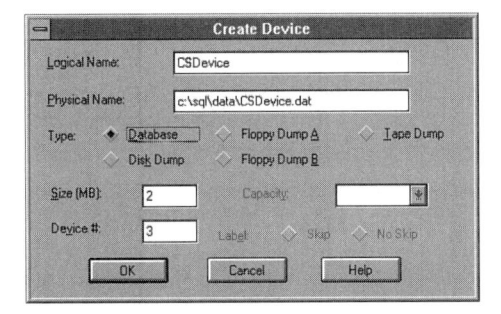

Now click the Database diamond button in the Device type area. This automatically fills in the Size (MB) fields and the Device # field. Note that the default size for the device is 2MB. This is also the minimum size required for a database.

Therefore, if more than one database is required in a device, be sure to allocate enough space. There is no general rule for estimating the required size of the database. Perhaps the best educated guess is to calculate the size of each record for each table and then estimate how many records will typically be stored in each table. This will provide a ballpark figure of how much space is required.

In your example case, the default values are just fine, so click the OK button. The new device now appears in alphabetical order in the Devices window. Once a device has been created, it can be mirrored, deleted (dropped), and specified as the default device in which databases will be created. The SQL Administrator, however, does not allow changes in its basic characteristics.

Creating the Database

Now that a device to store your database has been created, you must create the database structure. Click the icon labeled DB to show the Database Management window. Here, you can see the master database, which holds the system tables.

To create a new table, select the Manage menu (which once again changed because you had the Device window active), and select Database and then Create Database (see Figure 25.7). This displays the Create Database window.

FIGURE 25.7.
Creating a database.

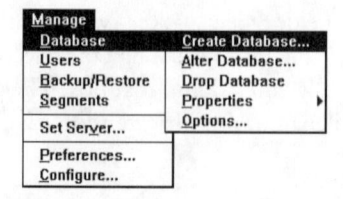

Enter CS_DB in the Database Name field (see Figure 25.8). The Data Device field defaults to the most recently created device, so the device you just created appears in this field. The Data Size defaults to 2MB, which is fine for your project.

FIGURE 25.8.
Entering CS_DB.

Note the Log Device field. This field enables the SQL Server to store the transaction log on another device (see the description of the transaction log). The selected default, (none), makes the log share the same space with the database. You may put the log in a separate device for the reasons stated previously. If so, it is recommended that you make the Log Size about 10 to 25 percent or more of the size of the database to which it is attached.

Click the OK button, and the SQL Administrator should display a message window saying the CREATE DATABASE command was successful and 1024 pages were allocated on the specified device. Clicking the OK button dismisses the message window and returns you to the Database Management window. Here, in alphabetical order, you will see the listing of the database just created.

Note that the 2MB that was specified for the database is merely reserved on the hard disk and not automatically used. In the Database Management window, the SpaceAvail column tells how much of this allocated space remains. In the case of a newly created database, almost all the space remains free. As tables and records are added to the database, the space available shrinks.

You're now finished with the SQL Administrator program. The database has been created on the database server. Use the File menu to exit and return to the Program Manager.

Two Ways to Create the Table

There are two ways to create the structure of your sample table: by using the SQL Object Manager program and by using direct SQL instructions. This chapter demonstrates both ways because each is required in different situations. Most often, the SQL Object Manager is used because of the easy graphical user interface, which makes modification simple, and because of the convenience of not having to do any coding.

However, creating the table in SQL enables the process to be automated (in case many tables must be created) and also produces fairly general SQL code, which may be used to create the same tables on other diverse systems, such as Oracle. A Create Table button is included in the Table Builder program. Use this button if you don't want to create the table with the SQL Object Manager.

Double-click the SQL Object Manager. After you enter your password and user name and connect to the server, you must select a database in which the new table will be created. Click the Current Database pop-down menu and select the CS_DB database you just created (see Figure 25.9).

FIGURE 25.9.
Selecting the CS_DB database.

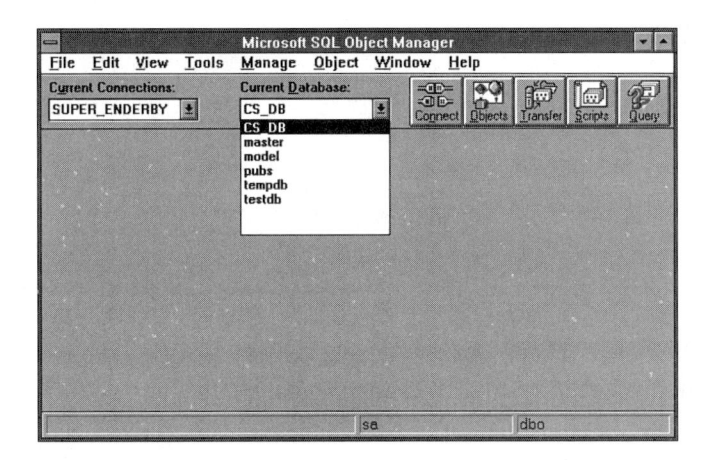

Now, click the Manage menu and select the Tables... option. The Manage Tables window will appear. The table should show the <New Table> heading for the selected table. This means that any new table information entered will be saved as a new table. If you already had the Current Database window open when you selected the Tables... menu option, you might have had to select the Tables pop-down menu and move the selection upward to reach the <New Table> designation (see Figure 25.10).

You will now create the QueryTable table that will be accessed by both the Table Builder and the Query Builder. Enter the field names and data types shown in Figure 25.11. As soon as the first field has been entered, the Alter button that is shown in Figure 25.11 will be labeled Create.

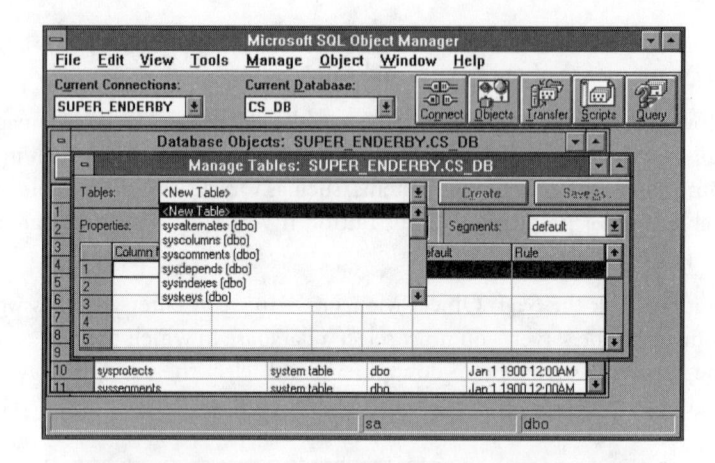

FIGURE 25.10.
Selecting <New Table>.

FIGURE 25.11.
The QueryTable structure.

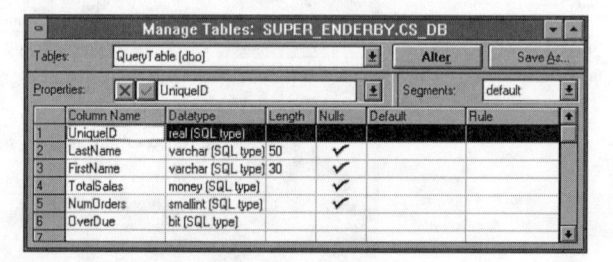

> **WARNING**
>
> Field names (column names) are case-sensitive. Make sure that they are entered exactly as shown. If any modifications are made, make sure that those same modifications are made to the query code in the Table Builder and the Query Builder.

When you have entered all the fields, click the Create button. The program will prompt you for the new table name. Enter `QueryTable` and click the OK button.

You're all done! You've now created a device that holds a database that holds a table. The device name is CSDevice. The database name is CS_DB. The table name is QueryTable. You will use all of these later.

Creating the ODBC Connection

Now that you've created a database to connect with, you must create the ODBC Connection so that the Table Builder program can access the necessary tables. To create a connection to the SQL Server, you will construct an ODBC data source. First, execute the ODBC

Administrator application by using the ODBC Administrator icon (see Figure 25.12). If you can't find such an icon, don't worry—the ODBC Administrator is probably somewhere on your hard disk.

FIGURE 25.12.
The ODBC Administrator icon.

Many of the various installers (such as Access, Visual Basic, and SQL Server) place the ODBC Administrator application in different directories. Therefore, use the Find File command in the Explorer to locate the program. Search for ODBCADM.EXE, starting from the C:\ directory. If the program is not on your hard disk, reinstall the ODBC drivers through one of the programs listed previously or download it from one of the Microsoft online sources listed in Appendix C, "Sources."

Now execute the ODBC Administrator so that you can create a data source. The ODBC application should execute and show a dialog box that displays all the current data sources available (see Figure 25.13). Note that when a new data source is created, information about the source is stored in the ODBC .INI file, so it is thereafter always available for access until it is specifically removed.

FIGURE 25.13.
ODBC data sources.

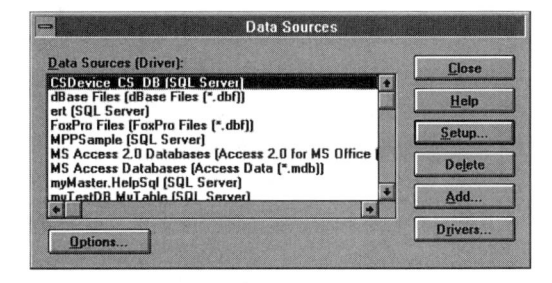

You're going to create a new data source to access the SQL Server. Select the Add... button in the ODBC window. This shows a list of ODBC drivers available for data sources. Select SQL Server and click the OK button (see Figure 25.14).

FIGURE 25.14.
The Add Data Source window.

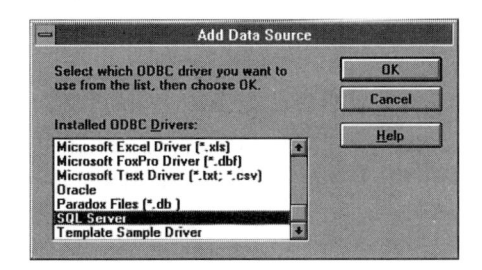

> **NOTE**
>
> If the SQL Server driver does not appear in the list, it probably wasn't installed when Visual Basic was originally set up. To install either the SQL Server or the Oracle ODBC drivers included with Visual Basic, the VB Setup application must be run.
>
> Execute the VB Setup application and select the drivers that are missing from the system. Note that you will have to use your Visual Basic install disks or CD-ROM from which the application will read the drivers.

The ODBC Administrator presents a window that enables entry of all information necessary for the data source connection (see Figure 25.15). Click the Options >> button to see all the parameters that might be entered for the connection. Most of the blank entry fields will be left to their defaults. A client/server designer may find it necessary to use them all for one project or another.

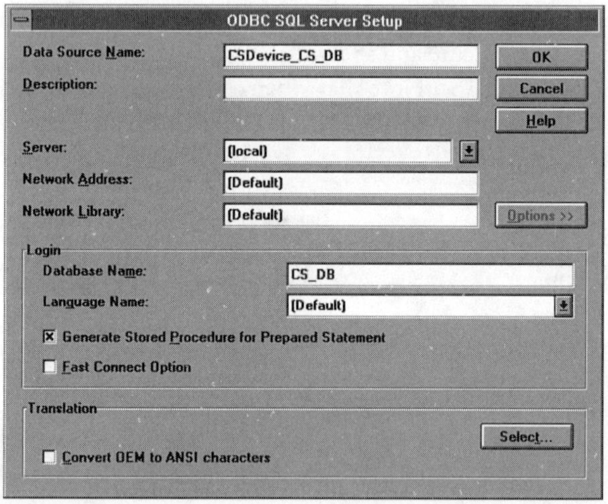

FIGURE 25.15.
Making the SQL Server data source connection.

Data Source Information

The Data Source Name field holds the name a program uses to access the data source. This does not have to be in any particular format, but be sure to name any data source carefully and explicitly. As more data sources are created, simple names such as DataS1 or Test can become confusing or misunderstood.

The Description field is a general text field that can be used to describe the connection more thoroughly. Many times, this field is used to detail what data is available through this data source, such as Sales History, Inventory, Customer List, and so forth.

The Server field describes the name that identifies the given SQL Server on the network. The simplest type of server is (local), which specifies that the SQL Server is running on a Windows NT network. To find out the specific way to access your server by using such protocols as Banyan Vines, Microsoft LAN Manager, Netware, or TCP/IP networks, see your SQL Server manual or the ODBC online help.

The Network Address and Network Library fields specify the location of the SQL Server program and the drivers needed to communicate with it, respectively. These fields may be left to (Default) in most cases.

The Database Name field specifies the database that the connection will access by default. This field is very useful for creating multiple connections to the same server, but still addressing various databases. For example, two connections might be created—one for the Sales database and another for the Inventory database. The user merely selects one without having to know all the information about the network address and so forth. This shields the user from confusion and provides a simplified interface for the client program.

The Language Name field enables the connection to use any of the standard languages available through SQL Server. This is recorded for individual data objects within the System Tables.

The Generate Stored Procedures for Prepared Statements field, when active (the default), compiles the stored procedures sent to it. Otherwise, the definition of the procedure remains uncompiled until it is called at execution time.

The Fast Connect Option field delays acquiring information and setting up structures as soon as the connection is opened. This enables quick connect time; the delayed processing is done later as it needs to be. This option was created to optimize programs that connect and disconnect repeatedly, especially transaction-based applications.

The Select button in the Translation frame enables you to place a DLL between the application and the data source. The DLL might do particular data filtering, compression, decompression, encryption, decryptions, or translation between various character set types. This function can also be used to provide a go-between to capture data meant for a custom program. For example, a connection can send a piece of data to the server that is meant for use only by a custom DLL. This DLL can examine all data being sent through this connection and use the custom packets meant for itself.

Creating a Data Source for the Query Builder

Now let's create the data source that will be used by both the Table Builder and Query Builder programs. Refer to Figure 25.15 for an example of the information that you will enter in the data source for this connection.

First, select the Data Source Name field and enter CSDevice_CS_DB. This title adequately describes the database that the connection will access. Remember, descriptive data source names are worth the time and trouble.

Press the Tab key to move to the next field or select the Description field and enter a brief description of the connection. This is a type of comment field so that the designer knows the type of connection.

In the Server field, click the pop-down menu arrow and select the (local) option. This uses the local SQL Server. If you're using the server from a remote location, specify the path to reach the server.

Move to the Database Name field and type `CS_DB`. This makes the connection access the database you created earlier as the default database. That means that once the connection is made, the path is automatically set to access any tables in the default database.

After all this information has been entered, click the OK button to create the data source. The screen should again show the window with all the listed data sources, but this time, you should find the connection you just created in alphabetical order. Now the connection can be easily accessed from within Visual Basic.

Creating the Table Builder Program

Next you will build the Table Builder program. When complete, it should look like the form shown in Figure 25.16. From top to bottom, the form contains the following: a Create Table command button, an Insert Records command button, a Build Indexes command button, a Picture Box (used for the text status), and a Gauge control (used for the status bar). Constructing this form is as simple as it looks.

FIGURE 25.16.
The Table Builder window.

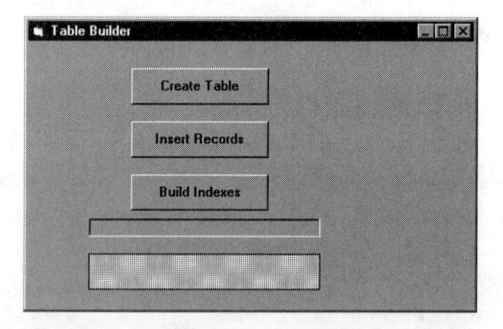

Execute Visual Basic and let it create a new project. Change the size of the form so that it roughly matches the one shown in the figure. Change the caption of the form to `Table Builder`.

Then draw the three buttons on the form and change their `Caption` properties to match those shown in the figure. Set the first button's `Name` property to `cmd_CreateTable`. Set the second `Name` property to `cmd_Insert`. Set the third to `cmd_Index`.

> **TIP**
>
> Remember to set the Name properties of the controls before you begin adding code, or it will become quite a hassle later.

Use the Picture Box control on the control palette (the icon with the cactus and the sun) to draw the box below the third button. Change the Name property to read pct_Status. Change the FontTransparent property from True to False. This enables new text printed in the box to write over older text so that the control does not have to be completely cleared.

Finally, use the Gauge control to draw the final box below the picture box. Change the BackColor property to a light shade so that the status is visible as the bar moves across the control. The BackColor property is light gray in this example, but feel free to use any color that is easily visible. Leave the Name property to read Gauge1.

You now have the basic form set up as it should be. This Table Builder user interface doesn't have to be slick or attractive, because this type of application is seen only by the designer.

> **TIP**
>
> Keep programs that the user doesn't have to use as simple as possible. It is a great temptation to add features that no one will ever use or spend excessive time making a form look good that will be used by only one person. Try to maximize the functionality.

General Declarations

Now that the form has been created, you can begin adding the code that makes it work. Double-click the form so that the code window is shown. Enter the following code in the General Declarations section:

```
Dim MyDB As Database
Dim SQLStmt As String

Const err_ODBCItemConnect = 3151

Const FT_TRUEFALSE = 1
Const FT_TRUEFALSE_Size = 1
Const FT_BYTE = 2
Const FT_BYTE_Size = 1
Const FT_INTEGER = 3
Const FT_INTEGER_Size = 2
Const FT_LONG = 4
Const FT_LONG_Size = 4
Const FT_CURRENCY = 5
Const FT_CURRENCY_Size = 8
```

```
Const FT_SINGLE = 6
Const FT_SINGLE_Size = 4
Const FT_DOUBLE = 7
Const FT_DOUBLE_Size = 8
Const FT_DATETIME = 8
Const FT_DATETIME_Size = 8
Const FT_STRING = 10
Const FT_STRING_Size = 10
Const FT_BINARY = 11
Const FT_BINARY_Size = 0
Const FT_MEMO = 12
Const FT_MEMO_Size = 0
```

You may use the pop-down menus to access General Declarations, but there is a quicker way. After you double-click the form and the code window is shown, notice the double line just below the pop-down menus. This enables you to split the code window. If you pull it down slightly, the General Declarations section is automatically shown and you can enter code there (see Figure 25.17).

FIGURE 25.17.
The General Declarations section.

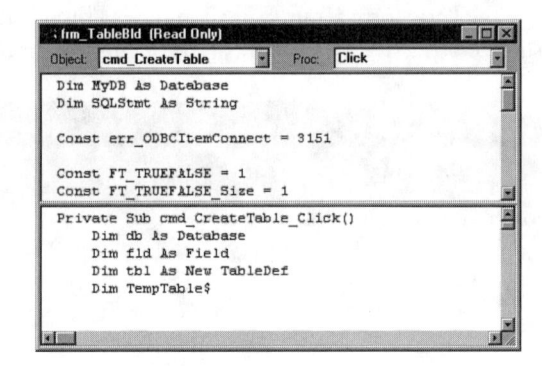

Notice that there are constants for all the field types and sizes. If you want to add fields to the QueryTable constructed by the Table Builder, simply use any of these constants. Once you entered the previous text in the General Declarations area, you can put the code in the various buttons.

The Create Table Button

Close the code window and double-click the Create Table command button. Now you're ready to enter the following code. You may skip the comment lines (denoted beginning with a single quote (') character), but it's not recommended. This program may become the basis for a program that you design in the future. Putting the comments in at the beginning is an excellent way to encourage continuing code documenting. Enter this code:

```
Private Sub cmd_CreateTable_Click()
    Dim db As Database
    Dim fld As Field
    Dim tbl As New TableDef
    Dim TempTable$
```

```
Pct_Status.Cls
Pct_Status.Print "Opening Database..."

' Setup error checking routine
On Error GoTo ErrorCheck_create

' Attempt to open the connection to the Database
Set MyDB = OpenDatabase("CSDevice_CS_DB", False, False, "ODBC; DSN=MyServer;
➥UID=sa")

' Make name of TableDefs match what the table
'    will be called by the SQL Server
tbl.Name = "QueryTable"

Pct_Status.Cls
Pct_Status.Print "Checking if table exists..."

' Check to make sure Table doesn't already exist
' It will be stored as dbo.Database, so add the dbo
TempTable$ = UCase("dbo." & tbl.Name)
For i = 0 To MyDB.TableDefs.Count - 1
    If UCase(MyDB.TableDefs(i).Name) = TempTable$ Then
       If MsgBox(tbl.Name & " already exists, delete it?", 4) = 6 Then ' 6 =
       ➥Yes Button
          MyDB.TableDefs.Delete tbl.Name
       Else
          Pct_Status.Cls
          Pct_Status.Print "Table creation aborted."
          Exit Sub
       End If
       Exit For
    End If
Next

Pct_Status.Cls
Pct_Status.Print "Creating Table..."

' Create the 5 fields: UniqueID,
Set fld = New Field
fld.Name = "UniqueID"
fld.Type = FT_SINGLE
fld.Size = FT_SINGLE_Size
' Add field to collection.
tbl.Fields.Append fld
Set fld = New Field
fld.Name = "LastName"
fld.Type = FT_STRING
fld.Size = 50
tbl.Fields.Append fld
Set fld = New Field
fld.Name = "FirstName"
fld.Type = FT_STRING
fld.Size = 30
tbl.Fields.Append fld
Set fld = New Field
fld.Name = "TotalSales"
fld.Type = FT_CURRENCY
fld.Size = FT_CURRENCY_Size
```

```
            tbl.Fields.Append fld
            Set fld = New Field
            fld.Name = "NumOrders"
            fld.Type = FT_INTEGER
            fld.Size = FT_INTEGER_Size
            tbl.Fields.Append fld
            Set fld = New Field
            fld.Name = "OverDue"
            fld.Type = FT_TRUEFALSE
            fld.Size = FT_TRUEFALSE_Size
            tbl.Fields.Append fld

            ' Append new table to the ODBC connected Database
            MyDB.TableDefs.Append tbl

            Pct_Status.Cls
            Pct_Status.Print "Finished."
            Exit Sub

ErrorCheck_create:
        If Err = err_ODBCItemConnect Then
            Set MyDB = OpenDatabase("", False, False, "ODBC; DSN=; UID=sa")
            Resume Next
        End If
        Msg = "Error# " & Err & ":" & Error(Err)
        MsgBox Msg       ' Display message.
        Exit Sub
End Sub
```

The program uses the TableDefs collection to add the table. A collection is an array of objects, in this case TableDef objects. The SQL command CREATE DATABASE is not supported through the Visual Basic engine. Instead, the accepted way of creating a table is by appending a table to the TableDefs. Visual Basic may also create a table by using the SQL command INSERT INTO, but this must build a table based on an existing table.

The Insert Records Button

Double-click the Insert Records command button and enter the following code:

```
Private Sub cmd_Insert_Click()
    ' Setup # of records to insert
    Const NumRecords = 1000

    On Error GoTo ErrorCheck

    ' Attempt to open the connection to the Database
    Set MyDB = OpenDatabase("CSDevice_CS_DB", False, False, "ODBC; DSN=MyServer;
➥UID=sa")

    ' Initialize progress bar to 0
    Gauge1.Value = 0
    Pct_Status.Cls
    Pct_Status.Print "Inserting Records..."

    ' Main insert loop
    ' Using Transactions greatly speeds the process
```

```
        BeginTrans
        For i = 0 To NumRecords
            ' Using Rnd formula: (upperbound - lowerbound + 1) * Rnd + lowerbound
            TempTotalSales = (12000 - 0 + 1) * Rnd + 0
            TempNumOrders = Int((300 - 0 + 1) * Rnd + 0)
            TempOverdue = Int((1 - 0 + 1) * Rnd + 0)

            ' Build SQL statement for insertion
            SQLStmt = "Insert Into QueryTable"
            ' Field list and order for values to be inserted
            SQLStmt = SQLStmt & " (UniqueID,LastName, FirstName,TotalSales,NumOrders,
            ↪OverDue)"
            ' Values: LastName and FirstName
            SQLStmt = SQLStmt & " values (" & Rnd & ",'LastName#" & i & "',
            ↪'FirstName#" & i & "',"
            ' Values: TotalSales and NumOrders
            SQLStmt = SQLStmt & TempTotalSales & "," & TempNumOrders & ","
            ' Values: OverDue flag
            SQLStmt = SQLStmt & TempOverdue & ")"

            ' Sample finished SQLStmt:
            '   INSERT INTO CSDevice_CS_DB (UniqueID,LastName, FirstName,
            '     TotalSales,NumOrders,OverDue) values (.2895625,'LastName#0',
            '     'FirstName#0',8467.275,160,1)

            ' Execute SQLStmt
            MyDB.Execute SQLStmt, dbSQLPassThrough

            ' Update Status to show progress
            Gauge1.Value = (i / NumRecords) * 100
        Next i
        CommitTrans

        Pct_Status.Cls
        Pct_Status.Print "Insertion Complete."
        Exit Sub

ErrorCheck:
        If Err = err_ODBCItemConnect Then
            Set MyDB = OpenDatabase("", False, False, "ODBC; DSN=; UID=sa")
            Resume Next
        End If
        Msg = "Error# " & Err & ":" & Error(Err)
        MsgBox Msg    ' Display message.
        Exit Sub
End Sub
```

The Insert Records button inserts a number of randomized data entries into the QueryTable. The number of records is determined by the constant NumRecords.

Notice that the PRINT command was used to display the status of the query instead of changing the Caption property of a Text Box control to the status text. Changing the Caption property doesn't cause an update immediately; instead, the update waits for a break in the event loop. The update doesn't occur until the entire loop has finished or it requires a DoEvents command to be called for every update (which has extreme performance penalties). In contrast, a PRINT command is immediately drawn to the screen. This keeps the user of the program informed as the insertion takes place.

The Create Indexes Button

Double-click the Create Indexes command button and enter the following code:

```
Private Sub cmd_Index_Click()
    Dim ind As Index

    ' Setup error checking routine
    On Error GoTo ErrorCheck_index

    Pct_Status.Cls
    Pct_Status.Print "Opening Database..."

    ' Attempt to open the connection to the Database
    Set MyDB = OpenDatabase("CSDevice_CS_DB", False, False, "ODBC; DSN=MyServer;
    ➥UID=sa")

    Pct_Status.Cls
    Pct_Status.Print "Creating UniqueIndex..."

    ' Creating 1st index: UniqueIndex
    Set ind = New Index
    ind.Name = "UniqueIndex"
    ' Set field that index will be created using
    ind.Fields = "UniqueID"
    ' Each UniqueID file will be different so set flag
    ind.Unique = True

    ' Search to ensure index name is not already in use
    For i = 0 To MyDB.TableDefs("QueryTable").Indexes.Count - 1
        If UCase(MyDB.TableDefs("QueryTable").Indexes(i).Name) = UCase(ind.Name)
        ➥Then
            If MsgBox(ind.Name & " already exists, delete it?", 4) = 6 Then ' 6 =
            ➥Yes Button
                MyDB.TableDefs("QueryTable").Indexes.Delete MyDB.TableDefs
                ➥("CSDevice_CS_DB").Indexes(i)
            Else
                Pct_Status.Cls
                Pct_Status.Print "UniqueIndex creation aborted."
                Exit Sub
            End If
            Exit For
        End If
    Next

    ' Append UniqueIndex to TableDefs
    MyDB.TableDefs("QueryTable").Indexes.Append ind

    Pct_Status.Cls
    Pct_Status.Print "Creating TotalSalesIndex..."

    ' Creating 2nd index: TotalSalesIndex
    Set ind = New Index
    ind.Name = "TotalSalesIndex"
    ind.Fields = "TotalSales"
    ' There may be duplicate totals, so flag is set to false
    ind.Unique = False
```

```
    ' Search to ensure index name is not already in use
    For i = 0 To MyDB.TableDefs("QueryTable").Indexes.Count - 1
        If UCase(MyDB.TableDefs("QueryTable").Indexes(i).Name) = UCase(ind.Name)
        ➥Then
            If MsgBox(ind.Name & " already exists, delete it?", 4) = 6 Then  ' 6 =
            ➥Yes Button
                MyDB.TableDefs("QueryTable").Indexes.Delete MyDB.TableDefs
                ➥("CSDevice_CS_DB").Indexes(i)
            Else
                Pct_Status.Cls
                Pct_Status.Print "TotalSales creation aborted."
                Exit Sub
            End If
            Exit For
        End If
    Next

    ' Append TotalSalesIndex to TableDefs
    MyDB.TableDefs("QueryTable").Indexes.Append ind

    Pct_Status.Cls
    Pct_Status.Print "Finished."
    Exit Sub

ErrorCheck_index:
    If Err = err_ODBCItemConnect Then
        Set MyDB = OpenDatabase("", False, False, "ODBC; DSN=; UID=sa")
        Resume Next
    End If
    Msg = "Error# " & Err & ":" & Error(Err)
    MsgBox Msg   ' Display message.
    Exit Sub
End Sub
```

This code connects to the SQL Server and adds two indexes to the QueryTable. The first index sorts the records by the UniqueID field and is labeled UniqueIndex. The second index sorts by the TotalSales field and is labeled TotalSalesIndex.

> **NOTE**
>
> The index names, like the field names in SQL Server, are case-sensitive. Be sure to enter them as they are printed in the next example.

The indexes are created by appending to the Indexes Collection, using the same type of operation with which a table is created. These indexes are single-tiered or simple indexes (based on a single field). To create a multi-tiered index, use a comma between the fields (for example, ind.Fields = "LastName,FirstName").

Executing the Program

Now that you've finished entering the code, save the project and form. You can name the project TABLEBLD.VBP and the form TABLEBLD.FRM. Always save before first running any new project. If the machine crashes for any unforeseen reason, all the previous work will be gone.

After saving it, execute the program. Click the Create Table button to make the connection by using the ODBC data source you created previously. Once the connection is made, the table automatically is created. If you've already created the table using the SQL Object Manager, there is no need to click this button. If you do, the program checks whether the table already exists. If the program finds a table with the same name, it prompts you on whether you'd like to delete it. Choosing to delete it eliminates the old table and begins creating the new one.

The Insert Records button attempts the same connection and then inserts 1,000 records into the table. The status bar shows the progress of the record insertion and notifies you when it is complete.

Finally, the Create Indexes button creates two indexes for the table. It also checks whether the indexes already exist and presents the option of deleting them.

Checking the Table

You can check that the data has been created properly by executing the iSQL/w Program. This program enables you to execute SQL commands and view resultant sets. Execute the program and select the Change Database... option under the Query menu. Change the selected database to the CS_DB database.

In the query window, enter this text:

```
Select * from QueryTable
```

Clicking the Execute button executes the query and shows a window with all the records contained in the table (see Figure 25.18). The program can be used to test various queries to ensure that they work properly before embedding them within a Visual Basic program.

To examine the indexes for the table, execute the SQL Object Manager program. Change the selected database to CS_DB. Now choose Indexes... under the Manage menu. A window describing the various indexes for QueryTable will appear (see Figure 25.19). In the figure, the two indexes for QueryTable are TotalSalesIndex and UniqueIndex. Notice the number 1 is present in the field that was selected for the index (for example, UniqueIndex has a 1 in the UniqueID field). If the index was multi-tiered, a 2 would appear in the second field that was indexed, and so on.

FIGURE 25.18.
Records using iSQL/w.

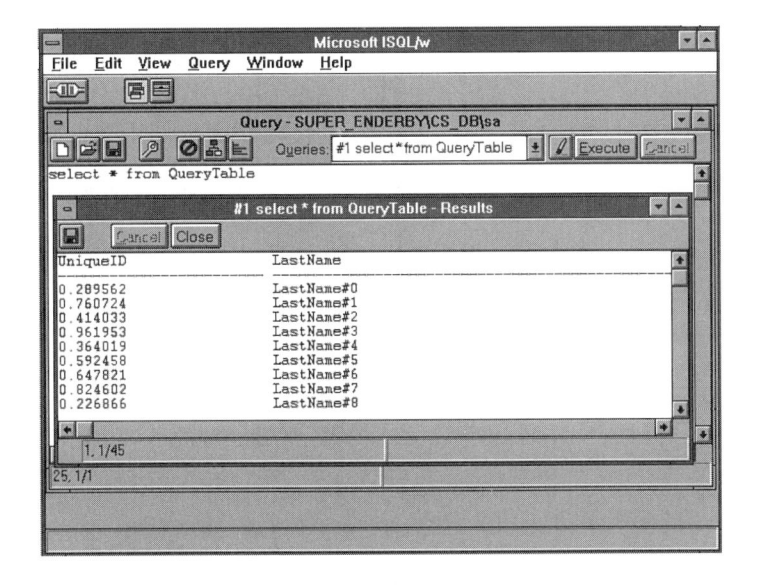

FIGURE 25.19.
Indexes for QueryTable.

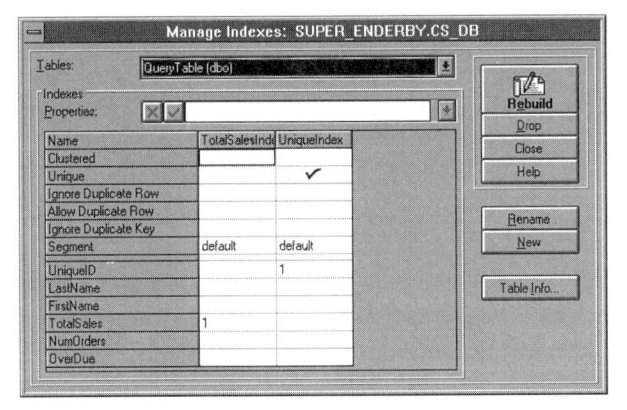

It is always a good idea to check the table creation by using these two programs. Sometimes data errors can be fairly subtle or unnoticeable, especially when you are in the process of developing a complex client/server system.

Creating the Query Builder

Now that the device, database, table, and data source connections have been created, you can construct the Query Builder (see Figure 25.20). The Query Builder enables the user to enter a number for the minimum sales to be shown, determine whether to show only the overdue accounts or all of them, and decide whether to order the display by the total sales volume. The Query Builder demonstrates how a simple screen with only three options can generate a myriad of resultant sets.

FIGURE 25.20.
The Query Builder window.

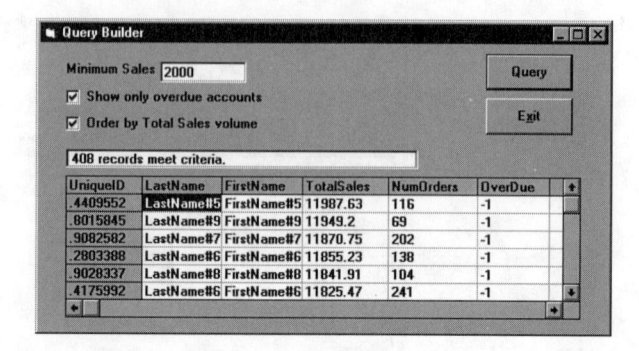

In the figure, the Minimum Sales figure shows how to build a SQL WHERE statement for querying. Additional comparison, such as a maximum sales level, can be added by tacking on additional AND statements.

The Show only overdue accounts option demonstrates the use of a check box to check a flag field. Additional enhancements can show how many days overdue the account is or whether the overdue amount is negligible.

The Order by Total Sales volume option orders the values returned by the query so that the highest total sales appears as the first record and decreases with each additional record. This uses the SQL command ORDER BY to sort the data automatically.

When the Query command button is pressed, the Query Builder checks the setting of these options and builds a SQL statement that will be sent to the SQL Server. The resultant set is returned in a Dynaset, which the Query Builder takes a record at a time and inserts into the grid control.

Note that the SQLPassThrough statement is used to send the query directly to the SQL Server. The queries are constructed to work through the JET engine as well and are sent through the SQLPassThrough for demonstration purposes and speed. To see the speed difference of sending the SQL statement through the JET engine, eliminate the SQLPassThrough option or set the SQLPassThrough constant to 0.

Form Construction

Start a new project by selecting New Project... under the File menu. This displays a blank Form1 and creates a new project. Change the Caption property on Form1 to Query Builder. Increase the size of the form until it roughly matches that shown in Figure 25.21.

Now you will construct the form as shown in the figure. The form is made up of eight controls: Label, Text Box, two Check Box, Picture Box, Grid, and two Command Button.

FIGURE 25.21.
The Query Builder form.

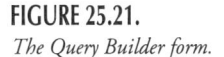

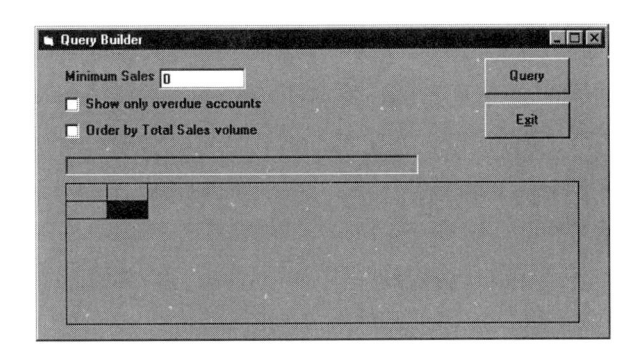

First, draw the Label control on the form and change the Caption property to Minimum Sales. Position it in the upper-left corner of the form. Next to it, create the Text Box control so that it is wide enough for five to six digits. Change the Text property to read 0, which is the default value for this field. The Query Builder automatically checks to make sure there is a number contained in the field before the query is constructed. Set the Name property to txt_MinSale.

Next, create the two Check Boxes controls as shown in Figure 25.21. Set the Name property of the top Check Box control to chk_Overdue. Set the Name property of the bottom one to chk_OrderBy.

Use the Picture Box control on the control palette (the icon with the cactus and the sun) to draw the box below the second Check Box control. Change the Name property to read pct_Status. Change the FontTransparent property from True to False. This enables new text printed in the box to write over older text so that the control does not have to be completely cleared.

Now draw a Grid control in the bottom of the form. Make the grid fairly wide, because it will display all the fields and fields data (columns and column data) that the query resultant set returns. You will use all the default values of the grid and change the ones you need to change programmatically.

Finally, create the two Button controls in the upper-right corner of the form. The top one should have a Caption property of Query and a Name property of cmd_Query. For the bottom Button control, set the Caption to E&xit (the & makes this button accessible with the Alt key), and set the Name property to cmd_Exit. Double-click the Exit button and enter one line of code:

```
Private Sub cmd_Exit_Click()
    End
End Sub
```

Now that the form layout has been created, the code for the individual parts may be entered. Note that because this is a single form application, no module creation was necessary. If this program is later modified to use multiple forms, move the Declarations in a module and label it GLOBAL so that each form may access the identical Data objects.

General Declarations

Insert the following code into the General Declarations portion of the form:

```
Dim MyDB As Database
Dim MyDS As Recordset
Dim SQLStmt As String
Dim i As Integer, j As Integer
Const err_ODBCItemConnect = 3151
```

The Database and Dynaset objects are used to access the database for the query. The variables i and j are used by the query loops as counters.

Building the Query

Double-click the Query button and enter the following code:

```
Private Sub cmd_Query_Click()
    Dim numfields As Integer
    Dim fieldTitle As String

    ' Make sure user input is a number
    If Not IsNumeric(txt_MinSale.Text) Then
        MsgBox "There must be a number in the Minimum Sales box for the Query to
        ➥continue.", 16, "Error in Minimum Sales"
        Exit Sub
    End If

    ' Setup Error Checking Routine
    On Error GoTo ErrorCheck

    ' Open connection to SQL Server Database
    Set MyDB = OpenDatabase("CSDevice_CS_DB", False, False, "ODBC; DSN=MyServer;
    ➥UID=sa")

    ' Print status for user to see
    pct_Status.Cls
    pct_Status.Print "Running Query..."

    ' Begin building query, selecting data from DummySource table
    SQLStmt = "Select * from QueryTable"
    ' Setup WHERE so that only records > Min. Sales input
    '    will be included in resultant set
    SQLStmt = SQLStmt & " WHERE TotalSales > " & txt_MinSale
    ' If Overdue is checked, add to WHERE statement
    If chk_OverDue Then
        SQLStmt = SQLStmt & " and OverDue = 1"
    End If
    ' If Order by TotalSales is checked, add to WHERE statement
    If chk_OrderBy Then
        ' Notice ORDER BY is made with the keyword DESC,
        '    which means Descending sort order. This will make
        '    the highest TotalSales show at the top of the Grid
        SQLStmt = SQLStmt & " ORDER BY TotalSales DESC"
    End If
```

```
    ' Create the Recordset with the SQLStmt that was built
    '    and the SQLPassThrough option for speed
    Set MyDS = MyDB.OpenRecordset(SQLStmt, dbOpenDynaset, dbSQLPassThrough)

    ' Clear the Status line
    pct_Status.Cls
    ' Find the number of fields for this table
    numfields = MyDS.Fields.Count
    ' Give grid enough columns to store all fields
    Grid1.Cols = numfields + 1

    ' For..Next loop will place field titles for all columns
    For j = 0 To numfields - 1
        Grid1.Row = 0
        Grid1.Col = j
        fieldTitle = MyDS.Fields(j).Name
        ' Set column heading to field name
        Grid1.Text = fieldTitle
        ' Make the column wide enough so the field name can be read
        Grid1.ColWidth(j) = pct_Status.TextWidth(fieldTitle) * 1.3
    Next j

    ' Reset record counter
    i = 0
    Do Until MyDS.EOF      ' Until end of file.
        ' Display status
        ' CLS is not used here because it would slow execution
        pct_Status.CurrentX = 0
        pct_Status.CurrentY = 0
        pct_Status.Print "Reading record #" & i; "    "

        ' Set number of rows to accomodate all records
        Grid1.Rows = i + 2

        ' Enter all fields for this record in Grid
        For j = 0 To MyDS.Fields.Count - 1
            Grid1.Row = i + 1
            Grid1.Col = j
            ' Enter field value into Grid
            Grid1.Text = MyDS.Fields(j).Value
        Next j

        i = i + 1
        MyDS.MoveNext       ' Move to next record.
    Loop

    ' Display final total of records displayed
    pct_Status.Cls
    pct_Status.Print Str$(i) & " records meet criteria."
    Exit Sub

ErrorCheck:
    If Err = err_ODBCItemConnect Then
        Set MyDB = OpenDatabase("", False, False, "ODBC; DSN=; UID=sa")
        Resume Next
    End If
    Msg = "Error# " & Err & ":" & Error(Err)
    MsgBox Msg     ' Display message.
    Exit Sub
End Sub
```

The Query button first checks to ensure that the number entered into the MinSale field is really a number. Then the query is constructed.

Notice that the query is broken into multiple lines using `SQLStmt = SQLStmt & code`. Even if the query does not require `If...Then` statements to build, you should use this technique to break a long query into multiple lines. This eases debugging, because the lines can be followed a step at a time, and also enables the designer to document each statement with a comment line.

When using this technique, be sure to include a separating space in the string before statements begin again (for example, `" where"`). This ensures that two commands won't run together and appear as a single command in the final string (for example, `"...QueryTableWhere..."`).

Finally, after the query uses a Dynaset to create a resultant set, this data is copied to the Grid control. This is done in two separate loops. The first loop inserts all the field names along the top row of the grid. As each field name is placed in a column, the column width is sized to accommodate the text width of the field name. Notice that the Picture Box control is used to return the text width. The Grid control lacks the `TextWidth` method, and therefore the Picture Control is used. The text width is then multiplied by 1.3 to give a small amount of extra room for the field name.

The second loop uses the Fields collection to insert all the individual data for the records into the Grid. The routine also updates the status text so that the user can see that work is being done. The number of rows for the grid is also incremented as the loop progresses so that all the records may be shown.

Suggestions for Improvements to Query Builder

Query Builder is a good example of how to begin to construct a Query front-end. If used as a foundation for future projects, there are a few limitations that should be noted.

Because we generated our own random data files, the number of fields was limited without great redundancy. Therefore, the Query Builder screen is fairly simple. In a real Query Builder client program, queries often cross multiple forms. For this reason, we have implemented the Query Builder to use Data Objects rather than the Data Control. The Database, TableDefs, and Dynaset objects can easily be made globally accessible by moving them to a module and using the `GLOBAL` keyword instead of `DIM` to create them.

For speed, instead of making the Data Objects global, you may choose to implement direct ODBC calls. Although the `SQLPassThrough` speed equals the speed of using direct ODBC calls, compatibility may be sacrificed.

You might notice that the rows for the grid are augmented with each added record. This is fairly inefficient. Probably the best routine is to increment the number of rows in the grid by some preset amount appropriate for the data. For example, if your resultant sets will be in the hundreds, the program sets the number of rows to 50. When these 50 are used, you increment the rows another 50. This can be done with a simple If...Then statement and an incremental variable.

The Grid control is not always the best way to display data. It is limited to 4,000 × 4,000 cells, so if the resultant set exceeds 4,000, the Grid control won't handle it without specialized programming. The Grid control does not enable on-screen editing if the program must do more than simple queries. All the data must be inserted into the grid at once, meaning long load times and substantial memory penalties. Some of the commercial Grid controls overcome all these limitations. See Chapter 29, "Third-Party Tools, Utilities, and Controls," for more information.

The error checking routines are rudimentary. They should provide more than simple error catching. However, some error routines are better than none. If you're tempted to skip the routine completely, don't. At least put in these simple routines, which tell the error number and a brief description of what error occurred.

The SQL statement GROUP BY can produce fantastic summary information. If the information in the client/server system that is being constructed lends itself to the technique of grouping, please consider adding this option to the Query screen.

The Query Builder currently is constructed to use only SQL commands native to the JET engine. That enables the Query to be directly portable to any other database type that has an ODBC driver. However, because the SQLPassThrough option is being used, system-specific commands and language functions may be freely included. Just realize that using native commands to your system (SQL Server, Oracle, Informix, and so forth) limits the program's later portability.

Finally, the Table Builder application used a BeginTrans and a CommitTrans to encapsulate all 1,000 insertions into a single transaction. In this case, building a single transaction was speedier and more convenient. In a real client/server system, transactions should probably be broken down into small batches of operations. The CommitTrans was never checked for an error, which it should be to ensure that the data was inserted correctly.

26

Remote Client/Server Access

Sometimes direct connection to a client/server system is not strictly practical. With the growth in power of portable computers and their dramatic reduction in price, having Remote Client programs is an attractive possibility. The freedom to enter and access data from anywhere decreases the cost of data entry, increases data currency for the enterprise information, and is a step toward ushering in the age of the paperless office.

However, having a remote machine also means that any data downloaded into the machine quickly loses its currency. Additionally, any updates to this data remain in the portable until it is reconnected to the system. Although remote systems substantially decrease the data problems of past paper-based systems, they also create problems of their own. The delay of information access (for both the client and the server) can be problematic, especially for a fast moving just-in-time enterprise.

To reduce the negative aspects of remote systems, there are many ways to access a data source remotely. The simplest way is to install a modem on the server and write a custom application to receive data transmissions from a remote modem-enabled machine. In this chapter we construct a Remote Server that does just that, incorporating it into the Pseudo Server application created in Chapter 14, "Pseudo Server." We then construct a Remote Client program to upload and access data on the Remote Server.

Messaging can also be used for data updates. The updated client information or information request can be sent encapsulated in an e-mail message. The server receives the e-mail and parses the data into update information. The server can also send a message back to the client containing the data confirmation or providing the information requested.

Messaging technology is in a tremendous state of flux at the time of this writing. Lotus Notes, a groupware product, can be used to achieve many of the remote access messaging needs required by business today. Lotus is working with AT&T to provide a global Notes Network so dial-in access to a Notes Server would be accessible and inexpensive.

Microsoft Exchange Server, another powerful groupware messaging product, is on the horizon and promises to provide many of the features available in Notes, as well as integration with the entire line of Microsoft products. Within the next year, Microsoft is also releasing Distributed or Network OLE, with an OLE database that can handle other remote data access needs (see Chapter 23, "Object Linking and Embedding (OLE)"). Even the protocol standards for messaging are currently changing, with several competing standards available.

For these reasons we have provided an overview of some of these technologies but have tried to avoid too many specifics. Many of these technologies are announced and in beta test phase but not yet released. This makes solid information difficult to obtain and often unreliable. However, the strategies for each are described so that as the products become available you can understand how they can be used.

Modem (Direct to Server) Connection

A modem connection is perhaps the simplest and most common method of remotely exchanging information between a server located at a central location and a Remote Client in the field. The data can be updated instantly as soon as the call is made from the client to the server. Data is confirmed while the client is online, allowing the client program to erase confirmed entries from its memory or hard disk, freeing limited system resources. The server can also send any news flashes or vital information to the client for immediate review.

Although this solution is simple and very powerful for information exchange, it has several disadvantages. The primary problem is one of maintenance. A phone line and modem must be put in for every access line needed for the system. If there are 1,000 remote salespeople, of which 20 need access at once, the logistics and programming for implementation become intimidating. A system (both hardware and software) must be constructed to juggle these numerous lines and connections.

Also, with each access number on a phone line, long-distance fees can become increasingly expensive, because each remote user must call from the remote location for data access. Bad phone lines might require frequent retransmissions, and convenient plug-in modem access to a phone line can be difficult in remote areas.

Despite any disadvantages, this method is most often chosen because of its simplicity and immediacy. An extremely low-cost, high-speed modem can be used for the updates. Almost every computer holds the capability to attach an internal or external modem. Writing a Remote Modem Client is extremely simple and can be created without any sophisticated operating system controls (a client could easily be created in MS-DOS). Because the communication is low speed (mostly 14.4KB and lower) compared with the processing power of even the average portable computer, Visual Basic can easily handle the task. Visual Basic for DOS could even be used to create clients for lower-power computing platforms.

Modem or Serial Port Connection

Using a modem with Visual Basic is an extremely simple task. Thanks to the Communications Custom Control included with Visual Basic 4, implementing a Modem Server is a fairly simple process. The communications control has most of the same features as the original communications control included with VB 3.0 Pro. It also provides a few additional settings and time-out properties.

Traditional access to the serial port (and hence the modem) is accomplished by opening the modem port with the characteristics (baud rate, synchronization, and so on) required to communicate with the modem. The modem is sent commands using the traditional Hayes or AT command set. Table 26.1 contains a list of some of the most common AT commands. There are also numerous extended and hardware-specific commands.

Table 26.1. AT command set summary.

Command	Description
AT	Attention
ATD	Attention dial
ATDT	Attention dial-tone
ATDP	Attention dial-pulse
ATA	Attention manually answer phone
A/	Repeat last command
ATB0	CCITT mode
ATB1	Bell mode (default)
+++	Switch from Data Mode to Command Mode
ATL0	Low speaker volume
ATL1	Low speaker volume
ATL2	Medium speaker volume (default)
ATL3	High speaker volume
ATM0	Internal speaker off
ATM1	Internal speaker on until Carrier Detect (default)
ATM2	Internal speaker always on
ATM3	Internal speaker on until Carrier Detect and off while dialing
ATN0	Connect only at DTE rate
ATN1	Automatic rate negotiation
ATO0	Return to Data Mode
ATO1	Return to Data Mode and initialize an equalizer retrain
ATQ0	Modem sends responses (default)
ATQ1	Modem does not send responses
ATSx	Read and display value in a register x (0 through 30)
ATSx=n	Set register x to value n
ATT	Set dial tone as default
ATV0	Numeric responses
ATV1	Word responses
ATY0	Modem does not send or respond to break signals
ATY1	Modem sends break signals four seconds before disconnecting
ATZ0	Reset and retrieve active configuration profile 0
ATZ1	Reset and retrieve active configuration profile 1

Through this command set, the modem can be configured, dial the phone, pick up the phone and send a carrier signal, and so forth. Although most of the simple commands such as dialing and answering the phone are standard, some of the more advanced commands are specific to particular vendor implementations. This is one of the reasons for the new approach (detailed in the following section) using the TAPI/MAPI interface to access the modem.

Unfortunately, the more advanced systems (using TAPI/MAPI) are just now becoming available and require large amounts of system resources. For now, sending data directly to the modem through the serial port and controlling interactions with the AT command set is the most common method.

Future Direct Connection (TAPI and MAPI)

Microsoft intends to dramatically change the way serial devices are accessed and used. Using a combination of two APIs, the new implementation will allow shared access to the serial ports and device-independent communication (see Figure 26.1).

FIGURE 26.1.
TAPI/MAPI coexistence.

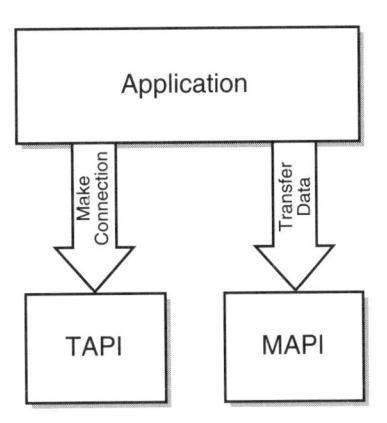

There are many disadvantages to using the serial port and the AT commands described earlier. In the current system arrangement, every computer has its own serial port with a modem hooked up. When a program wants to use the serial port, it must open the serial port connection, giving that program exclusive access to the port. Having a modem for each machine can be very inefficient (especially if the modem or fax/modem is used sporadically), and allowing only one program at a time to access the modem prevents more sophisticated use of it.

The new implementation (TAPI/MAPI) makes control of the serial port a system operation. This allows varying modems with different command sets to be used by simply plugging in a compatible driver. A modem would be accessed by any program in much the same way printers are used by any program—by adding the proper driver to the system.

The OS could then monitor and share the usage of the serial port. For example, a fax program, a BBS program, and a voice mail program could all monitor the serial port for their specific function. If a fax was incoming, the fax program could access the port and receive the fax. If data was coming over the line, the BBS program could be used. With the old implementation, only one of these programs could access and monitor the serial port for the necessary signal.

As an OS resource, the modem could also be shared over the network. Modem access and dialing capabilities could be routed to any user on the network, sharing a modem as printers are currently shared.

To accomplish this task, two different API interfaces are used together. The Telephony Application Program Interface (TAPI) is used to dial and open the line with the modem (see Figure 26.2). It can also handle a number of Telephony-based features, such as voice mail, call forwarding, and conference calling. After the connection is made using TAPI, the MAPI protocol can be used to transfer information content.

FIGURE 26.2.
TAPI access structure.

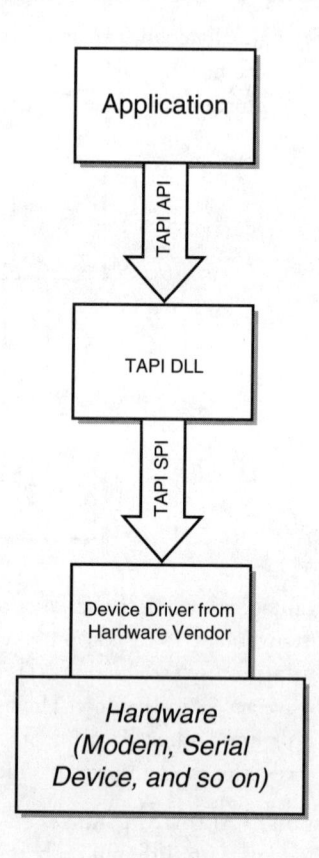

```
        ┌─────────────────┐
        │   Application   │
        └─────────────────┘
                 │ TAPI API
                 ▼
        ┌─────────────────┐
        │    TAPI DLL     │
        └─────────────────┘
                 │ TAPI SPI
                 ▼
        ┌─────────────────┐
        │ Device Driver from│
        │ Hardware Vendor │
        └─────────────────┘
                 │
        ┌─────────────────┐
        │    Hardware     │
        │ (Modem, Serial  │
        │ Device, and so on)│
        └─────────────────┘
```

Messaging Application Program Interface (MAPI) is a standard API to send messages and attached information. Using the connection established with TAPI, one or more messages can be sent to a server.

At the time of this writing, the TAPI/MAPI interface is in the beta stage, and documentation is scarce. The TAPI interface has been integrated into Windows 95, but only the most rudimentary access is provided through VB. OLE Messaging (described later) is also in beta but already shows the great potential power it will bring to client/server computing. For the near future, however, direct serial connections will remain the interface of choice.

Programming the Telephony API (TAPI)

The dialing capabilities of the TAPI interface are built into a DLL included with the Windows 95 system. (For more information, see Chapter 27, "Telephony.") They can be accessed through Visual Basic or VBA. Listing 26.1 shows sample code that demonstrates dialing the phone using TAPI.

Listing 26.1. TAPI sample dialer.

```
Sub cmd_Dial ()
    Dim strNumber As String
    Dim dwReturn As Long

    ' Set up a phone number to dial
    strNumber = "555-1212"

    ' Make sure TAPI DLL is present in the system
    If Not FileExists("C:\Windows\System\TAPI.DLL" Then
        MsgBox "No TAPI DLL could be found"
    Else
        'Attempt to make the call, display an error message
        'if not successful
        dwReturn = tapiRequestMakeCall(strNumber, 0&, 0&, 0&)
        If dwReturn <> 0 Then
        MsgBox "Error Occurred while dialing."
        End If
    End If
End Sub
```

Using the TAPI function `tapiRequestMakeCall`, the phone number set in `strNumber` is dialed. Before the TAPI function is called, the routine checks to see if the TAPI DLL exists on the system. If not, the routine exits.

Add the following code to the General Declaration section of a form. If you want TAPI access from all parts of the project, add these declarations to a module and make the constants global:

```
Declare Function tapiRequestMakeCall& Lib "TAPI.DLL" (ByVal DestAddress$,
➥ByVal AppName$, ByVal CalledParty$, ByVal Comment$)
Const TAPIERR_NoRequestRecipient = -2&
Const TAPIERR_RequestQueueFull = -3&
Const TAPIERR_InvalidDestAddress = -4&
```

The `FileExists` function is used to make sure the TAPI DLL exists before any calls are made to the DLL:

```
Function FileExists (fName As String) as Integer
    On Error Resume Next
    i = Len(Dir$(fName))
    If Err or i = 0 Then
        FileExists = False
    Else
        FileExists = True
    End If
End Function
```

Insert this code into a command button named `cmd_Dial`. The routine sets up a phone number, checks to ensure that the TAPI DLL exists in the WINDOWS/SYSTEM folder, and calls the TAPI routine to dial the number.

The preceding routines use Assisted TAPI. This is a severely limited version of the TAPI interface. Currently, full TAPI access is available only through C. With the inclusion of the TAPI DLL in Windows 95, expect to see integration of TAPI commands into a TAPI OLE Custom Control (OCX), giving full access to the TAPI interface.

Adding Remote Access to the Client/Server System

The client/server system we have constructed and enhanced in past chapters has been created to work over a network. As Remote Access Services (which simulate a direct network connection through a modem) become more common, special modem interfaces and security will become less common. However, by creating a custom modem interface, Remote Clients can even be created using foreign or under-powered computers (such as DOS-based machines or hand-held Personal Digital Assistants (PDAs)). These systems will not have access to full network protocol stacks.

Therefore, in this chapter we add Remote access capabilities to the client/server system. The Remote Client and the Remote Server are meant to be examples. Working telecommunications source code seems to be extremely difficult to obtain.

These programs can provide the basis for your telecommunications system. Note that very little transmission error checking is included, security is basic, and file transfers are not supported. All of these features can be added without tremendous additional work. Also, a basic error checksum routine is included, so retransmission routines can be added.

The programming we describe adds remote data update features to the Pseudo Server application and creates a new client called the Remote Client. These systems work together as the Remote Client calls through a modem to connect to the server modem (see Figure 26.3). Once the connection is established, the Remote Client exchanges information with the Pseudo Server program and then disconnects.

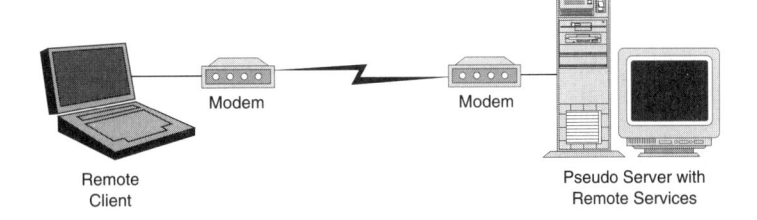

FIGURE 26.3.
Remote Client Access setup.

> **WARNING**
>
> This program makes little attempt to provide system security. As we stated earlier and would like to reiterate, beware of the security problems created by circumventing traditional security the way that this program does. These modifications have been provided as a demonstration, and anything that jeopardizes the security of a client/server system should be thoroughly examined before actual implementation.
>
> We have given the Pseudo Server access and modification privileges to the database. A Remote Client, theoretically, also has access to these privileges. This essentially circumvents most of the in-place security by providing a bridge to the outside world. Be sure to consider the implications of providing this type of remote access and its impacts on system-wide security.

The Remote Client calls in to the server system to upload Sales information and retrieve summary download data (see Figure 26.4). After a connection has been established, the Remote Client sends its identification (username and password). If this is verified, it uploads the necessary Sales information. With each piece of Sales information, a checksum is sent to ensure that data is sent properly.

After the uploaded data is confirmed by the server, the client can request summary Sales information. The server tabulates the necessary data and returns it to the Remote Client. The Remote Client can then hang up the phone and disconnect the port connection.

The Pseudo Server has the capability to answer the phone and supply information to the Remote Client. The Remote Client Access area has been added to the Pseudo Server (see Figure 26.5), which can answer the phone and exchange information. The Pseudo Server Administrator also has the power to disconnect the current Remote Client.

FIGURE 26.4.
The Remote Client process.

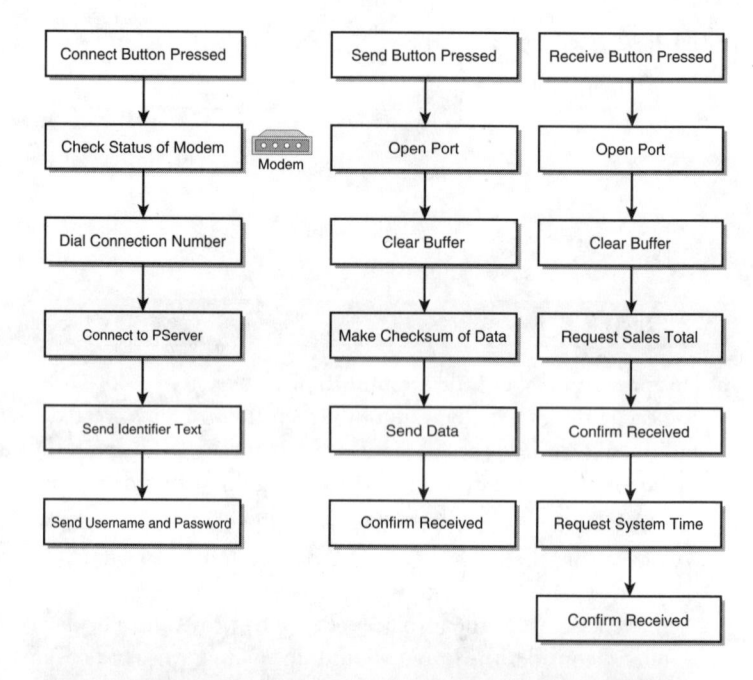

FIGURE 26.5.
Pseudo Server screen area.

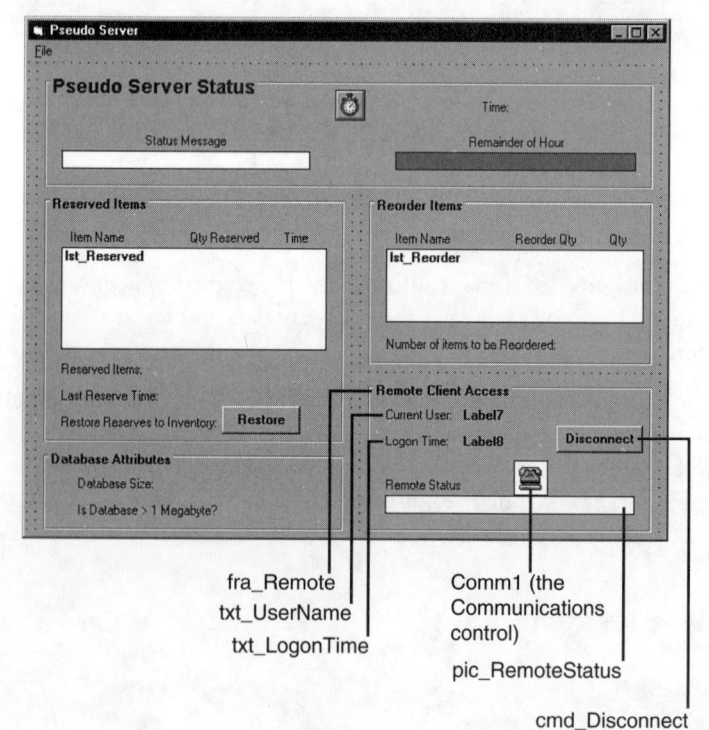

When the phone rings, the Pseudo Server tells the modem to pick up the line. Upon carrier detect, the Pseudo Server checks whether a Remote Client is on the other end (by awaiting a preset text line). After the connection has been established, communication between the two programs occurs. The Pseudo Server can receive Sales information for recording into the main database (WIDGETCO.MDB). It can also send requested Sales summary information.

Both programs expect a Hayes command-compatible modem (ATA, ATDT, and so on) to be attached to COM1. If your modem is attached to COM2, simply change all the access code to address COM2 instead.

Although the Remote Client talks directly to the Pseudo Server, a modem-based client program can essentially talk to any text-based server system. The Remote Client should provide a good sample foundation application for modem access. For example, with the correct sequence of commands, a client could be written to automatically retrieve such information as stock quotes or various news items from other data sources such as CompuServe or Dow Jones Online.

Likewise, the Pseudo Server could be programmed to occasionally retrieve information from various external sources and update the information in the company database. For example, if the Widget Co. relied on the raw material of tin for making finished products, the Pseudo Server might daily call an information source and retrieve the price of tin. Management reports could then track the price of the raw material tin versus the price that the supplier is paid, perhaps indicating that prices are over-inflated and a new supplier should be evaluated.

Additions to Pseudo Server

The Pseudo Server program provides a perfect platform to install the remote server. The Pseudo Server application is already made to be running continuously. It can therefore watch the modem for any incoming calls and provide the necessary data exchange.

Before we construct the Remote Client, we begin by adding the additional functionality required to the Pseudo Server application. In Figure 26.5, we have created a frame in the Remote Client Access area to hold the additional controls.

Begin by adding the Communications control to the control palette by selecting the Custom Controls option under the Tools menu. Now click the check box to the left of the Microsoft Comm Control line to add the control to the palette. Click the OK button. A Telephone icon should now appear in the palette (see Figure 26.5).

Adding the Frame to the Current PServer Form

Select the Frame control from the control palette. Draw and label the frame as shown in Figure 26.5. Add the controls shown and label them according to the figure. There are three labels: a Picture Box, the Comm control, and the Disconnect Command button. The Picture Box control displays the status messages generated as a client dials in.

Adding the Code

Now let's add the needed procedure to allow Remote Access. Constants and three routines need to be added. Add the variables and the constants shown in Listing 26.2 to the General Declarations portion of the PServer form. The constants are used to interpret the meaning of the OnComm event generated by the Comm control.

Listing 26.2. General declarations.

```
Dim Buffer$
Dim ConnectStatus As Integer

Const NotConnected = 1
Const NeedPassword = 2
Const Connected = 3

'Parse Line Column Numbers
Const plChecksum = 1
Const plSalesItem = 2
Const plQty = 3
Const plFinalPrice = 4

Dim ParseArray(5)
'---------------------------------------
'Comm Control
'---------------------------------------
'Handshaking
 Const MSCOMM_HANDSHAKE_NONE = 0
 Const MSCOMM_HANDSHAKE_XONXOFF = 1
 Const MSCOMM_HANDSHAKE_RTS = 2
 Const MSCOMM_HANDSHAKE_RTSXONXOFF = 3

'Event constants
Const MSCOMM_EV_SEND = 1
Const MSCOMM_EV_RECEIVE = 2
Const MSCOMM_EV_CTS = 3
Const MSCOMM_EV_DSR = 4
Const MSCOMM_EV_CD = 5
Const MSCOMM_EV_RING = 6
Const MSCOMM_EV_EOF = 7

'Error code constants
Const MSCOMM_ER_BREAK = 1001
Const MSCOMM_ER_CTSTO = 1002
Const MSCOMM_ER_DSRTO = 1003
Const MSCOMM_ER_FRAME = 1004
Const MSCOMM_ER_OVERRUN = 1006
Const MSCOMM_ER_CDTO = 1007
Const MSCOMM_ER_RXOVER = 1008
Const MSCOMM_ER_RXPARITY = 1009
Const MSCOMM_ER_TXFULL = 1010
```

Sub cmd_Disconnect_Click()

This command button function allows the Pseudo Server to disconnect a user. The modem automatically resets and awaits another caller.

```
Private Sub cmd_Disconnect_Click()
    Comm1.Output = "+++ATH" & Chr$(13)
End Sub
```

Sub Comm1_OnComm()

The `OnComm` event routine for the Comm1 control is the central routine to handle all modem events (see Listing 26.3). When an event occurs, the `OnComm` event is activated. The `CommEvent` property contains the type of event that occurred. Most of these cases do not need to be trapped, but we have included them so you can see the type of events registered with this control.

Listing 26.3. The OnComm event routine.

```
Private Sub Comm1_OnComm()
    Select Case Comm1.CommEvent
    ' Errors
        Case MSCOMM_ER_BREAK     ' A Break was received.
        ' Code to handle a BREAK goes here.
        Case MSCOMM_ER_CDTO  ' CD (RLSD) Timeout.
        Case MSCOMM_ER_CTSTO     ' CTS Timeout.
        Case MSCOMM_ER_DSRTO     ' DSR Timeout.
        Case MSCOMM_ER_FRAME     ' Framing Error
        Case MSCOMM_ER_OVERRUN   ' Data Lost.
            Beep
        Case MSCOMM_ER_RXOVER    ' Receive buffer overflow.
        Case MSCOMM_ER_RXPARITY  ' Parity Error.
        Case MSCOMM_ER_TXFULL    ' Transmit buffer full.
    ' Events
        Case MSCOMM_EV_CD   ' Change in the CD line.
            If Comm1.CDHolding Then
                pic_RemoteStatus.Cls
                pic_RemoteStatus.Print "Carrier Detected..."
                txt_LogonTime = Time$
            Else
                pic_RemoteStatus.Cls
                pic_RemoteStatus.Print "No Carrier."
                txt_LogonTime = "N/A"
                txt_UserName = "None"
                ConnectStatus = NotConnected
            End If
        Case MSCOMM_EV_CTS  ' Change in the CTS line.
        Case MSCOMM_EV_DSR  ' Change in the DSR line.
        Case MSCOMM_EV_RING ' Change in the Ring Indicator.
            pic_RemoteStatus.Cls
            pic_RemoteStatus.Print "Modem Ringing..."
            Comm1.Output = "ata" & Chr$(13)
```

continues

Listing 26.3. continued

```
            Case MSCOMM_EV_RECEIVE  ' Received RThreshold # of chars.
                Buffer$ = Buffer$ + Comm1.Input
                If InStr(Buffer$, Chr$(26)) Then
                    pic_RemoteStatus.Cls
                    pic_RemoteStatus.Print "Received Command..."
                    RemoteHandler
                End If
            Case MSCOMM_EV_SEND  ' There are SThreshold number of
                ' characters in the transmit buffer.
        End Select
End Sub
```

The three events that concern the Pseudo Server are the Ring event, the Change in Carrier Detect event, and the Receive Data event. These three events are used to provide the remote access.

When a Ring event occurs, this means that the modem has received a ring signal. The modem doesn't automatically pick up the phone when it is ringing. Therefore, when a ring is detected, an ATA command (Attention Answer) is sent to the modem. This makes the modem answer the phone and pick up the phone line.

If there is a change in the Carrier Detect line, the MSCOMM_EV_CD event occurs. The routine determines whether there is a carrier or not. If there is no carrier, the display settings and status are reset. If there is a carrier, the Pseudo Server is notified and the proper logon time is entered.

If a character is received, the MSCOMM_EV_RECEIVE event is activated. This event adds the received character to a buffer string. This string is then checked for a Chr$(26). We have chosen this character to indicate the end of a command line. In another application, a different character could be used, as long as it is an uncommon ASCII code. If a Chr$(26) is found in the string, the routine assumes it has a command from a Remote Client and activates the Remote Handler routine.

Function ParseLine()

The ParseLine routine takes a string that contains a number of values, separated by commas, and places each value in an array—ParseArray. Note that the final value in the string must contain a comma or it is not saved. The number of values found in the string is returned by the function.

```
Private Function ParseLine(tempStr As String) As Integer
    Dim CurrentBreak As Integer, LastBreak As Integer

    LastBreak = 1
    CurrentBreak = 1
    i = 1
    Do Until CurrentBreak = 0
```

```
        CurrentBreak = InStr(LastBreak, tempStr, ",")
        If CurrentBreak <> 0 Then
            ParseArray(i) = Mid$(tempStr, LastBreak, CurrentBreak - LastBreak)
            i = i + 1
            LastBreak = CurrentBreak + 1
        End If
    Loop
    ParseLine = i - 1
End Function
```

Sub RemoteHandler

The RemoteHandler routine, shown in Listing 26.4, is activated when the OnComm event receives one or more strings that end with a Chr$(26), signaling a remote command. This routine parses out as many remote commands as it is passed. For this we use a Do...Until construct.

Listing 26.4. The RemoteHandler routine.

```
Private Sub RemoteHandler()
    Dim Marker As Integer, DataBegin As Integer, DataLength As Integer
    Dim DataStr As String
    
    Marker = InStr(Buffer$, Chr$(26))
    Do Until Marker = 0
        RecLine$ = Left$(Buffer$, Marker)
        Select Case ConnectStatus
            Case NotConnected
                If InStr(RecLine$, "SalesClientLogon") Then
                    pic_RemoteStatus.Cls
                    pic_RemoteStatus.Print "Client Connected, waiting for
                    ➥password..."
                    Comm1.Output = "SERVERCONNECT" + Chr$(13)
                    ConnectStatus = NeedPassword
                End If
            Case NeedPassword
                templen = InStr(RecLine$, "Pwd:")
                If templen Then
                    TempPass$ = Mid$(RecLine$, templen + 4, Marker - (templen +
                    ➥4))
                    If TempPass$ = "Sales2,xxx" Then
                        pic_RemoteStatus.Cls
                        pic_RemoteStatus.Print "Password Verified. Waiting for
                        ➥command..."
                        Comm1.Output = "SR:Verified" + Chr$(26) + Chr$(13)
                        ConnectStatus = Connected
                        PwdBegin = InStr(TempPass$, ",")
                        txt_UserName = Left$(TempPass$, PwdBegin - 1)
                    Else
                        ' Password wrong or missing, disconnect
                        pic_RemoteStatus.Cls
                        pic_RemoteStatus.Print "Password wrong or missing,
                        ➥disconnect."
                    End If
                Else
```

continues

Listing 26.4. continued

```
                    pic_RemoteStatus.Cls
                    pic_RemoteStatus.Print "No Password Found."
                End If
            Case Connected
                templen = InStr(RecLine$, "SC:")
                If templen Then
                    pic_RemoteStatus.Cls
                    pic_RemoteStatus.Print "Executing Command..."
                    Select Case Mid$(RecLine$, templen + 3, 4)
                        Case "DATA"
                            pic_RemoteStatus.Cls
                            pic_RemoteStatus.Print "Receiving Data..."
                            ' Parse the line into individual pieces of data
                            DataBegin = templen + 3 + 4
                            DataLength = Len(RecLine$) - DataBegin
                            DataStr = Mid$(RecLine$, DataBegin, DataLength)
                            numitems = ParseLine(DataStr)
                            ' Make sure item number matches
                            If numitems = 4 Then
                                ' --- Save the data to the Database
                                ' To create a routine to save the data, consult
                                ' the CreateNewInvoice() routine in the Sales
                                ' Client
                                pic_RemoteStatus.Cls
                                pic_RemoteStatus.Print "Data received and
                                ➥verified."
                                ' Send back confirmation
                                Comm1.Output = "SR:Verified" + Chr$(26) + Chr$(13)
                            Else
                                ' Send back rejection
                                Comm1.Output = "SR:Rejected" + Chr$(26) + Chr$(13)
                            End If
                        Case "TOTL"
                            pic_RemoteStatus.Cls
                            pic_RemoteStatus.Print "Sending Sales Total..."
                            ' --- Create Sales Total
                            ' To create a real SalesTotal routine, simply
                            ' add the SQL query found in the Management Client
                            SalesTotal = 23010
                            Comm1.Output = "SR:TOTL" + SalesTotal + Chr$(26) + Chr$
                            ➥(13)
                            pic_RemoteStatus.Cls
                            pic_RemoteStatus.Print "Sent Sales Total."
                        Case "TIME"
                            pic_RemoteStatus.Cls
                            pic_RemoteStatus.Print "Sent System Time."
                            ' Return the system time
                            Comm1.Output = "SR:TIME" + Time$ + Chr$(26) + Chr$(13)
                    End Select
                Else
                    pic_RemoteStatus.Cls
                    pic_RemoteStatus.Print "No Command Found."
                End If
            Case Else
                pic_RemoteStatus.Cls
                pic_RemoteStatus.Print "No Command Found."
```

```
        End Select
        templen = Len(Buffer$)
        Buffer$ = Right$(Buffer$, templen - Marker)
        Marker = InStr(Buffer$, Chr$(26))
    Loop
End Sub
```

The first line within the loop takes a single command line from the buffer string and saves it separately in the RecLine$ (Received Line). The ConnectStatus variable is used with a Select Case statement to determine what level of progress the connection is currently in. For example, a user should not be able to send commands into the system until the password has been checked and verified. The ConnectStatus variable leads the user step-by-step through the verification process.

The first status level is the NotConnected level. This verifies that it is actually a Remote Client attempting to communicate with the system and not just a rogue modem. If the client has transmitted the value SalesClientLogon, the server responds with the value SERVERCONNECT to let the client know that it has reached a Remote Server.

The second status level is the NeedPassword level. At this level, the server waits for the client to broadcast a user name and password. As explained earlier, this is the most rudimentary system, accepting only a single password and user. A more sophisticated security routine might be required, depending on the needs of the organization. If the password is verified, the user is set to status level Connected and the username is displayed on the Pseudo Server screen.

The third status level, where actual commands are accepted, is called the Connected level. At this level, the Remote Client sends remote commands in the form of SC: (server command), followed by a four-letter command. The four-letter command may or may not also be followed with data or parameters.

Currently, three commands are accepted by the system: DATA, TOTL, and TIME. The DATA command actually accepts the Sales data sent by the Remote Client. This is just a dummy routine to show how data might be acquired. Because the data is parsed using the ParseLine() function, it would be a simple matter to add the other qualifying data and save a new invoice into the database.

The TOTL command sends back the total of today's sales. Once again, this is merely a dummy routine to show how data can be returned. Adding a query to the database and returning an actual figure would be a simple process.

The TIME command returns the time as set on the server system. This routine is an example of providing remote information on the server itself. Remote Clients could determine if system resources are getting low, or even possibly retrieve buffered messages on the system.

After completing the Select Case structure, the loop looks for another command. This routine provides for commands being sent as a batch. The proper markers are reset, and if another Chr$(26) is found in the buffer (signifying another command), the new command is processed.

All of these routines update the `RemoteStatus` picture so the Pseudo Server administrator can monitor what is happening. We highly recommend in any system you create to make sure plenty of status is provided.

Creating the Remote Client

The Remote Client, shown in Figure 26.6, is an excellent demonstration of the Communications control for use of Remote Communications using VB. Although many of the basic communications of Windows to Windows machines will be done in the future using Remote Access Services, TAPI/MAPI protocols, and various other communications layers, custom solutions will always be necessary.

FIGURE 26.6.

The Remote Client window.

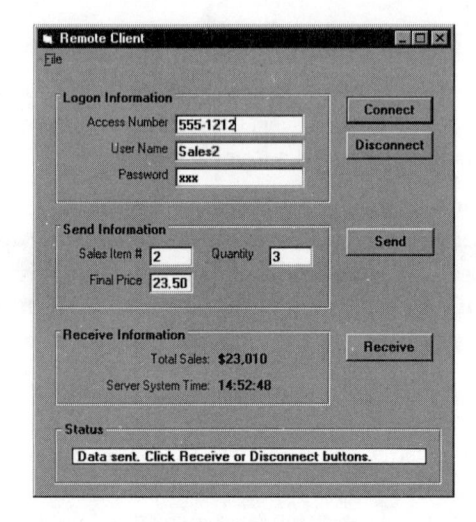

A serial port and modem have been the fundamental hardware for exchanging remote information. Although programs are available for specific information exchange (that is, fax programs or pcAnywhere-type products), client-specific data access is difficult without a custom solution.

The Remote Client uses the Communications control (see Figure 26.7), rudimentary error checking, and basic data access to exchange information with the host server system. In our Sales example, the Remote Client accepts a single item that was sold (identified by ID number) and the quantity of the item sold.

When the Connect button is clicked, the modem attempts to dial the number supplied. If a machine at the connection number answers and provides system identification, the Remote Client supplies a username and password. After the server verifies the user, the Remote Client commences sending data. If the server requests a resend, the data is resent until the server declares the data was received properly. The client then requests summary information and disconnects once the information is received.

Creating the Remote Sales Client

The Remote Sales Client is a simple single-form screen (see Figure 26.7). The top three text fields in the Logon Information frame are used to provide access information (access phone number, user name, and user password). The Send Information frame holds the item ID number, quantity, and final price of the item sold. The Receive Information frame contains the field to receive the summary information provided by the PServer.

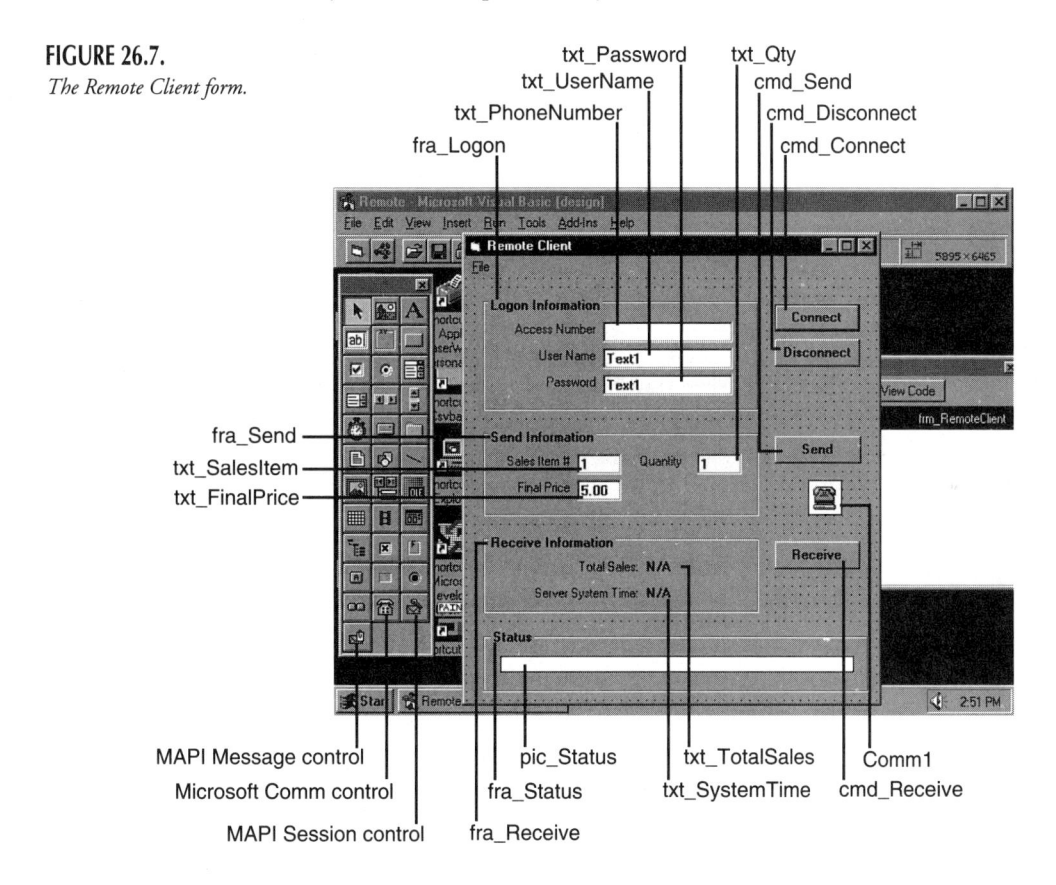

FIGURE 26.7.
The Remote Client form.

Finally, the Status frame displays ongoing information as the connection is made. Because communications have the tendency to have so many problems and errors (bad phone lines, bad connection, no dial tone, and so on), it is extremely important in a modem-based application to keep the user aware of the status of the communications.

Creating the Remote Client Form

Construct the form shown in Figure 26.7 using the information in the following sections.

The Remote Client form has many controls but is fairly similar to controls created on forms in previous chapters. Figure 26.7 shows what the completed form looks like after all the controls have been added and shows the Name properties of all the individual controls. Create each control on the form and set the properties to match the properties listed in the table for that property.

Setting the Properties

Table 26.2 shows where to place all the controls on the Remote Client form.

Table 26.2. Controls for the Remote Client form.

Table	Control	Location
Table 26.3	Form frm_RemoteClient	
Table 26.4	CommandButton cmd_Receive	Form
Table 26.5	Frame fra_Status	Form
Table 26.6	PictureBox pic_Status	fra_Status
Table 26.7	CommandButton cmd_Disconnect	Form
Table 26.8	CommandButton cmd_Send	Form
Table 26.9	CommandButton cmd_Connect	Form
Table 26.10	MSCommLib.MSComm Comm1	Form
Table 26.11	SSFrame fra_Receive	Form
Table 26.12	Label txt_SystemTime	fra_Receive
Table 26.13	Label txt_TotalSales	fra_Receive
Table 26.14	SSFrame fra_Send	form
Table 26.15	TextBox txt_FinalPrice	fra_Send
Table 26.16	TextBox txt_Qty	fra_Send
Table 26.17	TextBox txt_SalesItem	fra_Send
Table 26.18	SSFrame fra_Logon	Form
Table 26.19	TextBox txt_Password	fra_Logon
Table 26.20	TextBox txt_UserName	fra_Logon
Table 26.21	TextBox txt_PhoneNumber	fra_Logon

Table 26.3. Form frm_RemoteClient.

Appearance	0 'Flat
BackColor	&H00C0C0C0&
Caption	Remote Client

ClientHeight	5775
ClientLeft	1635
ClientTop	645
ClientWidth	775

Table 26.4. **CommandButton cmd_Receive**.

Caption	Receive
Height	375
Left	4320
TabIndex	24
Top	3600
Width	1215

Table 26.5. **Frame fra_Status**.

Caption	Status
Height	55
Left	240
TabIndex	20
Top	4800
Width	5415

Table 26.6. **PictureBox pic_Status**.

Appearance	'Flat
BackColor	&H80000005&
ForeColor	&H80000008&
Height	225
Left	40
ScaleHeight	195
ScaleWidth	4935
TabIndex	21
Top	360
Width	4965

Table 26.7. CommandButton cmd_Disconnect.

Caption	Disconnect
Height	375
Left	4320
TabIndex	16
Top	840
Width	215

Table 26.8. CommandButton cmd_Send.

Appearance	0 'Flat
BackColor	H80000005&
Caption	Send
Height	375
Left	4320
TabIndex	7
Top	2160
Width	1230

Table 26.9. CommandButton cmd_Connect.

Appearance	0 'Flat
BackColor	&H80000005&
Caption	Connect
Default	-1 'True
Height	375
Left	4320
TabIndex	6
Top	360
Width	1215

Table 26.10. MSCommLib.MSComm Comm1.

Left	4800
Top	2760

_Version	5536
_ExtentX	847
_ExtentY	847
_StockProps	0
CDTimeout	0
CommPort	1
CTSTimeout	0
DSRTimeout	0
DTREnable	-1 'True
Handshaking	1
InBufferSize	1024
InputLen	0
Interval	1000
NullDiscard	0 'False
OutBufferSize	512
ParityReplace	?
RThreshold	1
RTSEnable	-1 'True
Settings	"9600,n,8,1"
SThreshold	0

Table 26.11. SSFrame fra_Receive.

Height	1095
Left	240
TabIndex	8
Top	3480
Width	3855
_Version	65536
_ExtentX	6800
_ExtentY	1931
_StockProps	14
Caption	Receive Information
ForeColor	0

Table 26.12. Label txt_SystemTime.

Caption	N/A
Height	255
Left	2280
TabIndex	23
Top	720
Width	975

Table 26.13. Label txt_TotalSales.

Caption	N/A
Height	255
Left	2280
TabIndex	19
Top	360
Width	975

Table 26.14. SSFrame fra_Send.

Height	1215
Left	240
TabIndex	15
Top	2040
Width	855
_Version	65536
_ExtentX	800
_ExtentY	2143
_StockProps	14
Caption	Send Information
ForeColor	0

Table 26.15. TextBox txt_FinalPrice.

Height	285
Left	1320

TabIndex	5
Text	5.00
Top	720
Width	615

Table 26.16. TextBox txt_Qty.

Height	285
Left	3000
TabIndex	4
Text	1
Top	360
Width	615

Table 26.17. TextBox txt_SalesItem.

Height	285
Left	1320
TabIndex	3
Text	1
Top	360
Width	615

Table 26.18. SSFrame fra_Logon.

Height	1575
Left	240
TabIndex	11
Top	240
Width	3855
_Version	5536
_ExtentX	6800
_ExtentY	2778
_StockProps	14
Caption	Logon Information

Table 26.19. TextBox txt_Password.

Height	285
Left	1680
TabIndex	2
Text	Text1
Top	1080
Width	1815

Table 26.20. TextBox txt_UserName.

Height	285
Left	1680
TabIndex	1
Text	Text1
Top	720
Width	1815

Table 26.21. TextBox txt_PhoneNumber.

Height	285
Left	1680
TabIndex	0
Text	Text1
Top	360
Width	1815

Adding the Code

Place the following variables in the General Declarations section of the main form. The g_ErrorCode variable is used to contain an error code if the WaitforValue() routine has any problems. The two Wait constants define wait times for various routines.

```
Dim g_ErrorCode As Integer
Const WaitConst = 10
Const WaitConnectConst = 90
```

cmd_Connect_Click()

This routine, shown in Listing 26.5, is the main connection routine. It opens the modem port, ensures the modem is working, dials the specified access number, connects to the Remote Server, and sends the username and password. Note that each section contains error checking to make sure the step is complete. If an error occurs, the routine aborts and hangs up the phone.

A more sophisticated application would retry to send. On the other hand, often a bad or noisy connection is eliminated simply by redialing the server. We leave this up to you depending on how you want to implement a Remote System.

Listing 26.5. The `cmd_Connect_Click()` routine.

```
Private Sub cmd_Connect_Click()
    pic_Status.Cls
    pic_Status.Print " Checking Modem..."
    MyOpenPort
    ' Send the attention command to the modem.
    Comm1.Output = "AT" + Chr$(13)

    g_Error = 0
    Wait$ = WaitForValue("OK", WaitConst)

    If g_ErrorCode = 0 Then
        pic_Status.Cls
        pic_Status.Print " Modem OK."
    Else
        pic_Status.Cls
        pic_Status.Print " Modem Not Responding."
        AbortCall
        Exit Sub
    End If

    ' Send Dialing
    pic_Status.Cls
    pic_Status.Print " Dialing..."
    Comm1.Output = "ATDT " + txt_PhoneNumber + Chr$(13)

    Wait$ = WaitForValue("CONNECT", WaitConnectConst)
    If g_ErrorCode = 0 Then
        pic_Status.Cls
        pic_Status.Print " Connected. 8 second pause."
    Else
        ' Determine the problem
        If InStr(Wait$, "BUSY") Then
            pic_Status.Cls
            pic_Status.Print " Line is busy."
        ' Do a Case-Insensitive check
        ElseIf InStr(1, Wait$, "No Dialtone", 1) Then
            pic_Status.Cls
            pic_Status.Print " There is no dialtone."
        ElseIf InStr(1, Wait$, "No Carrier", 1) Then
            pic_Status.Cls
            pic_Status.Print " There was no carrier detected."
        Else
            pic_Status.Cls
            pic_Status.Print " There is a connection problem."
```

continues

Listing 26.5. continued

```
            End If
            AbortCall
            Exit Sub
    End If
    ' Connection was successful, pause for setup
    Pause 8
    ' Now send verification string
    pic_Status.Cls
    pic_Status.Print " Checking Remote Server..."
    Comm1.Output = "SalesClientLogon" + Chr$(13) + "SalesClientLogon" + Chr$(13)
➥+ "SalesClientLogon" + Chr$(26)

    ' SERVERCONNECT string should be sent by PServer
    Wait$ = WaitForValue("SERVERCONNECT", WaitConnectConst)
    If g_ErrorCode = 0 Then
        pic_Status.Cls
        pic_Status.Print " Connected to Remote Server."
    Else
        pic_Status.Cls
        pic_Status.Print " Not a Remote Server."
        AbortCall
        Exit Sub
    End If

    ' Send User name and password
    pic_Status.Cls
    pic_Status.Print " Sending Password..."
    Comm1.Output = "Pwd:" + txt_UserName + "," + txt_Password + Chr$(26) +
➥Chr$(13)

    Wait$ = WaitForValue(Chr$(26), WaitConnectConst)

    ' Server Responded, now check response
    If g_ErrorCode = 0 Then
        If InStr(1, Wait$, "SR:Verified", 1) Then
            pic_Status.Cls
            pic_Status.Print " Password verified."
        Else
            pic_Status.Cls
            pic_Status.Print " Password rejected, session ended."
            AbortCall
            Exit Sub
        End If
    Else
        pic_Status.Cls
        pic_Status.Print " No response, session ended."
        AbortCall
        Exit Sub
    End If

    pic_Status.Cls
    pic_Status.Print " Connected. Click the Send or Receive Buttons."
End Sub
```

Sub cmd_Disconnect_Click()

If the user clicks the Disconnect command button, call the `AbortCall()` routine. This hangs up the phone.

```
Private Sub cmd_Disconnect_Click()
    AbortCall
End Sub
```

Sub cmd_Receive_Click()

This routine, shown in Listing 26.6, requests data from the server. It sends the server a server command (`SC`) with a specific request. The first request sends a server command to gain the sales totals for the day. If the total is received, it is entered in the `txt_TotalSales` control. The system time is then requested with an `SC:TIME` command.

These are simple demonstrations of retrieving data from a remote system. Almost undoubtedly a system you implement will require more complex and robust commands, as well as more complicated data reception. However, these routines can provide a framework on which to build other command functions.

Listing 26.6. The `cmd_Receive_Click()` routine.

```
Private Sub cmd_Receive_Click()
    MyOpenPort
    Comm1.InBufferCount = 0

    Comm1.Output = "SC:TOTL" + Chr$(26)
    Wait$ = WaitForValue(Chr$(26), WaitConnectConst)

    ' Server Responded, now check response
    If g_ErrorCode = 0 Then
        Position = InStr(Wait$, "SR:TOTL")
        If Position Then
            txt_TotalSales = Format$(Mid$(Wait$, Position + 7, Len(Wait$) -
            ➥Position - 7), "$#,###")
        End If
    Else
        pic_Status.Cls
        pic_Status.Print " No response."
        Exit Sub
    End If

    Comm1.Output = "SC:TIME" + Chr$(26)

    Wait$ = WaitForValue(Chr$(26), WaitConnectConst)

    ' Server Responded, now check response
    If g_ErrorCode = 0 Then
        Position = InStr(Wait$, "SR:TIME")
        If Position Then
```

continues

Listing 26.6. continued

```
            txt_SystemTime = Mid$(Wait$, Position + 7, Len(Wait$) - Position - 7)
        End If
    Else
        pic_Status.Cls
        pic_Status.Print " No response."
        Exit Sub
    End If
    pic_Status.Cls
    pic_Status.Print " Data received. Click Send or Disconnect buttons."
End Sub
```

Sub cmd_Send_Click()

The Send command button sends the Sales data stored in the text box controls (see Listing 26.7).

Listing 26.7. The `cmd_Send_Click()` routine.

```
Private Sub cmd_Send_Click()
    MyOpenPort
    Comm1.InBufferCount = 0
    pic_Status.Cls
    pic_Status.Print " Sending Data..."

    SendData$ = txt_SalesItem + "," + txt_Qty + "," + txt_FinalPrice + ","
    checkval = GetChecksum(SendData$, Len(SendData$))
    SendData$ = "SC:DATA" + Str$(checkval) + "," + SendData$ + Chr$(26)
    Comm1.Output = SendData$

    Wait$ = WaitForValue(Chr$(26), WaitConnectConst)

    If InStr(Wait$, "SR:Verified") Then
        pic_Status.Cls
        pic_Status.Print " Data sent. Click Receive or Disconnect buttons."
    Else
        pic_Status.Cls
        pic_Status.Print " Data didn't verify, please click Send again."
        AbortCall
        Exit Sub
    End If
End Sub
```

Private Sub ExitItem_Click()

This is the Exit menu item under the File menu. It ends the execution of the program and closes all the forms. It is a good idea to have a File menu with an Exit command in even the simplest programs. This way the user can always go to the same place when he needs to quit.

```
Private Sub ExitItem_Click()
    End
End Sub
```

Private Sub Form_Load()

Set the various text fields to their defaults. These defaults should probably be kept in an .INI file rather than compiled into the Remote Client program.

```
Private Sub Form_Load()
    txt_PhoneNumber = "555-1212"
    txt_UserName = "Sales2"
    txt_Password = "xxx"
End Sub
```

Sub Form_Unload(Cancel As Integer)

If the user clicks the Close box, this ensures that any other forms that are open (even if hidden) are closed as well. It is a good habit to include this statement in the main form of all your applications.

```
Private Sub Form_Unload(Cancel As Integer)
    End
End Sub
```

Function GetChecksum(checkstr As String, checklen As Integer) As Long

This routine builds a checksum of a string. The checksum can then be sent with the string of data. At the other end, the data can use a similar routine to create a new checksum. If the two match, the data is most likely good. If not, it needs to be resent.

```
Private Function GetChecksum(checkstr As String, checklen As Integer) As Long
    Dim checknum As Long

    For i = 1 To checklen
        checknum = checknum + Asc(Mid$(checkstr, i, 1))
    Next i
    GetChecksum = checknum
End Function
```

Function WaitForValue(Wait$, WaitTime) As String

The `WaitForValue` routine, shown in Listing 26.8, is given a string receive in the input stream and a maximum time to wait for that string. After this time has passed, the routine aborts and returns an error.

Listing 26.8. The `WaitForValue` routine.

```
Private Function WaitForValue(Wait$, WaitTime) As String
    Dim Receive$, StartTime, EndTime, MyIn$, ErrCode%

    ' Setup to receive one character at a time.
    Comm1.InputLen = 1
    g_ErrorCode = 0
    Received$ = ""
    ' Begin timer for timeout if no response is received
    StartTime = Timer
```

continues

Listing 26.8. continued

```
        EndTime = StartTime + WaitTime
    Do
            ' Let the System handles other events
            DoEvents

            If Comm1.InBufferCount Then
                'Add character in the input buffer to In$
                MyIn$ = MyIn$ + Comm1.Input
                'Use the InStr function to detect whether the value matches what
                'we're waiting for.
                There% = InStr(MyIn$, Wait$)
                If There% Then
                    Exit Do
                End If
            End If

            ' Has it passed the timeout
            If Timer >= EndTime Then
                'Set the error code and exit
                g_ErrorCode = 1
                Exit Do
            End If
    Loop
    WaitForValue = MyIn$
End Function
```

Sub AbortCall()

This routine provides a central routine to terminate the connection. If the hangup on your modem is not working, check the Handshake parameters for the Comm control. Often particular modems need a certain type of handshaking setting to properly be called to attention with the +++ attention command.

```
Private Sub AbortCall()
    ' If port is not open, open so modem can be hung up
    MyOpenPort
    ' Hang up phone
    Comm1.Output = "+++ATH"
    ' Close Port
End Sub
```

Sub Pause(Seconds!)

This routine is necessary because many modems require time to initialize, even after the initial carrier connection is made. While this initialization is taking place, any characters sent to the modem are lost.

In the Remote Client program, we have set a delay of eight seconds (the recommended standard wait). We recommend putting the value of the delay in an .INI file. This way the delay can be tuned to the specific system that needs to be connected to the client. This minimizes the wait for connection.

```
Private Sub Pause(Seconds!)
    StartTime! = Timer
    EndTime! = Seconds! + Timer
     Do
         DoEvents
     Loop Until Timer >= EndTime!
End Sub
```

Sub MyOpenPort()

This routine centralizes the port configuration. Therefore, if needed, the application could be quit without severing the connection. Then, when re-executed, it could re-open the port and send and receive data.

```
Private Sub MyOpenPort()
    If Comm1.PortOpen = False Then
    ' Note that these settings could be put in an INI file
        ' Use COM1.
        Comm1.CommPort = 1
        ' 9600 baud, no parity, 8 data, and 1 stop bit.
        Comm1.Settings = "9600,N,8,1"
        ' Open the port.
        Comm1.PortOpen = True
    End If
End Sub
```

Messaging

A newer method that is becoming increasingly popular for remote communication is the use of standard e-mail as the carrier. The client dials into a local access number and sends an e-mail packet of all the update information. The e-mail can also be sent over a wireless service such as Cellular Modem, CDPD, or an Ardis wireless network. The server located at the central office can be connected directly to an e-mail carrier or can automatically check an e-mail account periodically for any updates. The message containing the information can be received by the server.

The message containing the data can be either routed to the proper user or automatically handled by the server. This information could be stripped out of the message and added to the central database. The server could also store a number of such data updates and handle them as a periodic batch to do all the updates at once.

This type of remote messaging is being increasingly advocated by the operating system vendors. Using MS Mail, Groupwise, Lotus Notes, or MS Exchange, such a mail-based remote update system can be created. Soon global groupware information networks will be dedicated to convenient exchange of data formatted in this way.

> **NOTE**
>
> Moss Micro, a custom application development firm, created an amazing example of a remote updating system. The system uses Microsoft Access, Microsoft SQL Server, ODBC, and Microsoft Mail to do remote client updates to an SQL Server database. The source code description of the project is included on the Microsoft Solutions Development Kit CD. The article describing the system is titled "Remote Database Synchronization with Microsoft Office and Microsoft BackOffice."
>
> We would highly recommend examining the system they have implemented for a sample of the advantages and difficulties in deploying such a system. ODBC, BackOffice, OLE Automation, and Messaging are all implemented in the project.

Although idealized by many software and hardware vendors, there are currently many disadvantages to this system. Communication is very asynchronous; an update sent might not be received at the server for hours, meaning costly delays in information currency that do not occur with a direct connection. The lack of direct exchange might also prevent the remote client program from obtaining crucial information.

For example, a salesperson might place an order for an item and send the update through e-mail. He might learn hours later, after he has left the customer, that the item is out of stock. This could create costly problems.

Through an e-mail based system, lost data is difficult to recover, and faulty data can be extremely inconvenient. If the client sends the information, and the e-mail somehow gets lost or garbled, the information must be resent. With a direct connection, the server asks for the client to resend the information and instantly gets an update.

In an e-mail system, the server must alert the client program through e-mail and wait for a resend. Meanwhile, to avoid possible data loss, the client program must keep all updates on file until the update is confirmed. Until verification is received, the portable must use disk storage and retain additional data clutter.

Finally, information requests, such as how many type C Widgets are in stock, can take the server an extremely long time to respond to. A message requesting the information must travel all the way through the system. The server must respond and send the information all the way back through the system. The client must then find a convenient place to re-access the e-mail carrier to receive the new data. All of this effort can be tedious and expensive.

> **NOTE**
>
> E-mail transmission rates are extremely inconsistent. As a test, we sent three pieces of mail through our Internet account to our America Online account. The first time, there was only a 15-minute delay. The second time it took four hours to receive the

> message! (We checked every 15 minutes.) The third time took about 45 minutes. We have also noticed a great time lag for mail sent between CompuServe and America Online accounts.
>
> Before setting up a messaging-based client/server system, be aware of the possible delay imposed by wide area network routing. Even tests such as the one described here are good only to see general variability. Send time almost certainly varies not only with internetwork services but also within a network, as the geographic source and destination vary.

We don't mean to berate the e-mail and groupware messaging solutions. They will increasingly become the standard means of communication. As speed increases, wide area networks are deployed, and error rates decrease, these services will provide unbeatable price, performance, and convenience advantages. Just be aware of the possible problems before committing your enterprise to any long-term deployment strategy.

Simple and Complex Messaging

Simple messaging is the form of messaging users traditionally use. Simple messaging is used by such systems as Microsoft Mail, cc:Mail, MHS, and Groupwise. This type of messaging is usually based on the file server metaphor. Messages are stored on a particular machine in a particular area or directory of the main hard disk. More advanced systems using simple messaging offer gateways for other e-mail formats. Most of the processing for message handling is done by the individual client machines.

Complex messaging is the newer form of messaging. Complex messaging is used by such systems as Lotus Notes, Microsoft Exchange, and HP Open Mail. Based on a client/server model, messages are stored in a mail server. Messages are centralized at the mail server, where they can be replicated, publicly accessed, and processed using server computing power. In a complex messaging system, most of the message processing occurs on the mail server, freeing the clients to concentrate on display and presentation.

Complex messaging has hierarchical storage so that messages can be transferred between stores (and folders) and sorted much like a database. Notification services have also been added so Messaging Clients can register with the server and be notified when system events occur (such as a new message or a message deletion).

Messaging Interfaces

There are several standards for sending e-mail in the industry. Each standard provides features missing from the other standards and achieves certain levels of market acceptance. The baseline standard for basic messages is know as the CMC standard. This standard is supported as a subset in most of the available messaging protocols. Many of the drivers available on machines support the calls of a particular standard but map these calls to their own messaging interface (see Figure 26.8).

FIGURE 26.8.
Various messaging APIs.

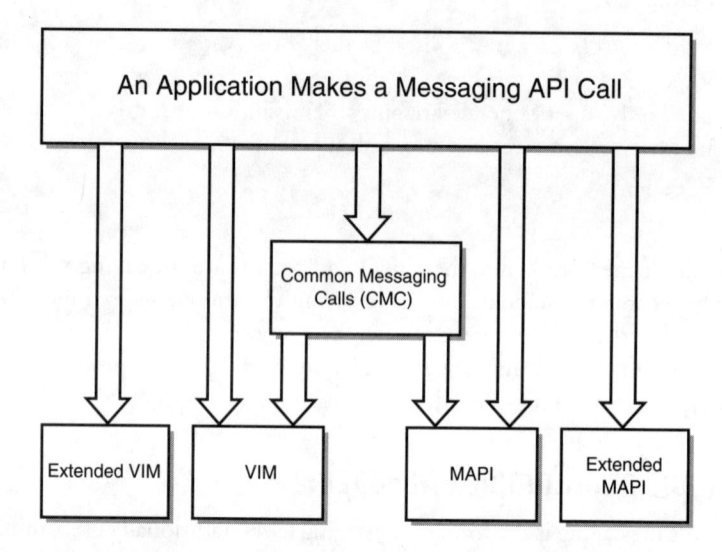

```
                    ┌──────────────────────────────────────────────┐
                    │  An Application Makes a Messaging API Call   │
                    └──────────────────────────────────────────────┘
                                         │
                                         ▼
                                 ┌──────────────┐
                                 │ Common Messaging │
                                 │  Calls (CMC)    │
                                 └──────────────┘
         │              │                │                │
         ▼              ▼                ▼                ▼
   ┌──────────┐   ┌─────────┐     ┌──────────┐    ┌──────────┐
   │Extended  │   │   VIM   │     │   MAPI   │    │ Extended │
   │   VIM    │   │         │     │          │    │   MAPI   │
   └──────────┘   └─────────┘     └──────────┘    └──────────┘
```

Common Messaging Calls (CMC) or X.400

Common Messaging Calls (CMC) are a set of API calls that have become a cross-platform function standard for Simple Messaging. The API is released by the X.400 API Association and is often referred to as the X.400 API standard. The X.400 Association has released many standards (five of which are directly related to messaging), and one of these is related to the CMC API support. Therefore, there is often confusion when referring to X.400 support as to how many of the standards the product actually supports.

X.400 consists of support for attachments, Electronic Data Interchange (EDI) support, Distributed Directories support (via the X.500 standard), security (through the X.509 standard), and CMC API support. Therefore, when evaluating a product advertising X.400 support, be sure to determine exactly what this means.

The CMC API has received the widest support of all the standards described by the X.400 Association. Because all the functions are standardized, a single program can use these functions and easily be ported to any machine that supports them. Most e-mail vendors support CMC services, including Microsoft, Lotus, HP, IBM, SoftSwitch, Tandem, and DEC.

The CMC API is originally based on Microsoft's Simple MAPI standard. The CMC has only 10 function calls to complete the basic messaging operations. The standard does not include file attachment capabilities. CMC is widely accepted and supported by Novell's Global Message Handling Service and MS Windows mail system and is included in the VIM mail interfaces.

CMC can be accessed through the MAPI DLL, which contains all the CMC functions. There is also an independent DLL for CMC. Microsoft has created a free CMC DLL, which contains all the common functions for CMC, including the common extension set. The DLL can be used from either C or Visual Basic. For a complete example of using the CMC functions, a sample project for VB is included on the Microsoft Developer CD and is available online (see Appendix C, "Sources").

The article briefly describing the project is called "Common Messaging Calls: Create Mail-Enabled Applications." A CMC Software Development Kit is available that contains tools and information about supporting CMC interfaces. The SDK is available on CompuServe or on the Developer Level 2 CD-ROM library.

Microsoft Exchange supports all the CMC functions (there is more information on Exchange later in this chapter). The CMC implementation is built on top of the MAPI interface and is therefore available to all design environments supporting MAPI. To support some of the capabilities of Extended MAPI, Microsoft has provided some of the CMC Extensions above the simple CMC interface. See Table 26.22 for a comparison of CMC and simple MAPI commands that can be used.

Interestingly, one of the seven requirements to qualify for the new Windows 95 logo program is the support of the CMC API so that Send and Send Mail options appear under the File menu. Because of this requirement, perhaps new CMC OLE Custom Controls will appear that support some of the advanced X.400 commands.

Table 26.22. A comparison of CMC and simple MAPI commands.

CMC Call	MAPI Call	Description
CMC_Logon	MAPILogon	Establishes a messaging session
CMC_Logoff	MAPILogoff	Terminates a messaging session
CMC_Free	MAPIFree	Frees the memory allocated for the messaging session
CMC_Send	MAPISendMail	Sends a mail message
CMC_SendDocuments	MAPISendDocuments	Sends a mail message, but first prompts user for recipient's name and other sending options
CMC_List*	MAPIFindNext	Finds information about messages meeting specified criteria
CMC_Read	MAPIReadMail	Reads a mail message
CMC_ActOn*	MAPISaveMail	Saves a mail message
CMC_ActOn*	MAPIDeleteMail	Deletes a mail message

continues

Table 26.22. continued

CMC Call	MAPI Call	Description
CMC_Lookup*	MAPIAddress	Creates and looks up addresses
CMC_Lookup*	MAPIDetails	Looks up e-mail address information
CMC_Lookup*	MAPIResolveName	Resolves "friendly" names with e-mail names
CMC_QueryConfiguration		Provides information on installing CMC service

*Indicates that the function is a CMC extension

Vendor-Independent Messaging (VIM)

Vendor-Independent Messaging (VIM) is a message protocol created by a coalition of companies, including Lotus, Apple Computer, Novell, Borland, IBM, MCI, Oracle, and Word Perfect. The standard was originally named Open Messaging Interface (OMI) and used in Lotus cc:Mail. It became a true open standard with its transition to VIM.

VIM supports the 12 standard CMC function calls as well as the following: the capability to attach documents to messages; services for creating, reading, and sending messages; keeping an address book; and linking to other message APIs (such as MAPI or SMF).

Standard Messaging Format (SMF)

Standard Messaging Format is the format used by Novell's Message Handling Services (MHS). SMF is the file format to store messages in for use with the MHS.

MHS is more comprehensive than a typical messaging interface. It can route and transfer files between systems, use routing tables on an MHS host, queue messages, use asynchronous connections, use inter-network connections, use gateway connections, and allow complete message attachment capabilities.

MHS uses store-and-forward technology, so the system can send messages as a batch at a predetermined time or interval. MHS can also be used for execution tasks such as querying a database, executing a remote procedure, workgroup scheduling, or network faxing.

Simple Mail Transport Protocol (SMTP)

Simple Mail Transport Protocol (SMTP) is the standard mail protocol used on the Internet, UNIX systems, and TCP/IP-based networks. SMTP is a protocol used to send and receive messages and can include attached files. The SMTP protocol uses control messages to communicate between the SMTP mailbox that holds the messages and the SMTP client application that retrieves them.

The protocol includes connection verification, password verification, negotiation of transmission parameters, and transmission and reception of messages. Messages are composed of ASCII characters or files encoded as a series of ASCII characters.

SMTP is not strictly an API in that it does not provide standard function calls. It is instead a protocol used to transfer and receive messages. The Internet community is working on a more robust messaging protocol called Multipurpose Internet Mail Extension (MIME). This new format allows the attachment of audio files, video clips, graphic images, and rich text.

MAPI Architecture

MAPI is a standard created by Microsoft; it is an open-ended programming interface. This means that additional drivers can be plugged into MAPI to provide access to new message protocols and formats (such as an ODBC interface for messaging). The Windows Messaging System (stored in the MAPI DLL) can receive function calls from any of three call sets: CMC, Simple MAPI, and Extended MAPI (see Figure 26.9). Therefore, MAPI is more like a set of interfaces than a single interface.

FIGURE 26.9.
The Windows Messaging System.

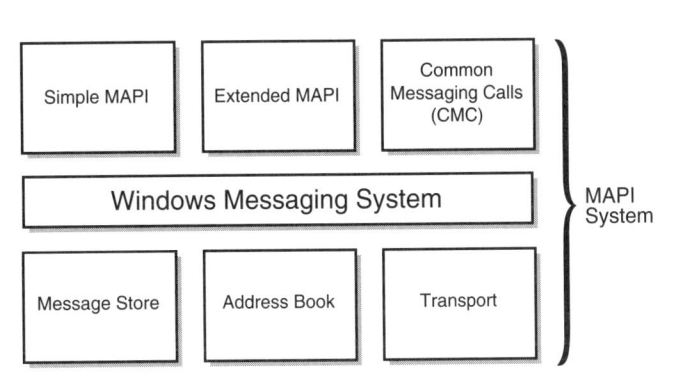

Because complete MAPI access is provided from Visual Basic, and there are hundreds of MAPI-compatible devices, we focus on the MAPI architecture of the present and future.

MAPI is an open API on both the client and the server sides. This means that a mail server, if MAPI server-compliant, can receive, store, and send any MAPI-compatible messages.

Simple MAPI

Simple MAPI is the version of MAPI supported by the Visual Basic Custom Controls. At the time of this writing, only Simple MAPI support is available through Microsoft Mail or Windows for Workgroups. As you can see in Table 26.23, there are only 12 MAPI function calls. These calls can be made directly to the MAPI.DLL or through equivalent commands available in the MAPI controls provided with Visual Basic.

Table 26.23. Simple MAPI functions.

Function	Description
MAPILogon	Begins a session with the messaging system
MAPILogoff	Ends a session with the messaging system
MAPIFindNext	Returns the ID of the next (or first) mail message of a specified type
MAPIReadMail	Reads a mail message
MAPISaveMail	Saves a mail message
MAPIDeleteMail	Deletes a mail message
MAPISendMail	Sends a mail message
MAPISendDocuments	Sends a standard mail message
MAPIAddress	Addresses a mail message
MAPIResolveName	Displays a dialog box to resolve an ambiguous recipient name
MAPIDetails	Displays a recipient details dialog box

Simple MAPI can be called to display appropriate user-interface dialog boxes or can be controlled entirely through programming.

Extended MAPI

Extended MAPI includes the expanded features for current and future groupware applications, Messaging Clients, workflow applications, rules-based agents, and Electronic Data Interchange (EDI) applications. Migration from a Simple MAPI implementation to one using Extended MAPI is fairly straightforward.

Whereas Simple MAPI is used primarily to send messages with or without attachments, Extended MAPI is for applications that make heavy use of messaging capabilities. These types of applications, called mail-reliant, depend on messaging for much of their functionality (such as a scheduling application). Extended MAPI applications can interact with and control the complete messaging operations of the system.

Extended MAPI provides a complete object foundation to messaging. Rather than traditional API function calls, Extended MAPI is based on messaging objects with methods and properties. Because the Extended MAPI interface directly passes parameters to the object interface (using the Microsoft Common Object Model), it is not used directly from Visual Basic. Instead, OLE Messaging provides access to many of the Extended MAPI functions.

Extended MAPI provides a vendor-independent interface to complex messaging functions. It has advanced features such as custom forms and smart forms. Also, Message Stores and Address Books are supported.

OLE Messaging

OLE Messaging is the future for any Visual Basic or VBA application accessing Extended MAPI services. Although Extended MAPI can be accessed only through a fairly complicated object-based API (and will probably be used mostly by C and C++ programmers), OLE Messaging allows any application access to most of the Extended MAPI functions.

OLE Messaging lacks the capabilities of Message Serving, which are more appropriate for high throughput integrated applications. The services missing from the OLE Messaging library include the ability to create new distribution lists, new folders, and new address book entries. These server features are included in the Extended MAPI instruction set but are missing from the OLE Messaging interface. Although not present in OLE Messaging Library 1.0, they might be added in the future.

OLE Messaging is simpler to use than the Extended MAPI services, because memory management, object tracking, and collection tracking are all done by the OLE Messaging objects. Also, the OLE Messaging features error-trapping that is integrated with the Visual Basic environment (trapped through normal On Error routines). The more complex the messaging application becomes, the easier it is to maintain using specific objects rather than API calls.

OLE Messaging is essentially a DLL that exposes Extended MAPI objects to OLE automation. The OLE Messaging Library contains seven primary objects: AddressEntry, Attachment, Field, Folder, Message, Recipient, and Session.

The high-level objects, those essential for primary creation, include the Session, Folder, and Message objects. All other objects are accessible only through these objects. Only the Session object is directly accessible from Visual Basic. Folder and Message objects are accessed in Visual Basic through the Session object.

OLE Messaging is used primarily by Visual Basic and VBA applications. For more information on programming the new OLE Messaging Library objects, see the section titled "OLE Messaging Library Access."

Visual Basic MAPI Interface

Visual Basic includes the two MAPI controls with the Professional Edition—the MAPI Session control and the MAPI Message control (see Figure 26.7). With these controls, a designer can give Simple MAPI capabilities to any Visual Basic program. For Extended MAPI capabilities, either the MAPI DLL must be called directly (fairly complicated) or the OLE Messaging capability can be used.

MAPI Controls

Visual Basic has two separate controls to access the MAPI interface: the MAPI Session control and the MAPI Message control. The MAPI Session control is used to make the connection with the MAPI services. The MAPI Message control accesses the system functions after the Session control establishes the connection.

There are no event activations for either control. Instead, the application must activate the controls directly through either methods (such as `SignOn` and `SignOff`) or the use of the `Action` property. For example, the Session control has only two action commands: `SESSION_SIGNON` and `SESSION_SIGNOFF`. When the `Action` property is set to either of these values, the appropriate action occurs.

All the properties for the MAPI Session control are described in Table 26.24. The methods for the control are described in Table 26.25. The `Action` property settings for the Session control are shown in Table 26.26. You will notice that the `Action` properties have parallel methods that do the same operations. The `Action` property is for backwards compatibility with VB 3.0. It is recommended you use the new methods for the functions you need.

Table 26.24. MAPI Session properties.

Property	Description
`Action`	Defines the action to be taken upon initiation of the MAPI Session control. This `Action` property is available only at runtime and provides only the write-only capability.
`DownloadMail`	Stipulates whether the mail server should download new messages for a designated user.
`LogonUI`	Stipulates whether a dialog box is available for sign-on.
`NewSession`	Defines whether to start a new mail session, even when a valid session is active.
`Password`	Defines which account password matches the `UserName` property.
`SessionID`	Takes the present messaging session handle and stores it. This property is active only at runtime and is read-only.
`UserName`	Defines the account user name.

Table 26.25. MAPI Session methods.

Method	Description
SignOff	Terminates a messaging session and logs the user off the account stipulated in the UserName and Password properties.
SignOn	Initiates a session by logging the user into the user's account using the UserName and Password properties and specifying a session handle, which is routed to the message subsystem.

Table 26.26. MAPI Session Action settings.

Action Setting	Value	Description
vbSessionSignOn	1	Initiates a session by logging the user into the user's account using the UserName and Password properties and specifying a session handle, which is routed to the message subsystem. This handle is saved in the SessionID Property.
vbSessionSignOff	2	Terminates a messaging session and logs the user off the account stipulated in the UserName and Password properties.

The MAPI Message control allows the programmer to access anything in the inbox of the system, create and send new messages, create attachments, save or delete messages, display the Address Book and Details dialog boxes, read attachments, and perform reply and forwarding actions.

The Message control properties are listed in Table 26.27. The methods for this control are in Table 26.28. The Action property settings that correspond with the methods are shown in Table 26.29. If you use the MAPI custom controls, make sure the system you are going to do the final installation on already has MAPI installed. If not, the MAPI DLL and system files must be included in your installation.

Table 26.27. MAPI Message properties.

Property	Description
Action	Defines the action to be taken upon initiation of the MAPI Session control. This `Action` property is available only at runtime and provides only the write-only capability.
AddressCaption	Identifies the caption shown at the top of the Address Book dialog box at the time the `Show` method is called and the `details` argument is missing or set to False.
AddressEditFieldCount	Stipulates how many of the edit controls are available to the user in the Address Book dialog box. This occurs when the `Show` method is called and the `details` argument is missing or set to False.
AddressLabel	Defines how the edit control looks in the address book at the time when the `Show` method is identified and the `details` argument is missing or set to False.
AddressModifiable	Defines whether the address book is capable of being modified.
AddressResolveUI	Defines whether a dialog box is available to display any ambiguous names that need to be resolved during addressing. This should occur at the time the `ResolveName` method is called.
AttachmentCount	Identifies the total number of attachments related to the active indexed message. This property is active only at runtime and is read-only. (It is not accessible at design time.)
AttachmentIndex	Attaches a number to this attachment that identifies it as a specific message attachment. (It is not accessible at design time.)
AttachmentName	Attaches a name to this attachment that identifies it as a specific message attachment. (It is not accessible at design time.) This property is active only at runtime and is read-only except when the `MsgIndex` property is set to −1.
AttachmentPathName	Attaches a full path name to this attachment that identifies it as a specific message attachment. (It is not accessible at design time.) This property is active only at runtime and is read-only except when the `MsgIndex` property is set to −1.

Property	Description
AttachmentPosition	Defines where to find the attachment identified within the message body. (It is not accessible at design time.) This property is active only at runtime and is read-only except when the MsgIndex property is set to –1.
AttachmentType	Defines the type of attachment identified as the currently active file attachment. (It is not accessible at design time.) This property is active only at runtime and is read-only except when the MsgIndex property is set to –1.
FetchMsgType	Defines the message type that makes up the message set.
FetchSorted	Defines the order that messages are loaded into the message set from the inbox.
FetchUnreadOnly	Decides whether restrictions should be placed on the messages in the message set, requiring them to be made unread messages only.
MsgConversationID	Identifies the conversation thread identification value corresponding to the active indexed message. This property is active only at runtime and is read-only except when the MsgIndex property is set to –1.
MsgCount	Shows how many messages are present in the message set at the time the current messaging session is in operation. This property is active only at runtime and is read-only. (It is not accessible at design time.)
MsgDateReceived	Identifies the date the indexed message that is presently active was received. This property is active only at runtime and is read-only. (It is not accessible at design time.)
MsgID	Defines with a string identifier the indexed message that is presently active. This property is active only at runtime and is read-only. (It is not accessible at design time.)
MsgIndex	Attaches an index number to the indexed message that is presently active. (It is not accessible at design time.)
MsgNoteText	Defines the message's text body. (It is not accessible at design time.) This property is active only at runtime and is read-only except when the MsgIndex property is set to –1.

continues

Table 26.27. continued

Property	Description
MsgOrigAddress	Shows the mail address of the originator of the indexed message that is presently active. As part of the messaging system operation, this property is set for you at message transmission time. This property is active only at runtime and is read-only. (It is not accessible at design time.)
MsgOrigDisplayName	Shows the name of the originator of the indexed message that is presently active. As part of the messaging system operation, this property is set for you at message transmission time. This property is active only at runtime and is read-only. (It is not accessible at design time.)
MsgRead	Provides the sender with an indication that the message has been read. This property is active only at runtime and is read-only. (It is not accessible at design time.)
MsgReceiptRequested	Used to define whether a return receipt is requested on the indexed message that is presently active. (It is not accessible at design time.)
MsgSent	Provides an indication that the message has been sent for distribution to the designated mail server. As part of the messaging system operation, this property is set for you at message transmission time. This property is active only at runtime and is read-only. (It is not accessible at design time.)
MsgSubject	Defines the subject line of the indexed message that is presently active. (It is not accessible at design time.) This property is active only at runtime and is read-only except when the MsgIndex property is set to −1.
MsgType	Defines the type of the indexed message that is presently active. (It is not accessible at design time.) This property is active only at runtime and is read-only except when the MsgIndex property is set to −1.
RecipAddress	Defines the e-mail address of the recipient of the indexed message that is presently active. This property is active only at runtime and is read-only except when the MsgIndex property is set to −1. (It is not accessible at design time.)

Property	Description
RecipCount	Defines how many recipients are identified to receive the indexed message that is presently active. This property is active only at runtime and is read-only. (It is not accessible at design time.)
RecipDisplayName	Defines the name of the recipient of the indexed message that is presently active. This property is active only at runtime and is read-only except when the MsgIndex property is set to –1. (It is not accessible at design time.)
RecipIndex	Attaches an index number to a message that identifies the message with a particular active recipient. (It is not accessible at design time.)
RecipType	Defines the type of presently active indexed recipients, such as message originator, primary or copy recipient, or blind copy recipient. (It is not accessible at design time.) This property is active only at runtime and is read-only except when the MsgIndex property is set to –1.
SessionID	Saves the specified messaging session handle of the current message. (It is not accessible at design time.)

Table 26.28. MAPI Message methods.

Method	Description
Compose	The process used to compose a message.
Copy	The process used to copy the presently active message to the compose buffer.
Delete	The process used to delete a message, recipient, or attachment.
Fetch	Generates a message set that is formed from selected messages in the inbox.
Forward	Forwards a message by copying it to a compose buffer and inserting an FW: at the beginning of the Subject line. This method changes the MsgIndex property to –1.
Reply	Replies to a message by copying it to a compose buffer and inserting an RE: at the beginning of the Subject line. This method changes the MsgIndex property to –1.

continues

Table 26.28. continued

Method	Description
ReplyAll	Replies to all message recipients specified. This is done by copying it to a compose buffer and inserting an RE: at the beginning of the Subject line and sending it to the originator and all recipients delineated on the TO: and CC: lines. This method changes the MsgIndex property to –1.
ResolveName	Performs a search of the address book to match the name with the currently active recipient.
Save	The process used to save the current message residing in the compose buffer.
Send	The process used to send a message, such as displaying to the user the components making up the message and transferring the message to the mail server for distribution.
Show	Displays a dialog box of the mail Address Book or information related to the currently active recipients.

Table 26.29. MAPI Message Action settings.

Action Setting	Value	Buffer	Description
vbMessageFetch	1	Compose/Read	Generates a message set formed with messages residing in the inbox. The message set uses these properties in its creation: FetchMsgType, FetchSorted, and FetchUnreadOnly.
vbMessageSendDlg	2	Compose	These messages are sent inside a dialog box. It prompts the user for the components needed and delivers it to the mail server for distribution.
vbMessageSend	3	Compose	Allows for sending a message without the use of a dialog box, by transferring the message directly to the mail server.

Action Setting	Value	Buffer	Description
vbMessageSaveMsg	4	Compose	Saves presently active messages residing in the compose buffer with `MsgIndex` equal to –1.
vbMessageCopy	5	Read	Copies the presently active message to the compose buffer. Also changes the `MsgIndex` property to –1.
vbMessageCompose	6	Read	Composes the presently active message and clears the entire compose buffer of components. Also changes the `MsgIndex` property to –1.
vbMessageReply	7	Read	Replies to a specified message recipient. This is done by copying the message to a compose buffer and inserting an `RE:` at the beginning of the Subject line and sending it to the originator and recipient delineated on the TO: line. Also changes the `MsgIndex` property to –1.
vbMessageReplyAll	8	Read	Replies to all message recipients specified. This is done by copying the message to a compose buffer and inserting an `RE:` at the beginning of the Subject line and sending it to the originator and all recipients delineated on the TO: and CC: lines. Also changes the `MsgIndex` property to –1.

continues

Table 26.29. continued

Action Setting	Value	Buffer	Description
vbMessageForward	9	Read	Forwards a message by copying it to a compose buffer and inserting an FW: at the beginning of the Subject line. Also changes the MsgIndex property to –1.
vbMessageDelete	10	Read	Deletes a presently active message with all its components and subtracts 1 automatically from the MsgCount property, along with decrementing the index of each of the remaining messages that follow the deleted one. When the deleted message is the last message in the set, this Action property decrements the MsgIndex by 1.
vbMessageShowAdBook	11	Compose/Read	Displays a dialog box of the mail Address Book or information related to the currently active recipients. Changes are not saved if outside the compose buffer and MsgIndex is not equal to –1.
vbMessageShowDetails	12	Compose/Read	Displays a dialog box that contains the information related to the currently active recipients. The messaging system determines the quantity of information that is displayed in addition to the recipient's name and address.

Action Setting	Value	Buffer	Description
vbMessageResolveName	13	Compose/Read	Performs a search of the address book to match the name with the currently active recipient. If a match does not occur, an error message is returned.
vbRecipientDelete	14	Compose	Deletes the presently active indexed recipient and subtracts 1 automatically from the `RecipCount` property along with decrementing the index of each of the remaining recipients that follow the deleted one. When the deleted recipient is the last recipient in the set, this `Action` property decrements the `RecipIndex` by 1.
vbAttachmentDelete	15	Compose	Deletes the presently active indexed attachments and subtracts 1 automatically from the `AttachmentCount` property along with decrementing the index of each of the remaining attachments that follow the deleted item. When the deleted attachment is the last attachment in the set, this `Action` property decrements the `AttachmentIndex` by 1.

Use of the MAPI custom controls continues. The controls are not memory-prohibitive (they don't require OLE Automation), they can be used on older Windows machines, and they work perfectly for simple messaging. We recommend you execute and examine the sample MAPI applications and source code included with Visual Basic. These examples provide excellent explicit implementations of current Simple MAPI features.

OLE Messaging Library Access

The Visual Basic controls can address only the functions of the Simple MAPI interface. Microsoft is centralizing access to most of the Extended MAPI functions through the OLE Messaging interface. This interface is stored as a DLL and can be controlled by any application that supports OLE Automation (see Figure 26.10). This will replace MAPI controls for Visual Basic.

FIGURE 26.10.
OLE Messaging.

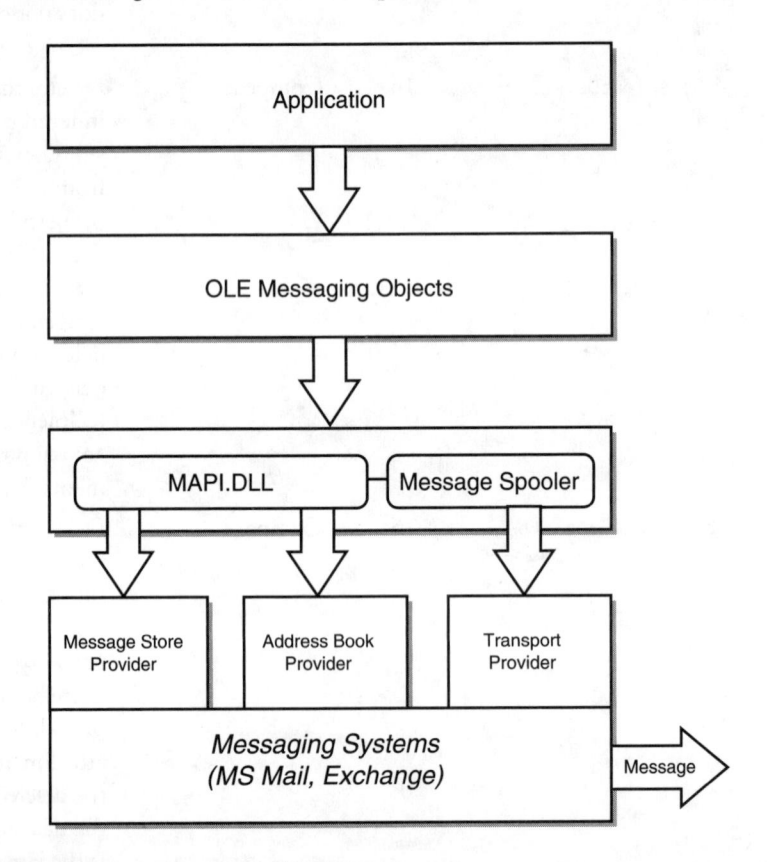

```
┌─────────────────────────────┐
│        Application          │
└──────────────┬──────────────┘
               ▼
┌─────────────────────────────┐
│   OLE Messaging Objects     │
└──────────────┬──────────────┘
               ▼
┌──────────────┬──────────────┐
│  MAPI.DLL    │Message Spooler│
└──┬────────┬──┴──────┬───────┘
   ▼        ▼         ▼
┌───────┬────────┬──────────┐
│Message│Address │Transport │
│ Store │ Book   │Provider  │
│Provide│Provider│          │
├───────┴────────┴──────────┤
│    Messaging Systems       │ ══▶ Message
│   (MS Mail, Exchange)      │
└────────────────────────────┘
```

The interface allows creations of message-specific OLE objects that are used to create and maintain e-mail messages and services. OLE Messaging is meant primarily for client access to messaging and therefore provides a subset of features available through Extended MAPI. For the creation of a true MAPI server, Extended MAPI must be used.

The OLE Messaging services create three basic objects: a Session object, a Folder object, and a Message object. Visual Basic, however, can completely access only the Session object. Therefore, from Visual Basic neither of the other two objects can be created, although they can be accessed. Figure 26.11 shows the object hierarchy of the Session object. VB can manipulate all these objects through a central Session object.

FIGURE 26.11.
OLE Messaging object chart.

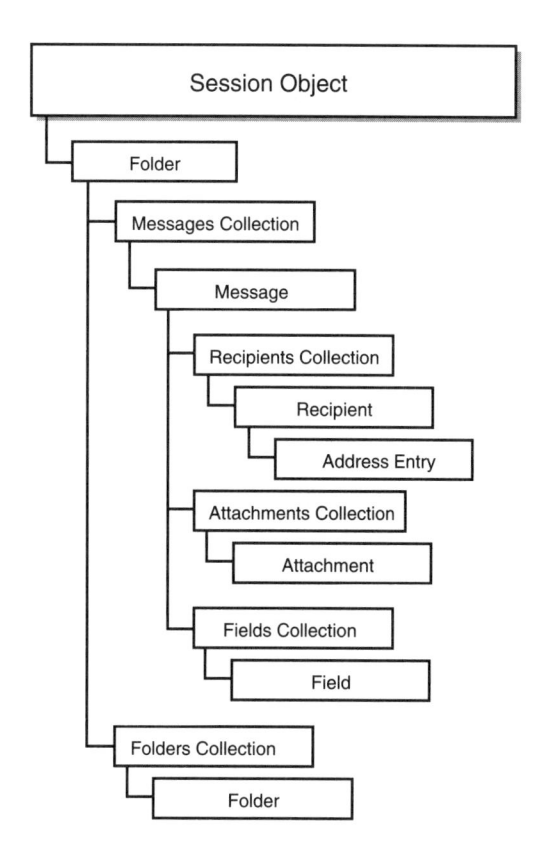

```
Session Object
 ├── Folder
 │    ├── Messages Collection
 │    │    └── Message
 │    │         ├── Recipients Collection
 │    │         │    └── Recipient
 │    │         │         └── Address Entry
 │    │         ├── Attachments Collection
 │    │         │    └── Attachment
 │    │         └── Fields Collection
 │    │              └── Field
 │    └── Folders Collection
 │         └── Folder
```

Sample OLE Messaging Code

The code sample in Listing 26.9 creates a Session, a Message, and a Recipient. It then sends a message. A Session object is accessed through OLE automation, and all the other objects, methods, and properties are manipulated through this central object. Note that the message object created is invalidated when the Send method is called. This routine should provide a sample of how OLE Messaging can be used from a VBA-compliant application.

Listing 26.9. OLE Messaging code sample.

```
Sub SampleOLEMess()
    Dim tempSession as Object
    Dim tempMessage as Object
    Dim tempDestination as Object

    Set tempSession = CreateObject("MAPI.Session")
    tempSession.Logon profileName := "myName"

    Set tempMessage = tempSession.Outbox.Messages.Add
    tempMessage.Subject = "Budget Request"
    tempMessage.Text = "Please have the Budget on my desk tomorrow morning."
```

continues

Listing 26.9. continued

```
    Set tempDestination = tempMessage.Recipients.Add
    tempDestination.Name = "Hugh Glass"
    tempDestination.Type = mapiTo
    ' Make sure email address has reference and is valid
    tempDestination.Resolve

    tempMessage.Update
    tempMessage.Send showDialog := False
    tempSession.Logoff
End Sub
```

Messaging Clients and Servers

Messaging can be created and maintained by various clients and servers. For example, a Microsoft Mail server can reside on a Window NT AS-based machine and receive and send mail created on a variety of hosts.

Messaging can be divided primarily into two groups: Simple Messaging and Groupware Messaging. Simple Messaging Servers can send and receive messages, often with attachments, and provide such functions as mail forwarding, basic distribution, and carbon copies. Examples of Simple Messaging Servers include cc:Mail from Lotus, MS Mail, and Novell MHS.

Complex Messaging is a new type of messaging that allows such capabilities as public message posting, replication, and group broadcasting. Groupware Servers include Lotus Notes, Novell's Groupwise, and MS Exchange.

cc:Mail

Currently, cc:Mail is the leading Simple Messaging system on the market. The cc:Mail product is produced by Lotus (now IBM) and is available for nearly every platform, including DOS, Windows, Macintosh, OS/2, and UNIX.

This e-mail system also has a gateway for Novell's MHS so that a cc:Mail system can be linked with other MHS-compatible systems such as AT&T Mail and MCI Mail. It supports the VIM messaging protocol.

Microsoft Mail

MS Mail Server automatically synchronizes directories and creates a global e-mail address list (with other MS Mail Servers). It can also store and forward e-mail messages if no permanent connection is available. Connections can be made over telephone or X.25 connections.

MS Mail Server provides complete mail password security, mail encryption and storage, and Server password protection for remote Server access. Gateways are available for IBM PROFS and OfficeVision, X.400, IBM SNADS, SMTP, MHS, MCI Mail, 3Com 3+Mail, AT&T Easylink, and fax.

Mail client programs are available for Windows, MS-DOS, Macintosh, and OS/2. The Microsoft Mail Remote Client program enables you to access messages on the network. Unfortunately, Remote Client is available only for Windows and MS-DOS machines.

Lotus Notes

Lotus Notes is the dominant supplier of Groupware Messaging Services. Lotus essentially invented Groupware as a market. Now that Lotus has been acquired by IBM, Lotus might remain an extremely important player in what will become a hotly contested market.

If you are unfamiliar with Lotus Notes, it is not simple to explain. In fact, Lotus often has difficulty explaining what it can do. Notes is essentially a message-based database that can manipulate complex data and links such as forms, tables, workflow, public posting of messages, rich-text fields, OLE fields, and more.

Because entire rich-text fields (including font styles and graphics) can be stored and searched, Notes can be used for document automation as well. Notes also includes a development environment (fairly simple but excellent), a macro language (called agents), and third-party tool support.

Notes databases are document-based and are not relational. Notes databases can be viewed like a traditional database with rows and columns. Each row or record in the database is known as a document. Each column is a field.

Notes databases can be viewed as a form-based resultant set, a view-based resultant set, or a document-based resultant set. A form is much like a Visual Basic form in that various fields are shown in a window, and data from each record appears in the fields. A view makes the database appear in row and column format like a spreadsheet or database browser. However, a view can also be hierarchical. Using a document view, various documents with different forms can be contained in the resultant set.

There are shortcomings to the Notes database model. Transactions are not supported, so there is no capability for locking, commits, or rollbacks. As mentioned previously, Notes also does not offer relational capabilities.

For Visual Basic programmers, Lotus Notes can be successfully integrated into an application with a minimum of difficulty. Two companies currently supply controls for Visual Basic that access the Notes API: Lotus and Brainstorm Technologies.

The VB/Link control encapsulates all the Notes functionality into three controls: the Notes Data control, the Rich Text control, and the HList Hierarchical control. The Notes Data control is the central piece of the VB/Link system and works essentially like the VB Data control. The Notes Data control determines what Notes Server will be connected and what database should be used. Most interaction with Notes takes place through the Notes Data control. The Rich Text control and the HList Hierarchical control are essentially bound to the Notes Data control.

The Lotus Notes HiTest Tools 2 is almost completely different from VB/Link in approach to interface. It provides 12 separate controls that are each linked to different objects. HiTest includes a complete object hierarchy and object API with properties and methods to access a Notes database. Although it is strong in data manipulation capabilities, it is weaker in its rich text capabilities and hierarchical viewing functionality.

Access to Lotus Notes can also be achieved through the Notes API. However, the API requires many callback routines (which VB cannot handle without extensions), so custom C glue programming (creating the "glue" routines to allow VB and the calls to communicate) is required. For more information on VB/Link and Lotus HiTest Tools 2, see Chapter 29, "Third-Party Tools, Utilities, and Controls."

Microsoft Exchange Server

Microsoft Exchange Server is the groupware structure that Microsoft intends to be the baseline for Windows communications of the future. A Microsoft Exchange Server runs on NT (like SQL Server) and provides complete groupware message access, replication, public message publishing, forms sharing, scheduling, scripting, and object and data sharing. It supports CMC, MAPI, SMTP, X.400, and X.500 formatted messages.

Microsoft Exchange is similar to Lotus Notes in that it integrates information sharing and e-mail into a single user interface. Exchange is a family of products that include capabilities for such functions as messaging, public posting, threaded discussions, integrated scheduling, and server-based rules for workflow.

MS Exchange Server provides a replication service that can distribute and maintain multiple copies of information across a distributed network. Exchange includes an application development environment that enables users or administrators to build simple Exchange-based process applications.

OLE automation can be used to access the Exchange system by using OLE Messaging to connect to the Exchange messaging and workgroup infrastructure. At the time of this writing, we have seen no general interface for Visual Basic that offers the access power available for Lotus Notes. Microsoft is committed to the support of Visual Basic and VBA, so by the time you read this, such a product could be announced.

Windows 95 Integrated Messaging

Windows 95 includes an integrated Messaging Client (which uses the Exchange API) that can be used as a peer-to-peer messaging server or can access other mail servers. The client provides an inbox, which is just like any other folder on the desktop (see Figure 26.12). Messages or faxes can be received in the inbox.

FIGURE 26.12.
Windows 95 inbox.

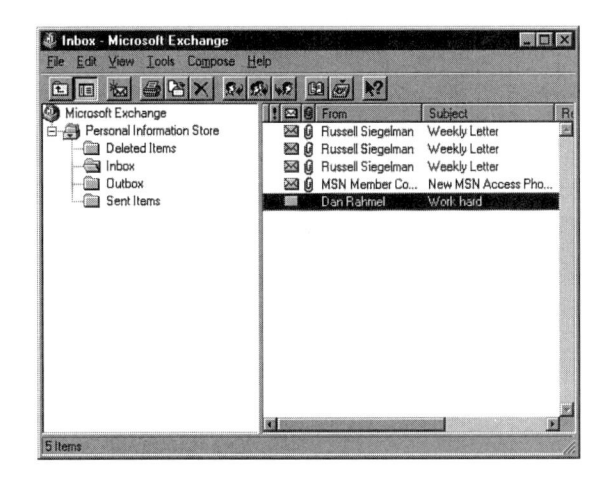

The inbox works with the MAPI interface. It can therefore receive any messages for which there is a Service Provider Interface (SPI). There are currently SPIs available for Microsoft Mail, Novell MHS, IBM PROFS, fax, DEC All-In-1 voice mail, AT&T, Easylink, CompuServe, and MCI Mail.

The MAPI address book included with Windows 95 (see Figure 26.13) can also obtain user and group lists for Windows NT Server, NetWare Bindery, and Microsoft (Online) Network. The Messaging Client can be used over a modem, standard network, Public X.25 WAN, or even ISDN connections.

The Messaging Client enables the user to organize incoming messages by Views and Rules. Views enable the user to specify various categories for the messages to be placed in. Rules automatically process and sort incoming messages and place the items in the specified view.

FIGURE 26.13.
Windows 95 Address Book.

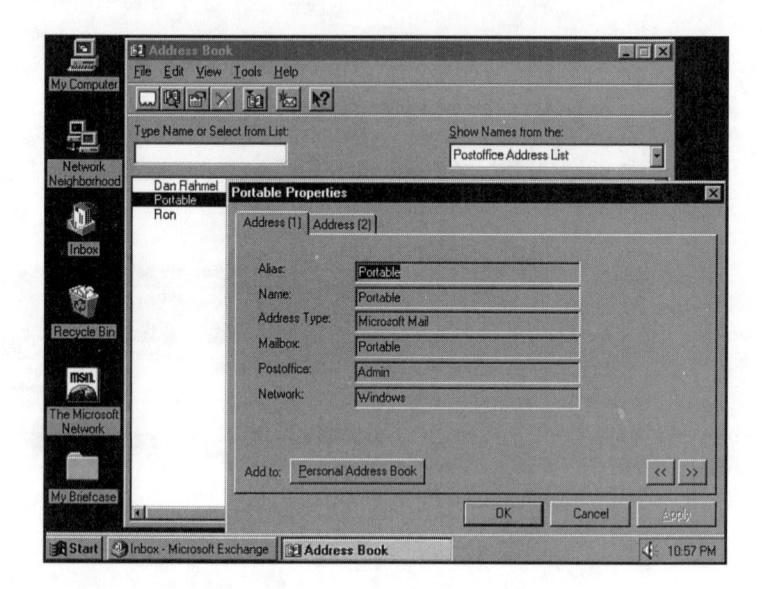

Private Messaging and Public Messaging

Messaging is currently split between the messaging activity that takes place within an organization and that which takes place outside. For various compatibility, expense, and security reasons, breaching the two domains was a difficult task. Increasingly, however, organizations want to send e-mail out into public systems and receive their public e-mail to their private inboxes (see Figure 26.14). Greater compatibility and cheaper costs are providing a way to accomplish this task.

E-mail systems are divided into two typical geographic types: public messaging and private messaging. Private e-mail consists of all the e-mail exchange that takes place within an organization. Usually cc:Mail, Microsoft Mail, MS Exchange, and Notes are used for private messaging. Public messaging usually consists of an online server (America Online, CompuServe, Prodigy) or the Internet.

Traditionally, most client/server applications have been engineered toward private messaging capabilities. With the growth of protocol stacks (such as WinSock, described at the end of this chapter), gateways, and LAN-to-WAN connectivity, there may be greatly increased use of public messaging.

The most popular method is to use a gateway to SMTP from the main mail server. This allows messages to be routed to and from the Internet. With increased MAPI/SMTP exchange interfaces, a gateway might become less necessary as the protocols are increasingly built into the networking API.

FIGURE 26.14.
Private and public messaging systems.

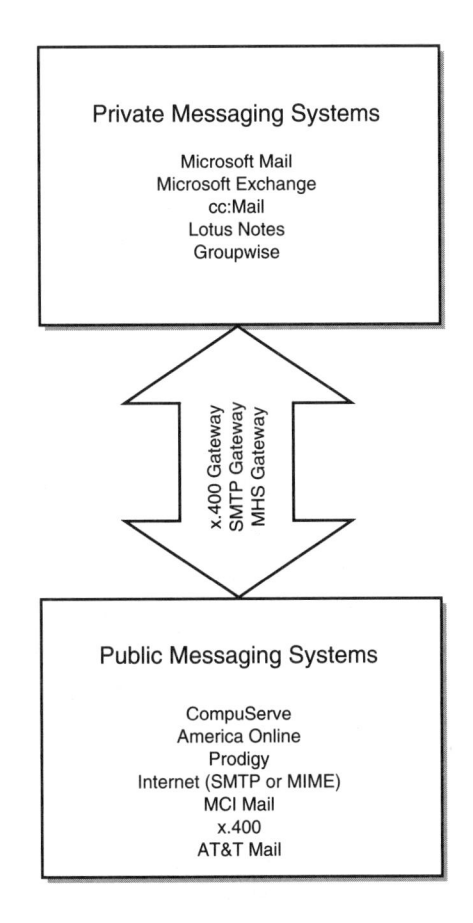

```
┌─────────────────────────────────┐
│    Private Messaging Systems    │
│                                 │
│        Microsoft Mail           │
│        Microsoft Exchange       │
│        cc:Mail                  │
│        Lotus Notes              │
│        Groupwise                │
└─────────────────────────────────┘
            ⇅  x.400 Gateway
               SMTP Gateway
               MHS Gateway
┌─────────────────────────────────┐
│    Public Messaging Systems     │
│                                 │
│        CompuServe               │
│        America Online           │
│        Prodigy                  │
│        Internet (SMTP or MIME)  │
│        MCI Mail                 │
│        x.400                    │
│        AT&T Mail                │
└─────────────────────────────────┘
```

With the increasing transparency of exchange between public and private messaging systems, it is important to consider what type of systems your client/server system will be required to transfer over. What are the delays involved? What is the expense when the communication occurs over a public system (per message or per KB charges are common)? What type of translation needs to take place for attached files?

All these questions must be taken into account as the system is designed. Bridges between the two types of systems will become more common, making some applications that were previously viable on a LAN too slow or expensive to scale to the new WAN-based client/server world.

Remote Access Service (RAS)

To increase the capabilities of the NT Server system, Microsoft has released Remote Access Services (RAS). This provides a gateway to the NT Server system through remote links (such as modems or ISDN lines) that preserve the security and integrity of the system (see Figure

26.15). The remote user logs onto the system as if present on the LAN. The Remote system, through RAS, believes that it is directly attached to the Server system and can access resources accordingly.

FIGURE 26.15.
Remote Access Service structure.

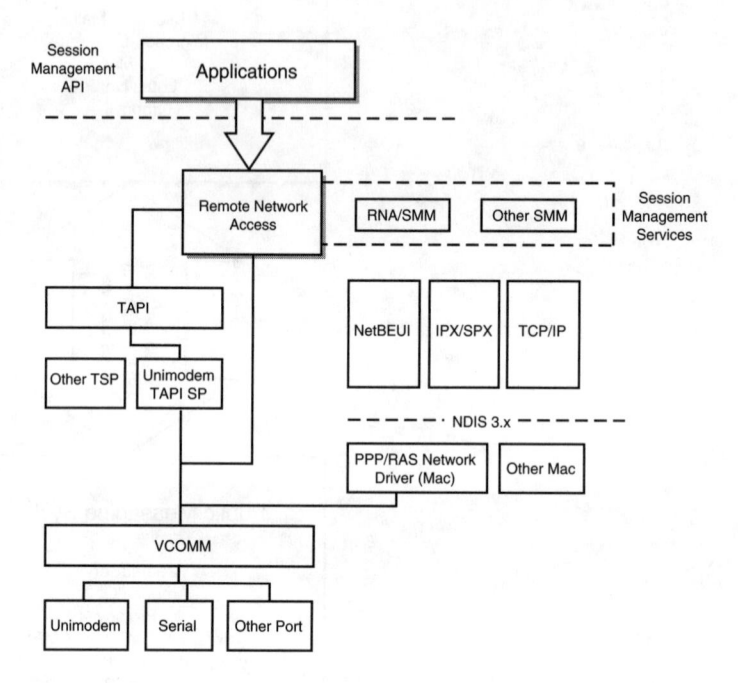

RAS has a complete API (available only to C and C++ programmers) that can be used to design custom transmission and serving interfaces. Although the programming aspects are not directly relevant to the Visual Basic programmer, the links to the server can be used by a remote VB program. Therefore, basic knowledge of possible remote system access is important.

Through the RAS, a remote access link is provided to a file server, a mail server, the network printers, or a database server. RAS works between any two RAS-enabled PCs or with Window NT Advanced Server or NetWare Connect. RAS also provides support for Point-to-Point Protocol (PPP). See Chapter 3, "Networks (Client/Server Foundation)," for more information on this and other protocols.

Available programming services include initiate, abort, or resume a connection, and gather data about the type and status of the connection. Remote access has an available user interface (similar in style to the ODBC interface) that enables the user to make explicit connections, or the connection can be accessed implicitly by a program or the system.

Connection Technologies

Other technologies will become increasingly important to remote access possibilities. As digital and Wide-Area Networks continue to grow around the world, digital access ports will become more common. For example, most of the available phone lines carry only analog signals. A transmitting modem turns digital information into analog (audio) information, broadcasts it over the phone line, and the receiving modem converts the analog signals back to digital data.

Networks such as ISDN are based entirely on digital transmission (see Chapter 3). As digital network connections become more available, users will be able to plug directly into a Wide-Area Network as if they were accessing their local LAN. For example, if an ISDN connector was available in the lobby of a hotel, a business traveler could plug directly into the digital network and access the LAN at his home office.

For this type of connection, traditional connection protocols (such as TCP/IP) will probably be commonly used. Therefore, remote connections will be able to directly use the same network protocol stacks as when connected to the local network.

To make programming for network protocols easier, Microsoft has introduced a network standard called Windows Sockets, or WinSock. WinSock provides a generic API through which connections are made, data is transferred, retransmissions occur, and so forth. WinSock allows a program to be designed to call the WinSock interface without regard to the networking protocol. The program can be transferring data over a TCP/IP, IPX/SPX, NetBEUI, or other protocol-based network. WinSock shields the program from the specifics of the protocol. New protocols are plugged into the WinSock interface (much like an electrical jack into a wall socket).

The WinSock specification is defined by a panel of 30 industry companies in the applications, networks, and operating system fields.

WinSock 1.1

The original WinSock 1.1 specification was a great step toward a vendor-independent network API. A program could call the WinSock API, and all the internal manipulations were handled by each driver. WinSock provides a networking API that offers binary compatibility between heterogeneous Windows-based protocol stacks and utilities vendors. WinSock is a multivendor standard, including companies such as 3COM Corp., Distinct Corp., FTP Software, Frontier Tech., IBM, JSB Corp., LAN Design, Microdyne, Microsoft, NetManage, Sun Microsystems, Walker Richer Quinn, and Wollongong.

WinSock supports both connection-oriented and connectionless protocols. There are sockets available for LAN Manager, TCP/IP, AppleTalk, and other protocols. An excellent book on WinSock programming is *Programming WinSock* (Sams Publishing, 1995). Appendix C lists Custom Controls available through Visual Basic to access the WinSock interface.

WinSock 2.0

At the time of this writing, the WinSock 2.0 specification had just been released. Already, companies are rushing to support the new interface. WinSock 2 does not run under Windows 3.1, only Windows 95 and Windows NT. The new API works with TCP/IP, IPX/SPX, DECnet, OSI, and other transports that are WinSock-compatible.

The new specification has the capability to share sockets across multiple tasks. This allows a data stream to be shared between multiple tasks or applications. Multitasking is becoming a dominant feature in client machines, where an OS can allow multiple programs to share the machine's hardware.

27

Telephony

Interfacing between the phone and computer is a growing market called *computer telephony*. The possibilities of such a system within the client/server architecture are incredible. Telephony does much more than enable a computer to dial the phone. Some of the applications used so far include

- Voice mail
- Call return
- Telemarketing
- Fax-back and fax-on-demand services
- Interactive information systems
- Voice signal processing
- Touch-tone-based database access
- Outbound call tracking
- Conference calling

Telephony systems give employees and customers easy access to information 24 hours a day. When combined with fax-back services or voice mail, telephony can greatly increase the responsiveness of an organization.

> **NOTE**
>
> One company we know just put its personnel system online through a telephony interface. This enables employees to dial into the system with a standard touch-tone phone. After punching in an identification number, they can instantly access information such as their remaining number of sick days or the amount vested in their retirement plans.

Telephony's great advantage over traditional modem-based information systems is its ability to access information over a traditional touch-tone phone. On-the-road salesmen can communicate with the office computer as easily as a customer, without needing any specialized hardware.

Businesses use telephony to provide conference calling, automated customer information systems, touch-tone surveys, call transferring, and other services. By either providing telephony services in-house or gaining access to sophisticated phone company-based services, a company can greatly increase efficiency in customer relations and its internal productivity.

In addition to telephony growth in the business community, individual users are beginning to equip their machines with basic telephony hardware. Such hardware usually consists of a card that integrates modem, fax, and voice mail. An individual computer can provide complete voice mail access as well as several mail boxes and even simple fax-back services for less than the price of a standard answering machine.

The most likely reason that telephony will become important in the information systems world is how inexpensively it provides services previously available only on a tremendously expensive and specialized custom phone system. Placing an entire PBX system in an organization has always been expensive in terms of both hardware and maintenance. The GUI-based telephony setup tools and the common interfaces and APIs dramatically reduce both of these costs.

With telephony, individual services can be added as they are needed. A beginning telephony system can be implemented by inserting a single inexpensive card into a desktop computer and plugging in a phone line. Options can be added and enhanced as needs increase. The standards that are being created will enable systems to integrate as they grow.

An Overview of Telephone Systems

The basic phone system may seem straightforward, but with the breakup of AT&T and the proliferation of alternative telephone technologies (ISDN, Digital Switching, and so forth), the world of the basic telephone has become increasingly complex.

When the phone system was originally implemented in the early twentieth century, phone operators used jumper wires to connect one phone user with another. For example, if an individual needed to call Joe's Plumbing across town, he would call the operator. The line coming out of the originator's house would be boosted, and through a centralized switchboard, the line signal would be connected with the line going into the plumber's store.

This is a simplified, yet essentially accurate, model of how the phone system still works. Now, however, that switching between lines is accomplished with electronic or digital switches. With the increasing use of fiber optics for long distance transmission, transmissions have changed from analog, where the actual signal is broadcast, to digital, where the signal is converted to a digital representation and then converted back to the actual signal.

In the past, companies had to buy a large, expensive system called a PBX to bring routing capabilities into an organization. This private system was attached to numerous phone lines from the phone company. Calls made into an organization were switched to their proper extension. The PBX could handle call transfer, hold, voice mail, and numerous other functions.

The growth of computer power on individual desktop machines made the integration of phone systems and computers attractive. Not only did desktop computers increasingly use communications to transfer data (by using modems, fax/modems, ISDN, and so on), people generally desired to use their sophisticated computer as a front-end for the phone.

A computer-telephone interface promised the ease of use of a graphical interface instead of numerous difficult-to-understand features accessed by buttons on an increasingly difficult-to-use phone. Likewise, integration with contact managers, personal information managers (PIM), and e-mail, modem, and fax services promised greater productivity for employees.

Small business could rarely afford a PBX setup, yet they had complete desktop computers with fax/modems and LANs. Personal users also had computers powerful enough to use some of the sophisticated features that a computer-based phone system could provide, such as voice mail and call forwarding.

Computer telephony seeks to fulfill this promise. By making the desktop computer the front-end for the telephone system, normal voice communications as well as data communications can become more powerful. There are numerous ways in which computer-telephone integration can be accomplished.

Types of Telephony Systems

Telephony systems may be implemented in a broad range of configurations. A telephony system is usually referred to as a *computer telephone interface* (CTI). A CTI system has many different forms, with different configurations providing for integration with current phone switching systems. There are four general types of telephony systems:

- PC-based
- Phone-based
- Server-based
- Voice server-based

Although each type of system is different, many enterprises employ a mixture of them. The new telephony protocols, such as Telephony API (TAPI) and Telephony Server API (TSAPI), seek to standardize the access to these various systems. A desktop machine could therefore use the same interface to place a call over a modem installed in the machine and to access voice mail stored on a voice server.

An often-used parallel is the use of printer drivers. The user can print to any printer using the same piece of software (word processor, spreadsheet, and so on). The user merely directs the program to the correct printer, and the document is printed within the printer's native capabilities. Telephony promoters seek to provide the same type of point-and-play capability to select and use telephony devices.

PC-Based CTI

The PC-based CTI is the most common type of interface that is familiar to most computer users. A piece of CTI hardware is added to a desktop machine, such as a fax/modem or voice mail modem. This hardware is then connected to the general system, such as a phone line, ISDN connection, or PBX. The desktop machines can set up connections—for example, dialing the proper phone number—and usually provide an on-screen graphical interface.

Phone-Based CTI

A phone-based system works with a PBX or phone company switching system. Typically, an interface is hooked to a computer via the serial or parallel ports that can control the local phone system. This provides the desktop computer with access to the advanced features in an organization's phone system instead of using a complex phone with many buttons.

A physical connection is used between the PC and the switching system. Commands are sent through the interface to the PBX system to control call transfers and so on.

With the growth of other types of interfaces, such as direct line control from the PC or through a network server, these interfaces will most likely become less common. These interfaces, as well as the advanced phones that can use the same feature set, are called *first-party call control devices*.

Server-Based CTI

A server-based CTI is typically used in a LAN-based enterprise. Modems, telephone switching, and other functions are shared. Resources are often centralized on the network server and can be accessed by any of the client machines. The individual desktop computers do not need a physical connection to the switching system.

The server-based CTI looks like another node on the LAN (see Figure 27.1). Call commands are sent to the LAN server or the LAN server device that activates the PBX for call control. The LAN server does the actual call routing. Because the PC itself does not control the switching—instead, it goes through the server—this is called *third-party call control*.

FIGURE 27.1.
Server computer telephony.

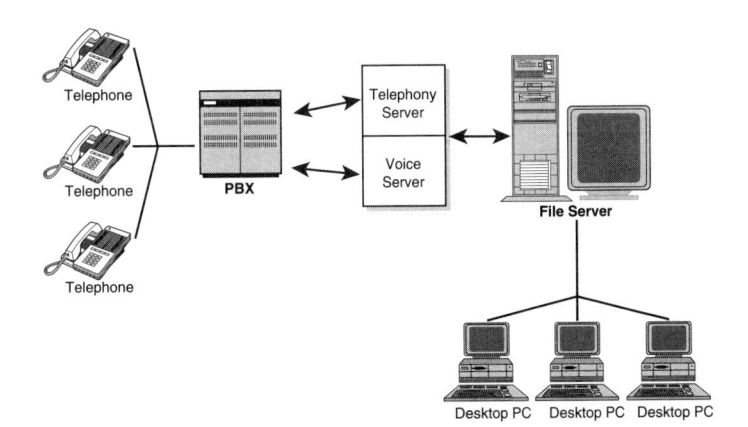

The PC that makes the call has no access to the actual line on which the connection occurs. A server-based system, therefore, gives the PC no access to the media stream. So in this type of system, the desktop machine has no direct access to the actual system. For example, the system can dial the number to a fax machine, but the desktop machine cannot send the fax over that connection through the PC modem.

Voice Server CTI

A voice server-based CTI uses a specific dedicated machine to handle voice calls, transfers, voice mail, fax-on-demand, and so forth. The voice server can control and provide access to the media stream, but it cannot control the connection. It relies on the PBX to make the necessary connections. The PBX receives incoming calls and routes the calls to the voice server.

Therefore, the system can do most of the functions that are available through a normal phone (such as hold, conference, and forward), but it cannot switch any of the lines—in other words, no call transfer and the like. It provides no centralized control of the incoming lines. The dedicated hardware tends to be more expensive than adding peripherals to a PC or network, but it often includes extra features and capabilities.

Telephony API Standards

As with most fields in the computer world, there are competing standards in the telephony market. The two primary standards are Telephony API (TAPI) and Telephony Server API (TSAPI). TAPI was created by Microsoft, Intel, DEC, and Novell; it is supported by more than 40 other vendors. TSAPI was created by Novell and AT&T; it is supported by many of the makers of phone switching systems.

Whether you decide to implement TAPI or TSAPI (or both) in a CTI system depends largely on the application and the existing system setup. The two standards were developed around different assumptions. TAPI was developed by Microsoft, making desktop operating systems the foundation. TSAPI was developing by Novell, giving it roots in the network server market.

TAPI is mostly a desktop-based or PC-based interface. Each individual machine can control the hardware that is attached to it, such as a modem, fax, or ISDN connection. TAPI does provide the potential interfaces for use of third-party call control devices, but that is not its primary strength. TAPI can be integrated with other services on the computer on which it runs. For example, a TAPI interface could be created to play a .WAV file for a musical hold or an answering announcement.

This integration with other interfaces on a machine is the reason that TAPI has greater line control capabilities than other interface standards. Each PC acts as an individual telephony server. Therefore, TAPI is based more on a peer-to-peer setup than a centralized server topology. Like most peer-to-peer systems, the weakness of the system lies in its decentralized architecture. This makes it perfect for some applications (voice mail, touch-tone menus, incremental expansion, and so on) and poor for others (centralized call transfer, conferencing, outbound call tracking, and so on).

> **NOTE**
>
> In the world of telephony, files with the .WAV file format are used extensively. For an example of recording a .WAV file, execute the Sound Recorder application included with the Windows OS and a multimedia configuration. Most Sound Blaster cards have a microphone port that will input sound for digitization.
>
> Many of the telephony programs have their own native format for storing sounds and messages. They usually provide a utility for converting .WAV files to and from their proprietary formats.

The TSAPI standard focuses on network telephony. TSAPI features call control, call routing, call/device monitoring, and phone management for workgroups. With a TSAPI application, an individual client computer sends control requests to a centralized phone server on the network server, which actually operates the phone switching. TSAPI, however, does not have direct access to the actual line media, which means that the interface is more for control and connection than for actual voice and data transmission.

TSAPI supporters include PBX manufacturers that have committed to develop device drivers for the equipment, including Alcatel, AT&T, Comdial, Ericsson, Fujitsu, Mitel, NEC, Nortel, and Siemens/ROLM. TSAPI support is available on most operating systems including Windows, OS/2, UNIXWare, and MacOS.

TSAPI, in contrast to the peer-to-peer configuration of TAPI, needs to be set up on a server with all the telephone resources funneled into the server. Individual desktop PCs send commands to the TSAPI server component. If there is currently an existing Novell server on the network, TSAPI will integrate well into such a LAN.

As with distributed data problems, deciding on a peer-to-peer or LAN-based system depends on the needs of the system and flexibility requirements. By keeping the configurations on desktop machines as TAPI does, expansion is simple, and the individual users can have varying options. This can make technical support within an organization simpler or more complex. Individual machines can be set up with exactly the specifications needed, but this means a proliferation of different configurations across the enterprise.

Network-based systems such as TSAPI require a larger up-front investment because the whole system must be integrated with a LAN. Adding options for individual users must be done at the network center. This provides more control for the system administrator, but it also adds more responsibility.

> **TIP**
>
> When making the decision about what CTI system to use, approach it as you would an information systems problem. Who needs access to what? What will the maintenance cost be? Is it more important to have heterogeneous solutions or one standard solution? Do the applications you have need individual line control or centralized access? Which system will integrate more easily with your existing phone system? Answering these questions should provide a fairly good idea of which system you should choose.

There are growing indications that organizations are interested in employing both standards. The standards tend to complement each other rather than act in a mutually exclusive fashion. The Nortel company is working on providing the necessary integration between the two systems. The interface, called *Tmap*, provides for interaction between the TAPI and TSAPI interfaces.

TAPI

Microsoft and Intel have been promoting the TAPI standard for telephony applications. TAPI provides a common way to integrate telephone networks, including analog, cellular, PBX, and ISDN systems (see Figure 27.2). It provides a single API for which programmers can write to access numerous phone services. It also provides the hardware vendor with a single standard for writing hardware drivers.

FIGURE 27.2.
A TAPI system configuration.

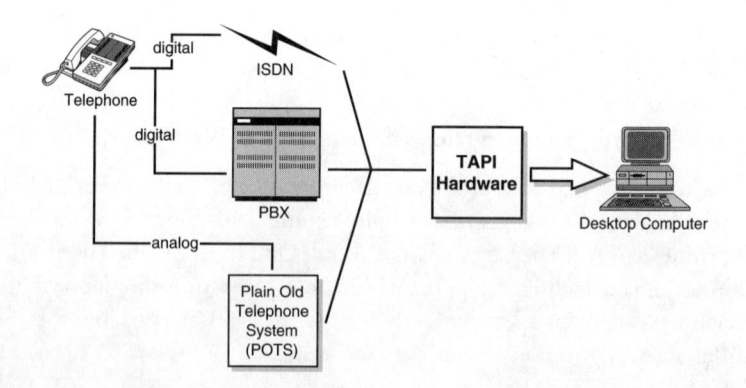

TAPI is a general API to telephony services. All the functions for the API are called through either TAPI.DLL or TAPI32.DLL (used on Win32s systems). The TAPI DLL loads the appropriate TAPI device driver and attempts to complete the function—to make a connection, alter a call, and so on.

The TAPI DLL accesses various TAPI drivers through the *service provider interface* (SPI). These drivers may provide access to such diverse hardware as a simple fax/modem or a complete PBX system (see Figure 27.3). A hardware vendor writes an SPI driver to be used with the TAPI system. Many of the common types of telephony hardware and PBXs have available SPI drivers. Some are included in the TAPI SDK.

FIGURE 27.3.
The TAPI service provider interface.

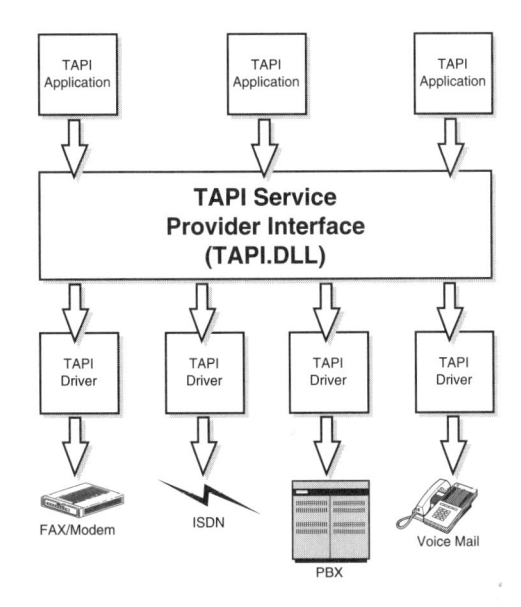

> **NOTE**
>
> TAPI is included as a standard service in Windows 95. As described in Chapter 26, "Remote Client/Server Access," TAPI is used by Windows 95 to create the connections to fax/modems and other devices on the system. There are TAPI drivers also available for Windows 3.1 and Win32. At the time of this writing, drivers for Windows NT are promised but not yet available. Be sure to include in your programming a routine to check that TAPI.DLL or TAPI32.DLL exists on the system before you attempt the various API calls.

TAPI, as described previously, is currently focused on providing desktop TAPI access. Microsoft's strategy is to expand into the server-based telephony market through Windows NT. Windows NT is to be the base platform to enable the centralization of resources.

Using Windows NT as a telephony network server, TAPI-compliant applications automatically have access to the network server. This transparent upgrade is the same strategy that Microsoft has pursued in implementing the capabilities of Remote or Distributed OLE.

Figure 27.4 provides a proposed structure for NT-based TAPI. Windows sockets (Winsock), in coordination with remote procedure calls, activates Remote TAPI and provides two-way communication between the client and the server. The server can then be interfaced with PBX hardware, direct outgoing analog or digital lines, or other compatible communications media. Microsoft has no announced date for shipping its already long-delayed release of NT TAPI.

FIGURE 27.4.
Windows NT TAPI implementation.

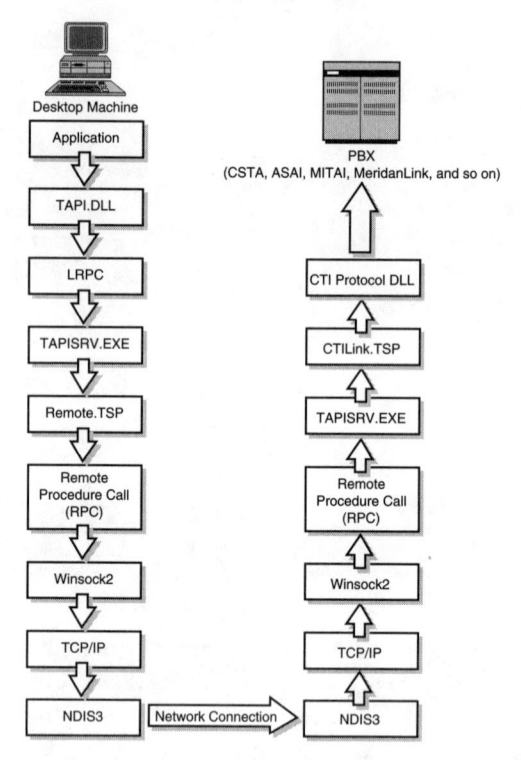

The connection that is made using the TAPI interface becomes a connection known as the *media stream*. The media stream can be accessed by other interfaces such as the Windows Sound System or data APIs (see Figure 27.5).

Interaction with the TAPI system occurs in three basic stages: initialization, asynchronous operations, and spontaneous events. *Initialization* is the setup of the TAPI services; it includes version negotiation, device characteristic queries, and procedure call-back registration. *Asynchronous operations* include events such as call transfer, call forwarding, and other switch-based functions. *Spontaneous events* include incoming calls, call progress, and so forth.

The TAPI interface is broken into two primary types: assisted telephony and full telephony (see Figure 27.6). *Assisted telephony* provides the most basic TAPI capabilities from any application. It can be easily used from VBA.

The more full-featured interface, called *full telephony*, contains numerous services. At the time of this writing, it must be accessed by using the TAPI API. Full telephony is broken down into three parts: basic services, supplementary services, and extended services. Basic and supplementary services can be used to access the full capabilities of a standard TAPI driver.

FIGURE 27.5.
Media stream interfaces.

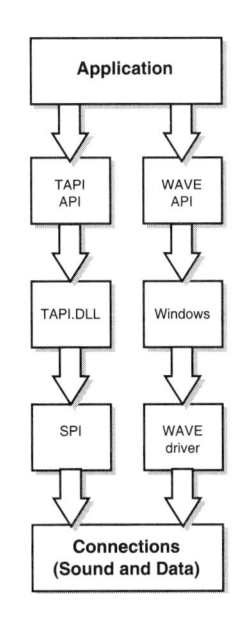

FIGURE 27.6.
TAPI interfaces.

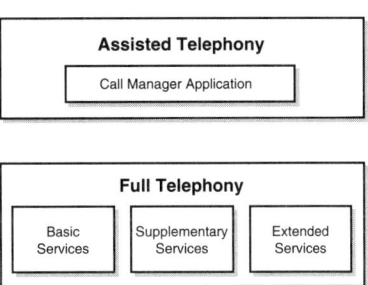

The extended services exist so that a program can access features that are not standard to the TAPI interface but are available for a particular driver or piece of hardware. This provides a similar interface to the ODBC PassThrough option, which enables a program to manipulate features found in only a particular database server.

The TAPI call structure uses TAPI.DLL (or TAPI32.DLL) to access the various functions that are included in the TAPI interface as well as those available only on specific hardware. As you can see in Figure 27.7, all the calls are made through the TAPI engine. System-specific functions are accessed through the extended services, which provide a function pass-through.

FIGURE 27.7.
The TAPI call structure.

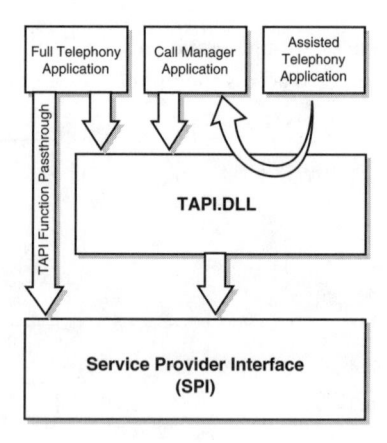

Assisted Telephony

Assisted telephony is the simplest way to access the TAPI interface. Assisted telephony uses a system-configured dialer application to make any connections requested by the TAPI calling program. Assisted telephony contains only four commands:

`tapiRequestCall`	Used to call a destination phone. Activates the call manager application.
`tapiRequestMediaCall`	Used to create a media stream connection.
`tapiRequestDrop`	Disconnects a media stream connection.
`tapiGetLocationInformation`	Returns the country code and city set in the control panel. Used to determine dialing prefixes.

> **WARNING**
>
> Microsoft recommends that developers avoid using the `tapiRequestMediaCall` function. The function will not be supported in future versions of the TAPI interface.

These functions can be called from Visual Basic, VBA, or any other program that contains access procedures to external DLLs. In Listing 27.1, the program dials the number 555-1212 to create a voice connection. If TAPI is not installed on the machine or the Call Manager application is unavailable, the program displays the appropriate message box.

Listing 27.1. A TAPI code example.

```
Declare Function tapiRequestMakeCall Lib "TAPI.DLL"(DestAddress$, AppName$,
↪CalledParty$, Comment$) As Long

Sub MAIN
   lResult = tapiRequestMakeCall("555-1212", "", "", "")
   If lResult <> 0 Then
```

```
    MsgBox "Sorry, Call Manager unavailable"
  End If
End Sub
```

The actual process when assisted telephony is called engages a dialing application specified by the system to place the call and make the connection. In this way, any service provider interface can be used to access various connection sources. For example, instead of the traditional dialer application, an application that makes an ISDN connection could be used.

Assisted telephony uses the most rudimentary services available to the TAPI driver to enable applications to implement basic TAPI functionality simply and easily. For more complex interaction with the TAPI system, the full telephony services must be used.

Full Telephony

For complete TAPI-enabled applications, use of the functions in full telephony is a must. All the more complex services, such as conferencing, call transfer, hold, and control, are available only through accessing the full telephony API.

Full telephony provides for three basic types of objects:

- Call objects
- Line objects
- Phone objects

Call objects are created dynamically by the system as incoming or outgoing calls occur. A call object can access the media stream of the call, the call progress, and the status notification. A call object corresponds to a connection that has a designated destination or endpoint.

Line objects represent connections to the phone network. A line usually represents a single connection or phone number, but it may represent multiple connections. These objects are configured statically by the service providers. Examples of line objects include a first-party telephone line, a set of channels (such as ISDN B-Channels), and third-party stations in a call center. Most of the TAPI functions access line object capabilities.

Phone objects represent an actual telephone. Through a phone object, the media stream for that particular phone can be accessed. Any features on the phone itself (such as the ringer, lights, line switches, displays, and status indicators) can be accessed through the phone object.

Basic Services

Basic services provide a parallel of the functions available on a Plain Old Telephone System (POTS). Calls can be dialed and answered, and basic connections can be manipulated. Basic services provide the core functions of the TAPI interface.

Basic services handle the original initialization and the final shutdown of TAPI services on a machine. The services provide the functions of version negotiation with the various SPI drivers. Basic services also enable you to configure the media stream, query the system's devices, and set various TAPI parameters.

Basic services handle dialing and answering calls, dropping calls, and configuring calling privileges. Also provided is the capability of sharing resources across multiple applications. For example, more than one application can watch a phone line. If a call occurs on that phone line, each program can determine the nature of the call. A fax call can be handled by the fax program, a data call by the data program, and so on.

Table 27.1 shows all the functions provided by basic services. Complete descriptions of each function are available in the TAPI SDK. The functions `lineGetAddressCaps` and `lineGetDevCaps` enable you to query the capabilities of the TAPI device.

Table 27.1. TAPI basic services.

Function	Description
lineAnswer	Answers the line call.
lineClose	Closes an open line device.
lineConfigDialog	Calls the driver for a specific line device to display an options dialog.
lineDeallocateCall	Deallocates a call handle.
lineDial	Dials a number.
lineDrop	Disconnects a call.
lineGetAddressCaps	Returns the capabilities of an address on a line.
lineGetAddressID	Returns the address ID associated with an address.
lineGetAddressStatus	Returns the current status of an address.
lineGetCallInfo	Returns the static information of a call.
lineGetCallStatus	Returns the current status of a call.
lineGetDevCaps	Returns the capabilities of a line.
lineGetDevConfig	Returns the current configuration of a line.
lineGetIcon	Returns the icon provided by the line driver.
lineGetID	Returns the device ID for a device class associated with a specific line, address, or call.
lineGetLineDevStatus	Returns the current status of an open line.
lineGetNewCalls	Returns handles to calls on a line.
lineGetNumRings	Returns the number of rings before the line is answered.
lineGetStatusMessages	Returns which notification messages the line is set to receive.
lineGetTranslateCaps	Returns the translation capabilities of an address.

Function	Description
lineHandoff	Transfers ownership of a call to a different application.
lineInitialize	Initializes the TAPI DLL.
lineMakeCall	Places a call to a destination address.
lineNegotiateAPIVersion	Negotiates which API version to use.
lineOpen	Opens a line when sent a device ID and returns a line handle.
lineSetAppSpecific	Allows the passing of application-specific information in a field of the call information record.
lineSetCallPrivilege	Sets the application's privileges for a call.
lineSetCurrentLocation	Sets the location used for context in address translations.
lineSetDevConfig	Sets the configuration of a line device.
lineSetNumRings	Sets the number of rings before a line is answered.
lineSetStatusMessages	Sets the types of status changes reported on a line.
lineSetTollList	Sets the capabilities of the toll list.
lineShutdown	Halts the application's usage of the line interface.
lineTranslateAddress	Converts between canonical and dialable address formats.

> **NOTE**
>
> TAPI functions accept any destination address, such as a phone number, in either canonical address format or dialable address format. Canonical address format—+1 (408) 555-1212—always stays the same; it is stored in such things as address books. The dialable address format—555-1212—is how the number will appear when it is actually dialed from a particular location. The lineTranslateAddress function is used to convert between the formats.

Interfacing these functions to Visual Basic can be tedious without a third-party telephony control. For more information on these products, see Chapter 29, "Third-Party Tools, Utilities, and Controls." Most of the TAPI functions are asynchronous. This means that most of the TAPI interface is based on the TAPI function returning a message when the operation is complete. Visual Basic cannot directly receive messages, so an additional driver is required.

Supplementary Services

Supplementary services in the TAPI interface provide access to the media of the call; they also provide access to PBX functions. The supplementary services can drive such features as holding calls, transferring calls (blind transfer and consultation transfer), conferencing, forwarding calls, parking calls, and picking up remote calls. The supplementary services functions can generate and detect Dual Tone Multifrequency signaling (DTMF). DTMF tones are the standard frequencies for a touch-tone phone plus the letters A through D. Valid digits for DTMF tones are 0 through 9, A, B, C, D, *, and #.

The supplementary services enable you to use camp-on, which places the call in a queue until it can be completed, and other automatic call completion features. Also supported are features to control incoming calls (accept, reject, or redirect), generate in-band (on a particular line) dial digits and tones, monitor the media stream (mode, DTMF digits, tones), route the media stream, control ISDN, and control features on the physical phone terminal.

The supplementary services are the heart of a true TAPI system. By providing complete control over the connections and the media stream itself, TAPI can provide all telephony services standard to a PC-based telephony system. The functions provided by the supplementary interface are shown in Table 27.2.

Table 27.2. TAPI supplementary functions.

Function	Description
lineAccept	Accepts a specific call onto a line.
lineAddToConference	Adds a specified call handle to a conference call.
lineBlindTransfer	Performs a single-step transfer of a call to a specified address.
lineCompleteCall	Specifies alternative ways of completing a call if normal resources are busy or unavailable.
lineCompleteTransfer	Transfers a call to another call.
lineForward	Specifies certain forwarding parameters for a line.
lineGatherDigits	Creates a buffer to gather digits on a call.
lineGenerateDigits	Generates specific digits into a particular line.
lineGenerateTone	Generates a tone of standard or custom frequencies.
lineGetConfRelatedCalls	Returns a list of calls associated with a conference call.
lineGetRequest	Returns the next by-proxy request by the type of request specified.
lineHold	Places the call on hold.
lineMonitorDigits	Sets whether the digits on a call will be buffered or unbuffered.
lineMonitorMedia	Sets whether the media mode for a call will be detected.
lineMonitorTones	Sets whether the in-band tones for a call will be detected.

Function	Description
linePark	Parks a call in a specified park mode.
linePickup	Picks up a call and returns a call handle.
linePrepareAddToConference	Prepares a conference call for the addition of another party.
lineRedirect	Redirects an incoming call to a specific address.
lineRegisterRequestRecipient	Registers the application as a receiver of specific types of requests.
lineRemoveFromConference	Removes a call from a specified conference call.
lineSecureCall	Secures a call from any interruptions specified by the media control actions.
lineSendUserUserInfo	Sends user-specified information over the line from one party to another.
lineSetCallParams	Sets the call privileges to either monitor or owner settings.
lineSetMediaControl	Sets whether the media control actions on a line are active.
lineSetMediaMode	Sets the media mode or modes for a specific call.
lineSetTerminal	Sets terminal routing information for a line, address, or call.
lineSetupConference	Sets up a conference call.
lineSetupTransfer	Sets up the consultation call to another address for transfer.
lineSwapHold	Swaps the active call with the call on hold.
lineUncompleteCall	Cancels the completion of a call requested on a line.
lineUnhold	Retrieves a call placed on hold.
lineUnpark	Retrieves a call parked at a specific address and returns a call handle.

Extended Services

Extended services contain only three functions, because the complete role of these services is to provide access to third-party extensions. The extended services perform essentially the same role as the SQLPassThrough function in the JET database engine. By providing a standardized way of passing system-specific functions through the general TAPI interface, no capabilities are lost by using the standard TAPI interface to access specialized hardware.

All the TAPI functions used by extended services are shown in Table 27.3. Applications need to format any commands to their devices as data. The TAPI functions can then pass the data through to the device. There must be a compatible SPI that can pass the necessary information to the device.

Table 27.3. TAPI extended functions.

Function	Description
lineDevSpecific	Calls a device-specific function.
lineDevSpecificFeature	Uses phone feature-button capabilities to activate device-specific features.
lineNegotiateExtVersion	Negotiates an extension version with a specific line device.

The TAPI Software Development Kit (TAPI SDK)

The TAPI SDK is available free for download from any of the online sources listed in Appendix C, "Sources." It also comes with the Microsoft Developer Network (MSDN) Level 2 CD.

The TAPI SDK provides many tools to learn about and understand the TAPI system. Included are sample files, such as Dialer (which dials the phone on a standard TAPI device), and numerous source code examples of TAPI client and service provider implementations. The installable drivers and the redistributable files are also provided.

Included with the TAPI SDK is the complete manual to the use of the TAPI interface. This includes the documentation on developing service provider interface (SPI) drivers. The SDK provides sample C and C++ code for accessing TAPI and interacting with its various features.

TSAPI

Telephony Server API (TSAPI), shown in Figure 27.8, is a competing API. Created by Novell and AT&T, the TSAPI standard has its supporters. Until recently, however, TSAPI lacked a solid connection component. Therefore, it could control the connection, but it had no access to the actual data stream.

Because of this shortcoming, unlike TAPI, TSAPI could not provide first-party fax services, direct answering machine access, and other media-specific services. Through the Versit company, the makers of TSAPI are attempting to eliminate some of these shortcomings.

FIGURE 27.8.
The TSAPI system structure.

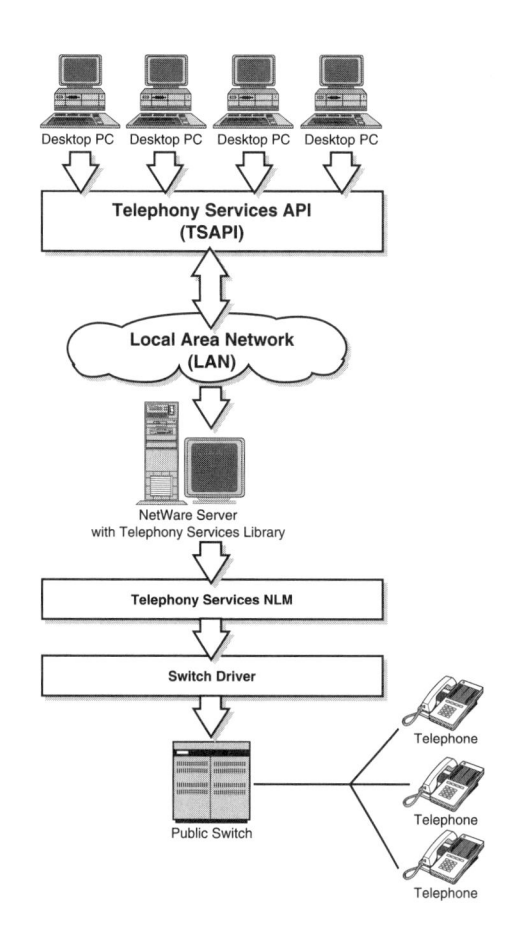

> **WARNING**
>
> NetWare telephone services that provide all the TSAPI connectivity can be prohibitively expensive for the small company. Because of all the PBX interface control and power that is introduced to the services, the NetWare services are complex. With unified messaging, at the time of this writing, the telephone services cost about $15,000. This is a much more substantial initial investment than the incremental TAPI implementation approach.

TSAPI allows centralization of call-control services on the NetWare server. This means that the legacy system at a large enterprise can often be upgraded to be used by the server. This can potentially provide nearly instant access of telephony services to all the PBX resources of the installed system.

Likewise, by putting the telephony services on the central server, the individual machines do not require any hardware or throughput upgrades. This can keep overall upgrade expenses down.

Additionally, because the organization can work with the PBX it is already familiar with, the expensive learning curve associated with installing new equipment is substantially shortened.

> **NOTE**
>
> The Tmap interface, created by Nortel (formerly Northern Telecom), bridges the gap between TAPI and TSAPI. Tmap maps the TAPI API calls to equivalent TSAPI calls. All the connection calls for which the TSAPI interface is optimized (call and routing control) are routed to the NetWare telephone services on the server.
>
> With Tmap, a TAPI-compatible application can be mapped to use an organization's central PBX through TSAPI telephone services.

Signal Computing System Architecture

Signal Computing System Architecture (SCSA) provides the driver/hardware standard to complement the TAPI software standard. Created by Dialogic (the dominant manufacturer of PC-based telephony hardware) and several other vendors, SCSA is increasingly becoming the *de facto* standard in the industry. It is supported by more than 260 companies.

The SCSA standard is meant to provide a standard implementation for switch manufacturers. It provides all the necessary standards for distributed computer telephony. Complete switching can occur with SCSA-compliant hardware and software. Therefore, a distributed call center can be set up that can switch the call to any of a number of endpoint connections (see Figure 27.9).

FIGURE 27.9.
A distributed call center.

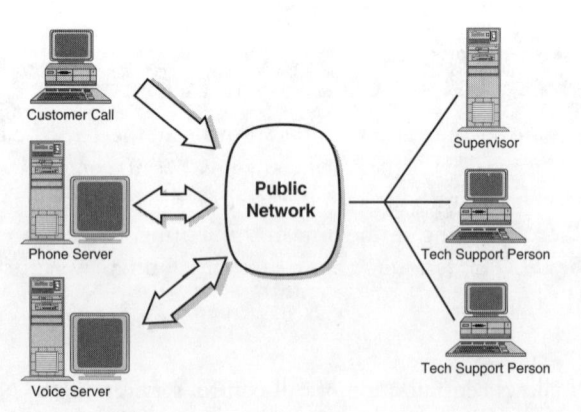

SCSA is both a hardware and a software interface standard. It is compatible with both TAPI and TSAPI. The software framework that makes up the interface standard is called the SCSA

Telephony Application Object (TAO). An SCSA compliant server can handle multiple calls and devices in real time. The standard even provides a shared bus, known as *SCbus,* which multiple servers can use to distribute the call load.

> **NOTE**
>
> An early competitor of the SCSA standard, Multi-Vendor Integration Protocol (MVIP), was created by Natural Microsystems, a leading voice-processing board manufacturer. MVIP is sometimes used in telephony servers and in distributed computer telephony systems. The MVIP standard is supported in the SCSA TAO framework.

Universal Serial Bus

The Universal Serial Bus (USB) is a standard created by Compaq, DEC, IBM, Microsoft, Intel, NEC, Nortel, and a host of other hardware vendors. The USB is meant to replace the traditional serial port as well as several other interfaces (such as the keyboard port, joystick port, and so on). The USB is meant for slower speed devices that do not need the tremendous speeds associated with interfaces like those used for hard disks (IDE, EIDE, SCSI, and so forth).

The throughput of the USB is a maximum of 12MB/second, providing an excellent bus for peripherals such as modems, fax machines, and ISDN connections. A normal serial port on a PC machine can run at a maximum of 115KB/second, so the USB is a significant improvement in throughput. USB offers a star-hub configuration so up to 63 devices can be attached to the bus.

Also offered is isochronous data transfer that enables an application to reserve specifically a certain amount of bandwidth on the port. Isochronous transfer is essential for certain applications such as video or audio transmissions. In traditional applications, a data delay is barely noticeable, but with a conversation or video broadcasts, the delay affects how the user interacts with the system.

> **NOTE**
>
> Apple has a competing serial bus structure called *Geoport.* The Geoport interface can handle up to a 2MB/second transfer rate. The Geoport is endorsed by the Versit company. It supports multiple simultaneous data streams, called *channels.* Up to several dozen channels can be supported.

Versit

Versit is a company jointly created by Apple, IBM, AT&T, and Siemens. The intention of Versit is to provide a complete set of integrated technologies for the telephony market. The company provides specifications to data formats, integration technology, and conferencing and messaging standards.

For example, Versit provides a standard data format for information on a business card. If this standard becomes widely used, an electronic business card could be attached to your e-mail that contains your phone number, fax number, e-mail, World Wide Web address, and other information.

Versit also intends to provide connectivity to Personal Digital Assistants (PDAs), such as Apple's Newton. PDAs are powerful handheld computers that will greatly benefit from the coming computer-telephone industry bridge. Versit keeps most of its progress updated online. See Appendix C for Versit's online access points.

Visual Basic Telephony

Now that you understand the basic structure of the telephony technologies, Visual Basic is an ideal platform for providing centralization and connectivity for these applications. With Visual Basic's strong connectivity to mission-critical data, information systems, and the reporting engine, the Visual Basic development platform provides the perfect foundation for a complete telephony system.

Rudimentary TAPI support is included in Visual Basic through the use of the assisted telephony application. Expect Microsoft to supply additional features in the future, perhaps through an OCX, as all the Windows environments gain access to the TAPI interface.

All the real telephony capabilities are currently provided by third-party manufacturers. Outstanding products such as Visual Voice give Visual Basic complete telephony access. For more information on these products, see Chapter 29. Also see Appendix C for other products and online resources.

28

Security for Client/Server

Security for client/server (C/S) systems will be discussed in two parts. The first part of this chapter gives an overview of the importance of security concepts, methods, and products used in making databases and networks secure. Threats, standards, directory services, operating systems (OS) and network operating system (NOS) security, database security, e-mail security (encryption), and security protection (firewalls) are addressed. Figure 28.1 shows a typical client/server system with firewalls connected over a wide area network (WAN) and the Internet. The second part of the chapter provides information on database security planning and examples of implementing security by using Visual Basic (VB) and Microsoft (MS) Access.

FIGURE 28.1.
Client/server systems with firewalls.

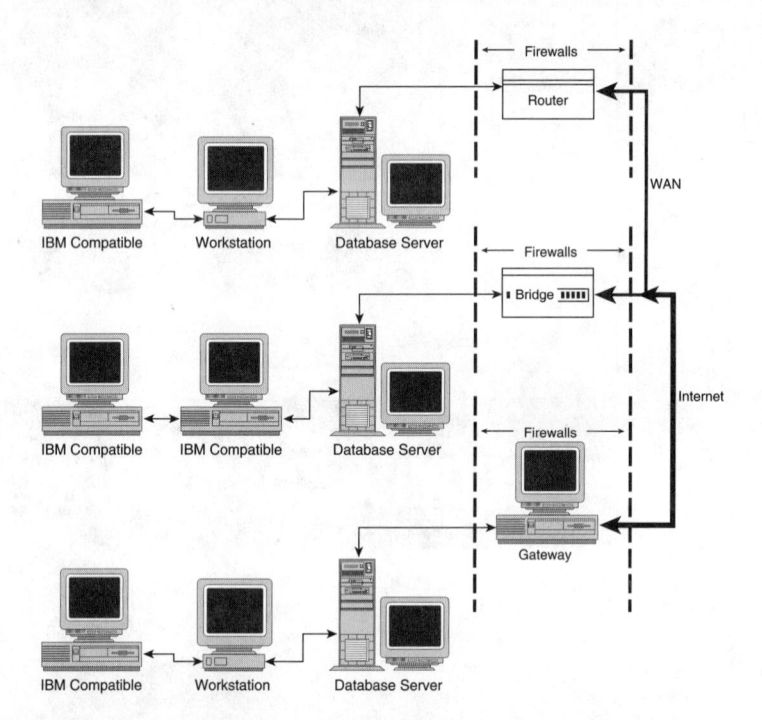

Why Is Client/Server Security Important?

C/S systems are designed to be cost-effective, to be secure, and to increase productivity to meet the business demands of all sizes of companies. These C/S systems are used to communicate and provide information services for internal and external business transactions throughout the business community. By tapping into the Internet resources, these businesses can expand their customer bases and provide these information services worldwide. Their information or data can be stored in a server on a local network or stored in a remote server located on the other side of the world.

The client communicates with the server over one of the various electronic mail (e-mail) systems available. Normally, e-mail is thought of as a message or letter-type of correspondence that is sent between two users on the Internet or through the network mail system. In the client/server environment, e-mail is used for transferring data between multiple users. These users may reside on the same network, or some may be located at remote sites. The e-mail discussed here focuses on the encryption techniques that can be used to make the client/server network communications more secure.

Protecting information sent on e-mail should have a high priority when you develop or use a client/server system because of the far-reaching effects it can have on the lives and futures of everyone involved. To be efficient and effective, businesses need to communicate across the Internet, through LANs and WANs, and be able to access and deliver valuable data and information in a timely manner. During this process, a network is vulnerable to access by unauthorized users. Maintaining network security and integrity, while still allowing public access and employee intercommunication, is vitally important to the client/server world.

It is understood, of course, that no system can be absolutely safe and secure. Many levels of system security can be implemented. The type of security used on a given system depends on the type of potential threat. Some military systems face different threats than commercial business; therefore, different security systems or tailored systems may be required. In the military, there are security levels or classifications such as Confidential, Secret, Top Secret, and so forth. Some of the client/server networks even require multilevel security, because they have users and systems with different levels of security clearances communicating at the same time over the same network.

Commercial client/server systems have the same operational conditions and circumstances, but may use different terms for security levels, such as Company Private or Company Confidential. These commercial C/S systems can also have confidential data traveling over a common network between secure and nonsecure areas with restricted access and use requirements. For example, some companies have specific areas, such as Personnel and Finance, which have sensitive data, so these areas are labeled Authorized Access Only.

What Are Security Risks and Threats?

Security risks and threats that can affect the client/server network and operation are extensive and beyond the scope of this book. Therefore, this is only a short overview of some of the current security risks and threats in the computer industry today.

There are countless risk possibilities, including data destruction, data contamination, viruses, and so forth. One of the highest risk conditions is networks or computer systems that are directly connected to the Internet through high-speed dedicated lines without a firewall or some other security system. These systems are very vulnerable to all forms of attack, from password guessing to spoofing. *Spoofing* is a way of deceiving security methods and procedures. Some types of threats include misuse of acquired information, theft of data or unauthorized access, and so forth. These threats can be internal, such as an unauthorized malicious user, or external (outside intruders). An external intruder can be a computer vandal, hacker, or highly soph-isticated and knowledgeable technical intruder performing industrial espionage, address-spoofing, or protocol-spoofing. There are also threats against physical components of the network, such as theft of user workstations or servers.

To locate or look up information (name and network address) about a person, two standard protocols are commonly used, *finger* and *whois*. The finger protocol was designed to search for and report back login names, personal information, the user login system, and account usage information. The whois protocol is limited in capability and reports only contact information, such as standard Internet-wide server names. This is the information hackers gather for spoofing.

> **WARNING**
>
> The finger and whois protocols are both a risk and a threat. These protocols are useful tools for network administrators, but if made accessible to all users of the network, they increase the risk of sensitive information leaving the network. That means the threat level to the network is increased, because that information can be used to gain unauthorized access through password guessing or spoofing.

The computer security industry has had knowledge of address-spoofing, IP-spoofing, and protocol-spoofing for a long time. It has now become common knowledge to the general public and becoming a concern to all computer users. Depending on an individual's definition of spoofing, all three terms for spoofing can describe the same event.

Spoofing, whether address-spoofing, IP-spoofing, or protocol-spoofing, is one of the most talked-about network security threats today. Spoofing is the process of generating counterfeit addresses to deceive the network security. Software tools are available to generate network addresses. These generated addresses are counterfeit addresses that can pass the authentication procedures used on the network. They enable the intruder to access the network under the pretense of being an authorized user.

Spoofing is becoming more of a concern to businesses as more information is stored in databases on client/server networked systems and as more systems are being developed. The main concern is the possibility of destruction or modification of data.

TCP/IP (IP stands for Internet Protocol) is a standard protocol and most commonly used on the Internet. Each message that is sent over the Internet is assigned an IP address. An intruder creates packets with source IP addresses that are capable of defeating the network's IP address-based authentication procedures. The intruder now has gained access to the network as a guest (but unauthorized) user or root (superuser) user, which enables the intruder to collect more information about the network, its users, and network configuration; it even enables the intruder to copy, steal, or destroy data.

In order to determine security risks and threats, knowledge is required of the networks, installed equipment, data stored and used, and network function. Without this knowledge, a security risk and threat analysis or evaluation probably is not valid.

Network Analysis Questions

The questions in this section can assist you in analyzing your current network configuration. From this information, you will have an idea of the strengths and weaknesses of your network, based on its configuration.

Keep in mind that securing a client/server system requires the following information: determining the operational concept, system configuration, communication links, current or proposed security level of link and system, how the security level is established, and what criteria are used to determine system security level. First, answer these questions:

- Is there one network (LAN), or are multiple networks joined together?
- If there are multiple networks, how are they interconnected?
- How large is the network, and how many connected components are there (users, servers, routers, and so forth)?
- Is the network cabling copper or fiber?
- Is the network configuration Ethernet, Token Ring, AppleTalk, or so forth?
- How many external entry points exist (routers, bridges, modems)?
- When multiple networks exist, is remote access required on each network?
- Do installed routers, bridges, or gateways have security features built in? What are they?
- How many servers are on the network?
- What kind of servers are on the network (directory, name, file, print, SQL, NT, NetWare, Oracle, and so forth)?
- What kind of network software is installed (Windows NT, NetWare, 3COM, LAN server)?
- What is used to monitor network traffic and status?
- What method, process, software, hardware, or combination of these will be implemented to protect the system?

Threat Analysis Questions

Once you have assessed the information from your answers to the questions in the last section, you are ready to consider the next set of questions:

- How many external entry points exist?
- What type of threat is envisioned?

Will the threat originate from inside the network?

Will the threat originate from outside the network?

Is the threat a hacker or knowledgeable technical intruder?

Is the threat industrial espionage?

What database, table, directory, or information are intruders trying to access?

Is the threat internal unauthorized use or removal of data?

Is data being corrupted or lost?

How is the network being attacked (internal or external unauthorized access, address-spoofing, IP-spoofing, protocol-spoofing, and so forth)?

Number your answers according to threat priority. After evaluating the answers, a basic security system can be designed. Priorities have to be given to the necessary and affordable steps that can be taken to make this network secure.

What Security Standards Are Available?

There are numerous lists of security standards developed for the military and for industry covering a wide variety of subjects and technologies that are used in the C/S IT environment. The following list, along with the subject matter addressed, includes only some of the ones available:

Network Security Models, Architecture, and Frameworks

ISO 7498-2	OSI Basic Reference Model, Part 2: Security Architecture
ISO 10745	Upper Layers Security Model
ISO 10181-2	Security Frameworks, Part 2: Authentication
ISO 10181-5	Security Frameworks, Part 5: Integrity

Integrity

IEEE 802.10B	Secure Data Exchange (DE)
ISO 11586-1	Generic Upper Layer Security (GULS)
ISO 11586-4	Generic Upper Layer Security (GULS)

Access Control and Authentication

NIST FIPS PUB 179	Government Network Management Profile (GNMP)
NIST FIPS PUB 180	Secure Hashing Standard (SHS)
NIST FIPS PUB 186	Digital Signature Standard (DSS)
IEEE 802.10B	Secure Data Exchange (SDE)

ITU (CCITT) X.509	X.500 Security (public key certificates)
ISO 10736	Transport Layer Security Protocol (TLSP)
ISO 11577	Network Layer Security Protocol (NLSP)
ISO 11586-1	Generic Upper Layer Security (GULS)
ISO 11586-2	Generic Upper Layer Security (GULS)
ISO 11586-3	Generic Upper Layer Security (GULS)
ISO 11586-4	Generic Upper Layer Security (GULS)
MIL-STD-2045-18500	Message Security Protocol (MSP)

Directory Services

DoD 5200.28-STD	Trusted Computer System Evaluation Criteria (TCSEC)
NCSC-TG-021	Trusted Database Interpretation (TDI)

Database Security

ISO 9594	X.500 Series Recommendations, SIA-11
IEEE 1224.2	Directory Services/Name Space API
ITU (CCITT) X.500	ISO 9594 (SIA-1)

Data Encryption

Orange Book	Military security
IEEE 802.10	Standard for Interoperable LAN Security (SILS)
NIST FIPS PUB 46-2	Data Encryption Standard (DES)
NIST FIPS PUB 185	Escrowed Encryption Standard (EES)

Security Association and Key Management

ISP 421	Security Association Management Protocol (SAMP)
ISO 10164-7	Security Alarm Reporting Function
ISO 10164-8	Security Audit Trail
ISO/IEC 9595	Common Management Information Service

Security Management

NIST FIPS PUB 179	Government Network Management Profile (GNMP)
ISP 421	Security Association Management Protocol (SAMP)
ISO 11586-1	Generic Upper Layer Security (GULS)
ISO 11586-2	Generic Upper Layer Security (GULS)

Internet Security

Industry is concerned about secure communications over the World Wide Web. To help in finding a solution, a developer's toolkit is being produced. It combines the Secure HyperText Transport Protocol (S-HTTP) and the Secure Sockets Layer (SSL) security standards. A team of companies, including Online Inc., CompuServe Inc., IBM, and Netscape Communications Inc., are supporting this development. The goal is to produce a single security standard that covers secure Web transactions.

Client/server versions of the developer's toolkit will be produced to make communications over the Internet cross-platform-compatible. These versions are being created to run on machines that support Microsoft Windows, Macintosh, and the UNIX platforms. The two Web security standards, S-HTTP and SSL, complement each other. Figure 28.2 shows the message flow when using these two Web security standards. S-HTTP provides document security through the use of public-key and private-key encryption, producing documents with different digital signatures. Then the SSL takes the secure document and adds a protective cover, keeping it a secure transaction as it transverses the Web network links.

FIGURE 28.2.
C/S Web security with S-HTTP and SSL.

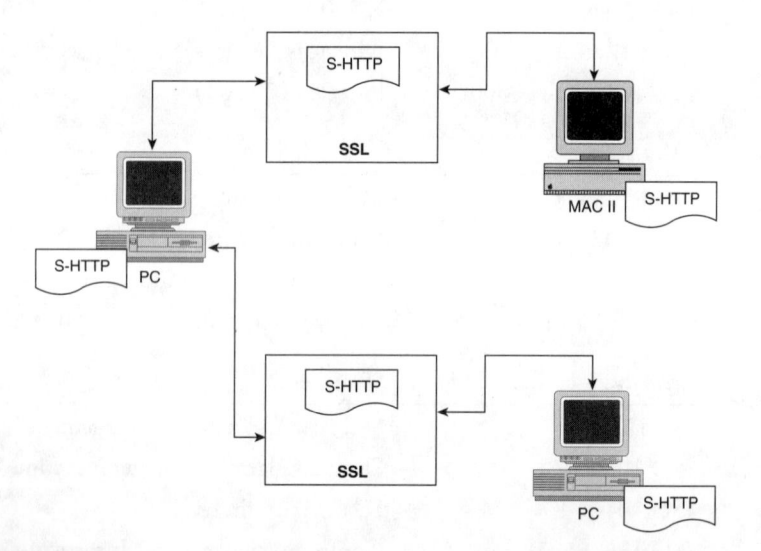

Security or Integrity?

Security is different from integrity. Integrity in the C/S Information Technology (IT) environment, is a concern that information and data contained in the C/S system is valid. *Data integrity* can be defined as the verification of the accuracy and completeness of the data that is transmitted, stored, or otherwise exposed to possible unauthorized modification. This also involves the processes to ensure data validity through preventing inconsistent or invalid updates to the stored data.

Security is protecting the C/S IT environment with both electronic and physical security from unauthorized access or alternation of stored information or data by internal or external users or intruders. C/S IT security is affected by, and interacts with, some of the operational functions performed in the network, operating system, data management, and system management areas.

Data Integrity

One method of protecting data integrity is mirroring. *Mirroring* is the process of making an identical backup of the complete server and Network Operating System (NOS). The mirroring process is done while the system is in operation, or at set time intervals, on another disk drive or completely different server machine. Figure 28.3 shows the mirroring process for a database server. In the event a failure occurs, automatic switchover can be done, replacing the primary system with the mirrored backup system and minimizing down-time and data loss. Novell has been using this method for years, but in the past, it was usually implemented as two identical disk drives or computer systems that were located in the same facility. In the C/S environment, the mirrored system can now be miles apart and linked over high-speed communication lines.

FIGURE 28.3.
The mirroring database process.

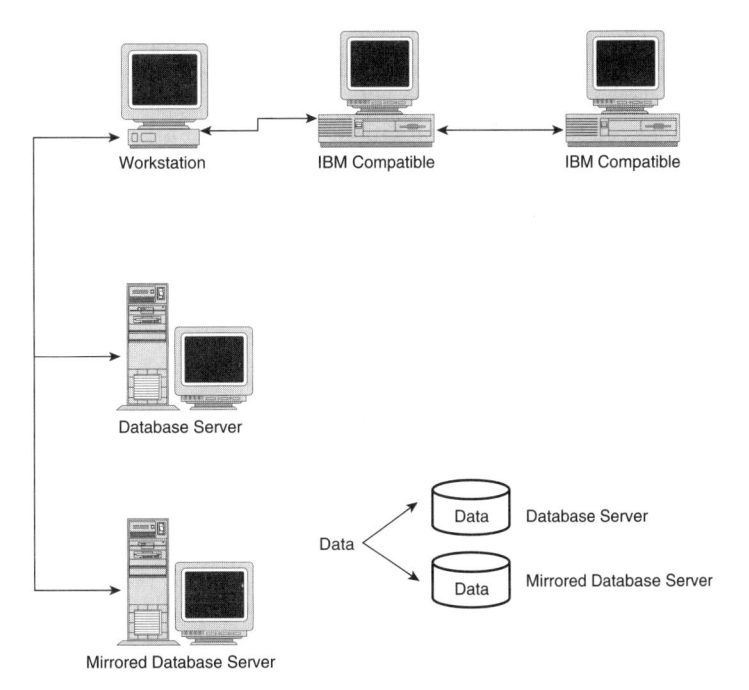

Data backup systems for networks have developed over the past years and are very reliable. The problem is that they aren't installed or used effectively in most networks. Backup systems have to be installed and set up properly. Backups should be automatic and back up new files and data at regular time intervals. Figure 28.4 shows a data flow process of a typical database backup. Periodic full-system backups should be completed at least once a week. The hardest part is making users aware of the importance of backing up data. Backup has to be completed at a convenient time so as not to affect productivity. A good administrator is the key to maintaining data integrity through data and system backups and monitoring network and C/S system operations.

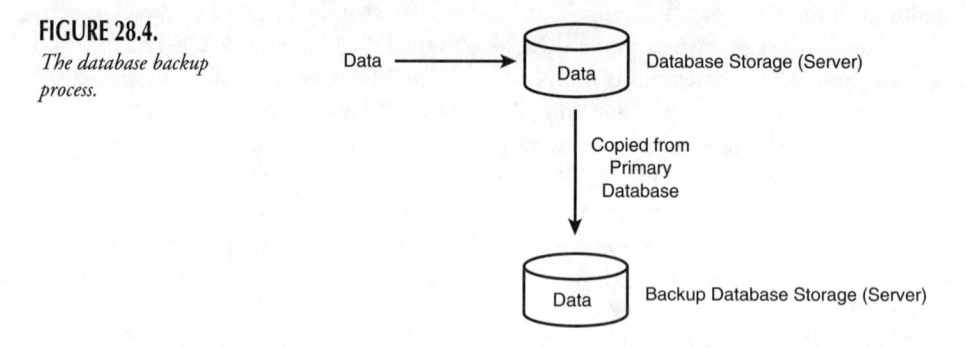

FIGURE 28.4.
The database backup process.

Data → Data [Database Storage (Server)]

Copied from Primary Database ↓

Data [Backup Database Storage (Server)]

Data Security

Data security involves protecting the C/S system both electronically and physically. Security involves protection from unauthorized access or alternation of stored information or data by internal or external users or intruders. Data security should be determined by the type of operational functions performed in the network operating system, data management, and system management areas. Most software produced (current operating systems, network operating systems, data management programs, and so forth) incorporates security mechanisms and procedures built into the products. These security mechanisms consist of passwords and user authentication systems or modules. Data encryption software and hardware is available, as well as firewalls and filters.

Data security is also linked to physical security. Physical security involves protecting your system equipment against theft or damage. Because of the value of the data stored on the server, the server is the most important part of the C/S system. Not only does the server store the data, it can manipulate data for multiple clients and databases. Physical security does not necessarily involve securing each individual computer system and does not have to entail a great expense. It can be attained through securing the facility wherein the server is located. This can include locks, security monitors, power strips, UPSystems or power backup systems, and so forth. Monetary loss is not limited to physical damage or loss of equipment. When C/S equipment is inoperable, all phases of business operations are affected.

Directory Services

Directory services can be defined as online information and distributed network user and resource services, built on a directory database. The database or multiple databases can be located on individual servers throughout the network. These directory databases contain the names and addresses of users and resources on the network and possibly some interconnecting networks. The directory is normally laid out and displayed in the form of a tree. Maintenance of the database is done by the network administrator, who also performs directory searches. Most major NOSs have, or are implementing, directory services, either by using the X.500 standard directory service model or its basic layout. These directory services require greater capability and capacity due to the steady rate of growth in client/server and distributed networking systems. Increased growth is caused by the addition of many new users and resources that are interconnected with the existing and new LANs. These LANs cover a wider geographical area and carry an ever-increasing traffic load.

There are three main pieces of information needed to locate a user: the name, the address, and the routing information to get to the address. This information is obtainable from three main services. The Name Service locates a user through his or her name. The E-Mail Service locates a user through a built-in address book. The Directory Service can search through lists of services to locate users or resources.

X.500 Directory Services

The X.500 Directory Services standard, first released in 1988, was developed jointly by the International Telecommunication Union (ITU formerly CCITT) and the International Standards Organization (ISO). The goal of these standards was to define a model and protocol that could be used to design a distributed global directory service. The global directory service model is a descriptive naming service, which is made up of known names (or objects) and special attributes to help users search for other users. These directory searches are performed by entering known features, such as a name, individual characteristics or attributes, or other identifying criteria.

This global directory service model was made up of three models: the Directory Model, the Information Model, and the Security Model. The Directory Model has two components: a Directory User Agent (DUA) and a Directory System Agent (DSA). A Directory User Agent is created in the client software, and its function is to access the directory and request DSA services on behalf of a user. The DSAs provide administrator access to the directory database for performing database maintenance.

To maintain directory databases effectively, multiple DSAs are required, with each DSA maintaining a separate part of that directory. Because these DSAs all perform maintenance on the database, interaction between DSAs is needed in order to respond to the DUA's requests for services. Figure 28.5 shows an X.500 directory search process.

FIGURE 28.5.
The X.500 directory search process.

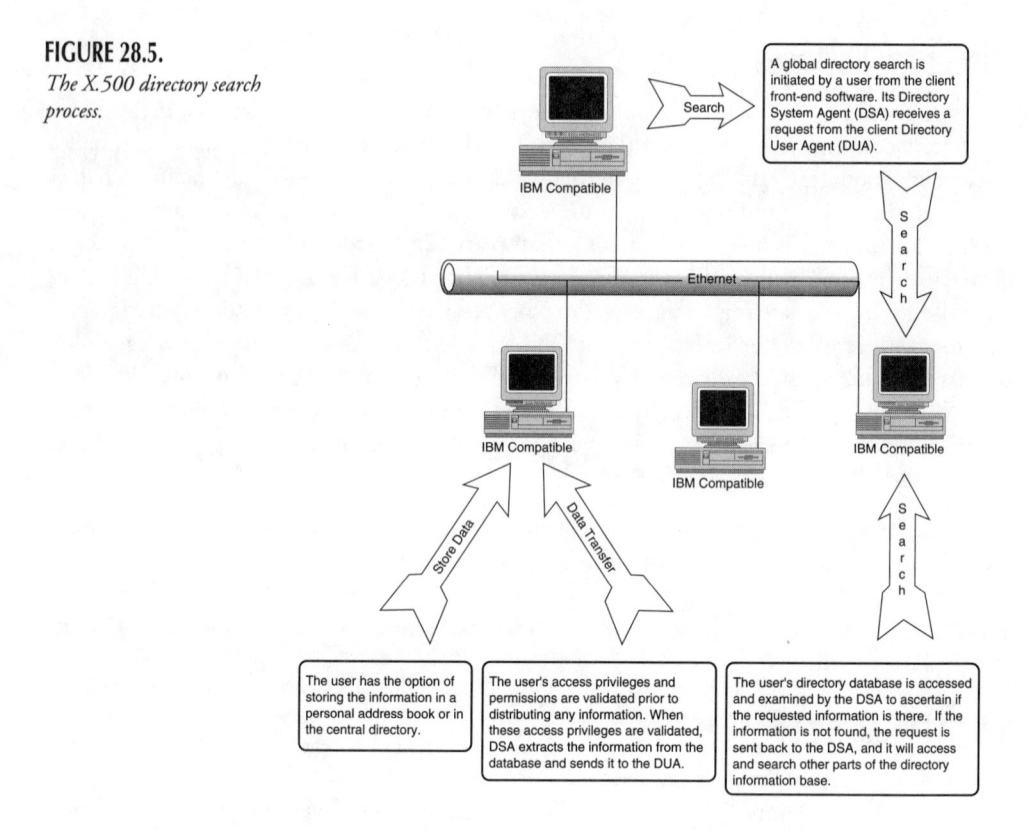

The Information Model provides the recommended structure to organize the directory information being entered and stored. These recommendations include the storage format and arrangement of data for efficient information retrieval from all X.500 directories. In 1988, when the first X.500 standard was released, most organizations felt that the standard was unacceptable due to deficiencies in the definition of the Security Model. Directory Service security was initially specified as some type of user password authentication check system. It was basically described as having two types of security: Simple Authentication, which used password identification type security, and Strong Authentication, which used cryptographic keys. Trying to implement a loosely defined security system over a global network didn't appeal to most businesses.

In 1993, a revised specification was released that contained important new features: replication, access control, and authentication. The new replication feature enables multiple copies of directory information to coexist and be stored throughout the network. Access control methods, which included adding the Access Control List (ACL) to Directory Service security, started changing the attitudes of businesses. Network developers and administrators were now provided the capability of controlling and limiting access to their network directories. With ACLs, password protection, and data encryption with public and private keys, X.500 Directory Service appears to be a secure and viable approach to implementing a global directory service.

X.509 is the standard for authentication and security for X.500. X.509 is a certificate-based model. Certificate management helps managers control security by tracking user access, resource access, and files being accessed. The standard also defines Access Control List (ACL), Certification Authority tools, database interfaces, and X.509 security, and includes cryptographic libraries. These features have been adopted at the international level as the standard for providing worldwide directory services.

X.500 Directory Services is the part of the Open Systems Interconnection (OSI) architecture standard that addresses some OSI management security. The goal for ITU and ISO was to create a secure directory services that is accessible to all users on local and global networks for operating in the OSI environment. The OSI standard was developed to define security of external interfaces of the OSI model. The standard is based on the assumption that the internal components of the system are secure, thus eliminating the need for addressing internal security requirements. This standards security focus is mainly on the security measures needed to protect the interface between the host (client or server) and the outside world. The main concern is to ensure that those interfaces, which interconnect open systems directory services, have a secure communication path or link.

X.509 Security and Cryptography

The ITU X.509 is a security and cryptography standards document. It covers the X.509 Security Library, which helps applications make use of cryptography, X.509 services, and the public-key certificates. By following the X.509 standard, the applications developed can communicate and be integrated into the X.500 Directory Services. X.509 describes the format for storing and maintaining public keys for a public-key system. This format is known as a *certificate*, which is the document that connects and binds a specific user to a specific key. The public-key certificate is essential in the formation of a secure public-key system. If a counterfeit certificate is mistaken for the real one, the counterfeiter can then decrypt all messages sent to that specific user. This can cause a real threat to that specific user, the user communication network, and all associates. Using X.509 as a standard helps ensure that the public-key package, format, and particular certification-generation scheme is the same between vendors. This helps in developing secure directory services for the C/S environment, based on X.500 and the X.509 key management system through certificate-checking at directory and network levels.

NetWare Directory Services

NetWare Directory Services (NDS) is a feature that was implemented in NetWare 4 to provide distributed directory services that contain user and resource data. In creating the NDS database, object and attributes definitions had to be generated. To become more compatible with the open systems type architecture, the X.500 Directory Services standard model was used. This, in turn, led to the predefined NDS schema that includes the base definition structure of the directory services supported.

A database is constructed according to a schema or plan with a definition of the contents of the database. Directory databases define objects as things such as user, printer, or server, and their object attributes as things such as name, ID, address, and phone number. This corresponds to a set of basic directory definitions that should present to the user a logical representation of the information and data organization. Additional NDS features are needed to make it an effective enterprise networking tool. Currently, there isn't an easy way of using NDS for applications to define their application-specific objects and attributes. There also isn't an easy way for the network manager (administrator) to modify or customize the management schema for covering directory databases.

Windows NT Directory Services

Windows NT has plans to incorporate global directory services, but has not indicated when this will occur. When Windows NT is installed, the Microsoft locator is automatically selected as the name-service provider. This name-service provider network software is selected by using Remote Procedure Call (RPC) service, and it can be changed any time through the Windows NT Control Panel. Currently, the NT Server supports only a Domain Name System (DNS), which is known for mapping IP addresses to user-friendly names. Domain can be defined as a group of users' computers that are interconnected and sharing a common database of user accounts and local and global group information. The DNS, which controls only user accounts, security, and names for file and print services, is not a dynamic system and has to be updated manually to stay current.

A domain controller is set up on a Windows NT Server. The controller maintains the database of user accounts for the entire domain and contains a copy of the domain controller's security information. The domain administrator creates user accounts, links passwords, and assigns permissions that can limit access to only the required files and resources designated for that user. Users logging on with a valid domain user account (user name and password) can be provided access to files and resources on all computers in the domain, but limited by permissions assigned by the administrator.

For user authentication, the Netlogon service processes logon requests. If the Windows NT workstation or NT Server is not a domain controller, Netlogon service attempts to find the domain controller. This process is called *discovery*. These requests can come from the local computers, and these login requests are passed through to a domain server. There is a three-step process that the Netlogon service uses to authenticate a logon request. The first step is discovery. If the domain controller is unknown, a search is made to locate the domain controller in its domain. If the computer is found to be part of a workgroup, not a domain, the Netlogon service terminates, and it is treated as a member of that workgroup. The second step is setting up a secure channel. After two NT computers are interconnected, their Netlogon service issues and verifies challenge and challenge response information. With the successful completion of this process, a secure channel or link has been established. The third step is pass-through authentication. This is used when a user account must be authenticated, but the local computer can't authenticate the account itself. The user name and password are forwarded to an NT Server computer that can authenticate the user and the user's information. After it has been authenticated, it is then returned to the requesting computer.

Current Operating System Security

As the network operating system software evolved, more security functions had to be implemented, due to increases in unauthorized network accesses that caused damage to network data and resources. NOSs have access rights or permissions that grant user-specific access privilege to network directories and files, as defined by the network administrator.

How Secure Is Windows NT 3.5?

Windows NT's security is designed for C-2 certification for operating systems. C-2-level security is a government standard for operating systems that requires all users and applications to have prior authentication and approval before allowing access to any operating system resources. To support this design, Windows NT incorporated software processes to help minimize affects from hardware failures and expedite recovery in case failure does occur. This is accomplished through the Windows NT File System (NTFS). NTFS maintains a transaction log to ensure the integrity of the disk structure if the system fails unexpectedly and provides hotfixing and a full recovery system to restore file integrity quickly.

NT security starts by providing users with individual accounts that require login with password identification. Tied to these accounts is a tracking system that records such things as login, logout, file accesses, and so forth. The SA has the capability of tracking and viewing auditable events. To keep directories and files secure in a multi-user environment, permissions must be installed and monitored by the NT OS on all shared directories and files.

How Secure Is NetWare?

NetWare is a NOS; therefore, security certification is for networks only. NetWare's security system is contained in NetWare Directory Services (NDS). There are four levels of security incorporated into NDS: login security, password security, file-system security, and server security. These levels can be implemented separately or combined to form an effective access management and control security system.

The first level of security protection in NetWare is the login password. The user selects a password. Then at login time, NDS processes the user password and validates it. After validation or authentication, privileges are granted to the user to access the network. A NetWare Loadable Module (NLM) called SmartPass is run by a network administrator, and it compares user passwords against 150,000 vulnerable passwords to identify weak passwords. When weak passwords are found, the administrator is notified and recommends that the user select a more secure password. Weak passwords also weaken the C/S network.

The other two levels of security, file-system and server, are security methods used to control users' access to the network's resources and services.

File-system security is divided into Rights security and Attributes security, which together control access to NetWare volumes, directories, and user's files. NetWare has designated that all users have certain rights, some of which are security rights. These rights regulate, limit, and control the user's ability to make changes on network stored directories, folders, and files.

How Are Network Interfaces Made Secure?

Network interfaces can be made secure through hardware or software or a combination of both. Software methods of securing interfaces will be addressed first. These methods are explained as they relate to database security and applications, ranging from passwords to software encryption techniques used on data prior to its being transmitted. The hardware used to secure interfaces is described second. It revolves around firewalls, which normally are an integration of the software (which may be firmware) and hardware.

Passwords

Passwords are one of the things that make most networks vulnerable to attack. Passwords are basically part of a user's identity on the network. Because others generally can't see or hear the user, they assume that it is the user that wrote the e-mail or message or sent the data. Passwords are generally transmitted in plaintext and can vary in length, but many programs follow the UNIX convention of eight characters. Weak passwords make a network more vulnerable to attack. A weak password is one that can be guessed easily—it is made up from personal characteristics or traits, a commonly used password, and so forth. The more secure the password, the more secure the network. One way to make a password more secure is to create it with a combination of alphanumeric characters, thus making it unique. Password encryption is another option for making the network secure. A drawback to encryption is the possibility of a lost or forgotten password, making it impossible to get back to the data.

Password Authentication (Kerberos)

Kerberos is an architecture, which means it can work on any application, protocol, platform, or encryption method. It is well known in the server-based systems environment. Kerberos was developed at the Massachusetts Institute of Technology (MIT) to protect its own network. It is distributed free of charge by MIT. Commercial versions are available that provide technical support and documentation, which is important to commercial users.

Kerberos is a primary standard used in the C/S and enterprise marketplace for authenticating identities. In its basic operation, two communication exchanges must occur before any user is granted access to an application. First, the client computer system must exchange information with the Security Server to authenticate being an authorized user of that system and network.

Second, the client is granted permission to communicate and have access to an application on the Application Server. Because all these operations are performed without transferring the user's password across the network, it keeps the password secure from intruders and the network is more secure. Kerberos does all identification, authentication, and grants prior to any data transfers occurring.

In today's world, Kerberos is found mostly on servers operating in the UNIX environment that are located on networks using the TCP/IP protocol and DES algorithm encryption technology. Kerberos is made up of three parts: the client software, the Security Server or Authentication Server software, and the Application Server software. Because each of these parts can be tailored for unique requirements, it makes the architecture very flexible and operational networks secure. The Security Servers are usually separate computer systems that are configured with the server software, database of users, and credentials. The Application Server software is normally loaded on the same computer system (such as a database or file server) as the system or network applications are loaded.

Database Security

Database security in the client/server market is complicated to implement in a distributed database environment because of the varying security needs of different types of databases and multi-architecture database designs. *Database security* can be defined as the methods or process used to protect data in a database system from unauthorized access, modification or destruction. The two database security approaches commonly used are the data-level and application-level approaches.

Data-Level Security

The data-level security approach is built on the data source, rather than the application. In this way, the database controls data access, eliminating the chances that the application's security will be bypassed. The implementation of data-level security is generally accomplished through setting up a relationship between a user and a role or a subschema. A *role* or *subschema* is a list of allowable data items and operations, which are checked by the database engine at the time data is requested.

Access to most relational databases are controlled by the use of a GRANT statement. Security administration can get very complicated depending on how this approach is implemented. Relational database applications may be made up of hundreds of tables, and each of these tables normally has four operations (select, update, insert, and delete). In addition, each application, each table, and each operation has an individual grant assigned to it. Implementing a process that can monitor, index, evaluate, and store all this information is quite complex and difficult to administer.

One way to simplify the administration task is to group tables into functional categories. This can be accomplished by assigning roles to users and/or sessions. These roles consist of a list of predefined table privileges that are controlled and managed by the end user. With these roles defined, Grants can be given to assigned users and/or sessions when applications are activated. If the database is remotely accessed, security is controlled and managed at the remote site, and privileges assigned at the source are irrelevant.

Application-Level Security

Application-level security uses access rules that are embedded in the application logic. These rules enable the application to control data access. This method is most effective when the user is attempting to access data in the application when security procedures are active. Trying to implement application-level data access control over a network in a client/server distributed database environment is difficult and ineffective. It is ineffective because application-level security can sometimes be bypassed in Structured Query Language (SQL) databases through the use of the online query tools. These tools enable the user to bypass application-level access control and obtain protected information.

dBASE Security

dBASE has two modes of operation. You can operate in dBASE itself, or in SQL mode. Security protection for dBASE databases in the dBASE mode is normally provided through the implementation of a password-protected login system, assigned access privilege to users, and encryption of data files. The dBASE IV software includes password security, which is activated by the system administrator during setup by using the PROTECT command. PROTECT consists of these three kinds of database protection:

- Login security prevents access to dBASE by unauthorized users.
- With file and field access security, access is restricted to defined files, or fields within those files, for individual users. Access is based on users' allocated privileges.
- Data encryption encrypts dBase files, preventing unauthorized personnel from reading the data even if access to the file is acquired

Once the PROTECT command is activated, any new data tables created are locked. The user creating the tables has exclusive privileges to view the data tables and make any necessary changes. Prior to entering the dBASE SQL mode, database security requires a list containing group names, user IDs (login names), and a password to be generated using the PROTECT command. To prevent a single point failure in data table administration, a user ID (designated as SQLDBA) must be created and placed in the security list to allow administration access to any of the dBASE tables. This security list is then referenced when the GRANT and REVOKE commands are implemented in the SQL mode.

Additional security protection can be implemented with dBASE IV software, which includes user-assigned access privileges and the capability of encrypting the data. The SA also assigns user privileges defining operations that the user can perform. These privileges are activated after user login has been successfully completed. To protect the data generated, dBASE has provided encryption algorithms that are used to protect the data files in the dBASE or SQL mode. These files are encrypted when data is being stored, and only authorized users have the decryption key.

When operating dBASE in the SQL mode, user privileges are designated through the implementation of the SQL GRANT and REVOKE commands. These dBASE data files may be defined as SQL tables. If the data files are defined as SQL tables, access can be accomplished only by using SQL commands. SQL security is also directly related to dBASE security, which is accessed through the security lists created as dBASE files.

SQL Security and Authorization

Security is a real concern in the database environment. SQL servers have their own security built in. When implemented, it is activated after a user has passed through the levels of OS or NOS and network security. SQL security's main requirement is controlling access to SQL databases and database objects. SQL security is based on control access features, such as SQL server control access levels, user authentication, grants and permissions, and data encryption.

SQL server controls access levels based on user authorization. The user is granted access to the server (server level) and, if authorized, access to the database (database level). Servers may contain multiple databases and each database may have a specific set of permissions. First, every user request enters the server for validation of the login ID and password. Then every valid server login ID is checked to make sure it matches with the valid database user name. Access is limited to the permissions assigned individual users. These permissions or privileges (read, read only, or write) may directly limit the capability of making changes to stored data.

E-Mail Security

E-mail security is mainly centered around two encryption algorithm packages: Privacy Enhanced Mail (PEM) and Pretty Good Privacy (PGP). PEM specifies that it uses the DES algorithm to encrypt its messages. PGP uses a combination of algorithms consisting of Rivest-Shamir-Adleman (RSA) for public-key encryption, IDEA for conventional encryption, and MD5 for hash coding.

The algorithms described here are block-type algorithms, which can operate in one of several modes. The three most common modes are Electronic Codebook (ECB) mode, Cipher Block Chaining (CBC) mode, and the Cipher Feedback (CFB) mode.

Electronic Codebook (ECB) mode operates or encrypts a block of data at a time. For example, in DES each 8 bytes is encrypted or decrypted independently. With an input of 8 bytes of plaintext, there is an output of 8 bytes of ciphertext and vice versa. To maintain maximum throughput, the ECB mode provides only minimal error propagation. This corresponds to the fact that transmission errors in current systems are very low. An error in one ECB mode block affects only that block, thus providing high-quality data transfers. One security problem is found in the ECB mode. It is possible to intercept a ciphertext message and modify it by substituting one ciphertext block, thus corrupting the original message. Upon retransmission of the message, the receiving site is unaware that the data it is receiving has been corrupted.

Cipher Block Chaining (CBC) mode operates by making cipher blocks dependent on each other. Therefore, any changes to the ciphertext by an intruder would be detected. This was done to correct the problem found in the ECB mode. Cipher Feedback (CFB) mode follows the CBC example by making the cipher blocks dependent on each other, but the feedback is different. In addition to the key in the CBC and CFB modes, an 8-byte long variable called the Initialization Vector (IV) is required. Due to ciphertext block interdependence in both the CBC and CFB modes, if an error occurs in one 8-byte block, part of the following 8-byte block is also affected.

Data Encryption Standard (DES)

Data Encryption Standard (DES) is a conventional cryptosystem used by the federal government. It was adopted in 1976 as the federal encryption standard for nonmilitary applications. Later, DES became the international encryption standard, but was renamed Data Encryption Algorithm-1 (DEA-1). DES can be referred to as an *iterated block cipher* or just *block cipher*. When using DES, the block cipher or encryption algorithm encrypts and formats the data into 8-byte blocks. Therefore, when an 8-byte plaintext block is delivered to DES, the output is an 8-byte ciphertext block. Figure 28.6 shows DES the encryption and decryption process using the 56-bit key.

FIGURE 28.6.
DES encryption and decryption with key.

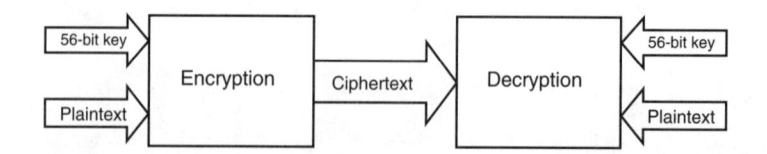

DES is implemented as a 56-bit single key concept that uses the same key for performing both encryption and decryption. This means that the key must be initially transmitted via a secure channel, link, or other secure means so that both the transmit and receive site have it prior to transmitting the message. The encrypted message can then be sent over a secure or nonsecure channel and be decrypted while it is being received. There are also double-key and triple-key concepts. In these concepts, the message is encrypted two or three times with different keys. Results from studies indicate that the double-key DES concept is no more secure than single-key. The triple-key concept has proven to be more secure than the single-key.

International Data Encryption Algorithm (IDEA)

International Data Encryption Algorithm (IDEA) was invented in Zurich Switzerland in 1991. This algorithm is an iterated block cipher like DES, but with a 64-bit block size and a 128-bit key size. IDEA performs its encryption in 8 iterations, as compared to the 16 iterations when it's done by using DES. To clarify the comparison, IDEA iterations are basically equivalent to a double-DES iteration, and its key length is over twice as long as DES. It is not yet known whether IDEA will provide a more secure message environment than DES, because it is such a new encryption algorithm.

Message Digest (MD)

Message Digest 5 (MD5) is a one-way hash function that generates a 128-bit hash value from an arbitrary-length input message. Because the one-way hash algorithm converts plaintext into unintelligible data that can't be decrypted, its function is to produce a unique identifier (similar to a fingerprint). The identifier is then linked to the digital signature to try to provide the receiving site with confidence that the signature and message are valid. This algorithm was designed to retain high security while being able to produce the required results rapidly.

ASCII Armor Format

ASCII is the American Standard Code for text characters (each character is represented by a 7-bit code). *ASCII armor* is the process of converting data files or messages made up of text characters and arbitrary binary data into a stream of ASCII printable text characters.

Encryption and other security processes commonly use arbitrary binary data to create secure files and messages. Most e-mail software can process only straight text files, causing a compatibility problem between security processes and e-mail. Using ASCII armor format, files and messages are converted to a text file that e-mail software can process, while still maintaining file security. ASCII armor format has been a cost-effective and efficient way of maintaining e-mail security and compatibility.

Privacy Enhanced Mail (PEM)

Privacy Enhanced Mail (PEM) is a draft Internet standard that defines message encryption and authentication procedures. With its adoption, the capability of providing secure e-mail network transfers can occur by using PEM services. PEM works with many of the e-mail schemes, such as X.400, but is most commonly implemented in conjunction with Simple Mail Transfer Protocol (SMTP).

Pretty Good Privacy (PGP)

Pretty Good Privacy (PGP) was developed to make communication between people, over e-mail and e-mail-transmitted data files, more secure. These communications are performed over nonsecure channels or links and require no prior exchange of keys. This was accomplished through public-key cryptography. PGP uses this technology to provide secure e-mail communications and file storage applications through PGP confidentiality and authentication services.

PGP features include key management, digital signatures, and data compression. It is also cross-platform-compatible, depending on the version of the software. There are versions for UNIX, DOS/Windows, Macintosh, and other operating systems.

The PGP software development was based on existing and tested encryption algorithms with a reputation of making information transfer secure. These algorithms consist of Rivest-Shamir-Adleman (RSA) for public-key encryption, IDEA (in the CFB mode) for conventional encryption, and MD5 for hash coding. PGP is available free via Internet bulletin boards and commercial networks such as CompuServe. It was primarily developed by Phil Zimmermann and is not controlled by any government agency or standards organization.

PGP was designed to provide the user with two services—encryption and authentication. They are implemented through the use of a digital signature. Encryption gives the user the capability of encrypting a file for either storage or electronic message transmission. By using the encryption service (algorithm), PGP has the capability of providing internal and/or external network security. The authentication service provides the user the ability to sign a document digitally prior to its transmission. Once the document is digitally signed, the receiver of the message can verify, with the PGP software, that the document has not been tampered with or altered. Figure 28.7 shows the process PGP uses to secure messages for transmission.

FIGURE 28.7.
The PGP secure message transfer process.

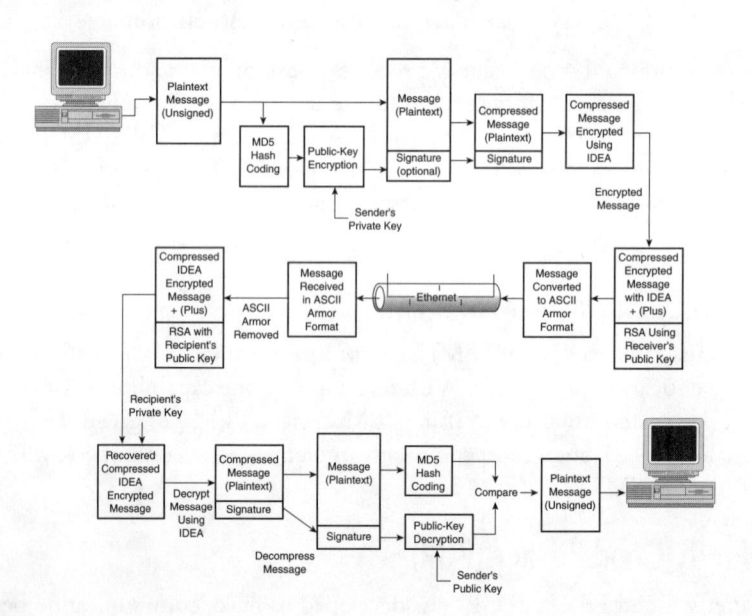

RSA Public and Private Key Data Security

Online application security is getting more attention. To accomplish this security, applications ranging from electronic data interchange and e-mail to document management are entering the marketplace. These products are providing secure transactions for messaging applications.

The RSA encryption algorithm is currently being used in systems to safeguard data transfers, and users' authentication and authorization. This same algorithm is being used to support the development of a digital signature. Integrating the digital signature into electronic forms, such as sale receipt, purchase orders, and so forth could expedite purchase orders and claim processing. By combining RSA's public-key encryption and digital signature technology, new products, such as secure data translators, are being developed to safeguard data transfers with authorization.

An alternative encryption algorithm to the government's DES, the RC5 Symmetric Block Cipher, was developed and is available from RSA Data Security Inc. RC5 is one of the online security products currently available.

Firewall Overview

A *firewall* (which may be referred to as a *screen*) is a security mechanism that restricts network access to authorized traffic only. Access is based on a security policy and plan. The original firewalls were developed by IT managers to protect their internal networks from external unauthorized traffic and still allow connection to the Internet. Firewalls are network barriers that are installed between two networks (LANs or WANs). Their specific function is to protect only the network behind it (a designated network) to the level defined in its security plan and policy. Each firewall consists of hardware and/or software that should collectively form the following set of properties:

- All traffic entering or leaving the network must pass through the firewall.
- All traffic transversing the firewall has to be identified and authorized within the security policy and plan.
- All firewalls themselves, in theory, must be designed to be impenetrable.

Due to the expanding market for network security products (including firewalls) and rapid installation with minimal down-time, plug-and-play firewalls are becoming available. One firewall can not protect against all possible threats.

Firewall Design or Selection

Firewall design or selection should first start with determining the value of the data you are trying to protect. This can be subjective, and different areas of the network may need different levels of security. The firewall design criteria, whether it's an original design or a selected existing one, is first governed by the level of security to be implemented. Next, the firewall design or selection has to match network interfaces and be optimized to protect against the network's perceived and real threats. Firewalls can be either hardware or software modules that can be integrated into bridges, gateways, or routers. Figure 28.8 is a diagram that shows the basic layout of a firewall.

With the proper level of security and firewall design specified, it becomes extremely expensive in time and money—and risky (because of possible exposure) for an intruder to attempt to access the network.

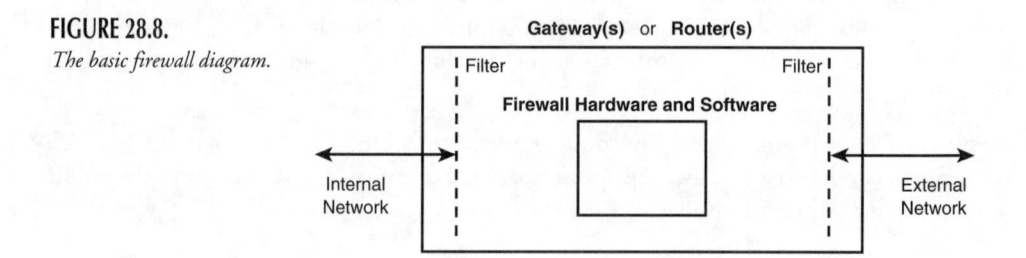

FIGURE 28.8.
The basic firewall diagram.

Filtering

> **NOTE**
>
> TCP is a virtual circuit protocol, and the filtering of TCP circuits is difficult.
>
> UDP is a datagram protocol, and filtering UDP packets is almost impossible while still retaining desired functionality.

Packet or protocol filtering is normally a function performed by bridges, gateways, or routers. These filters are designed to catch specific addresses, certain types of packets, and protocols such as Transmission Control Protocol/Internet Protocol (TCP/IP), Internetwork Packet Exchange (IPX), and AppleTalk. The filters analyze the type of packet, protocol, or destination address based on header information, and then they can be set up to prevent packets from entering or leaving the network. Packet or protocol filters are generally software-configurable modules with menu options that enable them to be reconfigured while remaining fully operational.

Routers

Routers are packet switches that perform their operations in the network layer and, with recent improvements in capabilities, have expanded by adding programmability. This programmability is in its routing and security software. The routing software is used to control and direct network traffic through the best route, thereby increasing throughput and reducing congestion. The security software is mainly focused on packet filtering, but can include protocol filtering. The packet or protocol filtering is implemented through software loaded into the router, giving it the capability of invoking a process of examining, rejecting, filtering, and/or logging every packet attempting to enter or leave the network.

Gateways: Packet-Filtering, Application-Level, Circuit-Level

A gateway is a computer system that performs the operational tasks of translating different communication protocols, data formats, structures, languages, and/or architectures between two systems or networks. Bridges, on the other hand, simply pass information between two systems or networks operating with the same architecture or protocols. Both gateways and bridges usually have packet or protocol filtering as a option. Network gateways operate at the application layer in the OSI protocol model. The gateways convert received information to match the format and protocol of the destination system or network.

Internal gateways interconnect and access networks that are normally located within one facility or building. The internal gateway is basically for cross-platform-compatibility between networked computer systems (Macintosh, IBM, Sun, HP, and so forth). External gateways connect and access the network to the Internet or external networks, such as WAN. External gateways are mainly concerned about network traffic compatibility and may operate under different conditions (protected or unprotected) when connected to the network. An external gateway that is not protected is one that is exposed directly to the network without an outside filter protecting it. This is also called an *exposed gateway* or *bastion host*.

Planning Database Security

Database designers often ask, "How do I design and develop a secure database?" This takes planning, knowledge of security threats and security products, and information about integrating those security products, methods, and procedures into the design. Many of development systems, operating systems, and current products have security mechanisms and features built in. Some products depend on accessing and activating them remotely. For example, Microsoft Access has security password protection and permissions built in. By using Visual Basic to develop the client/server system, the built-in security mechanisms of Microsoft Access can be activated remotely.

Here are some key things to keep in mind when designing a database and dealing with security:

- Develop a good security plan or scheme beginning with the database conceptual design.
- Follow the security plan or scheme, changing only to meet operational or design requirements. This ensures a secure database with a minimum of rework in the future.
- Assign permissions to groups, not to users.

Efficient, effective, and appropriate groups are also well thought out—an important aspect of security planning. A user's set of permissions for particular objects should match those of all the groups of which that user is a member. For example, if a user is a member of Group 1, which does not have permissions for an object, but is also a member of Group 2, which does have permissions for that object, the user will then have Group 2's permissions for that object.

Another benefit of careful planning of database groups is a significant decrease in redesign and maintenance work. This helps to complete the C/S database on time.

> **TIP**
>
> Here is a guideline for easier security management: When creating secure MS Access workgroups, the suggested maximum number is four or five groups.

Security management includes entering, storing, and using user names and passwords. MS Access has rules about case sensitivity when entering user names and passwords. Generally, user names aren't case-sensitive after logon procedure has been activated or a user name is typed to begin an MS Access session. However, when recreating a user account or group, each name letter must match the case of each letter in the name exactly, due to the format used in storing account information.

> **NOTE**
>
> User names aren't case-sensitive, except when re-creating a user account or group. Passwords are always case-sensitive.

Securing a Database

Protecting information is an important part of developing a C/S MS Access database. When you secure the C/S database, you gain control of what a user, or a group of users, can do with database objects. MS Access security consists of several parts, such as workgroups, user and group accounts, ownership, and permission assignments. In order to secure the database, each of these parts must be defined and in place. Security mechanisms in MS Access depend on a relationship between accounts in an MS Access workgroup and permission assignments in the database. MS Access stores account information with the workgroup and permissions assignments in the database file (.MDB).

To secure a database, follow these steps:

1. Define or select a workgroup in which the database will be used.

   From the system database, define the workgroup (typically, the SYSTEM.MDA file) that MS Access will use.

2. Establish one or more user accounts, or select one or more of the existing accounts, to administer the workgroup and to own the database and its objects.

   It is important to know that the Administrator and owner accounts have permissions that can't be removed. These designated accounts replace the predefined Admin user account, which is the default administrator and owner account. As part of the installation of every copy of MS Access, an Admin user account is set up.

3. Start up the logon procedure.
4. Make sure the owner account contains the database and object ownership.
5. Establish user accounts for each user of the database and establish groups to help manage user accounts.
6. Assign new permissions for the database and its objects, after removal of default permissions.

> **NOTE**
>
> Permissions must be removed from the Admin user and users group and all users currently in that workgroup. Until those permissions are removed, those users could have unintended permissions for objects. Upon removal of their existing permissions, the users can use only newly assigned permissions.

7. Install passwords to accounts where necessary.

    Passwords need to be installed on the Admin account and designated administrator and owner accounts to ensure the security of the database. Additional passwords should be installed on the accounts established for users, or you should instruct users to add their own passwords.

8. Implement database encryption.

    Database encryption makes it indecipherable by a normal utility program or word processor.

Converting Security Implemented in MS Access 1.x to 2.0

MS Access version 2.0 system databases include several internal security enhancements not included in version 1.x system databases. If you have an existing secure version 1.x application and want to take advantage of these enhancements, you must re-create your user and group accounts, passwords, and permissions in a version 2.0 workgroup. When recreating your user and group accounts, make sure that they are uniquely identified by specifying a personal identifier (PID).

If you continue to use the secure version 1.x application with your existing version 1.x workgroup, enhancements provided in the new version won't be available to those workgroups. Converting a version 1.x workgroup to version 2.0 format does require converting its system database. In order for a workgroup to take advantage of these enhancements, the following items have to be re-created: user and group accounts, passwords, and permissions. Figure 28.9 shows the Microsoft Access Permissions dialog box that is used to assign permissions to users and groups.

FIGURE 28.9.
The Access Permissions dialog box.

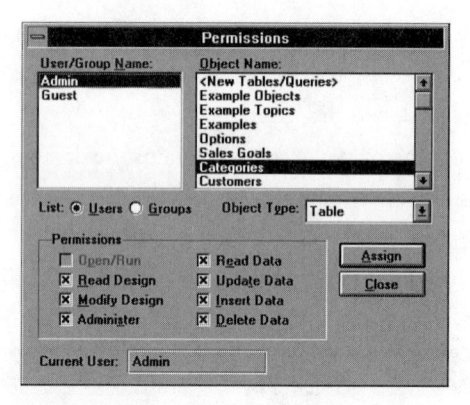

Handling Security with Visual Basic

The current versions of VB do not have a standalone VB security system. VB security is handled through the MS Access database engine that is included with Visual Basic 3.0 and above, both the Standard and Professional versions. The VB programming system for windows includes the syntax to access, operate, and control an MS access database—except in the area of security. Only MS Access can set up or change security options (such as login IDs and passwords for the system) and set up or change permissions on specific objects in a particular database. Through the use of two VB statements (SetDataAccessOption and SetDefaultWorkspace), VB applications can satisfy the security mechanism that MS Access implements and the login using VB code. These statements enable the programmer to obtain the permissions granted to a particular user.

> **NOTE**
>
> Microsoft Access security is implemented in two parts:
>
> - Unique Security ID (SID) code is assigned to each user and group.
> - The SID code is stored in the database with the associated permissions for that SID.

Security ID (SID) Code, User, and Group

Each user and group in Microsoft Access has a unique SID assigned to it in the form of a binary string. When a user logs on from MS Access logon dialog or code in VB, the Access engine reads the SIDs from the MSysAccounts table of the SYSTEM.MDA database. This database is created only by Access, and a new (empty) one is created if the original can't be found or was deleted.

> **CAUTION**
>
> Make a backup copy of both the database and the SYSTEM.MDA as soon as possible after the permissions are set up on the database.
>
> If the original SYSTEM.MDA was accidentally deleted, all the unique SIDs are lost. This means that access to those protected databases and its data is lost unless a backup copy of the original SYSTEM.MDA can be found.

When logging in, the user enters the user name and the password, which are then checked. If the name and password are correct, the SID of that user is retrieved and saved in a structure internal to the engine. The password is used only to validate the user. Once the user is validated, the password has no effect on security.

Due to VB's unique behavior and its relationship to the Access engine, the Access security mechanisms may be rendered inoperable. This could occur with the combination of the VB and Access engine defaults and if the following conditions exist with Admin and " " (" " means "nothing entered").

When activated, the default for the Access engine attempts to validate the user name and password of Admin and " ", respectively. This validation also occurs when the VB version 3.0 default is activated, without any code. By sending Admin and " " to the Access engine, even without using the VB security-related statements, the VB program gains access to the database, provided the "Admin" of the Group Admins password has not changed from the default of none (" "). Once logon is complete, the user's SID is retrieved and used for all subsequent operations performed within the Access engine.

SID and the SYSTEM.MDA Database

> **NOTE**
>
> Each user and group has a unique security ID (SID). The SID is stored in the SYSTEM.MDA database.

The unique SID is stored with all permissions granted to a particular user or group in the database itself. The VB program will gain entry to the database and have full permissions, seeming to ignore the MS Access security mechanism if either of the following is true:

- The program code doesn't contain any references to the location of the SYSTEM.MDA database.
- The password of user "Admin" has not changed from the default of none (" ").

In this case, overriding the security mechanisms is due to the default behavior of both the MS Access engine and Visual Basic. The effect of both defaults provides access to the database and its objects through the Visual Basic code.

> **NOTE**
>
> The following are MS Access object types: Table, Query, Form, Report, Macro, and Module.
>
> Visual Basic code has access to only two objects: Table and Query.

Because the VB code can access only the MS Access object types Table and Query, the others are omitted from any further reference. There are two Visual Basic security-related statements (`SetDataAccessOption` and `SetDefaultWorkspace`). These two VB statements provide an option of SYSTEM.MDA files and logon entries to an MS Access database, but the security is set by MS Access.

SetDataAccessOption: Syntax and Behavior

`SetDataAccessOption` has the following parameters:

```
SetDataAccessOption option, value
option is a numeric value with only one legal value (1).
```

Here is an example:

```
SetDataAccessOption 1, "E:\VBPROJ\MY.INI"
```

In the DATACONS.TXT file supplied at the root of the \VB directory, a constant is defined for this value:

```
Global Const DB_OPTIONINIPATH = 1
```

The name and path of an application's initialization (.INI) file is set by `SetDataAccessOption`. This application's .INI file goes into action only when `SetDataAccessOption` is implemented prior to loading and initializing the data access functionality. After data access has been initialized, the settings are locked and cannot be changed without first exiting the application. The value is a string expression. For the `DB_OPTIONINIPATH` option, the value argument contains a string expression providing the path and name of your application's initialization (.INI) file. Initialization files are normally stored in a user's \WINDOWS directory and have the same name as the executable file, but with an .INI extension. This statement should be used only if the application's initialization file has a different name or is in some directory other than the \WINDOWS directory.

The `SetDataAccessOption` statement is not required when running the VB project in the VB.EXE environment if the VB.INI file (in the \WINDOWS directory) contains the following lines:

```
[Options]
SystemDB=T:\ACCESS\SYSTEM.MDA
UtilityDB=T:\ACCESS\UTILITY.MDA
```

> **NOTE**
>
> Because the file SYSTEM.MDA is being shared by both MS Access and VB, the location or entry pointing to its location is important. As long as the application .EXE and .INI files share the same name and the .EXE file has its own .INI file in \WINDOWS, the `SetDataAccessOption` statement is not required.

SetDefaultWorkspace: Syntax and Behavior

`SetDefaultWorkspace` has the following parameters:

`SetDefaultWorkspace username, password`

If this statement is missing, VB sends the equivalent of the following line to the MS Access database engine that is included with VB:

`SetDefaultWorkspace "Admin" , ""`

The effect of this statement is to obtain a valid SID and gain entry to all the Table and Query objects in the database.

MS Access Security Mechanism

In order to understand the MS Access security mechanism, an understanding of the relationship between VB and MS Access security is essential. The following is a detailed explanation of MS Access capabilities provided for VB programmers who have not used MS Access extensively.

MS Access contains a hierarchy of permissions. Groups are at the top level, with users within a particular group. To grant permissions selectively to a particular user, all permissions must first be deselected or removed from the user's group. After that has occurred, permissions can then be granted or revoked for individual users.

Explicit permissions are lists of permissions for individual users. Implicit permissions are the permissions set for the group containing the user accounts. Implicit permissions take priority over explicit permissions. The Security menu can be used to set permissions in MS Access after a database has been opened and the user has logged on. From the Security menu, choose

Permissions to assign permissions on each object in the database. In VB, there are only two objects to which permissions can be assigned: Table and Query.

Suppose there is a group in the MS Access database named Analysts containing users Jon and Norma. If Jon is to be limited to Read Data only, and Norma is to be granted Full Permissions, follow these steps:

1. Login to MS Access as a user in the Admins group. For example, enter Admin or Dan.
2. Go to the Security menu and choose Permissions (Alt+S+P).
3. Table objects are the default type. The name of the table needs to be selected on which to set permissions. For example, select TestTbl.
4. Set the option in the User/Group frame to Groups. Then click the combo box list and click Analysts to select that group.
5. Clear all check boxes to revoke all permissions for the entire group.
6. Change the List option button back to Users and select Tom. Clear the check boxes for all of Tom's permissions.
7. Select Norma from the list, and check the Full Permissions check box.
8. Click the Assign button to apply the changes to the table.

Assume there is a VB program containing the following code in the form load event:

```
Sub Form_Load ()
    Dim db As database
    Dim ds As dynaset
    Dim scenario as integer

    scenario = 'insert a value between 1 and 4 here

    select case scenario
       case 1:
          ' Do nothing

       case 2:
          SetDefaultWorkspace "bob", "leftout"

       case 3:
          SetDataAccessOption 1, "E:\VB.INI"    ' not in \WINDOWS directory

       case 4:
          SetDataAccessOption 1, "E:\VB.INI"    ' not in \WINDOWS directory
          SetDefaultWorkspace "bob", "leftout"
    end select

    Set db = OpenDatabase("E:\DATACON\BASES\ACCESS11\ASAMPLE.MDB")   ' point 1
    Set ds = db.CreateDynaset("TestTbl")                             ' point 2

    autoredraw = True    ' to make Print  statement persist on the form
    Print ds(0), ds(1)

End Sub
```

The following scenarios are given to illustrate the relationship between VB and MS Access security:

Scenario One: The SYSTEM.MDA file has no reference location, and Windows and the MS Access engine can't find the .INI file. Therefore, the SYSTEM.MDA is ignored, and VB defaults to its default user and password combination (Admin, ""). However, previously, the default password for the User Admin was changed to something other than "". In addition, all permissions were revoked for the Group Admins and the User Admin in the Admins Group. Therefore, the following VB error occurs at point 2:

```
Couldn't read; no read permission for table or query 'f))'
```

Based on events, the back door was closed to VB and any VB application attempting to bypass the logons in the SYSTEM.MDA file.

Scenario Two: The SetDefaultWorkspace statement was invoked without having any pointer to the SYSTEM.MDA file. The VB MS Access engine continues to hunt for the SYSTEM.MDA file and, not finding it, gives the following error at point 0 in the code:

```
Couldn't find file 'SYSTEM.MDA'
```

> **NOTE**
>
> The errors that occur by moving, renaming, or deleting the SYSTEM.MDA file are the same in both Scenarios One and Two.

Scenario Three: The VB MS Access engine knows where the SYSTEM.MDA file is located, but is missing the user name and password combination. VB then supplies the only user name and password combination it knows (Admin, ""), which is no longer a valid combination since adding a password to the Admin User account. This results in VB identifying an error at point 1 in the code:

```
Not a valid account or password.
```

Scenario Four: Both parameters were entered correctly. Because Jon was given Read Data permission as well as Read Definitions to enable the VB MS Access engine to read, the VB application prints the first two fields in the first record of the table named TestTbl.

From the earlier example, these permission assignments were given. First, the group analysts were chosen and all user permissions were revoked at that time. Next, Jon was given permissions that allowed him only Read Data and Read Definitions, but all Norma's permissions were reinstated. Now if each of these scenarios is performed again by the user Norma, the results will remain the same, because Norma had the permissions to modify the table structure and the data.

> **TIP**
>
> The Admins group, along with any user in that group, is special when implementing database security. When a database and the Admins group is established at the same time, the Admins group's SID is stored in SYSTEM.MDA. A permit permission is then assigned to that group, which gives them the capability of changing the permissions on all objects in that database. This permission cannot be revoked and remains even if all other permissions have been revoked from the Admins group. This permission is not displayed in the Permissions dialog box. For this reason, it is important to keep a backup and be able to identify which SYSTEM.MDA was used to store the SID information when this database was created.

OwnerAccess Option in a SQL Query

The following example is given to try to remove possible confusion that could arise when using `With OwnerAccess Option` in a SQL query:

```
Sub Form_Load ()
    Dim db As Database
    Dim qd As querydef

    Set db = OpenDatabase("C:\ACCESS\DB1.MDB")

    ' Enter the following two lines of code as one single line:

    Set qd = db.CreateQueryDef("myQD", "select * from [TableDetails]
       with owneraccess option ;")
    db.Close
End Sub
```

This code results in this error:

`Invalid Database ID.`

The error occurred because `owneraccess` always refers to the owner as the creator of the database, not the owner (user or company) of the database. `owneraccess` may also describe or refer to the owner's user and password combination (unique SID), which is stored in the database (BD1.MDB in this case). However, the code is missing the two statements required to point to the SYSTEM.MDA file of a secured database, because only the `SetDefaultWorkspace` statement is essential if the compiled .EXE file's .INI file, containing a valid `[Options]` section, is in the \WINDOWS directory.

This code uses the back door, because the unique SID of the database owner was not supplied to the engine. The engine does not know whether the default name and password combination (Admin, "") of the user is different that the database owner's. In the event that the user Admin is the database owner, and the engine cannot verify that fact without being able to or having read the SYSTEM.MDA file, an error will occur and a message be generated.

Information for MS Access 2.0 Users

Visual Basic has the capability of gaining access to MS Access version 2.0 databases when using the MS JET 2.0/Visual Basic 3.0 Compatibility Layer.

When MS Access 2.0 is installed, it creates its own workgroup file (SYSTEM.MDA). If this installation happens to be in the same directory as version 1.x, the version 1.x SYSTEM.MDA file is renamed to SYSTEM1X.MDA. Because MS Access is backward-compatible, a version 1.x-secured database can be opened and still remain secure by either MS Access 1.x or 2.0. Even though the database can be opened by using MS Access version 2.0, changes or additional permissions to the database cannot be done, even by the administrator, until the database is converted to version 2.0. After the database is converted, making changes to the security involves creating identical groups and users (and identical PIDs) as the original SYSTEM.MDA in version 2.0 SYSTEM.MDA.

> **NOTE**
>
> PIDs (Personal IDs) in MS Access version 2.0 are the equivalent of PINs (Personal ID Numbers) in version 1.x.

Creating a Secure Workgroup

Use the MS Access 2.0 Workgroup Administrator tool to create a new workgroup and SYSTEM.MDA file. All the users and group accounts must be recreated by using the same names and PID numbers that were used in MS Access version 1.x. To create a secure workgroup, use the following steps:

1. The version 1.x database can not be in use when doing the conversion. Log on to MS Access 2.0 as a member of the Admins group who is not the Admin user.
2. From the File menu, choose Convert Database.
3. Choose the version 1.x database to be converted. When prompted, enter the version 2.0 database name.

> **NOTE**
>
> In order to convert a database from a version 1.x format to a version 2.0 format, in a secure workgroup, a user requires Modify Design permissions for all the objects contained in that database. Modify Design permissions must also be assigned to the version 1.x database in MS Access version 1.x, using the version 1.x workgroup.

> **CAUTION**
>
> The Convert Database command requires that a new name for the database be chosen. In renaming the database when it is being converted, the original version 1.x remains unchanged. Therefore, you now have a backup copy of your version 1.x database. Once the database has been converted from version 1.x to version 2.0 you *cannot* convert it back to version 1.x.

Users should now join the new version 2.0 workgroup (SYSTEM.MDA) by using the Workgroup Administrator tool.

> **TIP**
>
> You can also accomplish this by modifying the MSACC20.INI file in your Windows directory. In the [Options] section of the file, change the SystemDB entry to point to the version 2.0 SYSTEM.MDA file. The [Options] section of the file will be similar to this:
>
> ```
> [Options]
> SystemDB=<microsoft access path>\SYSTEM.MDA
> ```

Key Points

The following is a summary of key points to remember:

1. Only MS Access can create and modify the SYSTEM.MDA file.
2. The SYSTEM.MDA file contains the unique key (SID). This key is used in a database with its associated permissions to identify a user and enable the MS Access engine to enforce those authorized permissions. The key is acquired by giving the MS Access engine a valid user and password combination. The unique key is stored in memory, by the engine, to enforce security on an open database.
3. To gain access to databases that have security and permissions implemented, both MS Access and VB have to be directed to the location of the SYSTEM.MDA file.
4. Visual Basic application programs have a back door available to them, if the password for the default user in the Admins group (named Admin) is not changed from the default none (" ").
5. When using the phrase With OwnerAccess Option in the SQL query of a CreateQueryDef, CreateDynaset, or CreateSnapshot method, a pointer must be placed where it can be read by the engine in order to give the location of the SYSTEM.MDA

file. If, With OwnerAccess Option is being used in a SQL query and the back door (the default user and password combination of Admin and " ") is being used, it may seem as if SYSTEM.MDA file is not necessary. However, the SYSTEM.MDA file must be accessible for the engine to read so that it can match the SID of the database creator to the user who logs on.

6. The valid logon user and password combinations are stored in the SYSTEM.MDA file, and their permissions are being stored in the database (.MDB file) itself. To obtain the unique key (the SID) a valid user and password combination must be provided to either the MS Access engine (by the logon dialog in MS Access) or the code in VB.

Encryption of a Microsoft Access Database in Visual Basic

Database encryption is used to prevent someone from using a file or a disk editor to read and write data into a Microsoft Access .MDB file. Therefore, database encryption falls under data integrity rather than data security. Data integrity is important in the C/S environment because it can protect the data if an intruder gets in past the firewalls or other security protection products or procedures. The data can't be read or altered easily. The following information example shows how to encrypt an MS Access database file in Microsoft Visual Basic version 3.0 for Windows.

MS Access reads and writes all data a page at a time, with each page always being 2KB in size. Therefore, encryption is done at the page level, not at the data level. The encryption process is not concerned with what information is on a page, only that there is 2KB of data that has to be encrypted and written, or read and decrypted.

All data and information stored in an MS Access .MDB database file is encrypted, including tables, queries, forms, and indexes. To perform this database encryption, MS Access uses the RSA company algorithm. When encryption or decryption is used on these databases, there is overhead involved that causes a performance degradation of approximately 10 to 15 percent in operational speed. Once the flies are encrypted, these files cannot be compressed by using tools such as PKZip, Stacker, or MS-DOS version 6 DoubleSpace.

Step-By-Step Encryption Example in Visual Basic

To encrypt an MS Access database file from MS Visual Basic version 3.0 for Windows, the CompactDatabase statement must be used. This statement basically copies all the security permissions and data from one database into a new, more compacted database. An option is also provided that enables you to change the encryption or language locale while the compaction operation is being performed. The compaction process consists of organizing the data in the new database contiguously, which includes removing existing fragmented data files to recover disk space.

The following is the step-by-step example:

1. Start Visual Basic or, from the File menu, choose New Project (ALT+F+N) if VB is already running. Form1 is created by default.
2. Choose Data Manager from the Windows menu.
3. In Data Manager, choose New Database from the File menu. Then select either MS Access 1.0 or MS Access 1.1.
4. Enter the name TESTING.MDB as the name of the new MS Access file being created.
5. Click the New button and enter Table1 for the table name.
6. Click the Add button and enter First Name as the Field Name. Then select Text for the Field Type and enter 15 as the Field Size.
7. Click the Add button for Indexes, and enter First Name Index as the Index Name. Then select Unique, Primary and click Done.
8. Click the Open button, then the Add button. Next, enter a name (Jon, for example) into the First Name field. Then click the Add button.
9. Close the Data Manager and add a Command button to Form1.
10. Add the following code to the Command1 Click event procedure:

```
Sub Command1_Click ()
    Const DB_ENCRYPT = 2
    Const DB_LANG_GENERAL = ";LANGID=0x0809;CP=1252;COUNTRY=0"

    '** Enter the following two lines as one single line:
    CompactDatabase "C:\VB\TESTING.MDB", "C:\VB\NEWTEST.MDB",
        DB_LANG_GENERAL, DB_ENCRYPT
End Sub
```

11. From the Run menu, choose Start (Alt+R+S) to run the program. Click the Command1 button to encrypt the TESTING.MDB database file. To check the new NEWTEST.MDB file, choose Data Manager from the Window menu in VB 3.0. In the Data Manager, select Open Database from the File menu. Then select the NEWTEST.MDB file.

29

Third-Party Tools, Utilities, and Controls

Visual Basic has produced the first viable market for component software. Never before has a programmer or designer been able to choose from more than 3,000 shrink-wrapped programmer add-ons that are ready to use in commercial software. The benefits from using these tools are immense. Development time, money, and debugging time are dramatically reduced. Projects that were once impossible because of their scope are now within the grasp of even leisure-time hobbyists.

There are drawbacks to using some of the components, however. First is the expense. Each component costs between $50 and $1,000. Although this may seem expensive, once the package is purchased, it can be used in many products. It also is reasonable when you consider the programming time that would be required to duplicate these packages. Even so, it is a cost that must be taken into account, usually at the beginning of a project.

Another problem is memory and disk space. Most components have dozens or even hundreds of features. Often a particular application requires only a few of the available features. However, the entire component will be on the disk and loaded into memory for use. Plugging too many components into a single application can make the program bulky or slow on the client's machine. Be sure to consider this before you add an additional component.

A final consideration is the lack of control for bug correction when using a control. If you have discovered a bug in the component, you will have to report it to the company and wait for the company to fix it. If the component is simple, you may be able to create a workaround. If not, there is no choice but to wait or deal with the problem yourself somehow. In our experience with VBXs, this has not been a major problem. Because of the number of professional users requiring solid and well functioning components, companies are usually quick to fix problems that appear. Moreover, because thousands of users are actively using the component, odds are fairly good that bugs will be found and eliminated for all different platforms and hardware configurations. The components are, therefore, less likely to have bugs and incompatibilities than the programming you do yourself.

Now that you are aware of the potential pitfalls involved with using components, we highly suggest that you use them. Choose the components carefully, and make sure that they have the features you need before implementing a system around them.

The following sections briefly describe various components and tools that we have found most useful in the creation of client/server applications. This discussion is by no means exhaustive, and new products are coming out daily. It is also not a list of recommendations for these products. Where we have had direct experience or knowledge of them, we include some notes. The addresses and contact information for the companies that produce these products are listed in Appendix C, "Sources."

> **NOTE**
>
> At the time of this writing, most of these vendors had announced OCX versions of their controls but had not yet released them. Therefore, be sure to contact each vendor for specific upgrade information.

Help File Editors

Creating a help file by hand is a tedious process. A help file requires numerous codes to be placed in the text, so it is often best to purchase a help-generation program. These programs significantly decrease the time it takes to produce good, content-rich help files. They can also decrease the time it takes to generate your printed documentation.

Because more and more users use online help almost exclusively, make sure that yours is friendly and comprehensive. Whenever we begin the documentation for a new product, we examine existing help files for major products, such as Word and WordPerfect. These formats are familiar to users; they decrease the help learning curve.

> **TIP**
>
> On client/server projects, a dramatic variable is always technical support. If customers require constant help, your time and profits are reduced by the time you must spend with them answering simple questions. Spending a little extra time making help files and documentation better can significantly reduce technical support woes.

RoboHelp by Blue Sky Software Corporation

RoboHelp is the most popular of all the available help-creation systems. Primary among its capabilities is the seamless integration between RoboHelp and Microsoft Word. This enables the help file and the manual to be constructed at the same time with no duplication of effort.

RoboHelp can also be used in conjunction with Microsoft's multimedia tools to create multimedia training or help files. The potential for this is increasing as more multimedia-capable machines and CD-ROM burners become available.

Some additional features are HelpCheck Tools, a macro hotspot editor, two-way conversion between existing documentation and help systems, new templates, and a new visual interface. RoboHelp 3.0 supports MS Word 6.0 special features by letting the developer display smart quotes, em dashes (—), en dashes (–), and bulleted lists. To incorporate multimedia in Help projects more effectively, use RoboHelp with the WinHelp Video kit.

VB Helpwriter by Teletech Systems

This excellent program provides a tremendous number of features at an incredibly low price. In our opinion, it is the best of the low-end help creators that we have seen. If you need to write a manual, you might be better off going with a more expensive program that can exchange files back and forth with your word processor. VB Helpwriter exports RTF format but cannot read it back. Figure 29.1 shows a help display created in VB Helpwriter.

FIGURE 29.1.
A VB Helpwriter display.

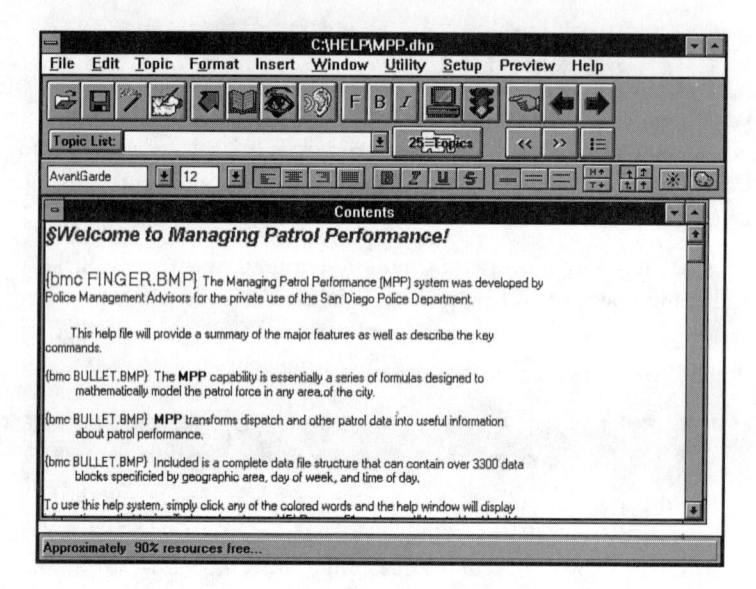

Multiuser Databases

Databases are the lifeblood of a client/server developer. Many small-to-medium offices use Microsoft Access on a file server to handle their database needs. However, many other databases are available.

Database servers are not covered in this chapter simply because the range of features at the time of each release varies dramatically. Therefore, the particular feature you may need (record locking, multiple database rules, database mirroring, and so on) may or may not be available on a particular system at the time you read this.

For example, with the introduction of distributed OLE, Microsoft SQL Server 6.0 is the only database server to offer object distribution capabilities. This will probably soon be remedied in other brands of database servers. We are on the edge of the object revolution. Database manufacturers are jockeying to add features and capabilities to their servers every month (in addition to compatibility with other servers, such as Oracle's Media Server).

> **TIP**
>
> When you're evaluating a database server product, make sure you go to a local user group. If one is not available in your area, check the online forums. You'll often be astounded by some of the rudimentary shortcomings or great hidden features that relate to your system deployment. This type of experience-based information is not available in product demos—only through other users who have already attempted what you are trying to do.

The best way to shop for a database server is to determine the types of features you need. What type of server will it be running on? Do you need cross-platform support? What are the per-seat charges? How does remote or wide-area network support affect the system's performance and cost? We recommend that you spend far more time evaluating a database server than you traditionally would evaluating a multiuser database. Most database products can convert data and definitions fairly easily between each other. Because of the complexity of a database server, however, switching systems is far more costly and time-prohibitive.

> **TIP**
>
> Visual Basic products work particularly well with Oracle servers and the Microsoft SQL server. For other database server products, we highly recommend that you find a local Visual Basic user group. You can probably talk to users who have already experienced a similar system and can provide recommendations.

Access by Microsoft

Access is one of the best database products that we have seen. It is easy to use and also powerful. We use Access extensively for many projects. It is completely compatible with the JET engine used in Visual Basic, so common database files can be used. It also provides security features that can be accessed programmatically from Visual Basic. Access 95 also has replication.

Access includes Rushmore indexing technology. This means nothing if you have only one index—or none—on your database. If multiple indexes are used, however, the speed increase is dramatic. Using an advanced synchronization technology, multiple indexes are coordinated to allow a multifield query to process very quickly.

> **WARNING**
>
> Note that the replication available in Access 95 is not compatible with replication in SQL Server 6.0. For many developers, this makes the replication features nearly useless. Perhaps, the coming Microsoft Exchange Server will remedy this problem.

Despite our love for this product, common complaints about Access include

- Slowed performance when working with very large numbers of records
- No cross-platform capabilities because there is no Macintosh, UNIX, or OS/2 version
- No available cross-platform ODBC drivers to manipulate an Access format database
- Its large memory footprint
- The Microsoft-proprietary data format

Visual FoxPro by Microsoft

Visual FoxPro is a complete development environment separate from Visual Basic. In addition to the large amount of legacy code and applications with Fox Pro, it is cross-platform (and will soon be available for both Windows and Macintosh). This means that you can develop a single application that will run in both the Windows and Macintosh environments without the need to rewrite any code.

If you need cross-platform support, or if you have substantial legacy FoxPro code, seriously examine this database system. If you don't, we recommend sticking with Access.

Visual/db from AJS Publishing

Visual/db provides a complete database engine written in Visual Basic. This product can be incredibly powerful, depending on your application. If you have a specific need to modify the engine, it is possible with this application—as opposed to most engines, which permit no modification. Visual/db is customized to use primarily xBase-type files.

ROCKET (SIxBase) by SuccessWare International

ROCKET stands for ROCK-solid Engine Technology. If you need to access xBase (dBase) or Clipper-type data files, we recommend this package. Visual Basic supports xBase file, but it doesn't support Clipper indexes or Clipper network-based record locking. It also doesn't have the same type of commands available to traditional xBase programmers. This makes porting legacy code an entire rewrite effort.

> **TIP**
>
> The term *xBase* is used to refer to the industry-standard database format pioneered by the dBase product from Ashton-Tate and now by Borland. Other databases such as Clipper use it as a standard format. The dBase database format became part of the public domain and has been generically renamed "xBase."

Successware has created a product that provides all of the traditional xBase calls as well as adding substantial new features to the engine. These include bound controls, support for graphics and other Binary Large Objects (BLOBs), a query builder, and a sophisticated bound grid control. This product also includes a data definition and manipulation tool that is more powerful than the Data Manager tool included with Visual Basic.

We have heard nothing but good things about the speed and reliability of this product. If you need to access these types of files, it is probably the ideal package.

> **TIP**
>
> Rocket has gotten extremely high marks from users, who say that it is not only extremely fast but also one of the most reliable database engines.

Components

Components come in many different variations. Some of the components are stored as dynamic link libraries (DLLs). Many of them are available as Visual Basic extensions (VBXs). The newest type of component, OCX, is purported to be the coming component standard. VBXs and the coming OCX implementations are the easiest extensions to use for Visual Basic designers. Many support such capabilities as bound controls and require little or no programming.

Not all DLLs can be used with Visual Basic. Some DLLs require something called a *call-back*. This requires that the DLL routine, when called, be passed a memory location where it can call-back into your code. Unfortunately, Visual Basic does not support call-back capabilities. Make sure that the DLL you want to use is compatible with Visual Basic before you purchase it.

> **NOTE**
>
> There are component plug-ins for Visual Basic that allow the use of callback routines. SpyWorks-VB from Desaware allows for subclassing, callbacks, window hooks, and so on. However, if the code you need requires numerous complicated system procedures, consider having a special DLL written for the specific task.

At the time of this writing, many VBX companies were planning to upgrade their VBX components to OLE custom controls (OCXs). An OCX would be available in both a 16-bit version (to run on Windows 3.x and Windows for Workgroups) and a 32-bit version (for Windows 95, Windows NT, and Win32). Check with the particular component vendor to see whether an OCX is available.

> **WARNING**
>
> Note that VBXs don't work on the 32-bit version of Visual Basic 4. Therefore, if you need to develop an application that uses a VBX that is unavailable as an OCX, you must stick with the 16-bit version of Visual Basic 4.

Some of the custom controls require royalties—either a per-copy royalty or a general royalty. Be sure to check with the control manufacturer before you begin distribution.

Printer and Report Components

Often one of the most difficult-to-implement parts of a Visual Basic program is the printer interface. Unless you have simple text and lines and know precisely the required layout for the printout, we highly recommend that you use one of the following programs.

Printers have more incompatibilities than any other piece of hardware that you will face. If an application must do particular functions such as printing a bitmap or drawing polygon shapes, this requires programming at the WinAPI level. Debugging is very difficult; even then there are broad and deep incompatibilities between printers, including those of the same brand.

The following components have been widely tested on all different types of printers. They take into account many of the peculiarities of dealing with them.

Crystal Reports Pro 4.5 Professional by Crystal

This excellent reporting package provides numerous capabilities for generating client/server reports. If you are currently using the Crystal Reports engine included with Visual Basic, we recommend that you purchase this package. It has significant upgrade features, such as live editing in the preview window, 80 additional chart types, and a more advanced user interface.

> **TIP**
>
> If you need to do graphs in your reports, buy Crystal Reports Pro 4.5 Professional. It has numerous graphs and significant graphing properties.

Crystal Reports Pro can display graphics as well as BLOB fields in Access and Paradox databases. It provides client/server report handling, cross-tab reports, fantastic pick-a-look wizards, a powerful formula generator, and a complete macro language. It is e-mail-enabled and supports both MAPI and VIM standards. (For more information on these messaging standards, see Chapter 26, "Remote Client/Server Access.")

> **NOTE**
>
> Potentially one of the most powerful features for the client/server developer is the ability to include a documented data dictionary with a report. That way, a user who needs access to specific data fields in order to generate a custom report can examine the definitions provided with the report.

The user interface for the reporting engine is extremely intuitive. Reports can simply appear in a window so that Crystal Reports Pro is transparent to the user, or the complete engine can be supplied for report editing. Crystal Reports Pro is also upwardly-compatible with the engine included with Visual Basic, so you can use the reports created with that version.

Crystal Info by Crystal

Crystal Info is essentially a full-featured report server. The main Crystal Info application is typically installed on a server machine, where it waits for instructions from various Crystal Info clients. In the simplest use of the server, an individual client can send a generate and print report command to the report server. The server begins generating the report, leaving the client machine free to continue working.

Reports can be scheduled to be done at particular times and are stored on the report server. Data can be stored with the report, so the query does not have to be redone. We think that Crystal Info is a potentially market-defining product. By providing robust client/server access to reports and report-generating capabilities, Crystal Info enables an organization to distribute vital information inexpensively, without incurring the great costs associated with custom reports.

For example, the report server can be setup to generate a particular report every week. This report remains stored in the report server and can be accessed by users across the network. Common financial and status reports can be centrally generated and located so that information about the company can be accessed quickly and consistently by any employees who need it.

R&R Report Writer by Concentric Data Systems

R&R Report Writer is one of the oldest report generation engines on the market. Versions are available for many platforms, which makes reports highly flexible if the people generating the reports are already familiar with R&R or if multiple platform compatibility is desired.

R&R is simple to use and is fairly powerful. However, it lacks the capability to do graphs or to provide OLE-inserted objects on a report. In the world of GUI, this seems like an oversight, but its multiple-platform focus precludes advanced graphics capabilities.

VSView by VideoSoft

VSView by VideoSoft is a fantastic utility that enables the simple creation of print previews, object pictures, and spooled-to-disk data files—and these are just the printer capabilities. The printer control can also format data in tables, allowing each individual cell to be customized. Also included are scrollable control views (so that a large picture or form can be displayed with scroll bars) and forms customization (so that a form can be given the Windows 95 look under Windows 3.1). We have used Videosoft components for quite a while now and cannot recommend them highly enough for quality, capability, and speed.

While you probably would not want to do numerous reports in VSView—they must be coded by hand—for most printing jobs it is essential. Graphics can be printed, including Windows metafiles. Text can be colored, rotated, and justified. Likewise, graphics such as polygons can be used freely. VSView also offers many other printing features not available from the traditional Printer object.

Links and Drivers

Visual Basic can be used effectively as a foundation where numerous components can be plugged together to form a whole application. Nowhere is this capability more evident than with its available links and drivers. Network protocols, groupware glue, database interfaces, and many more features are available. Visual Basic can connect to almost any device, protocol, or software component. The following list, therefore, is far from complete. We have listed the most useful extensions that we have used in our client/server projects. More drivers are listed in Appendix C.

VB/Link by Brainstorm Technologies

VB/Link is a VBX that enables programmers efficiently and effectively to create or customize applications to access Lotus Notes databases. With VB/Link, users can read, update, create, and delete existing Notes documents. It provides three controls: the RichText control, the HList Hierarchical control, and the NotesData control. Each one contains methods that give users bidirectional access to Notes data stored locally or on a Notes server.

The real power comes in its ability to join together the programming environment with groupware platform functionality. Other features that contribute to its power and usability are support of hierarchical Notes Views and Notes Mail. VB/Link can do full text searches, and it provides Notes rich text information. Based on the amount of custom controls available, it requires a developer to have more programming skills than some other products on the market.

Notes HiTest by Lotus

Lotus Notes HiTest Tools for Visual Basic was developed by Lotus Development Corporation. The purpose of HiTest Tools is to provide VB programmers with the capability to create, customize, and control Lotus Notes applications and data and to provide programmers with complete access to the Lotus Notes API. By using the 12 custom controls (VBXs) included in HiTest, you can create a complete object-oriented interface to a Lotus Notes system without writing extra code.

These controls were designed to work in the VB environment and give developed applications the ability to use the features of Lotus Notes and control the flow of Notes' data. Functions of the HiTest controls include server, database, and other selectors; database and document access; formula; item display; and edit and mail. Each control is designated by a Notes object in the object model and can be connected to other controls using the Piped property, which gives the programmer the ability to link controls through the click-and-drag process, thus avoiding additional code generation.

To make HiTest for VB more robust, Lotus added htGlue, a set of constants, structures, function declarations, and DLLs that provide an interface between VB and the C API originally developed for Lotus Notes. VB programmer access to the Notes API, custom control parameters, and the use of the Piped property make it possible to seamlessly integrate customized applications and APIs. Lotus Notes is becoming more important as its usage expands in the C/S and groupware environments. HiTest gives C/S developers a powerful set of tools for rapid development of customized applications that can link to Lotus Notes.

Distinct TCP/IP SDK by Distinct Corporation

This amazing package provides complete access to many of the most popular TCP/IP interfaces and protocols. Complete custom network applications can be constructed for file transfer, e-mail, news access, messaging, terminal emulation, remote execution, and other capabilities.

The library supports numerous interfaces through easy-to-use component plug-ins. Supported protocols include FTP, Telnet, VT220, SMTP (a standard Internet messaging protocol), POP2/3, NNTP (the protocol for Internet Usenet news), Rlib, TCP Server, and Remote Copy. This amazing range of capabilities lets you write a complete automated system using the Internet as a wide area network.

You could write a simple VB application to automatically scan news services, download and upload files, send messages, and perform other common tasks over the Internet. If you need specific network access, we highly recommend the Distinct libraries.

VBSQL/DBLibrary

VBSQL/DBLibrary can be used to optimize some connections with SQL Server. The people we talked to about this library felt that for Visual Basic development, it was largely historical. Because of the comparable performance of ODBC drivers, this library should be used only for particular projects that need porting capability to other systems that use the DBLibrary (such as C, Fortran, or other OS platforms). With the evolution of the ODBC access from Visual Basic (through the JET and Remote Data Object engines), there is little reason to use this library.

Client/Server Developers' Kits

In addition to components that may be added to Visual Basic, many development products add a whole dimension to the types of solutions that may be produced. These include development kits to build online and BBS services, data modeling systems, and object-oriented development environments. Development environments help extend the capabilities of the entire Visual Basic system, so the knowledge and skills you have acquired can be used to build systems not natively ideal for Visual Basic development.

Worldgroup by Galacticomm

Worldgroup is online, interactive software that takes bulletin board system (BBS) users into the world of client/server computing. Worldgroup software enables some of the tasks that used to be controlled by the host computer to be run from the BBS user's desktop instead.

The Worldgroup's client/server developer's kit enables developers to customize existing client-side applications and to develop new ones through the customization of Worldgroup software with Visual Basic. This customization provides a way to optimize the capabilities of the user's PC through the implementation of multitasking and multithreading along with the full use of system video capabilities.

While in the Worldgroup environment, links can be setup with other programs using OLE and DDE. Through the use of VBXs and Worldgroup software, JPEG images, WAV sound files, and AVI video capabilities will assist you in providing services in the world of multimedia.

Mindwire by Durand Communication Network

Mindwire is a complete communication system that provides both BBS and internetwork communications capabilities. This Windows and Windows NT-based system provides e-mail, messaging, chat, classified ads, and upload/download sections. A system created with Mindwire can also be hooked to the Internet for wide area network access.

The Mindwire system allows development of individual client programs through the use of several VBX components. This allows a programmer to include access to the BBS or network site within his own applications. The capabilities for feedback and user interaction and support are staggering. A user could simply pull down a menu to have access to the latest information or version of the client program he is using.

Automatic graphics downloading is supported for personalized site creation. Mindwire also sells numerous extensions for online scheduling, news, compression, database access, and remote filing.

Database Tools

A number of database tools are available to augment the capabilities of Visual Basic. These tools can significantly decrease not only original construction costs but also maintenance difficulties later on. Before you write a large amount of database code, verify whether there is already a commercial solution to solve the problem.

Choreo 1.1 for VB by CenterView Software

Choreo changes the way in which you construct a database system. Instead of following the typical *ad hoc* prototype approach, Choreo forces the designer to think about the construction of the database system. Choreo helps with all the traditional design problems, such as data normalization, to make the design process smoother (see Figure 29.2).

FIGURE 29.2.
Choreo for Visual Basic.

Choreo functions more like a data modeler (such as PowerBuilder or Data Modeler) that allows the database developer to focus on the structure of the database. Joins, lookups, and concurrent data refresh across forms are some of the features provided by Choreo with no coding. Choreo adds palettes to the Visual Basic Integrated Development Environment (IDE) to provide a transparent extension to the Visual Basic system.

Choreo includes its own more powerful grid control and navigation control that may be used to bind other controls. The Choreo system handles transactions, cursors, caching, security, and relations automatically. Choreo includes drivers for Sybase SQL Server, Microsoft SQL Server, Oracle, Gupta SQLBase, and ODBC connections.

Oracle Power Objects

Oracle has created a complete development system similar to Visual Basic called Oracle Power Objects. Instead of being a general development environment, this system is dedicated to producing client/server solutions. At the time of this writing, it could access any Oracle or SQL Server database; more are planned in the future.

One of the most fantastic features of this environment is its compatibility across the Windows and Macintosh platforms (and soon, OS/2). Programs are designed in an environment very similar to Visual Basic, and the code is syntax-compatible with VB 3.0 Basic code.

Power Objects provides an environment vaguely similar to VB but emphasizes the database end of operations. Rather than MS Access being its standard database engine, it supports something called BLAZE databases. Ideally, Power Objects should be hooked to a Personal Oracle 7 database or an Oracle Workgroups Server for development.

At the time of this writing, both the Windows and Macintosh versions seemed extremely slow and memory-intensive. Some good features were provided, but until OCX support is implemented, using it as a development environment will be expensive. Oracle appears committed to the product, so keep watching for improved future versions.

Source Code Tools

Managing projects and source code can be one of the most worthwhile investments that an organization can make. The number of hours lost to bugs for which there is no original version to check against, lost code, and code reinventing is staggering.

Some of these tools can significantly reduce or eliminate these costs. Integrating these tools into your working environment will be difficult at first because of the change in the way you work. Once they begin to be used, however, they will provide a significant amount of savings and peace of mind.

Visual Sourcesafe 4.0 by Microsoft

Visual Sourcesafe is included with the Visual Basic Enterprise edition. All the key features can be accessed without leaving Visual Basic; it is integrated into the environment. If you are doing team development and didn't buy the Enterprise edition, buy this product. This application is tremendously powerful for coordinating a project over a network.

> **WARNING**
>
> If you plan to modify the project file (VBP), be sure to check it out first. Checking out the project file reloads all of the individual forms. Therefore, if you've made some modifications to any of the forms but you haven't saved them, when you check out the project, these changes will be lost without warning.

Sourcesafe enables the coordination of a team working on a project. It can do version stamping, backups, and file check-in and check-out. It works with any development environment. Rebuilding older versions is a snap. The file changes are stored as differences between the two files (called *deltas*), so it does not eat up hard disk space. It also creates automatic login of all changes so that a complete paper trail for a project can be generated.

> **TIP**
>
> The best way to understand how Visual Sourcesafe works is to see a demo. The program is very graphical, and its ease of use cannot be described well in writing. We use Sourcesafe to track all our programming projects, including Visual Basic 3.0, Visual Basic 4, and Visual C++.

VB/Rig Professional by Avanti Software

VB/Rig Pro greatly simplifies adding all the on error routines for a project. This program processes every file (or specified selected files) in a project and adds on error routines to each procedure, event, and function. All the errors are trapped and sent to a central error routine and dialog box. This allows complete error reporting as well as traps that don't quit the program when an error occurs. VB/Rig maintains a procedure stack to show where the error occurred and provide explanations in English of which error faulted the program.

It can even log errors that occur to a file, including the function that was executing and the stack frame. This is perfect for beta testing. You can actually see the various errors that beta users encounter.

All of the error routines, as well as the common error dialog, may be freely modified. This tool is the one we use to provide error checking in our client/server projects.

Versions/VB by StarBase

Versions/VB is well integrated into the Visual Basic environment. The application completely integrates into the actual Visual Basic 3.0 application for seamless functioning. StarBase is supposed to release a new version for VB 4 compatibility that will be integrated into the VB IDE. Versions/VB also makes version-control tools for other development languages (such as C and Fortran) that integrate with this tool.

> **WARNING**
>
> The only problem with the version of Versions/VB that we used was that it backs up the entire changed file rather than just the changes in the file. This can quickly swallow disk space on a large project. Check the newest version to determine whether the program can save differences between the old and new files (often called *delta changes*).

User Interface

User interface components have seen the most proliferation since the introduction of Visual Basic. Beware of using too many interface controls. Otherwise, your interface might become nonstandard and, therefore, confusing.

These types of components also tend to be resource intensive. What might look excellent on a high-end development Pentium can bring a normal machine down to a crawl. Therefore, be sure to do a simple test install with the component on your target machine before you include it as a major part of your product.

VSVBX by Videosoft

This is a great control made by the same company that produces VSView and VSFlex. Elastic controls are essential for MDI-based applications. Elastic controls automatically resize each control within the elastic when the window size changes. Using this control allows, for example, placing a list box control that automatically expands and contracts as the user maximizes or resizes the window—all without coding!

The Tab control is superb and far superior to the one included with Visual Basic. Multiple color tabs, automatic or manual tab switching, multiple styles (including property sheet tabs and rounded tabs), multiple rows of tabs, and many more options are available. VSVBX offers an incredible number of options and flexibility. It also includes AWK (like the UNIX awk), which can quickly parse lines of data. This is great for those odd file formats that always seem to require conversion during a client/server project.

> **TIP**
>
> If you need increased flexibility for screen control, look at this control. It takes extremely little space—about 50KB to 70KB—and provides numerous incredible features.

VSFlex by Videosoft

VSFlex is a replacement control for the Grid control. Besides taking substantially less disk and memory space, this control allows individual cells to have different fonts, sizes, foreground colors, and background colors. The grid lines may be turned off. The user selection mode may be set to select only an entire row or column, providing a simulated list box.

The VSFlex control is code-compatible with the Grid control, so no recoding is necessary. The Flex control allows the user to modify the grid column and row widths.

> **TIP**
>
> Although the code is compatible, the control object is different. Therefore, if your code passes a reference to a grid to a routine (for example, `tempGrid As Grid`), these references will have to be changed. The flex object is called `vsFlexArray`.

VSFlex also includes a component called FlexString—a string-searching utility that provides complete pattern matching such as the searching engines found on UNIX machines. The control can find and replace complex string expressions.

Spread/VBX by FarPoint Technologies

Spread/VBX provides the developer with more than 250 properties and dozens of events and custom functions. It is a spreadsheet control with custom formulas and visual element control, fonts, line size, color, grid lines, and other data formatting capabilities.

Spread/VBX can be used as a bound control. Using a spreadsheet component in this way can be ideal for prototyping a system. A database can be instantly accessed and modified without any coding.

Featured with this control is an excellent tutorial and most of the features you will need from a grid-type control. Buttons, check boxes, combo boxes, and other types of fields can be shown in individual cells. It even features a learning mode, which can record actions that occur while the application is running and automatically generate Visual Basic code for these actions, which is pasted into the clipboard. This dramatically simplifies programming complicated cell interaction.

LeadTools by Lead Technologies

If you need imaging tools, LeadTools provides numerous graphic manipulation capabilities. This product can import and export over 40 standard image file formats, including JPG, PNG, BMP, TIFF, WMF, EPS, PCX, TGA, WinFax, CALS, IOCA, PICT, PCD, PSD, GEM, RAS, WPG, and more. This component also supports printing text or images, as well as scanning with any TWAIN-compliant scanning device.

Color conversion, bit manipulation, scrolling, zoom, color transformation, and other features are provided. Especially with the growth of Geographic Information Systems, many client/server systems are making increasing demands for image and document manipulation. Tools such as LeadTools may be used to give Visual Basic some capabilities for document processing.

Imageknife/VBX by Media Architects

Imageknife is also an image processing component. It provides a data-aware control that allows manipulation of numerous image formats. Support for multiple image features includes composing, masking, and integration. Imageknife also supports printing and TWAIN device scanning.

One of the best features of Imageknife is the ability to manipulate several images in off-screen image buffers. This allows background processing of memory- and time-intensive operations.

Media Architects also makes a multimedia product called MediaKnife. It's available as an OCX with complete Windows 95 feature support. The developers we've talked to highly recommend this product for multimedia development.

Gantt/VBX by ADDSoft

Gantt/VBX provides the client/server environment with the tools for planning and scheduling appointments, work, conferences, and other business activities. This VBX provides more than 100 properties and many event triggers, which enables a variety of applications to be created without losing programmatic control. The Gantt bar chart can be created from information retrieved from two types of databases: ASCII comma-delimited tables and Access database tables.

TrueGrid Pro by APEX Software Corporation

This is the most widely-used grid control that we have seen. It is powerful, has fantastic graphics controls, and can be instantly bound to a database. It has won many industry awards for its ease of use and power. TrueGrid also provides extensive printing capabilities. It might provide all the reporting features that you need for your project.

> **TIP**
>
> One of the most important things to consider when adding components to your project is how much memory they will require. On a development machine with plenty of RAM, a client program may appear to run fine. When it's deployed, however, memory can be a serious problem. Spreadsheet extensions such as True Grid Pro and Spread/VBX can use a substantial amount of RAM to provide their numerous features.
>
> Before integrating a component into your development, build a simple project with all of the controls you will use and attempt to execute it on a standard client machine. This will give you an idea of whether performance is acceptable.

Telephony

Telephony is an exploding market. The number of products available to the Visual Basic developer will mushroom in the next year with the inclusion of the TAPI interface with Windows 95. The coming Windows NT TAPI interface should provide complete client/server access to telephone services.

The following sections detail some of the market champions in the current world of telephony. Their slant toward using Visual Basic as the foundation for the telephony system provides a great deal of power to potential developers. Most of the telephony vendors have online access sites from which you can obtain the latest information on the products. See Appendix C for more information.

Visual Voice by Stylus Innovation

Visual Voice is the most widely used Visual Basic telephony application. Well thought out, user-friendly, and powerful, Visual Voice has been a leader in the Visual Basic community. Visual Voice can support voice mail, voice-based information systems, fax-on-demand, and even voice recognition features (see Figure 29.3).

There are two versions of Visual Voice: one that works with Dialogic-compatible telephony hardware (the professional industry standard) and another MWAVE-compatible version (which is usually available in the low-end voice/fax/modem cards).

FIGURE 29.3.
Visual Voice and Visual Fax.

> **NOTE**
>
> Dialogic-compatible telephony hardware has become the de facto industry standard. Most PC-based telephony software is written to interface to Dialogic-compatible boards. Therefore, when you're looking for telephony hardware and software, look for Dialogic standard compliance to ensure the widest range of product compatibility.

The Visual Voice product works through the Voice control, which is added to a Visual Basic project. The Visual Workbench enables the GUI creation of a telephony system that is then translated into Visual Basic code. Visual Voice will soon be TAPI-compatible, which will give it access to a much broader range of hardware.

Visual Fax by Stylus Innovation

Visual Fax has essentially the same interface style and implementation as Visual Voice (see Figure 29.3). Visual Fax has three controls that enable you to process faxes, change the status of jobs, and receive incoming faxes. It includes fax and line monitoring functions as well as other fax-specific functions.

Visual Fax is compatible with SatisFAXtion fax modems and GammaLink boards from Dialogic. Visual Fax is made for heavy-duty fax applications, such as complete fax-on-demand systems.

VBVoice by Pronexus

VBVoice integrates with the Visual Basic environment to provide a graphical construction system for telephony applications. VBVoice contains 18 controls that act as units. Outputs from one control placed on a form are connected to inputs on another control. In this way, a flowchart-like telephony system can be created.

VBVoice supports numerous voice boards, including Dialogic, Bicom, NewVoice, Rhetorex, and Pica. There is a different version of VBVoice for each type of board. VBVoice supports up to 32 lines.

VBVoice provides significant testing features and the ability to see the progress of a call. This can aid in determining where a call is being routed and in debugging incorrectly transferred calls. VBVoice will be TAPI-compatible soon.

VBFax by Pronexus

This is the complementary product to VBVoice. If you are using VBVoice and have a need for automated faxing capabilities, VBFax will add them to the system. VBFax consists of three controls: SendFAX, ReceiveFax, and FaxQueue. The FaxQueue control is used for fax monitoring and administration. VBFax works with SatisFAXtion fax modems. File formats that can be sent over VBFax include PCX, DCX (a multiple-page PCX format), and ASCII.

Installation Creators

Installation is an important point of consideration for many client/server developers. A full-featured installation program provides significant control during the installation process to avoid problems such as installation over vital files, version control, and installation of components unneeded by the user.

Despite Microsoft's significant upgrade to the Application Setup Wizard, control over the installation is still fairly limited. We highly recommend buying a commercial installation utility. Be sure that the installer you purchase can support all the new OLE features, the OLE registration, the Windows 95 Install/Uninstall, and various Remote OLE files.

Install Shield by Stirling Technologies

This application is the one used for most new Microsoft products, including Windows 95 itself. InstallShield is designed to run on 32-bit environments, including Windows 95. It can be used in a Windows NT environment running on an Intel-based, DEC Alpha, MIPS, or Power PC platform.

The version InstallShield3 runs under both 16-bit and 32-bit operating systems. The entry level 32-bit and InstallShield3 versions are completely compatible. Multiple user and network installation options are available.

> **TIP**
>
> The entry-level version of InstallShield is included with the Win32 SDK. If you are a Microsoft Developer Network Level 2 subscriber, you already have it.

WISE Installation System by Great Lakes Business Solutions

This installation program is the one most highly recommended by most Visual Basic developers we know. Powerful and easy to use, it provides all the features needed to make an advanced and attractive installer program. The program enables you to create complete installation scripts, including if...then statements.

The program's features include conditional install, billboards, uninstall application, compression, version checking, and old version file backup. A sample version of this application is available online.

Online Services

One of the most important tools to a developer is a good online service provider. By using a modem to call an online service, a developer gets instant access to the newest information, sample source code, various utilities, shareware libraries, and numerous other resources. We have found the most important feature of using online services is the informal peer technical support. If you have problems with a particular implementation issue, you can post the question to a message board and often receive an answer overnight.

Therefore, it is essential in terms of the time and money saved to have access to online information. A growing number of services are available; they include Microsoft Network, CompuServe, America Online, and various Internet services. The number of available Internet World Wide Web, FTP, and newsgroups available to client/server developers is tremendous and growing daily. Therefore, we have not attempted to make a comprehensive Internet review. We leave it to you to surf the Net.

Microsoft Network

Microsoft Network (MSN)—not to be confused with Microsoft Networks, the LAN communication system—is Microsoft's new online service. Support is provided for Visual Basic and the complete Microsoft Developer's Network (MSDN). The online service has promising features, such as the ability to create desktop shortcuts to online areas, over-the-phone OLE Automation, e-mail embedding of documents and shortcuts, and other advanced features not available through any other online service.

At the time of this writing, however, despite all its features, Microsoft Network was the poorest service we tested. Often unbearably slow, MSN lacked numerous features and content. This is sure to change. Microsoft Network is a fantastic foundation that, when brought up to the standards set by the other online services, will provide significant value. Additionally, Microsoft offers online authoring tools that provide individual users the ability to create online content. This is fantastic.

In short, MSN is currently a poor online service that should not be used as your primary online access. In the future, however, MSN may become the online service of choice for client/server developers.

CompuServe

CompuServe is probably the greatest single meeting place of Visual Basic users and programmers. With the Visual Basic forum (GO VBF), the Visual Basic Programmer's Journal (GO VBPJ), and various third-party vendors, a tremendous amount of source code, support, and tools is available.

America Online

America Online is the most aggressively-marketed online service at the moment. The number of users signing up for America Online is staggering. We have found, however, that America Online users are typically not the same sort as those on CompuServe. Judging by the number of messages posted and library uploads, America Online users do not seem to supply as much content as their tremendous numbers suggest.

The Visual Basic and client/server forums tend to be small, and the service's structure is significantly slanted toward Macintosh. At the time of this writing, all the PC and Windows forums were contained in one folder (out of more than 20) in the Computer Services section. America Online typically offers a free sign-up with a number of free test hours. Try it before you buy it.

OLE Broker

OLE Broker is a significant new service that provides access to numerous OLE controls. Like an online catalog of objects, OLE Broker is the first online resource we have seen that focuses on selling components. Do a Web search to find the OLE Broker site, which has information on this new service.

The End

You have reached the end of this tremendous book. We hope that you have enjoyed the material we've covered. We have tried to explain all the topics in a clear and comprehensive way. The client/server field changes so rapidly that new techniques and a new vocabulary are being invented all the time. This book should provide a foundation with which you can understand these new ideas, concepts, and products.

This book can also serve as an excellent reference work. The following appendixes provide information on user interfaces and error handling. Also included is a list of the tremendous number of new terms and acronyms in this field. Other chapters, such as "Remote Client/Server Access" and "Telephony," should prove handy as you incrementally build your client/server system. Thanks for joining us, and welcome to the world of client/server computing!

V

Appendixes

A
User Interface Guidelines

What Is Good User Interface Design?

One of the most difficult, yet most important, aspects of program creation is good user interface design. A good user interface should minimize the need for the user to reference the program's manual. The user interface should be simple to use but should enable the user to perform a wide variety of tasks.

In today's world of standard Graphic User Interface (GUI) operating systems (OS), such as Microsoft Windows and Macintosh OS, a program should conform to the standards set by the OS. This lets users approach and use a program they have never encountered before because of the way it is similar to standard OS programs. For example, a user knows to find the Cut, Copy, and Paste commands under the Edit menu. These functions shouldn't be placed in another menu.

Although it is possible that an excellent developer is also a good user interface designer, this rarely happens. Most often programmers and developers create an interface that is familiar to them and assume it is self-explanatory. Common problems include screen over-crowding, with every possible feature that will fit on a screen placed there, obscure keyboard commands or nomenclature, or odd program design flow (discussed later).

Because of the problems involved with designing your own user interface, we highly recommend consulting an expert. Although user interface specialists are almost impossible to find, usually in any organization there is one person whose skills at layout and design are superior. This is often a graphic artist or similar professional. Someone once said that the best art is created in a collaborative effort, usually with two people trying to realize a vision. Building a good user interface is an art.

One of the most effective ways to construct a user interface is to prototype it to fulfill all the required actions and features and then consult a professional. This enables you to decide what features and processes are necessary, and the user interface designer can help you put all the pieces together in one consistent interface.

Whether you work with a user interface designer or not, a few guidelines will make your application more useful to the users and easier to develop. These are general guidelines, not gospel. If your program violates them, make sure you know why you're not complying with them. User interface design is a constant balancing act between usability and utility. These guidelines provide a structure to ensure that usability is maximized.

Copy Other Programs

Look around your company or your client's company and see what programs are currently being used. If the people that will be using your client applications are comfortable with Word Perfect, try to emulate the design decisions used in that program. This eliminates half the training costs you will incur if you attempt to pioneer the way the user interacts with a program. The programs that are used most often and most effectively are the ones that require the least new training and new skills.

Replicating the look and feel of a commonly used program also supplies you with many hours of user interface research essentially free. Large companies like Novell and Microsoft spend thousands of dollars and commit tremendous resources toward the goal of making their programs simple to use but powerful. They have tried and eliminated many different interface possibilities that users are not comfortable with.

As with everything else, use this technique in moderation. A program that feels the same as a word processor, yet serves a completely different function, will most likely confuse and frustrate the user. Duplicate general interface concepts such as the tool bar and menu layout, standard function icons, and screen layout.

Try to follow the general guidelines for the menu titles that appear along the top of the screen (called the menu bar). File and Edit should be the first two menus. Even if the user doesn't interact with files in a standard way, include the File menu so the user can easily find the Exit command.

Remember to Be Consistent

To have an effective user interface, you should be consistent in terms of placement and function. Placement of various controls, menus, and options throughout an application enables the user to know where a particular feature is located without having to search for it. Functions of various items should work the same, so the user isn't confused about what interacting with a given object will do.

For standard types of menus and controls, try to keep them in the same location and appearance throughout the application. For example, if many forms have OK and Cancel buttons on them, try to keep these buttons in the same place on every form. That way the user knows where to find them. If the OK button is sometimes in the upper-right corner of the window and sometimes in the lower-left corner, this can be annoying and inconvenient.

Keep the function or interaction with a particular type of user interface consistent. The most effective way to illustrate this guideline is to describe programs that ignore it. One of the worst violations of this concept we have seen (even some of the VB demo files are guilty of it) is using a menu like a button. When a user clicks a menu, instead of that menu being displayed (often called dropping down), the program executes some type of function. Menus are supposed to display their menu lists, and that's all. The user then selects an item from that menu. Violating a standard like this makes the user suspect of the functions of all the other menus contained in your application.

Likewise, a radio button (see Figure A.1) is used to select among several options. If a radio button is placed within a frame (see Figure A.1), the frame automatically unselects the other radio buttons when the user selects a new one. We have seen applications use a single radio button to indicate True or False instead of a check box. Please do not do this. Use a check box for a True or False value, such as Check1 (see Figure A.1). Each type of control has a usage that is generally consistent throughout the popular widespread applications. If you comply with these standards, the enterprise or market you are creating the application for will appreciate it.

FIGURE A.1.
Radio buttons and a check box.

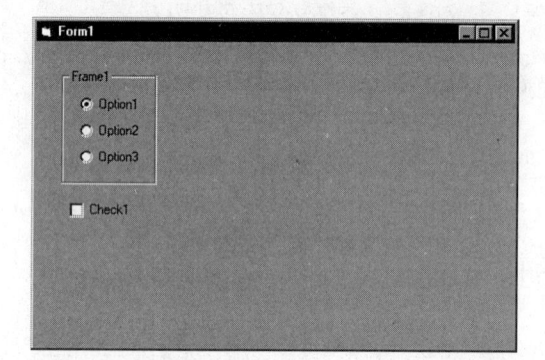

Keeping user interaction standard with controls that appear alike is important as well. The user shouldn't have to click a button on one screen and double-click the same type of button on another screen. There should be continuity and consistency within a program. If pressing Alt+O activates the OK button on one screen, try to ensure that key combination activates the OK button on all screens.

Keep the User Informed

Some of the applications that rate highest in overall user interface design fall down when it comes to keeping the user informed. A user finds it terribly irritating when a machine goes off to perform some calculated function or process and provides no clues to the user as to what it is doing. Creating all the routines that must be used to show the status of an operation can be tedious, but it is vitally important for the user to effectively understand what the application is doing.

Message Boxes

When an error occurs, an important function completes, or information is given, it is good design to show a message box to notify the user what has occurred (see Figure A.2). Visual Basic includes the MsgBox function to make this simple. Here is the code to create the message box in Figure A.2:

```
MsgBox "The replace routine has found 5 instances of the given string and
↪replaced them with the new string.", 64, "Replace complete"
```

FIGURE A.2.
A message box.

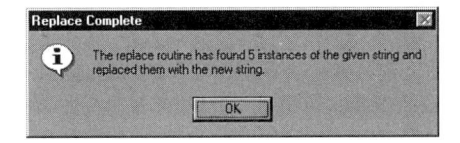

Try your best to make the message self-explanatory. You have undoubtedly seen countless cryptic messages (including those made by the Windows OS) that read something like "An Error of type −64 has occurred." Avoid these at all costs! They are disconcerting to the user, and they require tech support to look in a manual for the meaning of the code.

Make sure you also provide routines that make sure the user wants to complete a permanent action. If the user can simply press the Delete key to eliminate a record, make sure the program asks, "Do you want to delete the record: *Dummy*," where *Dummy* gives a clue to exactly what will be deleted. Many pieces of data have been lost over the years when a simple key like Esc can abort an entire record. If the user can easily damage the information they have been working on, this is the fault of the careless user interface designer, not the hapless user.

Providing error subroutines also ensures that the program doesn't unceremoniously quit and exit to Windows. For more extensive coverage of error routines and specifically how they relate to client/server applications, see Appendix B, "Error Handling."

Cursor Settings and Status Bars

The simplest type of process progress is the use of the clock or hourglass cursor. We have seen many programs that begin performing a lengthy process and simply leave the cursor as the standard arrow, making the user think they can proceed with operations. Visual Basic makes putting up an hourglass cursor extremely simple. At the beginning of a process, enter the following:

```
screen.mousepointer = 11
```

When the process has completed, reset the cursor to the default with this:

```
screen.mousepointer = 0
```

For general tasks (functions that require around 3 to 15 seconds to complete) the hourglass cursor is a perfectly convenient way to signal that processing is taking place. It also generally keeps the user from clicking various items that won't respond until the function completes. If a longer time is required, displaying a status bar is often recommended.

Almost everyone has experienced the frustration of seeing the hourglass cursor for several minutes. The user doesn't know whether to reset the machine because the program crashed or to just wait a little longer. Even if the user knows the program hasn't crashed, he has no idea whether the task is half complete, nearly complete, or just beginning.

Many designers don't implement status bars for three reasons:

1. The difficulty in creating a status bar
2. The extra processing time required for updating the status while transactions are occurring
3. The difficulty of isolating units to make the bar relevant

The designers of VB made sure that the first objection was eliminated. VB includes a gauge control at the bottom of the palette that makes it convenient to display the progress of a task. This control has Min and Max properties that are by default set to 0 and 100, respectively. Setting the Value property to a percentage number (for example, to 33) shows the desired progress (see Figure A.3).

FIGURE A.3.
A gauge control with the Value *property set to 33.*

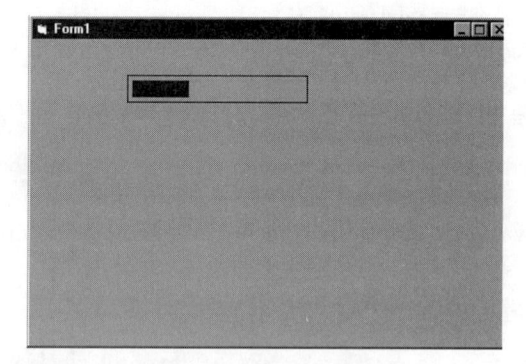

The second objection, of wasting processor time updating the status bar, has become less relevant as processor speeds have dramatically increased. The amount of time required for updating is a small fraction of the overall processing capability. Also, unless the calculation is truly time-critical, most users would gladly trade an extra few seconds of waiting to know the progress of a transaction that lasts two minutes or longer.

The third objection is still a primary obstacle. For example, if your routine must search all the directories for a particular file, it is fairly difficult to know how many total directories exist that must be searched. Without knowing the total number, finding a percentage is impossible. Likewise, a client/server programmer rarely knows the total number of records to be searched or updated. For these reasons, it is often a good idea to display a status box that shows overall progress. For example, a directory search might show the directory being searched, or the client/server application might show a "Number of Records Updated" area, which would increment with each updated record.

Keeping the user aware of progress is becoming increasingly important as multitask processing becomes available. Under Windows 95 multitasking, for example, a user might switch out of your client/server application while it is processing data to use a spreadsheet program. The user could then reactivate your application from time to time to check on its progress.

Screen Layout

How a particular form is set up depends on the particular role that screen is supposed to fulfill. One of the most common problems is the overuse of one particular type of control. For example, 20 radio buttons on the screen (see Figure A.4) is usually poor user interface design. When you need the user to select from 20 options, use a combo box. The number of options that must be selected from determines which type of control should be used. The progression goes something like this:

radio buttons (less than 10) → combo box (less than 20) → list box

FIGURE A.4.
Poor use of radio button controls.

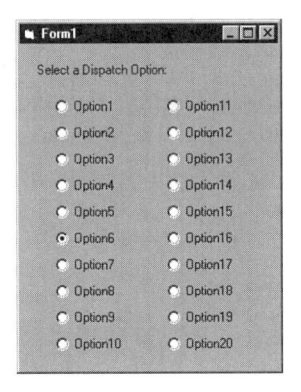

There are no hard and fast rules about when there are too many options for a given control. As a general guideline, if you have over ten radio buttons for selecting one property, you should probably be using a combo box. Likewise, if you have over 20 items listed in a combo box, you probably need to use a list box or a separate window that contains a list box.

Some people complain that these numbers are too high for the controls; others say they are too low. Use your best judgment. We have seen 20 radio buttons used effectively for one property in an application. We have also seen a combo box with around 100 items that was nearly unusable. Also, if you have too many options in one place, consider breaking the options into subcategories. This can often eliminate user confusion and increase the usability of your interface.

Think carefully about how the user needs to interact with the display. A combo box requires two mouse clicks to select an option. It also doesn't display the variety of choices the user can select from until it is clicked. This can be a blessing (it saves screen space) or a curse (users skip useful options because they don't notice them).

A list box can display many possible options on the screen at once and can also be scrolled to show more. If you have many options that need to be selected from the same list throughout the application, you might consider putting a list box in a floating window or palette. List boxes are also extremely useful when the user needs to indicate more than one selection from a list.

Consider how the options will be used and who will be using them. Screen space, simplicity, and general formatting determine which control you use for a given task. Take care to use these controls in a consistent manner, but don't use one type of control to fit every situation.

Multiple Forms or Windows

You can approach the way the user interacts with the application through many types of forms or windows. Some of these include dialog boxes, multiple forms, MDI (Multiple Document Interface), and floating palettes.

A primary design decision is whether to use the MDI form structure. MDI keeps all subforms, called children, within the main window (see Figure A.5). The MDI structure is typically used if the user will be opening multiple self-contained windows, usually with each window representing a different document. One central menu bar applies to all the windows. MDI gives the program great flexibility to do things such as tiling or auto arrangement. Also, when MDI child forms are minimized, the minimize icon appears at the bottom of the window (see Figure A.6).

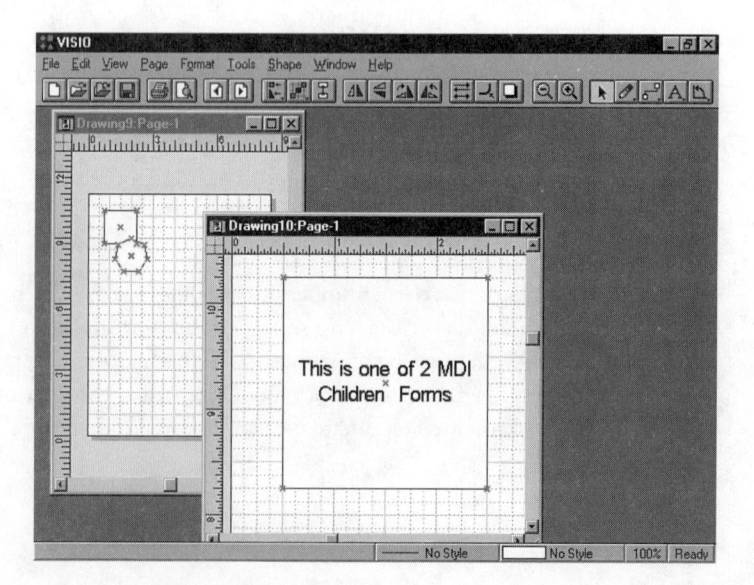

FIGURE A.5.
An MDI window and two child windows.

FIGURE A.6.
An MDI window and two minimized child windows.

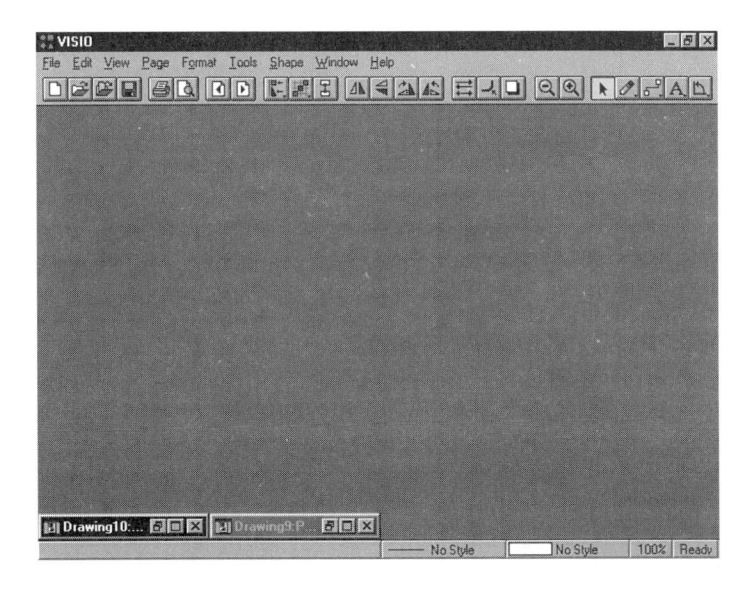

MDI applications are perfect for document-centered programs, such as word processors or spreadsheets, but this is not usually how a client/server application is organized. C/S programs traditionally access one homogenous database table or several heterogeneous database tables or servers. Therefore, most client/server programs simply use multiple forms to access the data.

Design Flow

Design flow is one of the most difficult aspects of a user interface to implement well. Design flow is building an application that can be used in the most convenient and natural way for the user. To complete an operation, a user should be able to easily complete a common process in the most simple and consistent way.

For example, the most common function in your customer client front-end is to add a new customer. Because the Add Customer function is called frequently and involves typing the name and address of the client, good design flow would make the function conveniently accessible from the keyboard. Requiring the user to press Alt+Shift+Ctrl+P to add a new customer would be a poor choice. A single key, perhaps the F5 key, would be the best implementation of this most used function.

Be Process-Consistent

If the operation requires using the keyboard extensively, make all the operations accessible from the keyboard. This provides continuity within the application. The same holds true for the mouse, touch-screen, pen, or any other input device. Switching back and forth from the mouse to the keyboard can be a tedious and unnecessary process for a common operation.

Luckily, Visual Basic includes many features to allow the mouse or keyboard to be used for a common function.

Make the Screen Layout Match the Process Flow

The screen should be designed for the flow that from the beginning to the end of any process works the way a user needs it to. For example, if a customer name and phone number must always be entered, but the address and other fields are optional, place the needed fields first on the screen (see Figure A.7). If the fields are placed in a more traditional order, the application is much more difficult to use routinely. For example, in Figure A.8 there are four optional fields between the two primary fields. This means the user must press the Tab key four times or move from the keyboard to the mouse to move quickly to the Phone field.

FIGURE A.7.
Important fields placed together at the top of the screen.

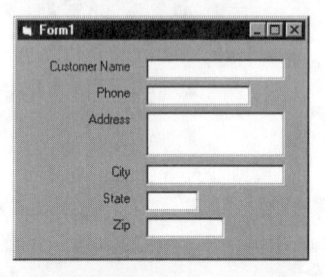

FIGURE A.8.
Important fields placed poorly.

To achieve the most process flow, consult the people that will be using the client application every day. What field order would they prefer? What are the most common operations they perform? You won't be able to please all the people all the time, but seek to make your application easy for the most people who are performing the most common functions.

Follow Common Direction Flow

Design the application so that the most common processes operate in a left-to-right and top-to-bottom fashion. People are used to this from reading books and newspapers. Programs designed for use in China should use the opposite flow, because that is what they are used to seeing in written and printed material.

Layout of the program like this does not apply only to field progression. For example, buttons should appear in the order they are most likely to be used (see Figure A.9). When a new screen appears, the user is most likely to look to the top-left corner to find where to begin.

FIGURE A.9.
Effective button order.

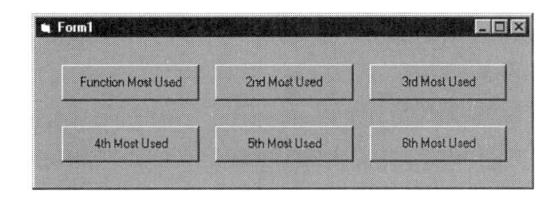

Icons and Menu Items

Icons and graphic user interfaces have become extremely popular because a large amount of information can be communicated and manipulated in a short period of time using graphics. For this reason it is good to attempt to make your user interface resemble items available in the real world, such as a printer icon indicating the user's desire to send the information to the printer.

Extremely relevant to current design metaphors is to not make the on-screen interface too much like the physical world, for the simple reason that it is not the physical world. The computer uses representations of the world to make communication with the user simpler, but a computer notepad is not a real notepad. Implementations that make the user's screen look too much like the real world (such as Microsoft's new BOB program) can be used only for simple operations.

The reason for this is simple: pictures show nouns most effectively, but they have a difficult time showing verbs. A printer icon is effective because the printer is a physical object. What is a query? A query is an action or process. Client/server computing in particular uses extensive processes and data abstractions, both of which are difficult to represent with nouns or pictures.

Menu items, on the other hand, should be mostly verbs. When the user selects a menu item, he usually wants the computer to do something, such as display a window, begin a query, or open a file.

Keep these distinctions in mind as you design your interface. Often when the correct icon cannot be found or the menu item doesn't seem natural for a particular feature, it could be that you are using the wrong item.

Tab Order

In Visual Basic, if an object has the focus, any operation (such as a key press) is sent to that object. For example, if the text box named `txt_Address` has the focus, any key strokes are entered into the `txt_Address` field.

The user of an application can press the Tab key to move the focus. Each press of the Tab key moves the focus to the next control in the tab order. Holding the Shift key while pressing the Tab key moves the focus backwards in the tab order.

Each control has both a `TabIndex` and a `TabStop` property. The `TabIndex` property is a number that determines what the given control's position is in the tab order. `TabStop` indicates whether the focus stops at this control when the user presses the Tab key. If `TabStop` is set to False, the Tab key skips that control.

Using the tab order, you can format the order the user moves through the screen for the best flow. For text box controls, you might want to put a routine in the `GotFocus` event routine that selects all the text in the box. That way the user can simply tab through an entire screen, changing the values as needed. This is done very simply by changing the `SelStart` and `SelLength` properties of the given text box. Listing A.1 includes sample code that selects all the text in the box.

Listing A.1. Sample auto-select code.

```
Sub Text1_GotFocus ()
    Text1.SelStart = 0
    Text1.SelLength = 65000
End Sub
```

You might want to use arrays of text boxes so the code has to be written only once, rather than once for each instance. Listing A.2 shows the sample code necessary for a text box control array.

Listing A.2. Sample auto-select code for a control array.

```
Sub Text2_GotFocus (Index As Integer)
    Text2(Index).SelStart = 0
    Text2(Index).SelLength = 65000
End Sub
```

Help Options

The online help available to a user is becoming increasingly robust. There are fewer reasons to look in the huge manuals included with many of today's programs. For the client/server developer, all this online help is heaven-sent. Providing extensive manuals to everyone who needs them in an organization is a tedious process. Often the manuals are brief and cryptic, because it is too expensive to produce a complete manual for in-house use. If the manual is produced, updates and upgrades are seldom included, and the manual can end up describing a program that looks nothing like the one in use.

Without a comprehensive manual, many functions of the in-house applications go completely undocumented. This creates increased training costs as well as less than full capacity use of features that took time, money, and energy to implement.

Online help solves most of these problems. Although the help must still be created, many tools are available to automate the process. Many of the forms of help are built into the program, so updates automatically include the new help. Distribution of new online help is often as simple as making the new file available on the server. Help files can also automatically generate a document that can be loaded into a word processor, so the time required to produce a paper-based manual is greatly reduced.

In addition to the savings to the company and the developer, online help is much more available to the users. A user can access online help using searches or even a point-and-click help interface for instant access to current help information. Online help can even incorporate digitized sounds to tell the user what to do, video to show the user, and various types of context-sensitive help to tell the user about the form that is currently displayed.

> **TIP**
>
> To assist you in creating help files, Microsoft provides some free tools. Microsoft Windows Help Authoring Guide and Microsoft Windows Help Authoring Tools are available either online from Microsoft or on CD as part of the Microsoft Developer Network CD-ROM package. For information on Microsoft's online services, see Appendix C, "Sources."

Help Files

When Microsoft built the Help engine into the Windows OS, making it standard on all Windows platform machines (see Figure A.10), the widespread use of online help exploded. Online help has become a standard feature with even the simplest Windows programs. Help files (files with the .HLP extension) can be accessed from Windows through the Help menu or from within a running application.

Now the Microsoft Help engine is also available on the Macintosh. The Macintosh version can read the same format files. Help files have become truly cross-platform. They can be viewed on any Windows machine, the Macintosh platform machines, and any computer that can run Windows NT.

A help file is a hypertext-like document, meaning the user can click a highlighted word or picture within the text, and the display jumps to the appropriate topic. A help file can hold text, graphics, hotspot images, various font types and styles, jump-to topics, and popup windows.

FIGURE A.10.
Microsoft online help for Visual Basic.

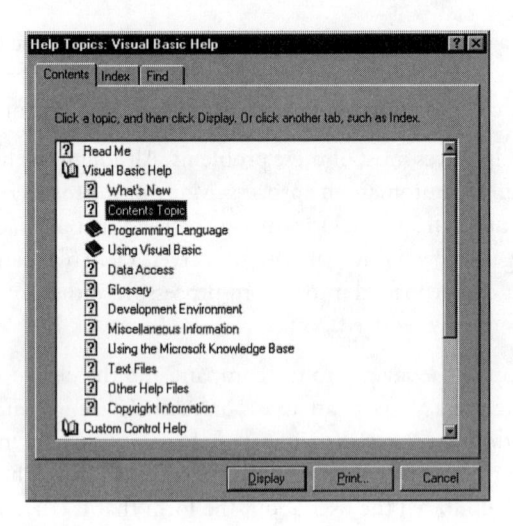

Included with Visual Basic is the Microsoft Help Compiler. The compiler takes a Rich Text File (RTF) created using help file formatting and compiles it into an .HLP file (see Figure A.11). We recommend that you use one of the excellent help file creators that set up the help file for you. This greatly simplifies the complex and tedious process of creating the .RTF file by hand. Look in Chapter 1, "Overview of Visual Basic," for an overview of the features and a general checklist for available help file creators.

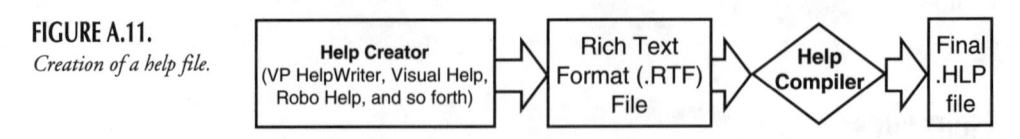

FIGURE A.11.
Creation of a help file.

From Visual Basic, the Help engine must be called using Windows API calls. Your program can instruct the Help engine to display a particular topic, display the Search window, show the Help window at a certain place on the screen, or display the main Contents page of the file.

Context-Sensitive Help

Context-sensitive help comes in many different forms. It can describe anything from tool tips (explained later) to a question mark cursor (this enables the user to click a control to get information on its function). In Visual Basic it enables the user to get information on any particular screen or control, usually by pressing the F1 key.

Topics in a Microsoft .HLP file are each given a `ContextID`. Using this `ContextID`, an application (such as a program you would write in VB) can call the Help engine and instruct it to display a particular topic. This way if the user wanted help on the data input screen, for example, the Help engine could be instructed to display the "Input Data Screen" topic.

Hotspot or SHED Files

Hotspot files (also known as Shape Editor or SHED files) are one of the most exciting aspects of the Help engine. Using the Hotspot Editor included with Visual Basic, a picture (or bitmap) can be used to construct many jump-to or popup links. For example, a picture of a map can be loaded into the Hotspot Editor. Then you can add rectangular hotspots that activate when you click them.

Figure A.12 shows a bitmap of the alphabet. There are hotspots on the letters A, C, and L. Double-clicking one of the hotspot rectangles shows you the information linked to that hotspot (see Figure A.13). By changing the information for the hotspot, you make the Help engine jump to another topic or show a popup when the user clicks within the rectangle.

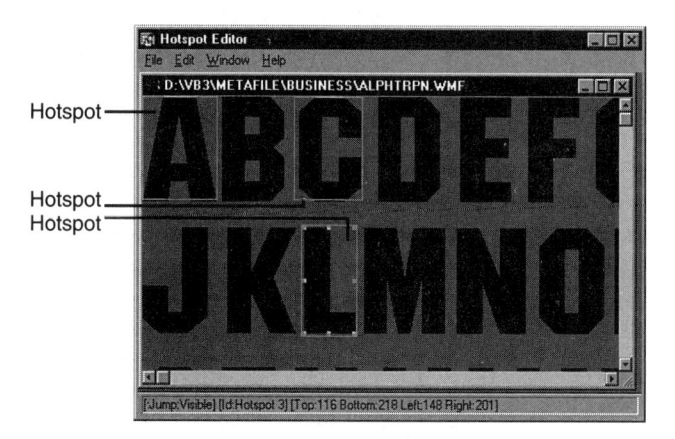

FIGURE A.12.
Hotspot Editor.

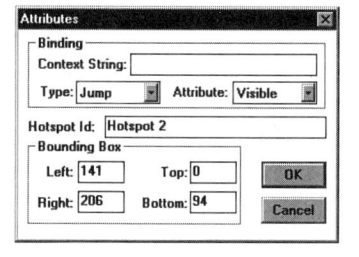

FIGURE A.13.
Hotspot rectangle information.

Component extensions are also available to incorporate these hotspot files into your application itself. Hotspot files promise to open a new way for the user to interact with online help. Category pictures can be placed within the help file, as well as active screen shots, sound and video links, and collapsible topics. These enable you to present your help files in a spatial manner, as well as textual.

Help Status Bar

A Help status bar is one of the simplest implementations of help available in Visual Basic. A Help status bar usually appears at the bottom of the screen (it can appear anywhere) and displays a given help message. This can be as simple as "Processing Data..." or it can describe the item the mouse cursor is currently placed over (see Figure A.14).

FIGURE A.14.
The Help status bar displays text for the control the cursor is placed over.

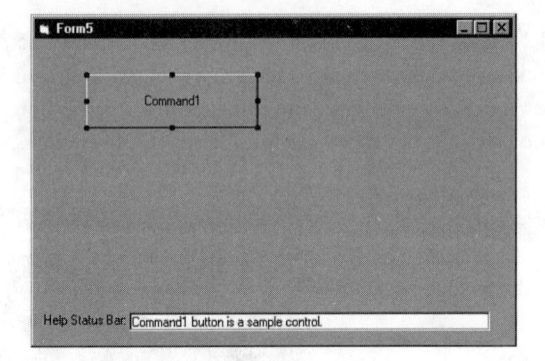

To implement this feature, simply create a text box or a label at the bottom of the form. Set the `Name` property of this control to `txt_Help`. To show status, have your routine set the `Text` or `Caption` property (for a text box or label, respectively) to the text you want it to display.

> **TIP**
>
> If you are designing for Windows 95 and Windows NT 3.51 and above, you can use the status bar control. This control can be placed at the bottom of a form and divided into up to 16 areas (see Figure A.15). The control supplies the ability to automatically display the time, date, and keyboard status information in specified panels. This control makes adding help incredibly simple, but it is available only for 32-bit operating systems. Similar panel controls are available for 16-bit systems from third-party vendors, see Appendix C.

FIGURE A.15.
The status bar control.

To make the Help status bar describe a control the cursor is placed over, put a routine to set the text in the `MouseMove` event routine. A `MouseMove` event is generated whenever the cursor moves over the given control. See the code in Listing A.3 for an example of how the Help status bar describes the Command1 button when the user moves the cursor over it.

Listing A.3. Sample Help status bar code.

```
Sub Command1_MouseMove (Button As Integer, Shift As Integer, X As Single, Y As
➥Single)
    txt_Help = "Command1 button is a sample control."
End Sub
```

Tool Tips

A Help status bar is one of the simplest implementations of help available in Visual Basic. Tool tips are small captions that display when the mouse moves over a particular area of the screen and remains still for a few seconds (see Figure A.16). One of the increasingly common uses of tool tips is to explain small on-screen icons whose function is not self-evident. This can save valuable screen area over using larger icons or permanent on-screen descriptions.

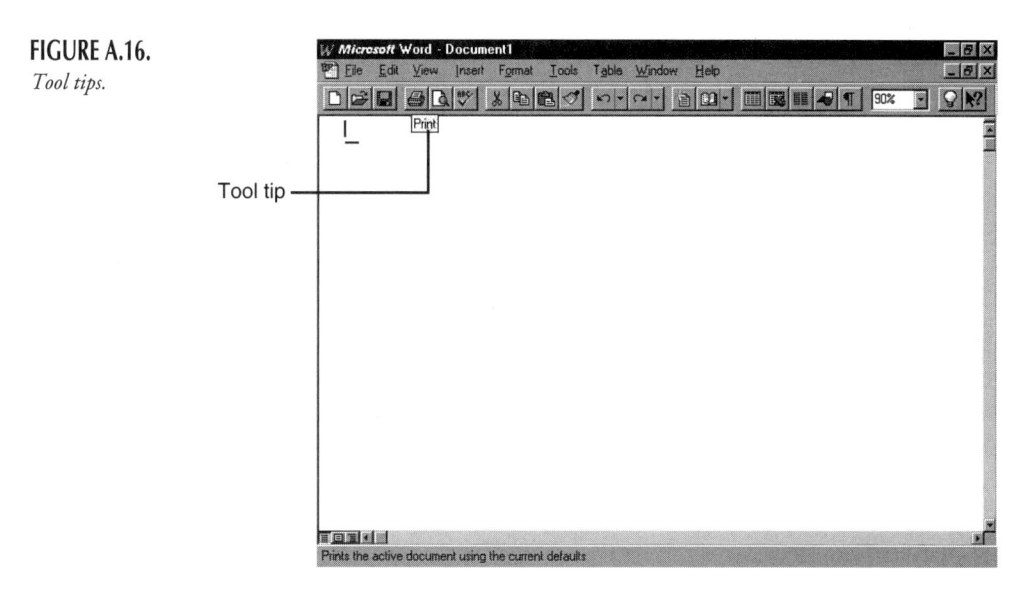

FIGURE A.16.
Tool tips.

Tool tips can be created by handle using a small text box control. When the mouse moves over a particular area, the text box is moved to that area, and the control property `Visible` is set to True. When the mouse moves away from the area, the property `Visible` is set to False. This method can be tedious, hard to maintain, and force a redraw of the current window, which can make the program extremely slow.

We recommend purchasing a third-party utility that provides tool tip capabilities. If you are developing for the Windows 95 or Windows NT 3.51 or above platforms, a tool tip control is included with VB 4 in the tool bar control. The property `ShowTips` in a tool bar must be set to True. Then simply add the text of the tool tip by setting the `ToolTipText` property to a particular string. Tool tips are available for buttons, tool bar buttons, and tabs on a tab strip.

B

Error Handling

Error Handling Routines

When running any program, errors are bound to occur. In client/server systems, this is particularly true. Connections can be broken, drivers can be missing, users can type values inappropriate for datatypes, the structure of the server database can be changed, another user can have the record locked, or any other numerous possible problems.

There are various types of error handling for different situations in which errors occur. A routine might return a value that contains an error return code. The routine (such as the CommDLOG routines) might cause a small system error that does not cause a system fault but can be checked with the System Error checking routines. All errors can be trapped by an On Error routine. These various error handling routines are described here.

Without error handling, any error displays a generic error dialog box, quits the program, and returns to Windows. This is the most disastrous result for the user. If any unsaved data is stored in the program, the smallest error can stop execution and flush the data and the program from the system. This is the worst-case scenario.

The best case of error handling includes recovery, reporting, suggestions, and access to more help. In the programs with the best handling, an error shows a detailed window of information on how and where the error occurred. The user should have access to help regarding the condition (for example, if the program couldn't find a file, what file was the program looking for?). The program should suggest a possible action to resolve the program (for example, "The value you entered is out of the available range—min: 0, max: 100. Please re-enter a value."). A Help button that shows the relevant portion of online help is also useful.

The error handler should then enable the user to continue the operation, modify the operation, or cancel the operation (Cancel, Ignore, Retry). Ideally, the user should be able to recover from any error and continue. Installation programs are the worst offender of this ideal. Often an installation process can reach the 31st of 32 disks, get an error, and abort the entire process. When designing a client/server system, the longer an operation takes, the more recovery possibilities should be available. An operation that takes 30 minutes to complete can be extremely frustrating when it aborts in the final stage.

Returned Error Processing

The simplest type of error processing occurs when a function returns a result code. For example:

```
' The value 1 below specifies an OK & Cancel button MsgBox
result = MsgBox "Do you want to continue?",1,"Error"
```

This routine retrieves the result from the user clicking the OK or the Cancel button. If the result equals 0, the user clicked the OK button. If the result equals 2, the user clicked the Cancel button. An If...Then operation can be used to handle the results of the function.

This is the type of error handling used most often by routines and functions that are designed and written by the programmer of the application. Functions can return values that denote the success or failure of a particular operation. Often, the results of these return codes are stored as constants in a module file so that all the routines can access them.

System Error Checking

The system itself can generate errors. These errors are retrieved using the Err, Erl, Error, and Error$ functions. These routines retrieve the error message from the operating system.

The Err function returns an integer value that is equal to the error variable of the system. The Erl function is a little-used function that returns a Long variable of the line number on which the error occurred. This function is excellent for an error logging function (described later).

The Error(errorcode) and Error$(errorcode) functions return the text for the generated error. If the errorcode variable is omitted, the text of the most recent runtime error is returned. The Error() routine returns the text in a Variant variable type, whereas the Error$() routine returns a string variable.

These routines are used in conjunction with the system error trapping functions to return information when an error occurs.

Error Trapping

Visual Basic provides the On Error command to trap any errors within a procedure. The simplest type of On Error routine can simply display the error and exit that particular routine. Listing B.1 demonstrates such a routine. The first line provides the jump to the CommandError part of the routine if an error occurs. The following Error statement generates an error, causing the CommandError routine to be activated.

Listing B.1. Basic On Error code.

```
Sub Command1_Click ()
    On Error GoTo CommandError
    Error 48
    Exit Sub

CommandError:
    MsgBox "An error of type: #" & Str$(Err) & "-" & Error & " occurred", 16,
    ↪"Error Occurred"
    Exit Sub
End Sub
```

The message box displays the error number (retrieved using the Err command) and the text description of that error (retrieved using the Error command). The dialog box displayed looks like the one shown in Figure B.1. After the user clicks the OK button, the next command exits the routine.

FIGURE B.1.
Basic `On Error` *dialog box.*

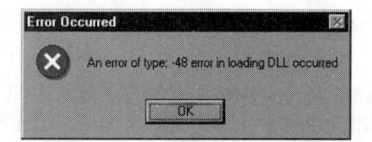

This routine uses the `Exit Sub` command to leave the subroutine after an error occurs. Also available is the `Resume` command, which, after any error processing occurs, reattempts the same command that generated the error. This can be used effectively in a system where record locking might cause an error to be generated one second but the record is free the next second. The `Resume Next` command resumes execution on the line following the statement that generated the error.

The `Resume` command can also be sent a specific line on which to continue. For example, `Resume MyResume` would restart execution at the label `MyResume`. The `Resume` command can be sent either a label or a specific non-zero line number.

This routine is an example of the simplest form of error checking and display. It lets the user understand what is happening and gives a general idea of what error occurred. Without this type of error checking, the user would have been presented with a generic error box, and the application would have stopped executing.

Error trapping can also be temporarily suspended. For example, in Listing B.2, the `On Error Goto 0` statement turns the error checking off. This can be useful for routines (such as common dialog boxes) that generate known errors for specific purposes (such as the user clicking the Cancel button).

Listing B.2. `Err` **suspend code demo.**

```
Sub ErrDemo ()
    On Error Goto Handler
    ' Error checking is turned on
    On Error Goto 0
    ' Error trapping is turned off
    On Error Goto Handler
    Exit Sub
Handler:
    MsgBox "Error"
    Resume Next
End Sub
```

The `On Error` routines might seem more tedious than traditional `If...Then` error checking and evaluation, but these types of routines will become increasingly common to development environments. As programs become more complex and use plug-ins (such as VBXs or objects), a program cannot expect to anticipate and program specific error-checking code for every possibility.

Fortunately, On Error type routines are becoming more sophisticated in development environments. Utilities are available that provide error code for an entire program. Some environments include global error trapping routines. We suggest becoming more proficient in designing code around this type of error checking because it will become increasingly common.

Generating Errors

One of the most useful functions for testing is the Error statement, which actually generates an error of the type sent to it. (Don't confuse this with the Error() function, which returns the text of an error that occurred.) This enables designers to manually generate errors to test all the error trapping and checking routines contained in the program.

In Listing B.1, the Error statement was used to generate a DLL loading error (error #48). The Error statement is followed by an errorcode variable that contains an error value between 1 and 32,767, inclusive. If the errorcode is equal to a Visual Basic error, that type of error is generated. Otherwise, a user-defined error is generated. Any error trapping routines that are in place are activated when this statement is executed.

> **NOTE**
>
> If you need to create a user-defined error number, the number cannot be between 1 and 1000. To make sure there is no conflict with other error codes, add the user-defined error number to the vbObjectError constant. This will prevent conflict with future versions of Visual Basic and other products. Custom controls may also add error numbers to the error list. Check the documentation of the custom controls that are included in your project to make sure that no conflict exists.

Unanticipated Errors

Visual Basic error routines work in a hierarchical fashion for a call chain (see Figure B.2). When an error occurs in a routine, if that routine has no On Error routine, Visual Basic searches up the calling chain until it finds an On Error routine or reaches the top routine. If it reaches the top routine, the generic basic error routine is activated.

If a debug breakpoint is set at the Error statement in the MyRoutineC procedure shown in the figure, the call chain can be examined. Selecting the Calls option in the Debug menu (or pressing Ctrl+L) shows the form in Figure B.3. Notice that MyRoutineC is at the top of the calling chain because it is currently executing. MyRoutineB is directly below it because it called the MyRoutineC procedure, and so on.

FIGURE B.2.
A call chain.

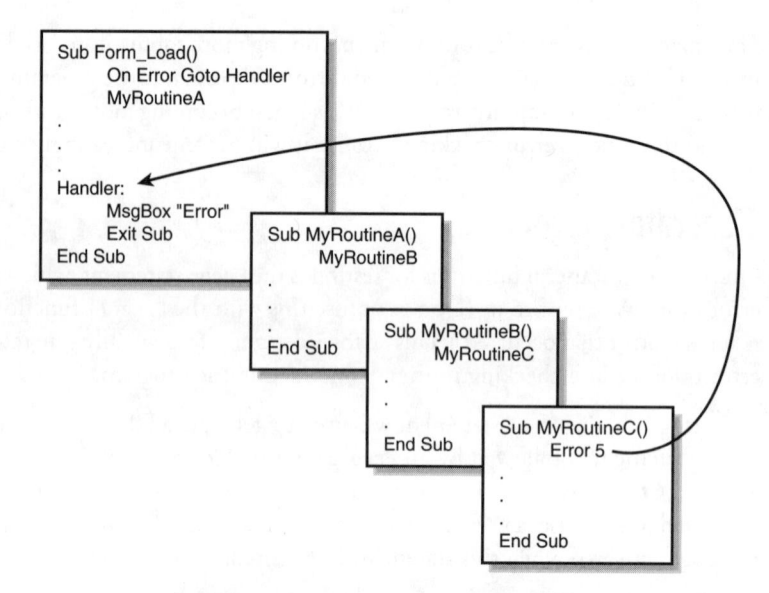

```
Sub Form_Load()
    On Error Goto Handler
    MyRoutineA
    .
    .
    .
Handler:
    MsgBox "Error"
    Exit Sub
End Sub
```

```
Sub MyRoutineA()
    MyRoutineB
    .
    .
    .
End Sub
```

```
Sub MyRoutineB()
    MyRoutineC
    .
    .
    .
End Sub
```

```
Sub MyRoutineC()
    Error 5
    .
    .
    .
End Sub
```

FIGURE B.3.
The Visual Basic call procedure stack.

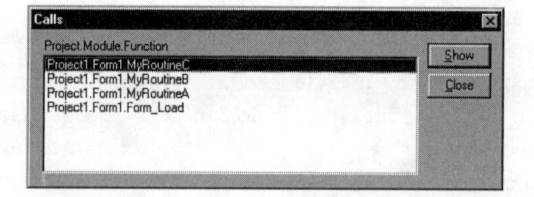

```
Calls
Project.Module.Function
Project1.Form1.MyRoutineC
Project1.Form1.MyRoutineB
Project1.Form1.MyRoutineA
Project1.Form1.Form_Load

[Show]  [Close]
```

> **TIP**
>
> Instead of using a traditional breakpoint, a `Stop` command can be inserted into your Visual Basic code to halt execution. The `Stop` statement does not generate an error but stops execution of the program so the calling chain, watches, and checkpoints can be examined. Make sure all `Stop` statements are removed before a final .EXE file is created. The `Stop` statement acts in the same way as an `End` command when executing alone.

Be aware of how your error routines are constructed. If they are very specific to the routine in which they are placed, confusion can occur if an error occurs in a routine that is called by the central routine.

Error Events

Some controls (such as the Data control) have an Error event. Rather than traditional On Error routines, a Data control executes the Error event when a problem occurs. This can be a useful feature for centralizing Error condition handlers relevant to that particular control. Many third-party controls have similar Error event routines. Check with the individual control for possible implementation.

Centralizing Error Handling

Putting a central error handling routine into a module is often the best way to implement error routines. Independent error routines are a maintenance nightmare and often present an inconsistent interface.

By having each On Error routine call a central routine, extensive work can be put into the main routine without performance or memory allocation difficulties that occur with hundreds of error routines in each project. Intensive text explanations can be used, logging can be enabled, help routines can be inserted, and user process direction can be more explicit.

> **NOTE**
>
> Although error handlers are ideal for finished applications, they can become bothersome when you're debugging an application. Instead of executing the VB debugger (so that you may examine variables, alter code, and so on), the main error routine is activated. Visual Basic provides a way to suspend the functioning of On Error routines during development. Select Options from the Tools menu and click on the Advanced tab. Selecting the Break on All Errors option will activate the debugger when an error occurs.

Error Handling Dialog Boxes

An Error Handling dialog box is placed in the central error handling routine. When an error occurs, this form is presented.

Figure B.4 shows an Error dialog box that is used in many of our system programs. This is actually a form generated by the VB/Rig Pro program that we have modified to suit our own uses. Notice the different parts of the form. The error is shown, along with a brief description of the error. The status of the procedure stack is included to show where the error occurred. At the bottom is a space for user comments. The user can add information to describe the environment the crash occurred in and other relevant details.

FIGURE B.4.
A common C/S Error dialog box.

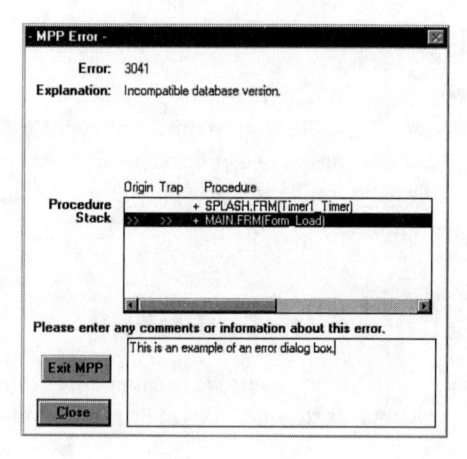

There are two buttons on the bottom left of the screen: the Close button and the Exit button. The Close button resumes execution of the program. If the error is recoverable, in the future the user can simply avoid activating the portion of the program that caused the error.

If the error occurs in a routine such as the `Paint()` event (which is called when the Error dialog box is closed), the user will be caught in an endless loop. As soon as the Error dialog box is closed, another error occurs that displays the Error dialog box again. The Exit button provides a way to exit the program gracefully. It can then be re-executed by the user.

Simple Error Routines

In Listing B.3, a general `ShowError` routine displays error messages using a message box. This routine uses a `Select Case` statement to find which error occurred and give it a text description. With this routine placed in a module, it is globally available, and any routine can execute it.

Listing B.3. General `ShowError` routine.

```
Sub ShowError (i_ErrorNum As Integer)
    Dim myError$

    myError$ = ""
    Select Case i_ErrorNum
        Case 3: myError$ = "Return without Gosub"
        Case 5: myError$ = "Illegal function call"
        Case 6: myError$ = "Overflow"
        Case 7: myError$ = "Out of memory"
        Case 9: myError$ = "Subscript out of range"
    End Select
    If myError$ = "" Then
        myError$ = "Unknown Type"
```

```
    End If
    MsgBox "An error of type: #" & Str$(i_ErrorNum) & "-" & myError$ &
    ➥" occurred", 16, "Error Occurred"
End Sub
```

The routine is sent an error code, which is checked in the Select Case statement against known error codes. If the code is nothing for which a specific error can be found, the system's error message for Unknown Type is displayed.

Listing B.4 provides a code example of how this might be called from one of your routines. The On Error function executes the given routine if an error occurs. The Error function generates an error of the type sent to it. In the example, this routine traps errors of type 48 because that error has particular relevance to this routine. Any other errors are sent the global ShowError subroutine for checking and display.

Listing B.4. Global Error routine.

```
Sub Command1_Click ()
    On Error GoTo CommandError
    Error 48
    Exit Sub

CommandError:
    Select Case Err
        Case 48
            MsgBox "Couldn't load the database DLL. Please move it into the
            ➥\WINDOWS\ directory and re-run this program", 16, "Couldn't
            ➥find DLL"
        Case Else
            ShowError (Err)
    End Select
    Exit Sub
End Sub
```

This type of code can be placed in each procedure and event of a program. Other programs can set up your entire application for error trapping, saving you time and energy (see Chapter 29, "Third-Party Tools, Utilities, and Controls").

Error Logging

For any global error routine, it is a good idea to log the errors into a text file. If the errors are written into a standard text file, any users that encounter problems can print or fax this text file to you. This way the designer can evaluate the problem remotely without having to be present at the site. This method also keeps a documented log of the problems that occur. Often users describe an error inaccurately or leave out crucial details about the error messages or condition of the machine.

The global routine used in a client program can easily append a general file with each error that occurs. A text file can be opened for appending by simply using the `Open` statement with extra append commands. For example:

```
Open LogFile For Append As #1
```

This code opens the text file as file #1. To append text statements, use the `Print #1, MyString$` command. In this way, all necessary data and values can be written to the text file for later retrieval.

> **TIP**
>
> In addition to logging errors, user suggestions can also be easily logged to the same file. For the simplest type of suggestion logging, make a menu item labeled Feature Suggestions. When the user selects this item, generate an error using the `Error()` function of a type unused by the system. Then the user can type any comments into the User Comments section of the Error dialog box. The suggestion is saved in the log file along with all the errors actually encountered.
>
> A user or beta-tester can then simply e-mail, upload, fax, or send the contents of the log file, and you will have a complete listing of all the errors encountered and suggestions made.

Client/Server Error Problems

Client/server systems have a large number of special errors they must handle. With connections and database access, the number of possible problems to a program is enlarged. Following are some specific areas in which C/S system designers often have problems.

Values Out of Range

One of the most tedious, but also most necessary, types of error handling is detecting inappropriate data. Often a client program has to access a data source that is not simply for its own use (such as a Decision Support System source) but also for various other clients. With multiple clients modifying the data, a Pandora's box of bad data can be created.

For example, a client might write the value "ext. TIPS" into a phone number text field, using a personal form of shorthand for the phone extension number. When another client tries to parse this into a standard (xxx) xxx-xxxx format, an error occurs. Often specific rules must be created to determine what can and cannot be entered into a particular data field.

Another example of inappropriate or erroneous data placed in a field occurs when the user violates an accepted range of values. For example, a field is supposed to hold a number specifying categories 1 through 6. Perhaps a division of the enterprise requires a catch-all category, which it enters as category 7. When your client program places all the variables in a six-cell array using the category number as the index, the number 7 generates an error.

There is no easy way to solve this problem. When retrieving data from a database held in common among many clients, be sure to use comparison operators when the data is read to ensure that it falls within acceptable limits. Always document the data structure of each table when creating a client/server system. Put as much error checking into the database itself as possible (using default values, triggers, data limits, business rules, and so forth).

Finally, make sure that when one of your clients stores data, it is within the accepted bounds. If the user enters a category 7 when only 1 through 6 are allowed, make sure this value is not written into the database. This might be frustrating at first, because in the beginning users request more modifications to the system (rather than creating their own workarounds), but you will benefit in data integrity and data consistency.

Various Error Types

Many of the routines and APIs that are used by a client/server developer have their own error codes. For example, ODBC, MAPI, MEF, and other APIs have separate error codes that are returned.

ODBC functions provide a return code for each of the functions to supply information on the success or failure of an operation. To get more information on an error, ODBC includes the `SQLError()` function. This function stores error information in data structures named `henv`, `hdbc`, and `hstmt`.

Because these routines have their own error codes, we recommended writing a separate global module routine to handle each API or set of functions. These routines can be called when an error is detected using an `If...Then` statement.

Business Rules

Business rules are becoming an increasingly dominant way of avoiding future data integrity problems and errors. A business rule specifies certain conditions when data is originally input. For example, the Sales application might allow input of particular Sales items. If the total price of the invoice is over $1000, extra information (such as credit history) might be required in the Customer record. If this information is not present, the transaction is stopped.

Business rules can be put in many places. They can be embedded in the actual application. A business rule can be placed on the database server, perhaps as a trigger routine. The advantage of putting a business rule on a server is the global nature of its implementation. In the preceding example, if the management of the enterprise decided to increase the limit before credit history was required to $2000, it would have to be changed in each application. If the rule was centrally located, it would have to be changed only once to take effect in the entire organization.

Having these business rules in a client/server system prevents users from entering information that is against company policy. It also allows global enterprise access to data such as tax rates (instead of being in stored in independent .INI files), general prices, and threshold levels for monetary policies. Business rules that are accessible through a network provide consistent policy for an organization in an automated way.

Microsoft has demonstrated sample Distributed OLE programs to act as network business rule Servers. If an OLE Server program is created that contains the necessary business rules, any application capable of OLE Automation could access this server to obtain the necessary information. This means that a word processor, spreadsheet, database, or any other type of program could base itself on a common set of business rules.

With the capabilities of Visual Basic 4 to create an OLE Server application, it might become the development platform of choice for business rule servers. When Distributed OLE becomes solid and usable on a day-to-day basis, OLE business rule servers might be the best technology to implement enterprise-wide business rule computing.

C

Sources

Books

Advanced Database Techniques. Daniel Martin. MIT Press. Copyright 1986 by the Massachusetts Institute of Technology. 377 pages.

Client/Server Computing with ORACLE. Joe Salemi. Ziff-Davis Press. Copyright 1993 by Joe Salemi. 232 pages.

Client/Server Programming with OS/2 2.1. Third Edition. Robert Orfali and Dan Harkey. Copyright 1993 by Van Nostrand Reinhold. 1142 pages.

Client/Server Technology for Managers. Karen Watterson. Copyright 1995 by Addison-Wesley Publishing Co. Inc. 235 pages.

Data Sharing: Using a Common Data Architecture. Michael H. Brackett. Copyright 1994 by John Wiley & Sons, Inc. 478 pages.

Database Developer's Guide with Visual Basic 3. Roger Jennings. Copyright 1994 by Sams Publishing. 1133 pages.

Design and Strategy for Distributed Data Processing. James Martin. Prentice-Hall, Inc. Copyright 1981 by James Martin. 624 pages.

Distributed Operating Systems. Andrew S. Tanenbaum. Copyright 1995 by Prentice-Hall, Inc. 614 pages.

E-MAIL Security: How to Keep Your Electronic Messages Private (covers PGP and PEM). Bruce Schneier. Copyright 1995 by John Wiley & Sons, Inc. 365 pages.

Essential Client/Server Survival Guide. Robert Orfali, Dan Harkey, and Jeri Edwards. International Thomson Publishing Co. Copyright 1994 by Van Nostrand Reinhold. 527 pages.

Firewalls and Internet Security: Repelling the Wily Hacker. William R. Cheswick and Steven M. Bellovin. Copyright 1994 by Addison-Wesley Publishing Co. Inc. 306 pages.

The Guide to SQL Server. Aloke Nath. Copyright 1990, fourth printing 1992 by Addison-Wesley Publishing Co. Inc. 306 pages.

Inside Windows 95. Adrian King. Microsoft Press. Copyright 1994 by Adrian King. 476 pages.

Insider's Guide to Personal Computing and Networking. Rick Segal. Copyright 1992 by Sams Publishing. 505 pages.

Interfacing to the PowerPC Microprocessor. Ron Rahmel and Dan Rahmel. Copyright 1995 by Sams Publishing. 476 pages.

Internetworking with TCP/IP: Volume I: Principles, Protocols, and Architecture. Douglas E. Comer. Copyright 1991 by Prentice-Hall, Inc. 547 pages.

Internetworking with TCP/IP: Volume III: Client/Server Programming and Applications. Douglas E. Comer and David L. Stevens. Copyright 1993 by Prentice-Hall, Inc. 498 pages.

LAN Times Encyclopedia of Networking. Tom Sheldon. Copyright 1994 by Osborne McGraw-Hill, Inc. 1006 pages.

NetWare 3.x: A Do-It-Yourself Guide. Charles Koontz. Copyright 1992 by Prima Publishing. 275 pages.

NetWare for Macintosh User's Guide. Kelley J. P. Lindberg. Copyright 1990 by M&T Publishing, Inc. 280 pages.

Network Security: How to Plan for It and Achieve It. Richard H. Baker. Copyright 1995 by McGraw-Hill, Inc. 456 pages.

Networking Standards: A Guide to OSI, ISDN, LAN, and MAN Standards. William Stallings. Copyright 1993 by Addison-Wesley Publishing Co. Inc. 646 pages.

Novell's Guide to Client/Server Applications and Architecture: The Enterprise. Jeffrey D. Schank. Copyright 1994 by Novell Press and SYBEX Inc. 455 pages.

Programming WinSock. Arthur Dumas. Copyright 1995 by Sams Publishing. 358 pages.

Protect Your Privacy: A Guide for PGP Users. William Stallings. Copyright 1995 by Prentice-Hall, Inc. 302 pages.

Relational Database Technology. Saud Alagic. Copyright 1986 by Springer-Verlag New York Inc. 259 pages.

Running Microsoft Access 2 for Windows. John L. Viescas. Microsoft Press. Copyright 1994 by Microsoft Co. Inc. 901 pages.

Running Microsoft Mail for Windows: Version 3.0. Russell Borland. Microsoft Press. Copyright 1993 by Microsoft Corporation. 188 pages.

Teach Yourself Visual Basic 3.0 in 21 Days. Nathan and Ori Gurewich. Copyright 1993 by Sams Publishing. 967 pages.

Teach Yourself...Windows NT: Covers version 3.1. Hayagriva Rao. Copyright 1993 by MIS:Press, a subsidiary of Henry Holt and Company, Inc. 476 pages.

Visual Basic for Windows: Release 3.0, Third Edition. Covers both Standard and Professional Editions. Steven Holzner and the Peter Norton Computing Group. Copyright 1993 by Steven Holzner and the Peter Norton Computing Group, Brady. 774 pages.

Visual Basic For Windows. Richard Mansfield. Ventana Press, Inc. Copyright 1993 by Richard Mansfield. 1254 pages.

Windows NT Answer Book. Jim Groves. Microsoft Press. Copyright 1993 by Microsoft Corp. 198 pages.

Magazines

ACCESS ADVISOR. Advisor Communication International, Inc., Access Advisor Subscription Dept., PO Box 469030, Escondido, CA 92046

ACCESS/VISUAL BASIC ADVISOR. Advisor Publications, Inc., ACCESS/VISUAL BASIC ADVISOR, Customer Service Dept., 4010 Morena Blvd., PO Box 17902, San Diego, CA 92177

Advanced Systems. Integrated Media, Inc., Advanced Systems, PO Box 41534, Nashville, TN 37204-1534

American Programmer. Cutter Information Corp., 37 Broadway, Suite 1, Arlington, MA 02174-5552, 800-964-8702

BYTE. McGraw-Hill. BYTE Subscriptions, PO Box 552, Hightstown, NJ 08520

Client/Server Computing. Sentry Publishing Company Inc., One Research Drive, Suite 400B, Westborough, MA 01581

Computer Telephony. Computer Telephony Magazine, 12 West 21st Street, New York, NY 10010, 800-677-3435

DATAMATION. Cahners Publishing Company, DATAMATION, 8873 South Ridgeline Blvd., Highlands Ranch, CO 80126-2329, 617-558-4281

Dr. Dobb's Journal. Miller Freeman, Inc., Dr. Dobb's Journal, PO Box 56188, Boulder, CO 80322-6188, 800-456-1215

INFORMATIONWEEK. CMP Publications, Inc., Circulation Dept., INFORMATIONWEEK, PO Box 1093, Skokie, IL 60076-8093, 800-292-3642

Microsoft Systems Journal. Microsoft Corporation, One Microsoft Way, Redmond, WA 98052-6399, 800-666-1084

PC MAGAZINE. Ziff-Davis Publishing Company. PC Magazine, PO Box 54093, Boulder CO 80322-4093

Software Development. Miller Freeman, Inc., Software Development, PO Box 469041, Escondido, CA 92046-9041

Software Magazine. Sentry Publishing Company Inc., One Research Drive, Suite 400B, Westborough, MA 01581

VB Tech Journal. PO Box 70127, Eugene, OR 97401-0107, 800-234-0386

Visual Basic Programmer's Journal. Fawcette Technical Publications. Visual Basic Programmer's Journal, PO Box 58872, Boulder, CO 80322-8872, 415-833-7100

Windows Tech Journal. PO Box 70127, Eugene, OR 97401-0107, 800-234-0386

Technical Manuals

Programmer's Guide. Microsoft Visual Basic, Programming System for Windows version 4.0 (TR5 release), Operating Environment. Volume I, Chapters 1 through 15. Document No. DB58499-0994. Microsoft Corporation. Copyright 1994.

Programmer's Guide. Microsoft Visual Basic, Programming System for Windows version 4.0 (TR5 release), Operating Environment. Volume II, Chapters 16 through appendixes. Document No. DB58499-0994. Microsoft Corporation. Copyright 1994.

Professional Features. Microsoft Visual Basic, Programming System for Windows version 4.0 (TR5 release), Professional Edition. Book 1 (this volume contains four separate books). Document No. DB58513-0994. Microsoft Corporation. Copyright 1994.

Professional Features. Microsoft Visual Basic, Programming System for Windows version 4.0 (TR5 release), Professional Edition. Book 2 (this volume contains two separate books). Document No. DB58514-0994. Microsoft Corporation. Copyright 1994.

Programmer's Guide. Microsoft Visual Basic, Programming System for Windows version 4.0 (TR6 release), Operating Environment. Volume I, Chapters 1 through 15. Document No. 58513-TR6. Microsoft Corporation. Copyright 1995.

Programmer's Guide. Microsoft Visual Basic, Programming System for Windows version 4.0 (TR6 release), Operating Environment. Volume II, Chapters 16 through appendixes. Document No. 58513-TR6. Microsoft Corporation. Copyright 1995.

Professional Features. Microsoft Visual Basic, Programming System for Windows version 4.0 (TR6 release), Professional Edition. Volume I (this volume contains two separate books). Document No. DB58499-0795. Microsoft Corporation. Copyright 1995.

Professional Features. Microsoft Visual Basic, Programming System for Windows version 4.0 (TR6 release), Professional Edition. Volume II (this volume contains Custom Control Reference). Document No. DB58499-0795. Microsoft Corporation. Copyright 1995.

Language Reference. Microsoft Visual Basic, Programming System for Windows version 4.0 (TR6 release), Volume I, (final documentation as of 11/9/94). Document No. 58500-0195. Microsoft Corporation. Copyright 1995.

Language Reference. Microsoft Visual Basic, Programming System for Windows version 4.0 (TR6 release), Volume II, (final documentation as of 11/9/94). Document No. 58500-0195. Microsoft Corporation. Copyright 1995.

Crystal Reports for Visual Basic User's Manual. Part of the TR6 release June 1995, of Microsoft Visual Basic, Programming System for Windows version 4.0., Microsoft Corporation.

Software Companies

Data Access and Report Writers

ACI US Inc., PO Box 20883, Stevens Creek Blvd. Cupertino, CA 95014
Phone: 408-252-4444
Fax: 408-252-4829
CIS: GO ACIUS

Products:

4D Open for Visual Basic, U.S. v1.0: An API made up of a set of Windows DLLs, providing applications with the ability to connect with 4D Server, ACI's C/S database. 4D Open allows the users to perform the following operations: adding, modifying, and rearranging data in a database.

ADDSoft Products, Inc., 11850 Nicholas Street, Suite 120, Omaha, NE 68154
Phone: 402-491-4141
Fax: 402-491-4152

Products:

Schedule/VBX: A scheduling and time management visually interactive control that provides developers with more than 100 properties, including fonts, color, resource bar, and more than 40 events.

Gantt/VBX: Provides the developer with a visually interactive Gantt control that allows project and task planning to be added to the application. It has more than 100 properties, including fonts, color, resource bar, and more than 40 events.

A.J.S. Publishing Inc., PO Box 83220, Los Angeles, CA 90083-0220
Phone: 310-215-9145
Fax: 310-215-9135
CIS: 70312,561

Products:

VB/Magic Controls 2.0: Lets programmers create new controls for embedding in VB applications; adds 3-D effects and shadows; includes over 40 modifiable controls.

Visual/db Database Manager, Single-user 2.0, Visual/db Network Database Manager 3.0: Relational database manager systems that can be used as a complete data storage and retrieval system. They contain features such as database access routines, database management forms, query language processor, help system, and library calls to make complete database systems.

Apex Software Corp., 4516 Henry St., Suite 202, Pittsburgh, PA 15213
Phone: 412-681-4343 / 800-858-2739
Fax: 412-681-4384

Products:

TrueGridPro: Provides enhancements to Microsoft's DataGrid such as splits, combo boxes, calculated columns, column summing, and style sheets.

BC Soft, AB Box 34176, S-100 26, Stockholm, Sweden
Phone: 46-8-657-91-90
Fax: 46-8-656-67-72

Products:

XFile Custom Controls 2.5: Provides simplified access to Dataflex, Powerflex, and all bound database files from VB, so VB can become an XFlex development platform.

Blue Lagoon Software, 6047 Tampa Ave., Suite 209, Tarzana, CA 91356
Phone: 818-345-2200
Fax: 818-345-8905
CIS: 70152,1601
BBS: 818-345-8433

Products:

DBProfiler SQL Inspector for MS/Sybase SQL Server, DBProfiler JET Inspector 2.0, DBProfiler ODBC Inspector 2.0, DBProfiler SQL Inspector 2.0, Oracle 7 version: These are performance optimizing and trace utilities for VB and other programming languages. They allow SQL queries, connects and disconnects, and other client operations to be monitored. Data can be analyzed and provide the user with a graphical performance analysis.

BlueRithm Software, 21823 N. Glen Dr., Colbert, WA 99005-9415
Phone: 509-468-1434
Fax: 509-467-2699
CIS: 72704,2273

Products:

Aeris for Windows 3.4: Allows users to visually access and change data from XBASE, ODBC, ASCII, EBCDIC, Print Files, Binary IEEE, Packed Cobol, Lotus, and others. Features include a large number of menu-driven processes such as Sort, Cut (Parse), Paste, Replace, Compare, Convert, and Search.

Classic Software Inc., 3542 Pheasant Run Circle, Suite 8, Ann Arbor, MI 48108
Phone: 313-913-8075 / 800-677-2952
Fax: 313-971-3287

Products:

VBtrv for DOS 1.1, VBtrv for Windows 1.2: Programmers can develop full-feature Btrieve applications that support networks and multiusers with VBtrv. This is accomplished without writing code by the provided function-call interface to Novell Btrieve that is used under VB.

CNA Computer Systems Engineering Inc., 1260 116th Ave. NE, Suite 100, Bellevue, WA 98004
Phone: 206-451-2727 / 800-235-4091
Fax: 206-451-2728

Products:

ConnX ODBC Driver for RMS: Provides VB-built applications with the capability to read and write to DEC VAX/VMS RMS files of ODBC-compliant products. C/S features are its data dictionary and advanced SQL optimization capability to increase performance.

Concentric Data Systems Inc., 110 Turnpike Rd., Westborough, MA 01581
Phone: 508-366-1122 / 800-325-9035
Fax: 508-366-2954
CIS: 71601,1465

Products:

R&R Report Writer, SQL Edition for Windows version 6, R&R Report Writer, Xbase Edition for Windows version 6: Powerful report creation tools with menu-driven data selection from SQL or Xbase files. Analysis capabilities with results summaries exported into professionally customized presentation reports. There are more than 25 ODBC drivers included, and the reports generated can be distributed via e-mail (MAPI).

Copia International LTD., 1342 Avalon Ct., Wheaton, IL 60187
Phone: 708-682-8898 / 800-689-8898
Fax: 708-665-9841
CIS: 71170,1014

Products:

AccSys for Paradox, AccSys for xBASE: Allow programmers using VB to access either Paradox or Xbase files, depending on the product. As applications are being developed, files and routines can be created, read, written to, modified, and updated as required, based on access privileges.

Coromandel Industries Inc., 70-15 Austin St., 3rd Floor, Forest Hills, NY 11375
Phone: 718-793-7963
Fax: 718-793-9710

Products:

Integra VDB for Visual Basic: A tool to assist visual database programmers in developing ODBC-compliant Windows database applications with little or no code. It contains database custom controls, a database class library, database functions, a visual query builder, a visual data manager, and an ODBC-compliant SQL engine.

ObjecTrieve/VB Professional: Made up of the ObjecTrieve data manager for VB, a BLOB manager for modifying binary large objects, and a set of high-level custom controls for use with VB in developing applications.

SQL Controls 1.x.x: Consists of high-level custom controls for use with VB in developing applications for SQL databases. These SQL controls let programmers associate VB forms with fields from one or multiple SQL database tables and perform queries and updates. Special extensions are provided for SQL and Oracle Servers; database connectivity is accomplished with ODBC.

Crescent Division of Progress Software Corp., 14 Oak Park, Bedford, MA 01730
Phone: 617-280-4000
Fax: 617-280-4025

Products:

QuickPak Professional for Access: Contains over 30 custom controls, 400 DLL routines, 2.7MB of sample code, 3MB of source code, and some time-saving utilities. Additional features include array searching routines, multikey array and file sorting, other file and directory services, string parsing, and formatting.

VBDD (Data Dictionary for Visual Basic 1.0): This utility makes the Microsoft Access engine available to VB developers, allowing them direct use of features such as parameterized QueryDefs. VBDD provides additional database features such as full referential integrity, pseudo-data arrays, and full-featured table maintenance.

Crystal, A Seagate Software Company, 1050 W. Pender St., Suite 2200, Vancouver, BC, Canada V6E 2M6
Phone: 604-681-3435
Fax: 604-681-2934
CIS: 72603,3352

Products:

Crystal Reports Professional 4.5: Crystal Reports is a powerful redesigned database report engine accessible through an enhanced OCX for use with new 32-bit systems and software such as Windows 95, Windows NT 3.51, and Visual Basic 4. It provides the user with an easy-to-use, versatile database presentation and report design, creation, and data analysis tool. Crystal Report SQL control features SQL pass-through and the ability to sort data on the SQL Server. Its support for stored procedures is a real benefit to IS professionals. In addition, it has more than 80 properties (direct Print Engine calls), including VBX, OCX with property page interface, Data Dictionary Builder, Extensible formula language, VCL, and Data API.

Data Translation Inc., 100 Locke Dr., Marlboro, MA 01752
Phone: 508-481-3700 / 800-525-8528
Fax: 508-481-8620
Internet: 538-9540@MCIMAIL.COM

Products:

Data Acquisition Custom Control 2.0: This control expands the capability of data acquisition functionality that can be added in new and redesigned applications. Being a DT-Open Layers product, it provides protection for developed software obsolescence, allowing minimal or no code changes when integrating new hardware.

DB Technologies, 2420 Briar Oak Circle, Sarasota, FL 34232
Phone: 813-378-3760
Fax: 813-378-3760
CIS: 72123,3661

Products:

DB Engine Custom Control VBX, DB Engine (version 3 releases) Custom Control VBX: These DB Engine VBXs provide developers with the capability to connect to Paradox 4.x and Paradox for Windows database tables. Additional features are compatibility with Paradox 3.x, Paradox 3.5 and 4.0 locking protocols, BLOB support, and Paradox 4.0 composite indexes and network compatibility.

Digital Equipment Corp., 110 Spit Brook Rd., ZK03-2/X46, Nashua, NH 03062
Phone: 603-881-0642
Fax: 603-881-0120

Products:

DECADMIRE for Visual Basic: A utility that provides a graphical application development environment for teams of programmers constructing large scale VB applications. Automatic output generation of VB/ODBC or VB/ACMS applications is built in, allowing application compatibility with different operating systems and databases without modification.

FarPoint Technologies Inc., 133 Southcenter Ct., Suite 1000, Morrisville, NC 27560
Phone: 919-460-4551 / 800-645-5913
Fax: 919-460-7606
BBS: 919-460-5771

Products:

Aware/VBX: Made up of 13 data-aware custom controls that were designed for database applications. Each control can be formatted and edited to meet customers' requirements for input data display. This VBX simplifies database front-end C/S application development by providing the programmer with more than 70 properties for each control. Other features are international and clipboard support, a variety of 3-D options, fixed and variable decimal points, and auto word-wrap.

Grid/VBX: A comprehensive grid control that has 10 cell types for individual cells or groups of cells, with the capability to lock or hide cells, columns, rows, or the entire grid, and to bind to the INTERSOLV DataDirect developer's toolkits or Access Engine. Grid/VBX allows designers to set runtime properties at design time.

Spread/VBX: A complete spreadsheet control developed for VB applications. It provides 12 flexible cell types with customization capabilities for each cell, and the spreadsheet size is supposed to have available billions of rows and columns.

Tab/VBX: A VBX control that allows easy insertion of tabs into VB applications. This control allows for complete customization of a tab's appearance in an application, with definition of ring type, size, and number, and the ability to insert bitmaps or icons on each tab.

Gilbert & Associates Inc., 705 Second Ave., Suite 710, Seattle, WA 98101
Phone: 206-223-7740
Fax: 206-223-7713
CIS: `75300,3650`

Products:

VIEWz VBX Custom Controls for Saros Mezzanine: Provides LAN users with a professional productivity and document management system for Windows. Users can focus on document creation, access, and management of the document, instead of computer and network file processes and operations.

Gradient Technologies Inc., 5 Mount Royal Ave., Marlboro, MA 01752
Phone: 508-624-9600 / 800-525-4343
Fax: 508-229-0338
Internet: `visual-dce@gradient.com`

Products:

Visual-DCE 1.0: Allows for easier development of DCE client applications, with the RPC interface control providing access to remote procedures. The RPC Binding control provides for making a valid connection to a server application, whereas the DCE login context control establishes a valid DCE login. Included is the extended IDL compiler that translates arguments between C and VB.

HiT Software Inc., 1174 Lincoln Ave., Suite 8, San Jose, CA 95125
Phone: 408-280-5795
Fax: 408-280-5792
Internet: sales@hit.com

Products:

SQL Fmt 2.0: A query formatter designed to handle large quantities of data while being able to use stored procedures and query files and perform data extraction. Other features include the management of headers, footers, page length, and page width.

Intersolv, 1800 Perimeter Park Dr., Suite 210, Morrisville, NC 27560
Phone: 919-461-4200 / 800-547-4000
Fax: 919-461-4526

Products:

Intersolv DataDirect ODBC Pack: A suite of ODBC drivers that provide the capability of connecting ODBC-compliant applications across multiple platforms to a majority of PC and SQL databases.

Intersolv DataDirect Developer's Toolkit 2.0: This tool kit is a high-level API providing DBMS-independent access, query, and data-handling functions to build ODBC-compliant SQL applications.

Intersolv Q+E 6.1: This product provides users with direct access to data in many database formats through the use of a single consistent and controllable interface. This is accomplished by the Intersolv enterprise-wide query and reporting system. This upgrade includes ODBC 2.0 drivers and more.

Marasco Newton Group Ltd., 1600 Wilson Blvd., Suite 1200, Arlington, VA 22209
Phone: 703-516-9100 / 703-247-4726
Fax: 703-516-9109

Products:

Advanced Database Environment (ADE) 1.0: Provides nine integrated 3-D custom controls for constructing ODBC database applications. Other features include its button-activated SQL query builder, editor, and the scrollable relational data control.

Micro Data Base Systems Inc. (mdbs), 1305 Cumberland Ave., PO Box 2438, West Lafayette, IN 47906-0438
Phone: 317-463-7200 / 800-455-MDBS
Fax: 317-463-1234

Products:

TITANIUM: This is a C/S database engine for ISVs and mainframe rehosting applications. With its active data dictionary, very complex real world models are supported whether working in single Windows systems or large networks. Other features include transaction processing and the use of stored procedures.

MicroHelp Inc., 4211 J.V.L., Industrial Park Dr. NE, Marietta, GA 30066
Phone: 404-516-0899 / 800-777-3322
Fax: 404-516-1099
CIS: 72420,2514

Products:

MicroHelp Report Generator 3: This help report generator is database-independent. Its layout editor allows reports to be designed in a process similar to VB's form construction, with the selection of an object type that is printed, positioned, and sized on the form. Other features include a print preview function and an end-user module to allow for customer customization of the report.

Microrim Inc., 15395 SE 30th Place, Bellevue, WA 98007
Phone: 206-649-9500 / 800-628-6990
Fax: 206-649-2785
CIS: GO MICRORIM

Products:

R:BASE SQL Engine 2.0 for Windows: The R:BASE SQL engine is a 32-bit PC-based database engine for use in Windows application development. It is compatible with those products developed in a Windows environment that support ODBC level 1 and can function on a LAN providing either single-user or multi-user engine support.

Nucleus Data Systems Inc., 7231 120th St., Suite 465, Delta, BC Canada V4C 6P5
Phone: 604-572-9892

Products:

DBStore for Windows: A script file database object manager for Windows. This utility is capable of displaying all database dependencies and permissions for all script objects prior to execution. Its store feature saves data at the time of table replacement and reapplies the existing dependencies and permissions for tables, triggers, stored procedures, and views.

Oracle Corp., 500 Oracle Pkwy, Redwood Shores, CA 94065
Phone: 415-506-7000
Fax: 415-506-7200

Products:

Oracle Objects for OLE: This product uses the Oracle Data Control/VBX with an OLE in-process server. This allows Windows applications to perform native Oracle 7 functions using its OLE plug-ins. Access of Oracle 7 data can be obtained directly and fed into Excel spreadsheets through its support of a VBA. The Oracle SQL Net Technology also provides applications with access to databases over TCP/IP, IPX/SPX, IBM SNA, DECnet, OSI, and other protocols.

Oracle Power Objects: Complete development system similar to Visual Basic. Compatible with Visual Basic syntax. Completely object-oriented. Cross-platform (Windows, Macintosh, and OS/2). Can connect to Oracle and Microsoft SQL Server database servers.

Platinum Software Corp., 195 Technology Dr., Irvine, CA 92718
Phone: 714-453-4000 / 800-426-0469
Fax: 714-453-4091

Products:

Platinum Publisher: A financial reporting tool that works with accounting software to create financial reports.

SeQueL Publisher: A financial data query and report generation tool designed for use by end users working with financial data.

Platinum FRx for Windows 2.0: A sophisticated financial report generation tool for creating reports with a high level of detail.

ProtoView Development, 2450 Rt. 130, Cranbury, NJ 08512
Phone: 609-655-5000 / 800-231-8588
Fax: 609-655-5353

Products:

ProtoGen+ Client/Server Suite: This suite contains ProtoGen+, WinControl custom controls, SQL View Database Access, the DataTable Spreadsheet Control with DataTable Lens Object, and the Report Writer Visual Coder with Crystal Report Writer Pro. It provides the tools for database access, forms building, report writing, application management, and quality code generation.

DataTable Spreadsheet Control 2.5, DataTable Spreadsheet Control NT 2.5: These products are sophisticated spreadsheet controls. The spreadsheet provides developers with information to control all aspects of their application development. Features include VBX control support, virtual memory management, column sorting, column locking, and check boxes and combo boxes as cells.

Revelation Technologies, 181 Harper Dr., Stamford, CT 06902
Phone: 203-973-1000
Fax: 203-975-8744

Products:

Open Engine: A powerful database engine that provides VB with a smart data access and transaction coordination tool for passing information between multiple back-end data sources. Included are a relational database, an active data dictionary, ANSI SQL implementation, and gateway technology to access distant data sources directly.

Sequiter Software Inc., 9644-54 Ave., Suite 209, Edmonton, Alberta, Canada T6E 5V1
Phone: 403-437-2410
Fax: 403-437-2999
CIS: 71321,1306
BBS: 403-437-2999

Products:

CodeControls 2.0: These are user interface controls that Xbase DBMS Windows application developers can use directly or interactively from the visual design tools of the development system compiler. Features built in provide formatted data entry and browse screen without additional coding and full data-aware capabilities.

CodeBasic 5.1: Provides a database management library for VB programmers that can be used to access FoxPro, Clipper, and dBase files in a multi-user environment.

Sheridan Software Systems Inc., 35 Pinelawn Rd., Suite 206E, Melville, NY 11747
Phone: 516-753-0985 / 800-VBDIREC
Fax: 516-753-3661
CIS: GO SHERIDAN

Products:

Data Widgets 1.0: A group of custom-bound data controls designed for the front-ends of VB database applications. These controls include a bound fully editable DataGrid similar to a Microsoft Access grid and a bound DataCombo that is editable with drop-down portions that can be linked to separate data controls.

Smithware Inc., 2416 Hillsboro Rd., Suite 201, Nashville, TN 37212
Phone: 615-386-3100
Fax: 615-386-3135
CIS: 75470,546

Products:

Controls for Btrieve 2.0: Consists of a set of VBX-bound controls and library routines that are used for Btrieve database access in VB for Windows. These Btrieve controls are a direct link to the Btrieve database, providing the developer with more control over record operations and better performance than is received by VB data controls or ODBC.

DDF Builder for Windows 2.0: This application provides the developer with a utility for creating and manipulating Btrieve data dictionary files and these DDFs to access Btrieve data. The DDF Builder comes with a file browser screen for viewing and modifying defined files and a DDF Wizard utility to assist in defining DDFs for Btrieve files with unknown file formats.

SuccessWare International, 27349 Jefferson Ave., Suite 101, Temecula, CA 92590-5611
Phone: 909-699-9657 / 800-683-1657
Fax: 909-695-5679

Products:

ROCKET (SlxBase/VB): A replaceable database engine DLL that simplifies development by allowing the use of common Xbase-style data management syntax. This allows applications to move between database environments with minimal or no code changes. Included are a Grid/Browse VBX and data-aware Access controls with new record level data encryption and an integrated query optimizer.

Sylvain Faust Inc., 880 Boulevard de la Carriere, Hull, Quebec, Canada J8Y 6T5
Phone: 819-778-5045 / 800-567-9127
Fax: 819-778-7943
CIS: 71162,1050

Products:

SQL-Sombrero/OCX for CT-Library, SQL-Sombrero/OCX for DB-Library, SQL-Sombrero/OLE2 Automation CT-Library, SQL-Sombrero/OLE2 Automation DB-Library, SQL-Sombrero/VBX for CT-Library, SQL-Sombrero/VBX for DB-Library: These are products that contain database libraries for SQL to communicate between a SQL database server and different database formats.

TechSmith Corp., 3001 Coolidge Rd., Sta. 400, East Lansing, MI 48823
Phone: 517-333-2100 / 800-517-3001
Fax: 517-333-1888
CIS: 75226,3136

Products:

Enterprise Wide 2.5: Provides high-performance remote access to C/S applications that use multiple X.25 or asynchronous connections. Through the use of ProtocolAssist, dynamic performance enhancements are offered with configuration options for multiplatform support and system management.

Graphics Utilities and Programs

AccuSoft Corp., 2 Westborough Business Park, Westborough, MA 01581
Phone: 508-898-2770 / 800-525-3577
Fax: 508-898-9662
Internet: simwiz@aol.com

Products:

AccuSoft Image Format Library 5.0/VBX, AccuSoft Image Format Library 5.0/VBX 32-bit, AccuSoft Image Format Library 5.0/VBX Pro Gold, AccuSoft Pro-Imaging Toolkit: These are custom controls that provide VB application developers with an image processing tool kit. These controls are capable of reading and writing raster file format, display, printing, scanning, image processing, special effects, and compression. The 32-bit version of the tool can process images two to four times faster than the standard version. The Pro Gold version adds the capability of JPEG image processing.

Media Architects Inc., 7340 SW Hunziker Rd., Suite 305, Portland, OR 97223
Phone: 503-639-2505
Fax: 503-620-5451
CIS: 71064,2344

Products:

ImageKnife/VBX Pro Pack 2.0: This is a data-aware custom control that can provide a VB application with easy-to-use complete image handling capabilities. These consist of displaying the image with built-in pan and zoom, format conversion (TIFF, BMP, DIB, PCX, GIF, Targa, and JPEG) and image processing (rotate, sharpen, and matrix filter). It supports true color (24-bit) through monochrome (1-bit) and contains many more features to simplify image processing.

System Development and Integration Tools

Avanti Software Inc., 385 Sherman Avenue, Palo Alto, CA 94306
Phone: 800-329-8889, extension 601

Products:

VB/Rig Pro: Automates the generation of error handling routines. Implemented in totally native Visual Basic code. Time-stamp and log runtime errors or route them to Avanti's PinPoint debugger.

CenterView Software Inc., 651 Gateway Blvd., Suite 1050, South San Francisco, CA 94080
Phone: 415-873-1295
Fax: 415-873-1298

Products:

Choreo for Visual Basic: A tool consisting of several components that integrate with Visual Basic and other industry standard tools to assist the programmer in developing scalable C/S applications. Choreo contains an object-oriented data access engine and drag-and-drop interface. The power of Choreo comes with its capability to develop database-independent applications easily. Applications can be designed and built for one type of database and used with others without code modifications.

Galacticomm Inc., 4101 SW 47th Ave., Suite 101, Fort Lauderdale, FL 33314
Phone: 305-583-5990
Fax: 305-583-7846
BBS: 305-583-7808

Products:

Worldgroup: Provides developers with the capability to customize the client-side applications or create new ones. This customization provides a way to optimize the user's PC's capabilities through implementing multitasking and multithreading along with full use of its systems video capabilities. While in the Worldgroup environment, links can be set up with other programs using OLE and DDE. Through the use of VBXs and Worldgroup software, JPEG images, WAV sound files, and AVI video capabilities will assist you in providing services in the world of multimedia.

Innovative Solutions & Technologies, 904 Jefferson Ave., Joplin, MO 64801
Phone: 417-781-3282
Fax: 417-781-3299
CIS: 74722,3231

Products:

OpenExchange VBX/Developer's Kit: Provides the developer with OpenExchange PRO that includes a VBX API for enabling the addition of custom data import/export capabilities to an application. The file formats supported by this kit are Access, FoxPro, Btrieve, Paradox, dBase, ASCII, Excel, and Lotus 1-2-3.

PageAhead Software Corp., 2125 Western Ave., Suite 301, Seattle, WA 98121
Phone: 800-967-9671
Fax: 206-441-9876

Products:

InfoPublisher Developer's Kit: Provides developers creating applications for production of high-quality price lists, catalogs, directories and other data-intensive documents with a utility to make a communication path for data transfer between databases and word processors.

Stylus Innovation, Inc., One Kendall Square, Building 300, Cambridge, MA 02139
Phone: 617-621-9545
Fax: 617-621-7862
E-mail: `info@stylus.com`
Home page: `http://www.stylus.com/~stylus`

Products:

Visual Fax: This is a custom control that can be integrated into a VB application to provide full fax capability, both sending and receiving over multiple lines (10 fax lines per PC). Visual Fax supports binary file transfers and transmit and receive of ASCII, PCX, DCX, and TIF file formats.

Visual Voice: Telephony Toolkit for Windows is the C/S approach of Visual Voice for setting up a network with many nodes. Visual Voice is a custom control available to VB application developers that allows them to integrate a sophisticated voice processing system with interactive voice response into their application. Examples of this are fax-on-demand, voice mail, and automated outbound dialing.

Other Visual Voice Products: Visual Voice Pro, Visual Voice for Mwave, and Visual Voice for TAPI.

XDB Systems Inc., 9861 Broken Land Pkwy., Columbia, MD 21046
Phone: 410-312-9300 / 800-488-4948
Fax: 410-312-9500

Products:

XDB-SQL for Visual Basic: A software development kit for VB application programmers that provides an easy way to create MS Windows operating system based database applications. These applications are multitasking and capable of supporting multiple concurrent Windows sessions.

Online Support

For more information on client/server topics, visit us (the authors) at our Internet World Wide Web page: `http://www.electriciti.com/~cvisual`.

America Online, 8619 Westwood Center Drive, Vienna, VA 22182-9806, 800-827-6364, extension 10121

Bennet-Tec Information Systems, on CompuServe: `GO BENNET-TEC`

Borland, produces Delphi development tools, on CompuServe: `GO BORLAND`, or Internet WWW page: `http://www.borland.com/`

Compaq Computer Corporation, Internet WWW page: http://www.compaq.com

CompuServe, 5000 Arlington Centre Boulevard, PO Box 20212, Columbus, OH 43220, 800-848-8990

Datamation, Internet WWW page: http://www.datamation.com

Desaware, on CompuServe: GO DESAWARE

Distinct, Internet WWW page: http://www.distinct.com

Dr. Dobb's Journal, on CompuServe: GO DDJ or Internet WWW page: http://www.ddj.com

Information Week, Internet WWW page: http://techweb.cmp.com/iwk

Lifeboat Publishing, BBS: 908-389-9783

Logic Works, makes Erwin for Visual Basic, Internet WWW page:http://www.logicworks.com

Microsoft Developer Services Area, on CompuServe: GO MSDS or Internet WWW page: http://www.microsoft.com or Gopher site at gopher.microsoft.com

Microsoft Visual Basic, Internet WWW page: http://www.microsoft.com/VBASIC/

Novell Incorporated, Internet WWW page: http://www.novell.com

Oracle, Internet WWW page: http://www.oracle.com

Pronexus, produces telephony products, BBS: 613-839-0034

Sams Publishing, Internet WWW page: http://www.mcp.com/sams/

Sheridan, on CompuServe: GO SHERIDAN

Simply Solutions, on CompuServe: GO SIMSOL

Software Interphase, Inc., makes Help Magician Pro, Internet WWW page: http://www.sinterphase.com

Summit Software Company, Internet WWW page: http://www.summsoft.com

VB Tech, on CompuServe: GO CLMFORUM or Internet FTP site: enf.org in the /pub/VBTech directory

Versit, an alliance between Apple, AT&T, IBM, and Siemens for telephony technology, Internet WWW page: http://www.versit.com

VBXtras, VB components and utilities at discount prices, Internet WWW page: http://www.vbxtras.com

Visual Basic Programmer's Journal, on CompuServe: GO VBPJ

D

List of Acronyms and Terms

Acronym or Term	Meaning
ACD	Automatic Call Distribution
ACL	Access Control List
ADPCM	Adaptive Differential Pulse Code Modulation
ADSI	Analog Display Services Interface
ADSL	Asymmetric Digital Subscriber Line
AIN	Advanced Intelligent Network
ALI	Automatic Location Identification
AMA	Automated Message Accounting
AMPS	Advanced Mobile Phone Service
ANI	Automatic Number Identification
ANSI	American National Standards Institute
AOL	America Online
API	Application Program Interface
ASCII	American Standard Code for Information Interchange
ATM	Asynchronous Transfer Mode
AUI	Attachment Unit Interface
AVI	Audio Video Integration
AVS	Audio and Video Services
BBS	Bulletin Board System
BER	Bit Error Rate
BETRS	Basic Exchange Telecommunications Radio Service
BISDN	Broadband Integrated Services Digital Network
BLOB	Binary Large Object
BNC	Bayonet Nut Connector (Thin Ethernet connector for coaxial cable)
BOA	Basic Object Adapter
BRI	Basic Rate Interface
BSTR	Basic String
Byte	A data unit composed of 8 bits
CAC	Carrier Access Code
CASE	Computer-Aided Software Engineering
CBC	Cipher Block Chaining mode
CBT	Computer-Based Training
CCITT	International Telephonic and Telegraphic Consultative Committee
CD	Carrier Detect
CDMA	Code Division Multiple Access
CFB	Cipher Feedback mode
CIM	CompuServe Information Manager

Cipher	Another name for an encryption algorithm
CIS	CompuServe Information Service
CMA	Concert Multithread Architecture
CMIP	Common Management Information Protocol
COM	Component Object Model
CORBA	Common Object Request Broker Architecture
CRC	Cyclic Redundancy Check
CSA	Canadian Standards Association
CSLIP	Compressed Serial Line Internet Protocol (SLIP)
CSTA	Computer-Supported Telecommunications Application
CSU	Channel Service Unit
CTI	Computer-Telephony Integration
C/S	Client/Server
C&M	Conferencing and Messaging
DAO	Data Access Object
DAP	Directory Access Protocol
dB	Decibel
DBCS	Double-Byte Character Set
DBList	Data-Bound list box
dBm	Decibel referenced to a milliwatt
DCE	Distributed Computing Environment
DCS	Digital Cross Connect
DDE	Dynamic Data Exchange
DDS	Digital Data Service
DEA-1	Data Encryption Algorithm -1
DEC	Digital Equipment Corporation
DES	Data Encryption Standard
DFS	Distributed File System
DHCP	Dynamic Host Configuration Protocol
DIB	Directory Information Base
DII	Dynamic Invocation Interface
DISI	Directory Information Services Infrastructure
DIT	Directory Information Tree
DLC	Digital Loop Carrier
DLL	Dynamic Link Library
DMF	Distribution Media Format
DMS	Digital Multiplex System
DNA	Digital Network Architecture (DEC's layered data communication protocol)
DNS	Domain Name System
DOC	Distributed Object Computing

continues

Acronym or Term	Meaning
DoD	Department of Defense
DPN	Data Packet Network
DSA	Directory System Agent
DSN	Data Source Name
DSOM	Distributed System Object Model
DSP	Directory Service Protocol
DSS	Digital Signature Standard
DTC	Decoder Time Clock
DTE	Data Terminal Equipment
DTMF	Dual-Tone Multifrequency
DUA	Directory User Agent
E-mail	Electronic Mail
E-TDMA	Enhanced Time Division Multiple Access
ECB	Electronic Codebook mode
ECC	Error Checking and Correcting
EDI	Electronic Data Interchange
EES	Escrowed Encryption Standard
EIS	Enterprise Information System
EMI	Electromagnetic Interference
Fax	Facsimile
FDC	Floppy Disk Controller
FDDI	Fiber-Distributed Data Interface
FDMA	Frequency Division Multiple Access
FDX	Full-Duplex Transmission
FEC	Forward Error Correction
FIPS	Federal Information Processing Standard
FL	10 Mb/second Ethernet fiber optic connector
FM	Frequency Modulation
FTP	File Transfer Protocol
Gbps	Gigabits per second
GGP	Gateway-to-Gateway Protocol
GIF	Graphics Interchange Format
GIS	Geographic Information System
GNMP	Government Network Management Profile
GPF	General Protection Fault
GSNW	Gateway Services for NetWare
GUI	Graphical User Interface
GULS	Generic Upper Layer Security
HCL	Hardware Compatibility List

HDLC	High-Level Data Link Control
HDM	Hierarchical Disk Management
HDX	Half-Duplex Transmission
HLM	Heterogeneous LAN Management
HSM	Hierarchical Storage Management
HTML	HyperText Markup Language
HTTP	HyperText Transport Protocol
IDEA	International Data Encryption Algorithm
IDL	Interface Definition Language
IEEE	Institute of Electrical and Electronic Engineers
IETF	Internet Engineering Task Force
IP	Internet Protocol
IPX	Internetwork Packet Exchange (packet format of NetWare transactions)
ISAM	Indexed Sequential Access Method
ISDN	Integrated Services Digital Network
ISO	International Standards Organization
ISV	Independent Software Vendor
IT	Information Technology
ITU	International Telecommunication Union
JET	Joint Engine Technology
JPEG	Joint Photographic Experts Group
KB	Knowledge Base
Kbps (Kb/s)	Kilobits per second
KBps (KB/s)	Kilobytes per second
KMP	Key Management Protocol
LAN	Local Area Network
LAT	Local Area Transport
LDAP	Lightweight Directory Access Protocol
MAN	Metropolitan Area Network
MAPI	Messaging Application Programming Interface
MAU	Medium Attachment Unit
Mb	Megabits
Mbps (Mb/s)	Megabits per second
MB	Megabytes
MBps (MB/s)	Megabytes per second
MCS	Multipoint Communication Services
MCU	Multipoint Control Unit
MD5	Message Digest 5
MDI	Multiple Document Interface
MHS	Message Handling Service

continues

Acronym or Term	Meaning
MIDI	Musical Instrument Digital Interface
MIME	Multipurpose Internet Mail Extension
MIS	Management Information Structure
MIT	Massachusetts Institute of Technology
MPEG	Motion Picture Experts Group
MPP	Massively Parallel Processor
MRBC	Multiple-Resolution Bitmap Compiler
MRU	Most Recently Used
MSP	Message Security Protocol
MSS	Maximum Segment Size
MTU	Maximum Transfer Unit
NBF	NetBIOS Frame
NBS	National Bureau of Standards (now NIST)
NDS	NetWare Directory Services
NetBEUI	NetBIOS Extended User Interface
NetBIOS	Network Basic Input/Output System
NIST	National Institute of Standards and Technology
NFS	Network File System
NLM	NetWare Loadable Module
NLSP	Network Layer Security Protocol
NOS	Network Operating System
NPA	Network Provider Architecture
NSA	National Security Agency
NWIP	NetWare Internet Protocol
OCX	OLE Custom Control
ODBC	Object Database Connectivity
ODBMS	Object Database Management System
ODL	Object Definition Language
OLE	Object Linking and Embedding
OMA	Object Management Architecture
OMG	Object Management Group
ORB	Object Request Broker
OSF	Open Software Foundation
OSI	Open Systems Interconnection
PBX	Private Branch Exchange
PDA	Personal Digital Assistant computing device
PDI	Personal Data Interchange
PEM	Privacy-enhanced Electronic Mail
PGP	Pretty Good Privacy

PID	Personal Identifier
POTS	Plain Old Telephone Service
PPP	Point-to-Point Protocol
PRI	Primary Rate Interface
PSTN	Public Switched Telephone Network
PWD	Password
RAID	Redundant Array Inexpensive Disk
RAM	Random-Access Memory
RAS	Remote Access Service
RDBMS	Relational Database Management System
RF	Radio Frequency
RFI	Radio Frequency Interference
RGB	Red Green Blue
RLE	Run-Length Encoding
RPC	Remote Procedure Call
RSA	Rivest-Shamir-Adleman
RTF	Rich Text Format
RTMP	Routing Table Maintenance Protocol
RTS	Request To Send
SAMP	Security Association Management Protocol
SAP	Service Advertising Protocol
SDE	Secure Data Exchange
SHS	Secure Hashing Standard
SIA	Stable Implementation Agreement
SID	Security ID
SII	Static Invocation Interface
SILP	Standard for Interoperable LAN Security
SLIP	Serial Line Internet Protocol
SMP	Symmetric Multiprocessing
SMS	Service Management System
SMTP	Simple Mail Transfer Protocol
SNA	Systems Network Architecture
SNMP	Simple Network Management Protocol
SOM	System Object Model
SONET	Synchronous Optical Network
SPX	Sequenced (or Sequential) Packet Exchange
SQL	Structured Query Language
STP	Shielded Twisted-Pair cable
SVD	Simultaneous Voice and Data
TAPI	Telephony API
TCP/IP	Transmission Control Protocol/Internet Protocol

continues

Acronym or Term	Meaning
TCSEC	Trusted Computer System Evaluation Criteria
TDI	Trusted Database Interpretation
TDM	Time Division Multiplexing
TDMA	Time Division Multiple Access
TFTP	Trivial File Transfer Protocol
TLSP	Transport Layer Security Protocol
tps	Transactions per second
TSAPI	Telephony Services API
TSI	Time Slot Interchange
UDP	User Datagram Protocol
UID	User Identification
UTP	Unshielded Twisted-Pair cable
VBA	Visual Basic for Applications
VBCL	Visual Basic Compatibility Layer
VBX	Visual Basic Extension
WAN	Wide Area Network
WAV	Waveform
WYSIWYG	What You See Is What You Get

Extension	Meaning
.AVI	Audio Video Integration
.BMP	Bitmap
.EXE	Executable file
.FRM	Form module file
.HLP	Help file
.HPJ	Help Project
.ICO	Icon
.INI	Initialization file
.MAK	Make file
.MRB	Multiple-Resolution Bitmaps
.OCX	OLE custom control
.OLB	Object Library file
.RES	Resource file
.RTF	Rich-Text Format
.SHG	HyperGraphics
.TLB	Type Library
.TXT	Text file
.VBP	Visual Basic Project

.VBX	Custom control
.WAV	Waveform
.WMF	Windows Metafile

Term	Meaning
AUI	Attachment Unit Interface (a 15-pin shielded twisted-pair Ethernet cable alternative to interconnect network devices and a MAU)
BNC	Thin Ethernet connector for coaxial cable
FDDI	Fiber-Distributed Data Interface
FL	10 Mb/s Ethernet fiber optic connector
RJ-21	Telephony 50-pin connector
RJ-45	Ethernet twisted-pair connector
SMA	Multimode fiber optic connector
ST	Single-mode fiber optic connector
STP	Shielded Twisted-Pair cable
UTP	Unshielded Twisted-Pair cable
10 Base-2	Standard specifying 10 Mb/s Ethernet characteristics over Thin Ethernet cable
10 Base-5	Standard specifying 10 Mb/s Ethernet characteristics over Thick Ethernet cable
10 Base-F	Proposed standard specifying 10 Mb/s Ethernet characteristics over fiber optic Ethernet cable
10 Base-T	IEEE 802.3 standard specifying 10 Mb/s Ethernet characteristics over UTP cabling
100 Base-T	Standard specifying 100 Mb/s Ethernet characteristics over twisted-pair Ethernet cable
100 Base-VG	Standard specifying 100 Mb/s Ethernet characteristics over voice-grade Ethernet cable

Index

Symbols

& operator, 145
* (asterisk), wildcard, 647
_ (underscore), VBA line-continuation character, 588
10BASE-2 (Thinnet) cabling, 56
10BASE-5 (Thicknet) cabling, 56
10BASE-T (Twisted Pair) cabling, 56
100BASE-T cabling, 57
16-bit Visual Basic, 161
32-bit Visual Basic, 161

A

AAL (ATM Adaptation Layer), 88
AbortCall routine, 820
Access, 915-916
  databases
    encryption, 909-910
    logons, 548-549
    upsizing to SQL Server databases, 668-680
  implementing SQL, 656-660
  NOS compatibility, 546
  security, 903-906
  SQL commands, 659
Access Basic, 561-563, 581-583
  code libraries, 581-583
  OLE Automation, 597
accessing
  data controls, 126
  databases, 122-131, 146
    from OLTP client applications, 357
    with custom drivers, 131, 135-136
    with data controls, 122-126
    with RDOs, 128-129
  DDE from Visual Basic, 192
  Excel objects, 609
  OLTP client applications, 269
  result sets with RDOs, 705-708
  tables, 269-270
acronyms (glossary reference), 988-995
Action settings
  MAPI Message controls, 836-839
  MAPI Session controls, 831
Activate method (Excel Workbook objects), 617
adapters (ATM networks), 92
ADD command, 193
Add-In Manager, 173
add-ons, 912-913
  creating, 175
  Gantt/VBX, 928
  Help File Editors, 913-914
  Imageknife, 928
  LeadTools, 928
  RoboHelp, 913
  Spread/VBX, 927-928
  telephony, 929-931
  TrueGrid Pro, 928-929
  VB Helpwriter, 914
  Visual Basic interfaces, 926-929
  VSFlex, 927
  VSVBX, 926-927
Addin objects (Excel), 622
AddRef function, 719
Administer permissions (databases), 558
Administrator accounts (databases), 553, 568
aggregate functions (SQL), 650-652
AIX (Unix operating system), 71
aligning labels in OLTP client application forms, 281
ALTER command (SQL), 647
America Online, 933
antimonikers, 723
API (Application Program Interface) functions, 16, 28, 135
  CMC, 824-826
  declaring, 17, 302
  ODBC, 121
  ODBC API, 698-704
API Viewer, 178-179
AppendChunk function, 140
Application Layer (TCP/IP), 63
Application objects (Excel), 612-615
application-level security (databases), 890
applications
  client applications, 189, 212
    common errors, 223-224
    creating, 199-206
    DSS systems, 217-220, 450-452
    error checking, 211
    executing, 204
    extending with other programs, 630

*Global modules,
    301-305*
*INI files, modifying,
    524-525*
install disks, 20-22
*installation setup files,
    modifying, 21-22*
*messaging services,
    842-847*
*OLTP systems, 212-
    216, 352-355*
registering, 750-751
routines, adding, 202
saving, 200
conditional compiling,
    177-178
incremental com-
    piling, 175
Pseudo Servers, 500-501
    *Change in Carrier
        Detect event, 802*
    *classes, creating,
        729-730*
    *converting to OLE
        Servers, 728-735,
        745-747*
    creating, 501-502
    *disconnecting
        users, 801*
    executing, 542-544
    forms, 502-518
    *forms, adding code,
        511-518*
    forms, loading, 516
    forms, unloading, 517
    forms, updating, 511
    *frame controls,
        adding, 799*
    INI files, 502, 572
    *installing remote
        servers, 799-806*
    *menus, adding
        code, 518*

*Receive Data event,
    802*
Ring event, 802
*timer controls,
    517-518*
Query Builder applica-
    tions
    creating, 781-787
    customizing, 786-787
    *tools required for
        creating, 754-756*
    registering in OLE
        Registry, 749-750
    server applications
        creating, 193-199
        executing, 196, 204
        *messaging services,
            842-847*
        *receiving client
            application com-
            mands, 188*
        routines, adding, 197
    Table Builder
        applications
        creating, 763-781
        saving, 780
        testing, 780
        *tools required for
            creating, 756*
    see also project files
**ARCNET transport
    protocol, 60**
**ASCII armor format
    (e-mail security), 893**
**assigning permissions to
    database objects,
    561-562**
**assisted telephony
    (TAPI), 862-863**
asterisk (*), wildcard, 647
AT commands, 792
**ATM (Asynchronous
    Transfer Mode) proto-
    cols, 89-93**

**ATM Adaptation Layer
    (AAL), 88**
**authenticating passwords
    with Kerberos, 888-889**
**Author property (Excel
    Workbook objects), 617**
**Autobuild Edit form
    (OLTP client applica-
    tions), 216**
**automatic links
    (DDE), 191**
**automatic procedures
    (Excel objects), 625**
**Automation Manager
    (Remote OLE), 740**
Avg function, 650

B

**B (Bearer) Channel,
    Narrowband ISDN, 84**
**B-ISDN (Broadband
    ISDN), 81, 87-89**
backbones (networks), 52
.BAS (module) files, 9
**Basic programming
    language operation
    codes, 5**
**Basic Rate Interface
    (BRI), Narrowband
    ISDN, 84**
**basic services (TAPI),
    863-865**
**BeginTrans com-
    mand, 141**
**BETWEEN command
    (SQL), 651**
**Binary Large Objects
    (BLOBs), 140**
**binding data controls to
    RDCs, 120**
**BLOBs (Binary Large
    Objects), 140**

BOFAction property
(data controls), 124
bonding architecture
(ISDN), 85
Border objects
(Excel), 615
bound controls, 119, 125,
171-172
BRI (Basic Rate Interface), Narrowband
ISDN, 84
bridges (networks), 65
Broadband ISDN (B-ISDN), 81, 87-89
buffers (databases), 127
flushing, 125
variables, 127
bus topologies, 55
business rules, 965
ByRef command, 751
ByVal command, 751

C

cabling
10BASE-2 (Thinnet)
cabling, 56
10BASE-5 (Thicknet)
cabling, 56
10BASE-T cabling, 56
100BASE-T cabling, 57
fiber optic cabling,
57-58
Calculate method (Excel
Application objects), 614
call objects (TAPI full
telephony), 863
Cancel operation (OLTP
client applications), 326
Caption property (Excel
Application objects), 613

Carrier Sense Multiple
Access with Collision
Detection (CSMA/CD), 58
cascade delete (database
referential integrity), 115
cascade relations
(records), 171
cascade update (database
referential integrity), 115
CBC (Cipher Block
Chaining) algorithm
mode, e-mail
security, 892
cc:Mail messaging
services, 842
CCITT (International
Consultative Committee
on Telegraphy and
Telephony), 74
CCSS7 (Common
Channel Signaling
System 7), 83
cells (ATM networks), 91
CenterForm routine, 304
centering OLTP client
application forms, 304
Central Processing Units,
see CPUs
centralized error handling, 961-964
centralizing databases, 116
CFB (Cipher Feedback)
algorithm mode, e-mail
security, 892
chain topologies, 53
chained transactions
(databases), 115
Change in Carrier Detect
event (Pseudo Server
remote access), 802

channels (ISDN), 82
Chart objects (Excel), 620
Chart Wizard, 606
ChartGroup objects
(Excel), 620
charts (Excel), 610-612
adding to DSS client
applications through
OLE, 634-640
creating DSS client
application forms for,
637-638
displaying in DSS client
applications, 638-640
running in DSS client
applications, 636-640
ChartTest macro, 608
ChartWindowItem_Click
routine, 639
checking system
errors, 957
CheckPServer( ) routine, 395
checksums, 36
Choreo database tool,
923-924
Cipher Block Chaining
(CBC) algorithm mode,
e-mail security, 892
Cipher Feedback (CFB)
algorithm mode, e-mail
security, 892
class modules, 162
classes
objects, 150
frameworks, 151
VBA, 153
Pseudo Servers, 729-730
clauses (SQL SELECT
command)
HAVING, 654-665
UNION, 655
WHERE, 649-651

client applications, 26-27, 189, 212
  common errors, 223-224
  creating, 199-206
  DSS systems, 217-220, 450-452
    creating, 453-454
    database access, 453
    executable files, creating, 522-523
    executing, 539-542
    files, 452
    INI files, creating, 454
    INI files, modifying, 571
    installation disks, creating, 524
    integrating with Excel through OLE Automation, 633-640
    upgrading with RDOs, 708-710
  error checking, 211
  executing, 204
  extending with other programs, 630
  flat transactions, 36
  forms, setup, 199
  Global modules, 301-305
  INI files
    modifications after database upsizing, 685-686
    modifying, 524-525, 570-572
  install disks, creating with Setup Wizard, 20-22
  installation setup files, modifying, 21-22
  logons, 570-574
  messaging services, 842-847
  modifying after database upsizing, 686-687
  OLE Clients, creating in Excel, 735-738
  OLTP systems, 212-216, 352-355
    accessing, 269
    Cancel operation, 326
    compiling as stand-alone executable files, 349, 447
    confirming transactions with OK command button, 329-331
    creating, 264-267, 358-359
    database access, 357
    directory paths, returning, 304
    executable files, creating, 522-523
    executing, 349, 447, 526-539
    exiting, 531
    files, 355-357
    forms, 267-269
    forms, creating, 273-349
    INI files, 268, 271-272, 305, 525, 571
    installation disks, 524
    updating, 322-324
  Password variables, 572
  properties, setting, 200-202
  registering, 750-751
  remote client applications, 796-799, 806-821
  requests, saving, 199
  routines
    activating on servers, 198
    adding, 202
  saving, 200
  storing, 523-524
  testing after database upsizing, 680-687
  transmitting data to servers, 205
  user accounts
    creating, 567
    permissions, 567-570, 684-685
  UserName variables, 572
  workgroups
    creating, 566-567
    permissions, 567-570
  workload responsibilities, 35-36
  see also databases; project files

Client Registration utility, 750-751
client/server applications, *see* **databases**
client/server computing, 26-30
  data warehousing, 37-38
  DDE (Dynamic Data Exchange), 191-192
  decision support systems, 36
  development kits, 922-923
  distributed data, 109-116
  distributed processing, 39-40
  e-mail support, 44-45
  EIS (Enterprise information systems), 37

errors, 964-966
integrating OOP, 158
intruders, 875
modem connections, 791-796
network setup, 526
OLTP (Online transaction processing), 36
progression, 30-34
remote access, 796-821
security, 565-573, 874-878
TAPI/MAPI connections, 793-796
three-tier, 38
values out of range errors, 964
workload breakdown, 34-36
ClipboardFormats property (Excel Application objects), 613
Clone function, 722
Close method (Excel Workbook objects), 617
cmb_BuildItem_Click routine, 435
CMC (Common Messaging Calls), 45, 824-826
cmd_Add_Click routine, 435
cmd_Cancel_Click routine, 326, 341, 347, 411-412, 430, 440, 446, 488, 495
cmd_Connect_Click routine, 814-816
cmd_Disconnect_Click routine, 801, 817
cmd_Exit_Click routine, 339, 420
cmd_Item_Click routine, 414-415

cmd_Next_Click routine, 329, 415
cmd_OK_Click routine, 329-331, 341-343, 347, 415-416, 430-431, 440, 446, 488, 495
cmd_Prev_Click routine, 331, 417
cmd_Print_Click routine, 331-333, 417
cmd_Receive_Click routine, 817-818
cmd_Remove_Click routine, 436
cmd_Restore_Click routine, 515
cmd_Send_Click routine, 818
code libraries (Access Basic), 581-583
Collection data types, 176
collections (objects), 163-165, 580-581
  accessing single objects from, 581
  Count property, 581
  navigating, 581
collisions (database data), 114
color, 173
COM (Component Object Model), OLE, 714-718
combo box controls (OLTP client application forms), 278, 284, 285, 292
Comm1_OnComm routine, 801
command buttons
  activating in client application forms, 202

  inserting in client application forms, 199
  OLTP client application forms, 214, 276-278, 280, 285, 294, 297, 300
commands
  ADD, 193
  ALTER (SQL), 647
  AT commands, 792
  BeginTrans, 141
  BETWEEN (SQL), 651
  ByRef, 751
  ByVal, 751
  CommitTrans, *323*
  COMPUTE, 664
  CREATE (SQL), 647
  CreateRecordset, 142
  DATA, 805
  dbOpenDynaset, 686
  dbOpenTable, 686
  DECLARE, 664
  DELETE (SQL), 647
  DROP (SQL), 647
  IN (SQL), 651
  INSERT (SQL), 647
  JOIN (SQL), 106, 655-656
  LIKE (SQL), 652
  On Error, 957-959
  OpenDatabase, 268
  PROTECT (database dBase security), 890
  Rollback, 141
  SELECT (SQL), 647-650
  Set, 632
  SHUTDOWN, 664
  SQL commands, 104
  TIME, 805
  TOTL, 805
  UNJOIN, 106

UPDATE (SQL), 647
With...End With,
586-587, 632
see also functions;
methods
**commercial online
services, 932-933**
CommitTrans command, 323
**Common Channel
Signaling System 7
(CCSS7), 83**
**Common Messaging Calls
(CMC), 45, 824-826**
**Common Object Request
Broker Architecture
(CORBA), 725**
**CompactDatabase
function, 133, 563**
comparison operators, 649
**compiled programming
languages, 5**
**compilers (Help files),
18-19**
compiling
applications
  *conditionally,
  177-178*
  incrementally, 175
OLTP client applications as stand-alone
executable files,
349, 447
**complex messaging
services, 823**
**Component Manager
(Remote OLE),
183-184, 742-745**
**Component Object
Model (COM), OLE,
714-718**
composite monikers, 723

compound documents, 713
displaying, 722
OLE, 721-722
compound links, 203
CompuServe, 933
COMPUTE command, 664
**computer telephone
interface,** *see* **CTI
systems**
computer telephony, *see*
telephony
**conditional compiling
(applications), 177-178**
**configurations (OLE
Servers), 732-734**
**confirming OLTP client
application transactions,
329-331**
**Connect property (data
controls), 122-123**
**connection technologies
(networks), 849-850**
**connection-oriented
protocols, 61**
connectionless protocols, 61
connections
MAPI to client/server
computing systems,
793-796
modems to client/server
computing systems,
791-796
TAPI to client/server
computing systems,
793-796
**consistency (database
transactions), 114-115**
constants, 232, 628

context menus, 173
**context-sensitive
Help, 950**
**control layers (TCP/
IP), 63**
Control Lock, 173
Control Nudge, 173
Control Palette, 7
controls
color, 173
custom controls,
  166-167
databases, 119
DSS client application
forms, 457-476
  *adding code, 483-484,
  488-490, 494-497*
  *screen default values,
  488, 494*
  *Tag properties,
  486, 490*
forms
  deleting, 8
  information displays, 7
  *primary event code,
  displaying, 8*
  properties, 7
  renaming, 8
inserting
  in forms, 7
  in server applications, 194
MAPI, 830-839
naming conventions, 194
OLTP client application
forms, 290, 296-298,
299, 373-392,
411-422
  *adding code, 341-342,
  347-349, 429-432,
  435-437, 440, 446*

■ *controls*

placing, 361-371
routines, 325-339
screen default values, 439, 445
setting to empty values, 347
tag properties, setting to text properties, 345, 438, 443
Pseudo Server application forms, 503-510, 515-518
Query Builder application forms, 782
remote client application forms, 808-814
see also add-ons

converting
flat-file databases to relational databases, 106-109
Pseudo Servers to OLE Servers, 728-735, 745-747

copying
OLTP client application form items, 339, 424
record data
to DSS client application form controls, 492
to OLTP client application form controls, 345, 439

CopyItem_Click routine, 339, 424
CopyTags routine, 345, 438, 443, 486, 490
CopyTo function, 722
CORBA (Common Object Request Broker Architecture), 725

Core functions
ODBC API, 699-701
ODBC SQL, 661-662
Count function, 650
Count method (Excel Workbook objects), 617
Count property (object collections), 581
counters (records), 239
CPUs (Central Processing Units), 67
CREATE command (SQL), 647
Create Indexes command button (Table Builder application form), 778-779
Create Table command button (Table Builder application form), 774-776
CreateObject function, 601
CreateRecordset command, 142
CreateWindow( ) function, 17
CreateXLChart routine, 634-640
Criteria Pane (Remote OLE Component Manager window), 743
cryptography (X.509 standards), 885
Crystal Info, 919
Crystal Reports, 23, 138, 181-182
Crystal Reports Pro 4.5, 918-919
CSMA/CD (Carrier Sense Multiple Access with Collision Detection), 58

CTI (computer telephone interface) systems, 854-856
cursors (GUI settings), 941-943
custom controls, 166-167
Custom Controls dialog box, 167
custom drivers (databases), 121, 131, 135-136
customizing Query Builder applications, 786-787
CutItem_Click routine, 339, 424
cutting
OLTP client application form items, 425
OLTP client application forms, 339

D

D (Data Channel) Channel, Narrowband ISDN, 83
DAO (data access objects), 118, 120, 579, 691
data collision (databases), 114, 223
DATA command, 805
data concurrency (databases), 112-113, 224
data constructs (SQL Server), 756-758
data controls (databases), 119, 122-126
accessing, 126
binding to RDCs, 120
drawbacks, 125-126
hiding, 124
properties, 122-125

data coordination (servers), 35
Data Definition Language (DDL), 656
data dictionaries, 110-111, 759
Data Encryption Standard (DES), e-mail security, 892
data entry (database tables), 233-234
data integrity (databases), 111-112, 881-882
Data Manager, 179-180
Data Manager utility, 136-137
Data Manipulation Language (DML), 656
data rule integrity (databases), 111
data security (databases), 882
data sources
    creating for Table Builder/Query Builder applications, 771-772
    information displays, 770-771
    ODBC, 693-694
data transfer protocols, 61-64
data transfer rates, 81-84
    ATM networks, 89-93
    Ethernet networks, 59
    Fast Ethernet networks, 59
    FDDI networks, 61
    Narrowband ISDN networks, 83
    Token-Ring networks, 60
data types
    Collection data types, 176

SQL data types for ODBC, 663
SQL Servers, 760-762
strings, 193, 197
data warehouses, 37-38
data-level security (databases), 889-890
database owners (SQL Servers), 758
database servers, 31
DatabaseName property (data controls), 123
databases
    Access
        encryption, 909, 910
        implementing SQL, 656-660
        logons, 548-549
    accessing, 122-131, 146
        with custom drivers, 131, 135-136
        with data controls, 122-126
        with RDOs, 128-129
    Administrator accounts, 568
    BLOBs, 140
    bound controls, 119, 125
    buffers, 127
        flushing, 125
        variables, 127
    catalogs, 759
    centralizing, 116
    client application logons, 570-574
    commercial software, 914-917
    controls, 119
    creating, 231-249, 557
        with automated routines, 250-255
        with Data Manager, 136-137

with Table Builder application, 765-766
custom drivers, 121, 135-136
DAOs, 120
data collision, 114, 223
data concurrency, 112-113, 224
data controls, 119, 122-126
    accessing, 126
    drawbacks, 125-126
    hiding, 124
data dictionaries, 110-111
data integrity, 111-112, 881-882
Data Manager utility, 136-137
data rule integrity, 111
data security, 882
DDE (Dynamic Data Exchange), 138
decentralizing, 116
decryption, 563
dependent key fields, 101-102
directories, creating, 230-231
display methods, 98
DSS client application access, 453
editing, 127
encryption, 559, 563
flat transactions, 112
flat-file databases, 99, 107
FlushTime, 515
importing/exporting information with ODBC, 705
indexes, 98-99, 139
ISAM drivers, 131, 133

databases

JET engines, 120, 131-134, 170-172
joins, 102-104
key fields, 101-102
locking, 141-142
monitoring free space, 220, 512
navigating
   with data controls, 122
   with Form_Paint ( ) routine, 343-344
normalization, 106-109
objects
   locking, 556-557
   ownership, 557-558, 562
   permissions, assigning, 561-562
   referencing, 145
   security, 574
ODBC, 120
   access, 549
   API, 134
   connections, 559-561, 768-772
OLE automation, 138
OLE objects, embedding, 140
OLTP client application access, 357
opening, 125
optimistic locking, 143
page locking, 143
pessimistic locking, 143
primary key fields, 101-102
printing software, 918-920
queries, 102, 139, 480
   building with Query Builder application, 784-786
   storing with QueryDef, 136
QueryDef objects, 140
RDOs, 120
recordsets, 125, 128
   creating, 142
   locking, 141
referencing, 101
referential integrity, 115-116, 170-171
relational databases, 99-104
reopening, 125
reports, 23, 138, 181-182
   printing, 564
   software, 918-920
result sets, 102, 126
scaling
   to SQL Server databases, 121
   with Upsizing Wizard, 137
searching, 198, 206
security, 564-565, 889-891, 908-909
   implementing, 898-899
   planning, 546-547, 897-898
   protocols, 551
   system-level security, 547-550
   testing, 573
   upgrading, 899
   via Visual Basic, 900-910
servers, 914-917
SQL programming language, 104-106
SQL security, 891
SQL Server databases
   client application permissions, 684-685
   creating, 668-670, 672-680
   devices, creating, 669
   exporting to other database servers, 687-688
   ODBC connections, 670-671
   user accounts, creating, 682-683
   workgroups, adding user accounts to, 683-688
   workgroups, creating, 681
storage devices, 757, 763-768
SyncPoints, 115
tables, 96-98
   accessing, 269-270
   creating, 221-223, 226-227, 231-249
   creating with automated routines, 250-255
   creating with Table Builder application, 766-768
   data access, 128
   data entry, 233-234
   joins, 655-656
   naming, 231
   normalizing, 229-230
   relations, 226
   security, 565-570
   splitting, 244
   upsizing to SQL Server databases, 675

testing after upsizing, 680-687
time stamps, 114
tool add-ons, 923-924
tools, 136-138
transactions, 141-144
   consistency, 114-115
   log files, 757
uninterpreted SQL functions, 145
updating, 141
upsized
   examining with attached tables, 678
   examining with SQL Object Manager, 679-681
   examining with SQL Server Browser, 678-679
upsizing to SQL Server databases, 668-680
Upsizing Wizard, 137
user accounts
   adding to workgroups, 555-556
   creating, 555, 561
   passwords, 563
   permissions, 557-559
   privileges, 556
   security IDs, 550-552, 900-902
workgroups, 546
   Administrator, 553
   creating, 554-555, 561
   naming, 554
   passwords, 563
   permissions, 557-559
   PersonalIDs, 554
   privileges, 556
   security, 907-908
   security IDs, 550-552, 900-902

workspace objects, 564-565
see also client applications
DataChanged property (bound controls), 171
DataField property (bound controls), 171
DataSource property (bound controls), 171
DateAdd function, 515
dBase security (databases), 890-891
dbOpenDynaset command, 686
dbOpenTable command, 686
DCE (Distributed Computing Environment), 40, 724
DDE (Dynamic Data Exchange), 188-192
   accessing from Visual Basic, 192
   databases, 138
   events, 192
   links, 191
   methods, 192
   OLE comparison, 189-190
   properties, 192
DDL (Data Definition Language), SQL, 656
debuggers (IDE), 173
Debugging tools (VBA), 594-595
decentralizing databases, 116
decision support system client applications, *see* **DSS client applications**
decision support systems (client/server computing), 36

DECLARE command, 664
declaring
   API functions, 17, *302*
   routines
      for DSS client application forms, 477, 486, 490
      for OLTP client application forms, 306, 340, 344, 428, 433, 437, 443
      for OLTP client applications, 392-393
      for Pseudo Server applications, 511
      for Pseudo Server remote access, 800
      for Query Builder applications, 784
      for Table Builder application forms, 773-774
   variables for forms, 8
DECODE function, 645
decryption (databases), 563
DELETE command (SQL), 647
Delete Data permissions (databases), 559
deleting form controls, 8
dependent key fields (databases), 101-102
dependent objects, 579
DES (Data Encryption Standard), e-mail security, 892
devices
   creating for database storage, 764
   SQL Server databases, creating, 669

dialects

dialects (SQL), 105, 644
dialog boxes
  Custom Controls, 167
  Error Handling, 961-962
  Project Preferences, 732
  References, 167
Dialog objects (Excel), 623
DialogFrame objects (Excel), 624
DialogSheet objects (Excel), 624
directories (databases), creating, 230-231
directory services (networks), 45, 883-887
DisplayAlerts property (Excel Application objects), 613
displaying
  compound documents, 722
  Excel charts in DSS client applications, 638-640
  fields in database tables, 235
  Load event methods for forms, 8
  macros, 591
  objects
    methods, 593
    properties, 593
  OLTP client application forms, *339,* 531
  primary event code for form controls, 8
DisplayXLChart routine, 638-640
DISTINCT statement (SQL SELECT command), 649

Distinct TCP/IP, 921-922
Distributed Computing Environment (DCE), 40, 724
distributed data (client/server computing), 109-116
Distributed OLE, 190, 724, 751
distributed processing (client/server computing), 39-40
DLLs (dynamic link libraries), 10, 14-16, 917-920
  memory size, 6
  simulating with Visual Basic, 169-170
  TAPI, 858
DML (Data Manipulation Language), SQL, 656
DocFile Explorer, 722
DocFile Viewer (OLE structured storage), 722
DoEvents routine, 423
DoFiveMinUpdate routine, 511
DoHourUpdate routine, 511
Drawing Objects (Excel), 621-622
drivers
  custom drivers, 121, 131, 135-136
  ISAM drivers, 131-133
  ODBC drivers, 120, 662-663, 694, 697-698
    JET engine compatibility, 704
    Visual Basic access, 691-693

DROP command (SQL), 647
DSS (decision support system) client applications, 217-220, 450-452
  creating, 453-454
  database access, 453
  displaying Excel charts in, 638-640
  executable files, creating, 522-523
  executing, 539-542
  files, 452
  forms
    activating, 489, 496
    adding code, 476-497
    controls, 457-476
    controls, adding code, 483-484, 488-490, 494-497
    controls, screen default values, 488, 494
    creating, 454-496
    creating for Excel charts, 637-638
    loading, 483-484, 489, 496
    menus, adding code, 484-486
    navigating, 452
    tab controls, 455
    unloading, 484
  INI files
    creating, 454
    modifying, 571
  installation disks, creating, 524
  integrating with Excel through OLE Automation, 633-640
  reports, 450, 539-542
  upgrading with RDOs, 708-710

Dynamic Data Exchange, *see* **DDE**
dynamic link libraries, *see* **DLLs**
Dynamic SQL, 645
dynasets, *see* **recordsets**

E

e-mail
    client/server computing support, 44-45
    messaging services, 821-827
    security, 875, 891-895
    transmission rates, 822
ECB (Electronic Codebook) algorithm mode, e-mail security, 891
editing
    databases, 127
    macros, 591
    OLTP client applications, 214-216
        forms, 531, 534, 536
        menus, 305
        text box controls, 405
    records, 269
Editing tools (VBA), 594-595
EIS (Enterprise information systems), 37
Electronic Codebook (ECB) algorithm mode, e-mail security, 891
embedding
    objects, 720
    OLE objects in databases, 140
encapsulation, 151-152
    protocols, 28
    transactions, 36
    variables, 9

encryption
    Access databases, 909-910
    databases, 559, 563
    e-mail, 891-895
Enterprise Edition (Visual Basic), 160
Enterprise information systems (EIS), 37
Entry SQL, 644
EOFAction property (data controls), 124
equi-joins, 656
error checking (client applications), 211
Error function, 957
error handling (centralized), 961-964
Error Handling dialog box, 961-962
error handling routines, 956-961
Error objects, 176
Error statement, 959
Error$ function, 957
errors
    client/server computing systems, 964-966
    events, 961
    generating, 959
    log files, 963-964
    OLE, 749
    returned processing, 956-957
    system errors, checking, 957
    trapping, 957-959
    unanticipated, 959-960
    values out of range, 964
Ethernet transport protocol, 58
event handlers (VBA), 590

events
    DDE events, 192
    errors, 961
    Excel objects, 624-626
    LinkExecute, 193
    Visual Basic orientation, 11-12
Excel
    Chart Wizard, 606
    macros
        ChartTest macro, 608
        exporting into projects, 626
        recording in VBA, 605-608
        running, 615
    objects
        Addin objects, 622
        Application objects, 612-615
        Border objects, 615
        Chart objects, 610-612, 620
        ChartGroup objects, 620
        Dialog objects, 623
        DialogFrame objects, 624
        DialogSheet objects, 624
        Drawing Objects, 621-622
        events, 624-626
        Font objects, 615
        forms, 608-610
        integrating with DSS client applications through OLE Automation, 633-640
        Interior objects, 615
        Menubar objects, 623
        Name objects, 616

Excel

Outline objects, 618
PageSetup objects, 616
PivotTable objects, 618
Range objects, 618
referencing, 609, 612
Routing Slip objects, 620
Scenario objects, 618
Toolbar objects, 623
user interface objects, 622
Workbook objects, 616-617
Worksheet objects, 617-619
OLE Automation, 598-599, 630-633
executable files (.EXE), 10-11
creating for client applications, 522-523
executing
client applications, 204
DSS client applications, 539-542
OLE Servers, 735
OLTP client applications, 349, 447, 526-539
Pseudo Server applications, 542-544
server applications, 196, 204
Table Builder applications, 780
exiting
OLTP client application forms, 339, 419
OLTP client applications, 424, 531
ExitItem_Click routine, 339, 424, 818
explicit permissions, 904

ExportChartItem_Click routine, 636
exporting
database data with ODBC, 705
Excel macros into projects, 626
SQL Server databases to other database servers, 687-688
Extended functions (ODBC SQL), 662
Extended MAPI, 45, 828
extended services (TAPI), 867-868
extending client applications with other programs, 630
extensions (filenames), 174

F

Fast Ethernet transport protocol, 59
FDDI (Fiber Distributed Data Interface) transport protocol, 60
fiber optic cabling, 57-58
fields (database tables), 98
displaying, 235
inserting, 232
null fields, 144-145
sorting, 268
file monikers, 723
file objects, 175
file servers, 31, 66-67
FileExists function, 796
filename extensions (project files), 174
files (DSS client applications), 452

filtering packets, 896
FindDBInfo routine, 512
FindFirst method, 269
finding records, 99, 269, 399, 438
finger protocol, 876
firewalls (networks), 895-897
flat transactions (databases), 36, 112
flat-file databases, 99
converting to relational databases, 106-109
drawbacks, 107
flushing database buffers, 125
FlushTime (databases), 515
Font objects (Excel), 615
For Each statement, 176
For...Each...Next loops (VBA), 586
Form_Activate routine, 333, 342, 348, 489, 496
Form_Click event routine, 590
Form_Load event routine, 202
Form_Load routine, 333-334, 343, 348, 419, 431-432, 436, 441, 447, 483-484, 489, 496, 516, 819
Form_Paint routine, 343, 432, 442, 447
Form_Unload routine, 334-335, 420, 484, 517, 819
formats (VBP files), 12
forms, 7-8
as objects, 169
client applications, 199-200

forms

controls, 7-8
creating to access Excel objects, 608-610
database normalization, 109
DSS client applications
   activating, 489, 496
   adding code, 476-497
   controls, 457-476
   controls, adding code, 483-484, 488-490, 494-497
   controls, screen default values, 488, 494
   creating, 454-496
   creating for Excel charts, 637-638
   loading, 483-484, 489, 496
   menus, adding code, 484-486
   navigating, 452
   tab controls, 455
   unloading, 484
GUIs, 944-945
Load event method, displaying, 8
naming conventions, 194
OLTP client applications, 267-269
   activating, 333, 342, 348
   adding code, 305-349, 392-447
   adding items to, 435
   centering, 304
   checking for modifications, 336
   combo box controls, 278, 284, 285, 292
   command buttons, 276-278, 280, 285, 294, 297, 300

   controls, 290, 296-299, 373-393, 411-422
   controls, adding code, 341-342, 347-349, 429-446
   controls, placing, 361-371
   controls, routines, 325-339
   controls, setting tag properties to text properties, 345
   controls, setting to empty values, 347
   copying, 339
   copying items from, 424
   creating, 273-349, 359-447
   cutting, 339
   cutting items from, 424
   declaring routines, 306, 340
   deleting items from, 436
   displaying, 339, 531
   editing, 531, 534, 536
   exiting, 339, 419
   frame controls, 279, 300
   grids, 279, 288, 321-322, 335, 407
   initializing, 333-334
   key press events, 336, 421
   labels, 278, 281, 286, 295, 301
   list box controls, 297, 300
   list box controls, loading, 340-341

   listbox controls, creating, 428
   loading, 343, 348, 420, 431-432, 437, 442, 447
   menus, adding code, 422-427
   menus, creating, 372
   navigating, 532
   navigating with Next command button, 415
   navigating with Previous command button, 417
   pasting, 339
   pasting items from, 424
   printing items from, 424
   properties, 276-278
   read-only text box controls, 283
   reports, 398
   saving, 276
   screen control default values, 406
   screen default values, 321
   storing, 296
   text box controls, 281-283, 285, 291-295
   text box controls, editing, 405
   text box controls, focus, 421
   text box controls, moving, 402
   text box controls, positioning over grids, 320

forms

text box controls, recovering lost focus, 337
text box controls, selecting all text from, 337
text box controls, shifting focus, 338-339
unloading, 335, 420
user interaction, implementing, 423
writing information from records, 317-320
Pseudo Server applications
  controls, 503-510
  controls, adding code, 515-518
  creating, 502-518
  loading, 516
  unloading, 517
  updating, 511
Query Builder applications, 782-783
remote client applications
  adding code, 814-821
  controls, 808-814
  creating, 807-808
  loading, 819
  unloading, 819
server applications, 193-195
Table Builder applications, 772-780
variables, declaring, 8
Visual Basic, 6
forms/controls objects, 175
fragile base class (objects), 154-155

fragmentation (packets), 62
frame controls
  OLTP client application forms, 279, 300
  Pseudo Server application forms, 799
Frame relay protocol, 78
frames (Token-Ring networks), 60
frameworks (object classes), 151
.FRM (text form) files, 7
FROM statement (SQL SELECT command), 648
.FRX (binary form) files, 7
Full SQL, 644
full telephony (TAPI), 863-868
functions
  AddRef, 719
  aggregate functions (SQL), 650-652
  API functions, 16-17, 135, 302
  AppendChunk, 140
  Avg, 650
  Clone, 722
  CompactDatabase, 133
  CopyTo, 722
  Core functions (ODBC API), 699-701
  Count, 650
  CreateObject, 601
  CreateWindow( ), 17
  DateAdd, 515
  Error, 957
  Error$, 957
  FileExists, 796
  GetAppPath( ), 304
  GetObject, 601

IsNull( ), 144
IStorage, 722
IStream, 722
IUnknown, 719
Level 1 ODBC API, 701-702
Level 2 ODBC API, 702-703
LoadResData, 176
LoadResPicture, 176
LoadResString, 176
Max, 650
Min, 650
MoveElementTo, 722
ODBC API functions, 129-131
ODBC SQL Core functions, 661-662
ODBC SQL Extended functions, 662
QueryInterface, 719
ReadINI, 305
Release, 719
RepairDatabase, 133
Set, 145
Simple MAPI functions, 828
SQL functions, 644-646
SQL PassThrough, 145
SQLGetInfo, 698
Sum, 650
TAPI basic services, 864-865
TAPI extended services, 868-872
TAPI supplementary services, 866-867
tapiRequestMakeCall, 795
uninterpreted SQL functions, passing to databases, 145
see also commands; methods; routines

G

Gantt/VBX add-on, 928
gateway ODBC drivers, 698
gateways, 52, 65-66, 897
General Protection Faults, *see* GPFs
generating errors, 959
Geoport telephony standards, 871
GetAppPath( ) function, 304
GetChecksum routine, 819
GetObject function, 601
Global Error routine, 963
Global modules
  adding code to, 301-349
  creating, 301
  DSS client applications, 453
global unique identifiers (GUIDs), OLE objects, 719
global variables, 9
GLOBAL.BAS files
  adding code to, 301-349
  creating, 301
Global.BAS files, 453
GPFs (General Protection Faults), 17
Graphic User Interfaces, *see* GUIs
grd_Main_Click routine, 335, 421
grd_Main_KeyPress routine, 336, 421
grids
  DSS client applications, 218
  OLTP client application forms, 214, 279, 288, 321-322, 335, 407

GROUP BY statement (SQL SELECT command), 653-655
grouping result sets, 653-655
groupware, 44
Groupware Messaging Servers, 842
groupware servers, 32-33
GUIDs (global unique identifiers), OLE objects, 719
GUIs (Graphic User Interfaces), 938
  consistency, 939-940
  cursor settings, 941-943
  design flow, 945-947
  forms, 944-945
  Help options, 948-953
  icons, 947
  menu items, 947
  message boxes, 940-941
  navigating with tabs, 947-948
  replicating, 938-939
  screen layout, 943-948
  status bars, 941-943
  windows, 944-945

H

H Channel, Narrowband ISDN, 84
hardware
  ATM networks, 92
  networks, 64-66
  switching, 91
  Windows NT Server requirements, 69
  Windows NT Workstation requirements, 69
HAVING clause (SQL SELECT command), 654-665

HDLC (High Level Data Link Control) protocol, 76
headers
  IP packets, 63
  IPX/SPX packets, 61
  TCP packets, 63
Help, 948-949
  context-sensitivity, 950
  files, 949-950
  form controls, 7
  hotspot files, 951
  SHED files, 951
  status bar, 952-953
  Tool tips, 953
Help file compilers, 18-19
Help File Editor add-ons, 913-914
Help method (Excel Application objects), 614
hiding data controls, 124
High Level Data Link Control (HDLC) protocol, 76
.HLP (Help) files, 10
Hot Spot Editors, 19
hotspot files (Help), 951
hubs (networks), 66
hypertext (Hot Spot Editors), 19

I

icons (GUIs), 947
IDE (Integrated Development Environment), 172-176
IDEA (International Data Encryption Algorithm), e-mail security, 892-893

IEEE (Institute of Electronic and Electrical Engineers), 72
Imageknife add-on, 928
imagelist control (Windows 95), 166
images (hot spots), 19
immediate replication (servers), 41
implementing
   SQL
      in Access databases, 656-660
      in ODBC, 660-663
   SQL Servers, 663-665
implicit permissions, 904
importing database data with ODBC, 705
IN command (SQL), 651
in-place activation
   menus, 168
   objects, 721
in-process objects (COM), 715
in-process OLE Automation servers, 162, 169-170
incremental compiling (applications), 175
Indexed Sequential Access Method drivers, *see* **ISAM drivers**
indexes
   database tables, 98-99, 139
   SQL Servers, 763
information hiding, 152, 178
inheritance (objects), 153-154, 715-716
.INI (Initialization) files, 10

changing settings, 582
client applications
   modifications after database upsizing, 685-686
   modifying, 524-525, 570-572
default settings, 582
DSS client applications
   creating, 454
   modifying, 571
JET engine settings, 132
ODBC, 696-697
OLTP client applications, 268
   creating, 271-272, 358-359
   modifying, 571
   reading, 305
   writing parameter values to, 305
Pseudo Server applications
   creating, 502
   modifying, 572
initializing OLTP client application forms, 333-334
inner joins (database queries), 104
INSERT command (SQL), 647
Insert Data permissions (databases), 559
Insert Records command button (Table Builder application forms), 776-777
inserting
   command buttons in client application forms, 199

controls
   in forms, 7
   in server applications, 194
fields in database tables, 232
objects
   as controls, 168-169
   in project file toolboxes, 167
routines
   in DSS client application form controls, 483-484, 488-490, 494-497
   in DSS client application form menus, 484-486
   in DSS client application forms, 476-497
   in OLTP client application form controls, 429-431, 435-437, 440-442, 446
   in OLTP client application form menus, 422-427
   in OLTP client application forms, 305-349, 392-447
   in Pseudo Server application form controls, 515-518
   in Pseudo Server application form menus, 518
   in Pseudo Server application forms, 511-518
   in remote client application forms, 814-821

text boxes in client
application forms, 200
**Install Shield utility,
931-932**
**installation disks (client
applications),
20-22, 524**
**installation utilities,
931-932**
**installing remote server
applications on Pseudo
Servers, 799-806**
instances, 9-10, 150
**Instancing property (OLE
objects), 729**
**instantiating objects from
classes, 715**
**Institute of Electronic
and Electrical Engineers
(IEEE), 72**
**Integrated Development
Environment (IDE),
172-176**
**Integrated Services
Digital Network,** *see*
ISDN
integrating client applications with other programs, 630
interfaces
GUIs, 938
consistency, 939-940
cursor settings, 941-943
design flow, 945-947
forms, 944-945
Help options, 948-953
icons, 947
menu items, 947
*message boxes,
940-941*
*navigating with tabs,
947-948*
replicating, 938-939
screen layout, 943-948
status bars, 941-943
windows, 944-945
messaging services,
823-827
networks (security),
888-910
OLE, 716-718
Visual Basic (add-ons),
926-929
Windows 95 (Visual
Basic support), 166
interfacing networks, 72
intergalactic networks, 42
**Interior objects
(Excel), 615**
Intermediate SQL, 644
**International Consultative Committee on
Telegraphy and Telephony,** *see* **CCITT**
**International Data
Encryption Algorithm
(IDEA), e-mail security,
892-893**
**International Standards
Organization (ISO), 72**
**International Telecommunications Union
Telecommuninication
Standard Sector (ITU-TSS), 74**
Internet security, 880
**Internet Layer
(TCP/IP), 63**
Internet Protocol, *see* **IP**
**Internetwork Packet
Exchange,** *see* **IPX
protocol**
**interpreted programming
languages, 5**
intruders (client/server
computing systems), 875
inventory client applications, 215-216
invoice client applications, *see* OLTP client
applications
**IP (Internet Protocol),
62-63**
**IPX (Internetwork Packet
eXchange) protocol,
61-62**
ISAM drivers, 131, 133
**ISDN (Integrated Services
Digital Network),
74-75, 849**
B-ISDN (Broadband
ISDN), 87-89
bonding architecture, 85
channels, 82
Narrowband ISDN,
81-86
NI-1 (National
ISDN 1), 81
NI-2 (National
ISDN-2), 81
NI-3 (National
ISDN-3), 81
ordering codes, 81
IsNull( ) function, 144
**ISO (International
Standards Organization), 72**
IStorage function, 722
IStream function, 722
item monikers, 723
**ITU-TSS (International
Telecommunications
Union Telecommunication Standard
Sector), 74**
IUnknown function, 719

J–K–L

JET (Joint Engine Technology) engines, databases, 120, 131-134, 170-172, 704
JET engine 2.5/3.0, 133-134
JOIN command (SQL), 106, 655-656
joins, 655-656

KB (Knowledge Base) files, 23
Kerberos password authentication, 888-889
key fields (databases), 101-102
key press events (OLTP client application forms), 336, 421
Knowledge Base (KB) files, 23

labels (OLTP client application forms), 278, 281, 286, 295, 301
LAN Server 4.0 for OS/2, 71
LANs (local area networks), 51
layers (TCP/IP), 63
LeadTools add-on, 928
Level 1 ODBC API functions, 701-702
Level 2 ODBC API functions, 702-703
libraries
 Access Basic code, 581-583
 see also DLLs
LIKE command (SQL), 652
line objects (TAPI full telephony), 863

line-continuation characters (VBA), 588
LinkExecute event, 193
LinkExecute event routine, 193
LinkExecute method, 193
linking objects, 720
links
 compound links, 203
 DDE, 191
list box controls
 creating for server applications, 195
 OLTP client application forms, 297, 300, 340-341, 428
List1_DblClick ( ) routine, 342
listings
 7.1 object groups for data access, 164-165
 10.1 MakeDB( ) routine, 250-255
 11.1 OLTP client application INI files, 272
 11.2 declaring routines for OLTP client application forms, 306
 12.1 OLTP client application INI files, 359
 12.2 declaring routines for OLTP client application forms, 393
 13.1 DSS client application INI files, 454
 14.1 Pseudo Server INI files, 502
 14.2 declaring routines in Pseudo Server application forms, 511

 15.1 OLTP client application INI file, 525
 16.1 creating database user accounts/ workgroups with Access Basic, 561
 16.2 assigning permissions to database objects, 562
 16.3 changing database object ownership, 562
 16.4 database account passwords, 563
 16.5 encrypting databases in Access Basic, 563
 16.6 modified INI files for OLTP client applications, 571
 16.7 modified INI files for OLTP client applications, 571
 16.8 modified INI files for DSS client applications, 571
 16.9 modified INI files for Pseudo Server applications, 572
 16.10 modified OLTP client application forms, 573
 17.1 Count property (object collections), 581
 17.2 INI file default settings, 582
 17.3 INI file settings, 582
 17.4 procedure-level variables, 584
 17.5 module-level variables, 585

17.6 project-level variables, 585
17.7 traditional location variables, 585
17.8 static variables, 586
17.9 traditional object reference, 586
17.10 With...End With object reference, 587
17.11 Nested With object reference, 587
17.12 With...End With interaction with other commands, 587
17.13 While...Wend loop, 588
17.14 Property Get routine, 589
17.15 Property Let routine, 589
17.16 Word Basic OLE Automation, 597
17.17 Excel OLE Automation, 599
17.18 Project OLE Automation, 600
18.1 Excel macros in VBA, 606
18.2 ChartTest macro, 608
18.3, Form_Load event code, 609
18.4 Command1 Click event, 610
18.5 exporting Excel macros into VB projects, 626-627
18.6 exporting Excel macros into VB projects, 628
19.1 CreateXLChart routine, 634-635

19.2 ExportChartItem_Click routine, 636
19.3 Form_Load routine for Excel charts in DSS client applications, 638
19.4 DisplayXLChart routine, 638-640
19.5 ChartWindowItem_Click routine, 639
21.1 client application INI files, 686
21.2 client application INI files after database upsizing, 686
21.3 client application routine modifications after database upsizing, 687
22.1 RegisterDatabase method, 708
22.2 opening ODBC data source connections, 709-710
24.1 OLE object class properties, 731
24.2 Property Get/Let routines, 732
24.3 OLE Client module code, 737
26.1 TAPI programming, 795
26.2 declaring routines for Pseudo Server remote access, 800
26.3 OnComm event routine, 801-802
26.4 RemoteHandler routine, 803-805
26.5 cmd_Connect_Click routine, 815-816

26.6 cmd_Receive_Click routine, 817-818
26.7 cmd_Send_Click routine, 818
26.8 WaitForValue routine, 819-820
26.9 OLE Messaging code, 841-842
27.1 TAPI code, 862-863
A.1 GUI controls, 948
A.2 GUI controls, 948
A.3 Help status bar, 953
B.1 On Error command, 957
B.2 suspending error trapping, 958
B.3 ShowError routine, 962-963
B.4 Global Error routine, 963
Load event method (forms), 8
LoadBuildList routine, 428, 433
loading
DSS client application forms, 483-484, 489, 496
list box controls for OLTP client application forms, 340-341
OLTP client application forms, 343, 348, 419, 431-432, 436, 442, 447
Pseudo Server application forms, 516
remote client application forms, 819
LoadItemList routine, 340-341, 429, 434

LoadLocation routine, 399, 438
LoadResData function, 176
LoadResPicture function, 176
LoadResString function, 176
local area networks, *see* LANs
local objects (COM), 715
local variables, 585
locking
  database objects, 556-557
  databases, 141-142
  objects, 174
  pages (databases), 143
  records, 144
    in database tables, 114
    optimistic locking, 560
  recordsets, 141
log files (errors), 963-964
logical operators, 650
logons
  Access databases, 548-549
  client applications, 570-574
  WFW workstations, 547-548
  Windows 95 workstations, 548
loops
  For...Each...Next loops, 586
  While...Wend loops, 588
Lotus Notes groupware servers, 32
Lotus Notes messaging services, 843-844

M

Macro Recorder, 590-592
macros
  displaying, 591
  editing, 591
  Excel
    ChartTest macro, 608
    exporting into projects, 626
    recording in VBA, 605-608
    running, 615
  recording in VBA, 590-592
mail servers, 44-45
.MAK files (Visual Basic 3.0), 12
MakeDB( ) routine (listing 10.1), 250-255
MANs (Metropolitan Area Networks), 51
manual links (DDE), 191
MAPI (Messaging Application Program Interface), 28, 45, 794, 827-829
  connections to client/server computing systems, 793-796
  controls, 830-839
  Extended MAPI, 828
  Simple MAPI, 827-828
  vs. CMC, 825
Max function, 650
MD5 (Message Digest 5), e-mail security, 893
media streams (TAPI connections), 860
memory
  runtime library size, 6
  Windows NT Server 3.51 requirements, 69

Menu Designer, 288
menu objects, 175
Menubar objects (Excel), 623
menus
  DSS client application forms, adding code, 484-486
  GUIs, 947
  in-place activation, 168
  OLTP client application forms
    adding code, 422-427
    creating, 288, 372
    editing, 305
    routines, 339
  Pseudo Server applications, adding code, 518
  user-interface negotiation, 168
merging result sets, 655
message boxes (GUIs), 940-941
Message Digest 5 (MD5), e-mail security, 893
message frames (Token-Ring networks), 60
messages, 152
messaging (client/server computing support), 44-45
Messaging Application Program Interface, *see* MAPI
messaging client applications, 842-847
messaging server applications, 842-847
messaging services, 790, 821-827
  complex, 823
  interfaces, 823-827

navigating 1019

OLE Messaging services, 829, 840-842
private, 846-849
public, 846-849
simple, 823
metacomputing (client/server computing), 40
methods, 7, 149
CompactDatabase, 563
DDE methods, 192
Excel Application objects, 614-615
Excel Workbook objects, 617
Excel Worksheet objects, 617-619
FindFirst, 269
LinkExecute, 193
MAPI Message controls, 835-836
MAPI Session controls, 831
objects, 578, 593
OLE object classes, 730-732
RegisterDatabase, 708
Metropolitan Area Networks, *see* **MANs**
Microsoft Access, *see* **Access**
Microsoft Developer Network, 23
Microsoft Exchange groupware servers, 32
Microsoft Exchange messaging services, 844
Microsoft Mail messaging services, 842-843
Microsoft Network (MSN), 932-933
Microsoft Project
OLE Automation, 599-600
VBA environment, 595

Microsoft Visual FoxPro, 916
middleware (client/server computing), 26-29
Min function, 650
Mindwire client/server development kit, 922-923
mirroring servers, 42, 881
modems, connections to client/server computing systems, 791-796
Modify Design permissions (databases), 558
module-level variables, 585
modules, 9
Global
  adding code to, 301-349
  creating, 301
  DSS client applications, 453
Visual Basic, 6
monikers, 722-723
monikers (OLE), 714
monitoring free space in databases, 220, 512
MoveElementTo function, 722
MoveTextBox routine, 316-317, 402-403
moving text box controls in OLTP client application forms, 319, 402
MSN (Microsoft Network), 932-933
Multiuser/ODBC option set (Access), 560
MyOpenPort routine, 821

N

Name objects (Excel), 616
Name property
OLE objects, 730
Workbook objects (Excel), 617
Worksheet objects (Excel), 619
naming
database tables, 231
database workgroups, 554
menus in OLTP client applications, 288
naming conventions (variables/forms/controls), 194
Narrowband ISDN, 81-86
National ISDN 1 (NI-1), 81
National ISDN-2 (NI-2), 81
National ISDN-3 (NI-3), 81
navigating
databases
  with data controls, 122
  with Form_Paint ( ) routine, 343-344
DSS client application forms, 452
DSS client application reports, 539-542
GUIs with tabs, 947-948
object collections, 581
OLTP client application forms, 532
  with Next command button, 329, 415

navigating

with Previous
command button
331, 417
result sets, 126
NDS (NetWare Directory Services), 885-886
nesting
SQL triggers, 665
With...End With statements, 587
NetBEUI (NetBIOS Extended User Interface) protocol, 64
NetBIOS Extended User Interface (NetBEUI) protocol, 64
NetWare, 70-71, 887-888
NetWare 3.11, 70-71
NetWare 4.*x*, 71
NetWare Directory Services (NDS), 885-886
Network Interface Layer (TCP/IP), 63
network operating systems (NOS), 45, 61-64
AIX, 71
LAN Server 4.0 for OS/2, 71
NetWare, 70-71
security, 887
Solaris, 71
Windows NT 3.51, 67-69
networks, 50
ATM, 89-93
backbones, 52
bridges, 65
Broadband ISDN, 87-89
cabling, 55-58
client/server computing setup, 526

components, 51-53
connection technologies, 849-850
directory sevices, 883-887
Ethernet, 58-59
firewalls, 895-897
frame relay, 78
gateways, 65-66, 897
hardware, 64-66
hubs, 66
IEEE standards, 72
interfaces
design, 72
security, 888-910
intergalactic, 42
ISDN standards, 74-75, 849
LANs, 51
Narrowband ISDN, 81-86
NetWare
directory services, 885-886
security, 887-888
nodes, 53
OSI reference model, 72
packets, 53, 896
passwords, 888-889
peer-to-peer, 46-47
routers, 65, 896
security, 877-879
spoofing, 876
Token-Ring, 60
topologies, 53-55
transport protocols, 58-61
WANs, 51, 73-74
Windows NT
directory services, 886-887
Remote Access Services, 847

Windows NT 3.5, 887
X.25, 77
Next property (Excel Worksheet objects), 619
NI-1 (National ISDN 1), 81
NI-2 (National ISDN-2), 81
NI-3 (National ISDN-3), 81
nodes (networks), 53
normal forms (database normalization), 109
normalization (databases), 106-109
normalizing database tables, 229-230
NOS (network operating systems), 45, 61-64
AIX, 71
LAN Server 4.0 for OS/2, 71
NetWare, 70-71
security, 887
Solaris, 71
Windows NT 3.51, 67-69
Notepad utility, creating INI files with, 271
Notes HiTest Tools, 921
notify links (DDE), 191
null fields (database tables), 144-145

O

Object Browser, 163, 593-594, 734
object servers, 33-34
object-oriented analysis (OOA), 725
object-oriented programming, *see* OOP

objects, 9-10, 150, 163-165, 578
  call objects (TAPI full telephony), 863
  classes, 150
    frameworks, 151
    VBA, 153
  collections, 163-165, 580-581
    accessing single objects from, 581
    Count property, 581
    navigating, 581
  compatibility between programming languages, 157
  creating
    through COM, 716-718
    with Visual Basic, 601
  databases
    locking, 556-557
    ownership, 557-558, 562
    permissions, assigning, 561-562
    referencing, 145
    security, 574
  dependent objects, 579
  embedding, 720
  Error objects, 176
  Excel
    Addin objects, 622
    Application objects, 612-615
    Border objects, 615
    Chart objects, 620
    ChartGroup objects, 620
    charts, 610-612
    Dialog objects, 623
    DialogFrame objects, 624
    DialogSheet objects, 624
    Drawing Objects, 621-622
    events, 624-626
    Font objects, 615
    forms, 608-610
    Menubar objects, 623
    Name objects, 616
    Outline objects, 618
    PageSetup objects, 616
    PivotTable objects, 618
    Range objects, 618
    referencing, 609, 612
    Routing Slip objects, 620
    Scenario objects, 618
    Toolbar objects, 623
    user interface objects, 622
    Workbook objects, 616-617
    Worksheet objects, 617-619
  file objects, 175
  focus, shifting, 948
  forms/controls objects, 175
  fragile base class, 154-155
  groups for data access (listing 7.1), 164-165
  heirarchy in OLE client/server computing systems, 748
  in-place activation, 721
  in-process objects, 715
  information displays, 163, 593
  inheritance, 153-154, 715-716
  inserting
    as controls, 168-169
    in project file toolboxes, 167
  instances, 150
  instantiating from classes, 715
  line objects (TAPI full telephony), 863
  linking, 720
  local objects, 715
  locking, 174
  menu objects, 175
  methods, 578, 593
  monikers, 722-723
  network sharing, 183
  OLE
    creating, 714
    global unique identifiers, 719
    information displays, 734
    Instancing property, 729
    Name property, 730
    Public property, 730
    reference counts, 719
    referencing, 719
  OLE automation, 596-601
  phone objects (TAPI full telephony), 863
  polymorphism, 155
  prioritizing, 167
  private objects, 715
  properties, 578, 593
  property procedures, 178
  RDO, 184
  rdoColumn, 707
  rdoConnection, 707
  rdoEngine, 706
  rdoEnvironment, 707
  rdoError, 707
  rdoParameter, 708

objects

rdoPreparedStatement, 707
rdoRecordset, 708
rdoTable, 707
referencing, 166-167
remote objects, 715
uniform data transfer, 721
version controls, 155-156
Visual Basic, 6
OCX (OLE Custom Controls), 14-16, 165-166
ODBC (open database connectivity), 118, 120, 690-691
   components, 693-698
   connections, 695
   data sources, 693-694
   database access, 549
   database connections, 559-561, 768-772
   drivers, 120, 662-663, 694, 697-698
     JET engine compatibility, 704
     Visual Basic access, 691-693
   exporting SQL Server databases to other database servers, 687-688
   implementing SQL, 660-663
   INI files, 696-697
   SQL Core functions, 704
   SQL data types, 663
   SQL Extended functions, 705
   SQL Server database connections, 670-671
ODBC Administration utility, 670, 694-695
ODBC API, 134, 691, 694
   Core functions, 699-701
   Level 1 functions, 701-702
   Level 2 functions, 702-703
ODBC Call-Level Interface, 692
ODBC Driver Manager, 694
OLE (Object Linking and Embedding), 712-714
   clients, creating in Excel, 735-738
   Component Object Model, 714-718
   compound documents, 721-722
   Distributed OLE, 190, 724, 751
   errors, 749
   in-process Automation servers, 162
   interfaces, 716-718
   monikers, 714
   objects
     creating, 714
     embedding in databases, 140
     global unique identifiers, 719
     information displays, 734
     Instancing property, 729
     Name property, 730
     Public property, 730
     reference counts, 719
     referencing, 719
   out-of-process Automation servers, 162
   Registry, 749-750
   Remote OLE, 724, 739-745
   servers, 728, 748-751
     configurations, 732-734
     creating, 162, 169-170
     executing, 735
     menus, 168
     registering, 734-735
     security, 752
     toolbars, 168
     version control, 749
   structured storage, 721-722
   vs. DDE, 189-190
OLE Automation, 596, 714, 724
   Access Basic, 597
   databases, 138
   Excel, 598-599, 630, 631-633
   in Visual Basic, 162-165
   Microsoft Project, 599-600
   Word Basic, 597-598
OLE Broker online service, 933
OLE Custom Control files, *see* **OCX**
OLE Messaging, 829, 840-842
OLTP (online transaction processing) client applications, 36, 212-216, 352-354
   accessing, 269
   Autobuild Edit form, 216
   Cancel operation, 326
   command buttons, 214

compiling as stand-alone
  executable files,
  349, 447
confirming transactions,
  329-331
creating, 264-267,
  358-359
database access, 357
directory paths, return-
  ing, 304
editing, 214, 216
executable files, creating,
  522-523
executing, 349, 447,
  526-539
exiting, 424, 531
files, 355-357
forms, 267-269
  *activating, 333,
    342, 348*
  *adding code, 305-349,
    392-447*
  adding items to, 435
  centering, 304
  *checking for modifica-
    tions, 336*
  *combo box controls,
    278, 284-285, 292*
  *command buttons,
    276-280, 285, 294,
    297, 300*
  *controls, 290,
    296-299, 373-393,
    411-422*
  *controls, adding code,
    341-342, 347-349,
    429-437, 440-442,
    446*
  *controls, placing,
    361-371*
  *controls, routines,
    325-339*

*controls, setting tag
  properties to text
  properties, 345*
*controls, setting to
  empty values, 347*
copying, 339
*copying items
  from, 424*
*creating, 273-349,
  359-447*
cutting, 339
*cutting items
  from, 424*
*declaring routines,
  306, 340*
*deleting items
  from, 436*
displaying, 339, 531
*editing, 531,
  534, 536*
exiting, 339, 419
*frame controls,
  279, 300*
*grids, 279, 288,
  321-322, 335, 407*
initializing, 333-334
*key press events,
  336, 421*
*labels, 278, 281, 286,
  295, 301*
*list box controls, 297,
  300, 340-341, 428*
*loading, 343, 348,
  419, 431-432, 436,
  442, 447*
*menus, adding code,
  422-427*
menus, creating, 372
*navigating, 415-417,
  532*
pasting, 339
*pasting items
  from, 424*

*printing items
  from, 424*
properties, 276-278
*read-only text box
  controls, 283*
reports, 398
saving, 276
*screen control default
  values, 406*
*screen default
  values, 321*
storing, 296
*text box controls,
  281-283, 285,
  291-295*
*text box controls,
  editing, 405*
*text box controls,
  focus, 421*
*text box controls,
  moving, 402*
*text box controls,
  positioning over
  grids, 320*
*text box controls,
  recovering lost
  focus, 337*
*text box controls,
  selecting all text
  from, 337*
*text box controls,
  shifting focus,
  338-339*
unloading, 335, 420
*user interaction,
  implementing, 423*
*writing information
  from records,
  317-320*
INI files, 268, 525
  *creating, 271-272,
    358-359*
  modifying, 571

reading, 305
writing parameter values to, 305
installation disks, creating, 524
menus
adding code to, 339
creating, 288
editing, 305
navigating, 329-331
reports, 215, 331-333
updating, 322-324
On Error command, 957-959
online services, 932-933
online transaction processing, *see* **OLTP client applications**
OOA (object-oriented analysis), 725
OOP (object-oriented programming), 9, 148-153, 156, 578-581
drawbacks, 157-158
in Visual Basic, 152-153
integrating in client/server computing environments, 158
Open Database Connectivity, *see* **ODBC**
Open Exclusive permissions (databases), 558
Open Systems Interconnection (OSI) reference model, 72
Open/Run permissions (databases), 558
OpenDatabase command, 268
opening databases, 125
operating systems
security, 887
see also NOS

operation codes (Basic programming language), 5
operators
& operator, 145
comparison operators, 649
logical operators, 650
optimistic locking
databases, 143
records, 560
Oracle Power Objects database tool, 924
ORDER BY statement (SQL SELECT command), 652-653
ordering codes (ISDN), 81
OSI (Open Systems Interconnection) reference model, 72
out-of-process OLE Automation servers, 162
outer joins (database queries), 104, 656
Outline objects (Excel), 618
OwnerAccess options (SQL queries), 906
ownership (database objects), 557-558, 562

P

packets, 53
bridges, 65
Ethernet networks, 58
filtering, 896
fragmentation, 62
IPX, 61
recommended sizes, 62
repeaters, 64
routers, 65, 896

SPX, 61
Token-Ring networks, 60
tunneling, 61
page locking (databases), 143
PageSetup objects (Excel), 616
palettes
color palette, 173
Control Palette, 7
parameters
client application INI files, 524
routines, 304
ParseLine routine, 802-803
passing uninterpreted SQL functions to databases, 145
Password variables (client applications), 572
passwords
database user accounts/workgroups, 563
Kerberos authentication, 888-889
networks, 888-889
PasteItem_Click routine, 339, 424
pasting
OLTP client application form items, 424
OLTP client application forms, 339
paths (OLTP client applications), returning, 304
Pause routine, 820
PC-based CTI systems, 854
peer-to-peer networks, 46-47

properties

PEM (Privacy Enhanced Mail), e-mail security, 893
periodic replication, *see* skulking
permissions
 Access databases, 904
 client application user accounts/workgroups, 567-570
 database objects, assigning, 561-562
 database user accounts/workgroups, 557-559
 SQL Server databases, 684-685
PersonalIDs (workgroups), 554
pessimistic locking (databases), 143
PGP (Pretty Good Privacy), e-mail security, 893-894
phone objects (TAPI full telephony), 863
phone-based CTI systems, 855
PivotTable objects (Excel), 618
plug-ins, 10, 14-16, 135-136
point-of-sale client applications, *see* OLTP client applications
Point-to-Point Protocol (PPP), 86
pointer monikers, 723
polymorphism (objects), 155
PPP (Point-to-Point Protocol), 86
Pretty Good Privacy (PGP), e-mail security, 893-894

Previous property (Excel Worksheet objects), 619
PRI (Primary Rate Interface), Narrowband ISDN, 84
primary event code (form controls), displaying, 8
primary key fields (databases), 101-102
Primary Rate Interface (PRI), Narrowband ISDN, 84
printing
 database security reports, 564
 OLTP client application form items, 424
 OLTP client application reports, 331-333
PrintItem_Click routine, 424
prioritizing objects, 167
Privacy Enhanced Mail (PEM), e-mail security, 893
private messaging services, 846-849
private objects (COM), 715
proactive servers, 189
procedural programming, 149
procedure-level variables, 584
procedures
 property procedures, 178, 588-589
 server storage, 35
Professional Edition (Visual Basic), 160
program files, 10-11
programming (TAPI), 795-796

programs, *see* applications
Project (Microsoft)
 OLE Automation, 599-600
 VBA environment, 595
project files
 directories, creating, 230-231
 executable files, creating, 522-523
 filename extension, 174
 registering in OLE Registry, 749-750
 resource files, 175-176
 storing, 523-524
 team coordination, 182
 toolbox objects, inserting, 167
 user privileges, 182
 see also client applications; server applications
Project Preferences dialog box, 732
project-level variables, 585
properties, 149
 bound controls, 171-172
 client applications, setting, 200-202
 data controls, 122-125
 DDE properties, 192
 Excel
  Application objects, 612-615
  DialogFrame objects, 624
  Routing Slip objects, 620
  Workbook objects, 617
  Worksheet objects, 617-619

1025

properties

form controls, 7
MAPI Message controls, 832-835
MAPI Session controls, 830
objects, 578, 593
OLE object classes, 730-732
OLTP client application forms, 276-278
server applications, 195-197
Property Get routine, 589, 731-732
Property Let routine, 589, 732
Property procedures (VBA), 178, 588-589
PROTECT command (database dBase security), 890
Protect method (Excel Worksheet objects), 619
protocols
ATM, 89-93
CCSS7, 83
connection-oriented protocols, 61
connectionless protocols, 61
data transfer protocols, 61-64
database security, 551
encapsulation, 28
filtering, 896
finger, 876
Frame relay, 78
hardware layer, 29
HDLC, 76
IP, 62-63
IPX, 61-62
NetBEUI, 64
PPP, 86
S-HTTP, 880
SMDS, 81
SMTP, 826-827
SNA, 64
SNMP, 61
SPX, 61-62
TCP, 63
TCP/IP, 62-63, 876
transport protocols
ARCNET, 60
Ethernet, 58
Fast Ethernet, 59
FDDI (Fiber Distributed Data Interface), 60
Token-Ring, 60
UDP, 62-63
whois, 876
X.25, 77
PServer (Pseudo Server) applications, 500-501
Change in Carrier Detect event, 802
classes, creating, 729-730
converting to OLE Servers, 728-735, 745-747
creating, 501-502
disconnecting users, 801
executing, 542-544
forms
adding code, 511-518
controls, 503-510, 515-518
loading, 516
unloading, 517
updating, 511
frame controls, 799
INI files
creating, 502
modifying, 572
installing remote servers, 799-806
menus, adding code, 518
Receive Data event, 802
Ring event, 802
timer controls, 517-518
public messaging services, 846-849
Public property (OLE objects), 730

Q

queries (databases), 102, 139, 480
building with Query Builder application, 784-786
DSS client applications, 218
joins, 102-104
SQL queries, 106
commands, 647-656
OwnerAccess option, 906
storing with QueryDef, 136
Query Builder applications
creating, 781-787
customizing, 786-787
tools required for creating, 754-756
QueryDef objects, 136, 140
QueryInterface, 156
QueryInterface function, 719
Quit method (Excel Application objects), 615-617

R

R&R Report Writer, 920
RACM (Remote Automation Connection Manager), 741-742
RAD (Rapid Application Development) tools, 273
Range objects (Excel), 618
Rapid Application Development (RAD) tools, 273
RAS (Remote Access Services), 847-848
RDCs (remote data controls), 120
RDO (remote data objects), 118, 120, 128, 184, 691, 705-706
  rdoColumn objects, 707
  rdoConnection objects, 707
  rdoEngine objects, 706
  rdoEnvironment objects, 707
  rdoError objects, 707
  rdoParameter objects, 708
  rdoPreparedStatement objects, 707
  rdoRecordset objects, 708
  rdoTable objects, 707
Read Data permissions (databases), 558
Read Design permissions (databases), 558
read-only text box controls (OLTP client application forms), 283

reading INI files for OLTP client applications, 305
ReadINI function, 305
ReadOnly property (data controls), 124
Receive Data event (Pseudo Server remote access), 802
recording macros, 590-592, 605-608
records (database tables), 98
  cascade relations, 171
  copying
    to DSS client application form controls, 492
    to OLTP client application form controls, 345, 439
  counters, 239
  editing, 269
  finding, 269, 399, 438
  finding with indexes, 99
  locking, 114, 144
  optimistic locking, 560
  refreshing to memory, 560
  restoring, 515
  snapshots, 128
  updating, 560
  writing data to OLTP client applications, 317-320, 403
recordsets (databases), 125, 128
  accessing table data, 128
  creating, 142
  locking, 141
RecordsetType property (data controls), 124

RecordSource property (data controls), 124
RecordToScreen routine, 317-320, 345, 403-405, 439, 444, 487, 492
reference counts (OLE objects), 719
References dialog box, 167
referencing
  databases, 101
  objects, 166-167
    database objects, 145
    Excel objects, 609, 612
    OLE objects, 719
  tables, 101-102
referential integrity (databases), 115-116, 170-171
refreshing records to memory, 560
RegisterDatabase method, 708
registering
  client applications, 750-751
  OLE Servers, 734-735
  project files in OLE Registry, 749-750
Registry (OLE), 749-750
relational databases, 99-104
Release function, 719
remote access (Narrowband ISDN), 86
Remote Access Services (RAS), 847-848
Remote Automation Connection Manager (RACM), 741-742
remote client applications, 796-799

remote client applications

creating, 806-821
forms
  adding code, 814-821
  controls, 808-814
  creating, 807-808
  loading, 819
  unloading, 819
remote client/server computing, 796-821
remote data controls, *see* **RDCs**
remote data objects, *see* **RDO**
remote objects (COM), 715
Remote OLE, 724, 739-745
Remote OLE Servers, 728, 745
remote processing (client/server computing), 39-40
remote server applications, installing on Pseudo Servers, 799-806
RemoteHandler routine, 803-805
renaming form controls, 8
reopening databases, 125
RepairDatabase function, 133
repeaters, 64
replication (servers), 41-42, 73
reports
  databases, 138, 181-182
    files, 23
    security, printing, 564
    software, 918
    upsizes, 677
  DSS client applications, 218, 450, 539-542

OLTP client application forms, 398
OLTP client applications, 215
printing, 331-333
requests (client applications), saving, 199
resource files, 175-176
RestoreReservedItems routine, 512
restoring records, 515
restricting access to variables, 152
Result Pane (Remote OLE Component Manager window), 743
result sets (databases), 102
  accessing with RDOs, 705-708
  grouping, 653-655
  limits, setting with SQL BETWEEN command, 651
  merging, 655
  navigating, 126
  retrieving with SELECT commands, 647-650
  sorting, 652-653
  SQL, 644
returned error processing, 956-957
Ring event (Pseudo Server remote access), 802
ring-topologies, 52, 54
RoboHelp add-on, 913
ROCKET software, 916-917
Rollback command, 141
rollbacks (database transactions), 115
routers, 52, 65, 896

routines, 149
AbortCall, 820
adding
  to client applications, 202
  to server applications, 197
CenterForm, 304
ChartWindowItem_Click, 639
CheckPServer, 394
client applications, activating on servers, 198
cmd_Add_Click, 435
cmd_BuildItem_Click, 435
cmd_Cancel_Click, 326, 341, 347, 411-412, 430, 440, 446, 488, 495
cmd_Connect_Click, 814-816
cmd_Disconnect_Click, 801, 817
cmd_Exit_Click, 339, 419
cmd_Item_Click, 414-415
cmd_Next_Click, 329, 415
cmd_OK_Click, 329-331, 341-343, 347, 415-416, 430-431, 440, 446, 488, 495
cmd_Prev_Click, 331, 417
cmd_Print_Click, 331-333, 417
cmd_Receive_Click, 817-818

cmd_Remove_Click, 436
cmd_Restore_Click, 515
cmd_Send_Click, 818
Comm1_OnComm, 801
CopyItem_Click, 339, 424
CopyTags, 345, 438, 444, 486, 490
CreateXLChart, 634-640
creating, 303-305
CutItem_Click, 339, 424
declaring
   for DSS client application forms, 477, 486, 490
   for OLTP client application forms, 306, 340, 344, 428, 433, 437, 443
   for OLTP client applications, 392-393
   for Pseudo Server applications, 511
   for Pseudo Server remote access, 800
   for Query Builder applications, 784
   for Table Builder application forms, 773-774
DisplayXLChart, 638-640
DoEvents, 423
DoFiveMinUpdate, 511
DoHourUpdate, 511
error handling, 956-961
ExitItem_Click, 339, 424, 818

ExportChartItem_Click, 636
FindDBInfo, 512
Form_Activate, 333, 342, 348, 489, 496
Form_Click event, 590
Form_Load, 343, 348, 419, 431-432, 436, 442, 447, 483-484, 489, 496, 516, 819
Form_Load event, 202
Form_Paint, 343, 432, 442, 447
Form_Unload, 334-335, 421, 484, 517, 819
GetChecksum, 819
Global Error, 963
grd_Main_Click, 335, 421
grd_Main_KeyPress, 336, 421
inserting
   in DSS client application form controls, 483-484, 488-490, 494-497
   in DSS client application form menus, 484-486
   in DSS client application forms, 476-497
   in OLTP client application form controls, 429-431, 435-437, 440-443, 446
   in OLTP client application form menus, 422-427
   in OLTP client application forms, 305-349, 392-447

   in Pseudo Server application form controls, 515-518
   in Pseudo Server application form menus, 518
   in Pseudo Server application forms, 511-518
   in remote client application forms, 814-821
LinkExecute Event, 193
List1_DblClick, 342
LoadBuildList, 428, 433
LoadItemList, 340-341, 429, 434
LoadLocation, 399, 438
MakeDB (listing 10.1), 250-255
MoveTextBox, 319, 402-403
MyOpenPort, 821
OLTP client application form controls, 325-339
parameters, 304
ParseLine, 802-803
PasteItem_Click, 339, 424
Pause, 820
PrintItem_Click, 424
Property Get, 589, 731-732
Property Let, 589, 732
RecordToScreen, 317-320, 345, 403-405, 439, 444, 487, 492
RemoteHandler, 803-805
RestoreReservedItems, 512

routines

ScreenToRecord, 318
ScreentoRecord, 346, 439, 444, 487, 493
SendEditMessage, 305
SetCell, 320, 405-406
SetOwnership, 562
SetPasswords, 563
SetPermission, 562
SetupDefaultScreen, 321, 347, 406, 439, 444, 488, 494
SetupGrid, 407
ShowError, 962-963
ShowInventoryItem_Click, 339
tab_Report_Click, 483
TestMacro, 591
text box control change event, 336
Timer1_Timer, 517-518
txt_GridText_GotFocus, 337, 425
txt_GridText_KeyPress, 337, 426
txt_GridText_LostFocus, 337-338, 426
txt_TabBefore_GotFocus, 338, 426
txt_TabNext_GotFocus, 338-339, 427
WaitForValue, 819-820
WriteINI, 305
see also functions; methods
Routing Slip objects (Excel), 620
RSA encryption algorithm, e-mail security, 895
rules (SQL triggers), 646, 965

Run method (Excel Application objects), 615
running Excel macros, 615
runtime library (memory size), 6

S

S-HTTP (Secure HyperText Transport Protocol), 880
sagas (database transactions), 115
saving
 client application requests, 199
 client applications, 200
 OLTP client application forms, 276
 Table Builder applications, 780
 VBP files, 13
scaling
 databases
  to SQL Server databases, 121
  with Upsizing Wizard, 137
 peer-to-peer networks, 47
Scenario objects (Excel), 618
Scope Pane (Remote OLE Component Manager window), 743
scope variables (VBA), 584-585
screen layout (GUIs), 943-948
ScreenToRecord routine, 318, 346, 439, 444, 487, 493

ScreenUpdating property (Excel Application objects), 614
SCSA (Signal Computing System Architecture), 870-871
searching databases, 102, 198, 206
Secure HyperText Transport Protocol (S-HTTP), 880
Secure Sockets Layer (SSL), 880
security
 Access, 903-906
 client/server computing, 565-573, 874-878
 databases, 564-565, 889-891, 908-909
  implementing, 898-899
  objects, 574
  planning, 546-547, 897-898
  protocols, 551
  system-level security, 547-550
  testing, 573
  upgrading, 899
  via Visual Basic, 900-910
 e-mail, 875, 891-895
 Internet, 880
 networks, 877-878
  interfaces, 888-910
  NetWare, 887-888
  operating systems, 887
  peer-to-peer networks, 46
 OLE Servers, 752
 remote client/server computing, 797
 reports (databases), printing, 564

SQL Servers, 891
standards, 878-879
tables, 565-570
Windows NT 3.5, 887
workgroups, 907-908
X.509 standards, 885
security IDs (SIDs), database accounts, 550-552
SELECT command (SQL), 647-650
self joins (database queries), 104
SendEditMessage routine, 305
sending Excel Workbook objects as e-mail attachments, 620
Sequenced Packet eXchange, *see* **SPX protocol**
server applications
creating, 193-199
executing, 196, 204
forms, setup, 193
messaging services, 842-847
properties, setting, 195-197
Pseudo Servers, 500-501
Change in Carrier Detect event, 802
classes, creating, 729-730
converting to OLE Servers, 728-735, 745-747
creating, 501-502
disconnecting users, 801
executing, 542-544
forms, 502-518
forms, adding code, 511-518
forms, loading, 516
forms, unloading, 517
forms, updating, 511
frame controls, adding, 799
INI files, 502, 572
installing remote servers, 799-806
menus, adding code, 518
Receive Data event, 802
Ring event, 802
timer controls, 517-518
receiving client application commands, 188
Remote OLE Servers, 739-745
remote server applications, installing on Pseudo Servers, 799-806
routines, adding, 197
server-based CTI systems, 855-856
servers, 26, 29-30
data coordination, 35
database servers, 31, 220, 914-917
file servers, 31, 66-67
groupware servers, 32-33
immediate replication, 41
mail servers, 44-45
mirroring, 42, 881
object servers, 33-34
OLE servers, 728, 748-751
configurations, 732-734
creating, 162, 169-170
executing, 735
menus, 168
registering, 734-735
security, 752
toolbars, 168
version control, 749
proactive servers, 189
procedure storage, 35
replication, 41-42, 73
skulking, 41
SMP (symmetrical multiprocessing servers), 30
specialized servers, 34
SQL Servers, 663-665, 756
TP (Transaction processing) monitors, 42-43
service providers, 932-933
Set command, 632
Set function, 145
SetCell routine, 320, 405-406
SetDataAccessOption statement, 902-903
SetDefaultWorkspace statement, 903-906
SetOwnership routine, 562
SetPasswords routine, 563
SetPermission routine, 562
setup
client application forms, 199-200
client/server computing on networks, 526
grids in OLTP client application forms, 321-322, 407

setup

server application forms, 193-195
Setup Wizard, 19-22
SetupDefaultScreen routine, 321, 347, 406, 439, 445, 488, 494
SetupGrid routine, 407
SHED files (Help), 951
shifting object focus, 948
ShowError routine, 962-963
ShowInventoryItem_Click routine, 339
SHUTDOWN command, 664
SIDs (security IDs), 550, 900-902
Signal Computing System Architecture (SCSA), 870-871
Simple Mail Transport Protocol (SMTP), 826-827
Simple MAPI, 827-828
Simple Messaging Servers, 842
simple messaging services, 823
Simple Network Management Protocol (SNMP), 61
simulating DLLs with Visual Basic, 169-170
single-tier ODBC drivers, 697
skulking servers, 41
SMDS (Switched Multimegabit Data Service) protocol, 81
SMF (Standard Messaging Format), 826
SMP (Symmetric MultiProcessing) servers, 30, 67

SMTP (Simple Mail Transport Protocol), 826-827
SNA (System Network Architecture) protocol, 64
snapshots, accessing table data, 128
SNMP (Simple Network Management Protocol), 61
software
database printing/ reports, 918-920
databases, 914-917
Solaris NOS, 71
SONET lines (ATM networks), 92
sorting
fields, 268
result sets, 652-653
SP&T (stored procedures and triggers), SQL, 646, 763
specialized servers, 34
splitting tables, 244
spoofing, 876
Spread/VBX add-on, 927-928
SPX (Sequenced Packet eXchange) protocol, 61-62
SQL (Structured Query Language), 104-106, 644
Access commands, 659
ALTER command, 647
BETWEEN command, 651
comparison operators, 649
Core functions in ODBC, 704

CREATE command, 647
Data Definition Language (DDL), 656
Data Manipulation Language (DML), 656
data types for ODBC, 663
DELETE command, 647
dialects, 644
DROP command, 647
Dynamic SQL, 645
functions, 644-646
aggregate functions, 650-652
Extended functions in ODBC, 705
ODBC Core functions, 661-662
ODBC Extended functions, 662
uninterpreted, passing to databases, 145
implementing
in Access databases, 656-660
in ODBC, 660-663
IN command, 651
INSERT command, 647
JOIN command, 655-656
LIKE command, 652
logical operators, 650
queries
commands, 647-656
OwnerAccess option, 906
result sets, 644
SELECT command, 647

SP&T (stored procedures and triggers), 646
standards, 644
Static SQL, 645
UPDATE command, 647
SQL PassThrough function, 145
SQL Servers, 756
  data constructs, 756-758
  data types, 760-762
  databases
    client application permissions, 684-685
    creating, 668-670, 672-680
    devices, creating, 669
    exporting to other database servers, 687-688
    ODBC connections, 670-671
    owners, 758
    user accounts, creating, 682-683
    workgroups, adding user accounts to, 683-688
    workgroups, creating, 681
  implementing, 663-665
  indexes, 763
  security, 891
  SP&T, 763
  system administrators, 758
  system tables, 758-760
  views, 762
SQLGetInfo function, 698
SSL (Secure Sockets Layer), 880
Standard Edition (Visual Basic), 160
Standard Messaging Format (SMF), 826
star-topologies, 52, 54-55
statements
  Error, 959
  For Each statement, 176
  SetDataAccessOption, 902-903
  SetDefaultWorkspace, 903-906
  SQL SELECT command
    DISTINCT, 649
    FROM, 648
    GROUP BY, 653-655
    ORDER BY, 652-653
  With statement, 176
Static SQL, 645
static variables (VBA), 585-586
status bars
  GUIs, 941-943
  Help, 952-953
StatusBar property (Excel Application objects), 614
stored procedures and triggers, *see* **SP&T**
storing
  client applications, 523-524
  database queries with QueryDef, 136
  OLTP client application forms, 296
strings (data types), 193, 197
structured programming, 149
Structured Query Language, *see* **SQL**
structured storage (OLE), 721-722
Sum function, 650
supplementary services (TAPI), 865-867
suspending error trapping, 958
Switched Multimegabit Data Service (SMDS) protocol, 79
switches (Token-Ring networks), 60
switching hardware (ATM networks), 91
Symmetric Multi-Processing (SMP), 30, 67
SyncPoints (databases), 115
system administrators (SQL Servers), 758
system errors, checking, 957
System Network Architecture (SNA) protocol, 64
system tables (SQL Server), 758-760

T

tab controls (DSS client application) forms, 455
tab_Report_Click routine, 483
Table Builder applications
  creating, 763-781
  executing, 780
  forms, creating, 772-780
  saving, 780
  testing, 780
  tools required for creating, 756

tables

tables (databases), 96-98
  accessing, 269-270
  creating, 221-223, 226-227, 231-249
  creating with automated routines, 250-255
  creating with Table Builder application, 766-768
  data access, 128
  data entry, 233-234
  fields, 98
    displaying, 235
    inserting, 232
    key fields, 101-102
    null fields, 144-145
    sorting, 268
  indexes, 98-99, 139
  joins, 655-656
  naming, 231
  normalizing, 229-230
  records, 98
    collisions, 114
    cascade relations, 171
    counters, 239
    editing, 269
    finding, 269
    locking, 144
    optimistic locking, 560
    refreshing to memory, 560
    restoring, 515
    snapshots, 128
    updating, 560
  referencing, 101-102
  relations, 99, 226
  searching, 102
  security, 565-570
  splitting, 244
  upsizing to SQL Server databases, 675

TAPI (Telephone Application Program Interface), 794, 858-868
  assisted telephony, 862-863
  basic services, 863-865
  connections to client/server computing systems, 793-796
  extended services, 867-868
  full telephony, 863-868
  programming, 795-796
  Software Development Kit, 868
  supplementary services, 865-867

tapiRequestMakeCall function, 795

TCP (Transmission Control Protocol), 63

TCP/IP (Transmission Control Protocol/Internet Protocol), 62-63, 876

Telephone Application Program Interface, *see* **TAPI**

telephony, 852-854
  add-ons, 929-931
  API standards, 856-872
  CTI systems, 854-856
  Geoport standards, 871
  SCSA standards, 870
  TAPI, 858-868
  USB standards, 871
  Versit standards, 872

Telephony API, *see* **TAPI**

Telephony Server API, *see* **TSAPI**

testing
  client applications after database upsizing, 680-687
  databases
    after upsizing, 680-687
    security, 573
  Table Builder applications, 780

TestMacro routine, 591

text box controls
  change event routines, 336
  inserting in client application forms, 200
  OLTP client application forms, 214, 281-285, 291-295
    editing, 405
    focus, 421
    moving, 319, 402
    positioning over grids, 320
    recovering lost focus, 337
    selecting all text from, 337
    shifting focus, 338-339

Thicknet (10BASE-5) cabling, 56

Thinnet (10BASE-2) cabling, 56

three-tier client/server computing, 38

three-tier ODBC drivers, 698

TIME command, 805

time stamps (database updates), 114

timer controls (Pseudo Server applications), 517-518

Timer1_Timer routine, 517-518

Tmap interfaces, 870

token frames (Token-Ring networks), 60

Token-Ring transport protocol, 60

Tool tips, 953
Toolbar objects (Excel), 623
toolbars (user-interface negotiation), 168
toolboxes (project files), inserting objects, 167
tools
  databases, 136-138
  RAD, 273
  see also add-ons
ToolTips, 173
topologies
  bus topologies, 55
  chain topologies, 53
  ring-topologies, 54
  star-topologies, 54-55
  wave topologies, 53
TOTL command, 805
TP (Transaction processing) monitors, servers, 42-43
transaction logs (databases), 757
Transaction processing (TP) monitors, servers, 42-43
transactions (databases), 141-144
  chained, 115
  consistency, 114-115
  encapsulation, 36
  sagas, 115
  rollbacks, 115
  SyncPoints, 115
Transmission Control Protocol/Internet Protocol, *see* TCP/IP
transmission rates (e-mail), 822
Transport layer (TCP/IP), 63

transport protocols
  ARCNET, 60
  Ethernet, 58
  Fast Ethernet, 59
  FDDI, 60
  Token-Ring, 60
trapping errors, 957-959
triggers (SQL), 646
  nesting, 665
TrueGrid Pro add-on, 928-929
TSAPI (Telephony Server API), 856-858, 868-870
tunneling packets, 61
Twisted Pair (10BASE-T) cabling, 56
two-tier ODBC drivers, 698
txt_GridText_GotFocus routine, 337, 425
txt_GridText_KeyPress routine, 337, 426
txt_GridText_LostFocus routine, 337-338, 426
txt_TabBefore_GotFocus routine, 338, 426
txt_TabNext_GotFocus routine, 338-339, 427

U

UDP (User Datagram Protocol), 62-63
unanticipated errors, 959-960
underscore (_), VBA line-continuation character, 588
uniform data transfer (objects), 721
uninterpreted SQL functions, passing to databases, 145

UNION clause (SQL SELECT command), 655
Universal Serial Bus (USB) telephony standard, 871
UNJOIN command, 106
unloading
  DSS client application forms, 484
  OLTP client application forms, 335, 420
  Pseudo Server application forms, 517
  remote client application forms, 819
Unprotect method (Excel Worksheet objects), 619
UPDATE command (SQL), 647
Update Data permissions (databases), 558
updating
  databases, 141
  multiple databases, 141
  OLTP client applications, 322-324
  Pseudo Server application forms, 511
  records, 560
upgrading
  database security, 899
  DSS client applications with RDOs, 708-710
upsized databases, examining
  with attached tables, 678
  with SQL Object Manager, 679-680
  with SQL Server Browser, 678-679

upsizing databases to SQL Server databases, 668-680
Upsizing Wizard, 137, 668, 674
USB (Universal Serial Bus) telephony standard, 871
user accounts
  client applications
    creating, 567
    permissions, 567-570
  databases
    adding to workgroups, 555-556
    creating, 555, 561
    passwords, 563
    permissions, 557-559
    privileges, 556
    security IDs, 550-552, 900-902
  SQL Server databases, creating, 682-683
User Datagram Protocol (UDP), 62
user interface objects (Excel), 622
user interfaces, *see* **GUIs**
user-interface negotiation, 168
UserName variables (client applications), 572
utilities
  Client Registration, 750-751
  Data Manager, 136-137
  Install Shield, 931-932
  installation utilities, 931-932
  Notepad, creating INI files with, *271*
  ODBC Administration, 670

VB/Rig Pro, 925-926
Versions/VB, 926
Visual Sourcesafe, 925
VSView, 920
WISE Installation System, 932
see also add-ons

V

values out of range errors (client/server computing systems), 964
variables, 149
  database buffers, 127
  encapsulation, 9
  forms, declaring, 8
  global, 9
  local variables, 585
  module-level variables, 585
  naming conventions, 194
  Password (client applications), 572
  procedure-level variables, 584
  project-level variables, 585
  restricting access to, 152
  scope variables (VBA), 584-585
  static variables (VBA), 585-586
  UserName (client applications), 572
VB Helpwriter add-on, 914
VB/Link, 920-921
VB/Rig Pro utility, 925-926
VBA (Visual Basic for Applications), 161, 578-595

  Debugging tools, 594-595
  drawbacks, 590
  Editing tools, 594-595
  event handlers, 590
  For...Each...Next loops, 586
  integration with Microsoft Office applications, 590-595
  line-continuation characters, 588
  Macro Recorder, 590-592
  Microsoft Project environment, 595
  Object Browser, 593-594
  object classes, 153
  Property procedures, 588-589
  scope variables, 584-585
  static variables, 585-586
  While...Wend loops, 588
  With...End With command, 586-587
VBCL (Visual Basic Compatibility Layer), 133
  see also JET engine 2.5/3.0
VBFax telephony add-on, 931
VBP (Visual Basic project) files, 12-13
  formats, 12
  installation setup files, modifying, 21-22
  saving, 13
  see also applications; project files
VBSQL plug-in, 135-136

VBSQL/DBLibrary, 922
VBVoice telephony add-on, 930-931
.VBX (Visual Basic Extension) files, 10, 14-16
Vendor-Independent Messaging (VIM), 45, 826
version controls (objects), 155-156
Versions/VB utility, 926
Versit telephony standards, 872
views (SQL Servers), 762
VIM (Vendor-Independent Messaging), 45, 826
virtual channels (ATM networks), 91-92
Visible property (Excel Worksheet objects), 619
Visual Basic
   16-bit, 161
   32-bit, 161
   accessing from ODBC drivers, 691-693
   DDE access, 192
   development, 4
   development environment, 160-161
   drawbacks, 184-185
   Enterprise Edition, 160
   events, 11-12
   forms, 6-8
   IDE, 172-176
   instances, 9-10
   interface add-ons, 926-929
   language enhancements, 176-177
   MAPI interface, 829-842
   modules, 6, 9
   objects, 6, 9-10
   OOP, 152-153
   Professional Edition, 160
   program files, 10-11
   source code tools, 924-926
   Standard Edition, 160
   telephony support, 872
   versions, 13-14
   Windows 95 interface support, 166
Visual Basic Compatibility Layer (VBCL), 133
Visual Basic eXtension files, *see* VBX files
Visual Basic for Applications, *see* VBA
Visual Fax telephony add-on, 930
Visual FoxPro, 916
Visual SourceSafe Administrator/Explorer, 182
Visual Sourcesafe utility, 925
Visual Voice telephony add-on, 929-930
Visual/db, 916
voice server-based CTI systems, 856
VSFlex add-on, 927
VSVBX add-on, 926-927
VSView utility, 920

W

WaitForValue routine, 819-820
WANs (Wide Area Networks), 51, 73-74
wave topologies, 53
WFW (Windows for Workgroups) workstations, logons, 547-548
WHERE clause (SQL SELECT command), 649-651
While...Wend loops (VBA), 588
whois protocol, 876
Wide Area Networks, *see* WANs
windows (GUIs), 944-945
Windows 95
   imagelist control, 166
   Integrated messaging services, 845
   interface (Visual Basic support), 166
   workstations, logons, 548
Windows API functions, *see* API functions
Windows for Workgroups (WFW) workstations, logons, 547-548
Windows NT
   directory services, 886-887
   Windows NT 3.5, 887
Windows NT 3.51, 67-69
Windows NT networks
   Remote Access Services, 847
   Windows NT Server, 67-69
   Windows NT SQL Server, 67
   Windows NT Workstation, 67-69
WindowState property (Excel Application objects), 614

WinSock 1.1, 849
WinSock 2.0, 850
WISE Installation System utility, 932
With statement, 176
With...End With command, 586-587, 632
wizards
   Chart Wizard, 606
   Setup Wizard, 19-22
   Upsizing Wizard, 137, 668, 674
Word Basic (OLE Automation), 597-598
Workbook objects (Excel), 616-617, 620
Workflow groupware servers, 33
workgroups
   client applications
      creating, 566-567
      permissions, 567-570
   databases, 546
      adding user accounts, 555-556
      Administrator, 553
      creating, 554-555, 561
      naming, 554
      passwords, 563
      permissions, 557-559
      PersonalIDs, 554
      privileges, 556
      security, 907-908
      security IDs, 550-552, 900-902
   SQL Server databases
      adding user accounts to, 683-688
      creating, 681
Worksheet objects (Excel), 617-619

workspace objects (databases), 564-565
workstations
   WFW, logons, 547-548
   Windows 95, logons, 548
Worldgroup client/server development kit, 922
WriteINI routine, 305
writing
   parameter values to INI files in OLTP client applications, 305
   record data to controls in OLTP client application forms, 403

X-Y-Z

X.25 protocol, 77
X.400 messaging service interface, 824-826
X.500 network directory services, 883-885
X.509 cryptography/ security standards, 885

PLUG YOURSELF INTO...

THE MACMILLAN INFORMATION SUPERLIBRARY™

Free information and vast computer resources from the world's leading computer book publisher—online!

FIND THE BOOKS THAT ARE RIGHT FOR YOU!

A complete online catalog, plus sample chapters and tables of contents give you an in-depth look at *all* of our books, including hard-to-find titles. It's the best way to find the books you need!

- **STAY INFORMED** with the latest computer industry news through our online newsletter, press releases, and customized Information SuperLibrary Reports.
- **GET FAST ANSWERS** to your questions about MCP books and software.
- **VISIT** our online bookstore for the latest information and editions!
- **COMMUNICATE** with our expert authors through e-mail and conferences.
- **DOWNLOAD SOFTWARE** from the immense MCP library:
    - Source code and files from MCP books
    - The best shareware, freeware, and demos
- **DISCOVER HOT SPOTS** on other parts of the Internet.
- **WIN BOOKS** in ongoing contests and giveaways!

TO PLUG INTO MCP:

GOPHER: gopher.mcp.com
FTP: ftp.mcp.com

WORLD WIDE WEB: http://www.mcp.com

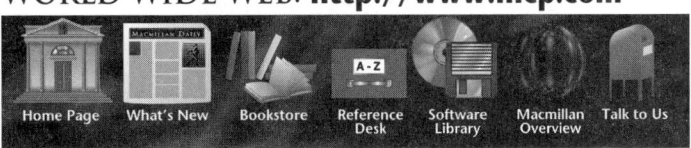

GET CONNECTED
to the ultimate source of computer information!

The MCP Forum on CompuServe

Go online with the world's leading computer book publisher! Macmillan Computer Publishing offers everything you need for computer success!

Find the books that are right for you!
A complete online catalog, plus sample chapters and tables of contents give you an in-depth look at all our books. The best way to shop or browse!

➤ Get fast answers and technical support for MCP books and software

➤ Join discussion groups on major computer subjects

➤ Interact with our expert authors via e-mail and conferences

➤ Download software from our immense library:
  ▷ Source code from books
  ▷ Demos of hot software
  ▷ The best shareware and freeware
  ▷ Graphics files

Join now and get a free CompuServe Starter Kit!

To receive your free CompuServe Introductory Membership, call **1-800-848-8199** and ask for representative #597.

The Starter Kit includes:
➤ Personal ID number and password
➤ $15 credit on the system
➤ Subscription to *CompuServe Magazine*

Once on the CompuServe System, type:

GO MACMILLAN

for the most computer information anywhere!

MACMILLAN COMPUTER PUBLISHING

CompuServe

Add to Your Sams Library Today with the Best Books for Programming, Operating Systems, and New Technologies

The easiest way to order is to pick up the phone and call

1-800-428-5331

between 9:00 a.m. and 5:00 p.m. EST.

For faster service please have your credit card available.

ISBN	Quantity	Description of Item	Unit Cost	Total Cost
0-672-30615-8		Peter Norton's Guide to Visual Basic 4 for Windows 95	$39.99	
0-672-30640-9		Master Visual Basic 4, 2E (Book/CD-ROM)	$49.99	
0-672-30596-8		Develop a Professional Visual Basic Application in 14 Days (Book/CD-ROM)	$35.00	
0-672-30837-1		Visual Basic 4 Unleashed (Book/CD-ROM)	$45.00	
0-672-30796-0		Visual Basic 4 Performance Tuning & Optimization (Book/CD-ROM)	$49.99	
0-672-30743-X		Gurewich OLE Controls for Visual Basic 4 (Book/CD-ROM)	$39.99	
0-672-30779-0		Real-World Programming with Visual Basic 4 (Book/CD-ROM)	$49.99	
0-672-30832-0		Teach Yourself Database Programming with Visual Basic 4 in 21 Days (Book/CD-ROM)	$39.99	
0-672-30782-0		Teach Yourself Excel Programming with VBA in 21 Days	$35.00	
0-672-30855-X		Teach Yourself SQL in 14 Days	$29.99	
0-672-30609-3		Teach Yourself ODBC in 21 Days	$29.99	
❏ 3 ½" Disk		Shipping and Handling: See information below.		
❏ 5 ¼" Disk		TOTAL		

Shipping and Handling: $4.00 for the first book, and $1.75 for each additional book. Floppy disk: add $1.75 for shipping and handling. If you need to have it NOW, we can ship product to you in 24 hours for an additional charge of approximately $18.00, and you will receive your item overnight or in two days. Overseas shipping and handling adds $2.00 per book and $8.00 for up to three disks. Prices subject to change. Call for availability and pricing information on latest editions.

201 W. 103rd Street, Indianapolis, Indiana 46290

1-800-428-5331 — Orders   1-800-835-3202 — FAX   1-800-858-7674 — Customer Service

Book ISBN 0-672-30789-8

Installing Your CD-ROM

System Requirements

The applications developed for this book were created using the 32-bit Edition of Visual Basic 4. To work with the source code, you must have the 32-bit Edition of Visual Basic 4 installed on your PC. (You can use the Standard Edition of Visual Basic 4 or the 32-bit compiler included with the Professional or Enterprise editions of Visual Basic 4.)

Since the applications are 32-bit, you must have Windows 95 installed as well. You cannot use Windows 3.1.

What's on the CD-ROM

The companion CD-ROM contains sample projects developed by the authors, plus an assortment of third-party tools and product demos. The disc is designed to be explored using a browser program. Using Sams' Guide to the CD-ROM browser, you can view information concerning products and companies and install programs with a single click of the mouse button. To install the browser, follow the next steps.

Windows 95 Installation Instructions

1. Insert the CD-ROM into your CD-ROM drive. If the AutoPlay feature of your Windows 95 system is enabled, the setup program will start automatically.
2. If the setup program does not start automatically, double-click the My Computer icon.
3. Double-click the icon representing your CD-ROM drive.
4. Double-click the Setup.exe icon to run the installation program. Follow the on-screen instructions that appear. When the setup ends, the Guide to the CD-ROM program starts, and you can begin browsing immediately.

Following the installation, you can restart the Guide to the CD-ROM program by clicking the Start button, selecting Programs, and selecting VB4 Client Server and Guide to the CD-ROM.

> **NOTE**
>
> The Guide to the CD-ROM program requires at least 256 colors. For best results, set your monitor to display between 256 and 64,000 colors. A screen resolution of 640 × 480 pixels is also recommended. If necessary, adjust your monitor settings before using the CD-ROM.